Property Law

CASES AND COMMENTARY

THIRD EDITION

Mary Jane Mossman
Osgoode Hall Law School
York University

Philip Girard
Osgoode Hall Law School
York University

2014
EMOND MONTGOMERY PUBLICATIONS
TORONTO, CANADA

Emond Montgomery Publications Limited
60 Shaftesbury Avenue
Toronto, ON M4T 1A3
http://www.emp.ca/lawschool

Printed in Canada.

We acknowledge the financial support of the Government of Canada through the Canada Book Fund for our publishing activities.

Emond Montgomery Publications has no responsibility for the persistence or accuracy of URLs for external or third-party Internet websites referred to in this publication, and does not guarantee that any content on such websites is, or will remain, accurate or appropriate.

Publisher, Professional division: Bernard Sandler
Director, editorial and production: Jim Lyons
Copy and production editor: Nancy Ennis
Proofreader: David Handelsman

Library and Archives Canada Cataloguing in Publication

Mossman, Mary Jane, author
     Property law : cases and commentary / Mary Jane Mossman and Philip Girard. — Third edition.

ISBN 978-1-55239-582-0 (bound)

     1. Real property—Canada—Cases.   I. Girard, Philip, author   II. Title.

KE625.M68 2013   346.7104'3   C2013-906566-0
KF560.M68 2013

Preface to the Third Edition

This third edition of *Property Law: Cases and Commentary* reflects a joint effort by us, as co-authors, to revise the earlier editions. Our revisions include not only updated cases and materials but also substantial rewriting and reorganization, as well as some new topics in several chapters. Significantly, Chapter 3 on the fundamental principles of land law has been entirely rewritten and Chapter 8 is now new, focused on the history and recent developments concerning Aboriginal title to land. At the same time, the book continues to be organized around basic themes in the law of property.

As with earlier editions, *Property Law* has two primary objectives: (1) to help students recognize, understand, and work with basic property principles; and (2) equally important, to enable students to become informed and imaginative critics of these principles and the ways in which they are used in differing societal contexts in the 21st century in Canada.

The cases and materials selected emphasize the role of property in a social context, exploring how property concepts define entitlement in ways that distinguish the rights of those who hold property interests from those who do not—and the consequences of these differences. In doing so, the materials focus on the contemporary coherence of traditional property principles within the legal system, as well as their connections to current public policy goals and to issues about race, class, gender, and sexuality. In addition, the book presents basic property principles in the context of their application to both chattels and land, thus challenging the continuing usefulness of traditional distinctions between personal and real property. The book also seeks to provide a basic foundation for upper-year courses in the JD curriculum, including real estate transactions, succession law, commercial law, family law, environmental law, trusts, and Aboriginal legal issues, offering a variety of additional references to academic literature and law reform studies for instructors and students interested in pursuing particular topics in more detail.

Although we have both been teaching property law for many years, we could not have written this book without the scholarly contributions of so many of our property colleagues in Canada; indeed, as will be evident, we have incorporated their published work at many points in the book. In addition to her colleagues at the University of New South Wales and at Osgoode Hall Law School, Mary Jane is grateful to Brian Bucknall, and Philip wants to express appreciation to his former colleagues at the Schulich School of Law at Dalhousie University for both intellectual insights and collegial support over many years. We both also acknowledge our enthusiasm for Bruce Ziff's scholarly work on Canadian property law.

We have worked together over several months in the preparation of this third edition of *Property Law*. However, we each took primary responsibility for four chapters: Mary Jane worked on Chapters 1, 2, 6, and 8; while Philip took on Chapters 3, 4, 5, and 7. As noted, Chapters 3 and 8 are entirely new chapters, and there are substantial revisions, updates, and new topics in other chapters in this edition. We are grateful to three research assistants who were significantly involved in the preparation of this new edition: Waleed Malik, Craig Mazerolle, and Althea Yip, and to a number of others who made useful contributions as well: Danielle Cornacchia, Gail Henderson, Thomas Hughes, Kalen Lumsden, and Deanne Sowter. We also thank Kent McNeil for his help with Chapter 8; the reference librarians at Osgoode Hall Law School; Miriam Spevack at Osgoode for her help with formatting; and Bernard Sandler, Nancy Ennis, and others at Emond Montgomery for their editorial support. Finally, we both acknowledge the many students who, over the years, have challenged us, provided useful examples of property law concepts in action, and always kept us thinking about how best to teach the first-year course in property law.

We welcome comments and suggestions.

Mary Jane Mossman and Philip Girard
November 2013

Preface to the Second Edition

The second edition of this casebook provides an opportunity, first of all, to express warm thanks to colleagues and students who have offered comments and suggestions about the first edition over the past six years. Many of them have been generous in their expressions of support for a casebook that attempts to explain traditional legal principles for first-year students, while, at the same time, identifying critiques and challenges for property law in 21st-century Canada. In addition to engaging with students on these issues, I have welcomed opportunities to discuss approaches to teaching property law with a number of colleagues across Canada: Douglas Harris (at the University of British Columbia), Sandra McCallum (formerly at the University of Victoria), Donna Eansor (at the University of Windsor), and Margaret McCallum (at the University of New Brunswick). My colleagues at Osgoode Hall Law School have also been helpful in making suggestions for the casebook: I am particularly grateful to Paul Emond, both as a colleague and as publisher, and to other property law teachers, including Kent McNeil, Eric Tucker, Stepan Wood, and Ben Richardson. I also want to express my appreciation for anonymous and thoughtful comments provided by several property law teachers at the request of Emond Montgomery Publications.

For this edition of the casebook, I have taken responsibility for Chapters 1, 2, 6, 7, and 8. With the help of student research assistants, I have tried to update cases and statutory references to ensure that the materials are current. To a limited extent, I have also reorganized some sections of these chapters to respond to suggestions for clearer presentation of some issues. In a few places, some new material or new issues have been introduced for further clarification of existing topics. However, I have not engaged in major reorganization of these chapters in the context of the casebook as a whole.

One issue, in particular, requires specific mention: the treatment of issues concerning Aboriginal property. One anonymous reviewer recommended a specific chapter on Aboriginal property issues, rather than the approach adopted in the first edition of the casebook. Although I considered this suggestion seriously, I remain convinced that there is merit in examining Aboriginal property issues within the context of concepts of property; first possession; the Crown as the basis for title, gifts and trusts, non-possessory interests, family property, and property and the constitution. For me, critical distinctions between European and Aboriginal conceptualizations about property issues, including land, become more sharply focused when these issues are approached comparatively. At the same time, I fully understand why some property law instructors might wish to teach a discrete unit on Aboriginal property, and I remain hopeful that it is possible for them to do so by pulling together parts of these different chapters. In this context, my co-author, Professor Flanagan, decided to include the *Delgamuukw* decision in his revisions to Chapter 3, and I fully concurred with him. As a result, the material in Chapter 8 concerning Aboriginal property issues and the constitution now includes commentary about the continuing impact of *Delgamuukw*, as well as references to similar developments in other common law jurisdictions. I will be interested, of course, to have further comments from colleagues and students as we work with these revised arrangements in the second edition.

Finally, I want to express my thanks to my property students, especially for their questions, their enthusiasm, and their willingness to grapple with legal concepts that are both hoary and traditional at the same time as they offer profound and controversial challenges to law in the 21st century. Four of these students provided able research assistance for the second edition: Christine Jenkins, LLB 2002; and Gail Henderson, Elissa Banach, and Jason Wang, all Class of 2005. My understanding of property law was also greatly enriched by the experience of working with students and faculty as Director of Osgoode's Part Time LLM in Real Property (1998-2001); and particularly by the opportunity to work in the program with Brian Bucknall, who continues to be the person with whom I have the best conversations about property law, and much else!

Mary Jane Mossman
June 2004

In this second edition of *Property Law*, I am responsible for Chapters 3, 4, and 5. In the first edition (1998), I was responsible for Chapters 3 and 4, and contributed, along with Professor Mossman, to the content in Chapter 5. Some of the material in Chapter 5 of this second edition includes material from the first edition; however, I am responsible for all changes and updates made to Chapter 5 in this second edition.

I am grateful to Professor Kent McNeil of Osgoode Hall Law School for his comments on Chapter 3.

It was a pleasure to participate in the second edition of *Property Law*. I welcome any comments or suggestions: wflan@sympatico.ca.

William F. Flanagan
June 2004

Preface to the First Edition

This casebook provides an introduction to the principles of property law and critical commentary on them. It is a published version of course materials that were developed over several years of teaching property law to students in the first year of the LLB program. The original course materials had two primary objectives—to help students recognize, understand, and work with basic property principles; and, equally important, to enable students to become informed and imaginative critics of these principles and the ways in which they are used in differing societal contexts.

The original materials emphasized the importance of property in law and society; they were designed to examine how property concepts define entitlement and distinguish the rights of those who hold property interests from those who do not. The materials examined traditional property principles in terms of their coherence within the legal system and in relation to public policy goals, and also took into account their impact on issues of race, class, family status, sexual orientation, and gender. Over a number of years, the materials were organized in order to present critical perspectives in the context of traditional legal principles, an approach that aspired to integrating (rather than segregating) accepted property principles with ideas that challenge them. For example, the materials included treatment of a number of important issues about Aboriginal property, introduced at relevant points throughout the casebook rather than being treated as a special topic separate from mainstream legal principles. In relation to Aboriginal property issues as well as other topics, the materials presented an introduction to concepts and critiques concerning property, and provided a foundation for further examination of these issues by students in their upper year courses.

In addition to these objectives, the original materials were designed to achieve a number of other related goals. First, the organization of the materials reflected a sense of the continuity of legal principles concerning real and personal property. Instead of presenting materials about personal property (such as finders, bailment, and gifts) within one unit, the materials presented these topics concerning personal property in conjunction with issues affecting real property—concepts of possession in relation to both finders and possessory title to land; the division of title and possession in relation to both bailment of personal property and leases; and transfers of proprietary interests by gift and sale of both real and personal property. This approach permitted an examination of property principles in the context of chattels and land, and an assessment of the continuing validity of the law's traditional distinctions between them. Second, the original materials were designed to provide an introduction to fundamental property principles as a foundation for more advanced courses in upper LLB curriculum, such as real estate law, succession law, commercial law, family law, environmental law, Aboriginal law, and others. In the published casebook, I have provided additional references, problems, and suggestions for further research that may be useful for instructors and students who want to pursue particular areas of interest. Third, the original materials deliberately provided some movement from introductory to more sophisticated analyses, with later chapters being somewhat more sophisticated than earlier ones, thereby giving students a sense of their own progression with respect to the development of their conceptual understanding and analytical skills within the first year program as a whole.

The origins and inspirations for this casebook reflect my experiences of teaching a first-year course in property law over a number of years in different law schools in Canada and Australia. In publishing this casebook, we have retained the original structure and organization of my course materials for the first-year property law course. I have benefited from the suggestions of Professor Flanagan, who has used my materials for his teaching for several years, and from a number of other property law teachers across Canada who have assisted me in "re-visioning" the materials that represent the core of this casebook. In deciding to publish these materials, I wanted to build on the organization and themes of the original materials, and to introduce additional notes and problems to assist student understanding of the principles in context. The exercises in Chapter 3, for example, are based on questions that Professor Flanagan and I developed together for our teaching in order to make the legal principles—and informed critique of them—more accessible to students. In preparing the work for publication, I also wanted to provide interested students and teachers with ideas about other sources and approaches that could broaden and deepen ideas about property analysis from a critical perspective.

The preparation of my property materials for publication has been a rewarding, even joyful, research and writing task. I take responsibility for all of Chapters 1, 2, 6, 7, and 8. Professor Flanagan prepared an early draft of Chapter 5, but I take responsibility for this chapter in its published form. Although my original materials focused on property law in Ontario, I have been delighted to be able to include cases and references to property law in the atlantic provinces, my place of origin. I have also tried to provide some references to property law in the western provinces, where the Torrens registration system is in place, and I hope that the casebook, perhaps with some supplementary materials, will be useful in these provinces as well. Thus, although this casebook has not been designed to be a national casebook on the law of property, I hope that it can be used successfully in many common law provinces.

As will be apparent, Chapters 1, 2, 5, 6, 7, and 8 have been arranged to focus on a series of major cases or problems in the law of property, with a number of questions and comments relating to them. the original materials were designed for a full-year course with three hours of classroom time in each week for both semesters. However, the arrangement of the materials permits instructors to choose specific topics, and to focus on all or part of the commentary relating to the cases and problems. In Chapter 1, for example, there are three interrelated case studies about the meaning of property—*Victoria Park*; *Harrison v. Carswell* and its subsequent development; and *Moore v. Regents of the University of California*. While the three case studies are designed to build on each other, they could be used individually to present particular principles of property law and to provide critical perspectives on them. In addition, while the overall organization of these materials reflects my objectives for a first-year property course, I hope that instructors with differing objectives can use the casebook successfully. The table of cases has been designed to assist those who may wish to use the casebook creatively for their own purposes.

No teaching materials are produced without relying on work that has gone before. I acknowledge gratefully the excellent efforts of other teachers and scholars of property law and the insights reflected in their teaching materials, law review articles, case commentaries, and monographs. In particular, I acknowledge with thanks the inspiration of texts and teaching materials in Canada, the United Kingdom, the United States, and Australia: Bruce Ziff, *Principles of Property Law*; W.B. Rayner and A.H. Oosterhof, *Anger and Honsberger Law of Real Property*; D. Mendes da Costa, R. Balfour, and E. Gillese, *Property Law: Cases, Text, and Materials*; A. Sinclair and M. McCallum, *Introduction to Real Property Law*; B. Laskin, *Cases and Materials on Property*; K. Gray and P. Symes, *Real Property and Real People: Principles of Land Law*; R. Chused, *Cases, Materials and Problems in Property*; and M. Neave, C. Rossiter, and M. Stone, *Sackville and Neave: Property Law, Cases and Materials*. I also warmly acknowledge the support and help of a number of property teachers and scholars in Canada and elsewhere: Brian Bucknall and Beverley Baines; Bruce Ziff, Kent McNeil, Chris Rossiter, Philip Girard, Ellen Zweibel, and Moe Litman; and all of those who have been involved in the (as yet unrealized) efforts to produce a national property casebook in Canada. I am grateful to my students in Australia and Canada whose questions spurred me to find ways to explain property principles in context, to a number of research assistants over several years whose help has been critical to the ongoing project, and to Tamara Barclay, Ned Djordjevic, and Naizam Kanji whose splendid research assistance is reflected in the published casebook. My chapters reflect the expert and often inspired assistance of librarians and staff of the Osgoode Hall Law School library, the support of the law school in funding research assistance for this project, word-processing talent and extraordinary patience on the part of Hazel Pollack at Osgoode, and the cheerful and unflappable editorial and other support at Emond Montgomery Publications and Words-Worth Communications.

I welcome comments and suggestions.

M.J.M.

Acknowledgments

A book of this nature borrows heavily from other published material. We have attempted to request permission from, and to acknowledge in the text, all sources of such material. We wish to make specific references here to the authors, publishers, journals, and institutions that have generously given permission to reproduce in this text works already in print. If we have inadvertently overlooked an acknowledgment or failed to secure a permission, we offer our sincere apologies and undertake to rectify the omission in the next edition.

American Society of Comparative Law   Slattery, Brian. "The Hidden Constitution: Aboriginal Rights in Canada" (1984) 32 Am J Comp L 361.

Brian Bucknall   Bucknall, Brian. "Two Roads Diverged: Recent Decisions on Possessory Title" (1984) 22 Osgoode Hall LJ 375. Reprinted with permission.

Canadian Bar Association   Arthurs, H. "Note" (1965) 43 Can Bar Rev 357.

Canadian Bar Assocation   McClean, AJ. "Severance of Joint Tenancies" (1979) 57 Can Bar Rev 1.

Chicago Law Review   Rose, Carol. "Possession as the Origin of Property" (1985) 52 U Chicago L Rev 73.

Copibec   Katz, Larissa. "The Moral Paradox of Adverse Possession: Sovereignty and Revolution in Property Law" (2010) 55 McGill LJ 47. Reproduced by permission of Copibec.

Emond Montgomery Publications Limited   Girard, Philip. "History and Development of Equity" in Faye Woodman & Mark R Gillen, eds, *The Law of Trusts: A Contextual Approach*, 2d ed (Toronto: Emond Montgomery, 2008). Reprinted by permission.

Irwin Law   Phillips, J & J Martin. "Manitoba Fisheries v The Queen: The Origins of Canada's De Facto Expropriation Doctrine" in Tucker, Muir & Ziff, eds, *Canadian Property Law Stories* (Toronto: Osgoode Society for Canadian Legal History and Irwin Law, 2012) 259.

Irwin Law   Tucker, Eric. "The Malling of Property Law?" in E Tucker, J Muir & B Ziff, eds, *Property on Trial* (Toronto: Irwin Law for the Osgoode Society for Canadian Legal History, 2012) 303.

LexisNexis   McCallum, Margaret E & Alan M Sinclair. *An Introduction to Real Property Law*, 6th ed (Toronto: LexisNexis, 2012). Copyright © 2012 Matthew Bender & Company, Inc, a part of LexisNexis. All rights reserved.

Oxford University Press   Gray, Kevin & Susan Francis Gray. *Elements of Land Law*, 5th ed (Oxford: Oxford University Press, 2009).

Oxford University Press   McHugh, PG. *Aboriginal Title: The Modern Jurisprudence of Tribal Land Rights* (Oxford: Oxford University Press, 2011).

J Rick Ponting   Little Bear, Leroy. "Aboriginal Rights and the Canadian 'Grundnorm'?" in J Rick Ponting, ed, *Arduous Journey: Canadian Indians and Decolonization* (Toronto: McClelland & Stewart, 1986).

Queen's Printer for Ontario   Ontario. *Report on Covenants Affecting Freehold Land* (Toronto: Ontario Ministry of the Attorney General, 1989). © Queen's Printer for Ontario, 1989.

Queen's Printer for Ontario   Ontario. *Task Force on the Law Concerning Trespass to Publicly Used Property as It Affects Youth and Minorities*, Raj Anand, Chair (Toronto: Ontario Ministry of the Attorney General, 1987). © Queen's Printer for Ontario, 1987.

Saskatchewan Law Review   McNeil, Kent. "Aboriginal Title and the Supreme Court: What's Happening?" (2006) 69 Sask L Rev 281.

Thompson Reuters Canada Limited   Bucknall, Brian. "Teis v Ancaster: Knowledge, the Lack of Knowledge and the Running of a Possessory Title Period" (February 1998) 13 RPR (3d) 68. Reproduced by permission of Carswell, a division of Thomson Reuters Canada Limited.

Thompson Reuters Canada Limited   Duggan, Anthony. "In the Wake of the Bingo Queen: Are Licences Property?" (2008-9) 47 Can Bus LJ 225. Reproduced by permission of Can Bus LJ & Canada Law Book, a division of Thomson Reuters Canada Limited.

Mary Ellen Turpel   Turpel, Mary Ellen. "Home/Land" (1991) 10 Can J Fam L 17.

University of British Columbia Law Review   Jackson, Michael. "The Articulation of Native Rights in Canadian Law" (1984) 18 UBC L Rev 255. Reprinted by permission.

University of Saskatchewan. Native Law Centre.   Montour, M. "Iroquois Women's Rights with Respect to Matrimonial Property on Indian Reserves" (1987) 4 Canadian NL Rep 1.

University of Toronto Faculty of Law Review   Johnston, Darlene. "The Quest of the Six-Nations Confederacy for Self-Determination" (1986) 44 UT Fac L Rev 1.

University of Toronto Press   McCallum, Margaret E. "The Sacred Rights of Property: Title, Entitlement, and the Land Question in Nineteenth-Century Prince Edward Island" in G Blaine Baker & Jim Phillips, eds, *Essays in the History of Canadian Law, vol VIII: In Honour of RCB Risk* (Toronto: University of Toronto Press for the Osgoode Society for Canadian Legal History, 1998).

Vancouver Bar Association   Lambert, Douglas. "The Tsilhqot'in Case" (2012) 70 Advocate 819.

The Vanier Institute of the Family   Ambert, Anne-Marie. *Divorce: Facts, Causes and Consequences*, 3d ed (Ottawa: Vanier Institute of the Family, 2009).

Wiley, American Bar Foundation   Harris, Douglas. "Condominium and the City: The Rise of Property in Vancouver" (2011) 36:3 Law & Soc Inquiry 694.

York University   McNeil, Kent. *Defining Aboriginal Title in the 90s: Has the Supreme Court Finally Got It Right?* (Toronto: York University, Robarts Centre for Canadian Studies, 1998).

Table of Contents

Detailed Table of Contents

Table of Cases

(Page numbers in boldface type indicate that the text of the case or a significant extract therefrom is reproduced in this volume.)

CHAPTER ONE

Concepts of Property in Law

I. INTRODUCTION: PROPERTY AS "RELATIONSHIP," NOT "THING"

Most people, including lawyers, define property as something that is owned by someone—for example, a book, a car, a house, or a block of land. Although this definition is acceptable in day-to-day social interactions, we need to recharacterize it for the purposes of examining property in law. By contrast with day-to-day usage, the legal concept of property concerns

Definition

the network of legal relationships prevailing between individuals in respect of things ... . Seen in this way, "property" comprises bundles of mutual rights and obligations between "subjects" in respect of certain "objects," and the study of the law of property becomes an inquiry into a variety of socially defined relationships and morally conditioned obligations.

(KJ Gray & PD Symes, *Real Property and Real People* (London: Butterworths, 1981) [Gray & Symes] at 8-9.)

This idea of property as relationship is well illustrated in Jeremy Waldron's description of Susan and her motor car, a Porsche: see Jeremy Waldron, *The Right to Private Property* (Oxford: Clarendon Press, 1988) at 26ff. As Waldron explained, our day-to-day description is that "Susan owns that Porsche." However, this description must be redefined for legal purposes so as to define the relationship between Susan and other people (the *subjects* of the legal relationship) and the Porsche (the *object* of the legal relationship):

> With regard to Susan's Porsche, there are all sorts of legal relations between Susan and other people ... . Susan has a legal liberty to use it in certain ways [but] she is not at liberty ... to drive it at all without a licence from the authorities ... . She has what Hohfeld called a "claim-right" against everyone else (her neighbours, her friends, the local car thief, everyone in the community) that they should not use her Porsche without her permission. But Susan also owes certain duties to other people in relation to her vehicle ... . She is liable to pay damages if it rolls into her neighbour's fence. These rights, liberties and duties are the basic stuff of ownership (at 27).

As Waldron further explained, Susan may alter these legal relationships by her dealings with the Porsche—by selling it, giving it away, bequeathing it in her will at the time of her death, or lending it to a friend for the day. If she fails to pay debts, it is possible that the car may be seized in satisfaction of her debts. As a result, the legal definition of Susan's relationship to the Porsche is that she has a "bundle of rights" that constitute a proprietary interest *in* the Porsche. (WN Hohfeld's analysis, referred to by Waldron, is more fully explained in his article "Some Fundamental Legal Conceptions as Applied in Judicial Reasoning" (1913) 23 Yale LJ 16.)

A. Property as Relationship: Implications

The concept of property as a relationship among people in respect of things is both complex and dynamic. It is complex because there are many different ways to assemble the "bundle of rights" in different contexts, especially where the *objects* of property differ. For example, Waldron asserted (at 31) that ownership of a Porsche is quite different from ownership of a piece of agricultural land, and different again from ownership of intangible ideas, like copyright. In this context, assertions that "X owns the car," "Y owns the land," and "Z owns the copyright" are not helpful legal statements because they cannot convey "any common content for these quite different bundles."

In addition to being complex, the concept of property as a relationship among people in respect of things is dynamic. CB Macpherson, for example, explained the dynamic quality of property as follows:

> The meaning of property is not constant. The actual institution, and the way people see it, and hence the meaning they give to the word, all change over time ... . The changes are related to

changes in the purposes which society or the dominant classes in society expect the institution of property to serve.

(CB Macpherson, "The Meaning of Property" in CB Macpherson, ed, *Property: Mainstream and Critical Positions* (Toronto: University of Toronto Press, 1978) [Macpherson] at 1.)

Macpherson also described (at 7) how the concept of property as "relationship" was well recognized in day-to-day language until the late 17th century. As the economy changed from feudalism to capitalism, the idea of property also changed, because "as rights in land became more absolute, and parcels of land became more freely marketable commodities, it became natural to think of the land itself as the property." According to Macpherson, current legal arrangements about property suggest that it is once again regarded as a "right," not a "thing," an approach that is consistent with the basic notion of property as a *relationship among people in respect of objects*.

B. Subjects and Objects of Property Relationships

The dynamic nature of both subjects and objects of property interests was also explored by Gray & Symes. They noted that some persons in the past, including serfs and married women, were excluded by law from holding—that is, being *subjects* of—property interests; and children under the age of 18 continue to be precluded from exercising certain kinds of property rights. In this context, Gray & Symes asserted (at 10) that the definition of who can be the "subject" of property interests has "an important political significance precisely because the delineation of potential right-holders fundamentally affects both the balance of power and the distribution of goods within a society." In the 21st century, few classes of people are *explicitly* precluded from holding interests in property. Yet the legal right to become the "subject" of a property interest has not resulted in equality among all persons in relation to property interests. In this way, there is an important relationship between property law and issues of social and economic inequality. For an examination of these issues in another historical period, see Jennifer Nedelsky, "Law, Boundaries and the Bounded Self" in Richard Chused, ed, *A Property Anthology* (Cincinnati, OH: Anderson, 1993) 28.

In addition to changing subjects of property, there is a dynamic quality about the objects of proprietary interests. For example, both slaves and married women were once considered objects of property relationships, but such arrangements are no longer legally recognized. By contrast, land has always been regarded as an object of property, although it may have less value now, by contrast with other objects of property, than in some former times. In the 21st century, there are also forms of "new property" that are often claimed as objects of property—professional licences, pensions, and even the right to a job or security of housing. As Gray & Symes pointed out (at 11):

> The things which are today of real value to the man [*sic*] in the street are assets like his job, his pension, and the right to undisturbed possession of his home. On the fringes of these new categories of property lie certain less well defined rights such as the right to education, the right to health and the right to a wholesome environment.

A classic formulation of these "new property" interests is found in Charles Reich, "The New Property" (1964) 73 Yale LJ 733. See also Mary Ann Glendon, *The New Family and the New*

Property (Toronto: Butterworths, 1981). We explore these issues more fully later in this and subsequent chapters.

C. Property Relationships in Context

The idea of property is often controversial. Philosophers and political economists have debated its merits and its justifications for a long time, as is evident in the differing points of view in the essays collected in Macpherson. In addition, these issues are reviewed in Carol Rose, *Property and Persuasion: Essays on the History, Theory, and Rhetoric of Ownership* (Boulder, CO: Westview Press, 1994) [Rose].

The law of property is particularly controversial in the context of 21st-century "new property" claims, which reflect desires to overcome insecurity or dependency in the lives of many people. Perhaps surprisingly, the law of property is also "old" law, much of it reflecting principles developed centuries ago in very different political, social, and economic contexts. In this way, property law provides a dual challenge for students: it is necessary to understand traditional property law principles in order to work with them effectively and, at the same time, it is critical to assess traditional property law principles in the larger context of modern life and its challenges. As Gray & Symes stated succinctly (at 9): "To confine property law to its mechanical aspects and to ignore the inevitable infusion of extra-legal factors, is to impoverish legal study by forcing it into a moral and social vacuum." Thus, in working with these materials, you need to become proficient in the use of traditional principles of property law and, at the same time, to understand how these principles work now in a different social, economic, and political context.

DISCUSSION NOTES

i. Differing Conceptions of Property

In considering the broader social, economic, and political context in relation to property law, it is important to note that there are differing conceptions of property and the meaning of "ownership." For some groups—Aboriginal peoples; Blacks, whose racial history meant that they were excluded from being subjects of property relationships; and women—some of these differing conceptions have been recognized, at least to some extent. For example, Aboriginal peoples developed a unique set of laws and customs concerning property interests; African Canadians were sometimes prohibited by law from holding property interests; and women sometimes "lost" their property rights upon marriage. For an introduction to the issues, see Leroy Little Bear, "Aboriginal Rights and the Canadian 'Grundnorm'" in J Rick Ponting, *Arduous Journey: Canadian Indians and Decolonization* (Toronto: McClelland & Stewart, 1986) at 243; Patricia Williams, "On Being an Object of Property" in Williams, *The Alchemy of Race and Rights* (Cambridge, MA: Harvard University Press, 1991) at 216; and Floyd Rudmin, "Gender Differences in the Semantics of Ownership: A Quantitative Phenomenological Survey Study" (1994) 15:3 Journal of Economic Psychology 487.

ii. Philosophical Perspectives About Property

The law of property may also reflect philosophical perspectives about the nature or purposes of property. In her introduction to *Property and Persuasion* at 1-7, Carol Rose briefly described some of these differing philosophical perspectives, and suggested a need to reconceptualize ideas of property to focus on "norms and narratives" and the links between them. As she explained (at 5-6):

> Community norms—the common beliefs, understandings, and culture that hold property regimes together—raise the issue of persuasion. Where do people get those understandings about property anyway, and what gets them over that peculiar gap between property-as-thing and property-as-relationship? Just as important, what persuades people to ease up on self-interest or convinces them to pay attention to the norms that let them manage property regimes as a whole, and in so doing become more prosperous? How do people *change* norms to accommodate different property arrangements that might enhance their well-being?

Rose's reflections emphasize the idea of property as a social concept, and we explore these and other ideas about property in this book. For an overview of different philosophical approaches to property, see also Bruce Ziff, *Principles of Property Law*, 5th ed (Scarborough, ON: Carswell, 2010) [Ziff] at ch 1.

iii. Property Law: Legal Principles and Commentaries

The cases presented in this and later chapters present basic legal principles about the law of property. However, because one of the important goals of this book is to examine principles in context, discussion notes provide information about other cases that have approached the same legal issues from different perspectives, as well as academic and other comments about the implications of legal decisions. Relationships between cases that define legal principles and these broader contextual materials are often complex, particularly because legal principles must always be applied to a variety of different factual situations. As a result, different contexts may influence the way that legal principles are applied.

In the introductory comments to an American casebook on property law, Joseph Singer explained how lawyers use legal principles, including gaps, conflicts, and ambiguities in these principles, "to define the law in ways that benefit their clients." As he noted, an examination of cases may reveal:

a. a rule of law that clearly defines the parties' respective rights;
b. no rule of law directly on point (a "gap");
c. a rule of law that does not clearly answer the question (an "ambiguity"); or
d. two or more rules of law that arguably govern the dispute (a "conflict").

In considering these possibilities, Singer suggested that it is important for students to consider

> what arguments the parties might have given to justify adopting their proposed rules, as well as what arguments they could have given against the rule proposed by the other side. These arguments should include considerations about the *fairness* of the proposed rules to the parties: which rule better protects individual *rights*? You should also consider the *social consequences* of the competing rules: which rule better promotes the *general welfare*?

(JW Singer, "How to Brief a Case and Prepare for Class" in Singer, *Property Law: Rules, Policies, and Practices*, 2d ed (New York: Aspen Law & Business, 1997) at liv.)

Thus, in relation to property law, it is important to focus on the analytical legal reasoning of the cases and the interpretation of statutes, but also to take account of the commentaries about these decisions to assess the validity and utility of legal principles in different contexts and in relation to contemporary concerns in Canada.

II. DEFINING "PROPERTY" IN CONTEXT

A. Historical Claims and Their Contemporary Themes: Victoria Park Racing and Recreation Grounds Co Ltd v Taylor

Although *Victoria Park* (1937), 58 CLR 479 was decided in the 1930s in Australia, it is a good example of the importance of *context* in the definition of "property." The case was litigated prior to the evolution of the modern communications industry, and likely provided a catalyst for the enactment of broadcasting legislation. In this way, it represents a good example of the *historical* context of 20th-century property claims.

In "Property in Thin Air" (1991) 50 Cambridge LJ 252 at 264, Kevin Gray described *Victoria Park* as "pivotal" for understanding property law:

> The case embodies one of the last great problems of property law and reverberates with a significance which has outlived its particular facts. With justification it may be said that the concept of property cannot be entirely satisfactorily explained without accounting, in some way or other, for the ruling in *Victoria Park Racing*.

The case concerned a suit for an injunction by the plaintiff, who owned the Victoria Park racecourse in Australia. The plaintiff sought the injunction against three defendants: Mr. Taylor, who owned land adjoining the racecourse and who had built a raised wooden platform so that one could see the racecourse and the notice boards with information about the races; Mr. Angles, who stood on the platform and commented on the races by telephone, announcing the winner of each race; and the Commonwealth Broadcasting Corporation, which broadcast the commentaries of Mr. Angles. Gray described the impact of the defendants' activities on the plaintiff's business as follows:

> The instant popularity of these transmissions stimulated an illicit off-course betting industry in Sydney, and there was unchallenged evidence that punters who would otherwise have attended the race meetings in person now preferred to follow those proceedings either from the comfort of their own homes or, even better, from their local hostelry. The plaintiff, perturbed by the catastrophic loss of business, sued for an injunction (at 265).

In the Supreme Court of New South Wales, Nicholas J refused the plaintiff's request for an injunction and this decision was then appealed to the High Court of Australia. Three justices (Latham CJ and Dixon and McTiernan JJ) dismissed the appeal, while two others (Rich and Evatt JJ) dissented.

According to Latham CJ, "Any person is entitled to look over the plaintiff's fences and to see what goes on in the plaintiff's land. If the plaintiff desires to prevent this, the plaintiff can erect a higher fence." Thus the majority concluded that there was no actionable nuisance claim in this situation. In addition, the judge indicated that it was not possible to find "property in a spectacle." The other majority judges concurred with this reasoning, and also con-cluded that it was preferable for the legislature, rather than the courts, to define rights and obligations in this new context of broadcasting. By contrast, the two dissenting judges focused on the need for flexibility in the common law, citing Lord MacMillan's words in *Donoghue v Stevenson* that "[t]he categories of nuisance are not closed." Rich J thus con-cluded that there were legal limits to the right to overlook a neighbour's land, and that the limitation required an "attempt to reconcile the right of free prospect from one piece of land with the right of profitable enjoyment of another." And, as Evatt J indicated, the absence of precedent for such a case was understandable because "simultaneous broadcasting or tele-vision [was] quite new."

DISCUSSION NOTES

i. Different Approaches to the Legal Category of "Nuisance"

As *Victoria Park* illustrates, a plaintiff's claim must typically fall within a defined legal category in order to succeed. In this case, the plaintiff wanted to establish the tort of nuisance—that is, interference with the plaintiff's "use and enjoyment" of his land. It seems, however, that the claim was unprecedented and that a majority of the judges did not want to overstep their role in relation to the law-making function of the legislature. To what extent should judges refrain from making decisions in novel contexts when there is no existing legal precedent? For some comments on this argument in a modern context, see Martha Minow, "Judging In-side Out" (1990) 61 Colo L Rev 795.

A number of legal scholars have suggested that common law principles may be applied by judges in ways that reflect prevailing political and economic ideas. In relation to the law of nuisance in the United States, for example, Morton Horowitz examined two interpreta-tions of 18th-century legal principles concerning the use of property. He described one as "an explicitly antidevelopmental theory" that limited property owners to what courts re-garded as the "natural" (mainly agricultural) use of land, a principle reflected in the maxim "*sic utere tuo*" in nuisance law. In addition, courts also developed a theory of property rights based on "priority of development"—that is, that someone with a prior developmental right (who had "developed" the land for industrial purposes) could arrest a future conflicting use on the part of an adjoining owner. By the 19th century, the potential for conflict between these principles began to surface and, in general, priority of development became "the dom-inant doctrine of property law in the early stages of American growth." Rejecting a Machiavel-lian explanation for this choice, however, Horowitz suggested that the judges were

> simply guided by the conception of efficiency prevailing at the moment. Practical men, they may never have stopped to reflect on the changes they were bringing about, nor on the vast differ-ences between their own assumptions and those of their predecessors.

(M Horowitz, *The Transformation of American Law, 1780-1860* (Cambridge, MA: Harvard Uni-versity Press, 1977) at 34.)

Assuming that legal principles may sometimes reflect prevailing political and economic ideas, what ideas might influence legal principles about land use in the 21st century? In considering this question, Eric Freyfogle suggested that the principle that landowners should not engage in uses that are harmful remains robust in American law:

Long embedded in American property law has been the understanding that landowners do not and should not have the right to engage in land uses that are harmful ... . Distilled to its essence, the current debate centers mostly on this issue of harm—what land uses are harmful, and when can they be banned in the name of community well-being ... ?

As a mode of understanding the human predicament, individualism has yielded many benefits, but its benefits have come with large and mounting costs, including costs to the land. Older rules of morality and even simple etiquette arose because a person was understood primarily in social or communal terms. But in these post-modern days, what is the community but a collection of parts? How do we best respect people today? We let them do what they want. How do we promote community today? We let people act out their own desires, the more publicly the better (or so it seems), and we assume naively that some societal good will be served thereby.

(Eric T Freyfogle, "The Construction of Ownership" (1996) 1 U Ill L Rev 173 [Freyfogle] at 181 and 183.)

To what extent do you think that these views are applicable with respect to the use of land in Canada? Assuming a need to rise above current political and economic ideas in the formulation of legal principles, how can this goal be achieved, if at all, in case-by-case decision making by courts? Is it appropriate to use different kinds of processes, different kinds of evidence, the participation of intervenors, or other measures? What are the consequences for courts and communities?

ii. Private Property, Common Property, and State Property

In *Victoria Park*, Latham CJ rejected the plaintiff's argument that, by the expenditure of money, he had created a spectacle that constituted "quasi-property." Using the analysis of property as a relationship among persons (subjects) in respect of things (objects), is it possible to find that there is property in a spectacle? Why or why not? How important was it that the property in question was intangible rather than tangible? What was the practical impact of the court's conclusion that the plaintiff's actions in this case did not create property?

According to Gray, *Victoria Park* offers "a rare opportunity to learn something of the tacit rules which govern the propertisation of resources." As he explained, if something is not an object of private property, then it must be "common property," and thus available to all. By contrast, if something is private property, the "owner" may exclude others from its enjoyment. By concluding that the plaintiff's spectacle was not his private property, the court in *Victoria Park* left the plaintiff without legal protection—in this way, the racecourse appeared to become common property. See Gray, "Property in Thin Air" (1991) 50 Cambridge LJ 252 at 268ff.

CB Macpherson also analyzed the distinction between private property and common property. According to him, private property means that there is an individual (or a corporate entity) that is the subject of the property relationship. By contrast, the concept of common property creates an entitlement for individuals, enforced by the state, so that all individuals are subjects of the property interest and no one is excluded. For Macpherson, common property should be available to be enjoyed only by natural persons, not by corporations or the state: see CB Macpherson, "The Meaning of Property" in Macpherson 1 at 4ff.

Using Macpherson's categories, how should we characterize the east coast fishery in Canada, a public park at the edge of Georgian Bay, or the rail lines abandoned by VIA Rail? In thinking about these issues, consider Wallace Clement's comment some years ago about the east coast fishery:

> As far as rights of access to fish, the sea has been transformed from common to private property for the most part. The state excludes some from the use or benefit of the products of the sea, not simply regulating its use (as can be the case with common property). The licences themselves, which are "tickets" to the amount of fish which may be gathered, the species, time and location, take on a value of their own. They become private property—the state grants the rights, individuals (or corporations) have the rights, and in the case of some fishing rights, these can be sold as private property. An important illustration of the state creating private property out of common property occurred in the initial stages of colonization in North America when the bulk of the land was alienated from the native people and turned into private property, often given over to corporations such as the Hudson's Bay Company.

(W Clement, *Class, Power, and Property: Essays on Canadian Society* (Toronto: Methuen, 1983) at 215.) See also A Bartholomew & S Boyd, "Toward a Political Economy of Law" in W Clement and G Williams, eds, *The New Canadian Political Economy* (Kingston, ON: McGill-Queen's University Press, 1989) at 212; and Michael Harris, *Lament for an Ocean* (Toronto: McClelland & Stewart, 1998). For an account of the history of the "commons" in England, see J Neeson, *Commoners: Common Right, Enclosure, and Social Change in England 1700-1820* (New York: Cambridge University Press, 1993).

Carol Rose also examined the classic economic argument that "the whole world of valuable things is best managed when divided among private property owners." In the absence of such a private property regime, the economic result is "the tragedy of the commons." From this perspective, "public property is an oxymoron: things left open to the public are not property at all but rather its antithesis": C Rose, "The Comedy of the Commons: Custom, Commerce, and Inherently Public Property" in Rose 105 at 106.

By contrast with this analysis, Rose examined the ways in which public access to common property—for example, roads and waterways—increased the value of the common property economically by fostering commerce. She also noted how common property in recreational parks was promoted in the 19th century by Frederick Law Olmsted as "a socializing influence and an education in democratic values." In *Higginson v Treasury*, 99 NE 523 (MA Sup Jud Ct 1912), the court asserted that parks are a public good because they "civilize" people living in urban congestion. (A good account of the history of Olmsted's views is found in Geoffrey Blodgett, "Frederick Law Olmsted: Landscape Architecture as Conservative Reform" (1976) 62 J Am History 869.) In the 21st century, parks are often owned by governments, so that they represent a third category of property—state property. According to CB Macpherson, state property is similar to private property because the state may grant or withhold access to it. How then does "state property" differ from "common property"?

According to Rose (at 110-12) different categories of private property rights and property are held (and managed) by government. In addition, Rose asserted that both English and American law historically recognized "public property." This category included government-held property and, in addition, "property collectively 'owned' by society at large, with claims independent of and indeed superior to the claims of any purported governmental manager":

> Thus it appears that older public property doctrine vested some form of property rights in the *un*organized public. But what could it mean for the unorganized public to have "rights" in any

property at all? How could its members possibly assert their rights except through a governmental body? And even if they could do so, how could the unorganized public be thought the best property manager, or even a manager at all … ? Nevertheless, strange though it seems, precisely this unorganized version of the "public" is strongly suggested in some of the earlier public property doctrine—as it is in some modern law as well.

For other arguments about the nature of property, including common property, see Bernard Rudden, "Things as Thing and Things as Wealth" (1994) 14 Oxford J Legal Stud 81; and Michael Robertson, "Reconceiving Private Property" (1997) 24:4 JL & Soc'y 465.

iii. The Right to Privacy

Another argument presented unsuccessfully by the plaintiff in *Victoria Park* was that the defendants' actions had interfered with a right of privacy on the part of the plaintiff. In his dissenting judgment, Evatt J pointed to cases that had decided that "systematic watching" on the part of trade union activists who were picketing an employer (without trespassing on the employer's property) constituted nuisance (*Ward Locke & Co (Ltd) v Operative Printers' Assistants' Society* (1906), 22 TLR 327 (CA)). For a classic argument about the need for a tort of invasion of privacy in the American common law, see Warren & Brandeis, "The Right to Privacy" (1890) 4 Harv L Rev 193.

iv. The Role of Precedent

All these arguments—the principles of nuisance, whether or not the spectacle was property, and the right to privacy—were considered by the justices in *Victoria Park* in relation to the common law doctrine of precedent. The role of precedent is fundamental to judicial reasoning in the common law and is the subject of much debate in practice, even though the principle is relatively straightforward—that is, like cases should be treated alike in subsequent decisions. In *Victoria Park*, however, Latham CJ concluded that there was no precedent applicable to the facts. By contrast, the dissenting judgment of Rich J stated clearly that "[i]t does not follow that because no precedent can be found a principle does not exist to support the plaintiff's right," and proceeded to provide a remedy to the plaintiff.

These two approaches demonstrate diametrically opposite approaches to judicial decision making. When there is no applicable precedent, some judges conclude that there is no legal remedy available, while others decide that the case must be decided on the basis of general principles, such as fairness or equity. Similarly, although judges are required to apply previous decisions as precedents, they may distinguish them (for a variety of reasons) and "make new law." According to one Australian academic, while the use of precedents maintains legal ideals of certainty, stability, uniformity, and order, legal analysis may also develop new principles in new contexts: see Julius Stone, *Legal System and Lawyers' Reasonings* (Stanford, CA: Stanford University Press, 1964) at 231; and Stone, *Precedent and Law: Dynamics of Common Law Growth* (Sydney: Butterworths, 1985).

These issues have been considered by many other legal scholars. In the United States, for example, Margaret Jane Radin considered similar arguments about precedent in relation to "facts," concluding that there is great flexibility in the process of deciding what are "the facts" of a case:

Many beginning law students assume that there is a world of hard facts out there waiting to be observed. Especially for the naive legal positivist, hard facts are needed to plug into the formalist equation: Rules + Facts = Decision. In the formalist equation, both rules and facts must be found objects, not malleable creations dependent upon who is observing them and the process of observation. …

Perception [By contrast, lawyers] need to know that perception is an active process, always dependent upon the person doing the perceiving and the social construction of the context in which she [*sic*] perceives. Perception depends upon [pre]conception. We tend to see what will make sense to us in light of our conceptions and in light of what we expect to see. Perception can also depend upon educational and class background, one's job or profession, and much else.

(Margaret Jane Radin, "'After the Final No There Comes a Yes': A Law Teacher's Report" (1990) 2 Yale JL & Human 252 at 259.) See also Peter Gabel, "Reification in Legal Reasoning" in James Boyle, ed, *Critical Legal Studies* (New York: New York University Press, 1994).

v. "Frame Shifting": Explaining Different Approaches?

Some scholars have approached these issues about differing approaches to judicial decision making with suggestions for first-year law students who have noticed that "when two judges write a majority and a dissent, … although both have looked at the same factual situation and the same progression of inquiry or line of precedent, each has reached a different conclusion": see Jennifer Jaff, "Frame-Shifting: An Empowering Methodology for Teaching and Learning Legal Reasoning" (1986) 36 J Legal Educ 249 at 251.

According to Jaff, this result occurs because judges "shift" their frame of reference from broad to narrow, or from narrow to broad, to construct rationales that justify differing results. Thus, for example, in a criminal law context, one judge may determine the issue of voluntariness of a confession by focusing on the state of mind of the accused at the moment in question, while another will assess the issue of voluntariness by looking at the broader context of the accused's sociological condition and the extent to which it may affect the accused's ability to take action voluntarily. According to Jaff (at 262), "frame shifting" provides a way of "seeing" different approaches to legal reasoning.

Jaff also focused (at 265ff) on psychological research about "male" and "female" perspectives on ethics undertaken by Carol Gilligan. Gilligan assessed the responses to an ethical issue posed to Amy and Jake, two 11-year-olds; the issue involved whether a man (Heinz) should steal a drug (because he could not afford it) in order to save his wife's life. For Jake, the issue was straightforward—life is more important than property, so Heinz should steal the drug. By contrast, Amy's response was much less definitive and suggested a need for Heinz to talk to the druggist and explain the situation. As Jaff reported in relation to this research:

Jake's reasoning sounds not unlike the weighing of interests that courts engage in to determine the nature and extent of procedural due process. Both analyses involve a balancing of the values of property and life.

Amy, on the other hand, in deciding that Heinz should not steal the drug, "considers neither property nor law but rather the effect that theft could have on the relationship between Heinz and his wife," [including the possibility that Heinz might go to jail and be unable to care for his wife].

Amy sees "a world comprised of relationships rather than of people standing alone, a world that coheres through human connection rather than through systems of rules." It remains, then, to translate this focus into legal analysis.

See Carol Gilligan, *In a Different Voice: Psychological Theory and Women's Development* (Cambridge, MA: Harvard University Press, 1982). Although Gilligan's work has been criticized by psychologists, especially for its highly gendered analysis of ethical reasoning, it has been influential in legal literature about dispute resolution—for example, see Carrie Menkel-Meadow, "Portia in a Different Voice: Speculations on a Woman's Lawyering Process" (1985) 1 Berkeley Women's LJ 39, and Shelley Wright, "Property, Information, and the Ethics of Communication" (1994) 9 IPJ 47.

vi. Property Claims and Courts Versus Legislatures: INS v AP

In the *Victoria Park* case, decided in Australia in 1937, Dixon J referred to a decision of the US Supreme Court in 1918 that raised similar issues. (Note that a US decision would be considered "persuasive," not "binding," in terms of precedent because it is from another jurisdiction.) In *International News Service v Associated Press*, 248 US 215 (1918), the plaintiff Associated Press (AP) sought an injunction to restrain certain activities on the part of its competitor in the news-gathering business, International News Service (INS). The case was complicated and controversial in the context of news reports during the First World War, especially because, in the absence of radio and television, people relied on newspapers almost exclusively for information. The owner of AP, Melville Stone, wished to establish the concept of "property in news," and sued in part to prevent INS's practice of "copying" news from early editions of AP newspapers on the eastern seaboard of the United States and then (taking advantage of the difference in time zones) selling these reports to INS customers on the west coast.

In general, the Supreme Court agreed to enjoin INS to some extent in relation to its practices, although there was no agreement that there was "property in the news," even though labour and money had been expended to create it. Brandeis J dissented (and Dixon in *Victoria Park* relied on his decision). His comments (at 250) about the nature of property, as well as the role of courts in defining new kinds of property interests, remain relevant today.

An essential element of individual property is the legal right to exclude others from enjoying it. If the property is private, the right of exclusion may be absolute; if the property is affected with a public interest, the right of exclusion is qualified. But the fact that a product of the mind has cost its producer money and labor, and has a value for which others are willing to pay, is not sufficient to ensure to it this legal attribute of property. The general rule of law is, that the noblest of human productions—knowledge, truths ascertained, conceptions, and ideas—become, after voluntary communication to others, free as the air to common use. Upon these incorporeal productions the attribute of property is continued after such communication only in certain classes of cases where public policy has seemed to demand it. These exceptions are confined to productions which, in some degree, involve creation, invention, or discovery. But by no means all such are endowed with this attribute of property. The creations which are recognized as property by the common law are literary, dramatic, musical, and other artistic creations; and these have also protection under the copyright statutes. The inventions and discoveries upon which this attribute of property is conferred only by statute, are the few comprised within the patent law. ...

The knowledge for which protection is sought in the case at bar is not of a kind upon which the law has heretofore conferred the attributes of property; nor is the manner of its acquisition or use nor the purpose to which it is applied, such as has heretofore been recognized as entitling a plaintiff to relief. ...

The rule for which the plaintiff contends would effect an important extension of property rights and a corresponding curtailment of the free use of knowledge and of ideas; and the facts of this case admonish us of the danger involved in recognizing such a property right in news.

Brandeis J also considered that the legislature was better suited to the task of finding an appropriate solution in this case, suggesting:

Legislators might conclude that it was impossible to put an end to the obvious injustice involved in such appropriation of news, without opening the door to other evils, greater than that sought to be remedied. ...

Or legislators dealing with the subject might conclude, that the right to news values should be protected to the extent of permitting recovery of damages for any unauthorized use, but that protection by injunction should be denied .... If a legislature concluded to recognize property in published news to the extent of permitting recovery at law, it might, with a view to making the remedy more certain and adequate, provide a fixed measure of damages, as in the case of copyright infringement. ...

Courts are ill-equipped to make the investigations which should precede a determination of the limitations which should be set upon any property right in news or of the circumstances under which news gathered by a private agency should be deemed affected with a public interest. Courts would be powerless to prescribe the detailed regulations essential to full enjoyment of the rights conferred or to introduce the machinery required for enforcement of such regulations. Considerations such as these should lead us to decline to establish a new rule of law in the effort to redress a newly-disclosed wrong, although the propriety of some remedy appears to be clear.

Do you agree with Brandeis J that it is more appropriate for legislatures to create new property, and that judges are not well-placed to consider such claims? What are the factors that were taken into account by Brandeis J in reaching his conclusion? How should courts balance the need for stability and certainty on the one hand with the need to do justice in appropriate cases on the other?

Broadcasting is a matter that is now generally regulated in Canada by legislation. See e.g. *Canadian Radio-Television and Telecommunications Commission Act*, RSC 1985, c C-22; *Broadcasting Act*, SC 1991, c 11; and *Telecommunications Act*, SC 1993, c 38. Does the existence of legislation show that Dixon and Brandeis were right to conclude that the courts should not provide a remedy in *Victoria Park* and in *INS v AP*? As a practical matter, if a litigant applies to a court for a remedy for which there is no existing precedent and is successful, who should pay the costs of the application?

For other assessments of these issues, see Richard Chused, *Cases, Materials, and Problems in Property* (New York: Matthew Bender, 1988) at 2ff; S Coval, JC Smith & Simon Coval, "The Foundations of Property and Property Law" (1986) 45 Cambridge LJ 457; S Felix Cohen, "Dialogue on Private Property" (1954) 9:2 Rutgers L Rev 357; and the collection of essays in CB Macpherson.

B. "Property" in the Context of Scientific Innovation: JCM v ANA

In *JCM v ANA*, 2012 BCSC 584, the litigants had begun a spousal relationship as lesbians in 1998, and they each eventually gave birth to one child, using therapeutic insemination with sperm from a single anonymous donor. In this way, their two children were biologically related through the anonymous sperm donor. The couple had purchased the sperm from a sperm bank in the United States for about $250 a unit (called a straw), and then stored the unused sperm straws in a Vancouver fertility centre.

However, in 2007, their relationship ended and they entered into a separation agreement that divided all joint property of the relationship and made custody and support arrangements. Unfortunately, the 13 remaining sperm straws were not addressed in their agreement. In 2010, after JCM began a spousal relationship with TL, this new partner wished to have a child with JCM who would be biologically related to JCM's child from her previous relationship. Unfortunately, by this date, it was not possible to obtain additional sperm straws from the anonymous donor, so JCM offered to buy out ANA's interest in the sperm straws. However, ANA was adamantly opposed to the use of the sperm straws by TL, and indicated her preference that the remaining sperm straws be destroyed. Thus, Justice Russell had to rule on whether the sperm straws were property and, if so, how they should be divided on separation pursuant to the provincial *Family Relations Act* in British Columbia.

The court analyzed arguments about whether sperm straws constituted property and concluded that they were property in this circumstance. Russell J relied on *CC v AW*, 2005 ABQB 290 and *Jonathan Yearworth & Ors v North Bristol NHS Trust*, [2009] 2 All ER 986, [2009] EWCA Civ 37 (Civil). In *Yearworth*, six men who stored their own semen (because they were undergoing chemotherapy and feared that the treatment would make them infertile) sued for negligent damage to property when their frozen samples thawed in the storage facility. The plaintiffs had to overcome the common law position that a human body and substances generated by it are incapable of being owned, a principle established in cases such as *Doodeward v Spence* (1908), 6 CLR 406 (Australia); *Moore v Regents of the University of California*, 51 Cal (3d) 120 (Sup Ct 1990); and *Hecht v The Superior Court of Los Angeles County*, 16 Cal App (4th) 836 (Ct App 1993). In *Yearworth*, however, the court held that it was necessary for the common law to keep up with scientific advancements and that, in the context of a negligence claim, the sperm stored by the plaintiffs was property because (1) it was being stored for the benefit and future use of the plaintiffs; (2) it was generated by their bodies; and (3) although the storage facility might have duties regarding the sperm that could conflict with the wishes of the plaintiffs, no one other than each plaintiff had rights in the sperm he had produced.

In *JCM v ANA*, the court also considered a number of American authorities: see e.g. *Davis v Davis*, 842 SW 2d 588 (Tenn Sup Ct 1992); *Kass v Kass*, 91 NY (2d) 554 (Ct App 1998); *AZ v BZ*, 431 Mass 150 (Sup Jud Ct 2000); *JB v MB*, 783 A (2d) 707 (NJ Sup Ct 2001); *Litowitz v Litowitz*, 146 Wash (2d) 514 (Sup Ct 2002); and *In the Matter of the Marriage of Dahl and Angle*, 222 Or App 572 (Ct App 2008). At the same time, the court noted that the respondent had argued that

> [39] … there is no Canadian legislation, federal or provincial, or Canadian case law that treats gametes as property. She argues the issue of treating sperm as property is a moral one. She states that the question of whether sperm is property should be answered in the negative.

The respondent identified academic literature to support her position, including B Steinbock, "Sperm as Property" (1995) 6:2 Stanford L & Pol'y Rev 57, and E Waintraub, "Are Sperm Cells a Form of Property? A Biological Inquiry into the Legal Status of the Sperm Cell" (2007-2008) 11 Quinnipiac Health LJ 1. The court then reviewed another article, as follows:

JCM v ANA
2012 BCSC 584

[53] Heidi P. Forester summarizes the case law in the U.S. regarding frozen embryo disputes in "Law and Ethics Meet: When Couples Fight Over their Frozen Embryos" (2000) 21:4 Journal of Andrology 512, at 514:

1. Embryos are considered neither persons nor property, but "special entities" that have the potential to become persons and, therefore, warrant respect;
2. Pre-procedural agreements between couples regarding the disposition of the embryos should be considered a binding contract;
3. In the absence of such an agreement, the party wishing to avoid procreation should be awarded the embryos, except in circumstances where the other party has no other way of becoming a parent; and
4. The rights of both donors should be considered equally.

[54] I will start this analysis by first commenting that I appreciate that this is a difficult situation for both parties. In determining whether the sperm donation they used to conceive their children is property, I am in no way devaluing the nature of the substance at issue. I do recognize that sperm used to conceive two children for two loving parents does not have the same emotional status as a vehicle or a home. Ultimately, however, this claim involves a dispute over the sperm straws and their disposition. The claimant wishes to use them to conceive another child; the respondent wishes to have them destroyed. I must, therefore, use the tools at my disposal to make a determination on whether the sperm straws are property and, if so, how they should be divided between the parties. There is no intent on my part to trivialize this matter.

[55] After careful consideration of the authorities provided to me, I am persuaded that on the facts of this case the sperm straws that remain at Genesis [the storage facility] should be treated as property and divided between the claimant and respondent as such. I rely mainly on the Canadian case of *C.(C.)* and the U.K. case of *Yearworth*, although I recognize that there are important distinctions between those cases and the facts before me.

[56] While the case of *C.(C.)* involved a dispute over frozen embryos, in my view many of its facts are analogous to the case before me. In *C.(C.)*, the sperm used to conceive the twins was given as a gift to the plaintiff. Here, the parties purchased the sperm. Either way, were the sperm to be considered property it would be the property of the person(s) to whom it was given or by whom it was purchased. The starting point is, therefore, the same in both cases.

[57] The court in *C.(C.)* had no reservations about finding that the sperm became the property of the plaintiff to do with as she chose once it was given to her. In my view, this simple approach is equally applicable to the facts of this case. Once the claimant and

respondent purchased the sperm straws, those sperm straws were their property to be used for their benefit.

[58] Further support for this position is found in the *Yearworth* case. This decision provided a much more detailed basis for a finding of sperm as property. As is acknowledged in that case, typically the common law did not allow for human beings, living or deceased, or their body parts and products to be considered property. This was, no doubt, for good reason. However, I agree with the court of appeal's finding that medical science has advanced to a point where the common law requires rethinking of this point. ...

[The court quoted from the Court of Appeal in *Yearworth* and continued:]

[60] Surely, here the parties, having purchased the sperm straws, have the choice to use them. In fact, unlike the circumstances in *Yearworth*, the parties here did use the sperm straws. They had two children from that use. While there may be a limit on the use the parties can make of the gametes and while they may be prohibited from certain uses of the sperm by the *Assisted Human Reproduction Act*, S.C. 2004, c. 2 (this point was not argued before me and, therefore, remains unclear) they still can use and have used the sperm. As well, I note that the plaintiffs in *Yearworth* were also limited in the use of their sperm by legislation.

[61] There are some difficulties with applying the *Yearworth* decision to the facts of the case before me. The court based its finding of the men's sperm as property on the basis that the men were the donors of that semen. They had ejaculated it. The intention was to use it for their benefit in the future if necessary: at para. 45(f).

[62] Furthermore, the court stated explicitly that "for the purposes of their claims in negligence, the men had ownership of the sperm": at para. 45(f). ...

[63] In this case, I am dealing neither with a claim in negligence nor sperm that came from either of the parties. I do not find, though, that this makes the need for advancements in the common law to keep up with medical science to be any less compelling. In fact, the Court of Appeal in *Yearworth* concluded that advances were needed in common law regarding the issue of ownership of body parts and products for the purposes of the negligence claim before them as well as for other purposes: at para. 45(a). Additionally, while the court was making a determination regarding semen samples intended to be used by the men who had produced them, they did not ignore that sperm could be owned by another; they simply pointed out they were not asked to determine this point: at para. 45(b). ...

[The court then held that along with the parties' right to use the sperm straws, they had an ownership interest, and that the US cases dealing with embryos were of limited assistance because, in this case, each party had contributed a gamete.]

• • •

[67] I do agree, however, with the claimant that the U.S. cases demonstrate the importance of balancing the right to procreate with the right to avoid procreation. But there is no need to balance these rights in this case. A.N.A. will not be the biological parent of any child conceived using the sperm straws. She will not have any parental obligations or responsibilities to any child conceived whether the child is conceived by T.L. or J.C.M.

A.N.A.'s right to avoid procreation is not being infringed by dividing the sperm straws between the owners as property.

[68] I have also considered the respondent's arguments, but I find I must reject them for several reasons. First, the court is ill equipped to handle moral and philosophical arguments ... .

[69] Second, it is clear to me in the context of this dispute that the sperm is the property of the parties. The sperm has been treated as property by everyone involved in the transaction, from the donor to Xytex [the company that collected the donor's sperm for sale], Genesis and the parties. It has been purchased; the parties have a right to deal with it. They have made use of it to their benefit. The respondent's moral objections to the commercialization of reproduction or the commoditization of the body seem to me to be too late. Certainly, they are interesting arguments for the respondent herself to make given she participated in purchasing and using a donation of sperm from an anonymous donor.

[70] I recognize that in Canada the federal government has prohibited the purchase of sperm (and ova) ... .

[The court cited s 7(1) of the *Assisted Human Reproduction Act*, and then continued:]

While much of this Act was recently declared *ultra vires* the federal government in the recent Supreme Court of Canada decision *Reference re Assisted Human Reproduction Act*, 2010 SCC 61, section 7 was not challenged: at para. 10. However, for the reason outlined above, that the sperm has been treated as property up until this point, in my view the legislation does not dictate or even influence whether or not the gametes in this case are property.

. . .

[The court also distinguished the views expressed in academic articles.

In addition, the court addressed whether the best interests of the existing children and any future offspring were a relevant consideration in deciding whether to award the sperm straws to JCM and concluded that analyzing the best interest of the children was "not appropriate to the circumstances of this case."

Russell J thus concluded that "these gametes should be treated as property for the purposes of dividing them upon the dissolution of the spousal relationship of the parties. The parties are the joint owners of the sperm they used in their successful attempts to conceive children" (para 75). The court also held:

> Consistent with their separation agreement, the 13 sperm straws shall be divided evenly between the parties. If not possible to split a sperm straw, then J.C.M. will buy out A.N.A.'s interest in that half. Furthermore, A.N.A. may sell her share to J.C.M. or otherwise dispose of the straws as she wishes (para 96).]

DISCUSSION NOTES

i. Property Concepts and New (Reproductive) Technologies

A number of factors have contributed to a sense of urgency about the need for legal regulation concerning human body parts—the pace of technological advances, the potential for
economic gain, and the international nature of biotechnology enterprises. Concern about
these issues in Canada resulted in the creation of the federal Royal Commission on New
Reproductive Technologies. Its report *Proceed with Care* (Ottawa: Minister of Government
Services Canada, 1993) adopted a broad ethical orientation, the "ethic of care," and eight
guiding principles—individual autonomy, equality, respect for human life and dignity, protection of the vulnerable, non-commercialization of reproduction, appropriate use of resources, accountability, and balancing individual and collective interests.

Significantly, the commission did not adopt a proprietary analysis. In relation to reproductive materials and services, for example, the report stated (at 55-56):

> [I]t is fundamentally wrong for decisions about human reproduction to be determined by a profit
> motive—introducing a profit motive to the sphere of reproduction is contrary to basic values
> and disregards the importance of the role of reproduction and its significance in our lives as hu-
> man beings. Commodifying human beings and their bodies for commercial gain is unacceptable
> because this instrumentalization is injurious to human dignity and ultimately dehumanizing. We
> therefore consider commercialization for reproductive materials and reproductive services to be
> inappropriate.

For a review of the commission's recommendations, see Diana Majury, "Is Care Enough?"
(1994) 17 Dal LJ 279. In addition, see B Dickens, "Living Tissue and Organ Donors and Property Law: More on Moore" (1992) 8 J Contemp Health L & Pol'y 73; B Knoppers, T Caulfield &
D Kinsella, eds, *Legal Rights and Human Genetic Material* (Toronto: Emond Montgomery Publications, 1996) [Knoppers, Caulfield & Kinsella]; and Margaret Davies & Ngaire Naffine, *Are
Persons Property? Legal Debates About Property and Personality* (Aldershot, UK: Ashgate/Dart-
mouth, 2001). In the United Kingdom, the Nuffield Council on Bioethics issued a report in
1995, recommending that human tissue, including blood, eggs, and sperm, should not be
bought and sold for profit and that hospitals should not be permitted to make money by
selling such material: *Human Tissue: Ethical and Legal Issues* (London: Nuffield Council on
Bioethics, 1995).

ii. The Assisted Human Reproduction Act

As noted in *JCM*, the federal government enacted the *Assisted Human Reproduction Act*, SC
2004, c 2. Section 7 of this statute provides:

> 7(1) No person shall purchase, offer to purchase or advertise for the purchase of sperm or ova
> from a donor or a person acting on behalf of a donor.

Although several provisions in this legislation were held to be *ultra vires* the federal jurisdiction in a legal challenge by a number of provinces, s 7 was not struck down: see *Reference
re Assisted Human Reproduction Act*, 2010 SCC 61, [2010] 3 SCR 457. (Note that the couple in
JCM v ANA had purchased sperm in the United States, perhaps as a way of avoiding the prohibition in s 7.) For some assessments of the challenges presented by reproductive technology,

see E Nelson, "Comparative Perspectives on the Regulation of Assisted Reproductive Technologies in the United Kingdom and Canada" (2006) 43 Alta L Rev 1023; MA Pieper, "Frozen Embryos—Persons or Property? Davis v Davis" (1990) 23 Creighton L Rev 807; and Margaret Jane Radin, *Reinterpreting Property* (Chicago: University of Chicago Press, 1993). See also Radin, "Property and Personhood" (1982) 34 Stan L Rev 957 and comments in the same volume responding to this article; and Radin, "Market-Inalienability" (1987) 100 Harv L Rev 1849.

iii. Humans Conceptualized as Objects of Property

Ideas about property and personhood must also take account of the impact on human beings who are conceptualized as objects, rather than subjects, of property interests. Consider, for example, an advertisement (on display at the Art Gallery of Ontario, 1993) that was published in a Toronto newspaper on 10 February 1806 by Peter Russell, a member of the Executive Council of Upper Canada:

> To Be Sold
>
> A black woman, named Peggy, aged about forty years; and a Black Boy her son named Jupiter, aged about fifteen years, both of them the property of the Subscriber [that is, Peter Russell].
>
> The woman is a tolerable Cook and washer woman and perfectly understands making soap and candles. …
>
> They are each of them servants for life. The Price for the Woman is one hundred and fifty dollars—for the Boy two hundred dollars, payable in three years with Interest from the day of Sale and to be properly secured by Bond, etc. But one fourth less will be taken in ready money.

Peter Russell's advertisement for the sale of slaves was published in the press after the enactment of legislation in 1793: *An Act to Prevent the Further Introduction of Slaves*. This legislation provided that no one would be enslaved after 1793, but those already slaves in that year were to continue as slaves until death. This compromise seems to have resulted because a number of members of the Assembly and of the Legislative Council of Upper Canada were themselves slave-owners, including Peter Russell who placed the advertisement above.

Slavery was eventually abolished in the British colonies in 1834 by an Act of the Imperial Parliament, although the practice of slavery had diminished somewhat as a result of judicial decisions before that date: see Robin Winks, *The Blacks in Canada* (Montreal: McGill-Queen's University Press, 1997); Jennifer J Nelson, "The Space of Africville: Creating, Regulating, and Remembering the Urban 'Slum'" (2000) 15:2 CJLS 163; Patricia Williams, *The Alchemy of Race and Rights* (Cambridge, MA: Harvard University Press, 1991); and Barrington Walker, ed, *The African-Canadian Legal Odyssey: Historical Essays* (Toronto: University of Toronto Press for the Osgoode Society for Canadian Legal History, 2012).

C. "Property" in a Statutory Context: Saulnier v Royal Bank of Canada

Saulnier v Royal Bank of Canada, 2008 SCC 58, [2008] 3 SCR 166 was an appeal by Saulnier, who held licences to fish for lobster, herring, swordfish, and mackerel, pursuant to the *Federal Fishery (General) Regulations*, SOR/93-53. (Saulnier's fishing boat was named the *Bingo Queen*.) Like most fishers, Saulnier required loans to finance his fishing business, and he had signed a general security agreement (GSA) with the Royal Bank in 1999. The GSA gave the bank a security interest in "all … present and after acquired personal property including …

intangibles" (as defined in Nova Scotia's *Personal Property Security Act* (the PPSA)). When his fishing business declined in 2004, Saulnier made an assignment in bankruptcy, pursuant to the federal *Bankruptcy and Insolvency Act* (the BIA). According to the bankruptcy legislation, Saulnier's assignment transferred his property (subject to statutory exceptions) to a trustee for Saulnier's creditors. At the time of the assignment in bankruptcy, Saulnier's debts amounted to about $400,000, although the market value of his four fishing licences was in excess of $600,000. Thus the trustee sought to include the fishing licences as property, available to discharge the debts to Saulnier's creditors.

As explored in more detail in Chapter 4, a licence is not generally regarded as a property interest. Instead, a licence provides permission to a person to enter someone else's land for a specific purpose, and the landowner is generally entitled to grant or to rescind this permission for any reason at any time. (As discussed later in this book, there are some circumstances in which a landowner may be estopped from rescinding permission, but these are usually quite narrow or specific situations.) Thus, a licence is often characterized as permission to do something that would otherwise be unlawful. Clearly, Saulnier wished to claim that his fishing licence was within this limited characterization as a licence that did not constitute a property interest.

At trial, the court examined the reality of the commercial context, and concluded that Saulnier's licences provided a bundle of rights that constituted marketable property, including for the purposes of the BIA. On appeal, the court concluded that the trustee had no property in the licences *per se*, but that the beneficial interest in the earnings from the licences was property pursuant to the BIA and PPSA. The Supreme Court of Canada then rejected Saulnier's appeal, although for different reasons.

Examine the SCC's decision, especially the interpretation of property in the statutory language at issue. To what extent is this analysis of statutory property the same or different from the approach in *JCM v ANA*?

Saulnier v Royal Bank of Canada
2008 SCC 58, [2008] 3 SCR 166

BINNIE J (for the court):

II. Relevant Statutory Provisions

[Binnie J first set out the definitions of "property" in the BIA and in the PPSA:]

Bankruptcy and Insolvency Act, R.S.C. 1985, c. B-3
>   s. 2 ...
> "property" means any type of property, whether situated in Canada or elsewhere, and includes money, goods, things in action, land and every description of property, whether real or personal, legal or equitable, as well as obligations, easements and every description of estate, interest and profit, present or future, vested or contingent, in, arising out of or incident to property;

. . .

Personal Property Security Act, S.N.S. 1995-96, c. 13
  2. In this Act,

> · · ·

  (w) "intangible" means personal property that is not goods, a document of title, chattel paper, a security, an instrument or money; [and]

> · · ·

  (ad) "personal property" means goods, a document of title, chattel paper, a security, an instrument, money or an intangible; …

III. Judicial History

A. Supreme Court of Nova Scotia, (2006), 241 N.S.R. (2d) 96, 2006 NSSC 34

[9] Kennedy C.J.S.C. found that "the fair and correct approach is to characterize the federal fishing licences [as property] based on the reality of the commercial arena" (para. 49). …

B. Nova Scotia Court of Appeal (Bateman, Hamilton and Fichaud JJ.A.) (2006), 246 N.S.R. (2d) 239, 2006 NSCA 91

[10] Fichaud J.A., writing for the court, found that while commercial reality and the market value attached to licences "may be a determinant in the accounting or appraisal contexts" (para. 17), the legal issue should be determined with reference to the definitions of "property" and "personal property" in the *BIA* and the *PPSA*.

[11] Based on his consideration of ss. 2 and 16(1) of the [*Fishery (General)*] *Regulations*, he concluded that the licence itself is the property of the Crown, and not of the holder. However, "during the term of a license a licensee has a beneficial interest in the earnings from use of the license. That interest, and the right to those earnings, pass to the trustee in bankruptcy of the license holder" (para. 38). An important issue, in his view, was whether Mr. Saulnier had any rights relating to the renewal or reissuance of his licences, and whether these rights pass to the trustee. He considered it important that the holder of a fishing licence not only had the right to request a renewal but a right not to be arbitrarily denied it. In these circumstances

> [t]he license holder has a legally recognized right—limited though it may be—that constitutes intangible personal property. … The security holder or trustee in bankruptcy takes the license holder's limited legal right or beneficial interest. The security holder or trustee takes [it] subject to all the risks of non-renewal that applied to the license holder—i.e. non-renewal on grounds that are not arbitrary. This ensures that the interest of the security holder or trustee in bankruptcy does not degrade the regulatory scheme of the [fisheries] legislation … . [para. 49]

[12] Fichaud J.A. cited cases in which bad-faith ministerial decisions had given rise to damages or had been judicially reviewed by the courts … [and concluded] that "[a] legal right to damages or to set aside a ministerial decision is, in my view, intangible personal property under the broad definition in s. 2 of the *BIA*" (para. 52). Moreover, while "[t]he PPSA's framework to define 'intangible' is less substantial than in the *BIA*," the result concerning the fishing licences is the same (para. 61). The holder's rights in the

fishing licences are also personal property ("intangibles") for the purposes of the *PPSA*, in his view.

IV. Analysis

[13] A commercial fisher with a ramshackle boat and a licence to fish is much better off financially than a fisher with a great boat tied up at the wharf with no licence. Financial institutions looking for readily marketable loan collateral want to snap up licences issued under the federal *Regulations*, which in the case of the lobster fishery can have a dockside value that fluctuates up to a half a million dollars or more. Fishers want to offer as much collateral as they can to obtain the loans needed to acquire the equipment to enable them to put to sea.

[Although the minister has a "more or less unfettered discretion" as to whether to renew a fishing licence each year, the court stated:]

[14] … [T]he stability of the fishing industry depends on the Minister's predictable renewal of such licences year after year. Few fishers expect to see their loans paid off with the proceeds of a single year's catch. In an industry where holding one of a very restricted number of licences is a condition precedent to participation, the licence unlocks the value in the fishers' other marine assets.

[15] Yet the appellants are correct to say that just because a "right" or "power" to fish has commercial value, it does not follow that licences also constitute property within the scope of the *BIA* or *PPSA*. Earlier trial level decisions in Nova Scotia had held that fishing licences were not property and were not claimable by the trustee in bankruptcy [e.g. *Re Jenkins* (1997), 32 CBR (4th) 262 (NSSC), and *Re Townsend* (2002), 32 CBR (4th) 318 (NSSC)]. We cannot wish away the statutory language however much practical sense is reflected in the result reached by the courts below.

A. A Question of Statutory Interpretation

[16] The questions before the Court essentially raise a dispute about statutory interpretation. We are not concerned with the concept of "property" in the abstract. The notion of "property" is, in any event, a term of some elasticity that takes its meaning from the context. The task is to interpret the definitions in the *BIA* and *PPSA* in a purposeful way having regard to "their entire context, in their grammatical and ordinary sense harmoniously with the scheme of the Act, the object of the Act, and the intention of Parliament" (R. Sullivan, *Sullivan and Driedger on the Construction of Statutes* (4th ed. 2002), at p. 1). Because a fishing licence may not qualify as "property" for the general purposes of the common law does not mean that it is also excluded from the reach of the statutes. For particular purposes Parliament can and does create its own lexicon.

[17] In determining the scope of the definition of "property" in a statutory context, it is necessary to have regard to the overall purpose of the *BIA*, which is to regulate the orderly administration of the bankrupt's affairs, keeping a balance between the rights of creditors and the desirability of giving the bankrupt a clean break … .

[18] Within this overall purpose an appropriate interpretation must be given to the following definition of "property" in s. 2 of the *BIA* … .

[19] The *PPSA*, on the other hand, is designed to facilitate the creation of a security interest to enable holders of personal property to use it as collateral, and to enable lenders to predict accurately the priority of their claims against the assets in question.

> Proceeding from the premise that all security agreements are designed to accomplish the same end and that borrowers usually have little bargaining power, the PPSA prescribes a detailed system for the regulation of default rights and remedies which is designed to provide consistency and fairness in the enforcement of security interests.

> (J.S. Ziegel, B. Geva and R.C.C. Cuming, *Commercial and Consumer Transactions: Cases, Text and Materials* (3rd ed. 1995), vol. III, at p. 18). ...

[20] Within that overall purpose, an interpretation must be given to the somewhat circular definitions given in s. 2 of the *PPSA* ... .

B. The Interest Conferred by a Fishing Licence

[22] The fishery is a public resource. The fishing licence permits the holder to participate for a limited time in its exploitation. The fish, once caught, become the property of the holder. Accordingly, the fishing licence is more than a "mere licence" to do that which is otherwise illegal. It is a licence coupled with a proprietary interest in the harvest from the fishing effort contingent, of course, on first catching it.

[23] It is extremely doubtful that a simple licence could itself be considered property at common law. See generally A.M. Honoré, "Ownership," in A.G. Guest, ed., *Oxford Essays in Jurisprudence* (1961). On the other hand, if not property in the common law sense, a fishing licence is unquestionably a major commercial asset [although ministerial policy precludes recognition of such licences as conferring a property interest on licence holders].

[24] ... [Yet, the] reality, as found by the courts below, is that the commercial market operates justifiably on the assumption that licences can be transferred on application to the Minister with the consent of the existing licence holder, that licences will be renewed from year to year, and that the Minister's policy will not be changed to the detriment of the existing licence holders. ...

[25] The jurisprudence indicates a number of different approaches.

(i) The Traditional "Property" Approach

[26] The appellants rely on the decision of the Ontario Court of Appeal in *Re National Trust Co. and Bouckhuyt* (1987), 61 O.R. (2d) 640 [(CA)]. In that case, the court dismissed the trust company's claim that a valuable tobacco quota listed in a chattel mortgage could properly be made the subject of Ontario *PPSA* registration. Cory J.A., as he then was, referred to some traditional *indicia* of rights of property and concluded that renewal of the tobacco quota year to year was subject to the "unfettered discretion of the [Tobacco Board]" and that the quota itself was "transitory and ephemeral" (pp. 647-48). Accordingly, the quota did "not constitute intangible personal property as that term is utilized" in the Ontario *PPSA* (p. 649). ...

[27] The *Bouckhuyt* approach has been followed in some of the Ontario *PPSA* cases ... but it has been criticized as insufficiently sensitive to the particular context of personal property security legislation, which (so the critics say) commands a broader concept of

intangible property if the purposes of that legislation are to be achieved. See, e.g. J.S. Ziegel and D.L. Denomme, *The Ontario Personal Property Security Act: Commentary and Analysis* (1994), at pp. 41-42. As discussed below, more recent cases have tended to restrict *Bouckhuyt* to its facts. ...

[28] In any event, there is a significant difference between a quota ... and a fishing licence, which bears some analogy to a common law *profit à prendre* which is undeniably a property right. A *profit à prendre* enables the holder to enter onto the land of another to extract some part of the natural produce, such as crops or game birds (B. Ziff, *Principles of Property Law* (2nd ed. 1996), at pp. 333-34; *The Queen in Right of British Columbia v. Tener*, [1985] 1 S.C.R. 533; M.J. Mossman and W.F. Flanagan, *Property Law: Cases and Commentary* (2nd ed. 2004), at p. 545). ...

[29] Fichaud J.A. in the court below noted numerous cases where it was held that "during the term of a license the license holder has a beneficial interest to the earnings from his license" (para. 37). ... This is another way of expressing substantially the same idea. The earnings flow from the catch which is lawfully reduced to possession at the time of the catch, as is the case with a *profit à prendre*.

· · ·

[The court then cited the comments of R Megarry & HWR Wade, *The Law of Real Property*, 4th ed (London: Stevens & Sons, 1975) at 779:]

> A licence may be coupled with some proprietary interest in other property. Thus the right to enter another man's land to hunt and take away the deer killed, or to enter and cut down a tree and take it away, involves two things, namely, a licence to enter the land and the grant of an interest (a *profit à prendre*) in the deer or tree. ...

[The court also referred to *Harper v Minister for Sea Fisheries* (1989), 168 CLR 314 (HC Aust), which noted the analogy of a commercial fishing licence to a *profit à prendre*, even though a fishing licence is nevertheless a statutory creation:]

> What was formerly in the public domain is converted into the exclusive but controlled preserve of those who hold licences. The right of commercial exploitation of a public resource for personal profit has become a privilege confined to those who hold commercial licences. This privilege can be compared to a *profit à prendre*. In truth, however, it is an entitlement of a new kind created as part of a system for preserving a limited public natural resource. ...

[33] In my view these observations are helpful. A fishing licence is, no doubt, a creature of the *Fisheries Act* and its *Regulations*. Our Court has already emphasized the broad scope and discretion of the Minister in relation to such licences in *Comeau's Sea Foods* [*Comeau's Sea Foods Ltd v Canada (Minister of Fisheries & Oceans)*, [1997] 1 SCR 12]. Nevertheless, there are important points of analogy between the fishing licences issued to the appellant Saulnier and the form of common law property called a *profit à prendre* ... . If the question were whether a fishing licence *is* a *profit à prendre*, the answer would almost certainly be no. But that is not the question. The question before us is whether the fishing licences thus conceived can satisfy the statutory definition of the *BIA* and *PPSA*, purposefully interpreted.

[34] My point is simply that the subject matter of the licence (i.e. the right to participate in a fishery that is exclusive to licence holders) coupled with a <u>proprietary interest
in the fish caught</u> pursuant to its terms, bears a reasonable analogy to rights traditionally
considered at common law to be proprietary in nature. It is thus reasonably within the
contemplation of the definition of "property" in s. 2 of the *BIA*, <u>where reference is made
to a "*profit*, present or future, vested or contingent, in, arising out of or incident to property."</u> In this connection the property in question is the fish harvest.

[35] Of course, the holder's rights under a fishing licence are limited in time, place
and the manner of their exercise by the *Fisheries Act* and *Regulations*. To say that the
fishing licence is *coupled* with a proprietary interest does not encumber the Minister's
discretion with proprietary fetters. The analogy used for present purposes does not prevail
over the legislation. The licence is no more and no less than is described in the relevant
legislation. Nevertheless, during its lifetime, however fragile, the fishing licence clearly
confers something more than a "mere" permission to do something which is otherwise
illegal.

(ii) The Regulatory Approach

. . .

[The court then reviewed cases concerning the degree of discretion available to the minister in relation to the renewal of licences and the impact of this issue with respect to their
status as property.]

[40] However, I do not believe the prospect of renewal, whether or not subject to an
"unfettered" discretion, is determinative. For present purposes the appellants do not have
to prove a renewal or even the reasonable prospect of it. The question under the *PPSA* is
whether the holder (in this case the appellant Saulnier) had a qualifying interest in the
licence either *at the time he entered into a General Security Agreement* with the Royal Bank
in April 1999, or at the time the Bank sought to realize on Saulnier's after-acquired property, and the question under the *BIA* is whether he had a qualifying interest within the
meaning of that Act *when he made an assignment in bankruptcy* on July 8, 2004.

(iii) The "Commercial Realities" Approach

[41] This approach is well illustrated by the trial decision of Kennedy C.J.S.C. in this
case, who put the argument succinctly:

> Th[e] evidence confirms my understanding, that on the east coast of Canada fishing licenses,
> particularly for lobster, are commonly exchanged between fishermen for a great deal of
> money.
>   Fishing vessels of questionable value are traded for small fortunes because of the licences
> that are anticipated to come with them.
>
>   . . .
>
>   To ignore commercial reality would be to deny creditors access to something of significant
> value in the hands of the bankrupt. That would be both artificial and potentially inequitable
> [paras. 51-52 and 58].

Similar views have been expressed in other licensing contexts … .

[42] The criticism of this approach is that many things that have commercial value do not constitute property, while the value of some property may be minimal. There is no necessary connection between proprietary status and commercial value. See generally T.G.W. Telfer, "Statutory Licences and the Search for Property: The End of the Imbroglio?" (2007), 45 *Can. Bus. L.J.* 224, at p. 238. I agree with the Court of Appeal that "commercial realities" cannot legitimate wishful thinking about the notion of "property" in the *BIA* and the *PPSA*, although commercial realities provide an appropriate context in which to interpret the statutory provisions. The *BIA* and the *PPSA* are, after all, largely commercial statutes which should be interpreted in a way best suited to enable them to accomplish their respective commercial purposes.

(iv) The Preferred Approach

[43] As described above, the holder of a [fishing] licence acquires a good deal more than merely permission to do that which would otherwise be unlawful. The holder acquires the right to engage in an exclusive fishery under the conditions imposed by the licence and, what is of prime importance, a proprietary right in the wild fish harvested thereunder, and the earnings from their sale. While these elements do not wholly correspond to the full range of rights necessary to characterize something as "property" at common law, the question is whether (even leaving aside the debate about the prospects of renewal) they are sufficient to qualify the "bundle of rights" the appellant Saulnier *did* possess as property for purposes of the statutes.

(a) Fishing Licences Qualify as Property Within the Scope of Section 2 of the BIA

[The court referred again to s 2 of the BIA, and continued:]

[44] … The terms of the definition are very wide. Parliament unambiguously signalled an intention to sweep up a variety of assets of the bankrupt not normally considered "property" at common law. This intention should be respected if the purposes of the *BIA* are to be achieved.

. . .

[46] I prefer to look at the substance of what was conferred, namely a licence to participate in the fishery coupled with a proprietary interest in the fish caught according to its terms and subject to the Minister's regulation. As noted earlier, the *BIA* is intended to fulfill certain objectives in the event of a bankruptcy which require, in general, that non-exempt assets be made available to creditors. The s. 2 definition of property should be construed accordingly to include a s. 7(1) fishing licence.

[47] It is true that the proprietary interest in the fish is contingent on the fish first being caught, but the existence of that contingency is contemplated in the *BIA* definition and is no more fatal to the proprietary status for *BIA* purposes than is the case with the equivalent contingency arising under a *profit à prendre*, which is undeniably a property interest.

. . .

[49] It follows that in my view the trustee was entitled to require the appellant Saulnier to execute the appropriate documentation to obtain a transfer of the fishing licences to the third party purchaser.

[The court also noted that a licence may expire, so that the trustee takes whatever rights were available to the fisher at the time of his assignment in bankruptcy:]

[50] … The trustee simply steps into the shoes of the appellant Saulnier and takes the licence "warts and all."

(b) The Fishing Licence Is Also "Personal Property" Within the Meaning of Section 2 of the PPSA

[51] … The definition of "intangible" [in the PPSA] simply describes something that otherwise constitutes "personal property" but is not one of the listed types of *tangible* personal property. "Intangible" would include an interest created by statute having the characteristics of a licence coupled with an interest at common law as in the case *of a profit à prendre*. Again, to repeat, I do not suggest that a fishing licence constitutes a *profit à prendre* at common law, for clearly there would be numerous conceptual objections to such a characterization. Our concern is exclusively with the extended definitions of "personal property" in the context of a statute that seeks to facilitate financing by borrowers and the protection of creditors. In my view the grant by the Fisheries and Oceans Minister of a licence coupled with a proprietary interest as described above is sufficient to satisfy the *PPSA* definition.

. . .

V. Disposition

[53] For these reasons I would uphold the result of the decision of the courts below and dismiss the appeal with costs in this Court to the respondents.

Appeal dismissed.

DISCUSSION NOTES

i. Fishing Licences: "Permission" or "Property"?

Saulnier is an example of judicial reasoning about whether an interest can be characterized as property in the context of statutory definitions, such as those in the federal BIA and the Nova Scotia PPSA. To some extent, the issue in *Saulnier* depended on the Supreme Court's analysis of the minister's powers to grant and to renew fishing licences, an issue concerning the validity of the exercise of administrative discretion. By concluding that the minister's power was appropriately constrained so that holders of fishing licences could be assured of renewal in the absence of major problems, the court construed the licences as a form of property that could be assigned to the trustee pursuant to the statutory provisions.

In doing so, the court briefly considered the fishing licence as an analogy to a traditional form of property, the *profit à prendre*. As is explored more fully in Chapter 7, the *profit à prendre* is a "non-possessory" property interest, which permits a person to enter someone else's land for the purpose of taking away something on the land. For example, a right to hunt or fish on private property, with permission of the landowner, creates a right to enter the land and take away the fruits of the hunting or fishing expedition. This property interest is also sometimes used to characterize mining rights as proprietary interests. For some assessments of licences and *profits à prendre*, see AJ Oakley, "The Licensee's Interest" (1972) 35 Mod L Rev 551, and MJ Mossman, "Developments in Property Law: The 1985-86 Term" (1986) 8 Sup Ct L Rev 319 (re *R v Tener*, discussed above in *Saulnier*). See also A Ceballos, "Fishing Licence Is Property, Says Supreme Court of Canada," *The Lawyers Weekly* (7 November 2008) at 1.

ii. Licences and Statutory Definitions

Although the court in *Saulnier* concluded that the definitions of "property" in the BIA and the PPSA were sufficiently comprehensive to include Mr. Saulnier's fishing licences, so that the value of the licences was transferred to the trustee at the time of the assignment in bankruptcy, courts must examine statutory language about property in relation to particular contexts. For example, as examined in more detail in Chapter 6, professional licences (such as licences to practise law, medicine, or dentistry) were held not to constitute property pursuant to Ontario's *Family Law Act*, RSO 1990, c F.3. As a result, the value of these professional licences was not included in the statutory requirement to share the value of property equally between spouses at marriage breakdown. Can you identify a possible rationale for distinguishing fishing licences and these professional licences in terms of whether they constitute property?

iii. Fishing Licences and Approaches to Defining "Property"

Consider the following critique of the *Saulnier* decision:

> The formal approach to the legal meaning of property is to construct a definition in the abstract, typically by a process of induction from earlier cases, and then to ask whether the entitlement in question falls within the definition. The exercise involves a search for the essential characteristics of a property right, which distinguish it from a contractual or other simply personal right. By contrast, the functional approach focuses on the reason why the entitlement holder in a given case wants a property right, and it compares the policy advantages and disadvantages of allowing the claim. In summary, the formal approach is precedent-driven, whereas the functional approach is policy-driven.
>
> The formal approach of reasoning by induction from earlier cases has produced a number of competing tests for determining whether an entitlement qualifies as property. The following is a short critical account of the various attempts .... One approach is to ask whether the entitlement has market value or, in other words, whether there are buyers willing to pay for it. This is sometimes called the "commercial reality test" and it is the test the trial judge in *Saulnier* applied to support the conclusion that Saulnier's fishing licence was property. The commercial reality test involves the following syllogism: (1) only proprietary entitlements are marketable; (2) the law should facilitate markets; (3) therefore, if there is proof of willing buyers for the entitlement in question, the court should say it is property. This is, of course, question-begging because a prospective buyer's willingness to pay for the entitlement is likely to depend on whether transfers are legally valid but, *ex hypothesi*, a transfer is not legally valid unless the entitlement is property. In other words, the commercial reality test defines property by reference to the reason for asking the question in the first place. ... [In addition, a formal approach uses tests of exclusivity, alienability, stability, and enforceability.]

The leading account of the functional approach to property rights is Hansmann and Kraak-man's "Property, Contract and Verification" [(2002) 31 J Legal Stud 373]. Their analysis can be summarized as follows. (1) The key distinguishing feature of a property right in an asset is that a property right runs with the asset or [that the right is enforceable against a subsequent holder]. (2) The main benefit of a property right is that it saves B transactions costs, ... by avoiding the need ... to negotiate a new agreement with [the subsequent holder] .... . (3) The main cost of property rights are verification costs, in other words, [the cost of discovering whether a party has a property right]. (4) The law's primary response to the verification costs problem is to assume that all property rights in an asset are held by a single owner, but the law allows partitioning of property rights provided there is adequate notice to potentially affected third parties .... . (5) The question whether to recognize a new property right, that is to say, a different method of parti-tioning, requires a comparison of the costs and benefits identified in (2) and (3), above. From this perspective, alienability is neither a necessary nor a sufficient condition of property rights.

(See A Duggan, "In the Wake of the Bingo Queen: Are Licences Property?" (2008-9) 47 Can Bus LJ 225 at 226-27 and 230-31.)

According to Duggan, the decision in the Supreme Court of Canada revealed an emphasis on the functional approach, but the decision also demonstrated aspects of the formal approach:

The functional argument was ... that treating a licence as property in the BIA and PPSA contexts facilitates access to credit and that any concerns about the potential for compromising the policy of the licensing statute are misplaced because [a transferee's interest is never greater than that of the transferor]. The formal argument was that a fishing licence is property in the BIA and PPSA senses because it is analogous to a *profit a prendre*.

Duggan recommended legislative reform to clarify the issue of licences and property in relation to issues of bankruptcy and security interests. In the context of legislative reform, should the definition use a formal or functional approach? Why? For other comments on *Saulnier*, see T Telfer, "Statutory Licences and the Search for Property: The End of the Imbro-glio?" (2007) 45 Can Bus LJ 224; and C. Weisenburger, "Digging Below and Looking Beside the Wall of Ministerial Discretion: Licences After Saulnier" (2007-8) 45 Alb L Rev 273 (comments on the decisions at trial and in the Nova Scotia Court of Appeal).

D. Property and Precedents

The three main cases in this section demonstrate a variety of different kinds of claims about property and differing approaches to resolving them. *Victoria Park* was a historical claim to protect the commercial viability of an activity taking place on an owner's land; *JCM v ANA* involved an issue about whether reproductive material constituted property in the context of family breakdown; and *Saulnier* required the interpretation of "property" in statutory provi-sions about bankruptcy to determine whether a fishing licence formed part of an assignment in bankruptcy. These cases represent some of the many contexts in which disputes about property may arise. They also reveal some differing approaches to determining property issues: in *Victoria Park*, the majority concluded that the issue was a matter for the legislature; the court in *JCM* chose to make a decision even though the context was relatively new; and Mr. Saulnier's efforts to preserve his fishing licences in the face of bankruptcy resulted in three different approaches (at trial, in the NS Court of Appeal, and then in the Supreme Court of Canada), although the judges were unanimous in their conclusion that the fishing licence was property. As you explore issues about property law in this book, it will be important to take note of different kinds of contexts for claims about property as well as different approaches to determining these claims.

In addition, these three cases reveal different approaches to the use of precedents. In *Victoria Park*, a majority of the Australian High Court concluded that there was no precedent to find "property in a spectacle," and that it was the responsibility of the legislature, rather than the court, to provide an appropriate remedy for the owner of the racecourse. By contrast, the court in *JCM v ANA* relied on a precedent in England and another in Alberta (both of which were merely persuasive) to conclude that sperm straws constituted property, while acknowledging that the facts in these precedent cases differed from the dispute in *JCM*. And in *Saulnier*, the court distinguished the Ontario decision in *Bouckhuyt* and did not follow earlier decisions in which courts had held that fishing licences did not constitute property. Recall the above discussion in relation to Singer's categories of precedents and Jaff's suggestions about frame shifting: do these views assist in understanding how judges approach the use of precedents and decision making more generally? These issues are also relevant for assessing the materials in this book.

III. PROPERTY AND THE "RIGHT TO EXCLUDE"

A. Shopping Centres: "Public" or "Private" Property?

It is fair to say that from the beginning, the Canadian state strongly protected the right to exclude. Not only did property owners enjoy common law rights, enforceable by damage actions and injunctions, but also criminal and regulatory legislation provided property-owners with quasi-criminal powers to protect their property against intruders. Clearly, protecting the right of private property owners to exclude was an important public policy that was never seriously contested—that is until the advent of the shopping plaza.

The [shopping] mall was the brainchild of Victor Gruen, a Jewish socialist who fled from Austria to the United States in 1938, after the Nazi *Anschluss*. Already a successful, innovative store designer, Gruen first proposed the idea for large regional shopping centres in a 1943 article. He envisaged numerous shops enclosed in a single building, surrounded by a landscaped area and parking lots. In addition to retail spaces, [Gruen envisaged that] these developments would contain public facilities, including a post office and library, and meeting rooms and auditoriums for community activities. ... [The author noted the creation of Northland, outside Detroit, in the 1950s and the increasing popularity of regional shopping malls, leading to the "hollowing out" of downtown retail areas. As a result, municipalities then began to promote the construction of malls in city centres. However,] as the mall became more popular, the public dimension of Gruen's vision increasingly fell by the wayside. ...

[A]t the heart of the mall concept was an unresolved tension between its public and private dimensions. [For private investors, the mall was private property and members of the public were simply licensees whose permission to be in the mall could be revoked at any time and for any reason. In city centres,] malls drew people off the streets into privatized spaces, [and] often literally entailed the privatization of public spaces, including the closing off of public streets and the sale of public lands to developers. … [As a Toronto planning commissioner stated in the mid-1980s,] "we have to be wary of giving up the public realm to the private sector."

(Eric Tucker, "The Malling of Property Law?" in E Tucker, J Muir & B Ziff, eds, *Property on Trial* (Toronto: Irwin Law for the Osgoode Society for Canadian Legal History, 2012) [Tucker, Muir & Ziff] 303 at 307-8.)

As the above excerpt about the emergence of shopping malls in the second half of the 20th century indicates, shopping centres may have been imbued with public purposes in Gruen's original conception, but, in practice, they have often reflected the interests of mall owners and their investors—quintessential private property. This material examines ideas about property as the "right to exclude" in the context of the emergence of shopping centres—particularly, the ways in which courts have interpreted the nature of shopping centres as property. Beginning with *Harrison v Carswell* in the early 1970s, and the different approaches of the judges in the Supreme Court of Canada about the "right to exclude" on the part of the owners of shopping centres, the material then looks at some later developments in which courts "distinguished" *Harrison v Carswell*. Although the case has never been overruled, and has often been distinguished in the context of the Charter's guarantee of freedom of expression, *Harrison v Carswell* remains significant for defining constraints on the use of public spaces.

Harrison v Carswell

[1976] 2 SCR 200

[In the 1970s, the Supreme Court of Canada considered the "right to exclude" in *Harrison v Carswell*, and the judges' decisions also considered the relevance of an earlier case, *R v Peters* (1971), 17 DLR (3d) 128, in relation to the doctrine of precedent. Examine the differing approaches to ideas about private and common property in this case. Because *Harrison v Carswell* was decided before the Charter (1982), these materials initially focus on the case before exploring subsequent developments that reveal the balancing of property rights with other interests protected by the Charter (particularly s 2 rights).]

Appeal by the prosecutor from the decision of the Court of Appeal for Manitoba, 17 CCC (2d) 521, 48 DLR (3d) 137, [1974] 4 WWR 394, setting aside the accused's conviction under the *Petty Trespasses Act* (Man).

DICKSON J (Martland, Judson, Ritchie, Pigeon, and de Grandpré JJ concurring):

The respondent, Sophie Carswell, was charged under the *Petty Trespasses Act*, RSM 1970, c. P-50, with four offences (one on each of four days) of unlawfully trespassing upon the premises of the Fairview Corporation Limited, trading under the firm name and style of Polo Park Shopping Centre, located in the City of Winnipeg, after having been requested by the owner not to enter on or come upon the premises. The appellant, Peter Harrison, manager of Polo Park Shopping Centre, swore the information. The charges were dismissed by the Provincial Judge, but on a trial *de novo* in the County Court, Mrs. Carswell was convicted and fined $10 on each of the charges. The convictions were set aside by the Manitoba Court of Appeal (Freedman CJM and Matas JA, with Guy JA, dissenting)

[(1974), 17 CCC (2d) 521, 48 DLR (3d) 137, 4 WWR 394] and the present appeal followed, by leave of this Court.

With great respect, I am unable to agree with the majority reasons, delivered in the Court of Appeal by Chief Justice Freedman, for I find it difficult, indeed impossible, to make any well-founded distinction between this case and *Peters v. The Queen* [(1971), 17 DLR (3d) 128], decided by this Court four years ago in a unanimous decision of the full Bench. The constitutional issue raised in *Peters* no longer concerns us; the only other issue was whether the owner of a shopping plaza had sufficient control or possession of the common areas, having regard to the unrestricted invitation to the public to enter upon the premises, as to enable it to invoke the remedy of trespass. The Court decided it did. That case and the present case came to us on much the same facts, picketing within a shopping centre in connection with a labour dispute. In *Peters*, the picketing was carried out by the president of the Brampton Labour Council and seven other persons, carrying placards and distributing leaflets in front of a Safeway store, seeking a boycott of Safeway for selling California grapes. In the present case, the picketing was carried out by Mrs. Carswell and 11 other persons, carrying placards and distributing leaflets, in front of the premises of their employer, Dominion Stores. In both instances the picketing was peaceful. Although the question posed in *Peters* did not recite the facts upon which the case rested, the question was worded thus:

> Did the learned Judges in appeal err in law in determining that *the* owner of *the* property had sufficient possession of *the* shopping plaza sidewalk to be capable of availing itself of the remedy for trespass under the *Petty Trespass Act*, RSO 1960, Chapter 294, Section 1(1)? (Italics are my own)

and in my view is so expressed, with repeated use of the definite article, as to relate the question to the circumstances in respect of which the Judges made their determination.

The judgment of the Ontario Court of Appeal in *Peters* [(1970), 2 CCC (2d) 336, 16 DLR (3d) 143, [1971] 1 OR 597] was delivered by Chief Justice Gale who said, p. 146 [DLR, 338 CCC]:

> With respect to the first ground of appeal, it is our opinion that an owner who has granted a right of entry to a particular class of the public has not thereby relinquished his or its right to withdraw its invitation to the general public or any particular member thereof, and that if a member of the public whose invitation to enter has been withdrawn refuses to leave, he thereby becomes a trespasser and may be prosecuted under the *Petty Trespass Act*. Here, the invitation extended by the owner was of a general nature and included tenants, employees, agents and all persons having or seeking business relations with the tenants. However, notwithstanding the general nature of the invitation, the owner did not thereby lose its right to withdraw the invitation from the general public or any particular member thereof. In addition, it is also our view with respect to trespass that possession does not cease to be exclusive so long as there is the right to control entry of the general public, and here the owner had not relinquished that right of control.

The brief judgment in this Court, answering in the negative the question asked, neither adopted nor repudiated the reasons delivered in the Court of Appeal, but it should not be overlooked that when the *Peters* case was before the Ontario Court of Appeal, counsel for Peters relied upon the decision of the Court of Appeal for Saskatchewan in *Grosvenor*

Park Shopping Centre Ltd. v. Waloshin [*et al* (1964), 46 DLR (2d) 750, 49 WWR 237]. That case arose out of injunction proceedings during a strike of employees of Loblaw Groceries Co. Ltd., in Saskatoon, who were picketing with placards on the sidewalk adjacent to store premises located in a shopping centre. The pertinent part of the judgment of the Saskatchewan Court of Appeal reads [at 755]:

> Learned counsel for the appellant argued that the respondent did not have that degree of possession essential to an action in trespass.
>
> The area upon which it is alleged the appellants have trespassed is part of what is well known as a shopping centre. While legal title to the area is in the respondent, it admits in its pleadings that it has granted easements to the many tenants. The evidence also establishes that the respondent has extended an unrestricted invitation to the public to enter upon the premises. The very nature of the operation is one in which the respondent, both in its own interests and in the interests of its tenants, could not do otherwise. Under the circumstances, it cannot be said that the respondent is in actual possession. The most that can be said is that the respondent exercises control over the premises but does not exercise that control to the exclusion of other persons. For that reason, therefore, the respondent cannot maintain an action in trespass against the appellants: *vide* 38 Hals., 3d ed., p. 743, para. 1212. Support, too, for this view may be found in *Zeller's (Western) Ltd. v. Retail Food & Drug Clerks Union, Local 1518* (1963), 42 DLR (2d) 582, 45 WWR 337.

Chief Justice Gale, in *Peters*, offered this observation with respect to *Grosvenor Park* [(1970) at 338-39 CCC, 146 DLR]:

> The solicitor for the appellant relied very heavily upon a decision of the Court of Appeal for Saskatchewan in *Grosvenor Park Shopping Centre Ltd. v. Waloshin et al.* (1964), 46 DLR (2d) 750, 49 WWR 237. If our view in this appeal does not harmonize with the reasoning of the Court in the *Grosvenor Park* case, we must respectfully disagree with that reasoning.

So when the *Peters* case came to this Court for consideration, the Court had before it the reasoning of the Court of Appeal for Ontario in that case and the reasoning, difficult to reconcile, of the Court of Appeal for Saskatchewan in *Grosvenor Park*; the reasoning of the Ontario Court prevailed. There has been no suggestion that *Peters* was wrongly decided; therefore, I would think it must be regarded as controlling unless it can properly be distinguished from the case at bar. No distinction can be made on the ground of contract; there is a copy of the lease from Fairview to Dominion Stores, among the papers, but it would not appear, nor has it been argued, that any distinction can rest on that document. As to a possible statutory distinction, the petty trespass acts of Manitoba and Ontario do not differ in any material respect and indeed s. 24 of the *Labour Relations Act, 1972* (Man.), c. 75 [continuing consolidation, c L10], specifically preserves rights against trespassers. Therefore it would seem the appeal must succeed unless a valid distinction can be drawn on the ground that the president of the Brampton Labour Council in *Peters* was a mere member of the general public from whom permission to remain on the premises could be withdrawn at will whereas Mrs. Carswell was an employee of one of the tenants of the shopping centre on strike in support of a current labour dispute, from whom permission to remain on the premises could not, as a matter of law, be withdrawn. I find myself unable to accept that any ground in law supports such a distinction.

The evidence discloses that distribution of pamphlets or leaflets in the mall of Polo Park Shopping Centre or on the parking lot has never been permitted by the management of the centre and that this prohibition has extended to tenants of the centre. The centre as a matter of policy has not permitted any person to walk in the mall carrying placards. There is nothing in the evidence supporting the view that in the present case the owner of the centre was acting out of caprice or whimsy or *mala fides*. In a comment entitled *Labour Law—Picketing in Shopping Centres*, (1965) 43 Can. Bar Rev. 357, at p. 362, H.W. Arthurs referred to the following as one of the legitimate concerns of the landlord of a shopping centre:

> … while public authorities may, on behalf of the community, strike a reasonable balance between traffic and picketing on public sidewalks and streets, the shopping centre owner can hardly be expected to make such a choice: he has no authority to speak for the community; to grant picketing or parading privileges to all would invite chaos, while to do so selectively would invite commercial reprisals. He is thus driven to adopt a highly restrictive approach to granting permission to groups who wish to parade or picket in the shopping centre.

It is urged on behalf of Mrs. Carswell that the right of a person to picket peacefully in support of a lawful strike is of greater social significance than the proprietary rights of an owner of a shopping centre, and that the rights of the owner must yield to those of the picketer. The American example has been cited, but I cannot say that I find the American cases to which we have been referred of great help. The facts in *Schwartz-Torrance Investment Corp. v. Bakery and Confectionery Workers' Union, Local 31* [394 P2d 921 (1964)], decided by the Supreme Court of California are almost identical with those in *Grosvenor Park*, but I think it not unimportant to note that in *Schwartz-Torrance*, Justice Tobriner, early in his judgment, drew attention to the fact that the Legislature of the State of California had expressly declared that the public policy of the State favoured concerted activities of employees for the purpose of collective bargaining and had enacted the policy into an exception to the criminal trespass law. Construing that exception, the California Supreme Court in a case antedating *Schwartz-Torrance* had concluded that the Legislature, in dealing with trespasses, had specifically subordinated the rights of the property owner to those of persons engaged in lawful labour activities. *Schwartz-Torrance* is, therefore, of small aid in this case and indeed can be said to support, in a negative sense, a position inimical to that of Mrs. Carswell. And one need only read *Amalgamated Food Employees' Union, Local 590 v. Logan Valley Plaza Inc.* [391 US 308 (1968)], and then read *Lloyd Corp. Ltd. v. Tanner* [407 US 551 (1972)], to apprehend the uncertainties and very real difficulties which emerge when a Court essays to legislate as to what is and what is not a permissible activity within a shopping centre.

The submission that this Court should weigh and determine the respective values to society of the right to property and the right to picket raises important and difficult political and socio-economic issues, the resolution of which must, by their very nature, be arbitrary and embody personal economic and social beliefs. It raises also fundamental questions as to the role of this Court under the Canadian Constitution. The duty of the Court, as I envisage it, is to proceed in the discharge of its adjudicative function in a reasoned way from principled decision and established concepts. I do not for a moment doubt the power of the Court to act creatively—it has done so on countless occasions; but manifestly one must ask—what are the limits of the judicial function? There are many and varied answers to this question. Holmes J said in *Southern Pacific Co. v. Jensen* [244 US 205 (1917)], at p. 221: "I recognize without hesitation that judges do and must legislate, but they can do it only interstitially; they are confined from molar to molecular actions." Cardozo, *The Nature of the Judicial Process* (1921), p. 141, recognized that the freedom of the Judge is not absolute in this expression of his view:

> [A] judge, even when he is free, is still not wholly free. He is not to innovate at pleasure. He is not a knight-errant, roaming at will in pursuit of his own ideal of beauty or of goodness. He is to draw his inspiration from consecrated principles.

[Dickson J also referred to comments made by the Chief Justice of the Australian High Court, Dixon CJ, in 1955, in which he argued against judges abandoning long-accepted legal principles "in the name of justice or of social necessity or of social convenience."]

Society has long since acknowledged that a public interest is served by permitting union members to bring economic pressure to bear upon their respective employers through peaceful picketing, but the right has been exercisable in some locations and not in others and to the extent that picketing has been permitted on private property the right hitherto has been accorded by statute. For example, s. 87 [since rep & sub 1975, c 33, s 21] of the *Labour Code of British Columbia Act*, 1973 (BC) (2d Sess.), c. 122, provides that no action lies in respect of picketing permitted under the Act for trespass to real property to which a member of the public ordinarily has access.

Anglo-Canadian jurisprudence has traditionally recognized, as a fundamental freedom, the right of the individual to the enjoyment of property and the right not to be deprived thereof, or any interest therein, save by due process of law. The Legislature of Manitoba has declared in the *Petty Trespasses Act* that any person who trespasses upon land, the property of another, upon or through which he has been requested by the owner not to enter, is guilty of an offence. If there is to be any change in this statute law, if A is to be given the right to enter and remain on the land of B against the will of B, it would seem to me that such a change must be made by the enacting institution, the Legislature, which is representative of the people and designed to manifest the political will, and not by this Court.

I would allow the appeal, set aside the judgment of the Court of Appeal for Manitoba and restore the judgment of the County Court Judge.

LASKIN CJC (Spence and Beetz JJ concurring) (dissenting):

I would be content to adopt the reasons of Freedman CJM and, accordingly, to dismiss this appeal without more if I did not feel compelled, in view of the course of argument, to add some observations bearing on the decision of this Court in *Peters v. The Queen* [(1971), 17 DLR (3d) 128], dismissing an appeal from the judgment of the Ontario Court of Appeal [(1970), 2 CCC (2d) 336, 16 DLR (3d) 143, [1971] 1 OR 597]. The observations I am about to make about the *Peters* case carry into two areas of concern respecting the role of this Court as the final Court in this country in both civil and criminal causes. Those areas are, first, whether this Court must pay mechanical deference to *stare decisis* and, second, whether this Court has a balancing role to play, without yielding place to the Legislature, where an ancient doctrine, in this case trespass, is invoked in a new setting to suppress a lawful activity supported both by legislation and by a well-understood legislative policy.

The factual setting for these issues in the present case needs no great elaboration. The locale is a shopping centre, in which a large number of tenants carry on a wide variety of businesses. The shopping centre has the usual public amenities, such as access roads, parking lots and sidewalks, which are open for use by members of the public who may or may not be buyers at the time they come to the shopping centre. There can be no doubt that at least where a shopping centre is freely accessible to the public, as is the one involved in the present case, the private owner has invested members of the public with a right of entry during the business hours of his tenants and with a right to remain there subject to lawful behaviour. Counsel for the appellant owner in this case stated that members of the public entered and remained in the shopping centre at the owner's whim, under what may be called a revocable licence, and were subject to liability for trespass if they did not leave when requested, regardless of how proper their conduct was at the time. This is an extravagant position. It is a sufficient demonstration of its hollowness to point out that a member of the public who came to the shopping centre at the express invitation of a tenant for business reasons could not lawfully be excluded by the private owner. I need not pursue the extreme of the appellant's submission, but put it to one side to deal with the specific trespass claim that arose here.

An employee of a tenant in the shopping centre participated in a lawful strike and then proceeded to picket peacefully on the sidewalk in front of the tenant's premises. The struck employer took no action to prohibit the picketing and, on the record, an action by the employer would probably have been unsuccessful. The owner of the shopping centre introduced himself into the situation and told the picketer, the respondent in this appeal, that picketing was not permitted in any area of the shopping centre, and if she did not leave she would be charged with trespass. He advised her to move to a public sidewalk which was some distance away. She continued to picket on the shopping centre sidewalk and charges against her under the *Petty Trespasses Act*, RSM 1970, c. P-50 followed.

The *Peters* case also involved picketing in a shopping centre. However, the picketing there arose not out of a labour dispute with an employer tenant of premises in the shopping centre, but was by way of a boycott appeal against the selling of California grapes. The oral reasons of Gale CJO, for the Ontario Court of Appeal, were undoubtedly geared to the specific facts before him, and it is therefore unfair, in my view, to read, without that context, his general statement [at 338 CCC, 146 DLR] that "an owner who has granted a right of entry to a particular class of the public has not thereby relinquished his or its right to withdraw its invitation to the general public or any particular member thereof, and that if a member of the public whose invitation to enter has been withdrawn refuses to leave, he thereby becomes a trespasser and may be prosecuted under the *Petty Trespass Act*." Be that as it may, the case came to the Supreme Court of Canada not at large but on two specific questions of law, the second of which concerned the constitutional validity of the provincial *Petty Trespasses Act*, a matter which did not become an issue here. That was made clear to the sole intervenant in the present case, the Attorney General for Saskatchewan, who appeared to defend the validity of such legislation.

The first question put to this Court in the *Peters* case was framed as follows:

Did the learned Judges in appeal err in law in determining that the owner of the property had sufficient possession of the shopping plaza sidewalk to be capable of availing itself of the remedy for trespass under the *Petty Trespass Act*, RSO 1960, Chapter 294, section 1(1)?

This question, a strictly legal one without any context of fact, was answered unanimously in the negative by the full Court of which I was a member. The Court gave the briefest of oral reasons (see 17 DLR (3d) 128), and I regarded the answer as a response to a narrow question of whether a shopping centre owner can have sufficient possession of a sidewalk therein to support a charge of trespass under the provincial Act. The question, to me, was whether the owner had divested itself of possession so as to make the shopping centre sidewalk a public way upon which there could be no trespass as against such owner in any circumstances.

It is, of course, open to others to read this Court's disposition of the *Peters* case differently, but I can say for myself that the brief reasons would not have sufficed had the question that was asked been put in a factual frame as is often done when questions are formulated for the consideration of this Court. For me, it follows that the *Peters* case is neither in law, nor in fact a controlling authority for the present case which came to this Court not upon specific questions of fact, but at large so as to enable this Court to consider both law and fact as they bear on the position *inter se* of the shopping centre owner and of the lawful picketer in a legal strike.

My brother Spence, who also sat as a member of this Court in the *Peters* case, associates himself with me in the view of it that I have put forward, and I would think that this should give pause to any suggestion that the *Peters* case has concluded the issue now before us, an issue arising on different facts and on a broader question of law than that to which an answer was sought and given in the *Peters* case.

This Court, above all others in this country, cannot be simply mechanistic about previous decisions, whatever be the respect it would pay to such decisions. What we would be doing here, if we were to say that the *Peters* case, because it was so recently decided, has concluded the present case for us, would be to take merely one side of a debatable issue and say that it concludes the debate without the need to hear the other side.

I do not have to call upon pronouncements of members of this Court that we are free to depart from previous decisions in order to support the pressing need to examine the present case on its merits. Pressing, because there are probably many hundreds of shopping centres in this country where similar issues have arisen and will arise. The Saskatchewan Court of Appeal has dealt with a picketing situation in a shopping centre in a different way than did the Ontario Court of Appeal in the *Peters* case, albeit on different facts and in respect of civil action rather than in a penal proceeding: see *Grosvenor Park Shopping Centre Ltd. v. Waloshin et al.* [(1964), 46 DLR (2d) 750, 49 WWR 237]. There are judgments in related cases, that were cited to us in argument, that need to be taken into consideration in order to enable this Court to begin to draw lines which Courts are habitually called upon to do. There should be, at least, some indication that the Court has addressed itself to the difficult issues that reside in the competing contentions that were made in this case and to which I will refer later on in these reasons. But, above all, this Court has not shown itself to be timorous in tackling important issues where it could be said, with some justification, that an important consideration was absent from an earlier judgment, even a recent one, upon which reliance was placed to foreclose examination of a similar issue in a subsequent case.

I refer to the judgment of this Court in *Brant Dairy Co. Ltd. et al. v. The Milk Commission of Ontario et al.* [(1972), 30 DLR (3d) 559, [1973] SCR 131] as evidence of the approach which I think is compelled in the present case. Of course, it was a different case and turns on the neglect of this Court to consider earlier conflicting decisions when deciding the case that was pressed as an authority to conclude the decision in the *Brant Dairy* case itself. What is important, however, is not whether we have a previous decision involving a "brown horse" by which to judge a pending appeal involving a "brown horse," but rather what were the principles, and indeed the facts, upon which the previous case, now urged as conclusive, was decided. I need only add that there can be no doubt on the question whether the present case provides a developed set of facts that raise the important issues of law that require decision here. It certainly does.

I come then to those issues, and they can only be understood if we look at the present case not only from the position asserted by the shopping centre owner, but as well from the position asserted by the lawful picketer. An ancient legal concept, trespass, is urged here in all its pristine force by a shopping centre owner in respect of areas of the shopping centre which have been opened by him to public use, and necessarily so because of the commercial character of the enterprise based on tenancies by operators of a variety of businesses. To say in such circumstances that the shopping centre owner may, at his whim, order any member of the public out of the shopping centre on penalty or liability for trespass if he refuses to leave, does not make sense if there is no proper reason in that member's conduct or activity to justify the order to leave.

Trespass in its civil law sense, and in its penal sense too, connotes unjustified invasion of another's possession. Where a dwelling-house is concerned, the privacy associated with that kind of land-holding makes any unjustified or unprivileged entry a trespass, technically so even if no damage occurs. A Court, however, would be likely to award only nominal damages for mere unprivileged entry upon another's private premises where no injury occurs, and it is probable that the plaintiff would be ordered to pay costs for seeking empty vindication. If the trespasser refuses to leave when ordered, he could be forcibly removed, but, more likely, the police would be called and the issue would be resolved at that point, or a basis for an action, or for a penal charge would arise. In short, apart from privileged entry, a matter to which I will return in these reasons, there is a significant element of protection of privacy in resort to trespass to exclude or remove persons from private dwellings.

The considerations which underlie the protection of private residences cannot apply to the same degree to a shopping centre in respect of its parking areas, roads and sidewalks. Those amenities are closer in character to public roads and sidewalks than to a private dwelling. All that can be urged from a theoretical point of view to assimilate them to private dwellings is to urge that if property is privately owned, no matter the use to which it is put, trespass is as appropriate in the one case as in the other and it does not matter that possession, the invasion of which is basic to trespass, is recognizable in the one case but not in the other. There is here, on this assimilation, a legal injury albeit no actual injury. This is a use of theory which does not square with economic or social fact under the circumstances of the present case.

What does a shopping centre owner protect, for what invaded interest of his does he seek vindication in ousting members of the public from sidewalks and roadways and parking areas in the shopping centre? There is no challenge to his title and none to his possession nor to his privacy when members of the public use those amenities. Should he be allowed to choose what members of the public come into those areas when they have been opened to all without discrimination? Human rights legislation would prevent him from discriminating on account of race, colour or creed or national origin, but counsel for the appellant would have it that members of the public can otherwise be excluded or ordered to leave by mere whim. It is contended that it is unnecessary that there be a reason that can stand rational assessment. Disapproval of the owner, in assertion of a remote control over the "public" areas of the shopping centre, whether it be disapproval of picketing or disapproval of the wearing of hats or anything equally innocent, may be converted (so it is argued) into a basis of ouster of members of the public. Can the common law be so devoid of reason as to tolerate this kind of whimsy where public areas of a shopping centre are concerned?

If it was necessary to categorize the legal situation which, in my view, arises upon the opening of a shopping centre, with public areas of the kind I have mentioned (at least where the opening is not accompanied by an announced limitation on the classes of public entrants), I would say that the members of the public are privileged visitors whose privilege is revocable only upon misbehaviour (and I need not spell out here what this embraces) or by reason of unlawful activity. Such a view reconciles both the interests of the shopping centre owner and [those] of the members of the public, doing violence to neither and recognizing the mutual or reciprocal commercial interests of [the] shopping centre owner, business tenants and members of the public upon which the shopping centre is based.

The respondent picketer in the present case is entitled to the privilege of entry and to remain in the public areas to carry on as she did (without obstruction of the sidewalk or incommoding of others) as being not only a member of the public but being as well, in relation to her peaceful picketing, an employee involved in a labour dispute with a tenant of the shopping centre, and hence having an interest, sanctioned by the law, in pursuing legitimate claims against her employer through the peaceful picketing in furtherance of a lawful strike.

The civil law doctrine of abusive exercise of rights provides, in my opinion, an apt analogue for the present case. I do not press it as having precise application, but in so far as it embraces a balancing of rights, a consideration of the relativity of rights involving advertence to social purpose as well as to personal advantage, it is the peaceful picketer who has cause for complaint against interference with her, rather than the shopping centre owner having a legally cognizable complaint: see, generally, Gutteridge, "Abuse of Rights" (1933-35) 5 Camb. LJ 22; Castel, *The Civil Law System of the Province of Quebec* (1962), pp. 409ff. The shopping centre owner has no overriding or even coequal interest to serve in intervening in the labour dispute, and, if anything, is acting as surrogate of the struck tenant in a situation where the latter has not and probably could not claim redress or relief.

It seems to me that the present case involves a search for an appropriate legal framework for new social facts which show up the inaptness of an old doctrine developed upon a completely different social foundation. The history of trespass indicates that its introduction as a private means of redress was directed to breaches of the peace or to acts likely to provoke such breaches. Its subsequent enlargement beyond these concerns does not mean that it must be taken as incapable of further adaptation, but must be applied on what I can only characterize as a level of abstraction which ignores the facts. Neither logic nor experience (to borrow from Holmes' opening sentence in his classic *The Common Law*) supports such a conclusion.

Recognition of the need for balancing the interests of the shopping centre owner with competing interests of members of the public when in or on the public areas of the shopping centre, engaged Courts in the United States a little earlier than it did the Courts in this country. Making every allowance for any constitutional basis upon which Courts there grappled with this problem, their analyses are helpful because they arise out of the same economic and social setting in which the problem arises here. Thus, there is emphasis on unrestricted access to shopping centres from public streets, and on the fact that access by the public is the very reason for the existence of shopping centres; there is the comparison drawn between the public markets of long ago and the shopping centre as a modern market place; there is the appreciation that in the light of the interests involved there can be no solution to their reconciliation by posting a flat all or nothing approach. ...

[Laskin CJC then cited the following US cases: *Schwartz-Torrance Investment Corp v Bakery & Confectionery Workers' Union, Local 31*, 394 P2d 921 (Calif 1964); *Amalgamated Clothing Workers of America v Wonderland Shopping Center, Inc*, 122 NW 2d 785 (Mich 1963); *Amalgamated Food Employees' Union, Local 590 v Logan Valley Plaza Inc*, 391 US 308 (1968); *Lloyd Corp Ltd v Tanner*, 407 US 551 (1972).]

A more appropriate approach, to which I adverted earlier, is to recognize a continuing privilege in using the areas of the shopping centre provided for public passage subject to limitations arising out of the nature of the activity thereon and to the object pursued thereby, and subject as well to a limitation against material damage. There is analogy in existing conceptions of privilege as an answer to intentional torts, such as trespasses. The principle is expressed in Prosser, *Handbook of the Law of Torts*, 4th ed. (1971), at pp. 98-9 as follows:

"Privilege" is the modern term applied to those considerations which avoid liability where it might otherwise follow. In its broader sense, it is applied to any immunity which prevents the existence of a tort; but in its more common usage, it signifies that the defendant has acted to further an interest of such social importance that it is entitled to protection, even at the expense of damage to the plaintiff. He is allowed freedom of action because his own interests, or those of the public require it, and social policy will best be served by permitting it. The boundaries of the privilege are marked out by current ideas of what will most effectively promote the general welfare.

. . .

Illustrations were given during the course of argument of situations which might put the respondent's activity in a different light relative to the place of picketing and to the object of picketing and which, correlatively, might provide some redeeming interest of the shopping centre owner in exercising control over the public areas. The character of a shopping centre, such as the one involved here, is one thing, and the nature and place of activities carried on there are something else. I would agree that it does not follow that because unrestricted access is given to members of the public to certain areas of the shopping centre during business hours, those areas are available at all times during those hours and in all circumstances to any kind of peaceful activity by members of the public, regardless of the interest being prompted by that activity and regardless of the numbers of members of the public who are involved. The Court will draw lines here as it does in other branches of the law as may be appropriate in the light of the legal principle and particular facts. In the present case it is the respondent who has been injured rather than the shopping centre owner.

I would dismiss the appeal.

Appeal allowed; conviction restored.

DISCUSSION NOTES

i. Facts and the Application of Precedents

Dickson J's and Laskin CJC's reasons illustrate differing approaches to the issue of whether the Supreme Court's previous decision in *R v Peters* constituted a precedent for this case. In reflecting on their differing views, consider the underlying assumptions that Dickson J and Laskin CJC demonstrate about whether a shopping centre should be characterized as fundamentally private or common property. Note that Dickson J concluded that it was not a relevant distinction that the picketer in *Peters* was "a mere member of the general public," while the picketer in *Harrison* was a striking employee of one of the tenants of the shopping centre. What factors supported this conclusion? What arguments were rejected?

Laskin CJC concluded that *Peters* was not a precedent for *Harrison*, but that even if it were, the Supreme Court should not be "mechanistic." Instead, he stated that the court should decide cases on the merits, even if that requires the court to reconsider its own precedent. Do you agree with Laskin CJC's suggestion that this case is not a case about a "brown horse," assuming that *Peters* was a case about a brown horse? Why, or why not? What kinds of factors should be considered relevant in the process of applying or distinguishing precedents? Should the existence of decisions of a number of provincial appellate courts that are not consistent be a relevant factor in such a context? Why is consistency in the treatment of picketers in shopping centres across the country a matter of importance that should be addressed by the Supreme Court of Canada? For a discussion about whether an appellate court like the Supreme Court of Canada should follow its own precedents (and what factors a court should consider before it decides to depart from one of its own precedents), see G Bale, "Casting Off the Mooring Ropes of Binding Precedent" (1980) 58 Can Bar Rev 255.

ii. Shopping Centres: Private or Public Property?

Is there a difference in the characterization of the shopping centre in the two judgments? Note that Laskin CJC identified different parts of the shopping centre, concluding that certain parts of the shopping centre were more public than private. How does such a characterization assist in supporting his conclusion in this case? What is the impact of his characterization on the potential effectiveness of striking picketers in a shopping centre? By contrast, if the shopping centre (as an entire entity) is characterized as private property, what is the impact on the potential effectiveness of striking picketers?

Does *Harrison* establish that the owner of private property has an absolute right to exclude? If the right is not an absolute one, what limits are recognized in *Harrison*? As noted above, some political theorists have argued that the concept of private property should be reconceptualized in terms of "a right not to be excluded": see CB Macpherson, "Liberal-Democracy and Property" in Macpherson 199 at 201:

> I shall argue that we have all been misled by accepting an unnecessarily narrow concept of property, a concept within which it is impossible to resolve the difficulties of any liberal theory. We have treated as the very paradigm of property what is really only a special case. It is time for a new paradigm, within which we may hope to resolve difficulties that could not be resolved within the old.
>
> As I have already shown, property, although it must always be an individual right, need not be confined, as liberal theory has confined it, to a right to exclude others from the use or benefit of some thing, but may equally be an individual right not to be excluded by others from the use or benefit of some thing. When property is so understood, the problem of liberal-democratic theory is no longer a problem of putting limits on the property right, but of supplementing the individual right to exclude others by the individual right not to be excluded by others. The latter right may be held to be the one that is most required by the liberal-democratic ethic, and most implied in a liberal concept of the human essence. The right not to be excluded by others may provisionally be stated as the individual right to equal access to the means of labour and/or the means of life.

How would such a characterization affect the outcome in *Harrison v Carswell*? For another analysis, see A Reeve, "The Theory of Property: Beyond 'Private' Versus 'Common Property,'" in D Held, ed, *Political Theory Today* (Stanford, CA: Stanford University Press, 1991) 91.

Consider the following application of Macpherson's concept of property as the right not to be excluded. RM Fischl described a typical employee making widgets in a company setting. At the end of the day, having built four widgets, the employee "tenders to her boss an amount in cash equal to the cost of the necessary materials and their procurement, the reasonable rental value of her workspace and tools, and the apportioned cost of other managerial expenses. She then leaves the shop and takes the widgets with her, planning to sell them and keep the profit." Fischl described how such an analysis is perplexing to most people who hear it because they think that the employee is guilty of theft. The author then suggests that, on the same basis, an employer may commit theft when the employer pays an employee a reasonable "rent" for her labour, "keeps the widgets for himself and sells them for his own profit." In response to the suggestion that the employer's actions do not amount to theft, by contrast with those of the employee, because "the law says that [the widgets] are his property," Fischl concluded that this result demonstrates how law generally reflects the interests of capitalism:

> The law reflects and enforces a core assumption about the relationship between employer and employee in a market economy: the employee's legally protected interest in the job is limited to his wage, while the employer is accorded the exclusive right to both the widgets and the profits to be earned from their sale.

(RM Fischl, "Some Realism About Critical Legal Studies" (1987) 41 U Miami L Rev 505 at 527.) For a critique of Fischl's analysis, suggesting that the employment relationship is justified in terms of arguments of economic efficiency, see RA Black, RS Kreider & M Sullivan, "Critical Legal Studies, Economic Realism, and the Theory of the Firm" (1988) 43 U Miami L Rev 343.

iii. The Context of Shopping Centre Picketing

In *Harrison*, the shopping centre's owner argued that it had established a policy, universally applied, prohibiting the distribution of pamphlets by anyone, including tenants of the shopping centre. How is this corporate policy relevant to the arguments in *Harrison*? Should such a policy override rights in provincial legislation that permit peaceful picketing by striking workers? If striking workers are permitted to picket on the grounds of shopping centres, should they also be permitted to do so on university campuses? Are there any differences in the "private" character of a shopping centre and a university campus?

In his reasons, Dickson J referred to an academic article that outlined the "legitimate concerns of the landlord of a shopping centre." The author, a respected labour-law academic, published this article as a commentary on the conflicting decisions across Canada in relation to picketing and shopping centres, reviewing US as well as Canadian decisions and assessing the competing interests of shopping centre owners and striking workers. In fact, as the following excerpt makes clear, the author reached a conclusion totally opposite to that excerpted in the reasons of Dickson J:

> There remains, then, the task of weighing up the competing interests of the labour union and the picketed tenant or landowner in the special context of shopping centre picketing. In the ordinary industrial dispute, of course, public policy acknowledges the union's interest in peacefully advertising the existence of a labour dispute through picketing. Such picketing is lawful even though it interferes with the use and enjoyment of the picketed property. To this extent, shopping centre picketing presents no special problem [and minor impediments to traffic or accidental inconvenience to adjacent shopowners] can be handled by requiring the pickets to confine their activities to the immediate vicinity of the dispute.
>
> The special factor in shopping centre picketing is the landlord, a neutral in the labour dispute. First, he is responsible for the maintenance of orderly traffic movement in the public areas of the shopping centre … . The landlord spends his own money on the public areas of the shopping centre, and does so for the sole purpose of making a profit. Second, while public authorities may, on behalf of the community, strike a reasonable balance between traffic and picketing on public sidewalks and streets, the shopping centre owner can hardly be expected to make such a choice: he has no authority to speak for the community; to grant picketing or parading privileges to all would invite chaos, while to do so selectively would invite commercial reprisals. He is thus driven to adopt a highly restrictive approach to granting permission to groups who wish to parade or picket in the shopping centre.
>
> Set against these two legitimate concerns of the landlord is the union's contention that unless picketing is allowed on the public areas of the shopping centre, it cannot take place at all. The theoretical alternative, of course, is picketing on the adjacent public highways. To such picketing there are both legal and practical obstacles. Legally, the risk is that picketing on the perimeter of the shopping centre will be construed as illegal pressure against all of its tenants [and, practically, many more pickets are needed to patrol the perimeter of a shopping centre].

> Weighing these considerations in the scales of public policy, it is hard to say that peaceful informational picketing should be forbidden in shopping centres. The flow of traffic may be protected by requiring that the pickets remain few in number, well-behaved, and in a confined area … . Happily the appellate courts of Saskatchewan and British Columbia appear to have struck this balance, whether consciously or otherwise.

(H Arthurs, "Note" (1965) 43 Can Bar Rev 357 at 362.)

How are the policy considerations identified in Arthurs's commentary reflected (in different ways) in the judgments in *Harrison v Carswell*? Does this case reflect differing views on the part of the two justices about the role of the courts as well as about policy concerns and the effects of precedent? Which of these concerns is most significant in terms of the outcome of the case?

iv. Litigation or Dispute Resolution?

Sophie Carswell was charged with four counts of trespass under the *Petty Trespasses Act* of Manitoba. The charges were initially dismissed by the provincial judge, but she was convicted on a trial *de novo* (a form of appeal that requires a new trial) in the County Court and she was fined $10 on each of the four charges. Her total fine was therefore $40. On appeal to the Manitoba Court of Appeal, the convictions were set aside, leading to this further appeal with leave of the Supreme Court of Canada. Why did Sophie Carswell's case, involving a monetary issue of $40, proceed to the Supreme Court of Canada? Were there important interests at stake for the parties? Were there important interests at stake for others who were not parties to this action?

Although the judgment does not address the issue of costs, it is likely that "costs followed the event," that is, the unsuccessful party bears the costs of the successful party. If there are important public issues at stake in this case, should normal rules about costs apply? In relation to a similar case about picketing in a shopping centre in the United States (*Hudgens v National Labor Relations Board*, 424 US 507 (1976)), Chused commented on the impact of the protracted proceedings in these cases and the general usefulness of litigation:

> The incredibly convoluted history of this litigation re-emphasizes several themes … . The legal system may be a disastrous place to take a dispute. The cost and length of some litigation is enormous. Perhaps that is why so many of the cases … [are] either grudge matches or, like *Hudgens*, test cases. Who, other than a "grudge" or a tester with outside financial support, would possibly pursue litigation far beyond the point justified by monetary loss or gain?

(R Chused, *Cases, Materials, and Problems in Property* (New York: Matthew Bender, 1989) at 344-45.) Do these comments appear to be applicable to *Harrison v Carswell*?

B. Distinguishing Harrison v Carswell: "Shifting the Paradigm"?

Since *Harrison v Carswell* was decided in 1975, the issue of the shopping centre owner's right to exclude has arisen in a number of other cases. Many of these cases have distinguished *Harrison v Carswell*. As a result, the definition of the shopping centre owner's private property interest must now take account of the reasoning not only in *Harrison v Carswell*, but also in several subsequent cases. These cases demonstrate the dynamic quality of common law decision making—a process that illustrates how later decisions may contribute to altering the current legal status of a landmark decision.

This process of ongoing refinement in the common law bears some similarity to Thomas Kuhn's theory of paradigm shifts in science. According to Kuhn, scientific theories replace earlier views because they answer questions that earlier views cannot answer: see J Moulton, "A Paradigm of Philosophy: The Adversary Method" in S Harding and MB Hintikka, eds, *Discovering Reality: Feminist Perspectives on Epistemology, Metaphysics, Methodology, and Philosophy of Science* (Boston: D Reidel, 1983) 149.

In the legal context as well, the process of common law decision making permits change to occur. Whether the decisions after *Harrison v Carswell* have added enough distinctions to the original decision so that we can say that a paradigm shift has occurred may be open to debate. Clearly, however, it is impossible to assert that the law is the same now as in 1975, and this result has occurred through judicial decision making, statutory reform, and the entrenchment of the Charter in the Canadian Constitution. As you examine the notes and cases that follow, assess the extent of a paradigm shift in the context of private property rights for shopping centre owners.

More practically, suppose that you are legal counsel for a shopping centre and must advise your client about the continuing relevance of *Harrison v Carswell*. What advice would be legally appropriate?

1. Contextual Differences: Provincial Statutes and Labour Board Decisions

The facts in *Wildwood Mall Ltd v Stevens*, [1980] 2 WWR 638 (Sask QB) were similar to those in *Harrison v Carswell*. However, the court distinguished *Harrison* on the ground that there was no legislation in Saskatchewan analogous to the *Petty Trespasses Act* in Manitoba, pursuant to which Sophie Carswell was charged. Why should this legislative difference be determinative? Why might a court in Saskatchewan have used this statutory difference to "distinguish" *Harrison v Carswell*?

Harrison v Carswell was also considered in *RWDSU v T Eaton Company Limited* (1986), 10 Can LRBR (NS) 289 (OLRB), where the union initiated a complaint before the Ontario Labour Relations Board (OLRB), alleging that Cadillac Fairview and the Eaton's store at the Toronto Eaton Centre had violated the rights of employees at the Eaton's store to belong to a union.

Cadillac Fairview managed and controlled the Toronto Eaton Centre shopping mall on a day-to-day basis, and it had adopted a "no-solicitation" policy for the shopping centre. When representatives of the Eaton's store notified Cadillac Fairview that union organizers were handing out informational material and leaflets on Eaton's premises, Cadillac Fairview informed the union organizers that, for example, distributing leaflets on mall property was prohibited. Because the Eaton's store was located entirely within the Toronto Eaton Centre, however, there were no public entrances to the Eaton's store available to union organizers except those clearly located on the shopping mall's premises.

In its complaint to the OLRB, the union asserted that Cadillac Fairview was in breach of s 64 of the Ontario *Labour Relations Act* (now SO 1995, c 1, s 70), a section that prohibits an employer or someone acting on behalf of an employer from interfering "with the formation, selection or administration of a trade union." In finding Cadillac Fairview in breach of the "unfair labour practices" section of the Act, the board specifically noted that this section "was not … before the Court in *Harrison v Carswell*, and we do not think that anyone would argue that the Court, by its decision, was granting to mall-owners a blanket exemption for unfair labour practices." As the board noted, although the owner of a shopping centre has an identifiable commercial interest in ensuring that mall traffic is not disrupted, its interest does not extend to situations where there is no interference or contact with the shopping public. In this context, the board concluded that Cadillac Fairview could not show any interference "with their own legitimate activities." An application to quash this decision of the OLRB was denied: *Re Cadillac Fairview Corp Ltd and RWDSU* (1988), 62 OR (2d) 337 (Div Ct), and this decision was affirmed by the Ontario Court of Appeal: (1988), 71 OR (2d) 206.

In the context of these subsequent decisions, can you identify the continuing impact of the Supreme Court's majority decision in *Harrison v Carswell*? Significantly, in the context of the OLRB decision, a prominent municipal councillor, Jack Layton, was arrested after refusing to leave the premises where he was leafleting Eaton's employees during a union organizing drive. Layton was charged under Ontario's *Trespass to Property Act*, 1980 (now RSO 1990, c T.21, as amended by SO 2000, c 30, s 11), and convicted.

Layton appealed his conviction, arguing that his actions were protected within the guarantee of freedom of expression under the Charter. On appeal, Scott J held that the method of distribution was an important factor, and that Layton was offering literature to employees in a "peaceful and friendly manner." Scott J overturned the conviction and expressly rejected the respondent's argument that allowing the accused's appeal would result in "a state of peril" for property rights in Canada: see *R v Layton* (1986), 38 CCC (3d) 550 (Prov Ct Crim Div). The Charter issue is discussed in more detail below. In addition, for discussion about the continuing litigation relating to challenges to the owner's claims of private property at the Toronto Eaton Centre, see Tucker, "The Malling of Property Law" in Tucker, Muir & Ziff, eds.

2. *Trespass in Ontario*

As Dickson J noted, legislation in British Columbia at the time of the decision in *Harrison* provided that, in relation to picketing, no trespass occurred in respect of real property "to which a member of the public ordinarily has access." Indeed, following the Supreme Court's decision in *Harrison v Carswell*, the Manitoba legislature amended the *Petty Trespasses Act* to permit informational picketing on "any walk, driveway, roadway, square or parking area provided outdoors at the site of or in conjunction with the premises in which any business or undertaking is operated and to which the public is normally admitted without fee or charge": see SM 1976, c 71, now CCSM, c P50, s 4. Does this legislative action confirm the view of Dickson J that the issue was better suited to the legislature rather than judicial decision making? For an excellent discussion of the issues in *Harrison v Carswell*, see P Girard & J Phillips, "A Certain 'Malaise': Harrison v Carswell, Shopping Centre Picketing, and the Limits of the Post-War Settlement" in J Fudge and E Tucker, eds, *Work on Trial: Canadian Labour Law Struggles* (Toronto: Irwin Law for the Osgoode Society for Canadian Legal History, 2010) 249.

In 1992, Ontario's legislation was similarly amended. The *Labour Relations and Employment Statute Law Amendment Act, 1992*, SO 1992, c 21 added s 11.1 to the Ontario *Labour Relations Act*. The 1992 amendment provided:

> 11.1(1) This section applies with respect to premises to which the public normally has access and from which a person occupying the premises would have a right to remove individuals.

(2) Employees and persons acting on behalf of a trade union have the right to be present on premises described in subsection (1) for the purpose of attempting to persuade employees to join a trade union. Attempts to persuade the employees may be made only at or near but outside the entrances and exits to the employees' workplace.

$$\cdots$$

(8) In the event of a conflict between a right described in subsection (2) [and other related sections] and other rights established at common law or under the *Trespass to Property Act*, the right described in those subsections prevails.

This legislation was later repealed and replaced by the *Labour Relations and Statute Law Amendment Act, 1995*, SO 1995, c 1. Section 11.1 was not included in the revised legislation. What is the explanation for the 1992 legislation and its repeal in 1995?

Ontario's *Trespass to Property Act*, RSO 1990, c T.21, as amended by SO 2000, c 30, s 11, currently defines the offence of trespass as follows:

2(1) Every person who is not acting under a right or authority conferred by law and who,
    (a) without the express permission of the occupier, the proof of which rests on the defendant,
        (i) enters on premises when entry is prohibited under this Act, or
        (ii) engages in an activity on premises when the activity is prohibited under this Act;
    or
    (b) does not leave the premises immediately after he is directed to do so by the occupier of the premises or a person authorized by the occupier,
is guilty of an offence and on conviction is liable to a fine of not more than $2,000.
    (2) It is a defence to a charge under subsection (1) in respect of premises that is land that the person charged reasonably believed that he had title to or an interest in the land that entitled him to do the act complained of.

This legislation is similar to statutes elsewhere: see *Protection of Property Act*, RSNS 1989, c 363, as am, and *Trespass Act*, SNB 2012, c 117, s 3(1). Consider the language of the Ontario statute in the light of the facts of *Harrison v Carswell*. Would the case have been decided in the same way pursuant to the Ontario legislation? Why, or why not?

3. The Continuing Impact of Harrison v Carswell

In an assessment of the continuing usefulness of *Harrison v Carswell* after the Charter, M Litman concluded that there were several reasons for being optimistic "that *Harrison v. Carswell* will be reconsidered and reversed":

The majority view in that case seems to have been based on the supposition that property is inherently absolute and that the dramatic step of depriving its owner, even to a limited extent, of its unbridled power is a matter for legislative policy. This supposition ... as a matter of historical record, is not entirely accurate. Proprietary rights of exclusion, like other private rights, have been modified or subordinated to accommodate a variety of interests since the early days of the common law, and continue today to yield to such interests ... . There is no reason in principle why free speech should not be part of the constellation of considerations which affect the determination of whether property rights exist and, if so, whether those rights are tempered by the public interest.

(MM Litman, "Freedom of Speech and Private Property: The Case of the Mall Owner" in D Schneiderman, ed, *Freedom of Expression and the Charter* (Scarborough, ON: Thomson, 1991) 361 at 407.) See also Lisa Loader, "Trespass to Property: Shopping Centres" (1992) 87 J L & Soc Pol'y 254; Stephanie M Robinson, "Revisiting the Eaton's Centre: Picketing on Quasi-Public Property in Ontario" (1999) LELJ 391; and JW Singer, "No Right to Exclude: Public Accommodations and Private Property" (1996) 90 Nw UL Rev 1283. Note, however, that although *Harrison v Carswell* has frequently been subjected to critique, it has not been expressly overruled.

4. Shopping Centres and Their Role as Public Spaces

The Ontario *Trespass to Property Act* was criticized by a task force report in 1987 that considered the law of trespass in relation to the experience of youth and minorities in shopping malls. The following brief extract provides arguments for conceptualizing shopping centres as public spaces, as originally envisaged by Victor Gruen. Consider the task force arguments and recommendations: do these arguments support legislative action to redefine the concept of trespass in shopping centres?

> **Ontario, *Task Force on the Law Concerning Trespass to Publicly Used Property as It Affects Youth and Minorities***
> Raj Anand, Chair (Toronto: Ontario Ministry of the Attorney General, 1987)
> at ii-x
>
> The traditional common law of trespass to property was predicated upon absolute notions of private property and its attributes, such as the right to exclude others. The last two centuries of industrialization and other social change have seen an accelerating process of limitation of private property rights where public and private interests in the use of such property have diverged. As late as the mid-1970's, the Supreme Court of Canada enunciated a "duty of common humanity" on property owners toward trespassers who suffered injury.
>
> Viewed in its common law context, the [*Trespass to Property Act* (TPA)] was unfortunate in certain respects. It took no account of the developing trends in balancing the competing social interests in publicly-used property. It instead crystallized the absolutist common law position in Ontario, and thereby foreclosed further development. The *TPA*, like its predecessors, makes no distinction between different types of property and the degree of public use. Under the Act, a shopping mall is no different than a private home, in that it carries with it a general right of exclusion of any visitor, and the exercise of this right is legally subject to the owner's whim. ...
>
> On its face, the *TPA* creates the potential for unduly restrictive or discriminatory enforcement against minorities and youth. An occupier or manager of publicly-used property or a security guard can require any member of the public to leave the property at any time, for any reason, or for no reason at all. This can be accomplished either orally or by written notice. If the person does not leave immediately, he or she commits an offence. ...
>
> The widespread public perception is that shopping centres are "public property" or "public places," in the sense that persons have the right to enter freely, walk around, converse

with others and remain within the common areas as long as they wish, much as they would conduct themselves in a city square. ...

The central role of shopping centres as a location for community interaction is reflected in the fact that in terms of time spent by the average citizen, shopping centres rank third, after (1) home and (2) work or school.

"Hanging out" is not a problem in itself. It is a healthy and indeed necessary pastime in a contemporary world which is increasingly dominated by the concerns of family and work. In earlier Ontario society and in many of the countries of origin of recent immigrants "hanging around" on street corners and squares has been indispensable to effective social participation. In Ontario, suburban areas frequently grew up without much planning for public spaces and social facilities, and malls became the accidental capitals of suburbia. In downtown areas, shopping malls literally displaced and enclosed city streets, street corners and plazas. Into the mall and onto its closed streets, have been added most of the amenities associated with community life; moreover, essential services are often found in shopping plazas and nowhere else in the neighbourhood. ...

The privatization of the town square must carry with it a corresponding obligation to provide for "non-productive uses." This obligation must be implemented through legal recognition in the *TPA* of the public use of such private property and by addressing design issues in the construction of publicly-used spaces.

This task force was created as a result of complaints from Toronto's Black community that its members were being unfairly banned from shopping centres, including those in the Jane-Finch area in Toronto: for some detail, see Parkdale Community Legal Services, "Submissions to the Task Force on the Law Concerning Trespass to Publicly Used Property as It Affects Youths and Minorities" (1997) 35:4 Osgoode Hall LJ 819. Although a bill was introduced to amend the *Trespass to Property Act*, it died on the order paper when an election was called and the government changed. Similar issues arose at the Scarborough Town Centre, with complaints filed to the Ontario Human Rights Commission as a result of the shopping centre's use of "trespass bans" against Filipino Canadians: see John Beaufoy, "Filipino Community Turns to OHRC After Members Banned from Mall," *Law Times* (25-31 October 1993) at 5. Some of these concerns were addressed in the context of Charter guarantees, discussed in the next section.

IV. PROPERTY RIGHTS AND THE CHARTER

With the advent of the *Canadian Charter of Rights and Freedoms*, Part I of the *Constitution Act, 1982*, 1982, c 11 (UK), Schedule B ("the Charter"), courts acquired new roles in examining legislation, with authority to strike it down if it infringed Charter-guaranteed rights (subject to s 1 of the Charter based on "reasonable limits," and s 32, the "legislative override" provision).

The Charter was significant for property law in two ways. First, because of the entrenched guarantees in s 2, including freedom of speech and freedom of assembly, issues about public access to shopping centres (and to similar places where the public is routinely invited) seemed to require new analytical approaches. As with Jack Layton's acquittal, discussed above, the cases reveal how courts were required to balance competing interests of owners of "private" property and persons who were invited to be present on the basis of the "quasi-public" aspects of such property. As you will recall, Laskin CJC identified the quasi-public nature of shopping centres in his dissenting judgment in *Harrison v Carswell*, and it is therefore also important to compare his approach to the reasoning in these later Charter cases. And, as these cases reveal, although the Supreme Court of Canada has never overruled *Harrison v Carswell*, the rights of owners of "public" property (including government-owned property) may now need to be balanced with the Charter's guarantees pursuant to a s 1 analysis.

The second aspect of the Charter that is of interest to property law is that "property" is not itself a protected interest in the Charter. Although there is protection for property in the US *Bill of Rights*, and in some comparable constitutional and international documents, Canada's Parliament debated and then rejected inclusion of protection for property in the Charter. By contrast, the US Constitution specifically provides for a right to compensation for a governmental "taking" of private property: see ss 5 and 14, discussed below. In the absence of such guarantees in the Canadian context, courts have tended to interpret quite strictly the provincial statutes concerning governmental expropriation of private land.

This section briefly examines issues about the impact of the Charter in relation to these two different aspects of the relationship between property and the Charter: to what extent do Charter guarantees provide citizens with access to "public" property; and is there a need for Charter protection for owners of private property in the context of governmental regulation affecting their property interests?

A. The Charter and Access to "Public" Space

Committee for the Commonwealth of Canada v Canada
[1991] 1 SCR 139

[In this case, the Committee (plaintiff) wished to distribute pamphlets about its organization at the Montreal airport at Dorval. The airport authorities prevented Committee members from doing so on the basis of federal regulations that expressly prohibited advertising or solicitation in the airport. The plaintiff initiated an action pursuant to s 2(b) of the Charter (protection for freedom of expression). The plaintiff succeeded at trial and on appeal in the Federal Court. The Supreme Court of Canada also dismissed the government's appeal, with a number of judges issuing reasons for the court's decision.

In her reasons, L'Heureux-Dubé J considered the government's argument that, as the owner of the airport, it had the "right to exclude" anyone for any reason, and that its proprietary rights were no different from those of other owners of private property. In rejecting this argument, L'Heureux-Dubé J stated:

> [If] the government had complete discretion to treat its property as would a private citizen, it could differentiate on the basis of content, or choose between particular viewpoints, and grant access to sidewalks, streets, parks, the courthouse lawn, and even Parliament Hill only to those whose message accorded with the government's preferences. Such a standard would be antithetical to the spirit of the Charter, and would stultify the true import of freedom of expression.

However, L'Heureux-Dubé J refused to decide the issue of the Charter's effect with respect to leafleting on *private* property, because she concluded that no such issue was before the court. Thus, in this case, the court did not *expressly* overrule *Harrison v Carswell*.

In the context of the Montreal airport, moreover, L'Heureux-Dubé J held that it was necessary to balance the interests of the government and members of the public:]

If members of the public had no right whatsoever to distribute leaflets or engage in other expressive activity on government-owned property (except with permission), then there would be little if any opportunity to exercise their rights of freedom of expression. Only those with large enough wealth to own land, or mass media facilities (whose ownership is largely concentrated), would be able to engage in free expression. This would subvert achievement of the Charter's basic purpose. …

On the other hand, the Charter's framers did not intend internal government offices, air traffic control towers, prison cells and judges' chambers to be made available for leafletting or demonstrations. It is evident that the right to freedom of expression … does not provide a right of access to all property whether public or private. …

The logical compromise then is to recognize that some, but not all, government-owned property is constitutionally open to the public for engaging in expressive activity. …

[After reviewing cases and principles in the American constitutional context, L'Heureux-Dubé J stated:]

… The logic of these cases is that airports have become "contemporary crossroads"; they are functionally equivalent to other public thoroughfares, and should therefore be on the same constitutional footing as streets and parks. …

[A]irplanes, even if publicly owned, could not be characterized as a public forum. People who find certain political expression unpleasant or disquieting in a park or on a street can easily move elsewhere. On planes the costs of premature exit are too high. However, bus stations and airports have much more in common with streets and parks …. These locations are "contemporary crossroads" or "modern thoroughfares," and thus should be accessible to those seeking to communicate with the passing crowds. …

While the symbolism of a courthouse lawn or Parliament Hill is self-evident, streets and parks have also acquired special significance as places where one can have access to and address his or her fellow citizens on any number of matters.

DISCUSSION NOTES

i. "Private" Property and Freedom of Expression

Committee for the Commonwealth of Canada was decided by the Supreme Court in 1991, a decade before the attacks on the World Trade Center in New York City. In this context, it seems clear that "public" space in airports has narrowed considerably since this case was decided, but the principle of balancing private property interests and opportunities for freedom of expression in "contemporary crossroads" may still be viable. For example, would the Committee for the Commonwealth of Canada be permitted to leaflet in a shopping centre? Why, or why not?

In reflecting on this question, consider some earlier US decisions with respect to freedom of expression. For example, in *Pruneyard Shopping Center v Robins*, 447 US 74 (1980), the US Supreme Court reviewed a decision of the California Supreme Court that had concluded that the state constitution protected persons soliciting petition signatures in a private shopping centre. In the Supreme Court, the shopping centre owner argued that the lower court decision constituted an unconstitutional "taking" by government of the mall owner's individual property rights. The US Supreme Court rejected this argument, concluding (at 83) that there was no basis for finding that "this sort of activity will unreasonably impair the value or use of their property as a shopping center." See also *Green Party v Hartz Mt Indus*, 752 A2d 315 (NJ S Ct 2000). For other comments on the nature of the public–private distinction in the property context, see M Horwitz, "The History of the Public/Private Distinction" (1982) 130 U Pa L Rev 1423; and D Kennedy, "The Stages of the Decline of the Public/Private Distinction" (1982) 130 U Pa L Rev 1349.

Is an airport owned by a government less "private" property than a shopping centre owned by a corporation? Why, or why not? The constitutional issues are complex, and you may want to reconsider the reasoning in this case in relation to subsequent materials in this chapter. For a good overview of the issues in the Montreal airport decision, see J Cameron, "A Bumpy Landing: The Supreme Court of Canada and Access to Public Airports Under Section 2(b) of the Charter" (1991) 2 Media & Comm Law Rev 91.

ii. Private Property and State Property

Consider the comments of CB Macpherson about property owned by the government— "state property":

> [State property] consists of rights which the state has not only created but has kept for itself or has taken over from private individuals or corporations … . Various enterprises, e.g., railways and airlines, are in many countries owned by the state. The rights which the state holds and exercises in respect of these things, the rights which comprise the state's property in these things, are akin to private property rights, for they consist of the right to the use and benefit, and the right to exclude others from the use and benefit, of something. In effect, the state itself is taking and exercising the powers of a corporation: it is acting as an artificial person … . State property, then, is not common property as we have defined it: state property is not an individual right not to be excluded. It is a corporate right to exclude. As a corporate right to exclude others it fits the definition of (corporate) private property.

(CB Macpherson, "The Meaning of Property" in Macpherson 1 at 5.)

Do you agree that state property is more like private property than common property? On what basis? Is this analysis consistent with *Committee for the Commonwealth of Canada* in relation to government property in Canada after the Charter? Is it possible to argue that the Charter introduced some limitations on government or state property?

In the light of *Harrison v Carswell* and *Committee for the Commonwealth of Canada*, what legal advice would you give to demonstrators at the provincial legislature whose activities were expressly banned by the Speaker? Is the legislature private property or government property? In *R v Behrens*, [2001] OJ no 245 (CJ), the court held (applying the reasoning of the Supreme Court in *Committee for the Commonwealth of Canada*) that the demonstrators could not be charged under the *Trespass to Property Act* so long as their demonstrations were peaceful and did not interfere with the function of the legislature.

By contrast, another 2001 decision concluded that there was no evidence that panhandlers begging for money on Toronto streets were intending to make a political point by soliciting for funds. According to the court, the activity of begging was "more akin to commercial than to political expression" so that it did not engage the core values of s 2(b) of the Charter: the "expression" in this case was characterized as "peripheral to the core values" of s 2(b). See *R v Banks* (2001), 55 OR (3d) 374 (CJ) at 409. This case was one of a number of constitutional challenges, in which the Canadian Civil Liberties Association intervened, with respect to Ontario's *Safe Streets Act*, SO 1999, c 8, legislation that prohibited soliciting in an "aggressive" manner and in relation to "squeegee" activity at road intersections. For an assessment of these issues, see N Blomley, "Begging to Differ: Panhandling, Public Space, and Municipal Property" in Tucker, Muir, & Ziff, eds, at 393.

The Supreme Court of Canada also applied the reasoning in *Committee for the Commonwealth of Canada v Canada* to a case involving secondary picketing activity: see *RWDSU, Local 558 v Pepsi-Cola Canada Beverages (West) Ltd*, 2002 SCC 8, [2002] 1 SCR 156 at paras 67 and 69. See also *United Food and Commercial Workers, Local 1518 v Kmart Canada Ltd*, [1999] 2 SCR 1083; *RMH Teleservices Inc v BCGEU*, 2003 BCSC 278; and *R v Marcocchio* (2002), 213 NSR (2d) 86.

B. Parks and "Public" Space

In *Committee for the Commonwealth of Canada*, L'Heureux-Dubé J identified different parts of the airport that might be more or less public areas, in much the same way that Laskin CJC identified different parts of the shopping centre as more or less public. Is it possible to regard parts of these properties as private or state property, while other parts are common property? Would such a resolution be more likely to be achieved by negotiation or by litigation? Why?

L'Heureux-Dubé J also identified parks as public property. Recall her statement that

> bus stations and airports have much more in common with streets and parks than they do with buses or airplanes which they service. These locations are "contemporary crossroads" or "modern thoroughfares," and thus should be accessible to those seeking to communicate with the passing crowds … . While the symbolism of a courthouse lawn or Parliament Hill is self-evident, streets and parks have also acquired significance as places where one can have access to and address his or her fellow citizens on any number of matters.

Consider this comment in relation to *Batty v Toronto*, which follows. Why did the court conclude that the Occupy Toronto protesters were not entitled to use a Toronto city park in relation to their Charter guarantee of freedom of expression?

Batty v Toronto (City)
2011 ONSC 6862, 108 OR (3d) 571

[In this case, protesters involved in the Occupy Toronto movement began to camp overnight in St James Park on October 15, 2011. The camp was used as shelter for the protesters, some of whom came from locations outside Toronto, and it provided a base for the protesters' periodic demonstrations. The court noted that the park was just over three acres in size and located three blocks east of the city's financial district, the target of many of the demonstrations. On November 15, the date when the City of Toronto issued a trespass notice, there were 300 tents, 3 yurts, approximately 10 larger tent structures used for purposes such as kitchen facilities, a library, meeting spaces, media, storage of basic necessities, and 25 porta-potty facilities. The protesters also permitted homeless persons to sleep in the camp overnight, thus "actively creating alternatives to inadequate government social assistance" (affidavit of Bryan Batty at para 28).

In response to the City of Toronto's trespass notice, the protesters applied for an injunction, preventing the city from evicting the protesters from the park. This claim was based on an infringement of the protesters' rights pursuant to ss 2(a) to (d) of the Charter (that is, their rights to freedom of conscience, expression, peaceful assembly, and association). In determining this application, the court concluded that there was an infringement of s 2 of the Charter, but that the city's infringement was saved by s 1. Examine the reasoning in this case and whether or to what extent it departed from the ideas about parks as public spaces in *Committee for the Commonwealth of Canada*.]

BROWN J:

[1] How do we live together in a community? How do we share common space? These questions have elicited quite different answers in different political communities at different times over the centuries. In our Canadian community we have crafted an understanding which has drawn on long strands tracing their roots back to both secular and religious sources. In the realm of political and civic relationships we have articulated that understanding most recently in the *Canadian Charter of Rights and Freedoms*. The Charter's Preamble makes two points: as a consequence of the "supremacy of God," we all must bring humility to our dealings with our fellow citizens; as a consequence of "the rule of law," we all must live subject to some rules—we are not unconstrained free actors.

[2] Now, of course, some dissent from that last point of view. Anarchism has a long political history. But, Canada has not chosen anarchism. Instead, when we collectively adopted [the Charter] some 30 years ago, we embraced, in a constitutional way, a political philosophy which places great emphasis on the liberty of the individual—as can be seen from the various rights and freedoms set out in [ss 2 to 15 of the Charter]—while at the same time re-iterating that those rights and freedoms are not absolute. Indeed, the first section of [the Charter] reminds us that individual action must always be alive to its effect on other members of the community: it states that limits can be placed on individual action as long as they are "reasonable limits prescribed by law as can be demonstrably justified in a free and democratic society."

. . .

[8] Four of the applicants filed affidavits which described part of the message of the Protesters as advocating the reform of democracy—render it more participatory, "direct," "horizontal," and ground it on "consensus-based decision making." As well, their message expresses a fundamental disagreement with the structure of the global economy. Those are most legitimate issues to raise in the public forum. The Protesters have every right to voice their critiques of the current political, economic and financial systems and to seek to bring others over to their point of view.

[9] Although proclaiming a message of participatory democracy, the evidence, unfortunately, reveals that the Protesters did not practise what they were preaching when they decided to occupy the Park. Specifically, they did not ask those who live and work around the Park or those who use the Park—or their civic representatives—what they would think if the Park was turned into a tent city.

[10] The Protesters now say, in effect, that the Charter did not require them to ask; that the Charter sanctions their unilateral occupation of the Park—which they intend to continue for an indefinite period of time—because of the importance of their message and the way in which they convey it—by taking over public property.

[11] With the greatest of respect to the Applicants and the Protesters, they are mistaken.

[12] The Charter offers no justification for the Protesters' act of appropriating to their own use—without asking their fellow citizens—a large portion of common public space for an indefinite period of time.

[According to the court, the Charter did not remove the need to apply common sense and balance in civic relationships, or in balancing competing rights in the contemporary Canadian polity. In addition, the court stated that the Charter does not permit protesters "to take over public space without asking, exclude the rest of the public from enjoying their traditional use of that space, and then contend that they are under no obligation to leave" (para 15).

The court provided details of the protesters and noted that the City of Toronto owned St James Park. The court also identified the intervention of the Canadian Civil Liberties Association as a friend of the court, and that proper service of notice of constitutional questions on the federal and provincial attorneys general had taken place, but that neither of these parties had appeared in the proceeding. The court then reviewed affidavits filed by the protesters, who had stated:

> My desire for a radically different society requires that I am able to learn through experience a new economic and social model. If we are to move forward as a country and world, citizens must have the opportunity to practice an alternative form of living and working, preparing for a more participatory, horizontal model of democracy [affidavit of Lana Goldberg at para 32].

> Creating reform within the city requires resources and a permanent space to facilitate this expression and civic engagement, our message would be significantly if not totally watered down by the dismantling of the encampment [affidavit of Bryan Batty at para 32].

The applicants also described their general assembly meetings twice each day and the extensive committee structure to oversee all the activities. They identified the camp as having a symbolic significance and as reflecting the motivation for change among the participants. They also noted the provision of services to the homeless and shelter for those from locations out of town, and then emphasized their creation of alternative services and their commitment to reform goals (affidavit of Bryan Batty at para 37).

The court then reviewed the affidavits of some of the residents in the area surrounding the park. The residents complained of altercations with the protesters in the use of the park, including as a place for children to play and dogs to be walked. They also identified the bad odours from the portable toilets, noise (including yelling, singing, and drumming), and smoke from campfires (para 42). In addition, the court referred to complaints to the city about the encampment, including one that described the occupation of the park as the "open theft and violation of the rights of the public" (para 43). Finally, the court also reviewed the concerns of the city, including destruction of grass and flowers, the noise of vans and trucks delivering goods, the smell of garbage, and littering (para 46). In this context, the city also noted how the encampment was a violation of a number of bylaws relating to city parks, including a prohibition on overnight activities (para 48). The court then turned to the applicants' claim of an infringement of s 2 of the Charter.]

. . .

[63] … Canada enjoys an enviable reputation amongst the world's nations for its public culture of political expression. Although public speech still sometimes stumbles against pockets of process and content-based restrictions in public institutions, by and large Canadian public streets and places remain open and available for the expression of a wide variety of political and social messages … . [According to s 2(b),] everyone has the fundamental "freedom of thought, belief, opinion and expression, including freedom of the press and other media of communication." The analytic approach adopted by the Supreme Court of Canada … requires a court to pose and answer three questions: (i) Does the applicant's conduct or statement have expressive content? (ii) If so, does the method or location of this expression remove that protection? (iii) If the expression is protected by [s 2(b)], does the government action or legislation infringe that protection, either in purpose or effect?

[The court noted that violent expression is not protected by the Charter, and then continued:]

Not all public or government-owned property is available for Charter-protected expressive activity. Public streets, however, "are clearly areas of public, as opposed to private, concourse, where expression of many varieties has long been accepted." Expressive activities on public streets are *prima facie* protected by the Charter.

[The court also noted that s 2 also related to lawful means of expression.]

[64] That the applicants are engaged in conduct expressing political and social messages is not in doubt. The content of their speech involves quintessentially political messages. What is distinctive about the claims the applicants make for their speech is two-fold. First, the applicants contend that one of the methods of their expression—occupying public land and creating a tent city—is essential to their exercise of Charter rights. Second, the applicants claim Charter protection for a "prolonged" exercise of their rights, indeed one which could be indefinite and will only end when they so choose.

[The court also presented the city's view that its trespass notice did not infringe the applicants' Charter rights.]

. . .

[66] The evidence in this case discloses that the applicants are using several methods or manners by which to convey their political messages: (i) posters and signs; (ii) marches or demonstrations; (iii) posting on internet sites; and (iv) erecting and periodically using structures, such as tents and yurts. The applicants place great emphasis on the link between the messages they wish to convey and the means by which they are attempting to convey them. The evidence shows that the applicants sincerely believe that the structures which the Protesters have erected in the Park are an important part of the manner by which they are expressing their messages.

[The court noted (at para 68) that the protesters believed that "the camp is the movement."

In its decision, the court accepted the protesters' argument that their encampment in a public park was activity that engaged s 2 of the Charter (para 70), quoting cases such as *Vancouver (City) v Zhang*, 2009 BCSC 84, 2010 BCCA 450. More specifically, the court held that the structures erected by the protesters in St James Park formed part of the manner of expressing their political message (para 72). The court then turned to the "central issue" in the case: "whether such an infringement can be justified under s 1 of the Charter":

. . .

[76] … In this case, the sole legal basis relied upon by the City of Toronto for the eviction, the *Trespass to Property Act*, does not contain specific legal authorization for the limitation of Charter-protected activity in St. James Park. The provisions of that Act provide no notice to the Applicants regarding what conduct is prohibited.

As the court noted, the applicants thus argued that the city's notice represented an administrative decision that was not "prescribed by law" (applicants' factum, para 77); however, the court then held that the city relied, in addition to the *Trespass to Property Act*, on the Parks bylaw (Toronto Municipal Code, Chapter 608) as authority to "invoke the enforcement mechanisms of the TPA and the issuance of its Trespass Notice" (para 82). The court also considered and rejected the argument that the limitation was overbroad or vague:]

. . .

[87] In the present case the Parks By-law quite clearly, and in considerable detail, identifies what types of conduct are impermissible or require a permit. If the applicants and other Protesters wanted to know whether their occupation was a permitted use of the Park under City ordinance, all they had to do was read the Parks By-law. The answer was crystal clear. Their occupation contravened the Parks By-law. There was no imprecision.

. . .

[91] Toronto is a densely populated city. Competing demands for the use of its limited parklands are numerous. Without some balancing of what people can and cannot do in parks, chaos would reign; parks would become battlegrounds of competing uses, rather than oases of tranquility in the concrete jungle. Or, parks would become places where the stronger, by use of occupation and intimidation, could exclude the weaker or those who are not prepared to resort to confrontation to carve out a piece of the park for their own use. The evidence filed before me from the residents indicates that that is precisely the

effect of the Protesters' occupation of the Park—the tents and other shelters hog the park land and non-Protesters who seek to use the Park face a chilly and somewhat intimidating reception.

[92] In addition, the permissible use of parks must take into account the effect on those living by and around the parks. If parks could be used without restriction to host all-night drumfests, folks who lived near the parks would not get much in the way of sleep. And we all have to sleep at some point of time.

[93] Finally, for folks in Toronto to continue to enjoy their parks, the City must maintain them in good condition. Having a picnic on a mound of bare earth is not the same experience as being able to stretch out a table cloth on some soft grass.

. . .

[96] I conclude that the regulation of the erection of structures in public parks and the use of parks during the midnight hours is a pressing and substantial objective.

[The court then considered the issue of proportionality, and concluded that the rational connection test was met.]

. . .

[104] … I accept the City's submission that the Trespass Notice which seeks to enforce two provisions of the Parks By-law would not result in an absolute ban on the Protesters' political expression or associational activities. As I observed earlier in these reasons, the Protesters employ several methods to convey their political messages: (i) signage; (ii) web postings; (iii) demonstrations and marches through City streets and to other public places; and (iv) occupying the Park. Compliance with the Trespass Notice would alter the Protesters' use of the Park—no structures, and absence during the midnight hours—but would not evict the protest from the Park. The Protesters would continue to be allowed to protest in the Park for close to 19 hours a day—hardly an absolute ban on their expressive activities. …

[105] The applicants submitted that because they regard the 24-hour a day occupation of the Park as an important part of their message, compliance with the Trespass Notice would result in an absolute ban of that form of their expressive and associational activities. This is where common sense must come into the picture. If I were to accept the applicants' argument, then any protest group could come along, assert that monopolizing a particular piece of public space was an important part of their political message, and the City would be powerless to object.

[106] The Charter does not create a world of such absolutes, rigidity, or lack of common sense with respect to the private use of public spaces. A few years back our Court of Appeal, in R. v. Banks—the "squeegeeing" case—had this to say about provisions in legislation which prohibited squeegeeing on public streets:

[T]he provisions impair the appellants' right of expression as little as possible. While the legislation does effectively ban squeegeeing on roadways, it does not prohibit the appellants from expressing their message that they are in need of help. I appreciate that the provisions of the Act not in issue in this appeal place other restrictions on where and how the appellants may solicit. Still, they are left with many alternatives. They can convey their message on the sidewalk. They cannot squeegee car windows, but to the extent that they may wish to provide a service in exchange for donations, there are other alternatives available [at para 131]. …

[108] I accept that part of the message the applicants and other Protesters seek to convey is that it is both possible and necessary to build a community structure different from that prevailing in most places of our society. The evidence shows that to that end the Protesters have appropriated public land to their exclusive, private use for the purpose of forming a residential community on public lands without complying with the rules governing the residential use of land in the City—zoning, sewage, water, etc.—or the rules governing the use of public parks. In sum, the applicants and the other Protesters want to create new rules through their General Assembly and ignore the existing rules that bind everyone else in this city. ...

[109] Part of our Constitution talks about "peace, order and good government." The Charter did not displace that organizing principle. When people come together to live in dense urban environments, flexibility and give-and-take must permeate everyone's actions, otherwise we would end up being at each other's throats—peace and order would go out the window.

· · ·

[114] In their submissions at the hearing the applicants argued that the City had failed to meet the minimal impairment test because it had not talked or consulted with the Protesters before issuing the Trespass Notice. As I understand their argument, the applicants contend that section 1 of the Charter imposed on the City a constitutional obligation to consult with them and to try to work things out before resorting to its by-law enforcement powers, such as the Trespass Notice.

[115] I see no merit in this argument. The applicants offered no jurisprudential support for the argument. That is not surprising. Such a constitutional obligation would paralyze municipal governments. Whether a municipality should consult with those who occupy public spaces before seeking to limit their use of those spaces is a matter of political prudence, not constitutional obligation [except with respect to Aboriginal rights and interests pursuant to s 35].

[The court also considered and rejected the argument in favour of a "political speech exemption policy" in the Parks bylaw.]

· · ·

[122] In sum, for the reasons set out above, I conclude that the City has demonstrated that its issuance and service of the Trespass Notice seeking to enforce two restrictions contained in the Parks By-law fell within a range of reasonable alternatives, tailored objective to infringement, and constituted a minimal impairment of the applicants' section 2 freedoms.

[Finally, the court also held that the requirement of proportionality between the measures and their salutary effects had been met by the city.]

· · ·

[124] For the reasons set out above, I conclude that the City has established that the limitations resulting from the enforcement of the Trespass Notice on the applicants' section 2 freedoms are "reasonable limits prescribed by law as can be demonstrably justified in a free and democratic society."

[The court thus dismissed the applicants' request for an injunction to prevent the city from enforcing the trespass notice. Because of the public importance of the issues raised, however, the court did not award costs.]

DISCUSSION NOTES

i. Balancing Public Space and Private (Governmental) Interests

As discussed in *Batty v Toronto*, a number of other cases have focused on balancing property rights and Charter-protected interests. In *Vancouver (City) v Zhang*, 2010 BCCA 450, for example, practitioners of the spiritual discipline Falun Gong (the respondents) had set up banners, posters, a billboard (8 feet high and 100 feet long), and a meditation hut on Granville Street, a main artery between downtown Vancouver and Vancouver International Airport; both the billboard and the hut encroached on the street. The protest was designed to create awareness about human rights abuses against Falun Gong practitioners in China. After discussions between the city and the respondents were unsuccessful, the city relied on s 71 of the revised bylaw no 2849, *Street and Traffic By-law*, which prohibits structures on city streets without permission of the city engineer, to remove the protesters.

At trial, the chambers judge held that the respondents breached s 71 by the construction and maintenance of their structures, that there were no exceptional circumstances preventing its enforcement, that the respondents' expression did not attract the protection of s 2(b) of the Charter (and in any event, was justifiable under s 1), and that the city was not engaged in an improper purpose. This decision was reversed at the BC Court of Appeal, where the court held that the respondents' method of expression did attract the protection of s 2(b) and that the bylaw was unconstitutional (*ultra vires* the city's powers) and could not be justified under s 1 of the Charter. The appeal court relied on *Committee for the Commonwealth of Canada*, and emphasized that the question to be asked was not whether the form of expression is compatible with the function of the street, but rather whether "the place is a public place where one would expect constitutional protection for free expression on the basis that expression in that place does not conflict with the purposes which s. 2(b) is intended to serve, namely (1) democratic discourse, (2) truth finding and (3) self-fulfillment" (para 35). Thus, the bylaw infringed freedom of religion in s 2 of the Charter, and it was not saved by s 1 because it did not meet the test of minimal impairment. The appeal court also took account of the need for the policy to include a procedure with clear guidelines for obtaining an exemption to balance the objective of controlling the streets while providing room for political expression. How does this case differ from *Batty v Toronto*?

Consider also *Victoria (City) v Adams*, 2009 BCCA 563, a case in which the BC Court of Appeal considered the constitutionality of a bylaw in Victoria, British Columbia, prohibiting homeless persons from setting up a "tent city" in a public park in a situation in which the number of homeless persons exceeded the shelter beds available in the city. Relying on its *Parks Regulation Bylaw* and *Streets and Traffic Bylaw*, the city applied for an injunction to remove the tent city from the park, and the respondents claimed Charter protection in relation to s 7 and the right to "life, liberty and security of the person."

The trial court acknowledged the difficulty inherent in this issue as a result of "the conflict between 'essential, life sustaining acts' and the 'responsibility of the government'" (para 4). The court also recognized the need for rudimentary shelter for the homeless when there are no other alternatives; in addition, it noted the city's responsibility to the public to preserve public property for all to use. In its decision, the court identified three main factors underlying its conclusion that the bylaw's absolute prohibition on the erection of temporary overnight shelters violated s 7 of the Charter, and that the violation was not justified as a reasonable limit pursuant to s 1: (1) the circumstances of the homeless in the city; (2) international human rights instruments that recognize adequate housing as a fundamental right; and (3) the failure of the bylaws to satisfy the minimal impairment requirement of the *Oakes* test.

The Court of Appeal affirmed the analysis at trial and struck down the provisions of the bylaw prohibiting homeless persons from erecting temporary shelters. In doing so, the court explicitly acknowledged that its judgment was based on the shortage of adequate shelter in the city for homeless persons, and that the bylaws were not in and of themselves unconstitutional. Is this decision consistent with the outcome in *Batty v Toronto*? Does *Adams* suggest that s 7 protection for homeless persons may be more effective as a Charter claim than freedom of expression for protesters? Consider also the extent to which the decision in *Batty v Toronto* is consistent with *Harrison v Carswell* in relation to an "owner's right to exclude." For further analysis of these issues, see S Hamill, "Private Property Rights and Public Responsibility: Leaving Room for the Homeless" (2011) 30 Windsor Rev Legal Soc Issues 91, and S Butler, "Cardboard Boxes and Invisible Fences: Homelessness and Public Space in City of Victoria v Adams" (2009) 27 Windsor YB Access Just 209.

More generally, see Parkdale Community Legal Services, "Homelessness and the Right to Shelter: A View from Parkdale" (1988) 4 J L & Soc Pol'y 35; R Sweeney, *Out of Place: Homelessness in America* (New York: HarperCollins, 1993); A Bennett, ed, *Shelter, Housing, and Homes: A Social Right* (Montreal: Black Rose Books, 1997); MO Herman, "Fighting Homelessness: Can International Human Rights Make a Difference?" (1994) 2:1 Geo J on Poverty L & Pol'y 59; and J Hohmann, *The Right to Housing* (Oxford & Portland, OR: Hart, 2013).

ii. Public Space and the "Public Interest"

Do you agree that the court in *Batty v Toronto* achieved a balance in its interpretation of s 2 Charter rights and an owner's right to exclude? The question is complicated, of course, by the fact that the owner of the park is a municipality and the purpose of public parks is to permit the enjoyment of all members of the public. Yet some scholars have argued that municipalities and other governments need to accept greater responsibility for the creation of "public" spaces for citizen engagement and discussion:

> When we press at the idea of public urban space, we find not only concerns with access and recreational use, but also an interest in the facilitation of a "public sensitivity," whether expressed in terms of "community" or, in urban history, "a civic polity." Deeply engrained into our expectations of public urban space is, or has been, a set of practices associated with politics and the democratic process. It was, and still to some extent is, on our streets and in our squares that we meet to organise, support or protest against, the decisions of government. From this perspective it is not only access to streets and squares which is important, but specifically access to significant sites, often ones which symbolically represent government or are centrally located. In this sense, even in big cities, we still seek the equivalent of the "market square" or "urban commons" which formed the privileged sites of civic protest in our history.

(Anne Bottomley, "A Trip to the Mall: Revising the Public/Private Divide" in H Lim & A Bottom-ley, eds, *Feminist Perspectives on Land Law* (Oxford: Routledge-Cavendish, 2007) 65 at 69.)

To what extent should values about democratic participation influence the balancing of property rights and interests such as freedom of expression in the Charter? Did the court in *Batty v Toronto* emphasize parks as places of urban leisure without sufficient consideration of the need for "public" space for democratic expression and protest? For example, if it had been demonstrated that there were insufficient public sites for protests in Toronto (as there were insufficient beds for the homeless in Victoria), would the outcome have been different? For one analysis of property and social participation, see AJ Van der Walt, "Protecting Social Par-ticipation Rights" in E Cooke, ed, *Property 2002*, vol 4 (Oxford & Portland, OR: Hart, 2003) at 27; see also N Blomley, D Delaney & R Ford, eds, *The Legal Geographies Reader: Law, Power, and Space* (Oxford: Blackwell, 2001); and D Mitchell, *The Right to the City: Social Justice and the Fight for Public Space* (New York: Guilford Press, 2003).

In *Batty v Toronto*, the Canadian Civil Liberties Association argued that, if St James Park was not available to the protesters, the city had an obligation to provide alternative space for their protest. Although the court considered this argument briefly, it was rejected:

> [113] [I]f the Protesters possess a constitutional right to occupy the Park and appropriate it
> to their use, then the next protest group espousing a political message would have the right to
> so occupy another park, say, Moss Park; and the next group the next park, and so on, and so
> forth. So, would result a "tragedy of the commons," another ironic consequence of a movement
> advocating greater popular empowerment.

However, in the light of Bottomley's arguments, is there a need for public space dedicated to democratic participation and protest?

C. The Right to Exclude: "Intellectual Property" and Freedom of Expression

How does the right to exclude affect intangible property interests, such as intellectual prop-erty? To some extent, the cases discussed above have addressed these issues. For example, the claim by the racecourse owner in *Victoria Park* that he held "property in a spectacle," in addition to his title to the land, represented a claim to intangible property; recall that the Australian High Court rejected this claim. The claims submitted to courts in other cases, in-cluding *INS v AP* and *Saulnier*, might also be characterized as claims to intangible property.

In this context, claims about intangible property in relation to copyright, trademarks, and patents (all forms of intellectual property) have become increasingly significant. For example, the Supreme Court of Canada considered an appeal relating to a patent application with re-spect to a mouse after its genetic composition was altered in relation to cancer research ("the oncomouse"): see *Harvard College v Canada (Commissioner of Patents)*, 2002 SCC 76, [2002] 4 SCR 45. Developments in technology have also resulted in claims about "property" in confi-dential information: see e.g. *R v Stewart*, [1988] 1 SCR 963, a case about whether it was an offence under the *Criminal Code* at that time when a person copied digital employee records without permission in the context of a union drive at a Toronto hotel; see also Ian Kyer, "Regina v Stewart: Is Information Property?" in Tucker, Muir & Ziff at 353. Earlier civil cases involved the "theft" of a university examination: see *Oxford v Moss* (1979), 68 Cr App R 183 (Div Ct) and *R v Offley* (1986), 28 CCC (3d) 1 (Alta CA).

Significantly, statutes create "exclusive rights" in relation to various kinds of intellectual property. For example, s 3(1) of the [former] *Copyright Act*, RSC 1985, c C-42 defined "copyright" as

the sole right to produce or reproduce the work or any substantial part thereof in any material form whatever, to perform the work or any substantial part thereof in public or, if the work is unpublished, to publish the work or any substantial part thereof … and to authorize any such acts.

Section 27(1) also defined an infringement of copyright: "It is an infringement of copyright for any person to do, without the consent of the owner of the copyright, anything that by this Act only the owner of the copyright has the right to do." Moreover, registration of copyright in a work created a presumption that a user had knowledge of the copyright at the time of his or her unauthorized use (see s 39(2)).

Similarly, the *Trade-marks Act*, RSC 1985, c T-13, s 2 defined a "trade-mark" as

a mark that is used by a person for the purpose of distinguishing or so as to distinguish wares or services manufactured, sold, leased, hired or performed by him from those manufactured, sold, leased, hired or performed by others.

In addition, s 19 of the *Trade-marks Act* provided that registration of a trade-mark gave the owner "the exclusive right to the use throughout Canada of the trade-mark," and s 20(1) defined infringement of a trade-mark as use by a person without entitlement "who sells, distributes or advertises wares or services in association with a confusing trade-mark or trade-name."

Although both copyright and trade-marks are considered "intellectual property," trade-marks serve commercial purposes, while copyright may serve either commercial or non-commercial purposes. In this context, what rationales or policy reasons justify treating copyright as private property? Why can a business, for example, hold both copyrights and trade-marks in its logos? Do statutory exemptions to infringement permit appropriation of a trade-marked or copyrighted design when it is used to further non-commercial goals? Might either of these "private" intellectual property interests interfere with freedom of expression?

Some of these questions were addressed in *Compagnie Générale des Établissements Michelin-Michelin & Cie v National Automobile, Aerospace, Transportation and General Workers Union of Canada (CAW-Canada)*, [1997] 2 FC 306 (TD) [*Michelin*]. The defendants were a labour union (CAW) and two of its representatives who organized a campaign to unionize employees at the Nova Scotia plants of Michelin North America—the Canadian subsidiary of the plaintiff, CGEM Michelin (a French manufacturer of tires). During February and March 1994, CAW members stood outside Michelin factory gates and distributed various union-organizing materials to workers. Among these materials was a leaflet produced by Larry Wark (the local CAW representative), who did not obtain permission from CGEM Michelin to display within the leaflets a caricature of the Michelin tire man ("Bibendum")—described in the decision as "a beaming marshmallow-like rotund figure composed of tires." The caricature was "meant to ridicule and mock 'Bibendum's' usual corporate image as a benign, smiling and safe father figure" by depicting him with a broad smile, crossed arms, and a raised foot that appeared ready to crush an unsuspecting Michelin worker. This content was also displayed in posters that occupied the windows of several CAW offices in Nova Scotia during the campaign. In March 1994, counsel for CGEM Michelin sent the CAW's National President Basil Hargrove a letter asserting its various copyright and trade-mark interests in the "Bibendum" figure. In response, CAW promptly took down all but one of its campaign posters, which remained visible to passersby until June 1994. CGEM Michelin subsequently initiated an action seeking damages for infringement of its trade-marks and copyrights in the term "Michelin" and the "Bibendum" design, and an injunction restraining the defendants from further use of its intellectual property.

The Federal Court discussed three issues in *Michelin*:

1. whether CAW infringed CGEM Michelin's trade-marks when it depicted the "Bibendum" design and the term "Michelin" on its organizing materials;

2. whether CAW infringed the plaintiff's copyrights in its modification of the "Bibendum" design that was reproduced in its campaign materials; and

3. whether the restrictions on CAW's use of the plaintiff's intellectual property set out in the *Trade-marks Act* and the *Copyright Act* infringed the defendants' freedom of expression guaranteed by s 2(b) of the *Canadian Charter of Rights and Freedoms*.

Michelin was the first case in Canada to address whether the "fair-dealing" defence to copyright infringement protected parody, a matter that was altered in more recent copyright legislation (see the *Copyright Modernization Act*, SC 2012, c 20, discussed after the *Michelin* extract). Examine the assumptions about intellectual property in *Michelin* in relation to the differing views about the right to exclude discussed in *Harrison v Carswell*, as well as the qualifications identified in relation to the Charter protection for freedom of expression.

Compagnie Générale des Établissements Michelin-Michelin & Cie v National Automobile, Aerospace, Transportation and General Workers Union of Canada (CAW-Canada)
[1997] 2 FC 306 (TD)

TEITELBAUM J:

I. The Trade-mark Issues

[At the outset, the court concluded that the defendants' actions did not fall under the ambit of "use" of marks in association with wares or services because the statute required "association during the ordinary course of trade." According to the court, handing out leaflets and pamphlets to recruit members into a trade union did not qualify as commercial activity. Nor did it qualify as advertising. There was thus no infringement of the *Trade-marks Act*.]

II. Copyright Issues

The defendants deny that there has been any infringement of copyright because the "Bibendum" on the leaflets and posters is an original work of the defendants that does not substantially reproduce CGEM Michelin's copyright. The defendants also argue that even if there has been reproduction of a substantial part, their "Bibendum" is a parody and therefore an exception to copyright infringement under paragraph 27(2)(a.1), fair dealing for the purpose of criticism. ... [Although "substantial part" is not defined in the statute, cases have held that the quality, more than quantity, of the reproduction is key.]

The message purportedly behind the union's "Bibendum" cannot overcome the fact that a substantial part of the copyright original has been reproduced. The threshold for whether an act constitutes reproduction of a substantial part and thus infringement is not so low that an upraised boot is enough to constitute a new creation. ... [Thus the burden was on the defendants to argue that parody is a form of "criticism," which creates an exception to copyright infringement (s 27(2)(a.1)).]

Under the *Copyright Act*, "criticism" is not synonymous with parody. Criticism requires analysis and judgment of a work that sheds light on the original.

[The court referred to the dictionary definition of parody as "a musical, literary or other composition that mimics the style of another composer, author, etc. in a humorous or satirical way."]

... In the Canadian and Commonwealth courts, parody has never been held to figure as criticism although the term criticism is not confined to "literary criticism."

[The court also noted that exceptions to copyright infringement should be strictly interpreted so that it was not appropriate to "read in" parody as a form of criticism to create a new exception. In addition, the court considered the exception for fair dealing, but concluded:]

The defendants held the "Bibendum" up to ridicule. Rather than the cuddly marshmallow creature of safety and responsibility, "Bibendum" became the boss's henchman about to stomp two workers into submission. The substantial quantity of the original work used in the leaflets and posters also casts doubt on the fairness of the defendants' treatment.

[The court thus concluded that the defendants had infringed the plaintiff's copyrights.]

• • •

III. Constitutional Issues

The defendants submit that their posters and leaflets depicting "Bibendum" are forms of expression protected by paragraph 2(b) of the Charter. The defendants further submit that if sections 3 and 27 of the *Copyright Act* limit their right to produce such pamphlets and leaflets, the sections are not saved under section 1 of the Charter as "reasonable limits prescribed by law as can be demonstrably justified in a free and democratic society."

I hold that the defendants' right to freedom of expression was not restricted. The Charter does not confer the right to use private property—the plaintiff's copyright—in the service of freedom of expression.

I take support for my position that the use of private property is a prohibited form of expression from the decision of the Supreme Court of Canada in *Committee for the Commonwealth of Canada v. Canada*, [1991] 1 S.C.R. 139 (hereinafter *Commonwealth*). In *Commonwealth*, ... the Supreme Court suggested that choosing a public forum of expression can possibly limit the scope of protection under paragraph 2(b). By analogy, I reason that use of private property to convey expression can also warrant removing the expression from the protection of paragraph 2(b).

[Citing *Harrison v Carswell*, the court also noted that private property cannot be used as a location or forum for expression.]

. . .

I have no hesitation in stating that I can find no merit in the defendants' characterization of the plaintiff's copyright as a piece of quasi-public property. The fact that the plaintiff's copyright is registered by a state-formulated system under the aegis of the *Copyright Act* in no way diminishes the private nature of the right. If one were to extend the defendants' test of "state sanctioned private property" to its logical extreme, no one in Canada could properly say that his or her house was "private property" since houses are also registered under various province designed systems of land title!

What then is the nature of copyright as private property? Copyright is an intangible property right. The owner therefore has a more challenging task in asserting his or her control over the use of the property … . But just because the right is intangible, it should not be any less worthy of protection as a full property right … . In *Commonwealth* at page 158, Chief Justice Lamer held that in instances of use of public property, expression is protected only if it is compatible with the primary function of the property. … By analogy to Chief Justice Lamer's reasoning on the use of public property, I hold that a person using the private property of another, like a copyright, must demonstrate that his or her use of the property is compatible with the function of the property before the Court can deem the use a protected form of expression under the Charter. In the present case, subjecting the plaintiff's "Bibendum" to ridicule as the object of parody is not compatible with the function of the copyright. A "Bibendum" about to stomp hapless workers into submission does not present the original author's intent of a favourable corporate image or provide an incentive for compensating artists for the integrity of their vision … . [Moreover, a] prohibition on using the plaintiff's "Bibendum" copyright does not therefore create undue hardship for the defendants in conveying their message to the Michelin workers.

DISCUSSION NOTES

i. Parody as Fair Dealing After Michelin

Sections 29 to 32.2 of the *Copyright Act*, RSC 1985, c C-42 set out statutory exceptions to copyright infringement, including the doctrine of fair dealing. The *Copyright Act* did not, however, provide a clear definition of what makes a dealing "fair." In contrast to Teitelbaum J's opinion in *Michelin*, the Supreme Court of Canada in *CCH Canadian Ltd v Law Society of Upper Canada*, 2004 SCC 13, [2004] 1 SCR 339 held unanimously (at para 48) that the exceptions in the *Copyright Act* "must not be interpreted restrictively."

Despite the SCC's ostensibly expansive approach to fair dealing in *CCH*, decided after *Michelin*, no Canadian court recognized a parody defence against allegations of copyright infringement. In *Michelin*, counsel for the defendant alluded (at para 64) to the fact that parody is protected under the American fair-use doctrine in s 106 of the US *Copyright Act* (17 USC §§ 101-810). Notwithstanding this argument, Teitelbaum J concluded (at para 71): "If Parliament had wanted to exempt parody as a new exception under the fair dealing provision, it would have done so."

Sixteen years after *Michelin*, Parliament "did so." The *Copyright Modernization Act*, SC 2012, c 20 (Bill C-11) introduced "education" and "parody or satire" to the purposes of fair dealing in the *Copyright Act*. Section 29 of the *Copyright Act* now reads: "Fair dealing for the purpose of research, private study, education, parody or satire does not infringe copyright." The exception of "criticism or review" in s 29.1 of the 1985 *Copyright Act* is unaltered by these amendments, and s 29.12 provides another new exception, permitting use of publicly available work for the purpose of creating a new work in some cases. To what extent would these amendments to the *Copyright Act* alter the outcome of *Michelin*, if it were litigated today?

For more analysis of the status of parody in copyright law in various jurisdictions (including Canada, the United States, and the United Kingdom), see Dinusha Mendis & Martin Kretschmer, *The Treatment of Parodies Under Copyright Law in Seven Jurisdictions: A Comparative Review of the Underlying Principles* (Newport, UK: Intellectual Property Office, 2013).

ii. Reconciling Intellectual Property Rights and Freedom of Expression

In *Compo Co Ltd v Blue Crest Music et al*, [1980] 1 SCR 357, Estey J declared (at 372-73) that "copyright law is *neither tort law nor property law* in classification, but is statutory law ... . Copyright legislation simply creates rights and obligations upon the terms and in the circumstances set out in the statute." In *Michelin*, these rights were subjected to claims by the defendants based on freedom of expression in s 2(b) of the Charter. What assumptions about "property" were reflected in Teitelbaum J's decision?

Some commentators have used *Michelin* to critique Canadian courts' treatment of intellectual property as "private" property, and their privileging of the latter over freedom of expression. In Teresa Scassa's view, for instance, Teitelbaum J incorrectly decided the s 2(b) Charter issue, likening the defendants' copyright infringement to physical trespass on private property (see T Scassa, "Trademarks Worth a Thousand Words: Freedom of Expression and the Use of the Trademarks of Others" (2012) 53:4 C de D 877 at 898-99). Carys Craig reached a similar conclusion about *Michelin*, arguing that Teitelbaum J's decision relied too heavily on principles of real property in this context of intangible property:

> Far from appreciating the difference between intellectual and physical property, the court [in *Michelin*] took pains to render this distinction meaningless, warning that recognition of the intangible nature of the plaintiff's property would distort the s. 2(b) balancing inquiry or, using Teitelbaum J.'s phraseology, would "colour our perceptions." ...
>
> If characterizing copyright as private property pits the copyright system against freedom of expression, then it follows that copyright ought not to be so characterized. Because the copyright system is concerned with maximizing the flow of meaning through cultural communication, copyright's very coherence is dependent upon its congruence with the principles of free expression. As such, conceptualizing the copyright system as inherently in conflict with free expression (such that it simply overrides free speech concerns) undermines copyright's own rationale and threatens its internal coherence.

(See Carys J Craig, "Putting the Community in Communication: Dissolving the Conflict Between Freedom of Expression and Copyright" (2006) 56:1 UTLJ 75 at 99-113.) To what extent do you agree that intangible copyright interests should be treated differently from other private property?

For additional commentary about intellectual property, see D Vaver, *The Law of Intellectual Property: Copyright, Patents, Trademarks* (Concord, ON: Irwin Law, 1996). In relation to copyright, see Ziff at 372-74; A Weinrib, "Information and Property" (1988) 36 UTLJ 117; S Wright, "A Feminist Exploration of the Legal Protection of Art" (1994) 7 CJWL 59; and D Magnusson, "Hell Hath No Fury—Copyright Lawyers' Lessons from Deeks v Wells" (2003-4) 29 Queen's LJ 680.

D. Rights to Private Property: Charter Protection?

Recall that Dickson J referred to the American context in *Harrison v Carswell*, stating:

> Anglo-Canadian jurisprudence has [traditionally] recognized, as a fundamental freedom, the right of the individual to the enjoyment of property and the right not to be deprived thereof, or any interest therein, save by due process of law.

In making this statement, Dickson J provided no support for his assertion, and indeed the language used seemed to paraphrase the US Constitution, which does provide protection for property, particularly in relation to governmental "takings" of private property for public purposes. Thus, pursuant to the constitution in the United States, governmental actions in relation to private property must be accomplished "with due process of law," and private property may not be taken for public use "without just compensation." These provisions have often been used in the United States to restrain governmental action to regulate property interests—for example, see *Village of Euclid v Ambler Realty Co*, 272 US 365 (1926), where the court upheld the general validity of state zoning laws so long as they were "reasonable" (even though zoning infringed on the rights of private property). This constitutional protection for property in the United States means that all statutes and judicial decisions must conform to the constitutional requirement. The "classic" case was *Pennsylvania Coal v Mahon*, 260 US 393 (1922); and see Joseph F DiMento, "Mining the Archives of *Pennsylvania Coal*: Heaps of Constitutional Mischief" (1990) 11 J Legal Hist 396.

According to Donna Christie, the absence of constitutional protection for property in the Canadian Constitution evidences a choice to make legislative bodies, rather than the courts, "the primary arbiters of the private property/public interest conflict": see D Christie, "A Tale of Three Takings: Taking Analysis in the Land Use Regulation of the United States, Australia, and Canada" (2007) 32 Brook J Int'l L 343 at 373. Moreover, according to Douglas Harris, the Charter has increased the role of courts in relation to many of its guarantees, so that protection for property remains the purview of legislatures:

> [T]he courts have become much more active than they were pre-*Charter* in patrolling the lines that mark the boundaries between individual rights and state authority …. How accurately the absence of a right to private property among enumerated constitutional rights reflects or manifests [an intention that the public and private aspects of property should be realized by federal and provincial legislative action] is debateable, … but the non-constitutional nature of property rights in Canada has situated the balancing of public regulation and private property in legislatures and the democratic process, and not in the courts.

(D Harris, "A Railway, a City, and the Public Regulation of Private Property: CPR v City of Vancouver" in Tucker, Muir & Ziff, eds, 455 at 474-75.) See also B Ziff, "'Taking' Liberties: Protections for Private Property in Canada" in E Cooke, ed, *Modern Studies in Property Law*, vol 3 (Oxford:

Hart, 2005) 347; A Alvaro, "Why Property Rights Were Excluded from the Canadian Charter of Rights and Freedoms" (1991) 24 Can J Political Science 309; and G Alexander, *The Global Debate over Constitutional Property* (Chicago: University of Chicago Press, 2006).

The material that follows provides some examples of "governmental takings"—that is, cases in which governmental action (by way of legislation or regulations) may interfere substantially with the rights of private property owners. Note especially the ways in which governmental objectives in the "public" interest may limit the rights of private property owners. How should these interests be "balanced" in the absence of Charter protection for property?

Manitoba Fisheries Ltd v The Queen
[1979] 1 SCR 101

[In this pre-Charter case, the plaintiffs owned and operated a fish exporting business, and did so quite successfully until the federal government enacted legislation giving the exclusive rights to carry on such a business to a statutory corporation. The governmental initiative was designed to promote better marketing arrangements for freshwater fish in order to enhance the very low incomes of (mainly) Aboriginal fishers who supplied the fish exporting businesses. The result was that fish exporters thereby became redundant. In this context, the plaintiffs claimed compensation for their property interests against the Crown. Should the plaintiffs succeed? On what basis? Would the plaintiffs' claim be more successful if protection for property rights were entrenched in the Charter?

In *Manitoba Fisheries Ltd v The Queen*, the court concluded that the plaintiffs were entitled to compensation for the governmental "taking" of the *goodwill* (a recognized property interest) of their business. Ritchie J stated (at 102) that he had great difficulty in following the reasoning of the Court of Appeal, which suggested that "implementation of the legislation had the effect of putting the appellant out of business but that result did not occur due to any deprivation of property of the appellant." (See Urie JA (1978), 78 DLR (3d) 393 at 400-1 (FCA).) By contrast, Ritchie J concluded (at 118):]

It will be seen that in my opinion the *Freshwater Fish Marketing Act* and the Corporation created thereunder had the effect of depriving the appellant of its goodwill as a going concern and consequently rendering its physical assets virtually useless and that the goodwill so taken away constitutes property of the appellant for the loss of which no compensation whatever has been paid. There is nothing in the Act providing for the taking of such property by the Government without compensation and as I find that there was such a taking, it follows, in my view, that it was unauthorized having regard to the recognized rule that "unless the words of the statute clearly so demand, a statute is not to be construed so as to take away the property of a subject without compensation": *per* Lord Atkinson in *Attorney-General v. De Keyser's Royal Hotel* [[1920] AC 508].

To what extent does this analysis depend on construing "goodwill" as a proprietary interest? How should it be valued? In awarding compensation, Ritchie J stated (at 118) that it should be valued as "the fair market value of [the plaintiff's business] as a going concern ... , minus the residual value of its remaining assets."

DISCUSSION NOTE

The Significance of Manitoba Fisheries

In spite of this outcome in *Manitoba Fisheries*, it seems that the case has had little effect on other court decisions in Canada. Indeed, most other governmental regulatory takings cases have failed, including cases concerning the regulation of land use, the introduction of rent controls, or governmental changes to marketing schemes. In all these cases, private property interests may have been compromised, but courts have generally failed to recognize these regulatory takings as requiring compensation. To some extent, the basis for these results is the high test established in *Manitoba Fisheries*. First, the case established that the taking must involve an identifiable interest in property ("goodwill" in *Manitoba Fisheries*), so that regulations changing the way that property can be used or that diminish its economic value are not sufficient to meet this test: there must be a taking of a property interest. In addition, *Manitoba Fisheries* required that the state must also acquire the property subject to the "taking," a test that creates a huge hurdle to overcome in contexts in which the government simply defines how private property may be used, but without actually "acquiring" it as a proprietary interest.

Consider the following comment about this case, particularly in relation to the language of the US Constitution:

> Thus since 1978 the courts have essentially confined *Manitoba Fisheries* to its rather unique facts. It is, in the words of one commentator, "one of the most liberal applications" of the *De Keyser's* compensation doctrine, and concerns that dire consequences for the ability of government to regulate were it to be expanded have not been borne out. Thus perhaps the best way to understand the case is to see it as a "palm tree justice" decision, a ruling in favour of a particular plaintiff for whom a group of Supreme Court judges had sympathy. It was a sympathy perhaps born of their small-c conservative politics, but one that has had to be restrained thereafter for fear of the consequences. … [According to the authors, it was the creativity of Ken Arenson, the lawyer for the plaintiffs, who identified the legal argument (that the government had taken the business's goodwill) that allowed the court to rule in the plaintiffs' favour.] The goodwill argument was crucial in that it provided a legal theory that could be married to the judges' "common sense" understandings of right and wrong, it turned an economic regulation case into one about property. [It appears that Manitoba Fisheries received approximately $300,000 to $400,000 in compensation, and other fish exporting businesses were also compensated.]
>
> But if we move beyond decided cases and speculate, it is possible that *Manitoba Fisheries* has been more significant, in two ways. First, it is possible that the decision has had the effect of making governments apprehensive about regulating areas of the economy when that regulation might produce similar litigation. We have no evidence for this, and indeed it would be difficult to find such negative evidence. But people always act "in the shadow of the law," and the shadow cast by *Manitoba Fisheries* could be a long one indeed.
>
> Second, *Manitoba Fisheries* may have been influential in the early 1980s when the details of Canada's new *Charter of Rights* were being fleshed out. The Charter does not contain a guarantee of property rights, unlike the American Bill of Rights or the [Canadian] Diefenbaker *Bill of Rights* of 1960. Right-wing politicians and pressure groups continue to press for its inclusion—in 1988 the House of Commons voted for it, albeit with only 124 members present. The issue is usually cast in simple left–right terms. But the fact is that in the early 1980s property rights were not a contentious

issue in the negotiations, and not an issue which saw a split between liberal/NDP provincial governments and conservative ones. While the federal government supported a right to property, all provincial governments, of whatever stripe, were opposed. In part they were concerned that such a right would trench on provincial power, "property and civil rights" being a very important aspect of provincial jurisdiction. But they also feared that the inclusion of a right to property would threaten a variety of regulatory schemes, from provincial crown corporations to Prince Edward Island's limitation of non-resident ownership of land. The fear was that a constitutionally entrenched right to property would introduce into Canada a version of American regulatory takings doctrine, which is much broader; rather than require the government to have acquired the property taken, it asks only if the owner has been denied "economically viable" uses [a much less stringent test]. The decision in *Manitoba Fisheries* showed a willingness in the Supreme Court to adopt an expansive approach to "takings," and could only have reinforced these concerns. In these two senses, *Manitoba Fisheries* may indeed have been a much more influential case than it would seem merely by looking at later judicial decisions.

(J Phillips and J Martin, "Manitoba Fisheries v The Queen: The Origins of Canada's De Facto Expropriation Doctrine" in Tucker, Muir & Ziff, eds, 259 at 291-92.)

Mariner Real Estate Ltd v Nova Scotia (Attorney General)
(1999), 179 NSR (2d) 213, [1999] NSJ no 283 (CA)

[In *Mariner Real Estate Ltd v Nova Scotia (Attorney General)*, the court considered whether the designation of private property as a "beach" under the *Beaches Act*, RSNS 1989, c 32 constituted an expropriation of private property. The case involved plaintiffs who owned land at Kingsburg Beach, a highly coveted beachfront area on the south shore of Nova Scotia. Because this land was designated as a beach, plaintiffs (who owned the land) were denied the necessary health and building permits required to build single-family residences on the lands. (The designation itself did not preclude construction of dwelling units, but permitted the government to have regulatory power over the beach for "the protection of the beaches and associated dune systems as environmental and recreational resources.") The minister's decision was based on an ecological study of Kingsburg Beach, which concluded that "maintaining the integrity of the present sand dunes is critical to reducing or preventing widespread flooding of the backshore lowland by the sea and to preventing erosion and narrowing of the beach face." In making its decision, the Nova Scotia Court of Appeal stated:]

[1] ... On one side, there are the interests of the respondents in the enjoyment of their privately owned land at Kingsburg Beach. On the other is the public interest in the protection and preservation of environmentally fragile and ecologically significant beach, dune and beach ridge resources. In the background of this case is the policy issue of how minutely government may control land without buying it.

. . .

[3] [T]he trial judge made two key findings. First, he decided that the respondents had been deprived of land within the meaning of the *Expropriation Act*. There were alternative bases for this finding. One basis was that the designation, on its own, was in

law, a taking of land. The alternative basis was that the taking resulted from the designation coupled with the application to the respondents' lands of the regulatory regime flowing from the designation. These, in combination, in the judge's view, took away virtually all of the land's economic value and virtually extinguished all rights of ownership.

[4] The second key holding by the trial judge was that the province acquired land within the meaning of the *Expropriation Act* because the regulation of the respondents' lands enhanced the value of the provincially owned property from the high watermark seaward.

[5] In my respectful view, the learned trial judge erred in each of these conclusions. For reasons which I will develop, my view is that the loss of economic value resulting from land use regulation is not a taking of land within the meaning of the *Expropriation Act*. Further, in my opinion, the respondents did not establish either the loss of virtually all rights of ownership, or that the Province had acquired any land as a result of the designation. I would, therefore, allow the appeal, set aside the order of the trial judge and in its place make an order dismissing the respondents' action.

[In arriving at its conclusions, the appeal court scrutinized: (1) the plaintiffs' claim of de facto expropriation, (2) the effects of regulation, (3) the loss of economic value of the land, (4) the loss of the "bundle of rights," and (5) the acquisition of land.

In relation to de facto expropriation, the court stated:]

[39] *De facto* expropriation is conceptually difficult given the narrow parameters of the Court's authority which I have just outlined. While *de facto* expropriation is concerned with whether the "rights" of ownership have been taken away, those rights are defined only by reference to lawful uses of land which may, by law, be severely restricted. In short, the bundle of rights associated with ownership carries with it the possibility of stringent land use regulation.

[40] I dwell on this point because there is a rich line of constitutional jurisprudence on regulatory takings in both the United States and Australia which is sometimes referred to in the English and Canadian cases dealing with *de facto* expropriation ... . The Fifth Amendment to the United States Constitution (which also applies to the States through the Fourteenth Amendment) provides that private property shall not be taken for public use without just compensation. In the Australian Constitution, section 51 (xxxi) prohibits the acquisition of property except on just terms. While these abundant sources of case law may be of assistance in developing the Canadian law of *de facto* expropriation, it is vital to recognize that the question posed in the constitutional cases is fundamentally different.

[41] These US and Australian constitutional cases concern constitutional limits on legislative power in relation to private property. As O'Connor J said in the United States Supreme Court case of *Eastern Enterprises v. Apfel* (1998), 118 S.Ct. 2131, the purpose of the US constitutional provision (referred to as the "takings clause") is to prevent government from "forcing some people alone to bear public burdens which, in all fairness and justice, should be borne by the public as a whole." Canadian courts have no similar broad mandate to review and vary legislative judgments about the appropriate distribution of burdens and benefits flowing from environmental or other land use controls. In Canada, the courts' task is to determine whether the regulation in question entitles the respondents

to compensation under the *Expropriation Act*, not to pass judgment on the way the Legislature apportions the burdens flowing from land use regulation.

[42] In this country, extensive and restrictive land use regulation is the norm. Such regulation has, almost without exception, been found not to constitute compensable expropriation. It is settled law, for example, that the regulation of land use which has the effect of decreasing the value of the land is not an expropriation.

. . .

[47] [T]he test that has developed for applying the *Expropriation Act* to land use restrictions is exacting and, of course … the plaintiffs at trial, had the burden of proving that they met it. In each of the three Canadian cases which have found compensation payable for *de facto* expropriations, the result of the governmental action went beyond drastically limiting use or reducing the value of the owner's property. In *British Columbia v. Tener*, [1985] 1 S.C.R. 533 (S.C.C.), the denial of the permit meant that access to the respondents' mineral rights was completely negated, or as Wilson J. put it at p. 552, amounted to total denial of that interest. In *Casamiro Resource Corp. v. British Columbia (Attorney General)* (1991), 80 D.L.R. (4th) 1 (B.C.C.A.), which closely parallels *Tener*, the private rights had become "meaningless." In *Manitoba Fisheries Ltd. v. R.*, [1979] 1 S.C.R. 101 (S.C.C.), the legislation absolutely prohibited the claimant from carrying on its business.

[Thus, the appeal court concluded that]

[48] … to constitute a *de facto* expropriation, there must be a confiscation of "… all *reasonable* private uses of the lands in question." … In other words, what is, in form, regulation will be held to be expropriation only when virtually all of the aggregated incidents of ownership have been taken away. The extent of this bundle of rights of ownership must be assessed, not only in relation to the land's potential highest and best use, but having regard to the nature of the land and the range of reasonable uses to which it has actually been put.

[Second, in evaluating a regulation, it is the "actual application in the specific case [that] must be examined, not the potential," and here the imposition of the regulatory regime did "not, of itself, constitute an expropriation [because the refusal for the respondents to build dwellings] was not an inevitable consequence of the designation of the lands as a beach, but flowed from the refusal by the minister of permission required to develop the lands" (at para 53).

Third, the court determined that loss of economic value of the land did not constitute loss of land under the *Expropriation Act*, based on the precedents of *British Columbia v Tener*, [1985] 1 SCR 533 and *Manitoba Fisheries Ltd v The Queen*, [1979] 1 SCR 101.

Fourth, the appeal court held that unless it was established that virtually all incidents of ownership were removed, the effects of the regulation would not amount to the loss of an interest in land. Here, the court commented that "[n]either the respondents nor the Province appear to have explored the possibility that development specifically designed in a way consistent with protection of the dunes might occur. The respondents, while asserting that all reasonable uses of the land are precluded by the operation of the Act and Regulations, have not shown that they would be denied the required permits with respect to such other reasonable or traditional uses of the lands" (at para 89).

Finally, the court concluded that only where a taking away of land is coupled with the acquisition of land by the expropriating authority can there be an expropriation within the meaning of the Act. In this case, "[t]here is no suggestion here that the Province acquired legal title or any aspect of it. The land remains private property although subject to the regulatory regime established by the *Beaches Act*." However, the plaintiffs raised the argument that the effect of the regulatory scheme was, for practical purposes, an acquisition of interest in land, but this argument was dismissed because it was determined that "for there to be a taking, there must be, in effect, … an acquisition of an interest in land and that enhanced value is not such an interest."

Ultimately, the court concluded that the designation of the plaintiffs' land and the subsequent refusal for them to build dwellings on that land did not constitute expropriation with the meaning of the *Expropriation Act*. Accordingly, there was no need to consider the issue of compensation.]

DISCUSSION NOTES

i. Rethinking Roles for Legislatures and Courts

Mariner Real Estate clearly reveals legislative supremacy with respect to restrictions on the use of private land in the interest of "public" purposes. To some extent, the case also shows governmental interest in protecting the environment. Recall the discussion above (following *Victoria Park*) with respect to whether courts or legislatures are better placed to determine emerging issues involving property claims. Does this case suggest that legislatures may sometimes be better able to consider the competing interests of private property owners and the preservation of significant and sensitive provincial lands, including beachfront lands? At the same time, is it fair to expect that developers whose plans are thwarted should be compensated for their commercial investments, even if such compensation must be provided by taxpayers? How should these issues be balanced? For some discussion, including the impact of NAFTA, see Ziff at 143-63.

ii. Private Property for Public Use

In *Canadian Pacific Railway v Vancouver (City)*, 2006 SCC 5, [2006] 1 SCR 227, the Canadian Pacific Railway Company (CPR), the petitioner-appellant, was granted a corridor of land by the provincial Crown in 1886 for the construction of a railway, known as the "Arbutus Corridor." However, with the increase of alternative methods of travel, rail traffic declined and, in 1999, CPR formally began the process of discontinuing rail operations on the corridor. CPR put forward proposals to develop the corridor for commercial and residential purposes or for the city or any other public body to acquire it by sale, but received no response. In the end, the city decided that it would not buy the land and instead adopted the *Arbutus Corridor Official Development Plan Bylaw*, which designated the corridor as a public thoroughfare for transportation and "greenways," such as heritage walks, nature trails, and cyclist paths.

In effect, the bylaw prevented redevelopment of the corridor and confined CPR to uneconomic uses of the land. CPR regarded this effect as unfair and unreasonable and argued: "(1) that the by-law is *ultra vires* the City and should be struck down; [and] (2) that the City is obligated to compensate CPR for the land" (at para 8). CPR succeeded, in part, before the chambers judge who held the bylaw to be *ultra vires* the city, but declined the declaration that the city must compensate CPR. In contrast, the BC Court of Appeal rejected both arguments and allowed the city's appeal. On further appeal to the Supreme Court of Canada, the appeal was dismissed.

In justifying its decision, the court provided detailed analysis of a number of issues, including whether the bylaw exceeded the city's statutory powers, and concluded that "the *Vancouver Charter* provides that the City is not liable to compensate landowners for loss as a result of these restrictions: s. 569" (at para 12). The court also rejected several related arguments, and then focused on the issue of CPR's entitlement to compensation.

In relation to compensation, CPR argued that "at common law, a government act that deprives a landowner of all reasonable use of its land constitutes a *de facto* taking and imposes an obligation on the government to compensate the landowner" (at para 29). In response to this argument, the court referred to the decisions in *Mariner Real Estate Ltd v Nova Scotia (Attorney General)* and *Manitoba Fisheries Ltd v The Queen*, which set out the two requirements that must be met in order to constitute a de facto taking requiring compensation at common law, including: (1) an acquisition of a beneficial interest in the property or flowing from it, and (2) removal of all reasonable uses of the property. The courts held that neither requirements of the test were met in this case:

> [33] CPR argues that, by passing the ... By-law, the City acquired a *de facto* park, relying on the observation of Southin J.A. [the BC Court of Appeal judge] that "the by-law in issue now can have no purpose but to enable the inhabitants to use the corridor for walking and cycling, which some do (trespassers all), without paying for that use" (para. 117). Southin J.A. went on to say: "The shareholders of ... CPR ought not to be expected to make a charitable gift to the inhabitants" (para. 118). Yet, as Southin J.A. acknowledged, those who now casually use the corridor are trespassers. The City has gained nothing more than some assurance that the land will be used or developed in accordance with its vision, without even precluding the historical or current use of the land. This is not the sort of benefit that can be construed as a "tak[ing]."
>
> [34] Second, the by-law does not remove all reasonable uses of the property. This requirement must be assessed "not only in relation to the land's potential highest and best use, but having regard to the nature of the land and the range of reasonable uses to which it has actually been put": see *Mariner Real Estate*, at p. 717. The by-law does not prevent CPR from using its land to operate a railway, the only use to which the land has ever been put during the history of the City. Nor, contrary to CPR's contention, does the by-law prevent maintenance of the railway track ... . Finally, the by-law does not preclude CPR from leasing the land for use in conformity with the by-law and from developing public/private partnerships. The by-law acknowledges the special nature of the land as the only such intact corridor existing in Vancouver, and expands upon the only use the land has known in recent history.

Ultimately, the court concluded that although "one may sympathize with CPR's position, none of its arguments withstand scrutiny. The City did not exceed the powers granted it by the *Vancouver Charter*. Neither the *Vancouver Charter* nor principles of common law require it to compensate CPR for the ... By-law's effects on its land" (at para 63). For a full assessment of this decision in context, see D Harris, "A Railway, a City, and the Public Regulation of Private Property: CPR v City of Vancouver" in Tucker, Muir & Ziff, eds, at 455.

iii. The Canadian Constitution, Protection for Property, and the Global Context

Although the Charter does not provide protection for property, a number of international covenants (in addition to constitutions in the United States and Australia) provide for some protection for property: see e.g. the *Universal Declaration of Human Rights* (1948), art 17, and the *European Convention on Human Rights* (1950), art 1 of the First Protocol. For some assessments, see J Kingston, "Rich People Have Rights Too? The Status of Property as a Fundamental Human Right" in L Heffernan, ed, *Human Rights: A European Perspective* (Dublin and Portland, OR: Roundhill Press in association with the Irish Centre for European Law, 1994).

Some scholars have argued that, although the "culture" of private property in the United States and Canada differed in the past, economic globalization may have effected significant change. For example, David Schneiderman reviewed the contexts for protection of private property in Canada and in the United States and suggested that commitments included in NAFTA might move Canada to a constitutional culture similar to the US style of limited government intervention: see D Schneiderman, "Property Rights and Regulatory Innovation: Comparing Constitutional Cultures" (2006) 4 Int'l J Const L 371. See also B Schwartz & M Bueckert, "Regulatory Takings in Canada" (2006) 5 Wash U Global Studies 477, part of a Symposium: "Regulatory Takings in Land-Use Law—A Comparative Perspective on Compensation Rights."

iv. Governmental "Confiscation" of Property

Proponents for recognition of property rights in s 7 of the Charter sometimes refer to the need to prevent confiscation of private property by the government, as occurred to citizens and residents of Japanese origin on the west coast of Canada during World War II. According to a Price-Waterhouse study in the mid-1980s, "the Japanese Canadian community suffered a total economic loss after 1941 of not less than $443 million [1986 dollars]," not including some kinds of economic loss that could not be quantified, such as disruption of education. For a detailed account of this confiscation of property, see K Adachi, *The Enemy That Never Was: A History of the Japanese Canadians* (Toronto: McClelland & Stewart, 1991) at 375 and Table 2.

Adachi described legal challenges and petitions during and immediately after the war, as well as the work of the Bird Commission, established in 1947 to assess compensation in cases where negligence could be proved on the part of the government officers involved in the process of confiscation. Although the Commission's terms of reference were later broadened, Adachi concluded:

> The awards came too late and were too little—despite Bird's claim that "rough justice" had been achieved. An old Issei in 1950 could stare at his cheque for $140.50 awarded as his recovery on a house in Vancouver for which he paid $3000 in 1930 and which was sold by the [governmental officer] for $1200 in 1943. He could stare and stare and wonder what remote connection it had with the destruction of his life's work and security.

In 1988, the Canadian government issued an acknowledgment of the injustice of governmental actions in relation to Canadians of Japanese ancestry during the Second World War, and entered into an agreement with the National Association of Japanese Canadians for "symbolic" redress payments: see Adachi, appendices XIV and XV. See also WP Ward, *White*

Canada Forever: Popular Attitudes and Public Policy Toward Orientals in British Columbia, 2d ed (Montreal and Kingston: McGill-Queen's University Press, 1990); and the "fictional" account in J Kogawa, *Obasan* (Toronto: Lester and Orpen Dennys, 1981). For a similar account in the United States, see L Broom & R Riemer, *Removal and Return: The Socio-Economic Effects of War on Japanese Americans* (Berkeley: University of California Press, 1949).

V. ALTERNATIVE VISIONS OF PROPERTY

As this chapter demonstrates, the concept of property is complex, revealing both doctrinal principles and policy concerns with respect to subjects and objects in proprietary relationships. At the same time, this concept of property in the western common law tradition is just one of many different ideas about property. For example, the former communist regimes in eastern Europe created a property regime quite different from common law arrangements, and political changes in eastern Europe in the 1990s have again influenced changing conceptions of private property. For some analysis of these issues, see George Ginsburgs, ed, *The Revival of Private Law in Central and Eastern Europe* (The Hague: Kluwer Law Int'l, 1996); and Andrew Cartwright, "Reforming Property Law in Eastern and Central Europe" in Elizabeth Cooke, ed, *Modern Studies in Property Law*, vol 1 (Oxford: Hart, 2001) 341.

Aboriginal peoples in North America also had their own distinctive conceptions about relationships to the land. Although these issues are examined in more detail in Chapter 8, this chapter provides an introduction to fundamental ideas about property among First Nations. The chapter concludes with a brief exploration of some emerging ideas about concepts of property.

A. Aboriginal Concepts of Property

In the North American context, it is critical to take account of Aboriginal concepts of property, particularly because they are fundamental to an understanding of land claims litigation. As an introduction to ideas about Aboriginal relationships with land, consider the recorded testimony of Chief Seattle at the ceremony to sign a treaty with Europeans in 1854:

Every part of this earth is sacred to my people.
Every shining pine needle,
every tender shore,
every vapor in the dark woods,
every clearing, and
every humming insect
are holy
in the memory and experience of my people.

The earth does not belong to the white man,
the white man belongs to the earth.
This we know.
All things are connected
like the blood
which unites our family.

(Ted Perry, inspired by Chief Seattle, "How Can One Sell the Air?" in Eli Gifford & R Michael Cook, eds, *How Can One Sell the Air? Chief Seattle's Vision* (Summertown, TN: The Book Publishing Co, 1992) at 31 and 46. "Seattle" is more correctly spelled "Seathl," although literary references are to "Seattle." These passages are from a speech given by Chief Seattle in Lushotseed, Seattle's native tongue, and then translated by Dr Henry B Smith.)

Some of the ideas in the words of Chief Seattle are more fully analyzed in the comments of Leroy Little Bear, which follow. To what extent can you identify similarities and differences between Aboriginal and common law concepts of property?

Leroy Little Bear, "Aboriginal Rights and the Canadian 'Grundnorm'"
in J Rick Ponting, ed, *Arduous Journey: Canadian Indians and Decolonization* (Toronto: McClelland & Stewart, 1986) at 244-47 (footnotes omitted)

The Aboriginal Peoples' Standard

In contrast to the Western (occidental) way of relating to the world—namely, a linear and singular conception—the aboriginal philosophy views the world in cyclical terms. A good example of linear thinking is the occidental conception of time. Time is conceptualized as a straight line. If we attempt to picture "time" in our mind, we would see something like a river flowing toward and past us. What is behind is the past. What is immediately around us is the present. The future is upstream, but we cannot see very far upstream because of a waterfall, a barrier to knowing the future. This line of time is conceptualized as quantity, especially as lengths made of units. A length of time is envisaged as a row of similar units. A logical and inherent characteristic of this concept of time is that once a unit of the river of time flows past, that particular unit never returns—it is gone forever. This characteristic lends itself to other concepts such as "wasting time," "making up time," "buying time," and "being on time," which are unique to occidental society.

Another characteristic of this linear concept of time is that each unit of time is totally different and independent of similar units. Consequently, each day is considered a different unit, and thus a different day. Every day is a new day, every year is a new year. From this we can readily understand why there is a felt need in Western culture to have names for days and months, and numbers for years. In general, Western philosophy is a straight line. One goes from A to B to C to D to E, where B is the foundation for C, and C is the foundation for D, and on down the line.

Native people think in terms of cyclicity. Time is not a straight line. It is a circle. Every day is not a new day, but the same day repeating itself. There is no need to give each day a different name. Only one name is needed: "day." This philosophy is a result of a direct relationship to the macrocosm. The sun is round; the moon is round; a day is a cycle (daylight followed by night); the seasons follow the same cycle year after year. A characteristic of cyclic thinking is that it is holistic, in the same way that a circle is whole. A cyclical philosophy does not lend itself readily to dichotomies or categorization, nor to fragmentation or polarizations; conversely, linear thinking lends itself to all of these, and to singularity. For example, in linear thinking there is only one "great spirit," only one "true rule," only one "true answer." These philosophical ramifications of Western habitual thought result in misunderstanding holistic concepts, as Westerners relate themselves to only one aspect of the whole at a time.

The linear and singular philosophy of Western cultures and the cyclical and holistic philosophy of most native peoples can be seen readily in the property concepts in each society. Indian ownership of property, like Indians' way of relating to the world, is holistic. Land is communally owned; ownership rests not in any one individual, but rather belongs to the tribe as a whole, as an entity. The members of a tribe have an undivided interest in the land; everybody, as a whole, owns the whole. Furthermore, the land belongs not only to people presently living, but also to past generations and future generations, who are considered to be as much a part of the tribal entity as the present generation. In addition, the land belongs not only to human beings, but also to other living things (the plants and animals and sometimes even the rocks); they, too, have an interest.

Although the native conception of title to land is distinct from the British concept in important ways, the two do have some points of overlap. The native concept of title is somewhat like a combination of different British concepts … . To Natives it is as though the Creator, the original one to grant the land to the Indians, put a condition on it whereby the land remains Indian land "so long as there are Indians," "so long as it is not alienated," "on the condition that it is used only by Indians," etc. In other words, the Indians' concept of title is not equivalent to what today is called "fee simple title" … ; it is actually somewhat less than unencumbered ownership because of the various parties (plants, animals, and members of the tribe) that have an interest in it and because of the above-noted conditions attached to the ownership. Finally, a point raised above must be emphasized: that is, the source of Indians' title to their land can be traced back to the Creator, who gave it not only to human beings, but to all living creatures. In other words, deer have the same type of interest in the land as does any human being.

This concept of sharing with fellow animals and plants is one that is quite alien to Western society's conception of land. To Western society, only human beings have a right to land, and everything else is for the convenience of humans. Yet, the concept of Indians sharing the land ownership with fellow living things is not entirely unrelated to the concept of social contract that has been put forward by such occidental philosophers as Rousseau and Locke. However, whereas Rousseau's and Locke's social contract encompasses human beings only, the Indian social contract embraces all other living things.

The question inevitably arises as to just what the Indians surrendered when they signed treaties with European nations. First, the Indian concept of land ownership is certainly not inconsistent with the idea of sharing with an alien people. Once the Indians recognized them as human beings, they gladly shared with them. They shared with Europeans in the same way they shared with the animals and other people. However, sharing here cannot be interpreted as meaning that Europeans got the same rights as any other native person, because the Europeans were not descendants of the original grantees, or they were not parties to the original social contract. Also, sharing certainly cannot be interpreted as meaning that one is giving up his rights for all eternity.

Second, the Indians could not have given unconditional ("fee simple") ownership to Europeans in any land transactions in which they may have engaged because they did not themselves have fee simple ownership. They were never given such unconditional ownership by their grantor (the Creator), and it is well known in British property law that one cannot give an interest greater than he or she has.

Third, Indians could not have given an interest even equal to what they were originally granted, because to do so would be to break the condition under which the land was granted by the Creator. Furthermore, they are not the sole owners under the original grant from the Creator; the land belongs to past generations, to the yet-to-be-born, and to the plants and animals. Has the Crown ever received a surrender of title from these others?

Fourth, the only kind of interest the native people have given or transferred must be an interest lesser than they had, for one can always give an interest smaller than one has. Thus, from all of the above we can readily conclude that, from their perspective, the Indians did not surrender very much, if they surrendered anything at all.

Thomas Berger, in a recent study of the *Alaska Native Land Claim Settlement Act*, summarizes the viewpoint of the native people of Alaska. His remarks can be applied readily to other native people. Writes Berger:

> The European discoveries, their descendants, and the nations they founded, including the United States, imposed their overlordship on the peoples of the New World. The Europeans came, and they claimed the land. No one has ever advanced a sound legal theory to justify the taking of native land from the Natives of the New World, whether by the Spanish, the Portuguese, the French, the Dutch, the Americans, or—in Alaska—by the Russians.
>
> Certain European powers claimed, by virtue of discovery, the exclusive right to purchase land from its original inhabitants. [However,] the rule of discovery depends upon the concept of native sovereignty: only if the original inhabitants had the right to sell their land could the discoverer exercise his right to purchase it. ...
>
> Before and after contact native peoples of the New World governed themselves according to a variety of political institutions; they were acknowledged to be sovereign as distinct peoples.

In summary, the standard or norm of the aboriginal peoples' law is that land is not transferable and therefore is inalienable. Land and benefits therefrom may be shared with others, and when Indian nations entered into treaties with European nations, the subject of the treaty, from the Indians' viewpoint, was not the alienation of the land but the sharing of the land.

DISCUSSION NOTES

i. Property as a Relationship Among Subjects and the Aboriginal Conception of Property Interests

Reconsider the idea of property as a relationship among subjects with respect to the objects of proprietary interests. How would an Aboriginal conception of property interests "redefine" this relationship?

In thinking about these issues, consider the comments of R Ross in *Dancing with a Ghost: Exploring Indian Reality* (Markham, ON: Octopus Books, 1992) at xxiii-iv:

> [W]e have not approached Native people with the expectation of difference which is essential for communication and understanding to commence. Not having perceived that a gulf divides us, we have never truly tried to bridge it. Unless we do, it is my fear that we are doomed to increasing mutual frustration and ... overt hostilities.

As an example of the failure to recognize differing conceptions of property, Helen Stone noted how lawyers who make claims on behalf of Aboriginal persons often try to show the "congruence" between ideas about time and history among Aboriginal people on the one hand and the dominant members of Canadian society on the other, even though (as Little Bear explained) there are major distinctions between them: see Helen Stone, "Living in Time Immemorial—Concepts of 'Time' and 'Time Immemorial': Why Aboriginal Rights Theory Is Problematic in the Courts and Around the Negotiating Table" (Carleton University, MA thesis, 1993). For other perspectives, see J Cruikshank, "Legend and Landscape: Convergence of Oral and Scientific Traditions in the Yukon Territory" (1981) 18:2 Arctic Anthropology 67; and J Webber, "Relations of Force and Relations of Justice: The Emergence of Normative Community Between Colonists and Aboriginal Peoples" (1995) 33 Osgoode Hall LJ 623.

Common law concepts of property provide the main focus of this book, but there is also discussion at relevant points of Aboriginal ideas and practices in relation to property, as well as a discussion of Aboriginal title to land in Chapter 8. For an overview of some of these issues, see K Hazlehurst, *Legal Pluralism and the Colonial Legacy: Indigenous Experiences of Justice in Canada, Australia, and New Zealand* (Aldershot, UK: Avebury, 1995); *Report of the Royal Commission on Aboriginal Peoples* (Ottawa: Commission, 1996); and D'Arcy Vermette, "Colonialism and the Process of Defining Aboriginal People" (2008) 31 Dal LJ 211.

ii. Rethinking the Concept of Property

Aboriginal concepts of property seem to recognize a concept of "land stewardship," by contrast with common law ideas of "dominion" in relation to land. In addition, Aboriginal concepts recognize the subjects of "property" as more than those who are human beings. How do these concepts alter the basic principles of property law? It is interesting that the new constitution of Ecuador provides for "nature rights" that change "the status of ecosystems from being regarded as property under the law to being recognized as rights-bearing entities": see Andrew C Revkin, "Ecuador Constitution Grants Rights to Nature" (29 September 2008), <http://dotearth.blogs.nytimes.com/2008/09/29/ecuador-constitution-grants-nature-rights>.

In this context, moreover, some scholars have been identifying current issues in relation to private property as a tension between ideas about "land ownership" and "land stewardship." Thus, even though legislatures (rather than courts) have had primary responsibility for issues relating to property, it has been suggested that

> [t]he absence of an ingrained ethic of stewardship has been a major deterrent to the shift toward responsible land management. … Legal and economic circumstances place the power to decide land use policies in those people who have the greatest incentive to regard land as a commodity and to discount noneconomic and long-range considerations. People committed to an ethic of stewardship and ecological sustainability continue to collide with those who make land use decisions upon a very different ethic, an ethic that regards economic development and monetary return as evidence of the land's highest and best use.

(L Caldwell, "Land and the Law: Problems in Legal Philosophy" (1986) U Ill L Rev 319 at 329.) For additional views, see Freyfogle; C Stone, "'Should Trees Have Standing?' Revisited: How Far Will Law and Morals Reach? A Pluralist Perspective" (1985) 59 S Cal L Rev 1; and C Rodgers, "Nature's Place? Property Rights, Property Rules, and Environmental Stewardship" (2009) 68:3

Cambridge LJ 550. Some of these issues are also discussed in relation to environmental and planning issues in relation to easements and covenants in Chapter 7.

iii. Delgamuukw: Common Law Recognition of Aboriginal Property

In *Delgamuukw v British Columbia*, [1997] 3 SCR 1010, the Supreme Court of Canada recognized Aboriginal title as a *sui generis* interest that is held on a communal (not individual) basis by Aboriginal peoples and that includes a right to exclusive occupation and use of defined land, on the basis of prior occupation of territory at the time when Europeans first arrived. This case was a landmark decision in relation to issues of Aboriginal title to land, and is discussed in more detail in Chapter 8. At the outset, however, it is important to take account of the impact of differing conceptions of property on the part of Aboriginal people and the European settlers in North America. These differences resulted in misunderstandings in relation to land negotiations in the past, but they also create legal challenges for the recognition of Aboriginal property interests by the common law, both in Canada and in other former British colonies. As one scholar noted:

> [R]especting Native peoples' own histories means being prepared, as a matter of principle, to abandon the law's search for a Western interpretation of aboriginal experiences and recollections that are alien to Western conceptions of reality. ...
>
> In [*Delgamuukw*,] the court was provided with an almost original opportunity to consider a radically different approach to historical knowledge from that which, in the past, has been applied almost without reflection ... . [However, the court was not able to set aside traditional Western ideas.] The history that [the trial judge] constructed from the testimony reflects the difficulty he had in conceiving of an historical knowledge that challenged his own so fundamentally ... . [Without] different conceptions of the past being allowed their day in court, ... the law is likely to do no more than entrench its own historicity and all the inequities of the past that it tries so hard to escape.

(Joel R Fortune, "Construing Delgamuukw: Legal Arguments, Historical Argumentation, and the Philosophy of History" (1993) 51 UT Fac L Rev 80 at 95 and 114.) For another view of the challenge of rethinking historical ideas, see George FG Stanley, "As Long as the Sun Shines and Water Flows: An Historical Comment" in Ian A Getty & Antoine S Lussier, eds, *As Long as the Sun Shines and Water Flows: A Reader in Canadian Native Studies* (Vancouver: University of British Columbia Press, 1983) 1.

iv. "Privatizing" Property on First Nations Reserves

Reserve lands for First Nations communities are regulated in Canada pursuant to the *Indian Act*, RSC 1985, c I-5. Although these reserve lands continue to be held in common, individual members of communities may obtain "certificates of possession" in relation to individual holdings. However, the federal government in Canada seems poised to introduce legislation that will create the possibility of private land ownership on First Nations reserve lands. According to the First Nations Property Initiative, the new legislation will generate business efficiencies, investment opportunities, and individual prosperity for First Nations people living on reserve lands. Although it appears that this legislation will be available on a voluntary basis, many First Nations communities and the Assembly of First Nations oppose this development as (once again) a policy of assimilation: see K Carsten Wyatt, "Losing the Land Again," *The Walrus* (March 2013) 17. The First Nations Property Initiative was proposed in T Flanagan, C Alcantara & A LeDressay, *Beyond the Indian Act: Restoring Aboriginal Property Rights* (Montreal: McGill-Queen's University Press, 2010). For a critique of Aboriginal relations with non-natives, see T King, *The Inconvenient Indian: A Curious Account of Native People in North America* (Toronto: Doubleday Canada, 2012).

B. Re-envisaging Property Interests as Human Rights

> Traditional property theory grants the private landowner a relatively unqualified right to decide who may or may not have access to his or her land and upon what terms. The problem, from a human rights perspective, is that this construction of the property right, in strict common law theory, is potentially totalitarian in its implications. This problem is already giving rise … to a clear conflict between common law property conceptualism and more inclusive, civic concerns arising from human rights values.

(Anna Grear, "A Tale of the Land, the Insider, the Outsider, and Human Rights (An Exploration of Some Problems and Possibilities in the Relationship Between the English Common Law Property Concept, Human Rights Law, and Discourses of Exclusion and Inclusion)" (2003) 23 LS 33 at 43.)

As this comment suggests, property provides power. Not surprisingly, a lack of property often creates vulnerability. As noted earlier, "homelessness" is the problem of "property-lessness." Or, as other scholars have suggested, property rights promote personal independence, while the absence of property often leads to dependency. For example, Pamela Symes suggested that the idea of property involves "a kind of personal power, power to effect change, power to exercise choice, to be a self-determining individual: [to have] independence": see P Symes, "Property, Power, and Dependence: Critical Family Law" (1987) 14 JL & Soc'y 199 at 201. Because individual autonomy and independence are important values in current western society, those who are without property are often dependent and may also be poor and powerless. Comparisons of those who have property with those who do not thus reveal some of the important elements of ideas about property. For example, see J Waldron, "Homelessness and the Issue of Freedom" (1991) 39 UCLA L Rev 295.

As noted in the discussion of *Harrison v Carswell*, ideas about property in relation to inequality represented an important aspect of the work of CB Macpherson. Macpherson suggested that liberal theory should reconceptualize property—instead of focusing on property as the "right to exclude," it should redefine property as including the "right not to be excluded from" the use or benefit of some thing:

> When property is so understood, the problem of liberal-democratic theory is no longer a problem of putting limits on the property right, but of supplementing the individual right to exclude others by the individual right not to be excluded by others. The latter right may be held to be the one that is most required by the liberal-democratic ethic, and most implied in a liberal concept of the human essence. The right not to be excluded by others may provisionally be stated as the individual right to equal access to the means of labour and/or the means of life.

(CB Macpherson, "Liberal-Democracy and Property" in Macpherson at 201.)

DISCUSSION NOTES

i. Property and Access to Jobs

Consider Macpherson's ideas in relation to *Local 1330, United Steel Workers v US Steel Corp*, 631 F2d 1264 (US Ct of Appeals 1980). In 1980, the US Court of Appeals reviewed a lower court decision concerning an application by a union to keep steel plants operating in Ohio, or sell the facilities to the union. One plant had been in operation since 1901, the other since 1918. Together, the two plants employed 3,500 workers. US Steel wanted to demolish the plants because they had become obsolete and the costs of modernization were greater than the costs of demolition. As the Court of Appeals subsequently noted (at 1265), the company's decision was likely to result in an economic tragedy for the community.

The union eventually initiated legal action, claiming a right on the part of the workers to purchase the plant. In the initial hearing, the trial judge made some comments about the possibility of a property interest arising out of the long relationship between the company and the employees. However, he subsequently concluded that there was no precedent for such a property right. The Court of Appeals agreed.

In "The Reliance Interest in Property" (1988) 40 Stan L Rev 614, JW Singer argued (at 621) that there was scope in this case for recognition of the workers' property rights arising out of their relationship with US Steel: "Such a new legally protected interest would place obligations on the company toward the workers and the community to alleviate the social costs of its decision to close the plant. Protection of this reliance interest could take a variety of forms."

What kinds of property analyses could be used to establish this entitlement? What forms would it take? In formulating your arguments, consider the importance of property as a social relationship as well as the connections between property, power, and poverty. For example, Singer suggested (at 662-63):

> The social relations approach asks us to be sensitive to the power inequalities within those relationships; some members of the common enterprise are more vulnerable than others. These inequalities are not natural; they are the direct result of the allocation of power determined by the assignment of legal entitlements. We should focus on the various ways in which vulnerable persons rely on relationships of mutual dependence. This perspective will give us a deeper understanding of how the legal system regulates economic life.

Consider how Singer's conception of "social relations" is dependent on a conception of property as a relationship among subjects with respect to objects. Reflect again on how this conception of property creates opportunities to reconsider social relations.

ii. Property Reform: What We "See"

Can you think of arguments about the nature of property that might be employed to challenge economic inequality? In reflecting on this challenge, consider the following comments by C Rose, "Seeing Property" in Rose 267 at 297:

> There is an old adage, told of plain people and plain things: what you see is what you get. Property seems plain in this way too: what you see is what you get. But things are more complicated than that. With property, the nature of "things" imposes their own quite fascinating constraints. Yet even with those, *what you see* in property is what you and others have talked yourselves into about those "things"; and given some imagination, you may always talk yourselves into seeing

something else—with all the effects on understanding and action that a new "envisioning" may bring.

In reflecting on Rose's suggestion, consider the following comments, which were inspired by careful observation of "property" relationships among the poor in Vancouver's downtown east side:

> I want to underscore the need to think more carefully about property relations in the constitution of social life. As a legal form, property seems remarkably important and pervasive, structuring a range of social issues, whether they be the constitution of the self, relations to nature, urban struggles, gender relations, colonial projects, or so on. With some notable exceptions, to my knowledge, relatively little empirical work has been done on this question … .
>
> I have tried here to attend to the ways in which property is constituted in and constitutive of everyday social and political relations in one particular urban context. I have tried to suggest that property is present but in some complex spatialized ways. My aim has also been to show the ways in which property is much more than Property Law, in the traditional legal sense, but is caught up in lived social relations in some surprising ways. If we wish to understand either—social relations or property—we need to think about both simultaneously … .
>
> In thinking through some of these complexities concerning property, then, we need an analytical framework that is sensitive to a number of issues. These include the dialectic between power and resistance, the manner in which property entails both practice and representation, the complex politics of place and the historical narratives and spatial mappings that underwrite property claims … . I do want to insist that a careful attention to space, place, and landscape is, at the very least, a necessary and important part of such a project.

(Nicholas Blomley, "Landscapes of Property" (1998) 32:3 Law & Soc'y Rev 567 at 608-9.) See also Anne Bottomley, "Figures in a Landscape: Feminist Perspectives on Law, Land, and Landscape" in A Bottomley, ed, *Feminist Perspectives on the Foundational Subjects of Law* (London: Cavendish, 1996) 124; and J Waldron, "Homelessness and the Issue of Freedom" (1991) 39 UCLA L Rev 295. In September 2013, an Ontario court rejected a Charter challenge launched by both the Centre for Equality Rights in Accommodation (CERA) and four individuals, who claimed that homelessness and inadequate housing violate s 7 (security of the person) and s 15 (equality). The court upheld a motion to strike the pleadings, filed by the Ontario and federal governments, on the basis that the court was not the proper place to resolve these issues: see *Tanudjaja v Canada (Attorney General) (Application)*, 2013 ONSC 5410, [2013] OJ no 4078, and further discussion in Chapter 4.

In this context, consider a decision from South Africa, *South Africa v Grootboom et al* (2000), CCT 11/00, a decision of the Constitutional Court, in which the court used a constitutional guarantee of "access to adequate housing" (s 26 of the South African constitution) to order the government to provide land for persons who had been evicted from their homes. Does this South African decision suggest that there is a need to enshrine rights to housing in a constitution in order to ensure that those who are rendered homeless have legal rights? What other measures might be appropriate here? As some scholars have noted, moreover, problems of homelessness may be increasingly a "middle-class" problem: see Rosy Thornton, "Homelessness Through Relationship Breakdown: The Local Authorities' Response" [1989] J Soc Welfare L 67; some of these issues are also discussed in Chapter 6.

iii. (Lack of) Property, Human Rights, and Section 7 of the Charter

The guarantee of "life, liberty and security of the person" in s 7 of the Charter has resulted in a number of challenges relating to dependency, although few of these cases have been entirely successful. For example, in *Masse v Minister of Community and Social Services* (1996), 134 DLR (4th) 20 (Ont Gen Div), the court held that it was within the government's competence to determine the level of welfare benefits, thus upholding the government's decision to reduce the level of benefits by 20 percent. The court concluded that this reduction in welfare benefits did not infringe the recipients' "life, liberty and security of the person" contrary to s 7: leave to appeal was denied ([1996] OJ no 1526 (CA), and [1996] SCCA no 373). Similarly, a Nova Scotia court held that the security of tenure of a public housing tenant was an economic interest and thus not protected by s 7: see *Bernard v Dartmouth Housing Authority* (1989), 88 NSR (2d) 190 (SC (AD)).

In addition, a 2002 decision of the Supreme Court of Canada upheld Quebec legislation that had lowered payments to welfare recipients under the age of 30 to one-third the usual amount, and had also created modest incentives for job training and education for them. In concluding that s 7 was not infringed by this legislation, even though welfare recipients under 30 did not have enough money to survive economically, a majority of the Supreme Court concluded that the facts did not support a claim under s 7 because the case did not involve interaction with the justice system and its administration. Moreover, even assuming that s 7 could apply to economic interests, the court held that there was no positive obligation on the province to ensure that all persons enjoyed "life, liberty and security of the person" and that s 7 related only to a *deprivation* of such rights: see *Gosselin v Québec (Attorney General)*, 2002 SCC 84, [2002] 4 SCR 429.

By contrast with these decisions, however, the Ontario Court of Appeal dismissed the government's appeal from a divisional court decision confirming a decision of the Social Assistance Review Board. The Board had upheld a challenge on the part of women welfare recipients in relation to a change in the statutory definition of "spouse": the change in the definition had disentitled women recipients to welfare benefits on the basis that they were in "spousal" relationships with men, even though their relationships were not lengthy and thus did not attract obligations of spousal support in family law: see *Falkiner v Ontario (Director, Income Maintenance Branch, Ministry of the Attorney General)* (2002), 212 DLR (4th) 633 (Ont CA). In this case, however, the appellate court relied primarily on s 15 of the Charter (the equality guarantee), and did not comment directly on s 7. For some discussion of the issues in *Falkiner*, see Tamara D Barclay, "Peering into the Bedrooms of the Province: An Examination of the Different Definitions of 'Spouse' in the Family Law Act and the Ontario Works Act, 1997" (2000) 15 J L & Soc Pol'y 1; and Diana Majury, "The Charter, Equality Rights, and Women: Equivocation and Celebration" (2002) 40 Osgoode Hall LJ 297.

Except for *Falkiner*, which was decided on the basis of s 15 rather than s 7, courts in Canada have generally eschewed arguments about protection for economic interests, particularly in relation to poverty and welfare entitlements pursuant to s 7. However, there is a good deal of academic commentary that suggests that there is much more scope in s 7 to protect the basic right to security of the person. For example, Michael MacNeil argued:

> The traditional difference between the economist and the lawyer in the use of the term "property" is that the former used it in respect to any relationship having an exchange value, while the latter used it to denote legal relations between persons, with respect to a thing .... [In this context, the

rise of law and economics studies has increasingly influenced how law interprets property rights. However, it is necessary to recognize that how property rights are protected] will have a direct bearing on the mechanisms that will be used by the state to distribute wealth and on the extent to which this [distribution] will be accomplished. ...

The rights which are being protected transcend the boundaries of property talk and go to the core of the fundamental essence of a right to life and full participation in a democratic society. The shortcoming of such protection is that the law is merely guaranteeing some form of security for those who have already acquired a share of the basic resources of society. There is a need to recognize that, if fundamental rights are to have any meaning, they must, above all, protect the claims of the poor to share in those resources, so that they can sustain a meaningful existence.

(See M MacNeil, "Property in the Welfare State" (1983) 7:3 Dal LJ 343 at 346-47 and 381-82.) See also G McGregor, "The International Covenant on Social, Economic, and Cultural Rights: Will It Get Its Day in Court?" (2002) 28 Man L Rev 321; C Scott, "The Interdependence and Permeability of Human Rights Norms: Towards a Partial Fusion of the International Covenants on Human Rights" (1989) 27 Osgoode Hall LJ 768; and M Jackman, "Poor Rights: Using the Charter to Support Social Welfare Claims" (1993) 19 Queen's LJ 65.

American scholars have also used ideas about property rights in relation to employment issues. For example, Beermann and Singer suggested that there is a "social vision" embodied in the common law of contract and property, and that "conceptualization of the worker–management relationship in terms of the prevailing social vision leads to common law categories that resolve conflicting claims between workers and management in favor of management": see JM Beermann & JW Singer, "Baseline Questions in Legal Reasoning: The Example of Property in Jobs" (1988-89) 23 Ga L Rev 911 at 916. See also JW Singer, "The Reliance Interest in Property" (1988) 40 Stan L Rev 614, arguing for legal recognition of workers' rights arising out of long-term employment relationships, especially in the context of corporate reorganization or restructuring.

C. The Organization of This Book: Real and Personal Property Interests

Historically, the classification of property interests as "real property" or "personal property" was critical to defining what rights and remedies were available to protect the interests. By contrast, in the 21st century, many of these historical distinctions have been abolished so that the principles of property apply more uniformly. Nonetheless, because statutes, judges, and lawyers continue to use traditional classifications, it is important to be able to recognize them and to understand their former significance.

The basic classification in property law was that relating to "real" property and "personal" property. This distinction derived from two different remedies available in medieval legal procedures for the return of property. In some cases, the plaintiff was entitled, by way of remedy, to the return of the object itself, or (in Latin) the "res." In this case, the plaintiff's action was called an action "in rem" or a "real" action, and property that could be recovered in such an action was called "real" property. Land, which was regarded as unique in the medieval period, was recoverable by a plaintiff using an action "in rem" so it became classified as "real property."

By contrast with land, other forms of property were not recoverable "in specie." Instead, the plaintiff was entitled to the value of the property, as damages for wrongful interference with

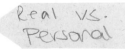

Real vs. Personal

it on the part of the defendant. This action was "*in personam*"—that is, it was an action against the defendant personally. Property for which the plaintiff could recover damages alone became known as "personal property." Because land was "real property," other forms of property became "personal property." Because an action *in rem* permitted recovery of the proprietary object, such an action was regarded as enforceable against the whole world. By contrast, because an action *in personam* resulted in damages only, it was regarded as enforceable merely between the parties to the dispute. Some of these ideas continue to be important in the principles concerning legal remedies, and these distinctions reflect, at least to some extent, the concepts of movable and immovable property recognized in civil law systems. For good overviews of the classification of real and personal property, see Ziff at 74ff, and D Jackson, *Principles of Property Law* (Sydney: Law Book Co, 1967) at 24ff. For an historical assessment, see AH Chaytor & WJ Whittaker, eds, *FW Maitland, The Forms of Action at Common Law: A Course of Lectures* (Cambridge: Cambridge University Press, 1965).

As the language demonstrates, this classification of property interests reflects the historical origins of the law of property. Moreover, the classification system really focuses on the *object* of proprietary interests, not on proprietary interests themselves, so that the classification may seem less useful to modern property analyses that focus on relationships among subjects with respect to proprietary objects. In addition, earlier distinctions between real and personal property sometimes have been changed by statute, and courts also have declared "*sui generis*" property interests, especially (but not only) in relation to Aboriginal property claims.

In this book, principles of real and personal property are examined together, wherever possible. Thus, the next chapter explores the concept of possession in relation to personal property in the "finders' cases" and in relation to land in the concept of "possessory title." Chapter 4 similarly examines the relationship between property law and contract law in the context of bailment (personal property) and leaseholds (a form of real property); and Chapter 5 explores the concept of transferring proprietary interests in relation to gifts of real and personal property and the sale of land. One purpose of this arrangement is to permit a critical assessment of the continued usefulness of the historical classification of proprietary interests, although you must also be attentive to important distinctions.

PROBLEMS

1. John Adams is the owner of a 100-acre parcel of land north of Toronto. Some years ago, he decided to discontinue his general farming operation on this parcel and instead create a wildlife reserve. This decision was consistent with Adams's lifelong fascination with wild animals and birds in North America. He was delighted to find that he could satisfy his own interests in wildlife and make a living at the same time by charging admission to visitors to the wildlife reserve. For the past decade, the wildlife reserve has provided him with a satisfactory livelihood.

Two months ago, Adams became aware of an intrusion to his wildlife reserve. For a six-week period, his neighbour on the adjoining property, Fred Bloggs, permitted a film crew to set up their equipment. On inquiry, Adams learned that Bloggs had agreed, in return for an undisclosed sum of money, to permit the film crew to use Bloggs's land as a base from which to film the background sequences for a documentary production about Canadian wildlife. The film crew, using special cameras and photographic techniques for filming at a distance, were able to simulate "life in the wild" by filming the birds and animals on Adams's wildlife reserve, although no one ever set foot on his land. For the film company, such an arrangement was both more efficient and much less costly than filming "in the wild."

John Adams wants to know whether the actions of the film company or of his neighbour Fred Bloggs are legally permissible, and what remedies may be available.

2. Ford-Fair is the corporate owner of a small shopping mall just outside the town of Vineyards, Ontario. As a result of recent extensive renovations, the mall is now a major commercial complex, with professional offices and services, as well as a department store and small shops.

Animal Heaven, a pet clinic providing vet services and overnight lodging for cats and dogs, is a relatively new tenant in the mall. The pet clinic is located beside KlikKliks, a hairdressing shop for men and women, which has been located in the mall for more than a decade. Joe Bright, who is the owner of KlikKliks and well-known for his fastidious ways, has been dismayed to see the usually serene ambiance of his hairdressing shop reduced—almost destroyed, according to him—by the animal sounds next door. He has complained to the mall owner without success. As a result, he has recently been considering whether he could take independent action against his neighbour in the mall, Animal Heaven.

In addition to his problem with the neighbouring pet clinic, Joe Bright has also decided to ask Ford-Fair to help him get rid of some demonstrators who have begun to picket in front of his shop, handing out leaflets decrying KlikKliks' wig business. The demonstrators are critical of his shop's use of "real hair" for wigs, claiming that it contributes to the oppression of poor women who must sell their hair at cut rates to provide for their families. Although the demonstrators have been quite peaceful for the past few days, Joe Bright has noticed a drop-off in business since they started to demonstrate in front of his shop. He wants to ask Ford-Fair to eject the demonstrators from the mall.

Can Joe Bright compel Animal Heaven to carry on its business in a way that does not interfere with the serenity of KlikKliks? (You may assume that there are no special issues related to the fact that these neighbouring shops are run by *tenants* in the mall.) Can KlikKliks request the mall owner to evict the "real hair" demonstrators?

3. In her article about frame shifting, Jennifer Jaff stated:

[D]ecision makers shift their frame of reference from broad to narrow, narrow to broad, to construct rationales that justify differing results ... . By using different frames of reference, two judges can arrive at two competing yet equally "legally sound" decisions in a single case.

Explain what Jaff means by "frame shifting," and show how frame shifting might be applied to explain the majority and dissenting judgments in *Harrison v Carswell*. Explain whether frame shifting helps to explain the problems of recognition (or non-recognition) of Aboriginal property concepts in Canadian law. To what extent is there a need to rethink the idea of "property" as dominion, or as stewardship?

4. Consider the impact of the Charter in relation to property rights in Canada, in relation to both the s 2 guarantees and the absence of protection for owners of private property. To what extent do cases such as *Batty v Toronto* and *Mariner Real Estate* suggest a need to reconsider the relationship between property interests and human rights? How should ideas about property and independence be balanced with the need to protect vulnerability?

CHAPTER REFERENCES

Adachi, K. *The Enemy That Never Was: A History of the Japanese Canadians* (Toronto: McClelland & Stewart, 1991).

Alexander, G. *The Global Debate over Constitutional Property* (Chicago: University of Chicago Press, 2006).

Alvaro, A. "Why Property Rights Were Excluded from the Canadian Charter of Rights and Freedoms" (1991) 24 Can J Political Science 309.

Arthurs, H. "Note" (1965) 43 Can Bar Rev 357 at 362.

Bale, G. "Casting Off the Mooring Ropes of Binding Precedent" (1980) 58 Can Bar Rev 255.

Barclay, Tamara D. "Peering into the Bedrooms of the Province: An Examination of the Different Definitions of 'Spouse' in the Family Law Act and the Ontario Works Act, 1997" (2000) 15 J L & Soc Pol'y 1.

Bartholomew, A & S Boyd. "Toward a Political Economy of Law" in W Clement & G Williams, eds, *The New Canadian Political Economy* (Kingston, ON: McGill-Queen's University Press, 1989).

Beaufoy, John. "Filipino Community Turns to OHRC After Members Banned from Mall," *Law Times* (25-31 October 1993).

Beermann, JM & JW Singer. "Baseline Questions in Legal Reasoning: The Example of Property in Jobs" (1988-89) 23 Ga L Rev 911.

Bennett, A, ed. *Shelter, Housing, and Homes: A Social Right* (Montreal: Black Rose Books, 1997).

Black, RA, RS Kreider & M Sullivan. "Critical Legal Studies, Economic Realism, and the Theory of the Firm" (1988) 43 U Miami L Rev 343.

Blodgett, Geoffrey. "Frederick Law Olmsted: Landscape Architecture as Conservative Reform" (1976) 62 J Am History 869.

Blomley, Nicholas. "Begging to Differ: Panhandling, Public Space, and Municipal Property" in E Tucker, J Muir & B Ziff, eds, *Property on Trial* (Toronto: Irwin Law for the Osgoode Society for Canadian Legal History, 2012) 393.

Blomley, Nicholas. "Landscapes of Property" (1998) 32:3 Law & Soc'y Rev 567.

Blomley, N, D Delaney & R Ford, eds. *The Legal Geographies Reader: Law, Power, and Space* (Oxford: Blackwell, 2001).

Bottomley, Anne. "Figures in a Landscape: Feminist Perspectives on Law, Land, and Landscape" in A Bottomley, ed, *Feminist Perspectives on the Foundational Subjects of Law* (London: Cavendish, 1996) 124.

Bottomley, Anne. "A Trip to the Mall: Revising the Public/Private Divide" in H Lim & A Bottomley, eds, *Feminist Perspectives on Land Law* (Oxford: Routledge-Cavendish, 2007) 65.

Butler, S. "Cardboard Boxes and Invisible Fences: Homelessness and Public Space in City of Victoria v Adams" (2009) 27 Windsor YB Access Just 209.

Caldwell, L. "Land and the Law: Problems in Legal Philosophy" (1986) U Ill L Rev 319.

Cartwright, Andrew. "Reforming Property Law in Eastern and Central Europe" in Elizabeth Cooke, ed, *Modern Studies in Property Law*, vol 1 (Oxford: Hart, 2001) 341.

Ceballos, A. "Fishing Licence Is Property, Says Supreme Court of Canada," *The Lawyers Weekly* (7 November 2008).

Chaytor, AH & WJ Whittaker, eds. *FW Maitland, The Forms of Action at Common Law: A Course of Lectures* (Cambridge: Cambridge University Press, 1965).

Christie, D. "A Tale of Three Takings: Taking Analysis in the Land Use Regulation of the United States, Australia, and Canada" (2007) 32 Brook J Int'l L 343.

Chused, Richard. *Cases, Materials, and Problems in Property* (New York: Matthew Bender, 1988).

Clement, W. *Class, Power, and Property: Essays on Canadian Society* (Toronto: Methuen, 1983).

Cohen, S Felix. "Dialogue on Private Property" (1954) 9:2 Rutgers L Rev 357.

Coval, S, JC Smith & Simon Coval. "The Foundations of Property and Property Law" (1986) 45 Cambridge LJ 457.

Craig, Carys J. "Putting the Community in Communication: Dissolving the Conflict Between Freedom of Expression and Copyright" (2006) 56:1 UTLJ 75.

Cruikshank, J. "Legend and Landscape: Convergence of Oral and Scientific Traditions in the Yukon Territory" (1981) 18:2 Arctic Anthropology 67.

Davies, Margaret & Ngaire Naffine. *Are Persons Property? Legal Debates About Property and Personality* (Aldershot, UK: Ashgate/Dartmouth, 2001).

Dickens, B. "Living Tissue and Organ Donors and Property Law: More on Moore" (1992) 8 J Contemp Health L & Pol'y 73.

DiMento, Joseph F. "Mining the Archives of *Pennsylvania Coal*: Heaps of Constitutional Mischief" (1990) 11 J Legal Hist 396.

Duggan, A. "In the Wake of the Bingo Queen: Are Licences Property?" (2008-9) 47 Can Bus LJ 225.

Fischl, RM. "Some Realism About Critical Legal Studies" (1987) 41 U Miami L Rev 505.

Flanagan, T, C Alcantara & A LeDressay. *Beyond the Indian Act: Restoring Aboriginal Property Rights* (Montreal: McGill-Queen's University Press, 2010).

Fortune, Joel R. "Construing Delgamuukw: Legal Arguments, Historical Argumentation, and the Philosophy of History" (1993) 51 UT Fac L Rev 80.

Freyfogle, Eric T. "The Construction of Ownership" (1996) 1 U Ill L Rev 173.

Gabel, Peter. "Reification in Legal Reasoning" in James Boyle, ed, *Critical Legal Studies* (New York: New York University Press, 1994).

Getty, Ian A & Antoine S Lussier, eds. *As Long as the Sun Shines and Water Flows: A Reader in Canadian Native Studies* (Vancouver: University of British Columbia Press, 1983).

Gilligan, Carol. *In a Different Voice: Psychological Theory and Women's Development* (Cambridge, MA: Harvard University Press, 1982).

Ginsburgs, George, ed. *The Revival of Private Law in Central and Eastern Europe* (The Hague, The Netherlands: Kluwer Law Int'l, 1996).

Girard, P & J Phillips. "A Certain 'Malaise': Harrison v Carswell, Shopping Centre Picketing, and the Limits of the Post-War Settlement" in J Fudge & E Tucker, eds, *Work on Trial: Canadian Labour Law Struggles* (Toronto: Irwin Law for the Osgoode Society for Canadian Legal History, 2010) 249.

Glendon, Mary Ann. *The New Family and the New Property* (Toronto: Butterworths, 1981).

Gray, Kevin. "Property in Thin Air" (1991) 50 Cambridge LJ 252.

Gray, KJ & PD Symes. *Real Property and Real People* (London: Butterworths, 1981).

Grear, Anna. "A Tale of the Land, the Insider, the Outsider, and Human Rights (An Exploration of Some Problems and Possibilities in the Relationship Between the English Common Law Property Concept, Human Rights Law, and Discourses of Exclusion and Inclusion)" (2003) 23 LS 33.

Hamill, S. "Private Property Rights and Public Responsibility: Leaving Room for the Homeless" (2011) 30 Windsor Rev Legal Soc Issues 91.

Harris, D. "A Railway, a City, and the Public Regulation of Private Property: CPR v City of Vancouver" in E Tucker, J Muir & B Ziff, eds, *Property on Trial* (Toronto: Irwin Law for the Osgoode Society for Canadian Legal History, 2012) 455.

Harris, Michael. *Lament for an Ocean* (Toronto: McClelland & Stewart, 1998).

Hazlehurst, K. *Legal Pluralism and the Colonial Legacy: Indigenous Experiences of Justice in Canada, Australia, and New Zealand* (Aldershot, UK: Avebury, 1995).

Herman, MO. "Fighting Homelessness: Can International Human Rights Make a Difference?" (1994) 2:1 Geo J on Poverty L & Pol'y 59.

Hohfeld, WN. "Some Fundamental Legal Conceptions as Applied in Judicial Reasoning" (1913) 23 Yale LJ 16.

Hohmann, J. *The Right to Housing* (Oxford & Portland, OR: Hart, 2013).

Horwitz, M. "The History of the Public/Private Distinction" (1982) 130 U Pa L Rev 1423.

Horwitz, M. *The Transformation of American Law, 1780-1860* (Cambridge, MA: Harvard University Press, 1977).

Jackman, M. "Poor Rights: Using the Charter to Support Social Welfare Claims" (1993) 19 Queen's LJ 65.

Jackson, D. *Principles of Property Law* (Sydney: Law Book Co, 1967).

Jaff, Jennifer. "Frame-Shifting: An Empowering Methodology for Teaching and Learning Legal Reasoning" (1986) 36 J Legal Educ 249.

Kennedy, D. "The Stages of the Decline of the Public/Private Distinction" (1982) 130 U Pa L Rev 1349.

King, T. *The Inconvenient Indian: A Curious Account of Native People in North America* (Toronto: Doubleday Canada, 2012).

Kingston, J. "Rich People Have Rights Too? The Status of Property as a Fundamental Human Right" in L Heffernan, ed, *Human Rights: A European Perspective* (Dublin and Portland, OR: Roundhill Press in association with the Irish Centre for European Law, 1994).

Knoppers, B, T Caulfield & D Kinsella, eds. *Legal Rights and Human Genetic Material* (Toronto: Emond Montgomery Publications, 1996).

Kogawa, J. *Obasan* (Toronto: Lester and Orpen Dennys, 1981).

Kyer, Ian. "Regina v Stewart: Is Information Property?" in E Tucker, J Muir & B Ziff, eds, *Property on Trial* (Toronto: Irwin Law for the Osgoode Society for Canadian Legal History, 2012) 353.

Lim, H & A Bottomley, eds. *Feminist Perspectives on Land Law* (Abingdon, Oxon: Routledge-Cavendish, 2007) 65.

Litman, MM. "Freedom of Speech and Private Property: The Case of the Mall Owner" in D Schneiderman, ed, *Freedom of Expression and the Charter* (Scarborough, ON: Thomson, 1991) 361.

Little Bear, Leroy. "Aboriginal Rights and the Canadian 'Grundnorm'" in J Rick Ponting, *Arduous Journey: Canadian Indians and Decolonization* (Toronto: McClelland & Stewart, 1986).

Loader, Lisa. "Trespass to Property: Shopping Centres" (1992) 87 J L & Soc Pol'y 254.

MacNeil, M. "Property in the Welfare State" (1983) 7:3 Dal LJ 343.

Macpherson, CB. "Liberal-Democracy and Property" in CB Macpherson, ed, *Property: Mainstream and Critical Positions* (Toronto: University of Toronto Press, 1978) 199.

Macpherson, CB. "The Meaning of Property" in CB Macpherson, ed, *Property: Mainstream and Critical Positions* (Toronto: University of Toronto Press, 1978) 1.

Macpherson, CB, ed. *Property: Mainstream and Critical Positions* (Toronto: University of Toronto Press, 1978).

Magnusson, D. "Hell Hath No Fury—Copyright Lawyers' Lessons from Deeks v Wells" (2003-4) 29 Queen's LJ 680.

Majury, Diana. "The Charter, Equality Rights, and Women: Equivocation and Celebration" (2002) 40 Osgoode Hall LJ 297.

Majury, Diana. "Is Care Enough?" (1994) 17 Dal LJ 279.

McGregor, G. "The International Covenant on Social, Economic, and Cultural Rights: Will It Get Its Day in Court?" (2002) 28 Man L Rev 321.

Mendis, Dinusha & Martin Kretschmer. *The Treatment of Parodies Under Copyright Law in Seven Jurisdictions: A Comparative Review of the Underlying Principles* (Newport, UK: Intellectual Property Office, 2013).

Menkel-Meadow, Carrie. "Portia in a Different Voice: Speculations on a Woman's Lawyering Process" (1985) 1 Berkeley Women's LJ 39.

Minow, Martha. "Judging Inside Out" (1990) 61 Colo L Rev 795.

Mitchell, D. *The Right to the City: Social Justice and the Fight for Public Space* (New York: Guilford Press, 2003).

Mossman, MJ. "Developments in Property Law: The 1985-86 Term" (1986) 8 Sup Ct L Rev 319.

Moulton, J. "A Paradigm of Philosophy: The Adversary Method" in S Harding and MB Hintikka, eds, *Discovering Reality: Feminist Perspectives on Epistemology, Metaphysics, Methodology, and Philosophy of Science* (Boston: D Reidel, 1983) 149.

Nedelsky, Jennifer. "Law, Boundaries, and the Bounded Self" in Richard Chused, ed, *A Property Anthology* (Cincinnati, OH: Anderson, 1993).

Neeson, J. *Commoners: Common Right, Enclosure, and Social Change in England 1700-1820* (New York: Cambridge University Press, 1993).

Nelson, E. "Comparative Perspectives on the Regulation of Assisted Reproductive Technologies in the United Kingdom and Canada" (2006) 43 Alta L Rev 1023.

Nelson, Jennifer J. "The Space of Africville: Creating, Regulating, and Remembering the Urban 'Slum'" (2000) 15:2 CJLS 163.

Nuffield Council on Bioethics. *Human Tissue: Ethical and Legal Issues* (London: Nuffield Council on Bioethics, 1995).

Oakley, AJ. "The Licensee's Interest" (1972) 35 Mod L Rev 551.

Ontario. Task Force on the Law Concerning Trespass to Publicly Used Property as It Affects Youth and Minorities, Raj Anand, Chair (Toronto: Ontario Ministry of the Attorney General, 1987).

Parkdale Community Legal Services. "Homelessness and the Right to Shelter: A View from Parkdale" (1988) 4 J L & Soc Pol'y 35.

Parkdale Community Legal Services. "Submissions to the Task Force on the Law Concerning Trespass to Publicly Used Property as It Affects Youths and Minorities" (1997) 35:4 Osgoode Hall LJ 819.

Perry, Ted, inspired by Chief Seattle. "How Can One Sell the Air?" in Eli Gifford & R Michael Cook, eds, *How Can One Sell the Air? Chief Seattle's Vision* (Summertown, TN: The Book Publishing Co, 1992).

Phillips, J & J Martin. "Manitoba Fisheries v The Queen: The Origins of Canada's De Facto Expropriation Doctrine" in E Tucker, J Muir & B Ziff, eds, *Property on Trial* (Toronto: Irwin Law for the Osgoode Society for Canadian Legal History, 2012) 259.

Pieper, MA. "Frozen Embryos—Persons or Property? Davis v Davis" (1990) 23 Creighton L Rev 807.

Radin, Margaret Jane. "'After the Final No There Comes a Yes': A Law Teacher's Report" (1990) 2 Yale JL & Human 252.

Radin, Margaret Jane. "Market-Inalienability" (1987) 100 Harv L Rev 1849.

Radin, Margaret Jane. "Property and Personhood" (1982) 34 Stan L Rev 957.

Radin, Margaret Jane. *Reinterpreting Property* (Chicago: University of Chicago Press, 1993).

Reeve, A. "The Theory of Property: Beyond 'Private' Versus 'Common Property,'" in D Held, ed, *Political Theory Today* (Stanford, CA: Stanford University Press, 1991) 91.

Reich, Charles. "The New Property" (1964) 73 Yale LJ 733.

Reiner, L & R Reiner. *Removal and Return: The Socio-Economic Effects of War on Japanese Americans* (Berkeley: University of California Press, 1949).

Report of the Royal Commission on Aboriginal Peoples (Ottawa: Commission, 1996).

Revkin, Andrew C. "Ecuador Constitution Grants Rights to Nature" (29 September 2008), online: *The New York Times*, The Opinion Pages <http://dotearth.blogs.nytimes.com/2008/09/29/ecuador-constitution-grants-nature-rights>.

Robertson, Michael. "Reconceiving Private Property" (1997) 24:4 JL & Soc'y 465.

Robinson, Stephanie M. "Revisiting the Eaton's Centre: Picketing on Quasi-Public Property in Ontario" (1999) LELJ 391.

Rodgers, C. "Nature's Place? Property Rights, Property Rules, and Environmental Stewardship" (2009) 68:3 Cambridge LJ 550.

Rose, Carol. *Property and Persuasion: Essays on the History, Theory, and Rhetoric of Ownership* (Boulder, CO: Westview Press, 1994).

Rose, Carol. "Seeing Property" in *Property and Persuasion: Essays on the History, Theory, and Rhetoric of Ownership* (Boulder, CO: Westview Press, 1994) 267.

Ross, R. *Dancing with a Ghost: Exploring Indian Reality* (Markham, ON: Octopus Books, 1992).

Royal Commission on New Reproductive Technologies. *Proceed with Care: Final Report of the Royal Commission on New Reproductive Technologies*, vol 1 (Ottawa: Minister of Government Services Canada, 1993), online: Canadian Women's Health Network <http://www.cwhn.ca/en/node/24428#sthash.SIKH1o2u.dpuf>.

Rudden, Bernard. "Things as Thing and Things as Wealth" (1994) 14 Oxford J Legal Stud 81.

Rudmin, Floyd. "Gender Differences in the Semantics of Ownership: A Quantitative Phenomenological Survey Study" (1994) 15:3 Journal of Economic Psychology 487.

Schwartz, B & M Bueckert. "Regulatory Takings in Canada" (2006) 5 Wash U Global Studies 477, part of a Symposium: "Regulatory Takings in Land-Use Law—A Comparative Perspective on Compensation Rights."

Scott, C. "The Interdependence and Permeability of Human Rights Norms: Towards a Partial Fusion of the International Covenants on Human Rights" (1989) 27 Osgoode Hall LJ 768.

Singer, JW. "How to Brief a Case and Prepare for Class" in Singer, *Property Law: Rules, Policies, and Practices*, 2d ed (New York: Aspen Law & Business, 1997).

Singer, JW. "No Right to Exclude: Public Accommodations and Private Property" (1996) 90 Nw UL Rev 1283.

Singer, JW. "The Reliance Interest in Property" (1988) 40 Stan L Rev 614.

Stanley, George FG. "As Long as the Sun Shines and Water Flows: An Historical Comment" in Ian A Getty & Antoine S Lussier, eds, *As Long as the Sun Shines and Water Flows: A Reader in Canadian Native Studies* (Vancouver: University of British Columbia Press, 1983) 1.

Stone, C. "'Should Trees Have Standing?' Revisited: How Far Will Law and Morals Reach? A Pluralist Perspective" (1985) 59 S Cal L Rev 1.

Stone, Helen. "Living in Time Immemorial—Concepts of 'Time' and 'Time Immemorial': Why Aboriginal Rights Theory Is Problematic in the Courts and Around the Negotiating Table" (Carleton University, MA thesis, 1993).

Stone, Julius. *Legal System and Lawyers' Reasonings* (Stanford, CA: Stanford University Press, 1964).

Stone, Julius. *Precedent and Law: Dynamics of Common Law Growth* (Sydney: Butterworths, 1985).

Sweeney, R. *Out of Place: Homelessness in America* (New York: HarperCollins, 1993).

Symes, P. "Property, Power, and Dependence: Critical Family Law" (1987) 14 JL & Soc'y 199.

Telfer, T. "Statutory Licences and the Search for Property: The End of the Imbroglio?" (2007) 45 Can Bus LJ 224.

Thornton, Rosy. "Homelessness Through Relationship Breakdown: The Local Authorities' Response" [1989] J Soc Welfare L 67.

Tucker, Eric. "The Malling of Property Law?" in E Tucker, J Muir & B Ziff, eds, *Property on Trial* (Toronto: Irwin Law for the Osgoode Society for Canadian Legal History, 2012) 303.

Tucker, E, J Muir & B Ziff, eds. *Property on Trial* (Toronto: Irwin Law for the Osgoode Society for Canadian Legal History, 2012).

Van der Walt, AJ. "Protecting Social Participation Rights" in E Cooke, ed, *Property 2002*, vol 4 (Oxford & Portland, OR: Hart, 2003).

Vaver, D. *The Law of Intellectual Property: Copyright, Patents, Trademarks* (Concord, ON: Irwin Law, 1996).

Vermette, D'Arcy. "Colonialism and the Process of Defining Aboriginal People" (2008) 31 Dal LJ 211.

Waldron, J. "Homelessness and the Issue of Freedom" (1991) 39 UCLA L Rev 295.

Waldron, J. *The Right to Private Property* (Oxford: Clarendon Press, 1988).

Walker, Barrington, ed. *The African-Canadian Legal Odyssey: Historical Essays* (Toronto: University of Toronto Press for the Osgoode Society for Canadian Legal History, 2012).

Ward, WP. *White Canada Forever: Popular Attitudes and Public Policy Toward Orientals in British Columbia*, 2d ed (Montreal and Kingston: McGill-Queen's University Press, 1990).

Warren & Brandeis. "The Right to Privacy" (1890) 4 Harv L Rev 193.

Webber, J. "Relations of Force and Relations of Justice: The Emergence of Normative Community Between Colonists and Aboriginal Peoples" (1995) 33 Osgoode Hall LJ 623.

Weinrib, A. "Information and Property" (1988) 36 UTLJ 117.

Weisenburger, C. "Digging Below and Looking Beside the Wall of Ministerial Discretion: Licences After Saulnier" (2007-8) 45 Alb L Rev 273.

Williams, Patricia. *The Alchemy of Race and Rights* (Cambridge, MA: Harvard University Press, 1991).

Williams, Patricia. "On Being an Object of Property" in Williams, *The Alchemy of Race and Rights* (Cambridge, MA: Harvard University Press, 1991).

Winks, Robin. *The Blacks in Canada* (Montreal: McGill-Queen's University Press, 1997).

Wright, Shelley. "A Feminist Exploration of the Legal Protection of Art" (1994) 7 CJWL 59.

Wright, Shelley. "Property, Information, and the Ethics of Communication" (1994) 9 IPJ 47.

Wyatt, K Carsten. "Losing the Land Again," *The Walrus* (March 2013) 17.

Ziff, Bruce. *Principles of Property Law*, 5th ed (Scarborough, ON: Carswell, 2010).

Ziff, Bruce. "'Taking' Liberties: Protections for Private Property in Canada" in E Cooke, ed, *Modern Studies in Property Law*, vol 3 (Oxford: Hart, 2005) 347.

CHAPTER TWO

The Concept of "Possession"

I. THE CONCEPT OF "FIRST POSSESSION"

"Possession is nine-tenths of the law." This old adage reflects the traditional importance of the concept of possession in the law of property, but possession continues to be an important concept in some modern property disputes as well. This chapter explores the concept of possession in relation to proprietary interests in chattels and in land.

At the outset, it is important to identify three related matters concerning possession. First, as was evident in the examination of the concept of "property," the everyday meaning of the word "possession" often differs from its legal concept. Courts and statutes frequently make important distinctions in defining possession—for example, as "actual possession," "constructive possession," a "right to possession," or "pedal possession." In the cases and examples that follow, take careful note of these different formulations of possession in law and how they affect the interpretation of proprietary interests.

Second, the concept of possession demonstrates the basic common law principle that property interests are *always relative*. Thus, even though someone may have "title" to a chattel or to land, a person who holds a possessory interest may nonetheless have a superior claim over someone who subsequently interferes with that possession (by theft, for example). This principle is often referred to as "the relativity of title": the plaintiff who can establish a right based on possession that is prior in time to the defendant's claim can succeed in an action against the defendant, even if there is a "true owner"—a person with a better title than the plaintiff's. Usually, the defendant cannot rely on the fact that someone else—a person not party to the suit—has a claim prior to or better than the plaintiff's claim. (The third party is sometimes referred to as the *jus tertii*.) Thus, it is always necessary to observe how a possible claim by a "true owner" affects litigation between a plaintiff and the defendant.

Finally, as is clear from this discussion of the "relativity of title" in property law, a person's possession of a chattel or land may, *by itself*, create a proprietary interest. This principle is sometimes expressed in terms of "possession as a root of title" or "possessory title." Although the common law historically recognized possession as creating proprietary claims in this way, the normative question why possession should continue to justify such legal claims remains a vexing one.

This chapter begins with an excerpt from Carol Rose's inquiry about the concept of possession as a basis for original claims to property (including land and chattels). In examining theories that scholars have used to try and understand why *something* comes to be owned by *someone*, Rose demonstrates how the current common law understanding of possession brings together two major, historical theories—that is, the labour theory and the societal consent theory. Arising from the works of philosopher John Locke, the labour theory of possession states that the original owner is the first person to combine his or her human labour with the thing that comes to be possessed—for example, the first person to fence in a piece of land owns the land. On the other hand, the societal consent theory of possession holds that people engage in an agreement within a community to define what any individual possesses—for example, democratically elected officials create rules about ownership regarding stocks.

Rose identified some of the criticism about these theories, and how they may not be satisfactory for the purpose of explaining the concept of possession. In this context, she proposed that the current understanding of possession at common law may help to overcome these difficulties. More specifically, the common law's "clear act" theory of possession combines an *act of labour* with an act that *clearly alerts society* with respect to a claim to possession of property. Although this theory seems to overcome many of the problems that plagued earlier conceptions of possession, Rose also highlights some continuing problems. For example, what acts should be considered "clear acts" for purposes of common law possession? This question is important in relation to many different kinds of claims to possession, but it has particular significance in relation to Aboriginal communities who were in "possession" of considerable territory at the time of European settlements in North America, an issue discussed briefly in this chapter and more fully in Chapter 8.

Carol Rose, "Possession as the Origin of Property"
(1985) 52 U Chicago L Rev 73 at 73-77 and 82-88 (footnotes omitted)

How do things come to be owned? This is a fundamental puzzle for anyone who thinks about property. One buys things from other owners, to be sure, but how did the other owners get those things? Any chain of ownership or title must have a first link. Someone had to do something to anchor that link. The law tells us what steps we must follow to obtain ownership of things, but we need a theory that tells us why these steps should do the job.

John Locke's view, once described as "the standard bourgeois theory," is probably the one most familiar to American students. Locke argued that an original owner is one who mixes his or her labor with a thing and, by commingling that labor with the thing, establishes ownership of it. This labor theory is appealing because it appears to rest on "desert," but it has some problems. First, without a prior theory of ownership, it is not self-evident that one owns even the labor that is mixed with something else. Second, even if one does own the labor that one performs, the labor theory provides no guidance in determining the scope of the right that one establishes by mixing one's labor with something else. Robert Nozick illustrates this problem with a clever hypothetical. Suppose I pour a can of tomato juice into the ocean: do I now own the seas?

A number of thinkers more or less contemporary to Locke proposed another theory of the basis of ownership. According to this theory, the original owner got title through the consent of the rest of humanity (who were, taken together, the first recipients from God, the genuine original owner). Locke himself identified the problems with this theory; they involve what modern law-and-economics writers would call "administrative costs." How does everyone get together to consent to the division of things among individuals?

The common law has a third approach, which shares some characteristics with the labor and consent theories but is distinct enough to warrant a different label. For the common law, *possession* or "occupancy" is the origin of property. This notion runs through a number of fascinating old cases with which teachers of property law love to challenge their students. Such inquiries into the acquisition of title to wild animals and abandoned treasure may seem purely academic; how often, after all, do we expect to get into disputes about the ownership of wild pigs or long-buried pieces of eight? These cases are not entirely silly, though. People still do find treasure-laden vessels, and statesmen do have to consider whether someone's acts might support a claim to own the moon, for example, or the mineral nodes at the bottom of the sea. Moreover, analogies to the capture of wild animals show up time and again when courts have to deal on a nonstatutory basis with some "fugitive" resource that is being reduced to property for the first time, such as oil, gas, ground water, or space on the spectrum of radio frequencies.

With these more serious claims in mind, then, I turn to the maxim of the common law: first possession is the root of title. Merely to state the proposition is to raise two critical questions: what counts as possession, and why is it the basis for a claim to title? In exploring the quaint old cases' answers to these questions, we hit on some fundamental views about the nature and purposes of a property regime.

Consider *Pierson v. Post*, a classic wild-animal case from the early nineteenth century. Post was hunting a fox one day on an abandoned beach and almost had the beast in his gun sight when an interloper appeared, killed the fox, and ran off with the carcass. The indignant Post sued the interloper for the value of the fox on the theory that his pursuit of the fox had established his property right to it.

The court disagreed. It cited a long list of learned authorities to the effect that "occupancy" or "possession" went to the one who killed the animal, or who at least wounded it mortally or caught it in a net. These acts brought the animal within the "certain control" that gives rise to possession and hence a claim to ownership.

Possession thus means a clear act, whereby all the world understands that the pursuer has "an unequivocal intention of appropriating the animal to his individual use." A clear rule of this sort should be applied, said the court, because it prevents confusion and quarrelling among hunters (and coincidentally makes the judges' task easier when hunters do get into quarrels).

The dissenting judge commented that the best way to handle this matter would be to leave it to a panel of sportsmen, who presumably would have ruled against the interloper. In any event, he noted that the majority's rule would discourage the useful activity of fox hunting: who would bother to go to all the trouble of keeping dogs and chasing foxes if the reward were up for grabs to any "saucy intruder"? If we really want to see that foxes don't overrun the countryside, we will allocate a property right—and thus the ultimate reward—to the hunter at an earlier moment, so that he will undertake the useful investment in keeping hounds and the useful labor in flushing the fox.

The problem with assigning "possession" prior to the kill is, of course, that we need a principle to tell us when to assign it. Shall we assign it when the hunt begins? When the hunter assembles his dogs for the hunt? When the hunter buys his dogs?

Pierson thus presents two great principles, seemingly at odds, for defining possession: (1) notice to the world through a clear act and (2) reward to useful labor. The latter principle, of course, suggests a labor theory of property. The owner gets the prize when he "mixes in his labor" by hunting. On the other hand, the former principle suggests at least a weak form of the consent theory: the community requires clear acts so that it has the opportunity to dispute claims, but may be thought to acquiesce in individual ownership where the claim is clear and no objection is made.

On closer examination, however, the two positions do not seem so far apart. In *Pierson*, each side acknowledged the importance of the other's principle. Although the majority decided in favor of a clear rule, it tacitly conceded the value of rewarding useful labor. Its rule for possession would in fact reward the original hunter most of the time, unless we suppose that the woods are thick with "saucy intruders." On the other side, the dissenting judge also wanted some definiteness in the rule of possession. He was simply insisting that the acts that sufficed to give notice should be prescribed by the relevant community, namely hunters or "sportsmen." Perhaps, then, there is some way to reconcile the clear-act and reward-to-labor principles. …

[It] turns out that the common law of first possession, in rewarding the one who communicates a claim, *does* reward useful labor; the useful labor is the very act of speaking clearly and distinctly about one's claims to property. Naturally, this must be in a language that is understood, and the acts of "possession" that communicate a claim will vary according to the audience. Thus, returning to *Pierson v. Post*, the dissenting judge may well have thought that fox hunters were the only relevant audience for a claim to the fox; they are the only ones who have regular contact with the subject matter. By the same token, the mid-nineteenth-century California courts gave much deference to the mining-camp customs in adjudicating various Gold Rush claims; the Forty-Niners themselves, as those most closely involved with the subject, could best communicate and interpret the signs of property claims and would be particularly well served by a stable system of symbols that would enable them to avoid disputes.

The point, then, is that "acts of possession" are, in the now fashionable term, a "text," and that the common law rewards the author of that text. But, as students of hermeneutics know, the clearest text may have ambiguous subtexts. In connection with the text of first possession, there are several subtexts that are especially worthy of note. One is the implication that the text will be "read" by the relevant audience at the appropriate time. It is not always easy to establish a symbolic structure in which the text of first possession can be "published" at such a time as to be useful to anyone. Once again, *Pierson v. Post* illustrates the problem that occurs when a clear sign (killing the fox) comes only relatively late in the game, after the relevant parties may have already expended overlapping efforts and embroiled themselves in a dispute. Very similar problems occurred in the whaling industry in the nineteenth century: the courts expended a considerable amount of mental energy in finding signs of "possession" that were comprehensible to whalers from their own customs and that at the same time came early enough in the chase to allow the parties to avoid wasted efforts and the ensuing mutual recriminations.

Some objects of property claims do seem inherently incapable of clear demarcation—ideas, for example. In order to establish ownership of such disembodied items we find it necessary to translate the property claims into sets of secondary symbols that our culture understands. In patent and copyright law, for example, one establishes an entitlement to the expression of an idea by translating it into a written document and going through a registration process—though the unending litigation over ownership of these expressions, and over which expressions can even be subject to patent or copyright, might lead us to conclude that these particular secondary symbolic systems do not always yield widely understood "markings." We also make up secondary symbols for physical objects that would seem to be much easier to mark out than ideas; even property claims in land, that most tangible of things, are now at their most authoritative in the form of written records.

It is expensive to establish and maintain these elaborate structures of secondary symbols, as indeed it may be expensive to establish a structure of primary symbols of possession. The economists have once again performed a useful service in pointing out that there are costs entailed in establishing *any* property system. These costs might prevent the development of any system at all for some objects, where our need for secure investment and trade is not as great as the cost of creating the necessary symbols of possession.

There is a second and perhaps even more important subtext to the "text" of first possession: the tacit supposition that there is such a thing as a "clear act," unequivocally proclaiming to the universe one's appropriation—that there are in fact unequivocal acts of possession, which any relevant audience will naturally and easily interpret as property claims. Literary theorists have recently written a great deal about the relativity of texts. They have written too much for us to accept uncritically the idea that a "text" about property has a natural meaning independent of some audience constituting an "interpretive community" or independent of a range of other "texts" and cultural artifacts that together form a symbolic system in which a given text must be read. It is not enough, then, for the property claimant to say simply, "It's mine" through some act or gesture; in order for the "statement" to have any force, some relevant world must understand the claim it makes and take that claim seriously.

Thus, in defining the acts of possession that make up a claim to property, the law not only rewards the author of the "text"; it also puts an imprimatur on a particular symbolic system and on the audience that uses this system. Audiences that do not understand or accept the symbols are out of luck. For *Pierson*'s dissenting judge, who would have made the definition of first possession depend on a decision of hunters, the rule of first possession would have put the force of law behind the mores of a particular subgroup. The majority's "clear act" rule undoubtedly referred to a wider audience and a more widely shared set of symbols. But even under the majority's rule, the definition of first possession depended on a particular audience and its chosen symbolic context; some audiences win, others lose.

In the history of American territorial expansion, a pointed example of the choice among audiences made by the common law occurred when one group did not play the approved language game and refused to get into the business of publishing or reading the accepted texts about property. The result was one of the most arresting decisions of the early American republic: *Johnson v. McIntosh*, a John Marshall opinion concerning the validity of opposing claims to land in what is now a large part of Illinois and Indiana. The plaintiffs in this case claimed through Indian tribes, on the basis of deeds made out in the 1770's; the defendants claimed under titles that came from the United States. The Court found for the defendants, holding that the claims through the Indians were invalid, for reasons derived largely from international law rather than from the law of first possession. But tucked away in the case was a first-possession argument that Marshall passed over. The Indians, according to an argument of the claimants from the United States, could not have passed title to the opposing side's predecessors because, "[b]y the law of nature," the Indians themselves had never done acts on the land sufficient to establish property in it. That is to say, the Indians had never really undertaken those acts of possession that give rise to a property right.

Although Marshall based his decision on other grounds, there was indeed something to the argument from the point of view of the common law of first possession. Insofar as the Indian tribes moved from place to place, they left few traces to indicate that they claimed the land (if indeed they did make such claims). From an eighteenth-century political economist's point of view, the results were horrifying. What seemed to be the absence of distinct claims to land among the Indians merely invited disputes, which in turn meant constant disruption of productive activity and dissipation of energy in warfare. Uncertainty as to claims also meant that no one would make any productive use of the land because there is little incentive to plant when there is no reasonable assurance that one will be in possession of the land at harvest time. From this classical economic perspective, the Indians' alleged indifference to well-defined property lines in land was part and parcel of what seemed to be their relatively unproductive use of the earth.

Now it may well be that North American Indian tribes were not so indifferent to marking out landed property as eighteenth-century European commentators supposed. Or it may be that at least some tribes found landed property less important to their security than other forms of property and thus felt no need to assert claims to property in land. But however anachronistic the *Johnson* parties' (ultimately mooted) argument may now seem, it is a particularly striking example of the relativity of the "text" of possession to the interpretative community for that text. It is doubtful whether the claims of any nomadic population could ever meet the common law requirements for establishing property in land. Thus, the audience presupposed by the common law of first possession is an agrarian or a commercial people—a people whose activities with respect to the objects around them require an unequivocal delineation of lasting control so that those objects can be managed and traded.

But perhaps the deepest aspect of the common law text of possession lies in the attitude that this text strikes with respect to the relationship between human beings and nature. At least some Indians professed bewilderment at the concept of owning the land. Indeed they prided themselves on not marking the land but rather on moving lightly through it, living with the land and with its creatures as members of the same family rather than as strangers who visited only to conquer the objects of nature. The doctrine of first possession, quite to the contrary, reflects the attitude that human beings are outsiders to nature. It gives the earth and its creatures over to those who mark them so clearly as to transform them, so that no one else will mistake them for unsubdued nature.

We may admire nature and enjoy wildness, but those sentiments find little resonance in the doctrine of first possession. Its texts are those of cultivation, manufacture, and development. We cannot have our fish both loose and fast, as Melville might have said, and the common law of first possession makes a choice. The common law gives preference to those who convince the world that they have caught the fish and hold it fast. This may be a reward to useful labor, but it is more precisely the articulation of a specific vocabulary within a structure of symbols approved and understood by a commercial people. It is this commonly understood and shared set of symbols that gives significance and form to what might seem the quintessentially individualistic act: the claim that one has, by "possession," separated for oneself property from the great commons of unowned things.

DISCUSSION NOTES

i. Possessory Rights: Subject and Object Revisited

As Carol Rose explained, the judgments in Pierson v Post, 3 Cai R 175 (NY Sup Ct 1805) illustrate legal reasoning about possession, and the philosophical limits of the labour theory and the consent theory in the context of claims based on first possession. Consider these arguments in relation to some of the theories in Chapter 1 used to justify property entitlement. Is the concept of first possession consistent with Macpherson's proposed formulation of a concept of property as the right not to be excluded? In thinking about how to conceptualize possessory rights from the perspective of those who have limited opportunities to acquire things, consider the following story told by Patricia Williams about Pierson v Post, as reinterpreted by a child, from the perspective of the fox. In reflecting on the story, Williams linked the perspective of the fox and the perspective of her great-great-grandmother who was a slave in the United States and the personal property of her slave-owner, Austin Miller:

> In reviewing those powerfully impersonal documents [the documents of her ancestor's sale as a slave to Austin Miller], I realized that both she and the fox shared a common lot, were either owned or unowned, never the owner. And whether owned or unowned, rights over them never filtered down to them; rights to their persons were never vested in them. When owned, issues of physical, mental, and emotional abuse or cruelty were assigned by the law to the private tolerance, whimsy, or insanity of an external master. And when unowned—free, freed, or escaped— again their situation was controllably precarious, for as objects *to be* owned, they and the game of their conquest were seen only as potential enhancements to some other self. (In *Pierson*, for example, the dissent described the contest as between the "gentleman" in pursuit and the "saucy intruder." The majority acknowledged that Pierson's behaviour was "uncourteous" and "unkind" but decided the case according to broader principles of "peace and order" in sportsmanship.)

They were fair game from the perspective of those who had rights; but from their own point of view, they were objects of a murderous hunt.

(Patricia Williams, "The Pain of Word Bondage" in *The Alchemy of Race and Rights* (Cambridge, MA: Harvard University Press, 1991) at 156ff.)

This analysis of those who are "owners" in the context of a principle of first possession reflects the distinction between subjects and objects of property interests, addressed in Chapter 1. Can the problems identified by Williams be solved by turning "objects" into "subjects" of property interests, or is the problem more fundamental?

ii. Problems of First Possession and Property

The case of *Pierson v Post* is one example, among several, of the concept of first possession as a basis for establishing a proprietary interest. Although *Pierson* involved fox hunting, there have been other cases concerning "first possession" of fish in Lake Erie (*Ohio v Shaw*, 65 NE 875 (OH Sup Ct 1902)); seals on the east coast of Canada (*MV Polar Star v Arsenault* (1964), 43 DLR (2d) 354 (PEISC)); whales (*Swift v Gifford*, 2 Lowell 110 (1872)); and bees (see the *Bees Act*, RSO 1990, c B.6, and CA Wright, "The Right to Pursue Bees" (1939) 17 Can Bar Rev 130). A US property casebook (A James Casner & W Barton Leach, *Cases and Text on Property*, 2d ed (Boston: Little, Brown, 1969) at 25) has suggested (facetiously) that the concept of first possession has even been used to deal with the problem of beached whales on Cape Cod:

> The whaling industry has long since disappeared from Cape Cod, but not the whales. They are periodically washed up on the beach where they first attract and later repel the tourist trade. The disposal problem is traditionally solved by waiting until a curious New Yorker approaches near enough to the whale to be charged with possession, and hence title, thereof; then requiring the New Yorker as owner to give the whale decent burial under the public health laws.

For another charming example of the problems of first possession in the context of ice-fishing holes, see Ted Russell, "Stealin' the Holes" in *Tales from Pigeon Inlet* (St John's: Breakwater Books, 1977) at 107. The author presents a fictitious account of a court case about a dispute that arose when Uncle Sol took advantage of holes cut in the ice for herring fishing by Skipper Lige Bartle. Part of Uncle Sol's (unsuccessful) defence was that "possession was nine pints (*sic*) of the law."

The question of animals as property is further complicated in relation to the domestication of wild animals: what actions are required to turn a feral animal into an objectified, domesticated pet? This question was central in a high-profile case concerning "Darwin the Ikea Monkey." In assessing the issue of "possession" of a primate (a wild animal) dressed in human clothing (which might suggest that he had become domesticated), after he was found running around an Ikea parking lot, the court was faced with a number of questions. Perhaps the most significant issue was whether Darwin was "found" in the Ikea parking lot as a "wild animal" or as a "domesticated pet." According to the court, a former owner may have a greater entitlement to (re)possession if a wild animal has become domesticated. In addition, the monkey's former owner suggested that the animal was actually a member of her family so that the court should use the principle for determining custody of children, that is, what is in the child's "best interests." The case attracted considerable media attention, of course: e.g. see

Laura Kane, "Darwin the Ikea Monkey's Former 'Mom' Weeps at Trial's End," *Toronto Star* (11 June 2013), online: Toronto Star <http://www.thestar.com>.

In *Nakhuda v Story Book Farm Primate Sanctuary*, 2013 ONSC 5761, the court reviewed how Yasmin Nakhuda, a lawyer, arranged to buy a Japanese snow macaque from an exotic pet dealer in the United States, even though she knew that a bylaw made it illegal to keep a monkey in the city of Toronto. She paid $5,000 for the monkey, which she treated as a member of her family, including dressing him in human clothing. According to the court, Ms Nakhuda experienced some problems with Darwin—the monkey had to wear diapers in the house and he hated wearing them and thrashed and bit her when she tried to change the diapers. At one point, she tried to return the monkey to the dealer, but Darwin then clung to Ms Nakhuda, and the dealer concluded that Darwin had bonded with her. Thus, Ms Nakhuda decided to keep him. A few weeks after this decision, however, Ms Nakhuda left Darwin in a double-locked crate in her locked car in a parking lot while she shopped in a store that did not permit pets. However, Darwin escaped and was picked up by Toronto Animal Services (TAS).

Ms Nakhuda then went to the TAS shelter, but the officer would not release Darwin to her because she was unable to prove that Darwin had been vaccinated, and it was thus necessary to test him to determine whether he carried diseases, some of which could be fatal to humans. After some delay, Ms Nakhuda signed a form surrendering and transferring the monkey to the TAS, which then placed him at the sanctuary the following day. The sanctuary refused to return Darwin to Ms Nakhuda, who then sued for his return.

At the outset, the court rejected Ms Nakhuda's argument that the monkey was a member of her family, so that the "best-interests" test relating to children did not apply. As the court stated:

> [4] … Callous as it may seem, the monkey is a chattel, that is to say, a piece of property.

The court then proceeded to determine entitlement to the monkey. First, it was necessary to decide whether the monkey was a wild animal or a domesticated animal, because different rules apply to each of these situations. After reviewing *Campbell v Hedley* (1917), 37 DLR 289 (CA), the court held that Darwin was a wild animal by virtue of his behaviour and qualities. The court then considered whether Darwin (as a wild animal) had the habit of returning after escaping from human control, a principle that would have increased Ms Nakhuda's entitlement on the basis that the monkey had become domesticated. On the facts in this case, it seemed that Darwin had not previously escaped, so that it was not possible to find that Darwin had a habit of returning to Ms Nakhuda. The court also considered other principles relating to wild animals, none of which assisted Ms Nakhuda's application for the return of Darwin. In addition, the court held that there was no inconsistency between these principles of common law and the city's bylaw, so that

> [33] … when the monkey ran away and Ms Nakhuda lost possession of him, she lost ownership of him. Accordingly, she has no right to have him returned to her.

In addition to this conclusion, the court also decided that Ms Nakhuda fully understood that she was transferring possession of the monkey to the TAS when she signed the form and was not unduly influenced when she agreed to sign it. See "Former Owner Loses Battle for Darwin," *The Globe and Mail* (14 September 2013), and Jacques Gallant, "Judge Rules Darwin's Wild and Belongs in Sanctuary," *Toronto Star* (14 September 2013). Issues about animals as property have become increasingly contested in recent years: e.g. see Maneesha Deckha, "Property on the Borderline: A Comparative Analysis of the Legal Status of Animals in Canada and the United States" (2012) 20 Cardozo J Int'l & Comp L 313, and Vaughan Black, "A Regulated Regard: Comparing the Governance of Animals and Human Experimentation" (2012) 24 RQDI 231.

iii. Rethinking Pierson v Post

Some recent assessments of *Pierson v Post* have challenged interpretations of the case, particularly in property law casebooks. For example, Angela Fernandez argued that the dispute occurred in a context in which fox-hunting enthusiasts in 19th-century New York were being challenged by those who were increasingly interested in engaging in agricultural pursuits (interests opposed to both foxes and fox hunting). As Fernandez argued: "This is not a case where custom was over-ruled; it is a case where there was a fight precisely because there was no shared custom" (see Angela Fernandez, "Fuzzy Rules and Clear Enough Standards: The Uses and Abuses of Pierson v Post" (2013) 63 UTLJ 97 at 100).

More significantly, Fernandez took issue with the interpretation of other scholars, such as Rose, in relation to *Pierson v Post*, particularly in law casebooks:

> There is a presumption in … Rose's … work that vagueness is bad … and a limited audience is bad … . This seems to translate into a different but related assumption that the greatest amount of clarity is best and the most extensively understood communication is best. However, neither of these positions seems to recognize that a signal that is clear enough (i.e. finding and starting a fox) is okay, as is a heterogeneous audience, so long as heterogeneity is not a barrier to communication and comprehension … . To use Rose's metaphor, the yell given was loud enough. … [C]ontext should be brought to bear when evaluating the varying degrees of importance of clarity and it should not automatically be assumed that more clarity and more certainty are always better … . Really, all the majority said was needed in order for there to be acquisition by first possession was a clear signal to take, and that signal (hunting with dogs and hounds), by Rose's own understanding of property as communication, was plenty clear enough … . Fact finding is fact finding, whether what is involved is finding out who killed and captured the animal or whether the original hunter was in hot pursuit with a reasonable chance of success.

(Fernandez at 119 and 121-22.)

As is evident from the title of Fernandez's article, her focus is on the ways in which the "rule" in *Pierson v Post* has created some modern problems. However, she also critiqued Rose's analysis in relation to the quality of "clear acts" and "clear communication" in differing contexts (and particularly in relation to fox hunting). Thus, Fernandez argued that "starting a fox" was a clear act and also a clear communication within the relevant community. For further analysis of *Pierson v Post*, see Bethany Berger, "It's Not About the Fox: The Untold History of Pierson v Post" (2006) 55 Duke LJ 1089; Andrea McDowell, "Legal Fictions in Pierson v Post" (2007) 105 Mich L Rev 735; and Angela Fernandez, "Pierson v Post: A Great Debate, James Kent, and the Project of Building a Learned Law for New York State" (2009) 34:2 Law & Soc Inquiry 301.

Consider a Canadian contribution to this jurisprudence about possession and wild animals in relation to the 19th-century sealing industry off the coast of Newfoundland and Labrador. According to Bruce Ziff, the traditional means of hunting seals off the coast of Newfoundland involved a process of killing the seals, marking the ice floe with an insignia (generally a flag), and then returning to the hunting grounds over a series of days to retrieve the pelts. By tracing a series of sealing cases in the 19th century, Ziff discovered that "salvagers" would sometimes recover the dead seals before the original hunters were able to do so. Because the uncollected seals were not in the physical possession of the original group of hunters, but were instead left on an ice floe in the middle of the Atlantic Ocean, courts had to decide whether killing a seal was a clear act to establish possession or whether physical possession of the pelts was necessary. Ziff focused on a number of cases, including *Clift v Kane* (1870), 5 Nfld LR 327.

Ziff reported that two basic theories arose during this period, with some cases sticking with the generic hunting rule from *Pierson v Post*—that is, whoever killed the animal had possession over the animal to the exclusion of all others. Other rulings, however, followed a theory of "deemed abandonment," which addressed the specific practices of sealing and the challenges facing hunters who might not be able to return to the ice floes where the dead seals remained and thus would be deemed to have "abandoned" their rights to the seals. Findings of deemed abandonment generally occurred when bad weather made it impossible for the original hunters to return to claim their seals because the movement of ice floes on the Atlantic Ocean made hunting sites difficult to track; or when hunters killed scores of seals but failed to make a reasonable, recognizable effort to establish ownership over the hunt. Ziff also suggested that the interplay of these two theories reflected economic pressures of the industry—for example, if the courts applied only a generic hunting theory without taking account of the context, sealers could go out and indiscriminately hunt this finite resource and then make no reasonable effort to bring the seals back to land. Overall, the cases reveal the importance of the context and the facts in determining issues about possession in law (see Bruce Ziff, "The Law of Property in Animals, Newfoundland-Style" in E Tucker, J Muir & B Ziff, eds, *Property on Trial: Canadian Cases in Context* (Toronto: Osgoode Society and Irwin Law, 2012) at 9).

iv. First Possession Principles: Determining Facts and "Evidence"

Clair Perry and Scott Gregory were avidly involved in the hobby of metal detecting for more than 20 years. They frequently went on metal-detecting expeditions together, sharing the cost of researching potential sites and transport to them; however, they did not operate in partnership and they did not share their findings. On one of their expeditions in late 2001 in a potato field in Prince Edward Island, with the permission of the owners, their efforts resulted in the discovery of a belt plate used by the PEI Regiment in the late 1700s; its value was unknown.

In subsequent litigation about entitlement to the belt plate (*Perry v Gregory*, 2003 PESCTD 73), the parties told different stories about its discovery. According to the plaintiff, he had received a signal from his machine, but, because he was using a new machine, he asked the defendant to verify the signal. According to the plaintiff, such a request was quite usual among metal-detecting enthusiasts. The plaintiff also asserted that when he requested the defendant to verify the signal, the plaintiff had already begun to dig at the site, and that the hole was two-thirds to three-quarters dug. When the defendant's machine confirmed the reading, the defendant finished digging the hole, revealing the belt plate. The plaintiff gave evidence that this procedure was also quite usual in metal detecting, and that it was understood that the results of the digging "belonged" to the person who had begun to dig the hole after such a reading. In addition, the plaintiff stated that, in order to prevent his machine from interfering with the defendant's machine, he stepped away about 15 to 25 feet, and after the defendant had retrieved the belt plate from the hole, the plaintiff reached for it and the defendant gave it to him, perhaps rather reluctantly. According to the plaintiff (at para 11), the belt plate belonged to him because "it was his signal and it was his hole." The plaintiff's assertions were supported by an experienced metal detector, who gave evidence (at para 12) that

> there was never a question in his mind that it was always the first person to receive a signal who owns the item found. ... [The] only exception to this is if the first person to get a signal walks away from and abandons the hole and someone subsequently comes along and digs in the hole. Then any item found belongs to that second person. He stated it is common courtesy and common sense that the first person to get a signal is the owner of any item found.

According to the defendant (at para 13), both men were proceeding separately with their metal detectors over the field. Then, at some point, they passed close to one another; according to the defendant, the plaintiff mentioned that he had received a signal but that he had "left the hole." Three minutes later, the defendant went to the hole, "got a signal and dug up the belt plate." He stated that he showed it to the plaintiff, who "grabbed" it from him, and that he told the plaintiff that "he had found it, that it was his."

How should the claims of the plaintiff and the defendant be resolved? To what extent is it helpful to analyze them in relation to ideas about a clear act or a reward for labour? Is evidence about common courtesy and common sense among metal detectors relevant here? Recall the dissenting judge in *Pierson v Post* who concluded that it was appropriate for those involved in fox hunting to decide the case. Obviously, the application of principles in this case was complicated by different views about "the facts," so that the case also demonstrates the interrelationship of facts and legal principles. In *Perry v Gregory*, the court decided that the plaintiff's version of the facts was more plausible. In reaching this conclusion, the court took into account that the defendant had subsequently "borrowed" the belt plate from the plaintiff and then returned it to him; and that the defendant had not made a claim to the belt plate until 10 months after its discovery and after consulting a lawyer. To what extent does this reasoning assist in defining the legal principles of "first possession"?

Interestingly, the plaintiff also testified (at para 10) that neither he nor the defendant had notified the owners of the potato field about the discovery of the belt plate, explaining that "owners generally do not ask about finds, and he [did] not make it a practice to inform them." After reviewing the *Parker* case below in this chapter, consider whether there are legal principles entitling the owners of the potato field to claim the belt plate.

v. Possessory Interests and Common Law Decision Making

The philosophical justifications for the concept of first possession as a root of title were also explored in Richard Epstein's article, "Possession as the Root of Title" (1978-79) 13 Ga L Rev 1221. Epstein concluded (at 1241) that the concept of first possession is justified in part because it has been "the organizing principle of most social institutions, and the heavy burden of persuasion lies upon those who wish to displace it." In reaching this conclusion, however, he suggested that it was not necessary to adopt the first possession principle with respect to things as yet unexploited by individuals or nations, such as the ocean bed or the Antarctic regions. In these cases, he asserted (at 1242) that we have the possibility of adopting "alternative systems of property rights that depart significantly from the first possession principle."

In considering the possibility of using different methods (instead of common law processes) to design new principles of first possession for "objects" that have not yet been possessed in law, Epstein also focused on some of the limitations of common law processes. For example, because courts have only a limited range of remedies to award in a litigated claim to possession, the remedies (such as damages) tend to be quite simple to enforce, rather than regulatory remedies that may require complex governmental machinery. In addition, claims are presented to courts on the basis of the needs of litigants so that common law principles are created accordingly, not always in the way that a philosophical method using first principles would create possessory interests: "The rule that possession lies at the root of title is one that a court can understand and apply; absent a better alternative it becomes therefore an attractive starting point for resolving particular disputes over the ownership of particular things." Moreover, courts define principles about possession in relation to the two litigants in front of the court—not in accordance with the rights of everyone who may be affected by the decision, perhaps particularly the government.

vi. Possession and the Claims of First Nations

As Rose suggested, *Johnson & Graham's Lessee v McIntosh*, 21 US (8 Wheat) 543 (1823) was significant for its definition of what constituted "possession" in the context of native land claims. According to Richard Chused, "*Johnson v. McIntosh* is the root case for almost all of modern tribal law" in the United States (Chused, *Cases, Materials and Problems in Property* (New York: Matthew Bender, 1988) at 106-7). The decision was also influential in cases about native title in Canada in the 19th and early 20th centuries.

For a different perspective on the concept of possession and First Nations in Canada, see Kent McNeil, *Common Law Aboriginal Title* (Oxford: Claredon Press, 1989) [McNeil], briefly excerpted below. In addition, in *Delgamuukw v British Columbia*, [1997] 3 SCR 1010, the Supreme Court of Canada recognized a *sui generis* Aboriginal entitlement to land. Issues about Aboriginal title to land are discussed in several parts of this book, and particularly in Chapter 8.

II. POSSESSION AND THE FINDERS OF "LOST" OBJECTS

In 1988, a Toronto newspaper reported that a lawyer who had recently purchased a 103-year-old house in the city experienced great surprise when the contractor whom she had hired to do renovations began tearing out the old plaster. According to the newspaper account, paper money started raining down on the renovation workers, eventually totalling between $46,000 and $50,000. The money was turned over to the police and was then held in trust pending a determination about who was entitled to it. Claims were made by the lawyer who owned the house, by the contractor whose workers found the money, and by the daughter of former owners of the house.

Assuming that none of these claimants was the "true owner" of the money, how does the concept of possession as a root of title assist in solving a dispute in the context of finding "lost" objects? What arguments support assertions of first possession on the part of each of these three claimants? (Remember that "possession" may be defined in differing ways.) What definition of first possession is most appropriate—that is, who has the best claim in this situation?

This case was settled, and the exact nature of the settlement has never been disclosed. In examining the materials that follow, try to assess the strength of each claim. What settlement is appropriate in light of the principles of possession?

A. Finders and First Possession

Armory v Delamirie
(1722), 1 Str 505, 93 ER 664 (KB)

PRATT CJ: The plaintiff being a chimney-sweeper's boy found a jewel and carried it to the defendant's shop (who was a goldsmith) to know what it was, and delivered it into the hands of the apprentice, who under pretence of weighing it, took out the stones, and calling to the master to let him know it came to three halfpence, the master offered the boy the money, who refused to take it, and insisted to have the thing again; whereupon the apprentice delivered him back the socket without the stones. And now in trover against the master these points were ruled:

1. That the finder of a jewel, though he does not by such finding acquire an absolute property or ownership, yet he has such a property as will enable him to keep it against all but the rightful owner, and consequently may maintain trover.

2. That the action well lay against the master, who gives a credit to his apprentice, and is answerable for his neglect.

3. As to the value of the jewel several of the trade were examined to prove what a jewel of the finest water that would fit the socket would be worth; and the Chief Justice directed the jury, that unless the defendant did produce the jewel, and shew it not to be of the finest water, they should presume the strongest against him, and make the value of the best jewels the measure of their damages: which they accordingly did.

DISCUSSION NOTES

i. The Principle of First Possession in Context

The first principle stated by the judge represents one formulation of the first possession principle. In considering it, think about the parties involved in the dispute in *Armory v Delamirie*. Were there others who might have had competing claims who were not parties to this suit? Consider the problem noted above where the claimants included the lawyer-owner, her contractor, the workers doing the renovation, and the daughter of the previous owners of the house. Does the principle of first possession permit an assessment of all these claims? To what extent?

ii. The Remedy of Trover

In *Armory v Delamirie*, the plaintiff sued in trover, a traditional common law action available to remedy an interference with chattels. The common law devised a number of different procedural actions to assist a plaintiff to (re)possess chattels that had been wrongfully "taken" by a defendant. These actions included trover, detinue, conversion, and trespass to chattels. The action in "trover," a term derived from Old French, meaning "to find," was used in cases in which there was an interference with the plaintiff's chattels in circumstances that permitted the law to adopt a fiction that the wrongdoer had "found" the chattels.

Although there have been a number of recommendations for reform, it seems that trover remains a "cause of action" in Ontario at the present time: see Ralph Simmonds & George Stewart, *Study Paper on Wrongful Interference with Goods* (Toronto: Ontario Law Reform Commission, 1989) [Simmonds & Stewart]. In British Columbia, a similar report recommended the abolition of different tort actions relating to interference with property and their replacement with a single tort: see Law Reform Commission of British Columbia, *Report on Wrongful Interference with Goods* (Vancouver: Ministry of the Attorney-General, 1992) at 55.

According to the judge in *Armory v Delamirie*, what was the measure of damages in an action in trover if the chattel itself were not returned? For further discussion of remedies, see the reports of the law reform commissions, above.

iii. Employers' Liability for Actions of Employees

This case also confirmed an employer's liability for actions of an employee or apprentice. This early example of an employer's liability for employees' (wrongful) acts is now recognized in other kinds of situations. For example, in *Janzen v Platy Enterprises*, [1989] 1 SCR 1252, the Supreme Court of Canada held an employer liable for sexual harassment when one employee harassed another. See also *Robichaud v Canada (Treasury Board)*, [1987] 2 SCR 84.

Parker v British Airways Board
[1982] 2 WLR 503 (CA)

DONALDSON LJ: On November 15, 1978, the plaintiff, Alan George Parker, had a date with fate—and perhaps with legal immortality. He found himself in the international executive lounge at terminal one, Heathrow Airport. And that was not all that he found. He also found a gold bracelet lying on the floor.

We know very little about the plaintiff, and it would be nice to know more. He was lawfully in the lounge and, as events showed, he was an honest man. Clearly he had not forgotten the schoolboy maxim "Finders keepers." But, equally clearly, he was well aware of the adult qualification "unless the true owner claims the article." He had to clear customs and security to reach the lounge. He was almost certainly an outgoing passenger because the defendants, British Airways Board, as lessees of the lounge from the British Airports Authority and its occupiers, limit its use to passengers who hold first class tickets or boarding passes or who are members of their Executive Club, which is a passengers' "club." Perhaps the plaintiff's flight had just been called and he was pressed for time. Perhaps the only officials in sight were employees of the defendants. Whatever the reason, he gave the bracelet to an anonymous official of the defendants instead of to the police. He also gave the official a note of his name and address and asked for the bracelet to be returned to him if it was not claimed by the owner. The official handed the bracelet to the lost property department of the defendants.

Thus far the story is unremarkable. The plaintiff, the defendants' official and the defendants themselves had all acted as one would have hoped and expected them to act. Thereafter the matter took what, to the plaintiff, was an unexpected turn. Although the owner never claimed the bracelet, the defendants did not return it to the plaintiff. Instead they sold it and kept the proceeds which amounted to £850. The plaintiff discovered what had happened and was more than a little annoyed. I can understand his annoyance. He sued the defendants in the Brentford County Court and was awarded £850 as damages and £50 as interest. The defendants now appeal.

It is astonishing that there should be any doubt as to who is right. But there is. Indeed, it seems that the academics have been debating this problem for years. In 1971 the Law Reform Committee reported that it was by no means clear who had the better claim to lost property when the protagonists were the finder and the occupier of the premises where the property was found. Whatever else may be in doubt, the committee was abundantly right in this conclusion. The committee recommended legislative action but, as is not uncommon, nothing has been done. The rights of the parties thus depend upon the common law.

As a matter of legal theory, the common law has a ready-made solution for every problem and it is only for the judges, as legal technicians, to find it. The reality is somewhat different. Take the present case. The conflicting rights of finder and occupier have indeed been considered by various courts in the past. But under the rules of English jurisprudence, none of their decisions binds this court. We therefore have both the right and the duty to extend and adapt the common law in the light of established principles and the current needs of the community. This is not to say that we start with a clean sheet. In doing so, we should draw from the experience of the past as revealed by the previous decisions of the courts. In this connection we have been greatly assisted both by the arguments of counsel, and in particular those of Mr. Desch upon whom the main burden fell, and by the admirable judgment of the deputy judge in the county court.

Neither the plaintiff nor the defendants lay any claim to the bracelet either as owner of it or as one who derives title from that owner. The plaintiff's claim is founded upon the ancient common law rule that the act of finding a chattel which has been lost and taking control of it gives the finder rights with respect to that chattel. The defendants' claim has a different basis. They cannot and do not claim to have found the bracelet when it was handed to them by the plaintiff. At that stage it was no longer lost and they received and accepted the bracelet from the plaintiff on terms that it would be returned to him if the owner could not be found. They must and do claim on the basis that they had rights in relation to the bracelet immediately *before* the plaintiff found it and that these rights are superior to the plaintiff's. The defendants' claim is based upon the proposition that at common law an occupier of land has such rights over all lost chattels which are on that land, whether or not the occupier knows of their existence.

The common law right asserted by Mr. Parker has been recognised for centuries. In its simplest form it was asserted by the chimney-sweep's boy who, in 1722, found a jewel and offered it to a jeweller for sale. The jeweller refused either to pay a price acceptable to the boy or to return it and the boy sued the jeweller for its value: *Armory v. Delamirie* (1722) 1 Stra. 505. Pratt CJ ruled:

> That the finder of a jewel, though he does not by such finding acquire an absolute property or ownership, yet he has such a property as will enable him to keep it against all but the rightful owner, and consequently may maintain trover.

In that case the jeweller clearly had no rights in relation to the jewel immediately before the boy found it and any rights which he acquired when he received it from the boy stemmed from the boy himself. The jeweller could only have succeeded if the fact of finding and taking control of the jewel conferred no rights upon the boy. The court would then have been faced with two claimants, neither of which had any legal right, but one had de facto possession. The rule as stated by Pratt CJ must be right as a general proposition, for otherwise lost property would be subject to a free-for-all in which the physically weakest would go to the wall.

Pratt CJ's ruling is, however, only a general proposition which requires definition. Thus one who "finds" a lost chattel in the sense of becoming aware of its presence, but who does no more, is not a "finder" for this purpose and does not, as such, acquire any rights.

Some qualification has also to be made in the case of the trespassing finder. The person vis à vis whom he is a trespasser has a better title. The fundamental basis of this is clearly public policy. Wrongdoers should not benefit from their wrongdoing. This requirement would be met if the trespassing finder acquired no rights. That would, however, produce the free-for-all situation to which I have already referred, in that anyone could take the article from the trespassing finder. Accordingly, the common law has been obliged to give rights to someone else, the owner *ex hypothesi* being unknown. The obvious candidate is the occupier of the property upon which the finder was trespassing.

Curiously enough, it is difficult to find any case in which the rule is stated in this simple form, but I have no doubt that this is the law. It is reflected in the judgment of Chitty J in *Elwes v. Brigg Gas Co.* (1886), 33 Ch. D 562, 568, although the chattel concerned was beneath the surface of the soil and so subject to different considerations. It is also reflected in the judgment of Lord Goddard CJ in *Hibbert v. McKiernan*, [1948] 2 KB 142, 149. That was a criminal case concerning the theft of "lost" golf balls on the private land of a club. The only issue was whether for the purposes of the criminal law property in the golf balls could be laid in someone other than the alleged thief. The indictment named the members of the club, who were occupiers of the land, as having property in the balls, and it is clear that at the time when the balls were taken the members were very clearly asserting such a right, even to the extent of mounting a police patrol to warn off trespassers seeking to harvest lost balls.

It was in this context that we were also referred to the opinion of the Judicial Committee in *Glenwood Lumber Co. Ltd. v. Phillips*, [1904] AC 405 and in particular to remarks by Lord Davey, at p. 410. However, there the occupier knew of the presence of the logs on the land and had a claim to them as owner as well as occupier. Furthermore, it was not a finding case, for the logs were never lost.

One might have expected there to be decisions clearly qualifying the general rule where the circumstances are that someone finds a chattel and thereupon forms the dishonest intention of keeping it regardless of the rights of the true owner or of anyone else. But that is not the case. There could be a number of reasons. Dishonest finders will often be trespassers. They are unlikely to risk invoking the law, particularly against another subsequent dishonest taker, and a subsequent honest taker is likely to have a superior title: see, for example, *Buckley v. Gross* (1863), 3 B & S 566. However, he probably has some title, albeit a frail one, because of the need to avoid a free-for-all. This seems to be the law in Ontario, Canada: *Bird v. Fort Frances*, [1949] 2 DLR 791.

In the interests of clearing the ground and identifying the problem, let me now turn to another situation in respect of which the law is reasonably clear. This is that of chattels which are attached to realty (land or buildings) when they are found. If the finder is not a wrongdoer, he may have some rights, but the occupier of the land or building will have a better title. The rationale of this rule is probably either that the chattel is to be treated as an integral part of the realty as against all but the true owner and so incapable of being lost or that the "finder" has to do something to the realty in order to get at or detach the chattel and, if he is not thereby to become a trespasser, will have to justify his actions by reference to some form of licence from the occupier. In all likely circumstances that licence will give the occupier a superior right to that of the finder.

Authority for this view of the law is to be found in *South Staffordshire Water Co. v. Sharman*, [1896] 2 QB 44 where the defendant was employed by the occupier of land to remove mud from the bottom of a pond. He found two gold rings embedded in the mud. The plaintiff occupier was held to be entitled to the rings. Dicta of Lord Russell of Killowen CJ, with whom Wills J agreed, not only support the law as I have stated it, but go further and may support the defendants' contention that an occupier of a building has a claim to articles found *in* that building as opposed to being found attached to or forming part of it. However, it is more convenient to consider these dicta hereafter. *Elwes v. Brigg Gas Co.*, 33 Ch. D 562, to which we were also referred in this context, concerned a prehistoric boat embedded in land. But I think that, when analysed, the issue really turned upon rival claims by the plaintiff to be the true owner in the sense of being the tenant for life of the realty, of the minerals in the land and of the boat if it was a chattel and by the defendants as lessees rather than as finders.

Again, in the interest of clearing the ground, I should like to dispose briefly of some of the other cases to which we were quite rightly referred and to do so upon the grounds that, when analysed, they do not really bear upon the instant problem. Thus, *In re Cohen, decd.; National Provincial Bank Ltd. v. Katz*, [1953] Ch. 88 concerned money hidden in a flat formerly occupied by a husband and wife who had died. The issue was whether the money belonged to the estate of the husband or to that of the wife. The money had been hidden and not lost and this was not a finding case at all. In *Johnson v. Pickering*, [1907] 2 KB 437 the issue was whether the sheriff on behalf of a judgment creditor had a claim to money which the judgment debtor took to his house at a time when the sheriff had taken walking possession of that house, albeit the sheriff had been unaware of the arrival of the money. This again is not a finding case. In *Moffatt v. Kazana*, [1969] 2 QB 152 the claimant established a title derived from that of the true owner. This does not help. Finally, there is *Hannah v. Peel*, [1945] KB 509. This was indeed a finding case, but the claimant was the non-occupying owner of the house in which the brooch was found. The occupier was the Crown, which made no claim either as occupier or as employer of the finder. It was held that the non-occupying owner had no right to the brooch and that therefore the finder's claim prevailed. What the position would have been if the Crown had made a claim was not considered.

I must now return to the respective claims of the plaintiff and the defendants. Mr. Brown, for the plaintiff, relies heavily upon the decision of Patteson J and Wightman J, sitting in banc in *Bridges v. Hawkesworth* (1851), 21 LJ QB 75; 15 Jur. 1079. It was an appeal from the county court by case stated. The relevant facts, as found, were as follows. Mr. Bridges was a commercial traveller and in the course of his business he called upon the defendant at his shop. As he was leaving the shop, he picked up a small parcel which was lying on the floor, showed it to the shopman and, upon opening it in his presence, found that it contained £65 in notes. Mr. Hawkesworth was called and Mr. Bridges asked him to keep the notes until the owner claimed them. Mr. Hawkesworth advertised for the true owner, but no claimant came forward. Three years later Mr. Bridges asked for the money and offered to indemnify Mr. Hawkesworth in respect of the expenses which he had incurred in advertising for the owner. Mr. Hawkesworth refused to pay over the money and Mr. Bridges sued for it. The county court judge dismissed his claim and he appealed.

Patteson J gave the judgment of the court. The decision is sufficiently important, and the judgment sufficiently short and difficult to find, for me to feel justified in reproducing it in full. In so doing, I take the text of the report in the *Jurist*, 15 Jur. 1079, 1082 but refer to the *Law Journal* version, 21 LJ QB 75, 77-78, in square brackets where they differ. It reads:

> The notes which are the subject of this action were incidentally ["evidently"] dropped by mere accident, in the shop of the defendant, by the owner of them. The facts do not warrant the supposition that they had been deposited there intentionally, nor has the case been put at all upon that ground. The plaintiff found them on the floor, they being manifestly lost by someone. The general right of the finder to any article which has been lost, as against all the world, except the true owner, was established in … *Armory v. Delamirie*, 1 Stra. 505, which has never been disputed. This right would clearly have accrued to the plaintiff had the notes been picked up by him outside the shop of the defendant; and if he once had the right, the case finds that he did not intend, by delivering the notes to the defendant, to waive the title (if any) which he had to them, but they were handed to the defendant merely for the purpose of delivering them to the owner, should he appear. Nothing that was done afterwards has altered the state of things; the advertisements inserted ["indeed"] in the newspaper, referring to the defendant, had the same object; the plaintiff has tendered the expense of those advertisements to the defendant, and offered him an indemnity against any claim to be made by the real owner, and has demanded the notes. The case, therefore, resolves itself into the single point on which it appears that the learned judge decided it, namely, whether the circumstance of the notes being found inside [word emphasised in *Law Journal*] the defendant's shop gives him, the defendant, the right to have them as against the plaintiff, who found them. There is no authority in our law to be found directly in point. Perhaps the nearest case is that of *Merry v. Green* (1841), 7 M & W 623, but it differs in many respects from the present. We were referred, in the course of the argument, to the learned work of Von Savigny, edited by Perry CJ; but even this work, full as it is of subtle distinctions and nice reasonings, does not afford a solution of the present question. It was well asked, on the argument, if the defendant has the right, *when* did it accrue to him? If at all, it must have been antecedent to the finding by the plaintiff, for that finding could not give the defendant any right. If the notes had been accidentally kicked into the shop ["the street" in *Law Journal*, which must be right], and there found by someone passing by, could it be contended that the defendant was entitled to them from the mere fact of their being originally dropped in his shop? If the discovery had never ["not"] been communicated to the defendant, could the real owner have had any cause of action against him because they were found in his house? Certainly not. The notes never were in the custody of the defendant, nor within the protection of his house, before they were found, as they would have been had they been intentionally deposited there; and the defendant has come under no responsibility, except from the communication made to him by the plaintiff, the finder, and the steps taken by way of advertisement. These steps were really taken by the defendant as the agent of the plaintiff, and he has been offered an indemnity, the sufficiency of which is not disputed. We find, therefore, no circumstances in this case to take it out of the general rule of law, that the finder of a lost article is entitled to it as

against all persons except the real owner, and we think that the rule must prevail, and that the learned judge was mistaken in holding that the place in which they were found makes any legal difference. Our judgment, therefore, is that the plaintiff is entitled to these notes as against the defendant; that the judgment of the court below must be reversed, and judgment given for the plaintiff for £50.

The ratio of this decision seems to me to be solely that the unknown presence of the notes on the premises occupied by Mr. Hawkesworth could not without more, give him any rights or impose any duty upon him in relation to the notes.

Mr. Desch, for the defendants, submits that *Bridges v. Hawkesworth*, 15 Jur. 1079 can be distinguished and he referred us to the judgment of Lord Russell of Killowen CJ, with which Wills J agreed, in *South Staffordshire Water Co. v. Sharman*, [1896] 2 QB 44. *Sharman*'s case itself is readily distinguishable, either upon the ground that the rings were in the mud and thus part of the realty or upon the ground that the finders were employed by the plaintiff to remove the mud and had a clear right to direct how the mud and anything in it should be disposed of, or upon both grounds. However, Lord Russell of Killowen CJ in distinguishing *Bridges v. Hawkesworth* expressed views which, in Mr. Desch's submission, point to the defendants having a superior claim to that of the plaintiff on the facts of the instant case. Lord Russell of Killowen CJ said, at p. 46:

> The principle on which this case must be decided, and the distinction which must be drawn between this case and that of *Bridges v. Hawkesworth*, is to be found in a passage in *Pollock and Wright, Possession in the Common Law*, p. 41: "The possession of land carries with it in general, by our law, possession of everything which is attached to or under that land, and, in the absence of a better title elsewhere, the right to possess it also. And it makes no difference that the possessor is not aware of the thing's existence. ... It is free to anyone who requires a specific intention as part of a de facto possession to treat this as a positive rule of law. But it seems preferable to say that the legal possession rests on a real de facto possession, constituted by the occupier's general power and intent to exclude unauthorised interference." That is the ground on which I prefer to base my judgment. There is a broad distinction between this case and those cited from *Blackstone's Commentaries*. Those were cases in which a thing was cast into a public place or into the sea—into a place, in fact, of which it could not be said that anyone had a real de facto possession, or a general power and intent to exclude unauthorised interference ... . *Bridges v. Hawkesworth* stands by itself, and on special grounds; and on those grounds it seems to me that the decision in that case was right. Someone had accidentally dropped a bundle of banknotes in a public shop. The shopkeeper did not know they had been dropped, and did not in any sense exercise control over them. The shop was open to the public, and they were invited to come there. A customer picked up the notes and gave them to the shopkeeper in order that he might advertise them. The owner of the notes was not found, and the finder then sought to recover them from the shopkeeper. It was held that he was entitled to do so, the ground of the decision being, as was pointed out by Patteson J, that the notes, being dropped in the public part of the shop, were never in the custody of the shopkeeper, or "within the protection of his house." It is somewhat strange that there is no more direct authority on the question; but the general principle seems to me to be that where a person has possession of house or land, with a manifest intention to exercise control over it and the things which may be upon or in it, then,

scene of event

if something is found on that land, whether by an employee of the owner or by a stranger, the presumption is that the possession of that thing is in the owner of the *locus in quo*.

For my part, I can find no trace in the report of *Bridges v. Hawkesworth*, 21 LJ QB 75, of any reliance by Patteson J upon the fact that the notes were found in what may be described as the public part of the shop. He could, and I think would, have said that if the notes had been accidentally dropped in the *private* part unbeknownst to Mr. Hawkesworth and had later been accidentally kicked into the street, Mr. Hawkesworth would have had no duty to the true owner and no rights superior to that of the finder.

However, I would accept Lord Russell of Killowen CJ's statement of the general principle in *South Staffordshire Water Co. v. Sharman*, [1896] 2 QB 44, 46-47, provided that the occupier's intention to exercise control over anything which might be on the premises was manifest. But it is impossible to go further and to hold that the mere right of an occupier to exercise such control is sufficient to give him rights in relation to lost property on his premises without overruling *Bridges v. Hawkesworth*, 21 LJ QB 75. Mr. Hawkesworth undoubtedly had a right to exercise such control, but his defence failed.

South Staffordshire Water Co. v. Sharman was followed and applied by McNair J in *City of London Corporation v. Appleyard*, [1963] 1 WLR 982. There workmen demolishing a building found money in a safe which was recessed in one of the walls. The lease from the corporation to the building owners preserved the corporation's right to any article of value found upon any remains of former buildings and the workmen were employed by contractors working for the building owners. McNair J upheld the corporation's claim. The workmen claimed as finders, but it is clear law that a servant or agent who finds in the course of his employment or agency is obliged to account to his employer or principal. The contractor similarly was bound to account to the building owner and the building owner, who was the occupier, was contractually bound to account to the corporation. The principal interest of the decision lies in the comment of McNair J, at p. 987, that he did not understand Lord Russell of Killowen CJ as intending to qualify or extend the principle stated in *Pollock and Wright, Possession in the Common Law* (1888), p. 41, that possession of land carries with it possession of everything which is *attached to or under* that land when the Chief Justice restated the principle, [1896] 2 QB 44, 47:

> … where a person has possession of house or land, with a manifest intention to exercise control over it and the things which may be *upon or in* it, then, if something is found *on* that land, whether by an employee of the owner or by a stranger, the presumption is that the possession of that thing is in the *owner* of the locus in quo. (My emphasis.)

[Donaldson LJ then summarized two Canadian cases referred to by the parties. The first was *Grafstein v Holme and Freeman* (1958), 12 DLR (2d) 727 (Ont CA), a case in which the defendants opened a locked box in the basement of a shop where they were employed, and discovered a large sum of money. These employees had actually found the locked box at an earlier point in time, and after drawing it to the attention of the shop owner, they had been directed by him to put it in the basement and leave it there. When their curiosity about the contents of the box led them to open it, and to find the money, they claimed entitlement to the $38,000 inside. In this case, the Ontario Court of Appeal held that the shop owner was entitled to the money because he had assumed possession of the box when it was found in his shop and because he had exercised control of the box when he told his employees where to place it in the basement.

The second Canadian case discussed was *Kowal v Ellis* (1977), 76 DLR (3d) 546 (Man CA), in which a person who was permitted to drive across rural land owned by another found an abandoned pump. Although the court conceded that there were strong arguments in favour of allowing a landowner to possess everything on his or her land, the finder was held to be entitled to possession in this case because the court was concerned about creating liability on the part of landowners with respect to all chattels lost or abandoned by original holders. Donaldson LJ then continued:]

One of the great merits of the common law is that it is usually sufficiently flexible to take account of the changing needs of a continually changing society. Accordingly, Mr. Desch rightly directed our attention to the need to have common law rules which will facilitate rather than hinder the ascertainment of the true owner of a lost chattel and a reunion between the two. In his submission the law should confer rights upon the occupier of the land where a lost chattel was found which were superior to those of the finder, since the loser is more likely to make inquiries at the place of loss. I see the force of this submission. However, I think that it is also true that if this were the rule and finders had no prospect of any reward, they would be tempted to pass by without taking any action or to become concealed keepers of articles which they found. Furthermore, if a finder is under a duty to take reasonable steps to reunite the true owner with his lost property, this will usually involve an obligation to inform the occupier of the land of the fact that the article has been found and where it is to be kept.

In a dispute of this nature there are two quite separate problems. The first is to determine the general principles or rules of law which are applicable. The second, which is often the more troublesome, is to apply those principles or rules to the factual situation. I propose to confront those two problems separately.

Rights and Obligations of the Finder

1. The finder of a chattel acquires no rights over it unless (a) it has been abandoned or lost and (b) he takes it into his care and control.

2. The finder of a chattel acquires very limited rights over it if he takes it into his care and control with dishonest intent or in the course of trespassing.

3. Subject to the foregoing and to point 4 below, a finder of a chattel, whilst not acquiring any absolute property or ownership in the chattel, acquires a right to keep it against all but the true owner or those in a position to claim through the true owner or one who can assert a prior right to keep the chattel which was subsisting at the time when the finder took the chattel into his care and control.

4. Unless otherwise agreed, any servant or agent who finds a chattel in the course of his employment or agency and not wholly incidentally or collaterally thereto and who takes it into his care and control does so on behalf of his employer or principal who acquires a finder's rights to the exclusion of those of the actual finder.

5. A person having a finder's rights has an obligation to take such measures as in all the circumstances are reasonable to acquaint the true owner of the finding and present whereabouts of the chattel and to care for it meanwhile.

Rights and Liabilities of an Occupier

1. An occupier of land has rights superior to those of a finder over chattels in or attached to that land and an occupier of a building has similar rights in respect of chattels attached to that building, whether in either case the occupier is aware of the presence of the chattel.

2. An occupier of a building has rights superior to those of a finder over chattels upon or in, but not attached to, that building if, but only if, before the chattel is found, he has manifested an intention to exercise control over the building and the things which may be upon it or in it.

3. An occupier who manifests an intention to exercise control over a building and the things which may be upon or in it so as to acquire rights superior to those of a finder is under an obligation to take such measures as in all the circumstances are reasonable to ensure that lost chattels are found and, upon their being found, whether by him or by a third party, to acquaint the true owner of the finding and to care for the chattels meanwhile. The manifestation of intention may be express or implied from the circumstances including, in particular, the circumstance that the occupier manifestly accepts or is obliged by law to accept liability for chattels lost upon his "premises," e.g. an innkeeper or carrier's liability.

4. An "occupier" of a chattel, e.g. a ship, motor car, caravan or aircraft, is to be treated as if he were the occupier of a building for the purposes of the foregoing rules.

Application to the Instant Case

The plaintiff was not a trespasser in the executive lounge and, in taking the bracelet into his car and control, he was acting with obvious honesty. Prima facie, therefore, he had a full finder's rights and obligations. He in fact discharged those obligations by handing the bracelet to an official of the defendants' although he could equally have done so by handing the bracelet to the police or in other ways such as informing the police of the find and himself caring for the bracelet.

The plaintiff's prima facie entitlement to a finder's rights was not displaced in favour of an employer or principal. There is no evidence that he was in the executive lounge in the course of any employment or agency and, if he was, the finding of the bracelet was quite clearly collateral thereto. The position would have been otherwise in the case of most or perhaps all the defendants' employees.

The defendants, for their part, cannot assert any title to the bracelet based upon the rights of an occupier over chattels attached to a building. The bracelet was lying loose on the floor. Their claim must, on my view of the law, be based upon a manifest intention to exercise control over the lounge and all things which might be in it. The evidence is that they claimed the right to decide who should and who should not be permitted to enter and use the lounge, but their control was in general exercised upon the basis of classes or categories of user and the availability of the lounge in the light of the need to clean and maintain it. I do not doubt that they also claimed the right to exclude individual undesirables, such as drunks, and specific types of chattels such as guns and bombs. But this control has no real relevance to a manifest intention to assert custody and control over lost articles. There was no evidence that they searched for such articles regularly or at all.

Evidence was given of staff instructions which govern the action to be taken by employees of the defendants if they found lost articles or lost chattels were handed to them. But these instructions were not published to users of the lounge and in any event I think that they were intended to do no more than instruct the staff on how they were to act in the course of their employment.

It was suggested in argument that in some circumstances the intention of the occupier to assert control over articles lost on his premises speaks for itself. I think that this is right. If a bank manager saw fit to show me round a vault containing safe deposits and I found a gold bracelet on the floor, I should have no doubt that the bank had a better title than I, and the reason is the manifest intention to exercise a very high degree of control. At the other extreme is the park to which the public has unrestricted access during daylight hours. During those hours there is no manifest intention to exercise any such control. In between these extremes are the forecourts of petrol filling stations, unfenced front gardens of private houses, the public parts of shops and supermarkets as part of an almost infinite variety of land, premises and circumstances.

This lounge is in the middle band and in my judgment, on the evidence available, there was no sufficient manifestation of any intention to exercise control over lost property before it was found such as would give the defendants a right superior to that of the plaintiff or indeed any right over the bracelet. As the true owner has never come forward, it is a case of "finders keepers."

I would therefore dismiss the appeal. *Ruling*

[Two judges also wrote concurring opinions. Eveleigh CJ reiterated that possession in law requires the two elements of control and *animus possidendi*. He also provided some additional suggestions about the factors to be used to determine these claims. In confirming that an occupier must "manifest" an intention to control, he stated:

concurring thoughts

A person permitted upon the property of another must respect the lawful claims of the occupier as the terms upon which he is allowed to enter, but it is only right that those claims or terms should be made clear. What is necessary to do this must depend on the circumstances. Take the householder. He has the key to the front door. People do not enter at will. They come by very special invitation. They are not members of a very large public group ... . I would be inclined to say that the occupier of a house will almost invariably possess any lost article on the premises. He may not have taken any positive steps to demonstrate his *animus possidendi*, but so firm is his control that the animus can be seen to attach to it. It is rather like the strong room of a bank, where I think it would be difficult indeed to suggest that a bracelet lying on the floor was not in the possession of the bank. The firmer the control, the less will be the need to demonstrate independently the *animus possidendi*.

Sir David Cairns also noted that, although the airport allowed only a fraction of the public to enter the executive lounge, this limited access did not reach the level of exclusivity that is found within a bank vault or private residence.]

DISCUSSION NOTES

i. Courts and the Evolution of Legal Principles

The *Parker* case is an example of a common law court consciously contributing to the "evolution" of legal principles about the concept of possession. What factors did Donaldson LJ identify as reasons for the court's action in this case? Do you agree that the absence of legislative action always warrants such judicial activism? What competing arguments might lead to the opposite conclusion? Would the role of a Canadian court in a factual case similar to *Parker* be the same as its role in a case involving a Charter claim? Why?

ii. Rights of Finders and Occupiers

As is evident in the reasoning of Donaldson LJ, some of the previous cases about finding lost objects were difficult to reconcile in terms of their doctrinal principles. On the one hand, there were cases that seemed to follow the basic principle of *Armory v Delamirie*—"finders keepers"—e.g. *Bridges v Hawkesworth* (1851), 21 LJQB 75; *Hannah v Peel*, [1945] KB 509 (TD); and *Kowal v Ellis* (1977), 76 DLR (3d) 546 (Man CA). On the other hand, some cases seemed to favour the occupier or owner of land where the lost object was found—e.g. *South Staffordshire Water Co v Sharman*, [1896] 2 QB 44 (AD); *Elwes v Brigg Gas Co* (1886), 33 Ch D 562; *Grafstein v Holme and Freeman* (1958), 12 DLR (2d) 727 (Ont CA); *Hibbert v McKiernan*, [1948] 2 KB 142 (CA); and *City of London Corporation v Appleyard*, [1963] 1 WLR 982 (QBD).

Examine closely the reasoning of Donaldson LJ in relation to these cases. To what extent do his conclusions depend on identifying differences "on the facts"? Note, for example, the significance of the finder's right to be in the place where the lost object is found. Does this factor satisfactorily explain the difference in the outcome of litigation in *Bridges v Hawkesworth* by contrast with *Hibbert v McKiernan*? Was the chimney sweep in *Armory v Delamirie* in a public or private place when he found the jewel?

How significant is the employer–employee relationship? Although the court did not rely on such a relationship in *Grafstein v Holme and Freeman*, it was a factor in *City of London Corporation v Appleyard*. What principle of possession justifies the conclusion that an employer is entitled to a lost object found on the premises by an employee? For another decision confirming an employer's entitlement to chattels found by an employee in the course of employment, see *White v Alton-Lewis Ltd* (1975), 49 DLR (3d) 189 (Ont Co Ct).

In thinking about these issues, consider the reasoning of Donaldson LJ in relation to the principle that an occupier has a relatively better claim than a finder when the object has become "attached to" the land or building. Is this principle in *Parker* consistent with Lord Russell's statement in *South Staffordshire Water Co v Sharman* that possession of land carries with it possession of all chattels "in or upon" the land? Consider the following assessment of this aspect of the *Parker* case:

> One is inevitably led to the conclusion that the distinction propounded by Donaldson LJ in *Parker* is one based upon the most tenuous authority, and that it is merely intended to rid the law of the earlier confusion. ...
>
> But a more serious difficulty with the distinction is that it is irrational. It seems absurd that the conflicting rights of finder and occupier to a lost chattel should be made to depend on such a fortuitous occurrence as the circumstances in which it was lost and subsequent events. For example, suppose that a chattel is lost in a field, and that at the time of losing it is lying on the land

surface. The conflicting rights of finder and occupier may then depend upon whether someone unwittingly later tramples upon it so that it becomes embedded in the soil. If it does become so embedded, the occupier will automatically have the superior title, if not, the finder or the occupier may have the superior title depending on whether the occupier had manifested an intention to possess the chattel prior to the finding.

(TJ Follows, "Parker v British Airways Board and the Law of Finding Chattels" (1982) 12 Kingston L Rev 1 [Follows].) The author offers a detailed critique of the decision in *Parker*.

Do you agree with this criticism of the distinction between chattels found "on" or "in or attached to" land? For example, consider the following situation. A man using a metal detector found a gold brooch beneath the surface of the ground in a park owned by the local council. He claimed "finders keepers" on the basis that the council did not occupy the park, because it was generally used by the public, and that he was a lawful visitor. The finder also argued that his rights should not depend on whether the brooch was found on the surface or just under it and that, in either case, it was necessary for the council to show an intention to exercise control over the park and things found in it. How should this claim be resolved, having regard to the principles in *Parker*?

In this English case, the trial judge held that the finder was entitled to the brooch, but the Court of Appeal allowed the appeal, applying the principle that the owner of land has better title than a finder to things "in or attached to" land. The appeal court also noted that metal detecting was not permitted in the park: see *Waverley BC v Fletcher*, [1996] QB 334, [1995] 3 WLR 772; 4 All ER 756.

iii. Possession, Policy Issues, and the Duties of Finders

Can the outcomes in *Parker* and in the previous cases be reconciled more satisfactorily on the basis of underlying legal policy? What is the legal policy promoting the finder's entitlement in *Armory v Delamirie*? What is the legal policy promoting the finder's entitlement in *Parker v British Airways Board*? What other policies might promote the entitlement of finders to claim title to lost chattels? Do the principles enunciated in *Parker* concerning the duties of finders tend to achieve these goals? For an excellent overview of doctrinal and policy issues (written prior to the *Parker* case), see DR Harris, "The Concept of Possession in English Law" in AG Guest, ed, *Oxford Essays in Jurisprudence* (Oxford: Oxford University Press, 1961) at 69.

In *Parker*, Donaldson LJ defined the duties of finders of lost objects. He also defined, apparently for the first time, the duties of occupiers who may discover lost objects on their property. How can these duties be enforced in practice? To what extent should the actions of finders (or occupiers) influence decision making about possession?

Consider the following cases. In British Columbia, a finder applied for an order entitling him to the return of $937,000 in cash that he had found in a garbage container in the middle of a park's baseball diamond while he was walking his dog. He had immediately called the police and handed over the money. After investigation, the police concluded that there was no evidence that the money represented the proceeds of crime and they were unable to identify the true owner. As a result of the finder's honesty, the court allowed the finder's application for return of the money, stating that it was important to encourage finders to fulfill their obligation to notify the police in such cases. See *Millas v British Columbia (Attorney General)*, [1999] BCJ no 3007 (Prov Ct). In this case, the finder was an off-duty police officer; however, the court found that he was not acting in his capacity as a police officer and should therefore be treated as any other member of the public. Do you agree with this outcome? Why?

In another case in 2006, Mr Thomas received an erroneous postal delivery of an envelope containing $18,000 that he handed over to the RCMP to seek the rightful owner. When the intended recipient did not claim the money (probably because it had been obtained by illicit means), Thomas attempted to regain control of the money on the basis of a claim to possession. Although Canada Post disclaimed any right to the money, the federal government attempted to assert a claim on behalf of Canada Post. This claim was *evaluate* because Canada Post was an independent agency. *criminality*

The federal government also argued that Thomas should not profit *in finding* (even though it was accidentally placed in his mailbox, he should not *the object* ope). In rejecting this claim, Trussler J analyzed cases involving the i*Thomas* activities and lost items, most notably *Baird v British Columbia* (1992), *Case* Fort Frances, [1949] 2 DLR 791 (Ont HC). In both these cases, finders h money obtained through criminal activities; in *Baird*, the finder was u finder in *Bird* was held entitled to the money. Although Trussler J admitt between these two cases remains somewhat ambiguous, she conclu between the results reflected the plaintiffs' relative levels of criminal intention. Specifically, she noted that *Baird* involved a cache of knowingly stolen travellers' cheques, while *Bird* involved a young boy trespassing in an abandoned building and then stumbling on a can full of money. Thus, considering the inadvertent acts that led Thomas to discover the money in his mailbox, as well as his subsequent efforts to find the true owner of the $18,000, the judge held that the criminality of opening the envelope was more similar to the accidental actions of *Bird* than to the facts in *Baird*. In the result, Thomas succeeded in his claim for the money (see *Thomas v Canada (AG)*, 2006 ABQB 730).

To what extent do *Millas* and *Thomas* confirm principle 5 in *Parker*, concerning the responsibility of a finder to make all reasonable efforts to discover the true owner of "lost" property? You may also want to consider both these cases in relation to the issue of "intention" in finders' cases, discussed below in this section.

iv. Interpreting Judicial Decisions and the Scope of Legal Advice

The principles in *Parker* establish rights to a lost object for an occupier of a building where the object is "upon or in, but not attached to" the building, but only if "before the object is found, [the occupier] has manifested an intention to exercise control over the building and the things which may be upon it or in it." What actions had been taken by British Airways in the *Parker* case—actions that were regarded as insufficient to demonstrate the airline's intention to exercise control over lost objects? What arrangements would have satisfied Donaldson LJ that the airline had manifested such an intent? What arrangements would have satisfied Eveleigh LJ, in terms of his stated requirements of "control and *animus possidendi*"? Is the principle of "manifest intent" in the *Parker* case consistent with ideas about property and human will as presented in Chapter 1? Is the idea of intent, in practice, the same for the finder and the airline in *Parker*? In a recent decision in Alberta, for example, the Court of Queen's Bench held that the finders of a cache of Canadian bills ($75,960 in total) on land that was a well site were entitled to the money because the lessee-occupier of the land had failed to manifest an intent to exercise control over it (*Trachuk v Olinek*, [1996] 4 WWR 137 (Alta QB)).

Parker is a good example of how a judicial decision results in a need for expert legal advice about exactly how a corporation can organize its affairs to meet legal requirements and avoid (further) litigation. After the decision in *Parker*, corporations such as British Airways probably requested advice from their lawyers in exactly this way. Reconsider your suggestions about arrangements that the airline should make to satisfy the test in *Parker*, taking account of additional issues of cost and practical effectiveness for a corporation such as British Airways. Is the legal principle in *Parker* sufficiently clear for you to provide the airline with a definite legal opinion? Why does Donaldson LJ identify how the airline's actions were insufficient rather than defining exactly how the airline could act to meet the legal test? As a member of the legal department of an airline like British Airways, how would you draft instructions to employees that satisfy the test in *Parker*?

v. Litigation and Negotiation as Processes for Problem Solving

The *Parker* case also raises an interesting question about why British Airways decided to pursue an appeal to the English Court of Appeal. In light of the costs of such an appeal, it seems clear that the value of the bracelet was not the reason for doing so. Why then was this appeal worthwhile for the airline? Is this a case where the unsuccessful appellant should have borne all the costs? Are there societal interests that benefited from the airline's decision to litigate? (In thinking about this question, you may want to imagine the task that law students and lawyers faced prior to *Parker* in resolving issues of finders' rights.)

This case also raises questions about whether Mr Parker and the airline attempted to negotiate a settlement prior to commencing litigation. How might such a process have occurred? What role do lawyers play in encouraging or discouraging out-of-court settlements? Do the legal principles set out in *Parker* encourage or discourage settlement of such claims? In thinking about the prospects for negotiating a solution in this case, you may want to reconsider the differing approaches of Amy and Jake in Carol Gilligan's analysis in Chapter 1. Although Jake's approach appears similar to typical legal reasoning in the law of finders, it may be more difficult to contemplate how Amy's approach would work in practice. According to her approach, the parties should talk to each other instead of to a third party, and they should find a solution that preserves relationships and connections important in the context of the dispute. How do these concerns apply to the dispute between Mr Parker and the airline? Is there a creative legal solution here that meets the needs of both parties, one that goes beyond being "just a compromise"? How would a lawyer using an "ethic of care," and approaching this problem from the perspective of both Jake and Amy, provide advice in a case such as *Parker*?

B. Joint Finding: A Critical Perspective?

The issue of entitlement to an object when more than one person is involved in the process of discovery presents a different challenge for judicial decision making. It is perhaps significant that some of these cases have been resolved by permitting all members of the group to share the bounty discovered. In the examples that follow, try to identify the definition of possession that resulted in group entitlement. Is this idea of possession similar to the concept used in *Parker*? How is the issue of intention defined? Is it the same as the definition of intention in *Parker*?

Keron v Cashman
33 A 1055 (NJ Ct Ch 1896)

[Five boys who were walking home from church along a railway track in the city of Eliza-beth found $775 in bills when an old stocking they were playing with broke open. The youngest boy, Crawford, stated that he found the stocking, which the oldest boy, Cashman, snatched from him. However, the other boys declared that Crawford threw the stocking down the embankment and then all the boys began playing with the stocking.

Because the police were unable to locate the true owner, Crawford claimed all the money, but the other boys claimed an equal division of the money.]

EMERY VC: Upon consideration of the evidence in this case, I reach the conclusion that the lost money which is the subject of the present controversy must be treated as legally found while in the common possession of all the defendants. This common possession arises from the fact that the old stocking which contained the money and other articles was, at the time the stocking burst open, in actual use by all the defendants as a plaything, and for the purpose of play only. The stocking itself, in the condition in which it was found, was not, in my view of the evidence, treated either by the boy who first picked it up or by any of the others as an article over which any ownership or possession was in-tended to be asserted for the purpose of examining or appropriating its contents. The evidence is conflicting as to whether the boy who first picked up the stocking threw it away again, or whether it was snatched from him by one of the older boys. The weight of evidence is that it was thrown away by him, and was then picked up again by Cashman. There is no sufficient evidence to establish that Crawford retained or desired to retain the stocking for the purpose of examining [it], or that it was taken from him for that purpose by the older [boy], Cashman. When Cashman first got the stocking, whether by picking it up or by snatching, he did not proceed to examine it, but commenced the play with it; and the only intention or state of mind in any of the boys in relation to the stocking and its contents, as found, established by the evidence, in my view, is that the stocking was treated by all of them only as a plaything, to be used as such, in the condition it was when found. In the course of the play with it, after it had passed from one hand to another, and while one boy was beating another with it, the stocking burst open, and it was then dis-closed to all of the boys that the stocking contained money. This money within the stock-ing was therefore the lost property, and as to this money the first intention, idea, or "state of mind," as it is called in some of the authorities, arose on this discovery. As a plaything, the stocking with its contents was in the common possession of all the boys; and inasmuch as the discovery of the money resulted from the use of the stocking as a plaything, and in the course of the play, the money must be considered as being found by all of them in common. Had the stocking been like a pocketbook, an article generally used for contain-ing money, or had the evidence established that Crawford, the boy who first picked up the stocking, retained it, or tried to retain it, for the purpose of examining its contents, or that it had been snatched from him by Cashman, another boy, for the purpose of open-ing or appropriating the contents himself, and preventing Crawford's examining, I think the original possession or retention of the stocking by Crawford, its original finder, for such purpose of examination, might perhaps be considered as the legal "finding" of the money inclosed, with other articles, in the stocking. But, inasmuch as none of the boys treated the stocking when it was found as anything but a plaything or abandoned article, I am of the opinion that the money within the stocking must be treated as lost property, which was not "found," in a legal sense, until the stocking was broken open during the play. At that time, and when so found, it was in the possession of all, and all the boys are therefore equally finders of the money, and it must be equally divided between them.

Edmonds v Ronella
342 NY Supp 2d 408 (SC 1973)

[While rummaging through trash in a supermarket parking lot on their way home from church, two boys aged 9 and 12 found a bag with a manila envelope containing $12,300 cash. Antoinette Ronella aged 15 was among the friends who came to the boys' assistance. She picked up the bag and the boys accompanied her to her house where her parents called the police who gave her a receipt as the "sole" finder of the money. At trial, the boys denied her testimony that they had disclaimed any interest in the money. Hammer J stated:

> A finder has been defined as the person who first takes possession of lost property but to be a legal finder, an essential element is an intention or state of mind with reference to the lost property.

On the basis of the principles of equity and the testimony given at trial, the court determined that the lost property was not found, in a legal sense, until the plaintiffs and defendant had removed it from the parking lot. Because possession was jointly obtained, the joint finders were entitled to an equal share of the money, a one-third share each.]

Popov v Hayashi
2002 WL 31833731 (Cal Sup Ct)

McCARTHY J:

[In this case, baseball fans assembled in PacBell Park in San Francisco on October 7, 2001, the day that Barry Bonds hit his 73rd home run (breaking the previous records of Babe Ruth (60), Roger Maris (61), and Mark McGwire (70)). As the court noted, "the event was widely anticipated," and baseball fans all realized that the winning ball would be worth a lot of money. The plaintiff, Alex Popov, and the defendant, Patrick Hayashi, were among a number of fans who positioned themselves in the arcade section of the ball park near right field. Barry Bonds hit the home run, and much of the action was captured on camera by another fan, Josh Keppel. In the subsequent litigation, 17 witnesses testified, although the court found that their testimony was somewhat variable. In its findings, the court stated:]

When the seventy-third home run ball went into the arcade, it landed in the upper portion of the webbing of a softball glove worn by Alex Popov. While the glove stopped the trajectory of the ball, it is not at all clear that the ball was secure. Popov had to reach for the ball and in doing so, may have lost his balance. Even as the ball was going into his glove, a crowd of people began to engulf Mr. Popov. He was tackled and thrown to the ground while still in the process of attempting to complete the catch. Some people intentionally descended on him for the purpose of taking the ball away, while others were involuntarily forced to the ground by the momentum of the crowd. Eventually, Mr. Popov was buried face down on the ground under several layers of people. At one point he had trouble breathing. Mr. Popov was grabbed, hit and kicked. People reached underneath him in the area of his glove. Neither the tape nor the testimony is sufficient to establish which individual members of the crowd were responsible for the assaults on Mr. Popov. [According to the court, this was an "out of control mob," engaged in violent, illegal behaviour.]

Mr. Popov intended at all times to establish and maintain possession of the ball. At some point the ball left his glove and ended up on the ground. It is impossible to establish the exact point in time that this occurred or what caused it to occur. Mr. Hayashi was standing near Mr. Popov when the ball came into the stands. He, like Mr. Popov, was involuntarily forced to the ground. He committed no wrongful act. While on the ground he saw the loose ball. He picked it up, rose to his feet and put it in his pocket. [Eventually, with Mr. Keppel's camera pointed at him, Mr. Hayashi held the ball in the air.]

Mr. Popov eventually got up from the ground. He made several statements while he was on the ground and shortly after he got up, which are consistent with his claim that he had achieved some level of control over the ball and that he intended to keep it. Those statements can be heard on the audio portion of the tape. When he saw that Mr. Hayashi had the ball he expressed relief and grabbed for it. Mr. Hayashi pulled the ball away. Security guards then took Mr. Hayashi to a secure area of the stadium.

It is important to point out what the evidence did not and could not show. Neither the camera nor the percipient witnesses were able to establish whether Mr. Popov retained control of the ball as he descended into the crowd. Mr. Popov's testimony on this question is inconsistent on several important points, ambiguous on others and, on the whole, unconvincing. We do not know when or how Mr. Popov lost the ball.

Perhaps the most critical factual finding of all is one that cannot be made. We will never know if Mr. Popov would have been able to retain control of the ball had the crowd not interfered with his efforts to do so. Resolution of that question is the work of a psychic, not a judge.

LEGAL ANALYSIS

[The court noted that the plaintiff pleaded several causes of action: conversion, trespass to chattel, injunctive relief, and constructive trust; as the court noted in relation to conversion: "If a person entitled to possession of personal property demands its return, the unjustified refusal to give the property back is conversion." Rejecting the possible claim of trespass to chattel, the court continued:]

Conversion does not exist, however, unless the baseball rightfully belongs to Mr. Popov. One who has neither title nor possession, nor any right to possession, cannot sue for conversion. The deciding question in this case then, is whether Mr. Popov achieved possession or the right to possession as he attempted to catch and hold on to the ball.

The parties have agreed to a starting point for the legal analysis. Prior to the time the ball was hit, it was possessed and owned by Major League Baseball. At the time it was hit it became intentionally abandoned property. The first person who came in possession of the ball became its new owner.

The parties fundamentally disagree about the definition of possession. In order to assist the court in resolving this disagreement, four distinguished law professors participated in a forum to discuss the legal definition of possession. The professors also disagreed.

[The court noted that the ambiguity in the term "possession" was related to the need to consider the concept in context. Particularly in relation to a commercial context, "a single definition of possession cannot be applied to different industries without creating havoc." The court then considered fundamental concepts of possession:]

It is possible to identify certain fundamental concepts that are common to every definition of possession. Professor Roger Bernhardt has recognized that "[p]ossession requires both physical control over the item and an intent to control it or exclude others from it. But these generalizations function more as guidelines than as direct determinants of possession issues. Possession is a blurred question of law and fact." Professor Brown argues that "[t]he orthodox view of possession regards it as a union of the two elements of the physical relation of the possessor to the thing, and of intent. This physical relation is the actual power over the thing in question, the ability to hold and make use of it. But a mere physical relation of the possessor to the thing in question is not enough. There must also be manifested an intent to control it." ...

We start with the observation that possession is a process which culminates in an event. The event is the moment in time that possession is achieved. The process includes the acts and thoughts of the would-be possessor which lead up to the moment of possession.

The focus of the analysis in this case is not on the thoughts or intent of the actor. Mr. Popov has clearly evidenced an intent to possess the baseball and has communicated that intent to the world. The question is whether he did enough to reduce the ball to his exclusive dominion and control. Were his acts sufficient to create a legally cognizable interest in the ball?

Mr. Hayashi argues that possession does not occur until the fan has complete control of the ball. Professor Brian Gray suggests the following definition, "A person who catches a baseball that enters the stands is its owner. A ball is caught if the person has achieved complete control of the ball at the point in time that the momentum of the ball and the momentum of the fan while attempting to catch the ball ceases. A baseball, which is dislodged by incidental contact with an inanimate object or another person, before momentum has ceased, is not possessed. Incidental contact with another person is contact that is not intended by the other person. The first person to pick up a loose ball and secure it becomes its possessor."

Mr Popov argues that this definition requires that a person seeking to establish possession must show unequivocal dominion and control, a standard rejected by several leading cases. Instead, he offers the perspectives of Professor Bernhardt and Professor Paul Finkelman who suggest that possession occurs when an individual intends to take control of a ball and manifests that intent by stopping the forward momentum of the ball whether or not complete control is achieved.

Professors Finkelman and Bernhardt have correctly pointed out that some cases recognize possession even before absolute dominion and control is achieved. Those cases require the actor to be actively and ably engaged in efforts to establish complete control.

Moreover, such efforts must be significant and they must be reasonably calculated to result in unequivocal dominion and control at some point in the near future.

[The court then reviewed cases about hunting and fishing of wild animals and salvage, noting that the rules applied in such cases are "contextual in nature" and "crafted in response to the unique nature of the conduct they seek to regulate." In the context of the hunting and fishing of wild animals and salvage activities, of course, it is "impossible to wrap one's arms around a whale, a fleeing fox or a sunken ship."]

The opposite is true of a baseball hit into the stands of a stadium. Not only is it physically possible for a person to acquire unequivocal dominion and control of an abandoned baseball, but fans generally expect a claimant to have accomplished as much. The custom and practice of the stands creates a reasonable expectation that a person will achieve full control of a ball before claiming possession. There is no reason for the legal rule to be inconsistent with that expectation. Therefore Gray's Rule is adopted as the definition of possession in this case.

The central [tenet] of Gray's Rule is that the actor must retain control of the ball after incidental contact with people and things. Mr. Popov has not established by a preponderance of the evidence that he would have retained control of the ball after all momentum ceased and after any incidental contact with people or objects. Consequently, he did not achieve full possession.

That finding, however, does not resolve the case. The reason we do not know whether Mr. Popov would have retained control of the ball is not because of incidental contact. It is because he was attacked. His efforts to establish possession were interrupted by the collective assault of a band of wrongdoers.

A decision which ignored that fact would endorse the actions of the crowd by not repudiating them. Judicial rulings, particularly in cases that receive media attention, affect the way people conduct themselves. This case demands vindication of an important principle. We are a nation governed by law, not by brute force.

[The court thus concluded that Mr Popov should have had an opportunity to try to complete his catch unimpeded; otherwise, the decision would be dictated by violence. As a result, the court considered and then decided that an action for conversion can proceed where the plaintiff has title, possession, or the *right to possession*. Noting that the remedies of injunctive relief and constructive trust were equitable remedies, the court decided that it had authority to fashion "rules and remedies designed to achieve fundamental fairness" (emphasis added):]

Consistent with this principle, the court adopts the following rule. Where an actor undertakes significant but incomplete steps to achieve possession of a piece of abandoned personal property and the effort is interrupted by the unlawful acts of others, the actor has a legally cognizable pre-possessory interest in the property. That pre-possessory interest constitutes a qualified right to possession which can support a cause of action for conversion.

Possession can be likened to a journey down a path. Mr. Popov began his journey unimpeded. He was fast approaching a fork in the road. A turn in one direction would lead to possession of the ball—he would complete the catch. A turn in the other direction would result in a failure to achieve possession—he would drop the ball. Our problem is that before Mr. Popov got to the point where the road forked, he was set upon by a gang of bandits, who dislodged the ball from his grasp.

Recognition of a legally protected pre-possessory interest vests Mr. Popov with a qualified right to possession and enables him to advance a legitimate claim to the baseball based on a conversion theory. Moreover it addresses the harm done by the unlawful actions of the crowd.

It does not, however, address the interests of Mr. Hayashi. The court is required to balance the interests of all parties. Mr. Hayashi was not a wrongdoer. He was a victim of the same bandits that attacked Mr. Popov. The difference is that he was able to extract himself from their assault and move to the side of the road. It was there that he discovered the loose ball. When he picked it up and put it in his pocket he attained unequivocal dominion and control.

[The court noted that Mr Popov did not establish a full right to possession, but that Mr Hayashi's right was "encumbered by the qualified pre-possessory interest" of Mr Popov; at the time of his acquisition, the ball had a "cloud on its title." Thus, the court concluded:]

An award of the ball to Mr. Popov would be unfair to Mr. Hayashi. It would be premised on the assumption that Mr. Popov would have caught the ball. That assumption is not supported by the facts. An award of the ball to Mr. Hayashi would unfairly penalize Mr. Popov. It would be based on the assumption that Mr. Popov would have dropped the ball. That conclusion is also unsupported by the facts.

Both men have a superior claim to the ball as against all the world. Each man has a claim of equal dignity as to the other. We are, therefore, left with something of a dilemma.

Thankfully, there is a middle ground.

The concept of equitable division was fully explored in a law review article authored by RH Helmholz in the December 1983 edition of the *Fordham Law Review*. Professor Helmholz addressed the problems associated with rules governing finders of lost and mislaid property. For a variety of reasons not directly relevant to the issues raised in this case, Helmholz suggested employing the equitable remedy of division to resolve competing claims between finders of lost or mislaid property and the owners of land on which the property was found. [See RH Helmholz, "Equitable Division and the Law of Finders" (1983) 52 Fordham L Rev 313.]

[The court then decided that it was appropriate to apply the equitable remedy of division (from ancient Roman law) because it provided a way to resolve equally strong competing claims, citing *Arnold v Producers Fruit Company* (1900) 128 Cal 637. The court also considered and applied *Keron v Cashman*, and concluded that the present case was similar because neither Popov nor Hayashi could present a superior argument. Thus, the court ordered the parties to appear before the court to come to an agreement as to how to implement the decision.]

DISCUSSION NOTES

i. Differing Perspectives on Popov v Hayashi

Following Justice McCarthy's order, the baseball was eventually sold for $450,000, a sum that was evenly split between the two parties. Several commentators have written about this interesting collision of sports and property law by viewing the pre-possessory interest/equitable division remedy as either a promising tool for adjudicating exceptional cases or a subversion of traditional jurisprudence about abandoned property. For instance, Michael Pastrick noted how the case's tension between honouring unwritten baseball customs and discouraging mob violence provided the inspiration needed to attempt this unique remedy:

> American jurisprudence has seen neither the adjudication of a specific claim of ownership to an abandoned baseball nor the incorporation of baseball custom concerning ownership of abandoned balls into common law. Clearly, law exists for the promotion of regulation of society and order. In matters involving the absence of binding precedent and a mere smattering of persuasive authority, courts *should* err on the side of caution in strengthening civility and order among the citizenry. Thus, any policy discouraging uncontrolled violence should trump any basis for maintaining the obscure or non-binding precedent discussed in *Popov*.

(See M Pastrick, "When a Day at the Ballpark Turns a 'Can of Corn' into a Can of Worms: Popov v Hayashi" (2003) 51 Buff L Rev 905 at 930-31.)

On the other hand, Jason Cielslik suggested that Mr Popov should have anticipated the dangerous situation he was entering. He further argued that an ordered society is better realized through commonsense, everyday conceptions of property, as opposed to new property interests that arise every time there is a unique set of facts:

> The *Popov* case was very unique. Situations such as this one can be anticipated and avoided. The difference between this case and previous games was the value of the baseball, the historic home run, and the area in which it was hit. An across-the-board rule cannot be formulated because of the complexity of the issue and the confined spaces at a sporting event. However, a clear-cut rule should have been addressed in the context of this case. First, possession of a baseball, whether it is a foul ball or a historic home-run ball, should not be defined by anything other than the simple definition of possession because … this would create certainty.
>
> As for the safety issue, those who assume the risk of injury because the circumstances are ripe for danger should not only be stripped of the right to sue for negligence, but stripped of any pre-possessory interest as well. This rationale is similar to denying a fireman the right to sue a homeowner, who, because of the homeowner's negligence, was injured while putting out the fire in the homeowner's home. The court in *Popov* should have constructed a holding that focused on the factors and dangers present that day in the arcade area by extending assumption of the risk. If the court had limited its holding to the particular facts, then there would not have been this slippery slope called a pre-possessory interest.

(See Jason Cielslik, "There's a Drive … Way Back … It Might Be … It Could Be … Another Lawsuit: Popov v Hayashi" (2003) 20 TM Cooley L Rev 605 at 636.) For further analysis of this case, see Patrick Stoklas, "Popov v Hayashi: A Modern Day Pierson v Post—A Comment on What the Court Should Have Done with the Seventy-Third Home Run Baseball Hit by Barry Bonds" (2002-3) 34 Loy U Chicago LJ 901; and Peter Adomeit, "Barry Bonds' Baseball Case: An Empirical Approach—Is Fleeting Possession Five Tenths of the Ball?" (2004) 48 Saint Louis ULJ 475.

ii. Shared Rights in Cases of Finding: A Different Voice?

If the concept of possession is sufficiently flexible to permit "joint" finders to share the value of their discovered chattel, could the same principle be used in disputes between a finder and an occupier? Such a recommendation was made, for example, in relation to the issue in *Parker* by Follows:

> A far more preferable rule, in the writer's view, would be one of equal division of the proceeds of sale of the lost chattel between occupier and finder, the sale being ordered by the court. The primary merit of such a rule would be its clarity. Such equality of treatment of finder and occupier would moreover accurately reflect the ethics of the situation, that unless the finder is dishonest or a trespasser, neither party has the morally superior claim. Admittedly the law must accord possession of the lost chattel to *someone* in order to avoid a "free-for-all situation" but it by no means follows that it must accord possession to one party to the exclusion of the other.

If this principle of sharing by a finder and an occupier were adopted, the result in *Parker* would be different. Should the principle be applicable to all such claims? Consider, for example, a finder's claim to a gold bracelet found in an apartment occupied by her friend. Were the claims of all the parties in these joint-finding cases of equal weight? What do these cases suggest about the institutional potential and limits of judicial decision making?

Are the joint-finding cases examples of "a different voice" in legal principles about possession and the law of finders? In Carol Gilligan's example of two children resolving their differing choices about whether to play "next-door neighbours" (the four-year-old girl's choice) or "pirates" (the four-year-old boy's choice), the little girl resolved the dilemma by suggesting a game called "the pirate who lives next door." According to Gilligan:

> She has reached what I would call *an inclusive solution* rather than *a fair solution*—the fair solution would be to take turns and play each game for an equal period. "First we will play pirates for ten minutes and then we will play neighbors for ten minutes." Each child would enter the other's imaginative world. The girl would learn about the world of pirates and the boy would learn about the world of neighbors. It is a kind of tourism on a four-year-old's level. Really, it's simple. But the interesting thing is that neither game would change—the pirate game would stay the pirate game, and the neighbor game would stay the neighbor game. ...
>
> Now look what happens in the other solution, what I would call *the inclusive solution*. By bringing a pirate into the neighborhood, both the pirate game and the neighbor game change. In addition, the pirate–neighbor game, the combined game, is a game that *neither* child had separately imagined. In other words, a new game arises through the relationship.
>
> That is basically my point: [t]he inclusion of two voices in moral discourse, in thinking about conflicts, and in making choices, transforms the discourse .... We are at the beginning of a process of inquiry, in which the methods themselves will have to be re-examined because the old methods are from the old game.

(Carol Gilligan, in the 1984 James McCormick Mitchell Lecture, "Feminist Discourse, Moral Values, and the Law: A Conversation" (1985) 34 Buff L Rev 11 at 45.) Are the joint-finding cases examples of an inclusive legal approach, or do they represent only a compromise? For another overview of possession, see Jonathan Hill, "The Proprietary Character of Possession" in Elizabeth Cooke, ed, *Modern Studies in Property Law, 2000*, vol 1 (Oxford and Portland, OR: Hart, 2001) 21.

C. The Issue of Intention

The issue of intention is relevant in a number of different ways in defining possessory interests in the law of finders. As has been shown, the principle entitling an occupier of a building to claim possession of a lost chattel is whether the occupier has "manifested an intention to exercise control" over the building and chattels found within it, a test not met by British Airways in *Parker*. As well, the finders' intentions were relevant to determining their claims to possession in the joint-finding cases. In addition to these examples, the issue of intention in defining rights to possession is relevant to disputes between a finder and someone who subsequently interferes with the finder's possession of a chattel. In the case that follows, note again how the concept of possession is defined in terms of competing claims to a lost object. Can you identify someone who is not a party to this action and whose claim might be relatively better than the claims of either the plaintiff or the defendant?

Bird v Fort Frances
[1949] 2 DLR 791 (Ont HC)

McRUER CJHC: This is an action brought to recover the sum of $1,430 from the defendant, the amount of a sum of money taken from the plaintiff by Chief Constable Gaston Louis Camerand, and subsequently handed over to the treasurer of the defendant municipality, and now held by him on deposit in a savings account in the local branch of the Dominion Bank.

In the month of May, 1946, the plaintiff, who was at that time about 12 years of age, was playing with a number of other boys in the rear of a pool-room built on private property in the Town of Fort Frances. As part of the game he attempted to crawl under the building and while doing so observed a can on a sill forming part of the understructure. On investigation he found this can to contain a large sum of money in bills. He took possession of it and after some incident in a coal bin, which was not clearly developed at the trial and is immaterial to this action, during which some of the money was lost, he took between fourteen and fifteen hundred dollars home, the substantial part of which he handed over to his mother, who hid it under the cushion of a chair. Some days later, as a result of the plaintiff's generous spending, the Chief Constable questioned him. The plaintiff gave a true account of the facts and disclosed that he had $60 on his person and where the balance of the money was. The Chief Constable went to the plaintiff's home, without a search warrant, and asked Mrs. Bird for the money, which she handed over without objection. The Chief Constable said in evidence that his purpose in securing the money was to return it to the rightful owner if he should be found. He says that he kept it for some time and, finding no owner, turned it over to the town treasurer. The town treasurer says that when he received the package of money from the Chief Constable the latter told him that it was money found and asked him to keep it in safe-keeping. It was eventually deposited, on December 23, 1946, in a special savings account to the credit of the Town of Fort Frances marked "Funds for Court disposal." The balance shown in the account on September 27, 1948 was $1,460.61.

The defendant in its statement of defence alleges that the moneys were found on premises owned by the late John Sandul and were rightfully retained by it as trustee for the true owner. Paragraph 2 reads as follows:

The Defendant submits that it has retained these moneys in good faith as trustee for the true owner and asks the direction of the Court with respect to the disbursement thereof, bearing in mind that the executor of the estate of the late John Sandul has already made a demand upon the Defendant for the return of the monies to him.

There was no evidence given at the trial of any demand made by the executor of the estate of the late John Sandul, and my understanding of what counsel said is that no such claim is made to the money. During the course of the trial counsel said that the executor wished to make a statement to the Court. I intimated that unless the executor was making a claim to the money, and would formally do so at the consequent risk of costs, I would not hear him. With that the matter was dropped. Whatever the rights of the estate of John Sandul may be, they cannot be considered or disposed of in this action as framed.

The facts are simple, but the law applicable has been a subject of absorbing interest to legal philosophers, jurists and textbook writers throughout the evolution of our jurisprudence, and in some aspects the British law cannot yet be said to be settled.

It is convenient first to consider the case in the following aspects: the rights of the plaintiff as the finder of the money; whether the removal of the money from the property of another was a felonious act; if so, how far his right to recover against this defendant is affected thereby; and whether the plaintiff's possession was subsisting at the time the money was handed over to the Chief Constable or had been so interrupted as to deprive him of a right to maintain this action.

The plaintiff's right of action, if any, depends on a finding that he was wrongfully deprived of possession of the money by the Chief Constable, and that the defendant continues to interfere wrongfully with his possession. I know of no better preface to a consideration of the law applicable than the chapter on "Possession" in Holmes, Common Law, 1948, from which I adopt the language of the learned author at p. 239 to express a cardinal principle of great antiquity: "The facts constituting possession generate rights as truly as do the facts which constitute ownership, although the rights of a mere possessor are less extensive than those of an owner."

Since *Armory v. Delamirie* (1722), 1 Str. 505, 93 ER 664, by the law of England the finder of a chattel, though he does not acquire absolute property or ownership, yet has such property as will enable him to keep it against all but the rightful owner (or at least one superior in title), and consequently may maintain trover. In that case a chimney-sweep found a jewel and carried it to the defendant's shop to know what it was. One of the defendant's employees, after a pretence of weighing it, refused to return the stone. Judgment was given in favour of the plaintiff.

Where the contest is between the finder and the owner of the premises on which a chattel is found the law still remains in an unsettled state, and I refer to it only as far as it throws some indirect light on the subject I have to consider, and not for the purpose of entering the lists of the legal debate that still continues on this subject.

In *Bridges v. Hawkesworth* (1851), 21 LJQB 75, the plaintiff found a parcel of banknotes which had been dropped on the floor in the part of a shop frequented by customers. He handed them to the shopkeeper to hold pending inquiry by the true owner. The true owner was not found and the plaintiff sued the shopkeeper to recover the notes. Judgment was given in his favour.

This case, together with all other relevant cases on the subject, has been the subject of consideration in two recent judgments in the English Courts. In *Hannah v. Peel,* [1945]

KB 509, the defendant was the owner of a house which he himself had never occupied. While the house was under requisition for war purposes the plaintiff, a soldier, found in a bedroom used as a sick bay, loose in a crevice on top of a window frame, a brooch, the owner of which was unknown. There was no evidence that the defendant had any knowledge of the existence of the brooch before it was found, but the police, to whom the plaintiff handed it for the purpose of ascertaining its owner, delivered it to the defendant, who claimed it as being found on the premises of which he was the owner. After a full discussion of the somewhat conflicting authorities, including *Elwes v. Brigg Gas Co.* (1886), 33 Ch. D 562, and *South Staffordshire Water Co. v. Sharman*, [1896] 2 QB 44, Birkett J followed the decision in *Bridges v. Hawkesworth, supra*, and gave judgment for the plaintiff.

In *Hibbert v. McKiernan*, [1948] 1 All ER 860, Lord Goddard CJ was required to consider the subject in a different aspect. McKiernan had been charged with the theft of eight golf balls, which had been lost and abandoned by their original owners and picked up and carried away by him while trespassing on the course. The Justices found that the balls had been abandoned by their original owners and only one was capable of being identified. They were of the opinion that the appellant took the balls for the purpose of selling them and that by taking the balls the appellant meant to steal them and did steal them, but stated a case on the questions of law which they considered arose, in the main whether the appellant, by finding them, acquired title to the balls which, as they had been abandoned by their original owners, would prevail against the owners of the land on which they were found.

After referring to *Bridges v. Hawkesworth, Elwes v. Brigg Gas Co.* and *South Staffordshire Water Co. v. Sharman*, the Lord Chief Justice said [at 861]: "These cases have long been the delight of professors and text writers, whose task it often is to attempt to reconcile the irreconcilable." He pointed out that "the Corpus Professor of Jurisprudence at Oxford and the Professor Emeritus of English Law at Cambridge have expressed the opinion that *Bridges v. Hawkesworth* was wrongly decided." He referred to the decision of Birkett J in *Hannah v. Peel* as having reinvigorated that "much-battered case" and leaves it to wiser heads than his to end the controversy "which will, no doubt, continue to form an appropriate subject for moots till the House of Lords lays it to rest for all time."

This discussion bears only on the case I have to decide in considering whether the plaintiff was a "true finder" as the term is used in the cases, or whether the owner of the land on which the money was found had an interest in it; and if he had whether the plaintiff was a mere wrongful taker or in law guilty of a felonious act. If the taking in this case amounted to a felony then for the first time in British law, as far as I can determine, the question must be expressly decided whether a thief can maintain an action for trover or conversion against one who has wrongfully deprived him of possession of the thing stolen. If the taking was "wrongful taking" with no felonious intent, the course to be followed is much more clearly defined.

[After reviewing a number of texts and cases, the court concluded:]

In applying the law I have discussed to the facts of the case before me I am convinced that the plaintiff was not a "true finder" within the meaning of the term as used by jurists and writers. The money was not found in a public highway or public conveyance or in any place to which the public had access by leave or licence, nor was there anything to lead one to believe that it had been lost in the true sense. It had been carefully put in the container for the purpose of hiding it in the place in which it was discovered. It may well be that it was hidden by a thief, or it may be that it was abandoned, but it was not lost in the sense that a wallet is lost if dropped in the street or that the bank-notes in *Bridges v. Hawkesworth, supra,* or the jewel in *Armory v. Delamirie, supra,* or the brooch in *Hannah v. Peel, supra,* were lost. The person who put the money where it was found put it there deliberately.

The plaintiff had no right to remove it from the property of another, and undoubtedly was a wrongful taker. The more difficult question to decide is whether he had a felonious intent and the taking was felonious; and if so, whether he would have the same rights as a wrongful taker who took under circumstances that it did not amount to a felony. The case is to be distinguished from *Bridges v. Hawkesworth* and *Hannah v. Peel* on the ground that in both those cases the plaintiff made immediate disclosure, on the one hand to the shopkeeper, and on the other hand to the police, which disproved any *animus furandi,* while in the present case every effort was made to conceal the fact that the plaintiff had taken possession of the money and removed it from the place where it was found.

A very comprehensive discussion of the law both ancient and modern on this aspect of the case is to be found in Pollock & Wright, *op. cit.,* pp. 171-87. The conclusion I have come to is that it is not necessary for me to decide whether the taking was with felonious intent or not, as I think in this case the same result flows. In my view the authorities with which I have dealt justify the conclusion that where A enters upon the land of B and takes possession of and removes chattels to which B asserts no legal rights, and A is wrongfully dispossessed of those chattels, he may bring an action to recover the same.

The next question to consider is whether the plaintiff had parted with possession of the money to his mother under such circumstances as to deprive him of his right of action. The mere fact that the plaintiff's possession may have been interrupted does not necessarily deprive him of the right to maintain an action against someone who wrongfully dispossesses his successor in possession. While it is not an authoritative statement of the law, I adopt the reasoning in Holmes, *op. cit.,* pp. 236-7:

> But it no more follows, from the single circumstance that certain facts must concur in order to create the rights incident to possession, that they must continue in order to keep those rights alive, than it does, from the necessity of a consideration and a promise to create a right *ex contractu,* that the consideration and promise must continue moving between the parties until the moment of performance. When certain facts have once been made manifest which confer a right, there is no general ground on which the law need hold the right at an end except the manifestation of some fact inconsistent with its continuance, although the reasons for conferring the particular right may have great weight in determining what facts shall be deemed to be so. Cessation of the original physical relations to the object might be treated as such a fact; but it never has been, unless in times of more ungoverned violence than the present. ... Accordingly, it has been expressly decided, where a man found logs afloat and moored them, but they again broke loose and floated away, and were found by another, that the first finder retained the rights which sprung from his having taken possession, and that he could maintain trover against the second finder, who refused to give them up.

In order to sue for the recovery of goods, the finder or wrongful taker must actually have taken possession, but when possession is once acquired it is not necessary, in order to retain it, that the effective control which must be used to gain possession originally should continue to be actively exercised. Possession will not be lost so long as the power of resuming effective control remains: Williams, *op. cit.*, p. 53. Any difficulty that might arise out of the contention that the plaintiff had voluntarily parted with possession of the money to his mother could be overcome by adding Mrs. Bird as a party in her personal capacity. This contention was not set up in the pleadings and I think it may be dismissed from further consideration.

There remains the question whether the police took possession of the money by due process of law. ...

I can find no authority for the police officer taking possession of the money as he did in this case as of right. That being so, the proper construction to be put on the transaction between him and the plaintiff's mother is that the police officer, believing that the true owner could be found, requested that the money be handed over to him to be held by him as the bailee of the plaintiff pending the search for the true owner. When he was unable to ascertain who the true owner was, in the absence of any other claim, he ought to have returned the money to the custody from which it came. The defendant can have no higher right than the police officer would have had, had he not handed the money over to the defendant and it is therefore liable for the amount of the money at the suit of the plaintiff.

Even, in the circumstances, if the money had been seized under a search warrant the constable would have been obliged to return it to the custody from which it was taken upon there being no conviction and no true owner found.

There will be judgment for the plaintiff for $1,430 together with the interest accrued in the bank account. The money will be paid into Court to the credit of the infant and paid out when he reaches the age of 21 years. Costs will follow the event.

Judgment for plaintiff.

DISCUSSION NOTES

i. Formulating the Concept of Intention: R v Christie

How did the court formulate the concept of intention on the part of the plaintiff in *Bird*? Recall also the discussion above about the actions required of finders—that is, attempting to locate the "true owner." To what extent did the young man's actions help to create his entitlement as a finder in *Bird*?

By contrast, consider the court's approach to the issue of intention in *R v Christie* (1978), 41 CCC (2d) 282 (NB SC App Div). In *Christie*, the police found marijuana in the trunk of the accused's car after an automobile accident. The accused told police that she had discovered the marijuana in the trunk and panicked, fearing that her children were involved with drugs. She had then driven around in a panicky state looking for friends. At trial, she was acquitted on a charge of possession of narcotics for the purposes of trafficking contrary to the provisions of the *Narcotic Control Act* (now RSC 1985, c N-1). On appeal, the Crown argued that the trial judge erred in failing to convict the accused of possession. Hughes CJNB dismissed the appeal, commenting as follows on the requisite intention for an accused in relation to a charge of possession under the *Criminal Code*:

This Court must ask itself whether on the whole of the evidence any rational hypothesis of innocence exists. Any such hypothesis must rest in the explanation given by the accused, and that amounted to this: that she had no intent to exercise control over the marijuana which she had found in the trunk of her car, and that at the time of the accident she had been driving about the city for about an hour looking for friends from whom she might obtain advice as to what she should do with it. The learned trial Judge did not think the defendant had consented to possession of the drug, and I infer that it was on this ground he acquitted her.

In my opinion, there can be circumstances which do not constitute possession even where there is a right of control with knowledge of the presence and character of the thing alleged to be possessed, where guilt should not be inferred, as where it appears there is no intent to exercise control over it. An example of this situation is where a person finds a package on his doorstep and upon opening it discovers it contains narcotics. Assuming he does nothing further to indicate an intention to exercise control over it, he had not, in my opinion, the possession contemplated by the *Criminal Code*. Nor do I think such a person who manually handles it for the sole purpose of destroying or reporting it to the police has committed the offence of possession. In the instant case the accused contended, under oath, that she was panic stricken and did not know what she should do when she found the narcotic in the trunk of her car, and that she drove around the city for about an hour before the accident in an attempt to find some of her friends from whom she might obtain advice as to what she should do with it. While the evidence is extremely suspicious I cannot say that the learned trial Judge erred in failing to convict the accused if he had a reasonable doubt as to whether she intended to exercise dominion or control over the narcotic.

For the foregoing reasons I would dismiss the appeal.

Are the tests of intention in relation to possession the same in *Bird* and in *Christie*? Why? For a case similar to *Christie*, where the accused was convicted of theft, see *R v Pace*, [1965] 3 CCC 55 (NSSC). Note that *Christie* was distinguished in *R v York*, 2003 BCSC 769.

ii. Intention and "Abandoned" Objects: Moffatt v Kazana

The issue of intention is also relevant to claims of possession in the law of finders in defining whether a chattel has been "lost" or "abandoned." In some cases, courts have denied a finder's claim on the basis that the chattel "discovered" was never really lost. Such reasoning suggests a continuing intention (perhaps implicit) on the part of a "true owner" to assert possessory title to the chattel. Compare the reasoning in relation to this issue in *Bird* with that in *Moffatt v Kazana*, [1969] 2 QB 152 (HC). In *Moffatt*, the defendant Kazana purchased a bungalow from Mr and Mrs Russell in 1961. Three years after the purchase, workers dislodged a biscuit tin from the main chimney, and discovered that the tin contained £1,987 in £1 notes. The money was turned over to the police, and in due course the police turned it over to the defendant Kazana. Moffatt claimed the biscuit tin and its contents on behalf of the Russells. Examine how Wrangham J defined "possession" in this case:

> Mrs. Russell testified that in 1951 when she and her husband drove their last load of furniture to their bungalow, No. 19 Northcliffe Avenue, which they had purchased in 1950, the biscuit tin was on the seat between them. Upon their arrival, her husband, carrying the biscuit tin, climbed into the false roof while she held the ladder. Then a few years later, Mr. Russell offered their son-in-law a loan for a car. The son-in-law remembered watching Mr. Russell climb into the false roof and reappear a few minutes later with £98 in £1 notes.

Mr. Russell died during the proceedings so his executors continued the action to determine whether the contents of the biscuit tin belonged to the plaintiffs or the defendant.

In discussing the issue of possession, Wrangham J stated, with respect to the quantity of notes:

It is not in dispute that, if it belongs to the plaintiffs, the plaintiffs are entitled to judgment for that amount. Of course, it is not disputed that if it belongs to the defendant the plaintiffs are not entitled to judgment for anything. It was first submitted to me on the part of the defendant that the evidence was not satisfactory enough to enable me to draw the inference that the money in the biscuit tin ever belonged to Mr. Russell at all. Of course, it is very odd that, if the money did belong to Mr. Russell, Mr. Russell did not think of it at the time when he sold the house to the defendant. One can only assume that he must have forgotten all about it. I have been given no evidence as to the mental or physical condition of Mr. Russell at the time of the sale or later; but he must then have been capable of doing business, otherwise he could not have sold the house. All I know is that he was within a few years of the end of his life. I know no more than that.

In those circumstances, the fact that this bungalow was sold to the defendant in 1961 without any reference to this biscuit tin, which according to the evidence of Mrs. Russell had been deposited there in 1951, does raise some doubt whether the evidence proffered on behalf of the plaintiffs is correct and accurate or not; but I have come to the conclusion that the evidence for the plaintiffs which seemed perfectly straightforward, is susceptible of only one reasonable inference, namely, that there was £1,987 or thereabouts in the biscuit tin belonging to Mr. Russell which was deposited by him in the false flue of No. 19 Northcliffe Avenue when he moved into that bungalow.

If one starts from that point, it is argued on behalf of the plaintiffs that Mr. Russell was the true owner of the money in the tin box in 1951 when he deposited it in the flue and that, as he had never done anything to divest himself of the property in that money, he remained the true owner of the money from beginning to end.

There are a certain number of cases in which the ownership or possession of articles which apparently had been lost and had been found has been considered. The first one which was cited to me was the case of *Merry v. Green* (1841), 7 M & W 623. The facts in that case were that a bureau was bought at a public auction and subsequently the buyer discovered a secret drawer in it which contained a purse and money. As a result of that there was litigation, the precise form of which is not relevant to my inquiry; but Baron Parke delivering the judgment of the Court of Exchequer said at p. 631:

But it seems to us, that though there was a delivery of the secretary—an early 19th century phrase for "bureau"—and a lawful property in it thereby vested in the plaintiff, there was no delivery so as to give a lawful possession of the purse and money. The vendor had no intention to deliver it, nor the vendee to receive it; both were ignorant of its existence ... .

The court then reviewed authorities about the relative rights of finders and occupiers, and concluded that all these cases recognized that the "true owner" had the best right of all. That is, only if the true owner was not asserting a claim would it be necessary to assess the relative merits of claims by a finder and occupier. In the result, the court concluded:

It is clear therefore that in the existing authorities there is an implication at least from the language in which the judgments are expressed that the true owner of a chattel found on land has a title superior to that of anybody else. Accordingly, having disposed of the authorities in that way, Mr. Appleby on behalf of the plaintiffs was able to say that the plaintiffs are, as representatives of Mr. Russell, the true owners of this money and they must be held to remain the true owners of the money unless they or Mr. Russell had divested himself or themselves of the ownership by one of the recognised methods, abandonment, gift or sale.

In *Moffatt*, the court held that the true owner's claim was relatively stronger than the finder's claim, concluding that there had been no gift or sale of the biscuit tin by the Russells. The court also concluded that Mr Russell had never abandoned the biscuit tin and 1£ notes, even though he seemed to have forgotten about them. By contrast with the court's conclusion, the defendant had argued that the court should conclude that the sale of the house should include a sale of "lost" property in it, so as to avoid the absurd result that the plaintiff would have no right to trespass to claim the chattel. The court declined to rule on this problem.

The problem of entering the land of another to recover a chattel, without the assistance of the legal process, is called "recaption." The right to recaption, at least in some cases, seems to permit a technical trespass to the land of another, so long as no damage is done to the land as a result. For a good overview of recaption, see Simmonds & Stewart, ch 8-10.

iii. Finders and Inappropriate Action: Weitzner v Herman

Reconsider the facts at the beginning of this section on possession and the rights of finders: how should the claims of the purchaser of the house, the contractor whose workers found the money, and the daughter of the previous owners be resolved? How do characterizations of "lost" and "abandoned" chattels affect the legal principles to be applied? In resolving the merits of these claims, consider the following case and its result.

An elderly widow in Stratford, Ontario sold the home in which she and her husband had lived for 40 years, and the purchaser hired a contractor to raze the property. In the course of the work, a fire extinguisher filled with $130,000 in old $50 and $100 bills was discovered. Initially, the purchaser and contractor decided to keep the money; they visited the widow in her retirement home and gave her some photos and other personal belongings found in the course of demolition, but they did not disclose that they had also discovered a large sum of money. However, the widow eventually heard about their discovery at the local hairdresser's when someone reported that about $12,000 had been found at her old home. The widow then requested a share, and the purchaser and the contractor agreed to hand over "one-third" of their find: $4,000. They asked her to sign a release saying that this amount represented full payment for any money found in or around the house.

In her subsequent litigation against them, the court held that the evidence clearly showed that the money belonged to the widow's husband: all the bills dated between the time when the couple moved into the house and the husband's death in 1989. As a result, the court ordered the purchaser to return $130,000 to the widow. In reaching this conclusion, the court decided that the "finders" had not behaved honestly in relation to the elderly widow. In light of this case, what advice would you give in relation to chattels that are found in the course of demolition and construction? See *Weitzner v Herman* (2000), 33 ETR (2d) 310 (Ont Sup Ct J) and Tracey Tyler, "Widow Wins Fight for Hidden Cash of Husband," *Toronto Star* (22 March 2000). In another case, a surviving spouse claimed entitlement to money found in a couch that she had sold after her husband died; according to the widow, her husband had a practice of stashing money away. The court held that she, and not the purchaser of the couch, was entitled to the money: see *Cranbrook (City) v Brown,* [1998] BCJ no 1144 (SC).

iv. AG of Canada v Brock

The issues of an accused's intention and the proper characterization of objects as "lost" or "abandoned" were canvassed in Canada in *AG of Canada v Brock* (1991), 67 CCC (3d) 131 (BC SC). Compare the approaches to these issues in the decisions at trial and on appeal. Which decision better reflects the legal principles? To what extent are the principles shaped by policy objectives?

A police officer stopped a car because of a minor traffic violation, and then arrested the driver because of discrepancies in the vehicle ownership and the driver's licence. When the car was searched, a bag containing nearly $300,000 in uncirculated US$100 and $50 bills was discovered. When questioned by the police, the driver denied any knowledge of the money. The next day, however, in the company of a lawyer, the driver made a claim to the sum of money "on behalf of offshore investors." A few weeks later, the driver was found dead as a result of cocaine overdose. The RCMP did not lay any further charges. Both the driver's estate and the municipality claimed the money.

At trial, MacDonell J held that the estate of the driver was entitled to the money. After reviewing numerous cases and particularly *Parker v British Airways Board*, MacDonell J held (at 140), referring to 35 Hals, 4th ed, para 1122:

> *Possession prima facie title.* The presumption of law is that the person who had *de facto* possession also has the property, and accordingly such possession is protected, whatever its origin, against all who cannot prove a superior title. This rule applies equally in criminal and civil matters. Thus, as against a stranger or a wrongdoer, a person in actual or apparent possession, but without the right to possession, has all the rights and remedies of a person entitled to and able to prove a present right to possession.

> In my opinion, an application of this principle to the facts of the case at bar results in a finding that Brock was in possession of the money at the moment he was pulled over. If he was aware of the hidden money, as I believe he was, in the absence of evidence to the contrary, the presumption is that he is the owner of that money. If he was unaware of its existence, the fact that it was concealed in a car lawfully owned by him would indicate that he was in *de facto* control and possession of the money and his right to title was superior to that of anyone other than the true owner.

The court then considered whether the money had been abandoned by Brock and held that it had clearly remained in his possession.

On appeal to the BC Court of Appeal, (1993), 83 CCC (3d) 200 (BCCA), Hinkson JA concluded that there was no (credible) evidence that the driver of the car was the owner of the money. Rather, the court held that the presumption of ownership relied on by MacDonell J was a rebuttable presumption and that it had been rebutted. The court stated (at 207):

> On this appeal the respondents did not contend that Brock was the owner of the money.
> Rather, the respondents relied upon the alternative conclusion reached by the chambers judge, namely, that Brock was in *de facto* possession of the money and hence his right to it was superior to that of the appellant.

The learned chambers judge said [at 142]:

> In conclusion, the case before the court is not one which involves the law of finding be-
> cause, on the facts, I do not believe the money was ever lost. The evidence indicates that,
> whether it was Brock who owned the money or whether he was merely holding it for
> others, it was Brock who hid the money and clearly had possession over it. The day follow-
> ing his release and without prompting, he was able to identify the quantity of money
> discovered and the manner in which it was packaged in two separate sums.

> If Brock was not the owner of the money, as I have concluded, then it is necessary to consider
> the respondents' claim that he had possession of the money at the time when the appellant
> found it and took it into its possession. Counsel referred to the leading cases in this field of the
> law, including *Bridges v. Hawkesworth* (1851), 21 LJQB 75, [1843-60] All ER 122 (QB); *South
> Staffordshire Water Co. v. Sharman*, [1896] 2 QB 44 (QB); *Corporation of London v. Appleyard*, [1963]
> 2 All ER 834 (QB); *Hannah v. Peel*, [1945] 2 All ER 288 (KB); *Bird v. Fort Frances*, [1949] 2 DLR 791,
> [1949] OR 292, [1949] OWN 223 (HJC); *Grafstein v. Holme & Freeman* (1958), 12 DLR (2d) 727,
> [1958] OR 296, [1958] OWN 161 (CA); *Kowal v. Ellis* (1977), 76 DLR (3d) 546, [1977] 2 WWR 761
> (Man. CA); *Parker v. British Airways Board*, [1982] 1 All ER 834 (CA).

> All of these decisions cannot be easily reconciled. Each turns on its own facts and each in-
> volves land rather than a chattel.

> In the present case the learned chambers judge relied upon the fact that Brock had posses-
> sion of his vehicle on January 18, 1990, and relying upon the land cases, concluded that he had
> possession of the contents of the vehicle whether or not he was aware of the contents.

> He went further and found that it was Brock who hid the money in the vehicle. The evidence
> does not support that conclusion. Rather the evidence indicates Brock did not know of the pres-
> ence of the money in his vehicle on that day. In my opinion, Brock did not have possession of the
> vehicle in a way that would entitle him to the money. Brock informed Detective Beatty that from
> time to time he loaned his vehicle to a buddy and that the last time was a couple of days before
> January 18, 1990. Thus, Brock was not exercising exclusive possession of the vehicle. He and
> others each used it independently.

According to the court, the evidence demonstrated that Brock was in possession of the
vehicle, but that he was not in possession of the money.

The BC Court of Appeal therefore allowed the appeal, and ordered the funds transferred
to the Corporation of the District of West Vancouver, noting that the Corporation must be
accountable should the "true owner" come forward and establish ownership. Is the court's
conclusion about Brock's absence of intention to exercise control in this case consistent with
that concerning Mr Russell in *Moffatt v Kazana*?

v. The Law of Finders and Treasure Trove

In relation to some kinds of chattels, especially those of historical significance, the intention
of the finder may be rendered irrelevant. For example, anyone who takes possession of a
wreck must deliver it to the government receiver of wrecks pursuant to the *Canada Shipping
Act, 2001*, SC 2001, c 26, s 155. There is also legislation concerning the log salvage industry in
British Columbia: see the *Forest Act*, RSBC 1996, c 157. The finding of treasure trove (cached
gold and silver in coin, bullion, or manufactured form) may also be subject to a claim by the

Crown: see NE Palmer, "Treasure Trove and the Protection of Antiquities" (1981) 44 Mod L Rev 178, and M June Harris, "Who Owns the Pot of Gold at the End of the Rainbow?" (1997) 14 Ariz J Int'l & Comp L 253.

As explained by Michael Nash in "Are Finders Keepers? One Hundred Years Since Elwes v Brigg Gas Co" (1987) 137 New LJ 118, the use of metal detectors in the field of archaeology and of sonar equipment in marine archaeology has created an urgent need for legislative regulation.

In reviewing the issues, Nash commented on *Elwes* (1886), 33 Ch D 562, a case decided using principles similar to those discussed in *Parker*. *Elwes* concerned the discovery in 1885 of a prehistoric boat, embedded in clay, by the lessee gas company in the course of its routine excavations. Both the lessee gas company and the landowner claimed a proprietary interest. The court considered many of the cases referred to in *Parker*, concluding that the lessor (the lord of the manor of Britt) had constructive possession of chattels, including the long-buried boat. According to the court, Elwes's awareness of the boat's existence was not necessary, and it was not part of the leasehold transferred to the gas company. For some years thereafter, Elwes exhibited the boat to the public in a specially constructed building and then later presented it to a museum in Hull. In 1943, it was destroyed in an air raid on the museum. For another comment on this case and the general problem of finders of such chattels, see PJ O'Keefe & Lyndal V Prott, *Law and the Cultural Heritage* (Abingdon, UK: Professional Books, 1984).

In Nova Scotia, the issue of treasure trove has particular significance. With an estimated 10,000 shipwrecks throughout the region, there are more underwater archaeological sites off the coast of Nova Scotia than in any other place in North America. Against this backdrop, the UNESCO Convention on the Protection of the Underwater Cultural Heritage pressed the province to create regulations that would stop this potentially harmful practice. Therefore, in 2010, Nova Scotia repealed its 1954 *Treasure Trove Act*, so that private treasure is now regulated by the pre-existing *Special Places Protection Act*, RSNS 1989, c 438, as amended by the *Oak Island Treasure Act*, SNS 2010, c 39, ss 14-15, legislation that requires explorers to hand over found artifacts to an appropriate museum or historical organization. In addition to these more comprehensive offshore regulations, the government's legislation is also meant to protect an important archaeological site in the province. Currently the home of a famous resort, Oak Island has long been the storied site of "pirate treasure," though nothing has been found in over two centuries of excavation. The new Act allows treasure-hunting parties to apply for excavation licences, licences that entitle them to keep a share of any treasure they might find.

To what extent do these regulatory arrangements alter the basic principles of possession in relation to lost objects? For more information about Nova Scotia's attempts to protect its underwater archaeological heritage, see: Natural Resources/Tourism, Culture and Heritage, "Changes to Treasure Hunting Regulations" (14 July 2010), online: Nova Scotia Canada <http://novascotia.ca/news/release/?id=20100714001>. For criticism of these government acts, see Katrina Pyre, "Treasure Pits Explorers Against Bureaucrats: Private Operators Say the Sea Will Destroy Nova Scotia's Shipwrecks Before the Government Gets Around to Salvaging Them," *The Globe and Mail* (4 May 2013) at A8.

D. Extinguishing the Rights of the True Owner

Extinguishment of an owner's rights to a chattel may occur where the owner has abandoned the chattel. In such a case, the finder's possessory interest (one which is good against all the world except the true owner) appears to be correspondingly more significant. For a case addressing the issue of when abandonment occurs, see *Simpson v Gowers* (1981), 32 OR (2d) 385 (CA). In addition to abandonment, provincial legislation, generically referred to as statutes of limitation, establishes time limits for bringing lawsuits. Thus, for example, the *Limitations Act*, RSO 1990, c L.15, as amended by SO 2002, c 24, Sched B, s 26, provides that an action (for example, against a finder with possession of a chattel belonging to a true owner) must be commenced by the person with title within two years after the claim arose. See also *Limitation of Actions Act*, RSNS 1989, c 258; *Limitation of Actions Act*, SNB 2009, c L-8.5; and *Statute of Limitations*, RSPEI 1988, c S-7.

Disposal of abandoned property

e usual problem is how to dispose of "lost property." In reviewing the *rt Act*, RSC 1985, c T-18, consider how and to what extent these regula- I the principles of possession in the law of finders.

Airport Personal Property Disposal Regulations
CRC, c 1563

Department of Transport Act

cting the Disposal of Personal Property Left at Airports

SHORT TITLE

1. These Regulations may be cited as the *Airport Personal Property Disposal Regulations*.

INTERPRETATION

2. In these Regulations,

"abandoned vehicle"

"abandoned vehicle" means a vehicle, other than a derelict vehicle, that has been abandoned at an airport or otherwise remains unclaimed at an airport for a period of not less than 30 days;

"airport"

"airport" means an airport or aerodrome under the administration and control of the Minister of Transport;

"Airport Manager"

"Airport Manager" means the Department of Transport official in charge of the airport or his duly authorized representative;

"Department"

"Department" means the Department of Transport;

"derelict vehicle"

"derelict vehicle" means a vehicle, other than an abandoned vehicle, that
    (a) has been abandoned at an airport or otherwise remains unclaimed at an airport for a period of not less than 14 days, and
    (b) has a market value less than $200;

"owner"

"owner," with respect to a motor vehicle, means a person who holds legal title to it or a person in whose name it is registered or is required to be registered by the laws of a province and includes a conditional purchaser, lessee or mortgagor who is entitled to or is in possession of the motor vehicle;

"personal property"

"personal property" means all property, other than a vehicle, not owned by Her Majesty;

"Regional Administrator"

"Regional Administrator" means the Regional Administrator, Canadian Air Transportation Administration, who has jurisdiction over the airport in question;

"vehicle"

"vehicle" means a self-powered device in, on or by which a person or property is or may be transported or drawn upon a road, except a device used exclusively on stationary rails or tracks.

PERSONAL PROPERTY

3. All personal property that has been lost or abandoned at an airport or that otherwise remains unclaimed at an airport shall, subject to reclamation by the owner thereof, be retained at the airport in the custody of the Airport Manager for a period of not less than 30 days and at the end of such period the Regional Administrator may dispose of that personal property, at his discretion, by one or more of the following methods:

    (a) by return to the finder, if the finder is not an employee of the Department;

    (b) by private sale or by sale at public auction;

    (c) by disposition, by gift or otherwise, to a charitable institution in Canada; or

    (d) by destruction where no other method of disposal is deemed appropriate.

ABANDONED VEHICLES

4(1) Every abandoned vehicle shall, subject to reclamation by the owner, be retained at the airport in the custody of the Airport Manager for a period of not less than 90 days.

(2) The Airport Manager shall, within the period referred to in subsection (1), send a notice by registered mail to the owner's latest known address or place of business advising that, if the vehicle is not claimed within 30 days of the date of such notice, the Regional Administrator may dispose of the vehicle by sale at public auction.

DERELICT VEHICLES

5(1) Any derelict vehicle shall, subject to reclamation by the owner, be retained at the airport in the custody of the Airport Manager for a period of not less than 30 days.

(2) The Airport Manager shall, within the period referred to in subsection (1), send a notice by registered mail to the owner's latest known address or place of business advising that, if the vehicle is not claimed within 20 days of the date of such notice, the Regional Administrator may dispose of the vehicle, at his discretion,

(a) by private sale;
(b) by sale at public auction; or
(c) by destruction.

DISPOSAL OF VEHICLES

6. Where a notice has been sent pursuant to subsection 4(2) or 5(2) and the vehicle is not claimed within the time specified in the notice, the Regional Administrator may dispose of the vehicle by a method specified in the notice.

PROCEEDS OF SALE

7. All proceeds realized from any sale pursuant to section 3, 4 or 5 shall be paid to the Receiver General.

DISCUSSION NOTES

i. The Disposition of "Found" Property in Airports

A loading supervisor for Air Canada found a packet of money on the floor in the cafeteria in the Dorval International Airport. He asked persons nearby whether the packet belonged to them, and when no one claimed it, he took it to the police. In his presence, the police counted the money in the packet, which held $10,000 in US$100 bills. The police officer gave the finder a receipt, telling him that if the bills were not claimed within three months, they would be returned to him; the receipt noted the date of finding and the date when the money could be returned. When the money was not claimed, the finder requested that it be handed over to him, but the airport refused, relying on s 3 of the *Department of Transport Act*, above. The regional administrator distributed most of the funds to charity, but offered the finder a reward of CAN$1,500. The finder rejected the reward and sued for the total amount of the funds CAN$12,330. How should the finder's claim be resolved?

In *Senecal v The Queen*, [1984] 1 FC 169, 3 DLR (4th) 684 (TD), the court rejected the claimant's argument that some of the charities that received donations from the regional administrator were not valid charities pursuant to the *Income Tax Act*, and focused more significantly on the finder's claim that s 3 of the Regulations provided too much discretion to the regional administrator (and were thus *ultra vires* according to the principles of administrative law).

After reviewing jurisprudence and case law, however, the court held (at para 14) that the regional administrator's decision to offer the finder $1,500 of the total amount of $12,330 "did not appear to be so shockingly low as to justify the Court in interfering with the valid exercise of his administrative discretion." The court also reviewed the provisions of the *Civil Code* and concluded that they did not create any entitlement in the finder. As well, the court rejected the argument that s 3 of the Regulations should be applied consecutively. The court thus dismissed the finder's claim. However, in light of the fact that the case raised new issues for determination, the court did not award costs.

To what extent do the Regulations respecting property found in airports in Canada affect the precedential value of *Parker v British Airways Board*? Do you prefer the outcome in *Parker* or that in *Senecal*? If you were asked to revise the Regulations concerning lost property in Canadian airports to achieve a different balance between the rights of the finder and the discretion of the airport administrators, how would you draft new Regulations?

ii. Finders' Rights and Rules About Lost Property

In 1983, the *Toronto Star* reported that a 16-year-old orphan in Florida found a bag of jewels alongside a railway track while playing hooky from school. He assumed that the jewels were costume jewellery and showed them off to other students and teachers at school until his aunt persuaded him to turn them over to police. The relevant police regulations provided that a person was entitled to claim found chattels if the owner had not appeared within 180 days. Thus, 183 days after finding the jewels, the young orphan received the jewellery, which was worth $1.3 million. The newspaper article declared "Honesty Does Pay," *Toronto Star* (21 September 1983) A19. For similar "lost property" arrangements of the TTC in Toronto, see Toronto Transit Commission <http://www.ttc.ca>.

III. POSSESSION IN RELATION TO LAND

A. "Possession" as a Property Interest in Land: "Possessory Title"

In 1907, a case was presented to the Judicial Committee of the Privy Council (JCPC) on appeal from the High Court of Australia. At issue was whether the plaintiffs, as trustees of the will of Frederick Clissold, could establish a *prima facie* case for compensation. The claim for compensation related to land resumed—that is, expropriated—by the state government for a public school site in 1891. At that time, the land was in the possession of Frederick Clissold, who had enclosed and fenced it in 1881 and been exclusively in possession of the land from that date until his death, which occurred just after the land was resumed by the state government. Clissold had leased the land to various tenants and, according to the official records of the municipalities, had regularly paid rates and taxes.

Assuming that the legislation provided for compensation to be paid to a claimant in respect of an interest in land, should this claim on behalf of Frederick Clissold have succeeded? On what basis? What is the legal principle applicable? In thinking about these facts, what is the relevance of the "true owner" to your analysis of Clissold's entitlement?

In *Perry v Clissold*, [1907] AC 73 (PC), the state government argued in the Privy Council that Clissold was "a mere trespasser, without any estate or interest in the land." The members of the JCPC disagreed, stating (at 79):

> It cannot be disputed that a person in possession of land in the assumed character of owner and exercising peaceably the ordinary rights of ownership has a perfectly good title against all the world but the rightful owner.

In the context of claims relating to land, Clissold had possessory title. Note the similarity in the conclusion of the Privy Council in Clissold's case to the reasoning in *Armory v Delamirie* with respect to the lost jewel. Clearly, the principles applied to claims about possession seem similar, whether the proprietary interest relates to chattels or to land. Yet, in a modern context, there may be good reasons to differentiate between a finder of a lost object, and a squatter's right to possession of land. For example, property interests in land are normally registered so that it is not difficult to know who holds title—although such a registration system may not have been fully in place in Australia in the early 20th century when Clissold enclosed his land.

Nonetheless, principles about possession of land, and the creation of possessory title—that is, title based on possession—remain part of real property law in the 21st century. This section first examines the history of possession in relation to land at common law, as well as some of the justifications for retaining possession as the basis for claiming title to land. The materials also examine how common law principles have been augmented by statutory provisions that must also be taken into account in relation to claims of possessory title. As will be seen, courts have attempted to deal with these principles in a variety of factual contexts, so that the application of principles about possessory title requires careful attention to facts and the interpretation of statutory language.

DISCUSSION NOTES

i. The (Medieval) History of Claims to "Possessory Title": Asher v Whitlock

After enclosing an unused plot of land belonging to a large manor and then residing there for more than 20 years, Thomas Williamson devised all of this land and the cottage he had built on it to his wife, Lucy Williamson. The will allowed the wife to take ownership of the property for as long as she lived, or until she remarried. In case of either occurrence, the property would go to their daughter, Mary Ann Williamson. Lucy remarried soon after Thomas's death, and then tragically—within the span of only a few months—both Lucy and Mary Ann died. Lucy's second husband continued to live in the Williamson cottage after these deaths.

Asher v Whitlock, [1865] LR 1 (QB) involved an attempt by Lucy's granddaughter (Mary Ann's daughter) to eject Lucy's second husband from the property. Essentially, the granddaughter argued that her grandfather's possessory interest in the land was first willed to her grandmother (Lucy), then transferred to her mother (Mary Ann) at the moment of the second marriage. As the heir-at-law of Lucy and Mary Ann, the granddaughter claimed she was entitled to her mother's interest in the property. However, Lucy's second husband argued that Thomas Williamson had never gained any proprietary interest in the land he had fenced in all those years ago, and so there was no interest that could have been devised to Lucy and then to her daughter.

Clearly, the issue was whether Thomas Williamson had an interest in the land (based on his possession of it) that was capable of being devised. In finding that Thomas Williamson had established a possessory title, which could be transferred by will, the court concluded that Lucy's granddaughter (rather than her second husband) was entitled to the land. As Chief Justice Cockburn stated:

> Here the widow was a prior devisee, but *durante viduitate* only, and as soon as the testator died, the estate became vested in the widow; and immediately on the widow's marriage the daughter had a right to possession; the defendant however anticipates her, and with the widow takes possession. But just as he had no right to interfere with the testator, so he had no right against the daughter, and had she lived she could have brought ejectment; although she died without asserting her right, the same right belongs to her heir …. On the simple ground that possession is good title against all but the true owner, I think the plaintiffs entitled to succeed.

Justice Mellor agreed with Cockburn CJ's final ruling, but by way of a subtly different line of reasoning. Basically, the judgment of Cockburn CJ (above) formulated the principle in the context of a possessory claim to land in the same way that the principle was stated in relation to finders of lost objects—that is, possession is good title against all but the true owner or someone claiming prior possession. By contrast, Mellor J stated that "the fact of possession is *prima facie* evidence of seisin in fee," a statement that seems to suggest that possession is merely *evidence* of seisin (see the paragraph below for an explanation of "seisin"), and that seisin was the basis for the plaintiff's entitlement to succeed in *Asher v Whitlock*. This formulation was regarded by some scholars as more accurate: see AD Hargreaves, "Terminology and Title in Ejectment" (1940) 56 Law Q Rev 376 [Hargreaves].

To understand the difference in the approaches of Cockburn CJ and Mellor J, the historical development of principles about possession needs to be explained. First of all, in the medieval period, few people could read or write and thus there were often few records of land ownership or title. In this context, the concept of "seisin" in early land law—that is, from about the 15th century—described the special nature of the possessory entitlement of an "owner" to land or real property. Not all persons "in possession" of land had seisin, the clearest example being the leaseholder or tenant who (according to historical principles) had "possession" but not "seisin." Entitlement to seisin was important in a context where procedural rights to recover land after being dispossessed depended on whether a claimant could show seisin prior to dispossession. Moreover, a transfer of an interest in land required a transfer of seisin, accomplished in medieval times by the ceremony of "livery of seisin," in which the grantor and the grantee stood together on the land to be conveyed. In the presence of witnesses, the grantor symbolically delivered seisin to the grantee by handing him a twig or handful of sod, while at the same time expressing appropriate words of transfer (a process discussed in Chapter 3).

According to K Gray & P Symes, *Real Property and Real People* (London: Butterworths, 1981) at 48-49:

> Seisin thus expressed the organic element in the relationship between man [*sic*] and land and as such provided presumptive evidence of ownership within the medieval framework of rights in land. Furthermore it was only the person seised of the land who could avail himself of an owner's rights in respect of the land.

Gray & Symes suggested that the concept of seisin significantly influenced the development of common law property principles, particularly the emphasis on rights flowing from factual possession, by contrast with abstract title. For a detailed analysis of the nature and development of the concept of seisin in English common law, see the classic studies by FW

Maitland: "The Mystery of Seisin" (1886) 2 Law Q Rev 481; "The Beatitude of Seisin: I" (1888) 4 Law Q Rev 24; and "The Beatitude of Seisin: II" (1888) 4 Law Q Rev 286.

In addition to the concept of seisin, it is important to understand how the procedural arrangements for recovering land after dispossession influenced common law principles relating to possession of land. Briefly, the early common law was characterized by highly technical "forms of action," and claims could be brought *only* in accordance with these technical, formalized processes. Inevitably, because the facts of individual claims differed widely from the formal actions available, the processes were often characterized by "fictions" as well. For more details about the forms of action at common law in this context, see JH Baker, *An Introduction to English Legal History*, 3d ed (London: Butterworths, 1990).

ii. The Jus Tertii Issue: Perry v Clissold

In *Perry v Clissold*, [1907] AC 73 (PC), the Privy Council also addressed the *jus tertii* issue—that is, the issue of whether the existence of a better claim by someone other than the plaintiff would defeat the plaintiff's claim against the defendant. The Privy Council rejected this argument, relying on the decision in *Asher v Whitlock*:

> Their Lordships are of opinion that it is impossible to say that no prima facie case for compensation has been disclosed.
>
> They do not think that a case for compensation is necessarily excluded by the circumstance that under the provisions of the Act of 1900 the Minister acquired not merely the title of the person in possession as owner, but also the title, whatever it may have been, of the rightful owner out of possession, who never came forward to claim the land or the compensation payable in respect of it, and who is, as the Chief Justice says, "unknown to this day."
>
> The Act throughout from the very preamble has it apparently in contemplation that compensation would be payable to every person deprived of the land resumed for public purposes ... . Even where the true owner, after diligent inquiry, cannot be found the Act contemplates payment of compensation into Court to be dealt with by a Court of Equity.

Although the court's analysis of the *jus tertii* plea was criticized by SA Wiren in "The Plea of Jus Tertii in Ejectment" (1925) 41 Law Q Rev 139, the accepted view now seems to be that the principle adopted in *Perry v Clissold* is the better view: see Hargreaves.

iii. Remedies for Recovering Possession of Land

In *Asher v Whitlock*, the plaintiff initiated legal action in ejectment as a means of recovering possession. Today, a similar legal action may be launched in Ontario through the *Rules of Civil Procedure*, RRO 1990, Reg 194, r 60.03: "An order for the recovery or delivery of the possession of land may be enforced by a writ of possession (Form 60C)." Form 60C instructs the local sheriff to take possession of the disputed lands so that they can be handed over to the plaintiff.

At common law, plaintiffs also have the alternative option of self-help—that is, a physical retaking of possession. However, this remedy is not encouraged by courts. For example, the UK Court of Appeal only tentatively allowed self-help remedies in *McPhail v Persons Unknown*, [1973] 3 All ER 393 (CA), while the Supreme Court of New York was less willing to endorse it in *City of New York v Utsey*, 714 NYS 2d 410 (2000).

iv. Possession and Aboriginal Title to Land

The idea of possession of land as the basis for a legally recognized claim is especially significant for Aboriginal land claims in North America. When Europeans first arrived in North
America, indigenous peoples were already occupying much of the territory that is now Canada and the United States (as well as Central and South America). In this situation, what
claims to "possessory title" existed for First Nations in Canada?

As explained in greater detail in Chapter 8, relationships between First Nations and the
British Crown evolved over several centuries. However, in cases before the Supreme Court of
Canada in the last decades of the 20th century, the court recognized a *sui generis* Aboriginal
interest in land: see *Guerin v The Queen*, [1984] 2 SCR 335, and *Delgamuukw v British Columbia*,
[1997] 3 SCR 1010 (discussed in Chapter 8). Prior to these decisions, however, title to land for
First Nations was a contested concept. As Kent McNeil has argued, part of the problem was
the assumption that British sovereignty in what is now Canada (at the conclusion of the Seven
Years War in 1759-1760) included title to land as well as sovereignty. As McNeil explained:

> [I]t must be remembered that at the time a territory was made British by settlement, the other
> principal claimant to lands occupied by indigenous people would be the Crown. Act of state apart,
> the Crown's claim could be based only on English law. Surely one cannot seriously argue that
> English law would apply to give title to the Crown, while at the same time denying the benefit of
> that law to the people who were actually on the land, using and occupying it as their ancestors
> had done for generations … . [In this context, this argument] proposes a return to fundamental
> common law principles [about possession]. … [I]f the conclusions reached in this book are correct,
> and by English law a right to fee simple estates did vest in indigenous occupiers, then (statutory
> bars aside) no one can contend that it is too late to declare the law, and enforce the right.

(See McNeil at 298
ff.) Significantly, McNeil also noted that present-day holders of Aboriginal lands that may
have been taken unlawfully are protected by registration systems and statutes of limitation.
At the same time, he recognized that issues of Aboriginal title to lands involve not just legal
rights but also economic, sociological, and other factors, so that just solutions to these issues
require compromise achieved through negotiation. Nonetheless, McNeil also argued that
establishing a clear legal right on the part of First Nations with respect to possessory interests would enhance the bargaining position of First Nations in these land claims
negotiations.

For a comparative analysis of Aboriginal land claims in Canada, Australia, and New Zealand, see K Hazlehurst, ed, *Legal Pluralism and the Colonial Legacy* (Aldershot, UK: Avebury,
1995), and J McLaren, AR Buck & N Wright, eds, *Despotic Dominion: Property Rights in British
Settler Societies* (Vancouver: UBC Press, 2005). See also K McNeil, "The Meaning of Aboriginal
Title" in M Asch, ed, *Aboriginal and Treaty Rights in Canada: Essays on Law, Equality and Respect
for Difference* (Vancouver: University of British Columbia Press, 1997) at 135. The Report of the
Royal Commission on Aboriginal Peoples expressly noted that Aboriginal peoples had "occupied specific territories and had systems of tenure, access and resource conservation that
amounted to ownership and governance—although those systems were not readily understood by Europeans, in part because of language and cultural differences": see Report of the
Royal Commission on Aboriginal Peoples, *Restructuring the Relationship*, vol 2, part 2 (Ottawa:
Minister of Supply and Services Canada, 1996) at 452.

B. Common Law Possession, Statutes of Limitation, and "Possessory Title"

1. Statutes of Limitation: History and Purposes

Statutes of limitation define the relationship between a person with an interest based on possession and the person who is the "true owner" (the person with "paper title"). The common law's historical emphasis on physical possession rather than "abstract title," and its insistence on the idea of relativity of title rather than absolute ownership, meant that a person with a possession-based interest was accorded the benefit of some legal protection and recognition (*Clissold*). Statutes of limitation built on this common law foundation of possessory title by providing that the right of the paper titleholder to bring an action to recover possession (against someone claiming entitlement by possession) did not last forever. At present, this right of the paper titleholder is limited to the period of time defined in the statutes of limitation in each province. Thus, for example, a paper titleholder (the true owner) in Ontario must bring an action to recover possession of land within 10 years after the possessory interest was established—for example, by a squatter. According to s 15 of the *Real Property Limitations Act*, RSO 1990, c L.15 (renamed by the *Limitations Act*, SO 2002, c 24, Sched B, s 26):

> 15. At the determination of the period limited by this Act to any person for making an entry or distress or bringing any action, the right and title of such person to the land or rent, for the recovery whereof such entry, distress or action, respectively, might have been made or brought within such period, is extinguished.

For comparable provisions, see *Limitation of Actions Act*, RSNS 1989, c 258, s 22; *Limitations of Actions Act*, SNB 2011, c 17, s 8; *Statute of Limitations Act*, RSPEI 1988, c S-7, s 26; and *Limitations Act*, SNL 1995, c L-16.1, s 17.

Section 15 of the *Real Property Limitations Act* provides for the extinguishment of the paper titleholder's right to bring an action to recover possession. It does *not* transfer the paper titleholder's title to the possessor. In the context of the common law's concept of relativity of title, however, it means that the possessor's interest may be less vulnerable because the true owner's interest is no longer enforceable. Yet the strength of the possessor's title in relation to other claims still depends on the nature of the possessory claim. In this way, the statutes of limitation simply add to the common law principles by defining time limits within which the paper titleholder must take action in order to preserve the relative priority of his or her claim.

The statutes of limitation also define the required time period within which the paper titleholder must initiate an action to recover possession and when the time period commences—that is, when time begins to run against the paper titleholder. For example, the Ontario *Real Property Limitations Act*, ss 4 and 5(1) provide:

> 4. No person shall make an entry or distress, or bring an action to recover any land or rent, but within ten years next after the time at which the right to make such entry or distress, or to bring such action, first accrued to some person through whom the person making or bringing it claims, or if the right did not accrue to any person through whom that person claims, then within ten years next after the time at which the right to make such entry or distress, or to bring such action, first accrued to the person making or bringing it.
>
> 5(1) *Where the person claiming such land* or rent, or some person through whom that person claims, *has, in respect of the estate or interest claimed, been in possession* or in receipt of the profits

of the land, or in receipt of the rent, *and has, while entitled thereto, been dispossessed, or has discontinued such possession* or receipt, *the right to* make an entry or distress or *bring an action to recover the land* or rent *shall be deemed to have first accrued at the time of the dispossession or discontinuance of possession*, or at the last time at which any such profits or rent were so received.

(Emphasis added.) The language of the statute is difficult, reflecting its historical origins, but by reading the emphasized words, it is possible to summarize the statutory principles, as follows:

s 4:   A person (who has a prior claim, including a "true owner") shall bring an action to recover land within 10 years after the right to bring such an action accrued to the person. (Note that the period in which an action to recover possession must be instituted differs from province to province; in Nova Scotia, for example, the limitation period is 20 years.)

s 5(1): Where the person claiming an interest in land was formerly in possession and was dispossessed *or* has discontinued possession, the right to bring an action to recover the land shall be deemed to have accrued at the time of the dispossession *or* discontinuance of possession.

Taking this formulation as a starting point, it is clear that it is necessary to define exactly what acts constitute "dispossession or discontinuance of possession" in order to define the moment when the limitation period begins to run. There may also be an issue about what acts are sufficient to qualify as "dispossession or discontinuance" of possession. Some of the judicial decisions in this chapter reflect differing views about how to interpret these provisions.

The decision in *Perry v Clissold* referred briefly to this issue of statutory bars to recover possession—that is, whether the true owner's right to recover possession from Frederick Clissold might have become barred by the effluxion of time:

It cannot be disputed that a person in possession of land in the assumed character of owner and exercising peaceably the ordinary rights of ownership has a perfectly good title against all the world but the rightful owner. And if the rightful owner does not come forward and assert his title by process of law within the period prescribed by the provisions of the Statute of Limitations applicable to the case, his [*sic*] right is forever extinguished, and the possessory owner acquires an absolute title (at 79).

Examine this statement closely. Can you define the rationale for the decision? Obviously, in circumstances where the true owner's interest is subsequently barred as a result of the passing of the limitation period, the *jus tertii* argument will be unavailable. This issue concerns the interpretation of legislation—for example, Ontario's *Real Property Limitations Act*, s 26(2)—and is sometimes referred to as the problem of "adverse possession." This chapter, however, refers to this issue as one of "possessory title," a phrase that is more accurate in relation to current legislation.

Statutes of limitation usually contain provisions relating to other legal claims, in addition to those concerned with the recovery of land. For example, such statutes may define the periods within which actions in contract or tort must be commenced. In Ontario, a new limitations act took effect on January 1, 2004: the *Limitations Act, 2000*, SO 2002, c 24. The statute introduced a uniform period of two years within which claims can be commenced (s 4), although there are some exceptions. In addition, although s 26 of the statute substantially repealed Parts II and III of the former *Limitations Act*, it did not affect Part I, which was renamed the *Real Property Limitations Act*: see s 26(2). Thus, for the purposes of a discussion of interests based on possession of land, the provisions of Part I of the former *Limitations Act* remain effective as the *Real Property Limitations Act*, and subsequent references focus on this legislation. The reform of limitations was initiated in Ontario in 1977: see "Discussion Draft on Proposed Limitations Act (1977)" (Toronto: Ministry of the Attorney General, 1977). For an overview of the changes in 2002, see Brian Bucknall, "Limitations Act, 2002 and Real Property Limitations Act: Some Notes on Interpretive Issues" (2004) 29 Advocates' Q 1.

Note that registration statutes may disallow claims of possessory title on land that the original owner has registered, regardless of how much time has passed. An example of this legislation is Ontario's *Land Titles Act*, RSO 1990, c L.5, s 51. However, Nova Scotia's *Land Registration Act*, SNS 2001, c 6, seems to preserve some limited claims to possessory title after registration, and the impact of registration on possessory title varies from province to province.

In thinking about the purposes of legal recognition of possessory title, and the statutes that extinguish the title of the true owner after the expiration of the limitation period, consider another excerpt from Carol Rose's article "Possession as the Origin of Property." In this excerpt, Rose examines the relationship between theories of possessory rights and the operation of statutes of limitation, focusing on the case of *Brumagim v Bradshaw*, 39 Cal 24 (1870).

Carol Rose, "Possession as the Origin of Property"
(1985) 52 U Chicago L Rev 73 at 77-82 (footnotes omitted)

Brumagim v. Bradshaw involved two claimants to a considerable amount of land that had become, by the time the litigation was brought, the residential and commercial Potrero district of San Francisco. Each party claimed ownership of the land through a title extending back to an original "possessor" of the land, and the issue was whether the first of these purported possessors, one George Treat, had really "possessed" the land at all. If he had not, his successors in interest could not claim ownership through him, and title would go to those claiming through a later "first possessor."

Those who claimed through Treat put a number of facts before the jury to establish his original possession. They noted particularly that Treat had repaired a fence across the neck of the Potrero peninsula—to which the other side rejoined that outsiders could still land in boats, and that, in any event, there was a gap in the fence. The Treat claimants also alleged that Treat had made use of the land by pasturing livestock on it—though the other side argued that the land had not been suitable for cattle even then, because San Francisco was expanding in that direction. The court ruled that the jury should decide whether Treat's acts gave sufficient notice to the public that he had appropriated the property. If so, he had "possessed" it and could pass it on as an owner.

This instruction would seem to come down clearly on the side of the "clear act" theory of possession. Yet that theory seems to leave out some elements of the evidence. The fence question, to be sure, bore on whether Treat's acts informed the public of his claim. But the parties' arguments over whether Treat's use was "suitable" seemed to reflect concern over an aim of rewarding useful labor. If suitable use were a relevant issue, why did the court's jury instruction ignore the value of rewarding labor?

The answer to this question may well be that suitable use is also a form of notice. If outsiders would think that a large area near a growing city was abandoned because it was vacant except for a few cows, they might enter on the land and claim some prime water-front footage for themselves. In other words, if the use that Treat made was unsuitable, his use would not give notice of his claim to others. Thus, to ask whether Treat used the land suitably is just another way of asking whether he informed others of his claim, particularly those others who might have been interested in buying the land from Treat or settling it for themselves. Society is worst off in a world of vague claims; if no one knows whether he can safely use the land, or from whom he should buy it if it is already claimed, the land may end up being used by too many people or by none at all.

Possession now begins to look even more like something that requires a kind of communication, and the original claim to the property looks like a kind of speech, with the audience composed of all others who might be interested in claiming the object in question. Moreover, some venerable statutory law obligates the acquiring party to *keep on* speaking, lest he lose his title by "adverse possession."

Adverse possession is a common law interpretation of statutes of limitation for actions to recover real property. Suppose I own a lot in the mountains, and some stranger to me, without my permission, builds a house on it, clears the woods, and farms the lot continuously for a given period, say twenty years. During that time, I am entitled to go to court to force him off the lot. But if I have not done so at the end of twenty years, or some other period fixed by statute, not only can I not sue him for recovery of what was my land, but the law recognizes him as the title owner. ...

Here again we seem to have an example of a reward to the useful laborer at the expense of the sluggard. But the doctrine is susceptible to another interpretation as well; it might be designed, not to reward the useful laborer, but to require the owner to assert her right publicly. It requires her to make it clear that she, and not the trespasser, is the person to deal with if anyone should wish to buy the property or use some portion of it.

Courts have devoted much attention to the elements of a successful claim of adverse possession. Is grazing livestock a continuous use, so as to entitle the livestock owner to claim full ownership of the pasture as an adverse possessor? How about farming (where intensive use may be merely seasonal) or taking care of a lawn? Is a cave that encroaches deep under my land something that is obvious to me, so that I should be required to kick out the trespasser who operates it as a commercial attraction? No matter how much the doctrine of adverse possession seems to reward the one who performs useful labor on land at the expense of the lazy owner who does nothing, the crucial element in all these situations is, once again, communication. "Possession" means acts that "apprise the community[,] ... arrest attention, and put others claiming title upon inquiry."

In Illinois, for example, an adverse possessor may establish his claim merely by paying taxes on the property, at least against an owner who is familiar with real estate practice and records. Why is this? Naturally the community likes to have taxes paid and is favorably disposed toward one who pays them. But more important, payment of taxes is a matter of public record, and the owner whose taxes are paid by someone else should be aware that something peculiar is happening. Just as important, the *public* is very likely to view the taxpayer as the owner. If someone is paying taxes on my vacant lot or empty house, any third person who wants to buy the house is very likely to think that the tax-payer is the owner because people do not ordinarily pay taxes on land they do not own.

If I want to keep my land, the burden is upon me to correct the misimpression. The possibility of transferring titles through adverse possession once again serves to ensure that members of the public can rely upon their own reasonable perceptions, and an owner who fails to correct misleading appearances may find his title lost to one who speaks loudly and clearly, though erroneously.

Possession as the basis of property ownership, then, seems to amount to something like yelling loudly enough to all who may be interested. The first to say, "This is mine," in a way that the public understands, gets the prize, and the law will help him keep it against someone else who says, "No, it is *mine.*" But if the original communicator dallies too long and allows the public to believe the interloper, he will find the interloper has stepped into his shoes and has become the owner.

Similar ideas of the importance of communication, or as it is more commonly called, "notice," are implicit in our recording statutes and in a variety of other devices that force a property claimant to make a public record of her claims on pain of losing them altogether. Indeed, notice plays a part in the most mundane property-like claims to things that the law does not even recognize as capable of being reduced to ownership. "Would you please save my place?" one says to one's neighbor in the movie line, in order to ensure that others in line know that one is coming back and not relinquishing one's claim. In my home town of Chicago, one may choose to shovel the snow from a parking place on the street, but in order to establish a claim to it one must put a chair or some other object in the cleared space. The useful act of shovelling snow does not speak as unambiguously as the presence of an object that blocks entry.

Why, then, is it so important that property owners make and keep their communications clear? Economists have an answer: clear titles facilitate trade and minimize resource-wasting conflict. If I am careless about who comes on to a corner of my property, I invite others to make mistakes and to waste their labor on improvements to what I have allowed them to think is theirs. I thus invite a free-for-all over my ambiguously held claims, and I encourage contention, insecurity, and litigation—all of which waste everyone's time and energy and may result in overuse or under use of resources. But if I keep my property claims clear, others will know that they should deal with me directly if they want to use my property. We can bargain rather than fight; through trade, all items will come to rest in the hands of those who value them most. If property lines are clear, then, anyone who can make better use of my property than I can will buy or rent it from me and turn the property to his better use. In short, we will all be richer when property claims are unᵉquivocal, because that unequivocal status enables property to be traded and used at its highest value.

DISCUSSION NOTE

Underlying Justifications for Possession as Title (and Statutes of Limitation)

The common law's historical focus on physical possession—recall the ceremony of livery of seisin, for example—may provide an explanation for statutes of limitation and their limiting of rights of true owners. In earlier centuries when records about interests in land were often non-existent or unreliable, the common law's protection of a person in actual possession may have been perfectly reasonable. Certainly by the late 20th century, however, when sophisticated electronic land-registry systems were becoming widespread, it is more difficult to explain why legal principles should continue to protect squatters' rights at the expense of the interests of the paper titleholder. Indeed, this issue raises numerous questions about the modern relationship between "owners" of land and resources and the rights of "users" of land. Should the law protect the rights of someone who owns land and who makes no use of it, especially when others have been using it for productive purposes, or may wish to do so?

As Rose argued, limitations statutes require owners of land to be vigilant about their interests as a means of ensuring clear titles to facilitate trade and minimize conflict. Others have also identified rationales to justify the underlying principles of statutes of limitation and the barring of the rights of action of "true owners." For example, Charles Callaghan examined three such justifications:

- The first possible rationale suggests that the law is punishing the owner for neglect in relation to the land, a theory rejected by Callaghan because punishment is the business of criminal law and should have no place in the context of statutes of limitations.
- The second possible rationale focuses on how limitation statutes serve to encourage the use of land by "rewarding" the active use of the possessor (rather than punishing the paper titleholder). In Callaghan's view, this justification begs the question whether we need to encourage the use of land and, even if one agrees with this view, whether statutes of limitation represent an effective means of accomplishing this purpose.
- Rejecting these two justifications, Callaghan conceded some validity to a third justification, the "clearing of title to land," a purpose identified in the opening words of the first Statute of Limitations in 1623—"For quieting of men's estates." As Callaghan admitted, a public registry of interests in land may not always be exactly in accord with what has occurred "on the ground." There may be a need for some legal means of "curing" titles, so that registered descriptions of parcels of land are congruent with the actual or "on the ground" location of boundary fences (see C Callaghan, *Adverse Possession* (Columbus, OH: State University Press, 1961) at 87ff).

What are the underlying concerns being addressed by the justifications proposed by Rose and Callaghan? Are all these justifications equally consistent with possessory claims that may occur in different fact situations? For example, should there be different justifications if the possessor acts innocently, negligently, or intentionally? That is, do these rationales "justify" the possessory claims of trespassers who assert "squatters' rights," as well as claims on the part of possessors who are just mistaken about their boundaries?

These questions are important because, as the cases below reveal, judicial interpretation of the plain words in statutes of limitation appears to have added an element of intention, and these judicial developments are sometimes explained by commentators in terms of underlying policies and purposes—for example, see Thomas Merrill, "Property Rules, Liability Rules, and Adverse Possession" (1985) 79 Nw UL Rev 1122 [Merrill].

This area of property law thus requires an understanding of common law principles of possession, the impact of statutory reform, and subsequent interpretation of the statutes by judges. The complex relationships among these principles may be better understood in the context of the underlying purposes of recognizing possession as a proprietary interest, as proposed by Rose and Callaghan. Keep their suggestions in mind when considering the cases that follow.

2. Acts of "Possession" and the Statutory Commencement of the Limitation Period

The cases that follow address a number of different aspects of possessory title. For example, it is important to define when the limitation period starts to run (the commencement of the limitation period, ss 4 and 5 of the *Real Property Limitations Act*), the quality of possession required for the running of the limitation period, and the relevance of intention on the part of both the possessor and the paper titleholder. Although these different issues sometimes overlap in the cases that follow, try to identify how these principles are applied in different kinds of fact situations. As will be apparent, moreover, the principles have been evolving in Ontario cases in recent decades, raising issues about the need for reform. Thus, the material also includes some information about recent reform legislation in England, one possible reform model.

This section focuses first on the test for determining when an action to recover possession commences and the nature of possessory actions that may trigger the beginning of the limitation period (that is, ss 4 and 5 of the *Real Property Limitations Act*). As noted earlier, these sections necessitate an inquiry to define exactly what acts constitute "dispossession or discontinuance of possession" in order to define the moment when the 10-year limitation period begins to run.

In thinking about these statutory provisions, consider the following fact situation. In September 1901, Ms Piper arranged for the fencing of six lots of land that she had purchased. In constructing the fence, it seems that she enclosed (apparently by mistake) not only these six lots but also two adjoining lots to which her neighbour claimed title. The eight lots enclosed by Ms Piper formed a block and were completely enclosed by her fences from September 1901 until her neighbour brought an action for trespass against her in June 1912. In the intervening years, Ms Piper had ensured that the eight lots were ploughed as one block, fertilized by manure, and sown and harvested. In 1905 and 1906, buildings were erected and Ms Piper moved in, continuously residing there to the time the suit commenced in 1912. Assuming that Ms Piper did not have title to the two extra lots, did her actions constitute "dispossession" pursuant to the *Limitations Act*? Which of her actions is determinative? Would it have been sufficient just to fence in the two extra lots? Also, was her farming activity necessary? Was it necessary for her to erect buildings and live there?

In *Piper v Stevenson* (1913), 28 OR 379 (AD), the trial judge concluded (at 382) that "until 1906 everything was done upon the land that an owner could do in reaping the full benefit of it; and since the spring of that year, everything was done that an owner in actual, constant occupation would do," thereby holding that Ms Piper had dispossessed her neighbour in 1901. Her actions constituted dispossession according to s 5(1) and the limitation period had thus commenced in September 1901, expiring 10 years later and prior to her neighbour's lawsuit in June 1912. The appeal was also dismissed, with Clute J commenting on the arguments presented against Ms Piper's entitlement and concluding (at 383) that "[she had] fenced them in, in September 1901; and her possession of them and of the land in question was continuous and exclusive from the date of fencing." In thinking about the judicial interpretation of ss 4 and 5(1) of Ontario's *Limitations Act*, consider the similarities and differences between *Piper v Stevenson* and *Re St Clair Beach Estates Ltd v MacDonald*, which follows. Is the judicial formulation of the test in the Ontario statute the same in both cases?

A.P. er llant
Appellant

Re St Clair Beach Estates Ltd v MacDonald
(1974), 5 OR (2d) 482 (H Ct J Div Ct)

[In this case, the St Clair Beach Estates Ltd wished to register a parcel of land (purchased from a previous owner, Mrs Grant) pursuant to the *Land Titles Act* in Ontario. As noted earlier, one effect of registering title pursuant to the *Land Titles Act* is that no claims of possessory title can then be recognized. It seems that the MacDonalds, adjoining neighbours of Mrs Grant, had used a portion of land to which Mrs. Grant held title, apparently without objection by Mrs Grant. Thus, when they received the required notice about the conversion of the title to their adjoining land, the MacDonalds initiated a claim of possessory title to the portion of the land that they had used for some years. The claim was dismissed by the deputy director of titles and also in a trial *de novo*; the MacDonalds then appealed. The land formed part of Gore Lot, West of Pike Creek, in the Village of St Clair Beach, County of Essex.]

PENNELL J: Issue
[The question to be determined is whether the appellants have established their claim to a possessory title of the land in question. Possession is a matter of fact depending on all the particular circumstances of the case. Therefore, I start from the facts as to which there is no dispute. Those facts, compendiously stated, are as follows:

1. The application for first registration by the respondent covered a large parcel of land in the Village of St. Clair Beach formerly known as the Grant Farm.

2. The Grant Farm was an irregularly shaped parcel some 3,100 ft. in depth lying between the south side of Riverside Dr. and the north side of St. Gregory Rd. The parcel has a width of approximately 900 ft. The Grant Farm excluded certain small residential parcels fronting on Riverside Dr. [See the figure on the next page.]

3. The respondent is the absolute owner in fee simple in possession of the Grant Farm subject to certain encumbrances which are not relevant to these proceedings. They purchased from the Grant estate in 1969.

4. The appellants purchased one of the residential parcels fronting on Riverside Dr. in August, 1961. Their title also comes from the Grant estate via a certain John Gazo and Mary Gazo. The appellants took possession of their parcel in August, 1961, and have occupied it to the present time.

5. The land in dispute abuts the southerly limit of the parcel of the appellants by the full width of the parcel and extends southerly to the northerly edge of a soybean field running in an irregular east–west line across the Grant Farm.

6. In August, 1961, the land in dispute was partly grass but generally was overgrown in weeds, trees and rubble. It is a rectangular piece of land 128.79 ft. wide running southerly from the southerly limit of the appellants' parcel for a distance of 50 ft. The area to the south was ploughed ground.

7. The house on the appellants' land was constructed in 1954. It has a septic tank for sewage and the weeping tiles for this tank are located on the lands in dispute.

This weeping tile was installed when the system was built in 1954 and was in place when the appellants purchased the property.

[The following figure is the author's—it is not part of the original case:]

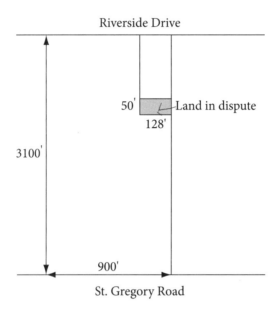

8. The appellants' use of the land in dispute was the normal domestic and recreational use which an owner would make of his own backyard. By way of illustration I refer to the following acts:

    (a) In the fall of 1961 they removed trees, brush and rubble.

    (b) In February, 1962, they bought a dog and set up a dog run of some 50 ft. in the south–west corner of the lands.

    (c) In 1962 they seeded the land with grass, fertilized it and cut it.

    (d) In the summer of 1962 they put a sand-box between the cherry trees on the land in question, installed swings and planted some flowers.

    (e) In 1963 a picnic table was placed on the land.

    (f) In the winter of 1964 they put in their first skating rink.

    (g) In the spring of 1965 they bought a 22-ft. boat hull and over the next two years they used the area in dispute to construct a boat and trailer for transporting it. Thereafter the boat and trailer were stored on the land in the fall and winter months.

    (h) In or about 1965 they erected a bird-house on a steel [post and] placed it on a temporary foundation on the land in question.

(i)   In 1967, at the latest, they built a dog-house and pole about 15 ft. high and embedded in a concrete foundation three feet deep and one foot across.

9. In so using the land the appellants never at any time had the permission or consent of the owners of the Grant Farm.

So much for the facts not in dispute. Counsel for the appellants contended that there was no evidence to support other findings of the learned trial Judge. I have carefully examined the evidence and I see no reason for differing from his findings. I adopt them as the basis of the conclusions which I have reached.

The following are the additional facts:

10.   The land in dispute was excluded from the conveyance by John Gazo and Mary Gazo to the appellants and this limitation on the actual extent of the conveyance was known to the appellants.

11.   There were a few cherry trees on the land in dispute and the Grants picked cherries from time to time from these trees.

12.   The predecessors in title to the respondent, Mrs. Annie Grant and her family, were never out of possession of the property in question, but continued to carry on farming operations on so much of the land as was arable having regard to its nature and characteristics. The reason the ploughing was limited was threefold. First, a hydro pole interfered with the equipment. Secondly, the cherry trees proved an obstacle, and thirdly, the sandy soil made it difficult to get on the land with farm equipment.

13.   Substantially speaking, the Grants and the appellants were on a friendly basis. The use of the land in question was in the nature of a neighbourly acquiescence by the Grants.

Two more findings of fact should be particularly set out.

14.   The title of the Grant family to the land in dispute was acknowledged by the appellants. On two occasions they attempted to purchase the property in question. They made an offer to purchase to Mrs. Annie Grant shortly before her death on May 14, 1966. In 1969 they renewed the offer to her estate at a price of $1,000. On the second occasion, the appellants deposited a certified cheque in that amount with their solicitor for completion of the transaction, but nothing came of it.

15.   In 1969 the respondent purchased the Grant Farm and caused a line of surveyor's stakes to be put in which clearly demarked the south boundary of the parcel owned by the appellants. At all times the appellants were aware of the presence of these stakes but did not deal with them except in silence until May, 1972. At that time the appellants became concerned about the location of the weeping tile of the septic system and then they tried to acquire part of the land in question from the respondent.

Those are the facts on which the learned trial Judge came to the conclusion that the respondent was entitled to an order for first registration. The contention between the parties depends far more on the inferences which are to be drawn from the facts of the case than in any different view as to the existence of the facts themselves.

The short basis of the case made for the appellants was that the learned trial Judge erred on three counts: (a) that he erred in failing to find that the appellants had acquired title to the land in question by adverse possession over the relevant statutory period within the meaning of the *Limitations Act*, RSO 1970, c. 246 [now *Real Property Limitations Act*]; (b) that he erred in finding that the appellants required an *animus possidendi* with the intention to exclude the titleholders from the property to acquire title by adverse possession; and (c) that he erred in finding that the acts of the Grants in picking cherries constituted actual possession on their part or, alternatively, that the evidence would not support a finding that the Grants picked cherries during the relevant period.

To understand what the law on the matter is, I must refer to the *Limitations Act* [now *Real Property Limitations Act*].

[Pennell J referred to ss 4 and 5, and continued:]

It is plain on its face that the *Limitations Act* [now *Real Property Limitations Act*] is a defence.

The Courts have been generous in elucidating the nature of the burden upon a party seeking to establish title by possession. From a long stream of cases I select, first, that of *Pflug and Pflug v. Collins*, [1952] OR 519, [1952] 3 DLR 681; affirmed [1953] OWN 140, [1953] 1 DLR 841. In that case, at p. 527 OR, p. 689 DLR, Wells J (as he then was) made it clear that to succeed the appellants must show:

(1) [a]ctual possession for the statutory period by themselves and those through whom they claim;

(2) that such possession was with the intention of excluding from possession the owners or persons entitled to possession; and

(3) discontinuance of possession for the statutory period by the owners and all others, if any, entitled to possession.

If they fail in any one of these respects, their claim must be dismissed.

As regards the "discontinuance" aspect which I have mentioned, a question arose at trial whether the Grants had discontinued their possession of the land north of the plough-line throughout the relevant period. In reaching a decision one must have regard to the particular circumstances of the case and the nature of the land in question (*Leigh v. Jack* (1879), 5 Ex. D 264).

The learned trial Judge answered the question in these words:

The Grant Farm (including the disputed land) was agricultural land prior to 1961, and was used solely for agricultural purposes at least to 1966. During that time, the Grants made such use of the disputed land as might reasonably be expected of an owner in possession, namely, ploughing as far north as the hydro pole, trees, and nature of the soil would permit. The area north of the plough-line was used for the only agricultural purpose possible, namely, picking cherries off the trees. The deedholders have constructive possession of the lands described in their deed, and it is not necessary for them (as contrasted with trespassers) to show that they have pedal possession. I find that the Grants were never out of possession prior to 1966. As to the lands south of the plough-line, actual possession was maintained by ploughing, and as to the lands north of the plough-line, actual possession was maintained by the simple act of picking cherries. There is no dispossession of the owner or discontinuance of possession by the owner within the meaning of s. 5 of the *Limitations Act*, RSO 1970, c. 246 [now *Real Property Limitations Act*], until there are acts by the claimants which interfere with the purpose to which the owner devoted the land. The smallest act by the owner would be sufficient to show that there was no discontinuance of his possession: *per* Bramwell LJ, in *Leigh v. Jack* (1879), 5 Ex. D 264 at p. 272. Where the land in dispute is unenclosed then the only safe rule to follow is to confine the trespasser to the actual area from which he has by visible occupation excluded the titleholder, but occasional use of the disputed land by the titleholder in a manner consistent with the uses to which such land may be put is sufficient to deprive the claimants of exclusive possession: *Walker et al. v. Russell et al.*, [1966] 1 OR 197, 53 DLR (2d) 509.

One of the questions on this appeal is whether there was evidence on which the learned County Court Judge could so find. The inference drawn by him from the evidence of the picking of cherries was impeached. In my view, the evidence on which the learned County Court Judge acted was sufficient evidence on which he could properly find that the respondent was never out of possession of the land north of the plough-line prior to 1966. In some cases possession cannot in the nature of things be continuous from day to day and possession may continue to subsist notwithstanding that there are sometimes long intervals between the acts of user. The owner of a farm cannot be said to be out of possession of a piece of land merely because he does not perform positive acts of ownership all the time.

The evidence led the learned trial Judge to the conclusion that at best the appellants had joint possession with the Grants. It is a small point but, for myself, I am doubtful that for the purposes of possession under the *Limitations Act* [now *Real Property Limitations Act*] it is strictly correct legal parlance to speak of concurrent possession. In this connection it seems to me possession is single and exclusive. No doubt the appellants occupied the land. With every respect to the opinion of the learned trial Judge, I think that the land should be regarded as in the possession of one or the other of the two parties concerned. On that footing it follows from the judgment of the learned trial Judge that the respondent, having picked cherries, remained at that period in possession of the land.

If this conclusion be right, it is enough to decide the case in the respondent's favour. I note, however, that a point much agitated before this Court was whether the learned trial Judge erred in law in finding that the appellants required an intention to defeat or exclude the true owners from the land. I think I ought to deal with this point, though the careful judgment of the trial Judge, with which I agree, absolves me from attending to the matter in great detail.

It is, I think, beyond the reach of controversy that the appellants never had any intention, nor claimed any intention of excluding the Grants. The dominant feature in the case is the fact that as late as 1969 the appellants offered to purchase the land from the Grant estate for the sum of $1,000. Counsel for the appellants, however, contended that the concept of adverse possession does not involve an intention on the part of the person in possession to acquire a right against a particular person. ...

[The court considered a number of precedents, including *A-G Canada v Krause*, [1956] OR 675 (CA), in which the court held (at 691) that a claim to possessory title required "(1) exclusive occupation in the physical sense, i.e., detention, and (2) the *animus possidendi*." In this context, the court agreed with the trial judge's determination that the issue of intention was relevant in relation to the MacDonalds' claim to possession.

In addition, the court considered two other points. The court did not resolve the issue of whether there was an easement in favour of the MacDonalds in relation to their septic tank located on the weeping bed, part of the land in dispute. The court also considered whether the 10-year limitation period had commenced as early as 1962, but adopted the decision in the trial *de novo* that it accrued at the earliest in 1965, when the birdhouse was erected and the hull and trailer were parked on the disputed property. Thus, Mrs Grant's right to recover possession accrued in 1965 and the limitation period had not expired at the time of the action taken by her successor, the St Clair Beach Estates Ltd.]

DISCUSSION NOTES

i. The Test for Dispossession

Identify the test used in this case to decide whether the appellants had established dispossession according to the *Real Property Limitations Act*. What is the effect of using the test of dispossession *and* discontinuance in the judgment as opposed to the test of dispossession *or* discontinuance, which is found in s 5(1) of the Act? What element of the test has been added by this decision? How would you describe the difference in the intent of the appellants here from that of Ms Piper in *Piper v Stevenson*? Is this difference critical to the reasoning or the outcome? Is this difference consistent with the common law principles regarding possessory interests or with the underlying purposes of adverse possession principles proposed by Callaghan and Rose?

ii. Possessory Titles and Registration

In cases where a person can show a title based on possession, an application may be made to register such an interest under legislation traditionally known as "quieting titles" legislation. In Ontario, such an application is made pursuant to the *Courts of Justice Act*, RSO 1990, c 11, s 208. A party may also obtain this declaration by filing an application through the *Courts of Justice Act*, RRO 1990, Reg 194, *Rules of Civil Procedure*, r 14.05(3)(e). In other provinces, such legislation continues to be known as quieting title statutes: see *Quieting Titles Act*, RSNS 1989, c 382; *Quieting of Titles Act*, RSNB 1973, c Q-4; *Quieting of Titles Act*, RSNL 1990, c Q-3; and *Quieting Titles Act*, RSPEI 1988, c Q-2. Note that intention was also considered in Alberta in *Lutz v Kawa* (1980), 112 DLR (3d) 271 (Alta CA), even though Alberta uses a Torrens system of title registration: issues about different regimes of title registration are explored in Chapter 5. See also A Bradbrook, SV MacCallum & AP Moore, eds, *Australian Real Property Law*, 4th ed (Sydney: Thomson Lawbook Co, 2008) at 670-76.

iii. The Quality of Possession Under Statutes of Limitation

There are many examples of cases where the issue was whether the acts of a possessor were sufficient to trigger the commencement of a limitation period. As well, there are cases about whether the possessor's actions were sufficiently continuous during the limitation period and whether the possessor's actions related to all or only part of the land held by the paper titleholder. These issues are generally considered in terms of the nature of the land and its appropriate use (including, for example, seasonal use), as was demonstrated by *Re St Clair Beach Estates Ltd v MacDonald* (1974), 5 OR (2d) 482 (H Ct J Div Ct). For other examples, see *Walker v Russell* (1966), 53 DLR (2d) 509 (Ont H Ct J) and *Georgia-Pacific Resins Inc v Blair* (1991), 121 NBR (2d) 349 (QBTD). There is also a helpful list of cases in Derek Mendes da Costa, Richard J Balfour & Eileen S Gillese, *Property Law: Cases, Text, and Materials*, 2d ed (Toronto: Emond Montgomery, 1990) at 12:34-35.

In *Leichner v Canada* (1997), 31 OR (3d) 700 (CA), the court allowed an appeal by the federal Crown, denying the plaintiff's claim to possession in relation to a strip of land along the Rideau Canal, part of the Federal Crown Reserve. In part, the decision was based on the absence of acts by the plaintiff sufficient to show actual possession and an intention to exclude the true owner. Even though the plaintiff's predecessors in title had fenced the property, Rosenberg JA held (at 709) that "line fencing to protect pasture or keep in cattle and not done for the purpose of taking possession is not sufficient to establish possessory title." In this case, the fencing was not along the shoreline and did not prevent members of the public from gaining access to the canal for swimming. Can you distinguish this case from *Piper v Stevenson*? How? For an English case that held that the purpose of a fence surrounding the disputed property was to keep sheep *in*, rather than to keep others *out*, see *Inglewood Investments Co v Baker*, [2002] EWJ no 5261 (CA).

iv. Possessory Claims Among Co-Owners

The issue of the commencement of the limitation period arises in a variety of circumstances. In two kinds of cases, for example, family "arrangements" may lead to such claims. First, where a number of persons are jointly entitled to property, but only a few of them have actual possession, those in possession may claim that the running of the limitation period has extinguished the rights of those out of possession to recover possession. This typically occurs when a parent dies, leaving a will designating joint interests to the children, and then some children remain at home while others leave. What is the appropriate test for determining whether those out of possession "discontinued" possession or were "dispossessed" by those remaining at home? Is mere possession sufficient, or do those in possession have to act so as to clearly show an intent to dispossess those not in actual possession? For a case that held that the limitation period started to run when two sisters remained in possession of the family farm after their father died, having left the farm to them and to other siblings jointly, and the other siblings remained out of possession, see *Paradise Beach and Transportation Co Ltd v Price-Robinson*, a decision of the Privy Council on appeal from the Bahamas, [1968] AC 1072 (PC). Lord Upjohn clearly rejected the idea that the statute required anything more than mere possession to start the limitation period, and stated that there was no requirement of "adversity" (an adverse intent), stating at 1084:

> It seems to their Lordships clear from the language of the Act and the authorities already referred to that subject to the qualification mentioned below where the right of entry has accrued more than 20 years before action brought the co-tenants are barred and their title is extinguished whatever the nature of the co-tenants' possession. That right of entry ... accrued in 1913 [the date of the father's death].

For relevant statutory definitions regarding joint possession and the commencement of the limitation period, see *Real Property Limitations Act*, s 11; *Limitation of Actions Act*, RSNS 1989, c 258, s 15; *Limitation of Actions Act*, SNB 2009, c L-8.5, s 8.1(5)(b); *Statute of Limitations*, RSPEI 1988, c S-7, s 33; *Limitations Act*, SNL 1995, c L-16.1, s 20.

In Ontario, the issue of possessory claims among co-owners was considered in *Re O'Reilly (No 2)* (1980), 28 OR (2d) 481 (H Ct J), aff'd (1981), 33 OR (2d) 352 (CA). In that case, the Ontario Court of Appeal applied the equitable principle of "laches" to bar the claim of beneficiaries "who had allowed their siblings to run a farm, with all its obligations for 33 years." For a good overview of the relationship between the equitable principle of laches and statutes of limitation, see G Creighton, "Equitable Limitations" in *Limitation of Actions* (Toronto: Canadian Bar Association—Ontario, 1985). According to Creighton (at 4), these equitable principles are not strictly limitations: "In no case is a certain period prescribed, following which no proceeding may be brought. Rather, on general principle it may become unconscionable to allow enforcement of a right in equity after an effluxion of time." Thus, because the basis for such a principle is unconscionability, there will be more flexibility (and less certainty) about when such a claim may be sustained. By contrast, the statutes of limitation provide greater certainty in defining the length of time after which claims by a true owner are extinguished. Is it accurate to say that there is no flexibility in the application of the statutes of limitation? Is there a continuing need for the equitable principle? In what circumstances? Issues about the rights of co-owners are also discussed in Chapter 6.

Periods of possession by a continuous succession of persons may be added together to create the statutory period of possession, a process often referred to as "tacking." For a critical reflection on the appropriate theoretical rationale for permitting tacking on the part of those asserting possessory claims, see Margaret Jane Radin, "Time, Possession, and Alienation" (1986) 64 Wash ULQ 739.

v. Possessory Claims and the Tenancy at Will

A second example concerning the commencement of the limitation period occurs in family arrangements to occupy land or premises with permission of the paper titleholder. Such a permission may create a form of tenancy known as a "tenancy at will." A tenancy at will is probably the most "fragile" form of tenancy, because the possession of the tenant at will may be terminated at any time by the lessor. In this context, s 5(7) of the Ontario *Real Property Limitations Act* provides that the 10-year limitation period begins one year after the tenancy at will was created; thus, a tenant at will will have a possessory claim after 11 years following the commencement of the limitation period. Issues about tenancies are discussed in more detail in Chapter 4.

In *MacLean v Reid*, the court considered a claim of possession based on an oral agreement between two brothers that had been in place for several decades. In Nova Scotia, the applicable legislation required a 20-year limitation period, so that a tenant at will had to be in possession for one year as a tenant at will and then remain in possession for a further 20 years—a total of 21 years of possession.

MacLean v Reid
(1978), 94 DLR (3d) 118 (NS SC App Div)

MacDONALD JA: At issue in this appeal is in effect the title to, ownership of, or possession of a farm property comprising approximately 50 acres located at Dean's Settlement, Upper Musquodoboit, Halifax County.

The respondent, David Reid, is now about 68 years of age and has resided on the property his entire life (it being the Reid homestead property) with the exception of a six-month period in the 1960's and another period around 1950 when he was working in Pictou County. On the latter occasion he returned to the homestead on week-ends.

The property was conveyed to the father of the respondent in 1915. By deed dated June 10, 1935, and registered on January 15, 1936, the parents of the respondent conveyed the lands to the latter's brother, Clarence Reid. Clarence Reid and his wife in turn deeded the property to the appellants Edward and Leona MacLean by conveyance dated November 8, 1971, and registered on July 31, 1972.

The appellants brought action against the respondent asking for an order requiring the latter to vacate the lands; an injunction restraining him from entering the lands and damages. The respondent raised as his principal defence that he had acquired title to the property by adverse possession. In other words, that Clarence Reid's title to the property was extinguished by virtue of the *Statute of Limitations*, RSNS 1967, c. 168, because the respondent had been in possession of the property as a tenant at will of Clarence Reid for a period in excess of 21 years. The respondent counterclaimed against the appellants for relief similar to that claimed against him by them.

The respondent testified that his brother Clarence told him in 1936 that "I could stay there [on the property] as long as I liked." The trial Judge, the Honourable Mr. Justice A.M. MacIntosh, found that the appellants were not *bona fide* purchasers for value without notice of the respondent's interest in the lands and held that the latter had an interest therein equivalent to a life tenancy. From such decision, the appellants appeal and the respondent cross-appeals.

In this reserved decision the learned trial Judge said in part:

> The plaintiff testified as to the movements of Clarence Reid vis-à-vis the Reid farm from the time he received the deed, i.e. 1935, until their purchase of same in 1971. Where there is any conflict of evidence, I accept the defendant's version as to the brother's whereabouts and his own dealings with the homestead.
>
> The defendant stated that he has spent all his life to the present time on this family farm. From 1935 until 1968 he farmed the property, raising cattle, sheep, poultry, grain and vegetable crops. He bought and paid for all the farm machinery. He kept the cattle in a lean-to he built onto the barn. He also purchased a horse stable and moved it onto the property. From 1935 onwards he paid the municipal taxes.
>
> From 1935 to 1940 the defendant's brother, Clarence Reid, worked as a woodsman, returning to the farm on week-ends. He never farmed the property. In 1940 he joined the Canadian Army and proceeded overseas. At the conclusion of hostilities he returned home for a short while, leaving to reside permanently in Ireland some time during 1946. Nothing was done by him relative to the farm until 1971 when he conveyed whatever interest he possessed to the plaintiffs.

[handwritten note: "lived on wlands moved to Ireland"]

The defendant stated that he was told by his brother that he, the defendant, could remain on the farm all his lifetime. He never knew that his brother had title by deed.

· · ·

In pursuance of his agreement with his brother, the defendant stayed on the farm property, operating, maintaining and improving same, and while they were living, provided a home for his mother and sister. This period of time commenced in 1935. In 1971 the brother conveyed whatever interest he had in the property to the plaintiff.

The learned trial Judge made no mention in his decision of the respondent's claim that he had acquired title to the lands by adverse possession. That issue is therefore at large before us and, in my opinion, for reasons I shall give, is decisive of this appeal. ...

[The court referred to the applicable *Statute of Limitations*, ss 9 and 10(f), which established the expiration of a tenancy at will at the end of one year, followed by an effective limitation period of 20 years, and then continued:]

At the time of the conveyance to Clarence Reid his father was not living on or farming the lands. After receiving the deed to the property Clarence Reid did not farm the lands but did live there on week-ends.

At the time of the conveyance of the lands to Clarence Reid the respondent was occupying and working them. Upon being told by Clarence that he could stay on the lands as long as he liked the respondent did so. The learned trial Judge has accurately detailed the nature of the respondent's occupation of the lands and the activities he carried on. ...

[MacDonald JA referred to a number of other authorities concerning tenancies at will and the operation of statutes of limitation and then continued:]

Returning to the present case the facts indicate:

1. *That* when Clarence Reid received the deed to the property in question the respondent was then in occupation of it as he had been all his life.

2. *That* in 1936 Clarence Reid told the respondent that he could live on the property as long as he liked.

3. *That* the respondent paid the real property taxes on the property from 1935-36 to approximately 1966 and made certain improvements and did the other things alluded to by the trial judge.

4. *That* the respondent did not pay rent to his brother Clarence nor was any demanded of him.

5. The respondent testified that about two years or "a little better than that" before the trial (January 21, 1977) he received a letter from his brother Clarence that he was planning on selling the land.

6. The appellant Edward MacLean testified that he purchased one piece of property from Clarence Reid in 1966 and that with respect to the property here involved Clarence wrote him in 1970 and "wanted to sell it to me."

7. Attached to the deed from Fred Reid and his wife to Clarence Reid, dated June 10, 1935, is a note dated May 17, 1971, written by either Clarence Reid or his wife. This note states:

To Whome [*sic*] it may concern

I, Clarence Reid, have sold the property in this will to:

Edward McLean
RR No. 1, Upper Musquodoboit,
Halifax Co.,
Nova Scotia
Canada

Signed

Clarence Reid
Ballyduff
Thurles
Co. Tipperary
Ireland

Obviously Clarence Reid thought he could convey the property to Mr. MacLean by attaching the foregoing note to the original deed to himself. Mr. MacLean advised him that the transfer could not be affected in such manner and had the deed of November 8, 1971, prepared and executed by Clarence Reid and his wife.

8. The appellant Edward MacLean had lived in the Dean Settlement area since the 1920s and was well acquainted with David Reid. Mr. MacLean testified that in 1935 Fred Reid, the father of David and Clarence lived across the road from the lands in question and in fact never occupied them thereafter.

9. The appellant Edward MacLean testified that he knew that the respondent David Reid lived on the lands in question from at least 1935 to the time of trial.

10. The appellant Edward MacLean said in evidence that he has been paying taxes on the property since 1966.

Section 12 of the *Statute of Limitations* of this Province provides:

12. No person shall be deemed to have been in possession of any land, within the meaning of this Act merely by reason of having made an entry thereon.

I refer to this section because there is evidence that Clarence Reid spent week-ends at the property during the years 1935 to 1940 and certainly made an entry on it upon his return from overseas in 1945. There is absolutely no evidence that the permission given by Clarence to David that the latter could stay on the lands as long as he liked was ever revoked or rescinded by Clarence unless the letter referred to earlier wherein he advised David that he was planning to sell the property could be construed as a determination of the tenancy. ...

[The court referred to *McCowan et al v Armstrong* (1902), 3 OLR 100 and then stated:]

The facts to which I have alluded, considered in light of the authorities cited, lead me to the conclusion that the respondent David Reid became a tenant at will of his brother Clarence in 1936 and that such tenancy by operation of s. 10(f) of the *Statute of Limitations* was determined one year later. If I am in error as to the time of determination of such tenancy because Clarence Reid made a re-entry onto the lands and possibly took possession of them in 1945 then, in my opinion, at that time a new tenancy at will was created which was determined by statute no later than 1947.

I would now refer to s. 21 of the *Statute of Limitations* which provides:

> 21. At the determination of the period limited by this Act to any person for making an entry, or distress, or bringing any action, the right and title of such person to the land or rent, for the recovery whereof such entry, distress, or action respectively might have been made or brought within such period, shall be extinguished.

In my opinion the respondent David Reid was a tenant at will of Clarence Reid from no later than 1946. That tenancy expired by operation of s. 10(f) of the *Statute of Limitations* a year later in 1947. From that time on the respondent had, to the knowledge of the appellants, actual, exclusive, continuous, open, visible and notorious possession of the lands in question. This possession extinguished the right and title thereto of the registered owner, Clarence Reid, and consequently of the appellants, no later than 1968. The result is that the respondent is entitled to possession of the lands in question with a title resting on the absence of the right of others to eject him.

For similar fact situations where courts have applied statutes of limitation in the context of family arrangements, see *Hoyt v Hoyt* (1990), 101 NBR (2d) 436 (QBTD); *Casey v Canada Trust Co* (1960), 25 DLR (2d) 764 (Ont H Ct J); and *Train v Metzger* (1974), 51 DLR (3d) 24 (H Ct J). For other provincial statutory provisions concerning limitation periods and tenancies at will, see *Limitation of Actions Act*, RSNS 1989, c 258, s 11(f); *Limitation of Actions Act*, SNB 2009, c L-8.5, s 8.1(4); *Statute of Limitations Act*, RSPEI 1988, c S-7, s 30(1); and *Limitations Act*, SNL 1995, c L-16.1, s 21(1).

vi. Possessory Title and Tenants' Rights to Possession of a Leasehold Estate

Issues about claims to possessory title are sometimes complicated in the context of leaseholds. As discussed in more detail in Chapters 3 and 4, when a lessor grants a lease to a tenant, the lessor retains a "right of reversion." This right means that, at the end of the lease period, the leasehold estate (granted to the tenant for the duration of the lease) terminates and the right to possession reverts back to the lessor.

The complication with respect to claims for possessory title arises because a grant of lease carries with it an "exclusive right to possession" on the part of the tenant. That is, when a lessor grants a lease to a tenant, the tenant is exclusively entitled to possession during the period of the lease, and the lessor's entitlement to possession is postponed until the termination of the lease and the reversion back to the lessor.

This principle means that a person may establish a possessory title claim against a tenant, and if the tenant takes no action before the expiration of the limitation period to recover possession, the claim will be enforceable by the possessor until the end of the lease. At that time, when the right to possession reverts to the lessor, a new claim to possession against the lessor arises, and the lessor must take action within the statutory limitation period to recover possession.

In *Fairweather v St Marylebone Property Co Ltd,* [1963] AC 510, the House of Lords considered a case in which a neighbour established possessory title over part of land occupied by a tenant. Because this was a long lease—for 99 years—the lessor was understandably concerned and arranged for the tenant to surrender his lease early; this arrangement meant that the lease would terminate early so that the right to possession would revert back to the lessor at the date of the surrender. In this case, the House of Lords concluded that the lease had been terminated, so that the lessor could then bring an action for possession to evict the possessor.

However, this conclusion is not entirely satisfactory because, as a matter of logic, if the tenant's right to possession has been eliminated by the possessor, the tenant has no right to possession to return to the lessor. This problem was reviewed by the UK Law Reform Commission in 1977, but without making a recommendation (see Law Reform Committee, *Twenty-First Report: Final Report on Limitation of Actions*, Cmnd 6923 (London: HMSO, 1977) [Law Reform Committee]). Two decades later, a consultation paper recommended that the running of time against the lessor pursuant to the *Limitation Act* should begin only when the lessor's interest falls into possession. For example:

> P2 lets land to P1. D starts squatting on the land in 1998. The lease comes to an end in 2003 and P1 leaves. The limitation period in respect of an action by P2 to recover the land would be ten years from the date on which P2's interest becomes an interest in possession, ending in 2013. [Note that the report also recommended changing the limitation period in the United Kingdom to 10 years instead of 12.]

See Law Commission, *Limitation of Actions: A Consultation Paper (No 151)* (London: The Stationery Office, 1998) at 13.118. This general recommendation was confirmed in Law Commission, *Limitation of Actions (Law Commission Report No 270)* (London: The Stationery Office, 2001) at 4.133 and 4.135(2).

In the *Fairweather* case, there is tension between principles of possession, on the one hand, and policy concerns about trespassers and squatters, on the other. How does the issue of intention affect this situation? Do the purposes identified by Rose and Callaghan for this area of property law point to any solution in this context?

In *Spectrum Investment Co Limited v Holmes*, [1981] 1 WLR 221 (Ch D), the facts were similar to those in *Marylebone*, except that the "squatter" registered his interest after expiry of the limitation period against the tenant. When the tenant attempted to surrender his lease to the lessor, the court held that the surrender was ineffective because the tenant was no longer in a position to make a surrender. The court did not, however, decide the question of whether the squatter had become the successor in title to the tenant.

vii. The Limitation Period and Leases in Ontario: Giouroukos v Cadillac Fairview Corp Ltd

In *Giouroukos v Cadillac Fairview Corp Ltd* (1983), 3 DLR (4th) 595, the Ontario Court of Appeal reviewed the issue of the commencement of the limitation period with respect to "successive" leases of the subject land. That is, what is the situation when there is a lease for 20 years and, at the end of the 20-year period, the lessor and tenant agree to a further 20-year lease of the same land? Especially if there is no "gap" between the two leases, and the tenant remains in possession throughout the successive lease periods, is it possible to conclude that there was a reversion of "possession" back to the lessor in between the two leases, so that the lessor acquired a right to recover possession in relation to a person who had established a posses-sory title against the tenant during the period of the initial lease?

In *Giouroukos*, the court focused on the lessor's grant of successive leases to the same tenant over a period of years; the tenant remained in physical occupation of the premises throughout the period, but on several occasions a short-term lease came to an end and the lessor and the tenant then entered into a new lease on the same terms. Technically, each time a current lease ended there was a reversion of possession to the lessor, with a regranting of possession to the tenant at the commencement of the next lease. The plaintiff, who was claiming possession against part of the lands subject to the lease, argued that time began to run against the lessor at the end of the first lease to the tenant because the lessor then be-came "notionally" entitled to possession; the plaintiff argued that there was possession against both the lessor and the tenant from that date.

Although the trial judge accepted this argument in favour of the plaintiff, the Ontario Court of Appeal reversed the trial judge's decision, stating that because the tenant had remained in actual possession, "more than a theoretical entitlement to possession" was required to show the commencement of the limitation period running against the lessor. According to the court, the lessor's entitlement to possession in the case of successive leases represented only a legal fiction. In reaching its conclusion, the court considered *Marylebone* and two other decisions in the United Kingdom relating to limitation periods and leasehold interests: *Eccle-siastical Com'rs of England & Wales v Rowe* (1880), 5 App Cas 736 (HL), and *President & Scholars of Corpus Christi College, Oxford v Rogers* (1879), 49 LJ Ex 4 (CA). These two decisions were not entirely consistent and, although the Ontario Court of Appeal in *Giouroukos* concluded that *Rowe* was more authoritative, it declined to follow this precedent. As a result, the plaintiff was not entitled to possession of the disputed lands. On appeal to the Supreme Court of Canada, the court released brief reasons concurring with the decision of the Ontario Court of Appeal: [1986] 2 SCR 707. For an assessment of the trial decision, see Brian Bucknall, "Comment: Giouroukos v Cadillac Fairview Corp" (1982) 24 RPR 307.

In *Giouroukos*, the Ontario Court of Appeal decided that it was unnecessary to consider the nature of the plaintiff's actions in relation to his claim to possessory title; the Supreme Court similarly declined to consider whether the plaintiff's actions were sufficient to establish possession. In fact, the plaintiff had used undeveloped lands to extend the parking area for his restaurant; in doing so, he had torn down an old fence, cleared the land, and spread gravel over the surface more than once. The tenant had no use for this section of the leased lands and, apparently, made no objection. The lessor was holding these lands for future re-development as a shopping centre, and thus the plaintiff's use of the lands did not interfere with the lessor's intention. It appears that the lessor's argument that the plaintiff's actions did not constitute an interference with the lessor's intended use of the lands may have influ-enced the conclusions of the Ontario Court of Appeal.

viii. Commencement of a Limitation Period in the Context of Legal Disability

There are numerous statutory provisions concerning the commencement of the limitation period when a person in possession is under a legal disability—for example, because of mental infirmity or because the person is a minor (a status that may differ among provinces based on the applicable legislation). For one example, see *Real Property Limitations Act*, ss 36-39.

C. The Element of Intention

Reflect again on the issue of intention that may have influenced the outcome in *Giouroukos*. Why is intention (on the part of the titleholder) relevant to a claim to possession or to the application of limitation statutes? In thinking about this question, consider the analysis of Wilson JA (and the intention of the true owner) in *Keefer v Arillotta* (1976), 13 OR (2d) 680 (CA). To what extent do the majority and dissenting views differ with respect to whether the test for possession is subjective or objective? Are these views consistent with the underlying purposes of statutes of limitation? How does the inconsistent user test, adopted in *Keefer*, resolve the tension between principles of possession and the court's interest in protecting the rights of titleholders?

Keefer v Arillotta
(1976), 13 OR (2d) 680 (CA)

WILSON JA: This is an appeal from an order of His Honour Judge Nicholls holding that the respondents [the Keefers] had acquired a possessory title to a portion of the appellants' land subject to an easement remaining in the appellants.

The facts are more fully set out in the reasons for judgment of the learned trial Judge but the more significant ones for purposes of this appeal may be summarized under the following headings:

1. The nature and location of the land in issue;

2. The chain of title;

3. The conduct of the owners.

The Nature and Location of the Land in Issue

It is unnecessary to describe the land by its metes and bounds description. Suffice it to say that it is a narrow strip of land 8 ft. wide by 105 ft. deep running between the residential property of the respondents to the south and the business premises of the appellants to the north. The most easterly 41 ft. of the strip running back from the street line is a stone driveway. Extending westward from the driveway is a grassy area running up to a frame garage owned by the respondents and located at the rear of the strip. A concrete walk-way adjacent to the appellants' store runs up the side of the store alongside the stone driveway to a set of steps which lead up to a concrete landing giving access to an apartment located over the store. To the west of the steps and concrete landing is an entrance door to an addition which was built on to the rear of the store in 1949 by the appellants' predecessors in title.

[The following figure is the author's—it is not part of the original case:]

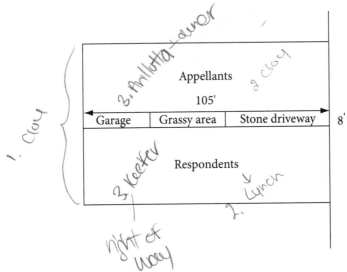

The Chain of Title

The appellants' and the respondents' properties were initially owned by one Martin Cloy. In 1918 Mr. Cloy conveyed the property now owned by the respondents to one Elzear Lynch together with a right of way of ingress and egress over a portion of his own property, the strip of land in issue on this appeal. In each subsequent conveyance of that property, including the conveyance made in July of 1957 to the respondents, the right of way over the appellants' [the Arillottas] land was granted.

When Mr. Cloy died in July of 1921, the land he had retained, now owned by the appellants, passed to his widow Maude Cloy who was also his executrix. As executrix she conveyed it to herself as devisee under the will but inadvertently included in the conveyance the lands already conveyed by her husband to Mr. Lynch. To rectify this error Mrs. Cloy made a new deed to Mrs. Lynch, who had acquired the land on her husband's death, and this deed made in April of 1926, included the grant of right of way over the strip of Mrs. Cloy's land. In November of 1952, Mrs. Cloy transferred her land to her son Douglas Cloy and again through inadvertence omitted to make that conveyance subject to the right of way in favour of Mrs. Lynch. Douglas Cloy remedied this in March of 1958 by a quitclaim deed in favour of the respondents who by that time had become the owners of the adjoining land. In August of 1972, when Douglas Cloy sold his property to the appellants' predecessors in title, he made the grant subject to the respondents' right of way and, when they in turn sold it to the appellants in February, 1973, they likewise made their grant subject to the respondents' right of way. …

The Conduct of the Owners

The learned trial Judge made a number of important findings with respect to the use of the strip of land made over the years by the owners of the two adjoining properties.

Keefer

(a) The Respondents and Their Predecessors in Title

Since the respondents' property has always been used as a dwelling-house, the main use of the strip made by the owners of that property has been as a driveway. Up until about 1956, the respondents' car was kept in the garage but since that time the garage has been used as a storage shed and the car has been left on the driveway at night. Although the respondent Mr. Keefer uses the car to go back and forth to work, it is also sometimes parked in the driveway during the day and so occasionally are the cars belonging to the respondents' friends when they come to visit. The trial Judge found that in the 1960s a disabled car was left at the rear of the driveway for some four years.

The trial Judge found also that the Keefers on several occasions had put gravel on the driveway at their own expense. They also kept it free of snow in the winter-time. This may not be significant since they have a right of way over it and the Cloys closed down the store every winter and went to Florida.

As far as the grassy area to the west of the stone driveway is concerned, the evidence disclosed that the grass had for many years been tended by the owners of the respondents' property, including the respondents themselves, and that the respondents occasionally held barbecues and picnics on it with no objection from the Cloys. The evidence that the Keefers made a skating-rink of part of the grassy area on three winters does not appear to be significant since it was when the Cloys were wintering in Florida. The evidence, however, that no objection was made by Mr. Cloy when in 1952 Mr. Keefer moved the garage located at the rear of his property over onto the rear of the strip in order to line it up with the driveway is clearly significant.

(b) The Appellants and Their Predecessors in Title

Arilotta

The appellants' premises have always been used for business purposes, first in Martin Cloy's time as a grocery store and later by Douglas Cloy as a marine supply store for vessels plying up and down the Welland Canal. Since 1972, when Douglas Cloy sold the property to the respondents' predecessors in title, it has been used as a general variety store. Douglas Cloy was assisting his father in the business prior to the conveyance to Elzear Lynch and gave evidence on behalf of the appellants as to the use made by his parents and himself of the property from 1918 to 1972. The Cloys never lived on this property.

The strip of land was used by the Cloys in the early days to give access to an ice-house at the rear of the store. The ice-house was filled in the winter with blocks of ice cut from the Welland Canal. Deliveries were made from it originally by means of a horse and wagon and later by truck. In 1949 the ice-house was removed and a one-storey addition was built on to the rear of the store. The addition was used partly as an office and partly for the storage of soft drinks. Access to the addition was through a door to the west of the stone steps and landing which provided access to the apartment over the store. Soft drinks were delivered by truck to the storeroom. If there was a car parked in the driveway, the soft drinks would be taken by a small hand-cart; if the driveway was clear, the truck would drive up to the entrance door to make its deliveries.

Mr. Cloy testified that he never parked his car in the driveway but that trucks parked there occasionally when unloading supplies if the driveway was clear. Mr. Cloy's customers also sometimes parked in the driveway for short periods of time when making purchases.

The tenants of the apartment above the store entered from the street by the concrete walk-way running alongside the driveway, but the one tenant who owned a car did not leave his car in the driveway. Moving trucks used the driveway and, when tenants were moving in or out, the Keefers always moved their car if it happened to be in the driveway at the time. The owners used the walk-way to visit the apartment. They also used a portion of the grassy area to get to and from the side entrance to the storage and office premises built on to the rear of the store in 1949.

Mr. Cloy testified that both he and his father had put gravel on the driveway over the years, but he acknowledged that the last time he had put gravel on was probably in 1956. Because of the store's being closed in the winters from December to March every year when he and his family went to Florida, no trucks or customers' cars would be parked in the driveway during the winter months. His evidence was that they had been wintering in Florida for the past 18 years.

The Issue

His Honour Judge Nicholls, after reviewing the evidence of user by both owners over the years, stated:

> The possession [of the plaintiffs and their predecessors in title] was not consistent with the rights accruing from the specific grant of right of way but far exceeded them. Counsel for the plaintiff expressed the opinion that the grant of right of way matured into a possessory title.

He also stated:

> The possession of the plaintiffs and their predecessors in title was open, visible and continuous for far more than the requisite number of years, but the question arises as to whether there was exclusive possession.

With all due respect to the learned trial Judge, I believe that the crucial question in this case is whether the respondents' possession challenged in any way the right of the legal owner to make the use of the property he wished to make of it. This is not a case where the Keefers could be viewed as trespassers on their neighbours' property so that any act of theirs on the property was a challenge to the constructive possession of the owners. Possession is not adverse to the extent it is referable to a lawful title: *Thomas v. Thomas* (1855), 2 K & J 79 at p. 83, 69 ER 701, *per* Sir William Page Wood VC. The Keefers were on their neighbours' property pursuant to their grant of right of way and, even if they exceeded the rights they had by virtue of the right of way, this would not necessarily mean that their right of way matured into a possessory title.

The use an owner wants to make of his property may be a limited use and an intermittent or sporadic use. A possessory title cannot, however, be acquired against him by depriving him of uses of his property that he never intended or desired to make of it. The *animus possidendi* which a person claiming a possessory title must have is an intention to exclude the owner from such uses as the owner wants to make of his property.

Viewed in this light the evidence that the Cloys never parked their car or truck on the strip of land, far from being helpful to the respondents' case, is harmful to it. It shows that the Cloys never intended or wanted to use the strip for parking. Indeed, this is clear from the fact that they gave the owner of the adjoining property a right of ingress and egress over it. Similarly, the fact that the respondents created a skating-rink on the grassy area in the winter-time when the appellants were in Florida has in my view no real significance in terms of the ouster of the true owner. The true owner was probably quite content to give the Keefers full rein on the property while the store was not in operation. The trial Judge was obviously correct in his finding that, even when the appellants were operating the store, the respondents were using the strip for more than just a means of ingress and egress to their property. I do not believe, however, that this is the test for the acquisition of a possessory title. The test is not whether the respondents exceeded their rights under the right of way but whether they precluded the owner from making the use of the property that he wanted to make of it: *Re St. Clair Beach Estates Ltd. v. MacDonald et al.* (1974), 5 OR (2d) 482, 50 DLR (3d) 650. Acts relied on as dispossessing the true owner must be inconsistent with the form of enjoyment of the property intended by the true owner. This has been held to be the test for adverse possession since the leading case of *Leigh v. Jack* (1879), 5 Ex. D 264.

The onus of establishing title by possession is on the claimant and it is harder for a claimant to discharge this onus when he is on the property pursuant to a grant from the owner. It was held in *Littledale v. Liverpool College*, [1900] 1 Ch. 19 that acts done on another's land may be attributed to the exercise of an easement, even an excessive exercise of an easement, rather than to adverse possession of the fee.

In *Pflug and Pflug v. Collins*, [1952] OR 519 at p. 527, [1952] 3 DLR 681 at p. 689 [aff'd [1953] OWN 140, [1953] 1 DLR 841], Mr. Justice Wells (as he then was) made it clear that a person claiming a possessory title must establish (1) actual possession for the statutory period by themselves and those through whom they claim; (2) that such possession was with the intention of excluding from possession the owner or persons entitled to possession; and (3) discontinuance of possession for the statutory period by the owner and all others, if any, entitled to possession. If he fails in any one of these respects, his claim fails.

In my view the respondents fail in both (2) and (3) above. I do not believe that while the Cloys owned the strip of property in issue the Keefers ever intended to oust them from the limited use they wanted to make of it. The evidence discloses that the relationship between the Cloys and the Keefers was excellent and that there never was any trouble with the respondents when delivery trucks occasionally used the driveway for unloading supplies, when customers parked for short periods on the driveway when making purchases at the store, when tenants were moved in and out of the upstairs apartment and when they came and went to the apartment. Nor did Douglas Cloy take any exception to the Keefers parking their car in the driveway. Why would he, even if it were an excessive use of the right of way, if it did not impede him in the use he wanted to make of the property? His whole posture appears to have been that of an accommodating neighbour anxious to avoid any trouble. This is clear from the one contentious incident disclosed by the evidence, i.e., the incident when one of Mr. Cloy's tenants in the upstairs apartment left his car in the driveway and had a "run-in" with Mr. Keefer. When his tenant reported this to him, Mr. Cloy told him to park somewhere else because "I do not want to fight with my neighbours."

The evidence of Mr. Keefer was "I never had any problems with Doug (Mr. Cloy) as far as the drive-way was concerned." He testified that on one occasion Mr. Cloy left his car in the driveway overnight so that he was unable to get his car out in the morning. He therefore pushed Mr. Cloy's car out onto the road and Mr. Cloy apparently made no objection to his having done that. I cannot attach great significance to this as evidencing an assertion of possessory title by the Keefers since the Cloys, having given the Keefers a right of ingress and egress, had no right to block Mr. Keefer's egress. Mr. Keefer was perfectly entitled to do what he did. I cannot find on the evidence that the Keefers' possession was with the intention of excluding the Cloys from the limited use they wanted to make of the property. I think that the issue of a possessory title is something that has arisen since the Cloy's property changed hands and the hitherto amicable relations between the adjoining owners disintegrated.

As far as proof of the discontinuance of possession by the owner is concerned, I do not believe that the Cloys did discontinue their possession of any part of the strip of land other than the portion at the rear occupied by the respondents' garage. I think that with respect to that portion the constructive possession of the owners was displaced by the actual possession of the Keefers for more than the statutory period. However, as far as the balance of the strip is concerned, I think the owners made such use of it as they wanted. It was used as an access to the apartment above the store and to the entrance to the addition at the rear of the store. It is true that the Cloys may not have used the full width of the strip for this purpose, but the authorities make it clear that the constructive possession which a legal owner has of the whole of his property is not ousted simply because he is not in actual possession of the whole. Possession of part is possession of the whole if the possessor is the legal owner: *Great Western R Co. v. Lutz* (1881), 32 UCCP 166. I find, therefore, that the respondents have not discharged the onus of proving discontinuance of possession of the strip (other than the portion occupied by their garage) by the owners for the statutory period.

I would allow the appeal and hold the respondents entitled to a declaration that the appellants' title has been extinguished only with respect to that part of the land occupied by the respondents' garage.

The appellants should have their costs of the appeal.

MacKINNON JA (dissenting): The plaintiffs asked for a declaration that they are the owners of an eight-foot strip of land lying between their residence, known municipally as 57 Chapel St. S in the Town of Thorold, and the lands of the defendants immediately to the north, known municipally as 53 Chapel St. S. The defendants counterclaimed for a declaration that they are entitled to absolute possession and ownership of the strip of land, and for an injunction restraining the plaintiffs from using the said strip except as a right of way.

The plaintiffs were granted the requested declaration based on a title acquired by prescription and the counterclaim was dismissed. The defendants now appeal.

The issue as to whether a prescriptive right has been acquired is a question of fact and an appellate tribunal must be careful not to re-try such an issue on appeal: *Johnston et al. v. O'Neill et al.*, [1911] AC 552; *Godson Contracting Co. v. Grand Trunk RW Co.* (1917), 13 OWN 241. In the instant case the learned trial Judge heard some 11 witnesses, seven of whom gave evidence on behalf of the plaintiffs. After thoroughly canvassing the evidence, and accepting the evidence given on behalf of the plaintiffs, he made his finding of fact. There is no suggestion that he misunderstood the evidence and unless it is clear that he misunderstood or misapplied the relevant law, this Court should not interfere with his finding. ...

The plaintiffs have shown the necessary *animus possidendi* to support their claim, having the clear intention from the evidence of excluding the owner as well as all others. In the course of his reasons for judgment the learned trial Judge stated that the plaintiffs, with regard to the right of way, "treated it and used it as their own, notwithstanding the grant of right of way in their favour." Clear findings of fact as found by the learned trial Judge with evidence to support them, ought not to be disturbed or varied by this Court on appeal except for the most cogent of reasons. Accordingly, upon a finding of possession and the requisite *animus*, in order to stop the time from running there has to be some act by the holder of the paper title made *animo possidendi*. The intermittent and desultory acts of the owner, through having soft drinks delivered by hand carrier from time to time, without more, were not such, under the circumstances found by the trial Judge, as to stop the time from running.

In my view, the learned trial Judge was correct in holding that the title of the servient owners had been extinguished and that the plaintiffs have gained title by the fact of uninterrupted possession. There is none now who has the right to eject them. The possession here clearly was not equivocal or for a temporary purpose. By 1956 the plaintiffs had abandoned the use of the lands in issue as a right of way and the owner was under an obligation to assert his title to the land to prevent the time running against him, or to ask for a declaration that, because of the abandonment of the use as a right of way, the land had now reverted to him as owner free from any such use. The use made by the plaintiff was no longer referable to a lawful title but rather was totally inconsistent with it: *Thomas v. Thomas* (1855), 2 K & J 79, 69 ER 701. ...

Counsel for the plaintiffs agreed it would make more sense to extend due east to the street line the line running from the north wall of the frame garage to the south face of the precast concrete landing and steps. Such a line would be the north boundary of the land acquired by prescription.

Subject to this variation, I would dismiss the appeal with costs.

Appeal allowed.

DISCUSSION NOTES

i. Possessory Title and "Intention"

The majority judgment in *Keefer* suggests that where the paper titleholder has no immediate wish to use land, a possessor's use will *never be inconsistent with* such (absence of) intention. Such a principle means that land held "for future development" can never be the subject of "dispossession" under statutes of limitation. Does this interpretation accord with the purposes of the statutes identified earlier in this chapter? What about the possessor's intention? Does it matter that the plaintiffs knew that they were using their neighbour's land? Would it have made any difference to the application of the inconsistent user test by Wilson J if the plaintiffs had been innocently mistaken as to the boundary of their lot? In thinking about these questions, consider the following article, which criticizes the use of (subjective) intention on the part of the true owner and advocates a return to the use of a more objective test in relation to claims of possessory title.

Brian Bucknall, "Two Roads Diverged: Recent Decisions on Possessory Title"
(1984) 22 Osgoode Hall LJ 375 (footnotes omitted)

I. Introduction

Let *Piper v. Stevenson* serve as a starting point. In 1901, Miss Piper purchased six lots from Mr. Whaley with the intention of setting up a farm. For some reason, Miss Piper fenced in eight rather than six lots and began to farm them. She lived on another farm during this period and went on the property only for the purposes of cultivating and harvesting. In 1905 and 1906 she had buildings constructed and moved to her new farm. In 1911, the holder of paper title to the two erroneously enclosed lots sold them to Mr. Stevenson. Mr. Stevenson knocked down Miss Piper's fences and himself fenced off the lands which Miss Piper thought she owned and Miss Piper sued successfully for a declaration that she had acquired a possessory title.

Compare that result to the decision over sixty years later in *Masidon Investments Ltd. v. Ham* [(1982), 39 OR (2d) 534 (HCJ), (1984), 45 OR 563 (CA)]. In 1958, Mr. Ham, a lawyer in Oakville, rented a 100 acre parcel of land with the intention of using it as his residence. The landlord apparently considered that the land was a long-term speculation in real estate and had little concern for the actual use made by Mr. Ham. Mr. Ham was a flying enthusiast and laid out a grassy airstrip suitable for use by light planes. It was a fair weather field, with no electric light, radar or radio assistance. The field did, however, become popular with other flyers and from time to time as many as twelve planes would be parked there. Around 1967, Mr. Ham's landlord defaulted on his mortgage on the property and an order of foreclosure was registered against the entire 100 acres. After some shuffling of papers, Mr. Ham's landlord re-acquired title to a fifty acre parcel at the west end of the farm, which was the parcel on which Mr. Ham lived, while Masidon Investments Ltd. held title to the fifty acre parcel at the east end of the farm, which was the parcel on which Mr. Ham had established his airstrip. From 1968 on, Mr. Ham continued to occupy the entire 100 acres. He continued to fly planes from the east half of the parcel, to use the buildings on that side of the parcel, to have the land cultivated by neighbouring farmers, to maintain fences and to make minor improvements to his airstrip. In 1979, the owners of the east half of the parcel realized what had been going on and brought action against Mr. Ham for a declaration that they owned the lands and sued for punitive damages for his trespasses. Masidon was successful in its suit for declaratory relief and it was held that Mr. Ham had not acquired possessory title.

The two cases provide some striking similarities. In both, vacant land was in question and the holders of paper title appeared to be indifferent to the steps taken by the persons in possession. The legislation governing the claims brought in each case, the *Limitations Act*, remained substantially the same over the entire period separating the two decisions. On the bare facts, none of the "distinctions" so beloved of lawyers will explain the contrast in results. One can only conclude that: *Piper v. Stevenson* was wrongly decided, or *Masidon v. Ham* was wrongly decided, or the law has changed.

The hallmark of the decision in *Masidon* is the reliance which Mr. Justice Carruthers, at the trial level, and Mr. Justice Blair on appeal, place on the doctrine of adversity. He concluded that whatever action Mr. Ham took could not be inconsistent with Masidon's intention to sell the land at a future date for development. Insofar as Ham did not and, indeed, could not, do anything inconsistent with Masidon's intentions—because Masidon had no intention—Masidon's rights were inviolable. This analysis, which on the face of it would appear to have been equally available in *Piper v. Stevenson*, was not even mentioned in the earlier case.

Before one can conclude that the law has changed in the decades following *Piper v. Stevenson*, one further decision should be considered. *Beaudoin v. Aubin* [(1981), 33 OR (2d) 604] concerned a dispute over a strip of land along the edge of a residential lot. Mr. Beaudoin and his wife rented the home adjacent to the disputed strip of property in 1951. In 1966, they purchased the home. From 1951 on, however, they had occupied the subsequently disputed strip on the assumption that it was their own. They learned at the time of their purchase that the strip had actually been registered in the name of the adjoining property owners but continued thereafter to use the lands as they had used them before. In 1979, the adjoining owners, by this time the Aubin family, became aware of paper title and disputed Mr. Beaudoin's rights. The parties brought the matter to court for declaratory relief. Mr. Justice Anderson specifically reviewed the Aubins' contention that, since the occupation of the land had arisen as the result of a mistake as to the boundary line between the parcels, no rights whatever could accrue. That is to say, in the absence of knowledge of the true state of title to the property, there could be no adversity and no intention to possess adversely. Mr. Justice Anderson rejected the intention test entirely and considered at length the question of whether the intention and adversity tests were, in fact, appropriate elements of the law in Ontario. He concluded that they were not and granted a declaration as to title to Mr. Beaudoin.

The decision in *Beaudoin v. Aubin* preceded the decision in *Masidon v. Ham* by over a year. Curiously enough, *Beaudoin* was not even discussed by Mr. Justice Carruthers in *Masidon* even though it had been relied upon by counsel for Mr. Ham. The divergence in approach is almost as striking as the divergence in result between *Piper v. Stevenson* and *Masidon v. Ham*. Nor are the two recent decisions uncharacteristic of the law in this area. Contrary to what might be professional expectations, the number of cases dealing with questions of possessory title does not seem to diminish year by year, nor does the jurisprudence used in those cases become more stable and consistent.

· · ·

As mentioned previously, the heart of the matter appears to have been that the use which Mr. Ham made of the property [in *Masidon Investments Ltd v Ham*] was not appropriate for the running of a limitations period. In this respect, Mr. Justice Carruthers relied heavily on the decisions of Madame Justice Wilson, then of the Ontario Court of Appeal, in *Keefer v. Arillotta* and in *Fletcher v. Storoschuk* [a case in which the court applied the inconsistent user test from *Keefer*]. One extract which Mr. Justice Carruthers took from the *Keefer* decision conveys the essence of the argument:

> The use an owner wants to make of his property may be a limited use and an intermittent or sporadic use. A possessory title cannot, however, be acquired against him by depriving him of uses of his property that he never intended or desired to make of it. The *animus possidendi* which a person claiming a possessory title must have is an intention to exclude the owner from such uses as the owner wants to make of his property.

Both Madame Justice Wilson and Mr. Justice Carruthers relied on the old English case of *Leigh v. Jack* for this proposition.

Madame Justice Wilson's words create the implication that possessory title is "acquired" by some ongoing process. Implicitly, the old doctrine that an estate in possession will either exist or not exist at any given instant in time, and will become indefeasible through the provisions of the statute, is ignored. Secondly, the quotation identifies not one but two tests of intention where a possessory interest is to be claimed. There is, first, the intention of the person in possession, which must be to "exclude the owner from such uses as the owner wants to make," and second, the intention of the owner, which may be to make some use, or no use, of the lands. To phrase the principle positively, a person in possession of lands which he does not own can "acquire" title only if he knows that he does not own the lands, knows who does own the lands, knows the intentions which the true owner has with regard to the use of the lands, and acts in a manner inconsistent with those intentions.

The phrasing of the principle in a positive form does, of course, display its weaknesses. Proof of any intention is difficult, especially over a ten year period. Certainly there would be few owners who would confess to having any immediate and consistent intention to use lands which they have not tried to occupy for over a decade. Mr. Justice Carruthers himself confessed that his approach to the doctrine may well mean that possessory title cannot be obtained against "development land which is in the holding stage." Further, the formulation is almost impossible to apply in what is the most common instance, situations where both the paper title holder and the possessor are simply mistaken about the nature and extent of their respective rights and cannot therefore establish an intention consistent with the proposed legal test.

[The author reviewed the judgment of Blair JA in the Ontario Court of Appeal and then compared the facts and the reasoning in *Beaudoin v Aubin*.]

The parties there proceeded on the basis of a mutual mistake with regard to their common boundary and their respective rights over the disputed land. The holder of paper title could form no intention with regard to lands which he did not know he owned nor could the possessor be expected to demonstrate that he was acting adversely to the true owner's interests since all he hoped to do was use the property which he thought he owned. Mr. Justice Anderson was called upon to consider the entire body of doctrine with regard to possessory title and, in a thorough and scholarly decision, he concluded that Mr. Beaudoin in fact, established an indefeasible title even though he had not acted with that intention. Mr. Justice Anderson began with a close analysis of the history of the *Limitations Act*. He pointed out that, prior to the passage of the *Real Property Limitation Act, 1833* in England, the common law for both Canada and England had employed the concept of "adversity" in a very technical sense when testing the question of whether or not a possessory title had been established. With the passage of the Act in 1833, the focus shifted to the question of whether or not an action against the possessor should have been brought by the true owner. The Act, after the manner of limitations acts generally, was simply procedural in its nature, not substantive.

Mr. Justice Anderson quoted Mr. Justice Smily in *McGugan v. Turner* to the effect that in the applicable section of the *Limitations Act*:

[N]o exception is made … of ignorance or mistake as to true ownership. In fact it has been held that a common error by the owners in regard to the true line of division between the properties does not prevent the statute running where the statute does not require it to be shown that possession was adverse and not with acquiescence or permission.

Justice Anderson pointed out that the change in the legislation led early commentators in Ontario to state that, for the purposes of this province, the concept of "adverse possession" in its original form had been abolished and the phrase had continued to be used only as a matter of convenience.

For at least fifteen years Mr. Beaudoin occupied land that he thought was his by right. Mr. Justice Anderson had to address directly the question of whether it was necessary to show that any particular intention was associated with his acts. He distinguished several cases, in which intention had been found to be an important element, by showing that they focused on factual situations in which the acts of possession were equivocal. He concluded that the possession of the lands by Mr. Beaudoin was certain and unequivocal and the *animus possidendi* could therefore be presumed. He ended his analysis with a condemnation of the doctrines requiring demonstration of some subjective intention:

> The application of judicial statements, without due regard for the facts of the case in which the statement is made, is a pregnant and perennial source of error. Upon such statements the defence has propounded the argument that, before a party can successfully rely upon sections 4 and 15 of the statute, he must establish a subjective intention, with knowledge of the rights of the plaintiff present in his mind, to occupy in defiance or denial of those rights. No case which I have considered, when one looks to the facts, supports that proposition and it is utterly inconsistent with the decisions in *Martin v. Weld, Babbitt v. Clarke, Nourse v. Clark,* and *McGugan v. Turner.*

· · ·

The doctrines of possessory title are, as suggested earlier, something of a hybrid in our law. The essential analysis goes back to medieval questions of who is seised of an interest and under what circumstances that person's seisin can be challenged. Onto this medieval root had been grafted a branch of statutory law limiting the time within which a challenge to the estate of the person in possession can be brought. Perhaps it would be useful to separate the two parts of the doctrine in order to see where the various tests of possessory usage arise and where they can be helpful.

The possessory estate, which the common law would have protected against all persons other than the true owner, was an estate established by the possessor acting as if he had an interest of indefinite duration (which was, therefore, a freehold interest and, furthermore, a seised estate) which was his as of right. A mere trespass across a piece of land, or a series of trespasses, would not give rise to the same sort of right. Hence, the requirement that possession be continuous. A person who asserted rights based on a stealthy or secretive use of a piece of property would, of course, face an evidentiary problem but was also thought not to be using the lands in a manner consistent with the assertion of a seised interest; thus the requirement that possession be open and obvious. Similarly, a person whose sole claim to property was that he was physically and violently keeping the true owner away was not seen to be enjoying any estate of his own in the lands. Finally, the common law recognized that a person who was in possession of property with the permission of the true owner was simply exercising the true owner's rights and not enjoying an independent estate of his own. The medieval shorthand for these doctrines was that the possession of land which was defensible as an estate in the land was possession "*nec calme, nec vie, nec precaria*" (without stealth, without violence and without permission).

While we have, in many cases, lost sight of the foundation for the tests which we now use, the principles remain the same. The tests for the running of a limitations period have been reformulated for modern application. The calls for "open, obvious and continuous" usage, "peaceful, open and obvious usage" and "usage as of right" are, however, all ways in which the court seeks to establish whether or not the claimant to a possessory title has in fact been enjoying the type of estate which the common law protected.

· · ·

Openness of possession was one of the indicia of the existence of a possessory estate. Similarly, an intention to possess can also be an indicium of a possessory estate in circumstances where the facts of possession are themselves ambiguous. Where the land is in such condition that a true owner would not be expected to constantly make use of it, a person who is making such use as a true owner would make may have his position advanced somewhat by showing that he had, in fact, intended to use the property as his own. The intention in such a case is an intention with regard to the use of an estate in land, not an intention with regard to the acquisition of an estate of land. The older law would not have recognized the idea that a person actually in possession had anything more to acquire. An intention test is, therefore, not wholly inappropriate in circumstances of ambiguity. It must not, however, be allowed to ripen into a threshold test for the assertion of a possessory interest. In the vast majority of instances, possessory interests arise through mistakes innocently made to which no intention whatever can be attached.

The statutory branch of the analysis is in many respects parallel to the common law doctrine. Just as the common law would focus on the question of whether an estate had been brought into existence, the statute focuses on the question of whether or not "an entry or distress ... or action to recover any land" can be brought. Just as a series of trespasses would not establish an estate at common law for which an "action for recovery" would be the appropriate remedy, a series of trespasses will not provide the foundation for such an action under the statute. (Trespasses to land are dealt with as "personal actions" under section 45(1)(g) of the Ontario *Limitations Act* and have their own separate limitations periods.) The tests used to establish whether or not a possessory estate exists are, therefore, appropriate as well to the question of whether or not the right to bring an action to recover land has existed. Again, open, obvious and continuous occupation are important considerations, as might be, in ambiguous situations, the establishment of an intention to use land as a true owner would use it.

The question of the true owner's intention with regard to the land is not definitive under either the common law or the statutory branch of the doctrine. As Mr. Justice Anderson pointed out in *Beaudoin v. Aubin*, the intention of the true owner is, in fact, a test peculiar to the jurisprudence of England.

If the analysis which I have been discussing is helpful, the law dealing with possessory interests might be set out under the following principles:

a)   The common law doctrine that a person in peaceful possession of land will himself have a species of seised estate from the commencement of such possession remains the foundation of our possessory doctrine.

b) The peaceful possession of land which is to be treated as amounting to a possessory estate is the type of possession which a true owner would himself wish to make. Note, however, that this principle is subject to the qualification that property which is not in its nature susceptible to some degree of open and continuous ownership will remain the estate of the paper title holder unless the claimant to a possessory estate takes unusual measures to establish the existence of his interests.

c) The establishment of a possessory estate can be demonstrated through a variety of indicia, none of which is either sufficient in its own right to establish the estate or necessary to establish the estate. Among these indicia are the enclosure of the lands in question, continuous possession, formal repudiation of claims by the true owner and a demonstrated intention to possess the lands as if the claimant were the true owner.

d) Where the facts with regard to open, obvious and continuous possession are well established an "intention to possess" (*animus possidendi*) will be presumed. Indeed, in such circumstances intention is not an issue. Where the facts with regard to possession are equivocal, and especially where the lands in question would not in normal circumstances be in continuous use, the subjective intention of the possessor may be a relevant factor in establishing the existence of a possessory estate.

e) The analysis which can be employed for the purpose of establishing whether or not a possessory estate would exist at common law is useful for the parallel purpose of establishing whether or not a suit to recover the land could (and therefore should) have been brought under the *Limitations Act*.

f) At common law a person in possession of land with the permission of the true owner did not run a possessory period. Similarly, except for the specific instances of tenancies and tenancies-at-will set out in the *Limitations Act*, the fact that a person is in possession without the authorization of the paper title holder is a necessary element in the establishment of a right to bring an action to recover the land and, therefore, a necessary element in the running of a limitations period. For the purposes of the law of Ontario, this is the entire extent of the "adversity" doctrine insofar as the rights and interests of the holder of paper title are concerned.

ii. Rethinking Possessory Title Claims in the United Kingdom: Rejecting Leigh v Jack

Reflect on the factual contexts in cases such as *Piper v Stevenson, St Clair Beach, Keefer v Arillotta, Masidon v Ham*, and *Beaudoin v Aubin*. Can you identify differences in these fact patterns that might explain the differing outcomes in the cases in relation to claims of possessory title? To what extent are the outcomes in these cases consistent with common law principles of possession, the language of the *Real Property Limitations Act*, or the underlying purposes of recognizing possessory title suggested by Rose and Callaghan?

In this context, it appears significant that the issue of the titleholder's intention with respect to the use of land, applied in *Keefer v Arillotta* and *Masidon v Ham*, relied on the English case of *Leigh v Jack* (1879), 5 Ex D 264, 42 LT 463, 28 WR 452 (CA). This case was later applied in *Williams Brothers Direct Supply Stores Ltd v Raftery*, [1958] 1 QB 159 (CA), and in *Wallis's Cayton Bay Holiday Camp Ltd v Shell-Mex and BP Ltd*, [1975] QB 94 (CA). In all these cases, the fact that the titleholder had no immediate intentions with respect to the use of land resulted in the courts' rejection of claims to possessory title. For the courts, these were all cases about "special purposes."

These cases were reconsidered by the English Court of Appeal in *Treloar v Nute*, [1976] 1 WLR 1295. In this case, the titleholder was the owner of a small parcel of rural land, and the trial judge had rejected the possessor's arguments that he had used this parcel for many years for the purposes of grazing animals and dumping excess soil. As the trial judge concluded, the possessor's actions were not inconsistent with the titleholder's (lack of) intentions with respect to the land. In the Court of Appeal, however, the possessor succeeded because the court held that the definition of possession in the limitations statute simply required "possession." As the court stated:

> It is not permissible to import into this definition a requirement that the owner must be inconvenienced or otherwise affected by that possession. Apart from the cases relating to special purpose no authority has been cited to us which would support the requirement of inconvenience to the owner and we are not ourselves aware of any such authority. On the contrary, so far as our own experience goes, the typical instance in which a possessory title is treated as having been acquired is that in which a squatter establishes himself upon a piece of land for which the owner has no use. Indeed, if inconvenience to the owner had to be established it would be difficult indeed ever to acquire a possessory title since the owner if inconvenienced would be likely to take proceedings.
>
> We conclude that, once it is accepted that the judge found, and could properly find, that the defendant's father took possession of the disputed land before the commencement of the limitation period, and in the absence of any evidence of special purpose on the part of the plaintiff, time began to run from such taking of possession, irrespective of whether the plaintiff suffered inconvenience from the possession, and that the defendant must be treated as having acquired a possessory title before the commencement of this action.

The UK Law Reform Commission subsequently confirmed the approach in *Treloar v Nute*, recommending legislation expressly providing that "possession" should bear its ordinary meaning in law for purposes of the *Limitation Act*: see Law Reform Committee. Parliament then enacted the *Limitation Act 1980*, 1980, c 58, s 8 to implement this recommendation:

> 8(4) For the purpose of determining whether a person occupying any land is in adverse possession of the land it shall not be assumed by implication of law that his occupation is by permission of the person entitled to the land merely by virtue of the fact that his occupation is not inconsistent with the latter's present or future enjoyment of the land.

The new legislation was interpreted, in accordance with the principles established in *Treloar v Nute*, in *Bucks County Council v Moran* (1989), 139 New LJ 257 (CA). In this case, the court confirmed that the word "possession" should be given its "natural and ordinary" meaning. This approach was later approved by the House of Lords in *JA Pye (Oxford) Ltd v Graham*, [2002] 3 All ER 865, a case in which a claim of possessory title was successful with respect to land with a potential development value of £10 million, even though the land was being held for future development and the titleholder had no immediate use for it. *JA Pye* is discussed later in this chapter, but it is significant to note here that the House of Lords held that the state of mind of the person dispossessed was essentially irrelevant.

In the context of the test developed in *Keefer v Arillotta* and applied in *Masidon v Ham* in Ontario, both of which relied on the English decision in *Leigh v Jack* (the case that was reviewed and rejected in *Treloar v Nute, Bucks County Council v Moran*, and *JA Pye*), how should Ontario courts now approach the inconsistent user test and the titleholder's intention?

It is interesting that the English approach, limiting the scope of *Leigh v Jack*, was also evident in cases involving squatters who had moved into abandoned council housing and repaired the premises (often also changing the locks): see *Lambeth London Borough v Blackburn*, [2002] 3 All ER 865 (CA). See also MP Thompson, "Adverse Possession: The Abolition of Heresies" (Sep/Oct 2002) 66 Conveyancer and Property Lawyer 480 [Thompson] (supporting the outcome in *JA Pye*); and L Tee, "Adverse Possession and Intention to Possess" (Mar/Apr 2000) 66 Conveyancer and Property Lawyer 113 (an argument for retaining the titleholder's intention in possession cases).

D. "Mistake": Reassessing the Inconsistent User Test

As is clear, judicial reliance on the inconsistent user test in cases such as *Keefer* and *Masidon* in Ontario now appears to diverge substantially from the use of principles to establish possessory title in the United Kingdom. As the facts in *Keefer* and *Masidon* reveal, however, the claims to possessory title were presented in these cases in a context in which the possessors were fully aware that they had no title to the lands involved. Consider, by contrast, situations in which the possessors were mistaken, including *Beaudoin v Aubin* and, probably, *Piper v Stevenson*. To what extent should the inconsistent user test apply to cases where the parties were mistaken?

In reflecting on this issue, consider how the Ontario Court of Appeal assessed the application of the inconsistent user test in the following case:

applicant   *respondent*

Wood v Gateway of Uxbridge Properties Inc
[1990] 75 OR (2d) 769 (Gen Div)

MOLDAVER J: ...

Brief Summary of Case

For almost 18 years, the applicants, Mr. and Mrs. Wood, have enjoyed the exclusive use of a two-acre parcel of land, abutting upon a large tract of land which they purchased in 1972. Until 1989, they honestly believed that the two acres belonged to them.

For almost 17 years, their neighbours to the south had no idea that they were the rightful owners of the two-acre parcel. They too honestly believed that it belonged to the applicants.

As it turns out, everyone was mistaken. This became apparent in 1989, when the respondent, a company known as The Gateway of Uxbridge Property Inc. (Gateway), purchased the land immediately south of the property owned by the applicants. At that time, a new survey was prepared. It established beyond doubt that Gateway held paper title to the two acres.

Nature of This Action

The applicants seek a declaration against the respondents extinguishing all of their rights and title to the two-acre parcel. The respondent Gateway opposes this. The other named respondents are mortgagees of the Gateway lands. They do not oppose the application.

In order to succeed, the applicants must establish that Gateway's right to recover possession of the two acres has been extinguished by operation of ss. 4 and 15 of the *Limitations Act*, RSO 1980, c. 240 ... . To do this, the applicants must show that for an uninterrupted period of ten years, they were in actual possession of the two-acre parcel; they intended to exclude the true owners from possession; and the true owners were in fact effectively excluded from possession. These are the tests set out in *Masidon Investments Ltd. v. Ham* (1984), 45 OR (2d) 563, 2 OAC 147, 31 RPR 200 (CA). In that case, after listing the three tests, Mr. Justice Blair stated, at p. 567 OR, p. 206 RPR:

> The claim will fail unless the claimant meets each of these three tests and time will begin to run against the owner only from the last date when all of them are satisfied.

In this case, the respondent Gateway conceded that the first test had been met. It was admitted that the applicants had been in actual possession of the two-acre parcel from 1972 to the present. However, the respondent submitted that the applicants had failed to satisfy the remaining tests.

The Issues

1. When mutual mistake exists, is it legally possible for the party seeking possessory title to establish the requisite intent to exclude the true owners from possession?
2. When mutual mistake exists, is it legally possible for the party seeking possessory title to establish effective exclusion of the true owners from possession?
3. Have the applicants, in fact, established the effective exclusion of the true owners during the requisite time frame?

The Facts

... Description of the Two-Acre Parcel

The two-acre parcel is found at the northwest corner of the lands purchased by the respondent Gateway. It is long and narrow and takes the form of a wedge. The parcel has been marked as Part 2 on the plan of survey prepared by H.F. Gander Company Limited, found at Appendix B.

It will be seen that the northern boundary of the two-acre parcel borders, in part, on the southern boundary of the large parcel of land which the applicants purchased in 1972. At the east end of the northern boundary is a post and wire fence which extends in a southerly direction for about 30 metres. This fence then proceeds along the southern boundary of the two-acre parcel in a north-westerly direction for approximately 150 metres. Where the fence stops, a row of poplar trees forming a natural boundary continues north-westerly to the western end of the parcel, forming the point of the wedge.

[The following figure is the author's—it is not part of the original case:]

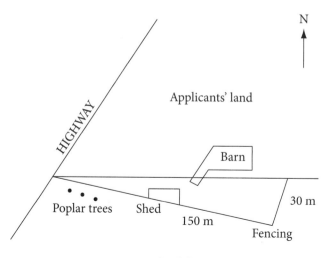

Applicants' Belief

In 1972, the applicants purchased the large tract of land immediately north of the two-acre parcel. However, at the time of purchase, they believed that the two-acre wedge formed part of their land. They had good cause for this belief because this is what they were told. Mr. Rhodes, the prior owner, testified that he believed that the two acres formed part of the land that he was selling. He so advised the applicants. Mr. Rhodes had treated the two-acre parcel as his from the time that he purchased the north parcel in 1968.

In addition, a gravel driveway existed entirely within the two-acre parcel. It commenced at the point of the wedge, that is, the western extremity, and extended easterly for a distance of several hundred metres. This driveway was located immediately north of the poplar trees. It provided access to a house and barn located, for the most part, just north of the two-acre parcel. (The survey prepared by the respondent Gateway in 1989 showed that the southern extremities of both the house and barn encroached slightly upon the north edge of the two-acre parcel.) In addition, a third building, referred to as a frame shed, was located entirely within the two-acre wedge. The gravel driveway also provided access to this building.

Activities of the Applicants on the Two-Acre Parcel

From 1972 until the present, the applicants have lived in the house which encroaches slightly on the two-acre parcel. The applicants have used the gravel driveway on a daily basis as a means of ingress and egress to and from the property.

For approximately 15 years, the applicants farmed the east half of the two-acre parcel. As part of this, they used the barn which also encroaches slightly on the two-acre parcel. As well, they housed farm employees in the frame shed located entirely within the two acres.

Sometime around 1987, the applicants ceased farming and commenced a lumber business on the property. Since that time, the eastern portion of the two-acre parcel has been used as a lumber yard. The barn has been used to store lumber and supplies. The frame shed has been rented out commercially to tenants.

During the 18-year period, the applicants have maintained the gravel driveway and all of the buildings. As well, they have mended the post and wire fence which encloses the entire eastern boundary and a significant portion of the southern boundary of the two-acre parcel.

In summary, for the past 18 years, the applicants have openly and continuously enjoyed the use of the disputed land. They have at all times maintained the buildings, two of which encroach upon and one of which rests exclusively within the two-acre parcel. They have actively and continuously conducted significant commercial operations on this property for the same period of time. They have also maintained and repaired the fence which encloses almost half of the property. They have left standing the row of poplar trees immediately south of the driveway which forms a natural southern boundary on the west half of the two acres.

History of the Property Purchased by the Respondent Gateway

The evidence indicates that the large parcel of land known as the south lot was purchased by Mrs. Hester in 1973. She and her husband initially intended to build a home on this property. However, in April of 1974, these plans changed and the Hesters decided to keep the land for long term investment. At no time during their ownership did the Hesters make any use of their lot.

However, in 1977, they leased the "vacant portions" of their property to the applicants. The agreement, contained in a letter dated May 12, 1977, provided for no rent during 1977 and 1978 and payment of $13.50 per acre for the successive three years. This arrangement was advantageous to the Hesters since the applicants would farm their property and thereby relieve the Hesters from maintaining it.

The evidence is clear that the Hesters at all times believed that the two-acre parcel belonged to the applicants. They had complete knowledge of the activities carried out by the applicants and understandably, registered no complaint. When they leased the "vacant lands" to the applicants, they did not intend for the agreement to cover the two-acre parcel.

The Hesters sold the south lot to Mr. Garro in May of 1987. Mr. and Mrs. Garro purchased the land with the intention of building a house but they too abandoned these plans. The Garros made no use of the property except to build a small chicken barn at the southeast corner of their lot. The Garros were holding the property as an investment when the respondent Gateway purchased it in 1989.

Throughout their tenure, the Garros honestly believed that the applicants were the true owners of the two-acre parcel. They too had full knowledge of the activities carried out by the applicants and again, understandably, made no complaint.

Discovery of the Problem

In 1989, before purchasing the south lot from Mr. and Mrs. Garro, the respondent Gateway had a survey prepared. The survey clearly revealed that the two-acre parcel was in fact part of the south lot.

Throughout the course of each of the prior transactions regarding the north and south lots, all of the parties had available to them a survey which had been prepared in 1967.

This survey was accurate as far as it went. However, it failed to demarcate the buildings, fences, poplar trees, driveway and the like, and therefore, no one knew how these related to the actual boundary lines. ...

[The court then examined the first issue—that is, whether it is ever possible for a person seeking possession, in a case of mutual mistake, to establish the requisite intent to exclude the true owners from possession. Citing Anderson J in *Beaudoin v Aubin* and Blair J in *Masidon v Ham* (among other cases), the judge concluded:]

Evidence of mutual mistake may justify an inference that the party seeking possessory title did in fact intend to exclude all others, including the true owners. This is an inference which may be drawn. It is not a presumption which must be drawn.

The trier of fact must look to the whole of the evidence to determine whether the claimant did, in fact, have the requisite intent to dispossess the true owners. However, in the absence of any evidence to the contrary, evidence of mutual mistake could alone justify such a finding.

For these reasons, I am satisfied that in cases of mutual mistake, it is legally possible for the party seeking possessory title to establish the requisite intent to dispossess the true owners. Issue one must therefore be answered "Yes."

Issue Two—The Law

When mutual mistake exists, is it legally possible for the party seeking possessory title to establish effective exclusion of the true owners from possession?

In *Masidon, supra*, Mr. Justice Blair held that a person seeking possessory title must establish the effective exclusion of the true owners from possession. To decide this, the court posed the following question at p. 568 OR, p. 207 RPR:

Was the use of the land made by the appellant inconsistent with that of the respondents? The question [is one] of "adverse possession."

In the next major paragraph, Mr. Justice Blair made the following observation [at 568 OR, 207 RPR]:

As a consequence of the reforming statutes of the 1830s, adverse possession is established where the claimant's use of the land is inconsistent with the owner's "enjoyment of the soil for the purposes for which he intended to use it": *Leigh v. Jack* (1879), 5 Ex. D 264 at p. 273, *per* Bramwell LJ, and see Megarry and Wade, *The Law of Real Property*, 4th ed. (1975), p. 1013.

His Lordship then continued p. 568 OR, pp. 207-08 RPR:

Recent decisions in this Court have established that not every use of land will amount to adverse possession excluding that of the owner. Madam Justice Wilson summarized the effect of these decisions in *Fletcher v. Storoschuk et al., supra*, at p. 724 as follows:

... [A]cts relied on to constitute adverse possession must be considered relative to the nature of the land and in particular the use and enjoyment of it intended to be made by the owner: see *Lord Advocate v. Lord Lovat* (1880), 5 App. Cas. 273 at 288; *Kirby v. Cowderoy*, [1912] AC 599 at 603. The mere fact that the defendants did various things on the ... land is not enough to show adverse possession. The things they did must be inconsistent with the form of use and enjoyment the plaintiff intended to make of it: see *Leigh v. Jack* (1879), 5 Ex. D 264; *St. Clair Beach Estates Limited v. MacDonald et al.* (1974), 5 OR (2d) 482, 50 DLR (3d) 650; *Keefer v. Arillotta* (1976), 13 OR (2d) 680, 72 DLR (3d) 182. Only then can such acts be relied upon as evidencing the necessary "*animus possidendi*" vis-à-vis the owner.

I must confess some difficulty applying this "test" to the case at bar. I say this because the true owners did not know that they were the rightful owners of the two-acre parcel during the requisite time frame. How then is it possible to determine what use they intended for the property when they at no time even contemplated its use? And if they had no intended use for the property, how can one compare the use of the applicants to find consistency or lack thereof with a non-existent intended use?

The respondent Gateway argued that the onus was upon the applicants to establish that the activities carried out by the applicants were inconsistent with the intended use of the property by the respondent or its predecessors. But since the respondent and its predecessors had no intended use for the property, the respondent submitted that the application must of necessity fail due to legal impossibility.

I cannot accept this proposition. If accurate, it would mean that in cases involving mutual mistake, no action could ever lie for a declaration of possessory title. And yet, there are numerous examples, already cited, where possessory title has been awarded in cases involving mutual mistake. These include: *Clarke v. Babbitt*; *Nourse v. Clarke*; *McGugan v. Turner*; *Laing v. Moran*; *Beaudoin v. Aubin*; and *Keil v. 762098 Ontario Inc.*, all *supra*. None of these cases even referred to the "inconsistency" test.

In *Masidon, supra*, it will be recalled that the court distinguished the facts in that case from a situation involving colour of right or mutual mistake. The extract bears repetition [at 575 OR, 215 RPR]:

> The appellant's occupancy of the land was not justified by any suggestion of colour of right or mistake as to title or boundaries. Occupation under colour of right or mistake might justify an inference that the trespasser occupied the lands with the intention of excluding all others which would, of course, include the true owners.

I do not read this to mean that in cases of mutual mistake, an application for possessory title must of necessity fail. Surely the Court of Appeal would have said so had this been the case. They did not because that simply is not the law.

The "Inconsistency Test"

As previously indicated, no mention of the "inconsistency" test is found in cases involving mutual mistake. In my opinion, this is so because the relevance of the "test," if it is a "test" at all, is restricted to situations where a trespasser seeks possessory title. Here, I refer to a trespasser as a person who uses land knowing that it belongs to someone else. This is a far different situation from a person who uses land under an honest, albeit mistaken, belief as to rightful ownership.

In cases of trespass, the law has placed a very high onus on those who would seek to dispossess the rightful owner. The reason for this is simple. It is a rather shocking proposition that a trespasser should be able to make use of property, knowing full well that it belongs to someone else, and then rely upon acts of illegitimate user to dispossess the true owner.

In *Masidon, supra*, this policy was clearly spelled out by Mr. Justice Blair at p. 574 OR, pp. 214-15 RPR:

> The policy underlying the *Limitations Act* was stated by Burton JA in *Harris v. Mudie* (1883), 7 OAR 414, as follows at p. 421:
>
>> The rule, as I understand it, has always been to construe the Statutes of Limitations in the very strictest manner where it is shewn that the person invoking their aid is a mere trespasser ... and such a construction commends itself to one's sense of right. They were never in fact intended as a means of acquiring title, or as an encouragement to dishonest people to enter on the land of others with a view to deprive them of it.

Robins JA speaking for this Court in the *Giouroukos* case, *supra*, reiterated this policy when he said at pp. 187-8:

> When all is said and done, this is a case of a businessman seeking to expand significantly the size of his commercial land holdings by grabbing a valuable piece of his neighbour's vacant property. The words of Mr. Justice Middleton used in denying the claim of an adverse possessor to enclosed land in *Campeau v. May* (1911), 19 OWR 751 at p. 752, are apposite:
>
>> It may be said that this makes it very hard to acquire a possessory title. I think the rule would be quite different if the statute was being invoked in aid of a defective title, but I can see nothing in the policy of the law, which demands that it should be made easy to steal land or any hardship which requires an exception to the general rule that the way of the transgressor is hard.

In my opinion, the "inconsistency" test arose in order to avoid apparent injustice to rightful owners and to prevent the unjust enrichment of wanton trespassers.

The test appears to have originated in the case of *Leigh v. Jack* (1879), 5 Ex. D 264, 49 LJQB 220, 28 WR 452 (CA), where the plaintiff retained a strip of land adjacent to the land conveyed to the defendant, intending that it be used at some future time as a street. For more than 20 years, the defendant used the strip as a refuse dump for his foundry. On these facts, the English Court of Appeal held that the defendant had not obtained possessory title. Bramwell LJ stated at p. 273 Ex. D:

> I do not think that there was any dispossession of the plaintiff by the acts of the defendant: acts of user are not enough to take the soil out of the plaintiff and her predecessors in title and to vest it in the defendant; *in order to defeat a title by dispossessing the former owner, acts must be done which are inconsistent with his enjoyment of the soil for the purposes for which he intended to use it*: that is not the case here, where the intention of the plaintiff and her predecessors in title was not either to build upon or to cultivate the land, but to devote it at some future time to public purposes. The plaintiff has not been dispossessed, nor has she discontinued possession, her title has not been taken away, and she is entitled to our judgment. (Emphasis added.)

There is a divergence in the jurisprudence as to the rationale for such a test. Some authorities related it to the quality of possession; others to the requisite intent to dispossess.

The "quality of possession" rationale was explained in *Wallis's Cayton Bay Holiday Camp Ltd. v. Shell-Mex & BP Ltd.*, [1975] QB 94, [1974] 3 All ER 575, [1974] 3 WLR 387 (CA), where Lord Denning MR said at p. 103 QB:

> The reason behind the decisions is because it does not lie in that other person's mouth to assert that he used the land of his own wrong as a trespasser. Rather his user is to be ascribed to the licence or permission of the true owner. By using the land, knowing that it does not belong to him, he impliedly assumes that the owner will permit it: and the owner, by not turning him off, impliedly gives permission. And it has been held many times in this court that acts done under licence or permitted by the owner do not give a licensee a title under the *Limitation Act 1939*. They do not amount to adverse possession: see *Cobb v. Lane*, [1952] 1 TLR 1037; *British Railways Board v. GJ Holdings Ltd.*, March 25, 1974; Bar Library Transcript No. 81 of 1974 in this court.

In my opinion, the approach taken by the Court of Appeal in *Masidon, supra*, reflected this rationale. Mr. Justice Blair related the "inconsistency" test to the question of the effective exclusion of the true owners, an important factor in assessing the overall quality of possession.

The "requisite intent" rationale was explained in *Keefer v. Arillotta* (1976), 13 OR (2d) 680, 72 DLR (3d) 182 (CA), where Madam Justice Wilson said:

> The use an owner wants to make of his property may be a limited use and an intermittent or sporadic use. A possessory title cannot, however, be acquired against him by depriving him of uses of his property that he never intended or desired to make of it. The *animus possidendi* which a person claiming a possessory title must have *is an intention to exclude the owner from such uses as the owner wants to make of his property*. (Emphasis added.)

This proposition was referred to again in *Fletcher v. Storoschuk* (1981), 35 OR (2d) 722, 128 DLR (3d) 59, 22 RPR 75 (CA), where Madam Justice Wilson said at p. 724 OR:

> … [A]cts relied on to constitute adverse possession must be considered relative to the nature of the land and in particular the use and enjoyment of it intended to be made by the owner: see *Lord Advocate v. Lord Lovat* (1880), 5 App. Cas. 273 at 288; *Kirby v. Cowderoy*, [1912] AC 599 at 603. The mere fact that the defendants did various things on the … land is not enough to show adverse possession. The things they did must be inconsistent with the form of use and enjoyment the plaintiff intended to make of it: see *Leigh v. Jack* (1879), 5 Ex. D 264; *St. Clair Beach Estates Limited v. MacDonald et al.* (1974), 5 OR (2d) 482, 50 DLR (3d) 650; *Keefer v. Arillotta* (1976), 13 OR (2d) 680, 72 DLR (3d) 182. *Only then can such acts be relied upon as evidencing the necessary "animus possidendi" vis-à-vis the owner*. (Emphasis added.)

Both of these cases involved trespassers as I have defined them.

To summarize, it would seem that acts of user carried out by trespassers which could not be said to be inconsistent with the rightful owner's intended use of the land would not suffice to establish possessory title because they either (1) carried with them the implied permission of the true owner, or (2) they negatived a finding of the requisite intent to dispossess.

It is of interest to note that although the "inconsistency" test originated in England as a result of cases such as *Leigh v. Jack, supra*, it has been the focus of a great deal of controversy in that country for many years. The nature and extent of this controversy is fully explored in Derek Mendes da Costa and Richard J. Balfour, *Property Law: Cases, Text and Materials* (Emond Montgomery, 1982), at pp. 614-19. Suffice it to say that as a result of the twenty-first Report of the Law Reform Committee (1977), the English *Limitations Act, 1939* (UK, 2 & 3 Geo. 6), c. 21, was amended as follows:

> For the purposes of determining whether a person occupying any land is in adverse posses-
> sion of the land it shall not be assumed by implication of law that his occupation is by per-
> mission of the person entitled to the land merely by virtue of the fact that his occupation is
> not inconsistent with the latter's present or future enjoyment of the land.
>
> This provision shall not be taken as prejudicing a finding to the effect that a person's oc-
> cupation of any land is by implied permission of the person entitled to the land in any case
> where such a finding is justified on the actual facts of the case.

See s. 8(4) of Part I of Schedule I to the *Limitation Act, 1980* (UK), c. 58.

For the purpose of this case, it need not be decided whether the "inconsistency" test is relevant to the quality of possession or the issue of intent or both. Furthermore, it need not be decided whether it creates a legal presumption against a trespasser seeking pos-sessory title or whether it should simply be a factor to be considered, along with all of the other evidence, in assessing either the quality of possession or the issue of intent. What-ever the case may be, in my opinion, it has no application in cases involving mutual mistake as to title.

For these reasons, I am satisfied that in cases of mutual mistake, it is legally possible for the party claiming possessory title to establish effective exclusion of the true owners from possession. Issue two must therefore be answered "Yes."

Issue Three

Have the applicants in fact established the effective exclusion of the true owners during the requisite time frame?

This issue arises from the evidence of Mr. Hester, who testified that he and his wife leased their vacant land to the applicants from 1977 to 1981. It will be remembered that the Hesters purchased the south lot in 1973. They sold the property to Mr. and Mrs. Garro in 1987.

The respondent submitted that [the] lease included the two-acre parcel. Thus, for a period of five years, the applicants used the two-acre parcel with the express permission of the rightful owners. The applicants were therefore precluded from establishing that they had, in fact, effectively excluded the true owners for a continuous and uninterrupted period of ten years.

In my opinion, this argument must fail for two reasons. First, the lease related to "vacant land." Minimally, the two-acre parcel contained a shed which the applicants initially used to house farm employees and later as a source of rental income. Second and of greater significance, the Hesters did not intend for the two-acre parcel to form a part of the leased property. Nor could they have. They honestly believed that it belonged to the applicants.

For these and other reasons which follow, issue three must also be answered "Yes."

Conclusion

Applying the three tests in *Masidon, supra*, to the case at bar, I am satisfied beyond any doubt that the applicants have established possessory title by way of adverse possession. Simply put, the possession of the applicants of the two-acre parcel has been open, notorious, constant, continuous, peaceful and exclusive of the rights of the true owners for almost 18 years. The applicants not only intended to exclude the true owners for this period of time; they in fact did so.

For 18 years the applicants carried out significant commercial activities on the property. They maintained and repaired the post and wire fence which encloses the entire east half of the two-acre parcel. They maintained the driveway on the western portion of the parcel and used it on a daily basis for ingress and egress to their house and barn, both of which encroach slightly on the two-acre parcel. Furthermore, the applicants have at all times used the shed located squarely within the boundaries of the parcel, first as a residence for farm employees, and more recently as a source of rental income.

Tracking the words of Mr. Justice Roach in *Laing v. Moran, supra*, the applicants for 18 years have asserted a claim to the soil. Within the statutory period, the true owners did not awake from their own inaction. It was only as a result of a new survey prepared for the respondent Gateway in 1989 that the problem came to light. By then, in my opinion, it was too late. The rights of the true owners to this land had been barred by statute.

In result, there will be an order as against the respondents extinguishing all of their rights and title to the two-acre parcel, more particularly defined as Part 2 in the plan of survey attached as Appendix B.

Further, there will be a declaration that the applicants are entitled as against the respondents to ownership of the said property in fee simple.

If counsel cannot agree, I may be spoken to as to the costs of this application.

Order accordingly.

DISCUSSION NOTES

i. Reassessing (Different) Tests for Possessory Title: Teis v Ancaster (Town)

In *Gateway*, the court clearly distinguished cases involving mutual mistake and those involving "knowing" trespass and limited the application of the inconsistent user test from *Keefer* to the latter. Is this distinction appropriate?

In considering this question, it may be helpful to consider the Ontario Court of Appeal's decision in *Teis v Ancaster (Town)* (1997), 35 OR (3d) 216. In this case, Teis applied for a declaration of possessory title in relation to two strips of land located at the edge of a public park in the town of Ancaster; the town held paper title to the strips of land. However, Teis had always considered the strip to be part of his field. Although there was some evidence that the town realized its vulnerability to a claim by Teis to possessory title, no action was taken within the limitation period. Teis was successful at trial, and the Court of Appeal confirmed the trial decision. In reviewing the facts and legal principles, the appellate court expressly confirmed the decision in *Gateway* (at 224), and its conclusion that "the test of inconsistent use did not apply to a case of mutual mistake about title." According to Laskin JA (at 225):

It makes no sense to apply the test of inconsistent use when both the paper title holder and the claimant are mistaken about their respective rights. The application of the test would defeat adverse possession claims in cases of mutual mistake, yet permit such claims to succeed in cases of knowing trespass. Thus applied, the test would reward the deliberate squatter and punish the innocent trespasser. Policy considerations support a contrary conclusion. The law should protect good faith reliance on boundary errors or at least the settled expectations of innocent adverse possessors who have acted on the assumption that their occupation will not be disturbed.

As a result of the Court of Appeal's decision in *Teis v Ancaster*, it appears that the inconsistent user test in *Keefer* is not applicable to cases of mutual mistake—e.g. see *Landmark Management Inc v Ouimet*, [2000] OJ no 230 (Sup Ct J). Yet, this distinction between cases of mutual mistake and knowing trespass may not be entirely satisfactory. For example, in an annotation to the Court of Appeal decision in *Teis*, Brian Bucknall argued:

> The key element in *Teis v. Ancaster (Town)* appears to be that both parties were mistaken about where the actual boundaries of their respective properties lay. Both parties acted as if the Teis were entitled to possess the now disputed property. If neither the Teis nor Ancaster knew that any trespass was occurring, how could the adversity test be met?
>
> On this point, Laskin JA offers a very helpful clarification of two streams of analysis that have sometimes appeared irreconcilable. Cases in Ontario began some years ago to divide themselves between situations of advertent trespass and situations of mutual mistake. The advertent trespass cases (*Masidon v. Ham* and *Giouroukos v. Cadillac Fairview Corp.* being the chief examples) raised a strict standard when a person in possession wished to assert that the rights of the holder of paper title had been terminated. Ontario courts advertently discourage any type of action in which a trespasser will be permitted to "steal" the property of a lawful owner. The possessor in any such case must convince the court that it knew who the owner was, that it knew what the owner's intentions were with respect to the property, and that it had acted in a manner advertently antithetical to the owner's rights.
>
> When both the holder of paper title and the possessor have been acting under a mistake with respect to the nature of title and the lawful boundaries, none of the foregoing tests can be met. Laskin JA holds, quite properly, that the adversity tests are inapplicable to a situation in which a mutual mistake has occurred. When the parties proceed under mutual mistake, it will be sufficient if the possessor is in open, obvious, and continuous possession for the applicable limitation period. For that conclusion, Laskin JA builds on, and amplifies, the decisions of Anderson J in *Beaudoin v. Aubin* and of Moldaver J in *Wood v. Gateway of Uxbridge Properties Inc.* One can be grateful to Laskin JA for clearly and forcefully stating those independent, and divergent, rules. One wonders, however, on what foundations those two rules are constructed.
>
> The test sometimes appears to be a moral one. A trespasser who knows that he or she is occupying property to which he or she is not entitled is acting contrary to moral and legal rules and is not entitled to any assistance from the court. When a trespasser demonstrates that his or her activities have been so blatant that the holder of paper title has been culpably negligent in protecting its interests, the court can, with apparent reluctance, declare that those interests have been lost.
>
> Moral tests, unfortunately, are difficult to articulate and even more difficult to apply. They lurk in the background of many contract, tort, and family law decisions, though a widespread adoption of moral criteria in judicial decision-making could paralyze commerce as we know it.

Perhaps the test, where a knowledgeable trespasser is concerned, is not the moral position of the trespasser but the subjective intention of the holder of paper title. Should the holder of paper title be forced into an aggressive, and potentially litigious, position (with all the expense that it might entail) when the holder sees no harm being done? Should the holder of paper title instead be allowed to assume that its rights are unimpaired until a genuine conflict develops?

The case that will test those issues will obviously be a case of *unilateral mistake*. What rule will apply when the person claiming a possessory title used property as his or her own on the assumption that he or she actually held legal title while the owner of paper title knew of, and ignored, the trespass because it had no apparent impact on his or her interests? Should the possessor, who acted in ignorance and is not fixed with moral blame, have the benefit of the running of a limitation period? Conversely, should the landowner, who saw no conflict, be permitted to assert that an adversity test applies and has not been met?

The latter situation may yet challenge the validity of the two new rules. My assumption is that the rule concerning advertent trespassers, will, in the light of an analysis of the third situation, be found to be unworkable in the context of a unilateral mistake and the law will settle again on one standard for the creation of a possessory title, which standard will be objective, rather than subjective, in its test of the steps taken by the person holding the possessory interest. (Emphasis added.)

(See Brian Bucknall, "Teis v Ancaster: Knowledge, the Lack of Knowledge and the Running of a Possessory Title Period" (1997) 13 RPR (3d) 68 at 70-72.) Note especially Bucknall's comment about the need to distinguish mutual mistake (as was evident in *Wood v Gateway* and *Teis v Ancaster (Town)* from unilateral mistake. What is the suitable approach in a case involving unilateral mistake? This issue is examined below in *Bradford Investments (1963) Ltd v Fama (Bradford)*.

ii. Morality and Possessory Title

Larissa Katz has argued that the position of a claimant to possessory title is a moral claim to "set the agenda" for land. Examine her argument in the following excerpt: to what extent do you agree with her claim? Note especially how societal consent (identified by Carol Rose, above) plays a central role in the agenda-setting theory of land "ownership":

On what grounds can we justify the transformation of squatters into owners? To understand the moral significance of adverse possession, we need to begin with the proper analogy. Much of the moral analysis of adverse possession has proceeded on the basis that adverse possessors are land thieves. I will begin here by explaining why it is inapt to think of adverse possessors as land thieves. Following that, I will present an analogy between adverse possession and revolution or, more precisely, a bloodless *coup d'état*, which better illuminates the nature of the adverse possessor's claim and also what justifies the law's recognition of it. The recognition of the adverse possessor's (private) authority solves the *moral* problem created by an agendaless object, just as the recognition of the existing government's (public) authority, whatever its origin, solves the moral problem of a stateless people. The morality of adverse possession, seen this way, does not turn on any particularized evaluation of the squatter's deserts or her uses of the land. I am thus not proposing that adverse possession is justified in the same way that some argue a conscientious revolutionary is justified in resisting an oppressive or otherwise unjust sovereign. Rather, the morality of adverse possession is found where we might least expect it, in its positivist strategy of ratifying the claims to authority of a squatter without regard to the substantive merits of her agenda or her personal virtue.

What distinguishes theft or robbery from adverse possession? Consider for a moment the characteristic *modus operandi* of the thief: the thief achieves his goals—permanent control of someone else's property—either by force or by stealth. The thief's method tells us something about the character of his claim to the object. The thief takes physical possession of the object with intent to deprive the owner permanently of possession without making a counterclaim of authority. The thief does not enter into a contest for legitimate authority over the object, but rather, as the robber's resort to force or the thief's secrecy reveals, it is an assertion of control *in spite of* their recognition of the owner's superior authority over the object. The thief aims to get away with wrongful possession in spite of someone else's acknowledged authority. What is significant about this is that the thief is not inviting an evaluation of a competing claim to authority nor is he demanding to be judged the owner as a result of his actions. Insofar as the thief controls the object of property, his aim is to dupe society into thinking he is the owner, which is something quite different from trying to elicit a judgment that he is in fact the owner.

Contrast the character of the thief's claims with the character of the adverse possessor's claims. The adverse possessor demands public recognition of her authority as owner, which she achieves only where she manifestly has authority over the land in place of the original owner. Thus, adverse possession is successful only where it is peaceful, open, and notorious. Stealth or force undermines the adverse possessor's claims because by sneaking or forcibly removing the original owner, she in effect reveals that she herself lacks effective authority.

The character of an adverse possessor's claim is much more like that of a new government following a *coup d'état* than that of a thief. An adverse possessor does not merely circumvent the authority of the original owner but rather displaces it by asserting his own claim to authority. The adverse possessor claims exclusive and supreme authority, as does a new government, whatever its origins.

(See Larissa Katz, "The Moral Paradox of Adverse Possession: Sovereignty and Revolution in Property Law" (2010) 55 McGill LJ 47 at 72-75.) To what extent do you agree that claims of possessory title to land can be compared to a bloodless coup to change government? Is it helpful to think about possessory title claims as efforts to "set the agenda" for land?

iii. Possessory Title, Mutual Mistake, and "Good Neighbours": Mueller v Lee

Mueller v Lee, [2007] OJ no 2543 (Sup Ct J), involved two adjacent properties in the Toronto neighbourhood of Humewood-Cedarvale. In this case, the court was asked to decide on a claim of adverse possession stemming from the actions of the lands' previous owners. Because property interests achieved through possessory title may be transferred, the Muellers claimed that the actions of their home's previous owners (the Mannis) granted them an interest in four small strips of land on the current property of Dr Lee (who bought the lot from the Allens). The four strips of land at issue included two small pieces of land on the Muellers' side of the dividing fence between the two houses, a part of the driveway connected to the Muellers' current driveway, and a concrete curb near that driveway.

Even though surveys and deeds showed that the Allen family was the true owner of the four pieces of land, both previous families had acted on the assumption that most of this disputed property belonged to the Mannis. Several examples of this acquiescence included that the Allens had no objection to the Mannis building two small fences that encroached on their land; the Mannis paved over the now-disputed driveway soon after moving in beside the Allens; and, when the Allens held their annual barbeque, they would always instruct their guests to avoid the now-disputed area. Furthermore, when the lot was first being described to the Mannis, their real estate agent pointed out the lands in question as being a part of their property. The court also explained that the only piece of land that did not fit this pattern of mistaken ownership was the concrete curb.

In the light of these facts, Justice Perell based much of his judgment on an application of the mutual mistake approach to possession, evidenced in *Wood*. Noting that mutual mistakes allow inadvertent trespassers to use a substantially lower threshold when demonstrating an intention to dispossess—that is, the inconsistent user test is inapplicable—Perell J found (at paras 53-56):

> The Mannis's exclusivity of possession was not interrupted by the very occasional intrusion by Mr. Allen or his children onto the driveway. These intrusions were not acts of control, and they were not acts of ownership because they were trivial, and, moreover, the Allens did not think they owned the driveway lands .... I find that the Allens shared the mistaken belief that the driveway lands and the small strips of land enclosed by the wood and chain link fences belonged to the Mannis. ...
>
> Dr. Lee argued that there was no adverse possession by the Mannis because the Allens were indifferent or permissive of the use being made by the Mannis of the driveway and that there was no dispossession of the Allens because the Allens would occasionally use the driveway lands near the side door of their home. These arguments, however, are answered by my finding that the Allens shared the belief that the Mannis owned the driveway [but not the use of the concrete curb].

The court also dealt with a line of reasoning raised by Dr Lee concerning the purpose of adverse possession—that is, "to give effect to the settled expectations of the parties" (para 62). Specifically, Dr Lee argued that because there were no issues with the deeds or surveys laying out the boundaries of the two properties, the court should use these documents as evidence of the settled expectations of the previous owners. Though Perell J did not deny the importance of deeds and surveys in judgments concerning adverse possession, he stated that the courts must mainly focus on the parties' actions and the expectations they produce (at paras 62-63):

> I have no quarrel with a submission that the deeds, surveys, and site plans are relevant to several aspects of the legal calculus of adverse possession, but if deeds and surveys were absolutely dispositive, then the doctrine of adverse possession would be abolished as is the case under the *Land Titles Act*. But the doctrine continues to exist for lands under the *Registry Act*, and it is available to the Muellers in the circumstances of this case. ...
>
> ... The law needs devices to settle boundary disputes, particularly in cases of honest mistakes and settled expectations. The law needs a way to do justice for the situation that neighbouring landowners by their words and conduct have for a lengthy period of time treated the ownership of lands in a settled way that is inconsistent with the registered ownership of the lands. In my opinion, that situation is what happened in the case at bar with respect to the driveway and the lands near the wooden and chain link fences but not with respect to the concrete curb.

Note that Perell J focused on the usefulness of principles of possession to alter title to conform to the "on the ground" usage of land. Recall the purposes of statutes of limitation in relation to possessory title, identified earlier by Rose and Callaghan. Does Perell's decision also suggest a need for titleholders to be vigilant about the boundaries with their neighbours' land? For another case in which the court granted a declaration of possessory title based on the possessor's use of the land, see *Murray Township Farms Ltd v Quinte West (City)* (2006), 28 MPLR (4th) 148.

E. Possessory Title and Mistakes: Mutual or Unilateral?

Wood v Gateway was a case of mutual mistake, and it seems that the Court of Appeal considered that *Teis v Ancaster* was also a case of mutual mistake. In addition, Perell J seemed to treat the litigants in *Mueller v Lee* as successors in title to neighbours who were mutually mistaken about their boundaries. In these cases, the courts rejected the application of the inconsistent user test, and in *Teis* there was some suggestion that the Court of Appeal was not comfortable with it more generally. As Bucknall has suggested, moreover, the issue of applying the inconsistent user test might be more challenging in a case of unilateral mistake.

In *Bradford*, the court considered a case involving unilateral mistake on the part of those claiming possessory title. In reviewing the case, note especially the court's examination of developments in the United Kingdom, and particularly the House of Lords decision in *JA Pye (Oxford) Ltd v Graham.*

Bradford Investments (1963) Ltd v Fama
(2005), 77 OR (3d) 127 (Sup Ct)

[The following figure is the author's—it is not part of the original case:]

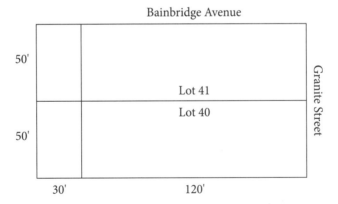

Bainbridge Avenue

[Bradford's evidence:

1. Bradford's evidence was given by Stanley Leibel, aged 77 and retired; he said that Bradford was one of the many corporations used in his real estate business, and that he had built "thousands" of homes in his lifetime (though he was at first unsure of his formal relationship to Bradford).

2. In addition, Leibel said that he had not visited this site for many years, probably since 1973; and that he had not paid any attention to these 30-foot strips other than paying realty taxes on them for the whole period since 1959.

3. Leibel also testified that Bradford discovered the statutory declarations on the title in 1999, when Bradford received an offer to purchase the 30-foot strips.

4. Leibel also gave evidence that he met the defendants at a meeting of a committee of adjustment in 1973 to consider severances of lots 40 and 41; however, he was unable to identify who spoke to him, and neither could his business partner, Mr. Freedman. Leibel remembered that the meeting involved the defendants complaining about garbage that had been left by the builders on the 30-foot strips, and they had asked him to remove it. Leibel said that he then visited the properties and agreed that the residents could extend their clothesline on to the 30-foot strip and keep a market garden. Leibel seems to imply that this deal was struck in exchange for the residents' promise to clear away the garbage from the lots. He was unsure whether there were fences on the properties and where they were located.

5. Freedman added that, although the two would not have concerned themselves with the usage of small, unimportant lots like 40 and 41, they would have been concerned if they had found that a fence had been erected.

Akerman and Fama evidence:

1. Mr and Mrs Fama and Mrs Akerman and her son gave evidence (Mr Akerman died before the trial).

2. Mr Fama testified that he thought he was purchasing the whole lot in 1963, and that the real estate salesman did not tell him anything different. He employed someone to remove a lot of garbage at the rear of the lot, which he thought had been left by the builders; in 1964, he built fences down both sides of his lot to a wooden fence at the western boundary (to prevent people taking shortcuts from Bainbridge Avenue); and in the same year, he planted a vegetable garden and fig trees. He had no idea that there was any problem with the 30-foot strip until Mr Akerman told him of this possibility; and then they both arranged the statutory declarations of 1975. He also testified that he never attended a meeting at which Mr Leibel was present, until the examinations for discovery in 2004.

3. Michael Akerman testified that the family had used the whole area back to the wooden fence at the western boundary as their own; they had planted trees, put up clotheslines, and planted grass. Much like the Famas, the Akermans also paid to have someone remove the debris that was left on their lot by the builders. In addition, by 1961, they had put up fencing that completely enclosed the lot; and, in 1964, Mr Akerman had begun a vegetable and flower garden on the 30-foot strip. Mrs Akerman also denied ever meeting Mr Leibel at a meeting in the early 1970s and that she had asked Mr Leibel's permission to use the 30-foot strip.

In this case, the judge concluded his assessment of the evidence as follows:

Overall, I have no hesitation in considering the defendants' evidence … to be more reliable than that of … Leibel … . He had been involved in thousands of real estate investments and developments, had attended numerous hearings and public meetings in connection with them, and the 30 ft strips were two of many very small pieces his corporation had retained on sales of other properties. … [T]he fact that someone connected with Bradford continued to pay realty taxes in respect of the 30 ft strips is not inconsistent with this conclusion.

The judge also found that the defendants were honest and truthful in their evidence, while Leibel may have formed a view, after examinations for discovery, with respect to matters of which he had no "clear recollection."

The judge then defined the issues as follows:

1. Did the defendants have actual possession of the 30-foot strips?

2. Did the defendants intend to exclude Bradford from possession?

3. Was the "true owner" effectively excluded from possession?]

CULLITY J:

. . .

4. Application of Section 4 to the Facts

I will consider, in turn, each of the three requirements stated by Blair J.A. in *Masidon*.

(a) Did the Defendants Have Actual Possession of the 30-ft Strips?

I believe the findings of fact I have made require a conclusion that the Famas have been in actual possession of the 30 ft strip at the rear of Lot 41 since February, 1964 and that Mrs Akerman and her husband were in possession of the other 30 ft strip from 1961 until his death in 1988—and that she has had actual possession since then. Their control and use of these properties commenced when they purchased the larger parts of Lots 41 and 40, respectively, under a mistaken belief about the location of their western boundaries. Their acts of user were made on their own behalf as purported owners of the 30 ft strips and were in no way equivocal, sporadic or transitory. Rather they were "open, notorious, constant [and] peaceful" and there is nothing to suggest that they were distinguishable in quality, or degree, from their possession of the lands they had purchased.

In *J.A. Pye (Oxford) Ltd v. Graham*, [2003] A.C. 419 (H.L.), at para 41, Lord Browne-Wilkinson stated that there are two elements necessary for legal possession:

1. A sufficient degree of physical custody and control ("factual possession"); and

2. An intention to exercise such custody in control on one's own behalf and for one's own benefit ("intention to possess").

Subject to the doctrine, or test, of inconsistent use that I will refer to in connection with the third of the requirements stated by Blair J.A., I have no hesitation in finding that the first of the requirements is satisfied.

(b) Did the Defendants Intend to Exclude Bradford from Possession?

To the extent that this requirement involves an inquiry into the actual intention of the defendants, I have no hesitation in finding that it, also, was satisfied. From 1961, in the case of the Akermans—and 1964 in the case of the Famas—until early in 1975, they thought they had purchased the 30 ft strips and it must, I believe, be presumed that they intended to have, and to exercise, over them the possessory rights of owners. Such rights would have included the right to exclude the whole world from possession—including the plaintiff. When they discovered the mistake with respect to the ownership of the strips in 1975, they moved promptly to assert their rights as persons who had been in possession for more than 10 years and the statutory declarations—which were sworn in April, 1975 and which the jurats suggest may have been prepared in March of that year—were made for that purpose. There is no evidence, or other reason, to infer that their intention to exclude the plaintiff has varied since that time

If it is the law that the intention to exclude the owner must be inferred, or corroborated, from the acts of user and control performed on the strips, I believe the following statements of Sharpe J. in *Raso v. Lonergan*, [1996] O.J. No. 2898 (G.D.), at paras 3 and 4 are equally applicable to the facts of this case:

> In the case at bar, the question involves a residential backyard property. It is difficult to imagine a more unequivocal act intended to exclude the true owner than to erect or maintain a chain-link fence along the entire boundary of the property. As has been frequently stated in the case law, "enclosure is the strongest possible evidence of adverse possession": *Seddon v. Smith* (1877), 36 L.T. 168 at 169. ... I would apply the statement of Anderson J. in *Beaudoin v. Aubin* (1981), 33 O.R. (2d) 604 at 617:
>
>> Where there is possession with the intention of holding for one's benefit, excluding all others, the possession is sufficient and animus is presumed. If it were necessary to say so, one can say of such a situation that the intention *ipso facto* included the intention to exclude the true owner even if his rights were unknown to the person in possession.
>
>> It was submitted in argument that this decision is of questionable authority in view of subsequent decisions of the Court of Appeal. In my view, those cases (*Masidon Investment*; *Fletcher*) are readily distinguishable as dealing with equivocal acts of possession.

I have placed the conditional "if" at the beginning of the preceding paragraph because of certain statements made in decisions of the Court of Appeal in connection with the doctrine of "inconsistent use." I will consider the meaning and significance of such statements, and the implications of the doctrine, when determining whether the third of the requirements recognised by Blair J.A. in *Masidon* has been satisfied.

Before considering that question, I note that, if I had accepted Stanley Leibel's evidence of his meetings with the defendants in 1973, and what was said at them, the possibility that the Famas were subsequently in possession pursuant to a licence given by him on behalf of Bradford would have arisen. This possibility would not be of the same relevance in the case of the Akermans as, by then, they had been in possession for more than 10 years. As I have found that the meetings and discussions between Leibel and the Famas did not occur, it is unnecessary to consider whether time that has commenced to run can be stopped by an intervening grant of permission to continue in possession. In principle, it seems it should have this effect by negativing the occupant's intention to exclude the true owner unless, and until, the former—to the actual or presumed knowledge of the true owner—repudiates the grant of the licence.

The evidence I have rejected would also have involved an express or implied acknowledgement of Bradford's title by the defendants. However, such an acknowledgement would be effective for the purpose of section 4 only if it was made in writing and delivered to the titleholder as contemplated by section 13 of the Act: *Shields v. Shields Estate*, 1923 CanLII 7 (SCC), [1924] S.C.R. 25, at page 33 *per* Anglin J. I doubt whether the terms of the statutory declarations in which the defendants asserted their claim to the 30 ft strips after they had been in possession for more than ten years could reasonably be considered to satisfy the requirements of the section—even if they had been delivered to the plaintiff.

(c) Was the True Owner Effectively Excluded from Possession?

There is no doubt that Bradford was, initially, the "true owner" of the 30 ft strips. If the question relating to the third of the requirements is to be determined solely from the nature and extent of acts of user or control performed by Bradford and the defendants after the defendants entered into possession, I believe the only possible conclusion is that Bradford was effectively excluded from possession.

I have not accepted Stanley Leibel's evidence of his visit to the properties and, apart from that, it is not suggested that anyone connected with Bradford had any physical contact with—or exercised, or attempted to exercise any control over—them. While the payment of realty taxes may have some relevance to the doctrine, or requirement, of inconsistent use that I have yet to consider—and, if made by the occupant, may have a bearing on the intention to exclude the true owner—such payments by the latter are, I believe, referable more to the ownership, than the possession, of the 30 ft strips.

The principal difficulty I have had in applying the law to the facts, as found, arises from the doctrine of inconsistent use which was accepted, and applied, by the Court of Appeal in *Masidon* and in the earlier decisions in *Keefer* and *Fletcher* to which Blair J.A. referred when delivering the judgment of the court in that case. The source of the doctrine is usually attributed to certain statements of Bramwell L.J. in what has been referred to in the Court of Appeal as "the leading case of *Leigh v. Jack* (1879), 5 Ex. D. 264 (C.A.)": *Keefer*, at page 691.

In *Leigh*, the plaintiff's predecessor in title, Mr Leigh, had conveyed lands to the defendant while retaining adjoining property that he intended to dedicate for public streets at some future time. The defendant—who was aware of Mr Leigh's title and intended use of the adjoining property—had subsequently, and for a period of years, placed various items of machinery and waste on it and, ultimately, enclosed it four years before the action was brought. It was held at that he had not acquired a title by adverse possession. The ratio of the decision is difficult to determine as Cockburn C.J. found that the defendant's acts prior to enclosing the property did not indicate an intention to infringe on the rights of the owner; Cotton L.J. found that acts done on the disputed property by Mr Leigh indicated that he had continued in possession; and, in the passage that has been influential in this jurisdiction, Bramwell L.J. stated:

> I do not think that there was any dispossession of the plaintiff by the acts of the defendant: acts of user are not enough to take the soil out of the plaintiff and her predecessors in title

and to vest it in the defendants; in order to defeat the title by dispossessing the former owner, acts must be done which are inconsistent with his enjoyment of the soil for the purposes for which he intended to use it: that is not the case here, where the intention of the plaintiff and her predecessors in title was not to build upon or to cultivate the land, but to devote it at some future time to public purposes. The plaintiff has not been dispossessed, nor has she discontinued possession, her title has not been taken away, and she is entitled to our judgment. (at page 273)

Although, as I have mentioned, there are several English decisions in which the dictum of Bramwell L.J. has been approved and applied, its correctness was, more recently, emphatically denied in the House of Lords in *Pye*, at para 45 where Lord Browne-Wilkinson stated:

The suggestion that the sufficiency of the possession can depend on the intention not of the squatter but of the true owner is heretical and wrong. It reflects an attempt to revive the pre-1833 concept of adverse possession requiring inconsistent user. Bramwell L.J.'s heresy led directly to the heresy in the *Wallis's Cayton Bay* line of cases to which I have referred, which heresy was abolished by statute. It has been suggested that the heresy of Bramwell L.J. survived the statutory reversal but in the *Moran* case the Court of Appeal rightly held that however one formulated the proposition of Bramwell L.J. as a proposition of law it was wrong. The highest it can be put is that, if the squatter is aware of the special purpose for which the paper owner uses or intends to use the land and the use made by the squatter does not conflict with that use, that may provide some support for a finding as a question of fact that the squatter had no intention to possess the land in the ordinary sense but only an intention to occupy it until needed by the paper owner. For myself I think there will be few occasions in which such inference could properly be drawn in cases where the true owner has been physically excluded from the land. But it remains a possible, if improbable, inference in some cases.

The retreat from *Leigh* in the English courts appears to have begun with the decision of Slade J. in *Powell v. MacFarlane et al*, [1977] 38 P. & C. R. 452 (Ch.D.) whose views were endorsed in *Buckinghamshire County Council v. Moran*, [1990] Ch. 623 (C.A.) and, ultimately, in *Pye*. The reasoning of Bramwell L.J.—or the interpretation that was previously placed on it—now appears to have been thoroughly discredited as far as English law is concerned. *Leigh* is, for example, no longer cited in the chapter on Limitations in the latest reissue of Halsbury available to me.

The suggestion in *Pye* that the requirement of inconsistent use based on the observations of Bramwell L.J. in *Leigh* tends to revive the concept of adverse possession that was thought to be abolished by the English legislation of 1833 would, I believe, be difficult to refute. In his *History of English Law* (volume 7, at page 80), Sir William Holdsworth described the effect of the 1833 Act as follows:

[The statute] takes away from every owner, not only his right of entry or action, but also his title to the property, if another has been in possession of it without acknowledging his title for the period fixed by the *Real Property Limitation Act*; and it operates in this way whether the possession of that other has or has not been adverse. ...

The same understanding of the effect of the legislation appears in the comment of Duff J. in *Hamilton v. Canada* 1917 CanLII 74 (SCC), (1917), 54 S.C.R. 331, at pages 369-70, where he said:

... The doctrine of "adverse possession" was so much modified that it might almost be said to have been abrogated; and the right to preserve title by "continual claim" was abolished.

The requirement of inconsistent use appears to have nothing to do with the question whether the true owner has been excluded from possession, if "possession" is to have its traditional meaning in land law. The inconsistency relates solely to the future intentions of the owner rather than to any existing factual contact or connection with the property. To a large extent this appears to be what was meant when it has been said repeatedly in the more recent decisions in this jurisdiction that the possession of a claimant under section 4 must be adverse to that of the true owner. It is, I believe, an accurate reflection of the effect of the independent use test if the statements in *Masidon* are, to use the words of Laskin J.A. in *Teis et al v. Ancaster (Town)* 1997 CanLII 1688 (ON CA), (1997), 35 O.R. (3d) 216 (C.A.), at page 224 to be "taken at face value."

In view of the decisions of the Court of Appeal in *Keefer, Fletcher* and *Masidon* in which the principle stated by Bramwell L.J. has been approved and applied—and notwithstanding the persuasive force of the reasoning in *Pye*—I do not believe it is open for me to conclude that the test of inconsistent use will necessarily suffer the same fate in this jurisdiction as in England. If I were free to do so, my task would be a lot easier.

In *Keefer* and *Fletcher*, the principle was understood to be that acts of a claimant to a possessory title will not be sufficient to demonstrate an intention to exclude the owner from possession unless they are inconsistent with the owner's intended use of the land. In *Masidon*, while citing, and quoting, from *Keefer* and *Fletcher*, the Court of Appeal related the inconsistent use test not to the question of intention but to the third of the requirements stated by Blair J.A.—whether the owner was excluded from possession. It was held that this had not occurred because the acts performed on the land by the trespasser were not inconsistent with the owner's use of the land during the statutory period. That "use" was to hold the land as an investment with a view to selling it at some indefinite future time.

The difference between the two approaches taken by the Court of Appeal was referred to by Moldaver J. In *Wood v. Gateway of Uxbridge Properties Inc et al*, (1990), 75 O.R. (2d) 769 (G.D.) at pages 780-1, but, as he held that the test of inconsistent use did not apply to cases of mutual mistake, he did not find it necessary to choose between them.

The limitation placed by Moldaver J. on the test of inconsistent user was approved by the Court of Appeal in *Teis*. Laskin J.A. referred to the fact that in each of *Keefer, Fletcher* and *Masidon*, the person claiming a possessory title had knowingly trespassed on the owner's land. In indicating his agreement with the reasoning of Moldaver J. he stated:

> Even accepting, however, that the test applies to cases of knowing trespass, it cannot apply to cases of mutual mistake. If it did apply, every adverse possession claim in which the parties were mistaken about title would fail. Inconsistent use means that the claimant's use of the land is inconsistent with the true owner's intended use. If the true owner mistakenly believes that the claimant owns the disputed land, then the owner can have no intended use for the land and, correspondingly, the claimant's use cannot be inconsistent with the owner's intended use ... . Therefore, if a claimant were required to show inconsistent use when both parties were honestly mistaken about the true boundary line, the claimant could never make out a case of adverse possession. Such a result would offend established jurisprudence, logic and sound policy. (at pages 224-5)

The difficulty I am faced with is that, on the facts as I have found them, this was neither a case of mutual mistake, nor a knowing trespass by the defendants. In view of Bradford's payment of realty taxes—and despite my belief that Stanley Leibel had most probably forgotten about the existence of these particular 30 ft strips—I do not believe I would be justified in concluding that Bradford, at any time during the period, no longer had a corporate intention to sell the land—was no longer "using" it by holding it as an investment. I do not know anything about Bradford except that Stanley Leibel is its President. There is no evidence of its shareholders, whether it owns the 30 ft strips beneficially or as a nominee or bare trustee, or whether it has any employees. I do not know who is receiving the assessments for land taxes and is ensuring that they are paid on its behalf. However, in the absence of any other relevant evidence, the fact that they have been paid throughout the period of the defendants' occupation excludes an inference that, at any particular time, Bradford, as a corporate entity, was no longer aware of the existence of the strips and in consequence had ceased to have any continuing intention to hold them as an investment.

Although both Moldaver J. in *Wood* and Laskin J.A. in *Teis* repeatedly contrasted cases of mutual mistake with those of knowing trespass—and did not consider cases of honest unilateral mistake on the part of the occupant—each of them placed emphasis on the law's refusal to provide "encouragement to dishonest people who enter on the land of others with a view to depriving them of it." In contrast to such cases—though again in a passage dealing with mutual mistake—Laskin J.A. stated:

> The law should protect good faith reliance on ... at least the settled expectations of innocent adverse possessors who have acted on the assumption that their occupation will not be disturbed. (at page 225)

I believe it is also fair to say that the reasons of Laskin J.A. appear to reveal a more muted enthusiasm for the test of inconsistent use accepted in the trilogy of earlier decisions of the Court of Appeal. At page 224, he stated:

> The test of inconsistent use focuses on the intention of the owner or paper title holder, not on the intention of the claimant. It is a controversial element of an adverse possession claim even when the claimant knowingly trespasses on the owner's land ... . Taken at face value, its application could unduly limit successful adverse possession claims, especially when land is left vacant. The paper title holder could always claim an intention to develop or sell the land, or could maintain that a person in possession cannot hold adversely to someone who does not care what is happening on the land.

The passage echoes a comment of Carruthers J. at first instance in *Masidon* to the effect that it might well be that land being held for development can never be subject to adverse possession.

I have referred to the difference in the approaches to the test apparent in *Keefer* and *Fletcher*, on the one hand, and in *Masidon* on the other and the reference to this made by Moldaver J. in *Wood*. The difference was also recognised by Laskin J.A in *Teis*. In neither case was it necessary to decide between them. If, however, the test is relevant only to the question of the occupant's actual intention, the absence of an inconsistent use would appear to do no more than give rise to a strong presumption that there was no intention to exclude the owner. Thus, in *Keefer*, Wilson J.A. stated that

The *animus possidendi* which a person claiming a possessory title must have is an intention to exclude such uses as the owner wants to make of his property. (at page 691)

On the facts of this case, I see no difficulty in inferring that persons—such as the defendants—who believe that they are the owners of property, and exercise all the possessory rights of owners over it, intend to exclude all uses of the property by any other person who may claim to be entitled to such uses by reason of a claim to ownership. When the learned judge subsequently stated that acts relied on as dispossessing the true owner must be inconsistent with the form of enjoyment of the property intended by the true owner, I believe she was referring to reliance for the purpose of drawing an inference with respect to the occupant's intention. The correctness of this interpretation is supported by the analysis of the same learned judge in *Fletcher* where, after making essentially the same statement, she added:

Only then can such acts be relied upon as evidencing the necessary "*animus possidendi*" vis-a-vis the owner. (at page 724)

The same approach was adopted by Slade J. in *Powell* when sitting as a judge of the Chancery Division and, therefore, bound by the decisions of the Court of Appeal that had followed *Leigh*:

I incline to the view that the *ratio decidendi* of all the various judgments in cases such as *Leigh v. Jack* … [other citations omitted] was either (a) that the necessary *animus possidendi* had not been shown or (b) that the acts relied on had been too trivial to amount to the taking of actual possession. … [I]n circumstances where an owner has no present use for his land but has future plans for its use (for example by development or by dedication to the public as a highway), then the court will, on the facts, readily treat a trespasser, whose acts have not been inconsistent with such future plans, as having not manifested the requisite *animus possidendi* or alternatively, as not having acquired a sufficient degree of exclusive occupation to constitute possession. (at pages 484-5)

Acts of user that are not inconsistent with the owner's intention to use the land in the future can be equivocal, when the occupant knows of that intention, in that they may support no more than an inference that the occupant intended to use the land until the owner needed it. Earlier in his Judgment, Slade J. referred to the evidential significance of the acts performed on the land by a person claiming a possessory title:

Though past or present declarations as to his intentions, made by a person claiming that he had possession of land on a particular date, may provide compelling evidence that he did not have the requisite *animus possidendi*, in my judgment statements made by such a person, on giving oral evidence in court, to the effect that at a particular time he intended to take exclusive possession of the land, are of very little evidential value, because they are obviously easily capable of being self-serving while at the same time they may be very difficult for the paper owner positively to refute. … [A]s Sachs L.J. said in *Tecbild Ltd v. Chamberlain*, "in general, intent has to be inferred from the acts themselves." (at pages 476-7)

In this case, however, I have accepted the defendants' evidence of their intention to have possession of the 30 ft strips as owners. This, I believe, was necessarily an intention to exclude the whole world including the plaintiff. Their use of the land was consistent with this intention and I do not believe that the fact that, following *Masidon*, it might not be considered to be inconsistent with the plaintiff's use—holding the strips as an investment—is sufficient to alter the conclusion I have reached about their intention on the basis of their evidence at the trial. The passage I have quoted from the reasons of Sharpe J.A. in *Raso* is, I believe, to the point.

If it were necessary, and permissible, to do so, I would follow the approach in *Keefer* and *Fletcher* in preference to that in *Masidon* which appears to treat inconsistent use by the occupier as a prerequisite to the actual dispossession of the owner. *Masidon* was, however, a case involving a knowing trespasser and this fact received considerable emphasis in the reasons of Blair J.A. Towards the end of his reasons the learned judge provided the following caveat:

> The appellant's occupancy of the land was not justified by any suggestion of colour of right or mistake as to title boundaries. Occupation and a colour of right or mistake may justify an inference that the trespasser occupied the land with the intention of excluding all others which would, of course, include the true owner. Such was not the case in this instance. (at page 575)

Blair J.A. did not confine his comment to cases of mutual mistake and neither did he say whether inconsistent user would still be required to establish the owner's exclusion from possession in the circumstances he mentioned. In consequence, I do not believe I am compelled by the decision in *Masidon* to find that Bradford was not excluded from possession in this case where:

1. the disputed lands adjoined, and were not physically separated from, residential properties purchased by the defendants;

2. the defendants enclosed the disputed lands and exercised the full possessory rights of owners of them for the statutory period under a *bona fide* belief that they owned them and, in consequence, with the intention to exclude the whole world; and

3. the owner of the disputed lands made no claim to them during the period and had no physical contact with them.

I note that a conclusion that Bradford was not "excluded" or dispossessed would mean that—contrary to my conclusion above with respect to the first of the requirements stated by Blair J.A.—the defendants have never been in factual possession of the 30 ft strips. As Slade J. stated—in a passage in his reasons that was subsequently quoted with approval in *Moran* and *Pye*:

> Factual possession signifies an appropriate degree of physical control. It must be a single and [exclusive] possession, though there can be a single possession exercised by or on behalf of several persons jointly. Thus an owner of land and a person intruding on that land without his consent cannot both be in possession of the land at the same time. The question what acts constitute a sufficient degree of exclusive physical control must depend on the circumstances, in particular the nature of the land and the manner in which land of that nature is commonly used or enjoyed … and everything must depend on the particular circumstances, but broadly, I think what must be shown as constituting factual possession is that the alleged

possessor has been dealing with the land in question as an occupying owner might have been expected to deal with it and that no one else has done so. (at pages 470-1)

To hold that, on the facts of this case, the plaintiff, and not the defendants, has been in legal possession of the 30 ft strips for more than 30 years would appear to me to give a new meaning to one of the most fundamental concepts of the law of property—a meaning that would dispense with factual possession and depend entirely on the intention of the plaintiff to hold the land as an investment. Presumably, the result would be the same if an owner had an intention to hold the land for any other purpose to be implemented in the future—such as, for example, an intention to provide an inheritance for the owner's descendants. There is, I think, a lot more than a hint of artificiality, and even mysticism, in the notion of a person "using" land by doing nothing other than to hold it in the hope and expectation of a profitable sale at some indefinite time in the future—whether or not realty taxes are being paid in the meantime.

The introduction and development of the requirement of inconsistent use, and its application in this jurisdiction, has led the courts to draw a distinction between knowing trespassers and other trespassers. To relate this to the terms of section 4 requires some intellectual effort. It means not only that the time that a true owner's right of re-entry will accrue will depend on the result of an enquiry into the purpose for which the property was held at different times within the statutory period, but also on the state of a claimant's knowledge. If the policy behind the statute is to provide certainty of land titles by protecting the settled expectations of those who have enjoyed undisturbed possession of land for what is considered to be a reasonable period, and to avoid litigation over titles that will require an inquiry into events—let alone subjective states of mind—in the distant past, the development could be considered regressive.

In any event, the three requirements recognised in *Masidon* are, in my judgment, satisfied on the facts of this case. Accordingly, the plaintiff's claim for a declaration that it is the owner of the 30 ft strips will be dismissed and the counterclaim of the defendants for declarations that the plaintiff has been dispossessed of the strips, that its title to them has been extinguished and that they are entitled to the exclusive possession of them will be granted.

[The court briefly considered arguments about s 113(1) of the Ontario *Registry Act* and the decision of the Ontario Court of Appeal in *1387881 Ont Inc v Ramsey* (CA docket C42118), and concluded that it was not necessary, in *Bradford*, to deal with these issues.

In addition, the court in *Bradford* considered evidence in respect to the payment of realty taxes by Bradford, and concluded that the plaintiff, and not the defendants, had paid these taxes. The court also considered the expert evidence of an experienced property tax consultant, who indicated that the additional amount of taxes payable by the defendants would have been "nominal" and that the amount actually paid by the plaintiff was based on an inflated current value assessment that might have been successfully appealed. On this basis, the court held that the defendants were each required to pay $1,326.15 to the plaintiff as "unjust enrichment."]

DISCUSSION NOTES

i. Revisiting JA Pye

JA Pye was discussed at some length in *Bradford* in relation to the issue of lands held for future development, although the court concluded that it was not appropriate to follow this decision in the United Kingdom. *JA Pye (Oxford Ltd) v Graham*, [2002] 3 All ER 865, involved a dispute about 25 hectares of agricultural land in Berkshire, England. Graham was the owner of land adjoining the disputed lands, and he had signed a formal agreement in 1983, which permitted him to use the disputed lands for a period of 10 months for grazing or mowing grass. Graham had the only key to the gate at the entrance to the disputed lands from a public highway. At the expiry of the agreement, an agent for the titleholder of the disputed lands wrote to Graham to request that he vacate the lands. Notwithstanding this request, Graham continued his farming activity and initially wrote a series of letters requesting a new agreement. However, he did not write any further letters after 1985 and he continued to farm the land until 1999.

At trial, Graham acknowledged he was quite aware that he did not have title to the disputed land, he remained willing to pay to use it, and his use in the absence of an agreement was somewhat "precarious." The titleholder argued that there was no discontinuance of possession and, because the lands were being held for future development, that Graham's activities on the disputed lands had not dispossessed the titleholder. The trial court concluded that Graham's actions constituted possession and that the right to recover possession on the part of the titleholder was precluded by the limitations statute. The Court of Appeal reversed this decision, but the House of Lords restored the trial decision.

The decision in the House of Lords reviewed a number of issues relating to possession of land. In particular, the court concluded that a willingness to pay for use of land on the part of a person in possession does not preclude the acquisition of possessory title. In addition, the court reviewed the law concerning intention on the part of the titleholder and upheld the approach in *Bucks County Council v Moran*, restricting the application of the principles of *Leigh v Jack* (cases noted above). In a note about the House of Lords decision, MP Thompson stated:

> [In relation to offers of payment by the possessor,] the squatter knows that he is squatting and that another person has a better right to the land. To insist upon an intention to own the property would preclude squatters from acquiring a possessory title when it is abundantly clear from the facts that the squatters intend to possess the land for as long as they legally can, which is a sufficient intention for the purpose of the *Limitation Act*.

(See Thompson at 488.)

According to *The Guardian*, the House of Lords decision in *Pye* meant that Graham was entitled to land with a potential development value of £10 million. Thus, after using the land without payment for 12 years, Graham received confirmation of title to the lands; in addition, Pye was saddled with legal costs. See Clare Dyer, "Britain's Biggest Ever Land-Grab," *The Guardian* (9 July 2002). Note that the decision in *Pye* occurred in a context in which the legislation contained language about "adverse" possession, in contrast to the Canadian statutes, which refer simply to "possession." Does this result suggest a need to revisit the reasoning in *Keefer*?

Pye appealed the House of Lords decision to the European Court of Human Rights, on the basis that the decision was incompatible with the company's human rights pursuant to the *European Convention on Human Rights*, Protocol 1, art 1. The ECHR concluded that Pye's right to peaceful enjoyment of its property had been infringed by the operation of statutory provisions in the *Land Registration Act 1925* and the *Limitation Act 1980*, and that this infringement was unjustifiable without compensation. By the time of the ECHR decision, however, Parliament had introduced changes in the *Land Registration Act 2002*, which require notice to a registered landowner about any claim based on possession and an opportunity for the landowner to object and take action to evict the claimant. The ECHR indicated that this new legislation addressed the potential injustice in cases like *Pye*, although it did not affect the decision of the House of Lords because the 2002 statute was not retrospective. See *JA Pye (Oxford Ltd) v United Kingdom* (2006), 43 EHRR 3.

Consider the court's assessment of *JA Pye* in relation to the facts in *Bradford*. What are the factual similarities and differences in the two cases? If the court had applied the principles in *Pye*, how would the result have been different in *Bradford*? To what extent was the award of compensation for the payment of taxes by Bradford required by the principles of possession?

ii. "Trespass" and "Mistakes" Revisited: Marotta v Creative Investments Ltd

Although it seems that the courts have concluded that the inconsistent user test does not apply in cases involving mistakes about title to land—including both mutual and unilateral mistakes—a careful assessment of these decisions suggests some uncertainty with respect to the nature of the mistakes that will lead to the rejection of the inconsistent user test. In *Marotta v Creative Investments Ltd*, [2008] OJ no 1399 (Sup Ct J), Tulloch J (as he then was) examined the evidence and denied a claim of possessory title, applying the inconsistent user test. In reviewing this case, identify the nature of the claimant's mistake: to what extent was this mistake different from the mistakes of the possessors in *Teis* and *Bradford*?

In *Marotta*, there was a dispute over a plot of land in a Toronto subdivision. Bought by Creative Investments in the mid-1960s, Block A was formed by the southern boundary of the Boyds' land and the northern boundary of what was to become the Marottas' land. Purchased with the intent of one day developing more single-family homes in the neighbourhood, Creative Investments paid property taxes on the land for several decades, recorded Block A in their ledgers, and even appealed a tax assessment on the property in 1986.

In 1975, the Marottas purchased their property in the subdivision and, although they were aware from the beginning that Block A was not their property, they were told by the real estate agent that they were allowed to use the property for their own purposes. Therefore, over the course of three decades, the family used Block A for parties, planting plum trees, building an extension on their deck, and clearing out snow and ice so that their neighbours could use the land as a path. The family even extended their fence into Block A in the early 2000s.

Over the years, the Marottas made several attempts to gain legal possession of the land. In 1982, the family wanted to build a sunroom on Block A, and yet, when they approached Creative Investments with an offer to buy, they heard nothing back. A similar attempt was made in 1995 (though this effort was based on a claim of possession), and again there was no response from Creative Investments. The Marottas did not pursue their claim based on possession because they could not afford litigation at the time. Therefore, other than a representative of Creative Investments occasionally driving by Block A during the course of the Marottas' residency (occasions when the representative would see the family using the lot), there was no interaction between the parties before this case was launched.

The case was based on an appeal from a decision of the deputy director of land titles who found that, although the Marottas could satisfy the actual possession requirement, the family could not show an intention to dispossess, because they did not meet the inconsistent user test. The land was being held by Creative Investments for development purposes, and the Marottas' actions, as knowing trespassers, did not frustrate this purpose. The appeal to the Ontario Superior Court of Justice was based on a claim that the inconsistent user test should not have been applied, because, although the Marottas could not rely on the mutual mistake doctrine from *Wood*, they alleged that they had made an honest unilateral mistake, "where the occupiers honestly believe that [they are] the 'rightful' owner[s] of the property," as opposed to the paper titleholder (para 29). That is, even though the Marottas knew they were not the titleholders of Block A (thereby distinguishing the honest unilateral mistake in *Bradford*), the Marottas used the land for several decades without Creative Investments asserting its ownership rights. The family therefore came to believe that they had obtained a *possessory interest* in the land, a "colour of right" belief giving rise to an honest, unilateral mistake; in this context, they argued that the inconsistent user test had no application.

After reviewing the relevant case law concerning possession in Ontario, the court concluded that there are only two situations where the inconsistent user test will not be applied by the courts: mutual mistakes and honest, unilateral mistakes. Tulloch J further concluded (at para 74) that an honest unilateral mistake will arise only

> in specific situations involving contiguous land, *a bona fide belief on the part of the adverse possessor that he or she owned the disputed lands*, and no claim by or physical contact of the owner in relation to the disputed lands (emphasis added).

Because the Marottas knew from the beginning that they did not own Block A, they were unable to meet the requirement of a bona fide belief for an honest unilateral mistake. Also, the court rejected the family's attempt at finding another means of avoiding the inconsistent user test, by asserting a colour of right.

Thus, although the court was willing to accept the deputy director of land titles' finding that the family had met the requirement of actual possession, the court applied the inconsistent user test to reject their claim to possessory title.

In addition to striking down the Marottas' appeal on the basis of their flawed colour of right argument, Tulloch J also reminded the parties that there are strong public policy considerations dissuading courts from extending possessory title claims in such cases:

> To extend *Bradford* to the facts of this case would facilitate claims for possessory title by knowing trespassers by presuming an intention to exclude the true owner. Persons asserting possessory title could argue that even though they knew they did not have legal title to the disputed lands, because they possessed lands beyond the limitation period, they believed they had acquired rights in the land. This type of reasoning defeats the intention of the legislation, which never intended to provide a means for knowing trespassers to acquire title. As stated by the Ontario Court of Appeal in the case of *Harris v. Mudie* (at para. 36):
>
> > The rule, as I understand it, has always been to construe the statutes of limitations in the very strictest manner where it is shewn that the person invoking their aid is a mere trespasser, having no colour of title, any such construction commends itself to one's sense of right. They were never in fact intended as a means of acquiring title, or as an encouragement

to dishonest people to enter on the lands of others with a view to deprive them of it. [*Harris v Mudie* (1882), 7 OAR 414 (CA) (QL) at para 84.]

To what extent do you agree with the court's assessment of the mistake in *Marotta v Creative Investments Ltd*? How do the facts in this case differ from those in *Bradford*? If you had been consulted by the Marottas earlier in their claim, what appropriate action might you have recommended, if any?

For an argument that possessory title should be understood in terms of the authority to set the agenda for land, rather than gatekeeping in relation to boundaries, see Larissa Katz, "Exclusion and Exclusivity in Property Law" (2008) 58 UTLJ 275. See also Mark Wonnacott, *Possession of Land* (Cambridge: Cambridge University Press, 2006).

IV. THE NEED FOR REFORM?

In the United Kingdom, the *Land Registration Act 2002* provided for a system of electronic conveyancing, but it also provided greater protection to registered landowners in relation to claims by squatters. According to Thompson, the statute requires that anyone claiming to be entitled to a possessory title must apply to be registered as proprietor of the land. In relation to such an application, the existing owner would be served with a notice and could object to the registration. Overall, the statute enhances the security of the register; it also makes it unlikely that a titleholder will lose land through inadvertence. As Thompson concluded:

> The implementation of the Land Registration Act 2002 will undoubtedly make the law substantively more satisfactory and meet to a considerable extent the objections of those who see the law of adverse possession as a means of enabling squatters to acquire another person's land without having to pay any compensation to the owner for having done so. Even under the new regime, however, it will still be necessary to determine whether the person claiming to be registered as the new proprietor was in adverse possession of the land within the meaning of section 15 of the Limitation Act 1980 and this will also be true in cases to which the Act does not apply [that is, cases of unregistered land]. The decision in *Pye v. Graham* is to be warmly welcomed in providing an authoritative statement of the principles underlying the subject and, in so doing, eradicating two long standing heresies which had previously blighted it.

(See Thompson at 492.)

Is it desirable to implement such reforms in Ontario and other Canadian provinces? Why is legislative reform appropriate, especially in contrast to judicial reform efforts such as those in *Gateway*?

Some years ago, a different reform proposal was advocated in the United States. The proposal was designed to respond to findings in an article about adverse possession, in which RH Helmholz reviewed a large number of US cases concerning claims for possession. Helmholz concluded that "the trespasser who knows that he is trespassing stands lower in the eyes of the law, and is less likely to acquire title by adverse possession than the trespasser who acts in an honest belief that he is simply occupying what is his already." See RH Helmholz, "Adverse Possession and Subjective Intent" (1983) 61:2 Wash ULQ 331 at 332. In response to these findings, Thomas Merrill examined the underlying principles regarding possessory claims and concluded that "subjective good faith" was an unstated element for their recognition. Thus, Merrill suggested that [courts] manipulate the common law doctrine of adverse possession in order to punish or deter those who intentionally dispossess others of their property. A less dramatic means of achieving a similar end would be to apply a liability rule in cases of bad faith possession. A rule of limited indemnification would in effect impose a fine on bad faith dispossessors equal to the value of the property at the time of original entry. Squatters and thieves would know that, even if they could obtain title to property after the passage of the statute of limitations … they would have to pay for their gain … . If courts knew that the bad faith possessor would be faced with an action for indemnification, they might not feel compelled to manipulate the traditional common law doctrine in order to "punish" those who acquired the property in bad faith, and "reward" those who acquired it innocently.

(See Merrill at 1152-53.)

Would Merrill's proposed solution have achieved a better result in cases like *Masidon*, *Giouroukos*, or *Keefer*? Is it helpful, as Merrill proposed, to separate the issue of entitlement (in relation to the traditional principles of possession) from the issue of remedy? To what extent are legal principles affected by the consequences of a possessor acquiring land without payment? Recall that the court ordered the successful possessors in *Bradford* to compensate the titleholder in relation to the corporation's payment of taxes on the disputed parcels of land over several decades. How would a proposal such as Merrill's be implemented by judicial reform; by legislative reform? Which kind of reform process is preferable to achieve such objectives? In considering these questions, it may be important to take account of the variety of contexts in which such claims may be presented—e.g. see *Gorman v Gorman* (1998), 36 RFL (4th) 448 (Ont CA), a claim concerning the family home; *Rodgers v Danielski* (2003), 9 RPR (4th) 97 (NB QB), a case about the boundaries of a garden; and *Ford v Kennie* (2002), 203 NSR (2d) 234, 4 RPR (4th) 230, var'd (2002), 210 NSR (2d) 50 (SC), a case concerning entitlement to a right of access across adjoining property in Kentville, Nova Scotia. To what extent should the context of claims for possession be a relevant factor?

Rethinking Fundamental Principles About Possession

In thinking about these questions, it may also be helpful to look once more at the "big picture" in relation to issues about ownership and possession. In this context, Kate Green argued that the law of possessory title is based on invisible, but very powerful values concerning land ownership:

> The ideal landowner constructed by the laws of adverse possession is clearly no threat to civilized society. On the contrary, he is settled and stable, and honours both man-made and natural laws. His cultivation involves hard work. The sturdy figure of the ideal English landowner as reflected and maintained in adverse possession law invests his physical, intellectual, and emotional energies in the ground: he has entirely committed himself, through his engagement with the earth, to his plot of land. He wants to be a figure in the landscape. He fences his land and locks his gates in order to exclude those who might detract from his hard labour—addressing the world outside as well as the land within his boundaries.
>
> His moral justification is equally plain. He may be apparently "stealing" land from his neighbour, but in practice he can do so only if the neighbour is a bad owner, a waster of the natural

national resource. Clearly, he cares more for the country than the mere holder of a piece of paper; his possible small dishonesty is justified by his reliability as a natural guardian of English earth.

(See Kate Green, "Citizens and Squatters: Under the Surfaces of Land Law" in Susan Bright & John Dewar, eds, *Land Law: Themes and Perspectives* (Oxford: Oxford University Press, 1998) 229 [Bright & Dewar] at 241-42.)

Does this characterization help to explain the decisions in the cases about possessory title? To what extent? In addition, it is important to examine these questions from the perspective of those who may be regarded by law as not entitled to possessory claims. For example, in an assessment of property law in relation to homelessness in the United Kingdom, David Cowan and Julia Fionda put forth the following argument:

> If land law is the law about land, then it is inconceivable that land law should not cover issues of *access* to land. The creation of rights in land is often covered only through a consideration of the boundaries between property and personal rights. In doing so, we (as land lawyers) mislead our students into believing that issues of access are routine matters which are outside the domain of land law.
>
> Put another way, land lawyers concern themselves with the "included" and not the "excluded." Land law is a subject where we consider the rights of the included, as consumers, but those unable to consume do not feature. The challenging notion of "citizenship," which might be defined in this context as "the ability to consume," assists us in our appreciation of a more radical approach. This preoccupation with consumerism is at odds with the more traditional socialist view of citizenship as social inclusion—a preoccupation with the welfare of the most marginalized and poverty-stricken in society in order to ensure their inclusion in the mainstream of society; that is, empowerment through social unity.

(See David Cowan & Julia Fionda, "Homelessness" in Bright & Dewar, eds, 257 at 260-61.)

Do these views suggest a need for a more fundamental review of the law of possession? To what extent is such reform within the mandate of the courts; the legislature? How might such reform be encouraged?

PROBLEMS

1. A week ago, Walter and Rosie went to the local shopping mall, the Penn Centre, to do their weekly shopping. They had several errands and split up for an hour or so to make their tasks more efficient. They agreed to meet at noon in the food court for a bite to eat before driving back to their farm. As agreed, they met at noon, each of them having done a number of errands. They were both a bit tired, but glad to grab a sandwich before heading back home. They sat down at a table with their tray of food and coffee and began to eat. Rosie had put a number of parcels down beside her chair and, after an inquiry from Walter about one of her purchases, she reached down to show him what she had bought. To her surprise, when she lifted up the parcel, it was not one of hers at all. "Oh dear," she said, "someone must have forgot this parcel when they finished eating and left this table." Walter was curious. He suggested that they see what was inside. Rosie was not so sure. She thought that it might be something private. However, as a result of Walter's curiosity, she handed the parcel to him and watched with interest as he opened it. There was a lot of string, and Rosie helped Walter to untie it. To their absolute astonishment, when the parcel eventually fell open, it revealed

a large number of $20 bills. They were quite overcome. Walter decided immediately that they should rewrap the package and try to look nonchalant. They did. When they had finished their lunch, they picked up all the parcels, including the mysterious parcel with $20 bills inside it, and drove home. When they got home they re-examined the parcel and discovered that it contained about $20,000. Walter decided right away that they should call the police, but Rosie objected, saying that such a fortune would be very helpful in relation to her aspirations to go to law school. Thus, the parcel of money is currently stowed under their bed.

Walter is in need of legal advice. He wants to know who is entitled to this money that they found.

Advise Walter as to his entitlement, Rosie's entitlement, and the possible entitlement of others in relation to the parcel of money discovered at the shopping centre.

2. Anne Abbott is the owner-director of a well-known wilderness camp for boys and girls several hours' drive north of Toronto. The camp is based on 2,000 acres of property bordering the edge of a large lake. Although there are comfortable cabins and other amenities at the camp headquarters beside the lake, some other parts of the camp acreage are quite wild, with rocky outcrops and few trees. One of the great attractions of the camp is the challenge of two- or three-day hiking expeditions away from the camp headquarters, with the necessity of carrying food and other provisions in order to be self-sufficient in nature.

Ms Abbott is currently seeking legal advice about an unusual discovery made by a group of campers a few months ago. In late August, a group of eight campers set off for a three-day hike with one of the camp leaders, Barb Bartoli. On the second day, the group stopped for the night beside a small river in a grove of pine trees. As they set up their tents, one of the campers, Jan Jung, felt a small depression in the earth, which she then discovered was a shallow cavity covered with a piece of birchbark over which moss had grown. Pulling up the birchbark covering, she found an old, discoloured, leather bag concealed in the cavity. Suddenly nervous, she called to her friend Petra for help. Petra immediately called their leader, Barb. Surrounded by the other campers, Barb Bartoli opened the bag to discover 18th-century French coins. The campers were astonished. They returned to camp headquarters the next day to report their find to Anne Abbott. On further inquiry with the local museum, Anne discovered that the location of the campsite where the cache was found was most likely on the route of French fur traders, and that the coins are now worth a great deal of money. Ms Abbott wants to know who is entitled to the value of the coins found by the campers.

Matters have become further complicated as a result of the publicity surrounding the unusual discovery. The 2,000 acres used by the camp are leased from the Great Northern Development Company, an investment company that owns large tracts of land in the area. Because of the discovery, there has been great interest in identifying the location where the cache of coins was found, especially on the part of those interested in old fur-trading routes. As a result, Anne Abbott has learned that the cache was found on land owned by the Great Northern Development Company. However, instead of being part of the 2,000 acres leased to her for the camp, the cache was actually located on adjoining land, currently unoccupied, and, of course, unfenced. Because of the recent publicity, Ms Abbott has now learned that the river beside which the campers had pitched their tents is not the boundary of her 2,000 acres—the boundary of her leased parcel is, in fact, 100 feet to the east.

Nonetheless, Ms Abbott has asserted a right to the land where the cache was found. She can demonstrate that campers have used the land continuously since 1963, the year the camp was established, assuming that the boundary of their 2,000 acres was the river. In 1963, the Great Northern Development Company created a 40-year lease of the camp land. In 1960, it had leased the adjoining land to a logging company for 20 years, but very little logging activity had taken place. In 1980, when the 20-year lease expired, Great Northern immediately entered into a two-year lease with a second logging company. It has continued to create two-year leases with a succession of tenants, some of whom have engaged in intermittent logging activity. However, Ms Abbott has claimed that, because there was no obvious sign of any logging near the river, she had no idea that the boundary of the land leased to the camp did not extend to the river. Thus, she is now claiming title to this land as well as to the cache of coins found on it. She is also asserting that neither the campers nor their leader, Barb Bartoli, are entitled to the cache because her rights as occupier of the land are superior to anyone else's.

Is Ms Abbott's claim to the parcel of land near the river valid? Assuming that she is the occupier of the land near the river where the coins were discovered, is her claim to the coins valid?

3. In *Kreadar Enterprises Ltd v Duny Machine Ltd* (1995), 42 RPR (2d) 274 (Ont Gen Div), the defendant used lands to which the plaintiff held paper title for about 20 years, and the defendant had made various minor improvements to it. In deciding that the defendant had not established the requisite criteria for a possessory interest, O'Connor J stated:

> The issue is whether the concept of acquiring title through adverse possession still exists in Ontario. If so, what are the modern criteria for successfully obtaining title to another's land by such methods? ... There would appear to be very limited circumstances, if they exist at all in Ontario, when a knowing trespasser, who has enjoyed the use of property over an extended period of time without payment of rent or taxes and who has made minimal improvements to it, would gain title to such property. In my view, that is how it should be.

Comment on the language used in this quotation, and its content, in relation to the principles of possessory title in Ontario at the present time.

4a. A took possession of Blackacre, but B subsequently ousted A. Can A now recover possession? Why?

Suppose that B claims to derive title from X, the person whom A ousted when A took possession? Can A now maintain his claim to possession? Why?

4b. K took possession of vacant land. Five years later, K died and his estate was inherited by Q. If Z ousts Q, can Q maintain a claim to possession? Why?

Suppose that K had left his estate to Q by will and Q remains in possession for six years. What is the position of the owner of the vacant land? Why?

4c. L held paper title to Redacre and leased it to T for four years in 1975. P took possession of Redacre in 1976. In 1979, when the lease ended, L leased it to T for a second four-year period, ending in 1983. In 1983, L leased the same land again to T for a further four-year period, ending in 1987. What is L's position in 1990? Why?

Assume the same fact situation, except that in 1979, L leased to M (a tenant unrelated to T); and in 1983, L leased to K (also unrelated to T or M). What is L's position as of 1990?

5. When her parents died in 1985, Alice Ames inherited their farm property, an irregular parcel of land comprising about 100 acres located just north of Kingston, Ontario. Although she works as a designer in Toronto, Alice has regularly used the farmhouse as a weekend retreat. Because she has no interest in farming, she has been leasing the arable land to neighbouring farmers. In the past year, however, Alice decided that she wanted to sell the farm (including the farmhouse) so that she could buy a cottage property closer to Toronto. Bob Bonville, one of the local farmers, has expressed interest in buying Alice's farm, but he said that he would like to see a survey of the farm before making an offer. As a result, Alice hired a surveyor and now needs legal advice about a number of aspects relating to the survey of the farm property.

The northern boundary of the farm property is a rather winding local road and its southern boundary is a narrow lake. Between the road to the north and the lake to the south, there are fences that mark the boundaries of Alice's farm and those of her neighbours to the east and west of her property. Just inside the fence at the western boundary is an old laneway, now somewhat overgrown, that has a row of old and valuable black walnut trees on either side of it. This laneway also provides the only easy access to the lake at the southern boundary of the farm property. To Alice's surprise, the recent survey shows that the fence is not located at the western boundary of her property. In fact, the survey shows that the laneway and the black walnut trees are not part of her land, but actually belong to her neighbour to the west. Alice is certain that the original fence was built by her father in the 1960s in consultation with his neighbour, Charles Cameron, who is still the current owner of the adjoining land to the west of Alice's farm. In a recent conversation, however, Charles told Alice that he will rely on the survey to establish his entitlement to the laneway, because he would like to supplement his farm income by developing public access to the lake for swimming in summer and snowmobiling in winter. It is clear that the value of Alice's land will be higher if the laneway is part of her farm property. Advise Alice in relation to her claim.

6. Marco Moran inherited 50 acres of land north of Highway 17 outside Ottawa about 30 years ago. Because much of the land is rocky and covered with forests and small lakes, Marco (who held a full-time civil service job in Ottawa) did not immediately have much use for this land. Although it was a 2-hour drive away, he did visit it to tap maple trees to make maple syrup, but this activity depended on the back roads being accessible in the early spring. Marco estimates that he may have tapped maple trees about half a dozen times in the past 30 years. However, he has faithfully paid property taxes on this land for 30 years, although the taxes are not significant because the land remains undeveloped. Marco's plan was to keep the land in its natural state in the hopes that either the government or a private developer might want to purchase it to create a wilderness park in the future.

Marco recently received an inquiry from Parklands Construction, a company that wants to purchase 25 acres bordering the western edge of the largest lake in this area, Lake Placid. With Marco's permission, Parklands ordered a survey of the proposed land for purchase. In doing so, Parklands discovered that Sunnyland Children's Camp (SC Camp) has been using about 5 acres of land on Marco's side of Lake Placid for at least 20 years. Although the main part of the SC Camp is located at the other side of Lake Placid on land clearly owned by the camp, the camp directors assert that they have always used the disputed land in a bona fide belief that their land also included these 5 acres bordering the lake on Marco's land. The camp directors are also adamant that their use of this land is continuous because they use it regularly not only during the summer months but also for camping for older children on winter weekends; in addition, camp employees regularly inspect the camp year-round to ensure that the camp buildings (including those erected on the disputed land) remain, for example, weather resistant. Parklands has advised Marco that it is not interested in purchasing his lands unless the acreage includes the 5 acres now claimed by SC Camp because it requires these acres of lake frontage to make its proposed park development marketable.

Assuming that the directors of SC Camp can establish their bona fide belief that they owned the 5 acres on Marco's land, advise Marco about his entitlement to succeed in claiming it. Give reasons for your conclusions.

AND

Assuming instead that Marco tapped maple trees on the 5 acres of land now claimed by SC Camp and that, when he encountered SC employees on these occasions, he advised them that he had no immediate use for the land, explain whether Marco would have a greater chance of succeeding in his claim to the 5 acres. Give reasons for your conclusions.

CHAPTER REFERENCES

Adomeit, Peter. "Barry Bonds' Baseball Case: An Empirical Approach—Is Fleeting Possession Five Tenths of the Ball?" (2004) 48 Saint Louis ULJ 475.

Baker, JH. *An Introduction to English Legal History*, 3d ed (London: Butterworths, 1990).

Berger, Bethany. "It's Not About the Fox: The Untold History of Pierson v Post" (2006) 55 Duke LJ 1089.

Black, Vaughan. "A Regulated Regard: Comparing the Governance of Animal and Human Experimentation" (2012) 24 RQDI 237.

Bradbrook, A, SV MacCallum & AP Moore, eds. *Australian Real Property Law*, 4th ed (Sydney: Thomson Lawbook Co, 2008).

Bright, Susan & John Dewar, eds. *Land Law: Themes and Perspectives* (Oxford: Oxford University Press, 1998).

Bucknall, Brian. "Limitations Act, 2002 and Real Property Limitations Act: Some Notes on Interpretive Issues" (2004) 29 Advocates' Q 1.

Bucknall, Brian. "Teis v Ancaster: Knowledge, the Lack of Knowledge and the Running of a Possessory Title Period" (1997) 13 RPR (3d) 68.

Bucknall, Brian. "Two Roads Diverged: Recent Decisions on Possessory Title" (1984) 22 Osgoode Hall LJ 375.

Callaghan, C. *Adverse Possession* (Columbus, OH: State University Press, 1961).

Casner, A James & W Barton Leach. *Cases and Text on Property*, 2d ed (Boston: Little, Brown, 1969).

Chused, Richard. *Cases, Materials and Problems in Property* (New York: Matthew Bender, 1988).

Cielslik, Jason. "There's a Drive … Way Back … It Might Be … It Could Be … Another Lawsuit: Popov v Hayashi" (2003) 20 TM Cooley L Rev 605.

Cowan, David & Julia Fionda. "Homelessness" in Susan Bright & John Dewar, eds, *Land Law: Themes and Perspectives* (Oxford: Oxford University Press, 1998) 257.

Creighton, G. "Equitable Limitations" in *Limitation of Actions* (Toronto: Canadian Bar Association—Ontario, 1985).

Deckha, Maneesha. "Property on the Borderline: A Comparative Analysis of the Legal Status of Animals in Canada and the United States" (2012) 20 Cardozo J Int'l & Comp L 313.

Dyer, Clare. "Britain's Biggest Ever Land-Grab," *The Guardian* (9 July 2002), online: The Guardian <http://www.theguardian.com/world/2002/jul/09/law.theguardian1>.

Epstein, Richard. "Possession as the Root of Title" (1978-79) 13 Ga L Rev 1221.

Fernandez, Angela. "Fuzzy Rules and Clear Enough Standards: The Uses and Abuses of Pierson v Post" (2013) 63 UTLJ 97.

Fernandez, Angela. "Pierson v Post: A Great Debate, James Kent, and the Project of Building a Learned Law for New York State" (2009) 34:2 Law & Soc Inquiry 301.

Follows, TJ. "Parker v British Airways Board and the Law of Finding Chattels" (1982) 12 Kingston L Rev 1.

"Former Owner Loses Battle for Darwin." *The Globe and Mail* (14 September 2013).

Gallant, Jacques. "Judge Rules Darwin's Wild and Belongs in Sanctuary," *Toronto Star* (14 September 2013).

Gilligan, Carol. 1984 James McCormick Mitchell Lecture, "Feminist Discourse, Moral Values, and the Law: A Conversation" (1985) 34 Buff L Rev 11.

Gray, K & P Symes. *Real Property and Real People* (London: Butterworths, 1981).

Green, Kate. "Citizens and Squatters: Under the Surfaces of Land Law" in Susan Bright & John Dewar, eds, *Land Law: Themes and Perspectives* (Oxford: Oxford University Press, 1998) 229.

Hargreaves, AD. "Terminology and Title in Ejectment" (1940) 56 Law Q Rev 376.

Harris, DR. "The Concept of Possession in English Law" in AG Guest, ed, *Oxford Essays in Jurisprudence* (Oxford: Oxford University Press, 1961).

Harris, M June. "Who Owns the Pot of Gold at the End of the Rainbow?" (1997) 14 Ariz J Int'l & Comp L 253.

Hazlehurst, K, ed. *Legal Pluralism and the Colonial Legacy* (Aldershot, UK: Avebury, 1995).

Helmholz, RH. "Adverse Possession and Subjective Intent" (1983) 61:2 Wash ULQ 331.

Helmholz, RH. "Equitable Division and the Law of Finders" (1983) 52 Fordham L Rev 313.

Hill, Jonathan. "The Proprietary Character of Possession" in Elizabeth Cooke, ed, *Modern Studies in Property Law, 2000*, vol 1 (Oxford and Portland, OR: Hart, 2001) 21.

Kane, Laura. "Darwin the Ikea Monkey's Former 'Mom' Weeps at Trial's End," *Toronto Star* (11 June 2013), online: Toronto Star <http://www.thestar.com>.

Katz, Larissa. "Exclusion and Exclusivity in Property Law" (2008) 58 UTLJ 275.

Katz, Larissa. "The Moral Paradox of Adverse Possession: Sovereignty and Revolution in Property Law" (2010) 55 McGill LJ 47.

Law Commission. *Limitation of Actions (Law Commission Report No 270)* (London: The Stationery Office, 2001).

Law Commission. *Limitation of Actions: A Consultation Paper (No 151)* (London: The Stationery Office, 1998).

Law Reform Commission of British Columbia. *Report on Wrongful Interference with Goods* (Vancouver: Ministry of the Attorney-General, 1992).

Law Reform Committee. *Twenty-First Report: Final Report on Limitation of Actions*, Cmnd 6923 (London: HMSO, 1977).

Maitland, FW. "The Beatitude of Seisin: I" (1888) 4 Law Q Rev 24.

Maitland, FW. "The Beatitude of Seisin: II" (1888) 4 Law Q Rev 286.

Maitland, FW. "The Mystery of Seisin" (1886) 2 Law Q Rev 481.

McDowell, Andrea. "Legal Fictions in Pierson v Post" (2007) 105 Mich L Rev 735.

McLaren, J, AR Buck & N Wright, eds. *Despotic Dominion: Property Rights in British Settler Societies* (Vancouver: UBC Press, 2005).

McNeil, Kent. *Common Law Aboriginal Title* (Oxford: Clarendon Press, 1989).

McNeil, Kent. "The Meaning of Aboriginal Title" in M Asch, ed, *Aboriginal and Treaty Rights in Canada: Essays on Law, Equality and Respect for Difference* (Vancouver: University of British Columbia Press, 1997).

Mendes da Costa, Derek, Richard J Balfour & Eileen S Gillese. *Property Law: Cases, Text, and Materials*, 2d ed (Toronto: Emond Montgomery, 1990).

Merrill, Thomas. "Property Rules, Liability Rules, and Adverse Possession" (1985) 79 Nw UL Rev 1122.

Nash, Michael. "Are Finders Keepers? One Hundred Years Since Elwes v Brigg Gas Co" (1987) 137 New LJ 118.

Natural Resources/Tourism, Culture and Heritage. "Changes to Treasure Hunting Regulations" (14 July 2010), online: Nova Scotia Canada <http://novascotia.ca/news/release/?id=20100714001>.

O'Keefe, PJ & Lyndal V Prott. *Law and the Cultural Heritage* (Abingdon, UK: Professional Books, 1984).

Ontario. "Discussion Draft on Proposed Limitations Act (1977)" (Toronto: Ministry of the Attorney General, 1977).

Palmer, NE. "Treasure Trove and the Protection of Antiquities" (1981) 44 Mod L Rev 178.

Pastrick, M. "When a Day at the Ballpark Turns a 'Can of Corn' into a Can of Worms: Popov v Hayashi" (2003) 51 Buff L Rev 905.

Pyre, Katrina. "Treasure Pits Explorers Against Bureaucrats: Private Operators Say the Sea Will Destroy Nova Scotia's Shipwrecks Before the Government Gets Around to Salvaging Them," *The Globe and Mail* (4 May 2013) at A8.

Radin, Margaret Jane. "Time, Possession, and Alienation" (1986) 64 Wash ULQ 739.

Report of the Royal Commission on Aboriginal Peoples. *Restructuring the Relationship*, vol 2, part 2 (Ottawa: Minister of Supply and Services Canada, 1996).

Rose, Carol. "Possession as the Origin of Property" (1985) 52 U Chicago L Rev 73.

Russell, Ted. "Stealin' the Holes" in *Tales from Pigeon Inlet* (St John's: Breakwater Books, 1977).

Simmonds, Ralph & George Stewart. *Study Paper on Wrongful Interference with Goods* (Toronto: Ontario Law Reform Commission, 1989).

Stoklas, Patrick. "Popov v Hayashi: A Modern Day Pierson v Post—A Comment on What the Court Should Have Done with the Seventy-Third Home Run Baseball Hit by Barry Bonds" (2002-3) 34 Loy U Chicago LJ 901.

Tee, L. "Adverse Possession and Intention to Possess" (Mar/Apr 2000) 66 Conveyancer and Property Lawyer 113.

Thompson, MP. "Adverse Possession: The Abolition of Heresies" (Sep/Oct 2002) 66 Conveyancer and Property Lawyer 480.

Tyler, Tracey. "Widow Wins Fight for Hidden Cash of Husband," *Toronto Star* (22 March 2000).

Williams, Patricia. "The Pain of Word Bondage" in *The Alchemy of Race and Rights* (Cambridge, MA: Harvard University Press, 1991).

Wiren, SA. "The Plea of Jus Tertii in Ejectment" (1925) 41 Law Q Rev 139.

Wonnacott, Mark. *Possession of Land* (Cambridge: Cambridge University Press, 2006).

Wright, CA. "The Right to Pursue Bees" (1939) 17 Can Bar Rev 130.

Ziff, Bruce. "The Law of Property in Animals, Newfoundland-Style" in E Tucker, J Muir & B Ziff, eds, *Property on Trial: Canadian Cases in Context* (Toronto: Osgoode Society and Irwin Law, 2012).

CHAPTER THREE

Fundamental Principles Governing Property Interests in Land

I. THE HISTORICAL BASIS FOR CURRENT LAND LAW

Land law has its roots deep in English social, economic, and political history. In medieval times, when land was the principal source of wealth, the configuration of rights in land was a major preoccupation of the legal order and political life. This was especially so after the Norman Conquest of England in 1066 by William the Conqueror; King William was regarded as owner of all land in England, such that any private landholder, no matter how important, held rights "of" the Crown in a tenant-type relationship. The protection of the possession of land and the articulation of rights in land became a major item in the jurisdiction of the royal courts created by William and his successors, courts that eventually created what we know as the common law. Early on, the common law thus developed a complex and sophisticated structure of rights to ensure that all three orders (or "estates") of medieval society—those who fought (nobility), those who prayed (clergy), and those who worked (everyone else)—could participate in the benefits of the land resource. Initially an outgrowth of feudalism as it developed in England after 1066, the common law of real property was later adapted to serve the commercial, imperial, and industrial needs of British society, and it continues to function in the post-imperial, post-industrial society of the 21st century. It may be useful to think of land law as a building, with its facade a carefully preserved, half-timbered structure from Tudor times, but whose interior has been fully equipped with modern conveniences. Some of the closets, however, may still contain the odd skeleton.

Continuity, marked by incremental change and punctuated by a few major reforms, has been the hallmark of land law in the common law world. This is why the only sensible starting point is 1066. In this way, the common law is quite distinct from continental systems of property law. The latter were originally based on concepts and structures similar to those in England, but underwent major conceptual change after the Napoleonic Code's revolutionary changes in property law were exported to the rest of Europe in the wake of the French Revolution. The Napoleonic Code of 1804 abolished pre-existing law and rebuilt property law from a *tabula rasa*. Continental property law, reflected in the *Civil Code of Quebec*, is a rational and functional system based on a few simple concepts centred on the notion of ownership. For example, art 947 of the *Civil Code of Quebec* reads:

> 947. Ownership is the right to use, enjoy and dispose of property fully and freely, subject to the limits and conditions for doing so determined by law.
>
> Ownership may be in various modes and dismemberments.

The common law of real property, although it recognizes a concept of ownership in practice, has never felt obliged to articulate it in theory. The main concepts of the common law of real property are those of tenure and estates, which are discussed in turn.

II. THE DOCTRINE OF TENURE

A. Tenure as a Land-Holding Relationship

The doctrine of "tenure" is a fundamental concept of land law in the common law. Although the word "tenure" (derived from the Latin word *tenere*, "to hold") is clearly related to principles of tenancies (discussed in Chapter 4), the doctrine of tenure needs to be understood as a separate concept that relates to land law generally.

Kevin Gray & Susan Francis Gray, *Elements of Land Law*
5th ed (Oxford: Oxford University Press, 2009) at 64-67
(footnotes omitted; emphasis in original)

Under the tenurial system of tiered or hierarchical landholding, all land in England (save unalienated crown land) was held, in pyramidal relationships of reciprocal obligation, either mediately or immediately of the crown. Whereas the concept of the estate systematised the relationship between the tenant and the physical land [see below], the concept of tenure characterised more closely the relationship between tenant and lord, it being "implicit in the relationship of tenure that both lord and tenant have an interest in the land." Under the original feudal principle the lord *seised* his tenant of his tenement. Unless the tenant failed in his service, the lord owed him enjoyment of his tenement as long as he lived.

1. Origins of Tenure

The theory of tenure identified the "radical title" at the back of all relationships in respect of land—the sovereign title of the king as paramount lord, achieved by conquest in 1066 and sustained by strong political control thereafter. Since the Normans had brought with them no written law of land, they initiated in their new territory what was effectively a system of landholding in return for the performance of services to a feudal superior. The fact of territorial subjugation provided the foundation for the theory that all lands were ultimately held of the king and could be granted to subjects of the crown only upon the continued fulfilment of certain conditions. Each landholder (or "tenant") therefore held his land in return for services to be rendered either to the king himself or to some intermediate baron or lord within a complex structure of lordship which had the king at its apex.

2. Classification of Tenures

It was left to the doctrine of tenures not only to spell out the complex tariff of services and duties owed within the network of feudal relationships, but also to delineate the valuable "incidents" or privileges which attached to tenure. The feudal services rendered by tenants were an integral part of early English land law, and in time became standardised and identifiable by the type of service exacted and performed. The different methods of landholding (differentiated according to the form of service required) were known as "tenures," each tenure indicating the precise terms on which the land was held. The tenures were themselves subdivided into those tenures which were "free" (and therefore formed part of the strict feudal framework) and those tenures which were "unfree" (and appertained to tenants of lowly status, some of whom were *adscripti glebae*—effectively little better than slaves).

3. Free Tenures

The kinds of service provided by those who enjoyed free tenure included, for instance, the provision of armed horsemen for battle (the tenure of "knight's service") or the performance of some personal service such as the bearing of high office at the king's court (the tenure of "grand sergeanty"). These tenures were known as "tenures in chivalry," and were distinct from the "spiritual tenures" of "frankalmoign" and "divine service" (by which ecclesiastical lands were held in return for the performance of some sacred office) and the somewhat humbler "tenures in socage" (which obliged the tenant to render agricultural service to his lord). With the passage of time, military and socage tenures were commuted for money payments, but all tenures carried with them incidents (or privileges enjoyed by the lord) which were often more valuable than the services themselves.

4. The Statute Quia Emptores 1290

Pollock and Maitland described the system of tenures in terms of a series of "feudal ladders," noting that "theoretically there is no limit to the possible number of rungs, and … men have enjoyed a large power, not merely of adding new rungs to the bottom of the ladder, but of inserting new rungs in the middle of it." This process of potentially infinite extension of the feudal ladder was known as *subinfeudation*. However, subinfeudation carried the disadvantage that it tended to make the feudal ladder long and cumbersome, and in time the process of alienating land by substitution became more common. Under the latter device the alienee of land simply assumed the rung on the feudal ladder previously occupied by the alienor, and the creation of a new and inferior rung was no longer necessary.

5. Prohibition of Subinfeudation

By the end of the 13th century a new concept of land as a freely alienable asset was beginning to displace the restrictive feudal order, and this evolution culminated in the enactment of *Quia Emptores* in 1290. The Statute *Quia Emptores* constituted a pre-eminent expression of a new preference for freedom of alienation as a principle of public policy [guaranteeing the tenant the right to alienate land without the consent of his lord]. The major innovation contained in the Statute was the prohibition for the future of alienation by subinfeudation. Following the enactment of 1290 only the crown could grant new tenures, and the existing network of tenures could only contract with the passage of time. Every conveyance of land thenceforth had the effect of substituting the grantee in the tenurial position formerly occupied by his grantor: no new relationship of lord and tenant was created by the transfer.

6. *The Levelling of the Feudal Pyramid*

It is the Statute *Quia Emptores* which—quite unnoticed—still regulates fee simple transfers of land today. Each transfer is merely a process of substitution of the transferee in the shoes of the transferor. The operation of the Statute during the last seven centuries has tended towards a gradual levelling of the feudal pyramid so that all tenants in fee simple are today presumed (in the absence of contrary evidence) to hold directly of the crown as "tenants in chief."

B. Reform of the Law of Tenures

The later history of tenure reflected the tumultuous history of early modern England. As you will see when we consider the emergence of the trust, below, major landowners always sought ways to evade the incidents (or taxes) that were attached to the tenure by which they held an interest in land. Those members of the nobility who held directly of the monarch were subject to the most onerous incidents. Before the emergence of a modern taxation system, these incidents represented an important part of state revenues. Thus monarchs, in turn, sought ways to plug the conveyancing "loopholes" used to escape the incidents of tenure; this contest became subsumed in the larger struggle between Crown and Parliament (which at the time represented mainly large landowners) over which of them exercised ultimate authority in the realm. (Although a history of this struggle between Crown and Parliament is beyond the scope of this discussion, it is important to keep in mind that this struggle was critical to the development of land law.)

The most important of the tenurial incidents were those relating to wardship and marriage, and escheat. Wardship was an incident of the tenures in chivalry, whereby on the death of a tenant leaving an heir under the age of 21, the lands of the minor were to be held by the monarch until the minor came of age. But unlike the later notion of fiduciary wardship (which required the Crown to be bound by the principle of "the best interests of the child"), the early notion of wardship permitted the monarch to keep the revenues produced by the lands, subject only to providing a living allowance to the heir and his or her family. A related incident was the right of the monarch to arrange the marriage of the minor heir of a deceased tenant in chivalry to a person of the monarch's choice. At a time when marriage among the nobility was a matter of intense political and economic significance, this incident was important and could itself be bought and sold.

Escheat came in two forms: escheat for failure of heirs (*propter defectum sanguinis*), and escheat for treason or felony (*propter delictum tenentis*). Escheat for failure of heirs addressed the situation where the holder of a fee simple estate died leaving no will and no blood relatives (in technical terms, no intestate heirs). In such cases, the fee simple was considered to have ended, and the doctrine of tenure directed that the estate would go to the feudal superior of the deceased holder of the fee simple. Escheat for treason or felony (serious crime) by the holder of an estate resulted in the forfeiture of the estate to the holder's feudal superior.

Even though the feudal order had largely disappeared by the 16th century, Henry VIII created the Court of Wards and Liveries in 1540 to provide a better mechanism for inquiring into and collecting such tenurial incidents as might be owing. A major task of this court was to collect the revenues of lands owned by wards of the king. Needless to say, Henry VIII's Court of Wards and Liveries was wildly unpopular with the nobility and the gentry: see HE Bell, *History and Records of the Court of Wards and Liveries* (Cambridge: Cambridge University Press, 1953). These and other grievances fuelled the English civil war (1642-1651), during which Charles I was executed and Oliver Cromwell ruled as "Lord Protector of the Commonwealth of England." During this time, the *Tenures Abolition Act* (also known as the *Statute of Tenures*) was passed, but the title of this statute is highly misleading. The Act did not "abolish" tenure as such, but rather converted *all existing free lay tenures* into socage tenure, which by that point had no onerous incidents attached to it. After the restoration of the monarchy in 1660 in the person of Charles II, most of Cromwell's legislation was declared ineffective. The *Tenures Abolition Act* was confirmed, however, subject to a provision compensating the Crown with an annual payment of £100,000 to be raised by a new tax on alcohol; the Act also abolished the Court of Wards and Liveries: see AWB Simpson, *An Introduction to the History of the Land Law* (Oxford: Oxford University Press, 1961) [Simpson] at 187.

C. Tenure in Canada

1. Early Grants: Knight's Service

Some early grants in Newfoundland under the Stuart kings were made in feudal tenures. James I granted Sir George Calvert (later Lord Baltimore, founder of Maryland) much of the Avalon Peninsula in 1623 "in Capite by Knights Service." After Calvert was deemed to have abandoned the settlement, Charles I named Sir David Kirke the "true and absolute Lord and Proprietor ... [of] that whole continent Island and Region ... commonly knowne by the name of Newfoundland," also in knight's service. Kirke and his heirs ruled the east coast of Newfoundland in a quasi-feudal way until the 18th century, when both his and the Calvert patent were ultimately declared invalid: see generally Keith Matthews, comp, *Compilation and Commentary on the Constitutional Laws of Seventeenth Century Newfoundland* (St John's: Memorial University of Newfoundland, 1975).

2. Post-1660 Grants: Socage Tenure

After the passage of the *Tenures Abolition Act*, all Crown grants in British North America and later Canada were made in free and common socage. The vast territories granted to the Hudson's Bay Company by Royal Charter in 1670, for example, were expressed to be "in free and common socage and not in knight's service or in capite." Socage was an easily marketable tenure and more popular with potential settlers. The *Constitutional Act, 1791*, 31 Geo III, c 31 (UK), which divided the old province of Quebec into Upper and Lower Canada, thus specified:

> 43. All lands which shall be hereafter granted within the said province of Upper Canada shall be granted in free and common soccage, in like manner as lands are now holden in free and common soccage, in that part of Great Britain called England.

The issue of the effect of grants under the French regime in what later became Upper Canada is discussed below.

D. Reception and Land Law

1. Reception of English Law in Canada

The reception of English law in Canada is a matter of particular importance for land law purposes because of the antiquity of the common law and the relevant statutes on the subject. The doctrine of reception deals with the question of what parts of English law became operative in England's colonial possessions. This is an issue that, in Canada, is dealt with at the provincial level: each province has a "reception date," sometimes established by statute, sometimes by common law, which declares the law of England as of a particular date to be the law of each colonial jurisdiction (now province or territory).

The reception date is understood to apply only to English legislation, not to the common law. The latter undergoes a kind of continuing reception: Canadian courts, even today, will refer to decisions of English courts if they find them persuasive, although they are not binding; see HP Glenn, "Persuasive Authority" (1987) 32 McGill LJ 261. However, English statutes passed before the reception date are considered to be in force in the province in question, unless they have been repealed or amended subsequently by the local legislature. This statement is subject to the qualification that the English statutes in question must be considered suitable for the province—for example, a statute dealing with the appointment of some parish officer in England with no equivalent in Canada will not likely be considered suitable, and thus will not be in force in Canadian jurisdictions. But all the statutes dealing with the fundamental principles of land law, such as *Quia Emptores* (1290), the *Statute of Uses* (1535) (considered below), and the *Tenures Abolition Act* (1660), are considered "suitable" under the reception doctrine and thus part of Canadian law. Some provinces, such as Ontario, re-enacted some of these statutes for convenience in the 19th century (see RSO 1980, App I, reproducing *An Act concerning Purchasers: An Act respecting Real Property (Quia Emptores, etc.)*, RSO 1897, c 330, and the *Statute of Uses: An Act respecting Uses*, RSO 1897, c 331), but their validity does not depend on such re-enactment or on inclusion within the Revised Statutes.

In Ontario, the first act passed by the legislature after the province was separated from the old province of Quebec specified the reception date. Originally enacted as SUC 1792, c 1, the *Property and Civil Rights Act*, now RSO 1990, c P.29, reads as follows:

> 1. In all matters of controversy relative to property and civil rights, resort shall be had to the laws of England as they stood on the 15th day of October, 1792, as the rule for the decision of the same, and all matters relative to testimony and legal proof in the investigation of fact and the forms thereof in the courts of Ontario shall be regulated by the rules of evidence established in England, as they existed on that day, except so far as such laws and rules have been since repealed, altered, varied, modified or affected by any Act of the Imperial Parliament, still having the force of law in Ontario, or by any Act of the late Province of Upper Canada, or of the Province of Canada, or of the Province of Ontario, still having the force of law in Ontario.

The Prairie provinces all adopted by statute the date 15 July 1870 as their reception date, while the relevant British Columbia statute specifies 19 November 1858 as the date of reception. The Atlantic provinces have not enacted reception statutes, Nova Scotia and Newfoundland and Labrador rely on a common law doctrine that indicates the opening day of the first sitting of the local legislature as the reception date: 3 October 1758 for Nova Scotia and 31 December 1832 for Newfoundland and Labrador. Prince Edward Island's reception date is considered to have been set by the Royal Proclamation of 1763 as 7 October 1763. The situation in New Brunswick is unsettled, with authority for different dates in 1660, 1758, and 1784: see JE Côté, "The Reception of English Law" (1977) 15 Alta L Rev 29; and *Scott v Scott* (1970), 15 DLR (3d) 374 (NBCA).

Although determining whether particular statutes have been received or not is of great importance to the practising lawyer, it is important to appreciate that the phenomenon of "reception" in general is of broad historical and cultural significance. English Canada received not just English laws but a set of ideas, expectations, and practices regarding law, often referred to as legal culture. Legal culture is a kind of soft law that conditions the application of formal law, and is especially important in cases where the latter is unclear or marked by conflicting lines of authority. See generally Philip Girard, "British Justice, English Law, and Canadian Legal Culture" in Phillip Buckner, ed, *Canada and the British Empire* (Oxford: Oxford University Press, 2008), and Bora Laskin, *The British Tradition in Canadian Law* (London: Stevens, 1969). Bruce Ziff argued that with regard to property law, Canadian legal culture (at least as revealed by judicial decision making) was highly conservative and deferential to the English model: "Warm Reception in a Cold Climate: English Property Law and the Suppression of the Canadian Legal Identity" in John McLaren, AR Buck & Nancy E Wright, eds, *Despotic Dominion: Property Rights in British Settler Societies* (Vancouver: UBC Press, 2005) [*Despotic Dominion*]. Quebec underwent two successive receptions, first of French law and then of English public and criminal law, and is often described as having a mixed legal culture: see Martin Boodman et al, *Quebec Civil Law: An Introduction to Quebec Private Law* (Toronto: Emond Montgomery, 1993).

2. The Interaction of English Law and Pre-Existing Law

In Canada, English law did not arrive in a vacuum—Aboriginal law and, in many places, French law existed before the reception of English law. In general, English law recognized the principle of continuity—that earlier legal traditions prevailed unless and until they were abolished or modified by the competent authorities.

a. The Impact of the Conquest on the Law and Land Titles of New France

Most land in New France prior to the Conquest of 1760 was held of the French king in seigneurial tenure, a tenure similar to those recognized under English feudalism. Neither the Conquest itself nor the *Treaty of Paris, 1763*, changed this fact. Although the *Royal Proclamation, 1763*, issued after the Treaty, purported to introduce English civil and criminal law to the entire conquered territory, resistance by the French inhabitants led to a reversal of policy a decade later. The *Quebec Act, 1774* extended the boundaries of Quebec into the Great Lakes region and the Ohio Valley, and declared that French civil law was to be used in relation to all matters of "property and civil rights." English criminal law, however, was to supersede French criminal law, and trial by jury was introduced: see WL Morton, *The Kingdom of Canada* (Toronto: McClelland & Stewart, 1963) at 148.

In 1887, Taschereau J of the Supreme Court of Canada described the effect of the cession by the French Crown as follows:

Now when by the treaty of 1763, France ceded to Great Britain all her rights of sovereignty, property and possession over Canada, and its islands, lands, places and coasts, ... it is unquestionable that the full title to the territory ceded became vested in the new sovereign, and that he thereafter owned it in allodium as part of the crown domain, in as full and ample a manner as the King of France had previously owned it.

(*St Catharine's Milling and Lumber Co v The Queen* (1887), 13 SCR 577 at 645, aff'd (1888), 14 AC 46 (PC-Ont).)

In other words, the effect of the British conquest of 1760 was considered legally analogous to the Norman conquest of England seven centuries earlier—it vested in the monarch both sovereignty and ownership of the land. This "ownership" did not, however, operate to invalidate the land titles of private parties granted under the former regime. Section 8 of the *Quebec Act, 1774* had thus provided that the King's "new subjects" (the French Canadians)

may also hold and enjoy their Property and Possessions, together with all Customs and Usages relative thereto, and all other their Civil Rights, in as large, ample, and beneficial Manner as if the said [Royal] Proclamation [1763, purporting to introduce English law] ... had not been made.

The issue of the validity of French-derived titles in what is now Ontario was considered in *Drulard v Welsh* (1906), 11 OLR 647 (Div Ct), rev'd on other grounds (1907), 14 OLR 54 (CA). The French settlement at Detroit, founded in 1701, straddled both sides of the Detroit River, such that the descendants of many grantees of the French crown found themselves on the "Canadian" side of the international border when it was fixed after the American Revolution. A grantee of the French Crown, Jacques Duperon Baby, had acquired 1,000 acres around the present site of Windsor, Ontario before the Conquest. He in turn disposed of lots to various purchasers under the French regime, and a successor in title of one of these purchasers found himself in a boundary dispute with a neighbour. In the course of his judgment in the Divisional Court, Chancellor Boyd remarked (at 652-53) on the continuing validity of French titles:

Patents [i.e. deeds from the Crown] were always granted [by the government at York/Toronto] to the occupants upon application being made, and proper proof of ownership furnished—and this at nominal fees. I do not know that the beneficial title to the land was enhanced by the patent; but it facilitated proof of legal ownership, and supplied more convenient means of transfer. The commutation or enlargement of title was taken advantage of by many proprietors, but till this day there is much land situate in Windsor which is held under a steady continuation of the old French occupancy. ...

As to this land, held by old [French] tenure, the Crown was really trustee of the legal estate for those occupants or owners who were beneficially entitled by possession and long enjoyment, and the grant and effect of patents so bestowed are not to be measured by rules applicable to grants which are made by the grace and bounty of the Crown. Before any patents issued in this (Essex) county bordering on the river, the land was occupied and practically possessed by the early French population and their descendants, and those holding under them: so that, in making the title of any one completer by patent, the Crown was limited by the prior valid titles of that one and his neighbours—on whose borders the grant might not impinge.

The Ontario Court of Appeal reversed Boyd C's decision in favour of Baby's successor in title, but on evidentiary grounds; it did not disagree with Boyd C's remarks on the continuing legal validity of titles based on pre-Conquest grants from the French crown.

b. Tenure and Aboriginal Title: The Royal Proclamation of 1763

In the context of land law, Aboriginal title is not tenurial. According to recent decisions of the Supreme Court of Canada, it is a *sui generis* interest, based on long possession, that was recognized (if not consistently) by the imperial and colonial authorities and, in particular, in the Royal Proclamation of 1763. Aboriginal title to land, in both its historical and contemporary dimensions, is discussed in detail in Chapter 8. The emphasis here is on the *Royal Proclamation* as a constitutional document that addressed how access to the land was to be governed as between the First Nations and settler societies of North America. In particular, it enshrined *consent* as the central principle that should govern Aboriginal–settler relations with regard to dealings with lands occupied by "the several Nations or Tribes of Indians" living under the Crown's protection. The main provisions of the *Royal Proclamation* (found at RSC 1985, App II, no 1) are as follows:

> And whereas it is just and reasonable, and essential to our Interest, and the Security of our Colonies, that the several Nations or Tribes of Indians with whom We are connected, and who live under our Protection, should not be molested or disturbed in the Possession of such Parts of Our Dominions and Territories as, not having been ceded to or purchased by Us, are reserved to them, or any of them, as their Hunting Grounds. We do therefore, with the Advice of our Privy Council, declare it to be our Royal Will and Pleasure, that no Governor or Commander in Chief in any of our Colonies of Quebec, East Florida, or West Florida, do presume, upon any Pretence whatever, to grant Warrants of Survey, or pass any Patents for Lands beyond the Bounds of their respective Governments, as described in their Commissions; as also that no Governor or Commander in Chief in any of our other Colonies or Plantations in America do presume for the present, and until our further Pleasure be known, to grant Warrants of Survey, or pass Patents for any Lands beyond the Heads or Sources of any of the Rivers which fall into the Atlantic Ocean from the West and North West, or upon any Lands whatever, which, not having been ceded to or purchased by Us as aforesaid, are reserved to the said Indians, or any of them.
>
> And We do further declare it to be Our Royal Will and Pleasure, for the present as aforesaid, to reserve under our Sovereignty, Protection, and Dominion, for the use of the said Indians, all the Lands and Territories not included within the Limits of Our said Three new Governments, or within the Limits of the Territory granted to the Hudson's Bay Company, as also all the Lands and Territories lying to the Westward of the Sources of the Rivers which fall into the Sea from the West and North West as aforesaid.
>
> And We do hereby strictly forbid, on Pain of our Displeasure, all our loving Subjects from making any Purchases or Settlements whatever, or taking Possession of any of the Lands above reserved, without our especial leave and Licence for that Purpose first obtained.
>
> And, We do further strictly enjoin and require all Persons whatever who have either wilfully or inadvertently seated themselves upon any Lands within the Countries above described, or upon any other Lands which, not having been ceded to or purchased by Us, are still reserved to the said Indians as aforesaid, forthwith to remove themselves from such Settlements.
>
> And whereas great Frauds and Abuses have been committed in purchasing Lands of the Indians, to the great Prejudice of Our Interests, and to the great Dissatisfaction of the said Indians; In order, therefore, to prevent such Irregularities for the future, and to the end that the Indians may be convinced of our Justice and determined Resolution to remove all reasonable Cause of Discontent, We do, with the Advice of our Privy Council strictly enjoin and require, that no private Person do presume to make any purchase from the said Indians of any Lands reserved to the said

Indians, within those parts of our Colonies where, We have thought proper to allow Settlement; but that, if at any Time any of the Said Indians should be inclined to dispose of the said Lands, the same shall be Purchased only for Us, in our Name, at some public Meeting or Assembly of the said Indians, to be held for that Purpose by the Governor or Commander in Chief of our Colony respectively within which they shall lie; and in case they shall lie within the limits of any Proprietary Government, conformable to such Directions and Instructions as We or they shall think proper to give for that Purpose; And we do, by the Advice of our Privy Council, declare and enjoin, that the Trade with the said Indians shall be free and open to all our Subjects whatever, provided that every Person who may incline to Trade with the said Indians do take out a Licence for carrying on such Trade from the Governor or Commander in Chief of any of our Colonies respectively where such Person shall reside, and also give Security to observe such Regulations as We shall at any Time think fit, by ourselves or by our Commissaries to be appointed for this Purpose, to direct and appoint for the Benefit of the said Trade.

Although there were treaties between individual First Nations and the governments of various settler colonies before the *Royal Proclamation*, the Proclamation may be seen as the foundation of the "treaty relationship" that is often said to exist between Aboriginal and non-Aboriginal peoples in Canada. On pre-1763 treaties, see William C Wicken, *Mi'kmaq Treaties on Trial: History, Land, and Donald Marshall Junior* (Toronto: University of Toronto Press, 2002), discussing treaties between the British Crown and the Nova Scotia Mi'kmaq in 1726 and 1760-61. On the "treaty relationship," see John Borrows, *Crown and Aboriginal Occupations of Land: A History and Comparison* (Toronto: Ipperwash Inquiry, 2005); and John Ralston Saul, *A Fair Country: Telling Truths About Canada* (Toronto: Viking Canada, 2008).

As you read the following extract analyzing the background and legal effect of the *Royal Proclamation*, consider the demands of the Idle No More movement that emerged in 2012-13. One of these is to "Honour the spirit and intent of the historic Treaties": <http://www .idlenomore.ca/calls_for_change>.

Brian Slattery, "The Hidden Constitution: Aboriginal Rights in Canada"
(1984) 32 Am J Comp L 361 at 368-72 (footnotes omitted)

The Royal Proclamation of 1763

By 1763, Great Britain's long struggle with France for American empire was over. At the Peace of Paris, France ceded all its remaining territories in Canada to the British Crown, as well as its territories east of the Mississippi River. Britain also obtained Florida from the Spanish Crown, thus completing its claims to the eastern and northern sectors of America. Only one area was left to another European power, namely the lands west of the Mississippi that France had relinquished to Spain the previous year.

These treaties temporarily sorted out the claims of the three main European rivals among themselves. But the French Crown could not give Great Britain what it did not possess itself, namely authority over the native groups inhabiting the ceded territories. These nations were, in many cases, trading partners of the French and sometime military allies. If they were not prepared to accept direct French authority, neither were they willing to accept that France might deposit them in the pocket of the English King.

As the Chippewa leader, Minivavana, told an English trader:

> Englishman, although you have conquered the French, you have not yet conquered us. We
> are not your slaves. These lakes, these woods and mountains, were left to us by our ancestors.
> They are our inheritance; and we will part with them to none.

A similar viewpoint was expressed by certain Wabash River Indians:

> You tell us, that when you Conquered the French, they gave you this Country. That no dif-
> ference may happen hereafter, we tell you now the French never conquered, neither did they
> purchase a foot of our Country, nor have [they a right] to give it to you[.] [W]e gave them
> liberty to settle for which they always rewarded us and treated us with great Civility.

Britain was well aware in 1763 of the precarious nature of its relations with the old
Indian allies of France, and the growing dissatisfaction of its own native allies and trading
partners. Since mid-century, the British government had been increasingly occupied with
Indian affairs, and the war with France had emphasized the importance of native friendship and support. For some time, a plan had been afoot to assure the Indians of the
Crown's good intentions by removing a principal cause of Indian discontent—white intrusion on Indian lands. This plan culminated in the publication of a Royal Proclamation on
7 October 1763. The interest of the document is not purely historical, for its main terms
have never been generally repealed in Canada. Although it must be read in the light of
later developments, it still forms a principal basis for aboriginal land claims in many areas.

The Proclamation is one of those legal instruments that does simple things in complicated ways. The central idea of its Indian provisions is simple: to ensure that no Indian
lands in America are taken by British subjects without native consent. This objective is
secured by three main measures: colonial governments are forbidden to grant any unceded
Indian lands, British subjects to settle on them, and private individuals to purchase them,
with a system of public purchases adopted as the official mode of extinguishing Indian
title. The British government was particularly concerned at the prospect of white settlement spreading indiscriminately into the American interior, and so the Proclamation
temporarily seals off much of that area to settlers, designating it an exclusive Indian territory. But the document's main measures are not confined to the Indian Territory; they
apply throughout British North America.

The Indian provisions of the Proclamation begin with a preamble, where the King
explains his basic aims:

> And whereas it is just and reasonable, and essential to our Interest and the Security of Our
> Colonies, that the several Nations or Tribes of Indians, with whom We are connected, and
> who live under Our Protection, should not be molested or disturbed in the Possession of
> such Parts of Our Dominions and Territories as, not having been ceded to, or purchased by
> Us, are reserved to them, or any of them, as their Hunting Grounds.

While the King asserts ultimate sovereignty over the Indians, he also acknowledges
their semi-autonomous status, describing them as Nations or Tribes "with whom We are
connected, and who live under Our Protection." He recognizes that the Indians are entitled to undisturbed possession of the lands reserved to them, and, in an important
formula repeated later in the text, defines these reserves as any Indian lands that have not
been ceded to or purchased by the Crown. The King claims these lands as part of his
dominions, but at the same time recognizes the existence of an Indian interest requiring

extinguishment by cession or purchase. In technical terms, the Indian interest constitutes a legal burden on the Crown's ultimate title until surrendered.

In 1763, most of the American territories claimed by Britain were unceded lands held by native peoples. Under the Proclamation, such lands were automatically deemed Indian reserves. Their boundaries were determined negatively by past Indian cessions and positively by current Indian possessions. Much of the unorganized American interior was still, of course, unceded. But other unceded lands lay within the undisputed boundaries of existing colonies, including the northern colonies of Rupert's Land, Quebec, Newfoundland, and Nova Scotia, now forming part of Canada.

It is sometimes argued that the Proclamation recognized aboriginal land rights only in the exclusive Indian Territory created in the American hinterland. On this supposition, Indian title was not recognized in areas specifically excluded from the Territory, such as the coastal belt east of the Appalachian Mountains, and the colonies of Quebec and Rupert's Land. But the text does not support this view. After describing the boundaries of the territory, the Proclamation orders the removal of all persons who have settled either within the territory "or upon *any other Lands*, which, not having been ceded to, or purchased by Us, are still reserved to the said Indians as aforesaid" (emphasis added). This provision clearly assumes that unceded Indian lands located outside the Indian Territory are reserved for Indian use. The King also forbids colonial Governors to make grants of "any Lands whatever, which, not having been ceded to, or purchased by Us as aforesaid, are reserved to the said Indians, or any of them." The ban applies to unceded Indian lands generally, wherever they happen to be located. Finally, the Proclamation provides that no private person shall make any purchases from the Indians "of any Lands reserved to the said Indians, within those Parts of Our Colonies where We have thought proper to allow Settlement," and specifies that if the Indians are ever inclined to dispose of such lands, they shall be purchased for the Crown in a public assembly. Since the provision only applies in areas where settlement was permitted, and the Indian Territory was, for the time being, expressly closed to "any Purchases or Settlements whatever," it could only refer to unceded Indian lands found outside the Territory, in eastern and northern colonies where settlement was still allowed.

In brief, the Proclamation recognized that lands possessed by Indians throughout British territories in America were reserved for their exclusive use, unless previously ceded to the Crown. Prior to a public cession of such lands, they could not be granted away or settled. These provisions applied not only to the Indian Territory, but to the full range of British colonies in North America, no matter how humble or peripheral. In this respect, Rupert's Land, Quebec, Nova Scotia, Newfoundland, the Thirteen Colonies, and the Floridas were brought under a uniform legal regime. The Indian Territory was placed in a special position. Whereas in other areas Indian lands might still be purchased by public authorities, in the territory such purchases were forbidden altogether for the time being. The idea was to divert the flow of white settlement from the American interior to the northern and southern colonies, which were still relatively sparsely settled. However, the Crown envisaged that in due course parts of the Territory might be opened up, in which case the standard regime governing purchase of Indian lands would take effect.

There has been some controversy whether the Proclamation applied to the far western reaches of the American continent, notably modern British Columbia and the Yukon Territory. The question has usually been treated as depending on how much territory

Great Britain claimed in 1763. Here, the historical evidence indicates that British claims extended indefinitely westward to the Pacific Ocean in latitudes now occupied by Canada. But a better basis exists for resolving the issue. Many of the Proclamation's provisions are framed in general terms, referring broadly to "Our Dominions and Territories" and "Our Colonies or Plantations in America." Imperial enactments using such terms were normally given a prospective application, so as to apply not only to colonies and territories held when the legislation was enacted but also to those acquired subsequently, unless this result was clearly excluded. The purpose of the Proclamation was to supply a uniform set of rules governing Indian lands throughout British territories in North America. There is no reason to think that Indian lands located in territories acquired after 1763 needed less protection than those acquired earlier. It is natural to infer that the Proclamation applied to both.

The Proclamation of 1763 has a profound significance for modern Canada. Under its terms, aboriginal peoples held continuing rights to their lands except where these rights have been extinguished by voluntary cession. Treaties of cession have been signed for large parts of Canada, notably in Ontario and the Prairie Provinces. But no such treaties exist for the Atlantic Provinces, and parts of Quebec, British Columbia, the Yukon, and the Northwest Territories, as well [as] for pockets of land elsewhere. Moreover, there is doubt whether Canadian legislatures were competent to override the Proclamation's terms prior to 1931, when the Statute of Westminster was enacted. So native peoples may today hold subsisting aboriginal rights to large tracts of Canadian land.

DISCUSSION NOTES

i. Tenurial Title: Current Significance and Reform

Today all land in Canada outside Quebec is held in free and common socage. In the words of the Ontario Law Reform Commission (OLRC), however, "in practice this tenurial relationship is of no importance": *Report on Basic Principles of Land Law* (Toronto: Ministry of the Attorney General, 1996) [OLRC *Basic Principles*] at 7. One remaining echo of the doctrine of tenure relates to the possibility of escheat. Escheat resulting from a failure of heirs—where a fee simple holder dies with no heirs and no will—is a situation that may arise in the 21st century, but it is now governed by statute rather than the tenurial relationship: see the *Escheats Act*, RSO 1990, c E20; *Escheats Act*, RSNS 1989, c 151; *Escheats and Forfeitures Act*, RSNB 1973, c E-10; *Unclaimed Personal Property and Vested Property Act*, SA 2007, c U-1.5. Some of these statutes apply to personal property as well as to interests in land. In Ontario, however, s 47(7) of the *Succession Law Reform Act*, RSO 1990, c S.26 makes any property (including personal property) of a person who dies intestate and without heirs the property of the Crown to which the *Escheats Act* then applies.

Escheat for treason or felony was abolished in the *Criminal Code* of 1892, SC 1892, c 29, s 965, although it has emerged in a new form in recent years with the adoption of statutes providing for the forfeiture of property that can be shown to be derived from the proceeds of crime or unlawful activity: see e.g. *Civil Remedies Act, 2001*, SO 2001, c 28, s 1(b) (aimed at "preventing persons who engage in unlawful activities and others from keeping property that was acquired as a result of unlawful activities").

A second echo of tenure, with somewhat more practical significance, arises with regard to leaseholds. As *Quia Emptores* does not apply to leaseholds, it is possible to create subtenancy arrangements that are reminiscent of the tenurial pyramid. Subtenancies are discussed in Chapter 4.

In spite of its conclusion as to the lack of practical significance of tenure, the OLRC was of the view that

> statutory abrogation of tenure of freehold land is unnecessary since it has become obsolete. …
> Tenure is not even indirectly important today. It does not have any impact on the drafting of legal documents. Nor does it have any continuing effect on the development of the law.

(OLRC *Basic Principles* at 19.)

This conclusion, although defensible as a technical principle of law, may not capture the more general significance of a tenure-based system of land as opposed to one not based on tenure; the latter is referred to as an allodial system of land law.

ii. Tenurial Title Versus Allodial Title

As noted earlier, the doctrine of tenure was based on the legal-political theory that the monarch owned all the land in England after the Norman Conquest. Such was not the case on the European continent, where some tracts of land were not subjected to a feudal order; these "allodial" lands were considered to be "owned" by those who lived and worked on them. In addition, as noted earlier, the Napoleonic Code (1804) abolished existing feudal relations of tenure in the civil law jurisdictions that adopted it. Moreover, after the American Revolution, the idea of a tenurial system was rejected in the newly independent "United States," along with the monarchy itself. As a result, many state constitutions declared that all lands in the state were to be considered as owned outright in allodial ownership. Consider, for example, the following provision of the Wisconsin state constitution:

> All lands within the state are declared to be allodial, and feudal tenures are prohibited. Leases and grants of agricultural land for a longer term than fifteen years in which rent or service of any kind shall be reserved, and all fines and like restraints upon alienation reserved in any grant of land, hereafter made, are declared to be void.

(Wisconsin State Constitution, § 14, <http://legis.wisconsin.gov/rsb/unannotated_wisconst .pdf>.)

Allodial title arguably encourages the holder to think in terms of "absolute" rights over land and to view himself or herself as the ultimate decision-maker with regard to it. It also encourages a stark division between the "public" and "private" spheres, with the private seen as a zone of minimal state interference. By contrast, a tenurial system may encourage (or at least reflect) a less dichotomous view of public and private, such that state regulation is not seen as an illegitimate incursion into a zone of individual privacy. In *Mariner Real Estate Ltd v Nova Scotia (Attorney General)* (1999), 177 DLR (4th) 696 (NSCA), for example (discussed in Chapter 1), Justice Cromwell observed (at 717):

> Considerations of a claim of de facto expropriation must recognize that the effect of the particular regulation must be compared with reasonable use of the lands in modern Canada, not with their use as if they were in some imaginary state of nature unconstrained by regulation. In modern Canada, extensive land use regulation is the norm and it should not be assumed that ownership carries with it any exemption from such regulation. … [T]here is a distinction between the numerous

"rights" (or the "bundle of rights") associated with ownership and ownership itself. The "rights" of ownership and the concept of reasonable use of the land include regulation in the public interest.

A land law based on tenure may also be more amenable to the practice of ideas of stewardship, where the landholder is seen as a kind of trustee for future generations. As Kevin Gray & Susan Francis Gray [Gray & Gray] explain in *Elements of Land Law*, extracted above:

> Tenurial theory has one further, indirect, significance for 21st century land law. In positing a mutuality of obligation, tenurial theory did at least reinforce the notion that right and responsibility are inseparable components of the deep theory of property. To the American scholar, John Cribbet, we owe the ironic reflection that the abolition of the incidents of feudal tenure, in freeing land from archaic and obsolete obligations, contributed towards a more general dissociation of entitlement and obligation in landholding. It is only in modern times that some element of the protective stewardship implicit within tenure has resurfaced as a basis for suggesting that, for environmental reasons, ownership of land is inherently qualified by social or community-oriented obligation.

(Gray & Gray at 68.)

Ideas of stewardship are discussed again in Chapter 7, in the context of the role of restrictive covenants and conservation "easements" in land-use planning. At this point, however, you may want to consider how ideas about "holding interests" in land may be important in the Canadian context. In particular, this concept may be more helpful in reflecting Aboriginal ideas with respect to "sharing" land and in relation to concepts of stewardship for future generations. In this way, it may be important to note how these ideas about relationships may be reflected not only in feudal times but also in contemporary relationships concerning title to land: see Margaret Ogilvie, *Historical Introduction to Legal Studies* (Scarborough, ON: Carswell, 1982) at 29ff.

E. Seisin

The concept of seisin functions as a bridge between the doctrine of tenure and the doctrine of estates. In early common law, seisin was a term that meant possession. Tenure relied on the concept of seisin in order to establish who was in possession and thus owed duties (and feudal incidents) to the person on the next higher rung of the feudal hierarchy. Seisin was also important in determining relative rights to possession of land and in conveyancing of estates in land (discussed below), thus implicating the doctrine of estates. In the early common law, it was possible to speak of being seised of a freehold or leasehold, or even a chattel: Simpson at 37-38. That is, whoever was currently in possession had seisin and every taking of possession, even an illegitimate one, gave rise to a new seisin. Thus (as discussed in Chapter 2), if A had seisin and was dispossessed ("disseised") by B, feudal law recognized that B had seisin. However, because A had prior seisin, the law entitled A to bring an action to recover the land. Nonetheless, B's seisin was also protected against any third party or subsequent disseisor, because B's seisin was prior and therefore better than the third party's. This principle about the relativity of title based on prior possession remains in effect as current law in relation to principles of "possessory title."

By the late Middle Ages, however, seisin had become a more technical concept. By then, it had become limited to freehold estates and was connected to complex and now obsolete legal "causes of action" called the "real actions." Real actions were technical legal processes by which possession of freeholds of land could be regained through litigation; because these actions resulted in regaining land (the "*res*" in Latin), land became known as "real property." By contrast, lessees of land and owners of personal property or chattels were no longer considered to be "seised." Thus, they had to rely on "personal actions" if they were "dispossessed"; the action in ejectment, developed to aid lessees in regaining "possession," is discussed in Chapter 4. This division between real and personal property has continued to the present; in fact, "the very distinction between real and personal property in one sense originates in the distinction between real and personal actions" for the recovery of land and chattels (Simpson at 42). However, as noted in Chapter 1, this book reflects the modern organization of property principles and their application to real and personal property; at the same time, it is often useful to note how these categories developed in relation to a more complex litigation process some centuries ago.

Seisin also played an important role in medieval conveyancing. As Simpson explained,

> The classic medieval conveyance was the feoffment with livery of seisin. ... [W]ith the Norman invasion, ... an actual physical delivery of land became the normal mode of private conveyance. Naturally one cannot hand over a tract of land in the same way as one hands over a horse, but the law encouraged alienors to make conveyances of land as like the delivery of a chattel as possible. The expression "feoffment with livery of seisin" does not indicate any twofold ceremony; a grant of a fee is implied by "feoffment," and livery, or delivery of seisin, is the mode in which the grant is made. ... It is obvious that this mode of conveyance gave to dealings in land a notoriety which no symbolic delivery or delivery of a deed could ever give.

(Simpson at 112.)

The nature of the public ceremony involved in livery of seisin is discussed in Chapter 2. Thus, although a transfer of land might be termed a "private" conveyance, the state of the title was rendered public. Particularly at a time when literacy rates were low, making land transfer depend on a type of public performance rather than a document made eminent sense.

However, because leases were not considered to involve seisin, they could be conveyed by private acts or writings and did not need to be publicized. This ability to keep one's land transactions private was often highly prized and led conveyancers to develop other modes of transferring freehold estates that could avoid the "public" ceremony of livery of seisin, discussed below. However, the public interest in information about land ownership and transfers eventually resulted in the *Statute of Frauds*, 1677, 29 Car II, c 3 (discussed in Chapters 4 and 5), which required that transfers of property interests in land be evidenced in writing, a requirement that eventually resulted in the elimination of livery of seisin as a method of transfer.

Although most provinces today have provisions abolishing feoffment with livery of seisin (see e.g. *Conveyancing Act*, RSNS 1989, c 97, s 10(3)), the *Conveyancing and Law of Property Act*, RSO 1990, c C.34 merely makes a written deed of grant a supplementary form of conveying estates in land:

> 2. All corporeal tenements and hereditaments, as regards the conveyance of the immediate freehold thereof, lie in grant as well as in livery.

In spite of this provision, there are no recent examples of a conveyance by livery of seisin.

III. THE DOCTRINE OF ESTATES

A. "Estates" and "Ownership" Contrasted

As the doctrine of tenure receded in importance, the related doctrine of estates took on more significance. Thus, while the law of tenure set out the general parameters for landhold-ing (for example, "holding" an interest in land), the doctrine of estates described the nature of the interest held—that is, the sets of rights that landholders (those in possession or with a right to future possession) could hold. As noted above, the common law did not identify an "owner" of land, but rather what "estate" in land an owner held. It stated that individuals owned not the land itself, but estates in land, where an estate was defined as a bundle of rights delimiting the period during which the holder was entitled to possession. It is import-ant to distinguish other uses of the word "estate":

- "estate" as a large tract of land
- the "estate" of a deceased person
- "estate" as a type of personal status

Although all these meanings are related to the word used in this chapter, none is identical. The first is an example of the confusion between rights and things that CB Macpherson, "The Meaning of Property" in CB Macpherson, ed, *Property: Mainstream and Critical Positions* (To-ronto: University of Toronto Press, 1978), identified in Chapter 1: the *land* is distinct from the *rights in the land*. The second refers to the totality of a deceased person's assets and liabilities, including interests in both land and personal property. And the third relates not to property as such but to personal status: historically, the first estate comprised the nobility, the second the clergy, and the third commoners. To what extent is this third meaning at all appropriate in the 21st century?

B. Freehold Versus Leasehold Estates

Estates were also divided qualitatively, between leasehold and freehold estates, with the lat-ter historically considered superior to the former—for example, although both privileges required the possession of a property interest, only freeholders had the vote and were en-titled to sit on juries. Leaseholders were seen as dependent on the will of others (for example, the lessor might not renew one's lease), while a freeholder's estate could be ended only by his or her own act, or by death in the special situation of a "life estate." This tension between freehold and leasehold estates was most evident in Canada during the century-long conflict generated by what was known as the "land question" on Prince Edward Island.

> **Margaret E McCallum, "The Sacred Rights of Property: Title, Entitlement,**
> **and the Land Question in Nineteenth-Century Prince Edward Island"**
> in G Blaine Baker & Jim Phillips, eds, *Essays in the History of Canadian Law,*
> *vol VIII: In Honour of RCB Risk* (Toronto: University of Toronto Press for the
> Osgoode Society for Canadian Legal History, 1999) at 360-62 (footnotes omitted)

Britain acquired sovereignty over Prince Edward Island by the *Treaty of Paris, 1763*. Formerly part of France's North American empire, Ile St-Jean, as it was called by the

French, was a small island in the Gulf of St Lawrence, heavily wooded and sparsely populated by Acadians and the Micmac. Considered valuable for its forests, fisheries, and potential as farmland, ... the imperial government decided to grant the island in large lots to proprietors whose payment of quit rents would provide the funds necessary to administer the new colony and whose tenants would turn the island into tidy farms. Accordingly, the island was surveyed and divided into sixty-seven lots of about 20,000 acres each. One lot was reserved as demesne lands of the Crown, and the remaining sixty-six were distributed in a single day to applicants selected by lottery [in 1767]. Three lots were given to the officers of the 78th Regiment of Fraser Highlanders, and the rest allocated among ninety-eight individuals, including high-ranking colonial administrators and military officers, members of Parliament, intimates of the establishment, merchants, and entrepreneurs. ... Grantees were required to settle their lands within ten years with one Protestant settler for every two hundred acres, and to pay quit rents to the Crown, of two, four, or six shillings per one hundred acres, depending on the quality of the land in the township lot. ...

[T]he proprietorial system remained in place for over a century. Not everyone who came to the Island became a tenant farmer on a short-term lease paying rent to an absentee landlord. ... By the 1830s, small freeholders were about one-third of the Island population and owned about one-fifth of its land. Resident proprietors remained the exception, particularly among those with the largest holdings; more than three-quarters of the twenty proprietors who owned one or more townships lived in the United Kingdom. The six largest proprietors owned four or more townships each, that is, more than 80,000 acres, an amount that one proprietor described as "a respectable family estate." Leasehold terms varied widely, from a few to a thousand years. The rents specified bore no direct relationship to the quality or productivity of the land ... . Some proprietors considered their estates only as long-term speculations, while others spent time, money, and attention on immediate development. But none of the proprietors complied with the conditions for settlement in their original grants, either as stated initially or as modified from time to time in response to proprietorial pleas of hardship. Given the proprietors' default, there was both popular and elite support for an escheat, or reversion to the Crown, of estates of proprietors who had failed to meet the conditions of their grants. Some escheat proponents assumed that when the Crown reclaimed the estates of defaulting proprietors, the land would be regranted without charge to the occupiers, while others hoped that the escheat would open up Crown lands for purchase.

McCallum then considered the ideas about property mobilized during the political campaign waged by various tenants' groups in the middle decades of the 19th century. She groups the main arguments advanced by the tenants' advocates around four main themes:

1. the thaumaturgic power of property ownership;
2. land belongs to those who make it productive;
3. property is historically contingent and socially constructed; and
4. property is never truly private.

Consider how these themes resonate with those discussed in Chapter 1 with regard to justifications for private property.

In fact, it was not until 1875, shortly after Prince Edward Island joined Canada, that the land question was finally settled by the *Land Purchase Act, 1875*, SPEI 1875, c 32. It provided for the expropriation of the proprietors' titles with compensation (the Dominion government providing $800,000 for this purpose) and the sale of the lands to their tenants. By the 1880s, an island of tenants had been largely converted to an island of owner-occupiers. For a study of the role of women landlords during the proprietorial era and their campaign to resist the passage and implementation of the *Land Purchase Act*, see Rusty Bittermann & Margaret Mc-Callum, *The Lady Landlords of Prince Edward Island: Imperial Dreams and the Defence of Property* (Montreal & Kingston: McGill-Queen's University Press, 2008).

At the present time, the "status" distinctions remaining between leasehold and freehold estates are minor. For example, as noted above, lessees do not have seisin. However, the *Constitution Act, 1867*, s 23(3) requires that a senator be "legally or equitably seised as of Freehold for his own Use and Benefit of Lands or Tenements held in Free and Common Socage ... within the Province for which he is appointed, of the Value of Four thousand Dollars," which means that a person holding only a leasehold interest in their province of appointment would not be entitled to appointment as a senator. Aside from such distinctions, however, lessees may often be more economically vulnerable than those with freehold estates, although freeholders whose properties are heavily mortgaged may also experience vulnerability. Leaseholds are considered in more detail in Chapter 4, and the remainder of this chapter deals with freehold estates in land.

C. Freehold Estates: Life Estate, Fee Simple, and Fee Tail

Estates were a feature of the land law and were not applied to personal property. (It is still the case that estates cannot be created in personal property at law, although they can be created in equity by using the trust device, considered below.)

1. An Overview of Estates

The common law recognized three main types of freehold estate in land: the life estate, the fee tail, and the fee simple. After a brief overview, we examine each type of estate in more detail with regard to how it can be created in modern law and what rights it affords the holder. The common law distinguished between estates according to whether or not they were inheritable—that is, estates "of inheritance" or "not of inheritance." The only estate not of inheritance is the life estate, while the fee simple and the fee tail are estates of inheritance. The life estate, as the name implies, lasts only for the lifetime of the holder. Consider the following disposition:

O grants "to A for life."

A's estate will cease immediately upon A's death. At that point, possession will revert to O, if he or she is still alive, or will pass to O's executor, if O is deceased, to be dealt with under O's will or by intestacy.

By contrast, the fee simple might last indefinitely, if B, the holder of the estate, had heirs to whom it could pass on B's death or had sold it during her lifetime. (Recall that after *Quia Emptores* (1290) any grantee from B would "step into the shoes" of B and thus take the same estate B had.) Because B or B's purchaser might have heirs forever, it is clear that the fee simple estate is one that may last a long time, even forever. In this respect, the fee simple estate may be comparable (for practical purposes at least) to allodial ownership.

At common law, the fee simple was created by the following formula:

O grants "to B and his heirs."

The fee simple was (and is) the largest estate known to the law. This formula contemplates that the estate will pass indefinitely to B's "heirs" as long as there continue to be heirs, broadly defined, of B.

The fee tail is a "shortened" type of fee simple, the name coming from the law French phrase *"fief taillé,"* or "cut fee." (Law French was a mixture of Norman French and English that was used in the English courts until the 14th century and by legal writers until the end of the 17th century.) It could only descend to a particular class of relatives, as indicated by the formula used to create it:

O grants "to C and the heirs of his body."

Anyone who takes the fee tail has to be a lineal descendant of C. If C died with no children, C's sibling, niece, or nephew could not inherit the estate. When "the heirs of the body" of C ended, possession would return to O, if he or she is still alive, or will pass to O's executor, if O is deceased, to be dealt with under O's will or by intestacy. Obviously, this form of estate was particularly important in earlier times, when holders of large estates in England wanted their lands to descend to a child connected by blood. It is important to note that fee tail estates can no longer be created in Ontario, an issue discussed below.

2. Significance of the Estate Concept

The estate concept, although developed in medieval times, remains a cornerstone of modern land law. Its significance is explained by Gray & Gray:

Kevin Gray & Susan Francis Gray, *Elements of Land Law*
5th ed (Oxford: Oxford University Press, 2009) at 61 (footnotes omitted)

A Functional Form of Land Ownership

The substitution of an abstract estate in land (in place of the land itself) as the object of proprietary rights has had the most profound influence on English law. The ingenious compromise of the doctrine of estates resolved at a stroke the apparent contradiction between the theory and reality in the ownership of land. At one level the estate in the land merely demarcated the temporal extent of the grant to a tenant within the vertical power structure emanating from the crown. In practice the conceptualism of interlocking estates facilitated a functional scheme of landholding which obviated any holistic theory about the wider phenomenon of ownership. Indeed, it was the concentration on the rights and powers appertaining to different kinds of "estate" which so sharply distinguished the common law view of real property from the continental emphasis on full ownership in the sense of *dominium*.

Flexibility in the Management of Wealth

From the earliest times the doctrine of estates equipped English land law with a range of highly manipulable constructs which conferred enormous convenience in the management of wealth. Through the doctrine of estates the common law was able to organise the allocation of certain powers of administration, enjoyment and disposition over land in respect of particular periods or "slices" of time. The conceptual legerdemain of estate ownership facilitated almost endless disaggregations of title through differentially graded grants of land. Proprietary rights over land could be fragmented and distributed in myriad ways: Greenacre could be allocated, say, to A for life, thereafter to B in tail, and then to C in fee simple. Such temporal distribution of fragments of title connoted a flexibility and versatility largely unknown to civilian systems of property law.

The Immediate Jural Reality of Successive Estates

It was possible, moreover, to accord an immediate conceptual reality to each "slice" of time represented by an estate. In other words, any particular slice of entitlement in the land could be viewed as having a present existence, notwithstanding that its owner was not entitled to possession of the land until some future date. In a world of jural abstractions it was quite easy to conceive of rights to successive holdings of the land as "present estates coexisting at the same time," albeit that the actual enjoyment of some was postponed. It was ultimately this feature of the time-related aspect of the estate in land which made it possible for the common lawyer to comprehend the feasibility of current dispositions of, and dealings with, *future* interests in land. Each successive interest had an immediate jural existence as of the date of the grant; each was freely commerciable (ie mortgageable) long before the estate in question came to vest "in possession."

The full significance of this discussion of consecutive interests in land will become apparent below in the discussion of "future interests" in land. For the moment, we will elaborate on each of the two main estates found in modern law—the fee simple and the life estate—and then turn more briefly to the fee tail, which is seldom encountered in 21st-century Canadian law. First, however, it is useful to briefly discuss the significance of the doctrine of estates for the lawyer.

3. Estates in Land: The Role of the Lawyer

Much of the work of the property lawyer is advisory rather than adversarial—it relates to the "solicitor" functions of the lawyer, as opposed to the "barrister" functions. This kind of law is often called "facilitative law"—it involves advising the client about the various options available to him or her with regard to structuring transfers of property, either *inter vivos* or by will. Although, as discussed below, the law does not allow entirely new forms of estates to be created, it does permit a high degree of flexibility with regard to varying existing forms of estates. The role of the lawyer is to carry out the intentions of the client as faithfully as possible while being aware of both the creative possibilities of the law and its limits. Thus, the bulk of this chapter is devoted to identifying and discussing the elements in the property lawyer's "toolkit," while at the same time raising larger questions about the way in which our legal order treats property rights.

The more complex a client's wishes are, the more attention must be paid to drafting the documents that will embody those wishes. Often the lawyer's role in drafting is to strike a balance between, on the one hand, trying to provide for every eventuality that may occur and, on the other, aiming for a simplicity that may prove to be ambiguous or illusory. In this regard, decided cases may be helpful as negative examples in pointing out phrases or terms that have been found to be ambiguous or ineffective to carry out a client's wishes.

Many of the cases in this chapter began as applications to the court by trustees or by executors of the estate of a deceased person asking for the advice and direction of the court with regard to the nature of the interests created under a trust deed or will. These cases were thus not triggered by any legal "wrong" committed by the defendant. This fact is often reflected in the style of cause—for example, *Re Walker* or *Re McColgan*. This style of cause indicates that the case did not originate in an adversarial format; rather, the trustee or executor has sought the advice of the court with regard to the interpretation of a will or conveyance of property. Such proceedings are provided for in the rules of civil procedure of all common law provinces. In Ontario, the relevant rule provides:

> 14.05(3) A proceeding may be brought by application where ... the relief claimed is
>
> (a) the opinion, advice or direction of the court on a question affecting the rights of a person in respect of the administration of the estate of a deceased person or the execution of a trust; ...
>
> (d) the determination of rights that depend on the interpretation of a deed, will, contract or other instrument, or on the interpretation of a statute, order in council, regulation or municipal by-law or resolution; [or]
>
> (e) the declaration of an interest in or charge on land, including the nature and extent of the interest or charge or the boundaries of the land, or the settling of the priority of interests or charges;

(*Rules of Civil Procedure*, RRO 1990, Reg 194.)

The standard of care expected of a trustee or executor when distributing property under a deed or will is one of perfection—a trustee or executor who misinterprets the interests created by the document, and gives to A what a court subsequently determines was meant for B, may be personally liable to B for the error. It is thus not surprising that when faced with any ambiguity in a deed or will, a lawyer will advise the trustee or executor to apply to court for advice and direction. Ideally, however, the document disposing of property should be drafted in a sufficiently clear manner that recourse to the court, with the attendant expense, is unnecessary.

When you have read the rest of this chapter you may wish to reflect further on this point. Is it appropriate that the court's time should be taken up in supplying legal advice to property owners outside the context of an actual dispute? Are there other ways in which the difficulty identified in the previous paragraph can be addressed?

4. The Fee Simple

The fee simple is the largest estate known to the law—largest with regard to both its duration (potentially indefinite) and the nature and extent of the rights granted to the holder. Each of these qualities is examined in turn.

a. Duration of the Fee Simple

With regard to duration, the very question "how long does a fee simple last?" has a strange ring to modern ears, because when we think of land transfer, we think mainly in terms of sale rather than inheritance. Even when purchasing a property for use as a family home, individuals are much more likely to think of selling it in future, rather than leaving it to the next generation. However, fee simple holders assume that, upon sale, they can pass on the totality of rights connected to the land in question, including the right to direct how title will pass in the future. That is what *Quia Emptores* guaranteed, and that is what duration means in this context: the right of a fee simple holder to transfer the same plenitude of rights that she acquired to the next holder. That holder can, in turn, pass on the same rights to another purchaser, and so on *ad infinitum*.

Although *Quia Emptores* guaranteed free alienation, in medieval times people thought of land transfer primarily in terms of inheritance rather than sale. The formula used by the common law to create the fee simple reflected this assumption: "to A and his (or her) heirs." (Note, however, that there were some restrictions in relation to women holding land, discussed in Chapter 6.) The "heirs" referred to here are A's intestate heirs—those who will take when there is no will. Indeed, willing of land was not permitted at common law, and only became possible in the 16th century by the *Statute of Wills* in 1540 (32 Hen 8, c 3), discussed below. At common law, land descended on intestacy by the rules of primogeniture, according to which the eldest son inherited all the parental land, and only if there were no male issue could daughters inherit; if there was more than one daughter, they inherited the land in co-tenancy as co-parceners (see Chapter 6 for further discussion of co-parcenary).

Unlike the situation in modern law, spouses were not heirs of one another: as explored further in Chapter 6, the surviving spouse held only a life interest in part or all of the deceased spouse's freehold lands. If the holder of a fee simple left no issue, the fee would pass on intestacy to the next closest relative(s). In theory, no degree of blood relationship was too remote as long as it could be proven by genealogical evidence. "Blood" relations were necessary because adoption was unknown at common law, but blood alone was insufficient: only "legitimate" kin, whose parents were married, could inherit. (The child of unmarried parents was considered *filius nullius*, the child of no one, and inherited from neither parent on intestacy.) If no "legitimate" blood relatives could be found, there would be an escheat to the Crown, as noted above. At that point, the fee simple would be considered to have "ended," and the Crown could add the land to its own domain, or regrant it to someone else. Although primogeniture was long ago replaced in Canada by partible inheritance (equal sharing among the children of the intestate), as noted below, the basic point remains that the fee simple ends whenever the holder dies intestate without any known heirs.

b. Rights Conferred by the Fee Simple

Turning to the rights enjoyed by the fee simple holder, these are perhaps best summed up by the terms used in Roman law, even though Roman law relied on the concept of allodial ownership and did not recognize estates in land as such. Roman jurists spoke of ownership as entitling the holder to *usus, fructus,* and *abusus*; P Van Warmelo, *An Introduction to the Principles of Roman Civil Law* (Cape Town, SA: Juta and Co, 1976) at 77-78. *Usus* is the right to use and possess the land, including the right of management and control. *Fructus* is the right to profit from the land, whether by exploiting it directly or leasing it out. It includes the right to whatever income is produced from the land. *Abusus* is the right to alter the land physically, even to the point of destruction. In addition to these three rights, Roman law from an early date recognized the full right of alienation, whether by sale or gift *inter vivos* or upon death.

It is difficult to destroy land, of course, but the Roman concept of *abusus* included, for example, cutting down trees, pulling down buildings, levelling hills, and opening mines. The fee simple holder has traditionally been able to physically alter the land at will, for worthy or unworthy purposes, subject to the restraints imposed by nuisance law in tort, respecting harm to neighbours, and any public law regulations that may be in place. This right to alter the landscape dramatically has been a key part of the exploitation of Canada's natural resources, from the earliest coal mines to the contemporary oil sands.

The right of alienation includes the right not only to transfer the fee simple itself, but also to create lesser estates, such as life estates or leases, and interests in land known as "incorporeal hereditaments"—easements, restrictive covenants, and *profits à prendre*—discussed in Chapter 7. It also includes the right to mortgage the fee simple—to create a security interest in it as collateral for a loan. Mortgages are discussed in Chapter 5.

Note that this account of the extensive rights associated with the fee simple is somewhat in tension with the suggestion above that the doctrine of tenure can promote ideas of stewardship, thus potentially limiting the rights of the fee simple holder in the interests of future generations. This tension has deep historical roots, and reflects the larger debate noted elsewhere in this book about whether property can ever be truly "private."

The expansive rights recognized as part of the fee simple led to its being equated with freedom and virtue in early America. Thus the Jeffersonian period in the early 19th-century United States is associated with the concept of the "fee simple empire." This phrase was coined by historians to capture the idea, associated with Thomas Jefferson, that the key to a vigorous and prosperous democracy was the virtuous yeoman farmer who owned his small holding in fee simple, which was equated with economic and political independence: see Henry Nash Smith, *The American West as Symbol and Myth* (Cambridge, MA: Harvard University Press, 1970) at 133. This state of affairs was in contrast to the situation Jefferson imagined in Europe, where aristocrats tied up enormous tracts of land in family entails for generations, and exercised disproportionate power as a result. Land is no longer the most prized asset in the global economy, but these ideas about the virtue inherent in the fee simple (particularly the owner-occupied fee simple) also circulated in Canada, motivated the debates on the "land question" in Prince Edward Island, as noted above, and continue to resonate in current political and legal discourse.

A countercurrent to this equation of the fee simple with freedom has emerged more recently, as Gray & Gray observed above (see their extract in section II.D). The emergence of a movement responding to the environmental degradation caused by industrialization has led to a renewed emphasis on the conservation and stewardship of land. In this context, the holder of a fee simple might be seen as subject to a responsibility to conserve the land for future generations, rather than exploiting it solely for short-term gain in his own lifetime. Instead of independence, this view stresses the interconnection of all landholders in space and time—a view that is particularly evident in Aboriginal ideas about land—and one that mirrors the ecological network underpinning all life on earth. At present, these views represent ideals more than current law, but legislation on conservation "easements," discussed in Chapter 7, provides some support for the emergence of concepts of stewardship in land law.

c. Freehold Estates and the Law of Succession

One of the most important rights attached to estates of inheritance is the right to transmit them by will; if the holder has no will, they will descend according to intestate succession. Transmission of property upon death is arguably a topic with a professional and educational profile inversely proportional to its social and economic importance. As US legal historian Lawrence Friedman observes,

> The law of succession is to the social structure in some ways what the genetic code is to the biological system. It perpetuates the social structure over time. It guarantees the persistence of the very shape of the social order: it helps define rich and poor, upper and lower class. If a society wiped out inheritance, or revamped its laws totally, it is a fair bet that the social structure itself would weaken and transform within two or three generations.

(L Friedman, Review of Carole Shammas, Marylynn Salmon & Michel Dahlin, *Inheritance in America: From Colonial Times to the Present* (New Brunswick, NJ: Rutgers University Press, 1987) [Shammas, Salmon & Dahlin] in (1988) 6 LHR 499 at 499.)

Upon the death of a fee simple holder, the individual will die either testate (with a will) or intestate (without a will). At common law, land descended upon intestacy to the "heir" according to one set of rules (primogeniture), while all other property descended to the surviving spouse and children or next of kin; the rules relating to personal property were formalized in the *Statute of Distribution*, 22 & 23 Car 2, c 10 (1670). Primogeniture was abolished in favour of partible inheritance early on in Nova Scotia, New Brunswick, and Prince Edward Island (in 1758, 1786, and 1787, respectively), a testament to the influence of the New England colonies in the Maritime provinces. For many decades, however, these provinces provided that, following the Massachusetts example and what was thought to be the Mosaic law, the eldest son was entitled to a double share: see Philip Girard, "The Maritime Provinces, 1850-1939: Lawyers and Legal Institutions" (1995) 23 Man LJ 379 at 381. Primogeniture had no impact in the Western provinces and was abolished, if it ever existed, in Newfoundland by the *Chattels Real Act, 1834*, 4 & 5 Will 4, c 18 (now RSNL 1990, c C-11).

In Ontario, more marked by its English inheritance, the abolition of primogeniture was more controversial and did not occur until 1851: see the *Act to Abolish the Right of Primogeniture in the Succession to Real Estate*, 14 & 15 Vict, c 6, which came into effect 1 January 1852. In fact, there were 18 bills to abolish primogeniture introduced after 1820, before that of 1851 finally succeeded: see AR Buck, "'This Remnant of Feudalism': Primogeniture and Political Culture in Colonial New South Wales, with Some Canadian Comparisons" in *Despotic Dominion* at 178-83. The 1851 Act had the effect of making personal and real property descend according to the same rules, and in 1886 Ontario took the next logical step: by the *Devolution of Estates Act, 1886*, SO 1886, c 22, all property of a deceased person, whether real or personal, was to be treated as a fund and vested in the personal representative of the deceased (that is, the executor where a will exists, or the administrator where one does not) for payment of the deceased's debts and distribution among those entitled according to law. These legal changes reflect a view of property appropriate to a capitalist, market-oriented society, where the form of property—whether land, chattels, or intellectual property—is less important than its exchange value.

Modern rules for intestate succession are contained in the *Succession Law Reform Act* [SLRA], RSO 1990, c S.26 and similar statutes in other provinces. It is useful to have some idea of the rules of intestate succession for a variety of professional purposes, because their slow transformation over time illustrates important changes in family relations and gender ideology, the nature of wealth, and the role of the state. After the abolition of primogeniture, the most important change over time has been the enhanced position of the spouse compared with that of the children and other relatives, reflecting the rise of "companionate marriage" and improvements in the social and legal status of women (Shammas, Salmon & Dahlin). The other important change has been the equalization of the status of children: adopted children and the children of unmarried parents are now recognized in the SLRA and other statutes as having the same rights as the natural-born children of married parents: see *Children's Law Reform Act*, RSO 1990, c C.12, ss 1-2.

The improvement in the status of married women began with the institution of the "preferential share" for a (childless) widow on the intestacy of a husband in Ontario in 1895, a legal innovation that gradually spread to other provinces: see *An Act making better Provisions for Widows of Intestates in Certain Cases*, 58 Vict c 21 (extended to widowers by the *Devolution of Estates Act*, SO 1960-61, c 22, s 2). The idea of the preferential share is that the widow(er) is entitled to take a certain sum "off the top" of the intestate's net estate. In Ontario this is currently set at $200,000: if the intestate's estate is less than this sum, the surviving spouse takes it all and no other heir takes anything. If there is a surplus above $200,000, the surviving spouse will take it all if there are no surviving issue of the marriage. If the intestate is survived by a spouse and a child or children, the spouse will share the surplus with them. This "distributive share" will be shared equally if there is a surviving spouse and only one child; if more than one child, the spouse takes one-third and the children share two-thirds. Where there is neither a surviving spouse nor children, other relatives will take according to specific statutory directions: SLRA, ss 46-47. The only way that this strict and mechanical scheme of distribution can be varied is pursuant to Part V of the SLRA, which provides for the support of "dependants":

> 58(1) Where a deceased, whether testate or intestate, has not made adequate provision for the proper support of his dependants or any of them, the court, on application, may order that such provision as it considers adequate be made out of the estate of the deceased for the proper support of the dependants or any of them.

Thus, in cases of intestacy, any fee simple (or other property) owned by the intestate at death may be subject to an order made under Part V, which may override in whole or in part the rights of those who would otherwise be entitled under the Act. All provinces provide for such applications to be made in cases of testate succession, but not all provide for them in the case of intestate succession: see e.g. *Testators' Family Maintenance Act*, RSNS 1989, c 465.

DISCUSSION NOTES

i. Primogeniture and Succession to the Crown

Until very recently, the British (and Canadian) Crown descended according to the rules of primogeniture. The one (obvious) exception is that the Crown cannot be held in co-parcenary, so that if there are no sons in a particular generation, an elder daughter will succeed ahead of a younger daughter (as did Queen Elizabeth II). In anticipation of the birth of an heir to Prince William and the Duchess of Cambridge in the summer of 2013, Parliament passed the *Succession to the Throne Act, 2013*, SC 2013, c 6; it incorporated by reference the following provision of the British *Succession to the Crown Act 2013* (2013, c 20):

In determining the succession to the Crown, the gender of a person born after 28 October 2011 does not give that person, or that person's descendants, precedence over any other person (whenever born).

In other words, had Prince George been a girl, she would not have been demoted in the line of succession had a brother been born later, as Princess Anne was on the birth of her younger brothers.

ii. Intestate Succession and the Definition of "Spouse"

The definition of "spouse" has been subject to review in the context of intestate succession in recent years. The SLRA currently defines a "spouse" in s 1(1) as including only formally married spouses. Thus, cohabitees in a conjugal relationship are not "heirs" of each other and do not inherit each other's property on intestacy. Under Part V of the Act (dealing with the support of dependants), however, there is a more expansive definition of "spouse": it includes either of two persons who are not married to each other and have cohabited continuously for a period of not less than three years, or are in a relationship of some permanence, if they are the natural or adoptive parents of a child. Thus, if the surviving cohabitee in a conjugal relationship was financially "dependant" on the deceased cohabitee, he or she is eligible to make a claim under Part V; otherwise, the surviving cohabitee has no rights under intestate succession to any of the deceased cohabitee's property.

d. Creation of the Fee Simple

As noted above, the common law recognized only one formula for the creation of a fee simple: "to A and his (or her) heirs." The words "to A" are considered "words of purchase," indicating *who* is receiving an interest under the grant. ("Purchase" has a technical meaning here, and it does not matter if this grant is gratuitous or for value.) The words "to his heirs" are "words of limitation": they indicate *what estate* A is taking. At first glance, "to A and his heirs" looks like a kind of joint gift, made to both A and his children. But that is not the case. The "heirs" take no interest in this disposition, and A can freely alienate the property without the consent or even knowledge of his "heirs." (In any case, no living person can have "heirs": the heirs of A will be known only on A's death.)

At common law, the effect of any phrase other than "to A and his heirs" in a conveyance, even one as seemingly obvious in intent as "to A in fee simple," was to create a life estate only. Thus, the presumption in any grant creating a freehold interest was for a life estate only. This principle reflected the idea that land was such a valuable commodity, and so crucial to the maintenance of family honour, that one would not normally want to convey it away. The presumption was to the effect that a grantor would want to convey away the smallest freehold estate possible, a life estate, rather than the complete fee simple.

In North America, with its active land market, such presumptions were much less apt. As a result, legislation reversed the presumption for both grants and wills. Almost all provinces have legislation similar to the following provisions.

Conveyancing and Law of Property Act
RSO 1990, c C.34

5(1) In a conveyance, it is not necessary, in the limitation of an estate in fee simple, to use the word "heirs."

(2) For the purpose of such limitation, it is sufficient in a conveyance to use the words "in fee simple" or any other words sufficiently indicating the limitation intended.

(3) Where no words of limitation are used, the conveyance passes all the estate, right, title, interest, claim and demand that the conveying parties have in, to or on the property conveyed, or expressed or intended so to be, or that they have power to convey in, to, or on the same.

(4) Subsection (3) applies only if and as far as a contrary intention does not appear from the conveyance, and has effect subject to the terms of the conveyance and to the provisions therein contained.

(5) This section applies only to conveyances made after the 1st day of July, 1886.

Succession Law Reform Act
RSO 1990, c S.26

26. Except where a contrary intention appears by the will, where real property is devised to a person without words of limitation, the devise passes the fee simple or the whole of any other estate or interest that the testator had power to dispose of by will in the real property.

Note that "conveyance" ordinarily refers to an *inter vivos* transfer, and thus does not include a will.

The New Brunswick *Property Act*, RSNB 1973, c P-19 adopts the first two subsections of s 5 of the *Conveyancing and Law of Property Act* (CLPA), but not the rest. Thus, if neither "and his heirs" nor "in fee simple" is used, the common law presumption of a life estate is still intact and will prevail unless the grantor can be shown affirmatively to have intended to pass the fee simple: *Thomas v Murphy* (1990), 107 NBR (2d) 165 (QB). What is the effect of using "and his heirs" in a province where it is not legally necessary? See *Re Ottewell* (1969), 7 DLR (3d) 358 (Alta SC (AD)), aff'd *Tottrup v Patterson et al*, [1970] SCR 318.

5. The Life Estate

a. The Nature of the Life Estate

While the fee simple is of potentially indefinite duration, the life estate is much more circumscribed, lasting only the length of one human life. Although the holder is often referred to as a "life tenant," the word "tenant" here does not indicate a leasehold interest. A life estate is necessarily a limited interest, in that the grantor must either have retained a reversion in fee simple or have granted that reversion to a third party. In the latter case, the interest is known as a remainder and the holder a remainderperson. Consider the following dispositions.

O grants to A for life.

A has a life estate. O retains a reversion in fee simple.

O grants to A for life, remainder to B in fee simple.

A has a life estate. B has a remainder in fee simple. O retains nothing.

(Note in this last example that even if B dies intestate and without heirs, the land does not revert to O—it will escheat to the Crown.)

A life estate is essentially an *income* interest, while a remainder or reversion is a *capital* interest. Consider, for example, a piece of land on which there is a small apartment building, the net rents of which amount to $50,000 per year. Assume further that the owner in fee simple has died, leaving the property "to A for life, remainder to B in fee simple." The life tenant (A) is entitled to possess the building, manage it, and keep the net rents each year for as long as she lives. The life tenant will be responsible for municipal taxes and for current, ongoing expenses relating to the property. B is entitled to none of the income while A is alive, but his remainder interest comprises the capital value of the property. He can sell or mortgage it even prior to A's death, subject of course to A's life estate. In what circumstances would B's remainder interest be attractive to a purchaser or a person lending money for a mortgage?

To the extent that the property in question produces income, a life estate can be seen as a revenue stream. For this reason it has historically been used to maintain dependants, such as widows, minor children, or persons incapable of supporting themselves. (Life estates are often created in conjunction with a trust, discussed below, pursuant to which the power to manage and control the property can be vested in a "trustee," who in turn will pay the net revenues to the holder of the "beneficial," or "equitable" life estate.) But life estates can also be created in property that is to be enjoyed in kind, such as a family home. In the era when the main family income was often earned by the husband, it was common for him to make a will leaving the family home to his widow for life, remainder to the children, with other income provided to the widow to enable her to pay the current expenses of the home during her lifetime. Even in the context of recent changes in income-earning roles for women, spouses may often make wills in which they leave a life estate in the family home to the surviving spouse, with the remainder interest for their children in fee simple.

b. Rights Conferred by the Life Estate

In Roman terms, the holder of a life estate has the *usus* and *fructus*—the right to possess the land and enjoy its current income—but not the full right of *abusus*. If the life tenant were allowed to physically alter the land in a significant way, the interests of B (and sometimes O) could be seriously compromised. The regulation of possible conflicts between a life tenant and a remainderperson is governed in the common law by the law of waste, which is "designed to protect those whose interests follow the life tenant, and specifically the reversioner or holder of the remainder, from acts of the life tenant which tend to injure or despoil the land": see Anne Warner La Forest, *Anger & Honsberger Law of Real Property*, loose-leaf, 3d ed (Aurora, ON: Canada Law Book, 2006) [La Forest] at 6-14. The life tenant cannot undertake acts that will damage the capital value of the land, such as pulling down buildings or engaging in acts that alter the land physically in significant ways. Waste is a tort which affords the reversioner or remainderperson the remedy of injunction if such acts are threatened. The law of waste also governs, albeit in a negative sense, the way in which expenses related to the maintenance of the property are shared between life tenant and remainderperson.

The common law distinguishes three types of waste—voluntary, permissive, and ameliorating. Voluntary waste is the prohibited kind—acts that damage the capital value of the property in a non-trivial way. Permissive waste occurs where the life tenant fails to maintain the property in a passive way—by not repairing the roof even though it is leaking, or by allowing a valuable orchard to deteriorate through lack of care. Replacing the roof is seen as protecting the remainderperson's capital interest in the property, and thus properly their responsibility. A life tenant is not liable for permissive waste unless the instrument creating the estate imposes such an obligation. Thus, the distinction between voluntary and permissive waste largely tracks the distinction between misfeasance and nonfeasance in tort law—the former normally leads to liability, while the latter does not. Ameliorating waste is that which alters the property for the better; although it is technically waste, it is unlikely that a remainderperson would be able to show sufficient harm to justify the issuance of an injunction or an award of damages: see La Forest at 6-14 to 6-18.

A fourth type of waste should also be mentioned here—equitable waste. A grantor was permitted to create a life estate that was "unimpeachable for waste," thus depriving the remainderperson of the normal protection of the law of waste. The Court of Chancery, however, which administered the principles of equity, would not permit such a clause to be used as a shield to permit acts of "wanton, malicious or unconscientious destruction." Such extreme acts of despoliation are thus referred to as "equitable waste": La Forest at 6-18. (The emergence of the Court of Chancery and its equitable jurisdiction are discussed below.)

Although the life tenant is not liable for permissive waste, she is responsible for expenses of a current and ongoing nature relating to her own occupation—for example, municipal taxes, the payment of mortgage interest, utilities, and snow removal. Expenses of a capital nature, such as the installation of a new furnace or a new roof, are the responsibility of the remainderperson: Bruce Ziff, *Principles of Property Law*, 5th ed (Scarborough, ON: Carswell, 2010) [Ziff] at 182.

Waste, a common law tort, is seldom required today because successive interests in land are normally held in trust, a concept discussed below. The trust instrument ordinarily provides the trustee with the necessary powers to ensure that the property is maintained for the benefit of all parties with interests in it and the authority to allocate responsibility for the expenses as between the life tenant and the remainderperson in whatever way the trust creator intended. The rules about waste and sharing expenses are thus "default rules" that can be displaced by the individual creating the interests, whether a grantor or testator, and whether the interests are created at common law or pursuant to a trust.

The life tenant can alienate the estate by sale or gift, though it cannot ordinarily be passed on by will because the estate terminates on death (see below, however, as to the life estate *pur autre vie*). She can also lease the property, although the lease will expire by operation of law on the death of the life tenant. A life tenant can even mortgage the interest, although the lender would be wise to insure the life of the life tenant to guard against premature death.

DISCUSSION NOTES

i. Sharing Expenses Between Life Tenant and Remainderperson: Estate of Peter P Ryan v Elizabeth Boulos-Ryan

In *Estate of Peter P Ryan v Elizabeth Boulos-Ryan*, 2007 NLTD 40, the deceased had entered into a marriage contract in which it was specified that his wife Elizabeth Boulos-Ryan would have the right "to use and occupy ... 104 Newtown Road ... during her lifetime, without charge." He further specified in his will that his trustees were to pay for any "major expenses" of the house required during the period of Elizabeth's occupancy. The marriage was a second marriage for each, and each spouse had children from prior marriages and substantial independent assets. After Mr Ryan's death, his widow argued that "without charge" meant that the trustees should cover all expenses relating to the house, including, for example, snow removal, lawn care, and utilities. The trial judge determined that "without charge" did not mean that Ms Boulos-Ryan was entitled to remain in the house without covering any expenses whatsoever. It meant, rather, that she was not to be charged any rent. The "default rules" for sharing expenses between life tenant and remainderperson would thus apply; she would be responsible for all periodic and current expenses in connection with the property, while Mr Ryan's estate would be responsible for any expenses of a capital nature. How would you have avoided this litigation if you had been acting for Mr Ryan? Do you think the result accurately captured his intention?

ii. Waste: Applying the Principles—MacDonald Estate (Re)

The principles of waste can be used as a shield by the life tenant rather than a sword by the remainderperson in an appropriate setting. In *MacDonald Estate (Re)* (2008), 268 NSR (2d) 193 (Prob Ct), 2008 NSSC 253 (CanLII) the testator had left his widow, GM, a life estate in the family home, with remainder to his stepson. The widow vacated the property and let it fall into disrepair, claiming poverty. The stepson, as executor, argued that these acts had terminated her life interest, and sought an order permitting him to sell the home. The court determined that GM had no duty to repair the property or to live in it personally; her actions constituted mere permissive waste, and did not disentitle her to her interest.

iii. Settled Estates

These problems with the unpredictability of the duration of life estates were dealt with in England by settled estates legislation, beginning in 1856. A "settlement" is a disposition creating successive interests in land, which may be as simple as "to A for life, remainder to B in fee simple," or may be much more complex. A large proportion of land in England being held in settlements, the legislation aimed to permit the leasing, sale, or mortgaging of land so as to bind the fee simple, even if carried out by a person, such as a life tenant, with a limited interest. Thus, the English *Settled Land Act, 1882*, 45 & 46 Vict, c 38, "accorded the holder of a life estate wide powers to lease, mortgage and sell. The monies received had to be held under a trust for the benefit of the life tenant as well as for those entitled to the remainder": Ziff at 185.

Canadian legislation is much more restrained. The Ontario *Settled Estates Act*, RSO 1990, c S.7, for example, gives few unilateral powers to the life tenant, except for a power to lease for 21 years (s 32). Such a lease will thus bind the remainderperson even if the life tenant dies before the 21 years have expired. Powers to grant longer leases, to sell, or to mortgage are subject to court approval, and all interested parties must consent unless the court dispenses with the need for such consent. This cumbersome regime has been virtually unused in Canada, probably because most settlements are created in trust documents where the trustee is given the necessary powers to sell, lease, and mortgage so as to bind all parties to the settlement and to give good title to third parties. For general commentary on the issue, and an argument that the Manitoba Court of Appeal incorrectly overlooked the presence of the *English Settled Estates Act, 1856* as forming part of Manitoba law via reception, see John Irvine, "Unsettled Estates: Manitoba's Forgotten Statute and the Chupryk Case" (2011) 35 Man LJ 49, commenting on *Chupryk v Haykowski* (1980), 110 DLR (3d) 108 (Man CA).

iv. Life Estates Pur Autre Vie

Although life estates can be alienated, doing so creates a variant of the life estate called the life estate *pur autre vie* (for the life of another). Thus, if A, the holder of a life estate, grants it to B, B takes an estate that is limited by the length of A's life. If A predeceases B, B's estate ends at that time. If A survives B, however, what happens to the property between B's death and A's? A cannot resume the property because she has already alienated all her rights. Modern law assumes that the right to the life estate during this period can be passed on by will or is included in the assets of a person dying intestate, even though Prince Edward Island is the only province to refer explicitly to "estates for the life of another" as being property capable of being willed: *Probate Act*, RSPEI 1988, c P-21, s 58; Bora Laskin, *Cases and Notes on Land Law* (Toronto: University of Toronto Press, 1964) at 68.

c. Creation of the Life Estate

As noted above, legislation specifying that the "default" presumption in creating estates in land is that of a fee simple in effect means that at present one must use some words of limitation in order to create a life estate. In most cases, "to A for his life" or "to B for her natural life" will suffice, but in more lengthy dispositions ambiguity can arise as to what the grantor or testator intended. In such cases, the court is the final arbiter of intent, which is determined against the backdrop of the statutory presumption. The following cases give some examples of the possibilities—and pitfalls—that can arise when testators try to create successive interests in the same property.

Re Walker

(1925), 56 OLR 517 (CA)

MIDDLETON JA (Latchford CJ and Orde JA concurring):

An appeal from the judgment of Mr. Justice Riddell pronounced on the 27th September, 1924, declaring that the estate of the late Ellen Fitze Walker does not include any part of the estate of the late John Walker undisposed of by her at the time of her death.

. . .

[23] John Walker died on the 27th March, 1903, and first made his will, bearing date the 17th November, 1902, which was in due course admitted to probate, his widow being his sole executrix. At the time of his death his estate amounted to approximately $16,000. By his will he provided as follows:

> I give and devise unto my said wife all my real and personal property saving and excepting thereout as follows namely my gold watch and chain I give to my nephew John Noble Walker son of my brother William Walker and all other jewellery I may have at the time of my decease I give to my nephews William Craig Walker and Percy Dugald Walker brothers of the said John Noble Walker share and share alike and also should any portion of my estate still remain in the hands of my said wife at the time of her decease undisposed of by her such remainder shall be divided as follows … .

[24] The widow survived until 1922. Her will has been duly admitted to probate. Her estate, including all that remained of her husband's estate, was valued at $38,000.

[25] Those claiming under the husband's will seek to have some portion of this estate earmarked as being an "undisposed of" portion of the husband's estate. Those claiming under the wife's will contend that under the provision of the husband's will the widow took absolutely. Mr. Justice Riddell decided in favour of those claiming under the husband's will. From this decision an appeal is now had.

[26] From the earliest times the attempt has been made to accomplish the impossible, to give and yet to withhold, to confer an absolute estate upon the donee, and yet in certain events to resume ownership and to control the destiny of the thing given: By conveyance this is impossible. Where there is absolute ownership, that ownership confers upon the owner the rights of an owner and restrains an alienation; and similar attempts to mould and control the law are void: *In re Rosher* (1884), 26 Ch. D. 801.

• • •

[30] When a testator gives property to one, intending him to have all the rights incident to ownership, and adds to this a gift over of that which remains in specie at his death or at the death of that person, he is endeavouring to do that which is impossible. His intention is plain but it cannot be given effect to. The Court has then to endeavour to give such effect to the wishes of the testator as is legally possible, by ascertaining which part of the testamentary intention predominates and by giving effect to it, rejecting the subordinate intention as being repugnant to the dominant intention.

[31] So the cases fall into two classes: the first, in which the gift to the person first named prevails and the gift over fails as repugnant; the second, in which the first named takes a life-estate only, and so the gift over prevails. Subject to an apparent exception to be mentioned, there is no middle course, and in each case the inquiry resolves itself into an endeavour to apply this rule to the words of the will in question. The sheep are separated from the goats; and, while in most instances there is not much doubt, in some instances the classification is by no means easy.

• • •

[38] Turning now to the will before the Court. I agree with the judgment in review that the words "undisposed of" do not refer to a testamentary disposition by the widow but refer to a disposal by her during her lifetime. I am, however, unable to agree with the construction placed upon the will otherwise. It appears to be plain that there is here an attempt to deal with that which remains undisposed of by the widow, in a manner repugnant to the gift to her. I think the gift to her must prevail and the attempted gift over must be declared to be repugnant and void.

[39] I would therefore allow the appeal and declare the construction of the will accordingly. Costs may well come out of the wife's estate.

• • •

MAGEE JA (concurring):

[41] My brother Riddell construed the will as giving to the wife all the testator's property except the watch and chain and jewellery and also except what property would not be disposed of by her, and the wording would lend itself to that interpretation—and it would have the merit of meeting the obvious wishes of the testator which he could readily

have effected by different wording. It would be desirable that his intention should be carried out. But to treat the property given over as excepted from the gift to the wife would allow her only an implied power of disposition and give her no life-interest, which obviously also it was intended she should have. The gift of realty to her would not necessarily carry the fee simple.

[42] On the whole I agree in the conclusion that there was an absolute gift to the wife and that what was undisposed of by her, if it can be said that there was any, was her property and not affected by the gift over.

Appeal allowed.

Re Taylor
(1982), 12 ETR 177 (Sask Surr Ct)

SCHEIBEL SURR CT J:

Facts

[1] This is an application by notice of motion on behalf of the executors of the estate of Kathleen Augusta Edith Taylor to determine the meaning, intent and effect of the following portion of the Last Will and Testament of John Hillyard Taylor namely:

> I Give, Devise and Bequeath all my real and personal estate of which I may die possessed to my wife Kathleen Augusta Edith Taylor, to have and use during her lifetime.
>
> Any Estate, of which she may be possessed at the time of her death is to be divided equally between my daughters namely ... .

[2] John Hillyard Taylor died on February 26, 1965 leaving his wife Kathleen Augusta Edith Taylor surviving. His will was probated on April 13, 1965. Mrs. Taylor used portions of his estate until her death.

[3] The testatrix Kathleen Augusta Edith Taylor died on December 27, 1981. In her will there is a general direction to her executors to convert the assets comprised in her estate into money and to establish two equal funds one of which is to go to charity with the remaining one half to go to 5 individuals.

Issue

[4] The question raised in this case is whether the testatrix takes an absolute interest under the will of John Hillyard Taylor or only a life interest. If she takes an absolute interest, then any property which she acquired by devise or bequest under the will of John Hillyard Taylor forms part of her estate for distribution according to the terms of her will. If she takes only a life interest, then any part of the estate of John Hillyard Taylor remaining in her hands at her death passes to the daughters upon a gift over under the will of John Hillyard Taylor. The executors of the testatrix seek to have these questions determined as affecting the administration of her estate.

Decision

[5] In my view, the meaning to be given to these clauses is clear. The language used evinces an intention on the part of the testator to give to his wife a life interest coupled with a power to encroach on capital for her own proper maintenance.

[6] Counsel for the executors argues that this construction should be rejected. He states that on a true construction of these clauses the words operate as a devise of the whole estate of the testator to his wife absolutely. Any attempt to cut down this absolute gift fails ex hypothesi for repugnancy. Counsel argues that an absolute gift must be presumed or inferred from that clause in the will of the testator by which a power to encroach on capital is given to the wife.

[7] It is argued that a right to encroach on capital which is not subject to any limitation and which may result in a depletion of the entire corpus of the estate amounts to an absolute interest. In such a case, the donee can by her own free act defeat the gift over so that the effect produced by the gift is the same as if it had been an absolute gift. In both cases the donee has the benefit of the entire estate. If the donee can have the whole estate, then the law presumes him to have what he can accomplish by his own free act. Several authorities are cited by counsel for the executors supporting this conclusion.

[8] I have no hesitation in reaching the conclusion that the line of reasoning advanced by counsel for the executors should be rejected. The initial premise on which the argument rests cannot be supported. It assumes that because the same result can be achieved by a gift of an absolute interest and by a gift of a life interest with a power to encroach on capital, the two interests are identical.

[9] The judgment of Thomson J. in *In Re Rankin Estate* (1951), 2 W.W.R. 562 is relied on as supporting this conclusion. In that case the testator gave the residue of his estate to his sister "to be used by her and at her death if any of the money is left ..." to X. Thomson, J. held that the sister took an absolute interest. The words used by the testator were found to be inadequate to create a life interest. There was no sufficient reference to the life of the donee as being a limitation on the enjoyment of the estate by the donee. This construction was confirmed for Thomson, J. by the fact that the donee was to have a right to encroach on capital with the possibility that there would be nothing left on which the gift over could take effect. At p. 563 of his judgment he states:

> It will be noted that the testator did not say that his sister was to have the use of the property for her life only. ... The use of the expression "if any of the money is left" makes it clear that the testator anticipated the possibility that none of the property would be left at the time of his sister's death. Obviously he intended that she should have an unfettered right to use up or wholly exhaust as she might see fit the capital or corpus of the property as well as the income therefrom. Ordinarily this would constitute an absolute or unconditional gift of the property ... .

[10] In my view, this case is not authority for the proposition that a life interest becomes an absolute interest when it is accompanied by a power to encroach on capital which may result in the depletion of the entire corpus of the estate. No intention to create a life interest was found in the words used by the testator in the *Rankin* case. Once that construction was placed on the words used by the testator the only conclusion left was that he intended the donee to take an absolute interest.

[11] No such difficulty arises here. The form of words used by the testator in this case evince a clear intention to give to the donee a life interest. The words "during her lifetime" operate as words of limitation. They define the size of the estate which the donee is to take. In their grammatical sense, they qualify the words "to have and to use." It is difficult to see how more apt words could be used to create a life interest.

[12] A reference to the life of the donee as a limitation of the enjoyment of the subject-matter of the gift necessarily suggests that the testator intended to create a life interest. In *Jarman on Wills*, 8th ed., vol. 2 at p. 1181 the form of words "for life" or similar words are said to have the effect of creating a life interest. The words "during her lifetime" must surely have the same effect. This is not because the law attributes any preconceived meaning to a particular form of words. Since this approach to the construction of wills was rejected by the House of Lords in *Perrin v. Morgan*, [1943] A.C. 399. It involves no more than giving effect to the plain and ordinary meaning of the words used by the testator.

• • •

[40] Counsel for the executors also relies on the case of *Re Walker* ... [(1925), 56 OLR 517 (CA)]. In that case the testator gave all his property to his wife excepting only certain items of personalty which were made the subject of specific bequests. This was followed by a gift over "should any portion of my estate still remain in the hands of my said wife at the time of her death undisposed of by her ... ." It was held that the wife took an absolute interest. Middleton J.A. took the view that the initial words of gift operated to pass the entire interest of the testator to his wife and that, therefore, the gift over should be rejected as repugnant. The testator was found to have had an intention to give an absolute interest and at the same time an intention to give a limited interest. This was said to give rise to a problem of repugnancy which could only be resolved by giving effect to what appeared to be the dominant intention of the testator.

[41] No such difficulty arises here. There is no logical inconsistency requiring the Court to choose between two alternative intentions which are opposed. The testator has used clear words to indicate an intention to give only a limited interest, and the gift over, far from being repugnant, completes the intention of the testator to dispose of all his property in the event that any should be left when the prior life interest comes to an end at the death of the donee.

[42] *Re Walker* has no application to a case such as this.

• • •

[65] Where the testator uses plain language to indicate an intention to give a life interest only, that interest is not enlarged to an absolute interest because the testator has declared that the donee is to have the right in her discretion to encroach on capital for her own proper maintenance. There is nothing in such a provision which can have the effect of displacing the clear intention of the testator.

[66] It should be noted that counsel for the executors also relies on the provisions of section 24 of The *Wills Act*, R.S.S. 1978, ch. W-14 [to the same effect as s 26 of the *Succession Law Reform Act*, above]. With respect, I fail to see how these provisions have any application to this case. The effect of the section is to pass to the donee the entire interest of the testator in any real property only where no words of limitation are used by the testator and where it does not otherwise appear from the will taken as a whole that the donee is to have only a limited interest. In this case, the testator has indicated an intention to give to his wife, Kathleen Taylor, only a life estate. The provisions of section 24 cannot have the effect of giving to her a larger estate than the testator declared she should have.

[67] I have no doubt as to the intention of the testator. The testatrix, Kathleen Taylor, was to take a life interest with a power to encroach on capital for her own proper maintenance. The daughters of the testator, John Hillyard Taylor, were to take that part of the estate of the testator remaining in the hands of Kathleen Taylor at her death. As a result the life estate of Kathleen Taylor was determined upon her death. Any property acquired by her under the will of John Hillyard Taylor remaining in her hands at the time of her death, passed to the daughters upon the gift over under the will of John Hillyard Taylor. Should the question arise whether any item of property forms part of the estate of John Hillyard Taylor for distribution to the daughters, or part of the estate of Kathleen Taylor for distribution according to the terms of her will, that question may be brought forward for determination by this Court.

[68] The applicant will have the costs of the application, payable out of the John Hillyard Estate on a solicitor–client basis after taxation.

DISCUSSION NOTES

i. Creating Life Estates: The Importance of Discerning Intention

Are you persuaded by Judge Scheibel's conclusion that *Re Walker* "has no application to a case like this"? Do you think that the testators in *Re Walker* and *Re Taylor* had different intentions? What do these cases suggest about the role of the lawyer when trying to discern the intention of testators in order to draft their wills?

ii. Life Estate Versus Licence

Another issue that can arise in the context of creating life estates is the distinction between a life estate and a licence. The concept of licence is discussed in Chapter 4; it is not an interest in land. However, it may sometimes be difficult to determine whether a testator intended to create a licence or a life estate. In *Re Waters* (1978), 21 OR (2d) 124 (H Ct J), the testator left a will containing the following clause:

> I give the use of 48 Walker Avenue, in the City of Toronto, to Mrs. Ellen Jones for as long as she lives, or until she re-marries, or gives to my executors and trustees a written notice that she no longer needs and desires the use of the property. Taxes, insurance, repairs and other upkeep expenses shall be paid by Mrs. Ellen Jones. Upon the death, remarriage, or notice being given by Mrs. Jones that she no longer needs or desires the property, it shall become part of the residue of my estate.

The executor of Mr Waters's will applied to court for advice and direction as to the nature of the interest of Mrs Jones. The residuary beneficiaries under the will argued that the devise created only a licence or personal permission to occupy the premises, such that Mrs Jones would not be able to rent out the property if she chose not to occupy it personally. Justice Pennell decided this issue as follows:

> I take it to be a cardinal rule of construction that the Judge must endeavour to place himself in the position of the testator at the time the will was made, and try to ascertain the intention of the testator, having regard to the language used, the context in which the language is used and the circumstances under which the will in question was made. This is the Geiger counter that must be passed over the whole of the will in order to ascertain what is the meaning of a part of it.

As regard to circumstances at the time the will was made, I notice that the testator states that the will was "made in contemplation of my marriage to ELLEN JONES" and he then goes on to direct that the provisions of "… this my will shall be applicable whether or not a marriage shall be solemnized by me with Mrs. Ellen Jones."

As I read the will before me, there is a clear interest given to Mrs. Ellen Jones for life in the words, "I give the use of 48 Walker Avenue … for as long as she lives." If the clause had ended there it would give a life estate. Is there anything in the will sufficient to prevent these words having their ordinary meaning or effect? It is to be observed that there is no gift over except if Mrs. Ellen Jones remarries or gives to the executors written notice that she no longer needs and desires the use of the property. If the testator had wished to introduce another proviso or exception, let us say that of personal occupation, he might easily have expressed it. He has expressed carefully what the provisos are on which the benefit is to cease. In my reading of the will as a whole, I see no condition annexed to her requiring personal occupation.

I am fortified in this view by the words of para. 7. In that clause the testator gives Mrs. Jones all the furniture and other household effects which are in 48 Walker Ave. and this bequest is entirely consistent with the devise of a life estate of the real property, and I would answer Q. 1 as follows: (1) Mrs. Ellen Jones was given a life estate under para. 6 subject to be determined by the proviso set out in the said paragraph.

By contrast, in *Re Powell*, [1988] AJ no 918 (QB), a will containing a similar clause was determined to create a licence and not a life estate. The testator directed that his daughter Verna

shall have the right to the occupation, possession and use of my house … for as long as she remains in possession of the said premises … and that in the event my said daughter ceases to remain in possession of the said premises or married [*sic*] or upon her death … the said premises … shall be held … in trust for my four (4) children. Marie Mitchell, William Albert Powell, Verna Powell and James Andrew Powell.

When her father died, Verna Powell was aged 42, unmarried, and suffered from schizophrenia. She lived in the testator's house until August 1986, when she was taken to hospital with a severe stroke. She was expected to require constant care for the rest of her life. The trustees under the will applied for direction from the court on the question of whether Verna's interest had ended. Justice Virtue found that it had:

[I]t is important to characterize what type of property interest was granted to Verna Powell in her father's will. The granting words are, "… shall have the right to the occupation, possession and use of my house … for as long as she remains in possession of the said premises … ."

If … the will simply gives to [Verna] Powell a licence to occupy, possess and use the premises for a period of time, and that period of time has passed, then her rights respecting the property have ended and the property will pass to the ultimate beneficiaries as provided in the will. A helpful analysis of these principles is to be found in *Re McColgan*, (1969) 4 D.L.R. (3d) 572.

I am satisfied that the language used in the will before me does not create an estate, that is, a vested interest in land, but rather a licence to occupy the premises for a limited time. That is the conclusion reached by the Supreme Court of Canada in *Moore et al v. Royal Trust et al* (1956) S.C.R. 880, where the language used was:

to permit my son … and his wife … as long as either of them shall occupy the same to have the use and enjoyment of my property, known as …

In considering the nature of the interest created by those words. Mr. Justice Cartwright concluded that:

> The true construction of the will was not to give to George Moore, Junior, and Frances his
> wife an estate for life in the property ... determinable on their ceasing to occupy such
> property, or indeed any estate therein, but merely a license to occupy such property personally ... From the death of the testator the legal estate in the property in question was
> in the trustees ... subject to the obligation to permit George and Frances, or either of
> them, personally to occupy the property ... (p. 883)

In the case before me the testator devised his property to his trustees; subject to the right of his daughter to use possess and occupy the house until she ceased to remain in possession of it, at which time he directed that the house be divided equally amongst his four children, of which his daughter [Verna] Powell was one.

This language does not, in my view, demonstrate an intent on the part of the testator, to create a vested estate in land, but rather an intent to simply give a license to use, possess and occupy the premises for a limited time. The estate was vested in his trustees for his four children of whom Verna Powell was one. ...

In the Powell will, which I have to consider there is, over and above the grant of the license to occupy, possess and use the house, the further proviso that "in the event my said daughter ceases to remain in possession of the said premises," the property is to be divided equally among the testator's four children. This additional proviso, in my view, takes this case one step beyond the facts in *Moore*. The testator has clearly expressed the intention that upon cessation of possession the house is to go into the residuary estate. The result is that the license terminates when Verna Powell is no longer in possession. I am satisfied that in the context of this will, possession means actual possession, not constructive possession. Having found as a fact that [Verna] Powell has ceased to be in possession—in the sense not only that is she not in actual possession now but she will not ever be—I am satisfied that the period of her license has ended.

Do you find the differing results in *Re Waters* and *Re Powell* justifiable? Again, what might one learn about the lawyer's role in advising testators after comparing these decisions?

6. The Fee Tail

The fee tail was a "shortened" version of the fee simple, as explained briefly above. In a grant "to A and the heirs of his body," only a lineal descendant of A could ever inherit the property; no ancestor of A, nor any collateral relative of A, such as a cousin or aunt or uncle, could ever do so. The advantage of the fee tail in a lineage-oriented society such as early modern England was twofold:

1. It was effectively inalienable, as few grantees would want to purchase an estate that would last only as long as A had lineal descendants. The "entailing" of an estate thus meant that the property was likely to descend in the grantee's family indefinitely.

2. The fee tail could be further refined such that it could be made to descend only to males ("to A and the heirs male of his body"), a possibility that was precluded with a fee simple. (It was also possible, though uncommon, to create a fee tail female.)

Recall that under the rules of primogeniture, if a father left no sons, his daughters would share his land equally. The fee tail male ensured that daughters would never inherit, although such an estate might also end prematurely through a failure of male heirs. Some scholars have argued that one of the main functions of the land law was to facilitate the exclusion of females from land ownership: see Eileen Spring, *Law, Land and Family: Aristocratic Inheritance in England, 1300-1800* (Chapel Hill: University of North Carolina Press, 1993). It has also been argued that when women did come into property, they tended to dispose of it differently from men, especially by providing enough for their daughters or nieces to live independently: see AL Erickson, *Women and Property in Early Modern England* (London: Routledge, 1993) at 20.

In the North American context, the fee tail was never as popular as in England. In theory it may still be created in Prince Edward Island, but has been abolished elsewhere at dates ranging from 1851 in Nova Scotia to 1956 in Ontario: see *Of Estates Tail*, RSNS 1851, c 112; *Conveyancing and Law of Property Act*, RSO 1990, c C.34, s 4. However, because these repeals were not retrospective, existing fee tails were not abolished and some remain in Ontario. Moreover, the fee tail remains a topic of popular fascination, if the appeal of the television series *Downton Abbey* is any indication. In it, the fictional Lord Grantham is the tenant in tail male of the landed estate known as Downton Abbey, but has three daughters and no son. Much of the narrative, in the manner of Victorian fiction, is driven by the possible romance between his eldest daughter, Lady Mary, and her cousin Matthew, who is Lord Grantham's heir.

EXERCISE 1 CREATING FREEHOLD ESTATES

This is the first of a number of exercises in this chapter that aim to challenge the student to apply the relevant principles discussed in the preceding section. The doctrine of estates works in a relentlessly cumulative way. A failure to master the early "building blocks" will prevent the student from understanding more complex material later on. Keeping in mind the common law rules and statutory reforms discussed above, consider the following dispositions and decide what estate(s) each of them creates. Does the grantor or testator retain an interest in any of these examples? If so, what kind of interest is it? In each case, be prepared to back up your answer with the appropriate authority for your conclusion.

1. As noted above, the common law presumption of a life estate in grants was altered by legislation. In Ontario, this alteration is found in the *Conveyancing and Law of Property Act*, RSO 1990, c C.34, s 5(5), effective as of 1 July 1886. Analyze the effect of the following grants before and after the effective date of the legislation. Does the grantor retain an interest in any of the following dispositions? If so, what is it?

Grant	Common Law	After 1 July 1886 (CLPA, s 5(5))
1. X grants to A and his heirs.	X has no interest	
2. X grants to A in fee simple.		
3. X grants to A forever.	fee simple	
4. X grants to A.	LE presumption	fee simple

Grant	Common Law	After 1 July 1886 (CLPA, s 5(5))
5. X grants to A for her natural life.	L E	L E
6. X grants to A for her natural life. One month later X grants to B and his heirs.		

2. Separate legislation was enacted to reverse the presumption of a life estate in wills. This modification is found in the *Succession Law Reform Act*, RSO 1990, c S.26, s 26. Analyze the effect of the following devises before and after the legislative change.

Devise	Common Law	SLRA, s 26
1. X devises to A.	Fee simple	
2. X devises to A and her heirs.	Fee simple	
3. X devises to A for life.	L E	

D. Variations on Estates

1. Absolute Estates and Conditions

So far we have been considering "absolute" estates. An absolute estate is one that has no conditions of any kind attached to it. An important feature of estates, however, is the ability to add conditions to them. Conditions allow the creator of an estate to control how an estate will be used in the future and to provide for eventualities that are unknown at the time the estate is created. Generally speaking, conditions are of two kinds.

1. Conditions of *forfeiture* are those that specify that if a certain event happens, the grantee will *lose the estate which she received*, by grant *inter vivos* or by will.

2. Conditions of *eligibility*, known as conditions precedent, are those that specify that a certain event must happen before the grantee *becomes entitled to receive* an estate.

These kinds of conditions can be added to any estate. The essential requirement of any condition is that it must refer to an event or state of affairs that may or may not ever happen. If an event is certain, it cannot be the subject of a condition.

Consider

"to A, and upon her death to B."

A's death is a certainty, and this grant would be construed as creating a life estate in A, with remainder to B. The death of A merely marks the end of her estate; it does not denote a condition of forfeiture. (Note too that this interpretation overcomes the presumption of a fee simple in favour of A that would otherwise flow from the *Conveyancing and Law of Property Act*, RSO 1990, c C.34, s 5(5). The wording used demonstrates a "contrary intention" within the meaning of s 5(4) of the Act.)

However,

"to A in fee simple if she survives B"

gives A a fee simple subject to a condition precedent. Although A's death is a certainty, whether she will survive B is not. That event can properly be the subject of a condition.

2. Conditions of Forfeiture

Conditions of *forfeiture* may be created in two ways: (1) an estate defeasible on condition subsequent, or (2) a determinable estate.

a. Estates Defeasible on Condition Subsequent

O grants Greenacre "to C in fee simple, but if she ceases to farm the land, I may re-enter."

C does not have an absolute estate. Her fee simple may be terminated prematurely if she breaches the condition. If she ceases to farm the land, the grantor has provided that he may re-enter and terminate her estate. C is said to have a fee simple defeasible on condition subsequent, and O retains an interest called a "right of re-entry." Note that the right of re-entry can be exercised at the grantor's option. Ceasing to farm the land does not *automatically* terminate C's estate. It will be terminated only if O exercises the right of re-entry, either by advising C that he regards her estate at an end or, if necessary, by commencing litigation.

b. Determinable Estates

The second way in which a condition of forfeiture may be imposed is by way of determinable limitation.

O grants Greenacre "to C in fee simple until she ceases to farm the land."

Although this disposition looks very similar to the preceding one, the law treats it differently. With a fee simple defeasible on condition subsequent, the grantee takes an "ordinary" fee simple subject to premature termination. With a determinable fee simple, the grantee takes a *modified* fee simple, and the grantor retains an interest known as a "possibility of reverter." The operation of the possibility of reverter is automatic: on the happening of the forbidden event, C's estate ends immediately and the fee simple reverts to the grantor. If C does not vacate immediately, she is considered a tenant at sufferance only, who can be evicted in a peremptory fashion. Strictly speaking, the clause "until she ceases to farm the land" is not a condition. A condition is considered external to the estate to which it is attached, while a determinable limitation is considered to define the estate itself. On this basis, it is important to use precise language to refer to either an estate "subject to condition" (or "defeasible estate") or a "determinable estate."

c. Defeasible and Determinable Estates Contrasted

These two types of interest are closely related in functional terms, but in property law they are understood as quite different interests in land. For example, different legal consequences flow from creating one or the other. In addition to the important differences between the right of re-entry and the possibility of reverter, defeasible and determinable estates differ with respect to the impact of the inclusion of an invalid condition or limitation, and with regard to the applicability of the rule against perpetuities. Both of these issues are discussed below. Understanding how to characterize a given disposition is critical; see generally Peter Devonshire, "Possibilities of Reverter and Rights of Re-entry for Conditions Broken: The Modern Context for Determinable and Conditional Interests in Land" (1990) 13 Dal LJ 650.

3. *Estates Subject to Conditions Precedent: Conditions of Eligibility*

O grants "to B in fee simple upon being called to the bar."

In this grant, becoming a lawyer is a condition precedent to B's entitlement to his estate, and B's interest is often called a "contingent" interest because B has the possibility of acquiring an estate only if he is called to the bar. If B dies before being called to the bar, there is nothing to go to B's estate. Because conditions precedent relate to future interests rather than present interests, they are discussed more fully below. However, it is important to appreciate that for purposes of interpretation, it may often be difficult in a given instrument to distinguish a condition precedent from a condition subsequent.

Thus, in *Re Down* (1968), 68 DLR (2d) 30 (Ont CA) the testator provided that when his son Harold "arrives at the age of thirty years, provided he stays on the farm," then all the testator's property was to go to Harold and his brother Stanley in equal shares. The court noted that the clause regarding staying on the farm could be interpreted as either a condition precedent or a condition subsequent. If it were construed as a condition precedent, then once Harold reached the age of 30 and was residing on the farm, he and his brother would be entitled to their father's property absolutely. If it were construed as a condition subsequent, then upon the same events occurring, Harold and his brother would be immediately entitled to their father's property; but should Harold cease to reside on the farm, he (and possibly Stanley) would stand to lose the property acquired under the will. The court decided that the clause was a condition subsequent, but that it was void for uncertainty (an issue discussed below); thus, Harold having reached the age of 30, Harold and Stanley took a fee simple absolute.

4. *Alienability*

All of these interests are now alienable: determinable and defeasible estates, contingent interests, rights of re-entry, and possibilities of reverter. The latter three were not alienable at common law, but have been made alienable by statute: *Conveyancing and Law of Property Act*, RSO 1990, c C.34, s 10.

Although these interests are alienable in theory, in practice there may be few purchasers. The rule *nemo dat quod non habet* ensures that grantees of determinable or defeasible estates can convey only the interests that they hold. Having an estate that is effectively subject to forfeiture through an event beyond the control of a purchaser is likely to render it inalienable in practice. The legislation is probably most useful in cases where a third party wishes to purchase the interests of both the holder of a fee simple defeasible on condition subsequent, for example, and the holder of the right of re-entry, in order to obtain a full fee simple absolute.

5. *Distinguishing Between Defeasible and Determinable Estates*

Re Tilbury West Public School Board and Hastie
[1966] 2 OR 20 (H Ct J)

GRANT J: This is a motion to pay out of Court to the applicant school board the sum of $1,500 paid in by the Department of Highways for the Province of Ontario when it expropriated for highway purposes certain lands used previously thereto for school purposes .... .

By deed dated May 3, 1890, one Alexander Craig Hastie conveyed to certain parties as Trustees of United School Sections No. 9 of the Township of Rochester and No. 14 of the Township of Tilbury West, a piece of land containing 85 perches and being part of the south half of Lot One in range north of the middle road in the said Township.

The form of the grant was as follows:

DOTH GRANT unto the said parties of the Third Part and their [heirs and assigns FOR EVER]: Successors as Trustees for so long as it shall be used and needed for school purposes and no longer. At the end of the description are the following words, "And the Trustees shall not build a brick building on the said site." The habendum was as follows:

TO HAVE AND TO HOLD unto the said parties of the Third Part, and their Successors [heirs and assigns to and for] as Trustees so long as used for school purposes [their sole and only use for ever], SUBJECT NEVERTHELESS, to the reservations, limitations, provisoes and conditions expressed in the original Grant thereof from the Crown.—also when the said piece or parcel of land is no longer used for school purposes it shall be returned to the owner of the said south half of lot number One North Range Middle Road Tilbury West.

There is added to the usual covenant for quiet possession the following words, "so long as used for school purposes and no longer." The release clause in the usual form has added to it, "except when no longer used or needed for school purposes." The words [printed in square brackets] in the above quotations were in the printed form but had been stroked out.

From the date of the grant until approximately September, 1961, the said lands and premises were used for teaching purposes in connection with the school which was erected upon the said lands and premises. Commencing in the fall of 1961, the school ceased to be used for teaching purposes, but use was continued to be made of the building and premises by the school board for the purpose of storing furniture and other school equipment therein.

On August 11, 1964, the Department of Highways for the Province of Ontario expropriated the whole of the said property for highway purposes, and compensation for the said lands and premises was agreed upon by all parties in the sum of $1,500 and was paid by such Department into Court pursuant to the *Expropriation Procedures Act*, 1962-63 (Ont.), c 43. ...

[Grant J then turned to the question of the nature of the interest created under Mr Hastie's will. If a defeasible fee simple with a right of re-entry was created, arguably the right of re-entry was void as contravening the rule against perpetuities. Under this interpretation the School Board would be entitled to the expropriation funds. If a determinable fee simple with a possibility of reverter was created, arguably the rule against perpetuities did not apply to the possibility of reverter and it was still valid. Using this interpretation,

Mr Hastie's sons would be entitled to the expropriation funds. The rule against perpetuities is discussed later in this chapter, but the focus here is Grant J's reasoning on how to distinguish between determinable and defeasible estates.]

It must be determined first if the grant in question was a determinable fee simple subject to a right of reverter or a fee simple subject to a condition subsequent, because the cases and authors are not in agreement as to whether the rule [against perpetuities] applies equally to both such forms of limitations. It is difficult to define the difference between a determinable fee and a fee simple defeasible by condition subsequent and often each cannot be readily put in its proper classification. The essential distinction appears to be that the determining event in a determinable fee itself sets the limit for the estate first granted. A condition subsequent, on the other hand, is an independent clause added to a complete fee simple absolute which operates so as to defeat it: Megarry and Wade [*The Law of Real Property*, 2d ed], p. 76. At p. 77 it is stated:

> Words such as "while," "during," "as long as," "until" and so on are apt for the creation of a determinable fee, whereas words which form a separate clause of defeasance, such as "provided that," "on condition that," "but if," or "if it happen that," operate as a condition subsequent.

In Cheshire [*Cheshire's Modern Law of Real Property*, 9th ed] at p. 280, the words "until," "so long as," and "whilst," are stated to be expressions creating determinable interests while phrases such as "on condition," "provided that," "if," "but if it happen," raise interests subject to condition subsequent.

Cheshire at p. 281, points out the difference in the following words:

> In short, if the terminating event is an integral and necessary part of the formula from which the size of the interest is to be ascertained, the result is the creation of a determinable interest; but if the terminating event is external to the limitation, if it is a divided clause from the grant, the interest granted is an interest upon condition.

Both authors refer to Challis's *Real Property* where examples of determinable fees are set out at p. 255 of the 3rd edition. At p. 256, examples 5 to 8 use the words "as long as," 9 uses "so long as," 10 to 18 use "till" or "until." ...

Different consequences arise if the limitation is considered a determinable fee as opposed to a condition subsequent. A determinable fee automatically determines when the specified event occurs and the land reverts to the grantor or if dead to the heirs of the grantor. A fee simple subject to a condition subsequent merely gives the grantor (or whoever is entitled to his interest if dead) a right of re-entry to determine the estate. Unless and until the entry is made a fee simple continues: Megarry and Wade, p. 77 and cases therein cited.

Thus a devise to a school in fee simple "until it ceases to publish its accounts" creates a determinable fee, whereas a devise to the school in fee simple "on condition that the accounts are published annually" creates a fee simple defeasible by condition subsequent: *Re Da Costa; Clarke v. Church of England Collegiate School of St. Peter*, [1912] 1 Ch. 337.

Goodeve and Potter's *Modern Law of Real Property* (1929) states at p. 124:

> With a fee simple determinable the estate determines *ipso facto* by the happening of the event but where there is a condition, external to the limitation, the estate is not determined until entry by the person entitled to take advantage of the condition.

It is my view that the deed in question created a fee simple determinable with a right of reverter. I am influenced to such a conclusion by reason that the words "so long as it shall be used and needed for school purposes and no longer" are used in the granting clause and they are words denoting a determinable fee. Another indication is that the limit of the estate granted is set in such granting clause itself as distinguished from a case where the fee absolute is qualified independently. It is also noted that the covenant for quiet possession is only for "so long as used for school purposes and no longer" and the regular release clause has added thereto the words "except when no longer used or needed for school purposes." The habendum is "To hold ... as Trustees so long as used for school purposes." While the latter words of such clause conclude with the words "also when the said piece or parcel of land is no longer used for school purposes it shall be returned to the owner of the said south half of Lot Number One North Range Middle Road Tilbury West" and might have some characteristics of a condition subsequent, it is a rule of construction that if there is any inconsistency in the deed the earlier direction governs. Consequently, if the words providing for a return of the lands are considered inconsistent the granting clause should control. The words in the habendum directing the return of the lands are consistent with the intention that the lands are to revert to someone as opposed to an intention that the owner of the land is to have the right of re-entry. ...

[Grant J then turned to the question of the applicability of the rule against perpetuities to possibilities of reverter. He found that it did not apply to such interests, with the result that the interest of the grantor's heirs was still valid. They were thus entitled to the money that had been paid into court.]

Judgment for respondents.

Re McColgan
[1969] 2 OR 152, 4 DLR (3d) 572 (H Ct J)

KEITH J: The Guaranty Trust Company of Canada, as the executors of the last will and testament and trustees of the estate of the late Dr. James W. McColgan, seek the advice and direction of the Court on eight questions arising out of the language used by the testator in one paragraph of his will.

The circumstances which gave rise to the present application are related in the affidavits of the respondent Mary Kovalchick and of David Ernest Morrow, a trust officer in the employ of the applicant. The respondent Mary Kovalchick states that she first became acquainted with the late Dr. McColgan as his patient in the year 1928 at which time she was 18 years of age and Dr. McColgan was the only medical practitioner in the Town of Sagamore, Pennsylvania. The respondent and the testator became, in her words, "great and good friends which relationship lasted up to the date of his death." The respondent says, however, that between the years 1928 and 1958 when Dr. McColgan retired and moved to Toronto permanently, "We were frequently in each other's company and the question of marriage was discussed between us on many occasions but because of religious differences no ceremony was ever performed." She continues in her affidavit sworn on November 22, 1968:

4. In 1958, Dr. McColgan retired from the practice of medicine and came to Canada for his retirement alone at which time he occupied his residence at 39 Arjay Crescent, Willowdale, which he had purchased in 1956 or 1957 and in which he resided up to the time of his death.

. . .

6. When the doctor retired to Ontario from Sagamore, Pennsylvania, he left me a power of attorney for the purposes of collecting his outstanding accounts and otherwise winding up his medical practice and, after the said medical practice was wound up, I visited with the late Dr. McColgan from 1959 to 1967 approximately three or four times each year at which time I would live with the doctor at 39 Arjay Crescent for several weeks at a time.

7. While I lived with the doctor in Toronto, I devoted myself completely to his comfort, well-being and needs and managed his home by supervising the housekeeper, day workers and repairmen, including the hiring and firing of such workers, attended to marketing and nursed the doctor and cooked his meals for him.

8. In 1965, the late Dr. McColgan insisted that I come to Ontario to stay with him permanently as he was alone and very sick and he had been informed that he had cancer.

9. My state of health at that time would not permit me to leave Sagamore, Pennsylvania for any protracted period in excess of two or three months and I was unable to accede to the doctor's request to come to Ontario to live with him permanently.

10. Throughout the period that I kept company with the late Dr. McColgan, he was at all times aware of my financial position and my state of health.

11. At the present time, I am suffering from a nervous condition which precludes the doing of heavy or extensive housework and my assets consist of the sum of approximately $14,000.00 cash, being the balance of insurance monies made payable to me directly upon the doctor's death and provided by the late doctor, and a pension of $380.00 per month from [the] US Government.

12. The premises at 39 Arjay Crescent consist of nine rooms and large grounds and I am unable to carry out the normal duties required to maintain housekeeping of the premises without a housekeeper.

Dr. McColgan died at Toronto on June 26, 1967. His will was executed on May 13, 1965, a year that is specially mentioned in para. 8 of the respondent's affidavit, above-quoted.

All the questions propounded to the Court related to the provisions of para. III(f) of the will which reads as follows:

III I Give, Devise and Bequeath all property of every kind and description wherever situate of which I may die possessed or over which I may have any power of appointment unto my Trustee upon the following trusts: …

(f) To hold my property at 39 Arjay Crescent, Willowdale as a home for Mary Kovalchick, of Sagamore, Pennsylvania until her death or until she is not residing therein personally, whichever shall first occur and thereafter to hold such property as a home for Carrie Leftdahl, of Plumville, Pennsylvania, until her death or until she is no longer residing therein personally, whichever shall first occur, when the said property shall fall into and form part of the residue of my estate; while such property is held for either of the aforesaid, all taxes, insurance, repairs and any other charges necessary for the general upkeep of the property shall be paid from a fund sufficient in the opinion of my Trustee to cover the same, which I direct it shall set aside upon my death and the balance of such fund shall fall into and form part of the residue of my estate as soon as the said property is no longer being held for either of the aforesaid.

Subparagraph (g) of said para. III contains the provisions with respect to the residue by way of remainder upon the termination of whatever the interests are of Mary Kovalchick and Carrie Leftdahl, as contained in subpara. (f).

I was informed by counsel that the value of Dr. McColgan's estate was approximately $231,000 of which $52,000 was accounted for by 39 Arjay Cres. There were also substantial insurance payments made out of this jurisdiction and which are not included in the above valuation. ...

Mary Kovalchick was residing with Dr. McColgan at the time of his death and had been so residing for some time prior thereto, really nursing him in his last illness. She continued to occupy 39 Arjay Cres. until about November 30, 1967, when she returned to Sagamore, Pennsylvania. On the same date she wrote to the solicitors for the applicant advising them that, due to illness, it was necessary to be under the care of a Dr. Wright in Sagamore for an indefinite period. She further said "however, I am not surrendering my rights to make my home at 39 Arjay Crescent." She returned to the said house on May 18, 1968, and has remained there ever since.

Questions have arisen between the executors and Miss Kovalchick as to the responsibility for various items of expense in connection with upkeep, heating and protection of the property and other incidental matters and as a result this application is now brought to settle these questions and to provide a comprehensive guide to the executors and others interested, for the administration of the property.

The questions propounded to the Court are as follows:

1. What estate or interest, if any, in 39 Arjay Crescent (hereinafter called the premises) passed to the said Mary Kovalchick under the provisions of the Will?

2. Has the estate or interest, in the premises, if any, which passed to the said Mary Kovalchick then terminated by reason of the facts adduced in evidence in support of this application, specifically her absence from the premises referred to in the affidavit of David Ernest Morrow?

3. Should this Honourable Court hold that the said Mary Kovalchick still has an estate or interest in the aforesaid premises, what conduct of the said Mary Kovalchick respecting the said premises would cause her estate or interest, if any, in the said premises, to become forfeited or to terminate?

[Question 4 asked whether Ms Kovalchick was entitled to rent out the premises to others and retain the rentals, and the remaining questions asked whether she or the estate was responsible for various expenses in connection with the property.]

The answer to Q. 1 will, of course, seriously affect the resolution of the remaining questions.

Question 1 itself raises four issues, as follows:

(a) is the interest of Miss Kovalchick and *a fortiori* the subsequent interest of Carrie Leftdahl upon the termination of the interest of Miss Kovalchick, a mere personal licence to use and occupy and enjoy the premises, 39 Arjay Cres.;

(b)   if the interest is more than a mere personal licence, does the language of the will create a determinable life estate or a life estate subject to a condition subsequent;

(c)   if what is intended to be created is a determinable life estate, is the language determining such life estate clear and unambiguous, or is it the converse rendering the gift void for uncertainty and,

(d)   if what is created on the other hand is a life estate subject to a condition subsequent, is the condition void for uncertainty thus leaving the life estate free of any condition.

In *Perrin v. Morgan*, [1943] AC 399, Viscount Simon LC, said at p. 406:

My Lords, the fundamental rule in construing the language of a will is to put on the words used the meaning which, having regard to the terms of the will, the testator intended. The question is not, of course, what the testator meant to do when he made his will, but what the written words he uses mean in the particular case—what are the "expressed intentions" of the testator.

And at p. 408:

I now turn to some of the reported cases, premising only that it seems to me a little unfortunate that so many of such cases should find their way into the books, for in most instances, the duty of a judge who is called on to interpret a will containing ordinary English words is not to regard previous decisions as constituting a sort of legal dictionary to be consulted and remorselessly applied whatever the testator may have intended, but to construe the particular document so as to arrive at the testator's real meaning according to its actual language and circumstances ... . In *Abbott v. Middleton* (1858), 7 HLC 68, 119, a decision of this House in which Lord Chelmsford LC, Lord Cranworth, Lord St. Leonards, and Lord Wensleydale all took occasion to expound the governing rule as to the interpretation of wills, Lord Wensleydale observed: "A great many cases were cited at the bar, as they always are, when the question is on the construction of wills. Generally speaking, these citations are of little use. We are no doubt bound by decided cases, but when the decision is not upon some rule or principle of law, but upon the meaning of words in instruments which differ so much from each other by the context, and the peculiar circumstance of each case, it seldom happens that the words of one instrument are a safe guide in the construction of another."

By way of illustration of the difficulties involved in construing the language of a testator in matters of this sort, one may well consider the case of *Moore et al. v. Royal Trust Co. et al.*, [1956] SCR 880, 5 DLR (2d) 152.

In that case one of the paragraphs of the will that was before the Court for construction was as follows [at 881 SCR, 156 DLR]:

6. I Direct my Trustees to permit my son George Moore Junior and his wife Frances as long as either of them shall occupy the same to have the use and enjoyment of my property known [words describing it] free of any duty rent or taxes and I Direct that my Trustees shall out of my Trust Fund pay the cost of maintaining any building thereon and the insurance of the same against damage by fire.

In the Court of first instance [[1954] 3 DLR 407, 13 WWR (NS) 113] it was held that these words intended to create a determinable life estate but since the language was ambiguous and uncertain as to the event that would terminate the estate, the whole gift failed for uncertainty.

In the Court of Appeal [[1955] 4 DLR 313, 16 WWR 204] (BC) it was unanimously held that these words did indeed create a determinable life interest and not a life estate subject to a condition subsequent but that there was no ambiguity or uncertainty in the words and therefore the gift was valid.

In the Supreme Court of Canada, however, it was equally unanimously held that all the Judges below were wrong and that what was created was not an estate or interest in the lands but a mere personal licence for the use, enjoyment and occupation of the property.

A similar situation arose in the Courts of New Brunswick in the case of *Re McLean*, [1940] 3 DLR 307, 14 MPR 475, where Baxter CJ held that the words of a gift in a will requiring trustees to hold property to allow the testator's daughter "to occupy and enjoy for her life, or for such shorter period as she wishes the above-named premises" gave her a mere licence to occupy the property. On appeal ([1941] 1 DLR 722, 15 MPR 338 *sub nom. Re McLean and Royal Trust Co.*) the majority of the Court held that what was conveyed to the daughter under the terms of the will was a life estate.

I have made reference to this case only to illustrate the difficulties mentioned by Viscount Simon and pointing out how essential it is to recall that the language in each will that requires consideration must be viewed in the context of the particular circumstances of the testator, beneficiaries and the estate itself.

Turning then to the first issue raised by Q. 1, it seems to me that the language of the will goes far beyond what one would deem appropriate to the creation of a mere personal licence. The obligations placed on the trustees "to hold my property at (*sic*) 39 Arjay Crescent, Willowdale, as a home for Mary Kovalchick of Sagamore, Pennsylvania, until her death" and to set aside a fund sufficient to cover the charges referred to in the will are much more consistent in the circumstances peculiar to this will and the persons involved with the intention to create an interest in the property rather than a mere licence. This property is to be held as a "home" not held subject to a mere permission to occupy. The interest created is a life interest.

In view of my opinion on the first issue let us now consider whether or not the interest created is a determinable life estate or a life estate subject to a condition subsequent.

[Keith J quoted the test for distinguishing between determinable and defeasible estates found in *Re Tilbury West Public School Board and Hastie*, [1966] 2 OR 20 at 21, 55 DLR (2d) 407 at 408, above.]

The author of Cheshire's *The Modern Law of Real Property*, 9th ed., puts the importance of the distinction for the purposes of this case as follows at p. 284:

> A condition subsequent which is void under the rules stated below or which becomes impossible of fulfilment by operation of law, is disregarded, and the gift takes effect as if the condition had not been imposed. On the other hand, a determinable interest fails entirely if the terminating event is void under the rules in question, for to treat it as absolute would be to alter its quantum as fixed by the limitation.

As already stated, I have come to the conclusion that the interest granted to Miss Kovalchick was a life interest since the words "until her death" are merely another way of expressing the intention that the estate created was to endure for the term of her natural life. The subsequent words in the will "or until she is not residing therein personally, whichever shall first occur" are to my mind "external to the limitation"—"a divided clause from the grant" thus creating an interest upon condition, to adapt the words quoted from Cheshire; and "they mark an event which, if it takes place ... will defeat an estate already granted," thus taking effect as a condition as the authors of Megarry and Wade put it.

It now remains to be considered whether or not the condition attached to the life estate is valid or void itself for uncertainty.

[Keith J found that the condition in question was void for uncertainty, applying *Sifton v Sifton*, [1938] AC 656 (JCPC), extracted below. The issue of when conditions are void for uncertainty is discussed in the next section, and Keith J's reasoning on this point is omitted.]

In the result, therefore, Q. 1 must be answered as follows: a life estate in 39 Arjay Cres. passed to Mary Kovalchick free and clear of any condition, the purported condition subsequent being void for uncertainty.

It follows that Q. 2 must be answered in the negative; that the answer to Q. 3 is simply that her life estate is not subject to disfeasance by any conduct of hers and that Q. 4 must be answered "Yes."

[The remaining questions were to be answered with reference to the wording of para III(f) of the testator's will, reproduced above, interpreted in light of the following circumstances:]

As has already been noted, the relationship between the testator and Miss Kovalchick was obviously an intimate one. He was familiar with the state of her health and her finances. The house is a large expensive nine-room house in an exclusive residential district and the income from his estate was ample to permit him in his lifetime to pay all the charges incidental to the enjoyment of the home without supplementing such income by working at his profession. In fact he had done so from retirement in 1958 until his death in 1967.

In the context of this will it is my opinion that he intended the enjoyment of the property as a home to be in no way dependent on the beneficiaries' own monetary resources.

[Keith J concluded that Ms Kovalchick was entitled to rent out the property and keep the rentals, but that "the expenses of the upkeep of the property so that it would at all times be in a suitable condition for her to occupy as a home, must be met by the estate."]

Order accordingly.

DISCUSSION NOTE

Reform of the Law of Defeasible and Determinable Interests

The distinction between defeasible and determinable estates has often been criticized as confusing, overly refined, and unnecessary. The OLRC recommended in 1996 that "the continuing distinctions between a determinable interest and an interest subject to a condition subsequent should be abrogated … by providing that language that at common law would create a determinable interest will instead create an interest subject to a condition subsequent" (OLRC *Basic Principles* at 64). Why might the OLRC have proposed the abolition of the determinable estate rather than the defeasible estate? What policy reasons underlie this choice?

6. Limitations on the Power to Create Qualified Estates

The basic principle with regard to creating conditions attached to property is a liberal one. Any condition may be attached provided that

- it does not amount to an impermissible restraint on alienation,
- it does not contravene public policy, and
- it is sufficiently certain.

If a condition contravenes one of these rules, it is void and of no effect.

There is a large body of law on these topics, almost all judge-made, although statutes have declared certain types of conditions void in recent years—notably, those that discriminate on racial, religious, or other grounds. All three concepts are sufficiently elastic that a high degree of judicial discretion is inevitable, and court decisions may depend ultimately on cultural assumptions that remain unarticulated in judicial reasoning. Consider, for example, clauses requiring a legatee to be "of the Jewish faith" in order to inherit property (sufficiently certain?); that a grantee never sell land "out of the family" (a permissible restraint on alienation?); or that a legatee will forfeit the property given if she marries a Catholic (against public policy?). One trend is clear, however—the older case law (prior to about 1900) in both England and Canada was more likely to uphold "dead hand control" than more recent case law, even though the older precedents have seldom been formally overturned: see generally Philip Girard, "Land Law, Liberalism, and the Agrarian Ideal: British North America, 1750-1920" in *Despotic Dominion* at 127-31. In this respect, the older precedents must be read with some caution.

a. Restraints on Alienation

Historically, the law allowed property owners a great degree of latitude in imposing restraints on the alienation of their property in the hands of the next generation. The older English authorities were reviewed in *Re Brown*, [1953] 2 All ER 1342 (Ch D), where Harman J noted that the following conditions had been held to be good: a condition not to alienate except to a class consisting of four sisters and their children (*Doe d Gill v Pearson* (1805), 6 East 173 (KB)), and a devise "to my brother John, on condition that he never sells it out of the family" (*Re Macleay* (1875), LR 20 Eq 186). Although neither case has been overturned, the authors of a prominent English text caution that "it would not be safe to treat these decisions as examples of the court's normal attitude to restraints on alienation": Robert Megarry & HWR Wade, *The Law of Real Property*, 5th ed (London: Stevens & Sons, 1984) [Megarry & Wade] at 72.

Older Canadian authorities similarly permitted a high degree of "dead hand control" to testators. In *O'Sullivan v Phelan* (1889), 17 OR 730 (Ch D), a devise to two nephews was upheld with the condition that neither was to be at liberty to sell to anyone "except to persons of the name of O'Sullivan in my own family." It turned out that there was only one such relative, but the court justified upholding the restriction by observing that it was limited to sale—thus, a gift, lease, mortgage, and testamentary disposition were still open. In the same year, a devise of farm land to the testator's son in fee with no power to sell or mortgage during his lifetime was upheld: *Re Northcote* (1889), 18 OR 107 (Ch D). In *Blackburn v McCallum*, however, the Supreme Court of Canada adopted a new, more rigorous approach to such restrictions.

Blackburn v McCallum
(1903), 33 SCR 65

[By his will dated 27 February 1887, Donald Chisholm devised a 50-acre farm in Ontario to each of his sons, William and Hugh Chisholm, in the following terms.

> I will that the aforesaid parcels of land shall not be at their disposal at any time until the end of twenty-five years from the date of my decease, and farther, I will that the said parcels of land shall remain free from all incumbrance, and that no debts contracted by my sons, William Chisholm and Hugh Chisholm, shall by any means incumber the same during twenty-five years from the date of my decease.

Mr Chisholm died soon afterward. Hugh Chisholm mortgaged his farm in 1896 as security for a loan, and defaulted on the loan. The land was sold at the mortgagee's (that is, the lender's) behest at a sheriff's sale, but a question arose as to whether the purchaser took good title because it appeared that the mortgage had contravened the clause in the will. (At this time, a mortgage operated as a conveyance of the legal title of the property and was thus considered an act of "disposal.") The Ontario High Court of Justice held that although the clause declaring that "no debts contracted by my sons, William Chisholm and Hugh Chisholm, shall by any means incumber" the land was void, the clause forbidding William or Hugh from disposing of the property for 25 years after their father's death was valid. Because the mortgage entered into by Hugh had contravened the clause, the devise was forfeit, the land went to the testator's intestate heirs, and the purchaser at the sheriff's sale took no title. The purchaser appealed directly to the Supreme Court of Canada, which was permitted at the time.]

DAVIES J: The question raised for our decision in this case is whether a general prohibition on alienation attached to a devise in fee of lands which prohibition would, if unlimited, be bad by the rules of Common Law, is made good by being limited as to time. I am of opinion that it is not. The will of Donald Chisholm after devising his farm of 100 acres to his two sons William and Hugh in fee and equally dividing it between them, contained [the provision cited above].

With the exception of the limitation as to time the restraint upon alienation by the devisees is general. The question is one of real property law, and it is a pure question of authority. The general rule avoiding conditions which prohibited a grantee in fee from alienating his land is to be found clearly laid down in all the earlier books of authority, and is founded upon principles about which there can be no doubt and which are easily intelligible. But there can be equally little doubt that upon this general rule there have been grafted several exceptions. The cases of *Gill v. Pearson*, 6 East 173, in which the judgment of the full Court of King's Bench was delivered by Lord Ellenborough, and the later case of *In re Macleay*, L.R. 20 Eq. 186, decided by Jessell M.R., establish the existence of exceptions to the general rule which it is not necessary for us to call in question. These two cases determine that a restriction upon alienation prohibiting it to a particular class of individuals is good. All the leading text writers upon real property law cite these cases with approval and in my opinion it is too late in the day now for us to call them in question. The whole subject is reviewed exhaustively by Pearson J. in the case of *In re Rosher*, 26 Ch. D. 801, ... [but he did not find that any rule existed that would validate] a general restraint on alienation [by reason of a] limitation of the time within which it is to be exercised. He [concluded] as follows:

> I find that the original rule which says that you cannot annex to a gift in fee simple a condition which is repugnant to that gift is a plain and intelligible rule. So far as I can find that an exception to the rule has been laid down and judiciously decided, I am bound by that exception. But I will not add other exceptions for which I can find no authority and the addition of which to my mind will only introduce uncertainty and confusion into the law which we have to administer.

If an exception to a general rule of law is well established by the cases I am not bound to inquire into the logical sufficiency of the reasons given. And so I do not feel it necessary to discuss the cases *Gill v. Pearson*, 6 East 173, or *In re Macleay*, L.R. 20 Eq 186, or to justify the reasons which underlaid these decisions. In allowing this appeal we are, it is true, following the decision of *Re Rosher*, 26 Ch. D. 801, but we are not over-ruling either of the other cases above referred to in which limited restraints upon alienation were allowed. The decision we have reached while not being contrary to any judicial decision in England follows that of Pearson J. in *Re Rosher*, 26 Ch. D. 801 and is in line with the late cases of *Re Parry v. Daggs*, 31 Ch. D. 130; *Corbett v. Corbett*, 14 P.D. 7; and also with *Renaud v. Tourangeau*, L.R. 2 P.C. 4; and the Irish case of *Martin v. Martin*, L.R. Ir. 19 Ch. 72. ...

The appeal should be allowed with costs and it should be declared that Hugh Chisholm took a fee simple absolute by his father's will in the lands devised to him and was able to convey the same in fee notwithstanding the restriction in the will. And also that the fee simple in the lands was subject to sale under execution as against Hugh Chisholm for his debts.

MILLS J: ... The question whether or not [the] absolute restraint of alienation, and the withholding of power to charge the land with the debts of the devisees, is a restraint allowed by law, is the question to be decided.

It is not necessary to enter into a very full discussion of the origin and history of estates in land which the English law permits, and how those estates arose, with the incidents which the law now attaches to them.

I may say that, at one time, the tenant held whatever estate he possessed from the lord of the fee, for his own life, upon condition of certain service, and he could make no transfer of his tenure to another without his lord's consent. He had sworn fealty to his lord, and was bound to render the necessary service for the estate which he held. Subsequently, the tenant of the fee was permitted to part with a portion of his holding, so long as he retained enough in his possession to give security for the service which, by his oath, he was bound to perform. All this was changed by the statute *quia emptores*, enacted in the eighteenth year of Edward I, and which, while it authorised the tenant to sell his estate in the land, forbade subinfeudation. Thereafter, the holder of the fee had the right to alienate his interest, and to grant an estate in fee simple, and the purchaser stood to the superior lord in the same position as the vendor had done before him. The holder of the fee has, by law, since then, the right to convey away his tenure, and any attempt to restrain him and to limit his exercise of power which are incident to the estate, are repugnant to it, and therefore void. Littleton, in his works on Tenures, says:

> Sec. 360. Also if a feoffment be made upon this condition, that the feoffee shall not alien the land to any, the condition is void, because when a man is infeoffed of lands or tenements, he has power to alien them to any person by the law. For if such condition should be good, then the condition should oust him of all the power which the law gives him, which should be against reason, and therefore, such a condition is void

But the following section qualifies this and says:

> But if the condition be such that the feoffee shall not alien to such a one, naming his name, or to any of his heirs, or of the issues of such a one, &c., or the like, which condition does not take away all power of alienation from the feoffee, then such condition is good.

This not a general restraint on alienation, but only a restraint which prevented the property from passing into the hands of one who might be an enemy. ...

I think when we trace the history of real property law, that it is not difficult to understand how the limited restraint mentioned by Littleton came into existence. It must not be forgotten that under the feudal system the right of alienation was restrained. That system established certain relations between the lord and his tenant. It was based upon an implied contract upon which the structure of society, as it then existed, rested, and it could not be departed from without the common consent of those concerned. The relaxations in the system are indicative of the changes which society itself was undergoing, and these relaxations did not proceed equally in the direction of all parties concerned. The law, as we would be inclined to make it so as to give to it logical consistency, did not at any time exist.

It is the scientific and systematised view that we get from looking back historically over the field after a good deal of progress has been made. It is reasonable to say that where an estate is bestowed, of which the power of alienation is an incident, that one conveying such an estate to another shall not have the power to alter its character, and to make it something wholly different from what it has been made by the law. To do so is to assume the power to make an estate unknown to the law. It is an attempt not simply to convey away an estate, but to exercise a legislative power, and to create a new form of property in land. It was decided in the Wiltes claim of peerage

> that the Crown could not give to the grant of a dignity or honour, a quality of descent unknown to the law, and much less can a private party create an estate in fee simple divested of an alienable character. ...

Where property is given absolutely a condition cannot be annexed to the gift inconsistent with its absolute character, and where a devise in fee is made upon condition that the estate shall be shorn of some of its necessary incidents, as that the wife shall not be endowed, or that the husband shall not have curtesy, or that the proprietor shall not have the power to alien, either generally, or for a time limited, such conditions are void, because they are repugnant to the character of the estate, *Sir Anthony Mildmay's* case, 6 Coke 40a; *Mary Portington's* case 10 Coke 35b; *Mandelbaum v. McDonell*, 29 Mich. 78.

In my opinion this appeal should be allowed, and it should be declared that Hugh Chisholm took an estate in fee simple, relieved from the restrictions imposed by his father's will upon the sale of the estate, and against incumbering it with any debts which he may contract.

TASCHEREAU CJC gave a separate concurring judgment. SEDGEWICK J concurred with DAVIES J, and GIROUARD J concurred in the result.

Appeal allowed without costs.

DISCUSSION NOTES

i. Restraints on Alienation and the Numerus Clausus

Justice Mills expressed his reasons for decision mostly in terms of precedent and historical necessity, but one part of his judgment raises an important policy issue, albeit somewhat obliquely. His observation that "one conveying ... an [absolute] estate to another shall not have the power to alter its character, and to make it something wholly different from what it has been made by the law [because that would] assume the power to make an estate unknown to the law" raises the issue of the *numerus clausus* in property law, an issue that recurs later in this book, especially in Chapter 7. This is the idea that "the common law, like the civil law, provides for a limited number of forms of partial property rights that can be created with relative ease and makes it difficult to enforce rights that differ from these accepted forms": see Henry Hansmann & Reinier Kraakman, "Property, Contract and Verification: The Numerus Clausus Problem and the Divisibility of Rights" (2002) 31 J Legal Stud S373 [Hansmann & Kraakman] at S376.

Thus, while the law of conditions provides property owners with considerable flexibility to regulate grantees' behaviour, it does not allow them to alter the basic characteristics of estates. One could not, for example, create a fee simple shorn of the ability to dispose of it by will, or that would descend on intestacy only to females, or that could not be leased (see *Re Winnipeg Condominium Corporation Corp No 1 and Stechley* (1978), 90 DLR (3d) 703 (Man QB)). While a variety of economic rationales are offered for this rule (the debates are reviewed in Hansmann & Kraakman), Bruce Ziff proposed an additional reason: property rights, when created, are difficult to abolish or reverse: see Ziff at 54; and B Ziff, "The Irreversibility of Commodification" (2005) 16 Stellenbosch L Rev 283. The legislature is not constrained by the *numerus clausus* rule: new forms of property such as condominiums (discussed in Chapter 6) and conservation "easements" (discussed in Chapter 7) have been created by legislation. However, according to Ziff, even legislatures "need to be cognisant of these reversibility barriers when creating new forms of property": Ziff at 54. Given that property is not protected under the *Canadian Charter of Rights and Freedoms*, do you agree that Canadian legislatures should be concerned with the "reversibility barrier"?

ii. Substantial Versus Partial Restraints

The current law on restraints on alienation is usually said to forbid "substantial" restraints on alienation, but to permit "partial" restraints: see Megarry & Wade at 72. In general, restraints may involve the mode of alienation, as in *Blackburn v McCallum*, above; the identity of the grantee, as in the cases limiting alienation to "family members"; or the price at which the grantee may sell; and all of these may be directed to last either indefinitely or for a set period of time. In deciding whether a given restraint is substantial or partial, the courts take a holistic view, considering what powers are left to the grantee as well as what powers are directed to be withheld. Inevitably, however, some line drawing must take place, and the cases are not necessarily all reconcilable. Total restraints on alienation meant to last in perpetuity will be struck down, as in *Lepage v Communist Party of Canada* (1999), 209 NRB (2d) 58 (Prob Ct), where the testatrix left land to the Communist Party of Canada with the proviso that it never be sold, as will those where the restraint is to last for a substantial period of time: see *Re Phillips Estate* (1995), 140 NSR (2d) 213 (SC), where a condominium was left to a granddaughter with the proviso that she could not sell for 30 years. Attempts to restrain alienation to a small circle of potential grantees will also be struck down, as in *Re Brown*, [1953] 2 All ER 1342 (Ch D), where a father's business was directed to be left to four sons who could only sell their shares to each other, and *Re Thibodeau* (1989), 100 NBR (2d) 156 (QB), where land was left by parents to their son James, who could not sell or will except to his son Luc, and Luc was permitted to sell only "in order to continue his education." Restrictions on price are addressed in *Laurin v Iron Ore Co of Canada* (1977), 50 APR 111 (Nfld SC (TD)), where employees leaving company employment were obliged to resell their houses to the company (which had built them) pursuant to a declining price formula. Such a clause was held to be a substantial restraint on alienation.

b. Public Policy

Although the law always recognized that there had to be some limits on freedom of contract and freedom to dispose of property ("to A provided that he murders B" could not be allowed), the English courts were historically reluctant to restrain these freedoms in any but the most obvious cases. According to a famous dictum justifying this stance, public policy was "an unruly horse, and dangerous to ride": *Mogul Steamship Co Ltd v McGregor Gow & Co*, [1892] 1 AC 25, *per* Lord Bramwell at 45. The very phrase "public policy" is one more often associated with the legislative sphere than the judicial, and seemed to afford the judiciary a quasi-legislative power that they were loath to admit, at least during the era of formalist jurisprudence. Well into the 20th century, it was debated whether the courts were even permitted to recognize new "heads" of public policy, beyond those already enshrined in precedent.

This debate was alluded to, although not resolved, in *Re Millar Estate*, [1938] SCR 1, the classic Canadian case on public policy until the late 20th century. Charles Vance Millar was an eccentric lawyer with no close relatives who, via a testamentary gift that even he termed "necessarily uncommon and capricious," left the bulk of his residuary estate to trustees to invest for 10 years. At the end of that time they were "to give it and its accumulations to the mother who has since my death given birth in Toronto to the greatest number of children as shown by the Registrations under the *Vital Statistics Act*." Mr Millar died in 1926, and "the Great Stork Derby," as it became known, became a staple of newspaper fare throughout the Depression years: see Mark M Orkin, *The Great Stork Derby* (Don Mills, ON: General, 1981). Millar's next-of-kin, who would inherit on an intestacy, challenged the devise as being contrary to public policy, but failed at all three levels of court. In the Supreme Court of Canada, Duff CJC stated (at 7):

We are asked to say that the tendency of this disposition is "against public policy" in the pertinent sense because, it is urged, its tendency is to give rise to a competition between married couples to bring about successive births of children in rapid sequence to the injury of the mothers' health, to the injury of the children, morally and physically, and to the degradation of motherhood and family life. It is even suggested that in cases in which the husband ceased to be fecund in course of the race, the contestants might be tempted to resort to other males to do his office.

The Supreme Court concluded that the line between mere eccentricity and violating public policy had not been crossed, and upheld the provision in Millar's will.

At about the same time as Millar's death, Colonel Reuben Wells Leonard was engaging in an act of philanthropy that would also raise questions of public policy. It would not be challenged until many decades later, however, as seen in the following case.

Re Canada Trust Co and Ontario Human Rights Commission
(1990), 69 DLR (4th) 321 (Ont CA)

ROBINS JA (Osler J (ad hoc) concurring): The principal question in this appeal is whether the terms of a scholarship trust established in 1923 by the late Reuben Wells Leonard are now contrary to public policy. If they are, the question then is whether the *cy-près* doctrine can be applied to preserve the trust. ...

[At first instance, McKeown J had found, on a motion by the trustee for the advice and direction of the court, that the terms of the trust did not contravene the Ontario *Human Rights Code* nor were they contrary to public policy: (1987), 61 OR (2d) 65 (H Ct J).]

The Trust Document

By indenture dated December 28, 1923 (the "indenture" or "trust document"), Reuben Wells Leonard (the "settlor") created a trust to be known as "The Leonard Foundation" (the "trust" or the "scholarship trust" or the "Foundation"). He directed that the income from the property transferred and assigned by him to the trust (the "trust property" or "trust fund") be used for the purpose of educational scholarships to be called "The Leonard Scholarships." The Canada Trust Company has been appointed successor trustee of the Foundation.

The indenture opens with four recitals which relate to the race, religion, citizenship, ancestry, ethnic origin and colour of the class of persons eligible to receive scholarships. These recitals read as follows:

> WHEREAS the Settlor believes that the White Race is, as a whole, best qualified by nature to be entrusted with the development of civilization and the general progress of the World along the best lines:
>
> AND WHEREAS the Settlor believes that the progress of the World depends in the future, as in the past, on the maintenance of the Christian religion:
>
> AND WHEREAS the Settlor believes that the peace of the World and the advancement of civilization depends very greatly upon the independence, the stability and the prosperity of the British Empire as a whole, and that this independence, stability and prosperity can be

best attained and assured by the education in patriotic Institutions of selected children, whose birth and training are such as to warrant a reasonable expectation of their developing into leading citizens of the Empire:

AND WHEREAS the Settlor believes that, so far as possible, the conduct of the affairs of the British Empire should be in the guidance of christian [*sic*] persons of British Nationality who are not hampered or controlled by an allegiance or pledge of obedience to any government, power or authority, temporal or spiritual, the seat of which government, power or authority is outside the British Empire. For the above reason the Settlor excludes from the management of, or benefits in the Foundation intended to be created by this Indenture, all who are not Christians of the White Race, all who are not of British Nationality or of British Parentage, and all who owe allegiance to any Foreign Government, Prince, Pope, or Potentate, or who recognize any such authority, temporal or spiritual.

The schools, colleges and universities in which the scholarships may be granted are described in the body of the indenture in these terms:

2. THE Schools, Colleges and Universities in which such Scholarships may be granted and enjoyed, are such one or more of Schools and Colleges in Canada and such one or more of Universities in Canada and Great Britain as the General Committee hereinafter described may from time to time in its absolute discretion select, *but subject always to the requirements, terms and conditions concerning same as hereinbefore and hereinafter referred to and set out,* and to the further conditions that any School, College or University so selected *shall be free from the domination or control of adherents of the class or classes of persons hereinbefore referred to,* whom the Settlor intends shall be excluded from the management of or benefits in the said Foundation:

PROVIDED further and as an addition to the class or type of schools above designated or in the Schedule "A" hereto attached, the term "School" may for the purposes of Scholarships hereunder, include Public Schools and Public Collegiate Institutes and High Schools in Canada of the class or type commonly known as such in the Province of Ontario as distinguished from Public Schools and Collegiate Institutes and High Schools (if any) *under the control and domination of the class or classes of persons hereinbefore referred to as intended to be excluded from the management of or benefits in said Foundation,* and shall also include a Protestant Separate School, Protestant Collegiate Institute or Protestant High School in the Province of Quebec.

PROVIDED further that in the selection of Schools, Colleges and Universities, as herein mentioned, preference must always be given by the Committee to the School, College or University, which, being otherwise in the opinion of the Committee eligible, prescribes physical training for female students and physical and military or naval training for male students.

(Emphasis added.)

The management and administration of the Foundation is vested in a permanent committee known as the general committee. The committee consists of 25 members, all of whom must be possessed of the qualifications set out in the indenture's recitals:

THE administration and management of the said Foundation is hereby vested in a permanent Committee to be known as the General Committee, consisting of twenty-five members, men and women *possessed of the qualifications hereinbefore in recital set out.* ...

(Emphasis added.)

The general committee is given, *inter alia*, the following power:

(c) *Power* to select students or pupils *of the classes of types hereinbefore and hereinafter described* as recipients of the said Scholarships or for the enjoyment of same, as the Committee in its discretion may decide.

(Emphasis added.)

The class of students eligible to receive scholarships is described as follows:

SUBJECT *to the provisions and qualifications hereinbefore and hereinafter contained*, a student or pupil to be eligible for a Scholarship shall be a British Subject of the White Race and of the Christian Religion in its Protestant form, as hereinbefore in recital more particularly defined, who, without financial assistance, would be unable to pursue a course of study in any of the Schools, Colleges or Universities hereinbefore mentioned. Preference in the selection of students or pupils for Scholarships shall be given to the sons and daughters respectively of the *following classes or descriptions of persons who are not of the classes or types of persons whom the Settlor intends to exclude from the management or benefit of the said Foundation as in the preamble or recital more particularly referred to*, but regardless of the order of priority in which they are designated herein, namely:

(a) Clergymen,

(b) School Teachers,

(c) Officers, non-commissioned Officers and Men, whether active or retired, who have served in His Majesty's Military, Air or Naval Forces,

(d) Graduates of the Royal Military College of Canada,

(e) Members of the Engineering Institute of Canada,

(f) Members of the Mining & Metalurgical [*sic*] Institute of Canada.

PROVIDED further that in the selection, if any, of female students or pupils in any year under the provisions of this Indenture, the amount of income to be expended on such female students or pupils from and out of the moneys available for Scholarships under the terms hereof, shall not exceed one-fourth of the total moneys available for Scholarships for male and female students and pupils for such year. ...

(Emphasis added.)

The trustee is empowered at the expense of the trust to apply to a judge of the Supreme Court of Ontario possessing the qualifications set out in the recitals for the opinion, advice and direction of the court:

9. THE Trustee is hereby empowered at the expense of the trust estate to apply to a Judge of the Supreme Court of Ontario *possessing the qualifications required of a member of the General Committee as hereinbefore in recital set out*, for the opinion, advice and direction of the Court in connection with the construction of this trust deed and in connection with all questions arising in the administration of the trust herein declared ... (Emphasis added.)

I should perhaps note that no challenge was put forth on this basis in either this court or the court below.

The Leonard Scholarships have been available for more than sixty-five years to eligible students across Canada and elsewhere, and are tenable at eligible schools, colleges and universities in Canada and Great Britain. Application forms are available upon request from members of the general committee. An applicant submits the application through a member of the general committee who conducts a personal interview of the applicant, completes the nomination and recommendation and forwards the application to the general committee.

The committee on scholarships meets in April or May of each year to consider all of the applications and to make recommendations to the general committee. Finally, the general committee meets and, after consideration of the recommendation of the committee on scholarships, approves the awards for the following academic year.

B. The Circumstances Leading up to the Application

The circumstances leading up to this application are described in the affidavit of Jack Cummings McLeod, a trust officer with Canada Trust Company who has been the secretary of the general committee since 1975. In light of the public policy aspects of the application, the circumstances described by Mr. McLeod become significant.

Mr. McLeod deposes that since 1975 he, as secretary, and various members of the general committee have received correspondence from students, parents and academics expressing concerns and complaints with regard to the terms of eligibility for scholarships under the trust. Since 1956, numerous press articles, news reports and letters to the editor have appeared in the daily and university press of Canada commenting on, or reporting on comments about, the eligibility conditions. Mr. McLeod is aware of approximately thirty such articles, all generally critical of the eligibility requirements. The tenor of these articles is evident from their headings, which include "A Sorry Anachronism," "Act Now on Racist Funding" and "Whites Only Scholarship is Labelled 'Repugnant.'" ...

Over the years 1975 to 1982, various schools and universities, including the University of Toronto, the University of Western Ontario and the University of British Columbia, have also complained, without success, to the Foundation about the eligibility requirements. In 1982, the University of Toronto discontinued publication of the Leonard Scholarship and refused to continue processing award payments because of the university's policy with respect to awards containing discriminatory or irrelevant criteria. The University of Alberta has taken similar action.

In January, 1986, the chairman of the Ontario Human Rights Commission advised the Foundation that the terms of the scholarships appear to "run contrary to the public policy of the Province of Ontario" and requested "appropriate action to have the terms of the trust changed." In response, the Foundation took the position that it was administering a private trust whose provisions did not offend the *Human Rights Code, 1981*. ...

In August, 1986, the Ontario Human Rights Commission, not satisfied with the response to its earlier letter, filed a formal complaint against the Leonard Foundation alleging that the trust contravened the *Human Rights Code, 1981*. This prompted the trustee to seek the advice and direction of the court. ...

The Public Policy Issue

A. Can the Recitals Be Considered in Deciding This Issue?

In holding that the provisions of the trust did not violate either the *Human Rights Code, 1981* or public policy, McKeown J. took into account only the operative clauses of the trust document and the second sentence of the fourth recital. In his view, the balance of the recitals were merely expressions of the settlor's motive and, hence, irrelevant to a determination of the issues before him. While he found the motives offensive to today's general community, he concluded that these recitals could play no part in interpreting the trust document or in resolving the question of whether the trust contravened public policy.

In my opinion, the recitals cannot be isolated from the balance of the trust document and disregarded by the court in giving the advice and direction sought by the trustee in this case. The document must be read as a whole. While the operative provision of an instrument of this nature will ordinarily prevail over its recitals, where the recitals are not clearly severable from the rest of the instrument and themselves contain operative words or words intended to give meaning and definition to the operative provisions, the instrument should be viewed in its entirety. That, in my opinion, is the situation in the case of this trust document. ...

To consider public policy issues of the kind in question by sterilizing the document and treating the recitals as though they did not exist, is to proceed on an artificial basis. In my opinion, the court cannot close its eyes to any of this trust document's provisions.

B. Does the Trust Violate Public Policy?

Viewing this trust document as a whole, does it violate public policy? In answering that question, I am not unmindful of the adage that "public policy is an unruly horse" or of the admonition that public policy "should be invoked only in clear cases in which harm to the public is substantially incontestable and does not depend on the idiosyncratic inferences of a few judicial minds": *Re Millar*, [1938] 1 D.L.R. 66 at p. 69, [1938] S.C.R. 1. I have regard also to the observation of Professor Waters in his text on the *Law of Trusts in Canada* (Toronto: Carswell, 1986), at p. 240, to the effect that:

> The courts have always recognized that to declare a disposition of property void on the ground that the object is intended to contravene, or has the effect of contravening public policy, is to take a serious step. There is the danger that the judge will tend to impose his own values rather than those values which are commonly agreed upon in society and, while the evolution of the common law is bound to reflect contemporary ideas on the interests of society the courts also feel that it is largely the duty of the legislative body to enact law in such matters, proceeding as such a body does by the process of debate and vote.

Nonetheless, there are cases where the interests of society require the court's intervention on the grounds of public policy. This, in my opinion, is manifestly such a case.

The freedom of an owner of property to dispose of his or her property as he or she chooses is an important social interest that has long been recognized in our society and is firmly rooted in our law: *Blathwayt v. Cawley*, [1976] A.C. 397 (H.L.). That interest must, however, be limited in the case of this trust by public policy considerations. In my opinion, the trust is couched in terms so at odds with today's social values as to make its continued operation in its present form inimical to the public interest.

According to the document establishing the Leonard Foundation, the Foundation must be taken to stand for two propositions: first, that the white race is best qualified by nature to be entrusted with the preservation, development and progress of civilization along the best lines, and, second, that the attainment of the peace of the world and the advancement of civilization are best promoted by the education of students of the white race, of British nationality and of the Christian religion in its Protestant form.

To say that a trust premised on these notions of racism and religious superiority contravenes contemporary public policy is to expatiate the obvious. The concept that any one race or any one religion is intrinsically better than any other is patently at variance with the democratic principles governing our pluralistic society in which equality rights are constitutionally guaranteed and in which the multicultural heritage of Canadians is to be preserved and enhanced. The widespread criticism of the Foundation by human rights bodies, the press, the clergy, the university community and the general community serves to demonstrate how far out of keeping the trust now is with prevailing ideas and standards of racial and religious tolerance and equality and, indeed, how offensive its terms are to fair-minded citizens.

To perpetuate a trust that imposes restrictive criteria on the basis of the discriminatory notions espoused in these recitals according to the terms specified by the settlor would not, in my opinion, be conducive to the public interest. The settlor's freedom to dispose of his property through the creation of a charitable trust fashioned along these lines must give way to current principles of public policy under which all races and religions are to be treated on a footing of equality and accorded equal regard and equal respect.

Given this conclusion, it becomes unnecessary to decide whether the trust is invalid by reason of uncertainty or to consider the questions raised in this regard in para. 23 of Mr. McLeod's affidavit which I reproduced earlier. Nor is it necessary to make any determination as to whether other educational scholarships may contravene public policy.

On the material before the court, it appears that many scholarships are currently available to students at colleges and universities in Ontario and elsewhere in Canada which restrict eligibility or grant preference on the basis of such factors as an applicant's religion, ethnic origin, sex, or language. None, however, so far as the material reveals, is rooted in concepts in any way akin to those articulated here which proclaim, in effect, some students, because of their colour or their religion, less worthy of education or less qualified for leadership than others. I think it inappropriate and indeed unwise to decide in the context of the present case and in the absence of any proper factual basis whether these other scholarships are contrary to public policy or what approach is to be adopted in determining their validity should the issue arise. The court's intervention on public policy grounds in this case is mandated by the, hopefully, unique provisions in the trust document establishing the Leonard Foundation.

TARNOPOLSKY JA: In this case there has been no difficulty over some six decades in ascertaining whether students qualify. The clause referred to above is sufficiently certain, except possibly for the "allegiance" exclusion. In my view, however, the clause as a whole meets the requirements established for a condition precedent and the provisions containing the conditions are sufficiently certain. If I am wrong, however, I would find only the clause referring to "allegiance" to be uncertain and I would hold that it is severable from the other restrictions as to class.

Turning now to the public policy issue, it must first be acknowledged that there has been no finding by a Canadian or a British court that at common law a charitable trust established to offer scholarships or other benefits to a restricted class is void as against public policy because it is discriminatory. In some cases, British courts have chosen to delete offensive clauses as "uncertain," as in *Re Lysaght*, [1966] 1 Ch. 191; *Clayton v. Ramsden*, [1943] A.C. 320 (H.L.), and *Re Tarnpolsk*, [1958] 3 All E.R. 479 (Ch. D.); or "impracticable," as in *Re Dominion Students' Hall Trust*, [1947] Ch. 183. In the latter case the court found a general charitable intention and then applied the trust property *cy-près*. The attitude of British courts, however, is probably best summed up in the words of Buckley J. in *Re Lysaght, supra*, at p. 206, quoted by McKeown J. at pp. 281-2:

> I accept that racial and religious discrimination is nowadays widely regarded as deplorable in many respects and I am aware that there is a Bill dealing with racial relations at present under consideration by Parliament, but I think that it is going much too far to say that the endowment of a charity, the beneficiaries of which are to be drawn from a particular faith or are to exclude adherents to a particular faith, is contrary to public policy. The testatrix's desire to exclude persons of the Jewish faith or of the Roman Catholic faith from those eligible for the studentship in the present case appears to me to be unamiable, and I would accept Mr. Clauson's suggestion that it is undesirable, but it is not, I think, contrary to public policy.

However, in considering these observations of Buckley J., it is necessary to keep in mind two points. First, the observations themselves indicate that they were made before the enactment of the first comprehensive statute in the United Kingdom to prohibit discrimination on racial grounds—the *Race Relations Act 1968* (U.K.), c. 71. Second, religion as a prohibited ground of discrimination is conspicuously left out of the anti-discrimination laws of the United Kingdom. I do not, therefore, find the English cases on point to be of any help or guidance.

In Canada the leading case on public policy and discrimination at the commencement of World War II was *Christie v. York Corp.*, [1940] 1 D.L.R. 81, [1940] S.C.R. 139, wherein the majority of the Supreme Court of Canada found that denial of service on grounds of race and colour was not contrary to good morals or public order.

After the war this court, in *Re Noble and Wolf*, [1949] 4 D.L.R. 376, [1949] O.R. 503, upheld a racially restrictive covenant in the course of deciding that there was insufficient evidence to conclude that racial discrimination was contrary to public policy in Ontario. In this the court specifically overruled Mackay J., in *Re Drummond Wren*, [1945] 4 D.L.R. 674, [1945] O.R. 778, who had found such covenants void as against public policy. The Supreme Court of Canada struck down the covenant in *Noble and Wolf v. Alley*, [1951] 1 D.L.R. 321, [1961] S.C.R. 64, on technical grounds, but did not refer to the public policy argument. [These cases are discussed more fully in Chapter 7.]

Subsequently, in *Bhadauria v. Board of Governors of Seneca College* (1979), 105 D.L.R. (3d) 707 at p. 715, 27 O.R. (2d) 142, 11 C.C.L.T. 121 (C.A.), in concluding that the common law had evolved to the point of recognizing a new tort of discrimination, Wilson J.A. referred to the preamble to the Ontario *Human Rights Code*, R.S.O. 1970, c. 318, the first two paragraphs of which then provided:

> WHEREAS recognition of the inherent dignity and the equal and inalienable rights of all members of the human family is the foundation of freedom, justice and peace in the world and is in accord with the Universal Declaration of Human Rights as proclaimed by the United Nations;

AND WHEREAS it is public policy in Ontario that every person is free and equal in dignity and rights without regard to race, creed, colour, sex, marital status, nationality, ancestry or place of origin;

She then observed:

I regard the preamble to the Code as evidencing what is now, and probably has been for some considerable time, the public policy of this Province respecting fundamental human rights.

That the *Human Rights Code, 1981* recognizes public policy in Ontario, was acknowledged a few years later by the Supreme Court of Canada in *Ontario Human Rights Commission v. Borough of Etobicoke* (1982), 132 D.L.R. (3d) 14 at pp. 23-4, [1982] 1 S.C.R. 202, 82 C.L.L.C. ¶17,005.

Therefore, even though McKeown J. referred to the caution of Duff C.J.C. in *Re Millar*, [1938] D.L.R. 65 at pp. 69-71, [1938] S.C.R. 1, to the effect that public policy is a doctrine to be invoked only in clear cases where the harm to the public is substantially incontestable and does not depend upon the "idiosyncratic inferences of a few judicial minds," the promotion of racial harmony, tolerance and equality is clearly and unquestionably part of the public policy of modern-day Ontario. I can think of no better way to respond to the caution of Duff C.J.C. than to quote the assertion of Mackay J. of nearly 45 years ago in *Re Drummond Wren, supra*, at p. 679:

Ontario, and Canada too, may well be termed a Province, and a country, of minorities in regard to the religious and ethnic groups which live therein. It appears to me to be a moral duty, at least, to lend aid to all forces of cohesion, and similarly to repel all fissiparous tendencies which would imperil national unity. The common law courts have, by their actions over the years, obviated the need for rigid constitutional guarantees in our policy by their wise use of the doctrine of public policy as an active agent in the promotion of the public weal. While Courts and eminent Judges have, in view of the powers of our Legislatures, warned against inventing new heads of public policy, I do not conceive that I would be breaking new ground were I to hold the restrictive covenant impugned in this proceeding to be void as against public policy. Rather would I be applying well-recognized principles of public policy to a set of facts requiring their invocation in the interest of the public good.

Further evidence of the public policy against discrimination can be found in several statutes in addition to the preamble and content of the *Human Rights Code, 1981*: s. 13 of the *Conveyancing and Law of Property Act*, R.S.O. 1980, c. 90; s. 4 of the *Ministry of Citizenship and Culture Act*, 1982, S.O. 1982, c. 6; s. 117 of the *Insurance Act*, R.S.O. 1980, c. 218; and s. 13 of the *Labour Relations Act*, R.S.O. 1980, c. 228. All of these indicate that this particular public policy is not circumscribed by the exact words of the *Human Rights Code, 1981* alone. Such a circumscription would make it necessary to alter what the court would regard as public policy every time an amendment were made to the *Human Rights Code, 1981*. This can be seen just by comparing the wording of the second paragraph of today's preamble with that considered by Wilson J.A. in 1979 and quoted above. Currently this paragraph reads:

AND WHEREAS it is public policy in Ontario to recognize the dignity and worth of every person and to provide for equal rights and opportunities without discrimination that is contrary to law, and having as its aim the creation of a climate of understanding and mutual respect for the dignity and worth of each person so that each person feels a part of the community and able to contribute fully to the development and well-being of the community and the Province;

It is relevant in this case to refer as well to the Ontario Policy on Race Relations (Race Relations Directorate, Ministry of Citizenship) as well as the Premier's statement in the legislature concerning that policy (Hansard Official Report of Debates of the Legislative Assembly of Ontario, 2nd Sess., 33rd Parliament, Wednesday, May 28, 1986, pp. 937-41). The Policy on Race Relations states:

> The government is committed to equality of treatment and opportunity for all Ontario residents and recognizes that a harmonious racial climate is essential to the future prosperity and social well-being of this province. ... The government will take an active role in the elimination of all racial discrimination, including those policies and practices which, while not intentionally discriminatory, have a discriminatory effect. ... The government will also continue to attack the overt manifestations of racism and to this end declares that: (a) Racism in any form is not tolerated in Ontario. ...

In introducing it in the legislature, Premier David Peterson said (Hansard, at p. 937):

> This policy recognizes that Ontario's commitment to equality has grown from benign approval to active support. It leaves no doubt that the path we will follow to full racial harmony and equal opportunity is paved, not just with good wishes and best intentions but with concrete plans and active measures.

Public policy is not determined by reference to only one statute or even one province, but is gleaned from a variety of sources, including provincial and federal statutes, official declarations of government policy and the Constitution. The public policy against discrimination is reflected in the anti-discrimination laws of every jurisdiction in Canada. These have been given a special status by the Supreme Court of Canada in *Ontario Human Rights Commission v. Simpsons-Sears Ltd.* (1985), 23 D.L.R. (4th) 321 at p. 329, [1985] 2 S.C.R. 536:

> The accepted rules of construction are flexible enough to enable the court to recognize in the construction of human rights codes the special nature and purpose of the enactment (see Lamer J. in *Insurance Corp. of B.C. v. Heerspink et al.* (1982), 137 D.L.R. (3d) 219 at pp. 229, [1982] 2 S.C.R. 146 at 157, 39 B.C.L.R. 145), and give to it an interpretation which will advance its broad purposes. Legislation of this type is of a special nature, not quite constitutional, but certainly more than ordinary—and it is for the courts to seek out its purpose and give it effect.

In addition, equality rights "without discrimination" are now enshrined in the *Canadian Charter of Rights and Freedoms* in s. 15; the equal rights of men and women are reinforced in s. 28; and the protection and enhancement of our multicultural heritage is provided for in s. 27.

Finally, the world community has made anti-discrimination a matter of public policy in specific conventions like the *International Convention on the Elimination of All Forms of Racial Discrimination, 1965*, and the *Convention on the Elimination of All Forms of Discrimination Against Women, 1979*, as well as arts. 2, 3, 25 and 26 of the *International Covenant on Civil and Political Rights, 1966*, all three of which international instruments have been ratified by Canada with the unanimous consent of all the provinces. It would be nonsensical to pursue every one of these domestic and international instruments to see whether the public policy invalidity is restricted to any particular activity or service or facility.

Clearly this is a charitable trust which is void on the ground of public policy to the extent that it discriminates on grounds of race (colour, nationality, ethnic origin), religion and sex.

Some concern was expressed to us that a finding of invalidity in this case would mean that any charitable trust which restricts the class of beneficiaries would also be void as against public policy. The respondents argued that this would have adverse effects on many educational scholarships currently available in Ontario and other parts of Canada. Many of these provide support for qualified students who could not attend university without financial assistance. Some are restricted to visible minorities, women or other disadvantaged groups. In my view, these trusts will have to be evaluated on a case by case basis, should their validity be challenged. This case should not be taken as authority for the proposition that all restrictions amount to discrimination and are therefore contrary to public policy.

It will be necessary in each case to undertake an equality analysis like that adopted by the Human Rights Commission when approaching ss. 1 and 13 of the *Human Rights Code, 1981*, and that adopted by the courts when approaching s. 15(2) of the Charter. Those charitable trusts aimed at the amelioration of inequality and whose restrictions can be justified on that basis under s. 13 of the *Human Rights Code, 1981* or s. 15(2) of the Charter would not likely be found void because they promote, rather than impede, the public policy of equality. In such an analysis, attention will have to be paid to the social and historical context of the group concerned (see *Andrews v. Law Society of British Columbia* (1989), 56 D.L.R. (4th) 1, [1989] 1 S.C.R. 143, 34 B.C.L.R. (2d) 273, *per* Wilson J. at pp. 32-3, and *per* McIntyre J. at pp. 19) as well as the effect of the restrictions on racial, religious or gender equality, to name but a few examples. ...

In this case the court must, as it does in so many areas of law, engage in a balancing process. Important as it is to permit individuals to dispose of their property as they see fit, it cannot be an absolute right. The law imposes restrictions on freedom of both contract and testamentary disposition. Under the *Conveyancing and Law of Property Act*, R.S.O. 1980, c. 9, s. 22, for instance, covenants that purport to restrict the sale, ownership, occupation or use of land because of, *inter alia*, race, creed or colour are void. Under the *Human Rights Code, 1981*, discriminatory contracts relating to leasing of accommodation are prohibited. With respect to testamentary dispositions, as mentioned earlier, one cannot establish a charitable trust unless it is for an exclusively charitable purpose: see Waters, *supra*, at pp. 601 and 626; and *Ministry of Health v. Simpson, supra*. Similarly, public trusts which discriminate on the basis of distinctions that are contrary to public policy must now be void.

A finding that a charitable trust is void as against public policy would not have the far-reaching effects on testamentary freedom which some have anticipated. This decision does not affect private, family trusts. By that I mean that it does not affect testamentary dispositions or outright gifts that are not also charitable trusts. Historically, charitable trusts have received special protection: (1) they are treated favourably by taxation statutes; (2) they enjoy an extensive exemption from the rule against perpetuities; (3) they do not fail for lack of certainty of objects; (4) if the settlor does not set out sufficient directions, the court will supply them by designing a scheme; (5) courts may apply trust property *cy-près* providing they can discern a general charitable intention. This preferential treatment is justified on the ground that charitable trusts are dedicated to the benefit of the community: Waters, *supra*, p. 502. It is this public nature of charitable trusts which attracts the requirement that they conform to the public policy against discrimination. Only where the trust is a public one devoted to charity will restrictions that are contrary to the public policy of equality render it void.

[The *cy-près* power is part of the inherent jurisdiction of a superior court to supervise and reform charitable trusts. If it is found that a charitable trust is void for any reason, the court asks whether the testator or settlor had a general charitable intent in creating the trust, or whether he or she intended that the trust be carried out in the specific manner contemplated and no other. If the trust creator is found to have had a general charitable intent, the court has the power to, in effect, rewrite the trust in a manner that is as close as possible ("*cy-près*") to his or her original intention. The court found the requisite general charitable intention here and allowed the trust to be reconstituted shorn of the discriminatory directions.]

Appeal allowed.

Re Ramsden Estate
(1996), 139 DLR (4th) 746 (PEI SC (TD))

[The testatrix, Eliza Jane Ramsden, created a trust in her will by which she directed that half of her residuary estate should be paid to the Board of Governors of the University of Prince Edward Island for the purpose of founding scholarships or bursaries for "protestant students," with preference to students intending to enter the field of ministry. Section 3 of the *University Act*, RSPEI 1988, c U-4 provided that "the government, management and control of the University shall be non-denominational and non-political and no religious or political tests or religious observance shall be required of any officer, member of the teaching staff, employee, or student of the University," while s 4(f) stated that the University could not accept gifts that would be "prejudicial to its non-denominational character" or require religious tests. The executors of the estate of Ms Ramsden sought the advice of the court as to whether they were permitted to make the gift to the University in light of these statutory provisions; they also sought a ruling as to whether the trust contravened public policy. Macdonald CJTD found that the gift violated ss 3 and 4(f) of the *University Act* because the University would have to administer a religious test to scholarship applicants. He then held that the *cy-près* power could be used to maintain the trust, provided that some entity other than the University could be found to act as trustee.]

If another group were to administer the Scholarship or Bursary, in my view, it would not be prejudicial to the non-denominational character of the University. I am strengthened in this view by the fact that three scholarships currently provided to students at the University have religious requirements, but are not administered directly by the University. The Saint Dunstan's University Board of Governors Scholarship is administered by that body, and requires that its recipient(s) be members of the Catholic faith. The Rogers-Cairns

Scholarships are based on academic standing, but preference is to be given to persons of Protestant or Catholic faith. The Ivan and Blanche Darrach Bursary requires "good Christian character." These latter two awards are administered by Trinity United Church. No concern about the status of these scholarships with respect to s. 4(f) has been raised. Therefore, in my view, if the trust were to be administered by a body other than the Board of Governors of the University, it would not violate the provisions of the University Act.

Therefore, I would declare that the applicants must find a suitable person or body, willing to administer the trust instead of the University, and that this person or body must be presented for the approval of the Court, within sixty days of the issuance of this declaration. Once the person or body receives the approval of the Court, that person or body will then replace the Board of Governors of the University as the administrator of the trust. ...

In *Re Leonard Foundation Trust* ... , a general educational trust with discriminatory conditions attached was held to fail on a ground of public policy. In my view, that case is distinguishable from the present one, in that the trust in that case was based on blatant religious supremacy and racism. There is no such basis for the trust in this case. Therefore, I can see no ground of public policy which would serve as an impediment to the trust proceeding, if it were administered by a body other than the University itself.

Order accordingly.

DISCUSSION NOTES

i. Religious Freedom and Public Policy

In *University of Victoria v British Columbia (Attorney General)*, [2000] BCJ no 520, the BC Supreme Court followed *Re Ramsden* and held that a testamentary trust providing for a scholarship to a "practicing Roman Catholic student" did not offend public policy. Nor did it offend the BC *Human Rights Code* because the relationship between the testatrix and the intended beneficiary was a "private" one beyond the reach of the Code. Do these two cases convincingly distinguish the *Canada Trust* decision? Consider, in this context, the following defence of decisions such as *Ramsden*:

> Testamentary freedom is precisely the freedom to choose [the] beneficiary and to set the conditions for the benefaction. As with any gift, the grounds of this choice are entirely personal to the benefactor ... . To invoke Charter values to upset what the testator has done strikes at the core of testamentary freedom in circumstances so personal that Charter values are peripheral.

(Lorraine E Weinrib & Ernest J Weinrib, "Constitutional Values and Private Law in Canada" in Daniel Friedmann & Daphne Barak-Erez, eds, *Human Rights in Private Law* (Oxford: Hart, 2001) at 43.)

In *Peach Estate (Re)*, 2009 NSSC 383 (CanLII), [2009] NSJ 643 the testator had, in a home-drawn will, provided that "My property at 89 Brookland St, Glace Bay is to be sold, to an Anglican or Presbyterian and the amount placed in the balance of my estate." The Nova Scotia Supreme Court found that such a provision contravened the relevant provisions of the Nova Scotia *Human Rights Act*, RSNS 1989, c 214, s 5(1), which states:

> 5(1) No person shall in respect of …
>   (c) the purchase or sale of property: …
> discriminate against an individual or class of individuals on account of …
>   (k) religion.

The court thus directed that the executor was not bound to sell to a purchaser of the Anglican or Presbyterian faith. Why did the judges in *Ramsden* and *University of Victoria* consider testamentary gifts to be "private" and thus beyond the reach of their respective provincial human rights codes, while the court in *Peach Estate* did not?

For a comment on the Leonard Foundation case, see Jim Phillips, "Anti-Discrimination, Freedom of Property Disposition, and the Public Policy of Charitable Educational Trusts: A Comment on Re Canada Trust Company and Ontario Human Rights Commission" (1990) 9:3 Philanthropist 3. For a book-length study of the background to the case and its impact on the law, see Bruce Ziff, *Unforeseen Legacies: Reuben Wells Leonard and the Leonard Foundation Trust* (Toronto: University of Toronto Press for the Osgoode Society for Canadian Legal History, 2000). See also Sheena Grattan & Heather Conway, "Testamentary Clauses in Restraint of Religion in the Twenty-First Century: An Anglo-Canadian Perspective" (2005) 50 McGill LJ 511 [Grattan & Conway].

ii. Restraints on Marriage and Public Policy

Certain restraints on marriage have been held to be contrary to public policy. The law is similar to that on restraints on alienation in this respect: *total* restraints on marriage are forbidden, although many *partial* restraints have traditionally been allowed. "Total restraint" refers only to clauses that seek to preclude a never-married person from marrying: *In re Muirhead Estate*, [1919] 2 WWR 454 (Sask KB). Presumably the policy basis of this rule is that the state has an interest in encouraging marriage. A restraint on *remarriage*, however, has been upheld as recently as 1969: *Re Goodwin* (1969), 3 DLR (3d) 381 (Alta SC). In that case the testator left property by will to his deceased son's widow, provided that she did not remarry, with a gift over to her son (the testator's grandson) if she did remarry. She did remarry and the executor of the testator's estate applied for advice and direction. The court found (at para 19) that "[t]he intention of the testator was only to provide for the daughter-in-law while she was in fact a widow and that upon her remarriage it was his intention to provide for his grandson on the basis that his daughter-in-law would then be provided for out of her subsequent remarriage." The court found that such a clause was not contrary to public policy. Do you think the result would change today in light of *Canada Trust Co and Ontario Human Rights Commission*?

Partial restraints that aim to prevent the grantee or devisee from marrying a particular person, or marrying "out" of a particular faith have often been upheld, although the Canadian cases on the topic are pre-1945 and may not be a reliable guide. In *Re Curran*, [1939] OWN 191 (H Ct J), for example, the testatrix, a devout Roman Catholic, provided that only those grandchildren should share in her estate who reached the age of 25 and were members of a Catholic parish, and if married at that time, were married to spouses of the same faith. The court held that the testatrix's wishes engaged no questions of public morality and upheld the condition precedent. Again, in light of *Canada Trust* and *Fox Estate* (discussed in the next section), such conclusions may be open to question.

With regard to the question of whether conditions that contemplate the ending of exist-ing marriages are valid, the courts have held that the testator's motive is key: if it is to break up an existing marital relationship, such a clause will be invalid. If the testator wishes only to provide financial support for a person in case of widowhood or divorce, however, such a condition will be valid: see *MacDonald v Brown Estate*, 1995 CanLII 4552 (NSSC). Why do the courts look at motive in this instance when they generally regard motive as irrelevant in property law?

iii. Public Policy and the Public–Private Distinction

In *Canada Trust*, Tarnopolsky JA drew a bright line between charitable trusts, which he char-acterized as "public," on the one hand, and "private, family trusts," on the other. The latter, he stated, were not affected by the doctrine of public policy, although this remark was *obiter* in the context of *Canada Trust*. In *Fox v Fox Estate* (1996), 28 OR (3d) 496 (CA), the issue of the applicability of public policy to a "private, family trust" arose squarely. As summarized by Grattan & Conway, *Fox* was a case where

> the testator appointed his wife as executrix of his estate and gave her a life interest in seventy-five per cent of the residue. His son, Walter, was given a life interest in the remaining twenty-five per cent and was to receive any unallocated residue if he survived his mother. The will gave the widow extensive powers to encroach upon the capital for the benefit of Walter's children, and she used these powers to allocate the residue away from the son, because she disapproved of his marrying a non-Jew. The Ontario Court of Appeal held that this was an improper exercise of the power, since the widow's decision had been influenced by extraneous matters, and she had dealt with the estate assets as if they were her own property.

The court based its decision on the doctrine of public policy. Referring to the reasons of Robins JA in *Canada Trust* and speaking for a majority of the court, Galligan JA observed (at 502):

> If a settlor cannot dispose of property in a fashion which discriminates upon racial or religious grounds, it seems to me to follow that public policy also prohibits a trustee from exercising her discretion for racial or religious reasons.
>
> I am of the view that in this case it would be contrary to public policy to permit a trustee ef-fectively to disinherit the residual beneficiary because he dared to marry outside the religious faith of his mother. While there were decisions in the past which have upheld discriminatory conditions in wills, in response to a query from the bench, counsel in this case were not prepared to argue that any court would today uphold a condition in a will which provides that a benefici-ary is to be disinherited if he or she marries outside of a particular religious faith.

The court in *Fox* did not expressly refer to the statement by Tarnopolsky JA in *Canada Trust* regarding the inapplicability of the doctrine of public policy to private family trusts. Which approach do you find more persuasive?

c. Certainty

As with the doctrines of restraints on alienation and public policy, the courts were historically rather generous in upholding dispositions with conditions or determinable limitations expressed in what might be considered less than clear terms. In *Pew v Lafferty* (1869), 16 Gr 408 (Ont Ct Ch), a mother left property to her son conditional on his "continuing to be a steady boy and remaining in some respectable family until he is of age"; otherwise, there would be a gift over. Aged 14 when his mother died, at age 16 the son, who had had virtually no formal education, signed up in the US army and fought in the Civil War. The court found not only that the clause was sufficiently certain, but also that the son had violated it by his actions and thus forfeited the property. Vice-chancellor Spragge declared that he had "exposed himself voluntarily ... not only to the danger but to all the temptations of a soldier's life under such circumstances, [and] chose as a mercenary to engage in a contest with which he had nothing to do" (at 410).

In *Re Jordan and Dunn* (1887), 13 OR 267 (HC), aff'd (1888), 15 OAR 744, a father left land to his son on condition that he was "to abstain totally from intoxicating liquors and card-playing, be kind and obedient to his mother, and be known among his friends as an industrious man ten years after the death of his mother," or face forfeiting the property. The conditions were found to be sufficiently certain and the forfeiture enforced when it was admitted that the son was a habitual drinker. In interpreting the clause, Justice Patterson observed (at 746):

> What did the testator mean by requiring Michael to abstain totally from intoxicating liquors? He used a common vernacular expression, and evidently meant that his son was to be a total abstainer in the well understood import of that term. That does not and cannot fairly be interpreted to preclude the use of alcoholic stimulants for bona fide medicinal purposes, any more than an injunction against the opium habit would forbid the proper use of Dover's powder or paregoric.

Why might the courts have been concerned to uphold such broadly worded clauses? What do these decisions reveal about the "interpretive community" and the legal culture within which these clauses were created and understood?

A different approach to certainty began to appear with the following decision of the Judicial Committee of the Privy Council.

Sifton v Sifton
[1938] AC 656 (JCPC)

[In this case, the trustees of the will of Clifford Sifton Jr sought the advice, opinion, and direction of the court with regard to certain provisions in the will. The case proceeded from the Ontario Court of Appeal directly to the Judicial Committee of the Privy Council by means of an exceptional procedure called a *per saltum* appeal. This type of appeal allowed the parties to bypass the Supreme Court of Canada.]

LORD ROMER: The testator died on June 13, 1928, leaving him surviving his widow, the respondent Mabel Cable Sifton, and his daughter and only child, the appellant, who was then of the age of thirteen years.

The will (dated July 12, 1926), after bequeathing the testator's furniture and effects to the appellant, continued as follows:

> I give, devise and bequeath all other property real and personal to my executors upon the following trusts namely—To manage the corpus of the estate in accordance with their best judgment

continuing any investments that exist at the time of my death if they see fit and to pay to or for my said daughter a sum sufficient in their judgment to maintain her suitably until she is forty years of age, after which the whole income of the estate shall be paid to her annually.

But the will then proceeded as follows: "The payments to my said daughter shall be made only so long as she shall continue to reside in Canada."

The principal question arising upon this appeal is whether this last mentioned direction is not void for uncertainty. ... The will contained no express direction as to what was to happen to the income of the estate during the rest of the appellant's life after she should have ceased to "reside in Canada."

The testator is stated in the evidence to have been "domiciled" in England during the years 1915 to 1925, but to have returned to Canada in the last mentioned year with his daughter, and to have taken up his residence (presumably with her) at Assiniboine Lodge, in the County of Leeds, Ontario, where he continued to reside, except for temporary absences on business or pleasure, until his death in 1928. After the death of her father the appellant appears to have remained in Canada continuously until the month of October, 1934, during the latter part of which period she was taking a course in modern languages at the University of Toronto. This course provided an option to take the third year thereof by traveling abroad, and the appellant accordingly spent the period between October, 1934, and September, 1935, in European countries, traveling and studying for the purpose of completing her education. Thereafter she returned to Canada, where she has remained down to the present time. Since June, 1936, she has maintained an apartment of her own, which she has taken on lease and fully furnished, in the City of Montreal. In February, 1937, however, she was desirous of going abroad again for the purpose of study and travel, but very naturally was anxious to know to what extent she could gratify that desire without any risk of it being held that she did not "continue to reside in Canada" within the meaning of the will. It was in these circumstances that the respondent trustees issued their originating motion for the determination by the Court of certain specific questions. ...

The motion in due course came on for hearing before Middleton J.A., the appellant being the only respondent to the motion. The only question argued before him was as to the meaning of the words "continue to reside in Canada." The point that such words were void for uncertainty was not raised on that occasion.

On February 18, 1937, the learned judge delivered judgment [in which he expressed the view that]

The questions as propounded in the notice of motion do not admit of categorical answers.

In the judgment as drawn up, however, an attempt was made to give the executors somewhat more specific directions. It [declared that the "true intent, meaning and construction of the clause" was:]

> (a) That the words "to reside in Canada" are equivalent to "spend substantially all of her time in Canada" but that mere temporary absences from Canada in certain circumstances would not bring about a forfeiture of the interest of the said daughter in the estate.
>
> (b) That any and all absences of the said daughter from Canada not exceeding two calendar months in the aggregate on one or more occasions during any one calendar year, or not exceeding two calendar months on one continuous occasion and one additional

calendar month on one or more additional occasions in one calendar year, be in all events incapable of constituting a failure to continue to reside in Canada. ...

(c) That the absence of the said daughter from Canada abroad between October, 1934, and September, 1935, does not work a forfeiture of such interest.

(d) That an absence from Canada for a period of eleven months during the next two or three years will work a forfeiture of such interest unless the executors ... are satisfied it is in good faith for the purpose of completing the education of the said daughter.

2. And this Court doth further order and adjudge that the questions propounded in the notice of motion do not now admit of categorical answers but the parties may apply to this Court from time to time, as circumstances arise, for the advice, opinion and direction of the Court on the matters in question.

Their Lordships realize to the full the difficulty of construing the words in question. But, with all respect to Middleton J.A., they cannot feel that his solution of the difficulty is a satisfactory one. It merely introduces further difficulties of construction. ...

[T]he learned judge had plainly stated that it was impossible to define with any accuracy what future conduct would fall within the terms of the will, and, although the judgment was a meritorious attempt to assist the parties, it abundantly confirmed the truth of that statement.

[Before the Court of Appeal, the appellant raised for the first time the argument that the clause containing the disputed words was a condition subsequent and, as such, was void for uncertainty.]

She had, in other words, determined to avail herself, if possible, of the principle enunciated by Lord Cranworth in *Clavering v. Ellison*. In that case a testator devised his real estate to the children of his son for what were held to be vested equitable estates in tail liable to be divested on breach of a condition subsequent [requiring that the son's children "be educated in England and in the Protestant religion according to the rites of the Church of England." Lord Cranworth held the condition void for uncertainty, stating:]

> I consider that, from the earliest times, one of the cardinal rules on the subject has been this: that where a vested estate is to be defeated by a condition on a contingency that is to happen afterwards, that condition must be such that the Court can see from the beginning, precisely and distinctly, upon the happening of what event it was that the preceding vested estate was to determine. ...

In the present case the appellant raised the contention before the Court of Appeal that it is impossible to tell with any certainty what she may do in the matter of absence from Canada without incurring the risk of losing her income under her father's will; and that the provision for cessation of payment of that income is a condition subsequent, which, in accordance with the principle laid down in the cases to which reference has been made, is void for uncertainty.

[The Court of Appeal made the following order:]

2. And this Court doth further order and adjudge that the questions propounded in the Notice of Motion do not now admit of categorical answers but the parties may apply to this

Court from time to time, as circumstances arise, for the advice, opinion and direction of the Court on the matters in question.

With the greatest respect to the majority of the Court of Appeal, their Lordships are unable to agree with their decision. If the clause in question be in truth a condition subsequent—a point with which their Lordships will deal later on—it can be of no validity unless, to use the words of Lord Cranworth, the Court and, their Lordships venture to add, the parties concerned, can see from the beginning precisely and distinctly upon the happening of what events it is that the payments to the appellant are to cease. In their Lordships' opinion, it is impossible to define these events precisely or distinctly.

It only remains to consider whether the words in question are a condition subsequent. As to this their Lordships feel no doubt. Henderson J.A. was of opinion that the words constituted a condition subsequent, and in this, as in other respects, their Lordships agree both with his conclusions and the reasons he gave for them. Where it is doubtful whether a condition be precedent or subsequent the Court *prima facie* treats it as being subsequent. For there is a presumption in favour of early vesting. ... It was further contended on behalf of the Official Guardian that the words in question merely limit the duration of the trust for payment, and are not in the nature of a condition at all. But the trusts for payment to the appellant are quite distinct from the words with which their Lordships are concerned, and which are in a separate clause. These words do not, in their opinion, qualify the trusts for payment. They are merely designed to abrogate the trusts in a certain event. In substance, no doubt, there is not much difference between a trust to pay until the happening of a certain event, and a trust to pay that is abrogated on the happening of that event. But the legal effect in the two cases of the event being described with insufficient certainty are widely different. In the first case the trust will fail altogether. In the second case the trust will remain, and it will be the clause of abrogation that will fail.

For these reasons their Lordships are of opinion, and will humbly advise His Majesty, that this appeal should be allowed; ... and that a declaration should be made that the clause in the will of the testator directing that the payments to the appellant should be made only so long as she continues to reside in Canada is void for uncertainty.

DISCUSSION NOTES

i. Uncertainty: The Effect of Invalidity

Recall the distinction between determinable and defeasible estates discussed above. Are you persuaded that the clause "so long as she continues to reside in Canada" indicates an estate defeasible on condition subsequent rather than a determinable estate?

Sifton v Sifton was applied in *Re Down* (1968), 68 DLR (2d) 30 (Ont CA). Recall that in *Re Down*, the testator had left a farm property in the following terms: "When my son, Harold Russell Down, arrives at the age of thirty years, providing he stays on the farm, then I give, devise and bequeath all of my estate both real and personal ... unto my sons Stanley Linton Down and Harold Russell Down ... equally." The court decided that the proviso regarding staying on the farm was a condition subsequent and void for uncertainty, such that upon attaining the age of 30, the brothers took a fee simple absolute. In doing so the court applied the "presumption in favour of early vesting" referred to in *Sifton*. What are the policy reasons that support such a presumption?

ii. Uncertainty and Conditions Precedent

Note that the certainty test is applied differently depending on whether the clause in question is a condition subsequent or a condition precedent. The test articulated in *Sifton* relates to a condition subsequent, where a high standard of certainty is required for validity. The law is not as strict with regard to conditions precedent. According to Ziff at 260, "[a]ll that need be shown is that the condition is capable of being given some plausible meaning. Moreover, a comprehensive mapping out of the full extent of the condition is not needed." Thus, in *In re Tuck's Settlement Trusts*, [1978] Ch 49 (CA), a condition precedent in an *inter vivos* settlement that each successor to the title of Sir Adolph Tucker should be paid a certain income "if and when and so long as he shall be of the Jewish faith and be married to an approved wife" was found to be valid. The court did not have to define "Jewish faith" in the abstract, but merely decide if a particular successor was of the Jewish faith or not. The settlement contained a definition of an "approved wife" and provided further that if any dispute arose the decision of the chief rabbi of either the Sephardic or the Ashkenazi community would be conclusive. This "arbitration clause" was upheld as a valid means of avoiding certainty problems, especially where the arbiter could be seen as possessing some special expertise that the courts would not possess: see Ziff at 261.

EXERCISE 2 QUALIFIED ESTATES

In the following dispositions, identify whether the interests created are determinable or defeasible, or subject to a condition precedent, and discuss whether any condition precedent, condition subsequent, or determinable limitation is invalid for any reason. Elaborate on the effects of the invalidity of any of these clauses where appropriate.

Grant	Analysis
1. X grants to A and his heirs so long as he remains on the farm.	
2. X grants to CNR, its successors, and assigns for so long as the land continues to be used for railway purposes, and subject to the understanding that, if the land ceases to be used for such purposes, the fee simple shall revert to the grantor and he shall be entitled to enter thereon. (See *Re McKellar* (1972), 27 DLR (3d) 289 (H Ct J).)	
3. X confirms that "the acre of land granted to the Village of Caroline Community Hall this day, shall revert back to the Thomas Roper Estate if used for other than a community centre." (See *Caroline (Village) v Roper* (1987), 37 DLR (4th) 761 (ABQB).)	

4. X devises to A, "if and when she shall attain the age of twenty-one years, provided that upon the attainment of such age she shall then be resident in one of the countries of the British Commonwealth of Nations." (See *Kotsar v Shattock*, [1981] VR 13 (SC Full Ct).)	
5. X devises a fund to trustees for scholarships "to support needy students entering the MD program at the University of X, provided that such students are of Protestant background."	
6. X devises "to A in fee simple if he has graduated from law school."	
7. X grants "to A in fee simple provided that the land continues to be used as a golf course; if not, their interest shall cease."	
8. X devises "to A for her natural life during widowhood."	
9. X devises "to A for life, but if she remarries, my executors may reclaim the property and transfer it to my daughter if, in their opinion, she is in need."	
10. X devises "to A in fee simple, but he shall not be permitted to mortgage the land within ten years of my death, otherwise it is to pass to his brother B."	

E. A Particular Problem in the Creation of Freehold Estates: The Rule in Shelley's Case

The rule in *Shelley's Case, Wolfe v Shelley* (1581), 1 Co Rep 93b, 76 ER 206, is a relic of early land law that continues to plague contemporary students and practitioners of law. It is most easily understood by considering a conveyance such as the following:

> "To A for life, remainder to the heirs of A in fee simple."

In the absence of the rule in *Shelley's Case*, A would receive a life estate and A's heirs would receive a remainder in fee simple.

However, the rule in *Shelley's Case* states that in such a disposition, the words "the heirs of A" are treated as "words of limitation" defining A's estate, not "words of purchase," granting an interest to the heirs. The two estates are thus merged in A, who takes an immediate fee simple, and the heirs take no independent interest. (Note, however, that merger is not a critical part of *Shelley's Case*—if there were an intervening life estate in favour of B, A would take a life estate and a fee simple remainder, but they would not merge until B's death.)

This result appears to frustrate the intent of the grantor or testator, who wanted to create only a life estate in A and a distinct interest in A's heirs. But the rule in *Shelley's Case* is a *rule of law*, not a *rule of construction*; it applies regardless of the intent of the wealth-holder creating the interest. It thus remains a trap for the unwary drafter. The rule is simply stated, but its application to a given disposition is often a matter of dispute. It is impossible to have recourse to the "policy" underlying the rule because even legal historians have difficulty understanding why it was initially articulated by the English courts: see AWB Simpson, *Leading Cases in the Common Law* (Oxford & New York: Clarendon Press, 1995). Bruce Ziff & MM Litman canvassed the varying theories that have been put forward justifying the rule, and concluded:

> Aside from its charm and fascination the only redeeming feature of the rule in *Shelley's* case is its value as a pedagogical tool. From that perspective it can be a useful device to assist in understanding problems concerning the reception of English law into Canada, the historical (feudal) underpinnings of modern Canadian land law, the rudiments of settlements and future interests, the interrelationship between law and social policy, and the interrelationship between common and statute law.

(B Ziff & MM Litman, "Shelley's Rule in a Modern Context: Clearing the 'Heir'" (1984) 34 UTLJ 170 [Ziff & Litman] at 174-85 and 196.)

With these goals in mind, consider the following case and the academic reaction to it.

Re Rynard
(1980), 31 OR (2d) 257, 118 DLR (3d) 530 (CA)

WILSON JA (Mackinnon ACJO and Goodman JA concurring):

[1] This appeal reminds us that the roots of some of our law are deeply embedded indeed. It concerns the application of the rule in *Shelley's Case* (1581), 1 Co. Rep. 93b, 76 E.R. 206, to a will made in 1933. The matter came before us by way of appeal from an order of Mr. Justice Walsh answering certain questions on a motion for construction of the will of the late Margaret Rynard of the Village of Cannington, in Ontario.

[2] The testatrix, Margaret Rynard, died on January 8, 1934, and was survived by her husband Philip Rynard and her two sons Bernard and Kennedy. These three are the sole beneficiaries of her estate which was apparently modest, the main asset being a farm in Scott Township which she inherited from her father in circumstances which will be referred to later. It is submitted by the respondents that these circumstances have a bearing on the issues in this appeal.

[3] The testatrix's husband, who was the residuary legatee under her will, died on April 23, 1960. Her two sons are the present executors of her will which is very short. After revoking all former wills and appointing her executors, she gives all her property to her executors upon the following trusts:

> 1. To carry on and conduct my Estate for three years after my death in the same manner as prior to my death.
>
> 2. To pay my just debts, funeral and testamentary expenses as soon after my death as possible.

(g) From and after three years after my death my beloved son, Kennedy Rynard shall have the use of my farm being the east half of lot No. twenty-seven in the sixth concession of the Township of Scott in the County of Ontario, until the death of his father, Philip H. Rynard and shall pay to his father annually for such use the sum of One Hundred and sixty dollars of lawful money of Canada, and out of such annuity my beloved husband shall pay to my sister, Mrs. Jessie McKnight the annuity of fifty dollars if she is entitled to it.

(h) And after my beloved husband's death my son, Kennedy shall continue to have the use of said lands until his death, subject to the annuity, if any, payable to Mrs. Jessie McKnight, and after my son Kennedy's death, my son Dr. Bernard Rynard shall be paid the sum of fifteen hundred dollars out of the said lands and the balance shall go to the heirs of my son, Kennedy.

The provisions in this clause shall prevail notwithstanding anything to the contrary contained in this Will.

My son, Kennedy Rynard, shall not have the right to sell or Mortgage his interest in the said lands or dispose of it in anyway and my Executors shall have full discretion to grant or withhold his life estate in the said lands, and should any creditor attempt to seize, attach or sell his life estate, then his said life estate shall cease and be determined and shall be null and void and his said life estate shall become possessed by my son Dr. Bernard Rynard and his heirs, executors administrators and assigns absolutely forever.

My desire and intention is that my son Kennedy, shall have a means of livihood [*sic*] but his said life estate shall not be anticipated, seized, attached or be taken under execution by any creditor of the said Kennedy Rynard.

All the Residue of my Estate shall be conveyed, assigned and assured to my beloved husband, Philip H. Rynard absolutely forever.

[4] It is immediately apparent that the major part of the will is given over to the specific devise of the farm contained in cls. 3, 4 and 5. It is on the language of these clauses that the appellant's counsel, Mr. Sheard, submits that the rule in *Shelley's Case* applies to vest the farm absolutely in his client, Kennedy Rynard.

[5] The rule provides that where the ancestor by any gift or conveyance takes an estate of freehold, and in the same gift or conveyance an estate is limited, either mediately or immediately, to his heirs in fee or in tail, in such cases the words "to his heirs" are words of limitation of the estate and not words of purchase. While this language was perfectly intelligible to conveyancers in the days of Edward II when the rule first made its appearance in the Year Books, it requires some explanation today.

[6] The rule had its origins in an even more ancient rule of law that whenever an ancestor received an estate for life, his heir could not under the same conveyance receive an estate "by purchase" but only "by descent." The reason for this was that in feudal times the lord of the manor received the fruits of his seigniory only when there was a descent of land upon the heir. If this descent were avoided by a purported direct gift to the heir on the death of the life tenant, the lord was viewed as having, in effect, been defrauded. Accordingly, the rule in *Shelley's Case* denied the effect of a remainder gift to the heirs of A and treated the gift of a life estate to A with remainder to his heirs on his death as a gift to A absolutely, his heirs taking only by descent on his death. Thus were the incidents of feudal tenure preserved to the lord of the manor and the invidious intent of the conveyancer frustrated.

[7] Mr. Sheard submits that the rule applies to cl. 4 of the testatrix's will. He says that, in effect, the farm is devised to Kennedy Rynard for life (subject to the payment of certain annuities) with the remainder "to the heirs of my son" on his death. This, says Mr. Sheard, is the classic language for the application of the rule. Mr. Gardner, for the respondents, the next of kin of Kennedy Rynard, says that it is very clear from cls. 3, 4 and 5 of the will that Kennedy Rynard's interest in the farm was very carefully circumscribed by the testatrix. He was to have "the use" of the farm until the death of his father. After that he was to "continue to have the use" of the farm until his own death. He was not to be able to sell or mortgage "his interest in the said lands" and, indeed, his interest was to be the subject of a protective trust for his benefit. How then, Mr. Gardner asks, can the rule apply in the face of such a clear expression of testamentary intention so as to give the farm absolutely to Kennedy? The testatrix, he submits, must have intended his heirs (next of kin) to take the remainder interest beneficially. The words "to the heirs of my son, Kennedy" must be words of purchase and not words of limitation. Mr. Beatty, representing infant, unborn and unascertained members of the class of Kennedy Rynard's next of kin, takes the same position.

[8] Much of the argument on this appeal dealt with the relevance of the testatrix's intention in determining whether or not the Rule applies. Mr. Sheard says it has no relevance. The rule is a rule of law, he submits, and not a rule of construction. It may, and frequently does, fly in the face of the testator's intention. Mr. Gardner and Mr. Beatty agree that it is a rule of law but they submit that there is a threshold question of construction which must be dealt with first, namely, when the testatrix used the word "heirs," did she mean the whole inheritable issue of her son down through the line of succession or did she merely mean her son's next of kin, those who would take under the *Devolution of Estates Act*, R.S.O. 1970, c. 129, in force at the time of his death as if he had died intestate?

[9] All counsel relied in their factums on Lord Davey's analysis of the rule in *Van Grutten v. Foxwell et al.*, [1897] A.C. 658. I quote what I consider to be the relevant part of his analysis at pp. 684-5:

> In my opinion the rule in *Shelley's Case* is a rule of law and not a mere rule of construction— i.e., one laid down for the purpose of giving effect to the testator's expressed or presumed intention. The rule is this: that wherever an estate for life is given to the ancestor or propositus, and a subsequent gift is made to take effect after his death, in such terms as to embrace, according to the ordinary principles of construction, the whole series of his heirs, or heirs of his body, or heirs male of his body, or whole inheritable issue taking in a course of succession, the law requires that the heirs, or heirs male of the body, or issue shall take by descent, and will not permit them to take by purchase, notwithstanding any expression of intention to the contrary. Wherever, therefore, the Court comes to the conclusion that the gift over includes the whole line of heirs, general or special, the rule at once applies, and an estate of inheritance is executed in the ancestor or tenant for life, even though the testator has expressly declared that the ancestor shall take for life and no longer, or has endeavoured to graft upon the words of gift to the heirs, or heirs of the body, additions, conditions, or limitations which are repugnant to an estate of inheritance, and such as the law cannot give effect to. The rule, I repeat, is not one of construction, and, indeed, usually overrides and defeats the expressed intention of the testator; *but the question always remains, whether the language of the gift after the life estate properly construed is such as to embrace the whole line of heirs or heirs of the body or issue, and that question must be determined apart from the rule, according to the ordinary principles of construction, including those which I have already referred to.*

The testator may conceivably shew by the context that he has used the words "heirs," or "heirs of the body," or "issue" in some limited or restricted sense of his own which is not the legal meaning of the words—e.g., he may have used the words in the sense of children, or as designating some individual person who would be heir of the body at the time of the death of the tenant for life, or at some other particular time. *If the Court is judicially satisfied that the words are so used, I conceive that the premises for the application of the rule in Shelley's Case are wanting, and the rule is foreign to the case. But I repeat, that in every case the words are to be interpreted in their legal sense as words of limitation, unless it be made plain to the mind of the Court that they are not so used, and in what sense they are used by the testator.*

(Emphasis added.)

[10] It seems to me that what Lord Davey is saying is that, while the rule is a rule of law, and *when applicable*, may well defeat the testator's intention, nevertheless it first has to be determined whether it *is* applicable and this involves a preliminary question of construction. The rule can only be applied if the words "to his heirs" are words of limitation and not words of purchase. This in turn hinges upon whether the testator in using these words was thinking of the whole line of inheritable issue of the tenant for life. If he was, then the tenant for life will take absolutely. But if the testator when he used the word "heirs" meant simply the children or issue or next of kin of the tenant for life then the tenant for life is confined to his life estate and his children or his issue or his next of kin take beneficially a remainder interest in the property. They are, in other words, "purchasers."

[11] So, following the course charted by Lord Davey, the Court is required to determine through the application of ordinary principles of construction what the testatrix had in mind when she devised the farm to her son Kennedy for life (subject to the payment of the annuities) with remainder "to the heirs of my son" on his death.

[12] Mr. Justice Walsh concluded that, if the devise to the heirs of Kennedy Rynard was a devise of real estate, he could not construe the word "heirs" in cl. 4 of the testatrix's will as meaning the whole line of Kennedy's inheritable issue because the *Wills Act*, R.S.O. 1927, c. 149, in force at the time she made her will contained a directive as to how the word "heirs" was to be construed in such a devise. Section 31 provided:

> 31. Where any real estate is devised by any testator, dying on or after the 5th day of March, 1880, to the heir or heirs of such testator, or of any other person, and no contrary or other intention is signified by the will, the words "heir" or "heirs" shall be construed to mean the person or persons to whom the real estate of the testator, or of such other person as the case may be, would descend under the law of Ontario in case of an intestacy.

The learned Judge concluded therefore that the rule in *Shelley's Case* could not be applied to the testatrix's will. The statute, in effect, compelled a construction of "heirs" which made the words "to the heirs of my son" words of purchase and not words of limitation.

[13] With respect, I think Mr. Justice Walsh was in error in giving to s. 31 of the *Wills Act* the effect of an implied repeal of the rule in *Shelley's Case*. I do not think the Legislature intended to repeal the rule by this section. I think it intended merely to negate the principle of primogeniture.

[14] At common law "heir" had a very technical meaning. It referred to the eldest son who, upon an intestacy, alone could inherit his ancestor's real property. When used in the plural, as in the phrase "to A and his heirs," the heirs encompassed the eldest son of each

successive generation of lineal descendants of A. Accordingly, a devise of real property "to A and his heirs" was absolute. The principle of primogeniture was, however, abolished in Upper Canada in 1852 by the Act of 14-15 Victoria, c. 6; (C.S.U.C., c. 82) commonly known as the *Act Abolishing Primogeniture*. Initially there was some confusion as to whether that Act applied only to determine who the heirs were upon an intestacy or whether it applied also to determine who the heirs were in the case of a testamentary devise to "heirs": see *Tylee v. Deal* (1873), 19 Gr. 601. This issue was resolved by the passage of the Act of 1880 (43 Vict., c. 14), which made it clear that the principle of primogeniture was abolished with respect to testamentary devises also. "Heirs" as used by the testator in his will no longer had reference to the eldest son but to his brothers and sisters as well: see *Baldwin v. Kingstone* (1890), 18 O.A.R. 63.

[15] However, in none of the case-law dealing with the effect of these legislative provisions is it suggested that the Act of 1880 was intended to have a more far-reaching effect, namely, to require the words "to his heirs" when used in a testamentary devise of real estate to be construed always as words of purchase. There is no suggestion that one of the purposes of the Act of 1880 was to repeal, either expressly or impliedly, the rule in *Shelley's Case* by precluding the use of the words "to his heirs" as words of limitation. Rather, it seems to have been assumed that all the section was intended to accomplish was that the word "heirs" when used as a word of purchase would not be confined to the common law heir or eldest son. The weight of the early authority following the enactment of the 1880 legislation seems to indicate that the rule in *Shelley's Case* was still very much a part of our law: see *Sparks v. Wolff* (1898), 25 O.A.R. 326; affirmed 29 S.C.R. 585. Quoting from the judgment of Maclennan J.A. in the Ontario Court of Appeal at pp. 335-6:

> ... [T]he word "heirs" may still be used technically, to limit or define an estate in fee simple or in fee tail as formerly, either in a deed or in a will. But here the word is not used as a word of limitation at all. It is a word of purchase. It is intended, not to limit or define the extent of the estate which is being devised, but to designate the person or class of persons to whom the estate is given.

Maclennan J.A. first resolved the preliminary question of construction as to whether the word "heirs" was used as a word of limitation or a word of purchase and then, having concluded that it was a word of purchase, he proceeded to apply the statutory definition.

[16] I am confirmed in the view that s. 31 of the *Wills Act* was not intended to effect a repeal of the rule in *Shelley's Case* by two considerations, firstly, the fact that the Legislature in England, despite the existence of a comparable section, found it necessary to abolish the rule expressly by the *Law of Property Act, 1925* (U.K.), c. 20; and secondly, the fact that our Courts continued to treat it as part of our law long after the enactment of the statutory definition of "heirs": see *Re Casner* (1884), 6 O.R. 282 (Ch. D.); *Re Cleator* (1885), 10 O.R. 326 (C.A.); *Re Thomas* (1901), 2 O.L.R. 660. Indeed, in *Re Gracey* (1931), 4 O.W.N. 1, Masten J.A. was reluctantly forced to the conclusion that the rule in *Shelley's Case* applied even although it probably defeated the testator's intention. He drew attention to the fact that the Legislature in England had abolished the rule in 1925 and expressed the hope that some day it would meet a similar fate in Ontario. This has not yet happened.

[17] Given then that the rule in *Shelley's Case* is still part of the law of Ontario and that s. 31 of the *Wills Act* applies only when it has first been determined that the words "to the heirs of my son" are words of purchase and not words of limitation, the preliminary

problem of construction must be resolved. And it must be approached, as Lord Davey pointed out, on the basis that "the words are to be interpreted in their legal sense as words of limitation, unless it be made plain to the mind of the Court that they are not so used, and in what sense they are used by the testator." Has it been made plain to the Court that the testatrix did not mean the whole line of inheritable issue of her son Kennedy? And if so, has the testatrix made plain to the Court in what sense she did use the word "heirs"?

[18] I think the testatrix has made it plain that she was not referring in cl. 4 to the whole line of inheritable issue of Kennedy, but rather to his next of kin living at his death. This is the only conclusion that can be drawn from a consideration of cl. 5 of her will and, in particular, the opening words of that clause. In my view, these opening words distinguish this case from those in which subsequent clauses inconsistent with an earlier devise have been disregarded as repugnant. In this will the testatrix states in cl. 5: "The provisions in this clause shall prevail notwithstanding anything to the contrary contained in this Will." She then goes on to make it clear that not only does she not intend her son Kennedy to take the farm outright under cl. 4 but even his life estate is to be determinable in certain circumstances.

[19] Mr. Sheard submits that, despite the opening words of cl. 5, we should disregard the clause on the repugnancy principle. I do not think we can. The doctrine of repugnancy is premised on the fact that certain interests in property must, of their very nature, confer upon anyone to whom they belong the right to do certain things. Accordingly, if a testator gives a person such an interest in property and, at the same time, by imposing a condition on the gift attempts to deprive him of a right which the law considers to be an essential characteristic of that interest, the condition is void as repugnant to the interest given. The principle, however, has no application to determinable interests. It does not prevent a testator from giving an interest the duration of which will be determined by certain events. I think this is what the testatrix has done here by giving cl. 5 paramountcy over cl. 4. This case is, in my view, clearly distinguishable from *Re Armstrong*, [1943] O.W.N. 43, in which Kelly J. found that the subsequent clause was merely an expression of desire on the part of the testator and not intended by him to limit the inheritance expressed in the earlier clause.

[20] The relevance of the determinable nature of Kennedy Rynard's life estate to the applicability of the rule in *Shelley's Case* is by no means clear-cut but it seems to me that an estate of inheritance cannot be executed in Kennedy under the rule when it will not be known until the death of Kennedy whether or not his life estate will be determined under cl. 5. I say that because of the underlying premise of the rule that, as soon as the ancestor is seized of his life estate, the inheritance limited to his heirs has the effect of turning his life estate into a fee simple absolute with all the incidents that adhere in law to such an interest. This interpretation of cl. 4 is totally inconsistent with cl. 5 to which the testatrix has in clear and unequivocal language given paramountcy. I appreciate that the rule, when applicable, may defeat the intention of the testatrix but, as Lord Davey pointed out, the first question to be determined is whether it applies at all and this must be ascertained by applying the ordinary principles of construction.

[21] I do not believe that the testatrix, when she used the word "heirs" in cl. 4, could have intended to refer to the whole line of inheritable issue of Kennedy when in the next clause she went on to specify the circumstances in which he would be deprived of his life estate and it would pass to his brother. There is no doubt about the fact that she intended her son Kennedy's life estate to be determinable. She makes this perfectly clear in the

concluding sentence of cl. 5. And, in my view, by giving cl. 5 paramountcy over cl. 4 she succeeded in doing so. The Court cannot, as Mr. Sheard suggests, discard cl. 5. We must look to it to discern the nature and extent of Kennedy's interest.

[22] In *Re Woods*, [1946] O.R. 290, [1946] 3 D.L.R. 394, the testator gave each of his daughters a share of his estate for life but with a restraint on alienation during coverture. The daughters were also given general powers of appointment over their shares and, in default of exercise of their powers, each daughter's share was to go to "her right heirs." Chief Justice McRuer held that the restraint on alienation during coverture made the rule in *Shelley's Case* inapplicable because the daughters did not have "complete life interests." He said at p. 294 O.R., pp. 398-9 D.L.R.:

> The premises for the application of the rule in *Shelley's Case* would require that there exist in the daughters a complete equitable life interest and in those who would in the due course of law take by descent in default of appointment a complete equitable interest in remainder.
>
> In such a case there would be a coalescence or merger of interest, so as to vest in each daughter an absolute equitable vested interest. However, I have been unable to find, in the legion of decided cases dealing with the rule in *Shelley's Case* in the English courts, authority for the proposition that where on a careful reading of the whole will there appears to be in the ancestor something less than a complete life interest, coalescence or merger can take place so as to vest in the ancestor an absolute interest.

And, again, at p. 295 O.R., p. 399 D.L.R. he says:

> In this case, the testator did not, by his will, vest in the daughters a complete life interest in the shares in question. The shares were given to the trustees and the income only was payable to the daughters, without power of alienation during coverture. They were restricted by the very terms of the gift from full enjoyment of an absolute life interest during coverture. Had the subject of the gift been real property, beyond question the daughters could not have disposed of their life estate during coverture. That being true, I cannot see how the rule in *Shelley's Case* can be applied to defeat the express terms of the trust imposed upon the trustees.

[23] It seems to me that Kennedy Rynard has something less than a complete life interest in this case. He has, in fact, a determinable life interest and it cannot on the basis of cls. 4 and 5 be said that Kennedy and his "heirs" together have the entirety. Accordingly, apart altogether from the question whether or not the testator intended when she used the word "heirs" to refer to the whole inheritable issue of Kennedy, the rule would be inapplicable on this ground. The two grounds are, however, in my view interrelated because cls. 4 and 5 have to be read together in order to determine the precise nature of the interest conferred on Kennedy and his heirs. In effect, the testatrix has made cl. 4 subject to cl. 5.

[24] In *Fetherston v. Fetherston* (1834), 3 Cl. & Fin. 67, 6 E.R. 1363, referred to in *Van Grutten v. Foxwell et al.*, *supra*, Lord Brougham discussed when words which appear *prima facie* to be words of limitation will, in the larger context of the will, be construed as words of purchase. He said at p. 1366:

> I take the principle of construction as consonant to reason, and established by authority, to be this, that where by plain words, in themselves liable to no doubt, an estate tail is given,

you are not to allow such estate to be altered and cut down to a life estate unless there are other words which plainly show the testator to have used the former as words of purchase, contrary to their natural and ordinary sense, *or unless in the rest of the provisions there be some plain indication of a general intent inconsistent with an estate tail being given by the words in question*, and which general intent can only be fulfilled by sacrificing the particular provisions, and regarding the expressions as words of purchase … *So again, if a limitation is made afterwards, and is clearly the main object of the will,—which never can take effect unless an estate for life be given instead of an estate tail,—here again the first words become qualified, and bend to the general intent of the testator, and are no longer regarded as words of limitation, which, if standing by themselves, they would have been.*

(Emphasis added.)

[25] To sum up, the key issue facing the Court on this appeal is whether, as Mr. Sheard suggests, the Court must discard cl. 5 on the basis that the rule applies to cl. 4 and cl. 5 is therefore repugnant to Kennedy's absolute interest under the rule in *Shelley's Case*, or whether the Court must look to cls. 4 and 5 together to discern the nature and extent of Kennedy's interest and then conclude that the combined effect of these two clauses renders the rule inapplicable. I have found no case on point but the approach taken by Kelly J. in the Armstrong case commends itself to me and compels me to the conclusion, applying ordinary principles of construction, that the testatrix has effectively limited Kennedy Rynard's interest to a determinable life estate. This being so, it is not open to the Court to apply the rule in *Shelley's Case* so as to convert his determinable life estate into a fee simple absolute.

[26] I made reference earlier to the circumstances in which the testatrix herself came to acquire the farm. In fact, she acquired it pursuant to the following provision in her father's will:

> … I give and devise to my daughter Maggie Rynard for her use and benefit during the term of her natural life, and after the decease of my said daughter Maggie Rynard to the heir or heirs of her body her surviving and failing such heir or heirs to my heirs surviving my said daughter Maggie Rynard.

There was no question on that language that the rule in *Shelley's Case* applied and accordingly it was necessary for the testatrix to execute a disentailing deed and have the lands reconveyed to her in order that she become the absolute owner. It would appear reasonable to conclude that in light of this experience the testatrix might be a little gun-shy of the rule in *Shelley's Case*. While I think the circumstances in which the testatrix herself acquired the farm are a legitimate and admissible guide to her intention as expressed in her own will, I would not attach as much weight to them as counsel for the respondents suggested.

[27] Having concluded on the preliminary question of construction that the rule does not apply to Mrs. Rynard's will, it is not necessary for me to deal at length with the alternative grounds on which Mr. Justice Walsh supported his conclusion that it did not apply. His primary basis for rejecting its application was s. 31 of the *Wills Act*. In this I think he was in error for the reasons already given.

[28] His second basis was that the remainder interest bequeathed to Kennedy Rynard's heirs was not a bequest of realty but a bequest of personalty to which the rule does not apply. The learned Judge pointed out that the bequest to them was of "the balance" after a lump-sum payment had been made to his brother. The use of the word "balance," he

felt, disclosed an intention on the part of the testatrix that the farm be sold on Kennedy's death. I am not persuaded that the language of cl. 4 is strong enough to give rise to a direction or trust for conversion of the real estate so as to preclude the application of the rule if the other conditions for its application are present.

[29] In *McDonell v. McDonell et al.* (1894), 24 O.R. 468, Street J. held that the direction of the testator to "pay" to each child his or her share of the residue on the life tenant's death, the residue consisting of realty, was not enough to require a conversion of the realty into personalty. Street J. stated the rule at p. 471 as follows:

> The rule is that in order to work a conversion of realty into personalty an imperative trust or direction to sell must be gathered from the terms of the will, not necessarily express, but at all events to be necessarily implied from its terms: *Hyett v. Mekin*, 25 Ch. D. 735. I have gone carefully through the cases cited to me upon this question and many more, and I can find no case in which a mere power of sale has been construed as a trust for conversion unless the duties imposed upon the trustee were inconsistent with the presumption that the real estate should continue to retain that character.

[30] Nor can I accept the learned Judge's third ground for rejecting the application of the rule, namely, that the interests of Kennedy and his heirs are not of the same kind or quality. I would have thought that they were both equitable being part and parcel of the trusts to which the entire estate is made subject in the hands of the trustees.

[31] For the reasons given I would dismiss the appeal and direct the costs of all parties except the respondent executor (who, having regard to his status as an appellant in his personal capacity, has taken no position on this appeal *qua* executor) to be paid out of the estate.

Appeal dismissed.

DISCUSSION NOTES

i. The Rule in Shelley's Case: Reception and Repeal

The courts decided that the rule in *Shelley's Case* was not received into Alberta: *Re Simpson*, [1927] 4 DLR 817 (Alta SC (AD)), aff'd on other grounds, *Simpson Estate (Re)*, [1928] SCR 329. It was repealed in England by the *Law of Property Act 1925*, 15 & 16 Geo 5, c 20 and subsequently in most common law jurisdictions outside Canada. Its repeal has been proposed in Ontario, where the OLRC recommended that "references to the heir or heirs of a person should in the case of *inter vivos* conveyances, as well as wills, mean the intestate successor or successors of the person" (OLRC *Basic Principles* at 71).

ii. Academic and Critical Reaction to Re Rynard

Ziff & Litman agreed with the result reached by the Court of Appeal in *Re Rynard*, but were critical of the reasoning in the decision on virtually every point. They also lamented that the court did not take the opportunity to judicially repeal the rule in *Shelley's Case*, or at least to minimize its incidence by adopting the interpretation of the word "heirs" in s 31 of the *Wills Act* (now s 27 of the *Succession Law Reform Act*, RSO 1990, c S.26) that had been adopted by the trial judge. On the latter point, they began by repeating the passage in which Justice

Wilson asserted that "Mr. Justice Walsh was in error in giving to s 31 of the *Wills Act* the effect of an implied repeal of the rule in *Shelley's Case*." They continued (at 191):

> This passage reflects the very heart of the Court of Appeal's misconceptions concerning the content of Walsh J's reasons for judgment and, more generally, indicates a confusion concerning the operation of *Shelley's* rule. First, section 31 compels nothing, and by her suggestion Wilson JA has overstated the trial judge's position. Section 31 creates only a rebuttable presumption as to the meaning of the word "heirs." Secondly, for the same reason, that section does not work an implied repeal of the rule in *Shelley's* case. Moreover, section 31 applies in the case of wills, whereas *Shelley's* rule has application to *inter vivos* conveyances, where the statutory presumption in section 31 cannot apply. ... It is also somewhat ironic that the Court of Appeal would consider [the possibly inadvertent abolition of the rule by s 31] to be unacceptable. For centuries the courts have been inventive in creating techniques to avoid the rigours of *Shelley's* rule. In this regard, section 31 provides a very useful avoidance technique which the Court of Appeal, without good reason, is apparently loath to embrace.

Ziff & Litman also conducted an empirical survey of over 300 lawyers (experts in the law of estates) across Canada to determine how they would interpret a will containing the clause "I hereby devise my Jasper Avenue home to Jill for life, remainder to Jill's heirs." Virtually all the respondents adopted an interpretation that was consistent with the restricted meaning of "heirs" that the trial judge found s 31 of the *Wills Act* to presume—that is, they replied that the word should be presumed to refer only to heirs of the first generation, not to an indefinite line of heirs. Such an interpretation would mean that the "threshold question of construction" articulated by Wilson JA would almost always be answered in a way that would exclude *Shelley's* rule. Only a contrary intention being expressed in the will would lead to the conclusion that an indefinite line of "heirs" was meant, and thus that *Shelley's* rule might apply.

Another scholar viewed Wilson JA's reasoning from a more sympathetic perspective, arguing that her primary goal was to implement the wishes of the testatrix as closely as possible. Mary Jane Mossman invoked a feminist perspective to argue as follows:

> [I]t is important to note that Justice Wilson's decision, with all of the technicalities of ancient principles, precisely implements the wishes of the testatrix, Margaret Rynard, [who] had made great efforts to enable her son Kennedy to have the farm as a means of support, while also ensuring that he could not destroy its intended purpose. From the perspective of feminist theory, Justice Wilson's decision arguably accorded agency to Margaret Rynard in relation to her intentions regarding her property and her children's well-being. By contrast, application of the rule in *Shelley's Case* would have undermined Margaret Rynard's efforts entirely, granting Kennedy Rynard an unfettered fee simple estate, which, in accordance with her fears, he might well have later lost.
>
>   Moreover, though judicial repeal of the rule in this case would also have accomplished Margaret Rynard's objectives, *a decision that the rule was no longer valid would not have accorded the same kind of recognition to her wishes.* ... Indeed, I sometimes speculate that Justice Wilson wanted, perhaps unconsciously, to promote the carefully considered intentions of Margaret Rynard; thus, in the face of a rule that denied significance to (anyone's) intention, she carved an exception, in the absence of direct precedent, out of the "threshold issue of construction" to implement Margaret Rynard's wishes, precisely and firmly.

(MJ Mossman, "Bertha Wilson: 'Silences' in a Woman's Life Story" in Kim Brooks, ed, *Justice Bertha Wilson: One Woman's Difference* (Vancouver: UBC Press, 2009) at 302-3 (emphasis in original).)

Are the views of Ziff & Litman, on the one hand, and Mossman, on the other, in opposition to one another; or can they be reconciled? Is this an example of the "frame shifting" discussed in Chapter 1? What is the appropriate judicial response when faced with the possible application of a rule that is arguably irrational and dysfunctional in a modern context?

iii. The Rule in Shelley's Case Revisited: Re Swenson Estate

Although Ziff & Litman expressed the view (at 172) that there were "very important reasons, which have implications beyond the rule itself, why *Re Rynard* should be the last Canadian case in which *Shelley's* rule is litigated," it appears that their hope was in vain. In *Re Swenson Estate*, 2012 SKQB 540, *Shelley's* rule was applied with regard to farm lands devised in the following terms:

> To my nephew, Randall Swenson. Upon his death, I DIRECT that the said land be transferred to one of his descendants, or a descendant of my parents, Charles Selmer, and Josephine Marie Swenson, for his or her use Absolutely during their lifetimes. It is my intention that the land not be sold but remain with my parents' descendants.

The executor applied to court to determine the meaning of the clause in question. The trial judge's reasoning was as follows:

> At the time of drafting the Will, in 2011, it must have been the intention of the testator to gift the property to a class larger than Randall Swenson's children as he would have known Ginger Christian, one of Randall Swenson's daughters, had children and he chose to use the word "descendants." The use of the term "descendants" creates a limitation upon the gift as contemplated in the rule in *Shelley's Case*. Furthermore, clause 3(c)(1) mentions the testator's intention to keep the land within his parents' descendants and not have the land sold outside of those descendants. This indicates that the term "descendants" means the whole blood line of inheritable succession as it was the testator's intention to continue passing a life interest in the real property throughout his family members for an indefinite amount of time. This limitation is not permissible.
>
> In order to avoid such an outcome, the term "descendants" in clause 3(c)(1) must be interpreted to mean children. In *Grant v. Fuller* (1902), 33 S.C.R. 34, [1902] S.C.J. No. 74 (QL) (Sup. Ct.), the term "children" was held not to have been a limitation warranting the vesting of real property in the first individual, as in that case, the beneficiaries were determinable.
>
> In the case before me, however, the term "descendants" cannot be interpreted to mean simply Randall Swenson's children because at the time the Will was drafted, the testator knew that Ginger Christian had children and still chose to use the term "descendants." It was the testator's intention to have the real property go to the "descendants" of the testator's parents, meaning the whole blood line.
>
> According to the second affidavit of Gerald Ignatiuk, there may be a significant number of descendants of the testator's parents throughout Canada and the United States. These individuals are unknown to the executor and are indeterminable, and thus the property is unable to be vested to the descendants of the testator's parents.

This is a clear case for the application of the rule in *Shelley's Case*. The law will not give effect to the clause leaving the land to the testator's parents' descendants. The effect of the rule in *Shelley's Case* is that the person given the life estate, namely Randall Swenson, shall receive the whole interest in the bequest.

Accordingly, Randall Swenson shall receive the land identified in clause 3(c)(1) of the Will for his own use absolutely.

Do you agree with the reasoning expressed by the trial judge? Were there arguments that might have been raised as to why *Shelley's* rule should not apply?

EXERCISE 3 SUCCESSIVE INTERESTS AND THE RULE IN SHELLEY'S CASE

Analyze the effect of the following grants and devises as of today's date, specifying the interests of all parties including the grantor or testator's estate. Indicate if the rule in *Shelley's Case* is applicable in any of the dispositions.

Grant or Devise	Analysis
1. X devises to A for life, remainder to the heirs of A in fee simple.	
2. X devises to A for life, and after her death to A's children.	
3. X grants to A for life, remainder to B for life, and then to C in fee simple.	
4. X grants to A for life, remainder to B for life, and then to the heirs of A.	
5. X grants to A for life, and then to such of A's descendants as my trustee shall select, it being my intention that the property shall remain in A's family.	

IV. "PRESENT" AND "FUTURE" INTERESTS

A. The Language: A Need for Precision

This section reviews the law of future interests. At the outset, it is important to define precisely why some interests in land are "present" interests, while others are "future" interests.

Although not all property books are entirely consistent with respect to these definitions, this book defines a "present" interest as one that is in existence, even though entitlement to possession may be postponed. For example, in the case of a grant "to A for life, remainder to B in fee simple," *B has a present interest*. She is, in effect, the "owner" of the fee simple, subject only to A's life estate. It is true that B may predecease A, and so never enjoy personal possession of the land; but B may direct by will who is to have the remainder after her death. And once A's life estate comes to an end, B will be entitled to possession. The situation is the same with regard to a grant by O "to A for life," with no remainder. O's reversion is a "present" interest, and even if A outlives O, O can direct by will who is to have the remainder after his death.

By contrast, an interest that is subject to fulfillment of a contingency is a "future" interest. For example, the grant "to B when he is called to the Bar" is, if B is a law student now, only a "future"—that is, "contingent"—interest.

In terms of language, an estate for which the holder has both the current title and the right to possession is referred to as an "estate that is vested in interest and in possession."

By contrast, an estate for which a person has current entitlement, but no right to current possession is an "estate vested in interest only."

And an estate that is "future" is identified as a "contingent interest."

An additional point of terminology: when referring to successive estates, the first estate in any series of interests is called the "particular estate" (it being a "particle" of the whole). A particular estate may be any estate of freehold short of a fee simple, but in view of the rarity of fee tails, it is almost invariably a life estate. Thus in "to A for life, remainder to B in fee simple," A's life estate is the particular estate.

This section considers contingent remainders, recognized at common law, as well as executory interests, a form of contingent interests recognized after the enactment of the *Statute of Uses* in 1535. That being said, we begin by examining vested and contingent interests.

B. "Vested" and "Contingent" Interests

All estates are either vested or contingent.

A vested estate is defined as one that satisfies two requirements:

1. it is held by an ascertained person or persons; and
2. it is ready to fall into possession forthwith, subject only to the ending of prior estates.

(See Megarry & Wade at 231-32.)

The first requirement is straightforward—a grant "to my first daughter to graduate from law school" cannot be vested if the grantor has no daughter who is a law graduate, because the grantee is not yet ascertained. The interest will be contingent until a daughter of the grantor fulfills the condition. If the grantor has no daughters, or has daughters, but none ever graduates from law school, the interest will never vest, and there will be a reversion to the grantor or his estate upon the death of the last surviving daughter.

The second requirement is less straightforward, because it requires distinguishing between "vesting in interest" and "vesting in possession." An estate that vests in *interest* is a present interest, but one in which possession is postponed. It is postponed because there are one or more prior estates that have not ended yet. We have already seen examples of such interests, but have not yet focused on this aspect in our analysis of them.

Thus, in the grant "to A for life, remainder to B in fee simple," B has a fee simple remainder that is vested *in interest* but not, so long as A is alive, *in possession*. When A dies, B will assume possession; if B predeceased A, B's heirs will be able to assume possession on A's death. In this example, vesting in *interest* takes place at the time the grant takes effect, and vesting in *possession* will take place at a later date. This is what is meant by the second requirement above—B's interest is ready to fall into possession as soon as A dies. There is no condition that B has to fulfill in order to take his interest. A's death is not a condition precedent to the *existence* of B's interest, only to its vesting *in possession*.

But vesting in interest and possession need not happen at different times. Consider "to N for life, upon his marriage." If N is unmarried at the time of the grant, N's interest is contingent, but on the day of his marriage, his life estate will vest in interest and in possession at the same time.

Of course, the vast majority of interests in land are conveyed as estates vested in possession. One need only be concerned about the distinctions between interests that are contingent, vested in interest, and vested in possession in grants or wills creating successive interests. These are more likely to be wills, but such interests can also be created by grant.

In contrast to a vested interest, a contingent interest arises in one of three situations:

- where the interest is subject to the fulfillment of a condition precedent before the interest can come into existence;
- where the holder is not yet in existence; or
- where the holder's identity is unknown.

Consider the following examples:

To A for life, and then to B in fee simple upon her graduation from medical school.

In this case the identity of the holder is ascertained—clearly it is B—but she must satisfy the condition of graduating from medical school before the fee simple will vest.

To A for life, then to B's first child in fee simple. (B has no children.)

Here B's first child is to take the interest, but no child is yet in existence. The interest must necessarily be contingent until a child is born.

To A for life, then to A's widow in fee simple.

The identity of A's widow will not be known until his death. He may be married at the time the grant is made (to C, say), but the marriage may end by death or divorce and A may marry D. If D survives A, she will fulfill the condition as "widow" and her interest will vest in interest and possession at the same time.

It often happens that the language in a will or grant is not entirely clear as to whether a vested or contingent interest was intended. In each case the "true intention" of the testator or grantor must be discerned. Fortunately, the courts have developed presumptions to assist in resolving this problem. One of the most important is that, in case of ambiguity, the court will prefer a "vesting construction"—that is, one presuming that a vested rather than a contingent interest was intended. What policy choices support this presumption?

**British Columbia (Public Guardian and Trustee of) v Engen
(Litigation Guardian of)**
2009 BCSC 24 (CanLII), [2009] BCJ no 33

[Mary Zalopsky died in 1971, leaving eight surviving children. Her will provided that her only asset, a house, be dealt with as follows:

[T]he said house at 5955 McKinnon Street, in the City of Vancouver, Province of British Columbia is not to be sold but is to be used, for the sole use and benefit, by my single, unmarried children which are living in it now namely, LENA ZALOPSKY, VICTORIA ZALOPSKY and ROSE ZALOPSKY. After the last of the said unmarried children would die, then it is my wish that the house be sold and the proceeds of the sale be distributed among my surviving children in equal shares.

Lena died in 1988 and Victoria died in 2007. In 2007, Rose was found incapable of managing her affairs because of dementia and was admitted to a care facility in early 2008. The Public Guardian and Trustee was appointed the "committee" of her estate, and also took over Rose's role as sole surviving executor of her mother's estate. Rose and another sister, Ann Engen, were the only two surviving children of Mary Zalopsky at the time the Public Guardian and Trustee applied to the court for advice and direction with regard to three questions arising under her will:

1. Did the named beneficiaries take life interests in the house?
2. Given that Rose was still alive, could the house be sold?
3. If so, to whom should the proceeds of disposition be paid?

The BC Supreme Court decided that the three sisters did take life interests and that Rose could disclaim her interest, after which the house could be sold. Ross J then turned to the question of entitlement to the proceeds of sale.]

[13] The primary purpose of the court in the construction of a will is to determine the intention of the testator having regard to the language used, and the circumstances in which the will was made. The general principles to be applied by the court were set out in *Re Campbell Estate*, 2005 BCSC 1561, 49 B.C.L.R. (4th) 148 as follows at para. 10 and 11:

. . .

> In the construction of wills the primary purpose of the court is to determine the intention of the testator. The court will only resort to rules of construction or presumptions when it cannot determine the testator's intention with certainty by giving his or her words their natural and ordinary meaning: *Fleury Estate v. Fleury Estate*, [1965] S.C.R. 817, 53 D.L.R. (2d) 700. In construing the will, the courts should give effect to the probable intent of the testator, taking into account the general scope and purpose of the will: *Cullen Estate v. Patricia L. Cullen Composers' Trust* (1997), 17 E.T.R. (2d) 197 (Ont. Gen. Div.). Where the testator's language is ambiguous, the court is entitled to consider not only the will itself but also the circumstances surrounding the making of the will at the time it was made: *Re Kline* (1980), 21 B.C.L.R. 273, 7 E.T.R. 176 (C.A.). ...

To Whom Are the Sale Proceeds to Be Distributed?

. . .

[20] Counsel submits on behalf of the estate of Mary Latva-Lusa [one of the deceased siblings] that the Will provides that the sale proceeds are to be distributed in equal shares to the children surviving at the date of the testator's death. Counsel submits that in respect to a plain reading of the words: "Surviving children" is commonly used in wills in British Columbia as a phrase that is effective at the time of the death of the testator. The ordinary definition of "surviving children" is children who survive the testator, not children who survive someone else. ... Thus counsel submits that a plain reading of the Will would suggest that the estate was to be divided among all the children alive at the testator's death. In respect to the intention of the testator, counsel submits that the intention of the testator was not to displace her children living in her house on McKinnon Street at the time of

her death. To this effect, she provides these children with a life estate in her house on McKinnon Street. Counsel submits that to interpret "surviving children" as "my children who survive my children Lena, Victoria, and Rose" is not what the Will intends. It is inconsistent with what appears to be an intention on the part of the testator to treat all her children equally. Counsel submits it is unlikely that the testator intended distribution to be determined by a "last man standing" principle such that one sibling's issue benefits, but another sibling's issue does not simply by the happenstance of how long the siblings survive in relation to each other.

[21] In my view, the answer to this question turns upon the date at which the recipients of the interest are determined. It is necessary to consider whether the gift was vested or contingent. Vested and contingent interests were defined by Mr. Justice Kelleher in *Re Campbell* as follows at para. 13:

> In order to determine the date at which the recipients of the interest are determined, it is necessary to determine whether the gift was vested or contingent. A contingent interest is one that is subject to the happening of an event that may never occur. A vested interest, on the other hand, is one the enjoyment of which is merely postponed, though it may be subject to subsequent divestment: see James MacKenzie, *Feeney's Canadian Law of Wills*, 4th ed, looseleaf (Markham, Ontario: Butterworths, 2000-) at para. 17.2. In other words, if the gift is subject to a condition precedent, then it is contingent; if it is subject to a condition subsequent (which will cause the interest to be divested if the condition is met), then it is vested subject to divestment.

[22] There is a presumption of early vesting—that is, whenever the words used in a will permit a construction that results in early vesting, the gift will be vested rather than contingent: see *Re Campbell* and cases cited therein. The presumption will be displaced by clear language in the will expressing a contrary intention. …

[24] I have concluded that the gift to the surviving children was vested. The gift was not subject to an event that might never occur, since it was inevitable that the life interests granted to the three single daughters would come to an end. I find that there is no contrary intention expressed in the Will to displace the presumption of vesting. There are, for example, no words of contingency such is "if" or "then surviving" used. Accordingly, I find that the proceeds of sale of the Property are to be distributed in equal shares to the children surviving at the date of the testator's death.

DISCUSSION NOTES

i. Engen: Revisiting the Reasoning and the Result

Do you agree with the result in this case? If the will directed that the house not be sold until the death of the last of the three sisters, how is it that all the siblings were determined to have an interest in it as of 1971? How would you describe their interest?

ii. The Significance of Characterization of Vested and Contingent Interests

Students often wonder why the law of property distinguishes interests that are vested (in interest or in possession) from those that are contingent. In addition to defining "entitlement" in cases such as *Engen*, above, it is also important to note differences in the degree of fragility among these property interests. An interest that is vested in both interest and possession permits the holder of the interest to exercise considerable freedom in relation to the land so vested. By contrast, an interest that is vested in interest only (and not also in possession) may permit the holder to transfer the interest by sale or by will, but not to exercise power in relation to the land itself, and never to do so if the interest does not vest in possession. And the holder of a contingent interest has nothing that is "sure" in the sense that it may or may not ever vest, and if it does not vest, it will likely terminate.

These differing degrees of fragility of property interests resulted in the creation of common law rules that affected their continuing viability over time. These rules are discussed in the next section, and, as noted above, there were competing interests with respect to whether fragile interests should be permitted to exist. It is thus necessary to understand whether interests are vested or contingent.

EXERCISE 4 DISTINGUISHING VESTED AND CONTINGENT INTERESTS

Identify all the interests created by the following dispositions, and specify whether they are contingent, vested in interest, or vested in possession.

Grant or Devise	Analysis
1. X devises to A for life, then to A's widow in fee simple.	
2. X grants to A for life, remainder to B in fee simple if she survives A.	
3. X grants to A for life, remainder to B in fee simple.	
4. X devises to A for life, then to B for life at 21, then to C in fee simple.	
5. X grants to A and B for their joint lives, remainder in fee simple to the survivor.	

C. The Common Law Legal Remainder Rules

**Margaret E McCallum & Alan M Sinclair, *An Introduction to
Real Property Law***
6th ed (Toronto: LexisNexis, 2012) at 72

The legal remainder rules were developed by the courts of common law to address two concerns: setting the time limit within which a contingent remainder must vest in interest, if it is ever to, and preventing gaps in seisin. ... In feudal times, the lord needed to know who was seised of an estate in land, in order to identify the person who was liable for feudal services and incidents. After enactment of the statute *Quia Emptores*, 1290 (UK),

18 Edw. 1, c. 1, enabled holders of estates in land to transfer those estates during their lifetimes without obtaining permission of the lord, courts developed rules to restrict attempts to impose conditions on transfers that would create uncertainty as to who was next in line for the property. Hence we have the legal remainder rules, which developed somewhat haphazardly but which remain valid in most common law jurisdictions today, setting limits on the creation of future interests.

Most texts identify four legal remainder rules, although not all texts present them in the same order. Some of the rules apply only to contingent remainders, some to all remainders. But all of the remainder rules apply only to interests created at common law. We call these interests "legal interests" in order to distinguish them from the "equitable interests" and "legal executory interests" that we will learn about [below]. To be a remainder, the legal interest must be created in the same instrument that creates a prior particular estate. [Thus, if there is] a grant of a life estate to A, and, in a separate instrument, the assignment of the grantor's reversion to B, ... B does not have a remainder and the remainder rules do not apply.

The rules are traditionally framed as follows:

Rule 1. A remainder is void unless, when it was created, it was supported by a particular estate of freehold created by the same instrument (no "springing interests").

Recall that a "particular estate" is an estate less than a fee simple that precedes a remainder. Thus, a grant "to A for life, remainder to B in fee simple" is valid according to this rule, because there is a particular estate that is less than a fee simple that supports and is prior to B's remainder in fee simple.

The following grants, however, would infringe this rule:

"To D and his heirs 10 years from today's date."

"To E's first daughter for life," where E has no daughter at the time of the grant.

D's and E's estates are meant to "spring up" in the future, which the common law does not allow them to do. There is no one who can receive the seisin from O, the grantor, at the moment of the grant, and this situation creates an impermissible (in the eyes of the common law) "gap in seisin."

Rule 2. A remainder after a fee simple is void.

This rule applies to any remainder, contingent or vested, that follows a fee simple. In part, this is simply a consequence of the rule *nemo dat quod non habet*—once the grantor has parted with the fee simple, he or she has nothing further to grant away. However, it also applies to determinable and defeasible fee simples. Thus the interest created in P in the following grant is void at common law:

"To M and his heirs so long as the land is farmed, and afterwards to P and his heirs."

With regard to defeasible and determinable interests, rule 2, in effect, reiterated the common law prohibition on rights of re-entry and possibilities of reverter being exercised by anyone except the grantor or his heirs.

Rule 3. A remainder was void if it was designed to take effect in possession by defeating the particular estate (no "shifting interests").

The concern for an orderly flow of seisin is at the heart of this rule. The following purported remainder to Z was thus invalid at common law:

"To W for life, but if she remarries, to Z and his heirs."

The remainder in Z purports to allow him to "cut in," to end W's life estate prematurely should she remarry. This attempt to cut short W's seisin and shift seisin over to Z was considered objectionable by the common law. The interest attempted to be created in Z is often referred to as a "shifting" interest, because it was to "shift over" from W to Z immediately on the happening of the event in question.

In relation to such "shifting" interests, however, the law distinguished between defeasible and determinable estates. The example just discussed featured a life estate defeasible on condition subsequent. A determinable life estate was not considered to run afoul of this rule. Consider the following:

"To W for life during widowhood, and then to Z and his heirs."

If W should remarry, her life estate would end, but this was seen as the "natural" end of her estate. Recall that a determinable limitation (here, the "during widowhood" clause) is seen as part of the very definition of the estate so delimited. Hence, seisin was seen to flow smoothly to Z whether W died or remarried, and the vesting of his estate was not considered to "cut in" to hers.

Rule 4. A remainder was void if it did not in fact vest during the continuance of the particular estate or at the moment of its determination.

The concern for an orderly flow of seisin was also at the heart of rule 4, but it was the only rule that had a "wait and see" component. The first three were rules of initial invalidity. This rule contemplates a standard disposition such as the following:

"To R for life, remainder to S and her heirs upon her marriage."

If S is married no later than the date of R's death—that is, before the particular estate has ended—her interest will vest in time. Note that while R is alive and S is unmarried, her remainder in fee simple is contingent; however, it vests in interest when she marries, and vests in possession at the death of R. Thus, rule 4 does not invalidate S's interest. How long can we wait to see if she does marry? Rule 4 says she must marry before R dies or she, S, will lose her interest through *natural destruction*. If she marries a year after R's death, no matter—the interest, once lost, cannot be resurrected. Upon R's death, if S is unmarried, there will be a reversion to the grantor or the grantor's estate.

Note, however, that it will suffice if the holder of the remainder is identified at the moment of the particular estate-holder's death. Thus the following grant is valid:

"To K for life and then to her eldest son alive at her death and his heirs."

K may have several sons and we will not know which will be the "eldest son alive at her death" until she dies. But that suffices for rule 4: the seisin will flow smoothly from K to her eldest son at the moment of her death. The remainder will only be void if K is survived by no sons at all.

DISCUSSION NOTE

Natural Destruction: Re Crow

The rules relating to legal remainders are seldom encountered today because most dispositions containing successive interests in property are created as equitable interests within a trust structure and, as noted by Margaret E McCallum & Alan M Sinclair, *An Introduction to Real Property Law* [McCallum & Sinclair], above, the legal remainder rules do not apply to equitable interests. As discussed below, frustration with these common law remainder rules was one impetus for the intervention of equity. Nonetheless, these rules remain part of the law in the 21st century, and they represent a trap for the unwary. As recently as 1984, a remainder interest under an Ontario will was held to have been "naturally destroyed" because it did not vest in time in accordance with rule 4: see *Re Crow* (1984), 48 OR (2d) 36 (H Ct J). *Re Crow* is discussed in more detail below in connection with the rule in *Purefoy v Rogers*.

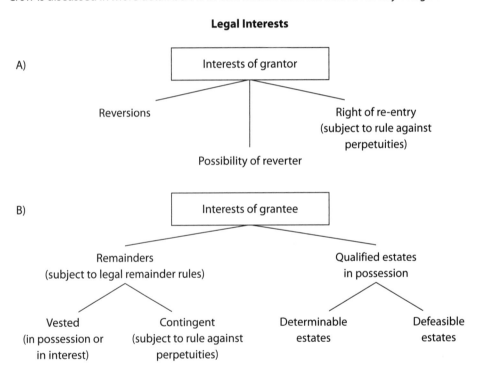

Legal Interests

A) Interests of grantor

Reversions

Right of re-entry
(subject to rule against
perpetuities)

Possibility of reverter

B) Interests of grantee

Remainders
(subject to legal remainder rules)

Qualified estates
in possession

Vested
(in possession or
in interest)

Contingent
(subject to rule against
perpetuities)

Determinable
estates

Defeasible
estates

D. Equitable Estates

The restrictions imposed by the common law on creating future interests, and the taxes levied on the holder of seisin, led medieval conveyancers to seek ways to avoid these inconveniences. They began to experiment with a device known as the "use," the ancestor of the modern trust. The use came to be recognized by the chancellor, an important position in the king's council from about the 14th century, and the court over which he presided, the Court of Chancery (the fourth court at Westminster by the 1430s). The following excerpt describes the development of the chancellor's jurisdiction over the body of law we now call "equity," and the emergence of the law of uses and trusts.

1. Origins of the Equitable Jurisdiction

Philip Girard, "History and Development of Equity"
in Faye Woodman & Mark R Gillen, eds, *The Law of Trusts:*
A Contextual Approach, 2d ed (Toronto: Emond Montgomery, 2008)
44-48 (footnotes omitted)

The origins of the modern body of law we call equity lay in the petitions that dissatisfied medieval litigants might address to the king. By the end of the 14th century, there were already thousands of such petitions. ... Petitioners appealed to the king because he was thought to possess a residuum of authority to do justice where the ordinary courts had failed to achieve it. These petitions came to be referred to the chancellor, because he was the senior member of the king's council and, in effect, the king's prime minister.

In its early life the Chancery was not a court of law but a department of state. Its head, the chancellor, had custody of the great seal of England. Much of the chancellor's work was administrative rather than judicial. The association of the chancellor with the administration of justice arose because the common law original writs needed to commence litigation in the royal courts had to be issued by Chancery. Indeed, the chancellor might create a new form of original writ in response to a petition if he felt that existing writs were inadequate. After 1350, the common law judges would quash such new writs, however, as not in conformity with the existing law. It was this premature rigidity of the common law that led, in large measure, to the chancellor's practice of responding to petitions with an individualized remedy.

Medieval chancellors normally held high ecclesiastical office as bishops, archbishops, or even cardinals. They were often trained in the civil (Roman) law, the canon law, or both, and it was from the canon law that the chancellor developed a procedure to deal with the investigation of these petitions, or bills, as they came to be known. From the 14th century, these bills and subsequent pleadings were permitted to be written in English, in contrast to the Latin that was the official language of record in the central courts at the time, or the law French in which legal treatises were written. Historians of English now believe that the Chancery clerks played a crucial role in the emergence of the modern English language. In particular, the clerks standardized the wide variety of spellings that existed at the time, and their choices have endured to the present day. ...

By later medieval times, [the chancellor] was being called on to supply equity in the Aristotelian sense, where a common law rule, just in itself, operated harshly in a particular case. The standard example was the case of the bond that had been paid by the debtor but not cancelled by the creditor. The common law treated the uncancelled bond as irrefutable proof that the debt was still due, but the chancellor would issue an injunction preventing the creditor from suing a second time on the bond if the debtor could prove by other means that the debt had been paid. In such cases, the chancellor did not say that the law applied by the common law court was incorrect, merely that in the particular circumstances of the case it would be inequitable for the defendant to collect the debt twice. His intervention was directed solely to the parties, and did not change the law for the future. This is what is meant by the maxims "equity acts in personam" and "equity follows the law." The common law's exacting approach was compounded by its highly exclusionary rules of evidence. Neither plaintiffs nor defendants were allowed to give evidence on the basis that it was tainted by their interest in the outcome of the cause. The chancellor recognized no such limitations and would allow both sides to tell their stories in great detail. This greater sensitivity to the context of a dispute allowed the chancellor to get at the real substance of the case and was embodied in the maxim "equity considers the substance, not the form." ...

Development of the "Use"

The origins of uses in English law and of the chancellor's jurisdiction over them remain elusive. An early example of the use can be dated to 1225, when land was conveyed to the town of Oxford "to the use of the [Franciscan] friars," who had arrived in England the previous year. The Franciscans were a mendicant order, forbidden from owning property but not from accepting hospitality, so that legal title to land might be conveyed to nominees to hold for their use and enjoyment. Today we would call this a charitable trust. The word "use" came from the Latin *opus* (benefit), which in law French became *oeps* and eventually *use*. If party A transferred lands to B to hold *ad opus* (to the use of) another, C, B was supposed to hold the land for C's benefit.

This apparently simple concept, however, created difficulty for the common law courts and opportunity for those wishing to avoid various restrictions and taxes that were part of the common and feudal laws. The difficulty for the common law courts was that once vested with seisin of certain lands, B was deemed to possess the sole interest in them. There was no room for legal recognition of the beneficial claim that A wished C to have, but this lack of recognition in itself could be very useful. As Maitland said, the use functioned as a hedge behind which the common law could not look. For example, A might wish to avoid creditors and transfer land to B to A's own use. In substance, A was still the owner, but the common law could not assist the creditor because it regarded B as the owner. To take another example, a landowner might create a use to avoid taxes. Most of the feudal taxes were imposed on a landowner at certain points in the life cycle, typically on death and at the age of majority. If A arranged for his land to be held by a group of adult trusted friends in joint tenancy, to the use of himself or of his own family members, there would never be a time when the landowner "died" or attained "majority," and the feudal taxes could be avoided indefinitely.

Creation of these kinds of uses became very popular by the 15th century, and by 1420 the chancellor's jurisdiction over them was established. His manner of intervention was the same as in other cases. If it was alleged that B, called the *feoffee to uses*, had without reason withheld profits from the lands in question from C, known as the *cestui que use* (beneficiary), the chancellor would subpoena B to appear and answer C's allegations. If unable to raise a good defence, B might be ordered to restore the lost profits to C. In such a case the basis for the chancellor's intervention was the fact that B had acted in bad conscience; having undertaken an obligation, B had knowingly breached it.

A case of lost profits was one thing. But what if B had parted with the legal title? Could B transfer title to a purchaser free and clear of C's claims? A series of cases presented themselves over the centuries. First, if B died and legal title descended to the heir, the chancellor would hold the heir bound to respect the use in C's favour. Even if the heir had not known that B held to C's use, the heir had not paid anything for the property. The "equities" of the situation were such that the heir should respect C's interest. The same situation obtained if B had alienated the property *inter vivos* by a gratuitous conveyance.

If B sold the property for valuable consideration to a purchaser, the purchaser would be bound if he or she had prior notice of C's use. Eventually this doctrine of notice was expanded to embrace three kinds of notice: actual, implied, and constructive.

Only in the case where the purchaser bought the legal title with no notice of any kind would he or she take full title free of C's claims. The combination of valuable consideration moving from the purchaser, plus the latter's moral innocence, meant that there was no basis for the chancellor's intervention. Today we say that the bona fide purchaser for value of a legal estate without notice of a prior equitable interest takes free of that interest. This reversal of the normal rule of priorities ("first in time, first in right") still applies today absent any question of registration and has its roots in the very nature of the distinction between legal and equitable interests.

[This extensive protection of the interest of the *cestui que use* led] Maitland to say that, while the claim of the *cestui que use* remained *in personam* in that it was only a claim to have the chancellor compel the feoffee to uses to do or not to do certain things, it came to look very like a proprietary (*in rem*) claim because it could (and can) be enforced against all third parties except the bona fide purchaser for value of the legal estate without notice.

For the reasons of family provision and tax avoidance alluded to earlier, conveying lands into use became popular, but the practice raised a number of problems. One was political and economic—the avoidance of tax was particularly unsettling for the monarch, who steadily lost revenue over the course of the 15th and 16th centuries. The second was more purely legal—the informality with which uses could be raised sometimes left the state of the title in some doubt. The common law demanded the formalities of a deed or a livery of seisin to constitute a proper conveyance of legal title to land, but uses might be raised through an informal writing or even orally, through a simple verbal direction to the feoffee to uses. The problems of proof that might arise in such situations are obvious.

Finally, Henry VIII tried to put a stop to the hemorrhage of feudal revenues through three statutes that he coerced Parliament into passing in the second quarter of the 16th century: the *Statute of Uses*, 1535, the *Statute of Wills*, 1540, and the *Statute in Explanation of Wills*, 1542. The first-named of this trio stated simply that where any use had been created, seisin—that is, the indicator of common law title—was to be taken from the feoffee to uses and vested in the *cestui que use*. The statute was said to "execute" the use. Once legal and beneficial title had been united in the *cestui que use*, the useful "hedge" disappeared and the feudal taxes could be levied once again against the person who actually enjoyed the property. The *Statute of Uses* allowed an exception in the case of active uses. Where the feofee to uses had active duties to perform, and was not just a "man of straw" inserted to frustrate the common law, the feoffee to uses was allowed to maintain seisin. It would have been very easy for settlors to manipulate this active–passive distinction to negate the intent of the statute were it not for further provisions on the subject contained in the statutes of 1540 and 1542. On the one hand, the *Statute of Wills* made a major concession to landowners by permitting willing of all land held in socage tenure and two-thirds of the land that a person might hold in knight's service. [Recall the discussion of the *Statute of Wills* earlier in this chapter.] On the other hand, it and the 1542 statute, in spite of their titles, attached tax consequences to *inter vivos* trusts, whether active or not, made for the preferment of wives, the advancement of children, and the payment of debts. After 1540, then, the purpose and nature of the trust, rather than its form (active versus passive), became the key consideration so that uses and trusts were no longer such a threat to royal revenue.

2. Equitable Future Interests Before the Statute of Uses, 1535

As Chancery's protection of uses became more regular and widespread, the "use" came to take on the characteristics of an "estate" in land. Chancery mimicked the language of the common law, such that it became common to speak of, for example, an equitable life estate and an equitable fee simple. However, Chancery did not follow all the technical common law rules restricting the creation of future interests, and thus presented wealth-holders with more flexibility in this regard. Simply put, the Court of Chancery was not concerned with seisin, which was the exclusive concern of the courts of common law. This stance liberated equitable remainders from the common law remainder rules and permitted the creation of new interests that could not exist at common law. Consider the following examples:

Example 1

X grants to T and his heirs to the use of A for life, remainder to the use of B and his heirs when he turns 21.

The interests are as follows:

- X: feoffor to uses, who holds the reversion in fee simple in equity (also called a "resulting use");
- T: feoffee to uses, who holds the legal fee simple and thus seisin;
- A: *cestui que use*, who holds an equitable life estate, vested in interest and possession; and
- B: *cestui que use*, who holds an equitable contingent remainder in fee simple.

Recall that rule 4 of the common law remainder rules required (in a common law conveyance) that B turn 21 before A died, or his interest would be naturally destroyed. Equitable contingent remainders did not have to observe this rule. If at A's death B was only 17, there would be a "resulting use" to X or his estate during the hiatus until B turned 21—that is, T would pay any income arising from the lands back to X during this period. Upon B turning 21, T would transfer legal title to the land to him and B would be the full owner in law and equity. Equity did not care that B's interest might "spring up" some years after A's death, and because T held seisin during this period, the common law was not concerned.

Note that if B died before he turned 21, T would hold the land for X or his heirs, because X retained the reversion in fee simple in equity. This too can be called a "resulting use": the phrase is used to describe the interest that arises when the equitable estate has not been fully disposed of; in such cases, the interest is said to "result" back to the grantor or testator, because he or she has not given it away. Other varieties of the resulting trust will be discussed in Chapters 5 and 6.

Example 2

X grants to T and his heirs to the use of Y and his heirs, but if he ceases to farm the land, to the use of Z and his heirs.

The interests are as follows:

- X: feoffor to uses;
- T: feoffee to uses, who holds the legal fee simple and thus seisin;

Y: *cestui que use*, who holds an equitable fee simple, defeasible on condition subsequent; and

Z: *cestui que use*, who holds an equitable "executory" ("shifting") interest in fee simple.

Recall that interests such as Z's infringed rule 3 at common law, because seisin could not be made to "shift over" on the happening of a future event. Equity, however, would permit Z to take the interest if Y ceased to farm the land. What Z has cannot thus be a legal remainder, and a new word was invented to describe this kind of interest: it was called an "executory" interest. The word "executory" means that the estate has not yet vested, and indeed may never vest. It is not yet "executed," in that Y may or may not cease to farm the land before his death. If Y ceases to farm the land, Z's interest will no longer be executory, but will vest.

EXERCISE 5 CONVEYANCES TO USES BEFORE THE STATUTE OF USES, 1535

It is useful to be able to identify the interests created in conveyances to uses prior to the *Statute of Uses*, 1535, because the Statute assumed a familiarity with them and used language that conveyancers of the day were accustomed to employ. Analyze the following dispositions, identifying the estates created, including any retained by the grantor, and specifying whether the estates are legal or equitable, vested or contingent.

Grant	Analysis
1. X grants to A and his heirs to the use of B and his heirs.	
2. X grants to A and his heirs to the use of B for life, remainder to the use of C and her heirs.	
3. X grants to A and his heirs to the use of B for life, but if B marries C, then to the use of D and his heirs.	
4. X grants to A and his heirs to the use of B and his heirs when B shall marry E (B is not yet married to E).	
5. X grants to A and his heirs to the use of X for life, remainder to the use of X's daughter Y and her heirs.	

3. The Statute of Uses, 1535: Passage, Impact, Legacy

The *Statute of Uses*, 1535, discussed above, is still part of Canadian law. Even though its initial rationale has long since disappeared, it is still an important part of the "story" of land law. The following extract provides some of the historical context of the Statute's passage and discusses its impact on the law of conveyancing, the law of future interests, and the evolution of the modern trust.

Margaret E McCallum & Alan M Sinclair, *An Introduction to*
Real Property Law
6th ed (Toronto: LexisNexis, 2012) at 83-90

Henry VIII could not govern without the consent of Parliament, where he was none too popular. But Parliament was full of common law lawyers, who did not like conveyancing work being handled by the Chancery bar. So they accepted Henry's proposal and in 1535 passed the *Statute of Uses*, 1535 (U.K.), 27 Hen. 8, c. 10, to take effect in 1536. Although repealed in England in 1925, the *Statute of Uses* was part of the received law of the Canadian common law jurisdictions and it, perhaps in a re-enacted version, is a key part of Canadian land law today. The operative section, a marvel of soporific repetition, can be summarized thus: where any person or persons is seised of any interest in land to the use, confidence, or trust of any other person, persons, or body politick, the person, persons or body politick who is to benefit from the use shall henceforth stand and be seised of the same estate in law as they had in equity; and the estate given to the person who stood seised to the use of another shall be deemed to be in the person, persons, or body politick who is to benefit from the use.

Thus, where, prior to the *Statute of Uses*, O conveyed "to A and heirs for the use of B and heirs," the state of the title was clear. A had a legal fee simple and B an equitable fee simple. A was seised to the use of another, B. The effect of the Statute is to drop A from the grant and move seisin to B. B now becomes the owner in fee simple of both the equitable estate, by the terms of the grant, and the legal estate, by the operation of the *Statute of Uses*. This process is called "executing the use." A is being written out, as it were, and B's interest is increased by the addition of A's.

The complete process involves two steps: first, the raising of a use and splitting of legal and equitable title by the conveyance; and second, the re-uniting of legal and equitable title when the Statute executes the use. Where O enfeoffs A and heirs to the use of B and heirs, the Statute cannot work until A gets the estate and is seised to the use of B. In a sense, therefore, A must have the estate long enough for the Statute to work on it and execute the use. In conveyances to uses that are executed by the *Statute of Uses*, the feoffee to uses will get the estate for a split second—a scintilla of time—then lose it to the various *cestui que usent*.

Sometimes surprising things can happen during that second, as *Pimbe's Case* (1585), 72 E.R. 528 illustrates. There, after committing treason, A received a conveyance of land from O, to the use of B. B then sold his interest to C. Once A was convicted of treason, any land of which A was seised at the time of the treason or thereafter was forfeited to the Crown. In the split second that A was seised of the legal estate before the *Statute of Uses* executed the use, the estate went to the Crown. Poor C had to accept that B had nothing to sell to C, as B had received nothing. But there is a happy ending—the monarch presented the land to C as an act of grace.

There then is the *Statute of Uses*. It seems brilliantly simple and straightforward, but within a century, conveyancers and courts had developed enough ways around the Statute that it failed utterly to eliminate conveyances to uses. Indeed, it may have given them new life by creating the possibility of interests in land previously unrecognized at common law or in equity.

Conveyances to Uses That Block the Statute of Uses

Recall that the Statute applies only where a person is seised of property to the use of another; that is, where the feoffee to uses has been granted a present freehold estate. Giving the feoffee to uses a leasehold estate thus protected the uses from the Statute. The estate in the *cestui que usent* cannot be greater than the estate given to the feoffee to uses, but, for most purposes, a grant to A for 999 years to the use of B for 999 years is almost as valuable to B as an equitable fee simple.

One could also block the Statute with a conveyance to a corporation. When describing *cestui que usent*, the Statute mentions persons or bodies politick—but persons only when referring to feoffees to uses. Bodies politick in this context means artificial persons—corporations or other legal entities that are treated as natural persons for the purposes of owning property. If the feoffee to uses was a corporation, the Statute was thus avoided, the uses were not executed, and the corporation retained the legal title subject to the obligations to the *cestui que use*.

A third way of blocking the Statute was to give feoffees to uses active duties to perform. Judicial interpretation of the Statute limited it to bare uses, where feoffee to uses did nothing but hold seisin. If, instead, feoffees to uses had to manage the property and pay the rents and profits to *cestui que usent*, the separation of legal and equitable title was maintained, for without legal title the feoffees to uses would be unable to carry out their responsibilities.

Conveyances to Uses That Exhaust the Statute of Uses

Evading the Statute by creating grants that the Statute only partly executed was not as straightforward as blocking its operation completely and so took a little longer to gain judicial acceptance. However, within a century and a half of passage of the *Statute of Uses*, it was possible, by adding a few words to a conveyance, to achieve what had been possible with a conveyance to uses prior to the Statute. One factor in this development was passage of the [*Tenures Abolition Act*, 1660], (U.K.), 12 Car. 2, c. 24, discussed [above in chapter], which, by abolishing feudal incidents, removed some of the significance of the *Statute of Uses* for the Crown.

In the early years after passage of the Statute, neither the common law courts nor the Chancellor would enforce a use on a use. A conveyance from O "to A and heirs to the use of B and heirs to the use of C and heirs" was interpreted as giving A the legal fee simple for a scintilla of time. Then the Statute executed the use and gave A's legal fee simple to B, who already had the equitable fee simple by the grant. Having both sides of the full fee simple, B had all that O had to grant and there was nothing left for C. The words of grant to C were treated as inconsistent with the rest of the grant, and ignored. But after passage of the [*Tenures Abolition Act*], the court of equity began to interpret this grant so as to give some meaning to all its words. The grant of the legal estate to A to the use of B was still executed, so that B got both legal and equitable title. But now the courts ruled that B held legal title for the benefit of C, so equitable title moved from B to C—but equitable title only. The Statute, having executed the first use of the fee simple to B, was exhausted and did not execute the second use of the fee simple to C.

Note that we are dealing not with all uses on a use, but with a use of a fee simple on a use of a fee simple. There is a difference between a use on a use and a use after a use. The Statute will execute fully a grant from O "to A and heirs to the use of B for life, and then to the use of C and heirs." Because C's use of a fee simple follows after B's use of a life estate, it is not a use upon a use. The Statute will execute any number of successive life estates; it is exhausted only by executing a use of a fee simple. ...

Return now to the grant of a use on a use: "to A and heirs to the use of B and heirs to the use of C and heirs." Once courts allowed the second use in fee simple to C, it became possible to eliminate B from the grant. Start with a grant "to A and heirs to the use of A and heirs," which was interpreted as giving A the legal fee simple to hold for the benefit of A. Regardless of the effect of the *Statute of Uses*, A would have both legal and equitable title. Now add another fee simple to this grant, so that it reads "to A and heirs to the use of A and heirs to the use of C and heirs." The use to C is a use upon the first use to A, so it is not executed by the Statute. But A was required to give up equitable title to C, since by the grant A was to hold the estate for the use of C. The cumbersome "to A and heirs to the use of A and heirs" was shortened to "Unto and to the use of A and heirs" which meant the same thing, and *voilà*—you had a form of conveyance with which to separate legal and equitable estates almost as if the *Statute of Uses* had not been passed. ...

The Statute of Uses and Testamentary Dispositions

In the first few years after its passage, the *Statute of Uses* was effective in preventing the use of conveyances to uses to make what were in effect testamentary dispositions. Prior to the Statute, O would enfeoff A to the use of O for O's lifetime, and then to the use of named beneficiaries on the terms and conditions that O specified to A. Loss of this power created such unrest that in 1540 Henry VIII agreed to passage of the *Statute of Wills*, recognizing the right of property owners to dispose by will of all their lands held in soccage tenure, and two-thirds of their lands held in knight service. Judges tended to interpret broadly the powers of disposition given in the *Statute of Wills*, so that it was possible in wills to grant a fee simple without using the magic words of limitation "and heirs." In addition, devises did not have to comply with the legal remainder rules, since they were treated as creating executory interests, regardless of whether the words of the devise expressly raised a use. ...

The Statute of Uses and Executory Interests

[Recall the discussion above regarding the emergence of "executory" interests prior to the *Statute of Uses*.]

... What is the effect of the *Statute of Uses* on executory interests ... ? If you understand the mechanical method by which the Statute operates, you will understand what happens to these interests after 1536. Where a use has been raised, ... the Statute executes the use. Therefore, where O conveyed to "D and heirs for the use of A and heirs but if A marries B then to the use of C and heirs," for a split second D has a legal fee simple, and A an equitable fee simple subject to C's equitable shifting executory interest in fee. The Statute then executes, D disappears, and A has a legal fee simple subject to a legal shifting executory interest in fee simple in C. ...

But how can we have legal shifting and springing interests despite the legal remainder rules? Because, when the Statute turns the equitable interests into legal interests, they are not common law remainders, but legal executory interests created by the operation of the *Statute of Uses*. And the *Statute of Uses* said that *cestui que usent* were to be seised of the same estate in law that they had in equity. Moreover, since purely equitable interests were not subject to the legal remainder rules, judges held that legal executory interests were exempt, too—with one exception that we will discuss soon. Henceforth, by raising a use that was executed by the *Statute of Uses*, conveyancers could create legal future interests that were not possible with common law conveyances.

And remember that by using a form of conveyance that blocked or exhausted the Statute, conveyancers could still create purely equitable interests not subject to the *Statute of Uses* at all. After 1536, then, it was possible to create three kinds of contingent future interests: legal remainders, equitable executory interests and legal executory interests. But be careful. Not all jurisdictions are uniform in their treatment of these possibilities. Nearly every common law jurisdiction, following the English precedent of 1540, now has wills legislation, whereby no use need be raised to create springing and shifting executory devises. In *inter vivos* transfers, however, one generally has to raise a use in order to bring in the *Statute of Uses* and create springing and shifting freeholds.

DISCUSSION NOTE

The Rule in Purefoy v Rogers

McCallum & Sinclair note in their penultimate paragraph that legal executory interests were exempt from the legal remainder rules, "with one exception." The rule in *Purefoy v Rogers* (1671), 85 ER 1181 is that exception. In *Re Crow* (1984), 48 OR (2d) 36 (H Ct J), Krever J described the rule as follows (at 44):

> The following concise and clear explanation of the rule, described in the paragraph preceding the explanation as the "notorious" rule in *Purefoy v. Rogers*, is taken from Megarry and Wade, *The Law of Real Property* (1957), at pp. 192-3:
>
>> This rule probably originated as a rule of construction, but it became a sanctified dogma of the law, to be applied without exception and without regard to the grantor's intentions. "Now, if there be one rule of law more sacred than another, it is this, that no limitation shall be construed to be an executory or shifting use, which can by possibility take effect by way of remainder." This meant that if any limitation, even though contained in a grant to uses or a will, was on any assumption capable of complying with the legal remainder rules, it was to be treated as a legal contingent remainder and not as an executory interest. Clearly this would not endanger limitations which were bound to comply with the rules when so treated. But equally clearly it endangered those limitations whose validity, when treated as contingent remainders, was placed in suspense by rule 4 [of the common law remainder rules]. If in the event such a limitation did not vest in time, it failed, because although it might have complied with the legal remainder rules it had not in fact done so. There were accordingly three possibilities. A contingent interest in a grant to uses or a will, when scrutinised as at the moment of its creation, might either
>>
>> (i)   defy the legal rules from the outset, and be certain to infringe them if it took effect at all, as did springing and shifting interests; or
>>
>> (ii) comply with them from the outset, and be certain to vest within the limits and in the way required at common law; or
>>
>> (iii) be capable of complying with them, but not certain to do so unless events turned out favourably.

Interests in class (i) were unaffected by the rule in *Purefoy v Rogers*; they remained legal executory interests, and were free from the legal rules.

Interests in classes (ii) and (iii) were required to conform to the legal rules and became legal contingent remainders. This could in no way injure class (ii). But class (iii) was exposed to the danger that if events turned out adversely the interest would be invalidated under the "wait and see" rule at some time in the future.

In *Re Crow*, the testator, who died in 1926, had devised a farm to his grandsons R and W for their lives, with remainder to their children. If they had no children, the children of two of the testator's other grandsons, J and C, were to share the remainder interest. W died without issue in 1944, at which point none of the three other grandsons had had children. J and C subsequently had children, and R died without issue in 1983. The court held that the interests were legal and subject to the remainder rules, and that although the half-share of R could be divided among the children of J and C, the undivided half-share of W was subject to the rule in *Purefoy v Rogers*. The remainder following his life estate was one that could have vested during his lifetime, but did not. It therefore could not be construed as a legal executory interest, fell into Megarry & Wade's category (iii), and was subject to natural destruction. In the event, it fell to be distributed as part of the testator's residuary estate.

Note that the rule in *Purefoy v Rogers* has no effect on equitable interests. Do you see why? *Re Crow* has been criticized on the basis that the interests in question should not have been considered legal, because the farm had never been conveyed out of the testator's estate by his executor and there was thus still a subsisting trust: see TG Youdan, "Annotation—Future Interests and the Rule in *Purefoy v Rogers*: The Unnecessary Application of Archaic and Capricious Rules" (1985) 17 ETR 3.

EXERCISE 6 CONVEYANCE TO USES AFTER THE STATUTE OF USES, 1535

After reviewing the extract from McCallum & Sinclair, identify as fully as possible the interests created in the following grants before and after the *Statute of Uses*, 1535. Take particular care to identify whether a given interest is legal or equitable.

Grant	Analysis
1. X grants to A and his heirs.	
Pre-1535	
Post-1535	
2. X grants to A and his heirs to the use of B and his heirs.	
Pre-1535	
Post-1535	
3. X grants to C and his heirs when C shall have attained 21 (C is 19 at the time of the grant).	
Pre-1535	
Post-1535	

Grant	Analysis
4. X grants to A and his heirs to the use of B and his heirs when B shall marry E (B is not yet married to E). Pre-1535	
Post-1535	
5. X grants to C and her heirs, but if C marries D, then to E and his heirs. Pre-1535	
Post-1535	
6. X grants to A and his heirs to the use of B and his heirs, but if B marries C, then to the use of D and his heirs. Pre-1535	
Post-1535	
7. X grants to A and his heirs to the use of B for life, then to the use of B's first child to marry and his or her heirs. Pre-1535	
Post-1535	
8. X grants to A and his heirs to the use of B for life, then to the use of B's first child to marry, before or after B's death, and his or her heirs. Pre-1535	
Post-1535	

4. Abolition of the Statute of Uses and Reform of the Law of Future Interests

The reaction of most students when they learn of the role of the *Statute of Uses* in modern conveyancing and estate planning is incredulity. Why is it that no Canadian province, with the exception of Manitoba, has enacted legislation similar to the *Law of Property Act 1925* in England, which repealed the *Statute of Uses* and made all estates in land equitable except the fee simple absolute in possession and the lease? Equitable estates are not subject to the common law rules regarding legal remainders, making the latter irrelevant in England since 1925. In Manitoba, the *Perpetuities and Accumulations Act*, CCSM c P33 (first enacted in 1984) did not actually repeal the *Statute of Uses*, but rendered it irrelevant by providing that all successive legal interests, "whether valid or invalid at common law or as executory interests," would take effect as equitable interests behind a trust.

Canadian provinces share their reluctance with regard to abolishing the *Statute of Uses* with Northern Ireland, various islands of the Commonwealth Caribbean, and, perhaps more surprisingly, many states in the United States.

OLRC *Basic Principles* suggested a reform of the law on future interests similar to that in Manitoba, advocating the imposition of a statutory trust whenever successive legal interests were created (at 47-60) and the abolition of the *Statute of Uses*. Such a move would, in effect, abolish legal remainders and make the common law rules regarding them irrelevant, along with the rule in *Purefoy v Rogers*.

Equitable Future Interests Before Statute of Uses 1535

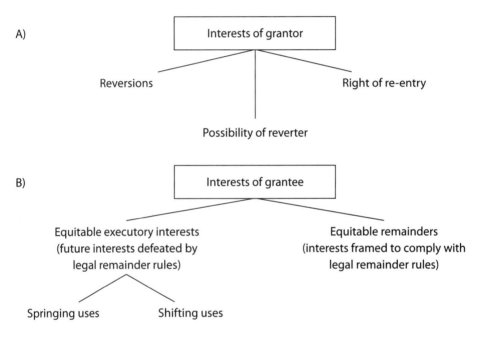

Future Interests After Statute of Uses 1535 and Statute of Wills 1540

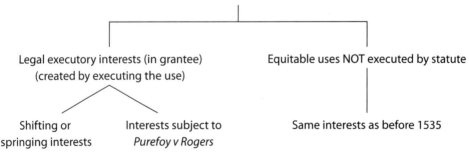

V. THE MODERN TRUST

A. Creating a Trust

Recall from the discussion above that through the device of the "use upon a use," the courts permitted conveyances that split legal and equitable title in the same way that had been allowed before the *Statute of Uses*, 1535. This device became the basis of the modern trust, where assets are conveyed to a trustee to manage on behalf of beneficiaries. With *inter vivos* trusts the *Statute of Uses* must still be invoked today in order to create a "use upon a use." The usual formulas are "unto and to the use of T in trust for A" or "to the use of T in trust for A," but for other possibilities see Ziff at 223-24. Recall, however, that corporations are exempt from the *Statute of Uses*, 1535 and thus trust deeds to corporate trustees do not need to use these formulas.

Modern testamentary dispositions are governed in most provinces by legislation that deems the "personal representative" of the deceased (the executor if there is a will, or the administrator if there is an intestacy) to be a trustee of all the deceased's assets. In Ontario, this provision is found in the *Estates Administration Act*, RSO 1990, c E.22:

> 2(1) All real and personal property that is vested in a person without a right in any other person to take by survivorship, on the person's death, whether testate or intestate and despite any testamentary disposition, devolves to and becomes vested in his or her personal representative from time to time as trustee for the persons by law beneficially entitled thereto, and, subject to the payment of the person's debts and so far as such property is not disposed of by deed, will, contract or other effectual disposition, it shall be administered, dealt with and distributed as if it were personal property not so disposed of.

In those provinces with such a provision, it may be accurate to say that the *Statute of Uses* has, in effect, been "repealed" with respect to testamentary dispositions. In provinces that do not have such a provision, the creation of a testamentary trust is simply a matter of intention, and no particular form of words need be used.

Note that although estates could not be created in personal property at common law (one could not create a life estate in a violin, for example), they can be created today in equity by using a trust. Thus one can convey a violin to a trustee in trust for A to use for her lifetime, and then to be given to A's son on her death. More frequently, the assets of a modern trust will be in the form of corporate shares, bonds, and other financial instruments, as well as realty.

This section deals with *express* trusts. Other kinds of trusts, such as those arising from implied intention (*resulting* trusts), and those imposed by the court in certain circumstances to prevent an injustice (*constructive* trusts), are discussed in Chapters 5 and 6.

B. The Trustee and Beneficiaries

Assuming a trust is validly created, the trustee has legal title to all the trust property, with the accompanying rights of disposition, management, administration, and possession. Note, though, that title to property the trustee holds in trust is totally distinct from title to the trustee's own property. Thus if the trustee experiences personal bankruptcy, none of the trust assets are available to the trustee's own creditors.

The beneficiaries have equitable title (sometimes called "beneficial title"), which involves mainly the right to enjoy the net profits of the trust property in the proportions set out in the trust instrument. Typically, a beneficiary will not have possession of the property, but the trust instrument may permit or direct the trustee to allow a beneficiary to have possession of an asset, such as a family home. The beneficiary's interest is fully alienable, liable to be mortgaged, and exigible for debts: see Sarah Worthington, *Equity*, 2d ed (Oxford: Oxford University Press, 2006) at 64-66. Moreover, there is nothing to prevent an individual from being both trustee and beneficiary at the same time—for example, a testator may leave property to her husband in trust for himself for life, remainder to their children equally. The husband will manage and invest the trust assets during his lifetime, pay the net profits to himself, and upon his death the property will be divided among the children.

The important distinction between a trust and a corporation is that a trust does not have legal personality, but a corporation does. An important corollary of this fact is that there is nothing like "shareholder democracy" in a trust. Unless the trust instrument otherwise provides, a trust beneficiary has no say whatever in the investment decisions or policy of the trustee.

The rights of the trustee noted above are only instrumental, in the sense that they are given to trustees to enable them to better carry out their duties. The main duty of the trustee is a fiduciary duty vis-à-vis the beneficiary that requires trustees always to put the beneficiary's interests ahead of their own, and never to allow their personal interests to affect the decisions made in their capacity as trustee. For example, even if the trustee runs a highly profitable company in his or her personal capacity that would likely provide a very good return for the beneficiaries, the trustee is not allowed to invest trust money in the company. Even technical conflicts of interest are treated very seriously by trust law: DWM Waters, Lionel Smith & Mark Gillen, *Waters' Law of Trusts in Canada*, 4th ed (Toronto: Carswell, 2012) [Waters] at 930-41. The fiduciary duty owed by the government of Canada to Aboriginal peoples with respect to dealings with their lands is discussed in Chapter 8.

The other principal duty of the trustee is to act as a "prudent investor" in the investment and management of the trust assets; this duty arose from the common law, but is also codified in the *Trustee Act*, RSO 1990, c T.23, s 27. Trustees are not insurers, and are not required to make good on all investment losses, should they arise. But they are required to meet the "prudent-investor" standard in their dealings with the trust assets.

Should the trustee fail in either or both of these duties, the trust beneficiary has important personal and proprietary remedies. If the trustee has fallen below the requisite standard of care regarding investment or management duties, the beneficiary has a personal action against the trustee (and many professional trustees carry trustee insurance to cover this risk). Should the trustee have dealt dishonestly with trust property, an action in breach of trust may be available against the trustee, while the beneficiary may follow the property into the hands of any third party who has acquired it, so long as he or she is not a bona fide purchaser for value of a legal estate without notice. This is where the concept of "equitable ownership" is perhaps most evident. These remedies were developed by the Court of Chancery, and provisions of the *Trustee Act* may also be relevant in establishing liability or in excusing the trustee from liability: see e.g. *Trustee Act*, s 35, authorizing a court to excuse certain breaches of trust where the trustee has acted honestly and reasonably; on remedies of the beneficiary generally, see Waters, chs 25 and 26.

C. Ending the Trust

A trust normally ends when the trust instrument specifies it should end. If the instrument creates an equitable life tenancy followed by a remainder to, say, three (adult) children in equal shares, it is common for the trust instrument to direct that the trustee shall sell the trust assets on the death of the life tenant and distribute the proceeds equally to the three children. Upon distribution, the trust would end, because the children would be the full owners in law and equity. There is one situation, however, where the beneficiaries can terminate the trust prematurely, contrary to the trust creator's intention. If all the beneficiaries of a particular trust are of the age of majority, of sound mind, and have no conditions attached to their interests, they may together demand that the trust be ended and that legal title to the trust assets be transferred to them in the proportions to which they are entitled under the trust instrument. This is known as the rule in *Saunders v Vautier* (1841), 4 Beav 115, and it illustrates once again the potency of the notion of equitable ownership.

D. Modern Functions of the Trust

The modern trust has a wide variety of functions. In addition to its traditional role in the protection of minors and incapable and vulnerable parties, the trust is widely used in the investment world (most mutual funds and many pension funds are structured as trusts) and in philanthropy (where the charitable trust is a familiar feature). Trusts of land, the favoured subject of earlier times, have given way to the trust of investments as the main type of modern trust. The change in the nature of trust assets transformed the trust itself. The trust's rationale shifted from conserving a particular asset over time (a landed estate) to managing a fund of constantly changing assets (bonds, stocks, mortgages) to derive the best possible income (consistent with risk tolerance) for the beneficiaries: see MR Chesterman, "Family Settlements on Trust: Landowners and the Rising Bourgeoisie" in GR Rubin & David Sugarman, eds, *Law, Economy and Society, 1750-1919: Essays in the History of English Law* (Abingdon, UK: Professional Books, 1984).

EXERCISE 7 THE MODERN TRUST

Identify the interests created in the following dispositions as fully as possible, including any interest retained by the grantor or testator, and briefly explain your reasons.

Grant or Devise	Analysis
1. X grants unto and to the use of A in fee simple in trust for B in fee simple.	
2. X grants to Canada Trust in fee simple in trust for A in fee simple.	
3. X grants to A in fee simple to collect the rents and profits for the benefit of B in fee simple.	

Grant or Devise	Analysis
4. X grants unto and to the use of T in fee simple in trust for my wife W for life and after her death in trust for my daughter upon her admission to the Bar of Ontario.	
5. X devises to P when she reaches the age of 25 (P is 15 at the time of X's death).	
6. X devises to T in fee simple in trust for A for life, then in trust for B, but if B is ever disbarred, then in trust for C.	
7. X devises to T in fee simple in trust for A for life, then 10 years after A's death, in trust for B in fee simple.	

VI. THE RULE AGAINST PERPETUITIES

The rule against perpetuities is in a sense the capstone of the law of future interests. Without the rule, property owners could create estates that might spring up at far distant times in the future, possibly rendering land or other assets inalienable for long periods of time. O might leave land to her first daughter for life, then to that daughter's first daughter for life, then to that daughter's first daughter for life, *ad infinitum*, with alternative gifts if there were no daughter in a particular generation. Likewise, conditions might be attached to property that would endure for generations—for example, "to B in fee simple, but if the land *ever* ceases to be farmed, my estate will have the right to re-enter."

Recall that the English courts had interpreted the *Statute of Uses* as permitting springing and shifting legal executory interests that could break the common law remainder rules and, in the 17th century, resurrected the "use" as the "trust," allowing springing and shifting equitable interests to be created that likewise did not need to follow the common law remainder rules. The judges then began to experience some unease about the unlimited amount of flexibility they had permitted wealth-holders to exercise. As a result, they created the rule against perpetuities, beginning with the *Duke of Norfolk's Case* (1681), 2 Swans 454, 22 ER 930; the rule did not take its modern form, however, until *Cadell v Palmer* (1833), 1 Cl & F 372, 6 ER 956 (HL). Until the mid-20th century there was no statutory reform of the rule, so that it is the product of nearly three centuries of judge-made law. The rule seems to have attracted a disproportionate share of academic commentary over the years, but for an excellent overview and critique, see Ronald H Maudsley, *The Modern Law of Perpetuities* (London: Butterworths, 1979) [Maudsley].

A. What Is the Rule Against Perpetuities?

The rule sets a maximum period within which any *contingent or executory interest* must vest, if it vests at all. It is framed negatively—if there is any *possibility* that the contingency might be satisfied *outside* (that is, beyond) the period, the interest will be *void ab initio* (that is, void from the moment the grant or will was supposed to take effect). For someone drafting a will or grant containing contingent or executory interests, this means that the interests must be framed so that the period within which any contingency may be satisfied must be restricted to the perpetuity period. This contingency is called the "vesting event."

B. What Is Meant by the "Vesting Event"?

Consider the following:

> To T in trust for A for life, then in trust for the first grandchild of A to marry.

The vesting event is the contingency that needs to be satisfied for the interest to vest. Thus, in this disposition the marriage of A's first grandchild to marry is the "vesting event."

In the case of a condition subsequent the "vesting event" will be the breach of the condition, which is the prerequisite to the exercise of the right of re-entry:

> To B in fee simple, but if the land ceases to be farmed, my executor is to have the right to re-enter the property and terminate B's estate.

The land ceasing to be farmed is the "vesting event," because it gives rise to the executor's right of re-entry.

In both these cases, the rule directs that the marriage of A's grandchild or the land ceasing to be farmed must happen, *if they happen at all*, within the perpetuity period and that there be no possibility that they could happen outside it.

C. What Is the Perpetuity Period?

The rule allows considerable flexibility to wealth-holders in creating contingent interests. It allows vesting to be suspended for a whole human generation plus the minority of the next generation, reflected in the formula "a life in being plus 21 years." In other words, the law allows property to be rendered inalienable in practical terms for a period of some 70 to 80 years or more.

D. How Is the Perpetuity Period Measured?

This is the most difficult aspect of the rule. It would have been easier if the common law had adopted a uniform period of, say, 80 years from the date of the grant or will within which all vesting events had to occur. (Some reform statutes adopt this approach, as we will see below.) Had it done so, to return to the examples above, we would then know that if no grandchild of A had married 80 years from the creation of the trust, the gift would be void at that time; or if the land had been farmed continuously for 80 years after the grant, the executor would lose the right to re-enter, and B's heirs or assigns would take a fee simple absolute at that time.

When the rule was adopted in the later 17th century, however, the courts were influenced by the type of disposition that was dominant at that time—for example, a disposition where a father O granted land to his son A for life, with remainder to A's eldest son at 21, whether that son turned 21 before or after A's death. In many cases the vesting event (the grandson turning 21) would occur within A's lifetime, but in a worst-case scenario (if A died around the time his son was born) vesting would be postponed until 21 years after A's death. The courts decided that this was a legitimate period within which to postpone vesting, and adopted the formula "a life in being plus 21 years" as the definition of the perpetuity period. In other words, *the period varies with every individual grant or will that creates contingent, executory, or conditional interests*. The "lives in being" will be different in each grant or will.

In the example just given, A is the life in being. If A is male, there is only one way in which the contingent interest of his (as yet unborn) eldest son could vest outside the period of A's life plus 21 years, and that is if A died with no sons but leaving his wife pregnant with a child who turned out to be a son. If those events actually happened, the law allowed the perpetuity period to be extended by the period of human gestation to see if the child was a boy. With this slight easing of the rule, it can be seen that there is no *possibility* that the grandson's interest will vest *outside* the perpetuity period. In other words, it is *guaranteed* to vest within it, *if it vest at all*. (Remember, the common law did not know anything about sperm straws or frozen embryos, and possibilities arising from these modes of reproduction are not taken into account when dealing with the common law rule.)

And what if A never does have a son? That is the significance of the words "*if it vest at all.*" It cannot be guaranteed that the vesting event *will* occur, and the rule does not require that. It was noted above that conditions attached to estates must be events that *may or may not* ever happen. So, by definition, the ultimate occurrence of the vesting event cannot be guaranteed. A may not ever have a son. If he does not, O's reversion will come into effect upon A's death. That has nothing to do with the rule. The rule's concern is to ensure that the grandson's interest was framed in such a way that the vesting event attached to it *could not occur* outside the perpetuity period. In this example, the grandson's interest is *valid* according to the rule, but he must still be born and reach age 21 to take his interest.

E. Who Is a "Life in Being"?

Anyone alive in the world at the time a grant or will takes effect is potentially a life in being, but that class is too large to be practical. Lives in being must be (1) human and (2) not so numerous as to be impractical to keep track of. Aside from that, anyone (there is a minimum of one) who can help answer the following question can be a life in being:

> Is it *guaranteed* that the vesting event in this disposition must occur, if it occur at all, within 21 years of the death of this person?

If there is at least one person about whom this can be said, the rule is satisfied and the gift is valid. The person does not have to be connected to the disposition in any way as long as he or she allows us to answer the above question positively.

Consider the following examples:

> A grants "to the first of my great-grandchildren to go for a walk with X."

A has no children at the time of the grant, and X is 40 years old. It is extremely unlikely that A will have a great-grandchild in sufficient time for him or her to go for a walk with X before X dies. But that is not the point. The perpetuities point is that the grant is framed so as to allow us to answer the above question positively. X is a living person, and the walk will happen, *if ever*, within X's own lifetime. X is the measuring life and thus the rule is satisfied. The unborn great-grandchild's interest is *valid* with regard to perpetuities, and it will only be extinguished if and when X dies without the requisite walk having occurred. But it will be extinguished because no one has satisfied the terms of the grant itself, not because of the rule. At that point there will be a reversion to A's estate.

Note that the disposition may not even refer to the lives in being—they can be *inferred*.

C wills all her property "to my first grandchild at 21."

Upon her death, C has left two children, D and E, but no grandchildren. One might say, there are no lives in being at all in this will, because no potential beneficiaries are born yet. But D and E are the lives in being. They allow us to answer the above question positively. No child could take this interest more than 21 years after the death of either D or E (allowing for the possibility of an extra nine months if necessary, as described above). Thus, the disposition satisfies the rule. There will be a resulting trust to C's intestate heirs if C's will has not provided what is to happen to the income in the interim.

Note that when the rule is satisfied, as in the above example, we are allowed to "wait and see" how events turn out. D and E may not have any children, such that on the death of the survivor of them, there will be no grandchildren and thus no one to receive the gift. But that has nothing to do with the rule. The gift will fail in this case because no one satisfied the conditions of being a grandchild of C and reaching 21.

If a grant is drafted so that there is *no* "life in being" within the meaning of the rule, then we are *not* allowed to wait and see how events turn out; the interest in question is then void from the outset (*ab initio*). This problem eventually led to reform of the rule in some jurisdictions, as discussed below.

F. Solving the Life in Being Problem: The Royal Lives Clause

Lawyers created a solution to the lives in being problem in the form of the "royal lives clause." Recall that the lives in being do not have to have any connection with the disposition and can be a class of people as long as it is not too large and its members remain ascertainable. Lawyers decided that the living descendants of a past or present monarch formed an ideal class satisfying these requirements. Consider the following example, drawn from *Laurin v Iron Ore Co of Canada* (1977), 82 DLR (3d) 634 (Nfld SC (TD)). In this case, Iron Ore had built houses for its employees and sold them at a discounted price. The company wished to be able to repurchase the houses once employees stopped working for it. The deed to each employee thus contained a *quid pro quo*: the company granted the fee simple to the employee, and the employee granted back to the company an option to purchase the estate exercisable by the company on the employee leaving the company. Options are considered interests in land subject to the rule. To comply with the rule, the following clause was added to the option:

> The option granted … shall … be open for acceptance at any time within the period commencing on the date hereof and ending on the twenty-first anniversary of the death of the longest lived of the descendants now living of Her Majesty Queen Elizabeth the Second.

The conveyance occurred in 1971, when the Queen did not yet have any grandchildren. At that time the class of "descendants now living" of the Queen would have been her four children, who ranged in age from 7 (Prince Edward, b 1964) to 23 (Prince Charles, b 1948). The perpetuity period would thus be measured by the life of the last survivor of these four royals, plus a period of 21 years. The option, by its own terms, could not be exercised after that date—it would not be "open for acceptance" after that date. Assuming Prince Edward was the survivor and lived to be 90, dying in 2054, the period would last until 2054 + 21 years, or 2075. It is highly unlikely that the company would be interested in invoking these option arrangements so far into the future, but use of the royal lives clause ensured that the option would not be struck down at the outset.

Using a royal lives clause today would mean that the class of the Queen's descendants would be much larger (13 members in 2013), but such a class would not be too large; in addition, the eventual deaths of its members will always be a matter of public record, so that there will never be a problem with deciding how long to "wait and see." The royal lives clause is a valid means of "perpetuity proofing" any contingent or executory interest in any jurisdiction where the rule still exists.

G. Problems with the Rule Against Perpetuities

The main problem with the common law rule is its requirement of a *guarantee* that the vesting event could not occur outside the period. This led the common law to consider all sorts of remote possibilities as violating that guarantee:

> "To A's first grandchild to reach 21," where A is an 80-year-old woman with two adult children and six grandchildren all under the age of 21.

There is a more than 99 percent probability that one of the existing grandchildren, who are all alive, will take this gift, and the first grandchild to turn 21 will obviously do so within his or her own lifetime. But according to the reasoning of the rule, all A's existing children and grandchildren might die, and A might have *another* child, born *after* the date of the grant (and thus *not* a life in being) who might produce the first grandchild to reach 21. The vesting event thus *might* happen more than 21 years after the deaths of all the possible lives in being (A, her existing children, and grandchildren).

One might object that it is impossible for an 80-year-old woman to have a child, but for the purposes of the rule the common law recognized no upper or lower limits on the age at which a woman might have a child (or a man might father one). In the academic literature on perpetuities, these are referred to as the "fertile octogenarian" and the "precocious toddler" cases. The grandchild's interest is thus *void* according to the rule. For a case very similar to this one, see *Ward v Van der Loeff*, [1924] AC 653.

Note that the maker of this disposition in all likelihood meant to say "to A's first grandchild (*being a child of one of her living children*) to reach 21," because the maker never dreamed A would have another child. Nonetheless, the common law interpreted the disposition in the way described above, according to the "rule of remorseless construction." This rule states that you must interpret the disposition in question in a literal manner, without trying to adopt a construction that might avoid a possible perpetuities problem: see Maudsley, 36-37. Many perpetuities problems can thus be avoided by careful drafting.

As a Nova Scotia judge observed recently,

> For many lawyers and judges, the rule against perpetuities is like a trip down Alice's rabbit hole to a land where things are not always what they seem. … [O]ne of the more vexing aspects of the rule is that it can invalidate a gift or interest even where the parties' intentions are clear and even if it is highly probable that the transfer will occur within the perpetuities period.

(*Silver v Fulton*, 2011 NSSC 127 at paras 18-20, *per* Coady J.) The perpetuities problem in this case was comparatively straightforward. The parties had entered into an oral agreement whereby one granted an option to purchase land to the other. As noted above, an option to purchase land is considered an interest in land subject to the rule. The agreement did not specify any life in being or any time period within which the option had to be exercised. Where no life in being is specified the perpetuity period is 21 years, but the parties must *explicitly* frame the interest so that it cannot vest or be exercised (in the case of an option) outside the 21-year period. Even though the parties expected the option to be exercised within 10 to 20 years, they did not specify this period in their agreement. As a result, the option was found to be void.

Note that the rule applies to all forms of property, not just land. In corporate and commercial transactions there are many instances in which parties may want to create contingent interests in personal property such as corporate shares, where there are no "obvious" lives in being. The rule will be applied to invalidate such agreements unless they expressly address the perpetuities problem.

H. Statutory Reform

The rule against perpetuities is an obvious candidate for statutory reform. Ontario was the first province in Canada to adopt a reform statute, the *Perpetuities Act, 1966*, SO 1966, c 113 (see now RSO 1990, c P.9). There are three main principles of the reform:

1. *Reverse the common law presumption of invalidity with a presumption of validity.* All contingent or executory interests are presumed *valid* until *actual events* establish that the vesting event cannot occur within the perpetuity period. This is called the "wait-and-see" principle. An interest may still be void because it did not vest within the period, but it will be void *at that future date*, not *ab initio*, as with the common law rule. Until then, the interest is potentially valid.

2. *Address the caricature cases with specific provisions.* For example, replace the possibility of the "fertile octogenarian" and the "precocious toddler" with presumptions regarding the age of child-bearing.

3. *Subject rights of re-entry and possibilities of reverter to a uniform period of 40 years, or a life in being plus 21 years if there are any relevant lives.* If the event in question does not occur within the relevant period, the right of re-entry or possibility of reverter will be rendered void and the grantee will take an absolute estate. Note that the statute makes the possibility of reverter subject to the rule, when it was exempt at common law.

There are sometimes disadvantages in being first in the field of law reform. There are two main problems with the Ontario reform. The first is that the reform is only prospective, such that all dispositions coming into effect prior to 6 September 1966 continue to be governed by the common law rule. The second, and larger, problem with the reform is that, with a few exceptions, it does nothing to change the perpetuity period itself.

6(1) Except as provided in section 9, subsection 13(3) and subsections 15(2) and (3), the perpetuity period shall be measured in the same way as if this Act had not been passed, but, in measuring that period by including a life in being when the interest was created, no life shall be included other than that of any person whose life, at the time the interest was created, limits or is a relevant factor that limits in some way the period within which the conditions for vesting of the interest may occur.

(2) A life that is a relevant factor in limiting the time for vesting of any part of a gift to a class shall be a relevant life in relation to the entire class.

(3) Where there is no life satisfying the conditions of subsection (1), the perpetuity period is twenty-one years.

The statute does not change the vague common law test on lives in being. Logically, however, we cannot know *how long* to wait and see unless we are absolutely sure who the lives in being are. In this respect, reform statutes such as that of British Columbia may be preferable. Pursuant to the *Perpetuity Act*, RSBC 1996, c 358, there are two choices for determining the perpetuity period:

1. If there are no lives in being, or if the parties have expressly selected a period of 80 years, the period is 80 years (s 7).

2. If there are lives in being, the period is a life in being plus 21 years, but the lives in being must be found in a closed list of such lives as found in s 10.

Other provinces, beginning with Manitoba in 1984, have taken the bolder step of abolishing the rule with retrospective effect: see *Perpetuities and Accumulations Act*, CCSM c P33; *Trustee Act*, SS 2009, c T-23.01 (rule against perpetuities abolished as of 1 January 2010); and *Perpetuities Act*, SNS 2011, c 42 (rule against perpetuities abolished as of 23 July 2013). These jurisdictions have not been persuaded that the original policy rationale of the rule is still valid. Recall that most assets that might be the subject of contingent interests are held in trust, where the trustee is under a duty to invest the assets and keep them productive. When a trust holds a constantly changing portfolio of assets there would seem to be little danger of property being rendered inalienable. In addition, variation of trusts legislation has existed for many decades to provide some flexibility in the management of trusts that may endure over long periods of time.

Still, abolishing the rule may give rise to its own problems. The spectre of perpetually valid rights of re-entry or executory interests springing up many generations in the future is one that has disturbed some reformers. Nova Scotia, in its perpetuities reform legislation, tried to anticipate these problems. Following the recommendations of the Nova Scotia Law Reform Commission, the legislation creates a mechanism to prevent such interests from becoming a clog on the alienation of property after the abolition of the rule against perpetuities: see Nova Scotia Law Reform Commission, *The Rule Against Perpetuities, Final Report* (Halifax: Commission, 2010) at 41-49. The Nova Scotia *Perpetuities Act*, SNS 2011, c 42, s 5 thus amends the *Real Property Act*, RSNS 1989, c 385, s 30 to provide that "a person interested in real property may apply to court for an order varying or terminating an interest in the real property to which this Section applies, whether the interest arose before or after the coming into force of this Section." The interests to which the section applies are declared to be "every contingent interest in real property ... *other than* a contingent interest in real property held on a trust under any will, settlement, or other disposition" (italics added). As in other provinces, variation of trusts legislation already clothes the court with such a power with regard to equitable interests: see *Variation of Trusts Act*, RSNS 1989, c 486 and *Variation of Trusts Act*, RSO 1990, c V.1.

EXERCISE 8 THE RULE AGAINST PERPETUITIES

Identify as fully as possible the interests in the following dispositions. For those that are contingent or executory, discuss whether they comply with the rule against perpetuities or not. Briefly explain your conclusions. In each case, indicate how the perpetuities problem would be analyzed under the common law rule, and under the reformed rule contained in the *Perpetuities Act* of Ontario. If you find any of the interests to infringe the rule against perpetuities, indicate how the instrument might be redrafted to comply with the rule.

Grant or Devise	Analysis
1. X grants to A so long as the land is used for school purposes, and then to B.	
Common law rule	
Perpetuities Act (Ontario)	
2a. X grants to A in fee simple, but if the land ceases to be used for school purposes, I or my heirs shall have the right to re-enter and end A's interest.	
Common law rule	
Perpetuities Act (Ontario)	
2b. X grants to A for life, remainder to B in fee simple when she reaches 25 (B is 15 at the time of the grant).	
Common law rule	
Perpetuities Act (Ontario)	
2c. X grants unto and to the use of T in trust for A 10 years from today's date.	
Common law rule	
Perpetuities Act (Ontario)	
3. X devises to T in trust for A for life, then in trust for A's nephews and nieces when the youngest shall have reached 21 (A has 5 nieces and nephews, all under 21; all A's siblings have died, as have A's parents).	
Common law rule	
Perpetuities Act (Ontario)	

Grant or Devise	Analysis
4. X devises to T in trust for A for life, then in trust for A's nephews and nieces when the youngest shall have reached 21 (A has 5 nieces and nephews, all under 21; all A's siblings have died, but A's mother is still alive). Common law rule	
Perpetuities Act (Ontario)	
5. X devises to T in trust for the first child of B to be called to the Bar of Ontario (B has 4 children at the date of X's death). Common law rule	
Perpetuities Act (Ontario)	

VII. THE FUNDAMENTAL PRINCIPLES OF LAND LAW AND LAW REFORM

The doctrine of estates in land, including its extension to personal property by means of the trust, provides wealth-holders with a great deal of flexibility in ordering their affairs. Yet it features many archaic rules that are capricious in their application and may operate to frustrate the reasonable intentions of those making dispositions of their property. In England the law of real property underwent a major reform with the enactment of the *Law of Property Act 1925*, but in Canada reforms have been piecemeal; only Manitoba has come close to undertaking a major reform, with the 1984 *Perpetuities and Accumulations Act*. Even in Manitoba, the rule in *Shelley's Case* survives, along with the troublesome distinction between determinable and defeasible estates.

There is no shortage of academic critique of the existing state of the law, or of proposals for change by law reform bodies, as noted at various points in this chapter. But a certain inertia with respect to law reform in this area exists at both the judicial and political levels. Judges seem unwilling to abolish outmoded rules, as noted in the discussion of the rule in *Shelley's Case* in *Re Rynard*, even though such rules are part of the common law and not found in statute law. Legislators also seem unwilling to take action. What explains this unwillingness to bring the law of real property into the modern era?

The reluctance of judges to reform or abolish these rules is perhaps understandable. The very antiquity of the rules suggests that if the legislature had wanted to abolish them, it would have done so by now. That the legislature has not yet done so suggests to judges that a deferential stance is warranted. It is also the case that judicial action alone cannot effect a major reform of the entire corpus of real property principles, as was accomplished by the English Act of 1925. Judicial action can only deal with one rule or principle at a time, following the hazards of litigation.

To what can we attribute the legislative inaction in this area? Legislative time is a scarce commodity, and it is not difficult to think of many pressing issues of public policy that require attention more urgently than basic land law principles. Yet Manitoba managed to enact a major reform, and more recently Saskatchewan and Nova Scotia have abolished the rule against perpetuities in spite of crowded legislative agendas. The common factor in these instances is the existence of a positive rapport between the provincial law reform commission and the government of the day. All three of these initiatives were preceded by careful study and consideration of various alternatives by the respective law reform commissions.

The governmental budget reductions of the 1990s, however, led to the disappearance of law reform commissions in some provinces, notably Ontario's in 1996 and British Columbia's in 1997. The timing of the decision in Ontario was particularly unfortunate, because the OLRC released its *Report on Basic Principles of Land Law* in 1996, just as the agency was being terminated. Although new law reform agencies of a non-governmental nature have been created in British Columbia (the BC Law Institute) and Ontario (the Law Commission of Ontario), it remains to be seen whether these bodies will be able to champion reform of the land law in a way that will capture legislative attention.

CHAPTER REFERENCES

Baker, G Blaine & Jim Phillips, eds. *Essays in the History of Canadian Law, vol VIII: In Honour of RCB Risk* (Toronto: University of Toronto Press for the Osgoode Society for Canadian Legal History, 1999).

Bell, HE. *History and Records of the Court of Wards and Liveries* (Cambridge: Cambridge University Press, 1953).

Bittermann, Rusty & Margaret McCallum. *The Lady Landlords of Prince Edward Island: Imperial Dreams and the Defence of Property* (Montreal & Kingston: McGill-Queen's University Press, 2008).

Boodman, Martin et al. *Quebec Civil Law: An Introduction to Quebec Private Law* (Toronto: Emond Montgomery, 1993).

Borrows, John. *Crown and Aboriginal Occupations of Land: A History and Comparison* (Toronto: Ipperwash Inquiry, 2005).

Brooks, Kim, ed. *Justice Bertha Wilson: One Woman's Difference* (Vancouver: UBC Press, 2009).

Buck, AR. "'This Remnant of Feudalism': Primogeniture and Political Culture in Colonial New South Wales, with Some Canadian Comparisons" in John McLaren, AR Buck & Nancy E Wright, eds, *Despotic Dominion: Property Rights in British Settler Societies* (Vancouver: UBC Press, 2005).

Buckner, Phillip, ed. *Canada and the British Empire* (Oxford: Oxford University Press, 2008).

Chesterman, MR. "Family Settlements on Trust: Landowners and the Rising Bourgeoisie" in GR Rubin & David Sugarman, eds, *Law, Economy and Society, 1750-1919: Essays in the History of English Law* (Abingdon, UK: Professional Books, 1984).

Côté, JE. "The Reception of English Law" (1977) 15 Alta L Rev 29.

Devonshire, Peter. "Possibilities of Reverter and Rights of Re-entry for Conditions Broken: The Modern Context for Determinable and Conditional Interests in Land" (1990) 13 Dal LJ 650.

Erickson, AL. *Women and Property in Early Modern England* (London: Routledge, 1993).

Friedman, Lawrence. Review of Carole Shammas, Marylynn Salmon & Michel Dahlin, *Inheritance in America: From Colonial Times to the Present* (New Brunswick, NJ: Rutgers University Press, 1987) in (1988) 6 LHR 499.

Friedmann, Daniel & Daphne Barak-Erez, eds. *Human Rights in Private Law* (Oxford: Hart, 2001).

Girard, Philip. "British Justice, English Law, and Canadian Legal Culture" in Phillip Buckner, ed, *Canada and the British Empire* (Oxford: Oxford University Press, 2008).

Girard, Philip. "History and Development of Equity" in Faye Woodman & Mark R Gillen, eds, *The Law of Trusts: A Contextual Approach*, 2d ed (Toronto: Emond Montgomery, 2008).

Girard, Philip. "Land Law, Liberalism, and the Agrarian Ideal: British North America, 1750-1920" in John McLaren, AR Buck & Nancy E Wright, eds, *Despotic Dominion: Property Rights in British Settler Societies* (Vancouver: UBC Press, 2005).

Girard, Philip. "The Maritime Provinces, 1850-1939: Lawyers and Legal Institutions" (1995) 23 Man LJ 379.

Glenn, HP. "Persuasive Authority" (1987) 32 McGill LJ 261.

Grattan, Sheena & Heather Conway. "Testamentary Clauses in Restraint of Religion in the Twenty-First Century: An Anglo-Canadian Perspective" (2005) 50 McGill LJ 511.

Gray, Kevin & Susan Francis Gray. *Elements of Land Law*, 5th ed (Oxford: Oxford University Press, 2009).

Hansmann, Henry & Reinier Kraakman. "Property, Contract and Verification: The Numerus Clausus Problem and the Divisibility of Rights" (2002) 31 J Legal Stud S373.

Irvine, John. "Unsettled Estates: Manitoba's Forgotten Statute and the Chupryk Case" (2011) 35 Man LJ 49.

La Forest, Anne Warner. *Anger & Honsberger Law of Real Property*, loose-leaf, 3d ed (Aurora, ON: Canada Law Book, 2006).

Laskin, Bora. *The British Tradition in Canadian Law* (London: Stevens, 1969).

Laskin, Bora. *Cases and Notes on Land Law* (Toronto: University of Toronto Press, 1964).

Macpherson, CB. "The Meaning of Property" in CB Macpherson, ed, *Property: Mainstream and Critical Positions* (Toronto: University of Toronto Press, 1978).

Macpherson, CB, ed. *Property: Mainstream and Critical Positions* (Toronto: University of Toronto Press, 1978).

Matthews, Keith, comp. *Compilation and Commentary on the Constitutional Laws of Seventeenth Century Newfoundland* (St John's: Memorial University of Newfoundland, 1975).

Maudsley, Ronald H. *The Modern Law of Perpetuities* (London: Butterworths, 1979).

McCallum, Margaret E. "The Sacred Rights of Property: Title, Entitlement, and the Land Question in Nineteenth-Century Prince Edward Island" in G Blaine Baker & Jim Phillips, eds, *Es-*

says in the History of Canadian Law, vol VIII: In Honour of RCB Risk (Toronto: University of Toronto Press for the Osgoode Society for Canadian Legal History, 1998).

McCallum, Margaret E & Alan M Sinclair. *An Introduction to Real Property Law*, 6th ed (Toronto: LexisNexis, 2012).

McLaren, John, AR Buck & Nancy E Wright, eds. *Despotic Dominion: Property Rights in British Settler Societies* (Vancouver: UBC Press, 2005).

Megarry, Robert & HWR Wade. *The Law of Real Property*, 5th ed (London: Stevens & Sons, 1984).

Morton, WL. *The Kingdom of Canada* (Toronto: McClelland & Stewart, 1963).

Mossman, MJ. "Bertha Wilson: 'Silences' in a Woman's Life Story" in Kim Brooks, ed, *Justice Bertha Wilson: One Woman's Difference* (Vancouver: UBC Press, 2009).

Nova Scotia Law Reform Commission. *The Rule Against Perpetuities, Final Report* (Halifax: Commission, 2010).

Ogilvie, Margaret. *Historical Introduction to Legal Studies* (Scarborough, ON: Carswell, 1982).

Ontario Law Reform Commission. *Report on Basic Principles of Land Law* (Toronto: Ministry of the Attorney General, 1996).

Orkin, Mark M. *The Great Stork Derby* (Don Mills, ON: General, 1981).

Phillips, Jim. "Anti-Discrimination, Freedom of Property Disposition, and the Public Policy of Charitable Educational Trusts: A Comment on Re Canada Trust Company and Ontario Human Rights Commission" (1990) 9:3 Philanthropist 3.

Rubin, GR & David Sugarman, eds. *Law, Economy and Society, 1750-1919: Essays in the History of English Law* (Abingdon, UK: Professional Books, 1984).

Saul, John Ralston. *A Fair Country: Telling Truths About Canada* (Toronto: Viking Canada, 2008).

Shammas, Carole, Marylynn Salmon & Michel Dahlin. *Inheritance in America: From Colonial Times to the Present* (New Brunswick, NJ: Rutgers University Press, 1987).

Simpson, AWB. *An Introduction to the History of the Land Law* (Oxford: Oxford University Press, 1961).

Simpson, AWB. *Leading Cases in the Common Law* (Oxford & New York: Clarendon Press, 1995).

Smith, Henry Nash. *The American West as Symbol and Myth* (Cambridge, MA: Harvard University Press, 1970).

Spring, Eileen. *Law, Land and Family: Aristocratic Inheritance in England, 1300-1800* (Chapel Hill: University of North Carolina Press, 1993).

Van Warmelo, P. *An Introduction to the Principles of Roman Civil Law* (Cape Town, SA: Juta and Co, 1976).

Waters, DWM, Lionel Smith & Mark Gillen. *Waters' Law of Trusts in Canada*, 4th ed (Toronto: Carswell, 2012).

Weinrib, Lorraine E & Ernest J Weinrib. "Constitutional Values and Private Law in Canada" in Daniel Friedmann & Daphne Barak-Erez, eds, *Human Rights in Private Law* (Oxford: Hart, 2001).

Wicken, William C. *Mi'kmaq Treaties on Trial: History, Land, and Donald Marshall Junior* (Toronto: University of Toronto Press, 2002).

Woodman, Faye & Mark R Gillen, eds. *The Law of Trusts: A Contextual Approach*, 2d ed (Toronto: Emond Montgomery, 2008).

Worthington, Sarah. *Equity*, 2d ed (Oxford: Oxford University Press, 2006).

Youdan, TG. "Annotation—Future Interests and the Rule in Purefoy v Rogers: The Unnecessary Application of Archaic and Capricious Rules" (1985) 17 ETR 3.

Ziff, Bruce. "The Irreversibility of Commodification" (2005) 16 Stellenbosch L Rev 283.

Ziff, Bruce. *Principles of Property Law*, 5th ed (Scarborough, ON: Carswell, 2010).

Ziff, Bruce. *Unforeseen Legacies: Reuben Wells Leonard and the Leonard Foundation Trust* (Toronto: University of Toronto Press for the Osgoode Society for Canadian Legal History, 2000).

Ziff, Bruce. "Warm Reception in a Cold Climate: English Property Law and the Suppression of the Canadian Legal Identity" in John McLaren, AR Buck & Nancy E Wright, eds, *Despotic Dominion: Property Rights in British Settler Societies* (Vancouver: UBC Press, 2005).

Ziff, B & MM Litman. "Shelley's Rule in a Modern Context: Clearing the 'Heir'" (1984) 34 UTLJ 170.

CHAPTER FOUR

Bailment, Licences, and Leases: Dividing Title and Possession

I. INTRODUCTION: TITLE AND POSSESSION

In Chapter 3 we saw how title to and possession of land could be divided via the doctrine of estates. The holder of a fee simple remainder, for example, has title but only a deferred right to possession if a life tenant is currently in possession of the land. In bailments, a similar although not identical division arises, with the bailor retaining title while the bailee has possession. In such cases, the law must regulate the rights of the parties with regard to each other and with regard to their rights against third parties who may damage the item in question, as when a negligent third party causes harm to an object that is in possession of a bailee. This chapter explores the theme of the division of title and possession through three common relationships: bailment, licences, and leases. Whereas Chapter 3 considered only land law, these three relationships extend to personal as well as real property. Bailments can exist only in chattels, but leases and licences can exist in either real or personal property. For reasons of space, however, this chapter considers only leases of land, and not chattel leases, such as car leases.

Because they are most often created by contract, the law of contracts plays an important role in understanding and shaping these relationships. In the case of bailment, licences, and leases, there is a division between "ownership," or title to the property, and lawful possession, or use of the property. Property law, occasionally supplemented by contract or tort law, governs the relationship between these parties, as illustrated in the following examples:

- a bailment arises when, for example, the owner of a car lends his or her car to a friend. The owner of the car is the *bailor*, and the borrower is the *bailee*. Although the owner retains title, he or she no longer has possession of the car; instead the bailee is in lawful possession of the car;

- a licence arises when the owner of real property, the *licensor* (for example, an owner of a movie theatre), agrees to permit another, the *licensee* (the moviegoer), to enter onto the property; and

- a leasehold estate arises when the owner of real property, the *landlord* (or *lessor*), agrees to lease his or her property for a period of time to another, the *tenant* (or *lessee*).

The principles of property law, contracts, and torts may apply to the various situations above. These principles may supplement one another or they may be in conflict. Where, for example, there has been no exchange of consideration between the bailor and the bailee—that is, the loan of the car is gratuitous—there is no contract between the parties and contract law does not apply. However, property and tort law may nonetheless impose some kind of obligation on the bailee to return the property in reasonable condition. Similarly, a licence may be granted without consideration (for example, when one person invites another into his or her home, he or she has granted a gratuitous licence to the invitee), or with consideration (as in the case of the moviegoer, above). If there is consideration, contract law will generally apply to the terms and enforcement of the licence. Because a lease is usually accompanied by consideration, it is also a contract. Both property law and contract law principles apply to the interpretation and enforcement of leases, and in some cases there may be conflict between these principles.

Unlike the areas of property law examined in Chapters 2 and 3, where *property* law generally governs the relationships in question, this chapter examines areas of law where property, contract, and tort law intersect. In addition, a layer of statutory regulation, particularly with regard to residential tenancies, may abolish or significantly modify the default rules that apply at common law. Thus, another important theme in this chapter is the relationship between public and private. As you read, think about why some of these relationships are left to the incremental and sometimes haphazard development of judge-made "private" law, while others are the object of the kind of intense and ongoing legislative consideration that we associate with "public" law.

II. BAILMENT AND ITS OBLIGATIONS

Bailment is a common transaction in daily life, arising any time an owner parts with possession of a chattel—for example, a car, a book, or luggage—for a specified purpose, such as repair, storage, loan, or transport. See generally Norman Palmer, *Palmer on Bailment*, 3d ed (London: Sweet & Maxwell, 2009) [Palmer]. A bailment may be contractual—for example, in the case of an agreement for the storage of furniture—or gratuitous—for example, borrowing a book from a friend. The relationship is typically consensual, although it may arise where there is no consent or agreement between the bailor and bailee—for example, the law considers the finder of lost property to be the bailee of the lost property. A bailment might also arise where one person is in possession of another person's goods, mistakenly thinking they are his or her own. Finally, there are "involuntary" bailments where, for example, a guest forgets property in the host's home. In all these cases, although there is no express agreement between the bailee and the bailor, the law imposes a relationship of bailment between the parties.

Bailment imposes certain obligations on the bailee with respect to the chattel in question. Originally, the bailee was held strictly liable for the loss or damage of the bailor's property, however caused: *Southcote's Case* (1601), 4 Co Rep 83b, 76 ER 1061 (KB). This onerous standard was later replaced as the law of negligence developed: *Coggs v Bernard* (1703), 2 Ld Raym 909, 92 ER 107 (KB). From this point on, bailees were generally held liable only on the basis of fault and a different level of care was imposed depending on the nature of the bailment. For example, in the case of a gratuitous deposit for safekeeping that benefited the bailor only, the bailee was said to assume a low duty of care and to be liable for gross negligence only. See e.g. *Remme v Wall* (1978), 29 NSR (2d) 39, 45 APR 39 (TD) and *Campbell v Pickard* (1961), 30 DLR (2d) 152 (Man CA). By contrast, where the bailment was for the sole benefit of the bailee—for example, a gratuitous loan of a car for the bailee's sole benefit—the bailee was said to assume a much higher duty of care and to be liable for slight negligence. See e.g. *Jenkins v Smith* (1969), 6 DLR (3d) 309, (1965-69), 1 NSR 728 (TD).

More recently, case law suggests that these various standards of care have been replaced with a general standard of reasonable care. See e.g. *Lifestyles Kitchens & Bath v Danbury Sales Inc*, [1999] OJ no 3097 (SCJ), where the court observed at para 34:

> [I]n modern law, there appears to be no material difference between the principles governing the [bailee's] potential liability as gratuitous bailee or as a bailee for reward. Although in some of the earlier cases it was said that the standard of care applicable for the purpose of determining whether a gratuitous bailee would be liable for loss or damage to the property of the bailor is gross negligence, more recent cases deprecate attempts to distinguish between degrees of negligence in this context … . At the most it is recognized that the standard of care required by a gratuitous bailee may be less exacting than that applicable to a bailee for reward.

This conclusion might be altered in either of the following situations. First, what might appear to give rise to a bailment may in fact only give rise to a licence. A mere licence to enter and place a chattel on another's property is a contractual agreement between the parties and will not generally impose any duty of care on the landowner to safeguard the chattel, unless the contract provides otherwise. The *characterization* of a given arrangement as a licence or a bailment is thus crucial, and often comes up in cases dealing with parking lots, as seen in *Heffron v Imperial Parking Co*, below. If there is only a licence, the parking lot will likely not be held liable for any damage done to the car while it is parked on the lot. However, if there is bailment, the parking lot owner may be liable for negligence.

Second, the duty of care that might typically arise may be altered by contract, even if a bailment can be established between the parties. A bailment for the mutual benefit of the parties is also a contract, and the terms of the contract may include a clause designed to limit the liability of the parties in the event of a breach of that contract. Such clauses are commonly included in standard form parking lot tickets. The extent to which the courts will recognize and enforce the clause limiting liability is a matter of contract law, not the law of bailment.

The following case examines these two issues. When reviewing the case, consider whether the court finds that the relationship in question gives rise to a licence or a bailment. Does the court accept that the obligations of the parking lot operators can be altered by a clause excluding liability? If so, on what grounds does the court make this finding?

Heffron v Imperial Parking Co
(1974), 46 DLR (3d) 642 (Ont CA)

ESTEY JA (for the court): This is an appeal from a judgment pronounced by His Honour Judge Shortt in the County Court of the Judicial District of York on March 29, 1973, wherein the plaintiff was awarded $1,251.92 as damages for the loss of an automobile left by the respondent with the appellants, the operators of a parking lot, together with costs.

The respondent on October 10, 1970, parked his motor vehicle in the parking lot of the appellants in downtown Toronto paying the evening flat rate charge and receiving in return a ticket whereon there was printed:

No. 49801

PARKING CONDITIONS

we are not responsible for theft or damage of car or contents, however caused

IMPERIAL PARKING CO.
237 Victoria Street—364-4611
Corner Bond & Dundas Sts.
Open 8:00 am—12.00 pm

At the request of the appellants' attendant the respondent left the keys in the automobile. The lot was marked with three signs on which the same message was set out as appeared on the ticket. The learned trial Judge came to the conclusion "that the defendants took reasonable steps under the circumstances to draw the conditions of parking to the plaintiff's attention even though, as he admitted, he had not read the parking ticket but merely slipped it into his pocket." In addition to these signs there was a sign announcing the hours in which the parking lot was open and which were the same as set out on the ticket described above. I can find no reason to disturb the learned trial Judge's conclusion that the appellant had taken all reasonable measures to communicate to the respondent the parking conditions including the hours of operation.

The respondent returned to the parking lot about one hour after it had closed and was unable to locate his car. Three days later it was discovered abandoned in a damaged condition. The evidence is that when the car was left with the appellants by the respondent it contained some personal property of the respondent including clothing, a tape player and an electric razor; there is no evidence to indicate that the tape player was affixed to or formed part of the car. These items of personal property were not in the car when it was recovered.

There was evidence indicating that the appellants operated a parking garage across the street from the parking lot in question and that it was a normal practice for the attendant when leaving the lot at midnight to take the keys of any cars remaining on the lot to the office of the parking garage across the street which was operated by the appellant. The keys to the respondent's car were not found in either the kiosk on the parking lot or in the office of the parking garage.

The appellants called no evidence to describe or explain any of the events which occurred. The attendant on duty at the parking lot was not called to give evidence and the only evidence presented by the defence was that of the manager of the appellants who testified to some of the normal practices followed in the operation of the appellants' parking lots. This witness was asked on this point:

Q. What was the procedure with regard to keys left for cars with respect to cars that hadn't been picked up at the time the attendant left the lot?

A. The procedure now?

Q. No. Then.

A. The keys were taken out of the car and taken—we have a parking garage across the street directly next to the Imperial Theatre and the cars are—we ask the people to pick up their keys at the parking garage. We have a man posted there until 2:00 am.

Q. Were any keys ever left in the cars or in the kiosk at that time?

A. Sometimes the—if the attendant would go out for coffee or something.

Q. No. I mean when he closed the lot.

A. I honestly can't say.

BY THE COURT:

Q. Just a moment. I am not clear. How would the customer know if he came back at one o'clock?

A. There is a note left on the car, sir.

Q. That he should go across to the parking lot?

A. "Please pick up your keys at the parking garage. ..."

Q. You mentioned that you have a lot in the immediate vicinity that is open until two o'clock?

A. Yes. We have a man posted until 2:00 am.

Q. So you retain custody of the car and the keys by taking the keys over to the other lot, is that right?

A. If the keys are left in the cars. If there are any cars on the parking lot left with keys, we try to do that.

The learned trial Judge in granting judgment in favour of the respondent stated:

The mere disappearance of the car does not of necessity import theft nor am I convinced that the admitted damage was done before the car left the parking lot. It would be going too far in view of "the magic words" to say that the defendant must negative negligence. It is, however, in my opinion, clearly necessary for the bailee to lead evidence to negative a fundamental breach or deviation from the contract of bailment which would render inoperative the exculpatory words: see *Williams & Wilson Ltd. v. OK Parking Ltd.*, [1971] 2 OR 151, 17 DLR (3d) 243.

The appellant relies upon the decision of this Court in *Samuel Smith & Sons Ltd. v. Silverman*, [1961] OR 648, 29 DLR (2d) 98, in support of its submission that the exculpatory condition in the ticket together with the same message in the signs posted on the parking lot are sufficiently broad in their terms to exonerate the appellant even when the damage occurred through negligence of the appellant, its servants or a third party. The appellant also submits that it is under no onus or obligation to advance any explanation for the non-delivery of the respondent's automobile and since the respondent was unable to show that its loss was occasioned by a fundamental breach of the contract by the appellant, the respondent's action should be dismissed. The appellant alternatively submits that the respondent in parking his automobile on the appellant's premises is a mere licensee and, consequently, no bailment arose and therefore no duty in the appellants to explain the loss.

In the *Samuel Smith* case the parties conceded and the Court proceeded on the basis that at least where the parking lot operator has asked the motorist to leave the keys in the car so that it may be moved around the parking lot for convenience of the operator "that this is a true case of bailment." In that case and the one before this Court the principal argument made was that the terms of the contract excluded liability in the parking lot operator. Neither in the *Samuel Smith* case nor in this case was evidence led by the parking lot operator to explain the disappearance of the automobile. Much of the discussion in the *Samuel Smith* case dealt with the communication of the ticket conditions to the car owner and the only direct reference in the judgment to the effect of the limiting conditions on the ticket is found in the concluding portion of the judgment at p. 652 OR, p. 102 DLR:

> The words printed on the ticket and the signs in question are not susceptible of this criticism. The clear declaration that the defendant was not to be responsible for theft or damage of car or contents *however caused*, is sufficiently broad in its terms to extend to a case where the damage occurred through the negligence either of the defendant or his servants, or the negligence or carelessness of a third party whether lawfully on the premises or not.

The Court thereupon concluded that the exclusionary clause applied to the claim of the plaintiff. The applicability of the doctrine of fundamental breach was apparently not advanced and in any case was not dealt with by the Court.

In another line of cases a relationship different from bailment was found to arise between the parties to such a transaction as parking a car in a parking lot. In *Ashby v. Tolhurst*, [1973] 2 All ER 837, Lord Greene MR found that a somewhat similar transaction resulted in the establishment of a licence relationship and not a bailment relationship. This Court followed and applied the *Ashby* judgment in *Palmer v. Toronto Medical Arts Building Ltd.*, [1960] OR 60, 21 DLR (2d) 181. The trial Judge had found that the plaintiff was a mere licensee and that there was no bailment of his automobile. In any case he found that any bailment which may have arisen was gratuitous bailment and without gross negligence no liability arose in the parking lot owner. As in *Ashby v. Tolhurst*, the Court found in the circumstances of the case the car had not been delivered to the defendants for safe custody but only for "parking" and nothing more. A circumstance of significance mentioned by Schroeder JA, speaking for the Court in the *Palmer* case at p. 69 OR, pp. 187-8 DLR, was the lack of a ticket system:

> The fact that there was no system of giving a card or parking ticket to the persons using this parking lot has vital significance and should have suggested to the plaintiff the absence of any arrangement for supervision or control over the cars left on the lot, since no person was required to surrender a ticket or produce any other form of identification when removing his car.

In that case the surrender of keys to an attendant was an unusual occurrence brought about by a heavy snowfall that morning which made the usual practice of car parking by its owner impossible. The attendant made it clear to the plaintiff that he could, if he wished, retain control over his car or he could remove it to some other parking lot or accept the attendant's offer extended as a voluntary courtesy to park the car for him when space became available. Sir Wilfrid Greene MR, in the *Ashby* case, *supra*, at p. 840, mentions a further circumstance which indicates the relationship which arises in law between the parties to such a transaction:

> The first thing to do is to examine the nature of the relationship between the parties, a matter upon which the character of the ground is, I think, not without importance, but the most important element is the document itself. It describes the place in which the car is to be left as a "car park," and the document is described as a "car park ticket." I myself regard those words as being in one sense, in a real sense, I think, the most important part of the document, because they indicate the nature of the rights which the proprietor of the car is going to get. "Car park ticket": you take a ticket in order to park you [*sic*] car, and parking your cars means, I should have thought, leaving your car in a place. If you park your car in the street, you are liable to get into trouble with the police. On the other hand, you are entitled to park your car in places indicated by the police or the appropriate authorities for the purpose. Parking a car is leaving a car and, I should have thought, nothing else. The right, therefore, which this document starts off by giving on its face is a right to park the car.

In that case the plaintiff locked his car and did not leave the keys with the attendant.

The respective characteristics of the bailment and the licence relationships are guides to the application of the appropriate relationship to the case at hand. Bailment has been defined as "a delivery of personal chattels in trust, on a contract, express or implied, that the trust shall be duly executed, and the chattels redelivered in either their original or an altered form, as soon as the time or use for, or condition on which they were bailed, shall have elapsed or been performed": *Bacon's Abridgement*, adopted in *Re S. Davis & Co., Ltd.*, [1945] Ch. 402 at p. 405. A licence on the other hand is simply the grant of such authority to another to enter upon land for an agreed purpose as to justify that which otherwise would be a trespass and its only legal effect is that the licensor until the licence is revoked is precluded from bringing an action for trespass. Romer LJ, speaking at p. 844 in the *Ashby* case, *supra*, distinguished a bailment from all other relationships when he stated: "… in order that there shall be a bailment there must be a delivery by the bailor, that is to say, he must part with his possession of the chattel in question."

While no single fact may be of controlling importance in the isolation and categorization of the relationship between the parties to this appeal, the combination of the following factors favour the relationship of bailor–bailee, rather than licensor–licensee:

(a)   the owner of the car delivered the keys and therefore the control over the movement of his automobile to the attendant at the attendant's request;

(b)   the parking ticket had a serial number which would indicate that the surrender of the specific ticket would be necessary in order to obtain delivery from the attendant of the automobile;

(c)   the provision of the attendant raises a reasonable inference that he is supplied by the owner of the business for more than the mere function of receiving money upon the parking of the car;

(d)   the parking lot closed, according to the conditions announced on the ticket and signs, at midnight and no conditions were imposed concerning the removal of cars prior thereto;

(e)   the notice of a closing hour reasonably infers an active operation of the parking lot rather than a passive allotment of parking stations from which the car owner could at any time, day or night, unilaterally withdraw his parked vehicle; and

(f)   the practice of the parking lot owner (although unknown to the owner of the car) was to place the keys left in automobiles at the end of the day in the office of the appellants' car parking garage across the road.

In my view, the special circumstances of this case, which I have summarized above, indicate that there was no mutual intention of a mere parking of the car by the respondent owner on the appellants' lot without any action required by the appellants beyond the collection of the fee. The appellants did not hold out a single identified unit of parking space for the exclusive use of the respondent nor did the appellants represent to the respondent that there would be identified a small rectangular island of land somewhere in the appellants' parking lot on which either the respondent or the appellants would place the respondent's vehicle as an alternative to leaving it at the side of the street. The ticket system, the hours of operation, the operating habits of the appellants, including the disposition of car keys at the close of business, and the stipulation that the keys be left in the car so as to enable the appellants to place and move the car at their convenience anywhere within the appellants' parking facility, all indicate a relationship quite different from that of a licence passively granted by the appellant as licensor to the respondent. In the *Ashby* case, *supra*, the car was placed by its owner in a designated spot and locked and the keys were left by the owner with the parking lot supervisor. Here the respondent surrendered and the appellant accepted (indeed required) control of this valuable and highly mobile item of property. I therefore conclude that there was a delivery of possession by the respondent to the appellants of the automobile under a contract of bailment.

The exculpatory clause I have set out above and observe that it is in words identical with those appearing on the ticket which came before this Court in *Mitchell v. Silverman*, [1952] OWN 130, where Robertson CJO, in an oral judgment found that the contract between the parties excluded any liability in the parking lot operator and placed no burden on that operator to account for the missing automobile. The appellant has submitted that should it be found that it was a bailee the exculpatory terms of the contract relieve it from any liability including negligence of the appellant's servants. The respondent in turn has argued that by reason of the fundamental breach of the contract of bailment by the appellant the contract has been terminated including the exculpatory term and the appellant is therefore liable to the respondent for damages thereby occasioned.

Linked inextricably with the answer to the question of applicability of the exempting clause in any such transaction, is the determination of what onus, if any, lies upon the bailee once the bailor proves non-delivery. Lord Denning in *J. Spurling Ltd. v. Bradshaw*, [1956] 1 WLR 461 at p. 466, stated:

> A bailor, by pleading and presenting his case properly, can always put on the bailee the burden of proof. In the case of non-delivery, for instance, all he need plead is the contract and a failure to deliver on demand. That puts on the bailee the burden of proving either loss without

his fault (which, of course, would be a complete answer at common law) or, if it was due to his fault, it was a fault from which he is excused by the exempting clause. ...

Vide also *Woolmer v. Delmer Price Ltd.*, [1955] 1 QB 291 at p. 294. The onus in the case of a licence relationship is of course quite different and the licensor is not ordinarily called upon to discharge any burden or onus other than to demonstrate that he has honoured the existence of the licence.

We are left, therefore, with the unexplained disappearance of the respondent's automobile and the last question remaining to be answered is whether the exculpatory clause exonerates the appellants notwithstanding the appellants' complete failure to explain the cause of disappearance, or whether the clause ceased to operate upon the happening of the unexplained loss of the automobile by reason of a breach of a fundamental term of the contract. At one time it was clear that loss by the bailee of the subject of the bailment without any demonstration of the cause was a fundamental breach going to the root of the contract: *Karsales (Harrow), Ltd. v. Wallis*, [1956] 2 All ER 866 at p. 868.

· · ·

[The court engaged in a lengthy discussion of fundamental breach and then continued:]

But there is a further circumstance in this case which requires examination to completely dispose of this transaction and the rights and obligations of the parties therein. As stated earlier, both the signs on the lot and the ticket referred to the closing of the lot at 12:00 pm, which the parties agreed in this instance means midnight. When the appellants asked the respondent to leave the keys in the car there arose the clearest implied duty in the appellants to take reasonable steps at the close of business to retain custody of the keys in a manner appropriate to the need of the respondent to recover his car and the necessity of protecting the keys and the car from loss. The appellants are unable to explain what became of the keys. They were never located in either the kiosk on the lot or in the appellants' parking garage across the road. Thus, the keys were either stolen during the day or after the lot closed. In either case the appellants must fail, in the first instance as bailee of the keys and the car for the reasons I have outlined earlier, and in the second instance for breach of duty to exercise reasonable care to safeguard the keys after the closing of the lot. This latter understanding and the duty arising therefrom are entirely unrelated to the exculpatory term set out in the parking ticket. It could not be otherwise as the law would then be unable to imply a duty to exercise reasonable care in the second stage of the custodial arrangement. ... In any case, the term of the bailment may expire but the consequential duty to make reasonable provision for the return of the keys to the owner continues. ... The appellants have not, and presumably cannot, relate the non-delivery to either time period and I know of no principle of law requiring the respondent to do so as plaintiff in order to recover his damages.

There was some evidence that the ignition of the car was faulty prior to the disappearance of the car from the appellants' lot but in any event there is no evidence to dispel the ordinary explanation that the keys were used to improperly remove the automobile.

Finally, we turn to the question of the contents of the automobile which, when the car was subsequently recovered in a damaged condition, were not in the car. This personal property consisted of some tools, clothing, and a radio and tape player for which the re-spondent claimed in all $308.10, calculated on the basis of the value of the goods at the time of loss. These goods were generally of a type which one might reasonably be expected to carry in an automobile. The evidence does not indicate whether these articles were located in the trunk or the body of the car. However, once the keys fall into the hands of a person intent upon stealing the automobile it makes no difference whether the personal property mentioned above is located in the trunk or inside the car.

Laidlaw JA, in dealing with a similar claim in *Brown v. Toronto Auto Parks Ltd.*, [1955] OWN 456, [1955] 2 DLR 525, found neither actual nor constructive knowledge in the bailee of the presence of a quantity of books in the car and, hence, the contract of bailment did not extend to cover the books in the car. On the facts in the case before this Court the goods are not of such an unusual nature that would not reasonably be expected to be regularly found in an automobile and it, therefore, is not unreasonable for a parking lot operator to assume that a great many of the cars left in his custody will contain this kind of personal property in reasonable quantity. On this basis I conclude that the items men-tioned above were constructively included in the bailment arrangement and were property included in the claims made by the respondent.

For these reasons I would dismiss the appeal with costs but in so doing wish to add that the Court was greatly assisted in the disposition of this matter by the thorough and detailed analysis of the authorities presented by both counsel.

Appeal dismissed.

DISCUSSION NOTES

i. Bata v City Parking Canada Ltd

In *Bata v City Parking Canada Ltd* (1973), 43 DLR (3d) 190 (Ont CA), the plaintiff parked his car in a parking lot and left his keys in the car at the request of the attendant. The car was stolen, and the plaintiff brought an action against the parking lot. The plaintiff was unsuccessful be-cause the court (at 194) determined that the relationship was a licence rather than a bailment:

> The words on the two signs and the words which appear on the parking ticket given the cus-tomer indicate in a very real sense the nature of the rights which the proprietor of a car may ex-pect to enjoy under the arrangement into which he is entering. The words "charges are for use of parking space only" exclude at once any notion that the arrangement entered into is one of bailment, and if there is any doubt on that score the words "[t]his company assumes no respon-sibility whatever for loss or damage due to fire, theft, collision or otherwise to the vehicle or its contents, however caused" should effectively remove any doubt in the matter.

In *Heffron*, the court distinguished *Bata* on its facts. The major distinction appears to be the express inclusion of the words "charges are for use of parking space only" in the parking ticket in *Bata*. Is this a reasonable ground to allow the plaintiff in *Heffron* to recover damages, but not the plaintiff in *Bata*?

ii. Minichiello v Devonshire Hotel (1967) Ltd

When a bailment exists, there will be constructive bailment of other items that might reasonably be expected to be in, or part of, the principal chattel. For this reason, the plaintiff in *Heffron* was able to recover the value of his personal property contained in the car, including some tools, clothing, a radio, and a tape player. In *Minichiello v Devonshire Hotel (1967) Ltd* (1978), 87 DLR (3d) 439 (BCCA), the plaintiff left his car (and his car keys) with the parking attendant. He paid 40 cents to park the car. He also informed the attendant that there were "valuables" in the car. In the car's trunk, there was a briefcase with over $16,000 worth of jewels. The briefcase disappeared, and the plaintiff was able to recover this amount on the grounds that the plaintiff's statement to the attendant was sufficient to enable the court to conclude that one could reasonably anticipate that property of such value might be in the car.

Is it reasonable to conclude that for a payment of 40 cents, the defendant parking lot should be held liable for the entire value of the lost jewels? What kind of legal advice would you offer to the defendant parking lot following this decision? Should the parking lot attendant be instructed to refuse to accept any cars, if informed that they contain "valuables"? Is this a feasible alternative? Should the parking lot ticket be amended to exclude liability for any damage or loss sustained while parked on the premises? Will this clause be effective in restricting the parking lot's liability?

iii. Clauses Excluding Liability

Exculpatory clauses are also commonly included in cloakrooms, where a sign will be posted stating something like, "Not responsible for lost goods." A similar statement may be printed on the cloakroom ticket. Courts frequently strain to ignore or restrict such clauses. For example, the clause will apply only if the bailor has accepted it. The bailor must have either actual or constructive notice of the clause at the time he or she entered into the bailment. Thus the placement of the exculpatory clause is critical. If the clause is not prominently and obviously displayed, it may not apply. See B Ziff, *Principles of Property Law*, 5th ed (Scarborough, ON: Carswell, 2010) [Ziff] at 328. Similarly, if the agreement is tainted by unconscionability, as might be the case with standard form contracts, the clause may be ineffective. See *Davidson v Three Spruces Realty Ltd*, [1977] 6 WWR 460, 79 DLR (3d) 481 (BCSC).

iv. Length of Term of the Bailment

Bailments may be for a fixed term—for example, the long-term lease of machinery—or at will—for example, a gratuitous loan. Where there is a contract providing for a fixed term, the owner's right of possession is postponed until the term has expired, unless the bailee is in such serious breach of the contract that the bailor is permitted to retake possession. A bailment at will can be determined at any time by the bailor, giving the bailor an immediate right to repossess the article. See Ziff at 321.

v. Burden of Proof

In most civil actions, the burden of proof rests on the plaintiff to establish all elements of liability. By contrast, in bailment cases, a presumption of negligence may arise, thereby shifting the burden of proof to the bailee, as Estey JA noted in *Heffron*, above. This presumption may arise if the plaintiff-bailor can establish that the act complained of—for example, the disappearance or damage of an article—occurred during the course of the bailment. Presumably, the bailee is in the better position to know the reason for the putative negligence. For this reason, the bailee bears the onus of proof to rebut the presumption of negligence. To evade liability, the bailee does not need to establish exactly what happened to the article. The bailee need show only that the system in place to safeguard the bailed goods was sufficient to meet legal requirements. See *United Refrigerator Parts Co v Consolidated Fastfrate Ltd*, [1974] 5 WWR 166, 46 DLR (3d) 290 (Man CA).

vi. The Bailor's Duties

The bailor may also owe a duty of care to the bailee. If the chattel is defective, the bailor may be liable to the bailee, much as the vendor of defective goods may be liable to the purchaser. A bailor for reward—for example, a car rental company—must ensure that the chattels are reasonably fit and suitable for the purposes of the hirer and is liable for any defects that are known, or ought to have been known, by the bailor. On the other hand, a gratuitous bailor is likely required only to inform the bailee of known defects. See Ziff at 327-28.

vii. Assignment and Sub-bailment

A bailee may assign or "sub-bail" his or her interest, providing that the terms of the original bailment expressly or impliedly permit it. Where the bailor has an immediate right to terminate the principal bailment—for example, when the goods have been lost—the bailor has a direct right of action against the sub-bailee: *Scott Maritimes Pulp Ltd v BF Goodrich Canada Ltd* (1977), 72 DLR (3d) 680, 19 NSR (2d) 181 (CA). The sub-bailee may seek to rely on exculpatory clauses contained in the contract between itself and the bailee, raising the question of when the head bailor may be bound by such clauses.

In *The Pioneer Container*, [1994] 3 WLR 1 (PC-HK), P contracted with freight carriers for the carriage of goods from Taiwan to Hong Kong. The freight carriers issued P with bills of lading providing that the freight carrier was entitled to subcontract "on any terms" the handling, storage, and carriage of the goods. The freight carrier subcontracted the carriage to D, the shipowners, who issued feeder bills of lading that incorporated an exclusive jurisdiction clause requiring that any dispute was to be determined in Taiwan. The vessel sank with the loss of all cargo and P commenced proceedings in Hong Kong. D applied for a stay of proceedings on the ground that P, by the exclusive jurisdiction clause, had agreed that any dispute should be determined in Taiwan. The limitation period in Taiwan had already expired when P commenced its action. The Court of Appeal of Hong Kong held that P was bound by the clause. P appealed to the Privy Council, arguing that it could not be bound by a clause in a contract to which it was not a party.

The Privy Council dismissed the appeal, holding that if a bailee sub-bails goods with the owner's authority, the relationship between the owner and sub-bailee is·that of owner and bailee, such that the owner is bound by the terms of the sub-bailment if the owner had expressly or impliedly consented to the bailee making a sub-bailment on those terms. Lord Goff of Chievely, delivering the judgment of their Lordships, observed that such a result was "both principled and just" (at 13):

They incline to the opinion that a sub-bailee can only be said for these purposes to have voluntarily taken into his possession the goods of another if he has sufficient notice that a person other than the bailee is interested in the goods so that it can properly be said that (in addition to his duties to the bailee) he has, by taking the goods into his custody, assumed towards that other person the responsibility for the goods which is characteristic of a bailee. This they believe to be the underlying principle. Moreover, their Lordships do not consider this principle to impose obligations on the sub-bailee which are onerous or unfair, once it is recognized that he can invoke against the owner terms of the sub-bailment which the owner has actually (expressly or impliedly) or even ostensibly authorized.

Here the terms of the contract between P and the freight carriers were wide enough to indicate that P consented to the freight carriers sub-bailing the goods to D on D's terms, including the exclusive jurisdiction clause. Accordingly, P was bound by the clause. The expiry of the time limit in Taiwan was not a reason for refusing to grant a stay.

viii. Strict Liability of Common Carriers and Innkeepers

As noted above, the law of negligence gradually replaced the historical standard of strict liability of the bailee. There are, however, two exceptions to this general rule. Common carriers and innkeepers remain strictly liable for damage to the property of persons for whom they provide their services. A common carrier contracts with other parties for the transportation of goods. Unless the common carrier's liability is altered by statute or the terms of the contract, the common carrier will be held strictly liable for any damage to the goods being transported: *Brookins v Canadian National Railway Co* (1974), 43 DLR (3d) 280 (PEISC).

At common law, innkeepers were also held to a strict liability standard, likely to protect the interests of medieval travellers who faced considerable risks. Today, this liability is typically altered by statute, as is the case in Ontario: *Innkeepers Act*, RSO 1990, c I.7. Section 4 provides that the innkeeper's liability for loss or injury to the guest's property is generally limited to $40, except where the goods have been stolen, lost, or injured "through the wilful act, default, or neglect of the innkeeper or the innkeeper's employee" or the goods "have been deposited expressly for safe custody with the innkeeper." Section 6 provides that the limited liability outlined in s 4 will not be available to the innkeeper unless the innkeeper "conspicuously" posts a copy of s 4 in the "office and public rooms and in every bedroom in the inn." This requirement was strictly enforced in *Laing v Allied Innkeepers Ltd* (1969), 8 DLR (3d) 708 (Ont HC), where $400 was stolen from the plaintiff's hotel room. Although a proper notice had been posted in the plaintiff's room, the hotel was nonetheless found liable because it was unable to establish that the proper notice had been posted in all the other locations required by s 6.

ix. Bailments and Third Parties

Although a bailee is merely in lawful possession of the bailor's property, he or she may nonetheless maintain a right of action against a third party who has damaged or wrongfully deprived the bailee of the bailed property: *The "Winkfield,"* [1902] P 42 (Eng CA). This follows from the fact that the bailee is in possession of the bailed goods and may recover possession from any wrongdoer, a point further explored in *Armory v Delamirie* (1722), 93 ER 664 (KB), discussed in Chapter 2. The common law allows the bailee in such cases to recover the full value of the chattels in question, and payment to the bailee of this amount by the tortfeasor constitutes a full defence to any subsequent claim by the bailor; the bailor must then look to the bailee to recover any damages that have been sustained. This is a clear exception to the general principle that tort damages are compensatory, based on the common law's treatment of possession as equivalent to title: see *Petrifond Midwest Ltd v Esso Resources Canada Ltd* (1996), 187 AR 107 at paras 30-36 (CA). The rule has been the subject of criticism, and in England the *Torts (Interference with Goods) Act 1977* effectively abolished it, allowing the tortfeasor to plead the bailor's *jus tertii* and thus reduce the amount of damages owing in any suit by a bailee. No Canadian province has followed suit to date.

Although not in possession of the bailed property, the bailor may nonetheless bring an action against a third party for any wrongdoing with respect to it on the ground that the bailor is entitled to recover for damage to his or her reversionary interest in the bailed property: *Chapman v Robinson* (1970), 71 WWR 515 (Alta Dist Ct). In the original case to recognize such a claim, *Mears v London and South Western Railway Co* (1862), 11 CBNS 850; 142 ER 1029 (CP), the court spoke of recovery only for "permanent injury done to [the] chattel." Subsequent case law has not been as stringent, and Palmer, at 304, suggests that if some injury enures to the bailor's detriment, that should be sufficient. However, this formulation still leaves some cases where the bailor's right to recovery may be less extensive than the bailee's.

III. LEASEHOLD ESTATES IN LAND: AN INTRODUCTION

Much as a bailment for the mutual benefit of the parties constitutes a contract, a lease for consideration also creates a contract between the parties. (Gratuitous leases are possible in theory, but rarely encountered in practice.) As examined above, the principles of contract law may apply to a bailment for the mutual benefit of the parties and an exculpatory clause in the bailment agreement may effectively alter the duty of care otherwise owed under the law of bailment. Similarly, the principles of contract law may apply to a lease.

As discussed in Chapter 3, a lease was historically regarded as a contract. The law did not recognize that a lease gave rise to any estate in land. Leases were primarily entered into as a means to avoid objections to usury laws, which prohibited lenders from charging interest on loans. See EH Burn and J Cartwright, *Cheshire and Burn's Modern Law of Real Property*, 18th ed (London: Butterworths, 2011) at 58-59. To repay a debt, the debtor would lease lands at a nominal rent to the creditor, enabling the creditor to obtain interest at an agreed rate from the profits of the land. The actual interest charged was thus hidden in the agreement. Because the lease was regarded as a contractual arrangement only, if the landlord (debtor) were in breach of the lease agreement and wrongfully evicted the tenant (creditor), the tenant was not regarded as having any interest in the land that might give rise to an action to recover the land itself. Instead, the tenant was limited to recovering a monetary award of damages in contract law, effectively recovering the debt due and no more. For this reason, leases were historically classified as personal property, not real property, because the lease did not give rise to an action to recover the land (the *res*) itself.

As the lease became a more popular legal device, this lack of security of tenure for the tenant, particularly the agrarian leaseholder, became increasingly problematic. Over time the courts gradually permitted the tenant to bring an action in *ejectment*, which permitted the tenant to recover the land itself when wrongfully evicted from the leasehold premises. As a result, the tenant gradually began to acquire an enforceable interest in the land itself and not merely a right to recover monetary damages for wrongful eviction. The leasehold interest thus began to resemble an estate in land. For this reason, the leasehold came to be known as a "chattel real"—that is, personal property, which nonetheless gave rise to a right to recover the property itself when the tenant was wrongfully evicted. At this point, the leasehold estate was developed; it effectively resembled an estate in land and, on the whole, was regarded as a proprietary interest in land governed primarily by the principles of property law (not contract law).

A. Contemporary Leaseholds and Contract Principles

In contemporary law this trend has been reversed. The principles of contract law have been increasingly applied to the leasehold estate, particularly in the context of remedies for breach of the leasehold agreement. The remedies developed by property law, which in effect relieved the landlord of any duty to mitigate in the face of the tenant's breach, have inefficient and undesirable results. Consequently, as illustrated in cases dealing with commercial tenancies, beginning with *Highway Properties Ltd v Kelly, Douglas & Co*, [1971] SCR 562 (examined later in this chapter), the courts have increasingly incorporated contract law concepts. With regard to residential tenancies, statutory reform has expressly mandated the adoption of contract principles in many instances. Thus, the Ontario *Residential Tenancies Act, 2006*, SO 2006, c 17, states in s 16 that "[w]hen a landlord or a tenant becomes liable to pay any amount as a result of a breach of a tenancy agreement, the person entitled to claim the amount has a duty to take reasonable steps to minimize the person's losses." As a result, the leasehold estate (rather like bailment) is now situated at the crossroads of property law and contract law and is subject to both bodies of law, although residential tenancies are also subject to detailed statutory regulation that is absent in the case of most bailments.

B. Leaseholds and Property Law: Assigning and Subletting

The estate concept has certainly not disappeared from the legal conceptualization of leasehold interests. It remains important, especially with regard to assignment and subletting of the tenant's interest, and an inability to assign or sublet may be an important clue that the parties have not intended to create a tenancy at all: see *Re Canadian Pacific Hotels Ltd and Hodges* (1978), 23 OR (2d) 577 (Co Ct), below. The tenant's interest is in principle as alienable as the landlord's, giving rise to the question whether assignees of the tenant's estate are subject to, and able to enforce, provisions in the initial lease to which they are not parties. Similar questions arise when a landlord grants its reversion to a third party. In general, the concept of privity of estate governs such questions. Privity of estate is based on the idea that the landlord–tenant relationship is tenurial—that is, the rights and obligations can flow to grantees of the original parties even if there is no privity of contract between them.

Thus, in the figures below, if a landlord (L) grants a ten-year lease to a tenant (T), and after four years T assigns the remaining six years to an assignee (A), there is no privity of contract between L and A, but there is privity of estate between them, meaning that a landlord–tenant relationship exists between them (top figure). Likewise, if the initial landlord grants its reversion to a second landlord (L2), there is a landlord–tenant relationship between L2 and the initial tenant via privity of estate, even though there is no privity of contract between them (middle figure).

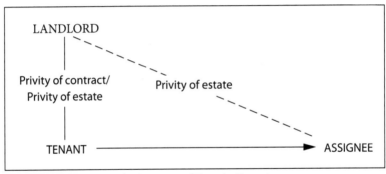

Assignment of Term by Tenant

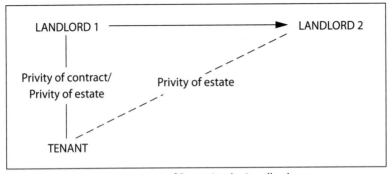

Assignment of Reversion by Landlord

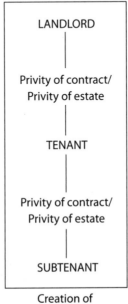

Creation of
Subtenancy by Tenant

The legal positions of landlords and tenants are not completely symmetrical in this regard, however. The *Grantees of Reversions Act 1540*, 32 Hen VIII, c 34 provided that the benefit and burden of all covenants in the initial lease passed to the grantee of the landlord's reversion (see now *Commercial Tenancies Act*, RSO 1990, c L.7, ss 4-8); later judicial interpretation limited this to covenants that "touch and concern the land," a matter discussed in Chapter 7: see Charles Harpum, Stuart Bridge & Martin Dixon, eds, *Megarry and Wade: The Law of Real Property*, 8th ed (London: Sweet & Maxwell, 2012) at 963. A tenant who assigns her interest to a third party, however, remains secondarily liable for the rent payable under the initial lease term. In other words, the landlord must look first to the assignee for the payment of rent, but if, for example, the assignee goes bankrupt the original tenant may be sued for any rent owing on the lease: see *Crystalline Investments v Domgroup Ltd*, 2004 SCC 3, [2004] 1 SCR 60.

A further distinction must be made between assignment and subletting. A tenant who grants away the remainder of her term has created an *assignment* and hence a new tenurial relationship between the original landlord and the assignee. A tenant who grants away less than the remainder of her term has created a *sublease*, which does not give rise to any privity of estate between the original landlord and the subtenant. The subtenant has privity of estate with the tenant, and the tenant has privity of estate with the landlord, but no new tenurial relationship is created between the landlord and the subtenant (see bottom figure). For this reason, when tenants seek permission to sublet, landlords are sometimes willing to allow them to surrender the balance of their term in order to enter a fresh lease directly with the potential subtenant.

Note that the positions of the subtenant of realty and the sub-bailee of personal property, considered above, are quite different with respect to their relationship (or lack thereof) with the head lessor/bailor. Can you explain why?

C. A Note About Terminology

The traditional language of leases used the terms "landlord" and "tenant," which, with their feudal overtones, suggested the social subordination that historically accompanied the status of tenant. When a property requirement for voting existed, for example, generally speaking the voter had to possess a freehold, and not a leasehold, estate. Section 23(3) of the *Constitution Act, 1867* still requires senators to be "legally or equitably seised as of Freehold … of Lands or Tenements held in Free and Common Socage" to the value of at least $4,000 above any encumbrances. As seen in Chapter 3, the tenant is not considered to hold seisin. In modern times, the more neutral terms "lessor" and "lessee" came into use, and are legally synonymous with "landlord" and "tenant," respectively. Both are used in this chapter, but note that in Ontario, the *Commercial Tenancies Act* uses largely the language of lessor–lessee, while the *Residential Tenancies Act, 2006* uses largely the language of landlord–tenant.

D. Leases: The Legislative Context

The common law imposed few obligations on the landlord and left virtually all terms of the lease arrangement, apart from the grant of bare possession, to the parties' negotiation. In addition, it gave the landlord the extrajudicial remedy of distress, which is the right to enter the leased premises and seize chattels as security for arrears of rent. By an act of 1689, the landlord was given the right to sell such chattels upon notice to the tenant, a situation that still obtains today with respect to commercial tenancies: *Commercial Tenancies Act*, s 53. However, by the 1970s the large numbers of tenants in major Canadian cities were able to exert a political force that resulted in major reforms to the law of residential tenancies. All Canadian jurisdictions now have separate statutory regimes for residential tenancies that are much more "tenant-friendly" than the common law. The reforms have three main features: (1) the transformation of the residential lease into a regulated contract that attempts to re-balance the inequality of bargaining power between the parties by imposing new duties on the landlord, such as the duty to repair, and curbing the ability to evict tenants except for cause; (2) the creation of new tribunals aimed at providing speedier and less costly resolution of residential tenancy disputes than the ordinary courts; and (3) the adoption of some form of rent control, although the details of the latter vary widely across Canada. These changes reflect worldwide shifts in attitudes toward shelter, which is now seen as an essential human right, rather than just another commodity bought and sold in the market. See e.g. Jessie Hohmann, *The Right to Housing: Law, Concepts, Possibilities* (Oxford and Portland, OR: Hart, 2013). In *Tanudjaja v Canada (Attorney General)*, 2013 ONSC 5410, however, the Ontario Su-perior Court of Justice decided that federal and provincial changes in housing policy that were alleged to increase the risk of homelessness did not engage either s 7 or s 15 of the *Canadian Charter of Rights and Freedoms*.

In Ontario, until January 1, 1970, when a new Part IV of the *Landlord and Tenant Act*, RSO 1970, c 236, dealing with residential tenancies came into effect, the *Landlord and Tenant Act* did not make any distinction between residential and commercial tenancies. It was, and re-mains, largely a codification of the common law, reflected in its antique wording. Since then residential and commercial tenancies have been regulated separately. At present, the *Resi-dential Tenancies Act, 2006*, SO 2006, c 17 and the *Commercial Tenancies Act*, RSO 1990, c L.7 are the relevant statutes. The *Residential Tenancies Act, 2006* replaced the *Tenant Protection Act*, SO 1997, c 24, which itself had replaced Part IV of the *Landlord and Tenant Act*. When the *Tenant Protection Act* was passed, removing residential tenancies altogether from the *Land-lord and Tenant Act*, the latter was renamed the *Commercial Tenancies Act*, but no substantive reform of the law relating to commercial tenancies was effected. The tribunal created in 1997 to deal with residential tenancy disputes was called the Ontario Rental Housing Tribunal, but the name was changed in 2006 to the Landlord and Tenant Board.

At a conceptual level, the estate concept remains rather more influential with commercial tenancies than with residential tenancies, where extensive statutory regulation has pushed it into the background. As you read the materials in this chapter, reflect on the public–private distinction as it plays out in the context of commercial versus residential tenancies.

IV. LEASES AND LICENCES

A. Contemporary Leaseholds and Contract Principles

The lease, a hybrid of property and contract law, must be contrasted with the licence, largely a creation of contract law. A lease is a grant of exclusive possession giving rise to an estate in land, whereas a licence is merely a contractual right to enter onto the land of another for a specified purpose and constitutes little more than a defence to an action in trespass: Anne Warner La Forest, *Anger & Honsberger Law of Real Property*, loose-leaf (Aurora, ON: Canada

Law Book, 2006) ch 16 at 18. The essence of a lease is that the tenant has a right to the exclusive possession of the leased premises and the right to exclude all other persons, including the landlord. A licence does not give rise to a right of exclusive possession, but merely permits the licensee to enter onto the premises.

The distinction between the two is crucial in a variety of contexts. In general, the remedies available to a tenant are more robust than those available to a licensee, leading landowners to try on occasion to characterize arrangements made by them as licences rather than leases. For example, in England, various landlords tried for some time to evade legal protections available to tenants, including English rent control legislation and residential tenancy legislation, by attempting to construe their lease agreements as "licences": *Street v Mountford*, [1985] AC 809, [1985] 2 All ER 289 (HL). To do so, some landlords drafted agreements that provided that the owner could enter the premises at any time without the "licensee's" permission and further provided that the owner reserved the right to assign additional lodgers in the premises. Either provision is, on its face, inconsistent with the right of exclusive possession enjoyed by a tenant. The inclusion of such provisions was specifically designed to ensure that a court would construe the agreement as a licence rather than a leasehold estate. In practice, the landlords seldom if ever exercised such extraordinary rights, and the occupants effectively enjoyed exclusive possession of the premises. However, these same occupants, technically licensees, were denied any of the protections available in applicable rent control legislation or residential tenancy legislation.

After much litigation, the House of Lords resolved the question largely in favour of the occupants in *Street v Mountford*. The court found that, notwithstanding the terms of the agreement, which seemed inconsistent with a grant of exclusive possession (such as the reservation of the right to assign additional lodgers), if the occupant in fact enjoys exclusive possession, and was meant to do so, then a tenancy will be found. The House of Lords was willing to recognize that such provisions were "shams" and not meant to reflect the reality of the situation. Accordingly, the ability of landlords in England to evade rent control laws and residential tenancy legislation has been restricted. Nonetheless, there is evidence that some English landlords have continued to issue such "licences" in the hope that the occupants will remain unaware that they are in fact tenants who are entitled to all the legal protections available to residential tenants. For a further analysis of this problem, see Peter Vincent-Jones, "Exclusive Possession and Exclusive Control of Private Rented Housing" (1987) 14 JL & Soc'y 445, and Charles Harpum, "Leases, Licences, Sharing and Shams" (1989) 48 Cambridge LJ 19.

There is no specific counterpart in Canadian law to the struggle between landlords and residential tenants in England, although the issue comes up at times in commercial contexts, as the cases below illustrate. This difference may be due to the fact that all residential tenancy legislation in Canada is broad enough to include licence-like arrangements. For example, the Ontario *Residential Tenancies Act, 2006*, s 2(1) defines "residential unit" as "any living accommodation used or intended for use as residential premises," including "a room in a boarding house, rooming house or lodging house and a unit in a care home." However, where the living accommodation requires its occupants to share a bathroom or kitchen facility with the owner or the owner's family, the Act does not apply: s 5(i). Such accommodation would presumably be only a licence and not a lease. All provinces and territories now adopt a functional definition of residential housing that does not depend on the legal characterization that might be given to the arrangement. The Nova Scotia *Residential Tenancies Act*, RSNS

1989, c 401, s 2(h), for example, defines "residential premises" simply as any "place ... occupied by an individual as a residence."

B. Long-Term Care Facilities: Lease or Licence?

Although Ontario residential tenancies legislation covers residents in boarding houses, until 1994 this legislation did not expressly cover residents in long-term care facilities, such as rest and retirement homes. These facilities provide some kind of supportive care for the residents and have typically enjoyed considerable power over who is admitted as a resident and under what conditions the resident may remain. For example, if the facility can no longer care for the resident, the resident may no longer be eligible to remain in the facility. For this reason, among others, the residential tenancy legislation that extended greater security of tenure to the tenant was not regarded as appropriate for this setting. This view came under re-examination, particularly in the light of cases where residents in such facilities were abused. In 1992, the issue was the subject of an Ontario commission of inquiry, whose report led to legislative amendments in 1994: ES Lightman, *A Community of Interests: The Report of the Commission of Inquiry into Unregulated Residential Accommodation* (Toronto: Ontario Government, 1992).

In its report, the commission of inquiry documented the lack of suitably regulated accommodation in Ontario for persons with psychiatric histories, adults with developmental disabilities, and frail elderly persons. Noting the closure of many large psychiatric hospitals in prior decades, the commission described the circumstances faced by Ontarians with psychiatric histories, "living six or more to a room, sleeping in bunk beds or on floors, with few protections from exploitation, abuse, and capricious behaviour by landlords, staff, and sometimes complete strangers." Similarly, the commission described the plight of many frail elderly persons who were required to enter retirement homes where unscrupulous operators might victimize them. According to the commission, many of these vulnerable persons lived in accommodation that was "uninspected and outside the protection" of rent control, tenant protection laws, and other regulatory legislation.

The 1994 amending legislation resulting from Professor Lightman's report generally extended tenant protections to residents in care homes: *Residents' Rights Act*, SO 1994, c 2. These protections are now incorporated in Part IX of the *Residential Tenancies Act, 2006*, s 1(1) of which provides that "residential unit" includes "a unit in a care home" defined as "a residential complex that is occupied or intended to be occupied by persons for the purposes of receiving care services, whether or not receiving the services is the primary purpose of the occupancy." Section 139(1) provides that tenancy agreements in care homes shall be in writing. Under s 150, a landlord must provide 90 days' notice of any increase in the charge for providing care services or meals. The written tenancy agreement must include a clause informing the tenant that he or she has the right to consult a third party with respect to the agreement and cancel the agreement within five days after it has been entered into: s 141. Under s 26, a landlord's right to enter leased premises is limited generally to emergencies and other specified circumstances. However, s 142(1) permits landlords to enter a rental unit in a care home at regular intervals to check the tenant's condition if the tenancy agreement requires the landlord to do so, while s 142(2) permits a tenant to revoke unilaterally any prior agreement to permit the landlord to do so.

Although residents of care homes have achieved some legislative protection, by and large, those suffering from mental health problems who were "deinstitutionalized" in the

1980s have not. They are the principal occupants of boarding houses in certain areas of major cities, such as Toronto's Parkdale, where their living conditions are sometimes deplorable. Their situation is analyzed by M McCreary, "Little House of Horrors: Discrimination Against Boarding Home Tenants—Human Rights Legislation and the Charter" (1998) 13 J L & Soc Pol'y 224.

C. Commercial Leases and Licences

The distinction between leases and licences remains important in Canadian law. In a commercial context, questions frequently arise regarding the characterization of various agreements as either leases or licences. These disputes tend to focus on (1) the question whether the owner or the occupant may avail itself of the provisions of the applicable landlord and tenant legislation, or (2) whether, on the sale of the land, the occupant's interest will bind the subsequent purchaser. In both cases, the characterization of the agreement is crucial in resolving this dispute. For example, in the case that follows, the landlord was seeking to employ the summary proceedings under the relevant landlord and tenant legislation to evict a commercial tenant. The tenant, in defence, argued that he was a licensee under the "lease" agreement, and not a tenant, because the agreement did not accord the occupant exclusive possession. Because he was not a "tenant," he argued that the court had no jurisdiction to evict him under the applicable landlord and tenant legislation. At the time of this case, both residential and commercial tenancies were governed by what was then called the Ontario *Landlord and Tenant Act*, as noted above. Today, a dispute similar to the case below could arise; however, the issue would be whether the relationship between the parties was a lease, and thus governed by what is now called the *Commercial Tenancies Act*, or a licence and not governed by this Act.

Re British American Oil Co v DePass
(1959), 21 DLR (2d) 110 (Ont CA)

SCHROEDER JA: On September 3, 1959, the appellant, the British American Oil Co. Ltd., as landlord, made application to His Honour Judge Macdonell in the County Court in the County of York for an order for a writ of possession directed to the Sheriff of the County of York, directing that official forthwith to place the applicant in possession of the service station premises located at 120 Fleet St. in the City of Toronto, which said premises were more particularly described in a lease entered into between the applicant as landlord and Jack Halpert as tenant on February 6, 1959. On the same date a similar application was made for an order for a writ of possession with respect to service station premises located at 929 Queen St. East in the City of Toronto, and more particularly described in a certain lease entered into between the applicant as landlord and the respondent, Richard DePass, as tenant, on February 6, 1959. The grounds of the said applications were that the leases entered into between the parties had been validly determined as of August 24, 1959, by service of a notice to quit dated July 25, 1959, given by the landlord pursuant to the terms of the said leases. It was alleged that the tenants, having wrongfully refused to go out of possession, were overholding tenants without permission of the landlord or right to possession or occupancy, and that they wrongfully held possession against the landlord. Each of the said applications was dismissed with costs. From these two orders British American Oil Co. now appeals.

The reasons for judgment of His Honour Judge Macdonell do not indicate the precise ground on which the applications were dismissed. He referred, without denominating them, to certain cases which had been cited which, in his view, were indistinguishable on the facts. One of those cases, we are now informed, was *Reliance Petroleum Ltd. v. Rosenblood*, [1953] OWN 115, decided by His Honour Judge Latchford in the County Court of the County of Wentworth in which a similar application under Part III of the *Landlord and Tenant Act*, RSO 1950, c. 199 was dismissed on the ground that the service station lease and the retail dealer sales agreement entered into between Reliance Petroleum Ltd. and Rosenblood, a service station operator, was to be construed not as creating the relationship of landlord and tenant, but the relationship of licensor and licensee. The County Court Judge decided in that case that the documents constituted "a mere device to secure the sale of McManus Petroleum Limited's products," [at 116] and further, that the service station operator had not been given the right to exclusive possession of the premises, but only a right to use them for the purpose of selling those products. We are informed that there were also certain unreported decisions of other County Court Judges cited to the County Court Judge in which the same reasoning was applied.

It is evident, therefore, that the reason for dismissal of the applications under review was that in the learned County Court Judge's opinion the true relationship between the parties was that of licensor and licensee and that he did not possess jurisdiction to hear the applications made by the landlord on the footing that the relationship was that of landlord and tenant.

On February 6, 1959, the parties signed a document described as a service station lease, and on the same date they signed a separate agreement described as an "equipment loan and retail dealer sales agreement." Both respondents are described in the former instrument as "tenant." It was provided in the leases that in consideration of the rents, covenants and agreements thereinafter reserved on the part of the tenant to be paid, kept, observed and performed, the British American Oil Co. did demise and lease unto the tenant the lands and premises therein described, followed by a *habendum* clause in the terms following: "To have and to hold the said premises for the term of one month to commence on the 1st January, 1959, and end on the 31st January, 1959, subject to earlier termination as herein provided." It was further stipulated that the leases should "automatically renew" themselves on the same terms and conditions (including this particular provision for automatic renewal) unless written notice of termination was given by either party to the other at least 30 days prior to the expiration of the term or any renewal thereof, or unless the lease or any renewal thereof had been terminated by the British American Oil Co. as thereinafter provided. The Retail Dealer Sales Agreement made on the same date obligated the lessee to sell only the products of the British American Oil Co. on the terms and conditions therein set forth, and also contained a list of the equipment furnished by the company to the tenants on loan upon the terms and conditions fully set forth in that contract.

The problem in this appeal is to decide what, upon the facts, is the true legal relationship between the parties. The County Court Judge thought that it was that of licensor and licensee and accordingly held that the summary procedure for which provision was made in Part III of the *Landlord and Tenant Act* could not be invoked by the appellant.

Counsel for the tenants submitted to this Court that the true legal relationship was that of licensor and licensee. He contended that on a proper construction of the formal documents and on an accurate appraisal of the proper inferences to be drawn from the surrounding circumstances and the conduct of the parties, the respondents should be held to have been given possession of the premises for the "limited purpose of selling the products of the appellants and for no other purpose"; that they had no effective control over the use of the premises, and if they attempted to use them for any purpose other than the sale of the appellant's products, their right of occupancy could be terminated forthwith; and that while the first mentioned document is in terms described as a lease and contains terms and conditions normally found in leases, that is not a decisive factor.

In support of his argument counsel referred to the several restrictive terms and conditions of the leases and retail dealers' agreements as hereinafter set out:

(a) The provisions in the leases that the tenant "will not use the demised premises for the storage or parking of motor vehicles nor will he permit the same, unless herein otherwise expressly authorized; he will indicate by signs, notices and such other methods as are satisfactory to BA that he is the sole proprietor of the business carried on in the demised premises; he will not erect any building or other structure on the said lands, and will not make any additions to or changes in the present buildings or equipment without the consent of BA in writing. ..."

(b) A covenant by the tenant "to execute BA's Retail Dealer Sales Agreement and further to observe and perform all the terms and conditions thereof. A breach of the terms of the Retail Dealer Sales Agreement aforesaid shall constitute a breach of the terms of this lease."

(c) A clause entitling the Oil Company "to erect and maintain such advertising signs on the demised premises as it deems advisable and a covenant that the Tenant will not erect or permit to be erected or to remain on the said premises any other signs or advertising except with the written consent of BA."

Counsel for the tenants also laid stress on certain provisions of the Retail Dealer Sales Agreements by which the company agreed to supply the dealer's entire requirements of gasoline, motor oil, greases and other petroleum products and anti-freeze compounds wanted for resale through the tenant's retail business. Reference was also made to cls. 4, 6, 7, 11 and 12 of the said Agreement which are reproduced hereunder:

> 4. The dealer covenants and agrees that during the term of this agreement he will, continuously and exclusively, by himself or his agents or tenants, purchase, sell, advertise, trade and deal in the particular kinds, grades, and brands of product marketed by the Company to the Retail Dealer Trade generally, at the time and point of delivery, and further covenants and agrees that during the term of this agreement no petroleum products other than those of the Company will be used, stored, sold or otherwise dealt in, on or about the above named premises or any other premises leased, owned or controlled by the Dealer within one mile of the said premises, said covenant being one of the main considerations for the Company entering into this agreement. The covenants set forth in this paragraph are to run with the lands comprising the above named premises.
>
> 6. The dealer agrees to provide and maintain without cost to the Company on the above named premises equipment and facilities for the storage, display, sale and delivery of the

petroleum products hereinbefore mentioned and agrees that the said equipment and facilities during the term of this agreement will be used exclusively for the handling of products purchased from the Company.

7. The dealer covenants and agrees to use the BA Record Keeper for keeping proper accounting records and the salesman of the Company shall have the right of access to these records at any time. At the Company's discretion provision may be made for the garage operators to use their own accounting books of record in place of the BA Record Keeper.

11. This agreement supersedes all retail dealer sales agreements heretofore made between the parties.

12. This agreement shall remain in force for ten (10) years from the 1st day of January, 1957; and shall renew itself automatically from year to year thereafter unless written notice of termination is given by either party to the other at least ninety (90) days prior to the expiration of the said term or of any renewal period.

It was contended by counsel for the tenants that these restrictive provisions were so completely inconsistent with a tenant's free use and enjoyment of property demised under a tenancy agreement as to constitute an effective derogation from that right of exclusive possession to which a tenant is by law entitled; that consequently the tenants had been granted no higher right than a mere right of occupancy as licensees for the purposes mentioned in the material documents.

Wherever the relationship of landlord and tenant exists there is present the element of permission or consent on the part of the landlord, and subordination to the landlord's title and rights on the part of the tenant. There must be a reversion in the landlord, the creation of an estate in the tenant, and a transfer of possession and control of the premises to the tenant. The reservation of rent to the landlord is usual but not in all cases essential, and whether the rent reserved is payable in money or through some other medium has no particular significance. It will be observed, therefore, that the transmission of an estate to the tenant is an essential characteristic of the relationship of landlord and tenant. No estate in the land passes to a licensee and this, on the authorities, is the principal distinguishing trait between the two relationships. An agreement which confers exclusive possession of the premises as against all the world, including the owner, is a lease, while if it merely confers a privilege to occupy under the owner, it is a licence. It is often difficult to determine whether a particular agreement is to be regarded as a lease or a licence. Broadly speaking, however, the general concept of a licence is that it is a mere permission to occupy the land of another for some particular purpose.

In *Thomas v. Sorrell* (1673), Vaugh. 330 at p. 351, 124 ER 1098, Vaughan CJ defined a licence in these words: "A dispensation or licence properly passeth no interest, nor alters or transfers property in any thing, but only makes an action lawful, which without it had been unlawful."

In *Errington v. Errington*, [1952] 1 KB 290, Denning LJ stated at pp. 296-7 that in distinguishing between these two relationships a crucial test had sometimes been supposed to be whether the occupier had exclusive possession or not; that if he was let into exclusive possession he was said to be a tenant, albeit only a tenant at will, whereas if he had not exclusive possession he was only a licensee. After referring to *Doe d. Tomes v. Chamberlaine* (1839), 4 M & W 14 at p. 16, 151 ER 7; *Lynes v. Snaith*, [1899] 1 QB 486;

Peakin v. Peakin, [1895] 2 IR 359; and *Howard v. Shaw* (1841), 8 M & W 118, 151 ER 973, Denning LJ stated: "The test of exclusive possession is by no means decisive."

The question was again considered by the Court of Appeal in England in *Addiscombe Garden Estates Ltd. v. Crabbe*, [1958] 1 QB 513. In that case the trustees of a members' lawn tennis club entered into an agreement with the owners of tennis courts and a club house, whereby the owners purported to "license and authorize" the trustees to use and enjoy the premises for 2 years from May 1, 1954 in consideration of monthly payments of "court fees." The agreement contained a number of clauses providing for repair and maintenance by the tennis club's trustees; for permitting the grantors to enter and inspect the condition of the premises, and for all other reasonable purposes. The owners also covenanted for quiet enjoyment, and the agreement provided that the grantors might "re-enter and determine the licence in the event of non-payment of any of the said payments of court fees ... or on any breach of ... the grantees' stipulations." The trustees continued to occupy the property after the expiration of the agreement, asserting that the agreement had granted them a tenancy which was protected by Part II of the *Landlord and Tenant Act* of 1954 which afforded security of tenure to any tenancy "where the property comprised in the tenancy is or includes premises which are occupied by the tenant and are so occupied for the purposes of a business carried on by him." It was held that the agreement taken as a whole, although described as a licence, on its true construction created the relationship of landlord and tenant and not that of licensor and licensee; that the true relationship was to be determined by the law and not by the label which the parties chose to put on it. At p. 528, Jenkins LJ referred to the statement of Denning LJ in *Errington v. Errington* (*supra*) that: "The test of exclusive possession is by no means decisive." In commenting upon that statement, Jenkins LJ stated: "I think that wide statement must be treated as qualified by his [Denning LJ's] observations in *Facchini v. Bryson*, [1952] 1 TLR 1386 at 1389, and it seems to me that, save in exceptional cases of the kind mentioned by Denning LJ in that case [*Errington v. Errington*], the law remains that the fact of exclusive possession, if not decisive against the view that there is a mere licence, as distinct from a tenancy, is at all events a consideration of the first importance. In the present case there is not only the indication afforded by the provision which shows that exclusive occupation was intended, but there are all the various other matters which I have mentioned, which appear to me to show that the actual interest taken by the grantees under the document was the interest of tenants, and not the interest of mere licensees."

I am unable to accept the submission of counsel for the respondent that the nature of the reservations or restrictions contained in the documents under review is such as to prevent the service station leases, as modified or qualified by the accompanying agreements, from being in law demises of the land. An answer to this contention is afforded by the proposition laid down in *Glenwood Lumber Co. v. Phillips*, [1904] AC 405. In that case the Government of Newfoundland had granted a licence to the respondent giving him an exclusive right of occupation of the land, though subject to reservations and to a restriction as to its user. Before the granting of this licence the appellants, who expected that they themselves would obtain the licence, commenced cutting timber on the land comprised therein and continued to do so until 3 days after its grant, notwithstanding the receipt of a formal notice from the respondent, and thereafter they removed the logs which had been cut. It was held that the lessee had lawful possession of the logs so cut which established a good title against the appellants with the right to consequent relief, namely, to recover the value of the logs removed. At p. 408, Lord Davey, who wrote the opinion of the Board, disposed of the appellant's contention that the instrument was only a licence which did not carry with it an interest in the land itself in these words: "The appellants contended that this instrument conferred only a licence to cut timber and carry it away, and did not give the respondent any right of occupation or interest in the land itself. Having regard to the provisions of the Act under the powers of which it was executed and to the language of the document itself, their Lordships cannot adopt this view of the construction or effect of it. In the so-called licence itself it is called indifferently a licence and a demise, but in the Act it is spoken of as a lease, and the holder of it is described as the lessee. It is not, however, a question of words but of substance. If the effect of the instrument is to give to the holder an exclusive right of occupation of the land, *though subject to certain reservations or to a restriction of the purposes for which it may be used*, it is in law a demise of the land itself."

I can perceive no analogy between the present case and such cases as *Edwardes v. Barrington* (1901), 85 LT 650 (HL); *Frank Warr & Co. v. London County Council*, [1904] 1 KB 713 and *Clore v. Theatrical Properties Ltd. & Westby & Co.*, [1936] 3 All ER 483, which involved agreements for what are frequently described as "the front of the house rights," under which the owner or lessee of a theatre grants to the licensee the use of refreshments rooms in the theatre for the purpose of supplying refreshments to and for the accommodation of visitors to the theatre during specified periods of the day. In those cases it was held that the contracts did not confer an interest in land, and that the documents creating the rights were not leases, but licences only, which created a purely personal right. Other instances of agreements which were held to create licences are stated in 23 Hals., 3d ed., p. 429, para. 1025. In those cases the persons granted the right to use the premises were held not to have become entitled to the exclusive possession thereof, and the circumstances and conduct of the parties indicated that all that was intended was that the grantee should be granted a personal privilege with no interest in the land itself.

In *Wells v. Mayor, etc. of Kingston-upon-Hull* (1875), LR 10 CP 402, the defendants, a municipal corporation, owned a dock of which they allowed the use to ships requiring repairs. The regulations governing the use of the dock provided that it should be "let" to parties requiring the same for the repair of vessels at rates to be fixed by the council of the borough. The regulations contained provisions that the defendants should be entitled to detain the vessel in the dock until the dockage was paid, that the corporation foreman should open and shut the dock gates, and various other provisions tending to show that the defendants intended to retain possession of and control over the dock while in use by vessels. The plaintiffs complained that the defendants did not admit their vessel into the dock in her turn, and it was held in an action for breach of contract by the plaintiff that the contract was not for an interest in land within s. 4 of the *Statute of Frauds* and therefore was not required to be in writing, nor was it required to be under the seal of the corporation. In deciding this question the Court had to consider whether the parties intended to create, or the terms of the contract did in fact create the relation of landlord and tenant, or give an exclusive right to the occupation of the dock, or any other such right as would amount to an interest in land. It was held that what was granted to the plaintiff was no more than a personal licence to use the dock notwithstanding the use of the word "let" in the regulations.

To determine whether an agreement creates the relationship of landlord and tenant or merely that of licensor and licensee, the intention of the parties must be ascertained. In the present case the whole of the documents signed by the parties must be carefully scrutinized and considered. The first document, known as the service station lease is couched in language peculiar to a lease, and contains terms which leave no doubt that it was the intention of the parties that the service station operators should have exclusive possession of the land demised, subject to certain reservations and restrictions which, in the circumstances, are not extraordinary. There is nothing in the leases or the retail dealers' agreements which suggest that the landlords intended to retain possession of and control of the service station premises in a manner which would be inconsistent with the grant of a right of exclusive possession to the lessees. Not only do the agreements in question give exclusive possession to the respondents in clear and unmistakable terms, but the very nature of the acts to be done and the business to be carried on by them required that they should have exclusive possession. In plain and simple terms these agreements impose on the grantees, in substance, the rights and obligations of tenants, and on the grantors in substance the rights and obligations of a landlord. There is nothing in the surrounding circumstances which in any way modifies or qualifies that determination. I cannot avoid the conclusion that the appropriate effect to be given to the agreements under consideration is to hold that they created a tenancy rather than a mere licence.

Considerable argument was directed to the point that s. 75(1) of the *Landlord and Tenant Act* deals with cases where a "tenant after his lease or right of occupation ... has expired ... wrongfully refuses or neglects to go out of possession."

Reference was also made to s. 1(b) of the Act where "landlord" is defined as follows: " 'landlord' includes lessor, owner, the person *giving or permitting the occupation of the premises in question*, and his and their heirs and assigns and legal representatives, and in Parts II and III also includes the person entitled to the possession of the premises."

In s. 1(d) "tenant" is defined as follows: " 'tenant' includes lessee, occupant, sub-tenant, under-tenant, and his and their assigns and legal representatives."

It was therefore argued that Part III of the Act and the summary procedure thereby authorized could be invoked against the respondents, even if they were licensees entitled only to a right of occupancy under a personal licence. Since I have decided that the relationship between the parties is that of landlord and tenant, it becomes unnecessary to consider this alternative contention and I express no opinion upon the point involved.

It was not contended that the notice given by the landlord did not fully comply with the terms of the lease. I would therefore allow the appeals with costs, set aside the orders in appeal, and order that writs of possession do issue directed to the Sheriff of the County of York commanding him forthwith to place the appellants in possession of the service station premises now occupied by the respondents as tenants. The respondents should pay to the appellant the costs of the respective applicants to the County Court Judge.

Appeals allowed.

DISCUSSION NOTE

Factors Defining a Lease or a Licence

List the factors that, according to the court, suggested that the agreement was a lease. What factors suggested a licence? What appeared to be the most legally significant facts that enabled the court to reach its conclusion that this agreement was a lease?

Metro-Matic Services Ltd v Hulmann
(1973), 48 DLR (3d) 326 (Ont CA)

[In the following case, consider the extent to which the expressed intention of the parties is relevant. Does it matter whether the parties describe their agreement as a lease or a licence, or do the courts instead look to the substance of the agreement rather than the name given it by the parties?]

BROOKE JA: This is an appeal by the plaintiff from the judgment of the Honourable Mr. Justice Houlden dated April 16, 1970, dismissing the plaintiff's action for loss of profit and damages for breach of a lease dated November 20, 1963, made between the appellant as tenant and 130 Jameson Apartments as the landlord, which lease was duly assigned to the defendant respondent on June 2, 1964.

The appellant carries on the business of leasing and operating coin-operated washing machines and in June of 1963, it installed a number of its machines in the apartment building located at 130 Jameson Ave. This building is a large 108-suite apartment building and was in 1963 owned by eight individuals as tenants in common, two of whom are S.J. Mendelson and Abraham Bleeman who were at all material times also officers of the appellant company.

On November 20, 1963, the document here in question being an agreement in writing entitled "Lease Agreement," was entered into between the appellant as the tenant and 130 Jameson Avenue as the landlord. By this agreement the landlord purported to "demise and lease" to the tenant the "laundry room or rooms located on the ground floor of the Landlord's premises." The document is now set out in full:

METRO-MATIC SERVICES LIMITED
Toronto, Ontario
LEASE AGREEMENT
THIS INDENTURE OF LEASE made the twentieth day of November, 1963, BETWEEN:
130 Jameson Apartments
hereinafter called "the Landlord"
—and—
METRO-MATIC SERVICES LIMITED
hereinafter called "the Tenant"

WHEREAS the Landlord is the owner of certain lands and apartment building(s), known as 130 Jameson Apartments located at 130 Jameson Avenue, in the City of Toronto, hereinafter called the "Landlord's premises."

NOW THIS INDENTURE WITNESSETH:

1. In consideration of the rents, covenants and agreements hereinafter reserved and contained on the part of the Tenant, the Landlord does demise and lease unto the Tenant the laundry room or rooms located on the ground floor(s) of the Landlord's premises.

2. To have and to hold the demised premises for and during the term of five (5) years to be computed from the 20 day of November, 1963; provided that this lease shall automatically renew itself for a further term of Five (5) years, unless either party, at least three months prior to the end of the term hereby granted or any renewal thereof, gives notice in writing to the other party of its intention to terminate this Lease.

3. Yielding and paying therefor during the term hereby granted, and any renewal thereof, unto the Landlord the sum of:
   ONE DOLLAR AND TWENTY-FIVE CENTS ($1.25) per suite per month payable quarterly, the first of such payments to become due and payable on the 31st day of December 1963.

4. The Tenant covenants and agrees that the demised premises shall be used only for the purpose of carrying on the business of an automatic laundry.

5. The Landlord covenants with the Tenant for quiet enjoyment.

6. The Landlord further covenants and agrees as follows:

   (a) the Tenant shall have the sole and exclusive right to install and maintain as many automatic washing machines and dryers, coin changers and soap machines as the Tenant in its absolute discretion shall deem necessary to properly serve the tenants of the Landlord's premises, as well as installing from time to time such other machines and equipment as the Tenant shall deem necessary.

   (b) the authorized employees and agents of the Tenant shall have free access to the demised premises at all reasonable times to install, inspect, service, repair or remove the said machines and equipment and to collect the monies deposited therein;

   (c) notwithstanding anything contained in the Landlord and Tenant Act, Revised Statutes of Ontario, 1960, Chapter 206, and amendments thereto (the benefit of which the Landlord hereby irrevocably waives) or any other Act of the Province of Ontario both present and future, the said machines and equipment referred to herein shall not be subject to distress or seizure by the Landlord or its agents by reason of any default whatever by the Tenant, its employees and agents; and the said machines and equipment shall not become fixtures of the Landlord, but shall remain the personal property of the Tenant;

   (d) to pay all charges for water and electricity incurred as a result of the use of the said machines and equipment;

   (e) to permit the tenants of the Landlord's premises to have free access to the demised premises and to have the use of the machines and equipment at all reasonable times;

   (f) in the event the Landlord's premises shall be sold during the term hereby granted or any renewal thereof, then the Landlord shall, prior to the closing of any such purchase and sale, obtain from the purchaser and remit to the Tenant a written acknowledgment by the purchaser that he agrees to be bound by the terms, covenants and conditions set forth herein;

(g) the Landlord will pay all taxes, duties and assessments whatsoever whether municipal, parliamentary or otherwise which during the said term may be charged upon the demised premises or upon the Landlord or Tenant in respect hereof;

(h) no part of the Landlord's premises shall during the term hereby granted or any renewal thereof, be leased, licensed or in any other way granted to any other person or corporation other than the Tenant for any of the aforementioned purposes.

7. Provided that the Tenant may remove the said machines and equipment.

8. Provided that in the event the demised premises are damaged by reason of fire, lightning, tempest or any of the other elements, then rent shall cease until the demised premises are rebuilt.

9. Provided that in the event the Landlord's premises other than the demised premises are rendered wholly unfit for occupancy by the tenants thereof, by reason of fire, lightning, tempest or for any other reason whatever, then the rent provided for herein shall cease until such time as the Landlord's premises are restored to the condition they were in prior to being rendered unfit for occupancy and the said Landlord's premises are again reoccupied to the extent of the occupancy prior to such damage; provided further that in the event only part of the Landlord's premises normally occupied by tenants are rendered unfit for occupancy, then the rent provided for herein shall abate in the proportion that the part of the Landlord's premises occupied by tenants after such damage bears to that part of the Landlord's premises ordinarily occupied by tenants.

10. Provided that if in the opinion of the Tenant, the Landlord has been in breach of any of the terms, covenants and agreements contained herein, the Tenant may terminate this Lease upon seven (7) days' written notice to the Landlord.

11. Any notice required or contemplated by any of the provisions of this Lease or which the Landlord or Tenant may desire to give to the other shall be sufficiently given to the Tenant by personal delivery or by registered letter, postage prepaid addressed to the Tenant at 153 Viewmount Avenue, Toronto 19, Ontario, and to the Landlord by registered mail postage prepaid and addressed to the said Landlord at

130 Jameson Avenue, Toronto, Ontario.

12. This Lease shall ensure to the benefit of and be binding upon the parties hereto, their heirs, executors, administrators, successors and assigns respectively.

IN WITNESS WHEREOF the parties hereto have executed these presents.

130 Jameson Apartments

SIGNED SEALED AND DELIVERED,
in the presence of

Per:
Landlord

(Seal)

METRO-MATIC SERVICES

Per:

(Seal)

On May 14, 1964, an offer was made by the respondent to S.J. Mendelson in trust for the eight tenants in common to purchase the building. It is clear from the evidence that before making this offer to purchase, the respondent had carried out an inspection of the building and was fully aware that the coin-operated laundry machines were in place on the premises and that they were not owned by the vendor, a fact which is set out in a schedule to the agreement of purchase and sale to the respondent's knowledge.

The offer to purchase provided in para. 12:

> The Vendor will deliver to the Purchaser's solicitor at least one week before closing date, all existing leases with sufficient assignment of leases, together with appropriate direction to all the tenants with respect of payment of rent to the Purchaser.

The respondent's offer was accepted and prior to closing the transaction the respondent's solicitors availed themselves of the opportunity of examining the lease agreement and other relevant leases. On June 1, 1964, the transaction was closed and at that time the respondent's solicitors received an assignment of the "lease agreement." The respondent took possession on June 2, 1964, and thereafter, while he accepted two rent cheques dated June 30, and September 30, 1964, almost immediately after taking possession commenced to negotiate for the supply of laundry equipment with another company and requested the appellant to remove its equipment from the premises. In October of 1964, the appellant contends that the respondent disconnected its equipment which the appellant then removed from the premises claiming damages arising from a breach of the lease and for loss of profit.

Houlden J dismissed the plaintiff's action, finding that the "lease agreement" did not constitute a valid lease between the parties named therein and that it was no more than a mere licence, as it failed to create any estate in the appellant. The appeal to this Court is upon two grounds; first, that the trial Judge erred in finding that there was no valid lease and secondly, and in the alternative, that the appellant had an equitable interest in the premises and, in the circumstances here present, the respondent had actual notice of the appellant's interest.

Turning to the first question, what is the effect of the "Lease Agreement" dated November 20, 1963?

After considering the authorities, the learned trial Judge considered the "Lease Agreement" and it appears directing his attention to the meaning and interpretation arising from the covenants, particularly cl. 6, held that the tenant had no exclusive possession of the premises or right to exclusive possession. Indeed, he found the right of occupation was not in the tenant but rather in the landlord and that the appellant's right to enter was limited to a right to enter at reasonable times to service its machines as set out. His view of the document was really that it was no more than a concession agreement to make laundry services available to the tenants in the 108 suites of the building.

Perhaps the most recent authoritative statement on the subject of the requirements of a lease and the interpretation of such documents is that of Schroeder JA in *Re BA Oil Co. and Halpert*, [1960] OR 71, 21 DLR (2d) 110 *sub nom. Re BA Oil Co. Ltd. and dePass*. This was a case in which conditions attached to agreements entitled leases were said to prevent them from being in law a demise of land. At p. 77 OR, p. 115 DLR, Schroeder JA said:

> Wherever the relationship of landlord and tenant exists there is present the element of permission or consent on the part of the landlord, and subordination to the landlord's title and rights on the part of the tenant. There must be a reversion in the landlord, the creation of an estate in the tenant, and a transfer of possession and control of the premises to the tenant. The reservation of rent to the landlord is usual but not in all cases essential, and whether the

rent reserved is payable in money or through some other medium has no particular significance. It will be observed, therefore, that the transmission of an estate to the tenant is an essential characteristic of the relationship of landlord and tenant. No estate in the land passes to a licensee and this, on the authorities, is the principal distinguishing trait between the two relationships. An agreement which confers exclusive possession of the premises as against all the world, including the owner, is a lease, while if it merely confers a privilege to occupy under the owner, it is a licence. It is often difficult to determine whether a particular agreement is to be regarded as a lease or a licence. Broadly speaking, however, the general concept of a licence is that it is a mere permission to occupy the land of another for some particular purpose.

He went on to consider the question raised by a statement in the judgment of Denning LJ in *Errington v. Errington and Woods*, [1952] 1 KB 290 at p. 297, a case which required consideration of the distinction between contractual or equitable rights as opposed to the rights of a tenant to remain in possession of property so long as conditions under a long term agreement of purchase and sale were fulfilled. In this context he said: "The test of exclusive possession is by no means decisive."

After considering the explanation of this statement quoted in the judgment of Jenkins LJ in *Addiscombe Garden Estates Ltd. v. Crabbe*, [1958] 1 KB 513, and the speech of Lord Davey in *Glenwood Lumber Co. Ltd. v. Phillips*, [1904] AC 405 at p. 408, the learned Judge concluded that to create the relationship of landlord and tenant the tenant must have exclusive possession of the demised premises and proceeded to examine documents there in question to determine if it was the intention of the parties to confer such an estate on the tenant. See also E.K. Williams, *Canadian Law of Landlord and Tenant*, 3d ed. (1957), pp. 4, 9, 11.

Turning then to the document before the Court entitled "Lease Agreement," it is significant that the parties have been careful to employ numerous words customarily used in leases but, perhaps more important, words traditionally required to create an estate or interest in land. One cannot ignore the important effect of the words "demise" and "lease" and of the *habendum* and the covenant for quiet enjoyment which I should think, in the absence of a clear statement of the parties' intention to the contrary, are conclusive of the intention to grant a lease of the land in question with exclusive possession and control thereof.

However, the document contained a restriction that the premises shall only be used for the purpose of carrying on the business of an automatic laundry. Relying upon this and cl. 6 of the agreement, Mr. Hately firmly contends that the parties' intention was to create nothing more than a concession to provide a service for tenants in the building and at the same time that the landlord retain the right to possession and to control the use of the premises. He points out that the document provides for automatic machines with no reference to attendants being provided or needed and that provision is made to assure that all of the tenants in the building will have free access to the laundry premises and the appellant has not the freedom of access to the building of an ordinary tenant but is restricted rather to "reasonable times" and then only for specific purposes. In the result, he contends that there can be in these circumstances no exclusive possession or control in the appellant.

With deference to these arguments and to the judgment in appeal, I am persuaded that the appeal must succeed. While it is true that the appellant has by its own covenant restricted the use to which it will put the premises, such a covenant does not affect the demise any more than would be the case when a tenant covenants to use his apartment as a dwelling place only. This does not make his possession any the less exclusive. I do not think that cl. 6 of the landlord's covenant should now be interpreted at his suit to change or modify an intention otherwise expressed in the document by important words as above set out so that he or his assigns can escape liability as now contended for. When in consideration of the tenant's covenant to pay rent and do those things required of him, the landlord demised the premises to the tenant surely except in unusual circumstances only an express restriction as to possession and control should be regarded and restrictions should not be read into the document because of positive covenants on the part of the landlord as are found in cl. 6.

This "Lease Agreement" provided for the demise of the premises and for carrying on of a business there. In such circumstances I should think that it was really unnecessary to include covenants to provide for the tenant's occupancy of the premises or the installation of the machinery and equipment needed for the business contemplated by the parties and the access to the premises in a multiple occupancy building should be implied with the demise and in circumstances such as these it was really unnecessary to require a covenant to permit the installation, maintenance, replacement and removal of the automatic machines. Further, perhaps because the appellant was a limited company and carried on business by its employees and agents, it considered it better to obtain the covenant cl. 6(b) and it was no doubt prudent to obtain the covenant cl. 6(a) when at the same time obtaining from the landlord its covenant with respect to competition. As to cl. 6(c) the tenants of the building were to be the appellant's customers and if the demised premises were to be kept locked and used only for the purposes as the parties intended at any hour of the night or day, it was also prudent for the appellant to obtain the covenant in cl. 6(c).

None of these covenants make the appellant's possession any the less exclusive; none of these covenants relinquish any control by the appellant to the landlord; indeed to the contrary, they assure the appellant's exclusive possession and assure its control and occupancy.

In the circumstances, I hold that the document was intended to and did in fact confer upon the appellant exclusive possession and exclusive control of the demised premises. Under this agreement the landlord had no right to possession and no right to control of the demised premises. Conversely, the appellant alone had these rights and with them all of the obligations and liabilities of a tenant. The document is a valid lease and the defendant has breached it as alleged.

Counsel contended that the document was ineffective because the lessor lacked the status to enter into such a contract. This issue was not raised at the trial. Having regard to all of the circumstances and the evidence, I am of the conclusion that the document was properly entered into by persons duly authorized to do so.

In the result, then, the appeal is allowed. The finding as to damages made by the learned trial Judge is not disputed in this appeal. Accordingly, the judgment below will be set aside and judgment will go for the plaintiff in the sum of $2,043.75. The appellant should have its costs at the trial and in this Court.

Appeal allowed.

DISCUSSION NOTES

i. A Lease or a Licence?

If the agreement in *Metro-Matic Services Ltd* was a "lease," why did the drafters of the agreement include clause 6(b) that provided that the tenant shall have "free access to the demised premises at all reasonable times"?

If this agreement was a licence only, could the occupier Metro-Matic still successfully argue that the licence, notwithstanding the absence of privity of contract, nonetheless bound the new owner of the building? Is it relevant that the purchaser took the building with actual notice of the agreement with Metro-Matic, and further accepted two cheques from Metro-Matic after the sale was completed? What legal arguments might Metro-Matic raise?

ii. Pacific Wash-A-Matic Ltd v RO Booth Holdings Ltd

In *Pacific Wash-A-Matic Ltd v RO Booth Holdings Ltd*, [1979] 6 WWR 458, 105 DLR (3d) 323 (BCCA), the plaintiff laundry company entered into an agreement, called a "location agreement," with the owner of an apartment building. The agreement granted Pacific Wash-A-Matic the exclusive right to install and maintain coin-operated laundry machines in the apartment building. Clause 16 stated that the agreement was binding on the parties and that, should the owner sell or assign his interest in the premises, his successor would be fully bound by the terms of the agreement.

The building was sold to a third party, the entire "location agreement" was attached to the agreement for sale, and the sales agreement made specific mention of the location agreement. Seven months later, the new owner attempted to terminate the agreement, eventually locking the laundry room and removing the machines to a storage area. At trial, the court found that the location agreement was a lease and consequently was binding on the new owner. On appeal, this decision was reversed, and the court held that there were no provisions in the present agreement such as those in *Metro-Matic*. In particular, the agreement did not provide for any demise of any portion of the apartment building. Instead, the court held that the agreement was merely a licence to place laundry machines in the building. The court thus concluded that the trial judge had been wrong and that the location agreement did not constitute a lease and was not binding on the new owner.

Why was clause 16 held to be of no effect by the court? Is it fair that the new owner should not be bound by this agreement?

D. "Residential" Leases and Licences

The following case considers circumstances that include aspects of both a commercial and a residential agreement, raising the question whether a long-term resident in a hotel can evolve from a mere licensee to a tenant. Consider the legal consequences of determining that a hotel resident can be a tenant. Is it fair that a long-term resident in a hotel should be accorded no more than the same legal rights provided to a short-term resident? Should it matter how long a person has been resident in the hotel? Why?

Re Canadian Pacific Hotels Ltd and Hodges
(1978), 23 OR (2d) 577 (Co Ct)

COO CCJ: Default judgment under the provisions of the *Landlord and Tenant Act*, RSO 1970, c. 236 having been set aside, this matter has come on again for formal and contested hearing.

The applicant, Canadian Pacific Hotels Limited, asks for judgment against the respondent, William E. Hodges, in the amount of $13,290 for rent owing for rooms nos. 11-297 and 11-299 at the Royal York Hotel in the City of Toronto.

The applicant claims that the relationship between the parties at all material times was that of landlord and tenant, there being a tenancy at will between the contracting parties.

The respondent takes the position that there was never in existence a landlord and tenant relationship, and that, in consequence, the applicant has no right to make use of the provisions of the *Landlord and Tenant Act* to attempt to recover rent owing.

There has been reserved for later disposition, if necessary, a defence upon which the respondent would seek to rely, if the landlord and tenant relationship is established, which defence, briefly set forth in Mr. Hodges' affidavit sworn September 19, 1978, is to the effect that the premises involved were dirty and unsafe, this presumably leading to a claim for abatement of rent. The alleged arrears of rent have not been paid into Court pursuant to the provisions of s. 106(6) [rep. & sub. 1975 (2d sess.), c. 13, s. 5(1)] of the *Landlord and Tenant Act*. Counsel for the respondent has argued that these proceedings ought never to reach the point where the strength and validity of the aforementioned defence of the respondent comes into issue, this in the light of the alleged inapplicability of all of the provisions of the *Landlord and Tenant Act* to the circumstances of this case. In addition, counsel for the respondent argues that the case of *Re Sam Richman Investments (London) Ltd. and Reidel et al.* (1974), 6 OR (2d) 335, 52 DLR (3d) 655, a decision of the Divisional Court, stands for the proposition that the only funds which in any event the respondent would be obliged to pay into Court under the provisions of s. 106(6), are those which might otherwise be said to be payable after notice of early termination was given by the applicant on June 26, 1978. In fact, Mr. Hodges and his family quit the two hotel rooms on July 22, 1978, which would mean, if counsel for the respondent is right, that the amount which ought to be paid into Court to permit the foregoing defence by his client to be presented would be at a daily rate of $54 for the period of time between the two above-mentioned dates.

The applicant of course takes the view that, assuming the landlord and tenant relationship to have existed, the amount of rent which would have to be paid into Court to permit the respondent to put forward the foregoing defence would involve the total amount allegedly owing, and not just the rent due for the approximate one-month period referred to by counsel for the respondent.

I have read the *Richman* case with some care and I do not accept that it stands for the proposition put forward by counsel for the respondent and, on this narrow issue, I would be prepared to rule that the respondent would be obliged, all other matters apart, to pay into Court the whole amount claimed as being arrears of rent, as a condition precedent to his being heard with respect to his other defences.

Counsel for the respondent also argued that the hotel rooms occupied over the years by the Hodges family were not "residential premises," to which kind of premises Part IV of the *Landlord and Tenant Act* applies. He referred to the definition section, s. 1(c) [rep. & sub. 1975 (2d sess.), c. 13, s. 12] and argued that the evidence supported the proposition that the rooms constituted "premises occupied for business purposes with living accommodation attached, ..." and that by reason of s. 1(c)(iii) the rooms could not constitute "residential premises."

On all of the evidence I cannot agree. I am satisfied that the rooms constituted "residential premises" as they are defined in the Act, and that, although the respondent did indeed engage in some business activities in the rooms, they were indeed "premises used or intended for use for residential purposes" as that phrase is used in s. 1(c)(i).

That leaves for determination the major problem, which is whether there was in existence between the parties to these proceedings a landlord and tenant relationship.

Essentially the facts are that the respondent and his family, as it was constituted from time to time over the years, have lived in the two hotel rooms for well over 15 years. There was at no time any agreement in writing with regard to this occupancy.

The respondent decided, for reasons which at least satisfied him, that it made sense to live in a well-constructed, well-managed hotel. The hotel was willing to provide to Hodges the two rooms which he and his wife ultimately selected. Hodges was charged on a *per diem* basis a somewhat lower rate than would have been charged to a transient guest. He was apparently generally billed monthly, for a long time, not only for room charges but also for room service, meals, and other sorts of services generally provided to its guest by a hotel. It is to be emphasized that the claim in these proceedings is limited to the amount allegedly owing for the rooms themselves.

There is really very little evidence indeed on the basis of which any meaningful, sensible and firm conclusions can be reached as to what was intended by the parties.

What seems to me to be fairly clear is that what was furnished to Hodges and members of his family was really in no way different from that which any guest at the hotel could reasonably expect to have had furnished to him. Daily maid service was provided and was available, although Hodges himself indicated that he was reluctant to have maids in the rooms at certain times.

Hodges introduced into at least one, and probably both of the rooms, some of his own furniture, this at least mostly coming from a room in the same hotel occupied by Hodges' mother for some years prior to her death. No one told me how much decorating was done of the two rooms over the period of 15 years, who did the decorating, who paid for it, or who was responsible for choosing the form and nature of the decoration. From the little evidence that was given on this point I gathered that the hotel took the view that they were entitled to decorate these rooms as they would the others, and that perhaps Hodges took a slightly different view.

The hotel kept putting up what one might call the usual standard innkeeper's signs within the two rooms. This I suppose might, to a very minor degree, tend to lead one towards one conclusion as to the relationship between the parties. The difficulty about the signs is that Mr. Hodges took it upon himself to remove the signs as soon as they were put up by the hotel forces which in, and of itself, would tend to lead to another conclusion.

Little or no cooking of any kind was done in either of the two rooms by the Hodges family during all the years they occupied the premises.

I gather that save for the introduction into the premises of some pieces of privately-owned furniture and, at the request of Hodges, a well-worn piano which the hotel was willing to place in the premises, and subject to the question of decoration, the two rooms were like any others which might be found in a hotel containing something between one and two thousand rooms.

Mr. Hodges had introduced into one of the two rooms and at one stage in his stay an extension of a telephone line which was introduced into a store in the basement arcade of the hotel building, at a time when that store was occupied by a company in which Hodges had a major interest. It is not clear from the evidence whether that telephone continued in existence after vacation of the store premises by the company. In any event, the rooms were serviced in the ordinary way and in accordance with ordinary custom by hotel telephones connected to the hotel switchboard.

When the Hodges family ultimately came to vacate the premises they "checked out" in pretty much precisely the same sort of way that anyone else would check out, save and except of course for the fact that there allegedly was owing by Hodges at the time he checked out many, many thousands of dollars.

The sum and substance of the evidence is to indicate that the Hodges family acted and were treated by the hotel and its staff as though they were just four more guests in the hotel. The only difference of any moment was that Hodges remained in the hotel for over 15 years.

Very few cases were cited by counsel in argument touching upon the problem which is before me now for determination. I have read all of them, and a very large number in addition, including some of the basic cases which are found referred to again and again in cases dealing with whether a particular fact situation reflects a true landlord and tenant relationship, a licenser and licensee relationship, or some other. I include in this much shorter list of cases such decisions as *Cobb et al. v. Lane*, [1952] 1 All ER 1199, *Errington v. Errington et al.*, [1952] 1 All ER 149, and *Abbeyfield (Harpenden) Society Ltd. v. Woods*, [1968] 1 All ER 352.

I have gone through all the textbooks on the subject which I thought might be of any guidance and I have read a very large number of the cases therein referred to. I have frankly not found any number of cases of any direct and conclusive guidance or assistance.

✳ It is relatively easy to state the principles. In determining whether an agreement between the parties constitutes a relationship of landlord and tenant or only that of licenser and licensee, the major consideration is the intention of the parties. If there is no formal agreement, in writing or otherwise, this intention must be gathered from all of the facts and circumstances and the conduct of the parties. The fact that the agreement grants a right of exclusive possession is, while important, by no manner or means conclusive.

Having reviewed again and again all of the factual circumstances of this case, including, but not to the exclusion of others, those elements to which I have made specific and direct reference, it has not been made out in this case that there existed at the material time a landlord and tenant relationship. It seems to me that essentially the only factual circumstance which points in this direction is the length of occupancy of the rooms by Hodges and his family. That is obviously of some importance but the difficulty is that whatever its length, the relationship between the parties was really no different than would have been that same relationship had Hodges' stay in the hotel lasted for a week. I do not and cannot accept that it was ever in the mind of either party to these proceedings that a legal estate of any kind had passed from the applicant to the respondent.

There was what might generally be described as exclusivity of possession but there remained a general, over-all control of the property by the applicant. While it is by no manner or means conclusive or even perhaps particularly important in this case, given the specific argument made on behalf of the applicant, I think, had the parties been asked before litigation became a possibility, both would have agreed that the occupant had absolutely nothing which he was entitled to assign or sublet to anyone else.

I have come to the conclusion on all of the evidence before me that the applicant has not made out its right to proceed under the provisions of Part IV of the *Landlord and Tenant Act*, and that it has not demonstrated that it was at the material time a "landlord" under the provisions of that statute. In this regard I should emphasize that counsel for the applicant specifically stated that he was not seeking to allege or argue that his client was a "person giving or permitting the occupation of the premises in question" thus qualifying to be considered as a landlord whether or not the applicant was a lessor. Similarly, counsel indicated that he did not wish to adopt the position that Mr. Hodges was an "occupant" and thus a tenant as that word is defined in the *Landlord and Tenant Act*. The whole case has proceeded and has been argued on both sides on the basis that the question for ultimate determination is whether there was a landlord and tenant relationship, that is, whether there was a lessor and lessee relationship involved between the parties during the period of time which is relevant to these proceedings and to the claim for arrears of rent now presented.

In the result, the applicant's claim must be dismissed with costs.

Claim dismissed.

DISCUSSION NOTES

i. The Issue of Intention

In *Canadian Pacific Hotels and Hodges*, the court concluded that the parties never intended that the occupant acquire an estate in land assignable to third parties and concluded that this indicated that the agreement was a licence only. It is not clear that either party ever put their minds to this question. Is it fair to base the decision on such speculation?

What are the most relevant facts identified by the court that led to the conclusion that the agreement in question was a licence only? How does this case differ from *British American Oil* and *Metro-Matic Ltd*?

ii. The Residential Tenancies Act, 2006

In Ontario, the *Residential Tenancies Act, 2006*, s 2(1) provides that a "residential unit" is "any living accommodation used or intended for use as rental residential premises." However, unlike the act in force at the time *Hodges* was decided, s 5(a) of the *Residential Tenancies Act, 2006* also specifically provides that the Act does not apply to "living accommodation intended to be provided to the travelling or vacationing public or occupied for a seasonal or temporary period in a hotel." It seems clear that the Act is not intended to apply to hotel accommodation; one can thus anticipate that the outcome of *Canadian Pacific Hotels v Hodges* would be the same under the new legislation. Is it still possible, however, to argue that, on the facts of *Canadian Pacific Hotels v Hodges*, the 15-year occupation period was not "temporary" and thus not covered by s 5(a) of the Act?

V. PRINCIPLES OF PROPERTY AND CONTRACT IN LEASEHOLDS: TERMINATION REMEDIES

The applicable legislation and common law governing leaseholds forms a large and complex body of law. This section of the casebook does not attempt to provide a comprehensive introduction to landlord and tenant law; for areas not covered here, see Christopher Bentley et al, eds, *Williams and Rhodes Canadian Law of Landlord and Tenant*, loose-leaf, 6th ed (Toronto: Carswell, 1988); Harvey Haber, *The Commercial Lease: A Practical Guide*, 4th ed (Aurora, ON: Canada Law Book, 2004); Jack Fleming, *Residential Tenancies in Ontario*, 2d ed (Markham, ON: LexisNexis, 2011) [Fleming]. Instead, this section focuses on one particular issue in landlord and tenant law—the termination of leasehold estates in relation to both commercial and residential leaseholds. It considers the variety of ways in which leasehold estates may be terminated, by either the tenant or the landlord, and some of the remedies available for wrongful termination or eviction.

A. Termination of Leasehold Estates: Introduction

The issue of termination is critical for a number of reasons. First, in the context of commercial leaseholds, the courts continue to struggle with the interplay of property and contract principles in shaping the remedies available to the landlord. Although contract principles have become more prominent, property concepts remain important. Second, in the context of residential tenancies, wrongful termination by the landlord has serious consequences for the tenant, who is frequently in a weaker bargaining position than the landlord. As examined below, residential tenancy legislation in Ontario attempts to balance the competing interests of tenant and landlord: on the one hand, there is the need to provide protection for residential tenants; on the other hand, there is the need to protect the landlord's reversionary interest over the leased premises.

A lease can be terminated in a number of ways—for example, a fixed-term lease will expire naturally at the end of the term in question, although, if the tenant remains in possession and the landlord accepts rent, tenant and landlord will be found to have created a new periodic tenancy based on the rental period, whether weekly, monthly, or yearly.

A lease may also be terminated by surrender. If the parties agree that the tenant will surrender the lease before the end of its term, the landlord is entitled to resume possession and both parties are discharged from all further obligations under the lease. Although a surrender is normally consensual, it can also occur by operation of law under certain circumstances, independently of the will of the parties and even against their will. In *Perasso v Perasso*, 2011 BCSC 230, a father granted his son a 99-year lease over a residential lot to allow the son to qualify for a provincial homeowner grant. Later, when the eligibility requirements changed, the father granted his son a three-year lease over the same lot, without any reference to the earlier lease. It was held that when the son accepted the later lease, the earlier lease was surrendered by operation of law, so that he could only claim a three-year lease. This result obtains, moreover, even where the subsequent interest is not a lease but merely a licence: see

AG for Saskatchewan v Whitehorse Salt & Chemical Co, [1955] SCR 43, [1955] 1 DLR 241. Abandonment of the premises by the tenant may also lead to an implied surrender, as will be seen in *Highway Properties*, below.

In a lease, if the tenant breaches an obligation that is framed as a condition, rather than a covenant, such an act allows the landlord to terminate the lease at his or her option. A covenant is a contractual promise, while a condition is a property law concept that limits the "absolute" character of the estate granted (recall the discussion of conditions in Chapter 3). The normal remedy for the breach of a covenant in a lease is damages, while, if the landlord chooses, breach of condition may lead to forfeiture. Tenants may seek protection from forfeiture by means of certain equitable doctrines and there is also legislative protection in some provinces: see Ziff, 305-7.

Alternatively, the tenant or the landlord can wrongfully terminate the lease before the end of its term. A tenant may wrongfully repudiate the lease, vacate the premises, and cease paying rent. On the other hand, the landlord may attempt wrongfully to evict the tenant before the end of the lease. These situations can arise in either a commercial or a residential context.

Section V.B examines the wrongful repudiation of a commercial lease by a commercial tenant and considers the various remedies available to the landlord, both in contract law and property law. These remedies have evolved and changed over time, raising important issues regarding law reform in a commercial setting. In addition, these property law and contract law remedies may occasionally be in conflict, raising the question of how this conflict should be resolved.

Section V.C considers the residential context, in particular the limits of the landlord's power to evict a residential tenant. The residential context raises an important question of social policy about the extent to which the law should enhance security of tenure in residential tenancies.

B. Termination Remedies: Commercial Leaseholds

Highway Properties, which follows, examines the various remedies available to commercial landlords in the event that the tenant wrongfully repudiates a lease and ceases to pay rent. When reviewing this case, take careful note of the remedies available under property law for wrongful breach by the tenant and compare this to the typical remedies available for breach of a contract—that is, the recovery of expectation damages. How do the three property law remedies differ from the recovery of expectation damages? Why did property law develop remedies so different from those developed in contract law? What rationale can be offered for this distinction? Do the various property law remedies result in the overcompensation or undercompensation of landlords? Do the property law remedies merely supplement the contract law remedies or do the contract law remedies now effectively replace the property law remedies?

Highway Properties Ltd v Kelly, Douglas & Co
[1971] SCR 562

LASKIN J: The issue in this appeal arises out of the repudiation of an unexpired lease by the major tenant in a shopping centre and the resumption of possession by the landlord with notice to the defaulting tenant that it would be held liable for damages suffered by the landlord as a result of the admittedly wrongful repudiation. This issue raises squarely the correctness of the decision of the Ontario Court of Appeal in *Goldhar v. Universal Sections and Mouldings Ltd.*, which was followed by the majority of the British Columbia Court of Appeal in the present case.

The substantial question emerging from the facts is the measure and range of damages which the landlord, the appellant before this Court, may claim by reason of the repudiation by the tenant, the respondent herein, of its lease of certain premises, and its consequent abandonment of those premises, where the landlord took possession with a contemporaneous assertion of its right to full damages according to the loss calculable over the unexpired term of the lease. It will be necessary, in dealing with this question, to consider the situations where, upon the tenant's repudiation and abandonment, the landlord does not resume possession but insists on enforcing the lease, or takes possession on his own or on the tenant's account. A common characterization of the problem in this appeal is whether it is to be resolved according to the law of property or according to the law of contract; but, in my opinion, this is an over-simplification.

The dispute between the parties stems from a lease of August 19, 1960, under which the landlord demised certain premises in its shopping centre to the tenant "to be used for grocery store and super market." A term of fifteen years from October 1, 1960, was specified at a prescribed annual rent, payable monthly in advance, plus an additional rent based on a certain formula which need not be reproduced here. The tenant covenanted, *inter alia*, to pay rent, certain taxes and maintenance costs; not to do or suffer anything to be done on the demised premises without the landlord's consent whereby insurance policies thereon might become void or voidable or the premiums increased; and to pay into a promotion fund to be used for the benefit of the shopping centre. There were covenants for repair and provisions for renewal but their terms are not germane to the disposition of this appeal. There was also a covenant by the landlord for quiet enjoyment. Clause 5(a), so far as relevant here, provided that if the rent or any part thereof be in arrears for 15 days or if any covenant by the tenant should be unfulfilled, and the failure to pay rent or fulfill the covenant should continue 15 days after notice thereof to the tenant, then the current month's rent and three months' additional rent should immediately become due and the landlord might forthwith re-enter and thereupon the demise should absolutely determine but without prejudice to any right of action in respect of any antecedent breach of the tenant's covenants.

Clause 9, which was central to the landlord's claim for damages, was as follows:

> The tenant further covenants and agrees that it will commence to carry on its business within thirty (30) days from the completion of the demised premises and will carry on its business on the said premises continuously. The demised premises shall not be used for any other purpose than as to conduct the Tenant's business in the said premises during such hours as the Landlord may from time to time require on all business days during the term hereby

created and in such manner that the Landlord may at all times receive the maximum amount of income from the operation of such business in and upon the demised premises. The Tenant shall install and maintain at all times in the demised premises first class trade fixtures and furniture adequate and appropriate for the business of the Tenant thereon. The Tenant further agrees to conduct its business as aforesaid in the said premises during such evenings and for such hours thereof during the term hereby created as permitted by the By-laws of the Corporation of the District of North Vancouver, BC and consistent with the practices generally accepted by retail outlets in the area.

The shopping centre built by the appellant consisted of eleven stores, including the supermarket premises let to the respondent. Before buying the land on which the shopping centre was later built, the appellant obtained the commitment of the respondent to lease space therein for a food supermarket to be constructed according to its specifications. This commitment was evidenced by a lease dated blank day of May, 1960, whose terms were carried into the document of August 19, 1960. The respondent went into possession through a subtenant (with the appellant's consent) on or about October 20, 1960. By February 1961, only five other stores in the shopping centre had been let, and the venture did not prosper. The supermarket subtenant indicated its intention to close the business down on March 24, 1962, and did so. The appellant drew the respondent's attention to clause 9 of the lease and received an assurance in a letter from the respondent of March 26, 1962, that it was standing by the lease and was endeavouring to sublet its leasehold. Nothing came of its endeavours.

The closing down of the supermarket adversely affected the other tenants in the shopping centre, and by November 22, 1963 (a date whose relevance will appear later) three of those tenants had moved out. The shopping centre began to take on a "ghost-town" appearance and suffered from petty vandalism. On April 13, 1962, following the closing down of the supermarket, the appellant's solicitors wrote to the respondent, again drawing attention to clause 9 of the lease, complaining that the appellant was suffering damage and advising that they would seek compliance to have the business reopened or would claim damages. The appellant learned in July 1962 that the respondent was removing fixtures, and its solicitors wrote in objection on July 11, 1962, relying on clause 9 and on the covenant in clause 10(a) permitting removal if the tenant is not in default. The letter threatened resort to an injunction unless the removal was halted.

The action, out of which this appeal arises, was commenced on July 16, 1962, and an interlocutory injunction was sought but refused. Rent was paid by the respondent to June 1963. The statement of claim, which was delivered on May 31, 1963, asked for a declaration that the lease was binding upon the respondent, asked for a decree of specific performance and for a mandatory order and an injunction, and also sought damages. The respondent delivered a defence and counterclaim on September 12, 1963. Paragraph 8 of the counterclaim said flatly: "The Defendant hereby repudiates the said agreement dated August 19, 1960." As a result of this repudiation, the appellant's solicitors wrote to the respondent's solicitors on November 22, 1963 (a date mentioned earlier in these reasons) in these terms:

> Dear Sirs: Re: Highway Properties Limited and Kelly Douglas & Co. Ltd.
>
> This is to advise you that in view of your pleadings, our client takes the position that your client has repudiated the lease in question.

Our client, therefore, intends to take possession of the premises and will attempt to lease these upon the same terms and conditions as set out in the lease of the 19th of August, 1960.

We would further advise you that our client intends to hold your client responsible for any damages suffered by them as a result of your client's breach and wrongful repudiation of the said lease.

Following this letter the appellant took possession of the supermarket premises and attempted, without success, to re-let them for the unexpired term of the lease of the respondent. Subsequently, the appellant subdivided the premises into three stores which were eventually rented, two under a lease of March 1, 1965, and the third under a lease of November 1, 1965. At the opening of trial on November 29, 1966, the appellant obtained leave to amend its statement of claim. The amendment referred to the respondent's repudiation of the lease and to the consequent rescission of the agreement thereunder in accordance with the letter of November 22, 1963, and claimed damages not only for loss suffered to the date of the so-called rescission but also, and mainly, for prospective loss resulting from the respondent's failure to carry on a supermarket business in the shopping centre for the full term of the lease.

The theory upon which the appellant claimed damages was rejected by the trial judge, Macdonald J, and by the majority of the Court of Appeal, Davey CJBC dissenting. The holding both at trial and on appeal was that there had been a surrender of the lease by reason of the repudiation and the taking of possession by the appellant; that the principles enunciated in the *Goldhar* case were applicable; that the lease and its covenants ceased to exist with the surrender; and that the appellant could recover only for breaches occurring to the date of surrender. The damages on this footing totalled $14,256.38, composed of five months' rent; the decline in rental income in 1962 and in 1963 to the date of surrender by reason of the closing of other stores; a portion of the taxes payable for 1963; a sum for increased insurance premiums for 1963; and a portion of maintenance costs for 1963 to the date of surrender.

It is common ground, as appears from the reasons of Davey CJBC in the Court of Appeal, that if it should be determined that damages must be assessed on the basis claimed by the appellant, the assessment should be remitted to the trial judge to be made on the evidence adduced before him.

I approach the legal issue involved in this appeal by acknowledging the continuity of common law principle that a lease of land for a term of years under which possession is taken creates an estate in the land, and also the relation of landlord and tenant, to which the common law attaches various incidents despite the silence of the document thereon. For the purposes of the present case, no distinction need be drawn between a written lease and a written agreement for a lease. Although by covenants or by contractual terms, the parties may add to, or modify, or subtract from the common law incidents, and, indeed, may overwhelm them as well as the leasehold estate by commercial or business considerations which represent the dominant features of the transaction, the "estate" element has resisted displacement as the pivotal factor under the common law, at least as understood and administered in this country.

There has, however, been some questioning of this persistent ascendancy of a concept that antedated the development of the law of contracts in English law and has been transformed in its social and economic aspects by urban living conditions and by commercial practice. The judgments in the House of Lords in *Cricklewood Property and Investment Trust Ltd. v. Leighton's Investment Trust Ltd.* are illustrative. Changes in various states of the United States have been quite pronounced as is evident from 1 *American Law of Property*, 1952, #3.11.

In the various common law Provinces, standard contractual terms (reflected, for example, in Short Forms of Leases Acts) and, to a degree, legislation, have superseded the common law of landlord and tenant; for example, in prescribing for payment of rent in advance; in providing for re-entry for non-payment of rent or breaches of other covenants exacted from tenant; in modifying the absoluteness of covenants not to assign or sublet without leave; and in blunting peremptory rights of termination or forfeiture. The contractual emphasis, even when reinforced by commercial clauses testifying to the paramount business considerations in a lease of land, has hitherto stopped short of full recognition of its remedial concomitants, as, for example, the principle of anticipatory breach and the principle governing relief upon repudiation. I note that this Court had no hesitation in applying the doctrine of anticipatory breach to a contract for the sale of land, even to the point of allowing an immediate suit for specific performance (but, of course, at the time fixed for completion): see *Kloepfer Wholesale Hardware and Automotive Co. v. Roy*. I think it is equally open to consider its application to a contractual lease, although the lease is partly executed. Its anticipatory features lie, of course, in the fact that instalments of rent are payable for future periods, and repudiation of the lease raises the question whether an immediate remedy covering the loss of such rent and of other advantages extending over the unexpired term of the lease may be pursued notwithstanding that the estate in the land may have been terminated.

The developed case law has recognized three mutually exclusive courses that a landlord may take where a tenant is in fundamental breach of the lease or has repudiated it entirely, as was the case here. He may do nothing to alter the relationship of landlord and tenant, but simply insist on performance of the terms and sue for rent or damages on the footing that the lease remains in force. Second, he may elect to terminate the lease, retaining of course the right to sue for rent accrued due, or for damages to the date of termination for previous breaches of covenant. Third, he may advise the tenant that he proposes to re-let the property on the tenant's account and enter into possession on that basis. Counsel for the appellant, in effect, suggests a fourth alternative, namely, that the landlord may elect to terminate the lease but with notice to the defaulting tenant that damages will be claimed on the footing of a present recovery of damages for losing the benefit of the lease over its unexpired term. One element of such damages would be, of course, the present value of the unpaid future rent for the unexpired period of the lease less the actual rental value of the premises for that period. Another element would be the loss, so far as provable, resulting from the repudiation of clause 9. I say no more about the elements of damages here in view of what has been agreed to in that connection by the parties.

There is no need to discuss either the first or second of the alternatives mentioned above other than to say, in respect of the second, that it assumes a situation where no prospective damages could be proved to warrant any claim for them, or even to warrant taking the third alternative. I wish, however, to examine the underpinnings and implications of the third course because they have a decided bearing on whether the additional step proposed by counsel for the appellant should be taken in this case.

Where repudiation occurs in respect of a business contract (not involving any estate in land), the innocent party has an election to terminate the contract which, if exercised, results in its discharge *pro tanto* when the election is made and communicated to the wrongdoer. (I agree with the opinion of such text writers as Cheshire and Fifoot, *The Law of Contract*, 7th ed., 1969, at p. 535, that it is misleading to speak of the result as rescission when there is no retrospective cancellation *ab initio* involved.) Termination in such circumstances does not preclude a right to damages for prospective loss as well as for accrued loss.

A parallel situation of repudiation in the case of a lease has generally been considered in the language of and under the principles of surrender, specifically of surrender by operation of law or implied surrender. It is said to result when, upon the material breach or repudiation of a lease, the innocent party does an act inconsistent with the continued existence of that lease. The *Goldhar* case applied the doctrine where, upon a tenant's repudiation of a lease, the landlord re-let the premises. The further consequence of this was said to be not only the termination of the estate in the land but also the obliteration of all the terms in the document of lease, at least so far as it was sought to support a claim thereon for prospective loss.

The rule of surrender by operation of law, and the consequences of the rule for a claim of prospective loss, are said to rise above any intention of the party whose act results in the surrender, so long as the act unequivocally makes it inconsistent for the lease to survive. Even if this be a correct statement of the law, I do not think it would apply to a case where both parties evidenced their intention in the lease itself to recognize a right of action for prospective loss upon a repudiation of the lease, although it be followed by termination of the estate. There are cases in other jurisdictions which have recognized the validity of covenants to this effect: see 11 *Williston on Contracts* (Jaeger) 3d ed., 1968, #1403. One of the terms of the lease in *BelBoys Buildings Ltd. v. Clark* was in the nature of such a covenant applicable to a guarantor, and the dissenting judgment of Allen JA of the Alberta Appellate Division recognized the enforceability of the guarantee notwithstanding the termination of the obligation to pay rent. I should add that the reasons proceeded on the ground that the guarantee obligation arose before there had been an effective surrender.

English and Canadian case law has given standing to a limitation on the operation of surrender, although there is a repudiation and repossession, if the landlord, before repossessing, notifies the defaulting tenant that he is doing so with a view to re-letting on the tenant's account. No such notice was given in the *Goldhar* case; and although it was argued in the present case that the letter of November 22, 1963, asserted that position, neither the trial judge nor the Court of Appeal accepted the argument. I agree that the letter is not sufficiently explicit to that end, but I would think that the recognition of such a modifying principle would suggest a readiness to imply that a re-letting was on the repudiating tenant's behalf, thus protecting the landlord's rights under the lease and at the same time mitigating the liability for unpaid rent. Some of the views expressed in *Oastler v. Henderson* point to a disposition to such an implication; and there is authority in the United States to that effect: see 11 *Williston on Contracts, supra*. I know that under the present case law the landlord is not under a duty of mitigation, but mitigation is in fact involved where there is a re-letting on the tenant's account.

Since the limiting principle under discussion is based on a unilateral assertion of un-authorized agency, I find it difficult to reconcile with the dogmatic application of sur-render irrespective of intention. One of the earliest of the cases in England which gave expression to this limiting principle was *Walls v. Atcheson*. I read it as indicating that a landlord upon an abandonment or repudiation of a lease by his tenant may qualify his re-entry to make it clear that he is not forgoing his right to insist on continuation of the tenant's obligation to pay rent. Since rent was regarded, at common law, as issuing out of the land, it would be logical to conclude that it ceased if the estate in the land ceased. But I do not think that it must follow that an election to terminate the estate as a result of the repudiation of a lease should inevitably mean an end to all covenants therein to the point of denying prospective remedial relief in damages.

I appreciate, however, that this principle of denial has been carried into modern doc-trine from the older cases that were founded on the relation of surrender to a continuing claim for rent. *Woodfall on Landlord and Tenant*, 27th ed., 1968, vol. 1, at p. 869 cites only the *Goldhar* case for the proposition, but it is evident from other English cases such as *Richmond v. Savill*, that the English law is to the same effect. I have the impression from a reading of the cases that the glide into this principle was assisted by translating repudi-ation or abandonment into an "offer" of surrender and by compounding this legal solecism by a further lapse into the language of rescission.

Nothing that was decided by this Court in *Attorney General of Saskatchewan v. White-shore Salt and Chemical Co. Ltd. and Midwest Chemicals Ltd.* bears on the issues now before it. That case was concerned with whether certain unexpired mining leases of Saskatchewan land, granted under federal authority before the 1930 transfer to Saskatch-ewan of its natural resources by Canada, must be taken to have been surrendered when in 1931 the leases were replaced by others granted by the Province, these being in turn replaced in 1937. On the answer to this question depended the liability of the lessees to increased royalties prescribed under provincial law. If there was no surrender, the lessees were protected by a provision of the National Resources Agreement of 1930. Kellock J, who spoke for the majority, was not addressing himself to any issue of damages such as is involved here when he referred generally to the proposition that on a surrender "the lease is gone and the rent is also gone" (a proposition which brooks no disagreement); or when he referred to *Richmond v. Savill, supra*, as standing for the principle that the lessee remains liable for rent accrued due or breaches of covenant committed prior to surrender. These observations were unnecessary for the determination of the question before him, and I do not regard them in any event as controlling for the present case.

As long ago as 1906, the High Court of Australia in *Buchanan v. Byrnes* held that upon an abandonment by a tenant, in breach of covenant, of the hotel property which he had leased, the landlord was entitled to claim damages over the unexpired term of the lease notwithstanding a surrender. It is coincidence that the lease in that case was for fifteen years and that it also included a covenant by the tenant, similar to the covenant here, to carry on the business for which the lease was given, for the full term of the tenancy. I quote two passages from the various reasons for judgment, one from those of Griffith CJ and the second from those of Barton J, as follows (found, respectively, at pp. 714 and 719):

> In this case he covenanted to carry on [the business] for fifteen years, and on 30th June he
> not only left the place, but he did so under such circumstances that he could not carry it on,

and he sold the furniture. That was as complete a breach of the covenant to carry on the business as it was possible for him to commit, and under these circumstances the plaintiff had at once a complete cause of action against him. He was entitled to bring an action forthwith for the breach of that covenant, and he was entitled to such damages as would properly flow from such a breach of covenant. The surrender, therefore, if accepted at all, took place after breach, and the defence is not proved. …

It must not be forgotten that a right of action had arisen on the termination of the correspondence on the 28th June, as the defendant had given distinct notice of his intention not to perform his covenant. There was at that time a renunciation which, at the plaintiff's option, amounted to a breach of the covenants that throughout the term he would carry on a licensed victualler's business upon the premises and keep them open and in use as an inn, & c., and of the covenant not to do anything which might entail forfeiture of the licence (*Licensing Act* 1885, sec. 101), as well as of the subsidiary covenants. The plaintiff was then entitled to claim in an immediate action, prospectively, such damages as would be caused by a breach at the appointed time, subject to any circumstances which might operate in mitigation of damages: *Leake on Contracts*, 4th ed., 617-618, and cases there cited, especially *Hochster v. Delatour*, 2 E & B, 678; 22 LJQB, 455, and *Johnstone v. Milling*, 16 QBD, 460. But it is said that the conduct of the plaintiff in resuming possession under the circumstances estops him from suing upon the covenants. I[t] must not be taken to hold that it has that effect as to the covenant to pay rent. But, however, that may be, can it estop him as to the other covenants which relate to the keeping [of] the premises as an inn throughout the term, and the doing of the other things necessary for that purpose? Conduct, to constitute an estoppel, must have caused another to believe in the existence of a certain state of things, and have induced him to act on that belief so as to alter his own position. How can that be said to be the effect of the plaintiff's conduct, when the act of the defendant, so far from having been induced by it, has preceded it? In my judgment the doctrine of estoppel cannot be applied against the plaintiff, and I am driven to the conclusion that the learned Judge who tried the case, and who held that the plaintiff was bound by estoppel, has based his judgment on facts which do not entitle a Court to apply that doctrine.

I note that *Buchanan v. Byrnes* was applied a few years ago by the Supreme Court of Western Australia in *Hughes v. NLS Pty. Ltd.*

The approach of the High Court of Australia commends itself to me, cutting through, as it does, artificial barriers to relief that have resulted from overextension of the doctrine of surrender in its relation to rent. Although it is correct to say that repudiation by the tenant gives the landlord at that time a choice between holding the tenant to the lease or terminating it, yet at the same time a right of action for damages then arises; and the election to insist on the lease or to refuse further performance (and thus bring it to an end) goes simply to the measure and range of damages. I see no logic in a conclusion that, by electing to terminate, the landlord has limited the damages that he may then claim to the same scale that would result if he had elected to keep the lease alive.

What is apparently the majority American view is to the same effect as the view taken in Australia and that I would take: see 4 *Corbin on Contracts*, 1951, #986, at p. 955. The *American Law of Property*, 1952, vol. 1, pp. 203-204, states that "If the lessee abandons the premises and refuses to pay rent, the cases quite generally hold, in accordance with the doctrine of anticipatory breach, that the landlord may sue for complete damages without waiting until the end of the term"; and I may add that, under the case law, this is so at least where the suit is for damages and not for rent as such.

There are some general considerations that support the view that I would take. It is no longer sensible to pretend that a commercial lease, such as the one before this Court, is simply a conveyance and not also a contract. It is equally untenable to persist in denying resort to the full armoury of remedies ordinarily available to redress repudiation of covenants, merely because the covenants may be associated with an estate in land. Finally, there is merit here as in other situations in avoiding multiplicity of actions that may otherwise be a concomitant of insistence that a landlord engage in instalment litigation against a repudiating tenant.

Lest there be any doubt on the point, clause 5(a) of the lease (previously referred to in these reasons) does not preclude the claim made herein for prospective damages. The landlord did not invoke the clause, and hence no question arises of an irrevocable election to rely on it.

I would, accordingly, allow his appeal, with costs to the appellant throughout, and remit the case to the trial judge for assessment of damages. It follows that I would overrule the *Goldhar* case.

Appeal allowed with costs.

DISCUSSION NOTES

i. Property Law Remedies for a Tenant's Repudiation of the Lease

Before the Supreme Court's decision in *Highway Properties*, there were three mutually exclusive options available to the landlord where a tenant vacated the premises and ceased paying rent before the end of term. These three options were developed in property law at a time when the lease was regarded primarily as a *conveyance* rather than a *contract*. First, the landlord could refuse to accept the abandonment and treat the lease as subsisting, suing for rent as it came due. Second, the landlord could terminate the lease and sue for rent accrued to the date of termination. Under this second option, the landlord was not entitled to rent or damages for any period after the termination. Third, the landlord could inform the tenant that he or she proposed to relet the premises on the tenant's behalf, and at the end of the term, the landlord would claim any deficiency between the rent payable by the tenant and the rent obtained by reletting the premises.

Why did the construction of a lease as primarily a conveyance, rather than a contract, lead to these three remedies? Why did property law develop remedies—for example, the first property law remedy—that effectively relieve the landlord from any duty to mitigate in the face of the tenant's wrongful repudiation of the lease? Compare this with the duty to mitigate as it has developed under contract law. For further discussion, see B Zarnett, "Damages for Breach of Lease" (1987) 8 Advocates' Q 257.

ii. Contract Law Remedies for a Tenant's Repudiation of the Lease

In *Highway Properties*, the Supreme Court added another option for a landlord faced with a tenant's wrongful repudiation of the lease, one modelled on contract law rather than property law. The Supreme Court held (at 570) that a landlord is entitled "to terminate the lease but with notice to the defaulting tenant that damages will be claimed on the footing of present recovery of damages for losing the benefits of the lease over its unexpired term." The court determined that a landlord was entitled to terminate the lease and still recover damages for the period after the retaking of possession. Under property law principles, a landlord was not entitled to recover damages for any period after the landlord had accepted the tenant's repudiation and terminated the lease. The court held that the normal rules relating to the recovery of expectation damages for a breach of contract ought to be applied to commercial leases. Why did the court adopt this fourth remedy modelled on contract law? Why did the court determine that the three property law remedies were inadequate?

iii. Landlord's Duty to Mitigate

Subsequent courts have held that where a landlord intends to rely on the fourth contract remedy in *Highway Properties*, the landlord is under an obligation to mitigate any loss, and his or her damages will be reduced accordingly if he or she fails to mitigate: *Adanac Realty Ltd v Humpty's Egg Place Ltd* (1991), 78 Alta LR (2d) 383, 15 RPR (2d) 77 (QB); and *West Edmonton Mall Ltd v McDonald's Restaurants of Canada Ltd* (1995), 50 RPR 9 (2d) 1, [1996] 3 WWR 191 (CA). In *Keneric Tractor Sales Ltd v Langille*, [1987] 2 SCR 440, where the court held that contract law remedies should be applied to a chattel lease (farm equipment in this case), the court also assumed that where the landlord seeks to obtain expectation damages pursuant to *Highway Properties*, the landlord must take reasonable steps to mitigate any damages.

If the landlord seeks to rely on the first property law remedy, however, and elects to treat the lease as remaining in force and sues for rent as it comes due, the landlord is not under a duty to mitigate. In *Almad Investments Ltd v Mister Leonard Holdings Ltd*, [1996] OJ no 4074 (CA), the Ontario Court of Appeal, citing *Highway Properties* as authority, held that a landlord who relies on the first property law remedy has no duty to mitigate. Likewise, in *Glenview Management Ltd v Axyn Corp*, [2003] OTC 43 (Sup Ct J), at para 18, the court held that in Ontario "the law is settled that there is no duty to mitigate where the landlord is found to have exercised the first option."

Is there any reason to relieve the landlord of a duty to mitigate when the landlord relies on the first property law remedy? What would be the outcome if only contract law principles were applied to this question? Should the landlord be permitted to shift to the defaulting tenant the costs of the landlord's failure to mitigate? Is this an efficient result? In *Toronto Housing Co Ltd v Postal Promotions Ltd* (1982), 39 OR (2d) 627, 140 DLR (3d) 117 (CA), aff'g (1981), 34 OR (2d) 218, 128 DLR (3d) 51 (HC), the landlord left the premises vacant for nine months after the tenant's wrongful repudiation of the lease. After nine months, the landlord terminated the lease and rented the premises at a much higher rent to a new tenant. Taking into account the income from the new, much higher rent, the landlord would receive enough from the new tenant to cover any loss suffered during the nine months when the premises were vacant and no rent was paid. In short, the landlord effectively mitigated and avoided any loss by entering into the new lease. Nonetheless, seeking to rely on the first property law remedy, the landlord sued for the rent due during the nine-month period before the lease was terminated. The Court of Appeal determined that the landlord was not entitled to these damages because the landlord had successfully avoided any loss. The court did not state that the landlord had a duty to mitigate in the face of the tenant's breach. But the case suggests that if the landlord does successfully avoid any loss, the landlord cannot then rely on the first property law remedy that would otherwise entitle the landlord to treat the lease as subsisting until termination. In "The Commercial Lease: Property or Contract?" (2000) 38 Alta L Rev 989 [Brock and Phillips], Jason Brock and Jim Phillips summarize the three post-*Highway Properties* decades of case law on mitigation (at 1002):

> [C]ourts have alternatively assumed that there is such a duty; have believed that there was not such a duty but that there should be; have refused to say whether they are enunciating such a new doctrine; and have contented themselves with a conclusion that it does not matter, providing that mitigation has actually taken place.

The legal position remains essentially the same today.

iv. Pacific Centre Ltd v Micro Base Development Corp

There are a number of problems with the property law remedies for a tenant's wrongful repudiation of a lease. The first property law remedy identified by the court in *Highway Properties* relieves the landlord from any duty to mitigate. The second and third property law remedies effectively prevent the landlord from recovering his or her entire prospective loss (expectation interest)—that is, the present value of the unpaid future rent for the remaining period of the lease, minus the actual rental value of the premises. For example, if the landlord seeks to rely on the third property remedy—that is, to relet the premises on the tenant's behalf—the landlord must relet the premises on the same terms as the original lease and not for a longer period. If the landlord relets for a longer term, the court may deem the landlord to have terminated the lease and the landlord will be able to recover only losses to the date of the termination (as in the second property remedy).

In *Pacific Centre Ltd v Micro Base Development Corp* (1990), 43 BCLR (2d) 77 (SC), aff'd on other grounds 49 BCLR (2d) 218 (CA), the landlord sought to rely on the third property law remedy, but (foolishly, as it turned out) relet the premises for a term that exceeded the original lease. The tenant argued that, on reletting for a longer term, the landlord had effectively terminated the original lease and therefore could not recover any further prospective damages subsequent to the termination, consistent with the second property law remedy. The tenant further argued that, when the landlord relet for a term expiring after the end of the term of the lease to the tenant, it could no longer have been acting as agent for the tenant because the agent cannot do something that is not within the power of the principal to do. The court accepted this argument. The landlord had relet the premises, but only at a lower rent. The result was that the landlord had sustained an expectation loss of over $46,000 over the course of the original lease. However, the court held that the landlord was able to recover only those losses sustained until the premises had been relet—in this case, only $1,400. In effect, because the landlord attempted to mitigate its loss under the third remedy, but had unwisely entered into a lease that exceeded the term of the original lease, the landlord could no longer recover its full expectation loss. The court also found that the landlord had failed to provide the tenant with the required notice that it would rely on the fourth contract law remedy in *Highway Properties* and, accordingly, the landlord was not able to recover its prospective loss under this fourth remedy either. Does this case effectively punish the landlord for having attempted to mitigate its loss? Does that result make any sense? What should the landlord have done to avoid this outcome?

v. Notice

In contract law, is the plaintiff required to provide the defendant with notice that the plaintiff intends to hold the defendant liable for any expectation loss arising from the defendant's breach? Why does the Supreme Court in *Highway Properties* suggest that such notice is required when the tenant is in breach of the lease and the landlord seeks to rely on the fourth remedy to recover its expectation loss? What function does such notice serve? Would it be unfair to hold the tenant liable for the expectation loss in the absence of any such notice? Under the first of the property law remedies, the landlord could refuse to accept the abandonment of the lease, refuse to mitigate any loss by attempting to relet the premises, and simply sue for rent as it comes due. Does it make sense that a landlord should be required to give the tenant notice if he or she seeks to recover expectation losses, and yet not be required to give notice if he or she chooses to refuse to accept the abandonment and sue for rent as it comes due? Under which remedy are the damages likely to be the highest?

Some courts continue to adhere to the view that some notice, even before the statement of claim, may be required if the landlord seeks to rely on the fourth remedy in *Highway Properties*. If the period of time between reletting the premises and the statement of claim is too long, the statement of claim may not be regarded as timely notice. In *Harvey v Burger*, [1994] OJ no 1175 (Gen Div), the landlord had not provided any notice until the delivery of the statement of claim, over three years after the reletting of the premises by the landlord. The court distinguished *North Bay TV & Audio Ltd v Nova Electronics Ltd* (1983), 44 OR (2d) 342 (H Ct J), aff'd (1984), 47 OR (2d) 588 (CA), where the statement of claim had been delivered approximately two months after the taking of possession by the landlord. In *North Bay*, the court found that this statement of claim itself was sufficient notice. In *Harvey*, the court held that the period of time between reletting the premises and the statement of claim was too great, and the notice requirement set out in *Highway Properties* had not been met. Accordingly, the landlord was not entitled to rely on the fourth remedy. For a review of the leading cases, see *Langley Crossing Shopping Centre Inc v North-West Produce Ltd* (1998), 20 RPR (3d) 112 (BCSC), rev'd on the facts (2000), 73 BCLR (3d) 55, 30 RPR (3d) 180 (CA). *Langley* also makes it clear that the content, as well as the timing, of the notice is important. At para 13 Esson JA observed that "[f]or the very reason that the landlord's remedies are mutually exclusive, it is not sufficient to simply give notice of its intention to exercise its 'rights' under the lease." In other words, a reference to "rights" does not clarify for the tenant which rights the landlord intends to enforce.

Perhaps the most that can be said at present on this issue is encapsulated in the following statement in *Learmonth v Letroy Holdings Ltd*, 2011 BCSC 143, aff'd 2012 BCCA 262: "The adequacy of both the content and timing of any purported notice will be informed by a consideration of the purpose that grounds the need for notice" (at para 52). In this case, the landlord was the defendant and notice of its claim for prospective damages was given in a counterclaim filed two months after the plaintiffs' notice of repudiation and one month after they commenced their action. This was held to be timely notice because the landlord's attempts to resolve matters without litigation were found to be valid reasons for its delay.

vi. Privity of Contract

Problems can arise when the landlord and the tenant are no longer in privity of contract. For example, in *Wing Lee Holdings Ltd v Coleman*, [1995] BCJ no 1847 (SC), the tenant had assigned his remaining leasehold interest to a third party. This third party was later in breach of the lease, and the landlord sought pursuant to *Highway Properties* to recover the present value of the unpaid future rent for the unexpired term of the lease, minus the rental value of the premises for that period. The court stated that "fundamental to the principle in *Highway Properties* is the existence of a contract between the parties." The court held that because there was no privity of contract between the parties in this case, the landlord could not rely on the fourth remedy in *Highway Properties*. How does this result illustrate the continuing interaction between contract law and property law remedies in this area of law?

vii. Conceptualization of Commercial Leases: Time for a Change?

Although some commentators have continued to herald *Highway Properties* as a major law reform decision, others are less sanguine about its impact. Brock and Phillips argue (at 998) that *Highway Properties*

> really represents not a reconceptualization of leasehold law, but a hybridization, importing a mix of contract rules into what is still a property-dominated paradigm. Its suggestion that the commercial lease is more properly conceived of as a contract than as an estate, while it is often cited, has not until very recently been used by the courts to rethink other important aspects of landlord–tenant law. The case has only been used once as a basis for further legal reform by the Supreme Court of Canada, and that was in the area of chattel leases [*Keneric Tractor Sales*, above].

The authors go on to make an argument for what they call "full contractualization" that would eliminate all remaining property elements in commercial leases. Recognizing that this would, in theory, enable landlords to evict tenants prior to the end of the lease term and pay only damages, the authors propose a number of ways in which this particular problem could be addressed. How do you think the continuing uncertainty in this area of the law should be resolved?

viii. Residential Tenancies and the Duty to Mitigate

With regard to residential tenancies, the question of the duty to mitigate is usually addressed in the legislation governing residential tenancies. For example, s 16 of the Ontario *Residential Tenancies Act, 2006* provides that when "a landlord or a tenant becomes liable to pay any amount as a result of a breach of a tenancy agreement, the person entitled to claim the amount has a duty to take reasonable steps to minimize the person's losses." In *190 Lees Avenue Ltd Partnership v Dew, Tanguay and Whissell* (1991), 2 OR (3d) 686 (Gen Div), the court applied *Highway Properties* in a residential tenancy context and held that the landlord could sue for prospective loss.

Interestingly, s 16 imposes an obligation to mitigate not just on the landlord but also on the tenant. How could it arise that a tenant is under an obligation to mitigate loss in the face of the landlord's breach? Under s 168 of the Ontario *Residential Tenancies Act, 2006*, landlord and tenant disputes are taken out of the hands of the civil courts and placed under the control of an administrative tribunal established under the Act, the Landlord and Tenant Board (formerly the Ontario Rental Housing Tribunal). Some Tribunal and Board decisions have considered the nature of the landlord and tenant's duty to mitigate. Although the case did not specifically consider s 16, in *Kawar v LT Greenwin Property Management Inc*, [2000] ORHTN no 75, the Tribunal found that the landlord had substantially interfered with the tenant's reasonable enjoyment of the premises while some repairs were being made to the building. However, the Tribunal also found that the tenant had failed to minimize the impact on himself by declining to take advantage of the landlord's offer of temporary alternative accommodation. As a result of the tenant's failure to mitigate, the Tribunal decided that the landlord's interference did not warrant an abatement of rent. See *Sawai v Cui*, [2003] ORHTD no 28 for a discussion of the landlord's duty to mitigate.

Other provinces generally impose on landlords only an express obligation to mitigate. For example, the New Brunswick *Residential Tenancies Act*, SNB 1975, c R-10.2, s 11(3), provides that where a tenant wrongfully terminates a lease, "the landlord shall, to the extent that a party to a contract is required generally to do so under the law relating to breaches of contract, mitigate any damages resulting from" such termination or from the tenant's abandoning the premises.

Where a duty to mitigate has been imposed on the landlord under the applicable residential tenancy legislation, a residential tenant is not liable for the entire amount of rental payments due for the remainder of the term of the residential lease, providing the premises have some market value. In effect, this legislation prevents residential landlords from relying on the first property law remedy, which otherwise permits a landlord to refuse to accept a tenant's repudiation of the lease and sue as rent comes due. Instead, pursuant to this legislation, the residential landlord will only be able to recover his or her expectation loss after taking into account the market rate for the premises in question and the loss that the landlord can reasonably avoid by mitigating appropriately. Should a similar rule govern commercial tenancies? Why should residential tenants be given preferential treatment over commercial tenants?

ix. Bailment and Prospective Loss

Under the law of bailment, is a bailor entitled to recover prospective losses after accepting a wrongful repudiation of the bailment? At one time, consistent with landlord and tenant law before *Highway Properties*, if a bailor accepted a bailee's repudiation, the bailment was brought to an end and the bailor had no right to sue for prospective loss. For example, if A leased a car from B for six months, and B accepted A's repudiation of the agreement after one month (by accepting the return of the car), B could not sue for prospective loss (B's expectation loss over the remaining five months in the agreement). As with the leasehold estate, consider the consequences of constructing a bailment primarily as a type of conveyance rather than a contract. Is there any reason why the law should prevent a bailor in this situation from recovering his expectation loss? As with *Highway Properties*, it is now clear that the bailor may sue for prospective loss even if the bailor accepts the repudiation: *Keneric Tractor Sales Ltd v Langille*, [1987] 2 SCR 440, 43 DLR (4th) 171.

C. Termination Remedies: Residential Leaseholds

Wrongful termination is also an important subject in the context of residential leaseholds. According to Statistics Canada, *Dwelling Characteristics and Household Equipment, by Province (Canada)* (2011), <http://www.statcan.gc.ca>, about 33 percent of all Canadians live in rental accommodation and most lower-income families live in rental accommodation. Residential tenancies are distinct from commercial tenancies for at least two reasons. First, the residential tenancy is the tenant's home and represents a considerable emotional investment. Wrongful or unfair eviction by the landlord can have a devastating impact on the tenant. Second, similar to other areas of consumer protection, there may be a disparity of bargaining power between the landlord and the tenant, and some measures to address this disparity are warranted. These policy goals have inspired considerable reform of residential tenancy law in Canada.

The *Tenant Protection Act, 1997*, SO 1997, c 24, predecessor of the *Residential Tenancies Act, 2006*, was the most comprehensive overhaul of residential tenancies legislation in the province in 20 years. Among other things, the legislation provided for the replacement of rent control guidelines with "vacancy decontrol," where tenants in most residential units are protected by statutory rent increases until they move, at which point the landlord can begin charging whatever the market can bear.

When the government first proposed these changes, it argued that the new law consolidated and improved the old system of rent controls and residential tenancies legislation in four ways. First, the government wanted to protect tenants from unfair rate increases and arbitrary evictions. Second, it wanted to improve maintenance of rental units across the province. Third, by allowing the price of rental housing to better reflect what the market would bear, it wanted to make Ontario a more attractive place for investment in rental housing, leading, it was hoped, to an increase in the number of available units in the province. Finally, the government wanted to cut red tape and create a faster and fairer system of administration of residential tenancies regulation in the province. These goals were set forth in s 1 of the *Residential Tenancies Act, 2006*, the first landlord–tenant statute in Ontario to include a purpose clause:

> 1. The purposes of this Act are to provide protection for residential tenants from unlawful rent increases and unlawful evictions, to establish a framework for the regulation of residential rents, to balance the rights and responsibilities of residential landlords and tenants and to provide for the adjudication of disputes and for other processes to informally resolve disputes.

(See Fleming at 15.)

There has been considerable debate about how well the legislation has met these goals. One commentator has argued that, since the legislation was passed, rental unit availability has decreased in the province, market rents in some urban areas have increased over 20 percent, eviction rates have increased, and it is at least as time-consuming to have a matter dealt with by the Board as it was under the old system: E Mahoney, "The Ontario Tenant Protection Act: A Trust Betrayed" (2001) 16 J Law & Soc Pol'y 261. Others have been more optimistic about the effect of vacancy decontrol, arguing that it will produce a two-tiered rent structure in the province and an initial spike in rents, but that over time the two tiers will merge and there will be a levelling off in rents: Lawrence B Smith, "Intertenancy Rent Decontrol in Ontario" (2003) 29 Can Pub Pol'y 213. See also Mary Truemner, "A Closer Look at Seemingly Pro-Tenant Provisions in the Residential Tenancies Act" (2009) 22 J Law & Soc Pol'y 27 for an argument that, in spite of some improvements, the legislation has not done enough to rebalance the inequality of bargaining power that still favours the landlord in the residential housing market.

The *Tenant Protection Act, 1997* contained a number of measures to enhance the tenant's security of tenure, which were continued in the *Residential Tenancies Act, 2006*. These include:

- statutory guidelines governing the standard obligations of the landlord (ss 20-32) and the tenant (ss 33-36) and a prohibition of the bargaining away of these statutory rights (s 4);
- an increase in the tenant's rights—for example, s 95 provides the tenant with a right to assign the premises and s 97 with a right to sublet, and in both cases the landlord cannot "arbitrarily or unreasonably refuse" consent to a proposed assignment or sublease;
- a prohibition on security deposits in excess of one month's rent (s 106);
- a curtailment of the landlord's remedies—for example, s 40 abolishes the "right of distress" whereby a landlord may impound the tenant's goods until payment of the rent is received;
- a voiding of any provision in a tenancy agreement that prohibits the presence of animals (s 14); and
- a general requirement of 24 hours' written notice, with some exceptions, before the landlord may enter the tenant's premises (s 27), with additional exceptions in the case of care homes (s 142).

For similar provisions elsewhere in Canada, see the Nova Scotia *Residential Tenancies Act*, the New Brunswick *Residential Tenancies Act*, and the Alberta *Residential Tenancies Act*, RSA 2004, c R-17.1.

The following materials focus on the termination provisions governing residential tenancies in the *Residential Tenancies Act, 2006*. Note the types of residences that are covered under this act and those that are not. The definition of "residential unit" is set out in s 2(1):

> "residential unit" means any living accommodation used or intended for use as residential premises, and "residential unit" includes,
>
> (a) a site for a mobile home or site on which there is a land lease home used or intended for use as a residential premises, and
>
> (b) a room in a boarding house, rooming house or lodging house and a unit in a care home.

Section 5 of the Act provides that the Act does not apply to a variety of living accommodations, including accommodation in hotels provided to the travelling public, accommodation where the occupant is required to share a bathroom or kitchen facility with the owner, and accommodation in a care home occupied for the purpose of receiving short-term respite care.

Section 4 of the Act provides that "a provision in a tenancy agreement that is inconsistent with this Act or the regulations is void." This section prohibits the parties from contracting out of any of the rights or obligations contained in the Act. As a result, even though a tenant may expressly agree to waive his or her rights under the Act, the agreement will be unenforceable.

D. Residential Leaseholds and Grounds for "Early Termination"

As was the case under prior legislation, a landlord's termination of the tenancy due to the tenant's breach of obligation (sometimes known as the "fault grounds") is treated differently from circumstances where the landlord has made an autonomous decision to terminate ("no-fault grounds"). In either case, termination can only occur in accordance with the Act: s 37. This usually means that a Board order will be required: s 39. There are seven major grounds for early termination of a tenancy:

- the tenant fails to pay rent: s 59;
- the tenant carries on an illegal act: s 61;
- the tenant has misrepresented his or her income to obtain public housing: s 60;
- the tenant commits wilful, negligent, or undue damage to the unit: s 62;
- the tenant causes substantial interference with the landlord's or another tenant's rea-sonable enjoyment of the residential complex for all usual purposes: s 64;
- the tenant's act or omission seriously impairs the safety of any person: s 66; and
- the tenant has too many persons in the unit: s 67.

There are various "no-fault grounds" for termination. These include good-faith possession where the landlord requires the premises for himself or herself or a family member (s 72), or demolition and conversion to non-residential use (s 50). Under s 69(1), a "landlord may apply to the Board for an order terminating a tenancy and evicting the tenant if the landlord has given notice to terminate the tenancy."

Under s 83, the Board enjoys a degree of discretion in determining whether to issue an eviction order:

83(1) Upon an application for an order evicting a tenant or subtenant, the Board may, de-spite any other provision of this Act or the tenancy agreement,

(a) refuse to grant the application unless satisfied, having regard to all the circumstances, that it would be unfair to refuse; or

(b) order that the enforcement of the order of eviction be postponed for a period of time.

(2) Without restricting the generality of subsection (1), the Board shall refuse to grant the application where satisfied that,

(a) the landlord is in serious breach of the landlord's responsibilities under this Act or of any material covenant in the tenancy agreement;

(b) the reason for the application being brought is that the tenant has complained to a governmental authority of the landlord's violation of a law dealing with health, safety, hous-ing or maintenance standards;

(c) the reason for the application being brought is that the tenant has attempted to se-cure or enforce his or her legal rights;

(d) the reason for the application being brought is that the tenant is a member of a ten-ants' association or is attempting to organize such an association; or

(e) the reason for the application being brought is that the rental unit is occupied by children and the occupation by the children does not constitute overcrowding.

The cases below examine how the Tribunal (now the Landlord and Tenant Board) has exercised this legal discretion. In the first case, *Cohen v Klein*, the landlord Cohen required the premises for his personal occupation and proceeded with eviction proceedings under s 51(1) of the *Tenant Protection Act, 1997* (now s 48(1) of the *Residential Tenancies Act, 2006*), which provides that "a landlord may, by notice, terminate a tenancy if the landlord in good faith re-quires possession of the rental unit for the purpose of residential occupation by the landlord." Section 70(1) (now s 72) provides that the Tribunal shall not make an order terminating a tenancy under s 51 (now s 48) unless the landlord files a declaration certifying that the landlord in good faith requires the rental unit for his or her personal use. On first review, the Tribunal issued an order for eviction. Upon judicial review, this order was overturned and the matter was remitted to the Tribunal for further consideration: *Klein v Cohen*, [2001] OJ no 299 (Sup Ct). Under s 196(1) of the *Tenant Protection Act* (now s 210), any person affected by a Tribunal order may appeal to the Divisional Court. The court overturned the decision because the Tribunal had failed to give the tenant adequate opportunity to present evidence on the application of s 84 (now s 83) to the order for eviction.

On remand, the case was considered again by the Tribunal and extracts of this reconsideration are reproduced below. The Tribunal considered the reasons that the landlord Cohen provided for seeking possession of the unit and found on the facts that he did in good faith require the unit for his personal occupation. As a result, the Tribunal concluded that there were sufficient grounds for eviction under s 70(1). The Tribunal then turned to the question of the application of s 84, specifically whether the Tribunal should exercise its discretion to refuse to grant an application for eviction. Those reasons are reproduced below. Note that the wording of the current s 83 of the *Residential Tenancies Act, 2006* is identical to that of s 84 of the *Tenant Protection Act, 1997*.

Cohen v Klein
[2001] ORHTD no 66

[1] Marcel Cohen and Hayim Kohen applied to the Tribunal for an order terminating the tenancy and evicting Joseph Klein and Malka Klein because one of the landlords requires the rental unit in good faith for residential occupation.

[2] After a hearing held on June 15, 2000, an Order was issued on July 7, 2000 in which the tenancy was terminated as of July 31, 2000, an extension of one month after the date specified in the notice of termination.

[3] On July 17, 2000, Joseph Klein and Malka Klein requested a review of the Order. After a hearing held on October 19, 2000, a Review Order was issued on October 26, 2000 which confirmed the original Order.

[4] Joseph Klein and Malka Klein appealed the Orders to the Divisional Court. After oral argument of the appeal, the Court released a decision on February 1, 2001. In this decision, the Tribunal Orders were rescinded and the matter was remitted back to the Tribunal for a new hearing.

. . .

Findings and Conclusions

Issues in This Application

[7]

1. Whether subsection 70(2) applies in this case and prevents the Tribunal from ordering an eviction;
2. Whether the landlord requires the rental unit in good faith for occupation by himself and his spouse;

3. Even if so, whether the landlord's reason for applying was to prevent the tenants from attempting to secure and enforce their rights, which would result in refusing the eviction; and

4. Whether it is more fair in all of the circumstances to make an eviction order or more fair to refuse or delay the eviction.

[8] In this Order, even though I need only give reasons for issues on which the decision rests, I will make findings about virtually all of the issues raised at the hearing. This is meant to assist the parties if there is a review or appeal of this Order, and recognize the significant time invested in the re-hearing.

Stages of Determination

[9] The factors should be divided into the categories in which they are properly considered. However, this is difficult because some factors considered in the first stage are also relevant in the second stage.

[10] The first stage is to determine whether the grounds exist for the eviction of the tenant because the landlord requires the unit in good faith for personal occupation. The second stage is to determine whether the grounds exist that require the Tribunal to refuse the eviction or whether an eviction order would be more unfair than a decision to refuse or delay the eviction.

Limits of the Issues Permitted

[11] Proceedings before the Tribunal are intended to be summary in nature where this is possible. This is clearly indicated by the genesis of the Tribunal, which evolved out of the transfer of the authority of the then Ontario Court (General Division) under Part IV of the Landlord and Tenant Act. Those proceedings were expressly summary.

[12] In further support of the notion of summary proceedings, section 171 of the Tenant Protection Act, 1997 ("the Act") directs in [a] similar vein that proceedings shall be expeditious, but fair. If there was any doubt that in most cases the determinations are to be made quickly where there are no significant issues raised to be determined, several provisions of the Act may be noted. The Act provides for only five calendar days for a respondent to file a written dispute to an application, one of the briefest in the quasi-judicial domain. The period of notice of a hearing is as little as five calendar days, even where the potential result is loss of shelter through eviction.

[13] The Divisional Court has shown its displeasure regarding Tribunal decisions in several cases which involve the potential impact of section 84 on eviction orders. In those cases, the Tribunal apparently gave no weight to its own Interpretation Guideline, and failed to recognize section 84 requests for relief from eviction, to properly hear and determine them, and/or to make findings about the issues in the order. Indeed in this case, the Divisional Court found that in the hearing held on June 15, 2000, the tenant showed the intention of relying on section 84, but the Tribunal failed to hear evidence regarding that claim. The Court found the Tribunal lacked procedural fairness, or at least appeared to do so.

[The Tribunal found that s 70(2) did not apply on the facts and also found that the landlord Cohen required the rental unit in good faith for occupation by himself. The Tribunal then went on to consider the application of s 84.]

First Stage Conclusion

[61] As such, I conclude that the grounds for eviction have been established, and it is necessary to turn to section 84.

Mandatory Relief from Eviction

[62] The mandatory relief from eviction claimed by Mr. Marzel [counsel for the tenant] for the Kleins is quoted here (clause 84(2)(c)):

> (2) Without restricting the generality of subsection (1), the tribunal shall refuse to grant the application where satisfied that: …
>> (c) the reason for the application being brought is that the tenant attempted to secure or enforce his or her legal rights; …

[63] The argument is that the landlord is threatening this unit precisely because of the rights which these tenants continue to possess under the legislation regarding their rent. Since they have occupied the same unit since the Rent Control Act, 1992 was repealed, the rent is lower for their unit than for other units. Further there are restrictions concerning rent increases the landlord can charge. Rent control now only applies to "sitting tenants" and if a tenant leaves the unit, whether voluntarily or not, and a new tenant enters into a tenancy agreement the rent will not be regulated. Thus [there are] many units for which the rents have been held down by rent restrictions over many years.

[64] I read the basis for refusal of an application in clause 84(1)(c) to be more active than simply being a tenant for a period of time. The verbs used are "secure or enforce," which are active verbs and "attempted" implies a past action. I find that this provision is meant to prevent landlords from evicting tenants merely because they have actively asserted their rights in some way. The Legislature could have said that an eviction would be refused where the landlord was interfering in the legal rights of the tenant, but it did not.

[65] If the Legislature intended a rule that landlords should not obtain evictions for personal use when the unit is "rent controlled" or the rent is below market to a certain extent, a specific ground for mandatory relief from eviction could have been added to subsection 84(2). It was not.

[66] I note that the Legislature made the test for mandatory relief from eviction more stringent in the Act than it was under the Landlord and Tenant Act. Under clause 121(3)(c) of that Act, the same words appeared as in clause 84(2)(c) but it was "a reason" rather than "the reason." The stress on "a reason" was part of the reasoning of the Divisional Court in Chin v. Hunt (1986), 17 OAC 267. Now, for clause 84(2)(c) to apply, the landlord's principal or only motivation in bringing the application must be to retaliate against a tenant.

Discretionary Relief from Eviction

[67] The same considerations possible under mandatory relief from eviction will be considered again under the discretionary determination. In addition, considerations of

fairness are appropriate. The scope of this consideration is dealt with in the Interpretation Guideline regarding section 84.

Disruption of the Tenants' Lives

[68] The vast evidence on this issue cannot be easily summarized.

[69] For Mr. Klein, he has a routine that involves praying in minions [*sic*] three times a day every day and studying each evening. This is required for a male Hassidic Jew or a "religious Jew," as the Kleins describe themselves. He goes to his favourite synagogue or shul, the Ger, at least once a day and the other times he attends the Bubov synagogue. He works part-time, earning a small salary, and uses the bus and walking for his travelling.

[70] Although Mr. Klein claimed to feel comfortable only in the Ger synagogue, he admitted that the Ger community was one of the smallest in Toronto. The shul was only established ten years ago. Yet he was able to practise his religion before it opened. As one witness said, this is the people of the Holocaust, and they are able to practise their religion in the face of incredible obstacles. It would be unreasonable to believe that there is not sufficient flexibility, even though there may be a loss of some comfort and "fit" within a particular community, to believe that travelling a short distance to another Orthodox community will be intolerable.

[71] For the whole family, they are prohibited by their religion from travelling on the Sabbath using any motorized vehicle, and thus they must live within walking distance of a synagogue. This places a significant constraint on the distance that they may live from a synagogue in which they will be able to pray. Reasonable limits must be placed on this particular consideration. Otherwise a tenant who lived beside their synagogue might be protected absolutely from eviction for the landlord's personal use.

[72] The degree of "fit" within a particular Hassidic community was described as depending on important differences of religious rites, but also differences of attire and hairstyle. Another witness said that the differences reflected the practices in the home country of that sect, and therefore reflected national origin. This is not to trivialize the differences in any way, because they affect a great deal of the life of a religious family. The Kleins' life as a family depends on the practice of their religion, and I find their insistence on this to be completely authentic.

[73] In some cases, a person will be forced by the options available to live near a reasonably amenable synagogue for walking purposes. For the rest of every week they could use a bus or car rides from friends to attend the most appropriate synagogue. If my decision forces the Kleins into such a situation, it is not that I wish to do so. It is simply that the existing advantages experienced by the Kleins cannot be guaranteed, and are not guaranteed by the legislation. I do not find that the Kleins will be so disadvantaged that they could not fully practise their religion as it is required to be practised. Convenience is not a factor to which I can give considerable weight.

[74] The circumstances of Ms. Klein are contradictory and complex. She feels at times that she is utterly without support, so that her home is crucial to her identity and essence. At other times she is dependent on the support she actively receives from the community, and could not leave her routine and her friends, even by moving a short distance. She lives close to the edge, ensuring that all her dependents are able to live their lives, and maintaining the family balance even when she must pay a personal cost in feelings and

emotional stability. Her family is so important that she cannot see how she could change any part of her life, or return to the world of outside work.

[75] The Kleins live on a subsistence income with support from their religious community in both financial and other matters. Mr. Wagman [counsel for the landlord] emphasized the choices that the family makes to stay in this position, for example requiring the four children to share a single bedroom. Ms. Klein works in the home and only earns about $20 a week from counselling. As stated, Mr. Klein works part-time and earns a modest amount. The two teenage boys are attending private Ger school in New York, and the girls (12 and 7) attend private Orthodox school.

[76] It was claimed that the Kleins are too old to make any changes in their lives, that their religion demands that they live in this way and that their existence is too "close to the edge" to be disturbed by any changes. Mr. and Ms. Klein are only 53 and 54 years old. Ms. Klein has been out of the workforce for 18 years but many women have viably returned to the workforce in the last few decades, not without difficulty. She tried to claim that she would be in the marginal service industry, but could at least handle office work with a little computer training. I was not convinced that the Kleins would fall apart as a family if they were forced to move anywhere from a few blocks to a kilometre, because they are a strong family from the best indications.

[77] It is part of every eviction that the life or lives of the person or persons displaced will be disrupted to some extent. The Legislature has provided that some tenants will be evicted where they have committed no fault whatsoever. The tenants do not accept this and expect to live in the unit without this disruption.

Other Options for the Tenants

[78] I agree with Mr. Wagman that the evidence showed that the tenants have done no serious investigation of their options for other accommodation in the area. Mr. Marzel said that there was no need for the tenants to do so because the landlord presented this evidence in the form of a list of sample units available as of March 31st, 2001. Mr. Cohen introduced this in response to questions put to him in cross-examination. He was not required to do this, and his list was seriously questioned through evidence led from Ms. Klein and Peter Miller who both called the numbers shown on that list. To a large extent Mr. Cohen's additional inquiries supported the original list, although there were a few discrepancies as noted above.

[79] The impact of this list is to show that the tenants would have to pay more for another rental unit that was comparable. This would probably be in the range of $200 to $300 per month, which is a considerable sum per year when the family income is so modest.

[80] The tenants have the burden of proving that they are entitled to consideration under subsection 84(1). They are fortunate that Mr. Cohen goes out of his way to provide information, to ensure that the wrong impression is not left. However, it is noted that the Kleins have done no serious investigation of other options for apartments, assistance that might be provided from friends or members of the same synagogues, or other changes in their lives that might reduce the degree of disruption from an eviction.

[81] Parties to disputes under the Act are required to reduce or mitigate their potential damages. By analogy, the tenants had some obligation, when seeking equitable relief, to act reasonably in searching out other possibilities.

The Rent-Controlled or Below Market Rent Factor

[82] I am not convinced that there is a presumption that a landlord must give notice to tenants of the unit most recently rented, as an employer might have to lay off the employee with the least seniority. If such a principle were intended, one would expect to find it expressed in the legislation. There are issues of fairness related to the length of occupancy, such as are evident in this case where the tenants have occupied the unit for 17 and 26 years. However, there are issues that may rank as being equal or greater in weight, such as illness of the tenant.

[83] Every tenant who has lived in the building for a year is rent controlled compared to what the landlord might be able to charge a new tenant. Thus it would be impossible to have a rule that would prevent a landlord from taking possession of a unit because the rent was lower due to a sitting tenant having some rights.

[84] There is no doubt that the landlord could charge a new tenant of Unit 4 more than these tenants pay, even with a guideline increase and potentially paying the same percentage "above guideline" increase to which the other tenants agreed. The tenants of two of the two bedroom units pay $860 per month, and I am not sure when their tenancies began. The Kleins still pay $647 monthly, although that could have been increased by now.

[85] Even though I find this difference in rent to be significant, I do not accept that there is a principle which prohibits landlords from evicting tenants who have the benefit of lower rents to some degree fixed by the legislation. It may be that a Member will not believe the grounds for the eviction, or the good faith of the landlord, if there seems to be other motivation. Nevertheless, there is no reason expressed in the statute why I would believe that landlords must be illogical about financial issues, or that tenants have a vested right forever to maintain units with rents below market levels.

[86] This should not be seen as encouraging landlords to evict tenants on any fabricated ground to maximize revenue. However, if the best unit in the building happens to have the lowest rent, the landlord should not be expected to evict the highest paying tenants in the least desirable unit first. I assume that the tenants have had the benefit for many years of rents that are below market.

[87] I am convinced that the landlord wishes to reside for years in this unit, and I will not consider it automatically unfair to these tenants that they will lose their low rent accommodation.

Property Rights as a Fairness Factor

[88] One question which I posed to Mr. Marzel is what a purchaser should do if he looked at a potential building purchase as a place to live as well as an investment. To follow the tenants' position, a purchaser would have to make inquiries about numerous issues before they made a significant investment. I would wonder if there should be any difference in standards which would relate to building size. According to Mr. Marzel's arguments, the requisite inquiries would involve how long tenants have occupied units, how low their rents are compared to market levels, other options for the tenants in the neighbourhood, the circumstances of their lives, their incomes, and many other factors. Unless the purchaser realized that this information was necessary at the time of signing

the agreement of purchase and sale, they would probably have no right to requisition this information before closing.

[89] In fact, following the tenants' position, a person may be unwise to buy a tenanted house, or building with a desirable but tenanted unit, without the prior consent of those tenants to eviction. Even with such consent, I wonder if it would be binding in view of section 2 of the Act.

[90] The position of the Kleins is that they could not possibly move from this unit. There was no end date ascribed to this. Apparently they believed that their rights related to the unit would last until their deaths. If that is so, then their rights begin to take on aspects of property rights but extending beyond the ownership of any particular owner. Their rights would be paramount unless and until a purchasing landlord could prove more prejudice than the tenants might suffer.

[91] What should be expressly stated is a factor that is largely implied in the decisions, although landlords and purchasers forcefully assert it. That factor is the property rights of the owner. It is true that the Legislature has qualified that right by section 84, but there is still a basic premise that a landlord, even of a mid to large sized building, has the right given by section 51. One might even say that the rights exists regardless of the statute, and it is merely qualified by section 51 in that there is a waiting period with notice, and a chance to question whether the reason given is genuine.

[92] If there were no such principle, many evictions would be refused without much need for analysis. The tenant almost always has less money and fewer options than the landlord. Fairness factors would weigh heavily in favour of the tenant unless the fact that the landlord invested money in the property is considered, as well as an implied right flowing from that. The implied right is that the landlord should be able to use the property as he or she wishes, subject to any laws that restrict that use. He or she should be able to reside in property they buy which is residential.

[93] Landlords and purchasers would wish this to be the end of the analysis, but it is not. Nevertheless it is a factor which should be stated.

[94] I accept that Mr. Cohen has many other housing alternatives, despite his denials and claims that he could not afford other options. However, this does not give the tenant a superior right to possession than that of the landlord. This is not a subjective statement but a reflection of what the law now is, in Ontario. The fairness arguments must go beyond the landlord's ability to choose somewhere else to live. The fairness aspect must go to the tenants' more restricted choices and/or misconduct by the landlord (which does not already bring into play mandatory relief).

Mr. Cohen as Deserving or Undeserving

[95] One of the many reasons why the tenants believed the landlord should not be given an eviction order was the insincerity of some of his stated reasons. I have already dealt with this issue in a different respect under "good faith," and found that some of the reasons were general beliefs rather than being beliefs based on well researched information.

[96] Mr. Cohen suggested that it was important to him that the area was a Jewish neighbourhood with synagogues and Jewish schools. The tenants wanted to deny this because Mr. Cohen is not Sabbath-observant and his wife is not Jewish. In the Jewish faith the children take on the religion of their mother, and this would restrict some choice of

denominational schools. None of the information I heard convinced me of anything more than that Mr. Cohen is being optimistic or positive about the prospects of his wife's conversion. He does not know that she ever will convert, and it seems reasonable to me that he would choose the neighbourhood without specifically picking the synagogue and school. I was not convinced that the community would reject Mr. Cohen or that he could not, with a car available, participate in religious life when he wishes to in this neighbourhood.

The Kleins as Good or Bad Tenants

[97] There was no evidence presented at the first hearing or in the proceedings since that would indicate that the Kleins were not model tenants. However, that was questioned in the re-hearing.

[98] I have set out above several lines of inquiry on which I set limits for Mr. Marzel's inquiries, such as the income of Mr. Cohen. However, I permitted Mr. Wagman to raise issues related to the conduct of the tenants. Although this would have been irrelevant and prejudicial if the only case to decide was the landlord's grounds for eviction, the fairness question raised by the tenants leads to the right of the landlord to answer with other fairness considerations. The fairness issues must cut both ways, as is suggested by the balancing approach described in the Guideline regarding Relief from Eviction.

[99] I heard evidence from Ms. Resurreccion in the unit below the Kleins and I found her to have very strong negative opinions about that family. The Kleins have disturbed the peace in her apartment on many occasions, although some of that is understandable given the number of children in Unit 4. However, the manner she has had of dealing with this has, until recently, been counter-productive. Recently she has decided not to sink to their level, as she put it. She should be pursuing the landlord or superintendent to witness the noise to facilitate action against the offending parties and, in the worst cases, calling the police.

[100] I believe that there has been friction coming back in the other direction. Neither side is blameless. The Kleins have less control over their children than is appropriate. Ms. Resurreccion may respond in a shrill way, which appears to be somewhat threatening to the children.

[101] The question is what effect this evidence should have on the decision. This evidence is an indication that the apartment might not be large enough for the Klein family. I am mindful of the fact that the police were only called once and the evidence of frequent complaints to the old and new landlords was not entirely convincing. I believe this factor does not disentitle the tenants to their arguments for discretionary relief from forfeiture, but they do contribute to the factors to consider in weighing the possible delay of the eviction.

Discretionary Relief Through Refusal or Delay of the Eviction

[102] In view of the property rights factor, I believe that it is only in exceptional cases that a landlord who wants possession in good faith for residential purposes should be denied forever. They would usually involve wrongdoing on the landlord's part, such as deception regarding the landlord's intention which caused the tenant to invest substantial

money in the unit. Other kinds of wrongdoing have prevented landlords from gaining possession.

[103] There are factors on the tenant side that have prevented landlords from obtaining possession within the foreseeable future, such as serious illnesses and a total lack of other options for the tenants. However, these must generally be matters beyond the control of the tenant. They will still not preclude a landlord forever from obtaining possession for personal or family occupation.

[104] In many cases, fairness factors in a personal use case will be considered as a proper basis for delaying the eviction. The original Member delayed the eviction by one month, which I will say I would find unreasonable in the circumstances of such a long tenancy and tenants with limited options. At the point of the original decision, I would have found something between four and eight months would have been an appropriate delay under clause 84(1)(b).

[105] The question now is what to do in the face of ten months' delay caused by the original decision, review process, appeal and the length of this re-hearing. Mr. Wagman argued that the tenants have already had ten additional months of notice, and thus a year since the original notice of termination. He submitted that they have had more than enough time, and should not be given more delay than the end of May.

[106] Mr. Marzel analogizes to unjust dismissal from employment cases, and suggests a month of delay for every year of tenancy. His concession at the end of the case was that the resulting 27 months could be reduced by the months already passed since the first notice.

[107] I believe that the Kleins' conduct as tenants comes into the balancing of interests at this point. On the other hand the limited range of options that are immediately available must be considered.

[108] I do not think it is fair to deprive the Kleins of the time spent in these proceedings, when making an equitable determination. They should not be forced to take another tenancy while they are exercising their right to defend the application, or the landlord would succeed without a decision on the merits. No landlord would have kept a tenancy open for eight months or even two. When they receive this decision, they should have considered their options and have a planned approach for apartment hunting ready. They should start immediately.

[109] There will be little choice now for the start of June. In a jurisdiction with two months' notice as the legal requirement to terminate, many tenancies still end after a month by agreement. Arranging a tenancy on a reasonable basis of choice can be done for month end one to two months later. That would indicate that it would be a futile search right now for the end of August, but tenancies at the end of June and July will be available shortly. Thus I start from the viewpoint that the end of July is the earliest date I would set.

[110] In this case, the tenants have to take some more fundamental steps to change their lives, whether it is searching for support within their community or looking at changing their family income, and the steps required to make that possible. In my discretion, I will give the tenants an extra month to permit the changes required by their circumstances. I do not think that this is unduly unfair to the landlord as he has not come to the Tribunal with entirely clean hands.

[111] I thank counsel for their assistance with all of the matters in issue, and in maintaining professional demeanour throughout the hearing.

[112] It is ordered that:

The Tribunal Orders issued on July 7, 2000 and October 26, 2000 have been rescinded and are replaced with the following Order:

1. The tenancy is terminated as of August 31, 2001.
2. Joseph Klein and Malka Klein shall move out of the rental unit by August 31, 2001.
3. The landlord may file this Order with the Court Enforcement Office (Sheriff) on or after August 10, 2001 and that Office may give any further notice to the tenants between August 10th and 31st.
4. The Court Enforcement Office (Sheriff) is directed to give vacant possession of the unit to Marcel Cohen and Hayim Kohen on or after September 1, 2001.

DISCUSSION NOTES

i. Mitigation Obligations

Do you agree with the outcome in *Cohen v Klein*? In para 81, the Tribunal notes that parties to disputes under the Act, including both landlords and tenants, are required to mitigate their potential damages. This principle is reflected in s 13 of the Act, which provides that when "a landlord or a tenant becomes liable to pay any amount as a result of a breach of a tenancy agreement, the person entitled to claim the amount has a duty to take reasonable steps to minimize the person's losses." Is it reasonable to impose a duty to mitigate on the tenants in this case? Could the landlord also minimize his or her loss by securing alternative accommodation?

ii. The Role of Discretion

The cases below found that there were sufficient grounds to exercise the discretion under s 84 of the Act. Consider whether these cases are consistent with *Cohen v Klein*. Is the Tribunal striking the right balance between the competing interests of the tenant and landlord? Note that the section numbers in the *Residential Tenancies Act, 2006* vary slightly from those of the *Tenant Protection Act, 1997* invoked in the decisions below, but the content of the sections in question remains the same.

Horst v Beingessner
[2002] ORHTD no 119

[1] Dawn Horst and Mike Horst (the "Landlords") applied for an order to terminate the tenancy and evict Annette Beingessner (the "Tenant") because they require possession of the unit. The Landlords also claimed compensation for each day the Tenant remained in the unit after the termination date.

[2] This application was heard in Kitchener on November 12, 2002. The Landlord Dawn Horst appeared, and the Tenant appeared.

[3] The evidence indicates that the father of Ms. Horst is recently separated, and has sold the matrimonial home. Mr. Horst filed as an exhibit the agreement of purchase and sale, and the closing date of the sale is December 6, 2002. I find the father in good faith is intending to move into the rental unit presently occupied by the Tenant. The residential complex consists of four units, and therefore qualifies for the purposes of this application.

[4] The Tenant has resided in the rental unit for 18 years, and the termination of her tenancy creates a real hardship to her. She submits that s. 84 of The Tenant Protection Act be invoked in the circumstances of this application. She states the reason they picked her unit is that she pays the lowest rent. She further states she has a medical condition, and a limited source of income that makes her ability to find alternate accommodation very difficult.

[5] The father states he does not wish to occupy a ground level apartment, and the Tenant's apartment is on the second floor, and this is suitable to him.

[6] I am satisfied the Landlord's father in good faith intends to move into the rental unit. Section 70(1) states:

> The Tribunal shall not make an order terminating a tenancy and evicting the tenant in an application under section 69 based on a notice of termination under section 51 or 52 unless the person who personally REQUIRES (my emphasis) the rental unit files with the Tribunal a declaration certifying that the person in good faith REQUIRES THE (my emphasis) rental unit for his or her own personal use.

[7] The Act uses the word "requires" and further "requires the rental unit." I am satisfied the father is intending to move into the rental unit. I am not satisfied the father "requires" this rental unit. There is uncontested evidence from the Tenant that her unit was picked due to ill feelings of the Landlords, and the modest amount of rent. I am not satisfied that another rental unit in the building could not have been picked by the Landlord. On a balance of probabilities, the evidence indicates this unit was picked by the Landlord as a convenient method to terminate this Tenant, in addition to satisfying the father's need to move into the complex.

[8] Section 84(2) lists reasons to refuse an application, and significantly states that 84(2) does not restrict the generality of subsection (1).

[9] It is therefore necessary to analyze the wording of s. 84(1) of the Act.

[10] Section 84(1) of the Tenant Protection Act states:

> Upon an application for an order evicting a tenant or subtenant, the Tribunal may, DESPITE ANY OTHER PROVISION OF THIS ACT (my emphasis), or the tenancy agreement,
> > (a) refuse to grant the application unless satisfied, having regard to all the circumstances that it would be unfair to refuse;

[11] Having regard to all the circumstances of this application, having regard to the extreme length of time the Tenant has occupied the rental unit, and considering the availability of three other units in the complex, I find it is fair to refuse the application. I make this finding on the basis that section 84 applies despite any other provision of the Tenant Protection Act.

[12] I further find the Landlord's father does not require this unit, as another unit in the four-plex would also be suitable. This unit was picked for reasons in addition to his

requirement to move into the residential complex. Latitude in picking a rental unit for the Landlord's own father to use is appropriate, however, in this case the picking of the Tenant who resided in the complex for 18 years is not fair nor is it reasonable.

[13] It is determined that:

1. The application for an order evicting the Tenant is denied pursuant to s. 84 of the Tenant Protection Act.

[14] It is ordered that:

The application of the Landlord is dismissed.

Valery Construction Ltd v Arno
[2000] ORHTD no 43

[1] Valery Construction Ltd. applied for an order to terminate the tenancy and evict Ari Arno because he or someone he permitted in the residential complex has caused damage to the premises; and because he, another occupant of the rental unit or a person Ari Arno permitted in the residential complex has seriously impaired the safety of others.

[2] This application was heard in Hamilton on February 24, 2000 and on March 14, 2000. The landlord appeared before the Tribunal by agent. The tenant was represented by counsel.

Introduction and Reasons

[3] The landlord relied on a Notice to Terminate which Notice listed the cause for termination as being damage. The landlord's agent significantly altered the form of the Notice such that its contents did not meet the requirements of section 63(2)(c) of the Tenant Protection Act, 1997. For this reason the said Notice is void and no termination will be granted based on this Notice.

[4] The landlord claimed compensation for damages caused by the tenant. The landlord's agent did not lead satisfactory evidence that established that the tenant had actually caused damage to the rental unit, nor did the agent file any evidence as to the cost of repairing the alleged damage. For these two reasons, the application in so far as it relates to damage will be dismissed.

[5] The landlord also relied on a Notice to Terminate which Notice listed the cause for termination to be impaired safety. Within the said Notice, the landlord set out three events that were sufficient, it was submitted, to constitute impaired safety.

[6] The first event was that the tenant had stuffed two baseboard heaters with paper and had taped them with duct tape. The evidence revealed that one of the baseboards did not work and the taping [of the] other did not constitute a hazard according to the local fire department. Accordingly, there will not be an order of termination based on this event.

[7] The second event was that the tenant had installed a homemade fan system. The evidence before the Tribunal did not establish that the system impaired the safety of anyone. Therefore there will be no order for termination base on this event.

[8] The third event was that the tenant had covered the smoke detector in his unit with a plastic bag. The tenant admitted doing this because the detector sounded an alarm whenever the tenant did normal household activities such as cooking and baking. The tenant had asked the landlord to provide a better ventilation system to stop the detector from sounding, but his request for such repairs went unanswered by the landlord.

[9] The covering of the smoke detector is an act that impairs the safety of not only the tenant and his family, but also the other tenants of the building. In other proceedings before this Tribunal, other landlords have been held strictly liable for the failure to install and maintain smoke detectors in rental units. There is no good reason why tenants should not be held to the same standard of strict liability when they alter, cover or otherwise tamper with smoke detectors in their respective units. Accordingly, the tenant has impaired the safety of others in the residential complex when he covered the smoke detector in his unit with a plastic bag.

[10] The tenant is married with a young family. He has been residing in the subject unit for over 2.5 years. He was described by the landlord as being a tenant who "pays on time, keeps the unit clean, has no social problems—and is a good tenant." The evidence indicates that the tenant has been a model tenant. When the landlord determined that the Notices were required to be served on the tenant, subsequent dealings between the tenant and the landlord have been satisfactory such that the tenant has co-operated with the landlord when the landlord was anxious to do repairs. It seems to me that the smoke detector is an isolated incident born from the landlord's failure to repair and the tenant's poor judgment. The tenant now clearly understands the gravity of his actions with respect to the detector. For the reasons set out above, I will exercise my discretion pursuant to section 84(1) of the Act and refuse to grant the application, as it is my view that in these circumstances, it is not unfair to the landlord for the application to be refused.

[11] For the reasons set out above, it is determined that:

Ari Arno has not willfully or negligently caused undue damage to the rental unit.
Ari Arno has seriously impaired the safety of other persons.
It is appropriate to refuse to grant the application pursuant to section 84(1) of the Act as it is not unfair to the landlord for the application to be refused.

[12] It is ordered that:

Valery Construction Ltd.'s application is dismissed.

DISCUSSION NOTES

i. The Rental Market

Are these cases consistent? Could the landlord in *Cohen v Klein* have also considered moving into another unit as was the case in *Horst v Beingessner*?

Disputes involving owners reclaiming rented units, such as those in *Cohen* and *Horst*, can affect a surprisingly large proportion of rental housing stock. Only 50 percent of the rental housing stock in Ontario in 2006 was "purpose-built"—that is, built to remain indefinitely as rental housing. Another 21 percent was social housing. In both these types of units, security of tenure is a reality as long as the tenant can continue to pay rent or maintain eligibility for social housing. The remaining 29 percent of rental stock consists of condominium rentals

(4 percent, mostly in the greater Toronto area) and houses, duplexes, townhouses, and the like (25 percent). In this "secondary market," tenants are much less secure because such units "may move more readily between owner occupation and rental and sometimes non-residential use": Jon Medow & Greg Suttor with assistance from Harvey Cooper, Sharad Kerur, and Margaret McCutcheon, *Where's Home 2013? Looking Back and Looking Forward at the Need for Affordable Housing in Ontario* (Toronto: Ontario Non-Profit Housing Association [ONPHA] and Co-operative Housing Federation of Canada, Ontario Region, 2013), 17-20, <http://chfcanada .coop/eng/pdf/ontdocs/WheresHome2013_WEB.pdf>. Like the Kleins, such tenants may find themselves displaced when the owner decides to take over the unit for personal occupation or for occupation by a family member or caregiver. Should this statistical evidence have any impact on the way that Landlord and Tenant Board adjudicators exercise their discretion under s 83?

ii. Affordable Housing and Legal Reform

Residential tenancies legislation holds out the promise of safe, secure, and affordable housing for all, but it is a promise that can be difficult to realize for significant sectors of the population, especially the disabled and those with low incomes. The ONPHA report just noted suggests that the supply of affordable housing, whether in the public or private sector, is not keeping pace with the large increase in the low-income population (from 8 percent of Ontarians in 1990 to 12 percent in 2010), with the result that "more people [are] finding less permanent, less private, and generally more insecure and unregulated rental arrangements" (*Where's Home 2013?* at 49). Are such needs likely to be addressed by incremental changes to residential tenancies legislation?

iii. Tenant Advocacy: An Ongoing Challenge

Advising and representing residential tenants forms a significant part of the work of some community legal aid clinics, whose staff have sometimes tried to use litigation strategically to advance law reform goals. Organizations such as the Advocacy Centre for Tenants Ontario, <http://www.acto.ca>, also work on behalf of low-income tenants. Accounts of their successes and failures are indispensable when reflecting on the possibilities for law reform in this area. Mary Truemner and Bart Poesiat recount the decades-long saga of the attempts by tenants of two apartment towers in the Parkdale area of Toronto to implement a groundbreaking Supreme Court of Canada decision, *Pajelle Investments Ltd v Herbold*, [1976] 2 SCR 520, dealing with the statutory obligation to keep leased residential premises in a good state of repair: see "The West Lodge Files: Joining Clinic and Community to Overcome Tenants' Subordination" (1997) 35 Osgoode Hall LJ 697. In spite of the ongoing assistance of staff at Parkdale Community Legal Services, an unprecedented rent strike, and active legislative lobbying, the tenants faced almost insuperable obstacles in having their claims effectively addressed.

PROBLEMS

1. Bob works for a large downtown insurance company, Insurco. The company provides Bob with a car and downtown parking facilities in a lot owned and operated by a local company, Park Inc. Insurco and Park Inc entered into an agreement under which Insurco rents a

number of underground parking spots from Park Inc for a small monthly fee. The agreement states that Park Inc may occasionally need to move one or more of Insurco's parked cars. For this reason, the agreement provides that Insurco employees are required to leave their keys in the ignitions of their cars whenever they park in the Park Inc lot. The agreement also states that Park Inc will provide certain security services in the parking lot. There will always be an attendant on duty, "no trespassing" signs will be posted, and members of the general public will be strictly excluded from the lot unless they have parked their cars there.

The agreement also provides that "Park Inc is not responsible for theft or damage to Insurco's cars, however caused."

Six months ago, Bob left work at approximately 7 pm and went to Park Inc to pick up his company car. He discovered that his car was missing and the Park Inc attendant had no idea where it was. Bob's company car has never been found. Insurco wants to know if it has any claim against Park Inc for the lost company car.

Advise Insurco.

2. Last week Ahmad decided to rent a car to drive to Ottawa. He went to "Rent-a-Lemon," a rather haphazard operation that rents lousy cars. Gail, the manager at "Rent-a-Lemon," handed Ahmad a standard-form contract to sign. A clever law student, Ahmad actually read the contract, which provided, among other things, that the lessee of the car was "absolutely liable for any theft of the car." For an additional $10 a day, the lessee could purchase theft insurance.

Ahmad was not happy with the "liability for theft" clause, because he believed that cars are frequently stolen in Ottawa, and he did not want to pay for the additional insurance. He told Gail that he would not rent the car unless the "liability for theft" clause were removed. He asked Gail to agree to the addition of the following clause to the agreement:

> Regardless of any negligence or gross carelessness on the part of the lessee, the lessee is hereby rendered free from any liability whatsoever for any theft of the rented vehicle.

Gail was on the verge of financial ruin and was desperate for business. The car was in poor shape and she could not imagine that anyone would steal it. She agreed to Ahmad's request. Ahmad struck out the liability clause and wrote in the additional clause as above. Both parties initialled the changes to the contract. Ahmad paid his money and drove off to Ottawa.

In Ottawa, Ahmad stayed with a friend. He had no use for the car there, so he left it with his sister, Sue, who also lives in Ottawa. Sue asked Ahmad to leave the keys in the glove compartment in case she needed to move the car, which was parked in her driveway. Of course the car was stolen, and it has never been recovered.

Gail has come to you for advice. She is devastated by the loss of this car, which was not insured for theft. If she cannot recover any money for the car, Gail is afraid she will have to close "Rent-a-Lemon." Gail leases the premises where she conducts her rent-a-car business. Gail's landlord, hearing of Gail's business troubles, has warned Gail that if she breaches the lease he will sue her for the entire amount due under the remainder of the lease—another 10 months at $2,000 per month.

Advise Gail.

3. Manchester Garages signed a "licence" with Shell-Mex to occupy a filling station. The agreement provided that Manchester was to occupy the premises for one year and to sell

only Shell-Mex products. The agreement also included a provision that allowed Shell-Mex's employees to visit the premises at their discretion. Shell-Mex attempted to terminate the agreement pursuant to the terms of the licence. Manchester argued that the licence was, in fact, a lease. Advise Manchester. See *Shell-Mex and BP Ltd v Manchester Garages Ltd*, [1971] 1 WLR 612 (CA).

CHAPTER REFERENCES

Advocacy Centre for Tenants Ontario. <http://www.acto.ca>.

Bentley, Christopher et al, eds. *Williams and Rhodes Canadian Law of Landlord and Tenant*, loose-leaf, 6th ed (Toronto: Carswell, 1988).

Brock, Jason & Jim Phillips. "The Commercial Lease: Property or Contract?" (2000) 38 Alta L Rev 989.

Burn, EH & J Cartwright. *Cheshire and Burn's Modern Law of Real Property*, 18th ed (London: Butterworths, 2011).

Fleming, Jack. *Residential Tenancies in Ontario*, 2d ed (Markham, ON: LexisNexis, 2011).

Haber, Harvey. *The Commercial Lease: A Practical Guide*, 4th ed (Aurora, ON: Canada Law Book, 2004).

Harpum, Charles. "Leases, Licences, Sharing and Shams" (1989) 48 Cambridge LJ 19.

Harpum, Charles, Stuart Bridge & Martin Dixon, eds. *Megarry and Wade: The Law of Real Property*, 8th ed (London: Sweet & Maxwell, 2012).

Hohmann, Jessie. *The Right to Housing: Law, Concepts, Possibilities* (Oxford and Portland, OR: Hart, 2013).

La Forest, Anne Warner. *Anger & Honsberger Law of Real Property*, loose-leaf (Aurora, ON: Canada Law Book, 2006) ch 16.

Lightman, ES. *A Community of Interests: The Report of the Commission of Inquiry into Unregulated Residential Accommodation* (Toronto: Ontario Government, 1992).

Mahoney, E. "The Ontario Tenant Protection Act: A Trust Betrayed" (2001) 16 J Law & Soc Pol'y 261.

McCreary, M. "Little House of Horrors: Discrimination Against Boarding Home Tenants—Human Rights Legislation and the Charter" (1998) 13 J L & Soc Pol'y 224.

Medow, Jon & Greg Suttor with assistance from Harvey Cooper, Sharad Kerur, and Margaret McCutcheon. *Where's Home 2013? Looking Back and Looking Forward at the Need for Affordable Housing in Ontario* (Toronto: Ontario Non-Profit Housing Association and Co-operative Housing Federation of Canada, Ontario Region, 2013), <http://chfcanada.coop/eng/pdf/ontdocs/WheresHome2013_WEB.pdf>.

Palmer, Norman. *Palmer on Bailment*, 3d ed (London: Sweet & Maxwell, 2009).

Smith, Lawrence B. "Intertenancy Rent Decontrol in Ontario" (2003) 29 Can Pub Pol'y 213.

Statistics Canada. *Dwelling Characteristics and Household Equipment, by Province (Canada)* (2011), <http://www.statcan.gc.ca>.

Truemner, Mary. "A Closer Look at Seemingly Pro-Tenant Provisions in the Residential Tenancies Act" (2009) 22 J Law & Soc Pol'y 27.

Truemner, Mary & Bart Poesiat. "The West Lodge Files: Joining Clinic and Community to Overcome Tenants' Subordination" (1997) 35 Osgoode Hall LJ 697.

Vincent-Jones, Peter. "Exclusive Possession and Exclusive Control of Private Rented Housing" (1987) 14 JL & Soc'y 445.

Zarnett, B. "Damages for Breach of Lease" (1987) 8 Advocates' Q 257.

Ziff, BH. *Principles of Property Law*, 5th ed (Scarborough, ON: Carswell, 2010).

CHAPTER FIVE

Transferring Property Interests by Gifts and Sale: The Role of Equity

I. INTRODUCTION: THE LEGAL CONTEXT

This chapter considers the transfer of interests in property and explores further the relationship between contract and property law, emphasizing the role of equity in shaping gift and sale transactions. The transfer of a property interest by contractual arrangement (sale) involves a mutual exchange of obligations that are enforced by way of legal and equitable remedies for breach. Such a transaction is often called a bargain promise. By contrast, transfer by way of gift involves a gratuitous, unilateral transaction, which is often referred to as a non-bargain promise. In general, non-bargain promises are unenforceable in the law of contract, although it may be possible to create a legally enforceable unilateral promise if the promise includes nominal consideration ("the peppercorn requirement").

Bargain promises typically occur in a commercial context where there is a need to enforce the expectations of contracting parties, while non-bargain promises, such as gifts among family members and friends, seem less important matters for legal regulation. Yet, some critics have suggested that to consider transfers by way of sale and gift only in economic terms is to miss the point. For example, wedding presents "transfer material capability, but also cement relations between groups and mark important changes of status for the partners to the marriage." See WT Murphy, S Roberts & T Flessas, *Understanding Property Law*, 4th ed (London: Sweet & Maxwell, 2004) [Murphy, Roberts & Flessas] at 184. In any event, even property interests transferred by way of gift may be enforced in some circumstances.

Principles of equity are important in the transfer of property interests. A number of modern equitable principles are relevant to an understanding of gift transactions. As well, equity is important in sale transactions, especially in the context of contracts for the sale of land and the doctrine of part performance and in relation to the recognition of "equities" in family property arrangements, a matter discussed in Chapter 6. Equity helped to create the modern law of mortgages and is also important in the context of priorities among competing interests in land and personal property. Both these topics are briefly considered along with registration schemes at the end of this chapter.

The legal regulation of transfers of property interests is a major focus of lawyers' work, although transfers of property interests do not always require lawyers. Most people, for example, give birthday presents without the help of a lawyer. However, even the giving of birthday presents may sometimes necessitate lawyers and, in some cases, even involve litigation. In *Michael Gruen v Kemija Gruen*, 68 NY 2d 48, 496 NE 2d 869 (CA 1986), a successful architect in New York, Victor Gruen, wrote to his son, Michael, to tell him that he was giving him a painting by Gustav Klimt to mark Michael's 21st birthday. A short time later, Victor Gruen sent a second letter (replacing the first one) to his son to announce the gift, explaining that his lawyer had concluded that the wording of the first letter would have attracted tax liability. (The painting had been purchased in 1959 for $8,000, but was valued at the time of the litigation in 1986 at $2.5 million.) The case suggests that the role of lawyers may be critical to the efficacy of such transactions.

II. TRANSFERRING PROPERTY INTERESTS BY GIFT

A. Gift Relationships

As a non-bargain promise, a gift does not attract legal regulation in the same way as a contract. Yet gifts may have great social significance:

> Lawyers look upon gift as at core a unilateral transaction, by contrast with the bilateral character of sale. Gift is not treated as a mode of exchange. In this respect the legal definition of gift differs sometimes quite sharply from the social meaning of gift in many cultures, including, perhaps, our own.
>
> In some societies, giving "buys" you prestige. As [the anthropologist Marcel] Mauss put it:
>
> > Between vassals and chiefs … the hierarchy is established by means of … gifts. To give is to show one's superiority, to show that one is something more and higher, that one is magister. To accept without returning or repaying more is to face subordination, to become a client and subservient, to become minister (1925; tr. 1966, 1969:72).

(Murphy, Roberts & Flessas at 192.)

Gifts and gift giving may also attract legal regulation. In Canada, for example, T Loo has analyzed amendments to the *Indian Act* (RSC 1985, c I-5), beginning in 1884, that made the "potlatch" an indictable criminal offence. "Potlatch" derives from the language of trade along the coast of British Columbia, a combination of English and a variety of Aboriginal languages, and means "to give." In traditional native culture in British Columbia, it is a ceremony given by a family to display its hereditary possessions, including dances, songs, and carvings, and ends with the distribution of gifts to those attending. The traditional ceremony of potlatch changed with increasing contact between First Nations people and European settlers and traders, so that the quantity and commercial value of gifts being distributed increased substantially. These changes attracted government attention and resulted in the enactment of a series of amendments to the *Indian Act* after 1884 that were designed to curtail potlatches. Although concerns were expressed about the wastefulness of the potlatch ceremonies, "the antithesis to the twin pillars of the Protestant work ethic: industry and sobriety," Loo identified anthropological interpretations of the potlatch that showed its similarity to European cultures:

> In [the anthropologists'] opinion, the law was flawed in part not because it was ethnocentric, but because its architects failed to appreciate the broad similarities between the potlatch and modern Western economic behaviour. …
>
> The problem with and the significance of the ceremony to white society lay in the distributive aspect of the ceremony. Accumulation was laudable, but the way Indians disposed of their goods stood as a radical counterpoint to the existing material order in white society … . Working to consume and accumulate was intelligible behaviour, but when Indians gave away or destroyed all they had worked for they debased the very commodity—property—around which white society was constructed.

(T Loo, "Dan Cranmer's Potlatch: Law as Coercion, Symbol, and Rhetoric in British Columbia, 1884-1951" in T Loo & L McLean, eds, *Historical Perspectives on Law and Society in Canada* (Toronto: Copp Clark Longman, 1994) [Loo & McLean] 219 at 231-32.) The prohibition against the potlatch was left out of the *Indian Act* in 1951 (Loo & McLean at 222).

As some critics pointed out in 1904, the feasting, dancing, singing, and use of masks at a potlatch were not so different from some European celebrations: "[T]he white man calls his friends at Christmas time & feasts them & has Xmas trees & gives presents & he dresses up a man & calls him Father Xmas & says he brings presents, etc." See Loo & McLean at 233-34, quoting correspondence. Others have suggested that one method of evading the law's prohibition of potlatches was to "[disguise them] as Christmas dinners and the gift giving as holiday presents." See D Cole & I Chaikin, "'A Worse Than Useless Custom': The Potlatch Law and Indian Resistance" (1992) 5:2 Western Legal History 187 at 209. For an overview of the policy of the *Indian Act*, see J Tobias, "Protection, Civilization, Assimilation: An Outline History of Canada's Indian Policy" in Loo & McLean 290.

Not all legal cultures treat gift and contract as mutually exclusive, as the common law does. The *Civil Code of Quebec*, SQ 1991, c 64, treats gifts under the heading of "obligations" not "property," and art 1806 of the Code states that "[g]ift is a contract by which a person, the donor, transfers ownership of property by gratuitous title to another person, the donee." A consequence of gifts being treated as bilateral transactions is that they may be revoked for ingratitude. Article 1836 states that "[i]ngratitude is a ground of revocation where the donee has behaved in a seriously reprehensible manner towards the donor, having regard to the nature of the gift, the faculties of the parties and the circumstances."

B. Requirements for a Valid Gift Inter Vivos

A gift of real property or personal property can be made by a deed of gift or by a declaration of trust. A gift of personal property may also be made by delivery, so long as there is intention to give on the part of the donor and acceptance on the part of the donee. Each of these arrangements is considered in turn.

A gift *inter vivos* is the most usual form of gift, but it needs to be distinguished from other kinds of gifts, including those made in contemplation of death, such as testamentary gifts and the *donatio mortis causa*, both of which are considered below.

1. Gifts Inter Vivos: The Deed of Gift

A deed is a document in writing that is signed by the donor, sealed, and delivered. The seal, representing the solemnity of the transaction, has long been held to take the place of consideration. Thus gift and contract do overlap in the context of a deed. The deed transfers title to the property in question to the donee from the moment of its delivery, but if the donor subsequently withholds possession of the item, the donee can sue for breach of covenant. The printed word "seal" on a document has been held to satisfy the requirement that the deed be sealed: *Bank of Nova Scotia v Hooper* (1994), 150 NBR (2d) 111 (QB), aff'd (1994), 155 NBR (2d) 132 (CA). For further analysis of deeds, see T Youdan, "The Formal Requirements of a Deed" (1979) 5 BLR 71. The traditional requirement that a deed had to be delivered to be effective has been interpreted to mean that there must be evidence that the person executing the deed intended to be immediately and unconditionally bound by it. See *Re Sammon* (1979), 94 DLR (3d) 594 (Ont CA). Delivery in this context does not mean physical delivery.

Consider a situation where a donor executed a deed conveying a one-half interest in fee simple to the donee; a few years later, after a discussion of marriage between the donor and donee, the donor executed a second deed conveying the remaining one-half interest as well.

The solicitor for the donee was expected to register it. Subsequently, the marriage plans fell through and the donor then sought to set aside the second deed of gift. How should the court determine whether there was a valid gift pursuant to the second deed? In *Schilthuis v Arnold*, [1991] OJ no 2212 (Gen Div), the trial court concluded that there was a valid and ir-revocable gift at the time when the donor executed the deed conveying the remainder of the property to the donee and left it in the office of the donee's solicitor. On the facts, the donor was a successful entrepreneur and had made several gifts to the donee over the years, and the court concluded that the gift was wholly separate from the discussion of marriage plans. As the court stated (at 2), a gift "is not a kiss in the dark. Unlike the memory of a kiss which fades in time, the giving of a gift has lasting consequences." Do you agree with this analysis?

Consider this problem in the context of the responsibilities of the donee's solicitor who drafted the deed of gift. If the donor did not intend his gift to be unconditional, how could this intention have been reflected in the document? On appeal, the Ontario Court of Appeal suggested that it would have been prudent for the donee's solicitor to have insisted that the donor execute the deed in his own solicitor's office. However, the court decided the appeal on the basis that the gift was conditional on marriage and that there could be no gift if the condition remained unfulfilled. The Court of Appeal also noted that the half-interest was val-ued at about $100,000. See *Schilthuis v Arnold* (1996), 95 OAC 196. Which decision do you find more persuasive—that of the trial judgment or that of the appellate court? Why? Is it relevant that the donor was 73 years old while the donee was just 44? In some cases, note that it may also be necessary to consider registration requirements that affect the validity of a transfer: see e.g. *Re Sammon* (1979), 94 DLR (3d) 594 (Ont CA). The principles of registration are exam-ined briefly at the end of this chapter.

In the United States, "the majority view today seems to recognize the validity of gifts by ordinary writings," whether or not the documents conform to the technical requirements for a deed. For an overview of the historical developments and analysis of US cases, see R Brown, *The Law of Personal Property*, 3d ed by W Raushenbush (Chicago: Callaghan & Co, 1975) [Brown] at 106ff. According to *Jones v Jones Estate* (1979), 5 Sask R 27 (QB), a written docu-ment that does not qualify as a deed will not be sufficient to transfer personal property—that is, a chose in possession. Is the US or Canadian approach preferable in the light of policy goals for the law of gifts?

2. Gifts Inter Vivos: Delivery, Intention, and Acceptance

In practice, a deed of gift is not often used for gifts of personal property, unless the items in question are highly valuable or physically bulky. In the absence of a deed, a gift of personal property is legally recognized if three requirements are met—the intention to make a gift on the part of the donor, acceptance of the gift by the donee, and a sufficient act of delivery.

The act of delivery provides tangible proof of a gift and helps to demonstrate the neces-sary intention to make a gift. It is, however, a distinct substantive requirement and not merely an evidentiary one. The delivery requirement marks an important difference between con-tract law and the law of gifts. A contract involves an exchange of promises. A gift, a unilateral act, does not. Contract law will enforce an exchange of promises ("a bargain promise") with expectation damages. On the other hand, the law of gifts attaches no significance to a uni-lateral promise in the absence of delivery. In other words, an exuberant declaration at a wed-ding in front of numerous guests that a donor has made or will make a gift to the newlyweds will not suffice in law to make an enforceable gift, unless the declaration is joined with an act of delivery before, during, or after the declaration: *Waite v Waite*, [1953] 3 DLR 142 (BCSC). The law of gifts in effect permits donors to change their minds and retract a gift, providing they do so before effective delivery of the gift. The common law has been traditionally suspicious of gifts and wants to "protect" the donor from acts of spontaneous generosity by requiring clear formalities for the gratuitous transfer of title. The deed is the most stringent type of formality, but physical delivery is also meant to serve the same goal of reminding the donor that he or she is parting with title permanently. The common law also protects the donor by putting the onus of proof of a gift on the donee in case of any dispute, as we will see below.

a. Delivery

The following cases illustrate the difficulties with the delivery requirement in a variety of contexts.

In re Cole
[1964] 1 Ch 175 (CA)

[In this case, consider the issue of delivery of a gift in a family context. Are there different factors to be taken into account in the case of gifts to family members? How can delivery of gifts be proved when family members reside together?]

HARMAN LJ: This is an appeal from an order of Cross J made on March 22, 1963, on a motion by the trustee in the bankruptcy of Theodore Cole by which the court declared that certain articles of furniture specified in the schedule to the notice of motion were the property of the applicant who is the bankrupt's wife. The value of these articles is comparatively small but we are told that the decision will probably cover other articles of very much greater value in respect of which a like claim has been made. These particular articles have been sold by the applicant and the order affects the proceeds of sale.

We first hear of the bankrupt and his wife in 1937 when they were living in a modest rented house at Hendon which, as well as its furniture, were the bankrupt's property. In July, 1940, the bankrupt, being Austrian by nationality, was apprehensive of internment as an enemy alien and he executed a deed of gift transferring the house to his wife and also gave her the furniture. The method of this latter gift is not known and is not in question. The family then moved to Clitheroe in Lancashire where they rented a house which was furnished largely from the Hendon house. The activities of the bankrupt during the war, apparently in the textile trade, resulted in his becoming before its end a very rich man indeed. In July, 1945, the war being over, he acquired a long lease of a large mansion at Hendon which he proceeded to furnish. A few articles were sent down from Clitheroe, three or four thousand pounds worth was bought from the vendor, and the rest to the tune of some £20,000 the bankrupt purchased himself and caused to be installed in the new house, to which he, together with two children and their nannie, removed in September, leaving the applicant and another child who was unwell at Clitheroe. In December, 1945, however, the wife came down to London with the other child and the bankrupt met her at the station and took her to the new home. He brought her into the house, took her into a room, put his hands over her eyes and then uncovered them saying "Look." He then accompanied her into other rooms on the ground floor where she handled certain of the articles—a silk carpet and an inlaid card table: next she went upstairs by herself and examined the rest of the house. When she came down again the husband said: "It's all yours." She now says that this was a gift to her of the furniture in the house, though apparently not of the house itself, and the judge accepted the evidence of the husband and wife that they had since believed that this was the position. We must accept the judge's finding in this respect, notwithstanding that the house and its contents and also £20,000 worth of furs and jewellery, said to have been other presents to the wife, remained insured in the bankrupt's name. Until the mid-'50s the bankrupt lived the life of a very rich man owning, among other things, a villa at Cannes and a fleet of cars, but the death of one of his associates, one Littman, was followed by a judgment against him by Littman's executors for a very large sum which remained unsatisfied; and in 1961 bankruptcy ensued and there is a very large deficiency. The trustee on behalf of the creditors resists the wife's claim to the furniture in the house, except the small items from Clitheroe, and that was the question tried on this motion: the judge acceded to the wife's claim: the trustee now appeals.

Mr. Megarry on behalf of the wife boldly put forward an entirely novel proposition to the effect that a perfect gift of chattels is constituted by showing them to the donee and speaking words of gift. It is enough, he says, that the donee should be brought to the chattels rather than the chattels to the donee and that she should be "near" the chattels (though what degree of proximity is needful remained vague) when the words of gift are spoken. This amounts to a change of possession, says Mr. Megarry, particularly if you are dealing with a collection of chattels, *a fortiori* if the chattels are or come under the physical control of the donee; and the case is strengthened if the donee handles some of the chattels in the donor's presence.

This remarkable submission is unsupported by authority and is in my judgment entirely heterodox. It is, I think, trite law that a gift of chattels is not complete unless accompanied by something which constitutes an act of delivery or a change of possession. The English law of the transfer of property, dominated as it has always been by the doctrine of consideration, has always been chary of the recognition of gifts. Witness the equitable doctrine of the resulting trust. In the early days when no clear distinction was made between what we now call real and personal property, transfer lay in livery and until a comparatively recent date the transfer of realty or chattels real lay in livery and not in grant. Indeed, until the *Statute of Frauds* no written instrument was required. I need not, I think, for the purposes of this judgment touch further on the question of the transfer of anything except chattels personal. Where consideration is given, possession of these is regulated by the *Sale of Goods Act* which, broadly speaking, causes possession to pass when the parties intend that it should; but in the absence of consideration, delivery is still necessary except in the cases of a gift by will or by deed, which latter itself imports both consideration and delivery. Attempts have been made to make use of the law of trusts to perfect gifts, particularly in the case of gifts *mortis causa*, but it has long been the doctrine of equity that it will not assist imperfect gifts by the introduction of the doctrine of trusts. In *Milroy v. Lord* Turner LJ thus stated the law:

> I take the law of this court to be well settled, that, in order to render a voluntary settlement
> valid and effectual, the settlor must have done everything which, according to the nature of

the property comprised in the settlement, was necessary to be done in order to transfer the property and render the settlement binding upon him. He may of course do this by actually transferring the property to the persons for whom he intends to provide, and the provision will then be effectual, and it will be equally effectual if he transfers the property to a trustee for the purposes of the settlement, or declares that he himself holds it in trust for those purposes; and if the property be personal, the trust may, as I apprehend, be declared either in writing or by parol; but, in order to render the settlement binding, one or other of these modes must, as I understand the law of this court, be resorted to, for there is no equity in this court to perfect an imperfect gift. The cases I think go further to this extent, that if the settlement is intended to be effectuated by one of the modes to which I have referred, the court will not give effect to it by applying another of those modes. If it is intended to take effect by transfer, the court will not hold the intended transfer to operate as a declaration of trust, for then every imperfect instrument would be made effectual by being converted into a perfect trust. These are the principles by which, as I conceive, this case must be tried.

The leading case on delivery is *Irons v. Smallpiece*, an action of trover for two colts said to have been given to the plaintiff by his father under an oral gift. This was rejected by the court, Abbott CJ saying that:

> … by the law of England, in order to transfer property by gift there must either be a deed or instrument of gift, or there must be an actual delivery of the thing to the donee.

Holroyd J said:

> In order to change the property by a gift of this description, there must be a change of possession: here there has been no change of possession.

The delivery may be what has been called "constructive delivery," as in *Winter v. Winter*, which was a case about a barge [a "lighter" used for unloading cargo from ships] which belonged to the plaintiff's father, a lighterman. It appeared that the plaintiff had been put into actual possession of the barge by his father and worked it as his father's agent or servant and was so doing when the father gave it him by word. It was held that this was sufficient, the delivery preceding the gift: and this it may do or it may accompany the gift or succeed it—see *Anderson v. Peel* and *In re Stoneham, Stoneham v. Stoneham*. In *Winter's* case Crompton J went so far as to cast doubt on *Irons v. Smallpiece* which had indeed been doubted in other cases about that time, but the leading case was fully re-established in the elaborate judgments in *Cochrane v. Moore*. This was a case about a quarter undivided share in a horse and the Court of Appeal held that the property did not pass by the gift because there had been no delivery. Fry LJ, in a judgment concurred in by Bowen LJ, reviewed the whole of the cases and came to this conclusion:

> This review of the authorities leads us to conclude that according to the old law no gift or grant of a chattel was effectual to pass it whether by parol or by deed, and whether with or without consideration unless accompanied by delivery: that on that law two exceptions have been grafted, one in the case of deeds, and the other in that of contracts of sale where the intention of the parties is that the property shall pass before delivery: but that as regards gifts by parol, the old law was in force when *Irons v. Smallpiece* was decided: that that case therefore correctly declared the existing law: and that it has not been overruled by the decision of Pollock B in 1883, or the subsequent case before Cave J.

Lord Esher concurred.

If the chattels be many or bulky there may be symbolical delivery, as, for instance, of a chair—*Lock v. Heath*, or the case about the gift of a church organ—*Rawlinson v. Mort*, where the donor put his hand upon it in the presence of the donee and accompanied his gesture with words of gift.

The question, therefore, for our decision is whether there has been anything here which amounts to an act of delivery or a change of possession either preceding or following or coincident with the words of gift so as to make it perfect. The judge dealt with this point very briefly. He assumed that there must be delivery and that words of gift alone are not enough, but he said he could not decide in the trustee's favour without deciding that a husband cannot give his wife the contents of the matrimonial home without executing a deed of gift. He said he did not see what more Mr. Cole could have done to put Mrs. Cole into the possession of the gift which he thought he was making. It seems to me that this was in fact a reliance on the word or words of gift which was the very thing which the judge said he could not do. Mr. Megarry, however, argued that when the question was of a gift to a wife of chattels in the matrimonial home, the introduction of the wife to the house was itself a putting of her into possession of its contents and that was a sufficient change of possession so that mere words of gift were enough. I reject this view. Mr. Megarry relied on two cases, *Ramsay v. Margrett* and *French v. Gething*. The former of these was a case under the *Married Women's Property Act* and decided that where the furniture is in the house where the husband and wife are living together, you cannot say in whose possession they are and, therefore, you must decide it by the title. In that case, however, the furniture had been bought by the wife from her husband and the property had passed to her for a good consideration. Similarly, in *French v. Gething* the furniture had been given to the wife by deed and that passed the possession to her and it was held that it was not in the apparent order and disposition of the husband. Those two cases, therefore, are no authority for Mr. Megarry's argument. *Bashall v. Bashall* shows that delivery is necessary to perfect a gift between spouses. This was an action by a wife for certain articles, notably a pony and trap, and Lord Esher MR said this:

> [I]t was clear law that in order to pass property in chattels by way of gift mere words were not sufficient, but there must be a delivery. And this requirement was as essential in a case of husband and wife as in a case of two strangers. But a difficulty arose when they came to consider how a husband was to deliver a chattel to his wife so as to pass the property in it. The difficulty arose, not from the legal relation between them, but from the fact of their living together. When a husband wished to make a present of jewellery to his wife, he generally gave it into her own hands, and then it was easy to see that there was a delivery. But in the case of a horse or a carriage, that would not be so. In such a case it was true the husband might wish to make an absolute gift to his wife, but, on the other hand, he might wish to keep the horse or carriage as his own property and merely to let his wife have the use of it. In an action by the wife it was necessary for her to show that the husband had done that which amounted to a delivery.

Similarly, in *Valier v. Wright and Bull Ltd.*, an action concerning a motor car said to be the subject-matter of a gift by a husband to a wife:

> *Held*, that after the gift no change had taken place in the custody of the car, and there had been no valid gift because there had been no actual or constructive delivery.

Mr. Megarry also relied on the old case of *Smith v. Smith*. This was a decision of Lord Hardwicke when Chief Justice and is merely an example of what amounted to a good delivery. There the donor had furniture and plate in the defendant's house where he lodged, which he was said to have given to the defendant's wife. I read this passage:

> And now in trover for the goods which were there at the intestate's death, it was ruled, that a parol gift, without some act of delivery, would not alter the property, and that such an act was necessary to establish a *donatio causa mortis*. Upon this opinion it came to the question, Whether there was any delivery? And to prove one, the defendant showed that the intestate, when he went out of town, used to leave the key of his rooms with the defendant: and that was insisted to be such a mixed possession that the law will adjudge the possession to be in him who has the right. And the Chief Justice ruled it so, and the jury found for the defendant.

This is merely a jury's view of what amounts to a sufficient delivery and is no authority here.

A stronger case is *In re Magnus, Ex parte Salaman*, where the husband settled furniture upon his wife by a marriage settlement and covenanted to add further furniture. He purchased a large amount of additional furniture which he installed in the house; he did not formally deliver it to the trustee of the settlement, but the trustee visited the house and saw the furniture there. It was held that this was a sufficient delivery to the trustee and that the wife was enjoying the furniture under the trusts of the settlement. This was enough to defeat the claim of the trustee in the husband's bankruptcy. It does not in my judgment cover the present case.

Perhaps the strongest case in the wife's favour is *Kilpin v. Ratley*. In that case furniture belonging to the husband and in the matrimonial home was purchased by his father-in-law who took an assignment of it by deed. Subsequently the father visited his daughter at the house and standing in one of the rooms orally gave her the furniture and then walked out of the house, leaving it behind him, and this was held to amount to a sufficient delivery to the wife. This furniture, until the time of the gift, was owned by the father and was in the possession of the son-in-law, but the father by pointing the furniture out to his daughter and then leaving the house put her and not her husband in possession of it and there was, therefore, a sufficient change of possession.

I cannot find that there was any change of possession here. It is argued that a wife living in her husband's house, and therefore having control to some extent of the furniture in it, is in possession of it, but this, I think, does not follow. In the ordinary case where a wife lives with her husband in a house owned and furnished by him, she has the use of the furniture by virtue of her position as wife, but that gives her no more possession of it than a servant has who uses the furniture. As to this, see Goddard LJ in *Youngs v. Youngs*. It is true that it may be doubtful who is in possession of the furniture and that you must look to the title, as in *Ramsay v. Margrett*, but in the absence of delivery there is no title in her, as was pointed out by Lord Evershed MR in *Hislop v. Hislop*.

I conclude, therefore, although I feel considerable sympathy with the wife who has believed this furniture to be hers, that it never became so because the gift was never perfected and that therefore she has no answer to the trustee's claim. I would allow the appeal.

PEARSON LJ: As to what is necessary to constitute delivery from husband to wife, guidance is afforded by the judgment of Lord Esher in *Bashall v. Bashall*. The earlier part of that judgment has been read by Harman LJ, and so I need only read the concluding part of it:

> In an action by the wife it was necessary for her to show that the husband had done that which amounted to delivery. If the facts proved were equally consistent with the idea that he intended to deliver the thing to the wife so as to be her property, and with the idea that he intended to keep it as his own property, then the wife failed to make out her case. He thought there was no sufficient evidence of delivery here, and the appeal must therefore be allowed.

As I understand that passage, it is dealing with delivery, and the effect of it is that an act to constitute delivery must be one which in itself shows an intention of the donor to transfer the chattel to the donee. If the act in itself is equivocal—consistent equally with an intention of the husband to transfer the chattels to his wife or with an intention on his part to retain possession but give to her the use and enjoyment of the chattels as his wife—the act does not constitute delivery.

In the present case the intended gift was from husband to wife. Be it assumed that he spoke words of gift—words expressing an intention of transferring the chattels to her, and not merely an intention to give her the use and enjoyment of them as his wife—and that in the circumstances the chattels intended to be given were sufficiently identified by the words of gift. There was no pre-existing possession of the donee in this case. The husband was the owner of the chattels and therefore considered in law to be in possession of them. No act of delivery has been proved, because the acts relied upon are in themselves equivocal—consistent equally with an intention of the husband to transfer the chattels to his wife or with an intention on his part to retain possession but give to her the use and enjoyment of them as his wife. ...

Pennycuick LJ agreed in a separate opinion.

> *Appeal allowed with costs in the Court of Appeal and below.*
> *Leave to appeal to the House of Lords refused.*

DISCUSSION NOTES

i. Delivery in the Context of Common Possession of the Donor and Donee

Given that many of the precedents cited by Harman LJ seem to treat the delivery requirement in a rather flexible manner, why do you think that the court was so concerned to find that it had not been satisfied here?

In a BC case, *Langer v McTavish Brothers Ltd*, [1932] 4 DLR 90 (BCCA), a man brought his fiancée to a new home, showed her an array of furniture, and declared, as the husband did in *In re Cole*, "It's all yours." The court held that there was a valid gift, taking into account the nature of the property and the circumstances of the parties. It was applied in *McLeod Estate (Re)*, 2012 ABQB 384, where the deceased was found to have given a large collection of wood, tools, and machinery to his wife even though most of it was located on premises that the two occupied jointly. The trial judge concluded (at para 92) "that physical delivery would have been 'unnecessary as an idle or purely artificial act.'" Are *Langer* and *McLeod* distinguishable from *Cole*? Is *Cole* still good law in Canada? For further analysis, see Bruce Ziff, *Principles of Property Law*, 5th ed (Scarborough, ON: Carswell, 2010) [Ziff] at 161-62.

In *Mackedie Estate v Mackedie*, [1998] BCJ no 2200 (SC), the deceased had owned five paintings worth $35,000 each. His son Graeme claimed that his father had given him the paintings as birthday presents, one painting each year over five years. On each birthday, a painting was taken off the wall, wrapped, and given to the son. Graeme's mother endorsed each gift with the written notation "Happy Birthday Graeme." After the painting was un-wrapped, it was agreed that the paintings would be kept in the possession of the deceased. The deceased died and in his will he left the paintings to someone else. The court found that the paintings belonged to Graeme because there was a clear intention by the deceased to make a gift, including the written endorsements that were known to the deceased. More-over, the court found that the presentation of the paintings as wrapped birthday gifts con-stituted delivery even though they remained in the possession of the deceased.

Suppose that Anne lives with her Uncle Robert, who owns a valuable Steinway piano. After two years of sharing a house with him, he tells Anne on her birthday that he no longer needs the piano and that she can have it as a birthday present. Both continue to play the piano; he plays Bach and Anne plays mostly Sondheim. A year after the alleged gift to Anne, she de-cides to move to her own apartment and makes arrangements for the piano to be moved. At this point, Uncle Robert furiously declares that Sondheim is a fraud and refuses to allow Anne to take the piano. Anne explains that he had made a valid gift of the piano, with sufficient intention and delivery of possession. Uncle Robert laughingly says that his words of intention meant "nothing" and that Anne has "no more a claim to possession of the piano than the cleaning attendant who dusts it once a week." Was there a valid gift? Assume that Uncle Rob-ert had taped a card to the piano with the words "Happy Birthday Anne" written inside. Would that make a difference? Alternatively, suppose that when Anne decided to move out, Uncle Robert agreed that he would lend Anne the piano; then, a year later, after Anne has had the piano in her apartment, he says that she can have it. If he subsequently asks for the return of the piano, can Anne argue that there was a valid gift? What are the relevant differ-ences in these fact situations? Define what issue of delivery is raised in each of them.

ii. Constructive (and Symbolic) Delivery

A valid gift does not require contemporaneous delivery of possession. An expression of in-tention that is preceded or followed by delivery may suffice. As well, courts have permitted constructive delivery where the chattel—for example, a car—is too large or difficult to trans-fer easily. In such cases, delivery of the "means of control"—for example, the keys to the car—may be sufficient, although the factual context will be examined carefully to ensure that the donor has done everything possible to part with possession. If a donor gives his daughter a set of keys to a new car, saying, "This is for you," but retains a duplicate set of keys, is there a valid gift to the daughter? In a case where a donor placed a gift in his safety deposit box, and gave a duplicate key to the donee, the court concluded that there was no change in the donor's control over the subject matter of the alleged gift. See *Bauernschmidt v Bau-ernschmidt*, 54 A 637 (Md CA 1903). By contrast, when a donor handed over the only set of keys to a safety deposit box to a donee, while stating that the donee could have whatever was in the box, the court held that the donee was entitled to the securities valued at over

$185,000 contained in the box. See *Thomas' Adm'r v Lewis*, 15 SE 389 (Va CA 1892). The use of constructive delivery seems to be restricted to the transfer of possession of goods that would be difficult or inconvenient to transfer *per se*. However, this area of the law of gifts remains controversial; as Brown suggested (at 92), there is no part of the law of gifts with "greater uncertainty and confusion than … the matter of constructive delivery."

By contrast with constructive delivery (delivery of the means of control), some cases have considered the idea of symbolic delivery. For example, if the donor delivers a photo of a new car, using words of gift, it may be argued that there has been symbolic delivery. According to Ziff (at 163), however, "there is little authority on which to base the view that symbolic delivery … is enough to complete a gift." Similarly, Brown concluded (at 92) that "[the] surrender of power and dominion is, as has been seen, the heart of the delivery concept, and without it a mere symbolic delivery is customarily declared to be insufficient." If Uncle Robert placed his hands on his piano and said to Anne, "This is now yours," and Anne enthusiastically thanked him for the wonderful gift, would there be a valid gift? How can a donor give "power and dominion" over a piano? Why was the husband's effort to transfer a gift to his wife in *In re Cole* ineffective because of a failure of delivery? Was he trying to make a constructive or symbolic delivery?

b. Intention

A second requirement for a valid gift is the intention to make a donative transfer. In reading the case that follows, note carefully which factors the court relied on to determine the donor's intent.

Thomas v Times Book Co Ltd
[1966] 1 WLR 911 (Ch D)

PLOWMAN J: This is an action by Mrs. Caitlin Thomas, who is the widow of the late Dylan Thomas and the sole administratrix of his estate, to recover from the defendants, the Times Book Company Ltd., the manuscript of Dylan Thomas's best-known work, "Under Milk Wood." The defendants claim that Dylan Thomas made a gift of this manuscript to Douglas Cleverdon, a British Broadcasting Corporation producer, and they claim title through him. It is also pleaded by way of defence that even if the plaintiff ever had a claim to the return of the manuscript it is a stale claim and barred by the *Limitation Act, 1939*.

The primary question with which I am concerned is, therefore, whether Dylan Thomas made a gift of this manuscript to Cleverdon. The manuscript in question consists of two parts. The first part, which is the earlier part of the play, is a fair copy in Dylan Thomas's own handwriting of some earlier draft, or drafts, or sketches. The latter part is a typescript, not made by Dylan Thomas, but made by a copyist of the later part of the play, and it contains emendations made by Dylan Thomas himself.

"Under Milk Wood" is a work which was commissioned by the BBC in, I think, 1943 or 1944. In 1946, when Cleverdon first enters this story, very little had been done by Dylan Thomas. About this time, that is to say, 1946, Cleverdon, who was on the staff of the BBC, inherited the "Under Milk Wood" project from another producer, one Burton, and Cleverdon, as he says, badgered and cajoled Dylan Thomas to get on with "Under Milk Wood."

The work proceeded slowly. There was a time, apparently, when Dylan Thomas got stuck with it, and there was an interval before it was restarted. But eventually, on Thursday, October 15, 1953, Dylan Thomas delivered the manuscript to Cleverdon at his office in the BBC. In that office there was also present Cleverdon's secretary, Miss Fox. Dylan Thomas was due to fly to America on the following Monday, October 19, and he was going there to try to raise some money by giving readings of "Under Milk Wood." He told Cleverdon that he wanted his manuscript back by Monday to take to the United States with him. Cleverdon told his secretary, Miss Fox, to cut a stencil of the manuscript as quickly as possible. She did so, and she gave Dylan Thomas his manuscript back on the morning of Saturday, October 17, and he lost it. He was perturbed about this loss; he had not any other copy of it, he was due to fly to America on the following Monday and he needed the manuscript for that trip.

Some time over the weekend Dylan Thomas telephoned Cleverdon at the latter's home and told him that he had lost the manuscript. Cleverdon told him not to worry about it because the BBC had had this script stencilled, and he, Cleverdon, would take three copies of it to the London air terminal at Victoria Station on Monday and hand them over before Dylan Thomas left for America. On the Monday Cleverdon told his secretary what had happened; he asked her to get three copies rushed off, and that was done. Cleverdon, in the early evening, took a taxi to the London air terminal and there he found Dylan Thomas in company with his wife and a Mr. and Mrs. Locke. Cleverdon handed over to him the three copies of the BBC script. I now quote the actual words of Cleverdon's evidence, which I read from a press cutting which is substantially the same, and is the same in all material respects as my own note. Cleverdon said that the poet was extremely grateful, and then I quote:

> The only words I can recall him actually saying were that I had saved his life. I said it seemed an awful pity that the original had been lost, and that it meant an awful lot to me. I had been working on it very closely over six or seven years, and it was the culmination of one of the most interesting things I had produced. He said if I could find it I could keep it. He told me the names of half a dozen pubs, and said if he had not left it there he might have left it in a taxi.

Either later that day or the next day—probably, I think, the next day—Cleverdon told his secretary, Miss Fox, what had happened. He told her that Dylan Thomas had given him the manuscript, which was still missing, and he told her that he was going to look for it. Within a day or two he found it, and he found it in one of the public-houses in Soho, the name of which he had been given by Dylan Thomas. He took possession of it and he retained it until 1961, when he sold it to one Cox, through whom it came to the defendants.

Two or three days after finding it, a friend of Cleverdon's, one Cranston, a reader in political science at the London School of Economics, and literary adviser to Messrs. Methuen's, the publishers, was having lunch with Cleverdon at his house. On this occasion Cleverdon told him the story of the loss of the manuscript; he told him how he had delivered copies of it to Dylan Thomas at the air terminal, that Dylan Thomas had said that if he could find the original which had been lost he could keep it, and he told him how he had found it.

To go back a little way, as I have already said, on Monday, October 19, Dylan Thomas flew to the United States. About three weeks later, namely, on November 9, 1953, he died in that country. On December 7, 1953, letters of administration were granted to the plaintiff in this action. On December 28, 1953, the plaintiff made a settlement of the copyrights in Dylan Thomas's works. There were three trustees of that settlement: namely, David Higham, who had been Dylan Thomas's literary agent; Dr. Daniel Jenkyn Jones, who was an old friend of Dylan Thomas's going back to school days, who wrote the music for "Under Milk Wood" and who edited the first published edition for Messrs. J.M. Dent & Sons Ltd., the publishers, and Stuart Thomas, a solicitor. The manuscript of "Under Milk Wood," as a chattel was not included in that settlement and, therefore, if there was no gift of it, and if the *Limitation Act, 1939*, is not a defence to this action, the plaintiff, as administratrix of the estate, is entitled to recover this manuscript.

The plaintiff submits that there was no gift of this manuscript to Cleverdon, but let me make it quite plain from the start that the onus is not on the plaintiff to disprove that it was a gift; the onus is on the defendants, and is accepted by their counsel as being on them, to prove affirmatively that a gift was made. But Mr. Sparrow, on behalf of the plaintiff, submits that there was no gift. He further submits, and I accept this submission, that in order to establish a gift the defendants have to prove two things, first of all, the relevant *animus donandi*, or the intention of making a gift, and secondly, a delivery of the subject-matter of the gift, this manuscript, to the donee. Mr. Sparrow submits that the gift claimed in this action fails on both scores: first, for the reason that there was no intention to give and, secondly, for the reason that there was no sufficient delivery of the subject-matter of the gift.

Let me first of all say something about the question whether the defendants have succeeded in establishing the necessary intention. It is said, first of all, and accepted by both sides, that in considering whether the defendants have discharged the onus of proof which is on them, I must approach the claim made by the defendants that there was a gift with suspicion. Reference was made in this connection to the decision of the Court of Appeal in *In re Garnett*, where Brett MR said this:

> Another point was taken. It was said that this release cannot be questioned because the person to whom it was given is dead, and also that it cannot be questioned unless those who object and state certain facts are corroborated, and it is said that that was a doctrine of the Court of Chancery. I do not assent to this argument; there is no such law. Are we to be told that a person whom everybody on earth would believe, who is produced as a witness before the judge, who gives his evidence in such a way that anybody would be perfectly senseless who did not believe him, whose evidence the judge, in fact, believes to be absolutely true, is, according to a doctrine of the court of equity, not to be believed by the judge because he is not corroborated? The proposition seems unreasonable the moment it is stated. There is no such law. The law is that when an attempt is made to charge a dead person in a matter, in which if he were alive he might have answered the charge, the evidence ought to be looked at with great care; the evidence ought to be thoroughly sifted, and the mind of any judge who hears it ought to be, first of all, in a state of suspicion; but if in the end the truthfulness of the witnesses is made perfectly clear and apparent, and the tribunal which has to act on their evidence believes them, the suggested doctrine becomes absurd. And what is ridiculous and absurd never is, to my mind, to be adopted either in law or in equity.

Therefore, not only in this case is the onus of proof on the defendants, but I am enjoined by authority to approach their story with suspicion having regard to the fact that the other actor in this story, the late Dylan Thomas, is dead and cannot therefore give his own version of what took place.

Then Mr. Sparrow submits that the story which is put forward on behalf of the defendants is so improbable as not to be credible. For example, it is said that the late Dylan Thomas was always hard up—and on the evidence it appears quite clearly that he was. It is said that he was setting off on this trip to the United States in order to try to raise some money, and that, no doubt, is equally true. It is said that this was the major work of a great poet; that he must have known that the manuscript was of considerable value; that he had had previous experience of using his manuscripts as a form, as it were, of currency; that he had sold manuscripts of poems previously for an odd pound or two; that the manuscript was a thing over which he had lavished great care and devotion over a number of years, and that in those circumstances it is really inconceivable that he should have made this present of it to Cleverdon.

In addition, it is said that when Dylan Thomas got to America he spent a good deal of time with a close friend of his, one Ruthven Todd—and Ruthven Todd has given evidence before me. His evidence was that Dylan Thomas used to come and see him at his house in Greenwich Village and that he remembers that Dylan Thomas told him on his arrival in the United States about the loss of the manuscript, and how upset he was; that he had said, "I have done it now"; that the manuscript contained material he wanted to refer to; that he hoped the manuscript was going to turn up, and that he would hear about it; that he had said that "Douglas"—that is to say, Cleverdon—had given him the scripts he had; that "Douglas" was looking for the other manuscript and that that was all that he said about it.

It is submitted by Mr. Sparrow that there, in effect, is Dylan Thomas giving evidence in this court, and that on that evidence, as it were, given by Dylan Thomas, I am bound to deduce that he had not made a gift of the manuscript to Cleverdon, because if he had done so he could not have said what he did to Ruthven Todd. Against that, of course, I have to remember this: while I have no doubt that Ruthven Todd was telling what he remembered to the best of his ability, what he was deposing to were conversations which took place over twelve years ago. It is hard enough to remember a conversation one had a week ago, let alone twelve years ago; and while those matters are no doubt matters which have remained in Ruthven Todd's recollection, the fact that these conversations were so long ago is a matter which I am bound to take into account in evaluating the evidence which he gave.

There is no contemporaneous record of the conversations that Dylan Thomas had with Ruthven Todd in the way in which there is an almost contemporaneous record by Cleverdon of the conversation which he had with Dylan Thomas, and on which the defendants base their claim that there was a gift.

I agree with Mr. Sparrow that it is right to weigh probabilities in assessing the weight of the affirmative evidence which is given. But I am bound to say that I think Mr. Balcombe was perfectly justified in saying that a great many of these matters which are now being put forward as establishing the inherent improbability of a gift are pure matters of hindsight.

At the time the alleged gift was made, that is to say, in October, 1953, Dylan Thomas was a comparatively young man; he was 39 years old, and he was still alive. "Under Milk Wood" had not then been performed in England. It had its first performance on the BBC in January, 1954. It had not been published in England. It is quite true, as Mr. Sparrow said, that Dylan Thomas was recognised as a considerable poet, but he was recognised as such by a comparatively small number of people. It was only after the BBC performance of "Under Milk Wood" that Dylan Thomas's name became known to the public at large. Although I do not think the question of the value of the manuscript has really very much to do with this case, it was only after the death of Dylan Thomas that this manuscript, with which I am concerned, became really valuable.

Another thing that I have to bear in mind in weighing the probabilities of the matter is this. When he made the alleged gift, he had not got the manuscript—it had been lost. Nobody knew whether it would ever turn up again. The character of Dylan Thomas, so far as it is delineated by the evidence that I have heard in this court, shows that he was generous, impulsive and capable of spontaneous gestures. It seems to me quite in keeping with that character—in so far as that has emerged in the course of this hearing—that he should have made the gesture of telling Cleverdon that if he found this manuscript he could keep it.

Let me just say a word about the word "keep," because a good many semantic points have been made about the actual words used, whether they were "keep it," or "have it," or "welcome to keep it," or "keep it for yourself." I shall not attempt to draw any distinction between them. They all seem to me to come to exactly the same thing, if Cleverdon is to be believed, because he was quite clear, and always has been quite clear, that the words used were not words by which Dylan Thomas was enjoining him to do something, but were words of gift.

There is another matter which seems to me to be relevant. Obviously, Dylan Thomas was very relieved to have these BBC manuscripts. He had even hinted that having lost his own manuscript there might not be any point in his going to America and now it was all right. He was clearly relieved. Cleverdon was not a stranger to him who had suddenly come on the scene. They had been working together for the past six or seven years, and for myself I see no inherent improbability at all in the story which the defendants put forward in this case through the mouth of Cleverdon.

Any question of probability or improbability fades into the background and disappears once I find myself forced to the conclusion that Cleverdon was telling the truth and that I ought to accept his evidence. Having seen him and listened carefully, and having approached this matter in, I hope, a proper state of suspicion, I find myself, in the end, forced to the conclusion that Cleverdon was speaking the truth, and I accept his evidence.

One of the reasons which certainly assists me very much in coming to that conclusion is this. I cannot believe that Cleverdon would have told Miss Fox and Cranston that Dylan Thomas had given him the manuscript if it were not true, because Dylan Thomas, at the time when he told both those persons, was still alive, and everybody was expecting him to come back from America within a short time. It would have been absolutely stupid to have invented a lie in those circumstances, and Cleverdon certainly is not a stupid person.

I think perhaps I ought to say a word about the evidence of Dr. Jones. As I have already said, it was he who edited the first published text of "Under Milk Wood" in this country.

As an editor, he would naturally be interested in any manuscript material which was available. As I understand it, the object of introducing his evidence into this case was to support the suggestion that from the death of Dylan Thomas until the year 1961, when the manuscript was sold, Cleverdon was concealing the existence of this manuscript from Dr. Jones. That does not seem to me to make sense. As early as January, 1954, Cleverdon was writing to one of Dr. Jones' co-trustees of the Dylan Thomas copyrights, telling him the story of the gift of the manuscript to him, just as it was told to me. And, incidentally, Higham, who was the trustee in question, had no hesitation in accepting that story. From that time on Cleverdon told the story of the recovery of the manuscript both in broadcasts and in press interviews, and I have been shown the reports of three press interviews in the year 1956 in which Cleverdon was telling the story of the gift, and how Dylan Thomas told him that if he could find the manuscript he could keep it, and how he found it. I am unable to find any foundation for the suggestion that Cleverdon was concealing this manuscript from anyone.

So much for the question of intention. It is then said on behalf of the plaintiff that even if Dylan Thomas intended to give this manuscript to Cleverdon, he did not succeed in giving effect to that intention because there was no delivery of the subject-matter of it to Cleverdon by Dylan Thomas. I feel bound to reject that argument. The fact is that Cleverdon got possession of this manuscript from the Soho public-house in which it had been left by Dylan Thomas and that he got that possession with the consent of Dylan Thomas. That, in my judgment, is sufficient delivery to perfect a gift in Cleverdon's favour. I can see nothing in *In re Cole, A Bankrupt* which was relied upon by Mr. Sparrow, which precludes me from taking what appears to me to be the common-sense view of the matter, and concluding that when Cleverdon got possession of the manuscript with the consent of Dylan Thomas, the gift was perfected.

In those circumstances, my conclusion is that the defendants have succeeded in establishing that Dylan Thomas made a gift of this manuscript to Cleverdon, and in those circumstances the plaintiff's action must fail.

Action dismissed with costs.

DISCUSSION NOTES

i. Evidence, Presumptions, and Onus

A determination of the donor's intention to make an *inter vivos* gift in *Thomas* was rendered especially difficult because the donor was not available to give evidence. Examine the court's analysis of the question of onus in establishing a valid gift. Why was the onus in this case on the defendant rather than the plaintiff? On what does the court rely in terms of evidence and presumptions to reach the conclusion that a valid gift was made in this case? Is the court defining Thomas's actual intention or deciding what intent it is reasonable to conclude was present at the time of the gift? According to Brown, the issue of intention requires a court to consider "the circumstances of the donor, the relationship between the parties, and the size of the gift and its relation to the total amount of the donor's property, in order to discover the reasonableness of the claim that the donor really intended to make the donation claimed." See Brown at 114. To what extent is the court's general knowledge of Dylan Thomas as a public figure a factor in its assessment of Cleverdon's claim that there was a valid gift? See comments on *Thomas*, "Property: Inter Vivos Transfers of Chattels Not in Possession of the Donor—Requirements for a Valid Gift" (1967) 53 Iowa L Rev 243 and RE Megarry, "Note" (1966) 82 Law Q Rev 304.

The general problem of claims involving a deceased person is addressed in some jurisdictions by statutory provisions concerning the need for corroborating evidence. For example, s 13 of the *Evidence Act*, RSO 1990, c E.23 provides:

> In an action by or against the heirs, next of kin, executors, administrators or assigns of a deceased person, an opposite or interested party shall not obtain a verdict, judgment or decision on his or her own evidence in respect of any matter occurring before the death of the deceased person, unless such evidence is corroborated by some other material evidence.

What is the purpose of this section? Would the outcome in *Thomas* be the same, taking into account this statutory provision? In *Brown v Rotenburg*, [1946] 4 DLR 139 (Ont CA), the court held (at 148) that it is sufficient to meet the test of s 13 if "the evidence relied upon as corroborative is evidence of some material fact or facts supporting the testimony to be corroborated." See also *Sands Estate v Sonnwald* (1986), 22 ETR 282 (Ont H Ct J) and similar statutory provisions in the evidence acts of other jurisdictions—RSNS 1989, c 154, s 45; RSPEI 1988, c E-11, s 11; and RSNL 1990, c E-16, s 16.

ii. Intention to Gift Versus Intention to Loan

Even where delivery is established, the intention to make a gift, as opposed to the intent to create some other form of legal relationship, such as a loan, must be proven. Such a question arose in a dispute between the UK Beaverbrook Foundation and the Beaverbrook Art Gallery in Fredericton, New Brunswick. Max Aitken of Newcastle, New Brunswick made a fortune in Canada in the early 20th century; he migrated to Britain, where he made another fortune in newspapers and was created a peer in 1917 with the title Lord Beaverbrook. In 1958 he established the Beaverbrook Art Gallery and endowed it with a valuable collection of paintings. For over 40 years, the gallery was of the view that the paintings were merely on loan, and that the title remained in the foundation created by Lord Beaverbrook. Upon a thorough investigation of the origins of the collection, by 2004 the gallery directors concluded that Beaverbrook had made gifts of many paintings to the gallery and then had the accession records altered to make them appear as loans.

The parties agreed to refer the dispute to arbitration and named retired Supreme Court of Canada Justice Peter Cory as arbitrator. There was no deed of gift, and the gallery's argument rested entirely on a gift by delivery—that in physically transferring the paintings to the gallery with a donative intention, Lord Beaverbrook had effected a gift, and then suffered "donor's remorse." The arbitrator deduced Beaverbrook's intention from media accounts, including some in his own newspapers, which lauded his generosity in making this "gift" to the gallery. Justice Cory's 2007 decision found the gallery's claims to be well-founded and awarded it 85 out of 133 paintings in dispute, including some of the most valuable, such as John Turner's *Fountain of Indolence*, itself valued at $25 million at the time: (2007), 325 NBR (2d) 1. The Foundation had argued that if a gift were found to exist, it could invoke as a defence either the *Limitations Act* or estoppel, asserting that the gallery could not now argue that it owned the paintings after agreeing that it was merely a bailee for 40 years. Justice

Cory found that Lord Beaverbrook's fraudulent concealment of the true situation and his breach of fiduciary duty as founding chair of the gallery's board suspended the limitation period and negated any estoppels that would otherwise have operated. Justice Cory also awarded $4.9 million in costs against the Foundation. The Foundation appealed to a panel of three retired Court of Appeal judges, as provided for in the original agreement to arbitrate, who in 2009 upheld Cory's ruling: see Appellate Arbitral Tribunal, online: <http://beta .images.theglobeandmail.com/archive/00218/Read_the_decision_218325a.PDF>. A separate dispute over 78 other paintings was still ongoing in 2013. Why do you think the parties chose arbitration, rather than going to the courts, as a means of dispute resolution?

iii. Intent Versus Motive in the Law of Gifts

In *McNamee v McNamee*, 2011 ONCA 533, the Ontario Court of Appeal had to consider an alleged gift that had taken place in the context of an "estate freeze." This is an estate-planning technique whereby the owner of a privately held business (usually a parent) transfers assets to another person (usually an adult child) with a view to deferring tax and achieving protection from creditors, while at the same time retaining control of the business. In this case, the father owned a successful trucking business; in 2003, by a written "declaration of gift" accompanied by delivery of the relevant share certificates, he transferred 500 common shares in the trucking company to his son. Four years later the son and his wife, who had always worked together in the business throughout their 18-year marriage, separated. It thus became relevant to know whether the shares should be included in the husband's "net family property" under the Ontario *Family Law Act*, RSO 1990, c F.3, s 4(2), which excludes some gifts during marriage from this calculation.

The trial judge found no gift because the father's main concern was not an altruistic one, but rather the desire to protect his business from creditors. The son's wife was thus entitled to half the value of the shares as at the date of the separation. The Ontario Court of Appeal reversed, pointing out that the trial judge had confused motive with intention: "The intention respecting the transfer of shares was to do so gratuitously. The transfer was part of the corporate structure putting the estate freeze in place. And the estate freeze was the ultimate motivation or purpose" (at para 34). Further, a donor does not need to be motivated by altruism: "A transfer of property by way of gift may equally be motivated by commercial purposes provided the transfer is gratuitous" (at para 37). Although this finding had the effect of excluding the shares from the husband's "net family property," the court directed a new trial on the issue of whether the wife, by her contributions to the trucking business, had established an interest in them by way of constructive trust. (Because there is no record of a subsequent trial of this issue, it is likely that the parties settled their family law action on the basis that the wife had some interest in the value of the shares at separation.) The doctrine of constructive trust in the family context is discussed below and also in Chapter 6.

c. Acceptance by the Donee

It is often said that a valid gift requires acceptance by the donee, but this is so only in an attenuated sense. As Justice Cory said in the Beaverbrook Art Gallery arbitration, above:

Although "acceptance" is referred to in some of the authorities, it is now apparent that it is not in fact a prerequisite … [to the gift vesting in the donee]. Further, the acceptance does not have to be express in order to be valid. See for example *Standing v. Bowring* (1885), 31 Ch.D. 282, *Halsbury's Laws of England* (4th Edition, vol. 20(1)) [which] states with regards to gifts at paragraph 50: "Express acceptance by the donee is not necessary to complete a gift. It has long been settled that the acceptance of a gift by a donee is to be presumed until his dissent is signified even though he is not aware of the gift."

At common law a gift vests in the donee as soon as the donor has done everything to transfer the legal and beneficial interest in the property to the donee. Ordinarily a gift of land will require a deed. However, there is no particular formality required to transfer tangible personal property such as a work of art.

((2007), 325 NBR (2d) 1, paras 211-12.) Thus, even though the Beaverbrook Art Gallery had for 40 years thought that the paintings in question were only on loan and not a gift, and hence could not have "accepted" them, the gift was still found to be valid.

A similar result was reached in the case cited by Cory J, *Standing v Bowring* (1883), 31 Ch D 282 (CA). The plaintiff wished to make a gift to the defendant and thus transferred certain stock into a joint account in the names of herself and the defendant. However, the plaintiff kept her gift a secret from the defendant. Some time later, when the plaintiff had married, she disclosed the gift to the defendant and asked him to transfer the stock to her. The defendant refused and the plaintiff sought to compel the transfer. The court held, however, that a gift vests immediately subject to the donee's right, on learning about the gift, to decide whether to accept it—that is, the donee has the right to repudiate it, but until doing so, the gift belongs to the donee.

The common law's theory of gift as a unilateral act compels it to treat "acceptance" as a less than essential requirement. To elevate it to the status of an essential requirement would transform the gift relationship into a bilateral one, where the donee's state of mind would be as important as the donor's. But the common law has always resisted this approach to gifts.

3. Gifts Inter Vivos: The Declaration of Trust

In addition to gifts by deed and (for personal property) gifts by delivery, intention, and acceptance, which deal with the legal title to property, it is also possible for the donor to retain the legal title and transfer only the equitable title to the donee. Here you may wish to review the material on trusts and equitable title in Chapter 3.

Watt v Watt Estate
(1987), 28 ETR9 (Man CA)

LYON JA (for the court):

At issue in this case is entitlement to ownership of a boat, "Thunderbird," valued at $40,000, formerly owned by a marina operator, Richard John Watt, who died March 14, 1984. Following his death, Shirley Watt, a friend who is not related to the deceased, produced a disputed holograph document, signed by R.J. Watt, purporting to declare that as of May 10, 1980, the boat "is now owned jointly by myself R.J. Watt and Mrs. Shirley

Watt." On June 8, 1984, Shirley Watt's solicitor wrote to Jean Ileen Watt, the widow and executrix of the estate of R.J. Watt, claiming possession of the boat. This claim was denied. Shirley Watt then brought action against the estate for possession of and title to the boat. The trial Judge awarded her sole title to the craft. It is from that judgment that the defendant executrix now appeals.

Much of the time of the trial was devoted to the evidence of two handwriting experts called by the plaintiff and defendant respecting the bona fides of the document signed by R.J. Watt. The learned trial Judge, rightly in my opinion, found that there was ample evidence to support the authenticity of the document. Even though the estate re-argued the forgery issue on appeal, I am fully satisfied that the trial Judge's finding was correct. That defence must therefore fail.

While several other grounds of appeal were advanced by the estate, the main issue remaining, as I see it, is what interest in the boat, if any, is Shirley Watt entitled to? Is she entitled, as the learned trial Judge found, to sole ownership by reason of being the surviving joint owner? Or is she entitled only to a one-half interest in common with the deceased? After consideration of the record and the law, it is my opinion that Shirley Watt is entitled to a one-half interest in the boat rather than to sole title as determined by the trial Court.

The facts are that over a period of approximately 20 years, Shirley Watt and her husband, Bill, formed a close friendship with R.J. Watt, the proprietor, at all material times, of Buchanan Marina located near the bank of the Red River in Winnipeg, Manitoba. A mutual interest in boating was the main ingredient in the long-standing relationship between Shirley Watt, her family and R.J. Watt. Indeed, Shirley Watt was present at the marina on almost a daily basis in the boating season, performing a variety of tasks including typing correspondence, bookkeeping, dealing with customers, gardening and other odd jobs. She became, in the words of one witness, R.J. Watt's "right-hand man." For all of this assistance, she received no remuneration.

During the 1970's, over a 4-year period, R.J. Watt and the plaintiff's husband, Bill, designed and built the superstructure and interior of the "Thunderbird." When the boat was completed, R.J. Watt gave Shirley Watt a set of keys for the boat and she and her family thereafter had free use of it for short or longer cruises until R.J. Watt's death. The logbook of the boat showed the owners as being Shirley Watt and R.J. Watt.

On May 10, 1980, after a discussion with Shirley Watt about his being "sued a couple of times by customers," R.J. Watt, in her presence, wrote out the following document:

To Whom it May Concern

I Richard John Watt of 25 Talbot Avenue and owner of Buchanan Marine boat yard being of sound mind & good health do hereby declare that on the 10 Day of May 1980 declare that [sic] the boat commonly known as the "Thunderbird" is now owned jointly by myself RJ Watt and Mrs. Shirley Watt of 330 Thompson Drive.

Signed
"RJWatt"

PS. If the boat is sold while under this joint ownership, moneys relized [sic] will be divided evenly.

"RJW"

He then gave the document to Shirley Watt in a sealed envelope telling her, "You know what this is about - put it away." She kept the envelope until after R.J. Watt's death without knowing its contents.

With respect to ownership of the boat, the evidence was that R.J. Watt's conduct at all times was consistent with his having given Shirley Watt an interest in the "Thunderbird." For example, on one occasion when a witness was interested in buying the "Thunderbird," R.J. Watt told him that he (Watt) would have to discuss any such sale with Shirley Watt. Another witness recalled R.J. Watt's conversations about Shirley Watt's interest in the "Thunderbird." During all of this time, however, the "Thunderbird" continued to be registered only in the name of R.J. Watt. Nonetheless, there can be no question about R.J. Watt's intention to make Shirley Watt a one-half owner of the boat from May 10, 1980, forward.

What effect, then, should the Court give to the document? The estate claims that, even if the document is not a forgery, there was no delivery and the gift was not completed. ... [A]nother alternative, not argued by the plaintiff in her factum on appeal but confirmed in response to questions, is that the document constitutes a declaration of trust and is enforceable as such against the estate. ... With respect, I find that the learned trial Judge was in error ... in the circumstances of this case in finding that delivery of a duplicate set of keys constituted sufficient delivery to perfect a gift. A review of the record indicates that the deceased also delivered keys to another boat to Shirley Watt without importing any suggestion whatsoever of ownership to that boat. Hence, I conclude that the delivery of the keys to "Thunderbird" was merely an indication by the deceased that Shirley Watt had the right to use the boat. He also gave duplicate sets of keys to other members of the family.

If not a gift, what did the deceased convey to the plaintiff by the written document and his words and actions subsequent to his death? It is clear that what he wrote, said, and did constituted an executed trust which made him and, subsequently, his estate a trustee of the one-half interest in "Thunderbird" on behalf of Shirley Watt. In *Cochrane v. Moore* (1890), 25 Q.B.D. 57 (C.A.), Benzon, who owned several race horses, gave a one-quarter interest in one of his horses to a friend, Cochrane, who accepted the gift which was unaccompanied by delivery. Subsequently, Benzon sold several horses to Moore, including the one in which Cochrane had an interest. Cochrane sued Moore for his interest and the Court of Appeal held (at p. 73) that "what took place between Benzon and Cochrane before Benzon executed the bill of sale to Cochrane, constituted the latter a trustee for Moore of one-fourth of the horse Kilworth."

Similarly, in the case at Bar, R.J. Watt became, on May 10, 1980, the trustee of the one-half interest in "Thunderbird" on behalf of Shirley Watt. The document signified the existence of the trust and the right to a one-half interest in the boat held by Shirley Watt. R.J. Watt's subsequent parol dealing with third parties corroborated that right in the plaintiff.

[Having found that a declaration of trust existed in favour of Shirley Watt, Lyon JA went on to consider whether she was a joint tenant or a tenant in common with RJ Watt. Discussion on this point is omitted here, but these issues are discussed in Chapter 6.]

In the result, I would set aside the judgment of the trial Court and would award the plaintiff an undivided one-half interest in "Thunderbird." The parties having agreed that the value of the boat is $40,000, there will be judgment accordingly for the plaintiff in the amount of $20,000. Since there was no gift inter vivos, the cross-appeal for conversion is dismissed without costs. Although the plaintiff has succeeded in part in her claim, the defendant has succeeded on the point raised in the appeal in reducing the amount recoverable and therefore is entitled to her costs in this Court.

Appeal allowed in part.

DISCUSSION NOTES

i. Gifts and Trusts

In *Cochrane v Moore* (1890), 25 QBD 57 (CA), the English Court of Appeal also examined the boundary between a gift by delivery and a declaration of trust. The case involved a valuable racehorse named Kilworth; the horse was owned by Benzon, but kept at a stable run by Yates. The jockey who rode Kilworth was Moore and, at some point, Benzon used "present words of gift" to give Moore an undivided one-quarter interest in Kilworth. Subsequently Benzon borrowed large sums from Cochrane, and Benzon executed a document that provided that a number of horses (including Kilworth) would be security for these loans to him by Cochrane—that is, if Benzon did not repay the money owed to Cochrane, the latter would take the horses instead. Thus, when Benzon fell into arrears, Cochrane arranged to have the horses sold at auction to satisfy the debts owing to him. In this context, Moore objected that his one-quarter interest in Kilworth could not be sold by Cochrane because this interest had been transferred to him by Benzon before Benzon had executed the security arrangement with Cochrane. The trial judge held that there was a valid gift because there was no requirement of delivery in the circumstances of this case.

In considering the arguments in this case, the appeal court reviewed the long history of the law of transfers by gift and also the later developments of bargain promises in the law of contract. In doing so, the court upheld a decision of the King's Bench in *Irons v Smallpiece* (1819), 106 ER 467, confirming a continuing requirement for delivery to make a valid gift. Thus, the appeal court concluded that there was no valid gift to Moore from Benzon because there had been no delivery. However, the appeal court then noted that at the time when Benzon and Cochrane were negotiating the security for the loans, they had reviewed a list of horses to be included as security, and that Cochrane was told of Moore's one-quarter interest in Kilworth, to which Cochrane had responded that it should be "all right." This statement was, according to the court, sufficient to constitute Cochrane a trustee for Moore of this one-quarter interest in this horse. Thus, Cochrane had to account to Moore for a quarter of the sale price of Kilworth.

Although the factual circumstances are very different, the courts in both *Watt* and *Cochrane v Moore* held that a trust was created in circumstances where the delivery requirement for a valid gift was not met. In the context of a well-known equitable maxim that "equity will not perfect an imperfect gift," it is clear that a court may not find a gift in the absence of the delivery requirement being satisfied. Does the creation of a trust evade this requirement? Is there a legal difference between the statements "I am giving you my car" and "I will hold my car (on trust) for you"? See Ziff at 159-60.

There is a well-known exception to the equitable maxim that equity will not perfect an imperfect gift, defined in *Strong v Bird* (1874), LR 18 Eq 315 (CA). This exception arises where a donor expresses an intention to make a present gift during his or her lifetime, fails to effect delivery, and then appoints the donee as executor by will. For another example, see *Re Bayoff Estate*, [2000] 3 WWR 455 (Sask QB).

ii. Express Trusts

As Chapter 3 explains, trusts were recognized in the 17th century, when courts of equity first provided protection for the grant of a "use upon a use." Today, the trust relationship is regarded as a remarkable and creative feature of modern property law. Because trusts can be created when a person transfers property to a trustee to hold it for named beneficiaries, there is an obvious similarity between the transfer of a gift and the creation of a trust. To create a trust, a person typically executes a deed of trust, defining the property that is to form the trust, identifying the trustee and the beneficiaries, and specifying the trustee's duties. For an express trust, three matters must be certain—the intention to create a trust, the subject matter of the trust, and the objects (beneficiaries) of the trust. However, there is no need for any physical delivery of trust property, and it is possible, although somewhat unusual, to create an express trust of personal property by means of an oral declaration as appears to have happened in *Cochrane* and *Watt*. For further analysis of trusts, see Eileen E Gillese & Martha Milczynski, *The Law of Trusts* (Toronto: Irwin Law, 2005), and Brown at 145ff. The trust relationship is also an important concept in modern legal analyses of the relationship between the Crown and First Nations. See *Guerin v The Queen*, [1984] 2 SCR 335, discussed in Chapter 8.

iii. Resulting Trusts and the Presumption of Advancement

In addition to express trusts, there are two other forms of trust relationships—the resulting trust and the constructive trust. Although both of these trusts are examined in more detail in Chapter 6, it is important to have a basic understanding of them in relation to gifts. A resulting trust arises when there is a transfer of property without an intention to create a gift—that is, there is a deed (or other valid instrument of transfer) or act of delivery, but no intention of gift. For example, A may fear being sued and having a judgment issued against his property. He may transfer land into the name of B, a friend or relative, in order to avoid this result, but with no intention of making a gift of the equitable interest to B. In a resulting trust, the recipient of the property holds it in trust for the transferor.

A resulting trust may also arise when one person purchases property in the name of another without intending to make a gift. In a family context, there was a traditional presumption against a resulting trust when a husband or father transferred property to his wife or children; in this context, the legal presumption was that the husband/father intended to make a gift to family members, a situation known as the "presumption of advancement." The presumption of advancement operates in a family context to create a presumption of gift rather than a presumption of resulting trust because of "the absence of any reason for assuming that a [resulting] trust arose." See *Martin v Martin* (1959), 110 CLR 297 at 303 and *Pettit v Pettit*, [1970] AC 777 (HL). Most family property statutes in Canada have repealed the presumption of advancement from husband to wife: see e.g. the *Family Law Act*, RSO 1990, c F.3, s 14; *Marital Property Act*, SNB 1980, c M-1.1, s 15; *Matrimonial Property Act*, RSNS 1989, c 275, s 21; *Family Law Act*, RSNL 1990, c F-2, s 31; and *Family Law Act*, RSPEI 1988, c F-2.1, s 14.

In *Pecore v Pecore*, 2007 SCC 17, [2007] 1 SCR 795, the Supreme Court of Canada clarified the situation regarding the presumption of advancement in the context of transfers between parents and adult children. As in *Pecore* itself, this issue often comes up in the context of joint bank accounts. An elderly father opened a joint bank account with his adult daughter Paula so that she could take care of his financial transactions when he was not able to do so. The father was the sole contributor to the account and deposited the bulk of his funds in the account. When he died, a dispute arose over the approximately $1 million remaining in the account. Could the daughter, the surviving account holder, claim the money, or was it part of the father's estate? The contract between the bank and the account holders allows the surviving account holder to withdraw the money, but the courts have generally held that the contract does not affect the legal relationship between the account holders themselves. The Supreme Court maintained this legal principle, while observing that the contract may nonetheless provide evidence of the alleged donor's intention.

Prior to *Pecore*, the law had been that any gratuitous parent–child transfer gave rise to a presumption of advancement, such that anyone arguing that the transaction was not a gift had the burden of proving it—a difficult task. In *Pecore*, the Supreme Court decided (Abella J dissenting on this point) that, henceforth, in cases of transfers between parents and *adult* children, the ordinary presumption of resulting trust will apply, requiring the adult child to prove that a gift was intended if he or she is to be able to assert full legal and equitable title to the transferred property. The court argued from history, observing that the original reason for the presumption of advancement was the parent's duty to maintain the child, and that such duty ceases in law on the child attaining majority. Abella J disagreed with the analysis and, in a manner more reminiscent of the civil law, noted that the natural love and affection of parents for their children of any age, and not just dependency, was the original rationale for the presumption of advancement. Which approach do you prefer? The court also considered and rejected the idea that the presumption of resulting trust should not apply in the case of dependent adult children, on the ground that it would be too difficult to distinguish factually between dependent and independent children.

In *Pecore*, Paula was the least financially secure of the father's children and the closest to him; he had assisted her and her family financially on a number of occasions; and in his will he had preferred her to his other children. In spite of the father's having written to financial institutions during his lifetime stating that the transfers to the joint account were *not* gifts to Paula, the court decided that he did so in order to avoid triggering capital gains tax by a disposition to her, and that a desire to maintain control of the account during his lifetime was not inconsistent with a gift of the balance of the account, whatever it should be, on his death. The father had continued to pay tax on all income produced by the account during his life. Paula succeeded in rebutting the presumption of resulting trust.

The court also clarified two points on which there had been some controversy. First, it confirmed that a gift of the balance of a joint account on the contributor's death is, in fact, an *inter vivos* gift and not a testamentary one. The gift is considered to be made at the time the account is opened and vests in the donee at that time. The donee's only right is to the balance, however, such that the donor could conceivably "revoke" the gift by draining the account of all funds prior to his or her death. Second, the court decided that in considering what evidence could be adduced regarding the intentions of the contributor/alleged donor, it was legitimate to look at evidence of events subsequent to the opening of the account, provided that such events shed light on the contributor's state of mind at the time the account was opened. The alleged donee is subject to the ordinary civil standard of proof, a balance of probabilities, in any attempt to rebut the presumption of resulting trust and prove a gift. For further analysis of *Pecore* in relation to joint tenancies, see Chapter 6.

iv. Constructive Trusts

Trust obligations can arise even in the absence of a specific intention to create a trust. For example, courts have recognized "constructive" trusts to ensure a just result in cases where a person without title to property has made a significant contribution to acquiring or maintaining it, thus preventing the "unjust enrichment" of the title holder. Canadian courts have frequently "constructed" such trust relationships in the context of cohabiting couples where the person without title has made valuable contributions of money or labour to the property such that it would be unjust not to recognize an interest on the part of the non-title holder. In these cases, the court declares that the title holder is a constructive trustee and the person who made the contribution is a beneficiary of a defined interest that corresponds to the contribution he or she has made. The Supreme Court of Canada first enunciated these principles for cohabiting couples in *Pettkus v Becker*, [1980] 2 SCR 834, 117 DLR (3d) 257, a case examined in detail in Chapter 6. The court held that Rosa Becker had not intended to make a gift of her money and labour over nearly 20 years to her cohabiting partner, Lothar Pettkus. However, a majority of the court concluded that there was no resulting trust in this case because Pettkus had denied that he had intended to hold the property for her benefit. For a discussion of the constructive trust, see L Rotman, "Deconstructing the Constructive Trust" (1999) 37 Alta L Rev 133.

4. Capacity

The requirement of intention may be relevant to both gifts and trusts. For example, a valid gift requires that the donor have the capacity to form the intention to make a gift to the donee. Consider *Csada v Csada*, [1985] 2 WWR 265 (Sask CA). In that case, the plaintiff brought an application to set aside two gifts to his brother, including a transfer of two quarter sections of land (valued at $150,000 to $200,000) and a cheque for $10,300. The plaintiff, who was 58 years old at the time, had requested that his older brother, aged 66, return to Canada from New Zealand (where he had made his home for some years) so that the two brothers could live together. Both were twice married but now divorced. The plaintiff paid for his brother's airfare and the expenses for both of them to move from the plaintiff's apartment to a house he had purchased for them. During a nine-month period, the plaintiff transferred large sums of money and land to the defendant and executed a power of attorney in his favour, in addition to the two gifts of land and money noted above. When the plaintiff later applied to set aside these two transactions, the trial judge considered evidence from several medical experts regarding the plaintiff's state of depression and their views that he was dominated by his older brother. The trial judge held that the plaintiff had the requisite intention to make these gifts to the defendant, that he had sufficient capacity, and that there was no undue influence. Thus the gifts were valid. The plaintiff appealed, arguing that the gifts should be set aside on the basis of undue influence. The reasons of the Saskatchewan Court of Appeal are reproduced below.

Csada v Csada
[1985] 2 WWR 265 (Sask CA)

The plaintiff has appealed on the ground that these gifts were made by reason of undue influence and should be set aside.

The equitable doctrine of undue influence has been well defined. Lord Justice Lindley in *Allcard v. Skinner* (1887), 36 Ch. D 145, expressed the principle on which the doctrine is founded in these words (at pp. 182-83):

> What then is the principle? Is it that it is right and expedient to save persons from the consequences of their own folly? Or is it that it is right and expedient to save them from being victimized by other people? In my opinion the doctrine of undue influence is founded upon the second of these two principles. Courts of Equity have never set aside gifts on the ground of the folly, imprudence, or want of foresight on the part of donors. The Courts have always repudiated any such jurisdiction. *Huguenin v. Baseley* is itself a clear authority to this effect. It would obviously be to encourage folly, recklessness, extravagance and vice if persons could get back property which they foolishly made away with, whether by giving it to charitable institutions or by bestowing it on less worthy objects. On the other hand, to protect people from being forced, tricked or misled in any way by others into parting with their property is one of the most legitimate objects of all laws; and the equitable doctrine of undue influence has grown out of and been developed by the necessity of grappling with insidious forms of spiritual tyranny and with the infinite varieties of fraud.
>
> As no Court has ever attempted to define fraud so no Court has ever attempted to define undue influence, which includes one of its many varieties. The undue influence which Courts of Equity endeavour to defeat is the undue influence of one person over another; not the influence of enthusiasm on the enthusiast who is carried away by it, unless indeed such enthusiasm is itself the result of external undue influence. But the influence of one mind over another is very subtle, and of all influences religious influence is the most dangerous and the most powerful, and to counteract it Courts of Equity have gone very far. They have not shrunk from setting aside gifts made to persons in a position to exercise undue influence over the donors, although there has been no proof of the actual exercise of such influence; and the Courts have done this on the avowed ground of the necessity of going this length in order to protect persons from the exercise of such influence under circumstances which render proof of it impossible. The Courts have required proof of its non-exercise, and, failing that proof, have set aside gifts otherwise unimpeachable.

Cotton LJ in the same case at p. 171 categorized the cases that fall under this doctrine, thus:

> These decisions [by the Court of Chancery in setting aside voluntary gifts on the ground of undue influence] may be divided into two classes—first, where the Court has been satisfied that the gift was the result of influence expressly used by the donee for the purpose; second, where the relations between the donor and donee have at or shortly before the execution of the gift been such as to raise a presumption that the donee had influence over the donor. In such a case the Court sets aside the voluntary gift, unless it is proved that in fact the gift was the spontaneous act of the donor acting under circumstances which enabled him to exercise an independent will and which justifies the Court in holding that the gift was the result of a

free exercise of the donor's will. The first class of cases may be considered as depending on the principle that no one shall be allowed to retain any benefit arising from his own fraud or wrongful act. In the second class of cases the Court interferes, not on the ground that any wrongful act has in fact been committed by the donee, but on the ground of public policy, and to prevent the relations which existed between the parties and the influence arising therefrom being abused.

These same principles have been variously expressed by Canadian courts. ...The Supreme Court of Canada in *Krys v. Krys*, [1929] SCR 153, [1929] 1 DLR 289, speaking through Newcombe J, approved (at p. 162) the following excerpt from the judgment of Lord Chelmsford LC in *Tate v. Williamson* (1866), LR 2 Ch. App. 55 at 61:

> Wherever two persons stand in such a relation that, while it continues, confidence is necessarily reposed by one, and the influence which naturally grows out of that confidence is possessed by the other, and this confidence is abused, or the influence is exerted to obtain an advantage at the expense of the confiding party, the party so availing himself of his position will not be permitted to retain the advantage, although the transaction could not have been impeached if no such confidential relation had existed.

The manner in which the presumption referred to in the second of the two classes delineated by Cotton LJ in *Allcard v. Skinner* may be rebutted is dealt with in the Privy Council case of *Inche Noriah v. Shaik Allie Bin Omar*, [1929] AC 127, 45 TLR 1, as follows (p. 3):

> [T]heir Lordships are not prepared to accept the view that independent legal advice is the only way in which the presumption can be rebutted; nor are they prepared to affirm that independent legal advice, when given, does not rebut the presumption, unless it be shown that the advice was taken. It is necessary for the donee to prove that the gift was the result of the free exercise of independent will. The most obvious way to prove this is by establishing that the gift was made after the nature and effect of the transaction had been fully explained to the donor by some independent and qualified person so completely as to satisfy the Court that the donor was acting independently of any influence from the donee and with the full appreciation of what he was doing; and in cases where there are no other circumstances this may be the only means by which the donee can rebut the presumption. But the fact to be established is that stated in the judgment already cited of Lord Justice Cotton, and if evidence is given of circumstances sufficient to establish this fact, their Lordships see no reason for disregarding them merely because they do not include independent advice from a lawyer. Nor are their Lordships prepared to lay down what advice must be received in order to satisfy the rule in cases where independent legal advice is relied upon, further than to say that it must be given with a knowledge of all relevant circumstances and must be such as a competent and honest advisor would give if acting solely in the interests of the donor.

The Supreme Court of Canada in *Krys* followed the *Inche* decision.

There is no express reference in the reasons for judgment of the trial judge in the present case to the principles of the equitable doctrine of undue influence as elucidated in the foregoing authorities, and specially, to the two-fold classification of cases by Cotton LJ, to the presumptions governing each class of case and to the relevant onus provisions. Nor is it implicit in the reasons for judgment that the judge directed himself in the manner prescribed by these authorities.

He resolved the issue of undue influence in these words:

> I am satisfied notwithstanding certain medical and other evidence called by the plaintiff (and which I will comment on later) that the plaintiff knew he was transferring the N½ 2-12-7-W3d to the defendant on 9th April 1980, that he intended to make a gift of the half section of land to his brother and that he carried out this conveyance free of any mental impediment and undue influence. The factors that influenced the plaintiff were his belief that the defendant should have received land from the father's estate, his desire to satisfy the defendant's complaints about his present circumstances and the plaintiff's wish to ingratiate himself with his brother. When differences later arose between the parties and the defendant threatened to sell the N½ 2-12-7-W3d and to leave the plaintiff, the plaintiff's distress was related, not to the fact that the defendant had title to the land, but that such action would prevent the parties from farming as the plaintiff understood they would with each other.

The judge appears to have examined the evidence from the standpoint of only the first of Cotton LJ's two classes of cases. Having found nothing in the evidence that he assessed as *express* influence used by the defendant for the purpose of acquiring the gifts, he reached the conclusion there was no undue influence. In other words, he found an intention on the part of the plaintiff to make a gift to the defendant, an intention not brought about through wrongful or improper acts of coercion by the defendant, and in consequence concluded there was no undue influence. It is a conclusion with which I respectfully agree. He failed, however, to examine the evidence from the standpoint of the second of the two classes of cases. Having determined that the plaintiff knew what he was doing, the judge failed to determine how the plaintiff's intention was produced. He failed to consider whether the circumstances presented a situation of confidence and dependence on one side and advice and persuasion on the other, and whether such advice and persuasion, although not wrong or improper, amounted to undue influence. The evidence clearly warranted an examination of those questions and the judge should have conducted such examination.

The provisions of s. 8 of the Court of Appeal Act, RSS 1978, c. C-42, empower this court to do what the trial judge should have done. The section reads:

> 8. Upon appeal from, or motion against, the order, decision, verdict or decree of a trial judge, or on the rehearing of any cause, application or matter, it shall not be obligatory on the court to grant a new trial, or to adopt the view of the evidence taken by the trial judge, but the court shall act upon its own view of what the evidence in its judgment proves, and the court may draw inferences of fact and pronounce the verdict, decision or order that, in its judgment, the judge who tried the case ought to have pronounced.

In doing what the trial judge omitted to do, it is important for this court not to disturb his findings of primary facts. No similar constraint, however, is imposed upon this court respecting the findings of inferential or evaluative facts. I proceed now to do what the trial judge should have done.

Did the defendant on 9th or 10th April 1980, the dates of the impugned gifts, occupy a position of natural influence in relation to the plaintiff? The evidence established beyond peradventure that although the plaintiff was not mentally incompetent on these dates, he was mentally weak, vulnerable and highly susceptible to influence from a domineering person. The evidence established with equal force that the defendant, the plaintiff's older brother, was just such a domineering person. As noted, the most potent evidence on these two questions was given by the defendant himself. That evidence is strongly reinforced by the testimony of the doctors, Mr. Stringer and the plaintiff. That the facts of this case present a situation of confidence and dependence on the side of the plaintiff and advice and persuasion on the side of the defendant is, in my respectful view, clear. This case, in other words, falls into the second of the two classes delineated by Cotton LJ. It follows then that the presumption of undue influence was engaged. It rested upon the defendant to rebut that presumption. Has he met the onus?

As stated in the *Inche* case, the best way to meet the onus is [to] furnish proof of independent legal advice having the quality described by the Privy Council. The defendant adduced no evidence of such legal advice. A careful perusal of Mr. Stringer's testimony discloses nothing that would meet the test prescribed by the Privy Council in this respect.

Does, nevertheless, the evidence establish that "in fact the gift was the spontaneous act of the donor acting under circumstances which enabled him to exercise an independent will and which justifies the Court in holding that the gift was the result of a free exercise of the donor's will"? It does nothing of the sort in my respectful view. Indeed, the trial judge expressly found the contrary. He found that the defendant's persistent complaints about his present circumstances and about not having received any land from his father's estate played a dominant role in the plaintiff's acting as he did. As already noted, he found:

> The factors that influenced the plaintiff were his belief that the defendant should have received land from the father's estate, his desire to satisfy the defendant's complaints about his present circumstances and the plaintiff's wish to ingratiate himself with his brother.

To paraphrase, the plaintiff at the time of the impugned transactions was well ensconced within the defendant's orbit of influence. The plaintiff's act does not have the quality of spontaneity and the circumstances under which he acted do not bear the mark of independence which would justify this court in holding that the gifts were the result of a free exercise of the donor's will. As noted, the question here is not one of wrongful acts committed by the defendant but whether the intention by the plaintiff was produced entirely free of the defendant's dominance. Exercising the "great jealousy" that a court must in these cases, I find that the defendant did not discharge the heavy onus placed upon him.

In the result, the appeal is allowed. The judgment of the trial judge insofar as it relates to the gift of lands and the gift of $10,300 made on 10th April 1980 is set aside.

The plaintiff will have judgment setting aside the transfer of the lands in question. The defendant is ordered to retransfer these lands at his own expense. Upon his failure to do so within 30 days, title to the lands will vest in the plaintiff subject to such encumbrances as are now registered against the lands. The registrar of the appropriate land titles office is directed accordingly. The plaintiff will have leave to apply to have removed such encumbrances as he is advised should be removed. There will be a further order entitling the plaintiff to judgment for $10,300 in addition to the sums awarded by the trial judge.

The appellant will have his costs here and below.

Appeal allowed.

DISCUSSION NOTE

Capacity and Undue Influence: Applying the Principles

Is the court's reasoning about intention to make a valid gift different in *Csada* by contrast with *Thomas*? What are the elements required to establish undue influence? Should there be a presumption of undue influence for gifts between family members? In general, courts have not recognized such a presumption except in some cases involving gifts made by children—see *Re Pauling's Settlement Trusts*, [1964] Ch 303 (CA). Similarly, there is no presumption that an elderly person is necessarily under the influence of others, although there are frequent examples of actions to set aside transactions entered into by elderly persons on the basis of undue influence: see e.g. *Kavanagh v Lajoie*, 2013 ONSC 7, which also contains a good review of the law at para 131, based on the Supreme Court of Canada's decision in *Geffen v Goodman Estate*, [1991] 2 SCR 353. Consider the responsibilities of the solicitor in *Csada*—what should have been done to ensure that the plaintiff understood the nature of the transaction? What precautions should be taken in such cases?

Consider a case in which an elderly woman executed a deed of gift of her house to one of her three daughters, at a time when the woman was in an advanced state of senile dementia. It was explained to her that she was making a gift of the house (her only major asset) but she was not told of the effect of the gift on her other daughters. Is this sufficient for a valid gift? See *Re Beaney*, [1978] 1 WLR 770 (Ch D), where the court declared that the purported transfer was void because the deceased was unable to understand that she was depriving her other children of a share in her estate.

Capacity issues may arise in the case of express trusts as well as gifts. If Mr Csada had transferred the lands in question to a trustee in trust for his brother, instead of making an *inter vivos* gift, the trust could have been set aside on the basis of undue influence. Or in *Watt v Watt Estate*, extracted above, if Shirley Watt had exercised undue influence over RJ Watt, the declaration of trust in her favour could have been set aside by Mr Watt's estate.

5. Intention and Future Enjoyment: Inter Vivos and Testamentary Gifts

A donor must have the intention to make a present gift, not an intention or promise to make a gift at some point in the future. However, a donor may make a present gift, the enjoyment of which is postponed to the future. In such a case, the title passes at the moment of the gift, but the donee's enjoyment may not occur until some time in the future. In one well-known case, for example, Gabriel Pascal, a theatrical producer who held 98 percent of the stock of a company that had exclusive world rights to produce a musical play based on GB Shaw's "Pygmalion," made a gift in writing to Marianne Kingman, his executive secretary, of a portion of the profits for a stage version in England and the United States and of the profits world-wide for the film version. At the time of the gift, the right to produce a musical version of "Pygmalion" remained unexercised so there were no profits to distribute. However, the court concluded that there was a valid, completed gift to Kingman, making an analogy between the expectancy of royalties in this case with contingent remainders in land. Subsequently, there was a highly successful production of "My Fair Lady." See *Speelman v Pascal*, 178 NE 2d 723 (NY CA 1961).

Speelman v Pascal is an example of an *inter vivos* gift in which there is a present gift with enjoyment postponed to the future. It is important to distinguish *inter vivos* gifts of this kind from testamentary gifts—that is, gifts that are not intended to take effect at all until the donor's death. Testamentary gifts must meet the requirements for succession of property interests at death, usually including a written document signed by the testator in the presence of two witnesses who sign the will in the presence of the testator and of each other: see e.g. Ontario's *Succession Law Reform Act*, RSO 1990, c S.26. See also the *Wills Act*, RSNS 1989, c 505 and RSNB 1973, c W-9 (although these statutes also permit a holograph will, one that need not be witnessed if it is "wholly" in the testator's handwriting and signed by him or her). A testator does not relinquish any rights to such property interests until the moment of death. However, it is sometimes difficult to distinguish cases such as *Speelman* from testamentary gifts, particularly when (as happened in *Speelman*) the donor died before his estate exercised the right to produce "My Fair Lady." For an analysis of some of these issues, see AG Gulliver & CJ Tilson, "Classification of Gratuitous Transfers" (1941) 51 Yale LJ 1.

The relationship between *inter vivos* gifts in which enjoyment is postponed and testamentary gifts must also take account of a special form of gift made in contemplation of death, the *donatio mortis causa*, discussed below.

C. Donatio Mortis Causa

A *donatio mortis causa* is a gift made in contemplation of death; the gift is subject to revocation if the donor recovers and does not die. The intention for a *donatio mortis causa* is different from that in a gift *inter vivos* because the donor of a *donatio mortis causa* has an automatic right to revoke the gift on recovery. There is also a requirement of delivery and there is some difference of opinion as to whether the test for delivery for a *donatio mortis causa* is similar to that for a gift *inter vivos* or whether it is less stringent. As well as the requirements of intention and delivery, there is also a need for acceptance of a *donatio mortis causa*.

To understand the *donatio mortis causa*, it is important to place it in a historical context. Brown has suggested that these gifts are of Roman origin and probably existed alongside testamentary dispositions in English law for some time in the feudal period. However, after the enactment of the *Statute of Frauds* in the 17th century, most transfers of interests in land were required to be in writing, thus placing severe restraints on the making of oral wills (sometimes called nuncupative wills). The Statute thus created problems for the beneficiaries of gifts made by deceased persons on their deathbeds (apparently a frequent practice), and these beneficiaries turned to the Court of Chancery for relief. After a number of years, the decision in *Ward v Turner* (1752), 28 ER 275, 2 Ves Sr 431 (Ch) held that such gifts could be sustained only when accompanied by an actual delivery of the subject matter of the gift. According to Brown:

> In this case [*Ward v Turner*] emerge gifts *causa mortis* as known to the common law. Like gifts *inter vivos* a delivery, or its equivalent, is required. The difference is in their conditional or revocable character. Like the testamentary disposition they do not take effect finally and irrevocably until the death of the donor. Until such time a power of revocation is reserved to him. Indeed if the donor survives the anticipated peril, the gift is automatically by operation of law revoked.

(Brown at 131.)

It is also possible for a person who may be dying to make a valid gift *inter vivos*; it is thus a question of intention whether the donor intended a present and irrevocable gift *inter vivos* or a *donatio mortis causa* revocable on recovery. As noted in *Ward v Turner*, delivery is required for a valid *donatio mortis causa*. Consider these issues in the case that follows. Is the test for delivery used here sufficient to meet the requirement of delivery for an *inter vivos* gift? If you conclude that it is a different test, identify the rationale for using a different test for delivery for a *donatio mortis causa* by contrast with a gift *inter vivos*.

Re Zachariuc; Chevrier v Public Trustee
(1984), 16 ETR 152 (Ont Dist Ct)

WARREN DCJ: At the outset of trial, counsel for the plaintiff advised the Court there would be a preliminary objection by counsel for the Public Trustee. Counsel for the Public Trustee argued that a District Court Judge did not have jurisdiction to hear a claim to property as having been the subject of a donatio mortis causa under the Surrogate Courts Act, RSO 1970, c. 451, s. 68, now RSO 1980, c. 491, s. 69, and referred to the case *Re Graham* (1911), 25 OLR 5, to support this contention.

The plaintiff, who was advised by counsel for the Public Trustee prior to trial of this objection, simultaneously, to expedite the disposition of this action, instituted an action in the District Court for the District of Algoma, no. 9393, 1983, styled *Re Zachariuc (a.k.a. Zachariuc and Macharuk)*; *Chevrier v. The Public Trustee* (the deceased hereinafter referred to as Zachariuc).

The Court reserved decision on the objection by counsel for the Public Trustee with regard to s. 69 of the Surrogate Courts Act and requested the plaintiff to proceed with the District Court action.

This is an action that arises as a result of the death of Zachariuc, who died sometime between the hours of 9:30 p.m. November 17, 1982, and 7:00 a.m. November 18, 1982, in his home in Wawa, Ontario. It is the contention of the plaintiff that he was given an inter vivos gift by the deceased, referred to in law as a donatio mortis causa.

The Facts

Counsel are in agreement as to the facts. Zachariuc and John Chevrier (hereinafter referred to as Chevrier) lived in Wawa as friends and neighbours for 33 years. They had worked together collecting scrap, had built three homes together, and Chevrier was constantly available to help Zachariuc at his request. They visited back and forth frequently on a daily basis.

The deceased at the time of his demise was in his 81st year and had no living relatives. He lived a very quiet, conservative existence, and associated socially with no one other than Chevrier.

Chevrier testified that he attended on Zachariuc on November 17, 1982, when he finished work, as he had done on many occasions. Zachariuc complained to Chevrier that he felt sick, was holding his head and thought he was poisoned. Chevrier suggested he should take him to a doctor, but Zachariuc stated he had no desire to see a doctor, and be confined to hospital. Mr. Chevrier testified that Zachariuc fashioned himself to be his own medicine man.

Mr. Chevrier testified while he was in attendance at Zachariuc's home that the paper-boy arrived, and Zachariuc, in the process of paying for the paper fell on the floor. With effort he got up and sat on a chair. In the opinion of Chevrier, Zachariuc seemed very strange and ill.

Chevrier suggested to Zachariuc that he was getting very old and asked Zachariuc if he had a will. Zachariuc replied to Chevrier, "No, I give what I have to you; you are my only friend." Chevrier further testified that Zachariuc commenced to reminisce and tell him things about the past that Chevrier had never heard before during their long acquaintance. In particular, he talked of things and locations that had happened years before while Zachariuc was a resident of Rouyn and Val d'Or in Quebec. Chevrier was about to leave for home at 8:30 p.m. when Zachariuc suggested they have a drink. They both had a drink and Zachariuc did a little jig and announced he was "not going to die tonight."

He then reiterated that Chevrier was his best and only friend, and that he had some money hidden which he was giving to Chevrier. He then explained in detail that the money was located in the crawl space under the two-room house. Chevrier was to look for barrels and underneath them, buried in the earth [were] jars full of money. He then gave Mr. Chevrier his house key and told Chevrier to check on him in the morning, and to bring a friend to witness a paper (presumably to act as a will), leaving his assets to Chevrier. Chevrier left for home at 9:30 p.m., had his supper and went to bed.

On the morning of the 18th of November, at 7:00 a.m., Mr. Chevrier went to Zachariuc's house as requested. He knocked on the door, went into the house, and saw a motionless body on the bed. I think it is essential to state that the witness Chevrier broke down in the witness box and cried when he gave this evidence, obviously very sad and emotional at the recall of finding his dear friend dead.

Chevrier immediately called the police station, and Constable Kennedy arrived shortly. Mr. Chevrier testified, "Officer Kennedy came over and found George dead. The old son of a gun died and no paper." Subsequently, he was officially pronounced dead by the doctor.

Later on that day Chevrier was made aware that the deceased's house would be torn down, then contacted Mr. Frank Macdonald, the Justice of the Peace, and told him about the money given to him by Zachariuc. Mr. MacDonald told Chevrier to contact Mr. Aquino who was appointed an agent for the Public Trustee.

If I may digress, Mr. Aquino gave evidence that he was appointed an agent for the Public Trustee on November 19, 1983. Aquino attended at the house of the deceased, did a thorough search of the house and contents. He testified the building and contents were of no value on November 20, 1982. Aquino secured the house and disposed of the contents of the home at the dump. He did however find four $100 bills in a cupboard, and $2,770 in a bag in the freezer.

Subsequently, on Saturday, around 5:00 p.m. he received a phone call from Mr. Chevrier who advised him that there was money in the house. They decided to attend with the police chief after church. They all attended, and on the instructions of Chevrier they found the jars which contained the sum of $16,280. I wish to add that Police Chief Egan testified and gave the same evidence as Mr. Aquino. They both stated that if it had not been for Mr. Chevrier they would not have found the money.

Counsel for the Public Trustee referred the Court to the *Ontario Evidence Act*, c. 145, s. 13, which states:

> In an action by or against the heirs, next of kin, executors, administrators or assigns of a deceased person, an opposite or interested party shall not obtain a verdict, judgment or decision

on his own evidence in respect of any matter occurring before the death of the deceased person, unless such evidence is corroborated by some other material evidence.

In *Brown v. Rotenberg*, [1946] OR 363, [1946] 4 DLR 139 (CA), Laidlaw JA at pp. 375-76 stated:

> It has been held that "it is sufficient if the evidence relied upon as corroborative is evidence of some material facts or facts supporting the testimony to be corroborated": *Ollson v. Fraser, Barned and Powell*, [1945] OR 69, [1945] 1 DLR 481. The evidence tendered in corroboration need not be in respect of the vital and essential portion of the respondent's evidence. "All that the statute requires is that the evidence to be corroborated shall be strengthened by some evidence which appreciably helps the judicial mind to believe one or more of the material statements or facts deposed to": *George McKean and Company Limited et al. v. Black et al.*, 62 SCR 290 at 308, 68 DLR 34; *Bayley v. Trusts and Guarantee Co. Ltd.* [(1930), 66 OLR 254, at 258; 1 DLR 500 (HC)].

In my view, the evidence of Chief Egan and Mr. Aquino corroborates the evidence of Mr. Chevrier, who was advised by the deceased the night before his death of the location of the money. In knowing the whereabouts of the money I am satisfied on a balance of probabilities that Zachariuc advised Chevrier the money was his.

There is no question in the Court's mind on the evidence, submissions by both counsel, and the witnesses that Mr. Chevrier is an honest, reliable witness. Someone lesser could easily have removed the money under the same circumstances, upon finding Zachariuc dead in his home on the morning of November 17, [*sic*] 1982, but not Mr. Chevrier.

The question to be answered: is this a donatio mortis causa, in other words a gift in contemplation of death? It is conceded by counsel that the case law appears to take the view that keeping in mind certain tests each case is settled on its own facts.

In 13 CED (Ont. 3d), Title 68 "Gifts," p. 68-8, para. 3, a donatio mortis causa is described as:

> … a gift made in contemplation of death intended to take effect only upon the death of the donor. There must be delivery of the subject of the gift. It is not necessary that the donor expressly state that the gift is effective only in the event of death since the condition may be implied from the circumstances. It is sufficient that the gift be made in contemplation of and not in expectation of death. …

In the case of *Brown v. Rotenberg, supra*, Laidlaw JA said at p. 368:

> It has been said that "for an effectual donatio mortis causa three things must combine: first, the gift or donation must have been made in contemplation, though not necessarily in expectation, of death; secondly, there must have been delivery to the donee of the subject-matter of the gift; and thirdly, the gift must be made under such circumstances as shew that the thing is to revert to the donor in case he should recover": per Lord Russell of Killowen CJ in *Cain v. Moon*, [1896] 2 QB 283 at 286.

Chevrier testified he had known the deceased for over 30 years and during this period of time the deceased showed no interest in the services of a doctor. The deceased was in his 81st year and in failing health, probably due to his age and was reluctant to see a doctor. On the night of November 17, 1982, when Chevrier visited Zachariuc, after he realized that Zachariuc was not well he asked him if he had a will, and Zachariuc replied, "No, what I have I give to you." Chevrier testified further that Zachariuc fell on the floor of his home and complained of being poisoned, and in his opinion Zachariuc looked very ill. Chevrier suggested Zachariuc should see a doctor immediately, but he refused.

Zachariuc advised Chevrier that he was his only friend and confidant, and reminisced at some length about his past, which Chevrier thought was unusual for his friend who was a very private person, but on the same evening he became specific as to the gift he intended his friend to have. At one point, Zachariuc remarked he "would not die tonight."

It is my view that taking into consideration the total conversation, the physical appearance of the deceased, and the fact that he made reference to his not dying tonight is indicative that he was contemplating the possibility of death. I am satisfied that the first rule for a valid donatio mortis causa has been established in that the gift was given in contemplation of death, though not necessarily in expectation of death.

Mr. Chevrier testified further that, before he had left on the evening of November 17, 1982 to go home, the deceased returned to the subject of his possessions and suggested Mr. Chevrier should return the following day with a witness, presumably to make a will leaving his estate to his friend Chevrier. However, this was not to be in that Zachariuc died in the interim.

During this conversation, Zachariuc became very specific as to the location of some of his personalty. In particular, he described to Mr. Chevrier in detail the location of a hidden cache of money that was buried in the ground in the crawl space under his two-room home.

It is my view he revealed this information because he realized if the location [were] not made known, upon his death the secret money cache would probably go undetected, and therefore Chevrier would not have received this gift.

Subsequent events bore out the deceased's thinking in that the agent for the Public Trustee, the day following Zachariuc's death, found money in the house which was put in an estate account. He arranged to have the remaining house contents taken to the dump. He advised Mr. Chevrier that the house would be razed, and it was at this juncture Chevrier spoke to Mr. MacDonald, the Justice of the Peace, regarding the alleged hidden cache of money.

It is significant to the Court that just prior to Mr. Chevrier's departure on the 17th of November 1982, the deceased for the first time in his life gave his house key to Chevrier and asked him if he would check on him in the morning. It is my view that the giving of the house key is similar to the line of cases that have established where the safety-deposit box key has been given to the donee this has been found to constitute delivery of the gift.

In the case of *Kooner v. Kooner* (1979), 100 DLR (3d) 76 (BC SC), Locke J said at p. 80:

> However, the second prerequisite of delivery has been relaxed by an anomalous doctrine peculiar to these gifts but established by the House of Lords in *Duffield v. Elwes* (1827), 1 Bligh NS 497, 4 ER 959. Choses in action may pass by gifts mortis causa in circumstances ineffective to constitute a valid transfer inter vivos: i.e., equity will in this case complete an imperfect gift: *Vaines, op. cit.* 318; *Re Dillon* (1890), 44 Ch. D 76; *Re Wasserberg*, [1915] 1 Ch. 195.

Brown v. Rotenberg was a case where the key to a safety-deposit box was given to the donee. Laidlaw JA at p. 370 asked the question:

Was there delivery to the donee of the subject matter of the gift? It is to be noted at once that an inchoate or imperfect delivery of chattels may be sufficient for effectuating a donatio mortis causa: In *Re Wasserberg; Union of London and Smith's Bank, Limited v. Wasserberg*, [1915] 1 Ch. 195; "... a transfer of the means of, or part of the means of, getting at the property" is sufficient.

It is my view when the deceased Zachariuc gave the location and description of the jars that contained the money and the key to his home, and advised Chevrier this money was his, that he gave up control and dominion of the cache of money and therefore Chevrier acquired title to the gift. Thus, the second essential has been satisfied in that there was a valid delivery of the cache of money.

The third essential to a valid donatio mortis causa is "... the gift must be made under such circumstances as shew that the thing is to revert to the donor in case he should recover: ... *Cain v. Moon, supra.*" In *Brown v. Rotenberg, supra*, Laidlaw JA said at p. 374:

> Was the gift to the respondent made in such circumstances as to show that the property was to revert to the donor in case he should recover? This question may be put in other language as follows: Was it intended that the gift should be effective only in the event of the death of the donor? It is not necessary that the donor should expressly state that term or condition at the time the gift is made. The inference may be drawn that the gift was intended to be absolute but only in case of death: *Gardner v. Parker et al.* (1818), 3 Madd. 184, 56 ER 478, cited in *In re Beaumont, supra*, and *Kendrick v. Dominion Bank and Bownas* (1920), 48 OLR 539 at 542, 58 DLR 309.

I am of the view that this inference can be made in this case in that the deceased, although ill, remained in the premises and did indicate that Chevrier could return the next day with a friend to witness the paper. The testimony of Mr. Chevrier was quite clear that he would only have considered the cache of money his on the death of Zachariuc. Thus, the last essential for an effectual donatio mortis causa is, in my opinion, satisfied.

I want to take this opportunity to express my thanks for the assistance which counsel have given the Court in their research and presentation of the law in argument.

There will be judgment for the plaintiff in the sum of $16,280, plus accrued interest from the time the Public Trustee deposited this sum to the estate account. The estate of Zachariuc will bear the costs of the plaintiff's solicitor and the solicitor for the Public Trustee on a party-and-party basis.

Judgment for plaintiff.

DISCUSSION NOTES

i. Delivery and the Donatio Mortis Causa

What factors did the court rely on in concluding that there was delivery of a gift to Chevrier in this case? If Zachariuc had told his friend about the secret cache, but had not provided a key to his home, would the court have held that there was sufficient delivery of a *donatio mortis causa*? Did Zachariuc give his friend a key to his home to enable him to obtain the cache of money, or for some other purpose?

Does the court's reasoning represent a different approach to the issue of delivery by contrast with *inter vivos* gifts? Do you agree that there was a "relaxation of the requirements for delivery ... as a dispensation in favour of the dying"? See R Brazier, "Death-Bed Gifts of Land" (1992) 43 N Ir Legal Q 35 at 48; and S Stoljar, "The Delivery of Chattels" (1958) 21 Mod L Rev 27. Most commentators agree that there was no requirement for delivery in the original *donatio mortis causa* of Roman law and this requirement was not introduced until Lord Hardwicke's decision in *Ward v Turner*, above. Is this history of *donationes mortis causa* important in understanding the standards applied to delivery in relation to such gifts?

In light of the reasoning in *Zachariuc*, consider a situation where a donor purports to make a *donatio mortis causa* in relation to money in a bank account by handing the donee the passbook to the account. Does this action constitute sufficient delivery? Is this constructive delivery? For some examples, see *McMillan v Brown* (1957), 12 DLR (2d) 306 (NSSC) and *Re Smith Estate*, 1995 CanLII 10500, 132 Nfld & PEIR 316 (Nfld SC (TD)). Consider also a purported *donatio mortis causa* where the donor handed the donee the key to a safety deposit box as a way of making a gift of the jewellery it contained. However, the donor did not provide the donee with the password or any written authorization, both required to open the box. Does this action constitute sufficient delivery? Is it relevant that the donor no longer has any control over the safety deposit box because there is only one key? See *Re Lillingston*, [1952] 2 All ER 184 (Ch D).

In *Zachariuc*, the court considered s 13 of the *Evidence Act*, discussed above following *Thomas v Times Book Co Ltd*. Why was this section relevant in *Zachariuc*? Is such a statutory provision adequate protection against fraud? Because the donor is not available to give evidence of a *donatio mortis causa*, is it appropriate to use a different standard of delivery, or is this a matter that should be addressed in relation to the donor's intention? For one analysis, see RG Murray, "Note" (1953) 31 Can Bar Rev 935.

ii. Intention and the Donatio Mortis Causa

The intention required for a *donatio mortis causa* reveals its historical roots as a "compromise" between an *inter vivos* gift and a testamentary disposition. It is both a present gift and one that nonetheless becomes irrevocable only on death. Its characterization is often stated to be *sui generis*. Consider, for example, the following description:

> [It] is not correct to characterize a *donatio* as a declaration of trust *inter vivos* immediately effective although conditioned in operation by reference to the death of the settlor. In truth the institution of the *donatio mortis causa* is peculiar and not to be understood by attempts to rationalize it within traditional ideas of trust, gift or legacy [testamentary gifts]; for while it has some attributes of each of these it has all of none.

(RP Meagher, JD Heydon & MJ Leeming, *Equity: Doctrines and Remedies*, 4th ed (Sydney: Butterworths, 2002) at 966.) Meagher, Heydon & Leeming also explore in detail the rights of the donee after the gift of a *donatio mortis causa* and before the death of the donor—see 965-76. See also DWM Waters, MR Gillen & LD Smith, *Waters' Law of Trusts in Canada*, 4th ed (Scarborough, ON: Carswell, 2012) [Waters] at 236-37.

Consider a situation where a donor, in immediate apprehension of death, gave a valuable ring to a longtime friend. However, the donor survived the peril and recovered, whereupon his friend urged him to take back the ring. The donor did so reluctantly and only after summoning witnesses to hear his declaration that the ring still belonged to the donee. The donor wore the ring until his death some years later, when the donee sought the ring from the donor's executor. The executor refused to give it to the donee. Was there a valid *donatio mortis causa*? Was there a valid gift *inter vivos*? What was the donor's intention? See *Newell v National Bank of Norwich*, 212 NYS 158 (CA 1925), where the court held that the donor's attempt to grant a *donatio mortis causa* was revoked automatically on his recovery. To give effect to the donor's obvious intent, the court characterized the original gift as a gift *inter vivos*. Is this reasoning satisfactory? According to Brown, this case might have been considered as one in which the donor made an *inter vivos* gift by means of his declaration while the ring was still in the possession of the donee, with a bailment to the donor until his death. See Brown at 141-43 and n 9.

As was evident in *Zachariuc*, a *donatio mortis causa* must be made in the contemplation (although not necessarily expectation) of death—the contemplation of a death more likely than that which all mortals expect. For some examples, see *Thompson v Mechan*, [1958] OR 357 (CA); *Canada Trust Co v Labadie*, [1962] OR 151 (CA); *Kooner v Kooner* (1979), 100 DLR (3d) 76 (BCSC). See also commentary by RE Megarry, "Note" (1965) 81 Law Q Rev 21 and Ziff at 163-64. If death is certain, should it be possible for a donor to make a *donatio mortis causa* or should the donor be required to make a will with its formal requirements? How should a court deal with a *donatio mortis causa* that was made in contemplation of death from one peril, but where the donor died as a result of another? See *Rosenberger v Volz* (1945), 12 ILR 34 (Ont HC), where the donor died in a railway accident in 1942, having "put his affairs in order" because of his enlistment in the armed forces. The purported *donatio mortis causa* was held to be valid.

In *Mennonite Trust Ltd v Good*, 2007 SKQB 351, James Good had a deathbed reconciliation with his daughter Elaine from whom he had been estranged for 21 years. In her presence and that of his other children, he declared that he wanted to change his will to include Elaine, but because this was unlikely to happen, he charged his son Arthur with delivering to Elaine $79,000 from a safety deposit box. James had put the box in his and Arthur's names in 1994, but had always accessed the box either alone or with Arthur; Arthur had never done so alone. After James's death, Arthur claimed that he was entitled to the $79,000 found in the box on the basis that his father had given it to him by putting the box in their joint names in 1994. He removed the money from the box, but later paid it to his solicitor in trust when James's executor, Mennonite Trust, claimed that the money belonged to the estate. The trial judge ordered that the money paid into court be given to Elaine. On what basis can such an order be justified? Was this an *inter vivos* gift; a testamentary gift; a declaration of trust; or a *donatio mortis causa*?

iii. The Donatio Mortis Causa: The Need for Reform

To some extent, these questions raise the issue of whether there is a continuing legal need for the *donatio mortis causa*. Although it is possible that such "deathbed gifts" were essential when many people lived in rural communities (without easy access to lawyers) and where the level of literacy was low, it is arguably now less fruitful to devote legal resources to such gifts. According to this argument, because it is preferable to encourage people to make proper testamentary gifts, the scope of *donationes mortis causa* should be more narrowly interpreted. Do you agree? What goals are achieved by preserving a wide scope for the *donatio mortis causa*? In considering these questions, examine the issues below concerning recent developments about *donationes mortis causa* of land.

iv. The Donatio Mortis Causa and Land: Sen v Headley

Traditionally, the scope of the *donatio mortis causa* was limited so that it was not possible to make a deathbed gift of land by the delivery of title deeds. In *Sen v Headley*, [1991] 2 All ER 636 (CA), however, the court held that the exclusion of land from *donationes mortis causa* was anomalous. In that case, the plaintiff, Mrs Sen, claimed to have received a *donatio mortis causa* of a house in Ealing worth £450,000 from the donor, Mr Hewett. She gave evidence that she and the donor were extremely close friends, and that when she had visited him in hospital shortly before his death and inquired about what was to be done with his house if he died, he replied:

> The house is yours, Margaret. You have the keys. They are in your bag. The deeds are in the steel box.

In this way, Mr Hewett gave Mrs Sen the only key to the steel box containing the title deeds to the house. She also had one of two keys to the house; Mr Hewett had the other. The court held that there was a sufficient parting with dominion in this case, although it did not resolve whether the case might have been decided differently if there had been two keys to the steel box and Mr Hewett had retained one. However, the central issue in *Sen v Headley* was whether English law recognized a *donatio mortis causa* of land, and the Court of Appeal held that there was no reason to distinguish land and other objects in relation to such gifts.

The decision in *Sen v Headley* has been critiqued extensively, both in terms of the court's reasoning about earlier decisions and in relation to underlying policy issues. According to P Sparkes, the decision represents "a revolutionary extension … with a wide and uncertain ambit":

> The Court of Appeal has validated a death-bed gift of a house, reportedly worth £450,000 made by the key to a deed box being slipped into the donee's handbag. There was no evidence apart from that of the donee, which [the trial judge] expressly found to be reliable and truthful. A door pushed open by an honest plaintiff, like Mrs. Sen, can be pushed further ajar by later dishonest claims. Land was not transmissible simply by delivery of title deeds, and should not be.

(P Sparkes, "Death-Bed Gifts of Land" (1992) 43:1 N Ir Legal Q 35 at 52.)

Because a full analysis of the issues in this case requires considerable knowledge about the principles of equity and the *Statute of Frauds*, you may need to reconsider this case in relation to these principles, discussed below. *Sen v Headley* has prompted recommendations for the abolition of all *donationes mortis causa* on the basis that there is no longer a need for them. See e.g. CEF Rickett, "No Donatio Mortis Causa of Real Property—A Rule in Search of a Justification?" (1989) Conveyancer and Property Lawyer 184, supporting the assessment of Waters, who argued:

> What has particularly concerned both courts and administrators, however, is that, while the whole object of the *Wills Act* is to eliminate fraud by requiring witnessed and signed wills or wills in the deceased's own handwriting [holograph wills, permitted by statute in some provincial jurisdictions], the doctrine of gift *mortis causa* reintroduces all the difficulties of oral and informal written evidence. …

There can be little doubt that the law of gifts *mortis causa* ought to be critically reviewed. The present law on the subject results in the drawing of lines between the valid and the invalid gift which is too often indefensible, and it is equally difficult to justify the position that a gift conditional on the donor's death is not testamentary. The truth is that the present law is largely a clutter of rules which have accrued over the centuries. … The preferable course may well be for those Canadian jurisdictions without the holograph will to introduce it, and for all Canadian common law jurisdictions to abolish the gift *mortis causa*.

(Waters at 238-40.)

Do you agree with this assessment? Note that it is not usual to keep deeds in a steel box in Canadian jurisdictions, a matter that is considered below in relation to registration systems. For statutory provisions concerning holograph wills, see *Succession Law Reform Act*, RSO 1990, c S.26, s 6 and *Wills Act*, 1996, SS 1996, c W-14.1, s 8. Ziff has identified a Canadian decision concerning a *donatio mortis causa* of land: see *Cooper v Severson* (1955), 1 DLR (2d) 161 (BCSC). He recommends abolition of any distinction between land and other gifts of *donationes mortis causa*; see Ziff at 163-64. In *Naylor v Naylor*, [1990] OJ no 287 (HC), the court dismissed an application for a declaration of a *donatio mortis causa*, but with little analysis of the fact that the subject matter of the alleged gift was real property. The appeal to the Ontario Court of Appeal was dismissed (1993), 1 ETR (2d) 308, leave to appeal to the Supreme Court of Canada denied (1994), 4 ETR (2d) 193n.

You may want to consider these issues concerning gifts of real and personal property, as well as the relationship between gifts *inter vivos*, *donationes mortis causa*, and testamentary gifts, after examining the remainder of this chapter.

III. TRANSFERRING INTERESTS IN LAND: LEGAL AND EQUITABLE INTERESTS

A. Conveyances and Contracts for Sale

Transfers of interests in land by sale are common legal transactions. Although they often involve multimillion-dollar developments and large corporations, many individuals are also familiar with such transactions as a result of purchasing a home. Typically, the vendor and purchaser first negotiate a contractual agreement, usually with the help of their real estate agents. The vendor and purchaser sign an agreement of purchase and sale that defines the terms of the sale, including the purchase price. In most respects, the negotiation of these contracts is similar to other kinds of contract bargaining. However, the validity and enforceability of contracts for the sale of land are subject to some special requirements, reflecting the historical role of land as a unique form of proprietary interest. This section focuses on basic principles of law and equity reflected in modern real estate transactions concerning the sale of land. For a more specialized analysis of real estate transactions, see Anne Warner La Forest, *Anger and Honsberger Law of Real Property*, 3d ed (Aurora, ON: Canada Law Book, 2006), and Paul Perell, *Lectures in Real Estate Transactions* (Toronto: Canada Law Book, 2011).

The history of conveyancing reveals a complex web of legal practices from the medieval period to the present, all designed to accomplish specified purposes of vendors and purchasers of land in the context of changing laws and policies. In addition to feoffment by livery of seisin (see Chapter 3) and grant by deed, conveyancers developed practices such as "bargain and sale" after the enactment of the *Statute of Uses* in 1535 and, later, a refined "lease and release" procedure that was used for conveying estates in possession in England from the 17th until the 19th century. Property reform legislation in England, the *Law of Property Act, 1925*, 15 & 16 Geo V, c 21, made conveyance by deed of grant virtually the only permissible means of conveyance.

Although ss 2 and 3 of the *Conveyancing and Law of Property Act*, RSO 1990, c C.34 use different (and perhaps less than felicitous) language concerning the use of feoffments by livery as well as by deed, it has been held that the effect of these sections and others in the *Registry Act*, RSO 1970, c 409 (see now RSO 1990, c R.20) requires a deed and registration to transfer interests in land so as to be enforceable against third parties: see *Bea v Robinson* (1977), 81 DLR (3d) 423 (Ont HC).

The modern process of real estate transactions in Canada usually involves two steps. After the vendor and purchaser have agreed on the basic terms for the sale, they sign an agreement of purchase and sale and the purchaser tenders a "deposit," a sum of money that represents consideration for the contractual agreement. Pursuant to the terms of this contract, and on a date fixed for "closing" the transaction, the vendor agrees to execute a deed conveying the vendor's proprietary interest to the purchaser and the purchaser agrees to pay the balance of the purchase price. The closing date is usually scheduled a few weeks after the signing of the agreement of purchase and sale. If all goes as planned, the vendor and purchaser agree that the vendor's title is satisfactory (perhaps after the purchaser has submitted a number of "requisitions on title"), the purchaser arranges details of financing, and on the closing date the vendor hands over the deed and the keys to the property in return for the balance of the purchase price. In some jurisdictions, it may be essential to register the purchaser's deed to ensure the transfer of title to the purchaser, a matter discussed briefly at the end of this chapter.

Not all real estate transactions go entirely smoothly, however. For example, the purchaser may not be able to pay the purchase price at closing, the vendor may die after signing the contract and before closing, or buildings erected on the land may burn to the ground between the date of the contract and the date set for closing. Thus, it is necessary to define exactly what interests are created for the vendor and purchaser at the time of the agreement of purchase and sale and what remedies are available to a vendor or purchaser in the event that the other party to the agreement fails to perform the terms of the contract at closing. These issues form a substantial part of the law of real estate transactions, a subject that can be pursued in detail in more specialized courses. The material that follows provides an introduction to these issues in terms of the role of law and equity in defining conveyances and contracts for the sale of land and offers some comparisons and contrasts with legal and equitable principles concerning gifts of chattels and land.

B. Conveying the Legal Estate: Requirements of the Statute of Frauds

The transfer of the legal estate occurs at closing, so long as the statutory requirements of transfer (and registration, if required) have been met. In addition to the statutory provisions identified above, the *Statute of Frauds*, 1677, 29 Charles II, c 3 was enacted to ensure written evidence of transfers of interests in land. As the authors of *Waters' Law of Trusts in Canada* have explained, a principal object of the 1677 Act was to reduce the opportunity for perjury, … [which] was easy enough when a contract for the sale of land, or a trust of land, could be created orally.

(Waters at 272.)

The *Statute of Frauds*, s 1(1) requires that the creation of a freehold estate must be in writing and signed by the parties, and that failure to meet these requirements will result in an estate at will only. Similarly, s 1(2) requires that leases "are void unless made by deed." Section 2 provides that no estate of freehold or leasehold can be "assigned, granted or surrendered" unless by deed or note in writing signed by the transferor. Leases (or agreements for leases) for a term not exceeding three years (with a rent that amounts to two-thirds of the value of the land) are excluded from the operation of these provisions by s 3—that is, they are valid even if not in writing. Other sections extend these requirements to the creation of trusts and other kinds of transactions relating to land. In particular, s 4 requires that any agreement to create or assign an interest in land—that is, any agreement of purchase and sale for land or any agreement to enter into a lease—must be in writing in order for an action to be brought to enforce the agreement. Reproduced below are the relevant provisions of the Ontario *Statute of Frauds*, RSO 1990, c S.19.

1(1) Every estate or interest of freehold and every uncertain interest of, in, to or out of any messuages, lands, tenements or hereditaments shall be made or created by a writing signed by the parties making or creating the same, or their agents thereunto lawfully authorized in writing, and, if not so made or created, has the force and effect of an estate at will only, and shall not be deemed or taken to have any other or greater force or effect.

(2) All leases and terms of years of any messuages, lands, tenements or hereditaments are void unless made by deed.

2. Subject to section 9 of the *Conveyancing and Law of Property Act*, no lease, estate or interest, either of freehold or term of years, or any uncertain interest of, in, to or out of any messuages, lands, tenements or hereditaments shall be assigned, granted or surrendered unless it be by deed or note in writing signed by the party so assigning, granting, or surrendering the same, or the party's agent thereunto lawfully authorized by writing or by act or operation of law.

3. Sections 1 and 2 do not apply to a lease, or an agreement for a lease, not exceeding the term of three years from the making thereof, the rent upon which, reserved to the landlord during such term, amounts to at least two-thirds of the full improved value of the thing demised.

4. No action shall be brought to charge any executor or administrator upon any special promise to answer damages out of the executor's or administrator's own estate, or to charge any person upon any special promise to answer for the debt, default or miscarriage of any other person, or to charge any person upon any contract or sale of lands, tenements or hereditaments, or any interest in or concerning them, unless the agreement upon which the action is brought, or some memorandum or note thereof is in writing and signed by the party to be charged therewith or some person thereunto lawfully authorized by the party.

The *Statute of Frauds* remains current law in most other provincial jurisdictions in Canada: see e.g. *Statute of Frauds*, RSNB 1973, c S-14; RSNS 1989, c 442; and RSPEI 1988, c S-6. The *Statute of Frauds*, 1677 "forms part of the law of Newfoundland by virtue of the reception of English law doctrine": see *Hollett v Hollett*, 1993 CanLII 8441, 106 Nfld & PEIR 271, 31 RPR (2d) 251 at 261 (Nfld SC (TD)). (It has, however, been repealed in Manitoba, effective 1 February 1988: *An Act to Repeal the Statute of Frauds*, CCSM, c F158.) With the spread of electronic conveyancing (see below, section V, A Note on Priorities and Registration), the relevance of writing and a physical document to land transactions is being superseded by electronic documents. Section 21 of the *Land Registration Reform Act*, RSO 1990, c L.4, as am by SO 1994, c 27, s 85(3) reads:

> 21. Despite section 2 of the *Statute of Frauds Act*, section 9 of the *Conveyancing and Law of Property Act* or a provision in any other statute or any rule of law, an electronic document that creates, transfers or otherwise disposes of an estate or interest in land is not required to be in writing or to be signed by the parties and has the same effect for all purposes as a document that is in writing and is signed by the parties.

In a modern real estate transaction, it is only when the vendor delivers a deed, or its electronic equivalent, to the purchaser at closing (along with registration, if required) that the legal estate in land is transferred to the purchaser. This conclusion may suggest that the purchaser has no recognizable interest in land between the signing of the agreement of purchase and sale and the time fixed for closing. Yet, although the purchaser may not have a legal estate, equitable principles have developed to provide protection for both the vendor and the purchaser in relation to their agreement. These principles reflect the historical economic importance of land and the availability of the remedy of specific performance in relation to contracts for the sale of land.

C. Equitable Interests in Agreements for Purchase and Sale

1. The Principle in Lysaght v Edwards

The classic description of the interests of a vendor and purchaser at the time of a contract for the sale of land is found in *Lysaght v Edwards* (1876), 2 Ch D 499. *Lysaght v Edwards* was decided shortly after the "fusion" of the courts of law and equity in England, described in Chapter 3, and in a context where courts were only beginning to decide some of the effects of a unified court of law and equity. In reading the decision, identify the nature of the interests acquired by the vendor and the purchaser at the time of their contract.

Lysaght v Edwards

(1876), 2 Ch D 499

[The vendor, Edwards, entered into an agreement dated 23 December 1874 to sell his interests in certain land to the purchaser, Lysaght, at a price of £59,750. The purchaser paid a deposit and the parties agreed on 11 October 1875 as the closing date. There was an investigation of the vendor's title and the parties agreed on all the issues of title, etc., before the date set for closing, and before the vendor's death on 1 May 1875. After the vendor's death, the purchaser brought an application for specific performance of the contract; the defendants were several heirs specified in Edwards's will. Much of the decision was concerned with the proper interpretation of provisions concerning the disposition of real and personal property under the will, but Jessel MR also considered (at 505) the effect of the contract for the sale of land entered into by the deceased and the plaintiff in December 1874.]

[T]he next point I have to consider is [w]hat is the effect of the contract? It appears to me that the effect of a contract for sale has been settled for more than two centuries; certainly it was completely settled before the time of Lord Hardwicke, who speaks of the settled doctrine of the Court as to it. What is that doctrine? It is that the moment you have a valid contract for sale the vendor becomes in equity a trustee for the purchaser of the estate sold, and the beneficial ownership passes to the purchaser, the vendor having a right to the purchase-money, a charge or lien on the estate for the security of that purchase-money, and a right to retain possession of the estate until the purchase-money is paid, in the absence of express contract as to the time of delivering possession. In other words, the position of the vendor is something between what has been called a naked or bare trustee, or a mere trustee (that is, a person without beneficial interest), and a mortgagee who is not, in equity (any more than a vendor), the owner of the estate, but is, in certain events, entitled to what the unpaid vendor is, viz., possession of the estate and a charge upon the estate for his purchase-money. Their positions are analogous in another way. The unpaid mortgagee has a right to foreclose, that is to say, he has a right to say to the mortgagor, "Either pay me within a limited time, or you lose your estate," and in default of payment he becomes absolute owner of it. So, although there has been a valid contract of sale, the vendor has a similar right in a Court of Equity; he has a right to say to the purchaser, "Either pay me the purchase-money, or lose the estate." Such a decree has sometimes been called a decree for cancellation of the contract; time is given by a decree of the Court of Equity, or now by a judgment of the High Court of Justice; and if the time expires without the money being paid, the contract is cancelled by the decree or judgment of the Court, and the vendor becomes again the owner of the estate. But that, as it appears to me, is a totally different thing from the contract being cancelled because there was some equitable ground for setting it aside. If a valid contract is cancelled for non-payment of the purchase-money after the death of the vendor, the property will still in equity be treated as having been converted into personalty, because the contract was valid at his death; while in the other case there will not be conversion, because there never was in equity a valid contract. Now, what is the meaning of the term "valid contract"? "Valid contract" means in every case a contract sufficient in form and in substance, so that there is no ground whatever for setting it aside as between the vendor and purchaser—a contract binding on both parties. As regards real estate, however, another element of validity is required. The vendor must be in a position to make a title according to the contract, and the contract will not be a valid contract unless he has either made out his title according to the contract or the purchaser has accepted the title, for however bad the title may be the purchaser has a right to accept it, and the moment he has accepted the title, the contract is fully binding upon the vendor. Consequently, if the title is accepted in the lifetime of the vendor, and there is no reason for setting aside the contract, then, although the purchase-money is unpaid, the contract is valid and binding; and being a valid contract, it has this remarkable effect, that it converts the estate, so to say, in equity; it makes the purchase-money a part of the personal estate of the vendor, and it makes the land a part of the real estate of the vendee; and therefore all those cases on the doctrine of constructive conversion are founded simply on this, that a valid contract actually changes the ownership of the estate in equity. That being so, is the vendor less a trustee because he has the rights which I have mentioned? I do not see how it is possible to say so. If anything happens to the estate between the time of sale and the time of completion of the purchase it is at the risk of the purchaser. If it is a house that is sold, and the house is burnt down, the purchaser loses the house. He must insure it himself if he wants to provide against such an accident. If it is a garden, and a river overflows its banks without any fault of the vendor, the garden will be ruined, but the loss will be the purchaser's. In the same way there is a correlative liability on the part of the vendor in possession. He is not entitled to treat the estate as his own. If he wilfully damages or injures it, he is liable to the purchaser; and more than that, he is liable if he does not take reasonable care of it. So far he is treated in all respects as a trustee, subject of course to his right to being paid the purchase-money and his right to enforce his security against the estate. With those exceptions, and his right to rents till the day for completion, he appears to me to have no other rights.

DISCUSSION NOTES

i. Equitable Interests and the Remedy of Specific Performance: Semelhago v Paramadevan

As Jessel MR explained, an enforceable contract for the sale of land results in the creation of a trust relationship between the vendor and the purchaser. With respect to the interest in land, the vendor holds the legal estate and the purchaser acquires the beneficial or equitable interest. Similarly, the vendor acquires a charge or lien on the purchase money and (unless the contract alters the arrangement) the right to remain in possession of the land until closing. In doing so, however, the vendor as trustee for the purchaser has an obligation to take reasonable care of the property. See *Clarke v Ramuz*, [1891] 2 QB 456 (CA) and *Earl of Egmont v Smith* (1877), 6 Ch D 469. Note also that any risk of loss also passes to the purchaser in equity at the time of the contract for sale although this result is sometimes expressly altered by the parties in their agreement for purchase and sale.

As the court declared, "a valid contract actually changes the ownership of the estate in equity." According to Gray & Symes, the explanation for this result is the availability of the remedy of specific performance to a purchaser in the event that the vendor fails to convey the legal estate in accordance with the terms of the contract for sale.

> The end result is that once a contract for the sale of a legal estate in land has been concluded, the eventual conveyance of that estate is virtually inevitable. Either the vendor will duly convey according to his contract or the purchaser will enlist the aid of equity towards this end by means of a decree of specific performance. The assistance of equity will normally be forthcoming in each case unless the purchaser has forfeited such help by reason of some unconscionable act or default or [unless] specific performance would prejudice the rights of third parties.

(Kevin J Gray & PD Symes, *Real Property and Real People: Principles of Land Law* (London: Butterworths, 1981) [Gray & Symes] at 84-85.) The remedy of specific performance for such a contract also reflects the equitable maxim that equity deems as done that which ought to be done, so that it is appropriate to award equitable remedies to enforce the agreement for sale. Gray & Symes described (at 85) the interests of the vendor and purchaser under a contract for sale, using a diagram similar to the one below:

	Before contract	Contract	Conveyance
Law	Vendor	Vendor	Purchaser
	(fee simple)	(fee simple)	(fee simple)
Equity	Vendor	Purchaser	Purchaser
	(fee simple)	(fee simple)	(fee simple)

Note too that the decree of specific performance is one that "compels the defendant personally to do what he promised to do." See *Lubben v Veltri & Sons Corp* (1997), 32 OR (3d) 65 (CA), where the court decided that a decree of specific performance required a purchaser personally to close a transaction and that the purchaser could not avoid this obligation by assigning the purchaser's rights under the agreement to an impecunious numbered company. See generally Robert J Sharpe, *Injunctions and Specific Performance*, 4th ed (Toronto: Canada Law Book, 2012) [Sharpe].

The purchaser's equitable interest in relation to an agreement for purchase and sale derives from the availability of the remedy of specific performance, a remedy developed by the Court of Chancery. Specific performance was normally granted only when the common law damages were shown to be inadequate. Historically, however, it issued as a matter of course in relation to a contract concerning land because each parcel of land was regarded as having a unique character such that damages would not be appropriate: see e.g. *Wroth v Tyler*, [1974] 1 Ch 30. This principle was revisited in the Supreme Court of Canada in *Semelhago v Paramadevan*, [1996] 2 SCR 415, a case where a vendor reneged on an agreement for sale of a home in the context of rising prices in the residential house market. The vendor's failure to complete the transaction meant that the purchaser was unable to complete the purchase of a home, which was worth $325,000 at the date of trial and for which he had agreed to pay $205,000 in the contract for sale. The value of the purchaser's loss was $120,000 and the purchaser sued the vendor successfully for $120,000 as damages in lieu of specific performance. At the same time, however, the purchaser's own home (which he had intended to sell to finance the purchase of the new home) had increased in value from $190,000 at the time of the agreement of purchase and sale to $300,000 by the time of the trial, an increase in value of $110,000. The trial judge characterized the result as a "windfall" for the plaintiff. The vendor appealed to the Ontario Court of Appeal, which made some adjustments but substantially confirmed the claim of damages of $120,000 as properly based on the value of a decree of specific performance to the plaintiff. On appeal to the Supreme Court of Canada, the appeal was dismissed. Sopinka J reviewed the principles concerning damages at common law and examined whether damages could be a suitable substitute for specific performance. Sopinka J suggested (in arguably *obiter* comments at 428) that "it is no longer appropriate ... to maintain a distinction in the approach to specific performance as between realty and personalty." Sopinka J quoted with approval the decision of the Newfoundland Court of Appeal in *Chaulk v Fairview Construction Ltd* (1977), 14 Nfld and PEIR 13 (Nfld CA), where the court stated (at 21):

> The question here is whether damages would have afforded [the plaintiff] an adequate remedy, and I have no doubt that they could, and would, have. There was nothing whatever unique or irreplaceable about the houses and lots bargained for. They were merely subdivision lots with houses, all of the same general design, built on them, which the respondent was purchasing for investment or re-sale purposes only ... . It would be quite different if we were dealing with a

house or houses which were of a particular architectural design, or were situated in a particularly desirable location.

Do you agree with Sopinka J's conclusion that there is no longer any need to treat real property as typically unique and thus usually giving rise to a remedy of specific performance? If a court finds that the circumstances do not justify an award of specific performance, should the court impose a duty to mitigate, as would normally be the case in any assessment of expectation damages for breach of contract? By selling his home in the rising market for $110,000 profit, did the plaintiff in *Semelhago* effectively mitigate some of his loss? Should the court have taken this into account by deducting this profit from the $120,000 loss suffered by the plaintiff?

Some commentators have been critical of *Semelhago* on the ground that there will be inevitable uncertainty as to what characteristics qualify as unique for the purposes of determining whether specific performance should be available. DH Clark, in "Will That Be Performance ... Or Cash?: Semelhago v Paramadevan and the Notion of Equivalence" (1999) 37 Alta L Rev 589, argues (at 589) that in *Semelhago* the court "unsettled not only established real estate law but also some of the basic principles governing contractual remedies in Canada." He adds that there is a "neatness about assimilating real estate transactions of all kinds to personalty," but it comes at a high cost:

> However, this symmetry has to be weighed against the considerable downside for both litigants and their legal advisors: inevitable *uncertainty* as to what characteristics or combination of characteristics will qualify as "unique" (for example, size, shape, view, proximity to shops/park/schools/relatives/friends, "character"), with the resultant dilemma of how much evidence to call and of what kind; the equally inevitable *inconsistency* of decisions on something so intangible as the attraction of a particular property; the *expense* of litigating this issue in every case; and the potentially severe financial penalty (in the rising market that often explains vendor default) that will be suffered if an assertion of uniqueness is rejected at trial. The whiplash effect of what would *ex post facto* be characterized as a failure to mitigate by purchasing an equivalent property within a reasonable time after the date of breach would be likely to constitute a major deterrent to attempting to keep such a contract alive.

(Clark at 592.)

OV Da Silva, in "The Supreme Court of Canada's Lost Opportunity: Semelhago v Paramadevan" (1998) 23 Queen's LJ 475, also takes the position (at 507) that *Semelhago* is "inconsistent with modern principles of contract law." Da Silva argues that damages in lieu of specific performance will frequently leave the purchaser of a home unfairly undercompensated because a damage award may fail to take into consideration the purchaser's unique or even idiosyncratic interest in the property. He adds (at 507):

> Sopinka J's criterion of objective "uniqueness" as the determinant of when specific performance will be available has the effect of treating consumer purchasers of homes in precisely the same fashion as commercial speculators purchasing investment properties, but without explicitly recognizing that consumer purchasers may have suffered vastly different losses that, though potentially significant, are still regarded by courts as nominal.

Da Silva noted (at 507) that, as a result of *Semelhago*, "no prudent lawyer would advise his or her client to seek specific performance of an agreement of purchase and sale (where there is no duty to mitigate) unless it is incontrovertibly and demonstrably clear that the property is objectively unique. Consumers will be encouraged to mitigate as opposed to litigate."

ii. Specific Performance and Land in a Commercial Context: John E Dodge Holdings Ltd v 805062 Ont Ltd

John E Dodge Holdings Ltd v 805062 Ont Ltd (2003), 63 OR (3d) 304 (CA), application for leave to appeal dismissed [2003] SCCA no 145, a decision of the Ontario Court of Appeal, considered the question of uniqueness in a commercial context. The defendant vendor had agreed to sell some commercial land to the plaintiff. The land was located close to Canada's Wonderland, a matter of considerable importance to the purchaser, who wanted to build a hotel. The vendor was in breach of the agreement of purchase and sale and the purchaser sought specific performance. The vendor argued that the commercial property in question was not unique and thus the purchaser should be limited to damages only, along with a duty to mitigate its loss by purchasing other comparable property available nearby as soon as the breach had become apparent—that is, the time of the "actionable wrong." On the question of uniqueness, the Court of Appeal held (at 317):

> In *Semelhago v. Paramadevan*, [1996] 2 SCR 415, 136 DLR (4th) 1 at para. 22, Sopinka J observed that specific performance will only be granted if the plaintiff can demonstrate that the subject property is unique in the sense that, "its substitute would not be readily available." Although Sopinka J did not elaborate further on this definition, in *1252668 Ontario Inc. v. Wyndham Street Investments Inc.*, [1999] OJ No. 3188 (Quicklaw), 27 RPR (3d) 58 (SCJ) at para. 23, Justice Lamek stated that he
>
> > [does] not consider that the plaintiff has to demonstrate that the Premises are unique in a strict dictionary sense that they are entirely different from any other piece of property. It is enough, in my view, for the plaintiff to demonstrate that the Premises have a quality that makes them especially suitable for the proposed use and that they cannot be reasonably duplicated elsewhere.
> >
> > I agree that in order to establish that a property is unique the person seeking the remedy of specific performance must show that the property in question has a quality that cannot be readily duplicated elsewhere. This quality should relate to the proposed use of the property and be a quality that makes it particularly suitable for the purpose for which it was intended. See also the comments of Low J in *904060 Ontario Ltd. v. 529566 Ontario Ltd.*, [1999] OJ No. 355 (Quicklaw), 89 OTC 112 (Gen. Div.) at para. 14.

On the facts in *John E Dodge Holdings Ltd v 805062 Ont Ltd*, the Court of Appeal held that the property in question was sufficiently unique to give rise to a remedy in specific performance.

> [43] The question then becomes whether the property was unique on the date of the actionable wrong. Magna [the defendant vendor] contends that the trial judge erred in finding that the property was unique. It submits that other comparable commercial properties were available and, in particular, a property owned by a group of persons including Mr. Sorbara (the "Sorbara property") and another at the Vaughan Mills Mall. At the date of the actionable wrong, May 11, 2000, the Sorbara property had been sold. The trial judge found that although the comparables from Magna's expert permitted a hotel to be built, none of them were in as close proximity to

Canada's Wonderland or the Vaughan Mills Centre, a planned $250 million retail mall to be located directly west of the site. At para. 69 of her reasons she found:

> The Magna site offers superior access, visibility, traffic patterns and location to each of the other sites that were under consideration. It also has a C7 commercial zoning designation that is more favourable for ancillary uses such as banquet halls and eating establishments. This was significant for Dodge as the hotel concept it was considering at the time of the contract and later pursued was for a Hilton Garden Inn. This concept does not require full restaurant facilities in the hotel. The ability to have an unrestricted, independent dining facility on the land to accommodate hotel guests, but also to serve patrons in the area, was another distinguishing feature of this site. None of the other sites offered this combination of attractive features at a comparable price.

> [44] The appellant has not shown that the trial judge misapprehended the evidence or committed any overriding and palpable error in her findings. The trial judge did not err in her conclusion that this particular piece of commercial real estate was unique.

The court arguably read the requirement of "uniqueness" quite broadly in this case, raising the question that it may still be fairly easy for plaintiffs to establish a unique interest in the property and thus claim specific performance. The commentators above are critical of *Semelhago* in part because the uniqueness test has injected too much uncertainty into the law at the expense of innocent plaintiffs. Does *John E Dodge Holdings Ltd* go some way toward addressing this concern? See also *Canamed (Stamford) Ltd v Masterwood Doors Ltd*, [2006] OJ no 802 (Sup Ct J), where specific performance of a purpose-built medical office building was ordered.

iii. Specific Performance and Land in a Residential Context: Marvost v Stokes

A recent Ontario decision, *Marvost v Stokes*, 2011 ONSC 4827 (CanLII), considered the "uniqueness" requirement in a case where specific performance of an agreement of purchase and sale for a $3.325 million home at 18 Glenorchy Road in Toronto's exclusive Bridle Path neighbourhood was sought. The plaintiff, his wife, and children had moved to Canada from Iran in July 2010. According to the trial judge, the plaintiff's wife deposed that the following criteria were important to them:

(a) They wished to buy a home in the Bridlepath area;

(b) They wished to have a home that backed onto a ravine;

(c) They did not want a pool because they did not intend to spend the summers in Toronto;

(d) They wanted a lot 100 feet wide;

(e) They wanted at least 5 bedrooms with a nanny suite on a separate level from the family bedrooms;

(f) They wanted the home to be in move in condition;

(g) They wanted a purchase price below $3.5 million;

(h) They wanted to be in the residential boundaries for St. Andrew's School because their daughter will be starting grade 7 in September, 2011. English is her second language and her best friend will be attending St. Andrew's School, upon whom she relies for assistance.

The defendants submitted that these criteria were an *ex post facto* rationalization aimed at proving that the home at 18 Glenorchy was unique. The defendants testified that shortly after entering into the agreement of purchase and sale, they changed their mind about selling their family home, to which they claimed to be emotionally attached and which was close to the wife's aging parent and her disabled nephew. They submitted that the plaintiff had not satisfied the burden of proving that 18 Glenorchy was unique:

> They submit that there are 28 properties available in the $2 to $4 million range, including 16 Glenorchy, the next door property to 18 Glenorchy, which is listed for sale for $3.7 million and meets the plaintiff's list of criteria. Five of these properties are in the Bridlepath area, the neighborhood in which the plaintiff and his family wish to reside. In her July 20th, 2011 affidavit, the wife addresses why these properties are not suitable replacements for 18 Glenorchy. In regard to 16 Glenorchy, she deposes that she and her husband did not like that it is a corner lot, and it was not acceptable because the children's bedrooms were in a separate wing of the house. She deposes that there is no nanny suite on a separate floor from the family bedrooms; the lot is an irregular shape with a smaller backyard; it lacks privacy because of a school next to it; the basement is only semi-finished; and they did not like either the exterior or the interior. On cross-examination, the defendants acknowledged that the style of the 2 homes is different.

The trial judge applied the law as follows:

> A moving party is entitled to specific performance of an agreement of purchase and sale where it can show that the property is unique to the extent that a substitute is not readily available. In *Semelhago v. Paramadevan*, [1996] 2 S.C.R. 415, 1996 CanLII 209, Sopinka J. stated at paragraph 20:
>
> > While at one time the common law regarded every piece of real estate as unique, with the progress of modern real estate development, this is no longer the case. Both residential, business and industrial properties are mass produced in the same way as other consumer products. If a deal falls through for one property, another is frequently, though not always, readily available.
>
> The burden of proof to establish that the property is unique and that damages are inadequate to do justice is on the plaintiff. There is a subjective aspect to uniqueness which will normally be more significant in residential purchases. (*De Franco v. Khatri*, 2005 CarswellOnt 1744 (Ont. S.C.J.) at para. 33) Uniqueness does not require proof that the property is entirely different from every other property nor does it require that the plaintiff must establish that the property is incomparable. (Mr. Justice Robert Sharpe, *Injunctions and Specific Performance*; Canada Law Book at para. 8.60)
>
> 18 Glenorchy is neither a condominium apartment nor a row house located in a mass produced subdivision. It is a custom built home which backs onto a ravine in one of Toronto's most expensive and exclusive neighbourhoods. The plaintiff and his wife spent months searching for this home. It satisfies their stated criteria and is particularly suited to their proposed use. The evidence proffered on behalf of the plaintiff that the other homes proposed as substitutes are not reasonably suitable alternatives satisfies me that 18 Glenorchy is unique both on an objective and subjective basis. 16 Glenorchy is also a custom built home with a different exterior and interior than 18 Glenorchy. It is smaller, more modern in design, less well situated and its floor plan is less suitable for the needs of the plaintiff and his family. On a subjective basis, they did not like the exterior or the interior. ...

The fact that the plaintiff made an unconditional offer the same day that he and his wife saw the house confirms that they were very taken by this particular property.

In all the circumstances, damages are not an adequate remedy. Specific performance is ordered. In addition, the plaintiff is awarded damages agreed upon by the parties in the amount of $37,500 to be deducted or abated from the purchase price agreed to in the agreement of purchase and sale.

On 2 February 2012, the Ontario Court of Appeal heard and dismissed an appeal from the trial decision: *Stokes v Marvost*, 2012 ONCA 74 (CanLII).

It was relatively easy for the plaintiffs to establish the unique character of the home in *Marvost v Stokes*, given their very specific requirements. Is the average purchaser likely to be in a position to outline his or her needs with such precision? If there is "a subjective aspect to uniqueness which will normally be more significant in residential purchases," what exactly does that mean? Will the subjective aspect be significant only if it is backed up by evidence of "objectively determined" uniqueness? See *Minto v Jones*, [2008] OJ no 3687 on this point, where the trial judge observed: "Viewed objectively, one might say that this was a typical home in a typical subdivision, but from the plaintiff's perspective, it had unique and attractive attributes that were ideally suited to her needs and those of her family." The trial judge ordered specific performance. Does this result suggest that a "pure" subjective test will suffice? One commentator has observed that *Semelhago* has not produced

> a dramatic change in practical results, particularly with respect to residential property [and that] [e]ven in commercial cases, the practical effect of *Semelhago* has been limited. Developers assembling related parcels of land have been granted specific performance [and] [i]n other commercial cases, there ha[s] been a tendency to apply a relaxed version of the uniqueness test [citing *John E Dodge Holdings*].

(Sharpe at para 8.60.)

In Sharpe's view,

> [w]hile the availability of specific performance was shaped and explained by the historical factors produced by the division between law and equity, courts are becoming less willing to justify decisions in terms of historical categories and more willing explicitly to recognize and state underlying principles.

(Sharpe at para 7.190.)

Thus, the real effect of *Semelhago* is seen as "open[ing] the door to a critical inquiry as to the nature and function of the property in relation to the prospective purchaser": *904060 Ontario Ltd v 529566 Ontario Ltd*, [1999] OJ no 355 (Gen Div).

iv. Specific Performance and Equitable Interests in Land

In the event that specific performance is available to enforce an agreement of purchase and sale, the creation of an equitable interest in land as a result of the contract for sale means that "[r]ights of mere *contractual* significance are elevated into rights of *proprietary* consequence." See Kevin J Gray & Susan Francis Gray, *Elements of Land Law*, 5th ed (Oxford: Oxford University Press, 2009) [Gray & Gray] at 1054. What consequences flow from characterizing the purchaser's interest as an equitable proprietary interest as of the date of the contract for sale?

Consider a situation in which a vendor (V) and purchaser (P) sign an agreement of purchase and sale, valid and enforceable in all respects. After signing the agreement of purchase and sale, but before closing, V executes and delivers a deed in favour of a third party (T) in relation to the same land that V had agreed to sell to P. What are the proprietary relationships among these parties? If P acquired an equitable interest at the time of the agreement of purchase and sale, and T subsequently acquired a legal estate, will P's equitable interest be enforceable against T's subsequent legal estate? Recall the discussion in Chapter 3 about the enforceability of equitable interests against everyone except a bona fide purchaser for value of the legal estate without notice. How should the purchaser ensure that there is notice of this interest to any subsequent third party dealing with the land?

Although this chapter deals with specific performance in the context of contracts for the sale of land, note that contracts for the sale of personal property are also capable of being specifically performed provided the requisite criteria are met. In *Van Damme v Gelber*, 2013 ONCA 388, the defendant had agreed to sell a valuable painting to the plaintiff art dealer pursuant to a contract subject to the law of New York. When the defendant resisted delivering the painting, a New York court granted the plaintiff an order of specific performance. The painting was hanging in the home of the defendant's son in Toronto, and the plaintiff sought a court order requiring the painting to be delivered to him. At both trial and appeal, the Ontario courts recognized the New York judgment and ordered the defendant to deliver the painting to the plaintiff. If you had been acting for the defendant in the New York action, what argument might you have tried to advance?

2. A Valid Contract

As *Lysaght v Edwards* indicated, a purchaser acquires an equitable interest in an agreement of purchase and sale if there is a "valid contract" that is capable of specific performance. The contract for sale must meet the usual requirements for a valid contract, including offer, acceptance, and consideration. The contract should also specify the basic matters of agreement, including a description of the property, identification of the parties to the contract, and definition of the purchase price. If the agreement fails to specify this information, it may be insufficiently precise to be a valid contract enforceable by specific performance. For examples of courts "reading in" provisions to contracts in this context, see *Connelly v 904 Water Street Ontario Ltd* (1994), 42 RPR (2d) 267 (Ont Ct J (Gen Div)); *Ryan v Cam-Valley Developments Ltd* (1993), 15 OR (3d) 24 (Gen Div).

3. The Statute of Frauds and Contracts for Sale

In addition to the requirements for a valid contract, a contract to transfer an interest in land must meet the requirements of the *Statute of Frauds*, s 4. As noted above, the *Statute of Frauds* defines the requirements for the creation and transfer of freehold and leasehold estates. In addition, s 4 of the *Statute of Frauds* (reproduced above) requires that any agreement to create or assign an interest in land—that is, any agreement of purchase and sale for land or any agreement to enter into a lease—must be evidenced in writing in order for an action to be brought to enforce the agreement.

Section 4 of the *Statute of Frauds* requires a contract for the sale of land, or any interest in or concerning it, to be in writing or evidenced by a "memorandum or note … in writing" that is "signed by the party to be charged" with contractual responsibility. Both these requirements have been the subject of litigation, particularly in a context of rising land prices. For example, consider the situation of a vendor who orally accepts an offer from a purchaser, but before this purchaser can deliver an offer in writing, the vendor "signs back" a written offer with a higher purchase price from a second purchaser. Why does the *Statute of Frauds* protect the vendor from liability to the first purchaser in this situation? Would the position of the first purchaser be improved if he or she had written out and signed an offer on a piece of paper and delivered it to the vendor, pending the formal written offer of purchase? Note that the *Statute of Frauds*, s 4 requires the signature of the person "to be charged therewith." Consider also situations where a purchaser may be able to avoid a conveyance if the vendor has signed a contract for sale and the purchaser has not yet done so.

The problem of vendors negotiating with multiple purchasers at the same time to obtain the highest sale price and using the *Statute of Frauds* to avoid the consequences of their oral agreements has been referred to in England as "gazumping." Partly in an effort to prevent the *Statute of Frauds* from being used for these somewhat shady dealings, the English Court of Appeal construed a solicitor's letter as meeting the requirements of the Statute when the letter contained the terms of the proposed agreement, but also expressed the view that the letter was "subject to contract": *Law v Jones*, [1974] Ch 112 (CA). However, this decision substantially altered usual conveyancing practices to such an extent that the same court (differently constituted) decided in *Tiverton Estates Ltd v Wearwell Ltd*, [1975] Ch 146 (CA) that the insertion of the phrase "subject to contract" prevented a written agreement from meeting the requirements of s 4 of the Statute. In *Tiverton*, Lord Denning stated (at 154) that the analysis in *Law v Jones* "virtually repealed the *Statute of Frauds*." The Law Commission of England and Wales approved the approach in *Tiverton*; see its *Report on "Subject to Contract" Agreements* (London: HMSO, 1975).

Note that equity has permitted the enforcement of oral contracts concerning land on the basis of the equitable doctrine of part performance, even though there has been no compliance with the *Statute of Frauds*. Part performance is addressed in more detail below.

4. The "Fusion" of Law and Equity: Walsh v Lonsdale

Walsh v Lonsdale (1882), 21 Ch D 9 (CA) demonstrates the legal effect of an agreement to lease (as opposed to a lease itself). Like *Lysaght v Edwards*, this case was also decided shortly after the fusion of the courts of law and equity in England and it provides another illustration of the procedural efficiency of a single court administering principles of both law and equity. In *Walsh*, the court considered an agreement for a seven-year lease of a weaving shed known as Providence Mill. The agreement for a lease, like a contract for the sale of land, evidenced the parties' agreement to execute a leasehold conveyance sometime later. It also stated that the lease itself would be prepared by the solicitor for the landlord and would contain other covenants "as are usually inserted in leases of a similar nature, and particularly those inserted in a lease of the Newfield Mills, Darwen." The Newfield Mills lease included a clause that the rent was payable in advance on May 1 each year. Although the parties never executed a deed of lease, the tenant went into possession and paid rent quarterly. As a tenant with an oral lease who paid rent that was accepted by the landlord, the common law regarded the tenant as holding a periodic tenancy—that is, a tenancy defined by the period of the rental payment, annual in this case. The tenant was thus a yearly tenant at law.

When the landlord subsequently demanded rent in advance (presumably as a result of the clause in the Newfield Mills lease that was to be incorporated in the deed of lease), the tenant refused. Accordingly, the landlord exercised the remedy of distress, discussed in Chapter 4. The tenant claimed that he had no obligation to pay rent in advance, because he was in possession under an oral lease only, and the formal lease, which included the requirement to pay rent in advance, had never been executed. By contrast, the landlord relied on the agreement to lease as an agreement capable of specific performance, so that the parties had equitable interests as if the deed of lease containing the requirement to pay rent in advance had been executed. At trial, Fry J ordered the tenant to pay into court the whole sum claimed as rent (including rent in advance and rent owing to date) in return for the landlord's cessation of his distress against the tenant. On appeal, Jessel MR stated (at 14):

> The question is one of some nicety. There is an agreement for a lease under which possession has been given. Now since the *Judicature Act* the possession is held under the agreement. There are not two estates as there were formerly, one estate at common law by reason of the payment of the rent from year to year, and an estate in equity under the agreement. There is only one Court, and the equity rules prevail in it. The tenant holds under an agreement for a lease. He holds, therefore, under the same terms in equity as if a lease had been granted, it being a case in which both parties admit that relief is capable of being given by specific performance. That being so, he cannot complain of the exercise by the landlord of the same rights as the landlord would have had if a lease had been granted. On the other hand, he is protected in the same way as if a lease had been granted; he cannot be turned out by six months' notice as a tenant from year to year. He has a right to say, "I have a lease in equity, and you can only re-enter if I have committed such a breach of covenant as would if a lease had been granted have entitled you to re-enter according to the terms of a proper proviso for re-entry." That being so, it appears to me that being a lessee in equity he cannot complain of the exercise of the right of distress merely because the actual parchment has not been signed and sealed.

The court concluded that the parties' rights should be determined *as if* there had been specific performance of the agreement to lease. Why did this conclusion result in the tenant owing rent in advance? Did the tenant also benefit from the court's characterization of the agreement to lease as one that created rights in equity for the landlord and the tenant? What advantage did the tenant gain from characterizing the agreement *as if* a lease had been executed? In thinking about this question, it is important to note that, as a yearly tenant with an oral lease, the tenant could have been evicted by the landlord on six months' notice. Was the tenant's position under the agreement preferable? Why? For an analysis of the principles in *Walsh v Lonsdale*, see S Gardner, "Equity, Estate Contracts, and the Judicature Acts: Walsh v Lonsdale Revisited" (1987) 7 Oxford J Legal Stud 60.

In *Walsh v Lonsdale*, the court treated the tenant and the landlord *as if* they had executed the lease. Does this mean that an agreement for a lease is always as good as a lease? Recall that an agreement will create equitable proprietary interests only if it is a valid contract with terms that are sufficiently certain such that specific performance is available. In addition, in some cases, an equitable remedy may be denied if the plaintiff is guilty of conduct that makes an equitable remedy inappropriate. For example, in *Cornish v Brook Green Laundry Ltd*, [1959] 1 QB 394 (CA), the English Court of Appeal refused to recognize an equitable interest where the tenant had failed to carry out repairs that were required, pursuant to the agreement, to be completed before the formal lease was executed. Finally, as illustrated above, recall that an equitable interest may be defeated by a bona fide purchaser for value without notice.

D. Equity and Part Performance: Beyond the Statute of Frauds

The equitable doctrine of part performance may make enforceable a contract for the sale of land even if the contract does not meet the requirements of s 4 of the *Statute of Frauds*. The doctrine arose after it became apparent that the Statute itself might be used as an "instrument of fraud":

> A party contractually obligated to sell or buy land could avoid the obligation by pleading that the contract was merely oral. … To meet the contract problem, courts of equity fashioned the doctrine of part performance as an alternative means of proving a contract, and for well over a century this doctrine has mitigated much of the bad faith which pleaders of the Statute might otherwise have been able to perpetrate. Provided an act has been done which can only be explained on the basis of the alleged oral contract, then the court will overlook that there is inadequate or no written evidence of the contract.

(Waters at 272.)

What kinds of situations might require the intervention of equity? Consider, for example, a situation in which a vendor makes an oral agreement with a purchaser to sell a parcel of land and, before the execution of the deed, the purchaser pays for improvements to the parcel. In doing so, the purchaser has relied on the vendor's oral promise and has enriched the vendor. If the vendor subsequently refuses to execute a deed, relying on the *Statute of Frauds*, on what basis can the purchaser claim that equity should intervene?

The principles of part performance were fully defined in a 19th-century case, *Maddison v Alderson* (1883), 8 App Cas 467 (CA). A later case referred to *Maddison v Alderson* as having stated the principle that

> in a suit founded on part performance of a parol contract relating to land the defendant is really charged "upon the equities resulting from the acts done in execution of the contract, and not (within the meaning of the Statute) upon the contract itself." It is clear from what the learned Lord Chancellor says [in *Maddison*] that in such a case the Court is not asked to give a better remedy in aid of a legal right, based on the contract, but is called upon to enforce an equity (independent of the Statute …) which has arisen by force of circumstances subsequent to the contract itself, namely by acts of part performance sufficient to attract the equitable jurisdiction of the Court. … [The] proper course in such a proceeding is that of "seeking to establish primarily such a performance as must necessarily imply the existence of the contract, and then proceeding to ascertain its terms." … No harm can arise from reversing that order as a matter of convenience in taking evidence, … [b]ut if the terms of the oral bargain are first ascertained and then the alleged acts of part performance are judged of merely by their consistency with and applicability to that bargain, grievous error may result.

(*McBride v Sandland* (1918), 25 CLR 69 at 77.)

Note that the principle of part performance is primarily based on the inequity arising out of the plaintiff's reliance on an oral promise and it is necessary, as a matter of evidence, to show the reliance first and then the existence of the terms of the promise that resulted in the plaintiff's actions.

The Supreme Court of Canada considered the elements of part performance in *Deglman v Guaranty Trust Co of Canada*, [1954] SCR 725 (indexed as *Deglman v Brunet Estate*). Quoting from *Maddison v Alderson*, Cartwright J stated (at 734) that "the part performance relied upon must be unequivocally referable to the contract asserted. The acts performed must speak for themselves, and must point unmistakably to a contract affecting the ownership or the tenure of the land and to nothing else." These principles were reconsidered in *Taylor v Rawana* (1990), 74 OR (2d) 357 (H Ct J). In *Taylor*, the plaintiff applied for a declaration of an interest in land owned by the defendants, stating that the defendant had agreed to sell the land to the plaintiff for $56,000 with a downpayment of 10 percent payable over two years. The plaintiff moved in and undertook repairs to the building and surrounding land. Although the plaintiff claimed that the defendant had signed an agreement incorporating these terms, he said that the defendant had retained the only copy of the agreement. The defendant stated that the plaintiff was only a tenant and that, while there had been some discussions about a sale, the price was higher and the time frame for submitting the downpayment was only six months. The defendant was a friend of the parents of the plaintiff.

In examining the evidence, the court found (at 359-60) that the plaintiff was more credible than the defendant. The judge also found that an agreement existed and that there were numerous actions on the part of the plaintiff that constituted "performance" of the agreement. The court held (at 362-64) that the situation in *Taylor* clearly satisfied the principles established in *Deglman*. As a result, the court in *Taylor* ordered a sale to the plaintiff at the price of $56,000.

In examining the case that follows, consider how the evidence of part performance was presented by the plaintiff and the extent to which the emphasis in the reasoning focuses on evidence of an agreement or on the inequity resulting from the plaintiff's reliance. Which approach is more consistent with the principles of part performance?

Starlite Variety Stores Ltd v Cloverlawn Investments Ltd
(1979), 92 DLR (3d) 270 (Ont H Ct J), aff'd 106 DLR (3d) 384 (Ont CA)

STARK J: This is an action for specific performance of a contract, or in the alternative for damages for breach of an agreement, brought by the plaintiff, called herein Starlite, against the defendant, referred to herein as Cloverlawn. The action against Mac's Convenience Stores Limited was discontinued.

Starlite is the operator of a chain of small variety stores, chiefly in Windsor and London, Ontario. It selects sites which are commercially suitable, leases the location, and then sublets the property on a franchise basis, to a tenant who uses the name and the goodwill, and the buying power of Starlite, in return paying to Starlite a royalty on gross sales, usually 2%. The tenants are known as franchisees.

The defendant Cloverlawn is a private company, which buys commercial land, builds shopping plazas, rents the stores in the plazas, and if required provides financing.

Among the plazas owned and operated by Cloverlawn was one situated at the corner of Grand Marais and Longfellow, in the City of Windsor. About 6,000 sq. ft. of this property was available for expansion and Cloverlawn decided to use this space if suitable franchisees could be obtained. Cloverlawn had frequently used the services of James Morrow, a well-known real estate salesman in Windsor, who had found commercial locations and franchisees for them, from time to time. Morrow was entrusted with a master key to all the plazas, checked on stores, sometimes collected rents, and investigated complaints. It was Morrow who in 1974 acted on the purchase by Cloverlawn of the land used by this plaza. Three years later, Morrow suggested that Cloverlawn build an addition to their plaza. Morrow found that a free-standing building of some 6,000 sq. ft. could be erected. The area was considered desirable, since it is surrounded by an upper middle class population and available commercial property was extremely limited.

Cloverlawn decided to proceed with the expansion. However, Cloverlawn told Morrow they would not commence construction until a certain 1,800-sq. ft. area adjacent to a sporting goods store in the new section had been leased.

These events occurred in the spring of 1977. In April of that year, Morrow approached Ray Myers, brother of Don Myers, who was the sole owner of Starlite. Ray Myers was the operation manager of his brother's company, and his duties consisted of general store supervision, promotion, office management and similar functions. Ray expressed great interest in the proposed location and told Morrow a suitable franchisee would have to be found. While the search for the franchisee was being conducted by Ray, Morrow suggested that his own wife would be qualified. Mrs. Morrow had at one time operated a Mac's variety store. The proposal was accepted.

In view of Morrow's close relationship with Cloverlawn, and in view of his own personal involvement through his wife, it was agreed that Morrow would do the negotiating with Cloverlawn's representative, Frank D'Amico, as to rent and terms. According to the evidence of Ray Myers and Morrow, which appears to have been grudgingly accepted by D'Amico in his evidence, a draft agreement on Cloverlawn's standard agreement to lease forms was drawn up, embodying the verbal terms they had discussed and presented to Morrow by D'Amico. The two men then went to Ray Myers' office. It was at this meeting that, according to Morrow, "Frank shook hands with Ray and said 'you've got a deal.' Then we had a liquid lunch." The agreement was then forwarded to Don Myers, for execution by Starlite, and was returned to the defendant with a deposit cheque as required by the agreement. The offer to lease agreement, ex. 1, was retained but was never executed by Cloverlawn.

During the course of the trial, considerable criticism was directed to Morrow, on the ground that his dealings constituted a conflict of interests. But I consider this criticism unjustified. His personal interest in the deal, through his wife, was well known to all concerned. He wanted to obtain the best arrangements he could for Starlite and for his wife, and since he would not be entitled to a real estate agent's fee, he asked for an equivalent amount by way of reduction from the rent, and this was accepted. It was evident that Cloverlawn was anxious to retain Morrow's goodwill, in view of the many services he had rendered in the past.

Construction on the addition to the plaza was now commenced. A well-known builder, one John Drazic, was asked to tender and in due course his bid was accepted. Construction began early in June of 1977. The store to be occupied by Starlite was designated on the plans as store no. 3. On August 16th, Ray Myers produced a sketch, known as a vellum drawing, which in effect provided for changes in the store front and in the location of certain electric conduits. These changes were made. Other changes were later requested. Drazic contacted Bairstow, an employee of Cloverlawn's who was supervising construction, and he gave verbal approval of the changes, and this approval was later confirmed in writing by Drazic, although Bairstow's letter of acceptance did not arrive until September 27th. The witness Drazic, whose records were very complete, testified that at all times he was given the impression from Bairstow and from other Cloverlawn employees that the tenant of store no. 3 was to be Starlite. The cost of the last-mentioned changes was $851.50. Certain additional changes had been requested but were refused by Cloverlawn.

Throughout the construction period, Starlite was busily engaged in preparing for the occupancy of the new store. They attended at the site and selected their colours. Ray Myers was at the location constantly, observing and pressing for progress. On June 16th, Starlite ordered their new advertising signs for the store, at a price of $1,540.80. On August 15th, Starlite ordered shelving for the new store at a cost of $3,697.74.

Viewing the evidence as a whole, it seems clear that the various managers of departments at Cloverlawn, acted on the understanding that a deal had been completed, with the single exception of Cloverlawn's president, Kenneth McGowen. Thus, Bairstow, the property manager, authorized structural changes. D'Amico was Cloverlawn's representative who negotiated the deal, just as he had previously negotiated deals on behalf of his company. I accept the evidence of Morrow and Myers that no suggestion was ever made to either of them that the deal as negotiated with D'Amico was conditional upon formal execution by the company.

The president of Cloverlawn, McGowen, admitted that on August 25th he accepted a better rental offer which he received from Mac's Convenience Stores Limited. He contended that his delay in formal acceptance of the Starlite deal was because of his dissatisfaction with Don Myers' handling of certain rental arrears on another property, leased by another company owned by Myers. McGowen said that he instructed D'Amico to get that settled and then he would consider the proposed lease. He also wanted Myers to take over a certain vacant store in another plaza. Nevertheless, he admitted that he authorized Bairstow to make the specific changes requested by Starlite which I have earlier described. He had also approved of the inclusion of air conditioning for store no. 3, a feature not ordinarily provided for tenants except when specially negotiated. Moreover, it also appeared from the evidence that one of McGowen's senior officers had already approved of a settlement of the rental arrears which had loomed large in persuading McGowen to delay his acceptance of the disputed deal. McGowen admitted his knowledge of the franchise deal with Mrs. Morrow. He said he felt sorry for Morrow but had no regrets for Starlite.

Two defences are raised by Cloverlawn. The first is that no agreement was ever reached between the parties, because the offer to lease was never formally accepted. The second defence is reliance on the *Statute of Frauds*, RSO 1970, c. 444.

In my view, a verbal agreement was in fact reached between the three men, Morrow, D'Amico and Ray Myers, subsequently accepted by Don Myers. The draft memorandum on Cloverlawn's standard forms, embodied certainly the principal points of agreement; and D'Amico's acting as representative of the defendant company never suggested that any formal or different kind of acceptance would be required. The conduct of all parties throughout was consistent with the completion of the deal and inconsistent with an unaccepted unilateral offer. I therefore reject that defence.

I turn now to the alleged failure to comply with the *Statute of Frauds*. Section 4 reads as follows:

4. No action shall be brought whereby to charge any executor or administrator upon any special promise to answer damages out of his own estate, or whereby to charge any person upon any special promise to answer for the debt, default or miscarriage of any other person, or to charge any person upon any agreement made upon consideration of marriage, or upon any contract or sale of lands, tenements or hereditaments, or any interest in or concerning them, or upon any agreement that is not to be performed within the space of one year from the making thereof, unless the agreement upon which the action is brought, or some memorandum or note thereof is in writing and signed by the party to be charged therewith or some person thereunto by him lawfully authorized.

To the defendants' reliance on this section, the plaintiff contends that in the case at bar, there is an oral agreement, that ex. 1 contains the terms of the oral agreement, and that the document does not require an actual signature. It is argued that the word "signature" in the statute has been very loosely interpreted. Thus, in 1862, Blackburn J, in *Durrell v. Evans* (1862), 1 H & C 174 at p. 191, 158 ER 848, said:

If the matter were *res integra*, I should doubt whether a name printed or written at the head of a bill of parcels was such a signature as the statute contemplated; but it is now too late to discuss that question. If the name of the party to be charged is printed or written on a document, intended to be a memorandum of the contract, either by himself or his authorized agent, it is his signature, whether it is at the beginning, or middle, or foot of the document.

Again, in the English case of *Leeman v. Stocks*, [1951] 1 Ch. 941, there is provided a more modern example of flexible interpretation. In that case the defendant had instructed an auctioneer to offer his house for sale. Before the sale the auctioneer partially filled in a printed form or agreement of sale by inserting the tenant's name as vendor, and the date fixed for completion. The plaintiff was the highest bidder, and after the sale the auctioneer inserted in the form the plaintiff's name as purchaser, the price and a description of the premises. The plaintiff signed the form. The defendant then refused to carry out the contract and the plaintiff sued for specific performance. The defendant pleaded failure to satisfy s. 40(1) of the *Law of Property Act, 1925* [the equivalent of s 4 of the *Statute of Frauds*] and in particular that he had never signed any document. It was held that there was a sufficient memorandum to satisfy the statute and that the defendant was liable. It was true that he had not "signed" it in the ordinary sense of the word. But his agent, acting with his authority, had inserted his name as vendor into the printed form, and this form was clearly designed to constitute the final written record of the contract made between the parties. However, I am not satisfied that the law in Ontario has gone this far. I therefore do not choose to base my decision on this argument.

The plaintiff contends further, that whether there was a verbal acceptance of the deal or not, there was an acceptance by conduct, by the alterations of the plans to suit the plaintiff's needs, by a continuing series of acts and of acquiescences to such an extent that any reasonable man would consider the deal accepted. The plaintiff points to the decision of the Manitoba Court of Appeal in *Greenberg v. Manitoba Hudson-Essex Ltd.*, [1934] 1 WWR 790, where it was held that if a person to whom an offer is made so conducts himself that a reasonable man would believe that he is accepting that offer, and the offeror acts upon that belief, the offeree will be held to have accepted the offer and therefore to have contracted on the terms proposed. However, that case dealt with the sale of an automobile, and does not in my view afford a sufficient answer to the defence raised by the *Statute of Frauds*, where the selling or leasing of real estate is concerned.

Finally, there is the doctrine of part performance. The essential elements required to establish the part performance which will exclude the statute are listed in 8 Hals., 3d ed., p. 110, para. 190, as follows:

> ... (1) the acts of part performance must be such as not only to be referable to a contract such as that alleged, but to be referable to no other title; (2) they must be such as to render it a fraud in the defendant to take advantage of the contract not being in writing; (3) the contract to which they refer must be such as in its own nature is enforceable by the court; (4) there must be proper parol evidence of the contract which is let in by the acts of part performance.
>
> The part performance, in order to take the case out of the operation of the statute, must be by the person seeking to enforce the parol agreement.

The leading Canadian authority is the decision of the Supreme Court of Canada in *Deglman v. Guaranty Trust Co. of Canada et al.*, [1954] SCR 725, [1954] 3 DLR 785, where the above principles are followed. That case made it clear that the mere payment of money, as occurred in the case at bar in the payment of the two deposit cheques, will not qualify as part performance. In view of the recent English decision in *Steadman v. Steadman*, [1974] 2 All ER 977, a case which reached the House of Lords, that may no longer be the fixed rule in England; and it seems logical that money clearly referable to the specific contract should no longer be treated as equivocal. However, I am bound by the *Deglman* decision.

As I have indicated there are acts of part performance on the part of Starlite which, in my view, meet the requirements of the common law so as to relieve the burden imposed by the *Statute of Frauds*. The preparation by the plaintiff of the plans to meet its peculiar requirements, the conduct of the plaintiff throughout the whole period of construction, the actions by the plaintiff in the preparation of its advertising signs and the shelving for its products, and the payment of various expenses concerned with these matters, all these are acts of part performance which meet the law's requirements. Accordingly, I hold that the agreement to lease is enforceable, and that the defendant breached the agreement, and that the plaintiff is entitled to damages in lieu of specific performance, which latter remedy is no longer available.

The matter of damages in a case of this kind is one which raises great difficulties. The plaintiff produced figures to show the revenue it receives from various other franchised stores in Windsor. This revenue in each case is based on 2% of the gross sales. The figures filed vary in amount from an annual volume of $5`76,000 to a low of $240,000. Thus, even if the low figure of $240,000 were accepted an annual income of about $5,000 continuing for the lease term of 10 years, would result in a claim for lost income of some $50,000. But there are many important contingencies before such a figure could be accepted. It was admitted that not all franchise stores succeed. Some fail in their attempts. The success of any new store is unpredictable. Much depends on the initiative and capabilities of the franchisee. Much depends on population changes and traffic conditions. Allowance must be made for expenses incurred by Starlite in the collection of its royalties and in the supervision of its franchises. It would be unrealistic not to discount any suggested figures by at least 50%.

One possible measure of the value to Starlite of the loss of the deal, is provided by the higher rental figures which Mac's Convenience Stores Limited undertook in their lease to pay. Exhibit 1 indicates that the total rent to be paid by Starlite for the 10-year period is $110,700. But the rent called for in Mac's Convenience Stores Limited lease, ex. 20, for the 10-year period is fixed at $126,000. Thus, it might be argued that Starlite, by the loss of its contract, has forfeited a property which was worth $16,000 more, over the 10-year period than they were required to pay under their agreement.

Under the above circumstances, and since in my view the plaintiff is clearly entitled to some relief by way of damages, even though those damages are ephemeral and difficult to determine, I would fix the amount to which the plaintiff is entitled for breach of contract at $20,000, as being a not unreasonable estimate of the damages he has suffered. The deposit payments of $790 should be returned to the plaintiff. I do not allow interest on that amount. Judgment for the plaintiff therefore should issue in the sum of $20,790 plus the costs of this action.

Judgment for plaintiff.

DISCUSSION NOTES

i. The Principles of Part Performance

In *Starlite*, the court concluded that all the elements were present for the application of part performance. Note that the first requirement is that the performance must be referable to the alleged contract. This requirement means that the court must be satisfied that the basic terms of the agreement can be determined with sufficient precision to enforce the parties' agreement. Evidence of reliance alone is not sufficient; there must be an agreement with identifiable terms to which the acts of reliance are referable. In *Britain v Rossiter* (1879), 11 QBD 123 (CA), it was held that the doctrine of part performance applies only to contracts in respect of which specific performance can be ordered. Similarly, in *Taylor v Rawana* (1990), 74 OR (2d) 357 (H Ct J), discussed above (section III.D, just before *Starlite*), the court noted (at 362) that it is necessary to find "acts done in performance" of a contract, and that "acts done in preparation" are not sufficient. The court suggested that "acts done in preparation" might include instructing a surveyor to prepare a valuation or a solicitor to prepare a conveyance. What acts on the part of Starlite did the court rely on to conclude that there were acts of part performance? Examine these actions carefully—were all of them "acts of part performance"? Are there any acts that might better be characterized as "acts of preparation"?

In *Starlite*, the court considered a number of arguments submitted by the plaintiff in response to the defendant's reliance on the *Statute of Frauds*—for example, that the requirements of the Statute had been met by the signature of the defendant company. Why was this argument rejected?

ii. Acts of Part Performance and the Payment of Money

As the court explained in *Starlite*, in *Deglman*, the Supreme Court held that the mere payment of money does not qualify as part performance. As well, quoting again from *Maddison v Alderson*, the court stated (at 733) that acts of part performance must be "unequivocally, and in their own nature, referable to some such agreement as that alleged." By contrast, the decision of the English House of Lords in *Steadman v Steadman*, [1974] 2 All ER 977 (HL) suggested (at 982) that it is sufficient for the acts of part performance to point, on a balance of probabilities, to *some* contract that is consistent with the alleged contract. The *Steadman* decision also indicated that, taking into account all the circumstances of a case, the payment of money might in itself amount to part performance under the doctrine. In *Starlite*, the court stated that it was bound by the *Deglman* decision. Can you identify the acts that were "unequivocally referable" to the agreement alleged by the plaintiff? What actions, in addition to the payment of money by the plaintiff, were relied on as sufficient acts of part performance?

The different approaches of *Deglman* and *Steadman* were considered in *Alvi v Lal* (1990), 13 RPR (2d) 302 (Ont H Ct J). The plaintiff brought an application for summary judgment in relation to an alleged oral trust arrangement in respect of land, relying on the payment of a deposit as part performance. In dismissing the application for summary judgment, the court reviewed the principles for establishing part performance, noting (at 312) that "the narrower view … has won repeated support of the Supreme Court of Canada," and citing *Deglman*; *McNeil v Corbett* (1907), 39 SCR 608; *Brownscombe v Public Trustee (Administrator of Vercamert Estate)*, [1969] SCR 658; and *Thompson v Guaranty Trust Co*, [1974] SCR 1023 (indexed as *Thompson v Copithorne Estate*). However, the court in *Alvi v Lal* also stated (at 313) that there were no known Canadian cases "specifically disapproving the more liberal English decision" and identified some cases (including *Starlite*) that favoured the approach in *Steadman*, including *Severin v Vroom* (1977), 15 OR (2d) 636 (CA), which referred to *Steadman* without expressing either concurrence or disapproval. The court concluded (at 313), however, that "[w]hatever may be the current judicial trend, it seems clear that until the Supreme Court of Canada accepts *Steadman*, the payment of money cannot constitute part performance of a contract involving land."

In *Neighbourhoods of Cornell Inc v 14401066 Ontario Inc*, 2003 CanLII 39477, (2003), 11 RPR (4th) 294 (Ont Sup Ct J), the court had another occasion to consider the different approaches of *Deglman* and *Steadman*. In this case, the court was urged to adopt the more liberal approach in *Steadman*, but declined:

> [69] As I stated in *Hunter v. Baluke* (1998), 42 OR (3d) 553 (Gen. Div.), I believe that I am bound by *Deglman* which clearly adopted the rule formulated in *Maddison v. Alderson* (1883), 8 App. Cas. 467. This rule requires that a plaintiff who relies on part performance to take an oral agreement respecting land out of the operation of the *Statute of Frauds* must show that the acts by themselves unequivocally refer to a dealing with land of the kind which is alleged to be the subject matter of the agreement sued upon. Notwithstanding the apparent trend in other provinces, the courts in Ontario appear to have consistently considered themselves bound by *Deglman*. See *Starlite* … , *Alvi v. Lal* (1990), 13 RPR (2d) 302 (H Ct J).
>
> [70] Even if *Deglman* did not bind me, I believe it would be unwise to relax the requirements of part performance in so far as agreements for the purchase and sale of land are concerned. I note that in 1989, the English legislation comparable to s. 4 of the *Statute of Frauds* was amended to require contracts in regard to the sale or disposition of interests in land to be made in writing: see s. 2 of the *Law of Property (Miscellaneous Provisions) Act 1989*. Thus the failure to have an agreement in writing goes to the question of validity rather than mere enforceability. The view has been expressed that as a result of this amendment the doctrine of part performance has been made inapplicable. See I.C.F. Spry, *The Principles of Equitable Remedies: Specific Performance, Injunctions, Rectification and Equitable Damages*, 6th ed. (Toronto: Carswell, 2001) at 250. It seems

to me that this is a salutary development that is likely to lead to greater certainty in this murky area of the law and a reduction in lengthy and expensive litigation.

Note that the court suggests not only that part performance should be read narrowly but that it might be a positive development if the doctrine of part performance were effectively eliminated so far as agreements for the purchase and sale of land are concerned. Do you agree? What concerns are reflected in such an approach? Are these concerns the same as those that resulted in the enactment of the *Statute of Frauds*? Does the approach in *Deglman* and the Canadian cases that follow it reflect a need to limit equitable intervention in the context of legislative action such as the *Statute of Frauds*? On the other hand, can the approach in *Steadman* also be justified as a balance between equitable intervention and legislative action? How? Which of these approaches is preferable?

Neighbourhoods of Cornell was appealed to the Ontario Court of Appeal (2004), 187 OAC 218, [2004] OJ no 2350, but the appeal was dismissed, leave to appeal to the Supreme Court of Canada denied, [2004] SCCA no 390.

iii. The Principles in Context: Hollett v Hollett

Consider the following situation. The defendant purchased several acres of land in 1965. He subsequently agreed verbally with the plaintiff, his brother, that the plaintiff could have one half of this land in order to construct a home; in return, the plaintiff would pay the defendant one half of the 1965 purchase price. The plaintiff made the payments by four installments throughout 1965 and 1966, and for each of these payments the defendant provided the plaintiff with a written receipt that stated, "For payment on land." The defendant, however, refused to issue a bill of sale to the plaintiff, contending that the plaintiff was not entitled to it until he built the home that had been agreed on. The plaintiff had started construction of the home, but had abandoned it, stating that he was concerned about not having proper title to the land. There was also evidence that the plaintiff's wife preferred to live closer to her family in another community. Twenty years later, in 1986, when the defendant planned to sell the land, the plaintiff brought an application for a declaration that he was entitled to a one-half interest in the land. Should the plaintiff succeed? Was there compliance with the *Statute of Frauds* in this case? In the alternative, can the plaintiff succeed on the basis of the principles of part performance in *Deglman*? Does it matter whether the court adopts the principles of *Deglman* or *Steadman*? Why?

In *Hollett v Hollett* (1993), 106 Nfld & PEIR 271, 31 RPR (2d) 251 (Nfld SC (TD)), the court concluded (at 282) that there was compliance with the writing requirement pursuant to the *Statute of Frauds*, noting that the four receipts

> establish the parties to the contract, the total consideration and the subject matter of the contract. All that is required is an identification of the material terms of parties, price and property. The only question here is whether or not the phrase "for payment on land" adequately describes the subject matter. In my view, the phrase implies a purchase; if the payment was for rental or usage, it is likely that in common parlance, a word such as rent would be used.

The court also considered the plaintiff's alternative argument that there were sufficient acts of part performance, stating (at 263) that it "is an open question as to whether the *Steadman* approach is the law in Canada," and citing the decisions of the Supreme Court of Canada, all of which were decided before the House of Lords decision in *Steadman*. The court also referred to Joseph T Robertson, *Discussion Paper on the Statute of Frauds, 1677* (St John's: Newfoundland Law Reform Commission, 1991), which (at 22) suggested that the Supreme Court's decision in *Thompson v Guaranty Trust Co of Canada*, [1974] SCR 1023, actually "applied a more liberal test while enunciating the stricter one." Noting that the *Steadman* approach had been adopted by a number of decisions in Newfoundland (including *Jenkins v Strickland* (1990), 10 RPR (2d) 17 (Nfld SC (TD)), the court concluded that it was appropriate to apply *Steadman* in the absence of any post-*Steadman* decision of the Supreme Court of Canada. The court continued (at 280 and 283):

> This case in many ways typifies the informal arrangements which frequently are involved in land holding in rural Newfoundland. It seems to me that a court ought to be sensitive to the fact that land holding, from a practical point of view, is often based upon arrangements which do not fit neatly into formal legal categories. If courts take too formalistic an approach to the application of property law concepts in such circumstances, the result may be the frustration of normal social expectations. ...
>
> Here, we have the acts of the payment of the purchase price which was acknowledged by the Defendant "for payment of land," and we also have the acts of the Plaintiff in entering on the property and commencing, with the concurrence and assistance of the Defendant, the excavation of a house basement. Neither of these acts would, in my opinion, satisfy the "unequivocally referable" test of *Maddison v. Alderson* [(1883), 8 App Cas 467 (CA), adopted by the Supreme Court of Canada in *Deglman*]. Even the construction of a basement on the property would not be unequivocally referable to the purchase of property because, in rural Newfoundland, it is common for family members to allow other members to build houses on their property without necessarily adverting to the question of whether this amounts to a gift or transfer of property. However, on the "equally consistent" test of *Steadman*, these two acts, taken together, in my view satisfy the test.

Consider the court's comments in light of the principles in *Deglman* and *Steadman*. Is it arguable that the acts of part performance in *Hollett* were in fact sufficient to meet the *Deglman* test? To what extent are the "common practices" of the community relevant in the application of the test?

iv. Principles of Part Performance: Further Developments

In *Hill v Nova Scotia (Attorney General)*, [1997] 1 SCR 69, the Supreme Court of Canada further developed the principles of part performance. The Ontario Court of Appeal applied and clarified these principles in 2009 in *Erie Sand & Gravel Ltd v Tri-B Acres Inc*, below, and also had occasion to refer to other aspects of the law of specific performance.

Erie Sand and Gravel Limited v Tri-B Acres Inc
2009 ONCA 709 (CanLII) (footnotes omitted)

GILLESE JA (Cronk and Armstrong JJA concurring):

[1] Two parties agreed on certain terms relating to the purchase and sale of farmland. Did their discussions amount to an agreement or merely an "agreement to agree"? If there was an agreement, were there sufficient acts of part performance to take the agreement

outside the requirements of s. 4 of the *Statute of Frauds*, R.S.O. 1990, c. S.19? If so, was specific performance properly ordered? This appeal depends on the answers to those questions.

Overview

[2] Erie Sand and Gravel Limited ("Erie") bought land from Seres' Farms Limited
("Seres' Farms") that lay to the north of County Road 18 in the County of Essex (the
"north side property"). It wanted to buy other land that Seres' Farms owned on the south
side of that road (the "south side property"). Erie wanted the south side property because
it contained aggregate and Erie's business depended on having an adequate supply of
aggregate. Seres' Farms told Erie that it was willing to sell the south side property to it on
the same terms as it had sold the north side property.

[3] Erie knew that the south side property was subject to a right of first refusal in favour
of Tri-B Acres Inc. ("Tri-B"). It had a copy of the right of first refusal and recognized that
giving Seres' Farms an offer for the south side property could trigger its operation.

[4] Erie and Seres' Farms met to discuss the purchase and sale of the south side property. Erie told Seres' Farms that because of the right of first refusal, it wanted to have all
the terms agreed to before it gave Seres' Farms a written offer. Over the course of four
meetings, the parties agreed that Erie would buy the south side property, consisting of
54.231 acres after allowing for the severance of a 180 ft. by 200 ft. piece of property on
which the Seres' family home stood, at a price of $22,000 per acre, with a closing date of
April 11, 2003. Seres' Farms asked Erie to give it a written offer that reflected their agreement and said that Erie would get the south side property unless Tri-B matched its offer.

[5] Erie prepared an offer in accordance with the agreed-on terms and delivered it to
Seres' Farms. Seres' Farms took the offer to Tri-B and Tri-B made an offer for the property
that did not match the Erie offer. Despite Seres' Farms promise to Erie, it accepted the
Tri-B offer.

[6] Erie immediately brought an action for specific performance of the agreement it
had with Seres' Farms and filed a certificate of pending litigation over the south side
property. Seres' Farms called Tri-B about the lawsuit and Tri-B said it would take care of
it for Seres' Farms. At Tri-B's suggestion, the agreement between Seres' Farms and it for
the purchase and sale of the south side property was closed. Tri-B was then added as a
defendant in the action.

[7] By judgment dated September 3, 2008 (the "Judgment"), among other things, Tri-B
was ordered to transfer the south side property to Erie.

[8] Tri-B appeals. Seres' Farms took no part in the appeal.

[9] For the reasons that follow, I would dismiss the appeal.

Background

[10] Erie is a family corporation whose current principals are two brothers, Allan
Koop ("Allan") and Randy Koop ("Randy"). Erie employs between 40 and 50 people. It is
in the business of mining sand and stone aggregate.

[11] Erie mines in Essex County, an area scarce in aggregate supply. It is estimated
that the south side property holds 50% of the total quantity of aggregate available in Essex
County, an amount that would satisfy Erie's needs for between 5 and 10 years. If Erie is

unable to purchase the south side property, it will not be able to replace the aggregate with other aggregate. Without aggregate, Erie will be out of business.

• • •

[16] The salient part of the right of first refusal reads as follows:

> If the Vendor [Seres' Farms] receives a *bona fide* arms length Offer to Purchase the said adjoining lands which the Vendor is willing to accept, the Vendor shall provide the Purchaser [Tri-B] with a copy of the Offer to Purchase, and the Purchaser shall have five (5) banking days following receipt to purchase the property by delivering to the Vendor a signed Offer to Purchase with the same deposit, terms and conditions, which the Vendor shall accept immediately.

• • •

[25] On January 9, 2003, Erie delivered a written offer to Seres' Farms' lawyer (the "Offer"), along with a certified cheque for the entire purchase price of $1,193,082.00. The Offer provides, in part, as follows:

> The Vendor [Seres' Farms] shall, on the day of acceptance of this Offer, deliver a copy of this Offer to Tri-B Acres and this Offer is conditional upon Tri-B Acres failing to exercise its right of first refusal within five banking days of receipt of a copy of this Offer. If Tri-B Acres purchases the property by delivering to the Vendor a signed Offer to Purchase with the same deposit, terms and conditions which the Vendor has accepted then this Offer shall become null and void and the purchaser's deposit shall be returned to the purchaser [Erie] without penalty, interest or deduction.

[26] The Offer reflected the terms that Erie and Seres' Farms had agreed to over the course of their four meetings. ... It also provided that if the Offer was not accepted by 4:59 p.m. on January 10, 2003, the Offer would become null and void and the deposit returned.

[27] Seres' Farms then delivered a copy of the Offer to Tri-B (Brunato). When Frank [Seres] delivered a copy of the Offer to Brunato, he told him the Offer was acceptable and that he had to match the Offer or he would sell the property to Erie.

[28] On January 10, 2003, Tri-B prepared an offer to purchase the south side property (the "Tri-B Offer"). The Tri-B Offer is the same as the Offer in all respects except that the deposit was $25,000.00—as opposed to $1,193,082.00—and the closing date was May 1, instead of April 11. ...

[29] Despite the fact that the Tri-B Offer did not match the Offer, on January 10, 2003, Seres' Farms accepted it.

[30] Erie immediately started the present action and filed a certificate of pending litigation against the south side property. ...

The Trial Decision

[The trial judge found that various acts by Erie "unequivocally referred to and supported the alleged agreement," and hence qualified as acts of part performance. He found that the offer was a "sufficient note or memorandum" of the essential terms of the contracts, satisfying s 4 of the *Statute of Frauds*, and that the property was unique, justifying an award of specific performance.]

. . .

Was There an Agreement Between Erie and Seres' Farms?

. . .

[45] In the present case, it cannot be said that the trial judge made a palpable and overriding error in finding that as of January 8, 2003, Erie and Seres' Farms had come to an agreement. There was no suggestion by either Erie or Seres' Farms that they intended that a written document was necessary in order for a binding agreement to come into existence. ... Indeed, Seres' Farms' statement of defence admits the Agreement.

. . .

[47] ... The agreement was not simply that Seres' Farms would sell the south side property, consisting of 54.231 acres, to Erie at a price of $22,000 per acre and a closing date of April 11, 2003. The agreement was that Erie would present Seres' Farms with a written offer containing those terms and that Seres' Farms would sell the south side property to Erie on those terms, unless Tri-B validly exercised its right of first refusal. When I refer to the "Agreement" hereafter, I am referring to this broader set of obligations that Erie and Seres' Farms undertook. As will become evident below, it is important to keep in mind the full terms of the Agreement between Erie and Seres' Farms.

Were There Sufficient Acts of Part Performance to Take the Agreement Outside Section 4 of the Statute of Frauds?

[48] To be enforceable, s. 4 of the *Statute of Frauds* requires that an agreement for the sale of lands (or some note or memorandum thereof) be in writing and signed by the party to be charged. ...

[49] The purpose of s. 4 of the *Statute of Frauds* is to prevent fraudulent dealings in land based on perjured evidence. However, Equity will not allow the *Statute of Frauds* to be used as an "engine of fraud." It created the doctrine of part performance to prevent the *Statute of Frauds* from being used as a variant of the unconscionable dealing which it was designed to remedy: see *Hill v. Nova Scotia (Attorney General)*, 1997 CanLII 401 (SCC), [1997] 1 SCR 69 at para 10. The requirements in s. 4 of the *Statute of Frauds* must give way in the face of part performance because the acts of part performance fulfill the very purpose of the written document—that is, they diminish the opportunity for fraudulent dealings with land based on perjured evidence.

[50] In the present case, the trial judge found that the Offer was a "sufficient note or memorandum" to meet the writing requirement in s. 4 of the *Statute of Frauds*. However, the second requirement in s. 4—that the "party to be charged" sign the written document—was not fulfilled because Seres' Farms never signed the Offer. Accordingly, the trial judge considered whether the doctrine of part performance operated to exclude the operation of s. 4.

[51] Tri-B submits that the trial judge erred in three ways in concluding that there were sufficient acts of part performance to exclude the operation of s. 4. First, it contends that Erie has not suffered a detriment such that it would be unconscionable to allow Tri-B to set up s. 4 of the *Statute of Frauds*. Second, it says that only acts of the plaintiff (Erie) can be considered when determining whether there are sufficient acts of part performance. Consequently, it submits that the trial judge erred by considering acts of Seres'

Farms, in addition to those of Erie. Third, it argues that the acts in question are not "unequivocally referable to dealings in land" and, therefore, cannot amount to sufficient acts of part performance.

[52] As *Hill v. Nova Scotia (Attorney General)* largely resolves this ground of appeal, a full examination of that decision is warranted before addressing Tri-B's three submissions.

Hill v Nova Scotia (Attorney General)

[53] The province of Nova Scotia (the "province") wanted to build a controlled access highway. To achieve this, it expropriated land which bisected a farm belonging to Ross Hill. The issue for the courts was whether, at the time of expropriation, the province granted Mr. Hill an equitable interest in the expropriated land which permitted him to move people, cattle and equipment back and forth across the highway.

[54] At first instance, the application judge found that the province had granted Mr. Hill an equitable easement and made an order accordingly. A majority of the Nova Scotia Court of Appeal held that Mr. Hill had retained no interest in the expropriated land and set aside the order. On further appeal, the Supreme Court of Canada allowed the appeal and restored the order of the application judge.

[55] Cory J., writing for the court, found that at the time of expropriation, the province (in the guise of the Department of Transport) promised Mr. Hill that he would have access to the highway so that he could move people, equipment and cattle back and forth across it. He found that the province acted on that promise—"[t]he Department of Transport by its actions in constructing fences, gates and ramps and maintaining them over 27 years recognized and confirmed its representation that Hill had an interest in land that enabled him to move cattle and equipment across the highway."

[56] In Cory J.'s view, the actions of the province were extremely telling: "The actions of the province speak louder than any written document."

[57] Justice Cory found that Mr. Hill relied to his detriment on the province's promise because consideration for his expropriated land would have been higher had there been a need to compensate him for injurious affection. He refused to permit the province to rely on the absence of writing saying, at para. 9:

> Where the terms of an agreement have already been carried out, the danger of fraud is averted or at least greatly reduced. To borrow a phrase from the law of tort, the thing speaks for itself. In the present case, for example, it does not matter so much what was said. What is critical is what was done; and what was done was the construction and maintenance of access ramps. There is no mistaking the purpose for which those ramps were constructed: it was to allow Mr. Hill a way of reaching and crossing the highway. Accordingly, in this instance strict adherence to the literal terms of the writing requirement would not serve the purpose for which it was devised. Fraud would not be prevented; rather, the appellants [the Hill family] would be defrauded.

[58] In para. 10 of *Hill*, Cory J. explains why Equity created the doctrine of part performance. He does so by quoting the following from *Steadman v. Steadman* (1974), [1976] A.C. 536 (U.K. H.L.) at p. 558:

> [This doctrine] was evoked when, almost from the moment of passing of the *Statute of Frauds*, it was appreciated that it was being used for a variant of unconscionable dealing,

which the statute itself was designed to remedy. A party to an oral contract for the disposition of an interest in land could, despite performance of the reciprocal terms by the other party, by virtue of the statute disclaim liability for his own performance on the ground that the contract had not been in writing. Common Law was helpless. But Equity, with its purpose of vindicating good faith and with its remedies of injunction and specific performance, could deal with the situation. … Where, therefore, a party to a contract unenforceable under the *Statute of Frauds* stood by while the other party acted to his detriment in performance of his own contractual obligations, the first party would be precluded by the Court of Chancery from claiming exoneration, on the ground that the contract was unenforceable, from performance of his reciprocal obligations; and the court would, if required, decree specific performance of the contract. Equity would not, as it was put, allow the *Statute of Fraud* "to be used as an engine of fraud." This became known as the doctrine of part performance—the "part" performance being that of the party who had, to the knowledge of the other party, acted to his detriment in carrying out irremediably his own obligations (or some significant part of them) under the otherwise unenforceable contract. [Citations omitted.]

[59] After noting that Equity recognizes as done that which ought to be done, Cory J. stated that a verbal agreement which has been partly performed will be enforced.

[60] In concluding that the doctrine of part performance operated to prevent the province from relying on the writing requirement, Cory J. stated at para. 16:

As the decision of the House of Lords in *Steadman, supra*, makes clear, the very purpose of the doctrine of part performance is to avoid the inequitable operation of the *Statute of Frauds*. … The writing requirement is specifically required to give way in the face of part performance or estoppel by conduct, because the part performance or conduct fulfils the very purpose of a written document.

[61] With these principles in mind, I turn now to consider Tri-B's arguments on the sufficiency of the acts of part performance.

Is It Unconscionable to Allow Tri-B to Take the Benefit of Section 4?

[62] Tri-B's first argument is that Erie has suffered no detriment that would render it unconscionable for it (Tri-B) to set up s. 4 of the *Statute of Frauds* and retain the ensuing benefit, namely, receipt of the south side property.

[63] In my view, *Hill* is a full answer to this argument.

[64] *Hill* stands for this principle: if one party to an otherwise unenforceable agreement stands by while the other party acts to its detriment by performance of its contractual obligations, the first party will be precluded from relying on the requirements in the *Statute of Frauds* to excuse its own performance. As I will explain, application of this principle leads to the conclusion that Seres' Farms is precluded from relying on s. 4 of the *Statute of Frauds* to excuse it from performance of its obligations under the Agreement. Further, in the circumstances of this case, Tri-B cannot stand in a better position than Seres' Farms.

• • •

[66] … Erie carried out its obligations under the Agreement. …

[67] But, Seres' Farms only partly fulfilled its obligations under the Agreement. As promised, it took the Offer to Tri-B. However, it did not sell the property to Erie when Tri-B failed to match the Offer. ...

[68] I reject the suggestion that Erie suffered no detriment because it got its deposit back. That suggestion ignores reality: Erie's real detriment is loss of the south side property, which it desperately wants because it contains the aggregate Erie needs to carry on its business. ...

• • •

[70] In conclusion, Equity will intervene because it would be unconscionable for the *Statute of Frauds* to be used when Erie acted to its detriment by irremediably carrying out its obligations under the otherwise unenforceable contract. Equity devised the doctrine of part performance to remedy precisely this kind of situation—it will not stand by and allow the *Statute of Frauds* to be used as "an engine of fraud."

Is the Doctrine of Part Performance Limited to a Consideration of Acts of the Plaintiff?

[71] Tri-B says that to constitute part performance, the acts relied on must be the acts of the plaintiff alone (the "Proposition"). Based on the Proposition, Tri-B argues that the trial judge erred because he considered the acts of Seres' Farms, as well as those of Erie, in finding that there were sufficient acts of part performance to take the agreement outside of s. 4 of the *Statute of Frauds*.

[72] Again, *Hill* is a complete answer to this argument. In *Hill*, the plaintiffs were Mr. Hill's sons, the successors in title to his farmland. The respondent—that is, "the party to be charged"—was the province. In finding that the requirements of the doctrine of part performance had been met, the Supreme Court relied primarily on the acts of the province in constructing and maintaining the access ramps, rather than on acts of the plaintiffs. In fact, the only act of the plaintiffs that is referred to is Mr. Hill's reliance on the province's promise.

[73] In the present case, Seres' Farms is "the party to be charged." As such, it stands in the same position as that of the province in *Hill*. Given that the Supreme Court considered the province's acts when determining whether the doctrine of part performance had been satisfied, it cannot have been an error on the part of the trial judge to have considered the acts of Seres' Farms in addition to those of Erie, the plaintiff.

• • •

[75] In sum, it appears to me that given the decision of the Supreme Court in *Hill*, it is now settled law in Canada that the acts of both parties to an alleged oral agreement may be considered when a court is called on to determine if sufficient acts of part performance take an alleged agreement outside the operation of the *Statute of Frauds*. ...

• • •

[79] ... [I]n my view, the Proposition flows from the conflation of two distinct, albeit related, aspects of the doctrine of part performance. The first aspect is detrimental reliance which, as has been noted, requires a party to prove its acts of performance. Without detrimental reliance there can be no inequity in relying on the *Statute of Frauds*, thus, it is the first hurdle to be met. The second aspect of the doctrine, however, relates to Equity's requirement that the acts of part performance sufficiently indicate the existence of the

alleged contract such that the party alleging the agreement is permitted to adduce evidence of the oral agreement. This latter requirement is discussed in the following section. For the purpose of this discussion, it is significant to note that these two aspects of the doctrine are not synonymous. The former is a matter of substantive law based on the rationale for the doctrine of part performance, whereas the latter is primarily evidentiary in nature.

· · ·

Are the Acts of Part Performance Unequivocally Referable to Dealings in Land?

[82] Relying on *Deglman v. Guaranty Trust Co. of Canada*, 1954 CanLII 2 (SCC), [1954] S.C.R. 725, Tri-B submits that the acts of part performance, as found by the trial judge, are insufficient to take the matter outside the operation of s. 4 of the *Statute of Frauds* because they do not "unequivocally refer to dealings with [the] land under the provisions of a pre-existing oral agreement." …

[After reviewing the *Deglman* case, Justice Gillese determined the proper test:]

[88] … [A]re the acts of part performance as found by the trial judge "unequivocally referable in their own nature to some dealing with the [south side property]"?

[89] In answering this question, the first step is to determine whether the acts of part performance are connected to the land. In this regard, the conduct in the present case stands in marked contrast to that in *Deglman*, [where] the acts of performance consisted of Mr. Constantineau doing chores on two properties, driving his aunt about and doing her personal errands—those acts are not referable to any particular piece of property. [Mr Constantineau had alleged that in return for doing these favours, his aunt promised to leave a piece of property to him in her will, which she did not do.] In this case, however, each act of part performance relates directly to the south side property. The Offer recites that it is for the south side property; the deposit, on which more is said later, is tied to the Offer; and the reason that Seres' Farms took the Offer to Tri-B is the right of first refusal over the south side property. Thus, it is undeniable that each of the acts of part performance relates to the south side property. Put another way, the conduct is unequivocally referable in its own nature to the south side property.

[90] However, it is not sufficient that the conduct is unequivocally referable to the property in question; the conduct must also, in and of itself, indicate that there had been "some dealing with the land."

[91] While there are a number of cases which make reference to this requirement, little guidance can be found on the analytical approach to be taken to this aspect of the requirement. *Haskett v. O'Neil*, [1939] 4 D.L.R. 598 (Ont. C.A.) pre-dates *Deglman* but, nonetheless, provides some assistance in this regard.

[92] In *Haskett*, as in the present case, the question was whether acts of part performance took an oral agreement outside the operation of the *Statute of Frauds*. …

[93] … Robertson C.J.O., on behalf of the court, stated at p. 601:

> To determine whether or not the acts relied upon in any particular case are within this description, one must have regard to all relevant circumstances in order to determine their true character.

· · ·

It is not necessary for respondent [plaintiff] to show acts of part performance that could not by any stretch of the imagination be referred to some other title than a contract such as that alleged. I think one must have regard to the way in which reasonable people carry on their affairs and if the acts relied on are of such a character that, judged by the standards in accordance with which reasonable people commonly act, they could not be done except in part performance of a contract such as is alleged, that is sufficient part performance to avoid the operation of the statute.

[94] There is much to be said for the commonsensical approach taken in *Haskett*. Based on that but modified to reflect the less stringent *Deglman* test, in my view, the proper approach to making such a determination is this. Begin by determining the context (or the "relevant circumstances" to use *Haskett* terminology). Then consider the acts of part performance having regard to the way in which reasonable people carry on their affairs. Indeed, although not stated explicitly, based on a full reading of the trial judge's reasons, he followed such an approach.

[95] What, then, were the relevant circumstances within which the trial judge viewed the acts of part performance? Erie established that it had a copy of the right of first refusal and knew that delivery of an offer to Seres' Farms could trigger its operation. It had also established that the south side property was critical to its financial viability because it contained a large store of aggregate, there were no other available properties in Essex County with aggregate, and its financial existence depended on an adequate supply of aggregate.

[96] It is within this context that the trial judge considered the acts of part performance to determine whether to admit evidence of the oral agreement. ...

[97] I accept that delivery of an offer to purchase land, with a deposit, will not normally amount to part performance. It happens every day and is not suggestive of a preexisting agreement in respect of the land. In fact, it suggests the opposite—namely, that the offeror is hoping to be able to enter into an agreement to purchase the property. But that is not this case. In this case, to the knowledge of all, there was a right of first refusal over the property. The right of first refusal is critical because it dictated that acts be performed in a particular sequence. Further, the Offer was not in standard form and the "deposit" was not a deposit in the ordinary sense of the word as it was for the full purchase price. In these circumstances, judged by the standards on which reasonable people act, was the trial judge entitled to conclude that the conduct reflected that there had been "some dealing" in the land? In my view, it was open to the trial judge to find that the acts were referable to "some dealing with the land," such that evidence of the oral agreement was admissible for the purpose of explaining those acts.

[98] The purpose of the doctrine of part performance is to avoid the inequitable operation of s. 4 of the *Statute of Frauds*. As I have explained, Erie acted to its detriment in reliance on the Agreement. It also proved acts of part performance sufficiently referable to some dealing with the land such that it would make it inequitable for the defendants to rely on s. 4 of the *Statute of Frauds* to avoid performance. That is especially true in this case where Seres' Farms openly and repeatedly acknowledges the Agreement and it is Tri-B that seeks to invoke the *Statute of Frauds* to render the Agreement unenforceable. Accordingly, I would not give effect to this ground of appeal.

Could Tri-B Purchase the Lands on Terms Different from Those in the Offer?

[Justice Gillese dismissed this argument summarily.]

• • •

Did the Trial Judge Err in Ordering Specific Performance?

[Justice Gillese concluded that the trial judge's finding that the land was unique was "unassailable."]

• • •

Disposition

[122] I would dismiss the appeal with costs to the respondent fixed at $25,000, inclusive of disbursements and G.S.T.

Appeal dismissed.

DISCUSSION NOTE

Part Performance, Specific Performance, and Damages in Lieu of Specific Performance

Reconsider *Walsh v Lonsdale* (1882), 21 Ch D 9 (CA) in relation to the principles of part performance. Why did the tenant in that case not plead part performance? Recall that the landlord and tenant had signed a written agreement to lease and thus, even though they never executed a deed of lease, the agreement to lease satisfied s 4 of the *Statute of Frauds*. As a result, there was no need for the landlord and tenant to rely on their actions to establish part performance in order to obtain a decree of specific performance. Consider a situation in which the facts are similar to *Walsh v Lonsdale*, except that the parties have entered into their lease agreement orally. Can the landlord and tenant be held to be in a relationship *as if* they had a deed of lease?

In *South Shore Venture Capital Ltd v Haas* (1994), 131 NSR (2d) 9, [1994] NSJ no 110 (SC), the tenant took possession under an oral lease for five years. No lease was ever executed and the landlord subsequently tried to evict the tenant, arguing that (in the absence of a written lease) the tenant was merely a periodic (monthly) tenant. On this argument, the tenant would have no right to remain in the premises for five years. The tenant claimed, however, that he could rely on part performance to establish an equitable leasehold and that, applying *Walsh v Lonsdale*, he was in the same position in relation to the landlord *as if* he had a deed of lease for five years. What is the appropriate result here? The court accepted the tenant's argument, in part relying on an unexecuted draft lease prepared by the solicitor for the landlord as well as the acts of the tenant. Is this result consistent with the principles of part performance required by *Deglman* or *Steadman*?

In *Starlite*, the court concluded that there were sufficient acts of part performance to permit a decree of specific performance. Yet, the court decided to order damages in lieu of specific performance because the latter remedy was no longer available. Why was specific performance precluded? Does this conclusion suggest that there are limits on the enforceability of Starlite's equitable interest? Can you explain why Starlite's interest was not enforceable against Mac's Convenience Stores Limited?

The issues concerning assessment of damages in lieu of specific performance in this case are similar to those addressed above in the Supreme Court of Canada's decision in *Semelhago v Paramadevan*, [1996] 2 SCR 415. In *Starlite*, the plaintiff had expended funds in anticipation of its occupancy of the space in the mall, amounting to approximately $5,000 or $6,000. Should this amount be recoverable? Why? How did the court actually calculate the damages to be paid by Cloverlawn? Is it appropriate to assess damages in lieu of specific performance according to the value of the proprietary interest at issue? Recall that equity granted specific performance for contracts for the sale of land on the basis that land was unique and an award of damages was therefore inadequate. To what extent is a commercial leasehold interest in a shopping mall sufficiently unique to justify this approach? Is your view different from that expressed by Sopinka J in *Semelhago* in relation to residential subdivision property? Recall the discussion in Chapter 4 in relation to *Highway Properties Ltd v Kelly Douglas & Co Ltd*, [1971] SCR 562, and whether a commercial lease should be characterized primarily as a proprietary or contractual interest for purposes of termination remedies. Are these arguments equally relevant in relation to the assessment of damages in lieu of specific performance? See generally Paul Perell, "Common Law Damages, Specific Performance, and Equitable Compensation in an Abortive Contract for the Sale of Land: A Synopsis" (2011) 37 Advocates' Q 408.

Assessing damages in lieu of specific performance often requires considering whether the plaintiff should have acted to mitigate its damages. In *Southcott Estates Inc v Toronto Catholic District School Board*, 2012 SCC 51, [2012] 2 SCR 675, the Supreme Court of Canada considered a situation where the defendant school board had breached an agreement of purchase and sale to sell 4.78 acres of land surplus to school purposes for residential development for $3.44 million. It was a condition of the agreement that the Board obtain a severance from the Committee of Adjustments on or before the closing date, as required by relevant planning legislation, which prohibits parcels of land from being subdivided without such permission. Where a contracting party agrees to attempt to obtain the consent of a third party, the law implies a term in the contract requiring that it use its "best efforts" to do so. As Karakatsanis J summarized the trial judge's findings on this point at para 14, the Board had "breached its best efforts obligation by failing to contact relevant city staff; delaying in processing the severance application; failing to include the proposed plan of use with the severance application; submitting an improper survey; failing to seek appropriate advice; ignoring the advice of the Committee of Adjustments; proceeding with the application for severance even after being advised that it was incomplete and failing to keep Southcott informed." To the Board's argument that Southcott should have mitigated its damages by purchasing other suitable property for development purposes, Southcott replied that it was not required to mitigate because it was a single-purpose corporation incorporated solely to pursue this particular development. It admitted that it had not made any efforts to mitigate.

The trial judge found that the Board had not shown that Southcott had failed to take advantage of any reasonable opportunity to mitigate its loss. The Court of Appeal decided that the trial judge had misapplied the law: once Southcott admitted it had not made any effort to mitigate, the burden shifted to it to show that it could not have done so if it tried. The fact that Southcott's "directing mind," the Ballantry Group, had purchased and developed other lands in the area showed that mitigation was possible. The Court of Appeal found that, although the Board had breached its contract, the plaintiff was not entitled to specific performance or damages in lieu and awarded nominal damages of $1. The Supreme Court of Canada agreed with this analysis and dismissed the appeal, observing that there was no legitimate reason for exempting a single-purpose corporation from the obligation to mitigate that is incumbent on all other entities seeking damages in lieu of specific performance. Is it fair that the Board should be able to breach its contract so egregiously and not be obliged to pay damages?

Note that part performance is relevant to oral contracts relating to interests in land. Thus, even though the contract is not in writing, it must nonetheless be a contract—that is, an agreement that includes offer, acceptance, and consideration. In other words, the principles of part performance do not apply to non-bargain promises. However, even in the case of non-bargain (unilateral) promises, there are some situations in which equitable property interests can be created, some of which are illustrated in Chapter 6.

IV. A NOTE ON MORTGAGES

A. Property as Security for Loans

One of the most important rights attached to property, real or personal, is the right to create a security interest in it—that is, to use it as collateral to secure repayment of a loan. By contrast, an ordinary contract debt for, say, $100, owed by Sarah to Ramesh is an *unsecured* debt—it is not guaranteed to be repaid in full or at all. It is *property* from Ramesh's point of view, but its *value* depends on Sarah's ability to pay. If Sarah should experience insolvency, Ramesh cannot claim any particular $100 bill that Sarah may have, or assert a right to any item worth $100 in her possession. If Sarah goes bankrupt, Ramesh and all Sarah's other unsecured creditors will have to share the value of her remaining assets in proportion to their claims. If those claims are worth, for example, 10 times more than what Sarah's assets could be sold for (a not uncommon situation), then her creditors will only be able to recover 10 percent of what they were owed. Ramesh will recover only $10 from Sarah's trustee in bankruptcy for his unsecured debt.

It is thus easy to see why those loaning money would not be satisfied with a mere unsecured debt. From an early date, the common law (like most legal systems) permitted debtors to pledge particular items of property (land or personal property) to their creditors as security for loans, on the understanding that if the debtor could not repay the loan and interest in full, the creditor could seize the item and either keep it or sell it, thereby extinguishing any interest of the debtor in the property. The word "mortgage" itself comes from law French and means "dead pledge" (gage = pledge). It refers to a particular kind of security interest in land, now obsolete, whereby the income produced by the land did not go toward reducing the principal amount; see Ziff at 431. Mortgages represent yet another example where the "bundle of rights" in property is divided between two or more persons.

Modern mortgages create a security interest in a particular asset or assets of the debtor, such that in case of default the creditor can satisfy the debt out of those assets without competing with unsecured creditors. Keep in mind, though, that while having a security interest in property increases the chances of recovering the debt in case of default, it does not guarantee it. If the lender has loaned money at a time when the value of the property subject to the security is declining, the debtor may default and disappear, leaving the creditor with an asset worth less than the outstanding amount of the loan.

This chapter includes a discussion of mortgages because most sale transactions involve the necessity of a loan or mortgage on the part of the purchaser to meet the vendor's sale price. In addition, however, the law of mortgages reveals the important role played by equity in developing the modern law. In fact, the role of equity in defining the respective rights of borrowers and lenders under a mortgage is evident even in ordinary speech—for example, we use the word "equity" to describe the net value of a home. If Ramesh paid $100,000 down on a home that was worth $500,000 and borrowed the other $400,000, we would say that he has $100,000 equity in the home. If he pays off $50,000 on the loan next year, he will have $150,000 equity in the home, and so on. The word "equity" here is an abbreviation of the legal term "equity of redemption," which is the technical name for the interest that Ramesh retains in his house under a traditional mortgage.

In legal terminology, the borrower is called the "mortgagor" and the lender is called the "mortgagee." It is important to keep in mind that a mortgage involves two distinct sets of rights. First there are those arising from the contract of loan, under which the mortgagor is obliged to repay the principal amount plus interest at the agreed rate over the agreed period of time. The obligation to repay the loan with interest—often called the "covenant to repay"— is purely contractual and does not involve property law. The mortgage proper is ancillary to the contract of loan, and will only be invoked if the mortgagor goes into default or does something contrary to the mortgagee's interest, such as damaging the property in which the security interest exists. The mortgage is also a contract, but it has an impact on the proprietary relations between the parties because the mortgagor agrees that on default, the mortgagor can obtain full rights in the property in which the security interest exists or can have the property sold to satisfy the outstanding debt.

This chapter does not aim to provide a comprehensive overview of the law of mortgages. Rather, it offers a brief account of the respective rights of mortgagors and mortgagees, providing another illustration of how crucial the interaction of law and equity has been in the development of modern property law. Even with the move to modern land registration systems, which treat the mortgage as a statutory *charge* rather than a conveyance of the legal estate, and increasing statutory regulation of mortgages—e.g. the *Mortgages Act*, RSO 1990, c M.40—the substantive law of mortgages remains strongly marked by the historic dynamic between law and equity.

B. Mortgages and Economic Power

The law of mortgages also illustrates another theme of this book: the relationship between property and power. Mortgages are and always have been a highly political topic. Even in ancient times, it was obvious that the power of moneylenders to claim title to mortgaged farms during times of economic depression, when borrowers could not make their scheduled repayments, would lead to an undesirable accumulation of agricultural land in the hands of a few. Thus, in the book of Leviticus (25:24), it is ordained that "in all the land of your possession, ye shall grant a redemption for the land."

Redemption is connected to the idea of the jubilee, outlined in verse 10. After every 49 years (seven cycles of seven years), the 50th year is to be a jubilee, and "when you shall return every man unto his possession"—that is, all properties lost through foreclosure must revert to their original owners (or their heirs), in an attempt to restore a fairer distribution of land. Some scholarship suggests that this was not merely a utopian ideal but was enforced to some extent in early Middle Eastern societies: see David Graeber, *Debt: The First 5,000 Years* (Brooklyn, NY: Melville House, 2011) at 81-84.

In the 20th century, during the Depression of the 1930s and again during the recession of the 1980s, state action was required to suspend mortgagee's remedies or to rewrite mortgage agreements to provide for lengthier periods of repayment to mitigate widespread economic distress. The *Farmers' Creditors Arrangements Act, 1934*, SC 1934, c 53 allowed insolvent farmers to make proposals for restructuring their debt and provided that any proposal concurred in by the secured creditors and three-quarters of the unsecured creditors would be binding. A board of review created by the Act had the power to impose new repayment arrangements where the creditors did not concur with a farmer's proposal. Similar provisions exist today under the *Farm Debt Mediation Act*, SC 1997, c 21. The Depression also inspired Alberta legislators to prohibit mortgagees from suing an individual on the covenant to repay in a loan agreement secured by mortgage; the mortgagee is left to its remedy against the property itself (the relationship between these two remedies is considered below): see Ziff at 441 and the *Law of Property Act*, RSA 2000, c L-7, ss 44-47. More recently, when interest rates exceeded 20 percent in the early 1980s, Saskatchewan passed the *Home Owner's Protection Act*, SS 1981-82, c H-4.2, which allowed homeowners to apply to have foreclosure proceedings suspended for a year.

The role played by mortgage debt in the modern economy was highlighted in the financial "meltdown" of 2008, when the bursting of the "bubble" in the US home-financing market is thought to have played a key role in generating a global recession. A period of rising home prices had created an environment where lenders in the early 2000s encouraged consumers, including high-risk or "subprime" borrowers, to take on additional mortgage debt or to purchase homes with little or no downpayment. The financial institutions offering these mortgages then sold them to others who bundled them into investments in which shares were widely sold. These mortgages often had adjustable rates, and when interest rates climbed in 2006 many of these mortgages went into default: by late 2009 nearly 14 percent of all US mortgages were delinquent or in foreclosure (<http://www.census.gov/compendia/statab/2012/tables/12s1194.pdf>). The fact that these overvalued mortgages were now widely held as investments created a domino effect that quickly spread through world markets: see Financial Crisis Inquiry Commission, *Final Report of the National Commission on the Causes of the Financial and Economic Crisis in the United States* (Washington, DC: US GPO, 2011). Yet, while large financial institutions were "bailed out," most ordinary citizens who lost their homes were largely left to fend for themselves.

Canada was spared the worst of the recession, in part because more stringent regulation of banks and financial institutions, and their own more conservative practices, meant that there were fewer "subprime" mortgages in the Canadian home-housing market. An important player in the Canadian market is the Canadian Mortgage and Housing Corporation (CMHC), created in 1946 to increase rates of home ownership among Canadian families. CMHC encouraged banks to offer mortgages to aspiring homeowners by agreeing to insure the loan, provided the borrower met certain criteria. In this way banks could lend money on homes with little risk. Typically borrowers would have to come up with a certain percentage downpayment and the loan would have to be paid over a maximum of 25 years. By 2006 CMHC had relaxed these requirements and was insuring loans with no downpayment and 40-year amortization periods, but in the wake of the 2008 crisis it tightened up eligibility again. At present, CMHC will insure mortgages where the buyer has a downpayment of between 5 and 20 percent, provided the amortization period is no more than 25 years and the price of the home is not more than $1 million (see <http://www.cmhc.ca>). The government has intervened frequently in recent years to "tweak" these rules to prevent the emergence of a Canadian housing bubble, illustrating the importance to the Canadian economy of the residential housing market and the mortgage market that underpins it.

C. The Development of the Modern Mortgage: The Role of Equity

The evolution of the modern mortgage has been described as follows:

> [The equity of redemption] arose as a response to the strict approach to mortgages taken by the common law. Mortgages typically involved a conveyance of legal title to land to the mortgagee together with an undertaking by the latter to reconvey title to the mortgagor on a specific date on repayment of the money borrowed together with interest. If the loan was not repaid, the property was forfeited to the mortgagee. A day's delay could result in the loss of the property, even where the mortgagor had paid off most of the debt. As part of its wider concern to provide relief against unconscionable penalties and forfeitures, equity began to accept applications from mortgagors seeking to reclaim their property. Equity theorized that the conveyance of title in a mortgage transaction was merely secondary to the principal obligation, which was the repayment of the debt. If it could be shown that the mortgagor would repay the debt, even after the originally agreed deadline, equity would order a reconveyance of the property after payment. The *legal* right to redeem the mortgage would expire on the agreed-on date, but in *equity* a right of redemption would continue for a reasonable period of time, which might last many years. Finally, equity developed the decree of *foreclosure*, whereby mortgagees could apply for a declaration that the equity of redemption was at an end, leaving them with the fee simple absolute. The better security provided for borrowers greatly encouraged the improvement of estates in the 17th and 18th centuries, and the equity of redemption remains the foundation of the modern law of secured transactions in England and in Canada. [Emphasis added.]

(Philip Girard, "History and Development of Equity" in Mark R Gillen & Faye Woodman, eds, *The Law of Trusts: A Contextual Approach*, 2d ed (Toronto: Emond Montgomery, 2008) at 51-52.)

The equity of redemption eventually came to be recognized as a distinct estate in land—indeed, as "ownership" in the eyes of equity—while the mortgagee's legal estate was regarded as secondary, because it was only ancillary to the contract of loan. Even the common law eventually recognized that this was not a true legal estate, treating the mortgagee's interest not as realty, but as personal property. Thus, if a mortgagee died before the loan was repaid, the right to be repaid would descend not to the heir through primogeniture, but to the mortgagee's next of kin as personal property. The mortgagee's right was, at its highest, a right to acquire full title to the land in the future should the mortgagor default for a sufficiently long period such that equity would grant a decree of foreclosure, cutting off the mortgagor's right to redeem. Legal historians have explained this "tenderness" toward borrowers on the part of equity by pointing to their class identity: it was mainly aristocratic owners of large English estates who found themselves obliged to mortgage their lands to raise cash and the commercial classes who were doing the lending. The Court of Chancery, presided over by the lord chancellor, was reluctant to permit large estates to be lost "merely" because their owners could not repay their loans and therefore developed the plethora of protections that came to characterize the equity of redemption. In these cases it was emphasized that the court's function was to ensure that ultimately land was returned to its "rightful" (often meaning historical or traditional) owner. … It was as if it were inconceivable that an English gentleman would give up his land, save in wholly exceptional circumstances. … From this perspective, for Englishmen to bargain away their land … and for "moneylenders" and "rogues" to acquire significant landholdings, was suspect, if not downright un-English.

(D Sugarman & R Warrington, "Land Law, Citizenship, and the Invention of 'Englishness': The Strange World of the Equity of Redemption" in J Brewer & S Staves, eds, *Early Modern Conceptions of Property* (London: Routledge, 1995) at 120.)

In Canada, although the mortgage device was imported into the common law provinces, it was not, at least initially, characterized by the same lenity as found in England. In Ontario, for example, there was no Court of Chancery until 1837 and hence no court that could enforce the protections inherent in the equity of redemption. This has been explained as an attempt by the colonial elite to entrench a highly creditor-oriented mortgage regime that would be favourable to them; it was not until the rise of the movement for political reform in the 1830s that the equity of redemption and a chancery court were introduced: see John Weaver, "While Equity Slumbered: Creditor Advantage, a Capitalist Land Market, and Upper Canada's Missing Court" (1990) 28 Osgoode Hall LJ 871. Thereafter, the Ontario courts tended to follow the more lenient jurisprudence of their English counterparts, and this trend, along with statutory intervention in the 20th century, has led to a law of mortgages that is not seen (in that province at least) as unduly weighted to either the creditor or the debtor interest. In its *Report on the Law of Mortgages* (Toronto: Ministry of the Attorney General, 1987), the Ontario Law Reform Commission found (at 5) that the law did not warrant wholesale reform, but that "existing procedures offered opportunities for both delaying legitimate realization procedures and overreaching on the part of lenders"—that is, there were problems from both the mortgagor's and mortgagee's points of view. The Commission recommended (at 21) the enactment of a new Land Security Act, mainly as a tool of legal rationalization, "designed to be a complete code that would … abolish many of the legal and equitable incidents of a 'mortgage,'" but to date no such legislation has been forthcoming.

In the Maritime provinces, chancery courts existed with jurisdiction over mortgages, but their judges imported a more creditor-oriented remedy from Ireland called "foreclosure and sale" that gave the mortgagee the best of both worlds: the right to take the property if it was worth more than the debt owed, while being able also to sue the debtor for any deficiency if the property was worth less than the debt. This process has survived intact, but has been subjected to severe criticism by the Nova Scotia Law Reform Commission, *Mortgage Foreclosure and Sale: Final Report* (Halifax: Commission, 1998). On the history of mortgages in Ontario and eastern Canada, see generally Philip Girard, "Land Law, Liberalism, and the Agrarian Ideal: British North America, 1750-1920" in J McLaren, AR Buck & NE Wright, eds, *Despotic Dominion: Property Rights in British Settler Societies* (Vancouver: UBC Press, 2005) at 131-35.

D. Mortgage Remedies

The traditional remedy of the mortgagee on default was foreclosure: if a reasonable period of time elapsed after default with no prospect of repaying the amount owing, a mortgagee could apply to have the mortgagor's equity of redemption extinguished. Recall that the mortgagee already held the legal estate: extinguishment of the equity of redemption resulted in the mortgagee becoming the absolute owner in law and equity of the mortgaged property. Foreclosure might result in either over- or under-compensation of the mortgagee, but in either case no further action was possible by either party. A decree of foreclosure extinguished the debt, so that if the mortgagee in turn sold the property and received less than the amount owed on the loan, the mortgagee could not sue the mortgagor for the deficiency. If, after resale, the mortgagee received more than what had been owed on the loan, the mortgagor could not sue for an accounting and the mortgagee could keep the full proceeds. Under the traditional English approach, the mortgagee could sue on the personal covenant to repay the loan or proceed against the property itself via foreclosure, but could not do both: the mortgagee had to choose between "the money and the mud"; see generally Ziff at 439-50.

Over time, mortgagees began inserting clauses in their mortgages creating what are known as "private powers of sale," which altered the binary approach to remedies just described. The private power of sale has become almost the universal mortgage remedy in Ontario, where it has been estimated that between 90 and 99 percent of defaults are remedied in this way; see JT Roach, "The Problem of Price Adequacy in Foreclosure Sales" (1987) 66 Can Bar Rev 671 at 678, n 25. A power of sale authorizes the mortgagee, upon default, to sell the property to a third party and apply the proceeds of sale to the satisfaction of the debt. If the proceeds are in excess of the debt and the expenses of the sale, the surplus must be returned to the mortgagor (and to this end the mortgagee is deemed a trustee of the surplus). If the proceeds are insufficient to cover the debt and expenses, the mortgagee is allowed to sue for the deficiency. These are called "private" powers of sale because the sale is not conducted under the authority of the court. However, the courts exercise control over the conduct of such sales indirectly, by setting aside sales that are determined to have been conducted in a manner not calculated to obtain the best price. In *Cuckmere Brick Co Ltd v Mutual Finance Ltd*, [1971] 2 All ER 633 (CA), the English Court of Appeal recognized (at 646) that a mortgagee has a "duty to take reasonable precaution to obtain the true market value of the mortgaged property at the date on which he decides to sell it." Some Canadian courts

> have adopted the principles in the *Cuckmere Brick* case and have imposed a high duty on the
> selling mortgagee to take all reasonable steps to ensure that the best possible price is obtained,
> taking into account the fact that it is a forced sale and, further, that market conditions may not
> be favourable.

(Walter M Traub, ed, *Falconbridge on Mortgages*, 5th ed (Toronto: Thomson Reuters, 2012) at 35-25.)

As the Law Reform Commission of Nova Scotia notes, however, "[o]nly Ontario and British Columbia have developed procedures which attempt to expose the property to the market and obtain as high a price as possible": *Discussion Paper: Mortgage Foreclosure and Sale* (Halifax: Commission, 1997) at 18. In the rest of Canada, the problems identified by Roach in his 1987 article remain mostly unremedied.

DISCUSSION NOTES

i. Landlord and Tenant Board

In Chapter 4 we noted that an important trend in recent decades has been the emergence of a division between commercial and residential leases, with enhanced regulation of the latter. In Ontario, a landlord's decision to evict a residential tenant can always be subject to review, and the Landlord and Tenant Board has the discretion to set aside an eviction notice even if the statutory requirements for eviction have been demonstrated. Although there are some distinctions between commercial and residential mortgages, mainly due to the role of the CMHC, in no province is there an administrative tribunal that supervises the exercise of the mortgagee's remedies in the residential context. Why is it that the actions of residential landlords are subjected (at least potentially) to a relatively high degree of administrative supervision, while the actions of those holding mortgages on residential properties are relatively unsupervised?

ii. The Impact of Registration Statutes

The next section outlines the differences between two types of land registration statutes: the older registry of deeds model, where the registry is simply a repository of documents that purchasers must interpret, and the newer land titles model, where the state guarantees whatever is recorded on the title register and title searching is, in general, unnecessary. Under a land titles system, the mortgage is not considered a conveyance of the legal estate, but merely a "charge" on title: the mortgagor remains the registered owner and retains the legal estate. Since the enactment of the *Land Registration Reform Act, 1984*, SO 1984, c 32 (now RSO 1990, c L.4), however, a mortgage is deemed to be a charge whether registered under the *Registry Act* or the *Land Titles Act*. Nonetheless, in s 6 the statute provides for legal continuity:

> 6(1) A charge does not operate as a transfer of the legal estate in the land to the chargee.
>
> . . .
>
> (3) Despite subsection (1), a chargor and chargee are entitled to all the legal and equitable rights and remedies that would be available to them if the chargor had transferred the land to the chargee by way of mortgage, subject to a proviso for redemption.

In spite of this continuity, the reconceptualization of a mortgage as a "charge" can have an impact in other areas of law. Some of these issues are considered in more advanced courses concerning real property issues.

V. A NOTE ON PRIORITIES AND REGISTRATION

As this and other chapters demonstrate, a number of different proprietary interests can exist at the same time in the same chattel or parcel of land. Principles for establishing priority are necessary in order to resolve conflicts among a number of competing interests. Recall from Chapter 2 how priority was determined among a number of claimants of chattels, using the concept of prior possession. Principles of priority were similarly developed by courts for legal and equitable interests, usually based on the order of their creation. These principles have been successively modified by statutes that create systems for the registration of property interests and that accord priority based on the order in which documents are registered. Principles of priorities form a substantial part of the law of real estate transactions and also affect legal relationships in commercial, securities, and bankruptcy law. Thus this note provides only a short introduction to issues that can be examined in greater depth in more advanced courses.

A. Priorities at Common Law

The basic common law principle *nemo dat quod non habet*, or one cannot give what one does not have, means that (with a few special exceptions) a transferor cannot confer on a transferee a title that is greater than that held by the transferor. In property law, the transferee thus needs to ensure that the title being conveyed is the same as that which the transferor purports to be able to convey. One reason for the development of systems of registration was the need to facilitate the process of determining the validity of a transferor's title. As we explain, however, there are in fact some registration systems that confer title by registration.

Initially, in the absence of systems of registration, courts developed principles for determining priority among competing legal and equitable interests; these principles continue to be important in determining the priority among unregistered interests in some situations. Essentially, where two claimants both hold legal interests, or where two claimants both hold equitable interests, the rule is that priority is determined in accordance with the order of creation of the interests: "first in time, first in right." For example, if A conveyed a legal estate to B, and then purported to convey the same legal estate to C, B's interest took priority. This result follows from the rule that the first of two legal interests takes priority. Can the result also be explained in another way? Consider the application of the *nemo dat* rule here, for example. Note also that C's problem, at least in theory, could have been avoided if C had properly investigated A's title, an easier process where there is a system for registering property interests. As is obvious, moreover, A has been either negligent or fraudulent in conveying the same interest to two transferees, a situation that might permit recovery by C against A, but which may not affect B's priority.

Where there are two equitable claims, the principle is somewhat modified—the rule is that the prior claim prevails, but only if the equities are otherwise equal: *Rice v Rice* (1854), 61 ER 646 (Ch D). Thus, in a contest between two equitable claims, a court examines all the equities between the parties before permitting the first-created equitable claim to prevail. If, for example, the earlier equitable interest was by way of gift and the later one for value, the later one will likely prevail, because the equities here are not equal. Where a legal claim is prior to an equitable claim, the legal claim generally takes priority—that is, where the equities are equal, the law will prevail, but there may be postponement of such a legal claim if the prior claimant has engaged in inequitable conduct. See e.g. *Tyrell v Mills*, [1924] 3 WWR 387 (BC Co Ct).

We have already considered the position of a prior equitable claim and a subsequent legal claim above and in earlier chapters. The prior equitable interest is enforceable against everyone except the bona fide purchaser for value without notice. This formulation includes the idea that a claimant in equity must come with clean hands (the bona fide requirement). As well, because equity will not assist "a volunteer," the holder of the subsequent interest must be a "purchaser for value," not a donee. Some commentators have questioned whether transactions in which land is conveyed for "$1.00 and other good and valuable consideration" will be sufficient to establish that the transferee is a purchaser for value—see e.g. GV La Forest, "The History and Place of the Registry Act in New Brunswick Land Law" (1970) 20 UNBLJ 1.

The necessity to show that the transferee is "without notice" is also significant. A transferee who inspects land before purchasing it may discover the existence of other inconsistent claims if, for example, someone other than the purchaser is in possession and the resident provides clear evidence of an inconsistent interest. Such notice is characterized as actual notice of inconsistent claims. However, in addition to actual notice, a transferee may be affected by imputed or constructive notice of inconsistent claims. In general, imputed notice means notice to any agent of the transferee. More significantly, constructive notice means that a transferee will be bound by anything that should have come to his or her attention. Thus, if a transferee fails to inspect premises or fails to make full inquiries with respect to the interests of any person in possession, the transferee will be subject to any interests that would have come to his or her attention in a proper inspection. For example, if a transferee inspects the premises and discovers someone other than the transferor in possession, the transferee will be bound by a claim asserted by such a person in possession, on the basis that there was an obligation to make full inquiries—see *Hunt v Luck*, [1902] 1 Ch 428 (CA). Even though the transferee may not have received actual notice, a court may find that the transferee had constructive notice.

The issue of constructive notice shows the extent to which purchasers bear the risk of ensuring that the transferor has title to convey. Consider a situation in which an elderly woman initially transferred title to her home to her male boarder, apparently so that he could take care of it for her. Pursuant to this understanding, they agreed orally that the boarder would hold the property as trustee for her benefit. Subsequently, the male boarder transferred legal title to a purchaser. When the elderly woman discovered the conveyance to the purchaser, she brought an application to enforce her equitable interest under the oral trust agreement against the purchaser of the legal estate. The purchaser had inspected the premises prior to the transfer, and had noticed that the elderly woman was present as well as the male boarder, but the purchaser had assumed (without asking) that she was the wife of the male boarder. Did the purchaser have constructive notice of the woman's interest under the trust agreement? See *Hodgson v Marks*, [1971] Ch 892 (CA), where the court held that the woman's equitable interest was enforceable against the purchaser because the transferee, although a bona fide purchaser for value, was not without notice of the prior interest.

Does this case mean that a prospective purchaser must question everyone on the premises in case there are "hidden" interests? Should a person in the position of the woman in *Hodgson v Marks* be permitted to enforce an interest when she remained silent during the purchaser's inspection (apparently because she did not understand the situation and was unaware of her boarder's fraudulent activity)? Does this case suggest a need to require registration of equitable interests as a condition of their enforceability?

As we will see in Chapter 6, in addition to recognized equitable interests such as those of the trust beneficiary, there is another class of emerging interests called "equities" that may give rise to priority problems. In *Inwards v Baker*, [1965] 2 QB 29 (CA), for example, a father encouraged his son to build a home on land that the father owned, and the son subsequently sought to enforce a proprietary claim against his father's widow and her children, who inherited the legal estate in the land after the father's death. The court concluded that, because they were not purchasers for value, the son's prior "equity" was enforceable against them. Thus it is clear that there are some cases in which an equity will be enforced as if it were an equitable interest. However, the nature of an equity, by contrast with an equitable interest, means that an equity may not always be so enforceable.

You may want to reconsider these issues in relation to the discussion of registration systems that follows, because some interests may be rendered unenforceable unless they are registered. For a further analysis of priorities at common law, see Ziff at 459-64 and AR Everton, "Equitable Interests and 'Equities': In Search of a Pattern" (1976) 40 Conveyancer and Property Lawyer 209.

B. Registration

The history of registration systems in England began with the *Statute of Enrolments* of 1535, enacted in conjunction with the *Statute of Uses*. There were subsequent efforts to establish systems for registering title to land, but many of them applied only to designated counties or to London. Registration reforms were introduced by the *Law of Property Act 1925*, 1925 15 and 16 Geo 5, c 20, but the reform process remains ongoing. See RRA Walker, "The Genesis of Land Registration in England" (1939) 55 Law Q Rev 547; HW Wilkinson, "I Have a Dream" (1993) Conveyancer and Property Lawyer 101; Gray & Gray at 187-210.

Registration systems for land title were introduced into Canada from an early period. According to Ziff (at 467), the earliest such system was introduced in Nova Scotia by imperial ordinance in 1752, and an early statute was enacted by the Nova Scotia legislature in 1759. Ontario enacted legislation concerning land registration in the *Registry Act 1795*, 35 Geo 3, c 5. For an account of the evolution of registration in Ontario, see T Youdan, "The Length of a Title Search in Ontario" (1986) 64 Can Bar Rev 507.

In general, these early registration statutes created systems of deeds registration. A deeds registration system creates a public record and place of deposit for documents relating to the title to all parcels of land. However, the deposit of title documents in a public register does not confer any additional validity on these documents; their validity and effect on the vendor's title must be satisfied by the purchaser's careful examination. In some situations, the failure to register may diminish the enforceability of an interest against another registered interest. Thus, although registration may not affect the inherent validity of a document, failure to register it may limit its enforceability, especially against a registered interest. Deeds registration statutes define how priority will be accorded to competing documents. For examples in relation to Ontario's *Registry Act*, see MA Neave, "Conveyancing Under the Ontario Registry Act: An Analysis of the Priority Provisions and Some Suggestions for Reform" (1977) 55 Can Bar Rev 500 and J Chapman, "A Stacked Deck: Specific Performance and the Real Estate Transaction" (1994) 16:3 Advocates' Q 273. As a result of amendments to Ontario's *Registry Act* introduced in 1981, there was some uncertainty for a period of time about the precise obligations of purchasers in searching titles, particularly in relation to the length of search required. In *Fire v Longtin*, [1995] 4 SCR 3, 46 RPR (2d) 1, the Supreme Court of Canada affirmed the interpretation of these provisions set out in the earlier Court of Appeal decision— (1994), 38 RPR (2d) 1 (Ont CA). For a full discussion (and a consensus opinion on the part of several real estate lawyers), see B Bucknall et al, "Title Searching Under the Ontario Registry Act After Fire v Longtin: A Consensus Opinion" (1996) 1 RPR (3d) 173.

Deeds registration systems were introduced in Ontario and the four Atlantic provinces. By contrast, the Western provinces legislated statutory registration systems that were based on a scheme developed by Robert Torrens and introduced in the state of South Australia in 1858.

(The *Land Titles Act* system was also implemented in northern Ontario after the beginnings of European settlement there in the late 19th century and gradually extended to the southern parts of the province.) In general, a Torrens registration system provides greater simplicity and cost-effectiveness and it is distinguished from deeds registration systems because the registration of an interest in Torrens registration confers validity. Thus, as Ziff explains:

> Under Torrens the register is supposed to be everything. That means that one should (in theory anyway) be able to examine an abstract of title for a specific parcel of land and see listed there all of the interests in land that pertain to that parcel. The register is said to be a *mirror* of all rights in relation to that land. (Since a mirror actually reverses the image being reflected, I would prefer to say that the register is a photo; but mirror is well-entrenched as the metaphor.) The failure to register a property interest alters the priorities that would otherwise govern that entitlement. A person registering without proper notice of a prior interest can claim priority over it.

(Ziff at 472.)

The idea that the register is a mirror is the basis for the concept of "indefeasibility" of title in Torrens registration systems, although both statutory provisions and judicial interpretation have somewhat qualified indefeasibility of title in most jurisdictions that have adopted Torrens registration schemes. A Torrens system of registration also includes a compensation fund, available to persons whose interests are compromised as a result of errors produced by the system. As is evident, a Torrens system of registration represents significantly more public or state involvement in defining the validity of titles to land, by contrast with the private process of land transfers reflected in a deeds registration system. In the United States, the deeds registration system is still the mainstay of the real estate industry, backed up by private title insurance to cover the risks involved in conveyancing.

In recent years, there have been a number of efforts to reform registration processes. For example, representatives of the Council of Maritime Premiers and other provincial jurisdictions published a draft Model Land Recording and Registration Act for real property in 1990. See also Joint Land Titles Committee, *Renovating the Foundation: Proposals for a Model Land Recording and Registration Act for the Provinces and Territories of Canada* (Edmonton: Alberta Law Reform Institute, 1990). In Ontario, the Province of Ontario Land Registration and Information System (POLARIS) introduced a computerized system for organizing and managing data related to land holdings, and in 1991 Teranet Inc was created as a public–private partnership with the Ontario government to convert and automate the province's land registration system. As of 2011 over 99.9 percent of all parcels in Ontario have been converted to the land titles system, and electronic conveyancing is also spreading rapidly: see <http://www.teranet.ca>.

In Alberta, the *Model Land Recording and Registration Act* has been used in establishing a Métis land registry system: see C Bell, *Alberta's Métis Settlements Legislation: An Overview of Ownership and Management of Settlement Lands* (Regina: Canadian Plains Research Centre, 1994). In the Maritimes, computerization has been key in the introduction of Torrens-type systems in both New Brunswick (1981) and Nova Scotia (2001); in both provinces all sales and mortgages of real property trigger a "migration" from the *Registry Act* to the new system, and in Nova Scotia half of all parcels of land in the province have now been migrated. See generally Greg Taylor, "The Torrens System in Nova Scotia and New Brunswick" (2009) 16 Austl Prop LJ 175. It appears that, with the exception of Prince Edward Island and Newfoundland and Labrador, the Torrens system has "conquered" common law Canada and will soon replace the registry of deeds system altogether; see generally Greg Taylor, *The Law of the Land: The Advent of the Torrens System in Canada* (Toronto: University of Toronto Press for the Osgoode Society for Canadian Legal History, 2008).

With its "mirror" principle and the availability of a government-backed assurance fund, one would expect that the spread of the Torrens system in Canada would make title insurance on the American model unnecessary. Such is not the case, however; title insurance has been growing in popularity in Canada in recent decades, along with the growth in Torrens. The explanation for this apparent paradox lies in the fact that the Torrens system does not eliminate all risks inherent in conveyancing—in particular, although it guarantees the *quality* of title, it does not guarantee the *quantity* or *boundaries* of the property that was bargained for. Section 140(2) of the *Land Titles Act*, RSO 1990, c L.5 states that "[t]he description of registered land is not conclusive as to the boundaries or extent of the land." Title insurance also covers other types of risks—for example, fraud, zoning bylaw non-compliance, and lawyer negligence—that would not necessarily be covered by the government assurance fund. Title insurance can only provide compensation if these risks materialize and does not entitle the holder to specific performance.

Note that although the emphasis in this section has been on registration schemes for title to land, similar schemes exist in relation to security interests in personal property. Under provincial acts such as the *Personal Property Security Act*, RSO 1990, c P.10, electronic registries have been set up under which security interests in virtually any form of personal property may be registered and made public. In this way, those seeking to purchase or loan money on valuable forms of personal property, such as cars, can verify whether prior security interests exist.

In spite of the spread of Torrens-type land registration systems and personal property security registries, however, it remains important to understand the basic concepts examined in this chapter that concern the transfer of interests by gift and sale. As Ziff stated, "Systems of registration ... [provide] a thin procedural veneer that covers the substantive law of property. ... [The rules concerning registration] presuppose existing entitlements and seek to determine only how they stand in relation to each other." See Ziff at 457. Although a full assessment of this statement requires a more sophisticated knowledge of real estate transactions, Ziff's statement reinforces the need to understand the fundamental principles concerning creation and transfer of property interests as the basis for more sophisticated work in advanced courses.

PROBLEMS

1. Aunt Mary lived alone in her large home after the death of her husband, a concert pianist of some note. She found it distressing and sad to see her deceased husband's piano in the living room each day. When her nephew Timothy came for his weekly visit on Saturday morning, she told him of her feelings about the piano and quite spontaneously said, "I want to give you the piano. Right this minute! Take it with you." Timothy expressed his delight and appreciation for such a wonderful gift, especially because it would provide such fond memories of his uncle. He looked in the telephone book for a piano mover and then called and made arrangements to have the piano moved as soon as possible, which turned out to be the following Monday afternoon. Timothy left his aunt's home very happy and spent the rest of the weekend rearranging the furniture in his home to make room for the piano.

On Monday afternoon, Timothy and the piano movers arrived at Aunt Mary's to find the piano gone. Aunt Mary explained that she changed her mind on Sunday after talking to the minister at her church, who expressed great enthusiasm about providing a suitable "public" place for her husband's piano in the church. Thus, with her consent, church movers came and took the piano on Monday morning.

Can Timothy claim the piano from the church? Consider the legal principles applicable here—are they congruent with social conventions or moral expectations? What concerns underlie legal principles about gifts? Is this a case involving undue influence, in the light of Aunt Mary's grief?

This situation may also require an analysis of contract remedies. For example, if Timothy had paid for the piano movers in advance, using his credit card, has he suffered detrimental reliance? Should his remedy be related to the cost he incurred for the removal of the piano or to his expectation loss—the value of the piano itself? Note that these issues show the relationship between principles in property concerning gifts and those relating to remedies in contract law.

2. A widow died intestate and without any known heirs, leaving an estate valued at $1 million. During the last years of her life she suffered from a number of illnesses, but continued to live alone. Her neighbours, a husband and wife who had known her for many years, assisted her with household maintenance, shopping, laundry, and chores. Before she was taken to the hospital for the last time, the widow gave this couple keys to her safety deposit boxes, stating that they should keep the keys and, if she ever needed them, she would ask for them to be returned. The safety deposit boxes contained a collection of stamps worth about $2,000, a receipt regarding an RRSP, and a state of title certificate regarding the widow's house.

The couple visited the woman in hospital and, on the day before she died, she told them they could have everything. A lawyer, who was summoned by the hospital, prepared a will making the couple executors and beneficiaries of the woman's estate, but the woman died before signing the will.

The couple claimed entitlement to the widow's estate on the basis of *donatio mortis causa*. What was the result? See *Costiniuk v Official Administrator*, 2000 BCSC 1372 (CanLII), 34 ETR (2d) 199, aff'd *Costiniuk v Cripps Estate*, 2002 BCCA 125 (CanLII).

3. Pam Cohen signed a document entitled "Agreement to Lease" that was dated 20 February 2014. Immediately after signing the document she made arrangements to do substantial renovations to the leased property and paid nearly $20,000 to the contractor who undertook to do the work for her. Since 1 March 2014, Pam has been using the premises as a trendy hair cutting salon for men and women. However, the landlord has recently advised her that she must move out because he wants to lease the premises to another tenant. Pam Cohen is therefore seeking advice about her legal position, having regard to the renovations she completed and in light of the document she signed. The document is short. It simply states:

> Pam Cohen hereby agrees to enter into a lease with the usual covenants with Dominion Investments Ltd. The parties agree that Pam Cohen will pay rent in the amount of $2,000 per month in respect of a lease of the premises at 2019 Bath Road (Suite 2), Kingston, commencing 1 March 2014, for a period of five years.
>
> (Signed) "Pam Cohen"

If the landlord had indicated an interest in leasing the premises to another tenant after Pam had signed the agreement to lease and completed the renovations, but before she had commenced her business, what would be her legal position? Would it make any difference if the landlord had granted possession to a subsequent tenant?

4. Hillcrest Farm has been in the Jordan family since 1830. It is 150 acres in size and located near Caledon, Ontario. Jack and Helen Jordan have farmed it since Jack was a young man in the 1960s. They gradually developed a herd of dairy cattle, but over time Jack became more interested in being a cattle buyer, which was remunerative but involved a lot of travel. Fortunately, his son Gary was willing to look after the dairy herd and tend to the daily business of farming. Gary did so for some 25 years prior to 2010. He received some wages from his father, which increased over time, and also a share of the profits of the farm business, though always less than 50 percent. His sister Louanne was not interested in farming and pursued a career in Toronto.

Jack was sole owner of the farm, which he had inherited from his father. His and Helen's wills were identical: each left all their property to the other, but the survivor left all their property equally to their children. However, two years before Jack's death, Jack and Helen had a discussion with both Gary and their tax adviser about turning over the farm to Gary. Jack and Helen felt that Gary deserved the farm because of all the work he had done over the years; they would leave other financial assets to Louanne. They wanted to treat their children fairly, if not necessarily equally. Soon after this discussion, however, Jack was diagnosed with cancer. He declined rapidly. A week before he died, he signed a document transferring into Gary's name all his (Jack's) Ontario Milk Marketing Board quota (owning this quota is necessary in order to be able to sell milk in Ontario, and is a highly valuable asset). Jack died late in 2010, and Helen, who had Alzheimer's disease, died a few months later. Neither had changed their will. Gary continued to work the farm until Louanne claimed her entitlement under the will in 2012. Gary's position is that there was an agreement between him and his parents that they would leave the farm to him on their deaths in return for his running the farm until they died or ceased farming. He seeks an order for specific performance of this agreement. Advise Gary as to his chances of success.

CHAPTER REFERENCES

Appellate Arbitral Tribunal. <http://beta.images.theglobeandmail.com/archive/00218/Read_the_decision_218325a.PDF>.

Bell, C. *Alberta's Métis Settlements Legislation: An Overview of Ownership and Management of Settlement Lands* (Regina: Canadian Plains Research Centre, 1994).

Brewer, J & S Staves, eds. *Early Modern Conceptions of Property* (London: Routledge, 1995).

Brown, R. *The Law of Personal Property*, 3d ed by W Raushenbush (Chicago: Callaghan & Co, 1975).

Bucknall, B et al. "Title Searching Under the Ontario Registry Act After Fire v Longtin: A Consensus Opinion" (1996) 1 RPR (3d) 173.

Chapman, J. "A Stacked Deck: Specific Performance and the Real Estate Transaction" (1994) 16:3 Advocates' Q 273.

Clark, DH. "Will That Be Performance … Or Cash?: Semelhago v Paramadevan and the Notion of Equivalence" (1999) 37 Alta L Rev 589.

Cole, D & I Chaikin. "'A Worse Than Useless Custom': The Potlatch Law and Indian Resistance" (1992) 5:2 Western Legal History 187.

Da Silva, OV. "The Supreme Court of Canada's Lost Opportunity: Semelhago v Paramadevan" (1998) 23 Queen's LJ 475.

Everton, AR. "Equitable Interests and 'Equities': In Search of a Pattern" (1976) 40 Conveyancer and Property Lawyer 209.

Financial Crisis Inquiry Commission. *Final Report of the National Commission on the Causes of the Financial and Economic Crisis in the United States* (Washington, DC: US GPO, 2011).

Gardner, S. "Equity, Estate Contracts, and the Judicature Acts: Walsh v Lonsdale Revisited" (1987) 7 Oxford J Legal Stud 60.

Gillen, Mark R & Faye Woodman, eds. *The Law of Trusts: A Contextual Approach*, 2d ed (Toronto: Emond Montgomery, 2008).

Gillese, Eileen E & Martha Milczynski. *The Law of Trusts* (Toronto: Irwin Law, 2005).

Girard, Philip. "History and Development of Equity" in Mark R Gillen & Faye Woodman, eds, *The Law of Trusts: A Contextual Approach*, 2d ed (Toronto: Emond Montgomery, 2008).

Girard, Philip. "Land Law, Liberalism, and the Agrarian Ideal: British North America, 1750-1920" in J McLaren, AR Buck & NE Wright, eds, *Despotic Dominion: Property Rights in British Settler Societies* (Vancouver: UBC Press, 2005).

Graeber, David. *Debt: The First 5,000 Years* (Brooklyn, NY: Melville House, 2011).

Gray, Kevin J & PD Symes. *Real Property and Real People: Principles of Land Law* (London: Butterworths, 1981).

Gray, Kevin J & Susan Francis Gray. *Elements of Land Law*, 5th ed (Oxford: Oxford University Press, 2009).

Gulliver, AG & CJ Tilson. "Classification of Gratuitous Transfers" (1941) 51 Yale LJ 1.

Joint Land Titles Committee. *Renovating the Foundation: Proposals for a Model Land Recording and Registration Act for the Provinces and Territories of Canada* (Edmonton: Alberta Law Reform Institute, 1990).

La Forest, Anne Warner. *Anger and Honsberger Law of Real Property*, 3d ed (Aurora, ON: Canada Law Book, 2006).

La Forest, GV. "The History and Place of the Registry Act in New Brunswick Land Law" (1970) 20 UNBLJ 1.

Law Commission of England and Wales. *Report on "Subject to Contract" Agreements* (London: HMSO, 1975).

Loo, T. "Dan Cranmer's Potlatch: Law as Coercion, Symbol, and Rhetoric in British Columbia, 1884-1951" in T Loo & L McLean, eds, *Historical Perspectives on Law and Society in Canada* (Toronto: Copp Clark Longman, 1994) 219.

Loo, T & L McLean, eds. *Historical Perspectives on Law and Society in Canada* (Toronto: Copp Clark Longman, 1994).

McLaren, J, AR Buck & NE Wright, eds. *Despotic Dominion: Property Rights in British Settler Societies* (Vancouver: UBC Press, 2005).

Meagher, RP, JD Heydon & MJ Leeming. *Equity: Doctrines and Remedies*, 4th ed (Sydney: Butterworths, 2002).

Megarry, RE. "Note" (1965) 81 Law Q Rev 21.

Megarry, RE. "Note" (1966) 82 Law Q Rev 304.

Murphy, WT, S Roberts & T Flessas. *Understanding Property Law*, 4th ed (London: Sweet & Maxwell, 2004).

Murray, RG. "Note" (1953) 31 Can Bar Rev 935.

Neave, MA. "Conveyancing Under the Ontario Registry Act: An Analysis of the Priority Provisions and Some Suggestions for Reform" (1977) 55 Can Bar Rev 500.

Nova Scotia Law Reform Commission. *Discussion Paper: Mortgage Foreclosure and Sale* (Halifax: Commission, 1997).

Nova Scotia Law Reform Commission. *Final Report: Mortgage Foreclosure and Sale* (Halifax: Commission, 1998).

Ontario Law Reform Commission. *Report on the Law of Mortgages* (Toronto: Ministry of the Attorney General, 1987).

Perell, Paul. "Common Law Damages, Specific Performance, and Equitable Compensation in an Abortive Contract for the Sale of Land: A Synopsis" (2011) 37 Advocates' Q 408.

Perell, Paul. *Lectures in Real Estate Transactions* (Toronto: Canada Law Book, 2011).

"Property: Inter Vivos Transfers of Chattels Not in Possession of the Donor—Requirements for a Valid Gift" at (1967) 53 Iowa L Rev 243.

Rickett, CEF. "No Donatio Mortis Causa of Real Property—A Rule in Search of a Justification?" (1989) Conveyancer and Property Lawyer 184.

Roach, JT. "The Problem of Price Adequacy in Foreclosure Sales" (1987) 66 Can Bar Rev 671.

Robertson, Joseph T. *Discussion Paper on the Statute of Frauds, 1677* (St John's: Newfoundland Law Reform Commission, 1991).

Rotman, L. "Deconstructing the Constructive Trust" (1999) 37 Alta L Rev 133.

Sharpe, Robert J. *Injunctions and Specific Performance*, 4th ed (Toronto: Canada Law Book, 2012).

Sparkes, P. "Death-Bed Gifts of Land" (1992) 43:1 N Ir Legal Q 35.

Sugarman, D & R Warrington. "Land Law, Citizenship, and the Invention of 'Englishness': The Strange World of the Equity of Redemption" in J Brewer & S Staves, eds, *Early Modern Conceptions of Property* (London: Routledge, 1995).

Taylor, Greg. *The Law of the Land: The Advent of the Torrens System in Canada* (Toronto: University of Toronto Press for the Osgoode Society for Canadian Legal History, 2008).

Taylor, Greg. "The Torrens System in Nova Scotia and New Brunswick" (2009) 16 Austl Prop LJ 175.

Teranet. <http://www.teranet.ca>.

Tobias, J. "Protection, Civilization, Assimilation: An Outline History of Canada's Indian Policy" in T Loo & L McLean, eds, *Historical Perspectives on Law and Society in Canada* (Toronto: Copp Clark Longman, 1994) 290.

Traub, Walter M, ed. *Falconbridge on Mortgages*, 5th ed (Toronto: Thomson Reuters, 2012).

Walker, RRA. "The Genesis of Land Registration in England" (1939) 55 Law Q Rev 547.

Waters, DWM, MR Gillen & LD Smith. *Waters' Law of Trusts in Canada*, 4th ed (Scarborough, ON: Carswell, 2012).

Weaver, John. "While Equity Slumbered: Creditor Advantage, a Capitalist Land Market, and Upper Canada's Missing Court" (1990) 28 Osgoode Hall LJ 871.

Wilkinson, HW. "I Have a Dream" (1993) Conveyancer and Property Lawyer 101.

Youdan, T. "The Formal Requirements of a Deed" (1979) 5 BLR 71.

Youdan, T. "The Length of a Title Search in Ontario" (1986) 64 Can Bar Rev 507.

Ziff, Bruce. *Principles of Property Law*, 5th ed (Scarborough, ON: Carswell, 2010).

CHAPTER SIX

Concurrent Interests and Family Property

I. THE CONCEPT OF CONCURRENT INTERESTS

The idea of shared or concurrently held interests in property—that is, more than one person having a property interest in the same object at the same time—occurs in a number of different contexts. Historically, the idea of shared ownership was a common feature of feudal property relationships. For example, recall the use of "joint tenants" in early grants to uses (explained in Chapter 3) that enabled the grantor to achieve the objective of transferring beneficial ownership to the grantee. The grant to joint tenants to the use of the grantee represented shared or concurrently held property interests among the feoffees to uses, and was designed to meet particular needs in feudal society. Although the 21st-century context is quite different, grants to joint tenants continue to offer one way of creating shared or concurrent property interests for two or more grantees. Thus, several decades ago, it was not unusual for farm property to be devised to surviving children of a testator "in common." In *Re O'Reilly (No 2)* (1980), 111 DLR (3d) 238 (H Ct J), aff'd (1981), 33 OR (2d) 352 (CA), for example, James O'Reilly's will devised the remainder interest in a dairy farm near Hawkesbury (including livestock, tools, and a milk quota) to his nine children as a shared or concurrent interest. The subsequent litigation, discussed in Chapter 2, occurred when disputes arose among the children in relation to their respective interests as co-owners.

The idea of shared or concurrent interests in property also represents an important challenge to dominant concepts of individual ownership and "private" property. In relation to environmental protection efforts, for example, it may be argued that interests in air or water are held "in common" by everyone. Moreover, as Chapter 1 explained, the basic concept of property for First Nations people in Canada is one of communal rather than individual "ownership," and property interests are shared not only among those currently living but also with members of past and future generations. According to this conception of shared interests in land, entitlement "in common" depends on membership in the community, and these entitlements cannot be alienated as "private" property.

Bruce Ziff has drawn comparisons between this conception of shared property interests in First Nations communities in Canada and some kinds of shared "customary" rights traditionally recognized at common law. In *Wyld v Silver*, [1963] 1 Ch 243 (CA), for example, the English Court of Appeal recognized a shared, customary right of the residents of Wraysbury to hold an annual fair. As well, Lord Denning MR noted the relationship between these customary rights and the concept of shared property interests among First Nations people in *R v Secretary of State for Foreign and Commonwealth Affairs, ex parte Indian Association of Alberta*, [1982] 1 QB 892 (CA). Indeed, as Ziff explains:

> Communal sharing systems are found all over the world. Within Canada, some groups have established communal arrangements within the strictures of the common law. In Hutterite communities, for example, all property is vested in the congregation. … Moreover, there was a time, not that long ago, when vast expanses of land on the prairies were regarded as being used and enjoyed, effectively, as commons.

(Bruce Ziff, *Principles of Property Law*, 5th ed (Scarborough, ON: Carswell, 2010) [Ziff] at 370, citing IM Spry, "The Tragedy of the Loss of the Commons in Western Canada" in Ian AL Getty & Antoine S Lussier, eds, *As Long as the Sun Shines and Water Flows* (Vancouver: University of British Columbia Press, 1983) 203.) Communal land-holding arrangements among the Hutterites in Western Canada also raised questions about the scope of federal and provincial constitutional authority when provincial legislators attempted to restrict them: see *Walter v Alberta (Attorney-General)*, [1969] SCR 383; see also J McLaren, "The Canadian Doukhobors and the Land Question: Religious Communalists in a Fee-Simple World" in AR Buck, J McLaren & N Wright, eds, *Land and Freedom: Law, Property Rights, and the British Diaspora* (Aldershot, UK: Ashgate/Dartmouth, 2001) at 135.

This chapter focuses on forms of concurrent interests as they have developed at common law, and are now frequently modified by statutory reforms. At the outset, it is important to distinguish the concept of concurrent interests (sometimes called "co-ownership") from other kinds of shared property interests. For example, recall the arrangements for "successive" interests (explained in Chapter 3) such as a grant to A for life with a fee simple remainder to B. Even though both A and B receive vested interests in this example, their rights to enjoyment of an *estate in possession* are successive, not concurrent—that is, B's right to possession is postponed until the termination of A's life estate. Shared interests in property are also created, of course, in bailment and leasehold arrangements and in the relationship of a trustee and beneficiary of trust property. In the leasehold context, for example, the tenant is entitled to exclusive possession for the duration of the leasehold estate. In all of these examples, the right to possession belongs to one party to the arrangement at a time. It is not shared. By contrast with these shared interests in property, concurrent interests identify a situation in which two or more people hold property interests entitling (and requiring) them to share possession.

Because concurrent property interests require grantees to share possession, they have been created more often among family members than among strangers. In this way, a study of concurrent interests requires some examination of family property relationships, both historically and in relation to 21st-century developments. Indeed, as this chapter illustrates, statutory reforms concerning property interests held by married couples (including same-sex couples) and judicial extension of the remedy of constructive trust to unmarried couples (including same-sex couples) have significantly transformed the nature of concurrent interests for these family members. Therefore, as will be explained, traditional common law principles concerning concurrent interests are now less often applied to married couples or cohabitees (although the principles do remain relevant to spousal relationships in some contexts). However, these common law principles remain relevant for concurrent interests held by other family members—for example, James O'Reilly's children—and by unrelated co-owners. This chapter also examines constitutional law principles that have prevented application of provincial statutory reforms concerning family property to First Nations peoples on reserve lands and recent federal legislation addressing this situation.

The concept of concurrent interests in property thus demonstrates connections between common law historical roots in feudal society and modern challenges—both legislative and judicial—in relation to their roles in family property. This chapter explores the ways that social and political ideas in the 21st century shape legal principles about concurrent interests, just as feudal ideas influenced traditional common law principles. In the United States, a similar assessment of the culture of legal reforms concerning married women and property is found in Richard Chused, *Cases, Materials and Problems in Property* (New York: Matthew Bender, 1988) at 251. See also Richard Chused, "Married Women's Property Law: 1800-1850" (1983) 71 Geo LJ 1359.

II. TRADITIONAL CONCURRENT INTERESTS

Four forms of concurrent interests were traditionally recognized at common law:

1. joint tenancy,
2. tenancy in common,
3. tenancy by the entireties, and
4. co-parcenary.

Joint tenancies and tenancies in common continue today as the usual forms for holding concurrent interests, although there are significant differences between them—differences in the rights and responsibilities of grantees of concurrent interests, differences in the language used to create them, and differences in how they are defined conceptually. (Note that the use of the word "tenant" in the co-ownership context is completely unrelated to a leasehold estate.)

A. Joint Tenancies and Tenancies in Common

Several decades ago, Finlay McEwen died, devising a life estate to his wife Helen in relation to lots 5 and 18 in the town of Carleton Place, Ontario. According to his will, he devised the fee simple remainder interest in lot 5 after his wife's death to his son Robert. His will also made provision for the remainder interest in lot 18 after his wife's death, as follows:

> [T]he said lot 18, that is the property fronting on Beckwith Street is to become the property of my daughters Bertha V. McEwen and Janet I. McEwen jointly and should they decide to sell the said property each of them is to have an equal share of the proceeds of the said sale.

It was clear that the testator intended to create concurrent interests in lot 18 for his two daughters, but after Bertha's subsequent death (when she devised her one-half interest in lot 18 to her brother Robert), a dispute arose within the family about exactly what form of concurrent interests had been devised to the two sisters by Finlay McEwen's will. Did they hold their concurrent interests as joint tenants or as tenants in common?

In this fact situation, the difference between holding a concurrent interest as joint tenant or as tenant in common is highly significant. According to traditional common law principles, one important feature of a joint tenancy is an inherent "right of survivorship." However, a tenancy in common did not include such a "right of survivorship." What consequences flowed from this distinction for Bertha and Janet? In reading the case, examine the court's approach to the language used in the will and how the words affect the judge's interpretation of the concurrent interest at issue.

McEwen v Ewers and Ferguson

[1946] 3 DLR 494 (Ont H Ct J)

BARLOW J: The plaintiff's claim is for a declaration that by the will of his father Finlay McEwen, lot 18 in section D of the Town of Carleton Place, in the County of Lanark, was devised to Janet I. Ewers and Bertha V. McEwen as tenants in common and that by a devise in the last will and testament of Bertha V. McEwen he became entitled to a one-half interest in said lot 18. In the alternative the plaintiff claims that if it is found that lot 18 was left to Janet I. Ewers and Bertha V. McEwen, as joint tenants, then the defendant Janet I. Ewers is put to her election because upon the death of Bertha V. McEwen she, (Janet I. Ewers) became the sole owner of lot 18, and Bertha V. McEwen having made certain bequests to Janet I. Ewers and also having bequeathed to the plaintiff one-half of lot 18, which belonged to Janet I. Ewers, the latter must elect which she must take under the will of the late Bertha V. McEwen.

The property in question, lot 18, has been sold. Exhibit 3 is an undertaking given by the defendant Janet I. Ewers, which provides that in the event of the Court finding that there was a tenancy in common, she will pay to the plaintiff one-half of the proceeds, namely $1,456.45.

The plaintiff is a son and Janet I. Ewers (formerly Janet I. McEwen) and Bertha V. McEwen were daughters of the late Finlay McEwen.

The paragraph in question in the will of Finlay McEwen (ex. 1) is as follows:

> I give devise and bequeath all my real estate to my wife Helen F. McEwen during the time of her life, said property consisting of the west half of lots No. 5 and 18 in Section D of the Town of Carleton Place in the County of Lanark. After her death the said lot 5 is to become the property of my son Robert L. McEwen and the said lot 18, that is the property fronting on Beckwith Street is to become the property of my daughters Bertha V. McEwen and Janet I. McEwen jointly and should they decide to sell the said property each of them is to have an equal share of the proceeds of the said sale.

After the death of the life tenant, Helen F. McEwen, Bertha V. McEwen the surviving executrix of the will of Finlay McEwen, purported to convey lot 18, being the property in question, to herself and Janet I. Ewers as joint tenants. This was merely purporting to carry out what was thought to be the terms of the will.

Bertha V. McEwen by her will (ex. 2) provides as follows:

> 2. I give and bequeath to my sister Janet Isobel Ewers, one thousand dollars and to my niece Helen Ruth Ewers three hundred dollars and my piano, to my brother Robert Latimer McEwen I direct that half of the lot no. 18, that is the property fronting on Beckwith Street to be given to him or the price of the same when sold in cash.

Does the bequest of part of lot 18 in the above-quoted paragraph from the will of Finlay McEwen create a joint tenancy or a tenancy in common? The specific words that fall for interpretation are as follows: "to become the property of my daughters Bertha V. McEwen and Janet I. McEwen jointly and should they decide to sell the said property each of them is to have an equal share of the proceeds of the said sale."

Under the common law it would probably be interpreted as the creation of a joint tenancy. However, under the *Conveyancing and Law of Property Act*, RSO 1937, c. 152, s. 12 [now RSO 1990, c C.34, s 13], unless an intention sufficiently appears on the face of the will, it must be interpreted that Bertha V. McEwen and Janet I. Ewers took as tenants in common and not as joint tenants.

Counsel for the defendant Janet I. Ewers cites *Re Campbell* (1912), 7 DLR 452, 4 OWN 221, and *Re Quebec* (1929), 37 OWN 271, where the word "jointly" was held to create a joint tenancy. In the case at bar the word "jointly" does not stand alone. The testator, in my opinion, shows his intention by the words following the word "jointly," *viz.*, "should they decide to sell the said property each of them is to have an equal share of the proceeds."

It appears to me that not only does the testator not show an intention to create a joint tenancy, but in the use of the words "equal share" he shows clearly an intention to create a tenancy in common. See Theobald on Wills, 9th ed., pp. 352-3, where cases are cited to show that where the words "jointly" and "equally" have been used the Courts have held the gift a tenancy in common. Also, that where there are words of division or distribution such as "to be divided" or "equally" it creates a tenancy in common. Further, that the use of the word "share" or similar words also imports a tenancy in common.

The Court undoubtedly leans towards a tenancy in common and will prefer it where there is a doubt. See also Jarman on Wills, 7th ed., vol. 3, pp. 1768-9, to the same effect as Theobald. Jarman says: "Anything which in the slightest degree indicates an intention to divide the property must be held to abrogate the idea of a joint tenancy, and to create a tenancy in common." I am, therefore, of opinion that the words in question must be held to have created a tenancy in common. This is sufficient for the disposition of this action.

[The court also considered an alternative claim relating to the obligation of a beneficiary under a will to "elect" between alternative legal entitlements.]

Counsel for the estate of Bertha V. McEwen merely submitted his rights to the Court. As Bertha V. McEwen in her lifetime was partially responsible for causing the situation which resulted in this litigation, I am of opinion that I should make no order as to costs in so far as she is concerned.

Judgment will go for the plaintiff for $1,456.45 and costs as against the defendant Janet I. Ewers.

Judgment for plaintiff.

1. Consequential Differences: The Right of Survivorship

The right of survivorship means that when one joint tenant dies, the interest of the deceased joint tenant is extinguished. In *Wright v Gibbons* (1949), 78 CLR 313, the court reviewed the status of a joint tenancy held by three sisters, Olinda Gibbons, Ethel Rose Gibbons, and Bessie Melba Gibbons. Latham CJ described the right of survivorship for a joint tenancy as follows (at 323):

> If one joint tenant dies his interest is extinguished. He falls out, and the interest of the surviving joint tenant or joint tenants is correspondingly enlarged.

The conceptual impact of the right of survivorship was also described in D Mendes da Costa, "Co-Ownership Under Victorian Land Law" (1961) 3 Melbourne UL Rev 137 [Mendes da Costa] at 153:

> It seems ... inaccurate to speak of the interest of one joint tenant "passing" on his death to the other. Although as a practical consequence of the death, considerable benefits do accrue to the survivor in that he alone is now exclusively entitled, it appears that the interest of a joint tenant

lacks the capacity to devolve upon that joint tenant's death, and so is thereupon exhausted, neither adding to nor subtracting from the seisin of the surviving joint tenants.

According to these principles, if Finlay McEwen's will created a joint tenancy (with a right of survivorship), then at Bertha's death, her interest was extinguished and Janet's interest was correspondingly enlarged—that is, her interest became an exclusive one. Note that it is not technically appropriate to say that Bertha's interest "passed" to Janet. The major consequence of a possible right of survivorship here, however, is that Bertha's death would have terminated her interest in lot 18 and thus she would have had no interest in lot 18 that could be devised by her will. If Finlay McEwen's will created a joint tenancy for Bertha and Janet, the right of survivorship required that Janet be recognized as holding an exclusive interest upon Bertha's death, the position asserted by Janet in the litigation that took place in this case.

By contrast, if Finlay McEwen's will created a tenancy in common, instead of a joint tenancy, then there was no right of survivorship. If Bertha and Janet were tenants in common, each had a devisable one-half share (as co-owners) in lot 18, and thus Robert was entitled to half the proceeds of sale of lot 18 in accordance with Bertha's will. This was the position asserted by Robert in the litigation in 1949 after Bertha's death.

DISCUSSION NOTE

Joint Tenancy or Tenancy in Common

Because a joint tenancy includes a right of survivorship and a tenancy in common does not, a grantor of concurrent interests must choose which form of concurrent interests to create for grantees. In what kinds of circumstances would it be preferable to create a joint tenancy rather than a tenancy in common? When might a tenancy in common be preferable?

Because the effect over time of a joint tenancy will be to reduce a number of co-owners to one remaining titleholder, a joint tenancy will be preferred in situations where there are advantages to (eventually) having only one owner. Historically, the common law preferred joint tenancy because the right of survivorship worked so as to reduce (over time) the number of persons from whom feudal dues had to be collected (a position reflecting a greater interest in easily identifying the payee responsible rather than in "spreading the risk" of non-payment among several persons). More recently, joint tenancies have sometimes been preferred because they eventually make title searching less complicated because there will (eventually) be only one remaining owner registered on title. By contrast with the shares of tenants in common (each of which can be devised), the interest of each joint tenant ceases at death, so that the title ultimately is consolidated in the last surviving joint tenant prior to being devised. Such objectives led to the 1925 legislative reforms in the United Kingdom that require that any legal concurrent interests must be held in joint tenancy: see *Law of Property Act*, 1925, c 20, s 1(6). Tenancies in common continue to exist only as equitable or beneficial estates. (See KJ Gray & PD Symes, *Real Property and Real People* (London: Butterworths, 1981) [Gray & Symes] at 240-41.)

According to Gray & Symes (at 241), the common law's preference for joint tenancy (also reflected in the 1925 statutory reform) was motivated by concerns of efficiency and convenience, especially in the context of title searching. By contrast, Gray & Symes suggested that equity preferred tenancies in common:

Tenancy in common represents certainty and fairness in the property relations of co-owners. Each tenant in common holds a fixed beneficial interest immune from the caprice of survivorship. Each share constitutes a tangible quantum of wealth which can serve as the subject matter of family endowment. Thus, whereas the law leaned in favour of joint tenancy largely for reasons of convenience, equity has leaned towards tenancy in common for reasons of fairness.

Do these arguments suggest a need for reforms in Canada? Is the context the same? Is there a similar need for joint tenancies to ensure "convenience" in determining legal title in Canada? What is the balance of convenience and fairness in the Canadian context?

2. Language: Statutory Presumption in Favour of Tenancies in Common

McEwen demonstrates that there are important consequences, depending on whether the interests of Finlay McEwen's daughters Bertha and Janet are characterized as those of joint tenants or tenants in common. As with other aspects of property law, it is necessary to take account of the language adopted by the testator in creating the interests for Bertha and Janet. Re-examine the language considered in the case when deciding which form of concurrent interests was created.

In considering the language of the will in *McEwen*, compare it with the wording of a will that devised the residue of an estate to three children "jointly in equal shares." The will also provided that if any of the three children predeceased their mother, the residue was to become the property of such child's "successors." According to the court in *Winchester v McCullough* (2000), 30 RPR (3d) 5 (NBQB), this will created a tenancy in common. The court reasoned that if the devisor had intended a joint tenancy, she would have used the word "survivors" rather than the word "successors," suggesting that the word "successors" was not consistent with the survivorship right inherent in a joint tenancy. On the basis of *McEwen*, what other reasons might have justified the court's conclusion that this will created a tenancy in common?

As these cases demonstrate, the words used to create concurrent interests are important. The common law's traditional preference for joint tenancies meant that ambiguity in language would be resolved in favour of the creation of a joint tenancy. This presumption was reversed by statute in the 19th century. Thus, the *Conveyancing and Law of Property Act*, RSO 1990, c C.34 now provides:

> 13(1) Where by any letters patent, assurance or will, made and executed after the 1st day of July, 1834, land has been or is granted, conveyed or devised to two or more persons, other than executors or trustees, in fee simple or for any less estate, it shall be considered that such persons took or take as tenants in common and not as joint tenants, unless an intention sufficiently appears on the face of the letters patent, assurance or will, that they are to take as joint tenants.

Note that this section was s 12 at the time of the *McEwen* case. See also *Property Act*, RSNB 1973, c P-19, s 20; *Real Property Act*, RSNS 1989, c 385, s 5; and *Estates Administration Act*, RSO 1990, c E.22, s 14.

As is apparent, the statutory provision (where it is applicable) resolves ambiguity in language in favour of tenancies in common. As a result, the creation of a joint tenancy now requires clear and specific language. Most often, a joint tenancy is created (in an *inter vivos* grant or in a will) by the words "To A and B in fee simple *as joint tenants and not as tenants in common.*" As is clear, this language attempts to avoid ambiguity and the presumption in s 13. Is it appropriate to have such a statutory presumption in favour of tenancies in common so that those who wish to create a joint tenancy must take care to ensure that they use appropriate language to achieve their objective? What are the assumptions on which such a policy is based?

DISCUSSION NOTES

i. The Interpretation of Section 13

Like many statutory reforms of property law, s 13 has been strictly interpreted. It does not apply to grants other than "after the 1st day of July, 1834." Nor does it apply to grants to "executors or trustees," as was demonstrated in relation to comparable legislation in Australia in *Mitchell v Arblaster*, [1964-65] NSWR 119 (SC). In that case, a will devised interests to co-owners (Harry and Nellie Mitchell) as executors and trustees of the will, and also to them as residuary beneficiaries. The statutory presumption did not apply to the grant to executors and trustees, but was applicable to the grant to Harry and Nellie Mitchell as beneficiaries. Thus, the same wording resulted in a grant to the executors and trustees as joint tenants (the legal interest as trustees) and to the same recipients as beneficiaries as tenants in common (the equitable or beneficial interest). See also *Robertson v Fraser* (1871), 7 Ch App 696 (CA), where the court interpreted words of sharing in a codicil to a will so as to conclude that the will devised a tenancy in common. Section 13 was also considered in *Choi Ki Yau Trust v Yau Estate* (1999), 29 ETR (2d) 204 (Ont Sup Ct J).

In *Campbell v Sovereign Securities and Holdings Co Ltd* (1958), 16 DLR (2d) 606 (Ont CA), the court held that s 13 was not applicable where the language creating concurrent interests was in an agreement for purchase and sale, on the basis that such an agreement is not an "assurance" pursuant to the wording in the section.

Note that the court in *McEwen* interpreted the testator's intention according to the language chosen to define the interests devised to Bertha and Janet. Having regard to Finlay McEwen's will as a whole, what arguments might be made in support of Janet's position that the will created interests for Janet and Bertha as joint tenants? Is there inconsistency in Bertha's actions (as executor of her father's will) in conveying lot 18 to herself and Janet as joint tenants, and then subsequently devising a one-half interest to her brother? How can this apparent inconsistency be explained? See also *Re Coughlin* (1982), 12 ETR 59 (Ont H Ct J), where the court held that the language of the will denoted an intention to dispose of the entire estate among the three named beneficiaries by means of the right of survivorship.

It is unclear from the case report in *McEwen* whether these family members were engaged in amicable litigation merely to confirm the title granted in the will or were in a bitterly contested family dispute involving other matters as well. In light of the impact of the right of survivorship, it is not surprising that joint tenancies are most often used in family property arrangements. Indeed, it has been suggested that many common law developments (perhaps including the concept of joint tenancy) were motivated originally by the needs of families, rather than those of commerce: "Historically, the demands of the family preceded the demands of commerce, and the manner in which they were met left an indelible and permanent mark upon the framework of the law." (See GC Cheshire, *The Modern Law of Real Property*, 7th ed (London: Butterworths, 1954) at v.) In any event, joint tenancy in Canada in the

21st century has frequently been used by spouses in their arrangements for holding interests in the matrimonial home. Such an arrangement appeared appropriate for couples who expected to remain married for their whole lives, so that the survivor would become sole owner by right of survivorship and then devise the interest to surviving children or others. However, in the context of rising divorce rates in recent decades, the right of survivorship in a joint tenancy may be more ephemeral. Moreover, there may be complicated problems where the spouses jointly own a farm or business, rather than just a matrimonial home: see M McCall, "Economic Security for Farm Women: A Discussion Paper" (Ottawa: National Association of Women and the Law, 1995). The relationship between the right of survivorship in joint tenancy and recent statutory reforms concerning family property is considered below.

Although joint tenancy is the form of concurrent interest often used by married couples, it is also available for use by cohabiting couples (same-sex or opposite sex). What factors would need to be taken into account by a cohabiting couple in relation to concurrent interests in property in choosing a joint tenancy or a tenancy in common?

ii. Simultaneous Death of Joint Tenants

In the *McEwen* case discussed above, if Bertha and Janet were joint tenants and Bertha died, Janet would become sole owner as a result of the right of survivorship. What if Bertha and Janet had died together in an accident, so that it was not possible to determine which of them died first? How would the right of survivorship operate in such a case? This situation is now regulated by statute. For example, in Ontario, the *Succession Law Reform Act*, RSO 1990, c S.26, s 55(2) provides that "unless a contrary intention appears," where two or more joint tenants die at the same time or in circumstances rendering it uncertain as to the order of death, each person is "deemed ... to have held as tenant in common." In some provinces, such legislation provides for a presumption that the younger person survived the older one—that is, that the deceased died in order of seniority: see RSNS 1989, c 454, s 3; RSNL 1990, c S-33, s 2; and RSPEI 1988, c C-12, s 1.

iii. Joint Tenancies: Corporations

Logically, one would expect that interests as joint tenants with consequent rights of survivorship could be held only by human beings, and not by corporations that have no natural life span although they may be subject to dissolution in other ways. At common law, therefore, it was not possible for a corporation and an individual to hold interests as joint tenants, but this principle has been revised by statute in Ontario. Section 43 of the *Conveyancing and Law of Property Act*, RSO 1990, c C.34 provides that two or more corporations, or a corporation and an individual, "are and have been" capable of holding property as joint tenants in the same manner as individuals (subject to the usual conditions for the acquisition and holding of property by a corporation in severalty). Section 43(2) provides that when a corporation that holds property as a joint tenant with an individual subsequently dissolves, "the property devolves on the other joint tenant"—that is, there is a right of survivorship for the individual when a corporate entity ceases to exist.

iv. Severance of Joint Tenancy

In the context of the right of survivorship in a joint tenancy, there may be situations where one or more of the joint tenants decides that it would be preferable for them to be tenants in common. The process for changing a joint tenancy into a tenancy in common can be accomplished by the severance of the joint tenancy, an issue discussed below.

3. Conceptual Distinctions: The Four Unities

In addition to the right of survivorship, which applies only to a joint tenancy, there are conceptual differences between joint tenancies and tenancies in common. A joint tenancy has four unities—unity of possession, interest, title, and time. By contrast, a tenancy in common has just one—unity of possession. Although holders of concurrent interests in joint tenancies and tenancies in common all have undivided rights to possession of the whole of the relevant property, their interests are conceptually different in other respects. In particular, the interest of a joint tenant is a unified interest in the whole, while that of a tenant in common is a fractional share—for example, one-half or one-third—of the whole. A tenant in common holds an "undivided" share. For example, a tenant in common who holds a one-third share in land cannot identify any particular part of the land as the one-third share, because of the unity of possession enjoyed by all the tenants in common.

A joint tenant holds an interest in the whole. According to Gray & Symes at 234:

> Indeed, the essence of joint tenancy consists in the dogma that each and every joint tenant is "wholly entitled to the whole" of the land. No joint tenant holds any specific share in the property himself, but each is (together with the other joint tenant or tenants) invested with the absolute interest in the land. In Bracton's expressive language, each joint tenant "totum tenet et nihil tenet": each holds everything and yet holds nothing. Joint tenancy is thus an amorphous kind of co-ownership in which the entire estate or interest in property—rather than any defined proportion or share in that property—is vested simultaneously in each and all of the co-owners.

Conceptually, therefore, the interest of a joint tenant is an interest in the whole estate, by contrast with the interest of a tenant in common, which is described as an undivided share in the whole.

The joint tenancy's unity of interest, title, and time means that joint tenants must have interests of the same quality and duration—for example, they must both hold life estates; they must derive them through the same title documents—that is, their joint title must not be created through different documents; and their interests must commence at the same time. The concepts were identified in the *Working Paper on Co-Ownership of Land* (Vancouver: Law Reform Commission of British Columbia, 1987) [BCLRC] at 2:

> Co-owners acquiring their title by separate instruments are not joint tenants. There is no unity of title. Similarly, where their interests are acquired at different times, there is no unity of time. If they have differing interests in property, there is no unity of interest. The absence of any of these unities means that co-ownership is by tenancy in common, not joint tenancy.

DISCUSSION NOTES

i. Unities of Possession, Interest, Title, and Time

In relation to Finlay McEwen's will devising concurrent interests in lot 18 to Bertha and Janet, were there unities of possession, interest, title, and time?

1. Were the sisters' interests the same in terms of size and duration (unity of interest)?
2. Were the sisters' titles derived from the same document (unity of title)?
3. Were the sisters' interests expected to commence at the same time (unity of time)?

Compare the concurrent interests in the *McEwen* case with the following:

- grant to A for life and to B in fee simple (are the interests the same?);
- grant to A and B in fee simple; and then grant from A to C (do B and C derive title from the same document?);
- grant to A for life, remainder to B and C when B and C graduate from law school (if B and C graduate at different times, there is no unity of time).

Note that there are some complex difficulties of interpretation in such grants. See Mendes da Costa for an informed discussion of some of the cases. Perhaps the most usual situation in which different interests preclude creation of a joint tenancy occurs when co-owners have differing shares. For example, in *Re Speck* (1983), 51 BCLR 143 (SC), two persons applied to register their interests in land as joint tenants with one party having an undivided $71/100$ interest and the other an undivided $29/100$ interest. The court denied their claim, stating that by trying to register a joint tenancy without a unity of interest, the applicants were trying to create "a monster unknown to the law." By contrast with the court's view in *Speck*, BCLRC has suggested that there may be cases where joint tenancies with undivided shares should be recognized—for example, the Commission explained (at 26-27) that

> a husband and wife may purchase a matrimonial home with the wife putting up 80% of the money. They find the notion of a joint tenancy attractive for its right of survivorship, but fear that if the husband's business activities should lead to his bankruptcy, the trustee [in bankruptcy] would be entitled to half the property. A form of joint tenancy which recognized unequal interests would seem to satisfy their needs.

BCLRC reviewed several options for achieving the needs of joint tenants in such cases, including the use of contractual agreements or trust arrangements. (The report also pointed out (at 27) that there are some cases recognizing tenancies in common with rights of survivorship, although there are a number of legal uncertainties in these cases because such interests can also be devised.) Having regard to the needs of joint tenants, however, BCLRC recommended legislation providing that "unity of interest is unnecessary to create a joint tenancy"—that is, joint tenants could hold interests that differ in extent.

In Ontario, the Law Reform Commission's *Report on Basic Principles of Land Law* (Toronto: Ontario Law Reform Commission, 1996) [OLRC, *Principles of Land Law*] briefly reviewed the requirements of unity of interest, time, and title in relation to joint tenancies and recommended (at 107) that *all* of them be abrogated as requirements. "Instead, the fundamental determining factor should (subject to the relevant presumptions) be solely one of intention: whether the parties intended the right of survivorship." In addition, OLRC, *Principles of Land Law* recommended changing the terminology for co-ownership: "co-ownership with right of survivorship" (formerly joint tenancy) and "co-ownership without right of survivorship" (formerly tenancy in common).

Do you agree that reform is necessary? If so, which of these reform proposals appears most appropriate? Why?

ii. Mutual Rights and Responsibilities Among Co-Owners

The unity of possession that applies to both joint tenancies and tenancies in common required the development of quite complex rules about mutual rights and responsibilities among co-owners, a topic considered below in relation to rights of accounting, and partition and sale.

B. A Note on Tenancies by the Entireties and Co-Parcenary

These forms of concurrent interests are uncommon, and there is some controversy about their continuing existence in practice. Both involve concurrent interests arising out of particular kinds of familial relationships, so that they too raise issues about the relationship between traditional common law principles and statutory reforms.

1. Tenancy by the Entireties

J Glenn has described tenancies by the entireties as follows:

> At common law, when property was conveyed to a husband and wife in any estate in such a way that had they been strangers they would have taken as joint tenants, they took rather as tenants by the entireties. This was so because of the doctrine of unity of legal personality, according to which husband and wife were considered in law as one: to the four unities of time, title, interest and possession was added a fifth unity, unity of the person. This unity was so complete that neither spouse was regarded as having even a potential share in the property; both were seised together as one individual of the whole, that is, of the entirety. They were, in other words, together tenants of the entirety. From this flows one of the most important features of a tenancy by the entireties: its unseverability. And it follows from this unseverability that the right of survivorship is indestructible.

(J Glenn, "Tenancy by the Entireties: A Matrimonial Regime Ignored" (1980) 58 Can Bar Rev 711 at 715.)

As is apparent, this form of concurrent interests is based on the traditional common law conception of a husband and wife as one person, with the wife's legal status "suspended" during coverture. Obviously, many legal reforms in the 20th century were intended to promote more equality for women in marriage, but there is some uncertainty about whether statutory reforms have repealed tenancies by the entireties in all Canadian provinces. Some provinces (including Prince Edward Island and Newfoundland) have expressly repealed such tenancies, while others (including Ontario) may arguably have done so by the combined effect of married women's property acts and family property statutes. In *Campbell v Sovereign Securities and Holdings Co Ltd* (1958), 16 DLR (2d) 606 (Ont CA), (1958), 13 DLR (2d) 195 (Ont H Ct J) it was suggested that tenancies by the entireties continued to exist in Ontario, although this view was distinguished later in *Demaiter v Link*, [1973] 3 OR 140 (Co Ct). Glenn provides a persuasive argument for the continuing utility of such tenancies in spite of substantial reform of family property arrangements in Canada. See also OLRC, *Principles of Land Law* at 74-77, and the recommendations about relying on intention to define exactly what concurrent interests are created (as well as the new terminology of "co-ownership with right of survivorship" and "co-ownership without right of survivorship").

2. Co-Parcenary

This form of concurrent ownership occurred at common law when there was an intestacy and the land would then devolve to the common law heir. If, however, no male heir existed, female heirs together were deemed to be the heir, and were together entitled as co-parceners. The right of survivorship did not apply and each co-parcener was entitled to a distinct undivided share. According to Gray & Symes (at 233), co-parcenary can arise now "only in certain highly anomalous situations." In Canada, however, it has been suggested that "co-parcenary may still arise upon the death of a tenant in tail who dies, without barring the entail, leaving no male heir and more than one female descendant in the same degree." See Derek Mendes da Costa, Richard J Balfour & Eileen S Gillese, eds, *Property Law: Cases, Text, and Materials*, 2d ed (Toronto: Emond Montgomery, 1990) at 18:10; and OLRC, *Principles of Land Law* at 77.

These forms of concurrent ownership clearly derive from traditional common law principles fashioned in a quite different context. Do you agree with Dixon J in the High Court of Australia when he said in *Wright v Gibbons* (1949), 78 CLR 313 (at 329) that joint tenancy was "a form of ownership bearing many traces of the scholasticism of the times in which its principles were developed"? If different kinds of concurrent interests were to be created now, what principles would be appropriate? Should there be different principles for family situations by contrast with commercial arrangements? Is it easier to adapt traditional principles or to fashion entirely new ones?

C. Severance of a Joint Tenancy

Because a joint tenancy requires that the four unities be present, acts that destroy these unities result in a severance of the joint tenancy and creation of a tenancy in common. In this way, severance of a joint tenancy eliminates the right of survivorship so that the co-owners, now tenants in common, hold undivided shares that are devisable. Where a joint tenancy exists among three persons, all three may join in a deed to sever the joint tenancy so that they become tenants in common instead. In the absence of agreement among all the joint tenants, however, common law principles have identified circumstances by which one joint tenant acting alone may effect severance of a joint tenancy, sometimes without notice to other joint tenants. Some commentators have suggested that there are good reasons for insisting that requirements for unilateral severance should be strictly interpreted because joint tenancies can be created only where express words are used to do so—that is, words sufficient to overcome the statutory presumption of tenancy in common. Significantly, courts may also conclude that severance has occurred because of a "course of dealing" with jointly owned property, and the element of fairness inherent in a tenancy in common seems to continue to be influential in judicial interpretation in some circumstances—see e.g. *Burgess v Rawnsley*, [1975] 3 All ER 142 (CA). Reconsider the balance between "convenience" and "fairness" in these forms of concurrent ownership in reviewing the general principles of severance in the following extract.

1. *General Principles of Severance*

AJ McClean, "Severance of Joint Tenancies"
(1979) 57 Can Bar Rev 1 at 1-4 (footnotes omitted)

A joint tenancy may be ended by severance, that is, by any act or conduct which, occurring during the lifetime of a joint tenant, has the effect of turning the joint tenancy into a tenancy in common. The same principles apply to interests in both realty and personalty, but most of the decisions deal with the application of those principles to realty … .

Despite the fact that joint tenancies have long been with us, there are still doubts about the operation of the common law rules on severance. In England and Canada these rules have been affected by legislation. The 1925 [UK] legislation made changes to the law of joint tenancy generally, and in one instance to severance in particular. Post 1925 English cases are therefore [irrelevant] in Canada, and will be considered here, only to the extent that they throw light on the common law principles. In Canada the common law has been modified by legislation, either expressly, or sometimes clearly, sometimes arguably, impliedly, and in some respects there is still uncertainty about the blending of common law and statute.

The starting point for any discussion of the modern law is the well-known passage in the judgment of Sir W. Page Wood VC in *Williams v. Hensman* [(1861), 70 ER 862 (Ch D) at 867]:

> A joint-tenancy may be severed in three ways: in the first place, an act of any one of the persons interested operating upon his own share may create a severance as to that share. The right of each joint-tenant is a right by survivorship only in the event of no severance having taken place of the share which is claimed under the *jus accrescendi*. Each one is at liberty to dispose of his own interest in such a manner as to sever it from the joint fund—losing, of course, at the same time, his own right of survivorship. Secondly, a joint-tenancy may be severed by mutual agreement. And, in the third place, there may be a severance by any course of dealing sufficient to intimate that the interests of all were mutually treated as constituting a tenancy in common. When the severance depends on an inference of this kind without any express act of severance, it will not suffice to rely on an intention, with respect to the particular share, declared only behind the backs of the persons interested.

In *Burgess v. Rawnsley* Sir John Pennycuick called the three propositions in this passage the three "rules" and, with the proviso that too much should not be read into the word rule, this is a convenient way of referring to them.

The reasons why these rules are effective to sever are clear. The first is based on the fact that generally a joint tenant, without the consent of or even notice to the other joint tenants, is as free to deal with his interest as any other owner, and may deal with it in such a way as to destroy one of the unities. If that happens it follows that the joint tenancy is severed. The second and third turn on the common intention of the joint tenants. And, if some recent English decisions are to be believed, rules one and three may also operate on the basis of the unilateral intention, express or implied, of a single joint tenant. In theory if one of the unities is destroyed, or if the common or unilateral intentions are shown to exist, there is a severance, and nothing else need be considered. This is generally the attitude taken by the Canadian courts, and in some cases the law is so well settled on this basis that it would be futile to debate the issues further. But there are two other factors which may be thought to be relevant, particularly where there is doubt about the destruction of the unities or the existence of the requisite intentions.

The first, and more general, consideration is the well-established judicial preference for the tenancy in common. This means that it can be expected that the courts will lean in favour of severance. It is arguable that in Canada, with respect to realty, there is no longer any justification for this attitude. Equity developed a preference for tenancies in common in light of the common law rule that, in the absence of a contrary intention, a conveyance or devise to two or more persons automatically created a joint tenancy. Thus, often without the parties realizing it, the right of survivorship, which runs contrary to equity's sense of equality, arose by implication. In Canada most jurisdictions have legislation reversing the common law rule; a conveyance or devise to two or more persons will create a tenancy in common, unless it is provided in the instrument that a joint tenancy is intended. Joint tenancies, therefore, need to be deliberately created, and it is doubtful if there should be any special preference for severance. This is particularly true in what is today probably the most common example of a joint tenancy—the conveyance of the matrimonial home to a husband and wife. We will have occasion to look at this argument at various places in the article.

The second, and more specific, consideration arises where a joint tenant and a third party engage in some type of dealing which in itself would not destroy any of the unities. In many such cases it is argued that in fairness to the third party there nonetheless ought to be a severance if the transaction is to be fully effective. Sometimes the argument is also put in terms of the presumed intention of the joint tenant himself to give full and faithful effect to the transaction. Therefore, although the point can arise in relation to other modes of severance, this consideration will be dealt with primarily in that part of the article where severance based upon the presumed intention of a joint tenant is discussed.

DISCUSSION NOTES

i. Severance of Joint Tenancies: Intention, Negotiation, and Completed Acts

Although the principles in *Williams v Hensman*, above, are often used as the starting point for judicial analysis concerning severance of a joint tenancy, application of the principles in practice may be more difficult. For example, although it is clear that a conveyance of an estate by one joint tenant to a third party (the first method set out in *Williams v Hensman*) will result in severance, the grant of a mere "encumbrance" such as an easement or a leasehold may not. The principles regarding one joint tenant's creation of a mortgage may depend on the applicable statutory principles concerning mortgages (and whether they constitute a conveyance of the fee simple or merely a charge) as well as on the principles of severance. See e.g. *Canadian Imperial Bank of Commerce v Muntain*, [1985] 4 WWR 90 (BCSC); *Re McKee and National Trust Co Ltd* (1975), 56 DLR (3d) 190 (Ont CA); *Frieze v Unger*, [1960] VR 230 (SC); *Re Sorensen and Sorensen* (1977), 90 DLR (3d) 26 (Alta SC (AD)); and Ziff at 342-44. See also

S Nield, "To Sever or Not to Sever: The Effect of a Mortgage by One Joint Tenant" [2001] Conv 462. It seems that an assignment in bankruptcy severs a joint tenancy: see *Royal Bank v Oliver (Trustee of)* (1991), 93 Sask R 161 (CA).

The second method identified in *Williams v Hensman*, mutual agreement, contemplates an agreement among joint tenants to sever the joint tenancy, and the cases have shown that even agreements not reduced to a registrable deed may suffice to sever a joint tenancy in equity. The "mutual agreement" basis for severance is particularly significant in the context of a married couple (and sometimes a cohabiting couple), who have separated but not finalized their property arrangements when one "spouse" dies. In *Robichaud v Watson* (1983), 147 DLR (3d) 626 (Ont H Ct J), for example, a cohabiting couple (who held property as joint tenants) separated, and their lawyers conducted "without prejudice" negotiations to settle June Watson's claim for her share of the value of a house, some household furnishings, and a car. Although an offer of settlement was made by Raymond Robichaud, it was rejected, and sometime later he was murdered. His mother applied for a declaration that the joint tenancy had been severed and that a one-half interest passed to Robichaud's estate. The Ontario High Court concluded (at 636) that "the negotiations carried on between the parties through their solicitors in this case clearly indicated that each regarded themselves as tenants in common, that their interests had been severed and what was at issue in the negotiations was the value only of their respective interests." See also *Re Walters and Walters* (1977), 16 OR (2d) 702 (H Ct J); and *Ginn v Armstrong* (1969), 3 DLR (3d) 285 (BCSC).

By contrast, in *Morgan v Davis* (1984), 42 RFL (2d) 435 (NBQB (Fam Div)), the court concluded that negotiations between a husband and wife in the context of their divorce did not effect a severance of their joint tenancy (the divorce decree was silent with respect to any property settlement). When the former husband died, the court held (at 440) that the right of survivorship operated in favour of his former wife (subject to the interpretation of sections of the relevant family property legislation in New Brunswick regarding the former husband's more extensive financial and other contributions to the maintenance of the property):

> I am satisfied that the divorce by itself did not sever the joint tenancy even though the relationship between Donald and Doreen Morgan was terminated …. There was simply an offer and an unreasonable counter offer, but no agreement. There was a presentation of documents for conveyance, which were never acknowledged. It seems clear the parties intended to return to the status quo and the matter was "to be held in abeyance and resolved at some later date." Having regard to their attitude and course of conduct, it is not difficult to infer that the parties, following the incomplete negotiations and the divorce, accepted the situation with respect to the joint tenancy as it was prior to the negotiations. I am satisfied they knew and understood the meaning and significance of the title being registered in their joint names and neither did anything to change that situation. Consequently, I find there was no severance and, by virtue of the joint tenancy, title to the property in question passed to Doreen Davis at the moment of Donald Morgan's death.

For a discussion as to the admissibility of "without prejudice" solicitors' letters written in the course of divorce negotiations, see *Kish v Tompkins* (1992), 86 DLR (4th) 759 (BCSC). See also OLRC, *Principles of Land Law* at 115ff.

The decision in *Robichaud v Watson* (above) may also be characterized as "a course of conduct," the third means of achieving severance set out in *Williams v Hensman*. Another example is found in *obiter* comments in *Murdoch v Barry* (1975), 10 OR (2d) 626 (H Ct J) where

Patricia Murdoch (a joint tenant with her husband of some cottage property) conveyed her estate to herself and then devised her interest in the cottage property to her sister just prior to her own death. One question in this case was the effect of a conveyance by a joint tenant to herself (an issue addressed in relation to *Knowlton v Bartlett*, discussed below). However, the court in *Murdoch* also considered the test for "a course of conduct," as set out in *Re Wilks; Child v Bulmer*, [1891] 3 Ch 59, requiring an act that precludes a joint tenant from claiming by survivorship any interest in the subject matter of the tenancy. In *Murdoch*, Patricia Murdoch executed a deed, declaring her intention to sever the joint tenancy in her affidavit of marital status on the deed, and then arranged for the deed to be registered. According to the court (at 633):

> That constituted an irrevocable act on her part, the purpose of which was to sever the joint ten-
> ancy and it was an act which, in my opinion, constituted more than a mere declaration of inten-
> tion but, rather, an endeavour on her part to carry out by her act the intention expressed in her
> affidavit ... . [These acts] effectively estopped her from claiming by survivorship any interest in
> the subject-matter of the joint tenancy in the event she had survived the applicant.

Accordingly, the court held that she had effectively severed the joint tenancy. Do you agree with this analysis? See also *Kissick Estate v Kissick* (1990), 90 OTC 306 (Ct J (Gen Div)); *Cormier Estate v Bourque* (2001), 233 NBR (2d) 92, 2001 NBCA 4 (a cohabiting couple); and *Havlik v Whitehouse* (2000), 262 AR 88, 34 RPR (3d) 128 (QB) (an uncle and niece). Such cases may also involve assessments of credibility and claims about undue influence: e.g. see *Sparks v Griggs et al*, 2000 BCSC 1164. See also *Presseau v Presseau*, 2010 NSSC 201, where the court held that a deed executed by a joint tenant wife to herself (without her husband's knowledge) prior to her death did not sever the joint tenancy because the *Real Property Act*, RSNS 1989, c 385, s 10 did not provide for a valid conveyance by the wife to herself.

Consider a recent case, where the Ontario Court of Appeal assessed whether the facts revealed a "course of dealing" on the part of married spouses prior to the husband's death. At separation, the spouses were joint tenants of the matrimonial home, and they were in the process of determining equalization under the *Family Law Act* when the husband died. In this context, the wife claimed title to the matrimonial home on the basis that they were still mar-ried at the date of her husband's death. However, prior to his death, the husband had final-ized a new will, leaving his estate entirely to his four daughters, and the daughters claimed that there was a "course of dealing" between the spouses that had severed the joint tenancy. The Ontario Court of Appeal concluded that the spouses had consulted lawyers to value their interests, that the husband had executed a will inconsistent with a right of survivorship, and that the spouses had maintained separate bank accounts:

> [57] When the evidence of [the parties'] course of dealing is considered as a whole, it is clear
> that the evidence is "sufficient to intimate that the interests of all were mutually treated as con-
> stituting a tenancy in common" [citing *Williams v Hensman*]. From the time the spouses separated
> until [the husband's] death, the spouses took a number of steps which reveal that they were each
> treating their interests in the property as distinct. In other words, their conduct demonstrated
> they were mutually treating their co-ownership as a tenancy in common and not as joint tenants.
>
>   • • •

[65] [The wife's assertion of a right of survivorship] is entirely inconsistent with the co-owners' mutual intention, as revealed by their correspondence and their conduct, to divide their interests in the property and hold their interests in common rather than jointly.

See *Hansen Estate v Hansen*, 2012 ONCA 112. Notice how courts must assess the evidence carefully to determine whether the test of a "course of dealing" has been met. For other cases, see *Jurevicius v Jurevicius*, 2011 ONSC 696; and *Su v Lam*, 2012 ONSC 2023, 213 ACWS (3d) 248.

ii. Severance of a Joint Tenancy by Murder

Severance of a joint tenancy has also been confirmed in circumstances where one joint tenant has murdered the other (although this result is usually characterized as a legal result outside the terms of *Williams v Hensman*). In *Schobelt v Barber* (1966), 60 DLR (2d) 519 (Ont HC), the court relied on a case comment of *Re Pupkowski* (1956), 6 DLR (2d) 427 (BC SC), written by R St J MacDonald, "Real Property—Joint Tenancy—Murder of One Tenant by Another—Share of the Survivor" (1957) 35 Can Bar Rev 966. In *Pupkowski*, which also involved the murder of a joint tenant, the court considered four options:

1. Permit the estate of the deceased to accrue to the survivor by right of survivorship (rejected because a person should not benefit from his own wrongful act).

2. Deprive the survivor of the right of survivorship (rejected because it is an inherent characteristic of a joint tenancy).

3. Vest the estate in the survivor, but the victim should be deemed to have died after the wrongdoer (rejected because it requires substantial change to property law and thus should be accomplished only by legislation).

4. Apply the normal rule so that the estate accrues to the survivor, subject to a constructive trust of an undivided one-half interest for the victim's estate.

The court adopted the fourth option, approved also by *Scott on Trusts*, and quoted from a statement by John W Wade in "Acquisition of Property by Wilfully Killing Another—A Statutory Solution" (1936) 49 Harv L Rev 715 at 720:

[T]he court is not taking away from the slayer an estate which he has already acquired, but "is simply preventing him from acquiring property in an unauthorized and unlawful way, ie, by murder."

Do you agree that the court's choice is the best way to resolve this problem? See also *Worobel Estate v Worobel* (1988), 31 ETR 290 (Ont HC); and *Brown v Ferguson*, 2010 BCSC 1890. For an assessment of policies about joint tenancy in the context of homicide, see Chris Triggs, "Against Policy: Homicide and Succession to Property" (2005) 68 Sask L Rev 117.

In *R v Ford*, 2010 BCCA 105, the court considered whether a criminal charge in relation to a marijuana grow-op on jointly owned land could result in severance of the joint tenancy. In this case, the court concluded that s 16 of the *Canada Drug and Safety Act* permitted the Crown to exercise forfeiture against the land, even though it was held in joint tenancy. The court concluded that it was appropriate to exercise forfeiture, but then to return a half-interest to the non-offending joint tenant; as a result, the joint tenancy was severed. The court also held that if the Crown could not come to an appropriate arrangement with the non-offending co-tenant, the Crown could apply for partition (a remedy for co-owners discussed later in this chapter).

iii. Unintentional Severance of a Joint Tenancy

As noted above, severance of a joint tenancy may also occur without an intentional act in the context of bankruptcy and in the execution of a judgment. In addition, a joint tenancy *at law* may also be held as a tenancy in common *in equity* in the context of partnership property or where the purchase price of property is advanced by joint tenants in unequal proportions. For example, if A and B are grantees as joint tenants and A has paid $30,000 while B has paid $10,000 of the total purchase price, A and B will be joint tenants in law and tenants in common in equity (with A having a three-quarter undivided share and B a one-quarter undivided share). What will be the result if A dies? For an example in relation to partnership property, see *Agro Estate v CIBC Trust Corp* (1999), 96 OTC 140, 26 ETR (2d) 314 (Sup Ct J).

iv. Severance: Conveyance by One or More Joint Tenants

Suppose that A, B, and C are joint tenants in fee simple. A conveys A's interest to D. This means that B and C are now joint tenants in relation to a two-thirds undivided share, which they hold together as tenants in common with D in respect to D's one-third undivided share. Explain why D takes as a tenant in common, and why B and C remain joint tenants. What happens when D dies? When B dies?

In relation to the above problem, assume that A conveys to B (another of the joint tenants) instead of to D (a stranger). What is the result? Similarly, assume that A conveys to B and B conveys to A, C taking no part in these transactions. It seems that A, B, and C are now tenants in common, each with an undivided one-third share. See *Wright v Gibbons* (1949), 78 CLR 313.

2. Severance in a "Family" Context: A Case Study

Knowlton v Bartlett
(1984), 35 RPR 182 (NBQB Fam Div)

JONES J: This comes before me on a notice of application wherein the applicant seeks an order for partition or sale of property.

The property in question is in the parish of St. Stephen, Charlotte County, and consists of a residence as well as approximately 47 acres of ground. It was formerly owned by the parents of the respondent. The respondent's parents deeded a substantial part of the property to the respondent in 1951 and in December of 1953 the respondent deeded that portion of the property to himself and his wife as joint tenants. A further lot of land abutting the original property was deeded by the respondent's mother to the respondent and his wife as joint tenants in December of 1965. The latter two deeds were recorded in the Charlotte County registry office in 1966.

The respondent and his late wife were married in the late 1940s and lived in the home on the premises until as a result of marital differences Mrs. Bartlett apparently left about 1971. On February 3, 1977, a decree absolute was granted with respect to this marriage in which the respondent was the petitioner and the late Mrs. Bartlett filed a counter-petition. One of the provisions of the decree absolute provided as follows:

> 2. AND THIS COURT DOTH ORDER AND ADJUDGE that Everett Eugene Bartlett shall pay to the said Laura Martha Bartlett a lump sum of $3,000.00 providing that Laura Martha Bartlett conveys to him all her interest in the property at RR #4, St. Stephen, NB, assessment code F1201019-2000.

It is common ground that the aforesaid sum of $3,000 was not paid and Mrs. Bartlett did not convey to her husband her interest in this property. It is further agreed that the property referred to in the decree absolute is the property in question in this matter. Mr. Bartlett stated that subsequent to the decree absolute he offered to his late wife the sum of money but that she "did refuse to accept such sums on the basis that she did not want to be bothered."

It further appears that the late Mrs. Bartlett became terminally ill sometime in 1979 and passed away December 22, 1982.

On October 6, 1981, Mrs. Bartlett executed a deed from herself to herself with respect to the aforementioned lands. This deed was recorded in the Charlotte County registry office on the 9th of October 1981. On the 15th of September 1982, Martha Laura Bartlett signed a last will and testament wherein she appointed her brother Kenneth Leon Knowlton to be her executor and also her sole beneficiary. Mr. Knowlton, the applicant in the within matter, makes this application asserting that he holds this property as a tenant in common with the respondent and seeking an order either for partition or sale. The respondent Mr. Bartlett opposes this application and raises several issues.

Joint Tenancy

It is common ground between the parties that certainly until Mrs. Bartlett executed the deed referred to, she and her husband owned this property as joint tenants and not as tenants in common. Had this interest continued it is the contention of the respondent that he as the survivor would be seised of full title in the property.

Joint tenancy consists of four unities, being that of title, interest, possession and time. The unity of time refers to the time of vesting but should any of the remaining unities cease to exist the joint tenancy and right of survivorship would cease. If the parties otherwise remain entitled to the property, it would be as tenants in common.

Joint tenancy can be severed by mutual consent or by conduct of the parties from which an intention to sever would be inferred. A joint tenancy may also be severed by the act of one of the joint tenants: see *Williams v. Hensman* (1861), 1 J & H 546, 70 ER 862 at 867, per Wood VC:

> A joint tenancy may be severed in three ways: in the first place, an act of any one of the persons interested operating upon his own share may create a severance as to that share.

At common law a party could not deed property to oneself but could employ the Statute of Uses, 1535 (Eng., 27 Hen. 8), c. 10, and thus a joint tenant could in this manner create a tenancy in common. The Law of Real Property, Megarry and Wade (2d ed., 1959), p. 423:

> The common law mitigated the uncertainty of the jus accrescendi by enabling a joint tenant to destroy the joint tenancy by severance, which had the result of turning it into a tenancy

in common. "The duration of all lives being uncertain, if either party has an ill opinion of his own life, he may sever the joint tenancy by a deed granting over a moiety [that is, conveying one-half] in trust for himself; so that survivorship can be no hardship, where either side may at pleasure prevent it." (*Cray v. Willis* (1729), 2 P. Wms. 529) "Severance" strictly includes partition, but the word is normally used to describe the process whereby a joint tenancy is converted into a tenancy in common, and it is used in this sense here.

Mrs. Bartlett of course did not deed to another for use of herself but rather conveyed directly to herself. Section 23 of the *Property Act*, RSNB 1973, c. P-19, provides as follows:

> 23(1) Freehold land may be conveyed by a person to himself jointly with another person by the like means by which it might be conveyed by him to another person.
>
> 23(2) Freehold land may, in like manner, be conveyed by a husband to his wife, or by a wife to her husband, alone or jointly with another person.
>
> 23(3) A person may convey land to or vest land in himself.

In the case of [*Murdoch v Barry*] (1975), 10 OR (2d) 626, 64 DLR (3d) 222, the Ontario High Court had to consider a circumstance somewhat similar to that in the present case. In that case a husband and wife owned property as joint tenants. The wife became ill in July of 1973. On July 20 of that year, she executed a deed to herself which was duly recorded. She died shortly thereafter, having made a will leaving her assets to her sister. The question before the Court was whether or not the execution of the deed constituted her termination of the unity of title so as to mean that the beneficiary of her will held a half interest in the property as tenant in common. The Court in that case reviewed the authorities and held that such conveyance did constitute a severance of the joint tenancy. In fact the provisions of the *Conveyancing and Law of Property Act* of the Province of Ontario are slightly different than those of New Brunswick on this particular point. The following is an excerpt of the pertinent portions of the *Conveyancing and Law of Property Act*, RSO 1970, c. 85 [see now RSO 1990, c C.34, ss 40 and 41]:

> 41. Any property may be conveyed by a person to himself jointly with another person by the like means by which it might be conveyed by him to another person, and may in like manner be conveyed or assigned by a husband to his wife, or by a wife to her husband, alone or jointly with another person.
>
> 42. A person may convey property to or vest property in himself in like manner as he could have conveyed the property to or vested the property in another person.

Counsel on behalf of the respondent makes the point that in the decision of [*Murdoch v Barry*] the trial Judge referred to a history of cases showing that a person may sever a joint tenancy by a conveyance to a third party which in fact the trial Judge in that case did do. Counsel then makes the point that in the Ontario statute, s. 42 provides that a person may convey property to or vest property in himself in like manner as he would have conveyed it or vested property in another person. For some reason s. 23(3) of the *Property Act* in this province does not make such a provision. In other words s. 23(1) provides that freehold land may be conveyed to the grantor jointly with another by the like means that it might be conveyed to another person. Section 23(2) indicates that conveyances described there may be done in like manner, i.e. in like manner to 23(1), but there is no such tie-in with respect to 23(3). I do not know nor can I interpret from the wording the reason for this particular variation on the face of the statute. Nevertheless it is clear that s. 23(3) provides that a person may convey land to or vest land in himself.

It was not necessary for the Court in [*Murdoch v Barry*] to consider this point as they had the Ontario statute available indicating that such conveyance would be in like manner as a conveyance to another person. As previously indicated in my reference to Megarry and Wade on the Law of Real Property, even at common law, if one proceeded by way of the Statute of Uses, one could sever a joint tenancy with a conveyance in effect to oneself and I see no reason why the same result would not obtain by simply conveying the property as authorised by s. 23(3) of the *Property Act* of this province.

In [*Murdoch v Barry*], the Court went a step further and found that in that case Mrs. Murdoch had made an affidavit with respect to her married status in which she had expressly indicated her purpose, "[T]his deed is given to sever the joint tenancy which existed with grantor's husband Alexander Murdoch." In that case, the Court found that even if the execution of the deed did not constitute a severance of title, that this affidavit was sufficient to constitute an irrevocable act on her part sufficient to sever the joint tenancy in that it would preclude her from claiming by survivorship the interest in the subject matter of the joint tenancy had she survived her husband.

In the present case, there is no documentation beyond the execution of the deed, and I find that this constituted a severance of the unity of title, and that following the execution and registration of the deed Mr. and Mrs. Bartlett held this property as tenants in common.

Divorce Decree

The provision in the decree absolute of the divorce action does not vest any title in Mr. Bartlett. Subject to any question as to the jurisdiction of the Court to deal with the title of land in the decree absolute, which question I do not need to address in this circumstance, the provision simply directs that Mr. Bartlett shall pay to his wife the sum of $3,000 and makes it a condition of his obligation that she convey him her interest in the property in question. He did not pay her the money, make any advance of the money, nor pay the money into Court which would have been a precondition of any right which he had to call upon her for a conveyance of her interest.

At the time of Mrs. Bartlett's demise, she was entitled to a half interest in the property as a tenant in common and her interest passed under the provisions of her will to the applicant Kenneth Knowlton.

[The court then considered the appropriate remedy in these circumstances—see the discussion about partition and sale, below.]

DISCUSSION NOTES

i. Severance: Statutory Principles and Interpretation

In *Knowlton*, the court compared the relevant New Brunswick statutory provisions (*Property Act*, RSNB 1973, c P-19, s 23(3)) to those in Ontario and concluded that there was no necessary distinction between them. Are there other arguments that might have been made in such a comparison? Are the policy considerations in *Knowlton* the same as those in *Murdoch v Barry*? What aspects of the facts of these two cases are significant in relation to these policy issues? To what extent is it relevant that the joint tenants are husband and wife? Although the *Real Property Act* in Nova Scotia does not appear to permit a conveyance to oneself (see RSNS 1989, c 385, s 10), such a conveyance is permitted in PEI (see RSPEI 1988, c R-3, s 13(2)).

ii. Severance: Principles About Notice

The issue of whether a joint tenant should be able to sever the joint tenancy without notice to other joint tenants remains a matter of some debate. McClean, extracted above, at 38-39, suggested that joint consent to any severance should be required when the joint tenancy involves a husband and wife and the matrimonial home, having regard to "the expectation of the spouses that the consent of both is needed to change the nature of their interests, and that, without that mutual consent, on the death of one the property will pass to the survivor." McClean suggested that this rule should apply to spouses who are joint tenants, leaving the traditional rules to apply to other joint tenants. However, he argued that if this proposal were too drastic, severance should not occur until other joint tenants have been notified of the proposed transaction, arguing (at 39):

> Severance may now take place without his [*sic*] even being informed. This element of secrecy is at the minimum unfair, and may also lead to a suspicion of fraudulent dealing. To require notice would achieve a fair balance between the competing interests of all the joint tenants.

See also *Stonehouse v AG of British Columbia*, [1962] SCR 103.

OLRC, *Principles of Land Law* reviewed McClean's assessment and suggested (at 116-18) that, although the consent of all joint tenants should not be required for severance, there should be a requirement of notice on the part of a joint tenant seeking to sever the joint tenancy to create a tenancy in common:

> The cardinal feature of joint tenancy, and the most important characteristic distinguishing it from a tenancy in common, is the right of survivorship. Ordinarily, this right of survivorship is only apt where the co-owners maintain harmonious relationships ... . When the relationship between joint tenants changes, ... they should be free to terminate the right of survivorship unilaterally by severing the joint tenancy. ... [However,] unilateral severance should not take effect unless notice of severance is given to the other joint owners.

For an example of legislation requiring notice for the severance of a joint tenancy, see Saskatchewan's legislation, the *Land Titles Act, 2000*, SS 2000, c L-5.1, s 36; see also *R in Right of Canada v Peters*, [1983] 1 WWR 471 (Sask QB).

In 1987, the BC Law Reform Commission reviewed the issue of "secret severance" in *Working Paper on Co-Ownership of Land* (Vancouver: Law Reform Commission of British Columbia, 1987), and proposed new legislation (at 48), providing in part that severance should be effected only by meeting specified conditions. More recently, in February 2012, the BC Law Reform Commission released a new report, documenting the problems of "secret severance," particularly in the context of spousal or long-term cohabiting relationships (at 19-21). According to this report, a decision that may deprive another party of the benefit of a right of survivorship (without that party's knowledge) is inconsistent with the interdependence arising from a family relationship. As the report argued (at 11), a secret severance may "overturn long-held expectations of future financial and perhaps physical security based on the right of survivorship." Thus, while the 2012 report agreed that consent of all the co-owners should not be required to effect a severance, it recommended that notice be given to the other joint tenant to achieve a legal severance:

> The *Land Title Act* should be amended to provide that in order to sever a co-ownership with survivorship in land unilaterally, the severing co-owner or other person receiving an interest under a severing transaction must give notice of the severing transaction, including a mortgage, to the other joint tenant(s).

See Real Property Law Reform (Phase 2) Project Committee, *Report on Joint Tenancy* (Vancouver: British Columbia Law Institute, 2012) at 21.

Do you agree that reform is necessary in relation to the principles of severance? If so, which reform proposal is most appropriate? Why?

iii. Severance and Consent in Relation to Family Property Statutes

The *Knowlton* case illustrates one aspect of the relationship between traditional principles about severance of joint tenancies and family property statutes. Many of these statutes contain provisions prohibiting dispositions of family property (especially the matrimonial home) without the consent of the other spouse. Where the matrimonial home is held in joint tenancy, such statutory provisions might thus preclude severance by one spouse without consent of the other. Although this issue has been resolved in different ways, the Ontario Court of Appeal in *Horne v Horne Estate* (1987), 45 RPR 223 held that a conveyance by a joint tenant to himself or herself for the purpose of severing a joint tenancy did not constitute a "disposition" for the purposes of the *Family Law Reform Act*, RSO 1980, c 152 [FLRA] (now *Family Law Act*, RSO 1990, c F.3 [FLA]) provisions. Confirming the earlier decision of the Ontario High Court in *Re Lamanna and Lamanna* (1983), 145 DLR (3d) 117, the court in *Horne* stated (at 231-32):

> In light of the scheme of these Acts and their very restricted and carefully defined effect on spousal rights to the matrimonial home after death, I cannot accept that the Legislature intended to include a joint tenant's "right of survivorship" in the class of "interests" in the matrimonial home to which the restrictions against alienation imposed by s. 42 of the FLRA and s. 21 of the FLA are applicable. These Acts do not purport to dictate the manner in which spouses may hold title to their matrimonial home. A severance of a joint tenancy neither interferes with nor affects the existing balance between spouses with respect to the ownership or occupation of their matrimonial home during their marriage. In practical terms, its only consequence is that the spouses' undivided one-half interests thereafter form part of their individual estates thereby permitting them to devise their respective interests as they wish. ...
>
> The right of a joint tenant to sever a joint tenancy unilaterally is a long-recognized common law right. In my opinion, the family law legislation in question ought not to be construed as restricting that right in the absence of express language to that effect. As the Acts are now framed, a severance is not inconsistent with the general scheme of the legislation or incompatible with the provisions respecting matrimonial homes. No policy considerations have been advanced which compel the conclusion that a party to a marriage, without the consent of the other party or a court order, should be barred so long as the marriage subsists (and regardless of the state of the marriage) from taking the steps necessary to ensure that this property interest form part of his or her estate and that the survivor, whichever party that might be, does not acquire sole ownership by operation of law. In my view, no matter how the "right of survivorship" may be characterized

in law, a deed from a joint tenant to himself or herself designed to remove that right does not constitute the "disposition" of an "interest" covered by s. 42 of the FLRA or s. 21 of the FLA. In sum, I agree with the result reached by Walsh J in *Re Lamanna and Lamanna* in this factual situation.

As discussed above, however, a Nova Scotia court concluded that a wife's conveyance to herself prior to her death did not sever the joint tenancy of the matrimonial home with her husband, because the Nova Scotia statute did not provide for a conveyance by a person to himself or herself: see *Presseau v Presseau Estate*, 2010 NSSC 201. Thus, the husband was permitted to set aside the deed executed by his late wife, without his knowledge, and he was entitled to the property by right of survivorship.

iv. Joint Tenancies: Parents and Children

In some cases, a parent may create a joint tenancy with a child as part of an estate-planning arrangement, assuming that the parent will die first and the child will "take" by right of survivorship. Such an arrangement was intentionally designed in *Pecore v Pecore*, 2007 SCC 17, [2007] 1 SCR 795, where the court considered whether the parent was using joint ownership as a tool of estate planning or merely as a tool of convenience to permit the child to manage the parent's funds. Because the parent in this case made it clear that he was fully in charge of the funds, so that the child had only a beneficial interest, the court held that the right of survivorship existed at the parent's death. Although such arrangements are often complicated by issues about taxation and estate planning, as well as by principles about intention, they may be useful ways of employing the concept of "joint tenancy" in some cases. For a different result, by contrast with *Pecore*, see *Madsen Estate v Saylor*, 2007 SCC 18, [2007] 1 SCR 838. See also Ann Elise Alexander, "The Ins and Outs of Joint Tenancy," *The Lawyers Weekly* (5 May 2006). Significantly, some comments suggested that the decision in *Pecore*, at least with respect to the issue of joint tenancy, may have "changed the law and created the right of survivorship as a separate and independent property right" in relation to *inter vivos* transfers: see James D Baird, *Estates: Out of the Ordinary Problems—Joint Tenancy* (Vancouver: Continuing Legal Education Society of British Columbia, June 2008) at 7.1.6. *Pecore v Pecore* was also discussed briefly in Chapter 5 in relation to principles concerning valid gifts and the presumption of advancement.

D. Rights and Obligations of Co-Owners: General Principles

Whether co-owners are joint tenants or tenants in common, their interests are characterized by unity of possession, the only unity common to both kinds of co-ownership. Unity of possession means that each co-owner is entitled, along with all other co-owners, to possession of the whole of the land. Such a possessory right among all co-owners often raises questions about the respective co-owners' rights—for example:

1. What happens if one co-owner remains in possession of a farm, while others leave to work elsewhere?

2. What if one co-owner wrongly excludes others from possession?

3. When are co-owners out of possession entitled to share in profits from the land? What about setoffs for expenses paid by the co-owner in possession?

4. If some co-owners are out of possession voluntarily, are they liable to contribute to the cost of improvements, or entitled to share in the increased value effected by improvements undertaken by the co-owner in possession?

Early common law principles provided that a co-owner in possession was required to pay "occupation rent" to co-owners out of possession in three situations:

1. where the co-owner in possession has excluded the other—that is, has effected an "ouster" of other co-owners; this concept was extended to "constructive exclusion" in a case where a wife left home because of her husband's continued violence: see *Dennis v McDonald*, [1981] 1 WLR 810 (Fam Div);

2. where the co-owners have made an agreement respecting occupation and occupation rent (co-owners are thus permitted to structure their relationship by contract); and

3. where the circumstances require that the co-owner in possession be regarded as "agent" for the other co-owners.

In addition to these common law principles about the rights and obligations of co-owners, the *Statute of Anne*, 1705, 4 Anne c 16, s 27 provided that a co-owner was required to account for benefits received as co-owner from third parties, but not for benefits that a co-owner achieved through the co-owner's own efforts. The effect of the *Statute of Anne* is found in Ontario in the *Courts of Justice Act*, RSO 1990, c C.43, s 122(2), as amended by 1993, c 27:

> An action for an accounting may be brought by a joint tenant or tenant in common … against a co-tenant for receiving more than the co-tenant's just share.

In *Henderson v Eason* (1851), 17 QB 701, the principles were applied so that a former co-owner was not required to share farm profits with absent co-owners who had not been excluded—that is, there had been no ouster of co-owners from possession. What should be the result where one co-owner uses the premises as a boarding house, collecting rent from boarders? Should the rent moneys be shared with absent co-owners? See *Spelman v Spelman*, [1944] 2 DLR 74 (BC CA).

For a case reviewing many of the authorities concerning the application of these principles, see *Osachuk v Osachuk* (1971), 18 DLR (3d) 413 (Man CA), where the court concluded (at 432):

> The law, as I have found it, respecting the rights of joint tenants, where one of them is in sole possession of the joint property, appears in some cases to operate unfairly, and some amendment, with proper safeguards, may be desirable. This would be a matter for the Legislature.

In Alberta, the principles for accounting among co-owners have been codified in the *Law of Property Act*, RSA 2000, c L-7, s 17. In a context where many co-owners are husband and wife, there may also be a need to reconsider these traditional principles, having regard to family property regimes. Once again, it may be important to decide whether it is appropriate to have the same principles applicable to co-owners who are married spouses or cohabitees and to those who are not. For example, issues about occupation rent and compensation for improvements were considered in the context of a divorce application in *McColl v McColl* (1995), 13 RFL (4th) 449 (Ont Ct J), a three-day trial in which the matrimonial home was the only issue in dispute other than child support. See also *Szuflita v Szuflita Estate* (2000), 4 RFL (5th) 313 (Ont Sup Ct J). To what extent would legislative principles (such as those in Alberta) help to resolve such disputes? Note that OLRC, *Principles of Land Law* recommended that co-ownership proceedings involving spouses should be subject to orders for exclusive posses-sion pursuant to Ontario's *Family Law Act*. For an example of proposed legislation see OLRC, *Principles of Land Law* at 109-13.

E. Termination of Concurrent Interests by Partition and Sale

When co-owners no longer wish to hold concurrent interests as joint tenants or as tenants in common, they may invoke the provisions of the *Partition Act*, RSO 1990, c P.4, s 2, which pro-vides that co-owners "may be compelled to make or suffer partition." This statutory provision permits a court to order the destruction of the co-owners' unity of possession by defining boundaries for each co-owner's entitlement to an individual parcel. The former concurrent interest (with unity of possession) is divided into separate units held as sole proprietary in-terests. See also *Partition Act*, RSNS 1989, c 333, s 4. Some provisions concerning partition are also found in the *Judicature Act*, RSNB 1973, c J.2.

One issue in such cases is how a court should choose between ordering partition, on the one hand, or judicial sale and division of the proceeds of sale, on the other. Such a problem was addressed in the case that follows, an appeal from an order that had granted an applica-tion for partition rather than sale.

Cook v Johnston
[1970] 2 OR 1 (H Ct J)

GRANT J: In this appeal from the Senior Master's report dealing with partition of prop-erty jointly owned by the parties, the appellant's contention is that the remedy ought to have been by way of sale rather than partition. Section 3(1) of the *Partition Act*, RSO 1960, c. 287, reads as follows:

> 3(1) Any person interested in land in Ontario ... may [bring an action or make an ap-plication] for the partition of such land or for the sale thereof under the directions of the court if such sale is considered by the court to be more advantageous to the parties interested. [See now *Partition Act*, RSO 1990, c P.4, s 3(1).]

In *Morris v. Morris* (1917), 12 OWN 80, Middleton J, in dealing with a similar matter, stated at p. 81: "Sale as an alternative for partition is quite appropriate when a partition cannot be made."

In *Gilbert v. Smith* (1879), 11 Ch. D 78, Jessel MR, at p. 81 stated:

> The meaning of the Legislature was that when you see that the property is of such a character that it cannot be reasonably partitioned, then you are to take it as more beneficial to sell it and divide the money amongst the parties.

In *Lalor v. Lalor* (1883), 9 PR (Ont.) 455, Proudfoot J, who was deciding whether parti-tion or sale should be ordered, stated:

> I do not think any party has a right to insist on a sale; and it will not necessarily be ordered, unless the Court thinks it more advantageous for the parties interested.

In *Ontario Power Co. v. Whattler* (1904), 7 OLR 198, Meredith CJ reviewed the legislation in the Province giving jurisdiction to the Court to order a sale instead of partition. In reference to the form for such remedies then adopted by the Consolidated Rules, he stated at p. 203:

> That form must be read in the light of the legislation by which jurisdiction has been conferred on the Court to order a sale instead of a partition; and the provision as to proceedings being taken for partition or sale is, I think, a compendious mode of saying that proceedings are to be taken to partition unless it appears "that partition cannot be made without prejudice to the owners of, or parties interested in, the estate," but that if that is made to appear proceedings are then to be taken for the sale of the lands.

The evidence taken before the learned Master in this case reveals that there are very few similar islands in the area that are now available. The appellant urged that the island was not of such an area as permitted two families to enjoy the same in separate cottages. The last survey, however, indicates the island is slightly over two acres in area. It is between 500 and 600 ft. in length and probably 150 ft. in width. The Master was quite justified on the evidence in coming to the conclusion, as I think he did, that it was actually more advantageous to the parties to partition the property than take the chances as to what might develop if it was sold. Even if the parties received more than the actual value of the property from a stranger, neither of them could readily find another suitable summer island home in that district. If one of them was successful in buying the property at a sale, the other would be deprived entirely of his right to spend vacations in the area where he had enjoyed summer vacations for some 30 years. As it stands under the Master's report, each of the parties will have the privilege of enjoying one-half for the whole summer of what they formerly enjoyed for only one-half of the summer. Under the report Cook is getting the portion of the island on which the cottage and dock are built. It was never contemplated that Johnston should contribute anything towards the erection of these. He lived in a tent while enjoying his vacation. The area adjoining the suitable swimming portion of the bay is equally divided between the parties. There may have to be some slight alterations made in the path that leads from the dock to the cottage but I cannot think this will be costly.

On the whole, it is my opinion that the division was more advantageous to Cook than to Johnston. I believe the Master has exercised his discretion properly. In any event it should not be interfered with lightly.

The motion by way of appeal will therefore be dismissed with costs, if demanded.

Appeal dismissed.

DISCUSSION NOTES

i. Partition and Sale: Judicial Discretion

Examine the exercise of discretion required in *Cook v Johnston*. Such discretion in the drawing of boundaries may often be required in co-ownership cases if the court concludes that sale is not appropriate in the circumstances. In *Ponvert v Wood*, [2006] OTC 197 (Sup Ct J), for example, the court ordered partition and identified three identical parcels for the tenants in common. Cases involving applications for partition and sale are frequently presented to courts: see *Peters v Peters* (2000), 32 RPR (3d) 121 (Ont Sup Ct J), and *Fellows v Lunkenheimer* (1998), 21 RPR (3d) 142 (Ont Ct J (Gen Div)).

For a case in which the court concluded that a sale was appropriate to serve the interests of both co-owners, see *Rouse v Rouse* (1999), 27 RPR (3d) 288 (Ont Ct J (Gen Div)). The co-owners were the first wife (aged 83) and the second wife (aged 71) of the deceased, James Rouse.

ii. Partition and Sale for Co-Owners Who Are Spouses

Where co-owners are or have been husband and wife, the considerations may be more complicated. For several years there was uncertainty about how judges should respond to an application for partition in such cases: for an analysis and recommendations, see JM Glenn, "Comment" (1976) 54 Can Bar Rev 149.

Some of these concerns were addressed in *Knowlton v Bartlett*, reviewed above, in which Mrs Bartlett secretly executed a deed to herself severing the joint tenancy with her husband. She died, leaving her one-half undivided interest as tenant in common to her brother, Kenneth Knowlton. The court then considered Knowlton's application for partition.

Knowlton v Bartlett
(1984), 35 RPR 182 (NBQB Fam Div)

JONES J: In the present case, the evidence before me indicates that this property as in most cases does not lend itself to partition. There is a residence on the property and some 47 acres of land. Therefore if an order is to be made in this matter, it would only be an order for sale of the property and an apportionment of the proceeds from such sale.

It is argued on behalf of the respondent that I have a discretion as to whether or not to order a sale at this time. Counsel for the respondent cites to me various authorities to this effect. In the case of *Davis v. Davis*, [1954] OR 23, [1954] 1 DLR 827, the Ontario Court of Appeal held that under the legislation then existing in their province there was a right to a partition or sale and that a Court should compel a partition or sale if no sufficient reason appears as to why an order should not be made. Laidlaw JA speaking for the Court at p. 830 [DLR] said:

> I do not attempt to enumerate or describe what reasons would be sufficient to justify refusal of an order for partition or sale. I am content to say that each case must be considered in the light of the particular facts and circumstances and the Court must then exercise the discretion vested in it in a judicial manner having due regard to those particular facts and circumstances as well as to the matters which I have said are, in my opinion, fundamental.

In that particular case, a wife was claiming partition or sale of a dwelling owned by her and her husband as joint tenants. The husband had been awarded custody of the infant children, and was residing in the house. The argument was made on behalf of the husband that this created a ground for hardship and that in any event the wife had a moral and legal duty to support the children and an order for partition or sale should be refused at that time. On the facts in that case the Ontario Court of Appeal held that there was not sufficient reason for refusal of an order for partition or sale.

There are other judgments subsequent to that where Courts applying this principle have found sufficient reasons or grounds to refuse an order at the time of application. In the case of *Re Yale and MacMaster* (1974), 3 OR (2d) 547, 18 CBR (NS) 225 (sub nom. *Yale v. MacMaster*), 18 RFL 27, 46 DLR (3d) 167 at 182 (Ont. HC), Galligan J held that

> … a consideration of relative hardship is a relevant consideration in determining how a Court ought to exercise the discretion conferred upon it by the *Partition Act*. …

In that case the trustee in bankruptcy of the husband was endeavouring to obtain an order for partition or sale of the property in which the wife and minor children were living. The Court in this case dismissed the application at that time, but a subsequent application when the circumstances had changed, i.e. the children were no longer dependent upon the home for shelter, might well have been successful.

This matter came before the Court of Appeal in New Brunswick in the case of *Melvin v. Melvin* (1975), 11 NBR (2d) 351, 23 RFL 17, 58 DLR (3d) 98 (NB CA). In that case the applicant was the former wife of a divorced man. She had deserted her husband and taken the three youngest children to British Columbia where she was living with and being supported by another man. The husband remained at the marital home along with the two older children. The trial Judge found that the plaintiff was not acting in good faith and was endeavouring to deprive her husband of use of the matrimonial home.

The Court of Appeal, in dismissing an appeal from the refusal of the trial Judge to exercise his discretion in ordering a partition or sale, approved the consideration of the relative hardships of the parties involved and held that real hardship would obtain to Mr. Melvin and his children if an order were made. The Court of Appeal judgment was based on the fact that no real hardship would obtain to the mother if this matter were delayed for such time as there remained minor children and observed at that time that in any event the value of interest in real estate was appreciating.

In the case of *Bruce v. Bruce* (1976), 14 NBR (2d) 422, 28 RFL 190, the New Brunswick Court of Appeal postponed the partition and sale of the home which was owned in joint tenancy by a husband and wife until such time as a minor son completed his education or until further order.

In the present case a property is involved which does not lend itself to partition. If the owners cannot agree as to disposition of the property then it can only be done by an order for sale. Prima facie either party to the ownership of property as in this case as tenants in common is entitled ultimately to have the property disposed of and the proceeds realized. The Court has a discretion to postpone the sale of property in these circumstances where it would result in hardship to one particular party.

In the present case, the house and property involved is the home of Mr. Bartlett. The property was originally that of his parents. He has lived in the property since 1946 and continued living there after his wife left in 1971. He still lives on the property and is now 63 years of age. I am satisfied that he planned to live in this property in the foreseeable future and probably the rest of his days.

Mr. Bartlett was apparently not aware of the fact that his wife had severed the joint tenancy in the property. His testimony is that in recent years he had made improvements to the home. These had included replacing the furnace, putting a cement floor in the basement, replacing some floors in the house, shingling of the roof, installing some insulation on one side of the house and rebuilding a rear porch. If I were to order a sale in this matter I would consider the amounts expended by Mr. Bartlett in considering the disposition of the proceeds of such sale: *Mastron v. Cotton*, 58 OLR 251, [1926] 1 DLR 767 (Ont. CA).

Mr. Bartlett has had of course the use and occupation of the premises since his wife left in 1971. On the other hand he has paid the charges against it including taxes and insurance and is taking care of ongoing maintenance. These would be offsetting. Tax bills filed in this matter indicate for example an assessed value of $9,450 in 1974 and an assessed value of $35,200 in 1984. A portion of this increase would be the result of inflation of values, but I feel I am justified in inferring from this increase in assessed value confirmation that the property has been maintained and in fact improved in value during this period of time.

There is no question that if I order a sale of this property at this time a very real hardship will be sustained by Mr. Bartlett at a relatively late stage in his life. No evidence was given by Mr. Knowlton. He resides out of the province. It is not suggested that he would have any particular use for the property but rather that he wishes to realize the value of his legal interest in the property. This is a legitimate desire.

It is open to a Court to exercise discretion with respect to granting or refusing an order for partition or sale. The cases to which I have referred have stated that a Court in exercising this discretion should consider the relative hardship to the parties.

I have considered these matters in the present circumstances. I am satisfied that at this time I should exercise my discretion and decline to order the sale of the property. Should circumstances change, a further application can be made to the Court and quite possibly a sale could be ordered at that time. Without predetermining or indicating what the decision of a Court might be on a future application, matters which might be considered are any failure of Mr. Bartlett to maintain the property at its present standard, or Mr. Bartlett no longer residing on the property or requiring it as his residence. It may well be that circumstances in the future would be such that Mr. Knowlton could satisfy a Court that failure to order the sale of this property is forcing a hardship on him.

This decision is simply that at the present time and in the present circumstances I find that an order for the sale of this property would constitute a very real hardship upon Mr. Bartlett and that I should exercise my discretion in these circumstances and decline to order a partition or sale of the property.

Under the circumstances each party will bear their own costs in this matter.

Application refused.

Courts have also considered the appropriate approach to an application for partition where the application is presented in the course of divorce proceedings that require the resolution of property issues between a husband and wife, now pursuant to family property statutes. In *Silva v Silva* (1990), 1 OR (3d) 436 (CA), the Ontario Court of Appeal decided that the *Family Law Act*, RSO 1990, c F.3 did not oust the jurisdiction of the *Partition Act*. However, the court concluded that an application under the *Partition Act* should be deferred where there is evidence that an order for partition would prejudice the rights of either spouse in relation to proceedings under the *Family Law Act, 1986*. In the circumstances of the *Silva* case, the court found no such prejudice, but the case also confirmed the existence of judicial discretion in such cases. See also *Kereluk v Kereluk* (2005), WDFL 323 (Ont Sup Ct J) and *Kanura v Simpraga*, 2011 ONSC 578. As is evident, therefore, traditional principles regarding concurrent interests may be substantially revised in the family property context.

iii. Partition and Sale in a Commercial Context

Applications for partition also occur in commercial developments in which co-owners are tenants in common. For example, in *Garfella Apartments Inc v Chouduri*, 2010 ONSC 3413, Garfella applied to the court pursuant to the *Partition Act* to force the sale of 23 units held by tenants in common with Garfella; Garfella was a co-owner (as tenant in common) of the remaining 147 apartment units in a 7-storey apartment building in Toronto. The building was not a condominium, although its ownership structure (which had become popular in the 1970s) was somewhat similar. However, unlike with a condominium, the unitholders did not hold title to their units, but rather a percentage interest in the overall building as tenants in common; they also had the right to occupy or to rent to others a specific apartment in the building. Because Garfella wished to redevelop the building, and the 23 unitholders were unwilling to transfer their interests to him, the corporation applied for a sale in accordance with the *Partition Act*. The application judge denied Garfella's application and the corporation appealed.

On appeal, the court reiterated the presumptive right of a co-owner to partition or, if partition is not appropriate, to a sale. Citing *Greenbanktree Power Corp v Coinamatic Canada Inc* (2004), 75 OR (3d) 478 (CA), the court concluded that there were only limited bases for denying such an application, including malice, oppression, vexatious intent, or hardship amounting to oppression. After reviewing the test for oppression in corporate law (see *BCE Inc v 1976 Debentureholders*, 2008 SCC 69, [2008] 3 SCR 560), the court noted that the oppressive conduct must both undermine the "reasonable expectations" of the parties and also meet the test of conduct that is "coercive, abusive, or unfairly disregarding of the minority interests." In *Garfella*, the court concluded that the test was met, and that Garfella was not entitled to the *Partition Act* remedy. In particular, the court considered the reasonable expectations of the holders of the 23 apartments, Garfella's abusive behaviour in relation to sales of units, and the hardship to long-term residents with limited financial resources to purchase equivalent properties.

Although Garfella did not succeed in its application pursuant to the *Partition Act*, it is important to recognize that there are only limited bases for refusing partition or sale pursuant to the legislation. For cases in which applications pursuant to the *Partition Act* succeeded in commercial contexts, see *CTV Diagnostics Inc v 2013871 Ontario Ltd* (2006), 39 RPR (4th) 60 (Ont Sup Ct J) (lands adjoining a department store), and *First Capital (Canholdings) Corp v North American Property Group*, 2010 ONSC 3196 (sophisticated parties who had purchased property together without a co-tenancy agreement).

III. CONCURRENT INTERESTS: CO-OPERATIVE HOUSING AND CONDOMINIUMS

In the context of widespread use of co-operative housing arrangements and condominium projects, it is important to note how these arrangements "build" on traditional principles about concurrent interests in land. Particularly in the context of condominiums, however, specialized statutes were enacted in the late 20th century to augment the traditional principles to make this form of property ownership attractive to unitholders and viable for developers.

In this context, although "co-operative housing" dates from the 1930s, it now represents a form of co-ownership that is a noticeable but not major form of housing in Canada. Most commonly, the land and buildings in a co-op housing complex are held by a corporation, with individual members holding shares in the corporation. A member's right to occupy a particular unit is defined in a separate occupancy agreement, and the corporation's board establishes rules relating to occupancy. Co-operative housing offers a community with shared amenities as well as exclusive occupancy of units, and the co-op members cooperate in the administration and governance of the project. Co-operative housing is similar to condominiums, but condominium projects have increased more quickly because, unlike co-operative housing projects, condominiums offer fee simple title to unitholders, an arrangement that may foster greater access to financing (see Ziff at 362-69).

As is evident in Canadian cities such as Vancouver and Toronto, however, the proliferation of condominiums has created a new option for home ownership for many people, especially since the enactment of legislation in the late 1960s and early 1970s. However, even though condominium arrangements are regulated by statute (for example, Ontario's *Condominium Act, 1998*, SO 1998, c 19), the conceptual basis for condominiums is essentially a more sophisticated co-ownership model in which individual units are held as fee simple estates, with unitholders sharing common amenities and structural elements of the condominium building as tenants in common. However, because positive covenants cannot be enforced in law or in equity (discussed further in Chapter 7), the enforcement of mutual obligations for unitholders in condominiums is dependent on the provisions of provincial condominium legislation.

Although this section of the chapter does not offer a full discussion of condominium law and practice, it is important to understand how traditional principles about co-ownership provided the basic elements of this new form of housing and commercial development.

A. Current Issues About Ontario's Condominium Act

Essentially, condominium legislation provides that each unitholder has a fee simple estate in an individual unit, while they all share, for example, common amenities as tenants in common. Although the first *Condominium Act* in Ontario was enacted in the late 1960s, the current legislation (enacted in 1998) is again under review, in part because of governance issues arising from the burgeoning growth of this form of concurrent home ownership. Thus, a review of Ontario's 1998 *Condominium Act* was commenced in 2012, with three stages to be completed. The stage one findings of the review, released in January 2013, concluded that there was a need to assess appropriate reforms to ensure the continued viability of condominium arrangements. As this report stated:

> Today, condominiums account for half of all new homes built in Ontario. With roughly 589,000 units in the province, about 1.3 million Ontarians call a condominium their home. As the sector has expanded, so has this housing option, the size and complexity of the market, and the number of people affected. ... [The report identified a number of particular issues relating to the "shared" nature of condominium projects and the need for unitholders to recognize their responsibilities as "co-owners" of the overall project. In this context, the report concluded that there was a need for more effective management] of relationships within the condominium sector itself, as

well as individual condominium communities ... . Owners and others with a stake in the condo-minium sector must see themselves as members of a single community who share common in-terests. Like good neighbours, they must learn to work together to manage their differences in order to achieve common goals.

(Public Policy Forum, *Ontario's Condominium Act Review: Stage One Findings Report*, Executive Summary (Ottawa, January 2013) at 5, online: Canada's Public Policy Forum <http://www.ppforum.ca/publications/ontarios-condominium-act-review-stage-one-findings-report>.)

According to the review, the condominium legislation in Ontario created the "framework" legislation for condominium projects. Thus, s 5 of the *Condominium Act* requires registration of a declaration, the essential "constitution" of the condominium project, but each individual cor-poration must then conduct regular meetings and create and administer bylaws and rules for each individual condominium community. There are also enforcement provisions (ss 130-37), by which the condominium corporation ensures that the declaration, bylaws, and rules are followed by all unitholders. Yet, according to the review, it seems that many people who purchase a fee simple unit in a condominium corporation may be unaware of all the obliga-tions pursuant to the bylaws and rules and also ignorant of the monthly costs of ongoing maintenance and other obligations relating to their participation in the condominium proj-ect. There is also some indication that a growing number of unitholders are absentee invest-ors who have rented their units, but neither the absentee investors nor the tenants of these condominium units participate in the corporate meetings of the condominium. Moreover, the lack of owner occupancy may create problems with respect to the enforcement of con-dominium bylaws and rules.

In this context, the review identified five primary issues of concern in relation to condo-miniums in Ontario:

1. governance of condominium corporations,
2. methods for more effective dispute resolution,
3. financial management arrangements for both operating and reserve funds,
4. transparency about the full costs of condominium living available to potential pur-chasers before they buy a condominium unit, and
5. qualifications and training for condominium managers.

In addition, as the review noted, there are now a variety of different kinds of condomini-ums, including timeshares (which create exclusive occupancy rights for defined periods of time) as well as combined hotel/condominium projects and condominium projects designed for commercial and retail developments. All these arrangements may provide greater flex-ibility for unitholders, but they also create a need for more sophisticated arrangements to ensure the viability of the projects in the mutual interests of all unitholders. For some addi-tional details about general principles and issues concerning condominiums, see Stephen M Karr, "Covenants and the Condominium" in *Covenants and the Use of Land* (Toronto: Ontario Bar Association, 2009); John G Sprankling, *Understanding Property Law*, 3d ed (New York: LexisNexis, 2012); Audrey Loeb, *The Condominium Act: A User's Manual*, 3d ed (Toronto: Cars-well, 2009); and Ziff at 362-69.

The review commenced stage two in March 2013, and its "solutions report" was released in September 2013: see Public Policy Forum, *Growing Up: Ontario's Condominium Communi-ties Enter a New Era* (Ottawa: Public Policy Forum, 2013) [*Growing Up*]. This report was based on the advice and recommendations of five working groups and a panel of experts who examined the five areas of concern identified in the stage one report: governance, dispute resolution, financial management, consumer protection (transparency re costs, etc.), and managers' qualifications and training. The stage two recommendations included several key recommendations; as identified on the website of the Public Policy Forum, they include:

- Creation of a Condo Office, an arm's length umbrella organization that could provide functions such as education and awareness, dispute settlement, condo manager licensing, and a condo registry.
- Improved consumer education and protection.
- Updated financial management rules and dispute resolution mechanisms.
- Stronger qualification requirements for condo boards, including mandatory training for first-time members.
- A new licensing program, managed by the condo office, to ensure that condo managers are properly trained and qualified.

(See *Ontario's Condominium Act Review: Stage Two Solutions Report* (Ottawa, 24 September 2013), online: Canada's Public Policy Forum <http://www.ppforum.ca/publications/ontarios-condominium-act-review-stage-two>.)

The recommendation for the creation of a condo office is particularly significant. Its responsibility for dispute resolution would include a separate dispute resolution office and a "quick decision maker," recommendations that are intended to alleviate the necessity for all disputes (large or small) to be referred to mediation, arbitration, or the courts. The office would be "at arm's length from government, but with authority delegated by government, [and it] would be funded by a combination of user fees and a modest levy (estimated at $1 to $3 a month) on each condo unit in the province" (see *Growing Up* at 7).

Following an opportunity for public input, there will be a final report with recommendations for governmental action, and possible reform of the *Condominium Act*, in early 2014.

DISCUSSION NOTES

i. Enforcement Costs for Condominium Corporations

Litigation on the part of condominium boards to enforce compliance with their bylaws and rules against individual unitholders often create both legal and financial challenges. Although the *Condominium Act*, s 134(5) permits the condominium corporation to recover damages or costs from a non-compliant unitholder in such litigation (secured by a lien against the unitholder's interest), courts have not always permitted a condominium corporation to recover all its litigation costs if the court regarded them as inappropriate in the circumstances: see *Metropolitan Toronto Condominium Corp No 1385 v Skyline Executive Properties Inc* (2005), 253 DLR (4th) 656, 197 OAC 144, 31 RPR (4th) 169 (CA); *Toronto Standard Condominium Corp No 1633 v Baghai Development Ltd*, 2012 ONCA 417 (CanLII); and *Royal Bank of Canada v Metropolitan Toronto Condominium Corp No 1226*, 2013 ONSC 239. See also Jeffrey Lem, "Condo Cost Rulings Tilting Away from Generous Awards," *Law Times* (13 May 2013) at 7.

ii. Human Rights in the Condominium Context

In addition to the problems discussed above, it seems that there are numerous human rights complaints filed by unitholders, both in relation to other unitholders and against the condominium corporation. In one successful human rights complaint in Alberta, for example, an elderly couple were challenged in relation to a "family only" bylaw when they hired a live-in caregiver in their condominium unit. At the time of the hearing of the complaint by the condominium corporation, the unitholders were Mr Davis, who was 87 years old and blind, and his wife, who was suffering from dementia. The couple had hired the live-in caregiver so that they could remain in their unit with her assistance. The condominium corporation's bylaws did not permit the unit to be used other than as a single-family dwelling (and it expressly prohibited "roomers" or "boarders"), and the corporation claimed that the live-in caregiving arrangement thus contravened the bylaws. The corporation's application for a declaration that the unitholders had violated the bylaws was dismissed on the basis that live-in caregivers were not within the definition of roomers and boarders, and that granting the declaration would be devastating to any unitholder in need of medical care. See *Condominium Plan No 9910225 v Davis*, 2013 ABQB 49. See also *Rosen v Corporation of the Town of Blue Mountains*, 2012 ONSC 4215 (Div Ct).

B. Condominiums and the Impact on Affordable Housing

Beyond these issues for individual unitholders and condominium corporations, there are broader concerns about the ways in which the proliferation of condominiums may affect traditional neighbourhoods and access to affordable urban housing. In the article that follows, Douglas Harris reviewed the history of condominium development in downtown Vancouver to assess some of these broader issues.

Douglas Harris, "Condominium and the City:
The Rise of Property in Vancouver"
(2011) 36:3 Law & Soc Inquiry 694 (footnotes omitted)

The statutes that introduced condominium to jurisdictions across North America and most of the rest of the common law world in the 1960s simplified the stacking of fee simple interests in land in a vertical column. They did so by coupling a fee simple interest in a defined area of a building with a common-property interest in the shared spaces and then by providing a structure of government for regulating the use of the private and common property.

The effect of this new statutory condominium regime was to detach the legal category of land from the surface of the earth, a feature that led to various playfully incredulous monikers: "Land without Earth" (Pitman 1962); "A Hybrid Castle in the Sky" (Schwartz 1964); "The Flying Fee" (Shiff 1970); and "Property in Thin Air" (Gray 1991). Playfulness aside, detaching the legal category of land from the earth's skin enabled the increase in density of private interests in land. Within the framework provided by condominium statutes, ownership of land could be layered in a column that was limited only by the height and depth of a building. Where there was once a single fee simple interest, there could, after statutory condominium, be several hundred. ...

[This article] focuses attention on a relatively new and increasingly prominent legal form, documents its arrival and spread across a city over forty years, and considers its contribution to the transformation of the urban landscape of a North American city and, perhaps, to the idea of property. It is a project that engages a legal form and its urban location. ...

According to [CB Macpherson, *Property: Mainstream and Critical Positions* (Toronto: University of Toronto Press, 1978) at 11], property as a legal right and, therefore, as an enforceable claim has always needed justification; property "depends on society's belief that it is a *moral* right," that it is "a human right" (emphasis in original). This is particularly true of private property, where the holder has a right to exclude others, or, as Larissa Katz (2008) recently argued, an exclusive right to set the agenda for an object. Seventeenth-century political philosopher John Locke offered one of the most influential of justificatory theories—that the right to private property arises in the state of nature through the mixing of one's labor with the material world (1988). The justifications for the regimes of statutory condominium, which fostered a massive increase in the density of private property in land, lay in other resonant justificatory traditions, particularly those that linked private property to freedom and economic efficiency.

From its introduction, many observers touted condominium and its capacity to increase the density of private interests as a legal mechanism with enormous potential to effect positive social change. Alvin Rosenberg, author of the first text on Canadian condominium law, published in 1969, described the possibilities of condominium in the following terms:

> In future years condominium may well be instrumental in effecting major changes. Large parts of the urban populations may be shifted to the city cores where costs of servicing, public facilities and transportation are at a minimum. A new class of responsible citizens may be created with a larger stake in the community because of their private ownership of their homes and working premises. The trend towards tenant living may be reversed. If the democratic, capitalistic society is to remain vital and vibrant, there is a need for the type of citizen who takes pride in owning his own home or business premises. In this period of rising land, servicing and construction costs the condominium may be the only way to fulfill this need. The condominium concept, if it is successful, will have reflected, or have been a response to, a need for social change and, in turn, will have promoted that change or at least made it possible.

This was a powerfully optimistic view of the transformative potential of a legal form. The basis for this optimism lay in the ability of condominium to facilitate the subdivision of land, opening the possibility of ownership to more people and increasing the density of private interests in the process. Home ownership fostered "responsible citizens" and encouraged an increase in population density to create more efficient cities. Condominium was the legal mechanism that made these goals possible. ...

Condominium arrived in Vancouver in 1970 and, measured by proliferation, became a remarkably successful legal innovation. A large and increasing proportion of Vancouverites live within condominium, which structures the ownership of land across a large swath of the city. Indeed, its concentration usefully defines the inner city. Condominium, a form of property characterized by private ownership of an individual unit in a multi-unit building, a share in the ownership of common property, and a right to participate in the collective governance of this property, is increasingly the way that people own land in cities. A creature of statute, it shares a similar legal structure to the community or neighborhood associations that have become prevalent in the suburbs of many North American cities. Condominium differs in that it subdivides a single building, facilitating the capacity to subdivide upward rather than outward. In so doing, it enables a massive increase in the density of private interests in land. Where there was once a single fee simple interest to a portion of the earth's surface, there might now be several hundred, each attaching to an area, defined in three dimensions, within a building. Condominium provides the legal architecture for this increase in density of private ownership and, in turn, for a potential increase in human densities.

Reflecting its success as a legal form, the "condo" has entered the lexicon to describe apartments owned under a condominium structure, but also to describe the location of modern, upscale, amenity-rich urban living. This usage reflects the perception of the legal form as the preserve of an affluent, professional class. In Vancouver, the tall, glass-sheathed condominium towers clustered on the downtown peninsula make this segment of the condominium market particularly visible. However, this visibility belies the diversity of structures built around the legal form and its capacity to make home ownership possible to a broad socioeconomic spectrum. Condominium has proliferated in Vancouver in all but the neighborhoods restricted to single-family residences.

As land values have risen in the city, condominium has extended the possibility of home-ownership to many otherwise excluded if the smallest spatial unit of ownership remained the standard city lot and the single-family residence. However, as a legal structure that operates to subdivide buildings into individually owned, three dimensional parcels, its success displaced other forms of tenure and those who might occupy buildings structured around those forms of tenure. In Vancouver, as elsewhere, the conversion of rental apartment buildings to condominium, coupled in most cases with a renovation of those spaces, has displaced tenants, pushing out those who might rent in older buildings but not purchase the renovated units. The association of condominium with affluence, therefore, reflects not just the visibility of "up-market" condos, but also the connection between the legal form and the displacement of tenants. Displacement need not be direct: changing forms of tenure in individual buildings affect land values more broadly, and wealthier owners demand different amenities and expect different streetscapes than those with fewer means. Neighborhoods will change with the arrival of condominium, and the mapping of condominium buildings in Vancouver reveals something of the reach of gentrification in the city. …

How much of the change in Vancouver over the past forty years can we attribute to a legal form of ownership? Certainly, an account of Vancouver's transformation would be incomplete without considering the role of condominium; it has become the principal form of residential property ownership in the inner city. In fact, its density now defines the inner city. However, I think we can go further: Vancouver without condominium would be very different from the city that has emerged. The legal form, introduced in the 1960s, enabled fuller rights of ownership to attach to a single unit in a multi-unit building than possible at common law or through cooperatives or residential tenancies. It is, at least in part, the opportunity to hold this fuller bundle of property rights that has brought people into the city as residents or as investors. Perhaps the cooperative might have been modified to satisfy lenders that its shares provided adequate security for a loan; perhaps greater security of tenure might have been extended to residential tenants and the tax system remade to create incentives to build large-scale rental accommodation; or perhaps another legal form might have emerged to play the role that condominium performs. Instead, governments across North America created statutory condominium and it became the preferred legal architecture for multi-unit residential buildings, nowhere more so than in Vancouver.

In a recent study of Toronto, Lehrer and Wieditz (2009) conflated the legal form and the processes of change, which they understand within the frame of gentrification, in describing the "condofication" of the city. Ley placed condominium with renovated property "as the landscape face of *embourgeoisement*" (1996, 48-49). However, perhaps it is the newness of the legal form and the fact that the buildings constructed around it are also new, or newly renovated, that has led many to associate condominium with gentrification. As the buildings age, the luster of many will fade, and the extent of renovation or rebuilding rather than the form of ownership will define the character of neighborhoods. In the longer term, the capacity of condominium to increase the density of private interests in land will endure. Whether this feature is a catalyst for continuing processes of urban upscaling remains in question, but the initial move to condominium has been a central part of a dramatic rearrangement of Vancouver's inner city.

Might the sudden rise of condominium challenge deeply rooted conceptions of what it means to own property? If the ownership of land remains the paradigm through which private property is understood, and an increasingly large proportion of land is held within condominium, which combines private and common property with collective governance, then it may become increasingly difficult to think of private property solely or even primarily in terms of, in Blackstone's famous caricature, "sole and despotic dominion." The legal form of condominium embeds private property within community, albeit a community that excludes all but owners. Does this embedding weaken an individualistic and detached sense of private property or enhance that detachment by limiting the community to a defined group of owners? These are few among many questions that one might ask of this relatively new, but increasingly ubiquitous and important form of ownership—condominium.

DISCUSSION NOTE

Linking the Rise of Condominium Housing and Homelessness?

In reflecting on these comments about condominiums and their impact on affordable rental housing ("condofication" of downtown neighbourhoods in major cities in Canada), recall the discussion in Chapter 1 about the right to housing as a human right. In this context, see also Jessie Hohmann, *The Right to Housing: Law, Concepts, Possibilities* (Oxford and Portland, OR: Hart, 2013); D Cowan & J Fionda, "Homelessness" in Susan Bright and John Dewar, eds, *Land Law: Themes and Perspectives* (Oxford: Oxford University Press, 1998) [Bright & Dewar] 257; and Nicholas Blomley, "Landscapes of Property" (1998) 32:3 Law and Soc'y Rev 567. For an earlier assessment, see Parkdale Community Legal Services, "Homelessness and the Right to Shelter: A View from Parkdale" (1988) 4 J L & Soc Pol'y 35.

IV. FAMILY PROPERTY: A STUDY IN LEGISLATIVE AND JUDICIAL REFORM

> There is a sense in which the law of matrimonial property is concerned, not with property at all, but with human relations and ideologies in respect of property. ... [The] law of matrimonial property "comprises a substantial portion of the secular definition of the institution of marriage." The law regulating the spouses' property relations is fundamentally an index of social relations between the sexes, and, for this reason, affords a peculiar wealth of commentary on such matters as the prevailing ideology of marriage, the cultural definition of the marital roles, the social status of the married woman, and the role of the state *vis-à-vis* the family.

(K Gray, *Reallocation of Property on Divorce* (Abingdon, UK: Professional Books, 1977) at 1, quoting Ontario Law Reform Commission, *Report on Family Law, Part IV: Family Property Law* (Toronto: Ministry of the Attorney General, 1974) [OLRC, *Family Property Law*] at 2.)

As Gray explained, the idea of family property offers useful insights about gender relations and property in a social and economic context. Moreover, as was evident in the first part of this chapter on concurrent interests, the traditional principles have been abridged from time to time where the co-owners were spouses. For practical purposes, because many co-owners are spouses or in relationships "tantamount to spousal," it is appropriate to examine the special principles applicable to property relationships in the family context. In looking at family property, the initial focus is on selected aspects of spousal entitlement to property at marriage breakdown, most of which now require interpretation of provincial legislative schemes specifically enacted for these purposes. In addition, the materials also examine judicial principles extending similar kinds of property entitlements to those in "marriage-like" (cohabiting) relationships. Finally, the situation of First Nations spouses on reserves and the issues arising from the limited application of provincial legislative schemes to their circumstances are explored.

By contrast with many other areas of property law, the issues of family property illustrate considerable legal reform, particularly in the last century or so. Thus, this area is one that has attracted the interest of legal historians and those interested in examining progressive social change movements. More specifically, because reform of family property has tended to coincide with greater equality for women (and others in spouse-like relationships), this area of law offers an important opportunity to reflect on gender and property, as well as the relationships between private family arrangements and the organization and structure of public life, including paid work. For an interesting analysis, see Wallace Clement & John Myles, "Linking Domestic and Paid Labour: Career Disruptions and Household Obligations" in Clement & Myles, *Relations of Ruling: Class and Gender in Postindustrial Societies* (Montreal: McGill-Queen's University Press, 1994) at 175:

> People experience class not only as individuals but through households, both *within* the household and *between* the household and the labour market. We say "people" but in fact the experience is specifically gendered. Men tend to be empowered by their households, while women have their powers diminished because of domestic responsibilities.

As you examine the materials that follow, assess the relationships between property and gender in households and in the labour market.

A. The Historical Background

1. The Concept of Coverture

The classic formulation concerning marriage and property is found in Blackstone's *Commentaries* (vol 1) at 442:

> By marriage, the husband and wife are one person in law: that is, the very being or legal existence of the woman is suspended during the marriage, or at least is incorporated and consolidated into that of the husband: under whose wing, protection, and *cover*, she performs everything; and is therefore called in our law-french a *femme-covert* … and her condition during her marriage is called her *coverture*.

The legal status of a married woman pursuant to the doctrine of coverture (described below) was a complex matter relating to many areas of law in addition to property: e.g. see CMA McCauliff, "The Medieval Origin of the Doctrine of Estates in Land: Substantive Property Law, Family Considerations, and the Interests of Women" (1992) 66 Tul L Rev 919. For an overview in the Canadian context, see M McCaughan, *The Legal Status of Married Women in Canada* (Scarborough, ON: Carswell, 1977) [McCaughan]; and in relation to restrictions on women's personal freedom, see M Doggett, *Marriage, Wife-Beating and the Law in Victorian England* (London: Weidenfeld and Nicolson, 1992). In relation to property, J Johnston Jr has succinctly explained the historical differences between single women (who were not subject to the restrictions of coverture) and married wives (who were subject to coverture), as follows:

> [A] *sui juris* single woman, like her male counterpart, was free to own, manage and transfer property; to sue and be sued; and to enjoy the income attributable to her property and personal labor. At the instant she was married, however, her status changed radically:
>
> (1) Her tangible personalty, subject to minor exceptions, instantly became her husband's property [as did personalty acquired by her after the date of the marriage].
>
> (2) She did not lose title to real property formerly held by her solely in fee, but her husband acquired an interest known as *jure uxoris*, entitling him to sole possession and control during the marriage. A fortiori, all income from this realty belonged to the husband, with no duty to account to the wife. His interest was alienable at his discretion and was subject to attachment by his creditors. [Property acquired after marriage was treated in the same way.]
>
> (3) [The husband had a right to an estate, if a child was born, called "curtesy," an arrangement explained below.]
>
> (4) After their marriage, all real property transferred to the spouses jointly was held in tenancy by the entirety; while the marriage lasted, the husband was entitled to sole control and enjoyment of this property. At the death of either party, the survivor assumed sole ownership.
>
> (5) During the marriage, the wife could not contract, sue or be sued on her own behalf.
>
> (6) Her husband was entitled to all of her earnings.

(J Johnston Jr, "Sex and Property: The Common Law Tradition, the Law School Curriculum, and Developments Toward Equality" (1972) 47 NYUL Rev 1033 at 1045-46.)

As Johnston stated, "In short, marriage converted the wife into a legal cipher, or nonperson." He also examined in detail a number of differing theoretical explanations for this legal treatment of women and men at marriage. For example, some commentators concluded that the legal principle of coverture reflected the biblical teaching that husband and wife become "one flesh," while others suggested that the principle represented a version of guardianship within marriage. After examining and rejecting these and other explanations, however, Johnston stated (at 1051) that "[u]nfortunately ... a general theory that will fully account for the common law system—and for female acquiescence in it over the years—has not yet been formulated."

In considering the materials that follow, note the kinds of explanations proffered for the treatment of married women in law and the assumptions underlying legislative and judicial reforms.

2. Dower and Curtesy: Common Law Entitlements

In addition to coverture, the rights of married spouses included dower (not to be confused with "dowry") and curtesy. Although these rights were not the same, they both provided life interests in some of the other spouse's property for a surviving spouse—that is, after the other spouse's death. Both dower and curtesy rights were available in most provinces until quite recently.

A wife's right to dower was technically described by B Laskin, in *Cases and Notes on Land Law* (Toronto: University of Toronto Press, 1958) at 72:

> At common law, whenever a husband became seised (otherwise than as a joint tenant) of an estate of inheritance during coverture[,] which issue of the marriage, if any, could inherit, the wife obtained an inchoate right of dower therein which became consummate on the husband's death survived by his wife. The dower right was a life interest in one-third of such freeholds of inheritance and constituted a clog on the husband's title even in his lifetime.

In practice, the wife's right to dower created problems for conveyancing. Unless the wife joined in barring her right to dower when her husband transferred any interest in real property by deed, a subsequent purchaser's interest would be subject to the wife's dower right. That is, long after the transfer occurred, a widow could claim, on the death of her husband, a life estate in one-third of any lands transferred to purchasers. Such an arrangement was obviously not convenient for purchasers, and measures to avoid this result were eventually devised. For example, because the dower right did not attach to an equitable interest, conveyances frequently utilized deeds to uses (explained in Chapter 3) to avoid dower rights. In other cases, a deed for a purchase and sale transaction might include a provision that "the vendor's wife joins in the deed to bar her dower." Yet these arrangements were sometimes fraught with conceptual problems that resulted in litigation: see *Freedman v Mason*, [1956] OR 849, 4 DLR (2d) 576 (H Ct J), rev'd [1957] OR 441 (CA), 9 DLR (2d) 262, appeal dismissed [1958] SCR 483; and *Re Hazell*, [1925] 3 DLR 661 (Ont CA). For further details, see GL Haskins, "The Development of Common Law Dower" (1948-49) 62 Harv L Rev 42 and OLRC, *Family Property Law* at 105-49. In most provinces, the wife's right to dower at common law was augmented by statute: e.g. see *Dower Act*, RSO 1970, c 135, repealed by *Family Law Reform Act*, SO 1978, c 2 (now *Family Law Act*, RSO 1990, c F.3). See also *Dower Act*, RSNB 1973, c D-13, repealed by *Marital Property Act*, SNB 1980, c M-1.1 (see now *Marital Property Act*, SNB 2012, c 107); *Dower Act*, RSNS 1967, c 79 and *Dower Procedure Act*, RSNS 1967, c 80, both repealed by *Matrimonial Property Act*, RSNS 1989, c 275; and *Dower Act*, RSPEI 1974, c D-17, repealed by *Family Law Reform Act*, SPEI 1978, c 6 (see now *Family Law Act 1995*, c 12, s 63 and RSPEI, c F-2.1). Dower was abolished in the United Kingdom by the *Administration of Estates Act, 1925*, c 23, s 45.

There are important historical differences between provinces in Eastern Canada (which received English common law, including dower) and some in Western Canada. For an account of the political movement to enact dower rights on the Prairies in the early 20th century (when the adoption of Torrens registration systems abolished them), see M McCallum, "Prairie Women and the Struggle for a Dower Law, 1905-1920" in T Loo & R McLean, eds, *Historical Perspectives on Law and Society in Canada* (Toronto: Copp Clark Longman, 1994) 306. For an account of modern "homestead" legislation that replaced dower in the Western provinces, see Ziff at 188-90.

The husband's right of curtesy was similar to but also different from a wife's dower right. McCaughan described curtesy as follows:

> Tenancy by the curtesy arose when a man married a woman seised of inheritable estates, that is of lands and tenements in fee-simple or fee-tail, and had by her issue born alive and capable of inheriting such estate: in such a case the husband, on his wife's death, held the lands for his life as tenant by the curtesy of England.

For further details, see McCaughan at 7.

3. Equitable Settlements and Statutory Reforms

The common law rights of dower and curtesy, as well as the doctrine of coverture, reflect the history of property and marriage relationships. For example, dower was the subject of one article of the *Magna Carta* in 1215. By the 17th and 18th centuries, however, the common law doctrine of coverture had been ameliorated to some extent by the use of family trusts or settlements, which enabled a married woman to retain some limited rights to property in spite of the requirements of coverture. Prior to marriage, for example, a woman's father could set up a trust, in which the father or the woman's brother would be the trustee, so that she could be the beneficial owner of her "separate estate"—and in this way, the trust property would not pass to her husband on marriage. Although such an arrangement successfully avoided the problems of the common law doctrine of coverture, it was not generally available to women in England unless their families were wealthy and had access to expert advice in drafting such settlements. In Canadian provinces in the 19th century, there was even less access to these equitable arrangements.

By contrast with these equitable responses to the common law doctrine of coverture, a significant movement emerged in support of statutory reform of the law of married women's property in the 19th century, both in England and in North America. A number of US states enacted married women's property legislation in the first half of the 19th century, and the first of these statutes in Canada was enacted in New Brunswick in 1851: see *An Act To Secure to Married Women Real and Personal Property held in their own Right*, SNB 1851, c 24. Similar legislation was enacted in Ontario in 1859: *An Act Respecting Certain Separate Rights of Property of Married Women* (1859), 22 Vict, c 73 (Ontario); and in Nova Scotia in 1866: *An Act for the Protection of Married Women in Certain Cases*, SNS 1866, c 33.

Yet, although these statutory reforms may have provided increased access to property rights for married women, some historians have argued that the reform statutes often were enacted at the behest of husbands involved in commercial activities who wished to thereby "preserve" their homes and other assets from bankruptcy or other debt-collecting processes. By ensuring that a wife held title to personal holdings (which the reform statutes enabled a husband to arrange), he could carry on commercial activities without fear of losing everything if these activities proved unsuccessful. In this way, the reform statutes were probably motivated more often by goals of enhancing husbands' commercial activities than by the desire to recognize equality for women. For some analyses of the purposes of such statutes in the United States, see N Basch, *In the Eyes of the Law: Women, Marriage and Property in Nineteenth-Century New York* (Ithaca, NY: Cornell University Press, 1982); P Rabkin, *Fathers to Daughters: The Legal Foundations of Female Emancipation* (Westport, CT: Greenwood Press, 1980); and Marylynn Salmon, *Women and the Law of Property in Early America* (Chapel Hill and London: University of North Carolina Press, 1986). In relation to the United Kingdom, see L Holcombe, *Wives and Property* (Toronto: University of Toronto Press, 1983). See also A Sachs & J Hoff Wilson, *Sexism and the Law* (Oxford: M Robertson, 1978); and Margaret Valentine Turano, "Jane Austen, Charlotte Brontë, and the Marital Property Law" (1998) 21 Harv Women's LJ 179. For a comparison of 19th-century assessments of the reform of married women's property in the United Kingdom and the United States, see MJ Mossman, "Women Lawyers and Women's Legal Equality" (2012) 87:1 Chicago-Kent L Rev 503.

Similar statutes concerning the reform of married women's property in Canada have also been subjected to critiques. According to Constance Backhouse, in "Married Women's Property Law in Nineteenth-Century Canada" (1988) 6 LHR 211, Canadian statutes fall into three categories. In the first and earliest group of statutes, the objective was to provide emergency relief for wives whose husbands had deserted them and whose well-being depended on their being able to regain control of their assets. Such statutes represented very little encroachment on traditional common law principles. In relation to later legislation, however, Backhouse suggests (at 212) that these statutes directly confronted traditional common law principles by means of the creation of "separate estates" for wives, thus insulating their property from control by their husbands (and their husbands' creditors). Only in the third wave of legislation did wives attain dispositive powers over their separate property and control of their earnings. According to Backhouse, judges were not always responsive to liberal interpretations of these reform statutes.

However, in another study about reforms to married women's property in Ontario, Lori Chambers reported some cases involving judicial sympathy to the plight of women in relation to their (lack of) access to property interests, and discretionary decision making by judges to overcome interpretive issues so as to accomplish the reform goals of married women's property legislation: see Lori Chambers, *Married Women and Property Law in Ontario* (Toronto: Osgoode Society for Canadian Legal History, 1997). See also S Ingram & K Inwood, "Property Ownership by Married Women in Victorian Ontario" (2000) 23 Dal LJ 406; and K Inwood & S van Sligtenhorst, "The Social Consequences of Legal Reform: Women and Property in a Canadian Community" (2004) 19 Continuity & Change 165.

In addition, in their study of married women's property reforms in Nova Scotia, Philip Girard & Rebecca Veinott suggest that both men and women may have generally accepted the traditional common law principles, so that the statutory reforms were enacted only for purposes of the "exceptional" cases when husbands were delinquent in their duties to their families.

For example, Girard & Veinott suggest a different understanding of the motivations for the reform statutes in Nova Scotia:

> The Nova Scotia experience is worthy of study because of the extent to which reform was propelled for much of the 19th century by conservative rather than liberal conceptions of the family. That this development occurred with the apparent support of Nova Scotia women sits uneasily with much of the existing literature, which tends to assume that a "harsh" common law was distrusted by women yearning for the adoption of separate property. The Nova Scotia experience makes us aware that in some jurisdictions at least, the application of liberal economic principles to family life possessed little appeal for much of the 19th century. Simultaneously, it reveals a perception by contemporaries that the conservative idea of the family, based on familial responsibility rather than individual independence, was capable of being transformed to serve the interests of women and children. Finally, it urges us to reconsider whether an explanatory paradigm based upon a movement from separate spheres to sexual equality adequately captures the dynamic of law reform in this instance.

(P Girard & R Veinott, "Married Women's Property Law in Nova Scotia, 1850-1910" in J Guildford & S Morton, eds, *Separate Spheres: Women's Worlds in the 19th-Century Maritimes* (Fredericton: Acadiensis Press, 1994) 67 at 67.) For another analysis of the legislation in Nova Scotia, see P Girard, "Married Women's Property, Chancery Abolition, and Insolvency Law: Law Reform in Nova Scotia, 1820-1867" in P Girard & J Phillips, eds, *Essays in the History of Canadian Law*, vol III: Nova Scotia (Toronto: University of Toronto Press, 1990) 80. As you read the late 20th-century cases in these materials, examine the assumptions they make about the role of statutory reform of "family property"—and the impact of differing approaches to judicial interpretation of modern statutory language.

4. *Property and the Impact of Divorce Reforms*

Regardless of the motives for the 19th-century reform statutes, they were generally enacted in Canadian provinces according to the models adopted in England in 1870 and again in 1882. More recently, however, it has become clear that the right to separate property was not always by itself a means of transforming women's access to wealth. In spite of women's rights to hold interests in property, the pattern of husbands being titleholders of family property frequently, but not always, remained intact.

This situation was not really addressed in the legal system until the enactment (for the first time) of federal divorce legislation in Canada in 1968. Thereafter, both federal and provincial law reform commissions began to examine the impact of divorce (rather than death) on married spouses and their property, and in relation to "spouses" in cohabiting relationships, and they made recommendations for changes in both property and financial support entitlements. Beginning with Ontario's *Family Law Reform Act*, RSO 1980, c 152, first enacted in 1978, all the common law provinces outside Quebec reformed provincial laws regarding spousal entitlements to property on marriage breakdown. Moreover, Ontario significantly altered its approach only eight years later in 1986 in adopting the *Family Law Act*, now RSO 1990, c F.3, as amended.

The issue of property entitlement is a complex one as a result of the process of reform over the past two decades and because of differing views about the rationale for these statutory reforms. It is also complex because of the socioeconomic implications of the creation of two economic units after divorce in place of one, with the inevitable need to stretch (sometimes limited or even non-existent) resources among former family members. Throughout the cases in this section, there is also an ongoing debate about the appropriate role for judges and the extent to which they must apply statutory provisions rigidly (to achieve consistency, predictability, and uniformity), on the one hand, or exercise discretion in each case (because "each spousal relationship is different"), on the other.

The recent reform developments were significantly influenced by the decision of the Supreme Court of Canada in *Murdoch v Murdoch*, [1975] 1 SCR 423. The Murdochs married in 1943, and Mrs Murdoch separated from her husband in 1968 after a marriage of 25 years. At separation, she filed claims for (among other things) financial support, and a declaration that her husband was trustee for her of an undivided one-half interest in several large tracts of ranch property owned by him and in relation to which she claimed that they were "equal partners." At trial, the judge concluded that there was no evidence of partnership and denied her claim to share in the property; he awarded her $200 per month by way of support. The Court of Appeal of Alberta dismissed her appeal.

In the Supreme Court of Canada, Mrs Murdoch's claim to share in the property was based, not on the idea of partnership, but rather on the doctrine of resulting trust, a doctrine then subject to numerous and sometimes conflicting judgments both in Canada and the United Kingdom. In an earlier case before the Supreme Court of Canada in 1960 (*Thompson v Thompson*, [1961] 1 SCR 3), for example, the court had stated its conclusion on the property issue (at 13-14) succinctly:

> [N]o case has yet held that, in the absence of some financial contribution, the wife is entitled to
> a proprietary interest from the mere fact of marriage and cohabitation and the fact the property
> in question is the matrimonial home.

On the facts of the *Murdoch* case, therefore, the court concluded that there had been no financial contribution by Mrs Murdoch that would sustain a declaration of resulting trust. Moreover, the court distinguished the cases in which a non-financial, but nonetheless valuable, contribution had been made by spouses to the acquisition of property because the claims of the non-titled spouses in all of those cases related only to property interests in matrimonial homes. In *Murdoch*, by contrast, the wife's claim related to the large ranch properties acquired by the couple during the marriage.

In discussing the previous cases, moreover, Mr Justice Martland for the majority reiterated the trial judge's conclusion that the work done by Mrs Murdoch during the 25 years of her marriage was *merely* "work done by any ranch wife," thereby distinguishing *Murdoch* from earlier cases. It was this characterization of Mrs Murdoch's contribution that provided the catalyst for reassessing the contribution of women at marriage breakdown, particularly because the majority judgment stood in stark contrast to the dissenting judgment of Mr Justice Laskin. The dissenting judgment concluded that the facts justified a declaration of constructive trust, recognizing the significant "contribution of physical labour beyond ordinary housekeeping duties" made by Mrs Murdoch.

Ironically, it was the majority judgment, and particularly the comment that seemed to trivialize women's contributions to farm labour, that provided the catalyst for statutory reform. Like many other comments, an editorial in the *Toronto Star* suggested that the decision was both "a warning to women and a cue to legislators." The editorial also cited the recommendation of the 1970 Royal Commission on the Status of Women in Canada that the law should be amended to recognize "the concept of equal partnership in marriage" and recommended law reform efforts to prevent other "'Irene Murdochs' [from being] left out in the cold with less than $60 a week to show for a quarter-century of labour."

The law reform process at both the federal and provincial levels also reflected public reaction to the outcome of the *Murdoch* decision. The federal Law Reform Commission [LRC] report, issued in 1975, stated pointedly:

> The need for some fundamental reorganization of the existing property laws … regulating the rights and obligations of family members was underlined in the recent decision of the Supreme Court of Canada in *Murdoch v. Murdoch*. The public reaction to that decision clearly indicates that the existing laws discriminate to the prejudice of the married woman and are no longer acceptable in contemporary society. A property regime must be devised that will promote equality of the sexes before the law.

(Law Reform Commission of Canada, *Studies on Family Property Law* (Ottawa: Information Canada, 1975) [LRC] at 3.) See also the recommendations in the *Report of the Royal Commission on the Status of Women in Canada* (Ottawa: Information Canada, 1975).

Indeed, the *Murdoch* decision became a "cause célèbre" for women in Canada when some women in Manitoba created a skit about the case to demonstrate wives' lack of entitlement to property. The skit, called "The Balloon Lady," started with a puppet of a woman holding a number of balloons naming legal rights; as the skit progressed to show the absence of each named right for women, the balloons burst, one by one, leaving just the puppet and the burst balloons at the end of the skit, a pointed comment on the lack of rights to "family property" for women. See Mysty Clapton, "Murdoch v. Murdoch: The Organizing Narrative of Matrimonial Property Law Reform" (2008) 20:2 CJWL 197; V Gruben, A Cameron & A Chaisson, "'The Courts Have Turned Women into Slaves for the Men of This World': Irene Murdoch's Quest for Justice" in E Tucker, B Ziff & J Muir, eds, *Property on Trial: Canadian Cases in Context* (Toronto: Irwin Law for the Osgoode Society for Canadian Legal History, 2012) 159.

Thus both public opinion and law reformers were in agreement about the need for reform after *Murdoch*. Turning away from the courts, which seemed to hold so little promise for appropriate decision making in this area, they focused attention on legislative reform. As a result, a number of statutes reforming family law were enacted in the common law provinces in the years after *Murdoch*. In the face of widespread enthusiasm for these new statutory reforms, the decision of the Supreme Court of Canada in *Rathwell v Rathwell*, [1978] 2 SCR 436 was not initially regarded as significant for divorcing couples, even though it finally recognized the appropriateness of Laskin's remedy of the constructive trust in the context of property rights for married couples at divorce.

On the other hand, because provincial statutory reforms applied only to married couples at divorce, and not to cohabiting couples at separation, the constructive trust remedy remained useful to cohabiting opposite-sex couples, and was adopted by the Supreme Court of Canada in *Pettkus v Becker*, [1980] 2 SCR 834. In addition, prior to recognition of same-sex marriage in Canada, the constructive trust remedy was also claimed by same-sex couples at separation.

In general, the provincial statutory reforms seemed to ensure property sharing at divorce as a matter of entitlement, based on the existence of the marriage relationship (subject to a few exceptions, including short marriages). By contrast with the right to ongoing spousal support (which is available in common law provinces to both married and cohabiting couples), however, property entitlement is still based on (marital) status in about half the common law provinces as well as in Quebec. Moreover, while spousal support focuses on goals of need and compensation, the right to share property at the end of a spousal relationship depends on marital status. In considering the cases that follow, try to identify the relationships between marital status, need, and compensation in relation to the claims of married spouses and cohabitees.

B. Legislating Family Property Reform for Married Spouses After 1968

Legislatures in the common law provinces in Canada enacted reform statutes defining entitlement to share in family property on the part of married spouses in the late 1970s. Some statutes, such as the Nova Scotia *Matrimonial Property Act*, RSNS 1989, c 275, permit judges to divide family assets equally at marriage breakdown. In practice, this approach means that judges have authority to transfer title to property owned by each spouse to achieve the overall goal of equality or equal sharing. By contrast, Ontario's *Family Law Act* requires that the *value* of all property acquired during the marriage by the spouses be shared equally at marriage breakdown. Although one approach shares "property" and the other shares "value," it is necessary in both cases to define what assets constitute "property" for purposes of this division or sharing at separation. Recall the brief discussion in Chapter 1 in the BC case *JCM v ANA*, 2012 BCSC 584, in which the court had to determine whether leftover sperm straws constituted "property" for purposes of division after a lesbian couple separated.

In Ontario, the *Family Law Act* defines "property" in general terms in s 4:

"[P]roperty" means any interest, present or future, vested or contingent, in real or personal property and includes,

    (a) [property relating to a power of appointment];

    (b) [property relating to a power to revoke disposition]; and

    (c) [the "imputed value" of a spouse's pension plan].

For property law purposes, the significant language is the very broad definition of "property" in s 4—that is, "*any* interest, present or future, vested or contingent, in real or personal property." The statute also provides for the valuation of these property interests, the exclusion of some interests—for example, gifts from third parties and property owned by each spouse prior to marriage, with the exception of the matrimonial home—and the calculation of each spouse's "net family property." After calculating each spouse's net family property in this way, it is possible to determine the total value of "property" owned by each of the spouses, and the court can then order the payment of a sum of money to "equalize" the spouses' entitlements. As noted above, provincial schemes across Canada all illustrate some form of equal sharing of property at family breakdown: e.g. see *Matrimonial Property Act*, RSNS 1989, c 275; *Marital Property Act*, SNB 2012, c 107, s 2; *Family Law Act*, RSPEI 1988, c F-2.1, s 6(1); and *Family Law Act*, RSNL 1990, c F-2, s 19.

These legislative arrangements require courts to interpret what constitutes "property." One important issue in the early years after the enactment of Ontario's *Family Law Act* in 1986 was whether a professional degree held by one spouse constituted property, requiring it to be valued for purposes of equalization between the spouses. Claims that professional degrees were property were made in several cases in Ontario, especially where a spouse had contributed through financial and other support to the acquisition of the other spouse's degree.

Thus, for example, in *Corless v Corless* (1987), 5 RFL (3d) 256 (Ont UFC), a wife claimed that her husband's LLB degree should be valued as property at the time of divorce. The couple had met as students and married when the husband had completed his second year of the LLB program at the University of Western Ontario (the wife had just completed her BA). The wife worked as a clerk in a printing company in London to support them while the husband completed his third year. He also worked part time as a carpet seller and then worked for the summer as a research assistant for a professor. When the husband got an articling position in Brantford, the couple moved there and the wife quit her job in London to take up a job in the customer relations department of a sporting goods company in Brantford. At the end of the articling year, the couple moved to Toronto so that the husband could attend the bar admission course. The wife quit her Brantford job and began to work in an employment agency in Toronto. On being called to the bar, the couple moved to Troy (near Brantford), rented (and later purchased) a home, and the husband went to work at the same firm at which he had articled, eventually becoming a partner there. The wife worked in Troy selling real estate and as a bookkeeper, and looked after the three children of the marriage. In 1981, the wife began a company called Canadian Living Accents, which had not shown any profits at the date of separation (after 12 years of marriage) in 1985.

In *Corless*, the court held that the husband's professional degree was property within s 4 of the FLA, but that it had no value and thus was not included in the calculation of the net family property. (The value of the husband's share in the law partnership was, however, included as part of his net family property.) This outcome was different from that in *Keast v Keast* (1986), 1 RFL (3d) 401 (Ont Dist Ct), where a wife had put her "mature student" husband through medical school. In *Keast*, the court awarded her extra "compensatory" spousal support, but did not include the medical degree as property. Similarly, in *Linton v Linton*, 11 RFL (3d) 444 (Ont H Ct J), the husband's PhD degree was not included as part of the net family property, even though his wife had supported him financially to enable him to acquire it. In this case, also, the wife was instead awarded substantial and ongoing financial support as compensation for her contribution.

By contrast with all these cases, in *Caratun v Caratun* (1987), 9 RFL (3d) 337 (Ont H Ct J), Van Camp J decided that a wife who had supported her husband's acquisition of a degree in dentistry was entitled to a beneficial interest, thereby recognizing a constructive trust in the husband's degree. Van Camp J calculated the value of the wife's beneficial interest as $30,000. Both *Linton* and then *Caratun* went to the Court of Appeal, where the appeal court held in each case that there was no "property" in a professional degree. Examine the reasoning of the Court of Appeal in *Caratun* about this property claim; to what extent does the analysis suggest a unique approach to the nature of "family property" claims?

Caratun v Caratun
(1992), 42 RFL (3d) 113 (Ont CA)

Contribution Towards the Obtaining of Appellant's Dental Licence

The reasons of the trial judge make it quite clear that Dr. Caratun's primary objective in marrying Mrs. Caratun and fathering their child was to assist him in immigrating to North America to practise dentistry. Mrs. Caratun worked extremely hard over a number of years in Israel and in Canada to assist Dr. Caratun in attaining his ultimate objective. Two days after attaining that objective, he rejected Mrs. Caratun as his wife, at a time when family assets were next to non-existent but his future income-earning ability was substantial.

Facts such as these raise difficult legal questions, given the purpose of the FLA, on the one hand, and its specific provisions, on the other. The combining of spousal efforts over a number of years to provide for the education and professional qualification of one spouse is not unusual in our society. The inevitable result, if there is a separation on attaining the joint objective, is that one family member is left with no assets and often very little in the way of educational or professional qualifications with which to sustain herself or himself in the future. The extreme unfairness of the situation is patent, but the possibility of a legal remedy is far from settled law.

Dental Licence as "Property"

Mrs. Caratun's position at trial, which was accepted by the trial judge, was that Dr. Caratun's dental licence is property within the meaning of that word as defined in s. 4(1) of the FLA, of which the relevant portion reads:

> "property" means any interest, present or future, vested or contingent, in real or personal property.

That definition is broadly framed, and includes all conceivable types of property in the traditional common law sense. However, it does not, by its terms, extend the meaning of property beyond those limits. The contrary argument is that in construing that definition one must keep in mind the FLA policy of marriage partnership, which requires, on final separation, the equal division of wealth accumulated during the marriage; and that a licence to practise a particular profession constitutes wealth in the matrimonial context.

Two important cases at the trial level have reached opposite conclusions on this issue—the trial decision in this case and the decision of Killeen LJSC in *Linton v. Linton* (1988), 11 RFL (3d) 444, 29 ETR 14, 64 OR (2d) 18, 49 DLR (4th) 278 (HC). Both decisions include detailed and thoughtful analyses of this issue, and substantial reference to authorities, both Canadian and American. The American decisions are so varied as to be of little assistance. Although all purport to be based on the wording of the particular statute involved, they reach varying results based on statutes with very similar wording.

In determining the issue of whether a professional licence constitutes "property," the cases and the numerous articles written on the subject concentrate primarily on two aspects of the problem: first, the nature or characterization of a licence, and, second, the difficulty of valuing a licence in the family property context.

(i) Characterization of Licence

The broad definition of property in the FLA clearly encompasses many forms of intangibles—a classification into which a licence must fall if it is to be considered property. The common law has never had any difficulty in dealing with property evidenced by pieces of paper representing bundles of rights—such as a share certificate with its attendant rights to dividends, voting privileges, and distribution of assets on corporate dissolution. If a licence to practise a profession is property, what are its attendant rights? Apart from possible benefits, such as the right to join professional groups and clubs—which are not relevant in this context—the only real right conferred on the holder of the licence is a right to work in a particular profession. That right, assuming it is held at the time of separation, is a present right to work in the future, and it will continue for as long as the holder of the right is professionally and personally able to perform the activity involved. It is the nature of the right given by the licence which, in my view, causes insurmountable difficulties in treating such a licence as property for matrimonial purposes. Those difficulties arise, first, because it is not a right which is transferable; second, because it requires the personal efforts of the holder in order to be of any value in the future; and, third, because the only difference between such a licence and any other right to work is in its exclusivity.

(a) Non-Transferability

One of the traditional indicia of property is its inherent transferability. That transferability may, of course, be precluded either by law or by contract. In contrast, the right or licence to practise a particular profession is, by its very nature, a right personal to the holder, incapable of transfer. It is very different in nature from the professional practice which may be built up by the licensee after attaining the licence. The practice itself is clearly capable of transfer for value, although the market is limited to other licensees. Where spouses separate before a practice has been built up, there is nothing available for transfer.

In *Brinkos v. Brinkos* (1989), 20 RFL (3d) 445, 69 OR (2d) 225, 60 DLR (4th) 556, 33 OAC 295, 34 ETR 55 (CA), Carthy JA speaking for this court, discussed the distinction between rights which are inherently inalienable and those which are rendered inalienable either by law or by agreement. At p. 451 he quoted the definition of "property" in *Jowitt's Dictionary of English Law*, 2d ed. by John Burke (London: Sweet & Maxwell, 1977), at p. 1447:

> In its largest sense property signifies things and rights considered as having a money value, especially with reference to transfer or succession, and to their capacity of being injured. Property includes not only ownership, estates, and interests in corporeal things, but also rights such as trade marks, copyrights, patents, and rights *in personam* capable of transfer or transmission, such as debts.

It is clear that many rights or things which are restrained from transfer by law are, by agreement or otherwise, inherently transferable and are of value to their owners. Such rights or things fall within the normal legal definition of property, and would clearly fall within the statutory definition of property in the FLA. However, rights or things which are inherently non-transferable, such as the right to practise a profession, clearly do not constitute property in any traditional sense.

(b) Requirement of Personal Efforts of the Licensee

Under the FLA the types of property included in the statutory definition are very broad-ranging. The definition is in the FLA for the purpose of determining the value of the property to be included in arriving at "net family property" to be equalized under s. 5. I see no way in which that definition can be interpreted to include work to be performed by either spouse in the future. It goes without saying that without the personal efforts of the licensee, the licence will produce nothing. The only provisions in the FLA that allow one spouse to share in the fruits of the other spouse's future labours are the support provisions, which do not form a part of the equalization payment under s. 5.

The policy of the FLA emphasizes principles of partnership during marriage, and self-sufficiency following its termination. When the marriage ends, the partnership ends. Placing a value on future labours of either spouse for purposes of the equalization payment would frustrate those policy objectives.

(c) Right to Work in General

The only difference between a professional licence and the ability and right of any individual to perform a particular type of work is in the exclusive nature of a professional licence. Only those who have successfully survived the rigours of professional training have the right to practise their profession. Nonetheless, the difference between the right to practise a profession and the right to work at any job which requires special skill or knowledge is a right which differs only in scope, but not in substance. A plumber, carpenter, or an electrician spends a substantial period of time in apprenticeship before becoming proficient at his trade; a salesman spends a substantial period of time developing a clientele in order to enhance his income; a business executive may spend a substantial period of time in university and then working his way up the corporate ladder to attain his level of income. Should the law consider all of these attainments as property for the purposes of determining the equalization payment under the FLA? Clearly not. I see no interpretation of the FLA, either specifically under s. 4, or generally, which would allow the court to treat such attainments as property.

(ii) Valuation of Licence

It is clear from the considerations referred to above that there are substantial difficulties, both practical and conceptual, in treating licences as "property." In addition, the valuation of such a right would be unfairly speculative in the matrimonial context. A myriad of contingencies, including inclination, probability of success in practice of the profession, length of physical and mental capability to perform the duties of the profession, competition within the profession, and many others, all render a fair valuation of the licence unusually difficult. But a further potential inequity arises: support orders may be varied if circumstances change, but no amendment of an equalization payment is possible regardless of changed circumstances.

The valuation approach approved by the trial judge in this case was to compare the appellant's actual professional income since attaining his dental licence up to September 1986 with the average earnings of an honours university graduate of the same age during the same period. His future professional income from 1986 until his expected retirement age of 65 was determined, based on his actual income level adjusted by the rate of growth of income for dentists according to the American Dental Association. The difference between his projected future earnings and those of honours graduates was valued at an annual discount rate of 2.5 per cent according to the *Rules of Civil Procedure*. Based on this approach, a valuation of the dental licence as of valuation date, July 18, 1981, was found to be $379,965. This valuation did not take into account any of the contingencies of the type referred to above. Another method of valuation, which resulted in the figure of $219,346, was to compare the expected career earnings of the average dentist obtaining his licence in July 1981 and retiring in November 2012, to the average earnings of honours university graduates for the same period.

Either valuation approach is logical, if the licence is "property." However, it would be equally logical to treat a university degree as property, and then value that degree by comparing incomes of university graduates with those of high school graduates. In the matrimonial context, the fallacy lies in treating a licence as property on valuation date, when most of its value depends on the personal labour of the licensed spouse after the termination of the relationship. That future labour does not constitute anything earned or existing at the valuation date.

For all of the above reasons, it is my view that a professional licence does not constitute property within the meaning of s. 4 of the FLA.

Constructive Trust

The trial judge decided that the appellant's dental licence was property within the meaning of s. 4 of the FLA. However, she did not include the value of the licence in the appellant's net family property, but rather decided that the licence would be held by the appellant subject to a constructive trust in favour of the respondent in the amount of $30,000—that amount representing the value of the respondent's contribution to the acquisition of the licence. Given a finding that the licence constituted property, it is my view that the court had no discretion as to whether or not to include its value in net family property under s. 5(1) of the Act.

The finding of constructive trust was based on cases involving circumstances substantially different than those in this case. The two decisions of the Supreme Court of Canada in *Rathwell v Rathwell*, [1978] 2 SCR 436, 1 RFL (2d) 1, [1978] 2 WWR 101, 1 ETR 307, 83 DLR (3d) 289, and *Becker v Pettkus*, [1980] 2 SCR 834, 19 RFL (2d) 165, 8 ETR 143, 117 DLR (3d) 257, 34 NR 384, were decided at a time when the relevant statutes of Saskatchewan and of Ontario would not have permitted appropriate recovery to the spouses. Both cases involved real property and other tangible assets which would clearly come within the definition of "property" under the Ontario FLA. Since the enactment of the FLA, cases have applied the constructive trust doctrine for the purpose of allowing a spouse, in appropriate circumstances, to share in the increased value of property from the valuation date until the time of trial. But, again, those cases involve tangible physical assets. The three BC decisions referred to by the trial judge—*Piters v Piters*, [1981] 1 WWR 285, (1980), 19 RFL (2d) 217, 20 BCLR 393, 3 Fam L Rev 123 (SC); *Underhill v Underhill*, 34 RFL (2d) 419, [1983] 5 WWR 481, 45 BCLR 244 (CA); and *Jackh v Jackh* (1980), 18 RFL (2d) 310, [1981] 1 WWR 481, 22 BCLR 182, 113 DLR (3d) 267 (SC)—are all cases dealing with the issue of a proprietary interest in a *professional practice*, as contrasted with the claimed proprietary interest in a *licence to practise*.

The trial judge stated that she did not see "any reason in principle why a professional licence cannot be subject to a similar proprietary interest in the form of a constructive trust" [at 355 RFL]. I agree that if the licence constituted "property," then there is no reason why, in a proper case, that property could not be subject to a constructive trust. However, if the licence does not constitute property, then there is nothing to which the constructive trust could attach. None of the cases relied on by the trial judge in this case assist in establishing that a licence is property to which a constructive trust can attach.

[The court then considered Mrs Caratun's entitlement to spousal support and ordered her husband to pay a lump-sum support award of $30,000.]

DISCUSSION NOTES

i. Property and Professional Degrees

In examining the reasoning of the Court of Appeal from a property perspective, consider whether or to what extent it resembles the idea of property as a "relationship among subjects with respect to objects." What other analysis might have been used in *Caratun*? Which reasons in the Court of Appeal seem to be the most persuasive?

This issue about whether a degree is property has been addressed by a number of courts in Canada and the United States. In a decision of the Michigan Court of Appeals, *Woodworth v Woodworth*, 337 NW 2d 332 (1983), for example, the court envisioned the husband's law degree as a "family asset" to which the wife had contributed. Thus the court decided (at 337) that she was entitled to realize "her expectation of economic benefit from the career for which the education laid the foundation." As the court stated (at 335):

> [W]hether or not an advanced degree can physically or metaphysically be defined as "property" is beside the point. Courts must instead focus on the most equitable solution in dividing among the respective parties what they have.

The approach of the Michigan court was adopted by courts in other US states and was also reflected in some state legislative provisions, but other states refused to recognize a professional degree as marital property: e.g. see *In re Marriage of Goldstein*, 423 NE 2d 1201 (Ill App Ct 1981). In reviewing the different decisions of courts in the United States, Lenore Weitzman identified three basic approaches:

1. a reimbursement of costs (usually including direct out-of-pocket expenses such as tuition, loans, and living expenses and sometimes such indirect costs as forgone opportunities);

2. a sharing in enhanced earning capacity or benefits gained as a result of the professional education (sometimes calculated by subtracting the present value of "pre-education earning capacity and the present value of the costs of education" from the present value of "post-education earning capacity"—the difference is the return on investment to be shared by both spouses); or

3. an equivalent opportunity—for example, the trial court in *Morgan v Morgan*, 366 NYS 2d 977 (1975), 383 NYS 2d 343 (1976) ordered a husband (who had been fully supported through college and law school by his wife) to support her attendance at medical school. The Court of Appeal, however, overturned this decision.

(See Lenore Weitzman, *The Divorce Revolution: The Unexpected Social and Economic Consequences for Women and Children in America* (New York: Free Press, 1985) at 131-35.) To what extent are these three approaches reflected, if at all, in the reasoning of the Court of Appeal in *Caratun*?

ii. A Critical Economic Perspective on Property and Professional Degrees

In addition to fulfilling the expectations of spouses, matrimonial property rules may also reflect "invisible" economic relationships adopted within households. For example, economist J Knetsch argued that households are often organized so as to maximize the overall economic well-being of the family *as a unit*, but without necessarily ensuring that the economic capacity of *each individual* is also maximized. Thus, if and when the unit dissolves, some individual family members will benefit more than others, an inequity, he argued, that matrimonial property rules should redress. Knetsch also suggested that the broader social and economic context constrains the kinds of real choices available to household units in maximizing the unit's well-being, arguing that there is a need for a more significant role for matrimonial property rules in adjusting inequities between men and women beyond an individual family context.

More specifically, in examining the connection between matrimonial property settlement and the division of labour within a household, Knetsch pointed to the principle of "maximization of family welfare via specialization"—for example, "the husband working in the job market and the wife in the household"—as the key rationale for traditional organizations of families. On the basis of this premise—that each partner specializing in complementary activities is the best means of contributing to the overall well-being of the family unit—Knetsch identified a need to ensure that individual contributions can be made compatible with equality in the allocation of marital assets if the relationship ends.

In addition to choices reflecting the maximization of family well-being, however, Knetsch also identified external variables that may influence how families are organized, in which case, specialization alone may not be sufficient to explain the traditional family arrangement. Some of these variables include:

1. the socialization process that encourages and discourages given interests and activities based on sex;

2. the tendency for women to make smaller investments in human capital (perhaps less now than in earlier times, but still present in some family situations);

3. the bias of tax laws that offer incentives for household-based production;

4. the lack of flexibility (to accommodate household responsibilities) in the job market;

5. the lack of market substitutes for household production;

6. discrimination against women in the labour market; and

7. a degree of self-imposed discrimination (women are more likely to choose lower-paying jobs if they provide a safe working environment).

Consequently, Knetsch concluded that "the fact that the traditional roles are so frequently observed may well have more to do with the biases in the system than to any natural ordering that prescribes this as more efficient." (See J Knetsch, "Some Economic Implications of Matrimonial Property Rules" (1984) 34 UTLJ 263 at 271-75.) In the light of this economic analysis, to what extent is it appropriate for principles of family property to contribute to goals of increased gender equality at family breakdown? Do Knetsch's arguments suggest a need to assess arrangements during marriage and to respond to gender inequality at marriage breakdown by permitting unequal sharing of property?

iii. Property and Family Relationships

Another criticism of the decision in *Caratun* focused on its misunderstanding of the idea of property relationships, particularly in the family context: see M McCallum, "Caratun v Caratun: It Seems That We Are Not All Realists Yet" (1994) 7 CJWL 197. Specifically, McCallum argued that the decision did not accord with the concept of "property as relationships" (discussed in Chapter 1). However, in addition, she critiqued the court's property analysis by analogizing the family context to a business partnership, suggesting a need to treat "property" in the family context more like property in commercial contexts. First, she explained how the *Partnerships Act* provides the remedy of repayment of all or some of a premium where "one partner pays premium to another on entering the partnership and the partnership is dissolved before the expiration of its term," a remedy not available to Mrs Caratun for her contribution to her husband's degree in the expectation that she would share in the future profits. (In this way, Mrs Caratun was the victim of fraud or misrepresentation.) McCallum also identified issues in business partnerships where a firm's good will is important to the determination of "who has to pay whom when a partner withdraws or is expelled from the partnership." Analogizing a business partnership to a marriage, she argued that in cases where the partnership owns few assets, "placing a high value on goodwill may be the only way to ensure that the partner's spouse is compensated for a contribution to the partner's ability to earn a good living." Ultimately, McCallum concluded that "a woman who sacrifices her own career opportunities in order to improve those of her husband is making a bad investment, unless she is able to obtain the benefits of her husband's career during the marriage." As she stated (at 207):

> Among the many meanings that one can draw from the result in *Caratun*, one stands out: a woman who sacrifices her own career opportunities in order to improve those of her husband is making a bad investment, unless she is able to obtain the benefits of her husband's career during the marriage. The wave of [statutory] family law reform following the decision of the Supreme Court of Canada in *Murdoch v Murdoch* profoundly altered the rights and obligations of spouses within marriage, and enhanced women's property and support rights on marriage breakdown. But the legislation works best for women who least need it, those who have resisted the idea that marriage is a partnership and have provided for themselves.

In the light of McCallum's critique, how might "property" be defined in the *Family Law Act* so as to lead to a different outcome in a case like *Caratun*? To what extent would a revised definition in the statute respond to McCallum's concerns? Are her concerns the same as those identified by Knetsch?

iv. Other Intangible and Non-Transferable Assets

In *Caratun*, the Court of Appeal ordered a lump-sum payment of support for Mrs Caratun of $30,000, having concluded that the husband's degree was not "property." By contrast with the court's unwillingness in Ontario to recognize a professional degree as property in *Caratun*, however, the Supreme Court of Canada decided in *Clarke v Clarke*, [1990] 2 SCR 795 that a spouse's pension constituted property under s 4 of the Nova Scotia *Matrimonial Property Act*, SNS 1980, c 9, even though there are equally difficult problems of valuation of a pension at the date of separation. Moreover, the Supreme Court reached its conclusion in *Clarke* in the context of the Nova Scotia statute, which did not expressly include pensions in the definition of sharable property. Even so, the trial court included future pension payments as property for purposes of the Act; and although the Nova Scotia Court of Appeal overturned the trial court's decision, the Supreme Court of Canada allowed the appeal unanimously.

Justice Wilson's decision in *Clarke v Clarke* expressly noted (at 811) the importance of pensions as family assets—sometimes the only significant assets—and the inadequacy of support payments by contrast with a pension asset:

> Discretionary support payments are a wholly inadequate and unacceptable substitute for an entitlement to share in the assets accumulated during the marriage as a result of the combined efforts of the spouses.

Wilson J specifically noted that the problems of valuation should not preclude the characterization of a pension as a matrimonial asset. Note also that her reasoning suggested that property sharing was preferable to spousal support payments (as ordered in the Ontario cases concerning professional degrees).

How should these comments in the Supreme Court of Canada be interpreted in relation to *Caratun*? What are the similarities and differences between professional degrees and pensions in relation to the goal of equal sharing of "family" property at separation? For further analysis of pensions as family assets, see A Bissett-Johnson, "Three Problems of Pensions—An Overview" (1990) 6 Can Fam LQ 137, and B Hovius & T Youdan, *The Law of Family Property* (Scarborough, ON: Carswell, 1991). Pensions as family property were addressed by the OLRC, *Report on Pensions as Family Property: Valuation and Division* (Toronto: Ministry of the Attorney General, 1995), and then by the Law Commission of Ontario (LCO), *Division of Pensions upon Marriage Breakdown: Final Report* (Toronto: Law Commission of Ontario, 2008). An amendment to the *Family Law Act*, effective as of 1 January 2012, enacted provisions concerning the valuation of pensions as "family property" in Ontario: see *Family Statute Law Amendment Act, 2009*, SO 2009, c 11.

In contrasting pensions and professional degrees, the American Law Institute in the United States similarly proposed that occupational licences and educational degrees be excluded from division, consistent with its general exclusion as "property" of spousal earning capacity, spousal skills, and post-dissolution spousal labour: see American Law Institute, *Principles of the Law of Family Dissolution: Analysis and Recommendations* (St Paul, MN: American Law Institute, 2002). According to the report, market data can establish a value for pensions, by contrast with professional degrees.

Do you agree with this analysis? In considering these differences between professional degrees and pensions, consider also the court's conclusion in *Clegg v Clegg* (2000), 188 DLR (4th) 365 (Ont Sup Ct J). During the marriage, the husband was involved in direct marketing of credit card applications to university students, but he sold the business just before the spouses' separation. At the time of the sale of the business, the husband entered into a non-competition agreement that was valued at $1,500,000. The wife claimed an entitlement to this "property" in relation to equalization, while the husband argued that the payments under the agreement related to a personal service not to compete and were therefore beyond the definition of "property" pursuant to the FLA. In this case, the court concluded that the payments owed to the husband were within the definition of "property" in the FLA, and that the fact that they were not transferable did not make them "non-property." Is this case consistent with *Caratun* and with *Clarke*?

v. The Context of Claims to Property in Degrees

As was evident in McCallum's critique of *Caratun*, the outcome of the decision left Mrs Caratun in a precarious economic situation by contrast with her husband. Part of the pressure to include "new property" in the family law statutory definitions clearly derives from increasing concern about post-separation rates of poverty, especially for women and children. For example, a research paper for the Vanier Institute of the Family reported in 2009:

> We have already seen that poverty increases the risk of divorce. In turn, divorce also increases the risk of poverty for a large proportion of women and their children (Finnie, 1993; Galarneau and Sturroch, 1997). Rotermann (2007) found that, within two years after a separation/divorce, 43% of women had experienced a decrease in household income compared to 15% of men. In contrast, 29% of men and only 9% of women had experienced an increase. Even three years after divorce, women's household income remains far below what it had been during marriage and far below their ex-husbands' current income. However, as more women are employed and earn better salaries, this income decline is less painful than before, even though it is still evident.
>
> Ex-husbands, compared to ex-wives, are less likely to be poor because their income is generally higher, they do not have full care of their children with all the attendant expenses, and their child support payments are usually not crippling. Nevertheless, in a decade when most families have two breadwinners, men who divorce lose far more economically than in the past, especially those married to a high-earning wife. As child support payments become better enforced, economic factors may contribute in the long run to dissuade some men from ending their marriage.
>
> For families already burdened by poverty, once separation takes place, the mother and child unit often becomes even poorer. The younger the children are at the time of parental divorce or common law dissolution, the more likely they are to be poor, as they have younger parents who typically earn less. On average, single parents who are poor have an income that is 40% below the poverty line. This is dire poverty. Another way of looking at this is to consider single-mother families. In 2002, according to the Vanier Institute of the Family (2004), 35% of all female lone-parent families lived in poverty while many more hovered just one precarious step above. Canada, the U.S., and England are the three western countries in which single-parent families experience elevated poverty rates and where a vast difference exists between the incomes of single- and two-parent families.

(See Anne-Marie Ambert, *Divorce: Facts, Causes and Consequences*, 3d ed (Ottawa: Vanier Institute of the Family, 2009) at 17-18, online: <http://thefamilywatch.org/doc/doc-0073-es .pdf>.)

Are these concerns relevant to the definition or interpretation of "property" interests in cases such as *Caratun*? How should they be addressed? For some analyses, see S Moller Okin, *Justice, Gender, and the Family* (New York: Basic Books, 1989); M Eichler, "The Limits of Family Law Reform" (1990-91) 7 Can Fam LQ 59; M Morton, "Dividing the Wealth, Sharing the Poverty: The (Re)Formation of 'Family' in Law in Ontario" (1988) 25 Canadian Review of Sociology and Anthropology 254; and MJ Mossman, "'Running Hard to Stand Still': The Paradox of Family Law Reform" (1994) 17 Dal LJ 5. For an interesting analysis of the relative wealth of men and women and differences in their respective approaches to the acquisition of property, see C Rose, "Women and Property: Gaining and Losing Ground" (1992) 78 Va L Rev 421.

vi. The History of the Concept of "Family Property"

The statutory reforms in common law provinces in Canada in the late 1970s borrowed a traditional civil law concept of "community property" from Quebec. Community property regimes
in many civil law jurisdictions often create some automatic joint ownership of family assets
during marriage. In this context, it is interesting that the LRC's study of family property in 1975
commenced with a long analysis of matrimonial regimes in Canada, including Quebec: see
LRC. However, most common law provinces adopted the idea of "deferred sharing" of community property—that is, recognition that married spouses have "separate property" entitlements during marriage, but a form of "community property" that is deferred to the time of
the couple's separation or divorce. Significantly, this idea of deferred community property is
also evident in the 1989 statute in Quebec: see *Act to amend the Civil Code of Québec and
other legislation in order to favour economic equality between spouses*, SQ 1989, c 55.

   However, the Civil Code in Quebec limits entitlement to community property to persons
who are married—that is, cohabiting couples have no entitlement to share property (or to
receive spousal support) at the end of their relationships. This conclusion was reinforced by
the Supreme Court of Canada's majority decision in *Québec (Attorney General) v A*, 2013 SCC 5.

C. Equity and Family Property Reform for Cohabitees

Provincial family property statutes focus on the entitlements of married spouses at separation or divorce. The statutory provisions concerning property have not applied to cohabiting
couples in provinces such as Ontario, even though there may be practical circumstances in
which cohabiting couples make similar kinds of family decisions that may disadvantage individual family members (as identified above by Knetsch). Yet, in spite of functional similarities
between married couples and cohabiting couples, the Supreme Court of Canada decided in
2002 that there was no Charter discrimination arising out of the exclusion of cohabiting
couples from provincial legislative schemes concerning property sharing at separation or
divorce: see *Nova Scotia (Attorney General) v Walsh*, 2002 SCC 83, [2002] 4 SCR 325, L'Heureux-
Dubé J dissenting. Following this decision, some provinces in Canada amended the definition of "spouse" for purposes of property sharing at the end of cohabiting relationships: for
example, see the BC *Family Law Act*, SBC 2011, c 25, s 3, which creates an entitlement to share
in property (according to the principles applicable to married couples) at the end of a cohabiting relationship that has existed for two years. Moreover, as noted above, a slim majority of
the Supreme Court of Canada also upheld provisions of the Quebec Civil Code, which entitled only married couples (and not cohabiting couples) to spousal support and property
sharing at the end of their relationships: see *Québec (Attorney General) v A*, above.

   In these circumstances, principles of equity were (re)fashioned by the Supreme Court of
Canada to achieve goals of equality for cohabitees in the common law provinces. As you review the cases in which these equitable principles have evolved in recent decades, note the
underlying assumptions about the acquisition of property in familial relationships.

Pettkus v Becker
[1980] 2 SCR 834

DICKSON J (Laskin CJC, Estey, McIntyre, Chouinard, and Lamer JJ concurring):

The appellant Lother Pettkus, through toil and thrift, developed over the years a successful bee-keeping business. He now owns two rural Ontario properties, where the business is conducted, and he has the proceeds from the sale, in 1974, of a third property located in the province of Quebec. It is not to his efforts alone, however, that success can be attributed. The respondent Rosa Becker, through her labour and earnings, contributed substantially to the good fortune of the common enterprise. She lived with Mr. Pettkus from 1955 to 1974, save for a separation in 1972. They were never married. When the relationship sundered in late 1974 Miss Becker commenced this action, in which she sought a declaration of entitlement to a one-half interest in the lands and a share in the bee-keeping business.

The Facts

Mr. Pettkus and Miss Becker came to Canada from central Europe separately, as immigrants, in 1954. He had $17 upon arrival. They met in Montreal in 1955. Shortly thereafter, Mr. Pettkus moved in with Miss Becker, on her invitation. She was 30 years old and he was 25. He was earning $75 per week; she was earning $25-$28 per week, later increased to $67 per week.

A short time after they began living together, Miss Becker expressed the desire that they be married. Mr. Pettkus replied that he might consider marriage after they knew each other better. Thereafter, the question of marriage was not raised, though within a few years Mr. Pettkus began to introduce Miss Becker as his wife and to claim her as such for income tax purposes.

From 1955 to 1960 both parties worked for others. Mr. Pettkus supplemented his income by repairing and restoring motor vehicles. Throughout the period Miss Becker paid the rent. She bought the food and clothing and looked after other living expenses. This enabled Mr. Pettkus to save his entire income, which he regularly deposited in a bank in his name. There was no agreement at any time to share either moneys or property placed in his name. The parties lived frugally. Due to their husbandry and parsimonious life-style, $12,000 had been saved by 1960 and deposited in Mr. Pettkus' bank account.

The two travelled to western Canada in June 1960. Expenses were shared. One of the reasons for the trip was to locate a suitable farm at which to start a bee-keeping business. They spent some time working at a bee-keeper's farm.

They returned to Montreal, however, in the early autumn of 1960. Miss Becker continued to pay the apartment rent out of her income until October 1960. From then until May 1961 Mr. Pettkus paid rent and household expenses, Miss Becker being jobless. In April 1961 she fell sick and required hospitalization.

In April 1961 they decided to buy a farm at Franklin Centre, Quebec, for $5,000. The purchase money came out of the bank account of Mr. Pettkus. Title was taken in his name. The floor and roof of the farmhouse were in need of repair. Miss Becker used her money to purchase flooring materials and she assisted in laying the floor and installing a bathroom.

For about six months during 1961 Miss Becker received unemployment insurance cheques, the proceeds of which were used to defray household expenses. Through two successive winters she lived in Montreal and earned approximately $100 per month as a baby-sitter. These earnings also went toward household expenses.

After purchasing the farm at Franklin Centre the parties established a bee-keeping business. Both worked in the business, making frames for the hives, moving the bees to the orchards of neighbouring farmers in the spring, checking the hives during the summer, bringing in the frames for honey extraction during July and August and the bees for winter storage in autumn. Receipts from sales of honey were handled by Mr. Pettkus; payments for purchases of beehives and equipment were made from his bank account.

The physical participation by Miss Becker in the bee operation continued over a period of about 14 years. She ran the extracting process. She also, for a time, raised a few chickens, pheasants and geese. In 1968, and later, the parties hired others to assist in moving the bees and bringing in the honey. Most of the honey was sold to wholesalers, though Miss Becker sold some door to door.

In August 1971, with a view to expanding the business, a vacant property was purchased in East Hawkesbury, Ontario at a price of $1,300. The purchase moneys were derived from the Franklin Centre honey operation. Funds to complete the purchases were withdrawn from the bank account of Mr. Pettkus. Title to the newly acquired property was taken in his name.

In 1973 a further property was purchased, in West Hawkesbury, Ontario, in the name of Mr. Pettkus. The price was $5,500. The purchase moneys came from the Franklin Centre operation, together with a $1,900 contribution made by Miss Becker, to which I will again later refer. 1973 was a prosperous year, yielding some 65,000 pounds of honey, producing net revenue in excess of $30,000.

In the early 1970s the relationship between the parties began to deteriorate. In 1972 Miss Becker left Mr. Pettkus, allegedly because of mistreatment. She was away for three months. At her departure Mr. Pettkus threw $3,000 on the floor; he told her to take the money, a 1966 Volkswagen, 40 beehives containing bees, and "get lost." The beehives represented less than ten per cent of the total number of hives then in the business.

Soon thereafter Mr. Pettkus asked Miss Becker to return. In January 1973 she agreed, on condition he see a marriage counsellor, make a will in her favour and provide her with $500 per year so long as she stayed with him. It was also agreed that Mr. Pettkus would establish a joint bank account for household expenses, in which receipts from retail sales of honey would be deposited. Miss Becker returned; she brought back the car and $1,900 remaining out of the $3,000 she had earlier received. The $1,900 was deposited in Mr. Pettkus' account. She also brought the 40 beehives, but the bees had died in the interim.

In February 1974 the parties moved into a house on the West Hawkesbury property, built in part by them and in part by contractors. The money needed for construction came from the honey business, with minimal purchases of materials by Miss Becker.

The relationship continued to deteriorate and on 4th October 1974 Miss Becker again left, this time permanently, after an incident in which she alleged that she had been beaten and otherwise abused. She took the car and approximately $2,600 in cash, from honey sales. Shortly thereafter the present action was launched.

At trial Miss Becker was awarded 40 beehives, without bees, together with $1,500, representing earnings from those hives for 1973 and 1974.

The Ontario Court of Appeal varied the judgment at trial by awarding Miss Becker a one-half interest in the lands owned by Mr. Pettkus and in the bee-keeping business.

[Chief Justice Dickson first considered the doctrine of resulting trust, suggesting that this case offered "an opportunity to clarify the equivocal state in which the law of matrimonial property was left" following the SCC decision in *Rathwell.*

To establish a resulting trust, Dickson CJ stated that it is necessary to show that there was a "common intention" on the part of the titleholder as well as the claimant that the property would be shared. After reviewing the cases and some of the academic literature that showed the artificiality of such a concept in the family context, Dickson CJ noted that the trial judge had found, as a fact, that there was no common intention in this case on the basis of Mr Pettkus's testimony. He continued:]

In the view of the Ontario Court of Appeal, speaking through Wilson JA, the trial judge vastly underrated the contribution made by Miss Becker over the years. She had made possible the acquisition of the Franklin Centre property and she had worked side by side with him for 14 years, building up the bee-keeping operation.

The trial judge held there was no common intention, either express or implied. It is important to note that the Ontario Court of Appeal did not overrule that finding.

I am not prepared to infer, or presume, common intention when the trial judge has made an explicit finding to the contrary and the appellate court has not disturbed the finding. Accordingly, I am of the view that Miss Becker's claim grounded upon resulting trust must fail. If she is to succeed at all, constructive trust emerges as the sole juridical foundation for her claim.

III

Constructive Trust

The principle of unjust enrichment lies at the heart of the constructive trust. "Unjust enrichment" has played a role in Anglo-American legal writing for centuries. Lord Mansfield, in the case of *Moses v. MacFerlan* (1760), 2 Burr. 1005, 97 ER 676, put the matter in these words: "[T]he gist of this kind of action is that the defendant, upon the circumstances of the case, is obliged by the ties of natural justice and equity to refund the money." It would be undesirable, and indeed impossible, to attempt to define all the circumstances in which an unjust enrichment might arise. (See A.W. Scott, "Constructive Trusts" (1955), 71 LQR 39; Leonard Pollock, "Matrimonial Property and Trusts: The Situation from Murdoch to Rathwell" (1978), 16 Alta. Law Rev. 357.) The great advantage of ancient principles of equity is their flexibility: the judiciary is thus able to shape these malleable principles so as to accommodate the changing needs and mores of society, in order to achieve justice. The constructive trust has proven to be a useful tool in the judicial armoury. See *Babrociak v. Babrociak* (1978), 52 DLR (3d) 146 (NS CA); *Douglas v. Guar. Trust Co.* (1978), 8 RFL (2d) 98 (Ont. HC); [and] *Armstrong v. Armstrong* (1978), 22 OR (2d) 223, 93 DLR (3d) 128 (Ont. HC).

How then does one approach the question of unjust enrichment in matrimonial causes? In *Rathwell* I ventured to suggest there are three requirements to be satisfied before an unjust enrichment can be said to exist: an enrichment, a corresponding deprivation and absence of any juristic reason for the enrichment. This approach, it seems to me, is supported by general principles of equity that have been fashioned by the courts for centuries, though, admittedly, not in the context of matrimonial property controversies.

The common law has never been willing to compensate a plaintiff on the sole basis that his actions have benefited another. Lord Halsbury scotched this heresy in the case of *Ruabon SS. Co. Ltd. v. London Assce.*, [1900] AC 6 (HL) with these words, at p. 10: "I cannot understand how it can be asserted that it is part of the common law that where one person gets some advantage from the act of another a right of contribution towards the expense from that act arises on behalf of the person who has done it." Lord Macnaughten, in the same case, put it this way, at p. 15: "There is no principle of law that a person should contribute to an outlay merely because he has derived a benefit from it." It is not enough for the court simply to determine that one spouse has benefited at the hands of another and then to require restitution. It must, in addition, be evident that the retention of the benefit would be "unjust" in the circumstances of the case.

Miss Becker supported Mr. Pettkus for five years. She then worked on the farm for about 14 years. The compelling inference from the facts is that she believed she had some interest in the farm and that that expectation was reasonable in the circumstances. Mr. Pettkus would seem to have recognized in Miss Becker some property interest, through the payment to her of compensation, however modest. There is no evidence to indicate that he ever informed her that all her work performed over the 19 years was being performed on a gratuitous basis. He freely accepted the benefits conferred upon him through her financial support and her labour.

On these facts, the first two requirements laid down in *Rathwell* have clearly been satisfied: Mr. Pettkus has had the benefit of 19 years of unpaid labour, while Miss Becker has received little or nothing in return. As for the third requirement, I hold that where one person in a relationship tantamount to spousal prejudices herself in the reasonable expectation of receiving an interest in property and the other person in the relationship freely accepts benefits conferred by the first person in circumstances where he knows or ought to have known of that reasonable expectation, it would be unjust to allow the recipient of the benefit to retain it.

I conclude, consonant with the judgment of the Court of Appeal, that this is a case for the application of constructive trust. As Wilson JA noted [at RFL 348]: "The parties lived together as husband and wife although unmarried, for almost 20 years, during which period she not only made possible the acquisition of their first property in Franklin Centre by supporting them both exclusively from her income during 'the lean years,' but worked side by side with him for 14 years building up the bee-keeping operation which was their main source of livelihood."

Wilson JA had no difficulty in finding that a constructive trust arose in favour of the respondent by virtue of "joint effort" and "team work," as a result of which Mr. Pettkus was able to acquire the Franklin Centre property, and subsequently the East Hawkesbury and West Hawkesbury properties. The Ontario Court of Appeal imposed the constructive trust in the interests of justice and, with respect, I would do the same.

IV

The "Common Law" Relationship

One question which must be addressed is whether a constructive trust can be established having regard to what is frequently, and euphemistically, referred to as a "common law" relationship. The purpose of constructive trust is to redress situations which would otherwise denote unjust enrichment. In principle, there is no reason not to apply the doctrine to common law relationships. It is worth noting that counsel for Mr. Pettkus, and I think correctly, did not, in this court, raise the common law relationship in defence of the claim of Miss Becker, otherwise than by reference to the *Family Law Reform Act*, 1978 (Ont.), c. 2.

Courts in other jurisdictions have not regarded the absence of a marital bond as any problem. ...

I see no basis for any distinction, in dividing property and assets, between marital relationships and those more informal relationships which subsist for a lengthy period. This was not an economic partnership, nor a mere business relationship, nor a casual encounter. Mr. Pettkus and Miss Becker lived as man and wife for almost 20 years. Their lives and their economic well-being were fully integrated. The equitable principle on which the remedy of constructive trust rests is broad and general; its purpose is to prevent unjust enrichment in whatever circumstances it occurs.

In recent years, there has been much statutory reform in the area of family law and matrimonial property. Counsel for Mr. Pettkus correctly points out that the *Family Law Reform Act* of Ontario, enacted after the present litigation was initiated, does not extend the presumption of equal sharing, which now applies between married persons, to common law spouses. The argument is made that the courts should not develop equitable remedies that are "contrary to current legislative intent." The rejoinder is that legislation was unnecessary to cover these facts, for a remedy was always available in equity for property division between unmarried individuals contributing to the acquisition of assets. The effect of the legislation is to divide "family assets" equally, regardless of contribution, as a matter of course. The court is not here creating a presumption of equal shares. There is a great difference between directing that there be equal shares for common law spouses and awarding Miss Becker a share equivalent to the money or money's worth she contributed over some 19 years. ...

VI

Causal Connection

The matter of "causal connection" was also raised in defence of Miss Becker's claim, but does not present any great difficulty. There is a clear link between the contribution and the disputed assets. The contribution of Miss Becker was such as enabled, or assisted in enabling, Mr. Pettkus to acquire the assets in contention. For the unjust enrichment principle to apply it is obvious that some connection must be shown between the acquisition of property and corresponding deprivation. On the facts of this case, that test was met. The indirect contribution of money and the direct contribution of labour is clearly linked to the acquisition of property, the beneficial ownership of which is in dispute. Miss Becker indirectly contributed to the acquisition of the Franklin Centre farm by making possible an accelerated rate of saving by Mr. Pettkus. The question is really an issue of fact: Was her contribution sufficiently substantial and direct as to entitle her to a portion of the profits realized upon sale of the Franklin Centre property and to an interest in the Hawkesbury properties and the bee-keeping business? The Ontario Court of Appeal answered this question in the affirmative, and I would agree.

VII

Respective Proportions

Although equity is said to favour equality, as stated in *Rathwell*, it is not every contribution which will entitle a spouse to a one-half interest in the property. The extent of the interest must be proportionate to the contribution, direct or indirect, of the claimant. Where the contributions are unequal, the shares will be unequal.

It could be argued that Mr. Pettkus contributed somewhat more to the material fortunes of the joint enterprise than Miss Becker but it must be recognized that each started with nothing; each worked continuously, unremittingly and sedulously in the joint effort. Physically, Miss Becker pulled her fair share of the load: weighing only 87 pounds, she assisted in moving hives weighing 80 pounds. Any difference in quality or quantum of contribution was small. The Ontario Court of Appeal in its discretion favoured an even division and I would not alter that disposition, other than to note that in any accounting regard should be had to the $2,600 and the car, which Miss Becker received on separation in 1974.

Appeal dismissed.

DISCUSSION NOTES

i. The Concurring Judgments in Pettkus v Becker

Ritchie, Martland, and Beetz JJ agreed with the conclusion of Dickson J, but for "substantially different" reasons. Ritchie J reviewed the cases concerning resulting trusts and the reasons of the Court of Appeal and decided (at 860) that

> the advances made by [Becker] throughout the period of the relationship between the parties [were] such as to support the existence of a resulting trust which is governed by the legal principles adopted by the majority of this court in [*Murdoch* and *Rathwell*].

Thus Ritchie J expressly held that Becker had made a financial contribution and there was a common intention that it be used for the benefit of both parties.

Martland J (Beetz J concurring) similarly concluded that the case could be resolved using the doctrine of resulting trust. After reviewing the idea of constructive trust in Anglo-Canadian law, moreover, he expressed serious concern about its use, concluding (at 859) that

> the adoption of this concept [of constructive trust] involves an extension of the law as so far determined in this court. Such an extension is, in my view, undesirable. It would clothe judges with a very wide power to apply what has been described as "palm tree justice" without the benefit of any guidelines. By what test is a judge to determine what constitutes unjust enrichment? The only test would be his individual perception of what he considered to be unjust.

To what extent do you think that the decision of the majority in *Pettkus v Becker* relied on (too much) judicial discretion? In this context, reflect on the different remedies available to married couples, by contrast with couples who cohabit. To what extent is it likely to be more difficult for a cohabitee such as Rosa Becker to acquire an interest in accumulated property using these principles of unjust enrichment and constructive trust? To some extent at least, difficulties of proof in such cases provided the impetus for provinces such as British Columbia to extend the legislative remedies available to married couples to those in cohabiting relationships—that is, those who meet the legislative definition of cohabitation for a continuous period of two years. What reasons may preclude similar legislative amendments in other provinces, including Ontario?

ii. Defining "Contribution": The Issue of Household Work

As *Pettkus v Becker* demonstrates, the Supreme Court of Canada applied the reasoning of its earlier decision in *Rathwell v Rathwell*, [1978] 2 SCR 436 (a case concerning property entitlement at divorce for married spouses) to the situation of a cohabiting couple. Even though the provincial legislature had excluded cohabitees from the application of its family property regime, the court decided that there was "no bar to the availability of an equitable remedy in the present circumstances." What is the fundamental basis for the remedy provided in *Pettkus v Becker*? How significant to the court's reasoning is the relationship between the parties, a relationship described in the judgment in the lower courts as "tantamount to spousal"? What factors are relevant to the conclusion in the Supreme Court of Canada that "Mr. Pettkus and Miss Becker lived as man and wife for almost 20 years"?

In some later cases, there were suggestions that a constructive trust would be awarded only where the non-titled spouse had performed exceptional work, especially work outside the home: e.g. see *Georg v Hassanali* (1989), 18 RFL (3d) 225 (Ont H Ct J), and *Stanish v Parasz* (1989), 23 RFL (3d) 207 (Man QB (Fam Div)). To some extent, the exceptional work done by Ms Becker (and by Mrs Murdoch a decade earlier) may have contributed to this limited precedential understanding of *Pettkus v Becker* in relation to principles of unjust enrichment in cohabiting relationships.

This issue was addressed again in the Supreme Court of Canada in *Peter v Beblow*, [1993] 1 SCR 980. In this case, Ms Peter sought an order declaring a constructive trust in relation to family assets at the end of a 12-year cohabiting relationship with Mr Beblow in British Columbia. She had done all of the domestic work, looked after the children, worked part time, and paid some of the costs of groceries and household supplies. However, title to most of the assets was in Mr Beblow's name.

The trial court in British Columbia allowed Ms Peter's action, concluding that there was an enrichment, a corresponding deprivation, and the lack of any juristic reason for the enrichment. However, the BC Court of Appeal allowed an appeal, concluding that there was an unjust enrichment, but no corresponding deprivation and no causal link between Ms Peter's contributions and the property owned by Mr Beblow at separation. On appeal to the Supreme Court of Canada, a unanimous court allowed the appeal, with judgments by McLachlin J (for La Forest, Sopinka, and Iacobucci JJ) and Cory J (for L'Heureux-Dubé and Gonthier JJ). In part of her judgment (at 992), McLachlin J addressed Mr Beblow's argument that

> some types of services in some types of relationships should not be recognized as supporting legal claims for policy reasons. More particularly, homemaking and childcare services should not, in a marital or quasi-marital relationship, be viewed as giving rise to equitable claims against the other spouse.

After reviewing legal principles and academic literature, McLachlin J concluded (at 993) that "this argument is no longer tenable in Canada, either from the point of view of logic or authority ... . The notion, moreover, is a pernicious one that systematically devalues the contributions which women tend to make to the family economy."

Is it appropriate to conclude after *Peter v Beblow* that household labour performed in a cohabiting relationship will always result in a finding of unjust enrichment? For further analysis of this issue, see *Nowell v Town Estate* (1994), 5 RFL (4th) 353 (Ont H Ct J), (1997), 30 RFL (4th) 107 (Ont CA), leave to appeal to SCC granted (1998), 35 OR (3d) 415, discontinued 8 September 1998; *Pelican v Karpiel* (1994), 20 OR (3d) 659 (CA), leave to appeal to SCC denied; and *Mariano v Manchisi* (1994), 8 RFL (4th) 7 (Ont H Ct J).

iii. Subsequent Refinements: Principles of Unjust Enrichment and Remedies

The award of a constructive trust in *Pettkus v Becker* and *Peter v Beblow* were not the only issues to be raised in relation to unjust enrichment principles and cohabiting relationships. In *Sorochan v Sorochan*, [1986] 2 SCR 38, for example, the Supreme Court of Canada held that a trust could be awarded where the non-titled cohabitee had contributed to the *maintenance* of property already owned by the other cohabitee at the beginning of the cohabiting relationship (thus, not requiring a claimant's contribution to the *acquisition* of property, as identified in *Pettkus v Becker*). There have also been different approaches to the nature of the causal connection between the contribution of the non-titled cohabitee and the property interests to be made subject to an award of a constructive trust, an issue addressed at some length in *Peter v Beblow*.

Peter v Beblow also focused on the issue of whether a constructive trust is the required remedy once there is a finding of unjust enrichment, or whether money damages must first be shown to be an inadequate remedy. On this question, McLachlin J held that, once a court has substantiated a claim of unjust enrichment, as the second step in its analysis, the court must consider the appropriate remedy. According to McLachlin J's (majority) judgment, it is first necessary to consider whether a money payment based on *quantum meruit* (money damages) is sufficient; and then only if such a remedy is inadequate, to consider whether there is a nexus between the contribution and the property to ground a remedy of constructive trust. In this context, a determination that there is unjust enrichment does not automatically result in the remedy of constructive trust; instead, a court must first assess the adequacy of the remedy of *quantum meruit* and only if this remedy is inadequate, proceed to consider the remedy of constructive trust. (In addition, the remedy of constructive trust is available only if there is a connection between the contribution and the property.) For some analyses of the remedy of constructive trust, see *Rawluk v Rawluk*, [1990] 1 SCR 70; R Scane, "Relationships 'Tantamount to Spousal,' Unjust Enrichment, and Constructive Trusts" (1991) 70 Can Bar Rev 260; L Smith, "The Mystery of 'Juristic Reason'" (2000) 12 Sup Ct L Rev (2d) 211; and J McCamus, "Restitution on Dissolution of Marital and Other Intimate Relationships: Constructive Trust or Quantum Meruit" in JW Neyers, M McInnes & SGA Pitel, eds, *Understanding Unjust Enrichment* (Oxford and Portland, OR: Hart, 2004) 359.

In 2011, the Supreme Court of Canada once again considered the appropriate remedy for unjust enrichment in the context of a cohabiting relationship. In *Kerr v Baranow* [and *Vanasse v Seguin*], 2011 SCC 10, [2011] 1 SCR 269, the court reviewed in detail the remedial context for unjust enrichment claims in the context of cohabiting couples and identified a third possible remedy, a monetary award based on a "joint family venture." In *Vanasse* (on appeal from Ontario, while *Kerr* was on appeal from British Columbia), the opposite-sex couple had cohabited for 12 years. For the first four years, they each had successful independent careers in Ottawa, but when the male partner decided to relocate to Halifax, the woman took leave from her employment to move there. In Halifax, the partners agreed to start a family, and the woman had two children and remained at home to care for them in the context of the man's very successful business, one that required him to travel a great deal. Eventually, the man sold his shares in the business for about $11 million and the couple moved back to Ottawa, where both were involved in childcare and household work for a few years, but they then separated. In the Supreme Court, Cromwell J held that a *quantum meruit* payment would not compensate the woman for her significant contribution, but a constructive trust remedy was not available because she could not show a connection between her contributions and property owned at separation. In this context, Cromwell J identified a new remedy based on the joint family venture:

> [60] [There are] cases in which the contributions of both parties over time have resulted in an accumulation of wealth. The unjust enrichment occurs following the breakdown of their relationship when one party retains a disproportionate share of the assets which are the product of their joint efforts. The required link between the contributions and a specific property may not exist [negating the possibility of a constructive trust]. However, there may clearly be a link between the joint efforts of the parties and the accumulation of wealth.

The court identified four factors to consider in determining whether a joint family venture exists: mutual effort, economic integration, actual intent, and priority of the family (paras 87-99). In *Vanasse*, the court held (at para 137) that Ms Vanasse had been "an equal contributor to the family enterprise," and ordered a monetary payment amounting to one-half of the prorated increase in Mr Seguin's net worth during the "period of unjust enrichment" (mainly the years in Halifax), less the value of some other family assets held by Ms Vanasse. (The *Kerr* decision was sent back for a new trial in British Columbia.)

The remedy based on a joint family venture was criticized because it requires a detailed and complex analysis of the work done by each member of the cohabiting couple as well as the need to link work to the accumulation of family wealth: see B Hovius, "Property Disputes Between Common Law Partners: The Supreme Court of Canada's Decisions in Vanasse v Seguin and Kerr v Baranow" (2011) 30 Can Fam LQ 129. As a result, claims based on the joint family venture require presentation of significant amounts of evidence and, if they are litigated, such claims may be subject to highly discretionary decision making by judges. In this context, the failure of some provinces (including Ontario, but not British Columbia) to extend their legislative regimes for property sharing to couples in cohabiting relationships (in addition to married couples) may require new law reform projects in future. For some assessments of reform options, see B Hovius, "Property Division for Unmarried Cohabitees in the Common Law Provinces" (2003-4) 21 Can Fam LQ 175; Simone Wong, "Property Rights for Home-Sharers: Equity Versus a Legislative Framework?" in S Scott-Hunt & H Lim, *Feminist Perspectives on Equity and Trusts* (London: Cavendish, 2001) 133; Marcia Neave, "Living Together: The Legal Effects of the Sexual Division of Labour in Four Common Law Countries" (1991) 17 Monash UL Rev 14; and H Conway and P Girard, "No Place Like Home: The Search for a Legal Framework for Cohabitants and the Family Home in Canada and Britain" (2005) 30 Queen's LJ 715.

iv. Same-Sex Cohabitees, Constructive Trusts, and Reform Proposals

Prior to parliamentary recognition of same-sex marriage in Canada (see the *Civil Marriage Act*, SC 2005, c 33, s 2), the principles of unjust enrichment and the constructive trust remedy were also used in the context of cohabiting relationships involving same-sex couples: e.g. see *Anderson v Luoma* (1986), 50 RFL (2d) 127 (BCSC); *Buist v Greaves*, [1997] OJ no 2646 (Gen Div). Moreover, as early as 1993, the OLRC recommended the extension of the family property regime of the *Family Law Act, 1986* to all heterosexual cohabitees, and to same-sex cohabitees if they were registered as "registered domestic partners," an arrangement proposed by the report: see OLRC, *Report on Family Property Law* (Toronto: Ministry of the Attorney General, 1993) and *Report on the Rights and Responsibilities of Cohabitants Under the Family Law Act* (Toronto: Ministry of the Attorney General, 1993).

Although the OLRC recommendations were never implemented in Ontario, same-sex couples who marry are now entitled, of course, to the *Family Law Act* regime for property sharing at the end of their relationships. OLRC, *Principles of Land Law* (1996) further recommended (at 108) that all property, both real and personal, co-owned by spouses should be presumed to be held in joint tenancy. In addition, the *Report on Family Property Law* recommended that the definition of "spouse" in relation to this presumption of joint tenancy should apply to cohabitees (as defined in the OLRC's 1993 *Report on the Rights and Responsibilities of Cohabitants Under the Family Law Act*). To what extent would the implementation of this recommendation have assisted Ms Becker in her claim against Mr Pettkus?

These issues about property arrangements at the end of different kinds of intimate relationships raise difficult questions for the law of property, both in Canada and elsewhere. In the United Kingdom, for example, some commentators have focused on concerns about the uncertainties of both constructive trusts and cohabiting relationships with respect to property principles. For example, John Mee characterized the constructive trust as "one of the imaginary beasts dreamed up by bored medieval minds, a nightmare synthesis of a number of real creatures": see John Mee, *The Property Rights of Cohabitees* (Oxford: Hart, 1999) 118, and Rebecca Probert, "Review" (1999) 19 LS 591. Others, such as John Dewar, have approached issues about property and families by focusing on the family home, suggesting a need to examine the content of property rights for families and to distinguish such rights in relation to the home: (1) a right of *control over dealings*; (2) a right of *occupation or enjoyment*; (3) a right of *capital entitlement on sale*; and (4) a right on the termination of the relationship to have *basic needs met out of the family resources represented by the family home*. According to Dewar:

> If ... we were to view the current maze of the law relating to the family home through the grid of the four rights mentioned above, and at the same time reduce our attachment to ownership as the sole vehicle for attaining these rights, we might get some greater clarity about proper policy in this important area of social and economic life.

(See John Dewar, "Land, Law, and the Family Home" in Bright & Dewar 327 at 355.) For another reform proposal, see Anne Barlow & Craig Lind, "A Matter of Trust: The Allocation of Rights in the Family Home" (1999) 19 LS 468; and Simon Gardner, "Rethinking Family Property" (1993) 109 Law Q Rev 263.

v. Problems of Enforcement in Pettkus v Becker

Although the decision in *Pettkus v Becker* appeared to provide Rosa Becker with a beneficial interest in one-half of the property held by her partner, subsequent newspaper reports indicated that there were problems in enforcing the judgment. On 13 November 1986, *The Globe and Mail* reported:

> After fighting in vain for six years to gain the fruits of a landmark 1980 court case—which awarded her a half-interest in her former common law husband's bee farm—Rosa Becker shot herself in the forehead. She had been working in Franklin Centre, Quebec as a $60-a-week housekeeper. At her bedside, Miss Becker left several letters, written in German, in which she described her death as a protest against a legal system that prevented her from seeing a penny of a Supreme Court of Canada award worth about $150,000.

The report further explained that a part of Pettkus's property was ordered to be sold in 1984 to comply with the decision of the Supreme Court of Canada, but the total amount ($68,000) went to pay the legal fees of Becker's lawyer. In a further report on 26 May 1989, *The Globe and Mail* indicated that the sum of $13,000 was paid to the trustees of Becker's estate, an amount agreed to by them and Mr Pettkus as a financial settlement of her claims. These reports illustrate the need, perhaps especially in the family property context, to appreciate that a court's decision may sometimes be difficult to enforce in practice. Thus, even though *Pettkus v Becker* may have established important principles about the use of the constructive trust as a remedy for contributions to family property in cohabiting relationships, the "successful" litigant did not benefit from the decision in any material way. Although this problem is one that has ramifications far beyond the instant case, it is salutary to remember the hidden limits of judicial decision making, reported cases, and law school casebooks.

In a final note about Rosa Becker, the *Lawyers Weekly* reported in September 1996 on a successful appeal by an artist living in Van Kleek Hill, Ontario, in relation to an action for libel initiated by L Pettkus. The action was initiated as a result of a letter to a newspaper written by the artist, along with a painting he advertised as "Homage to Rosa Becker." Rey J in the Divisional Court allowed the artist's appeal, holding that his statements did not constitute a libel: see *Cartwright v Pettkus* (10 July 1996, unreported).

V. INFORMAL PROPERTY TRANSACTIONS AND EQUITIES

A. Characterizing "Family Arrangements" in Law

Informal arrangements concerning family property—between spouses, between parents and children, among siblings, or in relation to others who are connected as family members—often create significant challenges when disputes arise about exactly what interests exist for family members. For example, family members may make informal arrangements about building a home on land owned by another family member, about the right to occupy residential premises even though another family member holds title, in relation to unwritten agreements about "loans" to pay mortgages or downpayments on land owned by another family member, or with respect to *inter vivos* "gifts" of land that are invalid because they were not conveyed by deed. Many of these informal arrangements are unproblematic in practice, but disputes may arise if, for example, the titleholder dies or becomes bankrupt or individuals become involved in other family disputes that lead to problems relating to the informal arrangements regarding land or homes. In such cases, the family member who has no proprietary interest, but who has contributed money or labour to land owned by another family member, may seek compensation for the contribution. In these cases, courts have sometimes recognized claims of unjust enrichment, but they may also rely on proprietary estoppel (based on a licence coupled with an "equity") to enforce the parties' arrangement in a way that seems to accord with fundamental fairness; such cases often involve judicial discretion because of the absence of written documentation of the informal arrangement. These cases are "at the boundaries" of property law, and although they most often involve family arrangements, there are also some examples of the use of proprietary estoppel in arm's-length commercial transactions.

As discussed in Chapter 5, equity plays an important role in transfers of interests in land. Recall that an agreement of purchase and sale conveys equitable title to the purchaser if certain requirements are met. In addition, if there is an oral agreement and sufficient acts of part performance, equity will enforce the agreement notwithstanding the *Statute of Frauds*. However, in many informal arrangements among family members, there may not be written documentation at all, and the existence of an oral agreement and sufficient acts of part performance may be difficult to prove. Thus, in this part of Chapter 6, the material focuses on selected examples of proprietary estoppel and equities—interests relating to land that are recognized and enforced even though there is no oral or written agreement. And, because most cases about equities appear to involve family property arrangements, it is appropriate to consider them in relation to other issues about co-ownership and family property in this chapter.

Not surprisingly, Lord Denning was particularly visible in many of these cases involving equities in England, and many of the decisions reflect his views about the remedial role of law, perhaps expressed most directly in *Hill v CA Parsons Ltd*, [1972] Ch 305 (CA) at 316:

> [It is a] fundamental principle that, whenever a man has a right, the law should give a remedy.
> The Latin maxim is *ubi jus ibi remedium*. This principle enables us to step over the trip-wires of
> previous cases and to bring the law into accord with the needs of today.

It may be helpful to consider this comment as you examine the cases and commentary in this section. It is also important to note that the concept of equities has developed significantly in recent decades, expanding beyond its origins in 19th-century cases. Indeed, the evolution of equities provides a good example of the continuing evolution of proprietary concepts, although this evolutionary character may sometimes present conceptual and practical difficulties within traditional principles of property law. As Gray & Symes suggested, "[D]evelopments in this area are occurring apace, and serve to demonstrate yet again the shifting nature of the concept of 'property'" (see Gray & Symes at 505).

This section examines the concept of equities arising out of family property arrangements, which may involve family members other than those who are in married or cohabiting couple relationships. In most cases, these informal property arrangements result from efforts to accommodate specific needs of family members. Moreover, as long as everyone continues to "get along," they present no major legal problems. When the relationships are no longer cordial, however, it becomes necessary to decide whether there was a valid gift, whether the court should "construct" a trust relationship in relation to the property interest, or whether there was a contractual licence or other recognized interest. In relation to these cases, Gray & Symes have suggested that the courts' increasing willingness in recent decades to recognize "equities" as proprietary interests may be resulting in "a new order of 'property' (at least in the residential sphere) in which the distinction between personal rights and proprietary rights is completely eliminated" (see Gray & Symes at 504-5). At the same time, concerns have been expressed about the uncertainty created in the context of so much judicial creativity. For one example, see *Re Sharpe (A Bankrupt)*, [1980] 1 WLR 219 (Ch D), and an analysis of the "conflicting social interests" in such cases in G Woodman, "Note: Social Interests in the Development of Constructive Trusts" (1980) 96 Law Q Rev 336.

As the following case demonstrates clearly, courts often have difficulty determining the appropriate legal category for some informal property arrangements. Examine the different views in *Hussey v Palmer*. What evidence supports the differing conclusions reached by different judges in this case? To what extent does this case represent "a new order of property"?

Hussey v Palmer
[1972] 3 All ER 744 (CA)

LORD DENNING MR: This case is of very considerable interest. Mrs. Emily Hussey, the plaintiff, is getting on in years. She is well over 70 and an old age pensioner. In 1967 she had a little house which was in a very dilapidated condition. It was condemned. She sold it for the sum of £1,100. She had a daughter who was married to a Mr. Palmer, the defendant. Mr. and Mrs. Palmer had two children and lived at no. 9 Stanley Road, Wokingham. It belonged to Mr. Palmer. When the mother sold her little house, the young couple invited her to go and live with them. That often happens. But there was not much room for them all. So they built on a bedroom as an extension for the old lady. She paid for it. She paid £607 for it in June and September 1967. She paid it direct to the builder, Mr. May. Nobody said anything about repayment. No doubt they all thought that the old lady would go and live there, using the bedroom, for the rest of her days. For a few months all went well. The old lady used to make payments to the daughter if she was short of money. But then differences arose. I am afraid that mothers and daughters do not always get on when they are living in the same house. After about 15 months they could not live in harmony any more in the house. So in March 1968, Mrs. Hussey went and lived elsewhere, leaving the Palmers there in their house. After a year or so, Mrs. Hussey wrote to her son-in-law and said she was very hard up. She asked if he could manage £1 or £1 10s. a week to help her out. He did not do it. He did not even reply. So she asked for the money back, the £607 which she had paid for the extension. They did not pay. She got legal aid.

In April 1970, she took out a default summons in the county court against Mr. Palmer. She claimed £607 for money lent. Mr. Palmer wrote a defence in his own hand. He said:

> The payments, made to a builder, were not a loan, but were paid by the plaintiff for her own benefit and at the time the question of repayment was not raised. I assumed that the payments were in effect a gift.

Later on, Mr. Palmer got legal aid too, and, with the help of legal advisers, he put in an amended defence in which he denied liability. He said that

> the moneys were only to be repaid in the event of the defendants' house, 9 Stanley Road, Wokingham, being sold within a short period of building works having been completed by

the said Mr. May. The said building works were mainly in respect of an extension to the said house, which extension was for occupation by the plaintiff.

He also said that "the said agreement was merely a family arrangement and was not intended to have legal consequences."

On February 10, 1971, the case came before the county court. The judge was fully occupied with another case. So it went before the registrar by consent. The registrar heard the evidence of Mrs. Hussey and also Mr. Palmer. He intimated a strong view that this was not a loan at all: but that it was a family arrangement. Mrs. Hussey's advisers were so impressed that they submitted to a non-suit and started a fresh action. This time they issued a plaint claiming £607 on a resulting trust. They said that, as she had contributed this £607 towards the extension of the building, at all events Mr. Palmer held the house on trust to repay it at some time or other to her: and that she would have an interest in the house to that extent in proportion to the amount she had contributed.

In July 1971, the fresh action came on for hearing before the county court judge himself. Mrs. Hussey went into the witness box and gave her story again. She said of Mr. Palmer: "… [H]e said he would build a bedroom on for me. He asked me if I would lend him the money. I agreed to lend it to him." In cross-examination she said: "They would give me a home for life, if I wanted it."

The defendant, Mr. Palmer, elected to call no evidence. The judge felt that, on Mrs. Hussey's own evidence, there was a loan, and not a resulting trust. After some discussion, Mrs. Hussey's counsel sought leave to amend the claim by adding an alternative claim for money lent. The defendant opposed the amendment. So the judge did not grant it. He made a note, saying: "The plaintiff's advisers decided to drop the claim for loan before the registrar and have in this action elected not to claim on a loan." So the claim remained on a resulting trust only.

On April 4, 1971, the judge decided in favour of the defendant. He said in his note for this court:

> I thought that the plaintiff was an honest witness, and at the end of her evidence I was satisfied that I ought to find that the money had been lent by the plaintiff and that there was no case for a resulting trust … . I … reserved judgment to see if I could find for the plaintiff on the case pleaded. I could not.

So Mrs. Hussey went away a second time taking nothing. Now she appeals to this court.

Mr. Owen, on her behalf, rests her case on a resulting trust. He says that, despite Mrs. Hussey's own evidence, there was no loan. I agree that Mrs. Hussey did not lend the £607 to Mr. Palmer. Test it this way: suppose that, a week or two later, Mrs. Hussey had demanded from Mr. Palmer repayment of the £607, and he had refused. Could she recover it as money lent, and have the house sold up to regain it? Clearly not. The courts would undoubtedly have said—as the registrar said here—that it was a family arrangement. There was no intention that it should be repaid on demand. Again, if she had stayed on in the house, making use of the bedroom, could she have sued Mr. Palmer for money lent? Clearly not. There was no intention that it should be repaid whilst she had the benefit of the bedroom. Suppose that she had stayed there until she died, could her executors have sued Mr. Palmer for money lent? Clearly not. There was no intention that it should be repaid after her death.

If there was no loan, was there a resulting trust, and, if so, what were the terms of the trust?

Although the plaintiff alleged that there was a resulting trust, I should have thought that the trust in this case, if there was one, was more in the nature of a constructive trust: but this is more a matter of words than anything else. The two run together. By whatever name it is described, it is a trust imposed by law whenever justice and good conscience require it. It is a liberal process, founded upon large principles of equity, to be applied in cases where the legal owner cannot conscientiously keep the property for himself alone, but ought to allow another to have the property or the benefit of it or a share in it. The trust may arise at the outset when the property is acquired, or later on, as the circumstances may require. It is an equitable remedy by which the court can enable an aggrieved party to obtain restitution. It is comparable to the legal remedy of money had and received which, as Lord Mansfield said, is "very beneficial and therefore, much encouraged" [*Moses v MacFarlan* (1760), 2 Burr 1005 at 1012]. Thus we have repeatedly held that, when one person contributes towards the purchase price of a house, the owner holds it on a constructive trust for him, proportionate to his contribution, even though there is no agreement between them, and no declaration of trust to be found, and no evidence of any intention to create a trust. Instances are numerous where a wife has contributed money to the initial purchase of a house or property; or later on to the payment of mortgage instalments; or has helped in a business: see *Falconer v. Falconer*, [1970] 1 WLR 1333; *Heseltine v. Heseltine*, [1971] 1 WLR 342; and *In re Cummins, decd.*, [1972] Ch. 62. Similarly, when a mistress has contributed money, or money's worth, to the building of a house: *Cooke v. Head*, [1972] 1 WLR 518. Very recently we held that a purchaser, who bought a cottage subject to the rights of an occupier, held it on trust for her benefit: *Binions v. Evans*, [1972] Ch. 359. In all those cases it would have been quite inequitable for the legal owner to take the property for himself and exclude the other from it. So the law imputed or imposed a trust for his or her benefit.

The present case is well within the principles of those cases. Just as a person, who pays part of the purchase price, acquires an equitable interest in the house, so also he does when he pays for an extension to be added to it. Mr. Owen has done a lot of research and has found a case in 1858 to that very effect. It is *Unity Joint Stock Mutual Banking Association v. King* (1858), 25 Beav. 72. A father had land on which he built a granary. His two sons built two other granaries on it at a cost of £1,200. Sir John Romilly MR held that the two sons had a lien or charge on the property as against the father, and any person claiming through him. The father had never promised to pay the sons £1,200. He was not indebted to them in that sum. He had never engaged or promised to make over the land to them or to give them a charge on it. Yet they had a lien or charge on the land. That case was approved by the Privy Council in *Chalmers v. Pardoe*, [1963] 1 WLR 677, 681-682, where it was said to be based on the "general equitable principle that ... it would be against conscience" for the owner to take the land without repaying the sums expended on the buildings. To this I would add *Inwards v. Baker*, [1965] 2 QB 29, when a son built a bungalow on his father's land in the expectation that he would be allowed to stay there as his home, though there was no promise to that effect. After the father's death, his trustees sought to turn the son out. It was held that he had an equitable interest which was good against the trustees. In those cases it was emphasised that the court must look at the circumstances of each case to decide in what way the equity can be satisfied. In some by an equitable lien. In others by a constructive trust. But in either case it is because justice and good conscience so require.

In the present case Mrs. Hussey paid £607 to a builder for the erection of this extension. It may well be, as the defendant says, that there was no contract to repay it at all. It was not a loan to the son-in-law. She could not sue him for repayment. He could not have turned her out. If she had stayed there until she died, the extension would undoubtedly have belonged beneficially to the son-in-law. If, during her lifetime, he had sold the house, together with the extension, she would be entitled to be repaid the £607 out of the proceeds. He admits this himself. But he has not sold the house. She has left, and the son-in-law has the extension for his own benefit and could sell the whole if he so desired. It seems to me to be entirely against conscience that he should retain the whole house and not allow Mrs. Hussey any interest in it, or any charge upon it. The court should, and will, impose or impute a trust by which Mr. Palmer is to hold the property on terms under which, in the circumstances that have happened, she has an interest in the property proportionate to the £607 which she put into it. She is quite content if he repays her the £607. If he does not repay the £607, she can apply for an order for sale, so that the sum can be paid to her. But the simplest way for him would be to raise the £607 on mortgage and pay it to her. But, on the legal point raised, I have no doubt there was a resulting trust, or, more accurately, a constructive trust, for her, and I would so declare. I would allow the appeal, accordingly.

PHILLIMORE LJ: I agree … . In all the circumstances here, in the absence of clear arrangements for repayment and in circumstances where repayment on demand might be very difficult for the son-in-law, I should have thought it was more appropriate to regard it as an example of a resulting trust; and I would accordingly entirely agree with Lord Denning MR that she has an interest in this house proportionate to the £607 which she paid. It follows that this appeal should be allowed.

CAIRNS LJ: I am afraid I differ from my Lords in this case; and, but for the fact that they have both taken the view that the plaintiff was entitled to succeed, I should have regarded this as a plain case where she had failed to establish the cause of action which she set up. Having in an earlier action alleged that this money was lent by her to the defendant, having elected to be non-suited in that action, she then starts this fresh action in which her case is based solely upon the claim of a resulting trust. She then gives her evidence and in the course of it she says:

> When I sold my house my son-in-law suggested that I should live with him as long as I liked to stay there. My daughter agreed. I went to see him one night and he said he would build a bedroom on for me. He asked me if I would lend him the money. I agreed to lend it to him.

Later she referred to going to the bank manager with her son-in-law, and said:

> My son-in-law told the bank manager that he would like me to lend him the money. As I lent the money, I expected to receive it back. As it was a loan I expected it back … . While living with my son-in-law he said he was going to Cornwall and would sell his Wokingham house, and try and buy a house and repay me what he owed me.

And in cross-examination: "I did not give my son-in-law the money—I lent it to him." In my view it is going a very long way to say that, all that evidence having been given by this lady, there was some misunderstanding by her of the legal position and that she was describing as a loan something which was not a loan at all. It is to my mind nothing to the point that in all probability no express terms as to repayment were ever agreed. It must be a common thing indeed for a parent or a parent-in-law to make a loan of money to a son or daughter or a son-in-law which both of them know is a loan, as to which it is obvious that there is no immediate prospect of repayment, but which in law is a loan repayable on demand. In my view that is the position here. As it was a loan, I think it is quite inconsistent with that to say that it could create a resulting trust at the same time. I accept as a correct statement of law the short passage in *Underhill's Law of Trusts and Trustees*, 12th ed. (1970), p. 210, in these words:

> Where the purchase money is provided by a third party at the request of and by way of loan to the person to whom the property is conveyed there is no resulting trust in favour of the third party, for the lender did not advance the purchase-money as purchaser ... but merely as lender.

... For these reasons I consider that the plaintiff was certainly not entitled to succeed on the evidence which she had given. As the particulars of claim stood, the only doubt that I could have had about the matter, if my judgment had been decisive, would be as to whether she should simply have the appeal dismissed or whether at this late stage she should have been given an opportunity of amending her particulars of claim and having a re-trial. I should have been anxious that she should have that opportunity, because I think the strong probability is that one way or another she ought to have got this money back. So far as concerns the inconvenience of having a third hearing, I do not think that is owing to anything done or omitted on the defendant's side. However, in the circumstances it is unnecessary for me to arrive at any final opinion as to which would have been the right course.

Appeal allowed.

Declaration that defendant held 9 Stanley Road, Wokingham, upon a resulting trust for plaintiff and that the plaintiff was entitled to a beneficial interest in the property of the value of £607.

Legal aid taxation of both parties' costs.

DISCUSSION NOTES

i. Informal Arrangements and Legal Categories

In *Hussey v Palmer*, the court considered whether the arrangement between Mrs Hussey and her son-in-law represented a gift or a loan, or whether it represented a contribution that should be reflected in a declaration of resulting or constructive trust. Why was it so difficult for the court to characterize the parties' arrangement? Are the judges in agreement about what arrangement was intended by the parties? To what extent does the plaintiff's evidence compound the difficulty of characterizing the arrangement? Is the result more dependent on concerns about the son-in-law's unjust enrichment or the intention of the parties? Do you agree with Gray & Symes when they suggest that "[i]t is extremely difficult to analyse the legal effect of informal family arrangements within the traditional categories of property and contract"? (See Gray & Symes at 473.)

What was Mrs Hussey entitled to as a result of this decision? Lord Denning MR suggested that "[the plaintiff] has an interest in the property proportionate to the £607 which she put into it," but he then went on to suggest that the son-in-law can extinguish the trust by a re-payment of £607. Are these statements consistent? It has been suggested, for example, that the case resulted in Mrs Hussey having a proportionate share in the increasing value of the house (due to inflation) rather than a mere right to have the amount of her contribution re-paid: see TC Ridley, "A Family Affair" (1973) 36 Mod L Rev 436. How might the uncertainty in this case have been avoided?

In *Hussey v Palmer*, the court seemed to conclude that the widow was entitled to a result-ing trust, a well-established equitable remedy. The court did not focus on proprietary estop-pel (an equity) in this case. However, consider a situation in which the owner of land gave oral permission to a woman, the widow of a former employee of the owner, to live in a cot-tage rent-free for the rest of her life. The woman continued to live in the cottage, which had been her home for over 50 years. Subsequently, the owner conveyed the property, expressly subject to the widow's right to live in the cottage, to a purchaser who obtained the land at a reduced price as a result of the widow's occupation of the cottage. In spite of the reduced price, the purchaser then initiated an action for possession against the widow. At the time of the action, the widow was 79 years old. How should this case be resolved?

In *Binion v Evans*, [1972] Ch 359 (CA), the Court of Appeal confirmed a trial court decision declaring that the purchaser held the cottage on trust for the widow for life or "as long as she desired." Note this language in relation to other cases (discussed below) in relation to equi-ties. To what extent is the remedy provided in this case different from the one awarded in *Hussey v Palmer*? See also commentaries on this decision, most of which focused on the equi-ties connected to the licence granted to the widow: J Martin, "Contractual Licensee or Tenant for Life?" (1972) 36 Conveyancer and Property Lawyer (NS) 266; RJ Smith, "Licences and Con-structive Trusts: 'The Law Is What It Ought to Be'" (1973) 32 Cambridge LJ 123; and AJ Oakley, "The Licensee's Interest" (1972) 35 Mod L Rev 551.

By contrast with the widow in *Binion v Evans*, and in spite of ambiguity about the precise nature of her proprietary interest, the court did not consider remedies that would have en-forced Mrs Hussey's right to remain in the house itself. Lord Denning MR referred to *Inwards v Baker*, [1965] 2 QB 29 (CA), in which the court resolved a family arrangement problem by mak-ing an order that permitted a non-titleholding family member to remain in possession for life or for as long as he wanted it as a home. Why was such an order inappropriate in *Hussey v Palmer*? As you consider *Inwards v Baker*, below, reflect on the extent to which the parties' wishes and circumstances may influence the scope of the court's (equitable) remedial action.

ii. Proprietary Estoppel: Estoppel by Acquiescence—Dillwyn v Llewelyn

Some courts have recognized equities because the actions of the parties result in estoppel. The context for these cases usually involves a request or encouragement by a titleholder to another (often, a family member), and subsequent action (such as the expenditure of money) by the other (family member) in reliance on the request or encouragement. The principles of proprietary estoppel are complex, especially in their application to diverse factual situations and in relation to the variety of remedies granted by courts to enforce them. According to Gray & Symes at 493-94, "the jurisprudence of proprietary estoppel provides an extremely flexible means by which the courts can so fashion discretionary relief as to do justice in the light of the interaction and expectation of the litigants." Moreover, although proprietary estoppel is similar to promissory estoppel, originally highlighted in Lord Denning's decision in *Central London Property Trust Ltd v High Trees House Ltd*, [1947] KB 130 (CA), proprietary estoppel may result in an interest binding on third-party purchasers with notice of the equity: see *ER Ives Investment Ltd v High*, [1967] 2 QB 379 (CA).

Recent decisions about equities are based on some 19th-century decisions involving informal family relationships. In one of these, *Dillwyn v Llewelyn* (1862), 45 ER 1285 (Ch D), a father made a will devising his real property in trust for his widow for life, remainder in trust for the plaintiff for life, and remainder in certain other trusts. After making the will (which would not take effect until the father's death), the father offered his son a farm property on which the son could build a home. Unlike in many family arrangements, the father actually signed a memorandum stating that he was presenting the farm to his son for the purpose of building a home. The son (the plaintiff) built a valuable house on the property, but no deed was ever executed by the father to transfer the fee simple interest to his son. Thus, after his father died, the son brought an application for a conveyance of the fee simple estate. The court granted the son's application, stating (at 1286):

> [I]f A puts B in possession of a piece of land, and tells him: "I give it to you that B may build a house on it," and B on the strength of that promise, with the knowledge of A, expends a large sum of money in building a house accordingly, I cannot doubt that the donee acquires a right from the subsequent transaction to call on the donor to perform that contract and complete the imperfect donation which was made. The case is somewhat analogous to that of verbal agreement not binding originally for the want of the memorandum signed by the party to be charged, but which becomes binding by virtue of the subsequent part performance.

What exactly was the basis for the court's decision to grant the son's application in *Dillwyn v Llewelyn*? Note how the court made an analogy to the principle of part performance. Why was this principle unavailable in *Dillwyn v Llewelyn*? As discussed in *Inwards v Baker*, which follows, *Dillwyn v Llewelyn* relied on an earlier decision, *Ramsden v Dyson* (1866), LR 1 HL 129, a case approved by the Privy Council in *Plimmer v Mayor, Councillors, and Citizens of the City of Wellington*, [1884] 9 App Cas 699. In reviewing *Inwards v Baker*, identify the extent to which this 20th-century decision represents an evolution of the principles applied in the earlier cases.

Inwards v Baker
[1965] 2 QB 29 (CA)

LORD DENNING MR: In this case old Mr. Baker, if I may so describe the father, in 1931 was the owner of a little over six acres of land at Dunsmore in Buckinghamshire. His son, Jack Baker, was living in those parts and was thinking of erecting a bungalow. He had his eye on a piece of land but the price was rather too much for him. So the father said to him: "Why not put the bungalow on my land and make the bungalow a little bigger." That is what the son did. He did put the bungalow on his father's land. He built it with his own labour with the help of one or two men, and he got the materials. He bore a good deal of the expense himself, but his father helped him with it, and he paid his father back some of it. Roughly he spent himself the sum of £150 out of a total of £300 expended. When it was finished, he went into the bungalow; and he has lived there ever since from 1931 down to date. His father visited him there from time to time.

In 1951 the father died. The only will he left was one he made as far back as 1922 before this land was bought or the bungalow was built. He appointed as executrix Miss Inwards, who had been living with him for many many years as his wife and by whom he had two children. He left nearly all his property to her and her two children by him. He left his son, Jack Baker, £400. Miss Inwards appointed her two children as trustees of the will with her. The trustees under the will did not take any steps to get Jack Baker out of the bungalow. In fact they visited him there from time to time. They all seem to have been quite friendly. But in the year 1963 they took proceedings to get Jack Baker out. Miss Inwards died during these proceedings. Her two children continue the proceedings as the trustees of the father's will.

The trustees say that at the most Jack Baker had a licence to be in the bungalow but that it had been revoked and he had no right to stay. The judge has held in their favour. He was referred to *Errington v. Errington and Woods*, but the judge held that that decision only protected a contractual licensee. He thought that, in order to be protected, the licensee must have a contract or promise by which he is entitled to be there. The judge said:

> I can find no promise made by the father to the son that he should remain in the property at all—no contractual arrangement between them. True the father said that the son could live in the property, expressly or impliedly, but there is no evidence that this was arrived at as the result of a contract or promise—merely an arrangement made casually because of the relationship which existed and knowledge that the son wished to erect a bungalow for residence.

Thereupon, the judge, with much reluctance, thought the case was not within *Errington's* case, and said the son must go.

The son appeals to this court. We have had the advantage of cases which were not cited to the county court judge—cases in the last century, notably *Dillwyn v. Llewelyn* and *Plimmer v. Wellington Corporation*. This latter was a decision of the Privy Council which expressly affirmed and approved the statement of the law made by Lord Kingsdown in *Ramsden v. Dyson*. It is quite plain from those authorities that if the owner of land requests another, or indeed allows another, to expend money on the land under an expectation created or encouraged by the landlord that he will be able to remain there, that raises an equity in the licensee such as to entitle him to stay. He has a licence coupled with an equity. Mr. Goodhart urged before us that the licensee could not stay indefinitely. The principle only applied, he said, when there was an expectation of some precise legal term. But it seems to me, from *Plimmer's* case in particular, that the equity arising from the expenditure on land need not fail "merely on the ground that the interest to be secured has not been expressly indicated ... the court must look at the circumstances in each case to decide in what way the equity can be satisfied."

So in this case, even though there is no binding contract to grant any particular interest to the licensee, nevertheless the court can look at the circumstances and see whether there is an equity arising out of the expenditure of money. All that is necessary is that the licensee should, at the request or with the encouragement of the landlord, have spent the money in the expectation of being allowed to stay there. If so, the court will not allow that expectation to be defeated where it would be inequitable so to do. In this case it is quite plain that the father allowed an expectation to be created in the son's mind that this bungalow was to be his home. It was to be his home for his life or, at all events, his home as long as he wished it to remain his home. It seems to me, in the light of that equity, that the father could not in 1932 have turned to his son and said: "You are to go. It is my land and my house." Nor could he at any time thereafter so long as the son wanted it as his home.

Mr. Goodhart put the case of a purchaser. He suggested that the father could sell the land to a purchaser who could get the son out. But I think that any purchaser who took with notice would clearly be bound by the equity. So here, too, the present plaintiffs, the successors in title of the father, are clearly themselves bound by this equity. It is an equity well recognised in law. It arises from the expenditure of money by a person in actual occupation of land when he is led to believe that, as the result of that expenditure, he will be allowed to remain there. It is for the court to say in what way the equity can be satisfied. I am quite clear in this case it can be satisfied by holding that the defendant can remain there as long as he desires to as his home.

I would allow the appeal accordingly and enter judgment for the defendant.

DANCKWERTS LJ: I agree and I will add only a few words. It seems to me the claim of the defendant in respect of this property is amply covered by *Errington v. Errington and Woods, Dillwyn v. Llewelyn* and *Plimmer v. Wellington Corporation*. Further, it seems to me to be supported by the observations of Lord Kingsdown in *Ramsden v. Dyson*. It is true that in that case Lord Kingsdown reached a result on the facts of the case which differed from that reached by the other members of the House of Lords, but Lord Kingsdown's observations which are relevant in the present case have received support since that case was decided; and, in particular, I would like to refer to the observations in the judgment of the Privy Council in *Plimmer v. Wellington Corporation*. It is said there:

> Their Lordships consider that this case falls within the principle stated by Lord Kingsdown as to expectations created or encouraged by the landlord, with the addition that in this case the landlord did more than encourage the expenditure, for he took the initiative in requesting it.

There are similar circumstances in the present case. The defendant was induced to give up his project of building a bungalow on land belonging to somebody else other than his father, in which case he would have become the owner or tenant of the land in question and thus have his own home. His father induced him to build on his, the father's, land and expenditure was made by the defendant for the purpose of the erection of the bungalow.

In my view the case comes plainly within the proposition stated in the cases. It is not necessary, I think, to imply a promise. It seems to me that this is one of the cases of an equity created by estoppel, or equitable estoppel, as it is sometimes called, by which the person who has made the expenditure is induced by the expectation of obtaining protection, and equity protects him so that an injustice may not be perpetrated.

I am clearly of opinion that the appeal should be allowed and judgment should be entered for the defendant.

SALMON LJ: I agree.

Appeal allowed.

DISCUSSION NOTES

i. Characterizing the Informal Family Arrangement

How did the court characterize the family arrangement in *Inwards v Baker*? Did the father make a promise to his son? What is the evidence before the court in relation to this family arrangement? Is it appropriate for the court to rely on Jack Baker's evidence after his father's death? Is the court's reasoning based on the parties' intentions or on Jack Baker's detrimental reliance? Are these facts different from the facts in *Dillwyn v Llewelyn*? How? On the basis of this case, how is a "licence coupled with an equity" defined?

What is the test used by the court to establish the equity? Does the test require "a request or permission" or merely "acquiescence"? What is the basis for equitable intervention based on a request, the granting of permission, or acquiescence by the titleholder? Are these different fact patterns equally deserving of equitable intervention? For example, what difference would it make if the evidence showed that Jack Baker's father had said to him: "If you build your bungalow on my land, I will transfer the land to you"? What if Jack Baker's father had simply said, "I give you this land"?

ii. Fashioning a Remedy for an Equity: Dodsworth v Dodsworth

Lord Denning MR concluded that Jack Baker could "remain there as long as he desires to as his home." What kind of property interest was thereby created? If the interest were simply a licence, rather than a licence coupled with an equity, what difference would it make? Recall that a licence is usually a contractual agreement—is it enforceable against third parties?

Why was Jack Baker's interest in *Inwards v Baker* enforceable against his father's widow and her children? Recall the discussion in Chapter 5 about priorities among competing interests in land and the impact of registration of interests. If an equitable interest is enforceable against everyone except a bona fide purchaser for value without notice, why was Jack Baker's interest enforceable against Ms Inwards and her children? Is the sphere of enforceability of an equity the same as that of an equitable interest?

Can Jack Baker sell or transfer his property interest? To what extent did the decision in this case fail to meet societal goals for alienability of land, because the decision both rendered the land unsaleable and discouraged Jack Baker from ever moving? See FR Crane, "Estoppel Interests in Land" (1967) 31 Conveyancer and Property Lawyer (NS) 332.

Consider also what other remedies were available to the court in this case. For example, in *Dodsworth v Dodsworth* (1973), 228 Estates Gazette 1115 (cited in Gray & Symes at 490), the plaintiff invited her younger brother and his wife to live with her. They did so, and spent about £700 on improvements to the plaintiff's house in the expectation, encouraged by the plaintiff, that they could remain there as long as they desired. Nine months after they had moved in and made the improvements, however, the plaintiff repented her invitation and brought an application for possession. The Court of Appeal concluded that there was an equity, and that it would be satisfied by securing the occupation of the defendants until the expenditure had been reimbursed by the plaintiff. Compare this result to the outcome in *Inwards v Baker*. What are the differences in the two cases that support these differing remedies: were there differences in the extent of the expenditures, in the length of cohabitation, in the family relationships, or other factors that justify the differing outcomes?

B. Judicial Discretion and Remedies in Relation to Equities: Pascoe v Turner

As seems clear, both the test for determining that an equity has been created and the scope of decision making about an appropriate remedy in particular fact situations require the exercise of judicial discretion. As the following case demonstrates, courts may sometimes use considerable discretion in assessing an appropriate remedy. Examine carefully the reasons adopted by the court in fashioning the remedy in *Pascoe v Turner*.

Pascoe v Turner
[1979] 1 WLR 431 (CA)

CUMMING-BRUCE LJ (for the court): This is an appeal from the orders made on April 21, 1978, by Mr. McKintosh, sitting as a deputy circuit judge in the Camborne and Redruth County Court, whereby he dismissed the plaintiff's claim for possession of a house at 2 Tolgarrick Road, Tuckingmill, Camborne in Cornwall, and granted the defendant declarations upon her counterclaim that the plaintiff held the house on trust for the defendant, her heirs and assigns absolutely and that the contents of the house belonged to her. The plaintiff asks for an order of possession, and that the counterclaim be dismissed.

The Issues

The appeal raises three issues about the house: (a) Did the defendant prove the trust found by the judge? (b) Did she prove such facts as prevented the plaintiff by estoppel from asserting his legal title? (c) If the answer to that question is yes, what is the equitable relief to which she is entitled? In respect of the contents of the house, did the defendant prove that they were given to her by the plaintiff's voluntary gift?

The Facts

The plaintiff was a business man in a relatively small way and at all material times was and had been building up some capital assets which he invested in purchases of private and commercial property. In 1961 or 1962 he met the defendant, a widow recovering from the distressing circumstances of her husband's death. She had invested about £4,500 capital and had some income from this and from an invalidity pension. They made friends. She was happy to help him in small ways in business activities. The relationship deepened and she took the plaintiff's young son under her wing, and helped to guide him through his problems. In 1963 she moved into the plaintiff's home, at first as his housekeeper. In 1964 the boy went away to his own mother, and shortly afterwards the plaintiff and the defendant began to share a bedroom and live in every sense as man and wife. The plaintiff's business was expanding, and she worked in the business as well as doing the housekeeping. She did all that a wife would have done. He offered marriage, but she declined. In 1965 they moved. He took her to see 2 Tolgarrick Road, and asked her if she liked it. He bought it. They moved in and continued living there as man and wife. He paid for the house and contents. He gave her £3 a week housekeeping. She used her own money to buy her clothes. She only bought small things for the house. Then she began to collect some rents for him and was allowed to keep part of them, bringing her housekeeping allowance up to £6 per week. He bought a place in Spain which they visited on holidays.

At some stage there was some mention of the position with regard to the plaintiff's property, including the house, and the defendant. There was what the judge describes as a sort of will on which there was mention of the defendant having the house if anything happened to the plaintiff. In 1973 Cupid aimed his arrow. It struck the plaintiff, who began an affair with a Mrs. Pritchard. All unknowing, the defendant went for a few days with her daughter to Capri. In her absence the plaintiff moved in for two days to the house with Mrs. Pritchard, but they removed themselves before her return. Immediately the defendant got back, he visited her. There was a conflict of evidence on what was then said. His version was that all he told her was that he would never see her without a roof over her head. The account given by the defendant and the witnesses called on her behalf was that he declared to her and later to them that she had nothing to worry about as the house was hers and everything in it. The judge rejected the plaintiff's evidence and accepted the evidence of the defendant and her witnesses. The plaintiff declared to the defendant not once but on a number of occasions after he had left her, "The house is yours and everything in it." He told a Mrs. Smejhal and a Mrs. Green the same thing. To Mrs. Smejhal he said that he'd put it in a solicitor's hands. Mrs. Green asked him at the end of 1973 if he'd given the defendant the deeds, and he replied that he hadn't yet but was going to see to it. In fact he never did. There was no deed of conveyance, nothing in writing at all. The defendant stayed on in the house. She thought it was hers and everything in it. In reliance upon the plaintiff's declarations that he had given her the house and its contents, she spent money and herself did work on redecoration, improvements and repairs. The judge found that the plaintiff as donor stood by knowingly while she improved the property thinking it was hers. In 1973 when he left and told her that the house was hers she had about £1,000 of her own capital left. She spent some £230 on repairs and improvements and redecoration to the house, and also paid a man an unspecified sum in cash for working on the house. She bought carpets for the lounge, stairs and hall and fitted carpets to the bedrooms. She bought curtains. Though the house was full of furniture, she got rid of a good deal and replaced it by purchases made out of savings. The work which she carried out in 1974 and 1975 was pleaded in a list given in further particulars of defence and counterclaim as follows. (1) Partly replumbing house, providing hot water from immersion system to kitchen and installing new sink unit and other fitments. Installing gas into the kitchen. (2) Joining outside toilet to rear door of premises by blockwork covered way. (3) Installing gas conduits and installing a gas fire into the lounge. (4) Repairing and retiling the roof where necessary and repairing lead valleys. (5) Repairing and redecorating interior. So she stayed on. He lived nearby and sometimes visited her. She continued to collect some rents for him. Then there was a quarrel. He decided to throw her out of the house if he could. On April 9, 1976, his solicitors wrote to her giving her two months' notice "to determine her licence to occupy," and demanded possession on June 10, 1976. She refused to go.

On August 25 he filed his plaint in the county court, claiming possession and mesne profits at £10 per week from June 10, 1976, until possession. On February 14, 1977, she filed her defence and counterclaim. She pleaded his declarations that the house and contents were hers and that in reliance on his statements she carried out extensive works on the house with the plaintiff's full knowledge and encouragement. By her counterclaim she sought a declaration that the house and its contents were hers, and that the plaintiff held the realty on trust for her, her heirs and assigns. Alternatively she sought a declaration that the plaintiff had given her a licence to occupy the house for her lifetime. She claimed that the plaintiff was estopped from denying the trust or the licence. By his reply and defence to counterclaim the plaintiff joined issue on the extent of the works alleged to have been done since 1973, denied that they had been done in reliance upon his promises, or that they were of sufficient substance to give rise to the estoppel alleged. The judge decided the issue of estoppel against him. It is implicit in his conclusion that he accepted the defendant's evidence about what was done to the house after 1973, and how the plaintiff knew all about it and advised and encouraged her.

The judge found that the plaintiff had made a gift to her of the contents of the house. I have no doubt that he was right about that. She was already in possession of them as a bailee when he declared the gift. Counsel for the plaintiff submitted that there was no gift because it was uncertain what he was giving her. He pointed to a safe and to the defendant's evidence that she had sent round an orange bedroom suite to the plaintiff so that he should have a bed to sleep on. The answer is that he gave her everything in the house, but later, recognising his need, she gave back some bits and pieces to him. So much for the contents.

Her rights in the realty are not quite so simply disposed of because of section 53 and section 54 of the *Law of Property Act, 1925*. There was nothing in writing. The judge considered the plaintiff's declarations, and decided that they were not enough to found an express trust. We agree. But he went on to hold that the beneficial interest in the house had passed under a constructive trust inferred from words and conduct of the parties. He relied on the passage in *Snell's Principles of Equity*, 27th ed. (1973), p. 185, in which the editors suggest a possible definition of a constructive trust. But there are difficulties in the way. The long and short of events in 1973 is that the plaintiff made an imperfect gift of the house. There is nothing in the facts from which an inference of a constructive trust can be drawn. If it had not been for section 53 of the *Law of Property Act, 1925* the gift of the house would have been a perfect gift, just as the gift of the contents was a perfect gift. In the event it remained an imperfect gift and, as Turner LJ said in *Milroy v. Lord* (1862), 4 De FG & J 264, 274: "[T]here is no equity in this court to perfect an imperfect gift." So matters stood in 1973, and if the facts had stopped there the defendant would have remained a licensee at will of the plaintiff.

But the facts did not stop there. On the judge's findings the defendant, having been told that the house was hers, set about improving it within and without. Outside she did not do much: a little work on the roof and an improvement which covered the way from the outside toilet to the rest of the house, putting in a new door there, and Snowcem to protect the toilet. Inside, she did a good deal more. She installed gas in the kitchen with a cooker, improved the plumbing in the kitchen and put in a new sink. She got new gas fires, putting a gas fire in the lounge. She redecorated four rooms. The fitted carpets she put in the bedrooms, the carpeting, and the curtains and the furniture that she bought are not part of the realty, and it is not clear how much she spent on those items. But they are part of the whole circumstances. There she was, on her own after he left her in 1973. She had £1,000 left of her capital, and a pension of some kind. Having as she thought been given the house, she set about it as described. On the repairs and improvement to the realty and the fixtures she spent about £230. She had £300 of her capital left by the date of the trial, but she did not establish in evidence how much had been expended on refurbishing the house with carpets, curtains and furniture. We would describe the work done in and about the house as substantial in the sense that that adjective is used in the context of estoppel. All the while the plaintiff not only stood by and watched but encouraged and advised, without a word to suggest that she was putting her money and her personal labour into his house. What is the effect in equity?

The cases relied upon by the plaintiff are relevant for the purpose of showing that the judge fell into error in deciding that on the facts a constructive trust could be inferred. They are the cases which deal with the intention of the parties when a house is acquired. But of those cases only *Inwards v. Baker*, [1965] 2 QB 29 is in point here. For this is a case of estoppel arising from the encouragement and acquiescence of the plaintiff between 1973 and 1976 when, in reliance upon his declaration, that he was giving and, later, that he had given the house to her, she spent a substantial part of her small capital upon repairs and improvements to the house. The relevant principle is expounded in *Snell's Principles of Equity*, 27th ed., p. 565 in the passage under the heading "Proprietary Estoppel," and is elaborated in *Spencer Bower and Turner, Estoppel by Representation*, 3d ed. (1977), chapter 12 entitled "Encouragement and Acquiescence."

The cases in point illustrating that principle in relation to real property are *Dillwyn v. Llewelyn* (1862), 4 De FG & J 517; *Ramsden v. Dyson* (1866), LR 1 HL 129 and *Plimmer v. Wellington Corporation* (1884), 9 App. Cas. 699. One distinction between this class of case and the doctrine which has come to be known as "promissory estoppel" is that where estoppel by encouragement or acquiescence is found on the facts, those facts give rise to a cause of action. They may be relied upon as a sword, not merely as a shield. In *Ramsden v. Dyson* the plaintiff failed on the facts, and the dissent of Lord Kingsdown was upon the inferences to be drawn from the facts. On the principle, however, the House was agreed, and it is stated by Lord Cranworth LC and by Lord Wensleydale as well as by Lord Kingsdown. Likewise in *Plimmer's* case the plaintiff was granted a declaration that he had a perpetual right to occupation.

The final question that arises is: to what relief is the defendant entitled upon her counterclaim? In *Dillwyn v. Llewelyn*, 4 De GF & J 517 there was an imperfect gift of land by a father who encouraged his son to build a house on it for £14,000. ...

[The court reviewed the facts and reasoning in the case, and continued:]

In *Plimmer's* case, 9 App. Cas. 699 the Privy Council pose the question, how should the equity be satisfied? (See pp. 713, 714.) And the Board declare that on the facts a licence revocable at will became irrevocable as a consequence of the subsequent transactions. ...

In *Crabb v. Arun District Council*, [1976] Ch. 179 this court had to consider the principles upon which the court should give effect to the equity: see Lord Denning MR at p. 189. Lawton and Scarman LJJ agreed with the remedy proposed by Lord Denning MR. On the facts of that case Scarman LJ expressed himself thus at pp. 198-199:

> I turn now to the other two questions—the extent of the equity and the relief needed to satisfy it. There being no grant, no enforceable contract, no licence, I would analyse the minimum equity to do justice to the plaintiff as a right either to an easement or to a licence upon terms to be agreed. I do not think it is necessary to go further than that. Of course, going that far would support the equitable remedy of injunction which is sought in this action. If there is no agreement as to terms, if agreement fails to be obtained, the court can, in my judgment, and must, determine in these proceedings upon what terms the plaintiff should be put to enable him to have the benefit of the equitable right which he is held to have. It is interesting that there has been some doubt amongst distinguished lawyers in the past as to whether the

court can so proceed … . But there can be no doubt that since *Ramsden v. Dyson* the courts have acted upon the basis that they have to determine not only the extent of the equity, but also the conditions necessary to satisfy it, and they have done so in a great number and variety of cases. I need refer only to the interesting collection of cases enumerated in *Snell's Principles of Equity*, 27th ed., pp. 567-568, para. 2(b). In the present case the court does have to consider what is necessary now in order to satisfy the plaintiff's equity.

So the principle to be applied is that the court should consider all the circumstances, and the counterclaimant having at law no perfected gift or licence other than a licence revocable at will, the court must decide what is the minimum equity to do justice to her having regard to the way in which she changed her position for the worse by reason of the acquiescence and encouragement of the legal owner. The defendant submits that the only appropriate way in which the equity can here be satisfied is by perfecting the imperfect gift as was done in *Dillwyn v. Llewelyn*. …

[The court noted that the plaintiff did not make submissions about the appropriate remedy.]

We are satisfied that the problem of remedy on the facts resolves itself into a choice between two alternatives: should the equity be satisfied by a licence to the defendant to occupy the house for her lifetime, or should there be a transfer to her of the fee simple?

The main consideration pointing to a licence for her lifetime is that she did not by her case at the hearing seek to establish that she had spent more money or done more work on the house than she would have done had she believed that she had only a licence to live there for her lifetime. But the court must be cautious about drawing any inference from what she did not give in evidence as the hypothesis put is one that manifestly never occurred to her. Then it may reasonably be held that her expenditure and effort can hardly be regarded as comparable to the change of position of those who have constructed buildings on land over which they had no legal rights.

This court appreciates that the moneys laid out by the defendant were much less than in some of the cases in the books. But the court has to look at all the circumstances. When the plaintiff left her she was, we were told, a widow in her middle fifties. During the period that she lived with the plaintiff her capital was reduced from £4,500 to £1,000. Save for her invalidity pension that was all that she had in the world. In reliance upon the plaintiff's declaration of gift, encouragement and acquiescence she arranged her affairs on the basis that the house and contents belonged to her. So relying, she devoted a quarter of her remaining capital and her personal effort upon the house and its fixtures. In addition she bought carpets, curtains and furniture for it, with the result that by the date of the trial she had only £300 left. Compared to her, on the evidence the plaintiff is a rich man. He might not regard an expenditure of a few hundred pounds as a very grave loss. But the court has to regard her change of position over the years 1973 to 1976.

We take the view that the equity cannot here be satisfied without granting a remedy which assures to the defendant security of tenure, quiet enjoyment, and freedom of action in respect of repairs and improvements without interference from the plaintiff. The history of the conduct of the plaintiff since April 9, 1976, in relation to these proceedings leads to an irresistible inference that he is determined to pursue his purpose of evicting her from the house by any legal means at his disposal with a ruthless disregard of the obligations binding upon conscience. The court must grant a remedy effective to protect her against the future manifestations of his ruthlessness. It was conceded that if she is granted a licence, such a licence cannot be registered as a land charge, so that she may find herself ousted by a purchaser for value without notice. If she has in the future to do further and more expensive repairs she may not be able to finance them by a loan, but as a licensee she cannot charge the house. The plaintiff as legal owner may well find excuses for entry in order to do what he may plausibly represent as necessary works and so contrive to derogate from her enjoyment of the licence in ways that make it difficult or impossible for the court to give her effective protection.

Weighing such considerations this court concludes that the equity to which the facts in this case give rise can only be satisfied by compelling the plaintiff to give effect to his promise and her expectations. He has so acted that he must now perfect the gift.

Appeal dismissed.

[The court further declared that the estate in fee simple in the house was vested in the defendant. The plaintiff was ordered to execute a conveyance at his expense within 28 days; in default, the registrar of the county court was authorized to execute it. Leave to appeal was refused.]

DISCUSSION NOTES

i. Remedies for Informal Family Arrangements: Clarke v Johnson

In *Pascoe v Turner*, the court had no difficulty concluding that the plaintiff made a valid gift of the contents of the house to the defendant. Why? Why was this reasoning not available to support a gift of the realty? Recall the discussion in Chapter 5 about gifts of personal and real property and the principle of *Milroy v Lord* (1862), 45 ER 1185 that "equity will not perfect an imperfect gift." How does this principle relate to the court's reasoning about the real and personal property in *Pascoe v Turner*?

As *Pascoe v Turner* reveals, such cases often involve unwritten arrangements that are ambiguous, especially when family members are defining their "intentions" long after the actual arrangements have been concluded. Consider, for example, the facts in *Clarke v Johnson*, 2012 ONSC 4320, in which there was a dispute between Don Clarke, who had been married to and then divorced from Victoria, the daughter of Martha Johnson.

In the 1970s, Martha and her late husband Bill, along with two of Bill's siblings and their spouses, had purchased an island (Johnson Island), which was shared by the families of the three siblings. (The arrangement seemed to create a one-third tenancy in common for each family in the title to the island, but there was also an unwritten agreement that each sibling's family would have exclusive control of a designated part of the island.) After Clarke married the Johnsons' daughter Victoria, Don and Victoria Clarke asked her parents for permission to build a camp on the part of the island under the control of Johnson and her late husband. The facts seemed to indicate that the Johnsons also loaned $17,000 to the couple to purchase and build a prefabricated cottage on this land. Although it was agreed that this loan was never repaid, there were other financial arrangements between the two couples that were similarly undocumented, perhaps because Clarke was a friend and also an employee of Mrs Johnson's late husband. The Clarkes had two children and the family used the camp on the Johnsons' section of the island for some years. However, the Clarkes then divorced, and Victoria abandoned any interest in the camp on the island, apparently on the basis that the land was owned by her parents. Clarke raised the two children and (eventually with his second wife) continued to use the camp; Clarke also paid, for example, hydro bills and property taxes. Both children grew up and moved away, and neither made any effort to occupy the building at the camp on the island for some years. In 2009, however, Clarke's son, Westley, returned to live in Ontario and wanted to use the camp again, but as a result of a disagreement with Westley, Clarke refused to give him permission to use the camp. Clarke's decision to refuse permission to Westley to occupy the camp on the island was strenuously objected to by Johnson, Westley's grandmother. Claiming that the camp formed part of the realty, title to which was held by her (as successor to her late husband's estate), and that Clarke held nothing more than a licence to occupy the camp on this land, Johnson issued a trespass notice against Clarke. In doing so, she reasserted the original intention expressed when she and her late husband participated in purchasing the island that it would always be available to family members and only to family members.

At trial, the court concluded that the evidence indicated that the camp was part of the realty of Johnson's part of the island and that Clarke had only a licence to occupy it with her permission, *unless he was entitled to an equitable remedy*. In this case, the court held that Johnson had been enriched (by the erection and maintenance of the home for 20 years), that Clarke had suffered a deprivation (through his financial contributions and labour), and that there was no juristic reason for the enrichment and deprivation. The court also concluded that the original loan had probably been forgiven or that any right to collect it had expired because of the limitation periods relevant to debt collection. Thus the court upheld Clarke's claim for unjust enrichment.

In addition, the court reviewed the test for a claim of proprietary estoppel on the basis of the Court of Appeal's decision in *Schwark Estate v Cutting*, [2010] OJ no 288 at para 16, in which the appeal court had stated the requirements as follows:

> [16] The law with respect to proprietary estoppel is well-settled. This court has accepted that Snell's Equity properly discloses the elements necessary to establish proprietary estoppel as:
>
> 1. encouragement of the plaintiffs by the defendant owner,
>
> 2. detrimental reliance by the plaintiffs to the knowledge of the defendant owner, and
>
> 3. the defendant owner now seeks to take unconscionable advantage of the plaintiff by reneging on an earlier promise.

The court concluded that Clarke had assumed that he would own the cottage, in the sense that he would be leaving it to his children, and that Johnson and her late husband induced, encouraged, or allowed Clarke to believe that he had this entitlement. In addition, the court held that in reliance on this understanding, Clarke contributed significantly to the construction, maintenance, and improvement of the camp. In finding this situation "unconscionable," the court then concluded:

> [38] The attachment between a person and his or her camp is unique and not easily described. Over time there comes to be an emotional attachment borne of the surrounding beauty, the investment of sweat equity, and the memories of times spent with family and friends. When one has been allowed to develop that attachment over the course of decades, and has directed

personal and financial resources to the property in the reasonable belief that it would continue, it is unconscionable to deny that benefit.

In the result, the trial court concluded that Clarke had established a claim for proprietary estoppel. The court then considered the appropriate remedy in this situation and stated:

> [42] ... Mr. Clarke is to have a licence to occupy the camp until he dies or is no longer phys-
> ically able to attend there. The licence to occupy is personal to him and his invitees and may not
> be assigned or conveyed in any fashion. It is a condition of the licence that he maintain the camp
> in a state of good repair and that he pay the taxes and utility costs associated with it. It is also a
> condition of the licence that he take no steps to materially alter the nature or quality of the camp
> during the licence period.

In April 2013, Martha Johnson filed an appeal to the Ontario Court of Appeal. In the context of the trial decision, consider what arguments are available in support of her appeal. Recall that there are two issues here: one is the existence of factors that support recognition of an equity. As in *Pascoe v Turner*, however, the more significant issue in this case may relate to the remedy fashioned by the trial judge. According to Martha Johnson's pleadings (at para 86), the remedy granted to Don Clarke in this case is "both disproportionate and excessive ... [and should be] re-fashioned to comport with the parties' reasonable expectations that require Don to share the use of the camp with his children."

How should the Ontario Court of Appeal determine the claims in this case—on the basis of unjust enrichment or proprietary estoppel? What is the appropriate remedy, if any? For another complex family property case in which the court recognized proprietary estoppel, see *Perasso v Perasso*, 2011 BCSC 230. In *Perasso*, a father leased land to his son, and the son and his cohabiting partner built a home on the land. (Recall the brief discussion in Chapter 4 relating to the lease issue in *Perasso*.) The land was mortgaged by the father, but it was agreed that the cohabiting couple would pay the mortgage; both the father and the couple made other contributions of money and labour. When the cohabiting relationship ended, the woman partner obtained an order that she was entitled to a one-half interest in the son's interest in the land, and litigation ensued to determine what interest, if any, the son had in the land. In the end, the court concluded that the son and his cohabiting partner were entitled to a three-fourths interest in the value of the improvements to the land, but the father retained title. In reaching this conclusion, the court considered both unjust enrichment and proprietary estoppel, stating:

> [151] In the present case the expectation that was created was not merely as to the expendi-
> ture of money but included conduct, such as waiver of rent, that was part of a long course [of]
> economic integration within the family unit. [The son] would certainly be entitled to assert the
> interest I have declared had the [father] attempted to repudiate the long course of mutually
> trusting dealings between them. In the circumstances, although [the son] does not assert a claim
> or defend the claim brought by [the father, the case requires this consideration].

Perasso reveals how issues about family relationships (including cohabiting relationships and parent–child relationships) may intersect with legal principles about title to land, leases, unjust enrichment, proprietary estoppel, and the courts' role in exercising judicial discretion with respect to appropriate remedies. In reflecting on the uncertainty in such situations, consider how the son and his partner could have avoided this litigation.

ii. Proprietary Estoppel and Unjust Enrichment

Clarke v Johnson and *Perasso* are also of interest because the courts considered the claims in terms of the principles of both unjust enrichment and proprietary estoppel. (Recall that the court in *Pascoe v Turner* also considered and rejected a trust relationship between the plaintiff and defendant as "unworkable.") Although these claims thus involved equitable intervention to overcome "injustice," some commentators have suggested that Canadian law more often focuses on unjust enrichment and the remedy of constructive trust, while English courts (which have traditionally used a narrower test for the constructive trust remedy) have tended to focus on proprietary estoppel and equities to achieve similar results. For example, Glenn argued that the underlying principles (especially the grounding in matters of conscience) are basically the same: see JM Glenn, "Promissory Estoppel, Proprietary Estoppel, and Constructive Trust in Canada: 'What's in a Name?'" (2007) 30 Dal LJ 141 at 161. Can you identify differences in the factual circumstances relating to unjust enrichment and proprietary estoppel? For example, recall the recent developments with respect to remedies for unjust enrichment in family contexts. Do these principles suggest that judges may have greater discretion in fashioning appropriate remedies in relation to proprietary estoppel (equities)?

iii. Equities and Informal Commercial Arrangements

In recent decades, Canadian courts have used principles of proprietary estoppel and equities more frequently, and often in cases that do not involve family property matters. As noted in *Clarke v Johnson*, the Ontario Court of Appeal identified the test for proprietary estoppel recently in *Schwark Estate v Cutting*, [2010] OJ no 288, a case in which neighbouring cottage property owners were unsuccessful in their claim to an easement over nearby land to access a beach. However, a proprietary estoppel claim to an easement was successful in *MacLean v Williams*, [2008] NSJ no 484 (a case in which the court quoted *Inwards v Baker*). For other cases concerning such claims other than in family cases, see *Eberts v Carleton Condominium Corp No 396* (2000), 136 OAC 317, and *Blatnick v Walklin Investments Ltd* (1990), 13 RPR (2d) 268 (Ont Ct J).

In British Columbia, the principle of *Inwards v Baker* was adopted in relation to a commercial agreement in *Stiles v Tod Mountain Development Ltd* (1992), 88 DLR (4th) 735, 64 BCLR (2d) 366, 22 RPR (2d) 143 (SC), and more recently in *Sykes v Rosebery Parklands Development Society*, 2010 BCSC 227 (CanLII), [2010] BCJ no 308. *Sykes* involved a residential development near a lake with several lots. All but one of the lots was sold and the remaining lot (lot 6) was retained as an easement to permit the landowners in the development (who did not have lake access) to have access by foot to the lake. Subsequently, a dispute arose with respect to whether this easement included permission for the owner of one of the other lots to construct a dock with rights of moorage on lot 6 (the lot that constituted the easement). Although the case was complicated by a number of other factors, the court held that the plaintiffs (owners of one lot) had a cause of action in proprietary estoppel:

> [45] [I]n my view, the plaintiffs have made out a cause of action in proprietary estoppel. The plaintiffs were unequivocally advised that they had the legal right to cross lot 6 and construct moorage facilities thereabouts; they reasonably believed in and relied upon these representations and expended funds as a result; [the defendant] encouraged this expenditure at the material time … ; and [the defendant] now seeks to resile from its earlier position and rely upon the

strict wording of the easement registered against title ... [which appeared to preclude moorage facilities].

[46] Having regard to the representations made, the conduct of the parties, and the detriment incurred by the plaintiffs in the course of their reliance on the [defendant's] unequivocal position, I find that an equity giving rise to proprietary estoppel has been established in the plaintiffs' favour, and that in all the circumstances it is unjust for the [defendant] to rely on its purported strict legal rights.

In this situation, the court granted a declaration that the lot owners had an easement that permitted them to have "private moorage tenure" (see para 82). And, although title to the easement land had been transferred by the defendant to a third party, the court concluded that the third party was not a bona fide purchaser for value without notice (applying *Stiles v Tod Mountain Development Ltd*) and, thus, the declaration was also binding on the third party.

In *Sykes*, the court also discussed the "broad and flexible" approach to proprietary estoppel in British Columbia, by contrast with the Ontario Court of Appeal's decision in *Schwark Estate*. In particular, the court noted the evolution of proprietary estoppel and appropriate remedies in three cases in the British Columbia Court of Appeal: *Zelmer v Victor Projects Ltd* (1997), 34 BCLR (3d) 125 (CA); *Trethewey-Edge Dyking District v Coniagas Ranches Ltd*, 2003 BCCA 197; and *Erickson v Jones*, 2008 BCCA 379, all of which relied on the English Court of Appeal's decision in *Crabb v Arun District Council*, [1976] 1 Ch 179 (CA), discussed above in *Pascoe v Turner*. In *Sykes*, the court relied on this broad and flexible approach to confirm the existence of an equity based on proprietary estoppel, even though the registered easement in the case (pursuant to BC's Torrens registration system: see Chapter 5) did not provide for such an interest. Although the Ontario Court of Appeal noted the approach of the BC Court of Appeal in *Schwark Estate v Cutting* in relation to proprietary estoppel, the Ontario court held that, on the facts in this case, there was no evidence to support a claim of proprietary estoppel. In particular, in relation to the final part of the test, the court stated:

[38] [T]here is nothing unconscionable about a property owner, who, having permitted his neighbor (*sic*) to use his property for a time, withdraws that permission.

Overall, however, and in spite of the denial of the claim in *Schwark Estate*, cases in Ontario and British Columbia, and elsewhere in Canada, suggest that, notwithstanding the availability of unjust enrichment principles in Canada (by contrast with their more stringent use in the United Kingdom), the use of proprietary estoppel is increasing in Canadian courts. Moreover, although it is often adopted in family property cases, proprietary estoppel has also been used in other cases involving informal arrangements that become the subject of later disputes. For further discussion, see R Wells, "The Element of Detriment in Proprietary Estoppel" (2001) 65 Conveyancer 13; S Bright & B McFarlane, "Proprietary Estoppel and Property Rights" (2005) 64 Cambridge LJ 449; and S Gardner, "The Remedial Discretion in Proprietary Estoppel—Again" (2006) 122 Law Q Rev 492.

iv. Proprietary Estoppel and Spousal Relationships

Pascoe v Turner can be distinguished from *Hussey v Palmer* and *Inwards v Baker* on its facts—unlike the parties in the latter two cases, the parties in *Pascoe v Turner* were a cohabiting couple. As a result, *Pascoe v Turner* must be considered in relation to Canadian cases involving the allocation of property interests—for example, *Pettkus v Becker*, *Peter v Beblow*, and *Vanasse v Seguin*. In all of these "spousal" cases, Canadian courts used principles of unjust enrichment and then discussed what remedy was appropriate in the circumstances. Clearly, however, the remedy awarded in *Pascoe v Turner* (the transfer of the fee simple in the land) was the most substantial remedy provided to a cohabiting spouse at family breakdown, and it was founded on the existence of proprietary estoppel (an equity). In this context, Gray & Symes characterized the decision in *Pascoe v Turner* as "remarkable," because

> the equitable jurisdiction of the court was effectively invoked to bring about a redistribution of assets on the breakdown of a *de facto* marriage relationship. The manner and extent of the redistribution lay entirely within the discretion of the court, and the common law wife was thereby enabled to circumvent the rule [in England] that a *de facto* spouse cannot claim property adjustment or financial provision from her partner on the demise of their relationship.

(Gray & Symes at 493.)

To what extent might the remedy in *Pascoe v Turner* be available in Canada? For example, in *Perasso v Perasso*, the cohabiting partner received a one-half interest. Should the remedy in *Pascoe v Turner* be available more often for cohabiting spouses?

VI. THE LIMITS OF FAMILY PROPERTY REFORM: FIRST NATIONS COMMUNITIES

In 1986, the Supreme Court of Canada considered two cases on appeal from British Columbia concerning the legal interests of Aboriginal women in matrimonial property on an Indian reserve—*Derrickson v Derrickson*, [1986] 1 SCR 285, and *Paul v Paul*, [1986] 1 SCR 306. In both cases, the court concluded that the statutory family property regime in British Columbia was not applicable because of the constitutional division of powers in Canada—that is, because of the federal *Indian Act*, which comprehensively regulates the lives of Indian peoples. In *Derrickson*, Rose Derrickson had petitioned for divorce and a division of family assets, including the matrimonial home located on the Westbank Reserve, for which her husband held a certificate of possession. In *Paul*, Pauline Paul had requested an order for exclusive occupancy of the matrimonial home, also on reserve land, under the BC *Family Relations Act* so as to avoid continuing violence on the part of her spouse, who held the certificate of possession.

ME Turpel criticized these decisions, on the basis that they represented the imposition of an alien political and legal culture on indigenous practices and institutions. In examining her arguments, consider the need to take account of the context in defining family property rights.

Mary Ellen Turpel, "Home/Land"
(1991) 10 Can J Fam L 17 at 21

I want to explore the colonial character of Canadian law and its capacity to silence aboriginal peoples through an analysis of two Supreme Court of Canada decisions, *Derrickson v. Derrickson* and *Paul v. Paul*. Both considered the legal interests of aboriginal women in matrimonial property on an "Indian reserve." I chose these cases for two reasons. First, they illustrate the formalist stream of discourse in the colonial legal framework as it affects aboriginal peoples. As such, they make interesting study of the hegemonic character of

Canadian law over aboriginal peoples. Secondly, these two cases invite analysis because they bring to light the violence inflicted upon aboriginal peoples in a colonial legal (and political) regime where there is little scope for the construction of an aboriginal vision of social and political relationships. The intermingling of several key factors in *Derrickson* and *Paul*—women, property and violence—facilitates an appreciation not only of the law's (in)capacity to situate aboriginal disputes in a social, political or cultural context, but also the price aboriginal people (in this case, aboriginal women) pay as a consequence of their subjugation to a colonial regime. ...

A brief explanation of the system of land holding for Indians pursuant to the federal *Indian Act* is required to provide the colonial history to the conflicts which arose in *Derrickson* and *Paul*. The *Indian Act* provides for a system of assignment of reserve lands to members of the reserves by band councils, municipal-style institutions also created by the Act. Final authorization for any assignment of land rests with the Minister of Indian Affairs. A band council allots a parcel of reserve land to an individual band member and this allotment is then approved by the Minister of Indian Affairs, at which time a "certificate of possession" for the land may be issued as proof of the band member's right to possession. For nearly a century before the 1951 amendments to the *Indian Act*, land holding on reserves was regulated by location tickets which were converted to certificates of possession. Alongside the issuance of certificates of possession are "certificates of occupation." These are issued for a period of two years in cases where ministerial approval for possession was denied. The Department of Indian Affairs maintains a "Reserve Land Register" on which the particulars of every certificate of possession or land allotment are recorded.

The system regulating Indian land allotments is not uniform across Canada. Some bands retained customary systems of land allotment and, while these are not expressly contemplated in the *Indian Act*, they have been recognized and continue to be followed. Under these systems, certificates are not issued and land holding is based on kinship and genealogy consonant with tribal practice. The provisions of the Act govern nearly all of the 633 bands in Canada. The system of land holding it decrees is a colonialist scheme designed for the complete regulation of Indian life in order to facilitate "orderly" Canadian settlement and the "protection" of the Indians. It was not devised in consultation with aboriginal peoples, nor does it coincide with any traditional practices. No tribe issued papers to its members to confirm possessory title: in close-knit tribal communities, everybody knows where each family lives, hunts or gathers food.

Alongside massive dispossession of aboriginal homelands, both through outright confiscation and breach of treaty, these colonial bureaucratic structures were imposed on a large number of aboriginal peoples (not the Métis or Inuit). In addition, elections, land surveys and allotments, criteria for membership and other administrative structures were established by the Act while traditional practices such as potlatches, longhouses and customary law were outlawed as offensive and anti-Christian. The certificate of possession system is part of the colonial effort to displace tribal structures, to confiscate tribal lands and to integrate Indians into Canadian society.

No Indian individual can own reserve lands in fee simple as reserve lands are set aside for the benefit of the band as a whole under the *Indian Act*. To some extent this might seem laudable as it fortuitously coincides with aboriginal beliefs regarding the land. Although varied by tribe, an all-sustaining relationship with the land is the foundation of a spiritual conception of social life for aboriginal peoples. This is based upon a non-exploitative protectorship or trusteeship of the earth in which land is not "owned," but shared and protected. Canadian law has yet to categorize this relation, or fully recognize its legitimacy as a distinct cultural conception, different but no less legally-significant than Anglo-European conceptions of property which have been imposed upon aboriginal peoples. The possessory nature of individual interests in reserve lands and the registration system is, of course, a convenient component of bureaucratic regulation as it ensures that the Department of Indian Affairs can keep tabs on every allotment in nearly every Indian community, while retaining final say on all of it.

The legal question framed in *Derrickson* (and *Paul*) was whether a partition of reserve lands under provincial family legislation would be an encroachment on the federal authority granted in the *Constitution Act, 1867*. This is a classic question of who does what in a colonial administration. In other words, is it up to the federal or provincial government to control Indians? The framing of the question focuses the issue into a division of powers conflict and erases the social and political context for the dispute. The basic issue of why the dispute is one of division of colonial powers over Indian lands and not a matter of aboriginal custom regarding family breakdown and land consequences upon breakdown is lost on all courts. The fact that it is never raised attests to the inability of colonial Canadian law to be anything but self-perpetuating. ...

C. The Supreme Court of Canada Judgments

In 1986 the Supreme Court of Canada released its judgments in the *Derrickson* and *Paul* appeals. They were both relatively brief decisions dismissing the appeals. The *Paul* judgment is particularly curt, applying the reasoning in *Derrickson*, with no reference to the violent conflict at the base of that particular dispute. Mr. Justice Chouinard wrote the unanimous judgment for the Supreme Court of Canada in the two appeals. Both reasons are adroitly evasive in confronting the underlying conflict in the cases and together provide a classic illustration of the colonialist approach to aboriginal conflicts utilizing formalist division of powers rhetoric.

In *Derrickson*, Mr. Justice Chouinard confirms the reasoning of the British Columbia Court of Appeal that the provincial *Family Relations Act* is inapplicable, either on its own or as a law of general application which would extend to Indians by virtue of section 88 of the *Indian Act*. He accepts that "[t]itle to reserve lands is vested in the Crown ... . So long as they remain as such, reserve lands are administered by the Federal Government and Parliament has exclusive legislative authority over them." The "very essence" of the exclusive federal jurisdiction over Indians, Mr. Justice Chouinard opines, is the right to possession of lands on an Indian reserve, consequently provincial legislation cannot apply. The *Family Relations Act* of British Columbia must, therefore, be "read down and given the limited meaning which will confine it within the limits of the provincial jurisdiction."

The issue of the extension of provisions of the British Columbia *Family Relations Act* to Indians in the province by virtue of section 88 of the *Indian Act* was one in which Mr. Justice Chouinard took a particular interest. He viewed the provincial family legislation as a law of general application eligible for extension according to section 88 of the [*Indian Act*]. Furthermore, he found that even if a court granted an order conditional upon ministerial approval under the *Indian Act*, this would not change the constitutional status of the provincial legislation as subordinate to the *Indian Act*.

Nevertheless, Mr. Justice Chouinard upheld the findings of the Court of Appeal on the issue of compensation in lieu of division of matrimonial property. The provisions of the *Family Relations Act* on compensation could be extended to Indians, he accepted, as these were not inconsistent with the property aspect of the *Indian Act*, particularly when awarded for the purposes of "adjusting the division of family assets between the spouses."

At no point in his decision does Mr. Justice Chouinard explore the consequences of his decision for aboriginal women, who are now without recourse for a just share of matrimonial property upon family breakdown. In passing he mentioned that he was "not unmindful of the ensuing consequences for spouses." He justified his disinterest in the consequences by borrowing a phrase from a noted constitutional publicist:

> Whether such laws are wise or unwise is of course a much-controverted question, but it is not relevant to their constitutional validity.

Mr. Justice Chouinard's reasons for judgment in *Paul* are similar. Following a brief statement of facts, he finds that

> ... this case is indistinguishable from *Derrickson*. To hold otherwise would mean that the husband by virtue of his Certificate of Possession would be entitled to possession and consequently to occupation of the family residence while the wife ... would be entitled to interim exclusive occupancy of the same residence.

He rejected the distinction between occupation and possession as too fine a legal argument to justify the extension of provincial family law to include Indian lands. Moreover, Mr. Justice Chouinard made no comment on the violent nature of the conflict which lead to the appeal.

III. Situating the Cases in Their Colonial Legal Context

The decisions in *Derrickson* and *Paul*, particularly at the Supreme Court of Canada level, project an image of a perfunctory division of powers conflict resolved by application of the constitutional doctrine of exclusivity of federal jurisdiction over Indians and lands reserved for the Indians. This style of reasoning masks the political complexity of the conflict(s) which were at the basis of *Derrickson* and *Paul*. The complexity stems from what can be called the "aboriginal dimension" of the legal dispute. This refers to the fact that the disputes that have arisen in these cases stem directly from the legacy of a colonial regime that continues to be imposed on aboriginal people by decontextualizing these conflicts and ignoring the impact of the law on aboriginal peoples' lives. To do otherwise would demand critical reflection on the inadequacy and oppressive nature of the colonial regime established by the *Constitution Act, 1867* and the *Indian Act*.

The chosen legal issue in *Derrickson* and *Paul* is which branch of the state should control which aspects of aboriginal life, not the very matter of state control itself. The state control of aboriginal life is the central political issue in these cases. Framing the issue in constitutional division of powers doctrine is an effective strategy for depoliticizing the cases and silencing any questioning of the overwhelming state control of (jurisdiction over) aboriginal peoples. The court, as an emanation of the colonial political regime for aboriginal peoples, is blinded to its role and to the political nature of the law it applies in this context.

A. *Insensitivity to Aboriginal Conceptions of Property*

The consequence of the *Derrickson* and *Paul* decisions is that an aboriginal woman who resides in a home on a reserve with her spouse cannot make an application under provincial family legislation for occupation or possession of the home upon marriage breakdown or in the event of physical and emotional abuse from her spouse. There is no federal family legislation to govern these conflicts. In the *Paul* case, for Pauline Paul, this meant she was denied legal access to the matrimonial home of sixteen years which she herself helped to build. With the sanction of constitutional law, she was, effectively, left out in the cold.

Even if an aboriginal woman holds a certificate of possession jointly with her spouse under the *Indian Act*, she will have no recourse under provincial family law (the only family law) for access to her home. Moreover, the situation on Indian reserves is such that the certificates of possession are invariably issued to male band members so an appeal to the Department of Indian Affairs or the band council would be equally futile in most, if not all, cases. The practice of issuing certificates to men is a carry-over from the late nineteenth century practice of issuing location tickets to males, an extension of Anglo-European patriarchal notions of land holding and succession. It was this same philosophy that infused the gender discrimination provisions in relation to Indian status.

The *Indian Act* requirement of ministerial approval for any transfer of reserve land likely forecloses the possibility of successfully pursuing a remedy for the situation at common law, although trust doctrines may have limited application. Applications pursuant to the *Canadian Charter of Rights and Freedoms* are possible, but fraught with another set of difficulties. Essentially, an aboriginal woman has no legally recognizable interest in her matrimonial home, unless she solely holds the certificate of possession. Even if this is the case, gaining an interim order for exclusive possession will be impossible as there is no legislation which will apply in this context. While this is an obvious injustice, there is another layer here which makes the injustice particularly cruel and oppressive: that is the cultural significance of property from an aboriginal perspective.

For aboriginal women, it is not the commodity character of property which is vital to her survival. The progressive literature on matrimonial property in Canada espouses the concept of the equality of the spouses and the notion of marriage as an economic partnership. The matrimonial home has been viewed in this light as the single most important unit of property in the relationship, of significance economically and perhaps even emotionally. The fair division of the matrimonial home upon marriage breakdown is seen to save women and children from financial breakdown and impoverishment. While this is undoubtedly the case for non-aboriginal people, when the context of aboriginal marriages is considered, especially when the spouses are living on the reserve, the situation must be appreciated as being different because of a combination of economic, cultural and linguistic factors.

Access to matrimonial property does not save aboriginal women from impoverishment because the value of a possessory interest in reserve land is circumscribed by restrictions on alienation and the limited interest (mortgagability [*sic*]) in the property. Moreover, aboriginal peoples on reserves already live far below the poverty line in Canada. Consequently, theories of economic partnerships and a woman's access to the home as an important commodity do not apply to aboriginal peoples as they would in a non-aboriginal context. Indeed these theories arguably devalue the significance of the matrimonial home for aboriginal women.

The significance of matrimonial property for aboriginal women must be understood in the context of what the reserve represents: it is the home of a distinct cultural and linguistic people. It is a community of extended families, tightly connected by history, language and culture. It is often the place where children can be educated in their language and with culturally-appropriate pedagogies. The reserve home is generally not that of a nuclear family—parents, grandparents, brothers, sisters and others in need will all share the home. The home may be the only access a woman and her children have to their culture, language and family. The economic value of the land is secondary to its value as shelter within a larger homeland—the homeland of her people, her family.

The second aspect of matrimonial property theory that infuses this area, the notion of equality of the spouses, is, similarly, not entirely applicable in the aboriginal matrimonial context. In most aboriginal communities, the belief is that women, children and elders come before men and the responsibility of the men is to live life as a good helper toward women, children and elders. Traditional tribal control of property did not lead to the victimization of aboriginal women. As one Mohawk lawyer suggests of property customs in the Iroquois Confederacy:

> The Iroquois woman's rights to the family property was based on political influence via the control over the economic wealth of the family ... she had real property rights even superior to those of her husband ... . The property situation of the modern day Iroquois woman is vastly different from her historical sister prior to European contact. Traditionally she had the control of the family assets and family life. There has been a complete demotion. If she is not the legal owner of the family asset situated on an Indian reserve, then upon marriage dissolution she has no possibility of real property rights ... . She is truly the forgotten victim in a matrimonial dissolution. Her situation is equivalent to that under the "separate as to property regime" which was remedied by provincial matrimonial legislation in the common law provinces. She has recourse only under common law trust doctrines and provincial compensation schemes. She no longer has her traditional real property rights over family assets.

The decisions in *Derrickson* and *Paul* sanction a situation which is completely opposite to that of the customs of many tribes. There are no obligations on aboriginal men now recognized at law to provide shelter for women, children or elders. Indeed, customary law has no place in matrimonial property disputes as Canadian law will not recognize it—it is the federal or provincial government which exercises jurisdiction over Indians upon marriage breakdown. The impact of this oppression of aboriginal custom on communities cannot be underestimated. When men no longer have to fulfil their responsibilities to women, children and elders, the social control network of the community disintegrates and respect for social responsibilities is lost.

B. Disregard for the Violence Aboriginal Women Endure

The cultural and spiritual conceptions of property held by aboriginal peoples find no recognition in the cases on matrimonial property. The social reality for aboriginal peoples also does not enter into the discourse of division of powers which has been seized upon by all levels of courts in these cases. The appellants had to structure their arguments into claims based upon alien property notions and legal doctrines foreign to the customs of their communities. Could a claim have been made on the basis of customary (that is, the aboriginal) practice of the community? Undoubtedly, this was the farthest thing in the minds of lawyers advising the appellants in *Derrickson* and *Paul*, or the court in examining the legitimacy of their claims under Canadian (i.e. federal or provincial) law. Moreover, it would be difficult, if not impossible, according to Canadian constitutional law.

The Canadian legal system is revealed, once again, as a thoroughly colonial regime. It is too busy trying to categorize jurisdictional matters between federal and provincial governments to step back and realize the oppressive and presumptuous nature of its exercise. To expect it to do so is to expect too much given that this branch of the state is an emanation and expression of a colonial state. In fact, the role of the judicial branch of the state is going to be, in such a regime, to justify the colonial mentality using legal doctrine. It is little wonder that the legal system enjoys a low level of respect from aboriginal peoples who see this exercise. The actors within the system and, even most academic commentators, often fail to see the violence this situation foists on aboriginal peoples. Aboriginal peoples have nowhere to turn to voice their grievances—taking them to court means accepting an alien system. Doing nothing has only meant continued oppression and an implosion of violence and social upheaval in communities. The violence of silence is difficult to ensure, and *it is violence*. The decisions in *Derrickson* and *Paul* mean that brutal victimization of aboriginal women and children will continue because of a "gap" in the colonial regime. The extent of this brutalization can only be fully appreciated if we reflect upon the situation in which Pauline Paul found herself and which a disproportionately high number of aboriginal women confront—family violence.

Pauline Paul wanted to stay in her home on the Tsarslip Reserve with her children and she sought protection from her abusive spouse. The law offered her no such protection because she is an Indian. Pauline Paul had to find shelter elsewhere, she had to leave the reserve because there was no mechanism to allow her to stay. She had to endure violence and banishment from the community in order to be safe.

This issue of protection was never addressed in *Derrickson* or *Paul*. The court was silent. The (in)appropriateness of the *Indian Act* in its provisions for dissolution of matrimonial property upon family breakdown or during violence was left unexamined. As noted earlier, the *Indian Act* does not provide for marriage breakdown, property division, or for situations of family violence and protecting the property rights of the abused in such situations. There is some scope for argument that the provisions of the Act empowering bands to enact bylaws would include jurisdiction over property. However, this is unlikely given the restrictive interpretation of band council bylaw jurisdiction and the common practice of disallowance of bylaws by the Minister of Indian Affairs when they come before the Minister for review.

The Supreme Court of Canada offered no analysis of the (in)adequacy of the present legislative scheme. Indeed, in reviewing the fact situations in *Derrickson* and *Paul*, one may wonder why the *Indian Act*, which is supposedly the comprehensive legislative enactment for Indians, does not regulate property division and access to the home in violent situations or during marriage breakdowns. However, this type of questioning further illustrates how the aboriginal dimension of *Derrickson* and *Paul* can be lost in a colonial legal framework. The *Indian Act* is not simply inadequate given its lack of comprehensiveness. Colonial gaps are not there just to be filled. The regime is problematic as a whole because it is a system which seeks to bureaucratically administer Indian people according to Anglo-European standards. Aboriginal peoples do not support the reform or tinkering amendments to the *Indian Act*. Aboriginal peoples do not want to continue as wards of the federal government with bureaucratic custodians. The problems of violence are connected with this model. Aboriginal peoples would like their inherent rights of self-government recognized by the Canadian state and their authority to deal with conflicts in their communities according to their customs recognized and respected.

Yet, the situation aboriginal women are left with after *Derrickson* and *Paul*, especially *Paul*, is one in which no law protects them. Given the magnitude of the problem of family violence in aboriginal communities, this is barbaric. The failure of the court to explicitly recognize the violence in the *Paul* case reveals a callous and wilful blindness. Recent empirical studies have suggested that the incidence of physical family violence perpetrated against aboriginal women is approximately 70% or seven times the national average. In a study, released in 1990 by the Ontario Native Women's Association, of the situation for aboriginal women in Ontario, 91% of respondents indicated that family violence occurs in their communities; 71% indicated they had personally experienced it. These are shocking findings. The reasons behind the figures are complex, as the Ontario Native Women's Association suggests:

> Living under bureaucratic control, with no real self-government or self-determination, means that we do not control our everyday affairs, including our family life, and as a result, the level of social problems in our communities is frequently severe. Alcoholism, drug and solvent abuse, family violence, and other crimes are uniform tragedies in aboriginal communities. The first and foremost place where the impact of these social problems is felt is in the family. The treatment of the members of the family is a reflection of the treatment of the community on a broader basis. This is especially true for us because we have an important cultural value in our communities which is the notion of the extended family.

As a consequence of *Derrickson* and *Paul*, aboriginal women who are abused will have to seek shelter off the reserve, usually in non-aboriginal run shelters for battered women, frequently at considerable distances away from the reserve. More likely, an aboriginal woman's economic situation would prohibit a move to a shelter and she may simply be trapped in an abusive situation with dim hopes for improvement. In situations where the marriage breaks down, the inability of a spouse (most frequently woman) to gain access to the matrimonial home is an aggreviously unjust one. An order for compensation is no redress. Indian reserves do not have cash economies and compensation awards would be nominal, if even enforceable. Moreover, where compensation was awarded in lieu of division, the task of obtaining another house on the reserve is a cumbersome endeavour. Housing lists on all Indian reserves are heavily backlogged and women will be forced to live in the already crowded homes of relatives, or more likely off the reserve, until housing can be obtained.

As noted above, the lack of recourse for protection of an aboriginal woman's interest in the matrimonial home may mean the loss of an entitlement to live in the community. When aboriginal women and children are forced to leave the reserve, with the hopes of returning only if and when housing becomes available, or violence subsides, they leave behind more than simply shelter or an asset. They leave behind their culture, language and family. Life in an urban centre is not the same as living on a reserve. It is difficult to maintain your language, educate your children, not to mention battle racism in attempts to secure housing and employment. The reserve represents the home of your people. It is a distinct cultural and linguistic community which cannot be found elsewhere.

In many ways, it seems that history is repeating itself for aboriginal women. In the 1970s and early 1980s, aboriginal people were engaged in a bitter struggle over section 12(1)(b) of the *Indian Act*; a section which provided that an Indian woman who married a non-Indian man was disenfranchised of her Indian status and lost, among other things, her privileges of residing on the reserve, her rights to education and to be buried on the reserve. Two well known cases came before the Supreme Court of Canada challenging this provision of the *Indian Act* as contrary to the *Canadian Bill of Rights. Lavell* and *Bedard* were turning points in constitutional legal history because they revealed the limitations of the *Canadian Bill of Rights*. In these cases, the Supreme Court of Canada failed to directly address the issue of sexual inequality or the predicament of aboriginal women as a result of section 12(1)(b) of the *Indian Act*. Their decision to uphold section 12(1)(b) in the face of challenge under the *Canadian Bill of Rights* rested upon a procedural ruling that the Bill could not be used to strike down federal legislation. In the course of their decision, some members of the court, particularly Mr. Justice Ritchie, articulated a concept of equality as equal application of the law to all persons similarly situated which was later vigorously criticized as misguided.

The predicament in which Indian women found themselves after *Lavell*, with the discriminatory section 12(1)(b) of the *Indian Act* intact for over a decade, led to outrage throughout Indian communities. It was not until international attention was drawn to the situation that changes were made. Sandra Lovelace, a Maliseet woman of the Tobique Reserve in New Brunswick, petitioned the United Nations Human Rights Committee alleging numerous violations on the part of Canada of international commitments under the *International Covenant on Civil and Political Rights*. Lovelace argued that section 12(1)(b) of the *Indian Act* denied her the right to live in her community and be with her people, a right she said was protected under the Covenant. Several years after filing the petition, and decades after suffering unjustly as a result of section 12(1)(b), the Human Rights Committee expressed its views on the petition. In finding Canada in violation of its international human rights obligations, they stated that:

> It has been considered whether Sandra Lovelace, because she is denied the legal right to reside in the Tobique Reserve, has by that fact been denied of the right guaranteed by article 27 to persons belonging to minorities, to enjoy their own culture and to use their own language in community with other members of their group.
>
> 15. … in the opinion of the Committee the right of Sandra Lovelace to access her native culture and language "in the community with other members" of her group, has in fact been, and continues to be interfered with, because there is no place outside the Tobique Reserve where such a community exists. …
>
> 16. In this respect, the Committee is of the view that statutory restrictions affecting the right to residence in a reserve of a person belonging to the majority concerned, must have both a reasonable and objective justification and be consistent with the other provisions of the Covenant, read as a whole. …

There are several interesting parallels between the Lovelace complaint regarding section 12(1)(b) of the *Indian Act* and the matrimonial property situation. Both situations affect aboriginal women by taking them and their children away from their communities. It is the loss of access to the aboriginal community, the place where aboriginal language and culture are vital, that reveals the discriminatory impact of these two situations. In the matrimonial property context, the absence of any law under which to claim protection is the problem which forces women off the reserve whereas with section 12(1)(b) of the *Indian Act*, the section disenfranchised women of their Indian status and forced them out of their homes and communities. The impact on women is uniform: they have to leave their homes and communities. The Supreme Court of Canada's decisions in *Derrickson* and *Paul* must be understood in this light.

IV. Conclusion

The complete silencing of aboriginal women's experiences and indeed of the aboriginal dimension of *Derrickson* and *Paul*, exposes the deleterious colonial character of Canadian constitutional law. The reasoning employed in the two decisions demonstrates the role played by the Canadian legal system in camouflaging the social and political aspects of aboriginal peoples' conflicts. Courts have been unable to grasp the impact of aboriginal peoples' treatment by a colonial legal system because this would require its dismantling and a critical examination of the function of the court and law in perpetuating the oppression. Dismantling it would require recognizing aboriginal peoples' presence as political communities in Canada with distinct cultural linguistic and social systems. It would require ending bureaucratic regulation of Indian life through the *Indian Act*. No court has been honest or reflective enough to acknowledge the colonial character of the regulation of aboriginal life in Canada. Meanwhile, aboriginal peoples have had to endure the violence of a colonial regime which silences aboriginal reality and displays disregard for aboriginal peoples' suffering. One cannot help wondering whether the courts and legislature would be as blind to the violence if it was endured by non-aboriginal women? Of course they would not be so blind because non-aboriginal women are "their" women and part of their cultural and imaginative world. Hence, doctrines of fairness and constructive trust could be stretched to soften gender bias.

There have been no initiatives taken since these decisions in 1986 to remedy the violence aboriginal women endure. How can this be explained? Has the colonial mentality become so engrained that non-aboriginal people in Canada are hardened to aboriginal peoples' suffering?

The decisions in *Derrickson* and *Paul* illustrate the need for highly contextualized readings of cases. Very little of the story in *Derrickson* and *Paul* can be found in the text of the decisions because the constitutional discourse which enveloped the cases silenced the colonial nature of those disputes. The system of white patriarchy is deeply embedded in Canadian legal thought, doctrine and jurisprudence. These two cases are clear and revealing examples of that system at work: a system which needs to be dismantled. The central question is whether we can expect the courts to accomplish this.

DISCUSSION NOTES

i. Litigation After Derrickson and Paul

In *Wynn v Wynn* (1989), 14 ACWS (3d) 107 (Ont Dist Ct), the court distinguished *Paul*. In *Wynn*, the plaintiff wife sought interim exclusive possession of the matrimonial home, which was located on reserve land. Wright DCJ acknowledged that the court could not grant an order under the provincial *Family Law Act* for exclusive possession of a matrimonial home that is located on an Indian reserve. Instead, he made an *in personam* order, without reference to the property, restraining the plaintiff's husband from interfering with her possession of the home.

In a number of other cases as well, although courts respected the principles enunciated in *Derrickson* and *Paul*, they nonetheless fashioned remedies for separating and divorcing spouses in First Nations' communities on reserves. For example, in *George v George* (1997), 139 DLR (4th) 53, [1997] 2 CNLR 62, the BC Court of Appeal confirmed that the trial judge had correctly concluded that there was no jurisdiction to award the wife an interest in the home located on a reserve; however, the Court of Appeal also affirmed the trial judge's decision to award the wife a compensation order pursuant to s 52(2)(c) of the *Family Relations Act*, RSBC 1979, c 121. (In this case, the appellate court also confirmed the husband's entitlement to the home on the reserve, even though he had never received a certificate of possession.) In *Dunstan v Dunstan* (2002), 100 BCLR (3d) 156, a judge in chambers similarly refused to make an order requested by the wife with respect to a ranch property located on a reserve, in which the husband was a part owner. However, the court did grant a restraining order with respect to the sale of cattle and horses, and in relation to a leasehold interest that was not on the reserve. In doing so, the court rejected the husband's argument that no such orders were possible because all the issues were governed by the *Indian Act*.

In *Darbyshire-Joseph v Darbyshire-Joseph*, 1998 CanLII 3522, [1998] BCJ no 2765 (SC), the wife brought an application for a compensation order in respect of a home on a reserve that was owned by the husband and wife as joint tenants. The husband had originally obtained the certificate of possession, and had then conveyed it to himself and his wife as joint tenants. In this case, the court concluded that it was not possible to make an order for compensation in relation to the home because the court had no jurisdiction to make a corresponding order transferring the wife's interest in the certificate of possession on payment of compensation. By contrast, in *Kwakseestahla v Kwakseestahla*, 1998 CanLII 5527, [1998] BCJ no 283 (SC), the husband applied to set aside consent orders issued at the time of the divorce, which granted the wife a life interest in a matrimonial home on a reserve. Rejecting the husband's argument that the court had no jurisdiction to make such orders, the court held that the consent orders were valid, because they were not based on the *Family Relations Act*, but rather on an agreement negotiated by the parties. In Ontario, a wife was granted an equalization payment of $10,000 in *VW v RNS*, [1998] OJ no 4889, 82 OTC 161 (Gen Div), but the court held that she was not entitled to a constructive trust order in relation to the home on the reserve, for which the husband held a certificate of possession.

Do these cases offer solutions to the problems identified by Turpel? Note that some courts in the United States have reached different kinds of solutions. For example, see *Lonewolf v Lonewolf*, 657 P2d 627 (NM Sup Ct 1982), and a brief discussion in MJ Mossman, "Developments in Property Law: The 1985-86 Term" (1987) 9 Sup Ct L Rev 419 at 430ff.

ii. Indian Self-Government and Family Property

Issues about land-holding arrangements on reserve lands constitute a longstanding problem in relation to land title issues for First Nations peoples, a subject addressed in more detail in relation to claims of Aboriginal self-government in Chapter 8. However, the problems are exacerbated in a context of family breakdown, and resolution of this issue requires an acknowledgment of gender issues and the ways in which they were reflected in some traditional Aboriginal cultures.

Some years ago, M Montour described women in traditional Iroquois family life and the ways in which the imposition of colonial culture transformed traditional roles. In addition to concluding that "the only recourse for spouses is under the trusts doctrine," she suggested the possibility of constitutional or international human rights challenges, as well as political action.

> The political route is for the woman to regain her former place in Iroquois society. But this requires that she have the same economic clout as in the past. This may be unrealistic as Iroquois women are generally dependent homemakers with no income of their own. This is the present day reality. The unemployment rate is high on most Indian reserves. Husbands will continue to be issued certificates of possession and to accumulate assets on the reserve in their name only.
>
> One could try to challenge the landholding scheme under the *Indian Act* as discriminatory under section 15 of the *Canadian Charter of Rights and Freedoms* … [but the author argued that this approach might not be successful].
>
> The most realistic solution is for the tribes to enact matrimonial property regimes as part of their right of self-government. If the federal government were to legislate on the matter under section 91(24) of the *Constitution Act, 1867*, it could possibly be challenged as a colourable attempt to legislate in the provincial jurisdiction over property and civil rights between spouses. But the regime could be upheld as being valid because it is essential to the use of reserve lands by Indian spouses whether enacted under Indian self-government or under the exclusive federal power of section 91(24).
>
> Another remedy is based on international law. In the *International Covenant on Civil and Political Rights*, Article 23 states, in part:
>
> > 4. States Parties to the present Covenant shall take appropriate steps to ensure equality of rights and responsibilities of spouses as to marriage, during marriage and at its dissolution. In the case of dissolution, provision shall be made for the necessary protection of any children.
>
> If neither the courts nor the government bodies rectify the inequity Iroquois women could appeal to the international arena. Spouses upon marriage dissolution have equal rights according to the Covenant. This should include an equal right to family property. Although this is not binding on Canadian courts, it can be politically embarrassing for Canada as a signatory to the Covenant. They are obliged to take the necessary steps to remedy any inequality of rights upon marriage dissolution. This may result in appropriate legislative action by the federal government or Indian governments. This was the result when Sandra Lovelace appealed to the international court because she had lost her rights as an Indian woman upon marriage to a non-Indian spouse. Her appeal was received and the federal government passed legislative amendments to the *Indian Act* ending sexual discrimination. (See "Selected Documents in the Matter of Lovelace versus Canada Pursuant to the International Covenant, 08/81.")
>
> If the legislative avenue is chosen it will be an opportunity to achieve an ideal matrimonial property regime. One could aim at restoring the influential position of the Iroquois women in the

social and economic life of their tribes by vesting real matrimonial property rights in them. However, this will only happen if women become politically and economically strong as they were in the past when they selected the political representatives and produced the necessities of life. Otherwise, they may have limited access to real property rights depending on the classification of divisible family property under any future regime for matrimonial reserve lands.

(M Montour, "Iroquois Women's Rights with Respect to Matrimonial Property on Indian Reserves" (1987) 4 Can NL Rep 1 at 6-8.) See also SD McIvor, "Aboriginal Women Unmasked: Using Equality Litigation to Advance Women's Rights" (2004) 16 CJWL 106; Christopher Alcantara, "Indian Women and the Division of Matrimonial Real Property on Canadian Indian Reserves" (2006) 18 CJWL 513; and Richard Bartlett, "Indian Self-Government, the Equality of the Sexes, and the Application of Provincial Matrimonial Property Laws" (1986) 5 Can J Fam L 188.

iii. Matrimonial Property on Reserves: Some Recent Developments

As discussed in greater detail in Chapter 8, some Aboriginal communities have asserted a right to sovereignty or self-government in relation to their traditional lands. Although the Supreme Court of Canada recognized Aboriginal title to land in its decision in *Delgamuukw*, the courts did not recognize claims to Aboriginal sovereignty. In this context, matrimonial property arrangements on reserve lands remained the responsibility of the federal government, in consultation with Aboriginal communities.

In 1999, Parliament enacted the *First Nations Land Management Act*, SC 1999, c 24. Pursuant to this statute, a First Nation may enter into a framework agreement with respect to land management with the federal government, and the First Nation (in consultation with its community) must then adopt rules about the use and occupation of lands. In accordance with this legislation, some First Nations communities have enacted rules about matrimonial property. For example, the Chippewas of Georgina Island adopted a *Matrimonial Real Property Law* in 2000: see Wendy Cornet & Allison Lendor, *Discussion Paper: Matrimonial Real Property on Reserve* (Ottawa: Indian and Northern Affairs Canada, 2002); L Rock & N Wallace, "The Division of Matrimonial Property on Reserve Lands" (Quebec: Quebec Native Women, 2004); and Assembly of First Nations, *Matrimonial Real Property on Reserves: Our Land, Our Families, Our Solutions* (Ottawa: Assembly of First Nations, 2007).

In recent years, a number of bills have been introduced into the federal Parliament concerning matrimonial property on reserve lands, but they have often failed to receive support. However, Bill S-2, *Family Homes on Reserves and Matrimonial Interests or Rights Act*, was introduced in the Senate in September 2011 and received third reading a few months later in December. It was then introduced in the House of Commons in the same month, and later received second reading and was referred to committee. According to the Library of Parliament Legislative Summary (at 1):

> Bill S-2 addresses issues relating to family real property on reserves by providing that a First Nation has the power to enact laws relating to "the use, occupation and possession of family homes on its reserves and the division of the value of any interests or rights held by spouses or common law partners in or to structures and lands on its reserves" (clause 7(1)). The federal provisional rules in the bill will apply until a First Nation has such laws in force.

As this summary indicates, Bill S-2 provided for First Nations to create their own matrimonial property arrangements, but, if they failed to do so, the default rules of Bill S-2 would apply.

On 19 June 2013, the Bill passed third reading in the House of Commons (by a vote of 149 to 125), as the *Family Homes on Reserves and Matrimonial Interests or Rights Act*, SC 2013, c 20. Both opposition parties had urged the government to take time to develop a more consultative Bill that included more detailed plans for enforcement of the rights set out in the Bill. The Assembly of First Nations also raised serious concerns about the Bill, and other Aboriginal persons decried the government's paternalistic role in enacting the legislation. However, Manitoba's Minister of Aboriginal Affairs and Métis member, Eric Robinson, endorsed it: see Josh Wingrove, "New Law Sets Out Rules for Divorces on Reserves Despite First Nations Opposition," *The Globe and Mail* (11 June 2013).

Recall Gray's quotation at the beginning of section IV concerning family property. To what extent do you agree that family property is concerned with "human relations and ideologies in respect of property"? In the context of First Nations in particular, you may want to consider this comment in relation to broader issues of Aboriginal title to land and self-government, discussed in Chapter 8.

PROBLEMS

1. Jane Turner, a widow, died in 1970. She left a will with somewhat complicated provisions about her extensive land holdings in Perth County—for example, in relation to a farm property of about 200 acres, her will stated:

> I hereby devise the old farm fronting on the Roberts sideroad (about 200 acres in all and including the farmhouse built by my grandfather in 1850) to two of my children—Esther and George in fee simple jointly; and if they should decide to sell the farm, they are entitled to share in the proceeds, share and share alike, equally.

Esther and George lived together in the old farmhouse after their mother's death. George farmed the property, continuing to raise some sheep on the pastureland and growing soybeans on the fertile acreage. He also started a modest Christmas tree business by careful management and replanting of the woodlot on the 200 acres. Esther managed the household for her brother, but she also went to work every day at a shop in Perth where she had been employed at the time of her mother's death. Esther and George generally contributed equally to their household expenses, and George used the proceeds of the farming operation to pay for seed, to transport the Christmas trees to the market in Ottawa, and to repair the farm buildings. By agreement between them, Esther kept her earnings from the shop separate from George and he kept the proceeds of the sale of Christmas trees.

Recently, George decided to get married. As part of the wedding arrangements, he wants to make a will; in particular, he wants to ensure that his interest in the farm will pass to his wife, should he predecease her. At the same time, Esther has decided that she should move to Perth. Accordingly, she and George want to know how to arrange their financial matters. Advise Esther and George about their respective entitlements and the consequences of George's marriage and Esther's decision to move to Perth.

2. In a search of the title to property in Brockville, the following documents were found:

    a. 12 January 1902: A deed of grant from Andrew Arthurs to his sons Bruce and Cameron in fee simple "as joint tenants and not as tenants in common."

    b. 18 December 1910: A deed from Bruce Arthurs to his wife Jane Seymour in fee simple.

    c. 22 August 1930: A deed from Cameron Arthurs to the local hospital, the Brockville General Hospital, in fee simple. This deed recited that this conveyance was from Cameron Arthurs as the surviving joint tenant, because Bruce had died in France during the First World War.

Explain what interest (if any) was received by the Brockville General Hospital pursuant to these documents. Give reasons for your conclusions.

3. Dorothy Dixon and Harriet Chong met five years ago and began to live together a year later. Both are lawyers. Dorothy is an associate lawyer in a thriving practice in London, Ontario. She was recently advised that she is likely to be invited to join the partnership next year. Harriet has a sole practice in a small community south of London from which she receives a steady but not large income. She is content with her work and her life with Dorothy, and would like to marry Dorothy.

Dorothy is seeking advice about the implications of marriage for the couple's property arrangements. At present, Dorothy owns the house in which they live, but Harriet has contributed to some major renovations, both financially and by means of work she has done on weekends. Harriet has also done most of the household chores because her hours are generally more regular than Dorothy's and she likes to cook and prepare meals more than Dorothy does.

What principles are applicable to assessing Harriet's entitlement at present to an interest in the home owned by Dorothy? To what extent would her entitlement change if Dorothy and Harriet were married? Note that the couple could also make a marriage contract and define property entitlement as they see fit. What arrangement would you recommend to Dorothy; to Harriet? Why? Do you think that these principles should be applicable to reserve lands? Why or why not? If you think that they are not appropriate, what principles would you recommend?

4. According to the terms of the last will and testament of Judge Matthews, his two children, Anna and Bruce, inherited his plot of land on Toronto Island "as joint tenants and not as tenants in common." After Judge Matthews's death, Bruce decided to convey his interest to his wife, Cathy, for tax purposes. A few years later, in March 2000, Anna was killed in a car accident. Cathy would like to build a house on the plot of land, but she needs to clarify her title to the land. Giving reasons, explain what interest Cathy holds in the Toronto Island property.

5. Consider the following quotation of Dickson CJ in *Pettkus v Becker* in relation to the remedy of constructive trust in the context of unjust enrichment claims by cohabiting spouses:

> The great advantage of ancient principles of equity is their flexibility: the judiciary is thus able to shape these malleable principles so as to accommodate the changing needs and mores of society, in order to achieve justice.

Assess the merits and disadvantages of using equitable principles in defining property interests in the context of family relationships. In doing so, *briefly* compare the approach to these issues in relation to married couples in Canada and to equitable principles in *Pascoe v Turner* in the United Kingdom.

6. Gisela Cicero is a recently graduated lawyer living in Toronto. She works hard and enjoys her law practice, but, because many of her clients are poor, her annual income is not high. Recently, however, her uncle in Italy died and left her a small inheritance of approximately $15,000. Gisela would like to use this money to invest in a house.

She has investigated the possibility of using the money as a downpayment on a house, but the sum is really too small. She is also concerned about monthly mortgage payments, because her earnings are somewhat uneven and precarious. Her good friend Sam Simmons has suggested that she could use the money effectively by moving into a house that he has inherited (mortgage-free). With her inheritance, she could afford to do necessary renovations to the kitchen and bathroom. Even though he does not have to pay a mortgage, Sam has no money to do these renovations because he is still a student and his funds are only sufficient to pay the taxes and monthly expenses on the house. Thus Sam thinks that the arrangement would suit both of them very well.

Sam has assured Gisela that they will marry when he completes his PhD in three years, and that he will pay back her $15,000 when he obtains a university teaching job. In the meantime, he says that she will have a good home and will have made an excellent investment with her uncle's inheritance.

Advise Gisela about her legal rights in relation to Sam's proposal, and explain how she can protect her potential investment.

CHAPTER REFERENCES

Alcantara, Christopher. "Indian Women and the Division of Matrimonial Real Property on Canadian Indian Reserves" (2006) 18 CJWL 513.

Alexander, Ann Elise. "The Ins and Outs of Joint Tenancy," *The Lawyers Weekly* (5 May 2006).

Ambert, Anne-Marie. "Divorce: Facts, Causes and Consequences," 3d ed (Ottawa: Vanier Institute of the Family, 2009), online: <http://thefamilywatch.org/doc/doc-0073-es.pdf>.

American Law Institute. *Principles of the Law of Family Dissolution: Analysis and Recommendations* (St Paul, MN: American Law Institute, 2002).

Assembly of First Nations. *Matrimonial Real Property on Reserves: Our Land, Our Families, Our Solutions* (Ottawa: Assembly of First Nations, 2007).

Backhouse, Constance. "Married Women's Property Law in Nineteenth-Century Canada" (1988) 6 LHR 211.

Baird, James D. *Estates: Out of the Ordinary Problems—Joint Tenancy* (Vancouver: Continuing Legal Education Society of British Columbia, June 2008).

Barlow, Anne & Craig Lind. "A Matter of Trust: The Allocation of Rights in the Family Home" (1999) 19 LS 468.

Bartlett, Richard. "Indian Self-Government, the Equality of the Sexes, and the Application of Provincial Matrimonial Property Laws" (1986) 5 Can J Fam L 188.

Basch, N. *In the Eyes of the Law: Women, Marriage and Property in Nineteenth-Century New York* (Ithaca, NY: Cornell University Press, 1982).

Bissett-Johnson, A. "Three Problems of Pensions—An Overview" (1990) 6 Can Fam LQ 137.

Blackstone, William. *Commentaries on the Laws of England*, vols 1-4 (Oxford: Clarendon Press, 1765-1769).

Blomley, Nicholas. "Landscapes of Property" (1998) 32:3 Law and Soc'y Rev 567.

Bright, Susan & John Dewar, eds. *Land Law: Themes and Perspectives* (Oxford: Oxford University Press, 1998).

Bright, S & B McFarlane. "Proprietary Estoppel and Property Rights" (2005) 64 Cambridge LJ 449.

Buck, AR, J McLaren & N Wright, eds. *Land and Freedom: Law, Property Rights, and the British Diaspora* (Aldershot, UK: Ashgate/Dartmouth, 2001).

Chambers, Lori. *Married Women and Property Law in Ontario* (Toronto: Osgoode Society for Canadian Legal History, 1997).

Cheshire, GC. *The Modern Law of Real Property*, 7th ed (London: Butterworths, 1954).

Chused, Richard. *Cases, Materials and Problems in Property* (New York: Matthew Bender, 1988).

Chused, Richard. "Married Women's Property Law: 1800-1850" (1983) 71 Geo LJ 1359.

Clapton, Mysty. "Murdoch v Murdoch: The Organizing Narrative of Matrimonial Property Law Reform" (2008) 20:2 CJWL 197.

Clement, Wallace & John Myles. "Linking Domestic and Paid Labour: Career Disruptions and Household Obligations" in Clement & Myles, *Relations of Ruling: Class and Gender in Postindustrial Societies* (Montreal: McGill-Queen's University Press, 1994).

Clement, Wallace & John Myles. *Relations of Ruling: Class and Gender in Postindustrial Societies* (Montreal: McGill-Queen's University Press, 1994).

Conway, H & P Girard. "No Place Like Home: The Search for a Legal Framework for Cohabitants and the Family Home in Canada and Britain" (2005) 30 Queen's LJ 715.

Cornet, Wendy & Allison Lendor. *Discussion Paper: Matrimonial Real Property on Reserve* (Ottawa: Indian and Northern Affairs Canada, 2002).

Cowan, D & J Fionda. "Homelessness" in S Bright & J Dewar, eds, *Land Law: Themes and Perspectives* (Oxford: Oxford University Press, 1998) 257.

Crane, FR. "Estoppel Interests in Land" (1967) 31 Conveyancer and Property Lawyer (NS) 332.

Dewar, John. "Land, Law, and the Family Home" in Susan Bright and John Dewar, eds, *Land Law: Themes and Perspectives* (Oxford: Oxford University Press, 1998) 327.

Doggett, M. *Marriage, Wife-Beating, and the Law in Victorian England* (London: Weidenfeld and Nicolson, 1992).

Eichler, M. "The Limits of Family Law Reform" (1990-91) 7 Can Fam LQ 59.

Gardner, Simon. "The Remedial Discretion in Proprietary Estoppel—Again" (2006) 122 Law Q Rev 492.

Gardner, Simon. "Rethinking Family Property" (1993) 109 Law Q Rev 263.

Getty, Ian AL & Antoine S Lussier, eds. *As Long as the Sun Shines and Water Flows: A Reader in Canadian Native Studies* (Vancouver: University of British Columbia Press, 1983).

Girard, P. "Married Women's Property, Chancery Abolition, and Insolvency Law: Law Reform in Nova Scotia, 1820-1867" in P Girard & J Phillips, eds, *Essays in the History of Canadian Law*, vol III: Nova Scotia (Toronto: University of Toronto Press, 1990) 80.

Girard, P & J Phillips, eds. *Essays in the History of Canadian Law*, vol III: Nova Scotia (Toronto: University of Toronto Press, 1990).

Girard, P & R Veinott. "Married Women's Property Law in Nova Scotia, 1850-1910" in J Guildford & S Morton, eds, *Separate Spheres: Women's Worlds in the 19th-Century Maritimes* (Fredericton: Acadiensis Press, 1994).

Glenn, JM. "Comment" (1976) 54 Can Bar Rev 149.

Glenn, JM. "Promissory Estoppel, Proprietary Estoppel, and Constructive Trust in Canada: 'What's in a Name?'" (2007) 30 Dal LJ 141.

Glenn, JM. "Tenancy by the Entireties: A Matrimonial Regime Ignored" (1980) 58 Can Bar Rev 711.

Gray, KJ. *Reallocation of Property on Divorce* (Abingdon, UK: Professional Books, 1977).

Gray, KJ & PD Symes. *Real Property and Real People* (London: Butterworths, 1981).

Gruben, V, A Cameron & A Chaisson. "'The Courts Have Turned Women into Slaves for the Men of This World': Irene Murdoch's Quest for Justice" in E Tucker, B Ziff & J Muir, eds, *Property on Trial: Canadian Cases in Context* (Toronto: Irwin Law for the Osgoode Society for Canadian Legal History, 2012) 159.

Guildford, J & S Morton, eds. *Separate Spheres: Women's Worlds in the 19th-Century Maritimes* (Fredericton: Acadiensis Press, 1994).

Harris, Douglas. "Condominium and the City: The Rise of Property in Vancouver" (2011) 36:3 Law & Soc Inquiry 694.

Haskins, GL. "The Development of Common Law Dower" (1948-49) 62 Harv L Rev 42.

Hohmann, Jessie. *The Right to Housing: Law, Concepts, Possibilities* (Oxford and Portland, OR: Hart, 2013).

Holcombe, L. *Wives and Property* (Toronto: University of Toronto Press, 1983).

Hovius, B. "Property Disputes Between Common Law Partners: The Supreme Court of Canada's Decisions in Vanasse v Seguin and Kerr v Baranow" (2011) 30 Can Fam LQ 129.

Hovius, B. "Property Division for Unmarried Cohabitees in the Common Law Provinces" (2003-4) 21 Can Fam LQ 175.

Hovius, B & T Youdan. *The Law of Family Property* (Scarborough, ON: Carswell, 1991).

Ingram, S & K Inwood. "Property Ownership by Married Women in Victorian Ontario" (2000) 23 Dal LJ 406.

Inwood, K & S van Sligtenhorst. "The Social Consequences of Legal Reform: Women and Property in a Canadian Community" (2004) 19 Continuity & Change 165.

Johnston, J Jr. "Sex and Property: The Common Law Tradition, the Law School Curriculum, and Developments Toward Equality" (1972) 47 NYUL Rev 1033.

Karr, Stephen M. "Covenants and the Condominium" in *Covenants and the Use of Land* (Toronto: Ontario Bar Association, 2009).

Knetsch, J. "Some Economic Implications of Matrimonial Property Rules" (1984) 34 UTLJ 263.

Laskin, B. *Cases and Notes on Land Law* (Toronto: University of Toronto Press, 1958).

Law Commission of Ontario. *Division of Pensions upon Marriage Breakdown: Final Report* (Toronto: Law Commission of Ontario, 2008).

Law Reform Commission of British Columbia. *Working Paper on Co-Ownership of Land* (Vancouver: Law Reform Commission of British Columbia, 1987).

Law Reform Commission of Canada. *Studies on Family Property Law* (Ottawa: Information Canada, 1975).

Lem, Jeffrey. "Condo Cost Rulings Tilting Away from Generous Awards," *Law Times* (13 May 2013) at 7.

Loeb, Audrey. *The Condominium Act: A User's Manual*, 3d ed (Toronto: Carswell, 2009).

Loo, T & R McLean, eds. *Historical Perspectives on Law and Society in Canada* (Toronto: Copp Clark Longman, 1994).

MacDonald, R St J. "Real Property—Joint Tenancy—Murder of One Tenant by Another—Share of the Survivor" (1957) 35 Can Bar Rev 966.

Macpherson, CB. *Property: Mainstream and Critical Positions* (Toronto: University of Toronto Press, 1978).

Martin, J. "Contractual Licensee or Tenant for Life?" (1972) 36 Conveyancer and Property Lawyer (NS) 266.

McCall, M. "Economic Security for Farm Women: A Discussion Paper" (Ottawa: National Association of Women and the Law, 1995).

McCallum, M. "Caratun v Caratun: It Seems That We Are Not All Realists Yet" (1994) 7 CJWL 197.

McCallum, M. "Prairie Women and the Struggle for a Dower Law, 1905-1920" in T Loo & R McLean, eds, *Historical Perspectives on Law and Society in Canada* (Toronto: Copp Clark Longman, 1994) 306.

McCamus, J. "Restitution on Dissolution of Marital and Other Intimate Relationships: Constructive Trust or Quantum Meruit" in JW Neyers, M McInnes & SGA Pitel, eds, *Understanding Unjust Enrichment* (Oxford and Portland, OR: Hart, 2004) 359.

McCaughan, M. *The Legal Status of Married Women in Canada* (Scarborough, ON: Carswell, 1977).

McCauliff, CMA. "The Medieval Origin of the Doctrine of Estates in Land: Substantive Property Law, Family Considerations, and the Interests of Women" (1992) 66 Tul L Rev 919.

McClean, AJ. "Severance of Joint Tenancies" (1979) 57 Can Bar Rev 1.

McIvor, SD. "Aboriginal Women Unmasked: Using Equality Litigation to Advance Women's Rights" (2004) 16 CJWL 106.

McLaren, J. "The Canadian Doukhobors and the Land Question: Religious Communalists in a Fee-Simple World" in AR Buck, J McLaren & N Wright, eds, *Land and Freedom: Law, Property Rights, and the British Diaspora* (Aldershot, UK: Ashgate/Dartmouth, 2001) 135.

Mee, John. *The Property Rights of Cohabitees* (Oxford: Hart, 1999).

Mendes da Costa, D. "Co-Ownership Under Victorian Land Law" (1961) 3 Melbourne UL Rev 137.

Mendes da Costa, Derek, Richard J Balfour & Eileen S Gillese, eds. *Property Law: Cases, Text, and Materials*, 2d ed (Toronto: Emond Montgomery, 1990).

Moller Okin, S. *Justice, Gender, and the Family* (New York: Basic Books, 1989).

Montour, M. "Iroquois Women's Rights with Respect to Matrimonial Property on Indian Reserves" (1987) 4 Can NL Rep 1.

Morton, M. "Dividing the Wealth, Sharing the Poverty: The (Re)Formation of 'Family' in Law in Ontario" (1988) 25 Canadian Review of Sociology and Anthropology 254.

Mossman, MJ. "Developments in Property Law: The 1985-86 Term" (1987) 9 Sup Ct L Rev 419.

Mossman, MJ. "'Running Hard to Stand Still': The Paradox of Family Law Reform" (1994) 17 Dal LJ 5.

Mossman, MJ. "Women Lawyers and Women's Legal Equality" (2012) 87:1 Chicago-Kent L Rev 503.

Neave, Marcia. "Living Together: The Legal Effects of the Sexual Division of Labour in Four Common Law Countries" (1991) 17 Monash UL Rev 14.

Neyers, JW, M McInnes & SGA Pitel, eds. *Understanding Unjust Enrichment* (Oxford and Portland, OR: Hart, 2004).

Nield, S. "To Sever or Not to Sever: The Effect of a Mortgage by One Joint Tenant" [2001] Conv 462.

Oakley, AJ. "The Licensee's Interest" (1972) 35 Mod L Rev 551.

Ontario Law Reform Commission. *Report on Basic Principles of Land Law* (Toronto: Ontario Law Reform Commission, 1996).

Ontario Law Reform Commission. *Report on Family Property Law* (Toronto: Ministry of the Attorney General, 1993).

Ontario Law Reform Commission. *Report on Family Law, Part IV: Family Property Law* (Toronto: Ministry of the Attorney General, 1974).

Ontario Law Reform Commission. *Report on Pensions as Family Property: Valuation and Division* (Toronto: Ministry of the Attorney General, 1995).

Ontario Law Reform Commission. *Report on the Rights and Responsibilities of Cohabitants Under the Family Law Act* (Toronto: Ministry of the Attorney General, 1993).

Parkdale Community Legal Services. "Homelessness and the Right to Shelter: A View from Parkdale" (1988) 4 J L & Soc Pol'y 35.

Probert, Rebecca. "Review" (1999) 19 LS 591.

Public Policy Forum. *Growing Up: Ontario's Condominium Communities Enter a New Era* (Ottawa: Public Policy Forum, 2013).

Public Policy Forum. *Ontario's Condominium Act Review: Stage One Findings Report*, Executive Summary (Ottawa, January 2013), online: Canada's Public Policy Forum <http://www.ppforum.ca/publications/ontarios-condominium-act-review-stage-one-findings-report>.

Public Policy Forum. *Ontario's Condominium Act Review: Stage Two Solutions Report* (Ottawa, 24 September 2013), online: Canada's Public Policy Forum <http://www.ppforum.ca/publications/ontarios-condominium-act-review-stage-two>.

Rabkin, P. *Fathers to Daughters: The Legal Foundations of Female Emancipation* (Westport, CT: Greenwood Press, 1980).

Real Property Law Reform (Phase 2) Project Committee. *Report on Joint Tenancy* (Vancouver: British Columbia Law Institute, 2012).

Ridley, TC. "A Family Affair" (1973) 36 Mod L Rev 436.

Rock, L & N Wallace. "The Division of Matrimonial Property on Reserve Lands" (Quebec: Quebec Native Women, 2004).

Rose, C. "Women and Property: Gaining and Losing Ground" (1992) 78 Va L Rev 421.

Sachs, A & J Hoff Wilson. *Sexism and the Law* (Oxford: M Robertson, 1978).

Salmon, Marylynn. *Women and the Law of Property in Early America* (Chapel Hill and London: University of North Carolina Press, 1986).

Scane, R. "Relationships 'Tantamount to Spousal,' Unjust Enrichment, and Constructive Trusts" (1991) 70 Can Bar Rev 260.

Scott, Austin W. *The Law of Trusts*, 2d ed (Boston: Little, Brown, 1956).

Scott-Hunt, S & H Lim. *Feminist Perspectives on Equity and Trusts* (London: Cavendish, 2001).

Smith, L. "The Mystery of 'Juristic Reason'" (2000) 12 Sup Ct L Rev (2d) 211.

Smith, RJ. "Licences and Constructive Trusts: 'The Law Is What It Ought to Be'" (1973) 32 Cambridge LJ 123.

Sprankling, John G. *Understanding Property Law*, 3d ed (New York: LexisNexis, 2012).

Spry, IM. "The Tragedy of the Loss of the Commons in Western Canada" in Ian AL Getty & Antoine S Lussier, eds, *As Long as the Sun Shines and Water Flows: A Reader in Canadian Native Studies* (Vancouver: University of British Columbia Press, 1983) 203.

Status of Women Canada. *Report of the Royal Commission on the Status of Women in Canada* (Ottawa: Information Canada, 1975).

Triggs, Chris. "Against Policy: Homicide and Succession to Property" (2005) 68 Sask L Rev 117.

Tucker, E, B Ziff & J Muir, eds. *Property on Trial: Canadian Cases in Context* (Toronto: Irwin Law for the Osgoode Society for Canadian Legal History, 2012).

Turano, Margaret Valentine. "Jane Austen, Charlotte Brontë, and the Marital Property Law" (1998) 21 Harv Women's LJ 179.

Turpel, Mary Ellen. "Home/Land" (1991) 10 Can J Fam L 17.

Wade, John W. "Acquisition of Property by Wilfully Killing Another—A Statutory Solution" (1936) 49 Harv L Rev 715.

Weitzman, Lenore. *The Divorce Revolution: The Unexpected Social and Economic Consequences for Women and Children in America* (New York: Free Press, 1985).

Wells, R. "The Element of Detriment in Proprietary Estoppel" (2001) 65 Conveyancer 13.

Wingrove, Josh. "New Law Sets Out Rules for Divorces on Reserves Despite First Nations Opposition," *The Globe and Mail* (11 June 2013).

Wong, Simone. "Property Rights for Home-Sharers: Equity Versus a Legislative Framework?" in S Scott-Hunt & H Lim, *Feminist Perspectives on Equity and Trusts* (London: Cavendish, 2001) 133.

Woodman, G. "Note: Social Interests in the Development of Constructive Trusts" (1980) 96 Law Q Rev 336.

Ziff, Bruce. *Principles of Property Law*, 5th ed (Scarborough, ON: Carswell, 2010).

CHAPTER SEVEN

Non-Possessory Interests in Land: "Private" Planning and the Use of Land

I. INTRODUCTION

This chapter provides an introduction to non-possessory property interests—that is, proprietary interests that do not include a right to possession. As explored in earlier chapters, possession is often fundamental to the creation of property interests, as in finders' cases or adverse possession of land, and it is possible to divide property interests on the basis of separate holders of possession and title, as in bailment and leases. In this chapter, we examine property interests that exist without a right to possession, a somewhat abstract but common and important set of proprietary interests in land.

Specifically, this chapter examines three kinds of non-possessory interests—*profits à prendre*, easements, and covenants. Conceptually, these non-possessory interests are often linked to a larger group of interests that "limit" the rights of landowners in their use of land—for example, rights of occupation in a licence or lease (Chapter 4), or other limits on landowners set out in fee simples that are determinable or subject to condition (Chapter 3). Similarly, the Supreme Court of Canada has recognized a right of the public in the nature of an implied licence in relation to government property, pursuant to the Charter's guarantee of freedom of expression—a right that constrains the rights of the landowner. See *Committee for the Commonwealth of Canada v Canada*, [1991] 1 SCR 139 (and Chapter 1).

Yet even though some aspects of *profits à prendre*, easements, and covenants share functional similarities with these other arrangements limiting a landowner's use of land, legal principles about these three interests have been regarded as conceptually distinct because they do not include rights to possession. In the United States, there have been lively debates about the appropriateness of maintaining easements and covenants as separate doctrinal categories and some persuasive arguments about adopting a redefined "law of servitudes" (including both easements and covenants) in their places. See e.g. U Reichman, "Toward a Unified Concept of Servitudes" (1982) 55 S Cal L Rev 1177 [Reichman (1982)] and the work of the American Law Institute, *Restatement of the Law, Third: Property—Servitudes* (St Paul, MN: American Law Institute, 2000) [American Law Institute (2000)], discussed at the end of this chapter. See also Ontario Law Reform Commission, *Report on Basic Principles of Land Law* (Toronto: Ontario Law Reform Commission, 1996) [OLRC *Report on Basic Principles*].

The limitations that can be imposed on subsequent owners by means of *profits à prendre*, easements, and covenants can, as property interests, be created to last in perpetuity or for some lesser period. As a result, over time they can have a powerful impact on the development, or non-development, of land. In one of the classic cases on easements treated in this chapter, *In re Ellenborough Park*, an agreement entered into in 1864 was relevant to the ability of landowners to develop their land in 1955, when the matter was litigated. When it was found that the agreement created an easement in law, the landowners were prevented from developing their land without buying out the rights of all easement holders. Although there are some doctrines that permit the early termination of easements and restrictive covenants, and legislative provisions in some provinces that authorize courts to discharge them in limited circumstances, in most cases the only means of ending them once created is by negotiation among the parties or expropriation by a public authority.

Easements and covenants have been characterized as mechanisms of "private" land-use planning. Before more widespread enactment of local planning statutes and zoning regulations, easements and covenants were used to achieve similar types of land-use restrictions. As will become clear, however, such private-planning devices could also be used to prohibit access to certain neighbourhoods on the basis of race and class, a result of the lack of public scrutiny inherent in private-planning activities. Because most private planning occurs in the context of privately negotiated contracts, non-possessory interests raise, once again, the intersection of property and contract law principles and the relationship between law and equity. As we explain below, non-possessory interests are also concerned with the public–private dichotomy in law, an issue that echoes throughout this book.

In this chapter, the balancing of private rights of landowners to "do as they like" with their land and the concomitant rights of others (including non-owners of land) to constrain landowners' choices is evidenced in the tension within some of the legal principles and their application in practice. As you consider the issues in this chapter, think about the following comment concerning US landowners, and assess the degree to which it applies in Canada as a description of the balancing of these interests:

> The property owner is the primary planner of land use. This statement may appear to conflict with the conventional notion that planning and resource management are public functions, to be exercised by government officials, boards, and professional staff. But the public role in the United States is essentially reactive to the decisions of the property owner. It is the owner who determines *how* to utilize his or her land in light of geographic, economic, legal and personal circumstances. It is also the owner who determines *when* a change in existing land use should occur. It is the owner's decision to change the use of land that triggers the public reactive role.

(R Platt, *Land Use and Society: Geography, Law, and Public Policy* (Washington, DC: Island Press, 1996) at 93.)

II. THE PROFIT À PRENDRE

According to R Megarry & HWR Wade, *The Law of Real Property*, 5th ed (London: Stevens & Sons, 1984) at 850, a "*profit à prendre*" is "a right to take something off another's land," including such things as timber, minerals, or wildlife. Bruce Ziff described a "*profit à prendre*" as entitling the holder of this non-possessory interest "to enter onto the land of another to extract some part of the natural produce, such as timber, crops, turf, soil, grass or animals." It may also entitle one "to extract oil and natural gas: this is the type of grant sometimes used in modern drilling and extraction operations." See Bruce Ziff, *Principles of Property Law*, 5th ed (Scarborough, ON: Carswell, 2010) [Ziff] at 394.

The idea of a *profit à prendre* was illustrated in a well-known decision about the doctrine of part performance (discussed in Chapter 5), *Mason v Clarke*, [1955] 1 All ER 914 (HL). Mr Mason paid £100 for the right to kill and take rabbits on the Holthorpe Estate for a year from 11 October 1950. When he tried to exercise this right, however, he was prevented from doing so by the respondent. In the suit that followed, Lord Morton of Henryton stated (at 923): "A *profit à prendre* is an interest in land." The court found for Mr Mason on the basis that he had an equitable interest arising from the doctrine of part performance. Thus, he had an equitable *profit à prendre*.

A *profit à prendre* can be distinguished from an easement: while an easement confers a right to use the land belonging to another, a *profit à prendre*

> confers a right to take from [another's land] some part of the soil of that [land] or minerals under it or some of its natural produce or the animals *ferae naturae* existing upon it. For example, the right to depasture cattle, or to graze sheep is a profit, and so is the right to take sea-washed coal from the foreshore. The subject-matter of a profit must be something which is capable of ownership.

(See Jonathan Gaunt & Paul Morgan, *Gale on Easements*, 19th ed (London: Sweet & Maxwell, 2012) [*Gale on Easements*] at 1-02 and cases cited. The authors provide a classification of profits at 1-143 to 1-147.)

The *profit à prendre* exhibits some similarities to a licence, since both permit the use of another's land for defined purposes. According to Derek Mendes da Costa, Richard J Balfour & Eileen S Gillese, *Property Law: Cases, Text, and Materials*, 2d ed (Toronto: Emond Montgomery, 1990) [Mendes da Costa, Balfour & Gillese] at 19:14, however, "a *profit à prendre* is not revocable in the sense of a licence, which is generally terminable at any time upon reasonable notice." As well, the nature of a *profit à prendre* is the right to remove something from land. And although fishing licences granted under statutory authority are not *profits à prendre*, the Supreme Court of Canada considered the close analogy between fishing licences and *profits à prendre* as an important factor in concluding that such licences could be considered "property," as noted in *Saulnier v Royal Bank of Canada*, 2008 SCC 58, [2008] 3 SCR 166, discussed in Chapter 1.

The Supreme Court of Canada considered the nature of the *profit à prendre* in *R v Tener*, [1985] 1 SCR 533. In this case, the plaintiffs sought compensation in respect of mining rights that were adversely affected by the enactment of provincial legislation establishing the subject lands in British Columbia as a provincial park. The judges in the court were not entirely in agreement about how to characterize the mining rights, but Madam Justice Wilson (with the concurrence of Chief Justice Dickson) concluded (at 540) that the claim should be characterized as a *profit à prendre*:

> I think the learned Chambers judge may have been in error in treating the respondents as having two separate and distinct interests in the land—the mineral claims and the right to go on the surface for the purpose of developing them .... I believe that what the respondents had was one integral interest in land in the nature of a *profit à prendre* comprising both the mineral claims and the surface rights necessary for their enjoyment.

This case focused on the basis for compensation to be awarded, and is interesting as an example of the intersection of private property interests and public regulatory issues. For further discussion of the case and these issues, see MJ Mossman, "Developments in Property Law: The 1984-85 Term" (1986) 8 Sup Ct L Rev 319 at 321-30.

A. Aboriginal Claims as Profits à Prendre

There are numerous cases where Aboriginal claims to hunt or fish on lands might also be categorized as *profits à prendre*, although jurisprudence in Canada has tended to recognize these claims on the basis of special principles applicable to Aboriginal rights. For example, in *R v Sparrow*, [1990] 1 SCR 1075, the Supreme Court of Canada recognized that the Musqueam band held an Aboriginal right to fish for food, going beyond mere subsistence and extending to fish consumed for social and ceremonial purposes. In its analysis, the court referred (at 1094) to *Guerin v The Queen*, [1984] 2 SCR 335 and the need to ensure the recognition of such Aboriginal claims as "*sui generis*" interests.

The Aboriginal Right

We turn now to the aboriginal right at stake in this appeal. The Musqueam Indian Reserve is located on the north shore of the Fraser River close to the mouth of that river and within the limits of the city of Vancouver. There has been a Musqueam village there for hundreds of years. This appeal does not directly concern the reserve or the adjacent waters, but arises out of the band's right to fish in another area of the Fraser River estuary known as Canoe Passage in the south arm of the river, some 16 kilometres (about 10 miles) from the reserve. The reserve and those waters are separated by the Vancouver International Airport and the Municipality of Richmond.

The evidence reveals that the Musqueam have lived in the area as an organized society long before the coming of European settlers, and that the taking of salmon was an integral part of their lives and remains so to this day. Much of the evidence of an aboriginal right to fish was given by Dr. Suttles, an anthropologist, supported by that of Mr. Grant, the band administrator. The Court of Appeal thus summarized Dr. Suttles' evidence, at pp. 307-308:

> Dr. Suttles was qualified as having particular qualifications in respect of the ethnography of the Coast Salish Indian people of which the Musqueams were one of several tribes. He thought that the Musqueam had lived in their historic territory, which includes the Fraser River estuary, for at least 1,500 years. That historic territory extended from the north shore of Burrard Inlet to the south shore of the main channel of the Fraser River, including the waters of the three channels by which that river reaches the ocean. As part of the Salish people, the Musqueam were part of a regional social network covering a much larger area but, as a tribe, were themselves an organized social group with their own name, territory and resources. Between the tribes there was a flow of people, wealth and food. No tribe was wholly self-sufficient or occupied its territory to the complete exclusion of others.
>
> Dr. Suttles described the special position occupied by the salmon fishery in that society. The salmon was not only an important source of food but played an important part in the system of beliefs of the Salish people, and in their ceremonies. The salmon were held to be a race of beings that had, in "myth times," established a bond with human beings requiring the salmon to come each year to give their bodies to the humans who, in turn, treated them with respect shown by performance of the proper ritual. Toward the salmon, as toward other creatures, there was an attitude of caution and respect which resulted in effective conservation of the various species.

While the trial for a violation of a penal prohibition may not be the most appropriate setting in which to determine the existence of an aboriginal right, and the evidence was not extensive, the correctness of the finding of fact of the trial judge "that Mr. Sparrow was fishing in ancient tribal territory where his ancestors had fished from time immemorial in that part of the mouth of the Fraser River for salmon" is supported by the evidence and was not contested. The existence of the right, the Court of Appeal tells us, "was not the subject of serious dispute." It is not surprising, then, that, taken with other circumstances, that court should find that "the judgment appealed from was wrong in ... failing to hold that Sparrow at the relevant time was exercising an existing aboriginal right." ...

Our earlier observations regarding the scope of the aboriginal right to fish are relevant here. Fishing rights are not traditional property rights. They are held by a collective and are in keeping with the culture and existence of that group. Courts must be careful, then, to avoid the application of traditional common law concepts of property as they develop their understanding of what the reasons for judgment in *Guerin*, supra, at p. 382, referred to as the "sui generis" nature of aboriginal rights. (See also Little Bear, "A Concept of Native Title," [1982] 5 Can. Legal Aid. Bul. 99.)

While it is impossible to give an easy definition of fishing rights, it is possible, and, indeed, crucial, to be sensitive to the aboriginal perspective itself on the meaning of the rights at stake. For example, it would be artificial to try to create a hard distinction between the right to fish and the particular manner in which that right is exercised.

DISCUSSION NOTE

R v Sparrow: Sui Generis Aboriginal Rights

Consider the nature of the Aboriginal claim asserted in *R v Sparrow*. Is it possible to characterize it as a *profit à prendre*? If it could be characterized in this way, what are the reasons for finding the right to be "*sui generis*"? For further discussion of these issues, see *R v Jack*, [1980] 1 SCR 294. See also B Slattery, "Understanding Aboriginal Rights" (1987) 66 Can Bar Rev 726; K McNeil, "The Constitutional Rights of the Aboriginal People of Canada" (1982) 4 Sup Ct L Rev 255; N Lyon, "An Essay on Constitutional Interpretation" (1988) 26 Osgoode Hall LJ 95; and W Pentney, "The Rights of the Aboriginal Peoples of Canada in the Constitution Act, 1982, Part II, Section 35: The Substantive Guarantee" (1988) 22 UBC L Rev 207; Phillip M Saunders, "Forum on R v Marshall—Getting Their Feet Wet: The Supreme Court and Practical Implementation of Treaty Rights in the Marshall Case" (2000) 23 Dal LJ 48; and the material in Chapter 8.

B. Profits à Prendre Versus Contractual Rights

While *profits à prendre* are often created by contract, it can be difficult to establish whether a contract creates a true property interest or merely a contractual right. This problem is similar to those discussed in Chapter 4 as to whether parties had created a bailment or a licence, or a lease or a licence. In *Robillard v Staaf*, 2008 BCSC 1266, such a dispute arose with respect to a *profit à prendre*. Four siblings owned 150 acres on Texada Island, British Columbia. Three of them agreed in 1958 that they would sell their shares to the fourth sibling, Ivan, so that he would be sole owner of the property, but a "condition precedent" of the agreement required that "the timber situate on ... the property ... shall be retained by the said ... four parties ... as to a one quarter interest each." At that time, the property had previously been logged and was used only as a hayfield; there was no timber on it. In the following decades, Melvin Staaf succeeded his father Ivan as sole owner in fee simple of the property, while the shares of the four siblings in the "timber rights" contemplated in the 1958 agreement eventually passed through inheritance and purchase into the hands of Melvin and his sister Barbara. Thus, by the time of the litigation, Melvin and Barbara held all the timber rights to the property, in two equal shares, while Melvin held the fee simple. By 2008, moreover, there was a stand of timber on the property worth some $400,000.

Barbara sought to register her interest in the timber rights as a *profit à prendre* and this action was opposed by her brother. Melvin agreed that Barbara had a contractual right, but denied that it created a *profit à prendre*. He argued that she was entitled to half the net profits from the sale of the timber, but that she was not entitled to be involved in the harvesting of the timber. According to Melvin, the burden was on Barbara to show that the agreement clearly and unequivocally created a *profit à prendre*. Because it did not specifically refer to any right to enter on the land and harvest the timber, it could not be construed as a *profit à prendre*.

The trial judge resolved the issue as follows:

> [39] There is no explicit reference in the 1958 Agreement authorizing the holder of the timber rights to enter upon the property and to effect harvest of the timber. Is it proper to imply this right of entry and harvest as part of the timber rights term of the 1958 Agreement?
>
> [40] The answer to that question is substantially informed by [the] fact that what the 1958 Agreement gave to the four persons who held the timber rights was *the timber*. It did not give them the right to the profits from the harvest of the timber, but, on a plain reading, gave them the actual trees. Accepting that proposition as a starting point, and recognizing that the 1958 Agreement is silent on the issue, the proper approach is to ask whether the right to enter upon the land and harvest the timber should be implied as necessary to give business efficacy to the contract. [The judge had previously canvassed contract law jurisprudence regarding the circumstances in which it is appropriate to imply terms in a contract.] In my view, this question must be answered in the affirmative.
>
> [41] If the 1958 Agreement did not confer such a right on the party who had the ownership of the timber, then the benefit of the timber rights would be essentially frustrated. The holder would have a right but no means of realizing upon it. Accordingly, I find it to be an implied term of the 1958 Agreement that the holder (or, in this case, holders) of the timber right is entitled to enter onto the property in order to harvest the timber situated thereon.

In response to the defendant's arguments that the finding of a *profit à prendre* would significantly interfere with his rights as titleholder, and that Barbara's non-payment of taxes on the property made the finding of a profit unfair, the court reasoned as follows:

> [57] Another argument advanced by the defendant was to the effect that if this Court concludes that the timber right includes the right to enter upon the property and harvest the timber, such entry and harvest constitute a very significant intrusion on the property rights of the title holder. He also argued that to accede to the position of the plaintiff would be to impose a dramatically different contract than was originally made.
>
> [58] The task of this Court is to determine as best it can what the 1958 Agreement actually meant. While the outcome may be dramatically different than the position advanced by the defendant, and the right to entry and harvest may indeed be a significant derogation from the absolute nature of the defendant's title to the property, it cannot be said that this Court is imposing any significant change. This is the agreement that I find was reached by the parties, and so that is the agreement to which effect must be given.

[59] The defendant's submission in regards to the payment of property taxes on the property is neither supported nor contradicted by any of the authorities. Payment of property taxes is not a requirement for holders of *profits à prendre*, and has no bearing on the ultimate determination of this issue.

The next question that arose was the duration of the *profit à prendre*. *Profits à prendre* may be created to last in perpetuity, for the lifetime of the holder, or for some defined period, but the agreement was silent as to duration. Here the trial judge again had recourse to the law of implied terms, finding that the profit related to only one "cycle" of timber growth, and that when the current stand of timber was harvested, the profit would cease.

DISCUSSION NOTES

i. Profits à Prendre and "Property" Interests

Do you agree with the trial judge's interpretation of the 1958 agreement? Is it the case that Barbara's ownership rights in the timber would be "frustrated" if she could not participate in the harvesting process? What assumptions are being made here about the nature and extent of ownership rights? In reflecting on these questions you may want to review the materials in Chapter 1 on the nature of property.

ii. Profits à Prendre and Aboriginal Rights

Why do you think that the BC court in *Robillard* was so willing to characterize Barbara's right under the 1958 agreement as a *profit à prendre*, but the Supreme Court was so resistant to treating the right asserted in *Sparrow* as a *profit à prendre*? Are there differences between the rights being asserted that justify these different characterizations?

III. EASEMENTS

A. Characterizing Easements: Gypsum Carrier Inc v The Queen

On 2 July 1968, the *Harry Lundeberg*, an ocean-going freighter (owned by Gypsum Carrier Inc, and carrying gypsum from Mexico to New Westminster, British Columbia), collided with the New Westminster Railway Bridge, which spanned the Fraser River near New Westminster. The bridge, owned by the federal government, was constructed in the early part of the 20th century for railway, vehicular, and passenger traffic. However, after the construction of the Pattullo Bridge upstream in the late 1930s, the New Westminster Railway Bridge was used only by railway companies, including the Canadian National Railway.

In the ensuing litigation after the collision, Gypsum Carrier Inc was held liable for damages to the federal Crown in respect of the cost of repairs and loss of profits. In addition, three railway companies made claims for their expenses in rerouting their trains during the bridge closure, but Gypsum Carrier Inc resisted these claims on the basis that "no damage or injury was caused to any property owned by the railway companies, or to any property in which they had a proprietary interest."

In evaluating the validity of the argument made by Gypsum Carrier Inc, the court reviewed the contractual agreements between each of the companies and the federal government.

The railway companies argued that, pursuant to the contracts, they each had an easement. In reviewing the contracts, the Federal Court in *Gypsum Carrier Inc v The Queen* (1977), 78 DLR (3d) 175 (FCTD) held that the railways were given the right to construct and maintain connections between their own tracks and those on the bridge and its approaches, and to run their trains over the bridge and its approaches, during the term of each agreement. The federal government, however, was given "full control over the maintenance and betterment of the property covered by this agreement" and had responsibility for repairing the bridge and its approaches at its own expense. Pursuant to the contracts, the railway companies agreed to pay 53 cents per car passing over the bridge.

In rejecting the claim that the contracts created easements for the railway companies, Collier J stated (at 180):

> An easement has been defined as
>
> > a right annexed to land to utilise other land of different ownership in a particular manner (not involving the taking of any part of the natural produce of that land or of any part of its soil) or to prevent the owner of the other land from utilising his land in a particular manner. [*Halsbury's Laws of England*, 4th ed, vol 14 at 4.]
>
> The railway companies contend that all the essential characteristics of an easement are here present. ...
>
> In my opinion, the agreements between the Crown and the railway companies did not create easements in favour of the railway companies. The documents, superficially, appear to contain the so-called essentials of an easement. But I think one must ascertain the intention of the parties. To my mind, when the agreements are read as a whole, there was no intention to create easements. The purpose was to create certain contractual rights whereby the railways, in return for stipulated fees, were permitted to run their trains over the bridge and approaches. There was no intention to create any rights annexed to land, or any interest in land.

DISCUSSION NOTE

Intention and the Principle of "Numerus Clausus"

The *Gypsum Carrier* case is an interesting illustration of property analysis about easements. Note, for example, that the court reviewed the substantive requirements for the creation of an easement and held that they were all present in these contracts. Nonetheless, the court declined to find that easements were created. Why? Compare Collier J's emphasis on the overall "intention of the parties" in *Gypsum Carrier* and cases examined below. What is the significance of "intention" in the characterization of easements? Why does the court characterize the relationships as merely contractual rather than proprietary as well? What form of agreement might have satisfied the court that the parties intended to create easements in their respective contracts? Does the decision reflect a concern for "form over substance"? Was *Gypsum Carrier* wrongly decided?

In exploring these questions, note also that claims about easements often raise the "numerus clausus" principle of real property law—that is, the general hesitancy to admit new forms of proprietary interests. This reluctance to create new interests has been especially evident in the law of easements:

English law is notorious for its reluctance to recognize new interests in land. Within the particular confines of the law of easements this reluctance has been illustrated by the fluctuation of opinion over the years on the question of whether or not new rights may be admitted to the company of the old and well recognized easements.

(AJ McClean, "The Nature of an Easement" (1966) 5 West LR 32 [McClean] at 32.) See also MM Litman & Bruce Ziff, "Easements and Possession: An Elusive Limitation" (1989) Conveyancer and Property Lawyer 296; and Jeremy Johnston, "Easements, Covenants, Licences, and Profits as Servitudes in Canadian Common Law: Escaping the Quagmire" (York University, D Jur dissertation, 2013).

To what extent did this general reluctance to create new easements appear to influence the decision in *Gypsum Carrier*? What options are available to assist a client who wishes to create an easement in such a situation? In *Gypsum Carrier*, the railway companies also submitted arguments that they had "some lesser proprietary interest," although the exact nature of that interest was not specified. The court concluded (at 181) that "at best, they may have had some kind of licence in respect of land (the bridge and approaches)," but concluded that interference with any such interest would not create liability here. How should an easement be distinguished from a licence?

B. The Four Requirements for Creating an Easement

Ziff stated the four requirements for the creation of an easement as follows:

1. there must be a dominant tenement, which enjoys the benefit of the easement, and a servient tenement, which is burdened;

2. the easement must accommodate the dominant tenement;

3. the dominant and servient tenements cannot both be owned and occupied by the same person; and

4. the easement must be capable of forming the subject matter of a grant.

(Ziff at 376-80.) See also *Gale on Easements* at 1-05 to 1-07 and OLRC *Report on Basic Principles* at 126-29.

1. Requirement of a Dominant and Servient Tenement

The requirement that there must be a dominant and a servient tenement means that an easement must be linked with two parcels of land, one over which the easement is exercised—the servient tenement—and one in favour of which the easement is created—the dominant tenement. Although this requirement is well-accepted in Canada and the United Kingdom, it does not apply in the United States, where it is possible for someone who does not hold an interest in adjoining land to hold an easement over a servient tenement. Such an easement is called an "easement in gross."

Traditionally, the authority relied on for the requirement of a dominant and servient tenement in English and Canadian law is *Ackroyd v Smith* (1850), 138 ER 68 (Common Pleas). In that case, the plaintiff's predecessor in title had entered into an agreement to permit the defendant's predecessor in title to use a road to cross the plaintiff's land. Subsequently, there was a dispute about whether this arrangement constituted merely a licence between the two original parties or was an easement and thus binding on the plaintiff (whose land would have been the servient tenement). The right had been granted to "owners and occupiers" of the defendant's land and "to all persons having occasion to resort thereto." The court held (at 77) that the right of way was a licence, not an easement, because the words of the grant were too broad and might have conferred rights on those other than the owner of the dominant tenement. The court thus confirmed that an easement cannot be granted in gross: "No one can have such a way but he who has the land to which it is appendant." (This case is also cited to support another requirement for an easement—that it must accommodate the dominant tenement. In *Ackroyd*, the court held that the interest granted was a right unconnected with the enjoyment or occupation of the land. This requirement is further examined below.) See also *Gale on Easements* at 1-08 to 1-22.

Even though the requirement of a dominant and servient tenement is well-accepted in English and Canadian law, both the authority for this requirement and its underlying policy rationale have been criticized. For example, McClean argued that neither *Ackroyd v Smith* nor other cases relied on in the texts as authority for the requirement are determinative, suggesting that *Ackroyd* is better cited for the proposition that an easement must accommodate the dominant tenement than for the requirement that there must be both a dominant and servient tenement. McClean was critical of Canadian judges who accepted the English decisions on this issue as if the principle were "self-evident," sometimes even without referring to any authority at all (citing *Pitman v Nickerson* (1891), 40 NSR 20 (SC); *Adamson v Bell Telephone Co* (1920), 48 OLR 24 (SC (AD)); and *Re Toscano and Dorien* (1965), 51 DLR (2d) 298 (Ont CA)). He suggested a need to re-examine the underlying policy rationale for such a requirement: see McClean at 38-39.

In *Ackroyd*, the court justified the approach it adopted, suggesting (at 68) that it was appropriate to limit the powers of vendors to annex rights to their interests in land, especially if the rights would render the land subject to "a new species of burthen, so as to bind it in the hands of an assignee." (This concern is also evident below, in the discussion of covenants and in relation to *Keppell v Bailey* (1834), 2 My & K 517, a leading case in the history of the law of covenants, used to support the conclusion adopted in *Ackroyd*. Recall also the concern about not allowing new kinds of estates to be created, examined in detail in Chapter 3.) By contrast with these arguments, McClean suggested (at 40) that there is no continued justification for such a limit on easements, especially in the light of the recognition of easements in gross in the United States:

> The argument in favour of the recognition of easements in gross is an extremely simple one. If to give effect to what is a socially desirable use of property it is necessary to have easements in gross, why should such easements not exist? If, to take Gale's example, A wants to grant to B a right, enforceable to the extent an easement is today, to land helicopters on A's property why should this be impossible if there is no dominant tenement? Similarly, if a long distance trucker wishes to acquire easements of parking along his routes, why should this not be possible?

According to McClean, concerns about the alienability of such interests can be satisfactorily resolved with modern registration systems, and there is no reason why easements, like *profits à prendre*, should not exist in gross. The OLRC *Report on Basic Principles* expressed agreement with this view (at 141-45). Which of these policy approaches do you find most satisfactory in relation to property principles? For further analysis of these issues, see MF Sturley, "Easements in Gross" (1980) 96 Law Q Rev 557. In the United States, the existence of the easement in gross has required some limiting principles to prevent "overburdening" of the servient tenement: see AD Hegi, "The Easement in Gross Revisited: Transferability and Divisibility Since 1945" (1986) 39 Vand L Rev 109.

Although McClean concluded that there was no real basis in legal authority or public policy for the principle that the existence of an easement requires both a dominant and servient tenement, he suggested that the principle was so well settled that it probably could not be changed without legislation. In practice, there are numerous examples of legislatively created easements where there is no dominant tenement. Most of these easements relate to public utilities such as water, sewage, and electricity. See e.g. *Ontario Water Resources Act*, RSO 1990, c O.40, s 14. Another approach was evident in *Vannini v Public Utilities Commission of Sault Ste Marie*, [1973] 2 OR 11 (Ont HC), where the court held that the commission's ownership of the waterworks system (even though the commission owned no contiguous land) constituted a "dominant tenement." How do these statutory provisions and cases affect your view about the desirability of permitting easements in gross in Canada? For a comparable approach in the United States, where easements in gross are recognized, see *Henley v Continental Cablevision of St Louis County, Inc*, 692 SW 2d 825 (Missouri CA 1985).

For an "exceptional" and rather macabre context concerning easements in gross, see *Hubbs v Black* (1918), 46 DLR 583 (Ont SC (AD)), where the defendant responded to an action for trespass against a cemetery plot by claiming that he had a right of easement. According to Riddell J (at 589), "while the right of burial is still called an easement, it is an exception to the general rule that an easement cannot be in gross." (This case also provides an interesting discussion of part performance and the equitable jurisdiction of the county court in Ontario.)

2. Requirement That the Easement Accommodate the Dominant Tenement

No right can qualify as an easement unless it can be shown that the right confers a significant benefit on dominant land as distinct from offering some merely personal advantage or convenience to the dominant owner. As always, the impact of the easement must be real rather than personal. The core idea is that an easement, properly so called, must make the use of the dominant land more beneficial or commodious in a way which applies indifferently to both the current dominant owner and all his successors in title.

(Kevin Gray & Susan Francis Gray, *Elements of Land Law*, 5th ed (Oxford: Oxford University Press, 2009) [Gray & Gray] at 607.) The requirement that an easement accommodate the dominant tenement was carefully considered in a decision of the English Court of Appeal: *In re Ellenborough Park*, [1956] 1 Ch D 131 (CA). In that case, there were a number of houses on a square in Weston-super-Mare with a garden or park in the centre (Ellenborough Park) enclosed by the houses. Title to the garden was vested in trustees and each of the owners of the houses around the garden paid a proportionate cost of maintaining the garden. In 1864, when subdividing the property, the owner had granted to the lot-owners

the full enjoyment ... at all times hereafter in common with the other persons to whom such easements may be granted of the pleasure ground [Ellenborough Park, and had covenanted that he would not] erect ... any dwelling-house and other building (except any grotto bower summer-house flower-stand fountain music-stand or other ornamental erection) within or on any part of the said pleasure ground … but that the same shall at all times remain as an ornamental garden or pleasure ground.

Only those who resided in the houses were entitled to use the garden or park. A question arose as to whether the owners of the houses surrounding the park had an enforceable right in respect of the use and enjoyment of Ellenborough Park. To validate such an enforceable right, given the absence of privity with the original owner, it was necessary to find that they had an easement.

The court considered all four requirements for an easement in reviewing the arguments in this case. In relation to this second requirement (that an easement must accommodate the dominant tenement), the court concluded that the right to use the garden or park conferred "a benefit on the dominant tenement" and not merely "a personal advantage upon the dominant owner." In examining the court's reasoning on this issue, try to distinguish the factors considered relevant in relation to *Ellenborough Park* by contrast with those in *Hill v Tupper* (1863), 2 H & C 121 (Ex Chamber), discussed in the court's reasoning. Are the distinctions drawn by the English Court of Appeal compelling?

In re Ellenborough Park
[1956] 1 Ch D 131 at 173 (CA)

EVERSHED MR: As appears from the map, the houses, which were built upon the plots around and near to Ellenborough Park, varied in size, some being large detached houses and others smaller and either semi-detached or in a row. We have already stated that the purchasers of all the plots, which actually abutted on the park, were granted the right to enjoy the use of it, as were also the purchasers of some of the plots which, although not fronting upon the park, were only a short distance away from it. As to the nature of the right granted, the conveyance of 1864 shows that the park was to be kept and maintained as a pleasure ground or ornamental garden, and that it was contemplated that it should at all times be kept in good order and condition and well stocked with plants and shrubs; and the vendors covenanted that they would not at any time thereafter erect or permit to be erected any dwelling-house or other building (except a grotto, bower, summer-house, flower-stand, fountain, music-stand or other ornamental erection) within or on any part of the pleasure ground. On these facts Mr. Cross submitted that the requisite connexion between the right to use the park and the normal enjoyment of the houses which were built around it or near it had not been established. He likened the position to a right granted to the purchaser of a house to use the Zoological Gardens free of charge or to attend Lord's Cricket Ground without payment. Such a right would undoubtedly, he said, increase the value of the property conveyed but could not run with it at law as an easement, because there was no sufficient nexus between the enjoyment of the right and the use of the house. It is probably true, we think, that in neither of Mr. Cross's illustrations would the supposed right constitute an easement, for it would be wholly extraneous to, and independent of, the use of a house as a house, namely, as a place in which the householder and his family live and make their home; and it is for this reason that the analogy which Mr. Cross sought to establish between his illustrations and the present case cannot, in our opinion, be supported. A much closer analogy, as it seems to us, is the case of a man selling the freehold of part of his house and granting to the purchaser, his heirs and assigns, the right, appurtenant to such part, to use the garden in common with the vendor and his assigns. In such a case, the test of connexion, or accommodation, would be amply satisfied; for just as the use of a garden undoubtedly enhances, and is connected with, the normal enjoyment of the house to which it belongs, so also would the right granted, in the case supposed, be closely connected with the use and enjoyment of the part of the premises sold. Such, we think, is in substance the position in the present case. The park became a communal garden for the benefit and enjoyment of those whose houses adjoined it or were in its close proximity. Its flower beds, lawns and walks were calculated to afford all the amenities which it is the purpose of the garden of a house to provide; and, apart from the fact that these amenities extended to a number of householders, instead of being confined to one (which on this aspect of the case is immaterial), we can see no difference in principle between Ellenborough Park and a garden in the ordinary signification of that word. It is the collective garden of the neighbouring houses, to whose use it was dedicated by the owners of the estate and as such amply satisfied, in our judgment, the requirement of connexion with the dominant tenements to which it is appurtenant. The result is not affected by the circumstance that the right to the park is in this case enjoyed by some few houses which are not immediately fronting on the park. The test for present purposes, no doubt, is that the park should constitute in a real and intelligible sense the garden (albeit the communal garden) of the houses to which its enjoyment is annexed. But we think that the test is satisfied as regards these few neighbouring, though not adjacent, houses. We think that the extension of the right of enjoyment to these few houses does not negative the presence of the necessary "nexus" between the subject-matter enjoyed and the premises to which the enjoyment is expressed to belong.

Mr. Cross referred us to, and to some extent relied upon, *Hill v. Tupper*, but in our opinion there is nothing in that case contrary to the view which we have expressed. In that case, the owner of land adjoining a canal was granted the exclusive right to let boats out for hire on the canal. He did so and then sought to restrain a similar activity by a neighbouring landowner. He sought to establish that his grant constituted an easement but failed. Pollock CB said in his judgment:

> It is not competent to create rights unconnected with the use and enjoyment of land, and annex them to it so as to constitute a property in the grantee.

It is clear that what the plaintiff was trying to do was to set up, under the guise of an easement, a monopoly which had no normal connexion with the ordinary use of his land, but which was merely an independent business enterprise. So far from the right claimed sub-serving or accommodating the land, the land was but a convenient incident to the exercise of the right.

For the reasons which we have stated, we are unable to accept the contention that the right to the full enjoyment of Ellenborough Park fails in limine to qualify as a legal easement for want of the necessary connexion between its enjoyment and the use of the properties comprised in the conveyance of 1864, and in the other relevant conveyances.

DISCUSSION NOTES

i. Defining the Nature of "Accommodation"

In a note about this decision, AL Goodhart & RE Megarry stated, "Plainly a right appurtenant to houses to use a garden for normal domestic purposes was beneficial to those houses, and so accommodated the dominant tenement." See Goodhart & Megarry, "Jus Spatiandi in a Pleasure Ground" (1956) 72 Law Q Rev 16 at 17. See also Elizabeth Cooke, "Re Ellenborough Park (1955): A Mere Recreation and Amusement" in Nigel P Gravells, ed, *Landmark Cases in Land Law* (Oxford and Portland, OR: Hart, 2013) [*Landmark Cases in Land Law*]. By contrast, other authors have criticized the distinctions created by *Ellenborough Park* and *Hill v Tupper*. For example, Ziff identified several possible ways of looking at the decision in *Hill v Tupper*:

[In that case,] it was decided that an exclusive right to place boats on a lake did not accommodate the dominant tenement, because such a monopoly was unconnected with the normal use and enjoyment of the land. *Hill v. Tupper* is an important case in the development of the law of easements, but the general principle it establishes is not obvious. If the ruling means that an easement does not meet the second requirement if it serves only to enhance business activity, then it seems both illogical and inconsistent with other authority [citing *Moody v Steggles* (1879), 12 Ch D 261]. In the case the dominant land was used in connection with the boating operations, and the monopoly obviously made that enterprise more viable, so the ruling might be too restrictive, even wrong. Another approach to this issue, one that would support the holding in the case, is to regard easements as serving to supply an attribute of ownership normally or frequently associated with land. Viewed in this way, the law of easements is designed to allow such deficiencies to be remedied. Because the bundle of rights over land does not include monopolies of the type found in *Hill v. Tupper*, the Court in that case was correct in rejecting the easement claim.

(Ziff at 378.) Ziff's criticism suggests that the English Court of Appeal might have seized the opportunity to clarify *Hill v Tupper* in the context of deciding *Ellenborough Park*. Note that Ziff's critique does not suggest that *Ellenborough Park* was itself wrongly decided, only that the basis for distinguishing it from *Hill v Tupper* may not withstand careful scrutiny. Do you agree? In a similar critique, Gray & Gray suggested that the issue of whether a right accommodates the dominant tenement (and therefore constitutes an easement) may reflect a value judgment about the specific interest claimed:

This test of "accommodation" is often heavily coloured by value judgments as to the propriety of conferring long-term protection on various kinds of land use: easements do not exist to safeguard purely personal or idiosyncratic advantage.

(Gray & Gray at 609.)

Is there a difference in the activity of the claimants in *Ellenborough Park* and *Hill v Tupper* that justifies this assertion on the part of Gray & Gray? Do you agree with their observation? For another discussion of this problem, see McClean at 44-45.

ii. Interpreting "Accommodation": Jengle v Keetch

Three cottage properties existed side-by-side. The lot that A owned was subject to an easement or right of way in favour of the adjoining lot, which B owned. B used the easement to gain access to his lot. C, who owned the lot adjoining B's lot, had no easement over the land of either A or B, and thus had to approach his own lot by water. After some years of living with the inconvenience of water access, and unsuccessful negotiations with A for an easement over A's lot, C leased a triangular portion of B's lot as "a parking area," for which C agreed to pay B $500 per year. As B's tenant, C began to use the easement across A's land, and A commenced an action for an injunction and damages for nuisance and trespass. Should A succeed?

In *Jengle v Keetch* (1992), 22 RPR (2d) 53 (Ont CA), the Ontario Court of Appeal reversed the trial decision and allowed A's appeal. Although the appellate court did not decide whether C's right was an easement or merely a licence, the court stated (at 58) that

> [in any event, C's] right of way over the appellants' servient tenement would be restricted to a means of access to and egress from their leased portion of the dominant tenement *for some purpose connected with the enjoyment of their portion of the dominant tenement* . . . . If therefore, [C's] object and purpose in entering into the lease was to park vehicles on [B's] property in order to reach his own property, it would constitute an unlawful user of the right of way. [Emphasis in original.]

Is this conclusion too restrictive as an application of the principle that an easement must accommodate the dominant tenement?

iii. Accommodation and Parking: Depew v Wilkes

In *Depew v Wilkes* (2002), 60 OR (3d) 499 (CA), the Ontario Court of Appeal reviewed the requirement that an easement must accommodate the dominant tenement. In *Depew*, a group of cottage owners was entitled, by way of easements granted to each of them, to use a lane called Willow Beach Lane to travel from a public roadway to their cottages on Lake Erie. Willow Beach Lane was part of lot 13, owned by the Depews. For many years, the cottage owners had used Willow Beach Lane not only to travel to their cottages but also to park their vehicles in front of their cottages; this use exceeded their rights pursuant to the easements. (In addition, one of the cottage owners had built a pier in front of the cottage, and there were other acts that were not consistent with their limited interests.) According to the Court of Appeal, the parking issue presented the main point of the dispute between the parties. The Depews argued that, although it was obvious that the cottage owners found it convenient to park in front of their cottages on lot 13, the requirement that an easement must accommodate the dominant tenement meant that the cottage owners had to show that the easement was "reasonably necessary for the better enjoyment" of the dominant tenement, citing *Ellenborough Park.* After referring to other recent decisions in the Ontario Court of Appeal, Rosenberg JA concluded (at para 24ff):

> In the present case, I agree with the respondents that the appellants had to establish that parking was, in the words of *Ellenborough Park*, "reasonably necessary for the better enjoyment" of the dominant tenements. The reasonable necessity requirement is fact specific and must be applied in a flexible manner … .
>
> The trial judge found that parking on Lot 13 does accommodate the dominant tenements:
>
> > Considering all of the evidence on the size of the lots and the availability of public parking, I would conclude that parking is reasonably necessary in this case. The lots are, for the most part, built in and only 50' by 60' in total. The public parking available is on Commercial

Road and, in the Court's view, a less than satisfactory alternative. I would conclude that parking is reasonably necessary.

. . .

I agree with that conclusion. The parking is connected with the normal enjoyment of the property. As the *Caldwell* case [*Caldwell v Elia* (2000), OAC 379, 30 RPR (3d) 295 (CA)] demonstrates, the fact that an alternative exists does not preclude a finding that the easement is reasonably necessary for the better enjoyment of that tenement.

In *Depew*, the appellants successfully claimed an easement by prescription (length of user), an issue addressed below. The Court of Appeal also reversed a requirement imposed by the trial judge that the cottage owners pay an annual fee to the defendant to park their vehicles on lot 13, observing that there would have to be some unconscionable conduct by the appellants in order to justify such an award, and that the court possessed no general discretion to force the acquirer of a prescriptive easement to pay for it. According to the lawyer who acted for the cottage owners, the outcome in the Court of Appeal did not represent a significant legal change, but was more consistent with current societal views about parking as "reasonably necessary and ancillary to rights of access." See Julius Melnitzer, "Ruling Clarifies Law on Easements," *Law Times* (28 October 2002) 10. The lawyer for the Depews, however, suggested that cottage owners "will have to be wary of neighbours parking on their property." Do you agree that the decision of the Court of Appeal simply reflects society's acceptance of the need for parking as "reasonably necessary"? Is a parking space at a cottage in Ontario similar to the court's assertion in *Ellenborough Park* in the United Kingdom that "the use of a garden undoubtedly enhances ... the normal enjoyment of the house to which it belongs"? You may want to reconsider these arguments in relation to issues about prescriptive easements discussed below.

Depew is similar to other recent cases concerning easements, many of which have attempted to clarify the scope of activities permitted on servient lands. For examples, see *Re Wouters v Forjay Developments Limited* (1998), 38 OR (3d) 369 (Gen Div): a dispute between successors in title to adjacent owners who had shared a driveway to gain access to cottages on Lake Huron; *Lefferty v Brindley* (2001), 8 RPR (4th) 279 (Ont Sup Ct J): parking of vehicles on a right of way held ancillary to the grant of right of way; and *MacKenzie v Matthews* (1999), 46 OR (3d) 21 (CA): a right of way was recognized, but subject to the installation of an unlocked gate to discourage access except by the owners of the dominant lands.

3. The Dominant and Servient Tenements Cannot Be Owned or Occupied by the Same Persons

This requirement appears to be common sense because there would typically be more extensive rights available to an owner of land than could be granted by an easement. However, this issue may arise in a context where two parcels of land have been owned by different persons (with an easement in place) and the owner of the dominant tenement subsequently acquires by purchase the servient tenement as well. What happens if the owner then sells the servient tenement to a third party? Similarly, issues may arise in the context of land development where there are good reasons for creating easements in relation to lots for sale, prior to the lots being transferred to individual owners. The problem has also arisen in the context of a tenant's easement where the landlord retains title to the property overall. For further discussion of these issues, see *Gale on Easements* at 1-31 to 1-35.

At common law, where the dominant and servient tenements both came into the hands of the same owner who also occupied both parcels, the easement was extinguished by reason of the doctrine of merger. However, statutory reform in some provinces has solved this problem by abolishing the doctrine of merger in such situations: see e.g. the Nova Scotia *Land Registration Act*, SNS 2001, c 6, ss 61(2) and (3):

> (2) A registered owner may create, by grant or otherwise, a right of way, restrictive covenant or easement for the benefit of the registered owner and that right-of-way, restrictive covenant or easement may be recorded pursuant to this Act.
>
> (3) Where dominant and servient tenement parcels are registered in the name of the same person, a right of way, restrictive covenant or easement referred to in subsection (2) is not merged by reason of the common ownership.

Do you think this reform should be adopted in other Canadian provinces?

4. *The Easement Must Be Capable of Forming the Subject Matter of a Grant*

Because an easement is a non-possessory interest, it cannot be created by a transfer of possession. Thus there is a need for a grant. However, as a number of commentators have suggested, this requirement presents some difficulty. According to McClean (at 61), for example, this fourth requirement for the creation of an easement is "both obscure and unhelpful." In *Ellenborough Park*, [1956] 1 Ch D 131 (CA), the English Court of Appeal identified three grounds for determining whether the rights in question met this fourth requirement and thus constituted an easement. The rights in question did not constitute an easement if they:

- were too vague;
- amounted to a claim to joint occupation of the park or would have substantially deprived the owners of proprietorship or legal possession; and
- were ones of mere recreation and amusement and were not of utility and benefit.

In *Ellenborough Park*, the court held that the rights claimed were not too vague, that they did not amount to claims to joint occupation, and that they represented claims beyond mere recreation and amusement and were of real utility and benefit. These factors have been important in recent litigation in Canada as well. In examining the following decision, consider how the fourth requirement (and particularly its relationship to an easement's "non-possessory" nature) was defined by the court.

Shelf Holdings Ltd v Husky Oil Operations Ltd
(1989), 56 DLR (4th) 193 (Alta CA)

[One issue in this case concerned a grant of easement in favour of the appellant, Husky Oil, to permit construction of a pipeline under lands owned by the respondent. The grant permitted the respondent, owner of the servient tenement, to continue farming the surface of the land. The issue of whether the interest was an easement or a possessory interest was relevant to the enforceability of the interest in light of the registration provisions of the *Land Titles Act*, RSA 1980, c L-5, ss 64 and 65(1)(g). The interest would be enforceable if it were an easement, but probably not if it were another kind of property interest. At trial, the court concluded that the interest conveyed, in spite of the language used in the grant, represented an interest in land rather than an easement because it conveyed a right to possession. The appellant appealed from this decision.]

HADDAD JA:

The Issue

With due respect to the considered reasons delivered by the learned trial judge, I am of the opinion that the interest conveyed in the grant of easement is a right of way in the form of an easement and not a grant of an interest in land yielding exclusive rights consistent with ownership. I construe the grant of easement as merely conferring upon Husky certain rights of occupation of a corridor for the purposes of a pipeline without divesting the owner of the servient tenement of its proprietary rights. Moreover, the easement attaches to the land by implication and without endorsement on the title by virtue of the provisions of the *Land Titles Act*, s. 65(1)(g).

The grant of easement must be recognized as a contract reflecting the terms of the agreement made by the contracting parties. It is elementary that any contract is the primary source of reference to determine a dispute involving the rights and obligations of those parties. Where a dispute arises over rights involving the acquisition of lands those rights are also subjected to and governed by legislative enactments regulating land titles.

The grant of easement provides that in consideration of the payment of a sum of money by the grantee (Husky) to the grantor (Peregrym) "and the grantee hereby covenanting to perform and observe all of the terms and conditions hereinafter mentioned on the part of the grantee to be performed and observed," the grantor does

> GRANT, TRANSFER and CONVEY unto and to the Grantee, for itself, its servants, agents and contractors, the right, license, liberty, privilege and easement to use so much of the said lands as may be necessary for a right-of-way for the laying down, construction, operation, maintenance, inspection, removal, replacement, reconstruction and repair of a pipeline together with all such stations, drips, valves, fittings, meters and other equipment and appurtenances as may be necessary or convenient in connection therewith, for the carriage, conveyance, transportation and handling of petroleum or petroleum products, water and/or gas through or by means of the same, and the right of ingress and egress for all purposes incidental to this grant as and from the date hereof and for so long hereafter as the Grantee may desire to exercise the rights and privileges hereby given, on the following terms and conditions: ...

> SECOND: The Grantor shall not without the prior written consent of the Grantee, excavate, drill, install, erect or permit to be excavated, drilled, installed or erected on or under the said right-of-way any pit, well, foundation, pavement, or other structure or installation, but otherwise the Grantor shall have the right fully to use and enjoy the said right-of-way except as the same may be necessary for the purposes herein granted to the Grantee.

> THIRD: The Grantee shall have the right to do whatever may be requisite for the enjoyment of the rights herein granted, including the right of clearing the said right-of-way of timber.

FOURTH: The Grantee shall compensate the Grantor and/or other interested parties, as their respective interests for the time being may appear, for damage done to any crops, pasture, fences or livestock on the said lands by reason of the exercise of the rights hereinbefore granted, and the Grantee will not at any time fence the said right-of-way, except as is hereinafter provided. ...

SIXTH: The Grantee shall, as soon as weather and soil conditions permit, bury and maintain all pipelines so as not to interfere with the drainage or ordinary cultivation of the said lands.

SEVENTH: Upon the abandonment of the said right-of-way and release of all of the rights hereby granted, the Grantee shall and will restore the surface of the said lands to the same condition, so far as may be practicable so to do, as the same were in prior to the entry thereon and the use thereof by the Grantee. ...

NINTH: The Grantee, performing and observing the terms and conditions on its part to be performed and observed, shall and may peaceably hold and enjoy the rights, license, liberty, privileges and easement hereby granted without hindrance, molestation or interruption on the part of the Grantor or of any person, firm or corporation claiming by, through or under the Grantor. ...

Although "easement" is a term to be found in various statutes, the trial judge quite rightly made the observation that neither the word "easement" or the expression "right of way" is given a statutory definition. A right of way is a form of easement. A definition of "right of way" is to be found in Halsbury's Laws of England, 4th ed., vol. 14, para. 144, p. 68:

... a right to utilise the servient tenement as a means of access to or egress from the dominant tenement for some purpose connected with the enjoyment of the dominant tenement, according to the nature of that tenement.

Gale in his text, *Gale on Easements*, 15th ed., at p. 6, is cautious about fixing a precise definition:

An easement was defined by Lord Esher MR in *Metropolitan Railway v. Fowler* as "some right which a person has over land which is not his own," but this definition lacks precision, as not every right which one has over another's land is necessarily an easement, and perhaps no precise definition is possible.

The Court of Appeal of England in *Re Ellenborough Park; Re Davies; Powell v. Maddison*, [1956] 1 Ch. 131 at p. 163, [1955] 3 All ER 667 at p. 673, approved the following characteristics proposed in Dr. Cheshire's *Modern Real Property*, 7th ed., p. 456, to properly identify an easement. He said:

... (1) there must be a dominant and a servient tenement: (2) an easement must "accommodate" the dominant tenement: (3) dominant and servient owners must be different persons, and (4) the easement must be capable of forming the subject-matter of a grant.

The first three characteristics present no problem in this case. The issue at hand concerns the fourth characteristic as the trial judge concluded that this requirement had not been satisfied. Evershed MR in *Re Ellenborough Park* dissected the fourth characteristic into the following three questions:

1. Is the right too wide and vague?

2. Is the grant inconsistent with the proprietorship or possession of the alleged servient owner?

3. Is it a mere right of recreation without utility or benefit?

The issue in this case can be narrowed to resolution of the second question.

The following statement by Lopes LJ in *Reilly v. Booth* (1890), 44 Ch. D 12 at p. 26, provides the premise upon which the learned trial judge proceeded: "[T]here is no easement known to law which gives exclusive and unrestricted use of a piece of land." This statement was quoted with approval in *Metropolitan R Co. v. Fowler*, [1893] AC 416 (HL), to which I will refer in due course. For the reader to better apprehend the statement of Lopes LJ, I will elucidate upon the context in which it was made. The report of that case reveals that certain land which embraced a large yard was conveyed absolutely to one W. A gateway gave access to the yard from a street known as Oxford Street. The conveyance to W was accompanied by the words "Together with the exclusive use of the said gateway into *Oxford Street*." ... The court examined the agreement to ascertain the intention of the parties and found the words "exclusive use" to be explicit and clear. The conveyance was therefore construed as saying that the right of W to the gateway was to be exclusive and consistent with ownership. The comments of Lord Justice Lopes contained this passage from which the foregoing extract as to exclusivity was lifted [(at 26)]:

> I think ownership passed. The exclusive use of the said gateway was given. The exclusive or unrestricted use of a piece of land, I take it, beyond all question passes the property or ownership in that land, and there is no easement known to law which gives exclusive and unrestricted use of a piece of land. It is not an easement in such a case, it is property that passes. Again, a mere easement can be conveyed, or may be conveyed, by words other than these, and would pass under general words.

In *Re Ellenborough Park* characteristic number 4 provided the issue. Unlike *Reilly v. Booth* no express intention could be found in the *Ellenborough* grant. At pp. 175-6 Ch., p. 681 All ER, of the *Re Ellenborough Park* report, Sir Raymond Evershed MR discussed the elements required to satisfy Dr. Cheshire's fourth condition. He said:

> We turn next to Dr. Cheshire's fourth condition for an easement—that the right must be capable of forming the subject-matter of a grant. As we have earlier stated, satisfaction of the condition in the present case depends on the consideration of the questions, whether the right conferred is too wide and vague, whether it is inconsistent with proprietorship or possession of the alleged servient owners, and whether it is a mere right of recreation without utility or benefit.

In reaching his decision in this action the learned trial judge was persuaded by the decision of the Saskatchewan Court of Appeal in *Re Interprovincial Pipeline Co.*, [1951] 2 DLR 187, 1 WWR (NS) 479, 67 CRTC 128, where the document before the court was similar to that under consideration in this appeal. The court there construed the terms of the document to mean that the rights conveyed went beyond the grant of an easement by giving the grantee exclusive use of a portion of the substratum in which the pipeline was buried—thereby conveying an interest in land sufficient to vest title.

The judgment in *Re Interprovincial Pipeline* relied on the decision handed down by the House of Lords in *Metropolitan R Co. v. Fowler, supra*, which adopted the principle expressed by Lopes LJ in *Reilly v. Booth, supra*. The learned trial judge also cited Canadian authorities which applied the same principle. In my opinion *Metropolitan R Co.* and other cases cited by the learned trial judge to support his conclusions are not applicable as they deal with absolute rights to land authorized by statute and can be distinguished.

The *Metropolitan R Co.* litigation was taken to determine the validity of a land tax assessed against the railway in respect of a tunnel it constructed under a highway for an underground rail line. The railway resisted the assessment contending that it merely acquired an easement. The House of Lords held that the railway was vested with more than an easement. It acquired a hereditament for its exclusive use and on that account it was liable for the tax assessed. To be precise, I distinguish this case from *Metropolitan* on the ground that Husky acquired its grant by private agreement which defines the rights of the parties whereas Metropolitan R Co. acquired land for its railway by appropriation pursuant to a statute authorizing the construction of the railway. The "appropriation" vested the land in the railway company for its exclusive use. Lord Herschell LC defines the railway's position in this way, at p. 423:

> Now, my Lords, the language used is this, that "the two companies may appropriate and use the subsoil and undersurface of any such roadway or footway." The word "appropriate" is one which seems to me clearly to point to a right of property becoming vested in the companies; they were to "appropriate and use"; and it seems to me that when they have thus made their appropriation and constructed the tunnel, that tunnel is as much their property as if it had been constructed upon land which they had purchased and paid for, and being their property held by them to the exclusion of any other person, it is as much a hereditament as if it had been constructed on land which they had purchased in the ordinary way.

And at p. 426 Lord Watson expressed the same view. He said:

> To appropriate, according to its natural meaning, is to take and keep a thing by exclusive right; and, as I construed their Act, the authority which it confers upon the company is to take and exclusively possess as much of the subsoil below highways as may be required for the purposes of the undertaking. There is no substantial distinction between the interest which they get by appropriation, and that which they acquire by purchasing in terms of the Lands Clauses Act.

Consumer Gas Co. of Toronto v. City of Toronto (1897), 27 SCR 453 at p. 457, is another tax assessment case. The validity of an assessment for taxes of the mains and pipes to supply gas laid under a highway was challenged and taken to the Supreme Court of Canada. The gas company was given the authority by statute to lay the gas pipes. Citing the *Metropolitan R Co.* case, Chief Justice Strong interpreted the governing statute at p. 457:

> I am of the opinion that the gas pipes of the appellants laid under the streets of the city were under this Act real property belonging to them, and as such liable to assessment. I regard the case of *The Metropolitan Railway Company v. Fowler* as conclusively showing that these pipes are not to be considered chattels placed beneath the public streets and highways, in the exercise of a mere easement, but being affixed to the land, as actual real property within the meaning of the interpretation clause.

Jarvis v. City of Toronto (1894), 21 OAR 395 at p. 400 is also a case of a compulsory acquisition by statute. Osler JA delivering the judgment of the Ontario Court of Appeal again cited the *Metropolitan R Co.* case for the principle that exclusive use of land cannot be equated with an easement. In that case a provincial statute empowered the municipal corporation to pass a by-law authorizing it to take land by compulsion for a sewer. A predecessor in title to the owner of the land through which the sewer was constructed gave his permission to the municipal corporation to acquire the land without the passing of a by-law. The court in these circumstances concluded that the corporation had acquired exclusive use of the land. Osler JA said at p. 400:

> What may thus be compulsorily taken from the owner by means of a by-law duly passed, may, of course, be acquired by agreement of the parties, and may be granted and assigned to the corporation by an appropriate conveyance. Property thus acquired for the permanent and exclusive use of the municipality for the construction thereon of a sewer is not properly described as an easement. ...

It is worthy of note that six months after the release of the judgment in this action MacPherson J gave judgment in the Court of Queen's Bench in the case of *Card v. Trans-Alta Utilities Corp.* (1987), 57 Alta. LR (2d) 155, where a similar issue arose. Mr. Justice MacPherson described [at 156] the issue there as "... whether an unregistered easement can be enforced and if so is there a proper easement in this case." The defendant TransAlta, pursuant to an agreement with a landowner, constructed a power line across the owner's land. The plaintiff subsequently purchased the land and acquired title free and clear of an endorsement for an easement. The plaintiffs contended, firstly, that the agreement did not create an easement and, secondly, that in any event it was ineffectual for lack of registration.

Mr. Justice MacPherson, rejecting the plaintiff's stand, held that the agreement did provide for an easement as it met the criteria set out in *Ellenborough Park, supra*. At the same time he also rejected the proposition that the right granted to TransAlta involved exclusive and permanent occupation to create a proprietary interest in the land. Moreover, he said that notwithstanding lack of registration the title was subject to the easement by implication pursuant to the exception provided by s. 65(1)(g).

Belanger v. CP Ltd. (1978), 93 DLR (3d) 734, [1979] 1 WWR 734; reversing 65 DLR (3d) 726, [1976] 3 WWR 235 (QB), like *Interprovincial*, is a decision of the Saskatchewan Court of Appeal and in that instance gave recognition to the implied exception to indefeasibility according to s. 71(c) of the *Land Titles Act* of that province, the provisions of which are similar to s. 65(1).

I have had the opportunity of perusing two articles from which I have derived assistance in the preparation of these reasons. I allude firstly to an article entitled "The Nature of an Easement," 5 Western L Rev. 32, by Albert J. McClean. The second article, "The Road Not Taken: Some Important Questions About the Nature of Easements," 57 Alta. LR (2d) 326 (1988), authored by M.M. Litman and B.H. Ziff, is a commentary on the judgment subject of this appeal. The influence of these articles will be reflected to some extent in the remarks which follow.

The key to resolving the issue at hand is to look at the grant of easement to assess the extent of the rights relinquished by Peregrym as opposed to the rights it reserved.

The simple test applied by Lindley LJ in *Reilly v. Booth, supra*, at p. 25, is this: "Now if we look at the matter we must see what has been granted and what has been reserved."

The author Gale in his book, *supra*, at p. 139, describes the modern interpretive approach:

> The modern tendency, as has been seen, is to rest the right to an easement on the supposed intention of the parties to the contract, or, if there was no contract, on the intention of the testator or grantor, irrespectively of the presence of general words in the conveyance.

In his article "The Nature of an Easement," Mr. McClean, at p. 51, puts into perspective the quality and extent of the limitations a grant will impose upon the servient tenement and the balancing process to be engaged to ascertain whether the grant is an easement or something more. I adopt these general observations:

> As was pointed out earlier, it follows from the general nature of the recognized interests in property that an easement cannot amount to a claim quite at variance with the proprietary rights of the servient owner. On the other hand, it is also quite obvious that an easement does to some extent detract from those rights. A right of way cuts down the servient owner's right to exclude people from his property or to develop it as he pleases; and a negative easement such as light, also hinders development. The issue in fact is the perennial one of drawing the line, of deciding when the point has been reached that the right in question detracts so substantially from the rights of the servient owner that it must be something other than an easement.
>
> Where this problem has been the most canvassed is in relation to the degree of occupation or possession of the servient tenement that is compatible with the existence of an easement.

The degree of occupation or possession will be governed by the document conceding the grant. I mention this simply to point out that Mr. McClean's approach, in effect, falls within the test adopted by Lindley LJ.

By the very nature of an easement it is inevitable that some measure of occupation by the easement taker is present in all cases—and that the dominant tenement will to some extent, at least, interfere with the servient tenement. Moreover, because of the rights it carries, an easement, for its limited purpose, is an interest in land.

By the character of its utility the purpose of an easement is to confer a benefit on the dominant tenement. At p. 17 of his text Gale reminds us that "An easement must accommodate the dominant tenement." This easement accomplishes that aim.

Examination of the grant in this case discloses, in my view, that the privileges granted to Husky do not detract from the servient owner's rights of ownership.

The tenor of the grant is such that it reflects the intention of the parties that the grantee Husky acquire a benefit subject to its compliance with certain terms and conditions. The right of Shelf as the servient owner to use the land free from interference has been curtailed to the extent only of prohibiting it from interfering with the subsoil or to erect works on the strip comprising the right of way "but otherwise the Grantor shall have the right fully to use and enjoy the said right-of-way except as the same may be necessary for the purposes herein granted to the Grantee."

I infer from the material filed and the comments of counsel that the lands are farm lands. It is apparent from the literal construction of the second term that curtailment of the appellant's use of its land does not deprive it completely of use of the surface of the right of way. All conventional rights of way will, to some degree, impair the use of the land.

The fourth term requires Husky to compensate the grantor (Shelf) for damages to crops, pasture, fences and livestock occasioned by the exercise of its rights and prohibits Husky from fencing the right of way thereby leaving Shelf free to cultivate and run cattle over the surface. This in effect allows Shelf full use of the entire parcel subject only to those limitations prescribed in the second term. Moreover, Husky in burying and maintaining its pipeline is prohibited from interfering with the drainage or ordinary cultivation of the lands.

The seventh term obliges Husky upon abandonment of the right of way to restore the lands to the same condition as they were prior to its use and entry thereon. This contemplates that the right of way will revert to Shelf after it has served Husky's purposes. I read this as confirmation that the parties intended the grant to create nothing more than an easement.

The ninth term is not consistent with the conveyance of an interest in land to Husky. It recognizes the mutual undertakings of the parties and it is explicit in providing that Husky is entitled to enjoy the rights it received under the grant subject to it "performing and observing the terms and conditions on its part to be performed and observed." I construe this paragraph to say that the rights conferred on Husky under the grant will be subject to termination in the event of its failure to perform and observe.

Husky acquired from Peregrym the privilege of using a corridor across a parcel consisting of 150 acres, and nothing more. The document reserves to the servient tenement a high degree of possession and control with only a low level of interference from the dominant tenement. The rights granted to Husky do not detract from the rights of the servient owner with the force required to raise the grant above the status of an easement. The grant is free of the words "appropriate" and "exclusive use" or words of that connotation. I view the document as having been devised to ensure that [the] servient owner's property rights in the corridor are preserved.

It is common knowledge that grants of easements for pipelines have been widely used in the development of the petroleum industry and accepted and operate as easements.

Accordingly in my judgment the grant to Husky is an easement valid and enforceable within the scope of s. 65(1)(g).

I would allow the appeal with costs to Husky here and at trial.

Appeal allowed.

DISCUSSION NOTES

i. "Exclusive" Possession and Intention

Do you agree with the analysis of the Court of Appeal? For a critique of the trial decision, see M Litman & B Ziff, "The Road Not Taken: Some Important Questions About the Nature of Easements" (1988) 57 Alta LR (2d) 326. According to Gray & Gray, the issue of whether an interest is an easement, using the test of "non-exclusive possession," has not been applied consistently in the cases. For example, see *Copeland v Greenhalf*, [1952] Ch 488, where the court held that the defendant's use for over 50 years of a strip of land (owned by the plaintiff) for storing vehicles being repaired was a claim of "joint user of the land," not an easement. See also *Ward v Kirkland*, [1967] 1 Ch 194; *Grigsby v Melville*, [1972] 1 WLR 1355; *Wright v Macadam*, [1949] 2 KB 744; and *Miller v Emcer Products*, [1956] 1 Ch 304. As Gray & Gray suggest (at 623), it may be difficult to reconcile all these cases:

> The courts may, on occasion, have used the supposed requirement of non-exclusive user as a smokescreen for judicial discretion, invoking the requirement in order to strike down claims felt to be unmeritorious while suppressing the requirement in cases where it has been thought that a remedy should be given.

Does this comment apply to the decision in *Husky Oil*? Why might the court have "thought that a remedy should be given" in this case? Are there other bases for reaching the same conclusion? Although the Federal Court decision in *Gypsum Carrier*, discussed earlier, did not analyze in detail the four requirements for the existence of an easement, consider whether you are in agreement with the court that all four requirements were met in that case. If you conclude that the four requirements were met, why did the court in that case conclude that the interest of the railway companies was not an easement? To what extent did the court in *Husky Oil* rely on the parties' intentions in defining the interest created as an easement? See also *820204 Alberta Ltd v McLarty* (2002), 6 RPR (4th) 146 (Alta QB), where the court gave detailed instructions about the use of land subject to an easement.

ii. The "Jus Spatiandi": Sufficiently Definite?

The requirement that an interest must be capable of forming the subject matter of a grant to be recognized as an easement has also been interpreted as a requirement that the nature of the interest granted must be sufficiently definite. This requirement was considered extensively in *Ellenborough Park* because the nature of the interest there permitted the owners of the surrounding houses to walk in the garden or park. Thus, there was a question as to whether the interest created was merely a *jus spatiandi*—that is, a right to wander at will—which could be regarded as indefinite in scope. The decision of the court was that the right granted was well defined and differed from that encompassed in the term "*jus spatiandi*" (although the court also seemed to approve of the *jus spatiandi* as capable of being an easement in some cases as well: see *Ellenborough Park* at 179-87). In this context, the court also adverted to the issue of whether the right was one of "mere recreation or amusement." In doing so it referred to a prior decision, *Mounsey v Ismay* (1863), 3 H & C 363, in which the inhabitants of a village claimed a prescriptive right to enter on a piece of land and hold horse races there once a year. Baron Martin found that such a right could not exist as an easement because it involved "mere recreation or amusement," to which the court in *Ellenborough Park* responded (at 179):

> [W]e do not think that the right to use a garden of the character with which we are concerned in this case can be called one of mere recreation and amusement, as those words were used by Martin B. No doubt a garden is a pleasure—on high authority, it is the purest of pleasures—but, in our judgment, it is not a right having no quality either of utility or benefit as those words should be understood. The right here in suit is, for reasons already given, one appurtenant to the surrounding houses as such, and constitutes a beneficial attribute of residence in a house as ordinarily understood. Its use for the purposes, not only of exercise and rest but also for such domestic

purposes as were suggested in argument—for example, for taking out small children in peram-bulators or otherwise—is not fairly to be described as one of mere recreation or amusement, and is clearly beneficial to the premises to which it is attached. If Baron Martin's test is applied, the right in suit is, in point of utility, fairly analogous to a right of way passing over fields to, say, the railway station, which would be none the less a good right, even though it provided a longer route to the objective. We think, therefore, that the statement of Baron Martin must at least be confined to exclusion of rights to indulge in such recreations as were in question in the case before him, horse racing or perhaps playing games, and has no application to the facts of the present case.

As appears from what has been stated earlier, the right to the full enjoyment of Ellenborough Park, which was granted by the 1864 and other relevant conveyances, was, in substance, no more than a right to use the park as a garden in the way in which gardens are commonly used. In a sense, no doubt, such a right includes something of a *jus spatiandi*, inasmuch as it involves the principle of wandering at will round each part of the garden, except of course, such parts as comprise flower beds, or are laid out for some other purpose, which renders walking impossible or unsuitable. We doubt, nevertheless, whether the right to use and enjoy a garden in this man-ner can with accuracy be said to constitute a mere *jus spatiandi*.

According to McClean, this conclusion shows "a willingness to look at the actual terms of the grant and a disposition not to judge certainty 'in the air' nor to assume that because the rights are wide in their scope they must '*ipso facto*' be uncertain": see McClean at 51.

For an example of a case in which this issue was considered by the Supreme Court of Can-ada, see *Dukart v District of Surrey*, [1978] 2 SCR 1039. In that case, the court examined in detail the wording of a document used by a development company in British Columbia, providing that the Foreshore Reserves (beside Boundary Bay) were to be held "for the pur-pose of giving free access to the waters of the Bay" to persons who owned houses in the surrounding subdivision. Prior to his examination of the documents to determine whether they created an easement, Estey J stated (at 1050):

> At one time there may have been some doubt as to whether a right to cross over or move gener-ally about on another's land was a right known in the common law as an easement, but this matter was put to rest [in] *Re Ellenborough Park*.

For a somewhat different view of the extent to which a right to wander over another's land meets the requirement of definiteness in the United States, see the American Law Insti-tute, *Restatement of the Law of Property* (1944) [American Law Institute (1944)], vol 5, s 450(e): Commentary.

C. The Creation of Easements: General Principles

In general, easements are expressly created by way of grant or by way of reservation. In the case of a grant, a vendor sells part of a larger parcel of land to a purchaser, granting the pur-chaser a right of way—for example, over the land retained by the vendor. In this example, the purchaser holds the dominant tenement and the vendor holds the servient tenement. By contrast, if the vendor sells the parcel to the purchaser, with a reservation of a right of way over the purchaser's land in favour of the vendor, the purchaser's land is the servient tene-ment, while the vendor holds the dominant tenement. A detailed analysis of the concept of "reservation" is beyond the scope of this chapter, even though it often raises important issues in relation to easements and related interests in land. For a good overview, see Ziff at 385-86; for an example, see *Polstra v Pierlot Family Farm Ltd* (2003), 227 Nfld & PEIR 84 (PEI SC (App Div)). The issue of whether a Crown patent had included a reservation, by contrast with an exception, was canvassed at great length in a dispute about the public's continued right to use a beach at Grand Bend on Lake Huron: see *Gibbs v Grand Bend (Village)* (1995), 26 OR (3d) 644 (CA), (1989), 71 OR (2d) 70, 64 DLR (4th) 28 (H Ct J).

1. Express Grant or Reservation: Hill v Attorney General of Nova Scotia

Many easements are created by express grant or express reservation and included as part of a deed transferring a fee simple estate to a purchaser. Such a grant or reservation must comply with requirements for the transfer of an interest in land, such as those in the *Statute of Frauds* (see Chapter 5). In addition, easements may be created in equity by an agreement to grant or reserve that is enforceable by specific performance, in accordance with the doctrine of *Walsh v Lonsdale* (1882), 21 Ch D 9 (CA). Although it may not technically appear to be an express grant or reservation, it is also possible to create an equitable easement pursuant to the doctrine of part performance. See Ziff at 382. Easements may also be created expressly by statute, especially in relation to public utilities.

In *Hill v Nova Scotia (Attorney General)*, [1997] 1 SCR 69, 142 DLR (4th) 230, considered in Chapter 5, the appellants claimed entitlement to compensation as a result of provincial expropriation of an easement. In 1966, the province had expropriated farmland, then owned by the appellant's father, in order to construct a section of the Trans-Canada Highway in Nova Scotia. In carrying out the expropriation, the province severed the farm with one parcel north of the highway and the other to the south. In constructing the Trans-Canada Highway, the Nova Scotia Department of Highways created two ramps from the north and south parcels to the highway, fences on both sides of the highway, and gateways across the ramps. Subsequently, in 1992, when the highway was expanded by the construction of two additional lanes (for which no additional land was required to be expropriated), the access ramps were removed, and the appellants were advised that access to the highway from these ramps was prohibited. The appellants claimed compensation on the basis of an expropriation of an easement as a result of the 1992 construction. Assuming that the documents relating to the expropriation in 1966 did not expressly refer to a grant of an easement, on what basis could the appellants succeed in claiming that there was a grant of an easement?

The appellants initially succeeded before Scanlan J in chambers, on the basis of affidavits describing the 1966 negotiations relating to the expropriation. The chambers judge held that the province had granted an equitable easement across the highway in 1966. This decision was reversed by the Nova Scotia Court of Appeal, but the Supreme Court of Canada allowed the appeal, citing (at 236) *Steadman v Steadman*, [1976] AC 536 (HL) in relation to the doctrine of part performance:

> In summary, there was then a representation made by authorized representatives of the Crown that Hill would have an interest orally and by letters ... permitting him to cross the highway with cattle and equipment. There was the compliance by the Crown with its representations by means of both construction and maintenance. It was contemplated that Hill would, as he did, rely upon them. He did so to his detriment. The words and actions of the Crown created an equitable interest

in the land in the form of a right of way over the highway. The Crown intended it to be used and it was for over 27 years. It would be unjust not to recognize the representations and actions of the Crown which created the equitable interest in land when they were relied upon by Hill.

Accordingly, the Supreme Court of Canada concluded that the appellants were entitled to compensation in relation to the 1992 expropriation of their equitable interest in land. In *Maritime Telegraph and Telephone Co v Chateau Lafleur Development Corp* (2001), 207 DLR (4th) 443 (NSCA), the Nova Scotia Court of Appeal confirmed the existence of an equitable easement created by a written but unregistered agreement between Maritime and the former owners of Chateau's property.

By contrast, in *Lanty v Ontario (Minister of Natural Resources)*, 2006 CanLII 1452, [2006] OJ no 239 (SC), aff'd 2007 ONCA 759 (CanLII), the trial judge found that "any reasonable reading" of the correspondence between the parties with respect to an alleged equitable easement did not support the plaintiff's claim. The plaintiff bought a cottage at Wasaga Beach Provincial Park in 1978. At that time, access to the cottage involved driving over 150 feet of beach after passing through a locked gate, to which the plaintiff was issued a key. Before purchasing the property Ms Lanty wrote to the Ministry of Natural Resources requesting confirmation that she would have a right of way for vehicles. She asserted that when the letter she received in reply from the park superintendent did not deny that such a right of way existed, she acted in reliance on it and purchased the property. In 1998, park officials changed the lock on the gate and denied Ms Lanty vehicular access over the beach, citing safety concerns to beachgoers. Ms Lanty continued to have pedestrian access and parking spots provided by the park, about 400 feet from the cottage, and vehicular access for emergency and maintenance purposes. The trial judge found that the letter did not constitute a representation that a right of way existed, nor had the Ministry made any other representations to that effect. Ms Lanty's access had always been by permission, never by right, and could be revoked by the Ministry at any time. Citing her "unreasonable and uncooperative behaviour," the trial judge awarded costs of $133,800 against Ms Lanty, an award upheld by the Court of Appeal.

2. *Implied Grant or Reservation: Necessity, Common Intention, and Non-Derogation—Hirtle v Ernst*

There are a number of different principles for implying the existence of an easement when none has been expressly created. For example, an easement of necessity has been recognized where a parcel of land has been transferred and is completely landlocked and without access, so long as there is adjoining land retained by the vendor over which an easement can be created. This principle may, however, be difficult to apply in practice—must the land be completely inaccessible, inaccessible by land but accessible by water, or inaccessible only with great difficulty or expense? In *Dobson v Tulloch* (1994), 17 OR (3d) 533 (Gen Div), the court concluded that the defendants were entitled to an easement in relation to their cottage property, which was completely landlocked except for a small portion that abutted the Mississagi River. They were thus entitled to an easement over land owned by a neighbouring owner who had initially brought an action for trespass against the defendants when she (the neighbouring owner) "became irritated with the increased traffic resulting from construction … and visits from family members" (at 538). In this case, the court declined to hold that access by way of the river made the defendants' lot accessible, distinguishing other authorities such as *Fitchett v Mellow* (1897), 29 OR 6 (H Ct J). An appeal from this decision was dismissed: (1997), 33 OR (3d) 800 (CA). (In *Dobson*, the trial court also held that there was an implied easement of "apparent accommodations," in addition to an implied easement of necessity, and that the defendants were entitled to succeed on the basis of s 15 of the *Conveyancing and Law of Property Act*, RSO 1990, c C.34. For a similar provision, see *Property Act*, RSNB 1973, c P-19, s 22.)

Recall *Jengle v Keetch*, referred to above in relation to the requirement that an easement must accommodate the dominant tenement. In *Jengle*, the essential problem was the lack of road access to C's cottage, although it was accessible by water: using *Dobson v Tulloch*, would C have achieved greater success by claiming an easement of necessity? In considering this possibility, it may be important to note that courts are generally cautious in concluding that an easement of necessity has been created. For example, in *Hough v Alberta* (2000), 284 AR 382 (QB), the Alberta Court of Queen's Bench denied the existence of an easement of necessity over an existing gravel road in circumstances where the claimant faced inconvenience and expense in constructing its own road; because the claimant had a means of access, it had not established the need for an easement of necessity. By contrast, courts appeared to recognize easements of necessity in *Babine Investments Ltd v Prince George Shopping Centre Ltd* (2002), 212 DLR (4th) 537, 49 RPR (3d) 187 (BCCA) and in *Canada Lands Co CLC Ltd v Trizechahn Office Properties Ltd* (2000), 31 RPR (3d) 39 (Alta QB).

Principles about the creation of an easement of necessity were reviewed in a Nova Scotia decision, *Hirtle v Ernst*, 1991 CanLII 4297, 21 RPR (2d) 95 (NSSC (TD)). The applicant was seeking a certificate under the *Quieting Titles Act*, RSNS 1989, c 382 in relation to his parcel of land, as well as a declaration of a right of way of necessity. The applicant had purchased a parcel of land bounded on three sides by Big Mushamush Lake and on the fourth side by a neighbouring parcel of land, without access to a roadway. The applicant purchased his lot knowing that it was landlocked and after making some unsuccessful attempts to purchase a right of way. He wished to build a home on the parcel and there was evidence that it would be difficult to transport all the needed materials by water because of a lack of docking facilities on the lake.

Nathanson J reviewed the principles concerning easements of necessity and held that when a larger parcel had been divided between two brothers in 1857, one brother (a predecessor in title to the applicant) received a landlocked parcel and, consequently, an easement of necessity had been created at that time. He considered *Fitchett v Mellow*, where an Ontario court had concluded that an inconvenient means of access by water meant that a lot could not be characterized as inaccessible. He also referred to two decisions in New Brunswick concerning landlocked cottage lots bordering on water, in which courts had recognized easements of necessity: see *Harris v Jervis* (1980), 31 NBR (2d) 264, 75 APR 264 (QB) and *Michalak v Patterson* (1986), 72 NBR (2d) 421, 183 APR 421 (QB), and a number of US decisions recognizing easements of necessity. Suggesting that the doctrine of easements of necessity had continued to evolve over the years, he formulated the following principles in reaching a conclusion (at 107) that the applicant was entitled to an easement of necessity in *Hirtle v Ernst*:

1. The doctrine of right of way of necessity is based on public policy—that land should be able to be used and not rendered useless (see Goddard, *A Treatise on the Law of Easements* ... , pp. 359-361; *Feoffees of Grammar School in Ipswich v. Proprietors of Jeffreys' Neck Passage* ... ; and *Hancock v. Henderson* ...).

2. Although there can be no right of way of necessity where there is an alternative inconvenient means of access, the requirement of an absolute necessity or a strict necessity has developed into a rule of practical necessity (see *Redman v. Kidwell* ... , and *Littlefield v. Hubbard* ...).

3. Water access is not considered to be the same as access over adjacent land (see *Harris v. Jervis* ... ; *Michalak v. Patterson* ... ; *Hancock v. Henderson* ... ; and *William Dahm Realty v. Cardel* ...). That is especially so in cases where the water access is not as of right, or would be contrary to law (see Megarry and Wade, *The Law of Real Property* ... , at p. 831), where access is not available for transportation of things needed for reasonable use of the land to be accessed (see *Feoffees of Grammar School in Ipswich v. Proprietors of Jeffreys' Neck Passage*, supra), where the water access does not have transportation facilities for carrying on the ordinary and necessary activities of life to and from the land (see *Cookston v. Box*, supra), or where the water is not navigable or usable as a highway for commerce and travel (see *Peasley v. New York (State)*, supra).

In the present case, I find: that without a right of way of necessity, the lot in question will not be able to be used and will be useless; that this is not a case where there exists an alternative, though inconvenient, means of access; and that water access over Big Mushamush Lake to the lot in question is not by right and, indeed, would probably be contrary to law pursuant to ss. 2(j) and 3 of the *Water Act*, RSNS 1989, c. 500. ...

I also find no evidence that Big Mushamush Lake can be used for transportation of things needed for reasonable use of the plaintiff's land, that Big Mushamush Lake has transportation facilities for carrying on the ordinary and necessary activities of life to and from the land, and that Big Mushamush Lake has been used or is usable as a highway of commerce and travel.

Conclusion

As previously indicated, the applicant's claim for a certificate of title pursuant to the *Quieting Titles Act* is granted.

The plaintiff has satisfied the court that, in the present circumstances, he is entitled to a right of way of necessity in order that he should have access to his land. An order will issue recognizing and granting a right of way over and along the so-called cottage road, in common with all other persons having use of the same road, with the plaintiff being required to pay the full cost of construction of any extension of the roadway as it presently exists, and a proportionate share of any cost of maintaining the roadway and keeping it in good repair and condition.

I consider it unnecessary to consider the plaintiff's alternative claim to a prescriptive right of way.

I consider the plaintiff's claim for damages to be inappropriate in the circumstances. Moreover, the plaintiff has not proved any general or special damages.

A claimant under the *Quieting Titles Act* usually bears the costs of the application, but where the application is contested unsuccessfully, such costs should be shared. Therefore, the plaintiff will have 50 per cent of his costs of the action to be taxed in accordance with Tariff A (the amount involved being $35,000 under Scale 3) and Tariff D.

Action allowed in part.

DISCUSSION NOTES

i. Judicial or Legislative Evolution of Easements of Necessity

What is the basis of the court's willingness to acknowledge the evolution of principles concerning easements of necessity? In light of the decision in *Hirtle v Ernst*, how would you formulate the test of necessity in this context? In reflecting on these issues, consider this proposal:

> [All] jurisdictions should develop a body of laws designed to ensure that its courts have the power to prevent land from remaining landlocked. The possibility of land remaining landlocked, as can occur in common law jurisdictions in the absence of legislation as a consequence of the limitations on the scope of the easement of necessity, is contrary to the basic tenet of real property law that land should be freely alienable .... It would also seem to be clearly in the public interest that land should not lie unused and that its potential for development should be fully realized.

(AJ Bradbrook, "Access to Landlocked Land: A Comparative Study of Legal Solutions" (1983) 10 Sydney L Rev 39.)

Is there any need for legislation in the light of *Hirtle v Ernst*? Why or why not? Are there other competing policy considerations that should be taken into account in formulating solutions to problems similar to those in *Hirtle*? Is it relevant that the market value of landlocked land may be less than it would be with access? Who should bear the cost of ensuring access? If there is a public policy interest in land development, should the cost of access be borne only by the owners of adjoining land? Is this issue one that can be resolved by common law principles, or is a legislative solution required?

Bradbrook's analysis examined different kinds of solutions to the problem of landlocked land in several jurisdictions in Australia, Europe, and the United States. For examples of legislative solutions, see *Property Law Act, 1974-1978*, s 180 (Queensland) and *Conveyancing and Law of Property Act 1884*, s 84j, an amendment added in 1978 (Tasmania). These statutes apply "where it is reasonably necessary in the interests of effective use in any reasonable manner of land" (Queensland), and generally provide for a court to order an easement where it is consistent with the public interest and where the owner of a servient tenement has unreasonably refused to accept the obligation but can be adequately compensated for doing so. See also H Tarlo, "Forcing the Creation of Easements—A Novel Law" (1979) 53 Austl L J 254; and A Bradbrook & S MacCallum, *Easements and Restrictive Covenants in Australia*, 3d ed (Sydney: Butterworths, 2012).

ii. Intention: Wong v Beaumont

In addition to easements of necessity, implied easements may be created by the common intention of the parties, taking into account the purpose for which land has been granted. It has been suggested that *Wong v Beaumont*, [1965] 1 QB 173, [1964] 2 All ER 119 (CA) is a good example of such an easement. In that case, Lord Denning held that an implied easement existed with respect to the construction of a ventilation duct in a restaurant because it was required by public health regulations. Even though the landlord objected to the tenant's need for the ventilation duct, the court held that the tenant was entitled to have it constructed because the landlord knew of the tenant's intended use of the premises as a restaurant when the lease was signed.

What is the difference, if any, between the basis for an implied easement of necessity and an implied easement based on the common intention of the parties? According to Ziff (at 383), *Wong* shows that "sometimes the two are treated as equivalent." He also suggested that the rationale for an implied easement based on common intention lies in the vendor's obligation of non-derogation—that is, "it would have amounted to a derogation from the grant not to recognize the easement over part of the property that had been retained by the landlord." In *Wong*, Lord Denning used the language of an easement of necessity. Is the language determinative here? For other examples, see *Duchman v Oakland Dairy Co Ltd*, [1929] 1 DLR 9 (Ont SC (AD)) and *Aircraft Maintenance Enterprises Inc v Aerospace Realties (1986) Ltd*, 1992 CanLII 7349, 94 Nfld & PEIR 271 (Nfld SC (TD)).

iii. The Principle of Wheeldon v Burrows

Easements may also be implied under the principle of *Wheeldon v Burrows* (1872), 12 Ch D 31 (CA). According to this principle, a vendor who holds a parcel of land, and who uses a path across one section to gain access to another, may create an implied easement at the time of a transfer of one section to a purchaser. Even though there was no easement so long as the whole parcel belonged to the vendor (remember that one requirement for an easement is that the dominant and servient tenements be held by different persons), the division of the parcel and its transfer to a purchaser "creates" an implied easement. The situation prior to the division of the parcel may sometimes be referred to as one of a "quasi-easement." According to Ziff (at 383):

> The *Wheeldon* rule is a pronounced application of the principle of non-derogation. It serves as a form of consumer protection, allowing a purchaser to acquire amenities (i.e., easements) that the purchased land appears to enjoy. As such, it is a minor deviation from the principle of *caveat emptor* (let the buyer beware).

See also AWB Simpson, "The Rule in Wheeldon v Burrows and the Code Civile" (1967) 83 Law Q Rev 240.

In *Barton v Raine* (1980), 114 DLR (3d) 702 (Ont CA), for example, such an implied easement was created when a vendor (who owned two adjoining city lots with a mutual driveway between them) conveyed one lot to his son and daughter-in-law. The son and his family had been living in the adjoining home for over a decade before the transfer of title, and thus the use of the mutual driveway had been established before the father's conveyance. After this transfer, both families continued to use the mutual driveway. The property line between the two houses meant that the owner of one house did not have sufficient room to drive a car to the garage at the back of the property without access to the mutual driveway. Some years later when both lots had been transferred to new purchasers, a dispute arose about the right to use the driveway.

According to Thorson JA (at 709), the trial judge had concluded that there was an implied easement in the deed transferring the adjoining lot to the son and daughter-in-law, suggesting that it could be supported either on the basis of the "mutual or reciprocal easement exception" in *Wheeldon v Burrows* or on the basis of the "broader, umbrella-like 'common intention' principle." After reviewing the authorities carefully, Thorson JA agreed, stating (at 709):

> In my opinion, the learned trial Judge was correct in the conclusion which he drew from the authorities referred to above, namely, that the development of the case-law since *Wheeldon v.*

Burrows has softened the rigour of the general rule set out in that case or has enlarged the scope of the exceptions to the rule. On the facts of the case at bar, I am satisfied that, although the 1952 conveyance made no mention of a right of way over the driveway between the two properties, there was, by necessary inference from the circumstances in which the conveyance was made, a common intention on the part of both the father on the one hand and the son and daughter-in-law on the other hand that, after the conveyance, each of them would continue to use the driveway in the same manner as, in fact, it had been used without interruption since the late 1920s.

In 1952 when the property next door was conveyed to them, the son and daughter-in-law of the grantor had been occupying the property for over a decade. The use of the driveway as a common passageway to and from the two garages was an accepted reality of their lives throughout the whole of their occupancy of the property, just as it had been an accepted reality for the owners of the two properties for many years before their occupancy of the property began. Were it not for the fact that the plaintiff's father became the owner of both properties in 1941, it is almost certain that the plaintiff's father would have acquired a right of way by prescription over the driveway well before the 1952 conveyance, since its use by him had been uninterrupted and had gone unchallenged throughout most of his lifetime as the owner of the originally-acquired property.

Throughout the whole of this period the driveway was a tangible physical fact, there to be seen by all who chose to see it, and the manner of its use would have been obvious to even the most casual observer of the physical features of the two properties. There could be no doubt that it was there to provide access to and from both garages near the rear of the two properties.

In my view, furthermore, it is not credible that when the son and daughter-in-law purchased the property which they had been occupying for over a decade with the father's permission, there could have been any misunderstanding by them about the basis on which the driveway was to be used thereafter by each of the parties to the conveyance, including of course, the father, with whom they had so long been sharing its use. That there was in fact no such misunderstanding seems evident. For example, it must be assumed that at the time they purchased the property next door, the son and daughter-in-law knew or were made aware of the location of the property line dividing the two properties, yet it is apparent from the known facts that at no time did they see it to be or treat it as being a consequence of their purchase of the property next door, any more than did the father, that thereafter the father would be obliged to have their permission to use the driveway in order to get to and from his own garage. In my opinion, the only reasonable inference to be drawn from all of the facts and circumstances surrounding the 1952 conveyance is that each of the parties had a common intention that the father would continue to have the right to use the driveway after the 1952 conveyance as he had before.

Quite possibly if, in 1952, the property next door had been purchased by some hypothetical third party who was a stranger to the father, the inference as to the intention of the parties would have been considerably less compelling, inasmuch as the property was then being severed from other property owned by the father, but in this case it is not necessary to indulge in speculation of this kind. Here the purchase was by the son and his wife from the father who, on all the evidence, borne out by the subsequent history of events, intended to and in fact continued to remain as owner and occupier of the retained property and to use it as he had used it before.

It follows that I agree with Killeen Co. Ct. J that an easement in the nature of a right of way over the driveway in question, in favour of the grantor of the property next door, was acquired by implied reservation from the 1952 grant. I also agree that the interruption in its use which occurred following the father's stroke did not impair that easement, which, once acquired, could only be lost by [a] non-user on evidence clearly establishing an intention to abandon it. As pointed out by the trial Judge, the circumstances of the non-user in this case were not consistent in any way with an intention to abandon the right.

In the result the defendants who purchased the property next door from the son and daughter-in-law in 1971 are, in my opinion, bound by the easement. It is well established (see, for example, *Israel v. Leith* (1890), 20 OR 361 (QB)) that the *Registry Act* does not interfere with legal rights, such as an implied grant of an easement, arising other than by a written instrument, and does not alter the priority of the grantee of the easement over a subsequent purchaser. In my view, there is no rational basis for distinguishing in this regard between an easement arising by implied grant and one arising by implied reservation. See, in support of this position, *Gale on Easements, supra,* at p. 113, and 9 CED (Ont. 3d), title 51, p. 51-38, §74, and the authorities referred to therein.

Do you agree that there was a "common intention" in *Barton*? What evidence was relied on to reach this conclusion? If the adjoining lot had been transferred by the father to an unrelated party instead of to his son and daughter-in-law, what difference would it have made, if any? Could this concept of common intention in relation to an implied easement have been considered in *Gypsum Carrier*, described above? What would have been the result? Remember that the court concluded that there had been no intention to create an easement in that case. What was the evidence relied on to support the court's conclusion?

In *Fife v Cohan*, 2007 CanLII 28324, 2007 OJ no 2844 (Sup Ct J), a situation similar to that in *Barton v Raine* arose. The owners of neighbouring properties had registered a mutual easement in 1923, allowing them to encroach on a 76-foot strip of each other's property in order to access parking spots in their respective backyards. In 1985 one of the successors in title, Mr Fife, added on to the back of his house, which meant that he needed to encroach on a further 39 feet of his neighbour's property to access his parking spot. He did so for over 20 years without protest from his neighbour, but at some point prior to 2005 the land was converted to the land titles system, which prevented him from acquiring a prescriptive easement. When the Cohans bought the neighbouring property in 2007, they indicated that they planned to fence in their portion of the additional 39-foot area. Owing to the construction of a garage elsewhere on their property, they no longer needed to access the backyard parking. Mr Fife argued that he was entitled either to an easement of necessity or to an implied easement based on common intention. With regard to the former, Justice Belobaba found that the necessity had to exist when the two parcels were initially severed and sold (1923). At that time there was no necessity because of the mutual deeded easement, and the necessity that arose in 1985 was due to Mr Fife's own act. Further, the absence of parking did not render Mr Fife's lot inaccessible; it was a serious inconvenience, but no more.

With regard to the argument of an implied easement based on common intention, Justice Belobaba accepted *Barton v Raine* as the starting point for analysis, but stated that it was impossible to find a common intention that the 76-foot encroachment would be extended indefinitely "as needed" in order to provide continued access to the backyard parking spots. Where the parties had initially specified the extent of the easement, there was no reason to extend it in the absence of any evidence pointing to this intention. In dismissing Mr Fife's application, Justice Belobaba made the following observation:

> Mr. Fife and the previous owners of 203 have been using the mutual drive amicably and in good faith for more than 20 years to access their backyard parking areas. Because of the *Land Titles* registration, Mr. Fife cannot be granted a prescriptive easement and the Cohans can legally build a fence across the top end of the laneway even though this will block the access to Mr. Fife's

backyard parking pad. In these circumstances, I would hope that Mr. and Mrs. Cohan would give Mr. Fife permission to park his car on the registered right of way. The Cohans no longer need this laneway and it would be the right thing to do.

If you were the lawyer for the Cohans, what would you advise them to do?

iv. Implied Easements and Law Reform in the United Kingdom

The rules regarding the situations where easements can be implied are somewhat complex, as illustrated in the material just considered. The Law Commission of England and Wales, in its report *Making Land Work: Easements, Covenants, and Profits à Prendre* (London: Stationery Office, 2011) [2011 Law Commission Report], recommended (at 37) that there be a single statutory mode of implying easements, such that an easement shall be implied as a term of a disposition where it is necessary for the reasonable use of the land at that date, bearing in mind: (1) the use of the land at the time of the grant; (2) the presence on the servient land of any relevant physical features; (3) any intention for the future use of the land, known to both parties at the time of the grant; (4) so far as relevant, the available routes for the easement sought; and (5) the potential interference with the servient land or inconvenience to the servient owner.

Do you think such a reform should be adopted in Canada? Are there good policy reasons for doing away with implied easements altogether?

v. Easements: Scope and Termination

Intention may also be important in determining the scope of easements. In *Giecewicz v Alexander* (1989), 3 RPR (2d) 324 (Ont H Ct J), for example, an express easement had been granted across the defendants' land in relation to land owned by the plaintiffs. The plaintiffs had no other access to a public highway. As a result of development some years later, however, the plaintiffs gained access to a new public highway, so long as they built a suitable driveway, and the defendants thereupon blocked the former access route by building on their land. The court dismissed the plaintiffs' application for a declaration of easement, holding that the extent of an express easement depends on the wording of the instrument, ascertainable by circumstances existing at the time of the grant and known to the parties or within their reasonable contemplation at the time (citing *Laurie v Winch*, [1953] 1 SCR 49. In addition, the court in *Giecewicz* held (at 335) that

subsequent changes in circumstances may alter the justifications for the use of the easement. A grant may be made for a limited purpose and when that purpose is accomplished, the right of way shall cease.

Accordingly, the court concluded that the right of way terminated when the plaintiffs acquired suitable access to a public highway. For further discussion of the termination of an implied easement of necessity, see *Holmes v Goring* (1824), 130 ER 233 (CP) and *BOJ Properties v Allen's Mobile Home Park Ltd* (1979), 108 DLR (3d) 305 (NSSC (AD)). By contrast, see *Peters v Morrison* (2001), 47 RPR (3d) 303 (Ont Sup Ct J), where the court granted the plaintiffs' motion for an interim injunction to prohibit the defendant from obstructing their right of way over his land. Even though other access routes were available, the court accepted that they were not viable, in part because of potential environmental damage.

Easements can also be terminated by abandonment, although there is a high bar for such a finding: see Ziff at 393. The parties may also negotiate for the release of an easement, but if the dominant tenement holder will not yield, there is no recourse except in British Columbia, where a statutory power to terminate easements (among other interests) exists under the *Property Law Act*, RSBC 1996, c 377, s 35.

There may also be important issues about the scope or extent of an easement—that is, assuming that an easement has been created, there may be disputes about the extent of the rights of the holder of the dominant tenement. For examples, see *Pearsall v Power Supermarkets Ltd* (1957), 8 DLR (2d) 270 (Ont HC) and *Malden Farms Ltd v Nicholson*, [1956] OR 415 (CA). See also P Huff, "Overburdening the Right of Way: Where the Right of Way Ends" (1991) 4:5 Nat'l Real PLR 49, and American Law Institute (2000).

D. Easements by Prescription

In addition to creating easements by express grant or implication, easements may be created by prescription. Basically, an easement by prescription is created as a result of "length of user" of servient land on the part of the owner of the dominant tenement. In this respect, the principles of prescription appear similar to ideas about the acquisition of title by possession (especially because possession may also be proved by acts of use). However, there are important distinctions, both in theory and in practice, between principles of prescription and those of possessory title.

First of all, prescription applies to non-possessory interests and thus usually requires acts that are less controlling than would be required to show a possessory title. Second, the acquisition of a possessory title extinguishes the right of the owner against whom possession has been established, and the new owner becomes solely entitled to use and possession of the land. By contrast, prescription provides for the encumbrance of the servient tenement by the owner of the dominant tenement, so that one landowner's options for using land may be constrained by the rights of the other. As well, the owner of the servient land obtains no compensation for the rights acquired by a neighbour in the servient land. On this basis, underlying concerns about the need to promote, not punish, neighbourly behaviour may influence judicial decisions concerning claims of prescriptive easements. Where one person permits another to use his or her land for a particular purpose, without compensation, it may not be appropriate to conclude that an easement has been created. For this reason, it may often be difficult to establish an easement by prescription. See e.g. *Tupper v Campbell* (1876), 11 NSR 68 (SC). See also S Anderson, "Easement and Prescription—Changing Perspectives in Classification" (1975) 38 Mod L Rev 641. It is also useful to consider *Keefer v Arillotta* (1976), 13 OR (2d) 680 (CA), discussed in Chapter 2, in relation to prescription. Might this claim have succeeded based on prescription rather than possessory title?

At common law, there were two methods of acquiring an interest by prescription. The first method involved proof of usage extending back to time immemorial (established by statute in England as the date of the beginning of the reign of Richard I, the year 1189). However, because any such claim could be rebutted by showing any period of adverse use since 1189, this method of acquiring prescriptive easements is of no use in Canada, except, perhaps, for First Nations. In *Abell v Village of Woodbridge* (1917), 39 OLR 382 (SCC) at 388, the court took judicial notice of the discovery of America as of 1492, thus denying the availability of this common law method of prescription to anyone except First Nations claimants.

The second method at common law, called the doctrine of "the lost modern grant," assumed the existence of a grant that had disappeared. According to this approach, continuous use for a period of 20 years raises a presumption of a lost "modern" (that is, post-1189) grant. This common law approach continues to exist in Canada, along with statutory provisions (a third method for the creation of prescriptive easements). According to the Ontario Law Reform Commission's report in 1969, the purpose of the *Prescription Act* was "to reduce uncertainties of establishing prescriptive easements at common law." The *Prescription Act* was adopted in Upper Canada in 1847 and the relevant provisions are now found in the *Real Property Limitations Act*, RSO 1990, c L.15. They were formerly contained in the *Limitations Act*, RSO 1990, c L.15, which was (retrospectively) renamed the *Real Property Limitations Act* by SO 2002, c 24, Sched B, s 26. However, these provisions are widely regarded as "ill-drafted," and the Law Reform Commission conceded that the prescription provisions of the Ontario limitations statute "remain a mystery to many a practising lawyer." For details about the operation of prescription in the Ontario legislation, see Ontario, *Report of the Ontario Law Reform Commission on the Limitation of Actions* (Toronto: Department of the Attorney General, 1969) at 143-48. See also the *Limitation of Actions Act*, RSNS 1989, c 258, ss 32-37 and the *Easements Act*, RSNB 2011, c 143. You may also wish to compare the doctrine of prescription with the law on adverse possession, discussed in Chapter 2.

Kaminskas v Storm
(2009), 95 OR (3d) 387 (CA)

[The appellant and respondent were neighbours in a residential area of Niagara Falls, Ontario. Their houses shared a common driveway that encroached three feet onto the property of the Storms. Mr Kaminskas had parked on this area since he acquired the property at 5087 Kitchener Street in 1991, and his predecessors had parked there since at least 1950. The Storms purchased the property in 2006 from the Angiers, who had owned it since 1950. Soon after, the Storms sought to build a fence that would prevent Mr Kaminskas from using the parking spot. On-street parking was not allowed in this part of the city, and Mr Kaminskas had no other place to park on his property, while the Storms had a driveway on the other side of their property. Mr Kaminskas sought a declaration that he had a prescriptive easement over the encroaching area, and injunctive relief. The main issue was consent: had Mr Kaminskas and his predecessors in title enjoyed the alleged easement as of right, or only with the consent of the servient tenement owners? The trial judge found in favour of Mr Kaminskas, and the Storms appealed. In this context, the Ontario Court of Appeal reviewed the requirements for prescriptive easements both under the doctrine of lost modern grant and under the *Real Property Limitations Act*.]

BLAIR JA (Rosenberg and Feldman JJA concurring): Mr. Angiers swore he and his wife "were always aware of the previous and current owners of 5087 Kitchener Street, using the single car driveway that encroached onto [their lands]." In fact, he said that to the best of his knowledge and recollection, the driveway "was already on the property" when he and

Mrs. Angiers bought it in 1950 and "had been in use of the then owners" at that time. ... He said that Mr. Kaminskas "has had the exclusive use" of the driveway and that he and Mrs. Angiers "had always given permission to the previous and present owners of 5087 Kitchener Street ... to the use of this single car driveway and the said encroachment."

In 1991, when Mr. Kaminskas acquired 5087 Kitchener St. from Mr. Parisi, the Angiers provided Mr. Kaminskas with a letter consenting to his use of the disputed driveway. This letter said:

> To: Janice Parker & John Kaminskas:
>
> We, Ross & Harriet Angiers give our consent to Janice and John for full use of the mutual driveway at 5087 and 5091 Kitchener Street.
>
> Sincerely,
>
> [Signed] Ross S. Angiers

The Grounds of Appeal

The appellants make two principal submissions.

They argue, first, that the application judge erred in the manner in which she calculated the time required for a prescriptive easement claim pursuant to the *Real Property Limitations Act*, R.S.O. 1990, c. L.15, ss. 31 and 32. The application judge determined that Mr. Kaminskas had established an absolute 40-year right that crystallized before the 1991 letter was provided and, therefore, that the letter of permission could not defeat what was already an absolute prescriptive easement. The appellants submit, however, that the relevant time period for a prescriptive easement under the Act is "the period next before some action wherein the claim ... was or is brought into question," i.e., from the date of the commencement of the application in these proceedings. The 1991 letter of permission therefore operates to defeat the prescriptive right, they say.

I agree with the appellants' submission that Mr. Kaminskas's claim under statute is defeated by the written consent provided to him by the Angiers in 1991. Further, the evidence failed to establish that the user was "as of right."

Law and Analysis

In law, there are three ways in which an easement may be acquired by prescription:

(a) prescription at common law;

(b) prescription by the doctrine of lost modern grant; and

(c) prescription by statute (*Real Property Limitations Act*).

[Blair JA outlined the nature of the prescription at common law and under lost modern grant, and continued:]

The *English Prescription Act 1832* (U.K.), 2 & 3 Will. 4, c. 71 may have been enacted, at least in part, to overcome [difficulties with earlier modes of prescription]. Its preamble states that it was enacted to prevent common law claims from being defeated by evidence of the commencement of use after 1189 (the very rationale for the development of the doctrine of lost modern grant). Sections 31 and 32 of the Ontario *Real Property Limitations Act* echo the language of the 1832 legislation.

The wording of these sections is tortuous at best. Stripped to their essentials, for purposes of this appeal, they read as follows:

Right of way, easement, etc.

31. No claim that may be made lawfully at the common law, by ... prescription or grant, to any way or other easement ... when the way ... has been actually enjoyed by any person claiming right thereto without interruption for the full period of twenty years shall be defeated or destroyed by showing only that the way ... was first enjoyed at any time prior to the period of twenty years, but, nevertheless the claim may be defeated in any other way by which it is now liable to be defeated, and where the way ... has been so enjoyed for the full period of forty years, the right thereto shall be deemed absolute and indefeasible, unless it appears that it was enjoyed by some consent or agreement expressly given or made for that purpose by deed or writing.

How period to be calculated, and what acts deemed an interruption

32. Each of the respective periods of years mentioned in [section] 31 shall be deemed and taken to be the period next before some action wherein the claim ... to which such period relates was or is brought into question, and no act or other matter shall be deemed an interruption within the meaning of those sections, unless the same has been submitted to or acquiesced in for one year after the person interrupted has had notice thereof, and of the person making or authorizing the same to be made.

Sections 31 and 32 do not displace the right to establish a prescriptive easement based on the doctrine of lost modern grant, which continues to exist in this province: *Henderson v. Volk* [(1982), 35 OR (2d) 379] at p. 382; *MacRae v. Levy*, [2005] O.J. No. 313, 28 R.P.R. (4th) 291 (S.C.J.), at para. 59; Graeme Mew, The Law of Limitations, 2d ed. (Markham, Ont.: LexisNexis Butterworths, 2004), at p. 237. Moreover, the nature of the enjoyment necessary to establish a prescriptive easement under the doctrine of lost modern grant is precisely the same as that required for a prescriptive easement under the statute: *Henderson v. Volk*.

Characteristics of Prescriptive Easements

In addition [to meeting the four requirements for an easement at common law], for an easement to be created by prescription, the user of the alleged right (for the applicable time period) must be shown to have been (i) continuous and (ii) "as of right."

Here, there is no real issue that the proclaimed easement meets the four essential criteria of an easement at common law, or that the use of the driveway by Mr. Kaminskas and his predecessors was continuous. The appeal hinges on whether the user was "as of right." User "as of right" means that the use has been uninterrupted, open, peaceful and without permission for the relevant period of time. It is often described using the Latin maxim *nec vi, nec clam, nec precario* (i.e., without force, without secrecy and without "*precario*"). "*Precario*" in this sense is taken to mean "[t]hat which depends not on right, but on the will of another person": *Burrows v. Lang*, [1901] 2 Ch. 502 (Ch. Div.), at p. 510. *Nec precario*, therefore, means "without permission."

Differences Between Prescriptive Easements Under Statute and Lost Modern Grant

There are three important differences between a prescriptive easement arising by statute and a prescriptive easement arising by lost modern grant, however. First, in order to establish a prescriptive right by statute, it is necessary for the use to have been continuous, uninterrupted, open, peaceful and without permission for a period of 20 or 40 years immediately preceding the commencement of the action or assertion of the claim—in the language of s. 32, during the 20- or 40-year "period *next before* some action wherein the claim ... to which such period relates was or is brought into question" [emphasis added]. For the right to accrue under the doctrine of lost modern grant, however, the requisite user need not be for the period "next before" the action, but may exist during any uninterrupted 20-year period or longer.

While the "next before" requirement may give rise to unfairness in some circumstances, there are policy reasons founded in the need to promote certainty and stability in conveyancing law that support its existence. As the authors of a leading text, Robert Megarry & William Wade, *The Law of Real Property*, 6th ed., by Charles Harpum (London: Sweet & Maxwell Ltd., 2000), observe, at p. 1138, footnote 76:

> It should be noted that, for all its shortcomings, prescription under the *Prescription Act 1832* is, from a conveyancing point of view, preferable to prescription by lost modern grant. Because it has to be exercised without interruption "next before some suit or action," it may be easier for any purchaser of the servient tenement to discover. If an easement has been acquired by lost modern grant ... [a] purchaser may be bound by it even though he could not have discovered its existence.

In addition, the "next before" requirement under the legislation confines the courts review to a relatively recent period of time, when the evidence will be easier to obtain and evaluate, and therefore may be preferable to the lost modern grant regime for that reason: see U.K., "Easements, Covenants and Profits à Prendre," The Law Commission Consultation Paper No. 186 (Belfast, Ireland: The Stationery Office, 2008), at p. 80, para. 4.213.

Secondly, a statutory claim to a prescriptive easement based on 40 years' use can be defeated by permission only where that permission was given in writing. This is established by the closing words of s. 31, which, for convenience, I repeat:

> [W]here the way ... has been so enjoyed for the full period of forty years, the right thereto shall be deemed absolute and indefeasible, unless it appears that it was enjoyed by some consent or agreement expressly given or made for that purpose by deed or writing.

Under the statute, a 40-year right will not be considered permissive ("*precario*") unless it is enjoyed by written permission. However, claims to a prescriptive right based on the doctrine of lost modern grant (or with respect to the statutory right based on 20 years' use) can be defeated by consent or permission, whether written or oral.

Finally, it is noteworthy that the 40-year concept is a creature of the statutory prescriptive right. It has no application to the doctrine of lost modern grant, which requires only an appropriate use of 20 years or more without permission.

Application of the Principles to This Case

In light of the foregoing review of the principles underlying prescriptive easements, it is apparent where the dilemma for Mr. Kaminskas arises. His claim under statute is defeated by the written consent provided to him by the Angiers in 1991, less than 20 years "next before" the commencement of his application. It is also defeated by the permission—by inference, an oral permission—that Mr. Angiers says he and his wife "had always given" to the owners of the Kaminskas property, whether the claim is based on statute or on the doctrine of lost modern grant.

[With regard to lost modern grant, which was not argued at trial but was raised on appeal, Blair JA reasoned as follows:]

Although permission can defeat a 40-year period of use for purposes of a prescriptive easement by statute only if evidenced in writing, oral permission is sufficient to defeat a prescriptive easement by lost modern grant. Here, the evidence is that the Angiers at all times gave permission to the use of the driveway for parking. It is not said whether that permission was oral or written, but since the 1991 letter is the only reference on the record to consent in writing, it is a reasonable inference that, prior to the letter, the ongoing permission was oral. In any event, a prescriptive right by lost modern grant cannot be established if the use was by permission, whether written or oral—it can only arise where the use is "as of right."

This result may seem unfair to Mr. Kaminskas. It is apparent that he and his predecessors in title have had the continuous, open, uninterrupted, peaceful and exclusive use of the driveway for purposes of parking over a period of at least 56 years before the commencement of these proceedings. Everyone was in agreement, except for the current occupants and owners of the Storm property. But it is also apparent that this use was with the permission of the predecessors in title to the Storms. And permission defeats a prescriptive easement.

Appeal allowed.

DISCUSSION NOTES

i. Prescriptive Easements: The Concept of Consent

As can be seen in *Kaminskas v Storm*, the distinction between consent and acquiescence is at the heart of the law of prescriptive easements. Yet disagreement remains about the parameters of this key concept. In *1043 Bloor Inc v 1714104 Ontario Inc*, 2013 ONCA 91, Dr S operated a medical practice at 1045 Bloor Street from 1966, when he purchased the building, until his retirement in 1997. There was a narrow laneway between his property and the property at 1043 Bloor, by which parking in the rear of both properties could be accessed, but the lane was entirely on his property. Successive owners of 1043 had used the laneway for some years without any permission from Dr S, and in 2008 the current owner, V, sought a declaration that he was entitled to a prescriptive easement based on 20 years' user prior to 2003, when the parcels were converted to the land titles system. The case turned on the effect of an attempt in 1987 by V to get Dr S to sign a document acknowledging that he (V) had no easement over the land and granting him an easement over the lane in return for an annual payment of $300. Dr S refused to sign the document, but V and his tenants continued to use the lane.

In the Court of Appeal, Justice Gillese interpreted the offer made by V as an acknowledgment that he had no right to use the land and, therefore, that his user was not "as of right." This acknowledgment thus interrupted any prescription that had begun, and had the effect of making any subsequent user by V permissive. Justice Laskin took the opposite view: that by not signing the agreement, Dr S was *not* granting permission to use the lane, and therefore any subsequent user was not permissive and did not interrupt the prescription that had already begun. He came to the same result as Justice Gillese, however, because of some subsequent acts by Dr S that he found had the necessary character of interrupting prescription. Justice Macpherson agreed in the result but did not choose between the two sets of reasons.

Which reasoning do you prefer? Which one best furthers the policy goals in this area of the law?

The overuse of a deeded easement can itself ripen into a separate easement through the doctrine of prescription. This occurred in *Depew v Wilkes* (2002), 60 OR (3d) 499 (CA), where cottagers had a deeded right of way over a 20-foot strip of land on the servient tenement to provide access to their cottages, but regularly parked on a further 10-foot strip for over 20 years. They were found to have a prescriptive easement over the 10-foot strip. For a similar result, see *Tasker v Badgerow*, 2007 CanLII 23362, [2007] OJ no 2487 (Sup Ct J), where the use of a right of way to construct a well and well cover was found to exceed what was granted in the original 1925 deed of easement, but upheld on the basis of a prescriptive easement as the servient tenement owners had not complained about the well since 1946.

ii. Reform of the Law of Prescription

In its 2011 report, the Law Commission of England and Wales recommended that the three modes of prescription currently recognized there be reduced to a single statutory mode (2011 Law Commission Report at 41-62). It recommended that the "next before" requirement contained in the *Prescription Act 1832* (and found in Canadian limitations acts) be abolished, in effect codifying the doctrine of lost modern grant. This would be balanced, however, by a requirement that a prescriptive easement not used in the year before a transfer of land, and thus not apparent on inspection, not be binding on the purchaser.

iii. Prescriptive Easements in Practice

Review the arguments about the need for principles recognizing the creation of title by possession in Chapter 2. To what extent do these arguments apply in the context of prescriptive easements? What are the consequences of recognizing prescriptive rights in terms of goals of neighbourly cooperation? Should courts interpret prescriptive claims broadly or narrowly? For different approaches, see *Temma Realty Co Ltd v Ress Enterprises Ltd* (1968), 69 DLR (2d) 195 (Ont CA) and *Brass Rail Tavern (Toronto) Ltd v DiNunzio* (1979), 12 RPR 188 (Ont HC). Should prescription be part of the modern law of property in Canada? Note that it has been abolished in Alberta, British Columbia, and Saskatchewan: see *Limitations Act*, RSA 2000, c L-12; *Land Title Act*, RSBC 1996, c 250; *Land Titles Act, 2000*, SS 2000, c L-5.1. It has also been abolished (prospectively at least) in the land titles systems of those provinces where both land titles and registry systems coexist, such as Ontario, Nova Scotia, and New Brunswick. In its 1996 *Report on Basic Principles*, the OLRC recommended (at 148) abolition of the creation of easements by prescription. After reviewing reform recommendations in British Columbia and Manitoba, and taking into account the fact that prescriptive easements may not be created on land registered under the *Land Titles Act*, the OLRC concluded that there was no justification for recognition of prescriptive easements.

In *Monaghan v Moore* (1966), 31 OR (3d) 232 (CA), the court concluded that the claimants could not acquire an easement by prescription in relation to a road allowance because they were entitled by law to use public highways. Thus, when the road allowance was closed and sold to a purchaser, the claimants could not continue to use it to gain access to a beach on Lake Muskoka. Does this case reveal some limits in relation to prescriptive easements?

If it is possible to obtain rights by prescription, should the opposite also be possible—that is, the extinguishment of rights through non-use? In the United States, for example, easements may be extinguished by prescription: see American Law Institute (2000), s 7.7. In thinking about these issues, consider the legislative law reform process. Why might reform on these issues be comparatively slow?

Recall *Depew v Wilkes*, discussed above in relation to the requirement that an easement must accommodate the dominant tenement. In *Depew*, the Court of Appeal confirmed the trial judge's decision that the cottage owners had acquired a prescriptive easement over lot 13, owned by the Depews, in relation to the parking of cars in front of their cottages. However, the Court of Appeal overturned the trial judge's order with respect to the obligation of the cottage owners to pay an annual fee to the Depews; as a result, the cottage owners acquired the easement by prescription without any requirement to compensate the owner of the servient tenement. According to Rosenberg JA (see *Depew v Wilkes* (2002), 60 OR (3d) 499 (CA) at paras 14-16):

> [14] The trial judge found that, because of the expiration of the 20-year limitation period provided for in ss. 31 and 32 of the *Limitations Act* [now renamed the *Real Property Limitations Act*], the appellants had acquired prescriptive easements to park their cars in front of their cottages on Lot 13 .... These were legal rights. It was nevertheless open to the trial judge to grant the respondents an equitable remedy, provided that he found assertion of these strict legal rights unconscionable.
>
> [15] The trial judge made no such finding and it is difficult to see any basis for doing so. The appellants and their predecessors in title had been parking on Lot 13 for many decades without charge and with the acquiescence of the respondents and their predecessors in title .... The only reasons given by the trial judge for imposing the licence fees were that the respondents presumably were paying taxes on Lot 13 and that "equity to the titleholder of the land requires that a reasonable annual fee be paid to the titleholder for the use of the land." There was no evidence of how much, if anything, the respondents were paying in taxes.
>
> [16] While I appreciate that the trial judge turned to equity in order to effect what he thought was a fair result, I have concluded that he erred in doing so. His approach is based on nothing more than his sense of justice or fairness and could be applied in virtually every case where a prescriptive easement is made out. Adopting this approach would make the law of easements unpredictable. As Cory JA said in *Henderson v Volk* (1982), 35 OR (2d) 379 at p. 384, 132 DLR (3d) 690 (CA), the courts ought to proceed with caution before finding title by prescription because "[i]t tends to subject a property owner to a burden without compensation." However, notwithstanding that result, absent a finding of unconscionability there is no basis for proceeding to

consider some further equitable remedy where a prescriptive easement has been found to exist. In the result, I would set aside the licence fees for parking.

Do you agree with this result? To what extent does this decision appear to "punish" rather than to "promote" neighbourly behaviour?

Prescriptive easements have often been recognized in recent cases in relation to cottage properties: see *Caldwell v Elia* (2000), 30 RPR (3d) 295 (Ont CA); *Rose v Kreiser* (2002), 58 OR (3d) 641 (Ont CA); and *Wouters v Forjay Developments Ltd* (1998), 38 OR (3d) 369 (Gen Div).

By contrast, in *Jennings v Redmond* (2000), 34 RPR (3d) 91 (Ont Sup Ct J), the court held that there was no prescriptive easement in relation to the location of drain pipes. However, in *Fu v Khan*, [2001] OTC 975 (Sup Ct J), the court held that the owner of the dominant tenement had acquired a prescriptive easement in relation to a stairwell. The owners of adjoining properties at 645 and 647 Yonge Street in Toronto were held to be subject to part of an agreement entered into by their respective predecessors in title, relating to the preservation and maintenance of a stairwell located partly on each property for the mutual use of the owners of each. Although the court held that some parts of the covenants were unenforceable as positive covenants (an issue discussed later in this chapter), and that there was no basis for an easement of necessity (because there was an alternative access route), it concluded that the use of the stairwell had continued since 1951 so that there was an easement by prescription. As a result, the owner of the servient tenement was not entitled to demolish the stairwell. How do cases concerning easements acquired by prescription, like easements of necessity, affect relationships between neighbours?

Do you agree with the OLRC that there is a need for reform? If so, what kind of reform is appropriate? In this context, two English authors have addressed these issues: see Susan Bright, "Of Estates and Interests: A Tale of Ownership and Property Rights" and Graham Battersby, "Informally Created Interests in Land" both in Susan Bright & John Dewar, eds, *Land Law: Themes and Perspectives* (Oxford: Oxford University Press, 1998) at 529 and 487, respectively.

E. Negative Easements: The Relationship Between Easements and Covenants

Phipps v Pears
[1965] 1 QB 76 (CA)

LORD DENNING MR (Pearson and Salmon LJJ concurring): In the 1920s there were two old houses in Warwick, standing side by side, Nos. 14 and 16, Market Street. They were both owned by Ralph Spencer Field. About 1930, he pulled down No. 16 but left the old No. 14 standing. He erected a new house at No. 16, Market Street, with its flank wall flat up against the old wall of No. 14. He did not bond the two walls together, but the new wall was built up touching the old wall of No. 14.

On July 17, 1931, Ralph Spencer Field conveyed the new No. 16, Market Street to Helena Field, but remained himself owner of the old No. 14. Helena Field disposed of No. 16 and eventually in 1951, the plaintiff bought it, as it was, standing then alongside the old No. 14. Ralph Spencer Field died and his personal representative in 1957 conveyed No. 14, Market Street to the governors of the Lord Leycester Hospital.

So there were the two houses—new No. 16 and old No. 14—standing side by side. In 1962, the Warwick Corporation made an order for the demolition of old No. 14, Market

Street because it was below the required standard. It was, I suppose, unfit for human habitation. In consequence, in September, 1962, the governors of the Lord Leycester Hospital demolished it. And when they did so, there was left exposed the flank wall of new No. 16. This was in a very rough state. It had never been pointed. Indeed, it could not have been because of the way it was built, flat up against the old No. 14. It had never been rendered or plastered. So it was not weatherproof. The result was that the rain got in and during the winter it froze and caused cracks in the wall. The plaintiff seeks to recover for the damage done.

In his particulars of claim the plaintiff alleged that No. 16 had a right of support from No. 14 and that the defendant had withdrawn that support. But he failed on this point because the judge found that No. 16 did not depend on No. 14 for its support. "There was, in fact, no support the one for the other. They were independent walls, untied one to the other."

Then the plaintiff said—or rather it was said on his behalf—that at any rate his house No. 16 was entitled to protection from the weather. So long as No. 14 was there, it afforded excellent protection for No. 16 from rain and frost. By pulling down No. 14, the defendant, he said, had infringed his right of protection from the weather. This right, he said, was analogous to the right of support. It is settled law, of course, that a man who has his house next to another for many years, so that it is dependent on it for support, is entitled to have that support maintained. His neighbour is not entitled to pull down his house without providing substitute support in the form of buttresses or something of the kind, see *Dalton v. Angus*. Similarly, it was said, with a right to protection from the weather. If the man next door pulls down his own house and exposes his neighbour's wall naked to the weather whereby damage is done to him, he is, it is said, liable in damages.

The case, so put, raises the question whether there is a right known to the law to be protected—by your neighbour's house—from the weather. Is there an easement of protection?

There are two kinds of easements known to the law: positive easements, such as a right of way, which give the owner of land *a right himself to do something* on or to his neighbour's land: and negative easements, such as a right of light, which gives him *a right to stop his neighbour doing something* on his (the neighbour's) own land. The right of support does not fall neatly into either category. It seems in some way to partake of the nature of a positive easement rather than a negative easement. The one building, by its weight, exerts a thrust, not only downwards, but also sideways on to the adjoining building or the adjoining land, and is thus doing something to the neighbour's land, exerting a thrust on it, see *Dalton v. Angus, per* Lord Selborne LC. But a right to protection from the weather (if it exists) is entirely negative. It is a right to stop your neighbour pulling down his own house. Seeing that it is a negative easement, it must be looked at with caution. Because the law has been very chary of creating any new negative easements.

Take this simple instance: Suppose you have a fine view from your house. You have enjoyed the view for many years. It adds greatly to the value of your house. But if your neighbour chooses to despoil it, by building up and blocking it, you have no redress. There is no such right known to the law as a right to a prospect or view, see *Bland v. Moseley* cited by Lord Coke in *Aldred's* case. The only way in which you can keep the view from your house is to get your neighbour to make a covenant with you that he will not build so as to block your view. Such a covenant is binding on him by virtue of the contract. It is also binding in equity on anyone who buys the land from him with notice of the covenant. But it is not binding on a purchaser who has no notice of it, see *Leech v. Schweder*.

Take next this instance from the last century. A man built a windmill. The winds blew freely on the sails for thirty years working the mill. Then his neighbour built a schoolhouse only 25 yards away which cut off the winds. It was held that the miller had no remedy: for the right to wind and air, coming in an undefined channel, is not a right known to the law, see *Webb v. Bird*. The only way in which the miller could protect himself was by getting his neighbour to enter into a covenant.

The reason underlying these instances is that if such an easement were to be permitted, it would unduly restrict your neighbour in his enjoyment of his own land. It would hamper legitimate development, see *Dalton v. Angus*, *per* Lord Blackburn. Likewise here, if we were to stop a man pulling down his house, we would put a brake on desirable improvement. Every man is entitled to pull down his house if he likes. If it exposes your house to the weather, that is your misfortune. It is no wrong on his part. Likewise every man is entitled to cut down his trees if he likes, even if it leaves you without shelter from the wind or shade from the sun; see the decision of the Master of the Rolls in Ireland in *Cochrane v. Verner*. There is no such easement known to the law as an easement to be protected from the weather. The only way for an owner to protect himself is by getting a covenant from his neighbour that he will not pull down his house or cut down his trees. Such a covenant would be binding on him in contract: and it would be enforceable on any successor who took with notice of it. But it would not be binding on one who took without notice.

There is a further point. It was said that when the owner, Ralph Spencer Field, conveyed No. 16 to Helena Field, the plaintiff's predecessor, there was implied in the conveyance all the general words of section 62 of the *Law of Property Act, 1925*. The conveyance included all "easements, rights and advantages whatsoever appertaining or reputed to appertain to the land." On the conveyance of No. 16, Market Street, to the plaintiff's predecessor, there passed to him all these "advantages" appertaining to No. 16. One of these advantages, it was said, was the benefit of having the old No. 14 there as a protection from the weather. I do not think this argument avails the plaintiff for the simple reason that, in order for section 62 to apply, the right or advantage must be one which is known to the law, in this sense, that it is capable of being granted at law so as to be binding on all successors in title, even those who take without notice, see *Wright v. Macadam*. A fine view, or an expanse open to the winds, may be an "advantage" to a house but it would not pass under section 62. Whereas a right to use a coal shed or to go along a passage would pass under section 62. The reason being that these last are rights known to the law, whereas the others are not. A right to protection from the weather is not a right known to the law. It does not therefore pass under section 62.

In my opinion, therefore, the plaintiff has not made out any right to the protection he seeks. I find myself in agreement with the county court judge: and I would dismiss the appeal.

Appeal dismissed with costs. Leave to appeal refused.

DISCUSSION NOTES

i. Negative Easements: The Policy Context

In *Phipps*, Lord Denning stated that the law has been "very chary of creating any new negative easements." What justification did he offer for the law's concern about negative easements? It is important to understand the nature of these concerns in relation to *Phipps* and in the context of covenants, discussed below. Are these concerns applicable only to negative easements? Consider, for example, the positive easements recognized by courts in cases discussed above—would any of these easements have tended to restrict the owner of the servient tenement "in his enjoyment of his own land" or "hamper legitimate development"? If so, why should there be a distinction between positive and negative covenants?

In thinking about these issues, consider the definitions of positive and negative easements in the American Law Institute (1944):

451: Affirmative Easement

An affirmative easement entitles the owner thereof to use the land subject to the easement by doing acts which, were it not for the easement, he would not be privileged to do.

452: Negative Easement

A negative easement assures to the owner thereof a particular use or enjoyment of the land subject to the easement by enabling him to prevent the possessor of the land from doing acts upon it which, were it not for the easement, he would be privileged to do.

Do these definitions suggest that negative easements may interfere more substantially than positive easements with the activities of the owner of the servient land? Why or why not? Is it always perfectly clear that an easement is negative or positive? Should the enforceability of an easement depend entirely on the way it is drafted or characterized by a court? You may want to re-examine these questions in the context of the enforceability of positive and negative covenants, discussed below.

Lord Denning's restrictive approach to the recognition of negative easements illustrated in *Phipps* may have resulted from his view that, if the owner of no 16 Market Street had wished to protect the wall of the house from damage from the weather, an easy method was available to accomplish such a purpose—an agreement between the two householders, referred to by Lord Denning as a covenant binding on the parties in contract, and binding on subsequent purchasers with notice. If the owner of no 16 Market Street had wished to enter into such a contract with the owner of no 14, it is possible that it would have been necessary to provide some consideration for the assumption of this obligation on the part of the owner of no 14. Is Lord Denning's real concern not to create an interest without compensation for the owner of no 14, or are there other considerations as well? For example, how would a subsequent purchaser know of the existence of such an easement? Is Lord Denning's concern really about problems of notice? Are there other ways of dealing with these concerns?

By contrast with English law, US law in the 19th century embraced negative easements as a method of enforcing subdivision controls, and it has been suggested that negative easements were generally more useful than covenants for achieving these purposes:

The negative easement was reluctantly acknowledged by English law, which recognized only four negative easements: the rights to air, light, support, and water in an artificial stream. But negative easements came to be used expansively in the United States, not only for protecting light and air, but also for enforcing setback lines and limiting noxious uses. The easement was superior to the covenant as a restrictive tool because it was not subject to a requirement of privity. ...

As actions for injunctions to enforce subdivision deed restrictions became more common, it became increasingly clear that courts were not particularly concerned with the legal classification of restrictions, only with whether the restrictions ought to be enforced at equity. Thus, [another] kind of restriction enforceable at equity, variously called an equitable servitude, equitable easement, or sometimes an (equitable) negative easement, came to the fore as the primary tool the courts recognized for enforcing subdivision restrictions.

(R Chused, *Cases, Materials and Problems in Property* (New York: Matthew Bender, 1988) [Chused] at 971.) This analysis suggests that the underlying rationale for the enforcement of such obligations (including those in negative easements) in the United States was an equitable one. As will be seen in the next section, negative or restrictive covenants were also enforced in England on the basis of equity, although separate principles concerning the enforceability of easements and covenants have been largely maintained in England and Canada, by contrast with the United States. Indeed, as suggested above, some commentators in the United States support the recognition of just one form of servitudes. In spite of these apparent differences among common law jurisdictions, it has been argued that in more recent times, English decisions (like decisions in the United States) have tended to emphasize equitable considerations in injunction actions initiated to preserve a view—for example, of the sea. See P Polden, "Views in Perspective" (1984) 48 Conveyancer and Property Lawyer 429 [Polden]. Moreover, in spite of Lord Denning's concerns to limit the range of negative easements recognized in law, courts have nonetheless enforced a wide range of positive easements. For a useful catalogue, see Mendes da Costa, Balfour & Gillese at 19:36-37. See also K Scott, "Comment" (1964) 22 Cambridge LJ 203.

ii. The Issue of Prescriptive Rights to Light and Air

The appropriateness of recognizing easements in relation to light, air, and unobstructed views may need to be assessed in the context of prescriptive rights. For a case in which a US court rejected a claim to prescriptive rights of access to light and air, see *Fontainebleau Hotel Corp v Forty-Five Twenty-Five, Inc*, 114 So 2d 357 (Fla CA 1959). In that case, a luxury hotel owner brought an injunction application to prevent a rival luxury hotel next door from building a 14-storey addition, on the ground that the new addition would create a shadow after 2 pm every day in the winter over the area of the plaintiff's cabana, swimming pool, and sunbathing areas. Although the trial court had issued a temporary injunction based on nuisance principles, the appellate court reversed this decision. There was no suggestion at trial or on appeal that the plaintiff in this case had any prescriptive rights to light, air, or an unobstructed view of the Atlantic Ocean.

The issue of prescriptive rights to light and air has also been considered frequently in the context of solar energy facilities: e.g. see *Prah v Maretti*, 108 Wis 2d 223, 321 NW 2d 182 (SC 1982). While this case was pending, the Wisconsin legislature adopted a statute permitting local communities to create a land-use permit system for those installing solar energy systems. See JO Grunow, "Comment: Wisconsin Recognizes the Power of the Sun: Prah v Maretti and the Solar Access Act" (1983) Wis L Rev 1263. For a good review of the principles in Canada, see MA Bowden, "Protecting Solar Access in Canada: The Common Law Approach" (1985)

9 Dal LJ 261. According to Bowden, current interpretation of nuisance principles may present some difficulties in preventing subsequent interference with a householder's solar energy facility, and she recommended legislative action. In addition, while suggesting that restrictive covenants may be the most useful device, she also commented on the usefulness of a solar easement (at 286):

> An individual solar user should attempt to negotiate a solar easement with his neighbour to secure the long-term viability of his home heating alternative. Once again the enforceability of such an easement demands a liberal attitude in the courts. However, if the easement is carefully drafted to meet the technical requirements of this tool, if the acceptability of solar easements in other jurisdictions can be outlined, and the perceived social need highlighted, the hesitancy of the courts to accept new easements should be overcome.

Do you agree with this advice? You may want to reconsider it after examining the material concerning covenants in the following section of this chapter.

No Canadian province has yet taken up the challenge of enacting solar easement legislation, but see Law Reform Commission of Saskatchewan, *Background Paper: Solar Access Legislation* (Regina: Commission, 2008).

iii. Easements and Title Registration

In most provinces with Torrens-type land titles legislation (Manitoba being an exception), new prescriptive easements are forbidden once land is brought under that system. East of Manitoba, however, the bulk of conversions into the land titles system has occurred relatively recently, as noted in Chapter 5. If the conditions for a prescriptive easement against a particular servient tenement were met prior to the registration of that parcel under the land titles system, depending on the particular legislative provisions, it may be that the easement can still be enforced as an "overriding interest"—that is, one that is still valid even though it does not appear on the land titles register. In Ontario, "land which has been transferred from Registry into Land Titles by administrative conversion ... may bring with it mature easement by prescription entitlements where there has been 20 years of use prior to the conversion": Marguerite E Moore, *Title Searching & Conveyancing in Ontario*, 6th ed (Toronto: LexisNexis, 2010) at 14. In "new" Torrens jurisdictions, then, prescriptive easements will continue to cast a long shadow over the integrity of the register for some time.

Apart from prescriptive easements that predate the conversion of a parcel to land titles, express legislative provision and judicial interpretation have provided that implied easements, easements of necessity, and possibly easements created by estoppel may also be enforceable as overriding interests against Torrens land: see *Fife v Cohan*, 2007 CanLII 28324, 2007 OJ no 2844 (Sup Ct J), discussed above. In a sense these are even more significant, because new prescriptive easements cannot generally be created in Torrens jurisdictions, while easements of necessity and implied easements arising from transfers of land remain an ongoing possibility. See generally BH Ziff, "A Matter of Overriding Interest: Unregistered Easements Under Alberta's Land Titles System" (1991) 29 Alta L Rev 718.

IV. COVENANTS AND THE USE OF LAND

Most home owners in Ontario would likely be surprised to learn that, if they agree with their neighbour, for example, that the neighbour and her successors in title will maintain a common boundary fence, or a common driveway, the obligation will not bind subsequent owners of the neighbour's property … . [This is an example] of the generally unsatisfactory state of the law of covenants related to land.

(Ontario Law Reform Commission, *Report on Covenants Affecting Freehold Land* (Toronto: Ministry of the Attorney General, 1989) [OLRC *Report on Covenants*] at 1.) Why are subsequent owners not bound by the promise made by the homeowner and his or her neighbour? What are the consequences for homeowner and neighbour, for subsequent purchasers of their land, and for other homeowners in the same neighbourhood? To what extent should the law permit the enforceability of such promises beyond the sphere of privity of contract and on what basis?

These questions are fundamental to understanding why some covenants have been recognized as proprietary interests. Although, as the above quotation from the OLRC *Report on Covenants* illustrates, such covenants may not always bind successors in title, they may be effectively enforced as proprietary interests in other cases. For example, consider again the adjoining landowners at nos 14 and 16 Market Street, discussed above in *Phipps v Pears*. In that case, the owner of no 16 Market Street claimed a right of protection from the weather from the adjoining building, no 14 Market Street. Lord Denning concluded that there was no easement of protection from the weather because any such easement would be a negative easement and, for the reasons discussed there, the law would not recognize any new negative easements. At the same time, Lord Denning suggested that the owner of no 16 could have accomplished the same objective by entering into a covenant with the neighbour at no 14. According to Lord Denning, the covenant would have been enforceable in contract between the parties. In addition, Lord Denning asserted that it would have been binding in equity on subsequent purchasers with notice. In this way, the contractual agreement relating to land entered into by the owners of nos 14 and 16 would bind their successors in title, at least with notice in equity, even though the successors in title to nos 14 and 16 were not involved in the original contract nor in any contract with each other. This means that privately negotiated promises about land, "operating outside the realm of contract, may effectively impose controls over the use of land which bind all parties into whose hands the land may come at any future time." (KJ Gray & PD Symes, *Real Property and Real People: Principles of Land Law* (London: Butterworths, 1981) [Gray & Symes] at 605.)

Covenants in relation to land, like easements and profits, create non-possessory interests in land. Like easements, covenants affect the rights of owners of neighbouring, although not always contiguous, parcels of land; covenants may also limit the scope of activities on servient land, similar to the impact of other non-possessory property interests and licences. In addition, the principles of covenants relating to land reflect the historical development of property law and contract, principles of law and equity, and social changes in land use and development over the past two centuries. Because many of the principles were fashioned by courts on a case-by-case basis, they may appear highly technical and, according to OLRC *Report on Covenants* (at 1) "unnecessarily complex and occasionally illogical." Indeed, Lawrence Berger suggested some years ago that they were "so complex that only a very few specialists understand them"; he recommended that, rather than just relying on legal pre-cedents, the principles should be re-examined in relation to underlying policies. See L Berger, "A Policy Analysis of Promises Respecting the Use of Land" (1970) 55 Minn L Rev 167 for an overview of principles and policies concerning covenants relating to land in the United States. The OLRC's review of the law of covenants also resulted in recommendations to sim-plify and rationalize the principles but, to date, there has been no legislative response to the Commission's recommendations.

This introduction to the law of covenants provides an overview of legal and equitable principles in the context of public policies concerning the use and development of land. In the 19th century, covenants provided an important means of private land-use planning in common law jurisdictions. For example, Timothy Jost examined early US legal techniques for controlling land use, particularly the defeasible fee simple estate, and the reasons why it was eventually rejected in favour of covenants (and other kinds of servitudes) and, in the 20th century, zoning legislation: see Timothy Jost, "The Defeasible Fee and the Birth of the Modern Residential Subdivision" (1984) 49 Miss L Rev 695. For further examination of the develop-ment of these legal policies, see OL Browder, "Running Covenants and Public Policy" (1978) 77 Mich L Rev 12 and U Reichman, "Residential Private Governments: An Introductory Survey" (1976) 43 U Chicago L Rev 253. Significantly, covenants have continued to be important as private planning techniques into the 21st century in spite of legislation enacting municipal zoning and other kinds of public regulation of land use. Indeed, in response to suggestions that modern statutory controls on land use make continued reliance on private covenants unnecessary, OLRC *Report on Covenants* concurred (at 99) with recommendations of the Law Commission of England and Wales that

> it would not be realistic to extend the ambit of planning law to take the place of private restric-tions. Planning law paints with an extremely broad brush, and it is therefore unsuited to the task of resolving the finer details. The planning authorities do not have the wherewithal to regulate the interests of adjoining landowners, and it would be unreasonable to expect them to do so.

Accordingly, it is important to consider the law of covenants in relation to the enactment, especially after the Second World War, of significant statutory changes concerning the use of land, developments that have attempted to balance landowners' freedom of contract with broader interests of public policy. Some of these policy debates are reviewed in Gregory S Alexander, "Freedom, Coercion, and the Law of Servitudes" (1988) 73 Cornell L Rev 883, spe-cifically assessing competing approaches in Reichman (1982); and R Epstein, "Notice and Freedom of Contract in the Law of Servitudes" (1982) 55 S Cal L Rev 1353. See also S Sterk, "Neighbors in American Land Law" (1987) 87 Colum L Rev 55, and Keith Aoki, "Race, Space, and Place: The Relation Between Architectural Modernism, Post-Modernism, Urban Planning, and Gentrification" (1993) 20 Fordham L Rev 699.

The tension between landowners' freedom of contract and broader interests of public policy has frequently occurred in relation to discriminatory covenants, an issue addressed in more detail below. Similar issues were discussed in Chapter 3 with respect to the tension between freedom of *inter vivos* and testamentary disposition, on the one hand, and the non-discrimination values in public policy, on the other. These concerns also require an assessment of the extent to which rationales of encouraging land use and productive development, so apparent during the Industrial Revolution in the 19th century, remain relevant in the 21st century in the context of ideas about the need for conservation and environmental protection.

Indeed, the law of covenants has provided the model for statutes in several Canadian provinces, permitting the creation of "conservation easements" as part of a strategy for protecting the natural environment. It is important to consider the principles and policies of covenants relating to land, not only as technical aspects of the law but also in terms of their impact on social and economic policies about land use. For an overview of some of these issues, see B Rudden, "Economic Theory v Property Law: The 'Numerus Clausus' Problem" in J Eekelaar & J Bell, eds, *Oxford Essays in Jurisprudence*, 3d series (Oxford: Clarendon Press, 1987) 239; and the 2011 Law Commission Report.

A. General Principles: Privity of Contract and Estate

Ontario Law Reform Commission, *Report on Covenants Affecting Freehold Land*
(Toronto: Ministry of the Attorney General, 1989) at 6-8

Historically, a covenant bound only the parties to it. At a relatively early date, however, it was determined that an action for breach of the contract (then an action in *assumpsit*) could be transmitted to the personal representatives of the parties upon their deaths. The right of action could also be released, but it was not generally assignable at common law, because that was thought to encourage maintenance. Although choses in action did later become assignable, in part, in equity, and although they are now generally assignable by statute, it does not follow that covenants are capable of running with land when it is transferred. In this context, the law has developed peculiar and complex rules.

Since covenants relating to land involve both contract law and land law, the principles of both must be considered throughout our discussion of covenants. The two leading principles emerging from these areas are privity of contract and privity of estate. Privity of contract means simply that the parties stand in direct contractual relation to each other and may enforce their rights under the law of contract. Privity of estate, on the other hand, connotes a relationship of tenure between the parties. In modern law, disregarding the relationship between the Crown and subject, a tenurial relationship exists only between lessor and lessee.

Functionally, three basic situations may be identified in connection with these principles. The first is a situation in which privity of contract exists between the parties. The second is one in which privity of estate, but not privity of contract, exists between the parties. The third is a situation in which neither privity of contract nor privity of estate exists between the parties. The fundamental rules, applicable in each of these circumstances, will be discussed in turn.

Privity of contract exists between a lessor and a lessee, the original parties to the lease, and between a vendor and a purchaser upon a transfer of freehold land. If privity of contract exists, the parties to the contract and, as we have indicated, their personal representatives, can bring action against each other to enforce the contract. An action lies either at law for damages for breach of the contract, or sometimes in equity for an injunction or specific performance. It should be noted that the benefit of the contract, that is, the right to sue upon it, is assignable, but the burden, that is, the liability under it, is not.

Privity of estate (as well as privity of contract) exists between a lessor and a lessee, because their relationship is based on tenure. Moreover, if the lessor assigns the reversion, or the lessee assigns the term of the lease, privity of estate will exist between the following: (1) an assignee of the lessor and the original lessee; (2) an assignee of the lessee and the original lessor; and (3) an assignee of the lessor and an assignee of the lessee. As we noted above, privity of estate exists only between lessor and lessee (and their respective assignees). Privity of estate does not exist, therefore, between the lessor and a sublessee, since no direct lessor–lessee relationship exists between them. Nor does privity of estate exist in the context of freehold land.

If privity of estate exists, but privity of contract does not, an assignee of the term or of the reversion may enforce only those covenants that "touch and concern," or relate to the subject-matter of, the lease. As we discuss below, these are covenants that concern the relationship of lessor and lessee. Covenants that do not touch and concern the land are not enforceable by the assignees of the original parties. It must be remembered, however, that such covenants would be enforceable by the original parties themselves.

Since privity of contract continues notwithstanding an assignment of the lease or the reversion, the original parties remain liable to each other for breaches of covenant during the entire term of the lease. On the other hand, since privity of estate continues only so long as the relationship of tenure exists, an assignee of the term or of the reversion is liable only for breaches of covenants that occur while she holds the estate in the land.

Neither privity of estate nor privity of contract exists, in the leasehold context, between a lessor and a sublessee, that is, a person to whom the lessee has sublet part of the term, rather than one to whom he has assigned the remainder of the term. In the freehold context, where the vendor of freehold land has retained adjoining or other land, there is neither privity of contract nor privity of estate between the following: (1) the vendor and the purchaser's assignee; (2) the vendor's assignee and the purchaser; or (3) the vendor's assignee and the purchaser's assignee.

If there is neither privity of contract nor privity of estate between the parties, a covenant is not enforceable, subject to two exceptions. First, in equity, the benefit and the burden of a restrictive covenant, that is, a covenant that is negative in substance, can run with the land. Secondly, at law, the benefit, although not the burden, of a positive or restrictive covenant that touches and concerns the land can run with an estate in the land. Moreover, the benefit of any covenant, whether or not it touches or concerns the land, can be assigned in equity or, more recently, at law by virtue of statute. By contrast, in Ontario, the burden of a covenant cannot be assigned, either at law, in equity or by statute.

DISCUSSION NOTES

i. Covenants and Privity of Contract

There is now general agreement that a "covenant" is simply a contractual promise. As Ziff explained, a covenant was formerly a "promise under seal," but the requirement for a seal in land transactions has now been discarded in many Canadian jurisdictions—e.g. see Ontario's *Land Registration Reform Act, 1984*, SO 1984, c 32 (now *Land Registration Reform Act*, RSO 1990, c L.4), s 13(1). See also Ziff at 399-405 and Anne Warner La Forest, *Anger and Honsberger Law of Real Property* (Aurora, ON: Canada Law Book, 2006) [La Forest] at 16-1. However, because a covenant represents only a contractual promise, it is generally enforceable only where there is privity of contract between the maker of the promise (the covenantor) and the person who benefits from it (the covenantee). The concept of privity of contract is fundamental to common law analysis; see generally V Palmer, *The Paths to Privity: A History of Third Party Beneficiary Contracts at English Law* (San Francisco: Austin & Winfield, 1992).

ii. Terminology of Covenants: "Benefit" and "Burden"

Before proceeding to analyze the principles of covenants, it is important to become familiar with the terminology. Consider *Phipps v Pears* again. In relation to Lord Denning's suggestion that the owners of nos 14 and 16 Market Street might have negotiated a promise, no 16 would have received the "benefit" of such a covenant, while no 14 would have had the "burden" of it. If the owner of no 16 had transferred his estate to a subsequent purchaser, the issue would have been whether the "benefit of the covenant had passed" to the subsequent purchaser (the "assignee of the benefit") along with the fee simple estate. Similarly, if the corporate owner of no 14 had transferred its estate to a subsequent purchaser, the issue would have been whether the "burden of the covenant had passed" to the subsequent purchaser (the "assignee of the burden" of the covenant) along with the fee simple estate. As is apparent, it is necessary to determine in what circumstances the benefit of a covenant will run and, similarly, in what circumstances the burden of a covenant will run with the estate in land that is being transferred.

Consider a vendor who wishes to sell a portion of a block of land, retaining the remainder. The vendor may negotiate with the purchaser that, in relation to the parcel being transferred, the purchaser may not "build any structure on the land except a single-family dwelling." Who has the benefit of the covenant in this case? Who has the burden? If both the vendor and the purchaser subsequently convey their respective blocks to assignees, will the covenant be enforceable? Note that the assignee of the vendor and the assignee of the purchaser have no privity of contract. Why do they not have privity of estate? If the purchaser's assignee decides to build a 40-storey apartment building, what can the vendor's assignee do to prevent this action?

This legal problem is complicated by the fact that the principles concerning the running of the benefit of a covenant are different from those concerning the running of the burden. Moreover, the legal principles for the running of benefits and burdens are somewhat different from the equitable principles, especially in relation to the running of the burden of a covenant. Thus, it may be necessary to define, as a matter of technical application of the principles, whether legal or equitable principles should be used. Moreover, because it is possible for landowners to enter into "mutual covenants," so that each party has both benefit and burden when the original promise is made, it may also be necessary to determine whether both the benefit and the burden have passed. Because the principles concerning the running of the benefit and the burden may differ, the position of subsequent purchasers in such cases may not be exactly the same as that of the original contracting parties. It is thus important to any analysis of covenants to determine at the outset which land is benefited and which is burdened (just as it was necessary to decide, in the context of easements, which land was the dominant tenement and which was the servient land).

The principles concerning covenants also require an analysis of the nature of the covenant and whether it "touches and concerns the land" or is merely a personal covenant. In some cases, the benefit or burden of a covenant will bind a successor only if the covenant touches and concerns the land. The question when a covenant touches and concerns the land is explored in more detail in the following sections.

B. Leasehold Covenants: An Overview

A lessor and lessee have privity of contract, so they are usually entitled to enforce all the covenants in a lease for the duration of the leasehold estate. Even if the lessee transfers the leasehold estate to an assignee, the original lessee generally remains liable for the covenants, although the lessee may be able to seek indemnification from the assignee. Similarly, as noted in Chapter 4, the original lessor generally remains liable on the covenants for the duration of the leasehold estate even if the reversion is assigned.

If either the lessor or the lessee makes an assignment, the parties may have privity of estate. For example, if the lessor assigns the reversion, the assignee of the reversion and the lessee will have privity of estate. Similarly, if the lessee assigns the leasehold, the assignee of the leasehold and the lessor will have privity of estate. As explained above, the benefit and burden of some covenants may be enforceable between parties who do not have privity of contract if they have privity of estate.

The principles concerning the enforceability of the benefit and burden of a covenant in relation to the assignment of the leasehold estate were established in *Spencer's Case* (1583), 77 ER 72 (KB). According to *Spencer's Case*, both the benefit and burden of covenants that "touched and concerned" the land passed to the assignee. The legal test to determine whether a covenant touches and concerns the land is whether the covenant affects the lessor as lessor or the tenant as tenant. However, the application of this definition in practice is sometimes perplexing. For example, in *Regent Oil Co v JA Gregory (Hatch End) Ltd*, [1966] Ch 402 (CA), a clause in a lease providing that the tenant in a commercial establishment would purchase products from the landlord was held to touch and concern the land. By contrast, a covenant by a lessor to repay a security deposit provided by the tenant was held not to be enforceable against the assignee of the lessor, because "the covenant did not touch and concern the land in the sense of affecting the landlord and tenant relationship." See *Re Dollar Land Corp Ltd and Solomon*, [1963] 2 OR 269 (H Ct J). For further analysis, see La Forest at 16-11 to 16-13.

The principles concerning the enforceability of the benefit and burden of a covenant in relation to the assignment of the reversion were established by the *Grantees of Reversion Act* in 1540, thus predating *Spencer's Case*. According to this legislation, the benefit and burden of covenants "having reference to the subject matter of the lease" run with the reversion. This legislation is now contained in the *Landlord and Tenant Act*, RSO 1990, c L.7, ss 4-8 (renamed the *Commercial Tenancies Act*); see also *Landlord and Tenant Act*, RSNB 1973, c L.1, ss 2-3. According to *Davis v Town Properties Investment Corporation Ltd*, [1903] 1 Ch 797 (CA), the phrase "having reference to the subject matter of the lease" has the same meaning as covenants that "touch and concern" the lease. For further analysis of the effect of an assignment of the leasehold and the reversion, and recommendations for reform, see OLRC *Report on Covenants* at 9-11.

These principles apply in relation to assignments of the reversion and the leasehold estate. As the OLRC *Report on Covenants*, excerpted above, explained, they do not apply in relation to a sublease by the lessee. In a sublease arrangement, the lessee transfers only part of his or her leasehold estate, creating a new lessor–lessee relationship between the lessee and the sublessee. By contrast, when the lessee assigns the leasehold estate, the new assignee takes on the entire interest of the lessee. Thus, when a lessee assigns the leasehold estate, there is privity of estate between the lessor and the assignee of the leasehold. However, when the lessee creates a sublease, there is no privity of estate between the lessor and the sublessee. As a result, the lessor cannot directly enforce covenants in the original lease against the sublessee, although the lessor can do so indirectly by enforcing them against the lessee (with whom there remains both privity of contract and privity of estate). In addition, as in the context of freehold covenants discussed in the next section, it may be possible for the lessor to enforce the benefit and burden of negative covenants against the sublessee if they touch and concern the land and meet the other requirements established in equity.

C. Freehold Covenants: Enforcement at Law

Freehold covenants are sometimes created by contractual agreements between two adjoining landowners to achieve particular objectives (as Lord Denning suggested in *Phipps v Pears*, discussed above). However, they are more often created when a vendor (or developer) transfers one or more lots to purchasers and, as part of a transaction, creates a burden on a purchaser's land in favour of the land retained by the vendor. If the purchaser subsequently breaches the agreement, the vendor may sue for damages for the breach and, in some cases, obtain an injunction in equity preventing a breach from occurring or continuing to occur. As is apparent, the vendor's entitlement in such cases is based on privity of contract between the vendor and purchaser. There are also common law principles and statutory provisions in some provinces that provide that personal representatives and others may be bound by such covenants according to contract principles. For a summary, see the OLRC *Report on Covenants* at 15. See also Department of Education, *Easements and Restrictive Covenants* (Toronto: Law Society of Upper Canada, 1989).

The legal principles concerning the enforcement of covenants by or against assignees of freehold interests are more straightforward than those in equity. In general, according to the legal principles, the benefit of a covenant may pass in defined circumstances, but the burden of a covenant cannot pass with the assignment of a freehold interest under any circumstances. The reasons for these principles, as well as underlying policy considerations, are explained in the material that follows.

1. The Benefit of the Covenant

In relation to legal principles for the passing of the benefit of a covenant with the assignment of the freehold, two requirements are relatively clear. First, the covenantee (the landowner for whom the covenant provided a benefit) must have a legal interest in land. Second, traditionally it has been suggested that the covenantee and the assignee of the covenantee must have the same legal estate in the land, although this requirement may have been altered by s 24(1) of Ontario's *Conveyancing and Law of Property Act*, RSO 1990, c C.34 and by s 78 of the English *Law of Property Act 1925* (15 & 16 Geo 5), c 20.

More complex is the principle that the benefit of a covenant can pass at law only if it touches and concerns the land. As Gray & Symes suggested (at 609), this requirement means that "it must be shown that the covenant was entered into for the benefit of the land owned by the covenantee and not merely for his personal benefit." In *Smith and Snipes Hall Farm Ltd v River Douglas Catchment Board*, [1949] 2 KB 500 (CA), the court stated (at 506) that a covenant that touched and concerned the land "must either affect the land as regards the mode of occupation, or it must be such as *per se*, and not merely from collateral circumstances, affects the value of the land." Thus, where the board had covenanted to keep the banks of a river in good repair, an assignee of the covenantee was able to require the board to undertake needed repairs because the covenant "touched and concerned the land."

By contrast with equitable principles, it is important to note that the legal principles for the running of the benefit of the covenant set out above make no distinction between positive covenants (requiring the covenantor to take some action) and negative covenants (requiring the covenantor to refrain from defined activities). As is evident, the covenant that was held to be enforceable by an assignee of the covenantee in *Smith*, above, was a positive covenant, requiring the board to undertake action to repair the banks of the river to prevent flooding. As well, the running of the benefit of the covenant at law may occur even if the covenant does not concern the covenantor's land. The classic illustration cited for this principle is *Pakenham's Case* (1368), YB 42 Edw 3, Co Litt 385a. In that case, the covenantee entered into an agreement with a prior who undertook to celebrate divine service each week in the covenantee's chapel. Some years later, the covenantee's great-grandson, as assignee of the covenant, sued to enforce the covenant successfully. As in *Smith*, the covenantor did not have to own land to make the covenant enforceable.

2. The Burden of the Covenant

As stated above, the burden of a covenant relating to land cannot pass at law. Although this principle is simple, it is also important to understand the rationale for this approach. The principle has existed for centuries, but the justification for the common law's approach is usually explained by reference to a 19th-century case, *Keppell v Bailey* (1834), 39 ER 1042 (Ch). In this case, the occupiers of an ironworks covenanted for themselves and their assigns to transport all limestone along a specific railroad, and then the original covenantors assigned their interest to the defendant. When the plaintiffs sought to enforce the covenant, it was held that the burden of a covenant did not run with the land at law. In stating this conclusion, Lord Brougham explained the policy underlying the legal principle (at 1049):

> [It] must not … be supposed that incidents of a novel kind can be devised and attached to property at the fancy or caprice of any owner. It is clearly inconvenient both to the science of the law and to the public weal that such a latitude should be given … . [Great] detriment would arise and much confusion of rights if parties were allowed to invent new modes of holding and enjoying real property, and to impress upon their lands and tenements a peculiar character, which should follow them into all hands, however remote.

Note that this is another way of discussing the *numerus clausus* problem, considered in Chapter 3 and elsewhere. *Keppell* is discussed in this context in Ben McFarlane, "Keppell v Bailey (1834); Hill v Tupper (1863): The Numerus Clausus and the Common Law" in *Landmark Cases in Land Law*.

As the OLRC *Report on Covenants* stated (at 20-21), the burden of such covenants was not permitted to run with freehold land "because property titles would become heavily encumbered, and, consequently, the assignability of the land would be impeded." In addition to rendering land less alienable, persons subsequently dealing with the land "would have great difficulty in ascertaining the existence of such covenants because they do not normally have a physical manifestation." Interestingly, the legal principle was adopted in Canada even though the existence of land registration systems in most provinces has never presented an obstacle to determining whether there was a covenant affecting land, by contrast with the situation in England at the time that *Keppell v Bailey* was decided. Moreover, in relation to Lord Brougham's concern about covenants making land less alienable, there may be other arguments suggesting that land that is subject to restrictions may, in some cases, become more valuable and thus more alienable.

DISCUSSION NOTES

i. Applying the Principle: Parkinson v Reid

The OLRC *Report on Covenants* described (at 21) the consequences of the legal principle concerning the running of the burden of a covenant in *Parkinson et al v Reid*, [1966] SCR 162:

> [The] owners of adjoining lots entered into an agreement under which the defendant's predeces-
> sor in title covenanted for himself, his heirs, executors, administrators and assigns (1) to construct
> a stairway on his lot to serve as a common entrance for the buildings on both lots; (2) to repair
> and replace the stairway as needed; and (3) to permit the plaintiff's predecessor in title free and
> uninterrupted access via the stairway. The lots subsequently having passed into the hands of the
> plaintiff and the defendant and the stairway having been destroyed, the plaintiff brought action
> to require the defendant to replace the stairway. The Supreme Court of Canada refused to grant
> a mandatory injunction.

Why did the court conclude that the plaintiff was not entitled to an injunction in the context of the legal principles concerning the running of the burden of covenants? What effect would the court's conclusion have on the value of the plaintiff's land? Would it be more or less alienable? What effect would the decision have on the defendant's land? Is this covenant negative or positive? You may want to reconsider this case after examining the principles for the running of the burden of covenants in equity below in this section.

The Ontario Court of Appeal applied *Parkinson v Reid* in *Durham Condominium Corp No 123 v Amberwood Investments Ltd* (2002), 58 OR (3d) 481 [*Amberwood*]. At issue was a covenant for payment of expenses in relation to a condominium development. According to Charron JA (at 488):

> The rule that positive covenants do not run with the land has been a settled principle of English
> common law for well over a century and it is undisputed that it has clearly been adopted in Can-
> ada: *Parkinson v. Reid* ... . It appears to be equally undisputed that the rule at times causes in-
> convenience, that its application in some cases may even result in unfairness, and that the present
> state of the law should be modified to meet the needs of modern conveyancing. However, it is
> my view that the call for reform is not one for the courts to answer but for the legislature. Any
> change in the law in this area could have complex and far-reaching effects that cannot be accur-
> ately assessed on a case-by-case basis. The need to preserve certainty in commercial and property
> transactions requires that any meaningful reform be achieved by legislation that can be drafted
> with careful regard to the consequences.

In *Amberwood*, a majority of the Court of Appeal also rejected arguments about "exceptions" to this rule, reviewed below. For further analysis of *Parkinson*, see the OLRC *Report on Covenants* at 21-22. Both *Parkinson* and *Amberwood* relied on the principles established in a 19th-century English precedent: *Austerberry v Corporation of Oldham* (1885), 29 Ch D 750 (CA).

ii. Austerberry v Corporation of Oldham

In 1837, John Elliott conveyed a part of his land to trustees who undertook to make a toll road and keep it in good repair. The trustees made the road and maintained it until it was taken over by the Corporation of Oldham. In 1881, the corporation sought to recover the costs of repairing this road from the landowners, including the plaintiff Austerberry, the assignee of John Elliott. Both Austerberry and the Corporation of Oldham had taken their conveyances with notice of the covenant. The plaintiff initiated an action to determine his rights pursuant to the covenant, requesting an injunction to restrain the Oldham Corporation. When the court found in favour of the defendant corporation, the plaintiff Austerberry appealed to the Court of Appeal. The court concluded that the burden of the covenant to maintain the road made by the trustees could not pass to their successor, the Oldham Corporation, because it involved positive obligations, but gave little in the way of policy analysis as to why this result should flow. The main reason advanced by the court was the absence of any precedent affirmatively stating that the burden of positive covenants could run with the land. In spite of its rather weak foundation, *Austerberry* has continued to be followed in England and the Commonwealth for well over a century.

D. Overcoming the Common Law Principle About the Burden of Covenants

As the court's decision in *Parkinson v Reid*, above, demonstrates, there are some circumstances in which plaintiffs may wish to enforce covenants relating to land, even though the legal principles do not permit them to be enforced directly. Not surprisingly, a number of methods were developed to achieve the result that could not be achieved because of the common law's intransigence with respect to the running of the burden of covenants. As described in the OLRC *Report on Covenants* (at 22-24):

> The inconvenience of the rule that the burden of a covenant cannot run with the land at law, particularly as it applies to positive covenants, has resulted in the development of a number of methods by which the effect of the rule may be circumvented.
>
> One such method of avoiding the rule is to rely on a chain of personal covenants, and thereby maintain privity of contract. For example, if a vendor exacts a covenant from a purchaser to maintain a watercourse running across the land sold and the land retained by the vendor, the purchaser can require a similar covenant from the person to whom he subsequently sells. The purchaser will do so because he will remain liable to the vendor for any breach of covenant, even after the subsequent resale, by reason of privity of contract. Although the vendor may not sue the transferee, he may sue the original purchaser who, in turn, can sue the transferee. The longer such a chain grows, however, the less likely it is to remain effective. It can be broken by the death, insolvency, or disappearance of one of the parties, or by the failure of one of them to take a covenant from his assignee. Moreover, the only remedy available in these cases is damages, whereas injunctive relief might be preferable in certain circumstances.

In England, a variety of other devices has been employed to avoid the problem. The first involves the use of a rentcharge, which is a periodic payment charged on land. The device is useful in the enforcement of positive covenants because it is possible both to annex a right of entry, and impose a positive covenant, under a rentcharge. Indeed, it is common for the payment to be a nominal amount only, the purpose of the rentcharge being simply to enable the enforcement of the positive covenants. Such covenants are then enforceable in perpetuity. It would appear that such a right of entry would also be exempt from perpetuities in Ontario.

A third method of avoiding the rule is to rely upon the doctrine in *Halsall v. Brizell*. This doctrine is based upon the old rule, relating to deeds, that a person who claims the benefit of a deed must also take it subject to the burdens. In the *Halsall* case, the purchasers of lots in a subdivision were entitled, under a trust deed, to use private roads and other amenities. Each purchaser covenanted to pay a share of the cost to maintain the amenities. The court held that their successors were liable to pay their share of the cost. The usefulness of the doctrine, however, is somewhat limited. It will operate only if there is a benefit to be claimed under the deed, and further, it will operate only so long as the assignee of the covenantor continues to claim that benefit.

In addition to the devices discussed above, the burden of certain positive covenants made in favour of public bodies can be made to run by statute. For example, provisions to this effect are contained in the *Planning Act, 1983*. Under this Act, a person who purchases or otherwise acquires land in a community improvement area from a municipality must covenant to maintain the land and buildings and the use thereof in conformity with the plan until a zoning bylaw is passed for the area. Similarly, an owner of land may be required to enter into an agreement with a municipality respecting the provision of facilities, services or matters in return for an increase in the height or density of a development.

Either of the above agreements may be registered on title to the land, and the municipality is entitled to enforce the agreement against the other party or, subject to the provisions of the *Registry Act* and the *Land Titles Act*, against subsequent owners of the land. ...

The rule prohibiting the running of the burden of positive covenants with freehold land presents a particular difficulty in the context of condominiums. Accordingly, legislation has been enacted to permit the enforcement of such covenants for condominiums governed by the legislation. Under the *Condominium Act*, each unit owner is bound by the Act, the declaration establishing the condominium and the condominium corporation's bylaws and rules, and each has a right to the compliance thereof by the other owners. Thus, for example, the unit owners are required to contribute to common expenses in the proportions specified in the declaration, which obligation is enforceable by lien. Furthermore, a unit owner has a duty to maintain, and may have a duty to repair, his unit.

(Some of these issues were discussed in Chapter 6.)

DISCUSSION NOTES

i. Applying the Principles: Lohse v Fleming

In *Lohse v Fleming*, 2008 ONCA 307, developers, as part of a land development at Port Albert, Ontario, drilled a well on their property and covenanted to supply water via underground pipes at an annual fee to purchasers of lots. Over the years, both the developers and the initial lot-owners had changed. After the Walkerton water disaster of 2000, the respondents, owners of the lot on which the well existed, began to advise lot-owners in the development that they no longer wished to supply water to them. The appellant lot-owners applied for a declaration that they had obtained an easement or covenant entitling them to be supplied with water. Their deed contained the following clauses:

> The vendor covenants to supply water from a central water system for domestic purposes only at an annual rate to be paid on or before May lst in each year. This covenant will not be applicable if the water system is taken over by either a municipal or any provincial agency.
>
> It is agreed that these restrictions and covenants shall run with the land hereby conveyed and shall bind and also enure to the benefit of the heirs and assigns of the various parties to whom any part of the lands so made subject to the above restrictions and covenants shall at any time become or belong to. All covenants and agreements herein and rights hereby granted to the said parties shall extend to and be binding on their heirs and executors.

The trial judge found that, having regard to the nature of the water system and the steps required to ensure the flow of water to the neighbouring properties, the supply of water entailed positive acts on the part of the respondents. According to the Court of Appeal at para 17,

> [h]aving made that finding, the trial judge was on solid ground in concluding that the positive nature of this obligation prevented the appellants from obtaining an easement, and that absent privity of contract, this positive covenant could not run with the land: see *Nordin v. Faridi*, 1996 CanLII 3321 (BCCA), [1996] 5 W.W.R. 242 (B.C.C.A.) at para. 45; *Parkinson v. Reid*, 1966 CanLII 4 (SCC), [1966] S.C.R. 162 at 167; and *Amberwood Investments Ltd. v. Durham Condominium Corp. No. 123*, 2002 CanLII 44913 (ONCA), (2002), 58 O.R. (3d) 481 (C.A.).

Why did the court not apply the clause stating that the covenants "shall bind and also enure to the benefit of the heirs and assigns of the various parties"? Is it fair that parties who have purchased a property in reliance on water being supplied pursuant to such clauses should have their expectations disappointed?

A somewhat similar situation arose in *Black v Owen*, 2012 ONSC 400 (Div Ct), regarding the levying of fees for the use and maintenance of private roads in a Toronto development. Wychwood Park was created in the 1880s as an artists' colony, and currently comprises some 60 properties in an area of central Toronto near Bathurst Street and St Clair Avenue. Under a trust deed of 1891, trustees were appointed to hold "the roadways, drives and the park reserve ... as private property for the benefit of the owners." They were also required to maintain the roads and given the authority to levy annual fees on the lot-owners in the development for that purpose. The trustees sought to recover the fees levied against Mr Owen for 2008 and 2009, which he had not paid. They succeeded in Small Claims Court and Mr Owen appealed. The Divisional Court dismissed the appeal on the basis that Mr Owen was bound by the terms of the trust deed because he had actual notice of it. Mr Owen raised the argument that the burden of the covenant to pay the fees could not run to him from his predecessor in title, but because this argument had not been raised at trial, the court declined to deal with it. For the same reason, it also declined to deal with an argument based on the rule against perpetuities. To what extent might the argument about positive covenants have succeeded had the court considered it in this context?

ii. The Principle of Halsall v Brizell: The Amberwood Decision

The principle of *Halsall v Brizell*, [1957] Ch 169 (Ch D), referred to in OLRC *Report on Covenants*, excerpted above, represented an important development, challenging the legal principle that prevented the running of the burden of a covenant. As Ziff pointed out, however, the case had limited value as a precedent because the judgment in the case was *obiter* on this point and the benefit–burden issue had not been fully argued by counsel. In spite of these limitations, however, *Halsall v Brizell* was subsequently used to support the judgment in *ER Ives Investment Ltd v High*, [1967] 2 QB 379 (CA), another English case involving estoppel by acquiescence in relation to the benefit and burden of covenants.

The most significant application of the principle of *Halsall v Brizell*, however, occurred in *Tito v Waddell (Ocean Island)*, [1977] Ch 106 (Ch D). In that case, the discovery of large deposits of high grade phosphate on the British South Pacific colony of Ocean Island (Banaba) resulted in an exclusive mining licence being granted to a British company. The company then set up arrangements to obtain the right to remove phosphate and trees in the late 19th century. By the time of the First World War, the existing arrangements had fallen into disfavour, and after 1913 they were replaced by a new set of agreements with landowners on Ocean Island that, among other matters, required the company to replant the lands subject to mining operations with coconut and other food-bearing trees at the conclusion of the mining operations. After the war, the original company was bought out by other interests and, in 1971, a number of Banabans (including Rotan Tito) filed suit, successfully seeking performance of the replanting obligations that were then due. As Ziff explained:

> The liability of [the assignees of the covenantor] could not be founded on contract *simpliciter*; they were not parties to the original contracts or deeds …. Moreover, under orthodox views the benefit but not the burden of a contractual promise may be assigned, and equally, the burden of positive covenants cannot run with land at law or in equity. Therefore, the liability of the defendants … had to rest on some other footing: enter [the principle in *Halsall v Brizell*].

(Bruce Ziff, "Positive Covenants Running with Land: A Castaway on Ocean Island?" (1989) 27 Alta L Rev 354 at 356.)

The decision in *Tito v Waddell* was expressly rejected in *Government Insurance Office v KA Reed Services Pty Ltd*, [1988] VR 829 (SC Full Ct) in Australia; the court also attacked the principle of *Halsall v Brizell* directly, suggesting that it was based on an illusory foundation. Do you agree with this analysis? How important are traditional concerns about the problems of the running of the burden of covenants, as established in cases such as *Keppell v Bailey*? To what extent is there is a need for more flexibility and creativity in the principles?

According to Ziff, the current controversy illustrated in the different outcomes in *Tito v Waddell*, on the one hand, and *Reed Services*, on the other, suggests a need for legislative reform concerning covenants relating to land. Ziff compared these cases to the situation in the early 19th century when there was a need for parliamentary reform of the law of covenants in England, but no such reform occurred. As a result, there was a dramatic new development in equitable principles concerning the running of the burden of covenants in the case of *Tulk v Moxhay* (1848), 41 ER 1143 (Ch):

> In 1832, the Real Property Commissioners recommended that legislation be introduced to make it clear that affirmative and restrictive covenants could be effectively annexed to land. Parliament did not act but the mantle of reform was taken up in 1848 in the landmark case of *Tulk v. Moxhay*.

In the years which followed, the scope of the new doctrine was refashioned and constricted. In a curious way, history may be repeating itself. Calls for reform of the law pertaining to the running of positive burdens have so far fallen on deaf ears, but there has been movement in this area nonetheless, through *Tito v. Waddell*. Even if that judgment is deficient—and *Reed Services* points to some of its vagaries and flaws—*Tito* as with *Tulk* may yet prove to be a valuable first step in the reform process.

(Ziff at 372.)

In this context, reconsider the decision in *Amberwood*, referred to above. In *Amberwood*, a developer constructed a condominium project in Whitby, Ontario; it was registered as Durham Condominium Corporation. In addition, the developer constructed a recreational facility on this land, which was intended to be used by residents of the Durham Condominium Corporation project and by a second condominium project to be constructed on adjacent lands. The developer and Durham Condominium Corporation signed an agreement that provided, *inter alia*, for the sharing of use and maintenance expenses of this recreational facility; the agreement stated expressly that these provisions were intended to be binding on successors of the parties. The developer eventually experienced financial problems and the adjacent lands were acquired through power of sale by Amberwood Investments Limited. No building was constructed on Amberwood's lands, and Amberwood ceased to make the payments pursuant to the agreement. In subsequent litigation, the trial judge held that the principles of *Austerberry v Oldham* were applicable and that the burden of a positive covenant did not run with the land. The trial judge also concluded that, in the absence of legislative reform, the principle of *Halsall v Brizell* was not available to compel Amberwood to make the payments required by the agreement.

On appeal, a majority of the Ontario Court of Appeal concluded that it was not appropriate for the court to overturn the common law principles established in *Austerberry*. After reviewing the analysis and recommendations of the OLRC *Report on Covenants* (dated 1989), Charron JA concluded (at 496):

> In my view, the sheer number and complexity of issues that would have to be considered in order to address the various concerns relating to such reform of the law make it abundantly clear that any significant change requires a legislative initiative. A case-by-case approach would create unmanageable confusion and uncertainty in the law.

As Charron JA also noted, there were a number of other precedents confirming that it was not appropriate for the courts to extend principles about the running of the burden of covenants: e.g. see *Rhone v Stephens*, [1994] 2 All ER 65 (HL) and *R v York (Township), Ex Parte 125 Varsity Rd Ltd*, [1960] OR 238 (CA).

In addition, Charron JA considered the application of the principle of *Halsall v Brizell*. However, because the court concluded that the appellant had failed to show any use and enjoyment of the benefit on the part of Amberwood, the majority held that the principle was not applicable on the facts. In addition, the majority noted that the principle had been subjected to criticism as well as refinement (and limitation) by subsequent cases, including the decision of the House of Lords in *Rhone v Stephens*, above. As a result, Charron JA concluded on this issue (at 507):

> In my view, the case law does not support the [trial judge's] finding that the benefit and burden principle (*Halsall v. Brizell*) has been clearly adopted by the English courts as an exception to the

rule that positive covenants do not run with the land. Indeed, had *Rhone v. Stephens* been brought to his attention, the [trial judge] undoubtedly would have held that the "pure" principle of benefit and burden, relied upon by [Durham Condominium Corporation] in this case and identified as an aspect of the doctrine in *Halsall v. Brizell* by Megarry V-C in *Tito's* case, was later expressly rejected by the English courts.

In a dissenting judgment, MacPherson JA questioned (at 513) whether "the law of real property in Ontario should recognize qualifications on, or exceptions to, the rule in *Auster-berry*." Citing both historical and practical issues, he suggested that it was appropriate for the courts to do so. In addition, he concluded that the comments in *Rhone v Stephens* were not compelling in rejecting the principle of *Halsall v Brizell*. Finally, MacPherson JA suggested (at 525) that Amberwood had notice of the covenant and appeared to accept it at the time of its negotiations:

> In summary, I would apply the benefit–burden exception to the rule in *Austerberry* in the present case. Since Amberwood had notice of the burdens, since the benefits are "real and substantial," and since Amberwood elected to accept them, it must also accept the burden of paying its share of the interim costs.

In assessing the benefit to Amberwood, the dissenting judgment suggested that the maintenance and 24-hour security provided by Durham Condominium Corporation consti-tuted the "real and substantial benefit."

As is evident, there was a difference of views in the majority and dissenting decisions with respect to *both* the existence of the principle of *Halsall v Brizell* in Canadian law *and* its applic-ability to the facts in *Amberwood*. These two aspects of the "exception" are, of course, often closely linked in the cases. In addition, however, the majority and dissenting judges differed with respect to the need for reform to be accomplished by legislation rather than by judicial intervention. You may wish to review this issue after considering the reform instituted by a 19th-century court in *Tulk v Moxhay*, below.

According to Bruce Ziff, the Ontario Court of Appeal's decision in *Amberwood* was "the most important decision on the subject of positive covenants running with the land in the history of Canadian jurisprudence." His assessment was contained in an affidavit in support of Durham's application for leave to appeal to the Supreme Court of Canada (discontinued [2002] SCCA no 208); others involved in the development of large commercial projects agreed with Ziff's further view that there are important practical consequences for clients and lawyers involved in negotiating these development agreements: see Julius Melnitzer, "The Most Important Decision on the Subject of Positive Covenants," *Law Times* (3 June 2002). For further analysis of the principle of *Halsall v Brizell*, see FR Crane, "Comment" (1957) 21 Conveyancer and Property Lawyer 160, and Christine Davis, "The Principle of Benefit and Burden" (1998) 57 Cambridge LJ 522.

For commentaries on the *Amberwood* case, see Paul Perell, "A Commentary on Amber-wood Investments Ltd v Durham Condominium Corp No 123" (2002) 50 RPR (3d) 52 and Peter A Simm, "Time to Drain the Swamp? Case Comment on Amberwood Investments Ltd v Durham Condominium Corp No 123" (2002) 50 RPR (3d) 63. See also Jeffrey W Lem, "Annota-tion" (2002) 50 RPR (3d) 4.

For other comments on enforcing positive covenants, see A Prichard, "Making Positive Covenants Run" (1973) 37 Conveyancer and Property Lawyer (NS) 194; RE Megarry, "Note"

(1957) 73 Law Q Rev 154; RJ Smith, "The Running of Covenants in Equitable Leases and Equitable Assignments of Legal Leases" (1978) Cambridge LJ 98; WH Lloyd, "Enforcement of Affirmative Agreements Respecting the Use of Land" (1928) 14 Va L Rev 419; and SF French, "Servitudes Reform and the New Restatement of Property: Creation Doctrines and Structural Simplification" (1988) 73 Cornell L Rev 928.

E. Freehold Covenants: Enforcement in Equity

1. The Burden of the Covenant

The legal arrangements adopted to overcome the common law principle that the burden of a covenant does not run with the land occurred in a changing social and economic context in 19th-century England. As Gray & Symes at 614 explained:

> The mid-19th century was a period of significant expansion, when the tension was greatest between the desire to keep land unfettered by private covenant (and therefore profitable for industrial development) and the conflicting desire to curb the effects of commercial and urban growth (by preserving residential amenity for the private householder). These conflicting policies were reflected in the case law of the period [including *Keppell v Bailey*, discussed above].

In the absence of public regulation of land use and development, the inability of private landowners to make enforceable arrangements to preserve the character and amenities around them resulted in considerable pressure for reform. As SI George noted, real property commissioners were appointed in the 1830s to examine English law on real property, and their third report in 1832 considered the state of leasehold and freehold covenants. In relation to freehold covenants, the report of the commissioners recommended that they should be enforceable in equity. In this context, the decision in *Tulk v Moxhay* represented a judicial response to a problem in the absence of any legislative action, although there continued to be disagreements among members of the judiciary after *Tulk v Moxhay* as to the scope of the decision. For an account of the legal context in which *Tulk v Moxhay* was decided, see SI George, "Tulk v Moxhay Restored—To Its Historical Context" (1990) 12:2 Liverpool L Rev 173 [George], and cases cited there.

In examining the decision in *Tulk v Moxhay*, consider the extent to which the case represents a departure from previous authority about the running of the burden of covenants.

Tulk v Moxhay

(1848), 41 ER 1143 (Ch)

[Tulk held the fee simple of the enclosed gardens and several houses in Leicester Square. In 1808, he conveyed in fee simple the enclosed garden called Leicester Square to Elms and his heirs and assigns. A covenant in this deed stated that Elms and his heirs and assigns would at their own expense maintain in sufficient and proper repair the square garden with the equestrian statue in the centre in an open state and uncovered with any buildings. For the payment of a reasonable rent, Tulk's tenants (the inhabitants of Leicester Square) and their heirs and assigns would have keys and the privilege of admission into the garden. Many years later, the gardens were conveyed to Moxhay and his heirs, but this conveyance did not include the covenant in the 1808 deed. Nonetheless, Moxhay admitted that he had had notice of the covenant in the deed of 1808 at the time of the conveyance to him. Moxhay intended to cut down the trees and shrubs in the garden, remove the equestrian statue and the iron railing around the garden, and erect a building on the square. According to Moxhay, the square had totally altered in character since the original covenant and was in a neglected and ruinous condition at the time of his conveyance. Tulk brought an application for an injunction preventing Moxhay from carrying out his plans. The master of the rolls granted the application to restrain Moxhay from converting or using the garden, and the iron railing around it, for any purpose other than as a square garden in an open state and uncovered with buildings. See *Tulk v Moxhay* (1848), 18 LJ Ch 83 (Ch D). Moxhay then brought a motion to discharge that order.]

COTTENHAM LC: … That this Court has jurisdiction to enforce a contract between the owner of land and his neighbour purchasing a part of it, that the latter shall either use or abstain from using the land purchased in a particular way, is what I never knew disputed. Here there is no question about the contract: the owner of certain houses in the square sells the land adjoining, with a covenant from the purchaser not to use it for any other purpose than as a square garden. And it is now contended, not that the vendee could violate that contract, but that he might sell the piece of land, and that the purchaser from him may violate it without this Court having any power to interfere. If that were so, it would be impossible for an owner of land to sell part of it without incurring the risk of rendering what he retains worthless. It is said that, the covenant being one which does not run with the land, this Court cannot enforce it; but the question is, not whether the covenant runs with the land, but whether a party shall be permitted to use the land in a manner inconsistent with the contract entered into by his vendor, and with notice of which he purchased. Of course, the price would be affected by the covenant, and nothing could be more inequitable than that the original purchaser should be able to sell the property the next day for a greater price, in consideration of the assignee being allowed to escape from the liability which he had himself undertaken.

That the question does not depend upon whether the covenant runs with the land is evident from this, that if there was a mere agreement and no covenant, this Court would enforce it against a party purchasing with notice of it; for if an equity is attached to the property by the owner, no one purchasing with notice of that equity can stand in a different situation from the party from whom he purchased. There are not only cases before the Vice-Chancellor of England, in which he considered that doctrine as not in dispute; but looking at the ground on which Lord Eldon disposed of the case of *The Duke of Bedford v. The Trustees of the British Museum* (2 My. & K 552), it is impossible to suppose that he entertained any doubt of it. …

With respect to the observations of Lord Brougham in *Keppell v. Bailey*, he never could have meant to lay down that this Court would not enforce an equity attached to land by the owner, unless under such circumstances as would maintain an action at law. If that be the result of his observations, I can only say that I cannot coincide with it.

I think the cases cited before the Vice-Chancellor and this decision of the Master of the Rolls perfectly right, and, therefore, that this motion must be refused, with costs.

DISCUSSION NOTES

i. Covenants and the Creation of "Property" Interests

Tulk v Moxhay is regarded as a significant departure from previous authority:

> The doctrine in *Tulk v. Moxhay* … had a dramatic effect upon both the law of contract and the law of property. As a consequence of equitable innovation, both covenantor and covenantee under a freehold restriction could justifiably assert that each held some form of "property" in the servient land, albeit graded by differing degrees of intensity. By virtue of his durable right of control over user the covenantee could claim that his *contractual* interest in the performance of the covenant had mutated or enlarged into a *proprietary* interest in the covenantor's land. In reality the proprietary relationship created by restrictive land-related obligations gave both covenantor and covenantee a strategic stake in the constructive coordination of their respective user-preferences. [Moreover,] the covenantee's entitlement was capable of binding all third parties into whose hands that land came, until such time as the covenantor's land was conveyed to a bona fide purchaser of a legal estate for value without notice of the covenant.

(Gray & Gray at 261-62.) The decision in *Tulk v Moxhay* thus extended the enforceability of the burden of covenants in equity, beyond privity of contract and privity of estate. How would you formulate the principle for the running of the burden of covenants in equity, pursuant to *Tulk v Moxhay*? You may want to reconsider your formulation of the principle in the light of subsequent developments in later cases, explained below.

ii. Policy Rationales for Enforcing Covenants

As SI George noted, there were other cases similar to *Tulk v Moxhay* before the courts in the early years of the 19th century. An interesting case concerned an application by the Duke of Bedford to restrain the British Museum from building an extension to house the Elgin Marbles. The Duke's application for an injunction to restrain the museum was based on an alleged breach of a covenant entered into in 1675 by predecessors in title of the Duke and the museum: *The Duke of Bedford v The Trustees of the British Museum* (1822), 39 ER 1055 (Ch D). The Duke's application was unsuccessful because "the character of the adjoining lands had been so altered with reference to the land conveyed, that the restriction in the covenant had ceased to be applicable according to the intent and spirit of the contract." See George at 176, quoting S Atkinson, *The Theory and Practice of Conveyancing*, 2d ed (London: Sweet, 1839), vol I at 447. In *Tulk v Moxhay*, above, the master of the rolls distinguished the Duke of Bedford's case (at 85-86) as follows:

> First of all, that there is such a change of circumstances that performance of the covenant ought not to be required. It was likened to the case of *The Duke of Bedford v. The Trustees of the British Museum* (3). I think Mr. Palmer, with the ability and sense with which he has conducted the whole of this business, did not press that strongly in his reply: and he was perfectly right in doing so, because there is a manifest and plain difference between the two cases. In the case of *The Duke of Bedford v. The Trustees of the British Museum* the party who was seeking against the other the performance of the covenant, had himself, by his own acts, placed the property under such different circumstances that it was perfectly manifest there was no reciprocity; the parties were not in any way in the same situation.

Do you agree with this analysis? In reviewing *Tulk v Moxhay* in the context of these early cases, George concluded (at 183):

> It is submitted that, while there may have been some legal foundation for the rules which developed, they were essentially formulated as a matter of public policy to give "business efficacy" to long-standing arrangements. It matters not what the foundation is thought to be: if the result is desirable the injunctions will be awarded.

Do you agree with this assertion? Why would the courts have wished to respond to public policy in these cases?

As George also suggested, the breadth of the principle enunciated in *Tulk v Moxhay* resulted in subsequent disagreements among judges about the basis for the decision, and in some judicial efforts to narrow the scope of the ruling in *Tulk v Moxhay*. Thus, it is evident that although courts established a new principle for the running of the burden of covenants in equity in *Tulk v Moxhay*, they then continued to develop the principle in subsequent cases. As a result, these principles provide a good illustration of judicial law reform activity in relation to private planning by landowners.

iii. The Requirement of Notice

Tulk v Moxhay firmly established the requirement of notice to an assignee of the covenantor in order for the burden of the covenant to run in equity. As it has developed, this requirement means that the covenant will not be enforceable if the assignee of the covenantor is a bona fide purchaser for value without notice. Consider the position of a squatter who takes possession of a covenantor's land. Will the covenant be enforceable against the squatter? It was held in *Re Nisbet and Potts' Contract*, [1905] 1 Ch 391 (Ch D) that even though the squatter may not have notice, the squatter does not qualify as a bona fide purchaser for value, and thus the covenant will be enforceable. The concept of notice must also take account of the requirements of provincial registration statutes, and the extent to which they may define the process for establishing effective notice. For an example, see *White v Lauder Developments Ltd* (1975), 60 DLR (3d) 419 (Ont CA).

iv. The Requirement That the Covenant Be Negative

As the principles developed in later cases, additional requirements for the running of the burden of covenants were established. For example, in *Haywood v The Brunswick Permanent Benefit Building Society* (1881), 8 QBD 403 (CA), the court held that it did not have the jurisdiction to enforce a positive covenant to build and repair, but it was able to enforce those covenants that restricted the use of land. Thus, the court distinguished positive covenants, unenforceable against an assignee of the covenantor in equity, from those that were negative or restrictive that could bind successors in title of the covenantor. The test for deciding whether a covenant is positive or negative is substantive, so that a covenant may be phrased positively and yet be negative in substance—for example, a covenant "to use the property for residential purposes only."

Recall the covenant in *Tulk v Moxhay*—was it positive or negative? According to George (at 188) it was a "hybrid" one in that the covenantor undertook not to build on the land and also to maintain it "in neat and ornamental order." OLRC *Report on Covenants* agreed, stating (at 26) that the covenant in *Tulk v Moxhay* was "positive in form, insofar as the covenantor agreed to maintain Leicester Square in an open state uncovered by any buildings, but it was negative in essence, since it was designed to prevent the covenantor from building in the square." Whether the covenant is positive or negative in substance may create problems of interpretation for courts because only negative covenants are enforceable against the assignee of the covenantor in equity.

In *Aquadel Golf Course Ltd v Lindell Beach Holiday Resort Ltd*, 2009 BCCA 5, the predecessor in title of the petitioner company agreed in 1978 "that he [would] not use the Whitlam land for any purpose other than as a golf course," and that such restriction would endure until 2076 or a date determined according to a "royal lives clause," whichever was earlier. In 2008 the covenantor sought to have the covenant discharged in order to redevelop the lands as a residential community. The BC Court of Appeal ordered the covenant to be removed from title on the basis that it was a positive covenant, the burden of which did not run to the petitioner. According to the court, the covenantor did not have the option of leaving the land idle—it was obliged to maintain it as a golf course, thus clearly indicating the existence of a positive covenant.

As OLRC explained, it may be possible for covenants to be severed to be enforced in some cases. For other examples and analysis, see Ziff at 405-10, the OLRC *Report on Covenants*, and George.

v. Reforming the "Positive Covenant" Requirement

Is there any justification for limiting the enforceability of covenants against assignees on the basis of whether they are negative in substance? Recall that the court in *Keppell v Bailey*, discussed above, seemed concerned about the enforceability of the burden of all covenants on the basis that it would render land less valuable and affect alienability, and also that it would be difficult for subsequent purchasers to obtain clear notice of such covenants. According to the OLRC *Report on Covenants* (at 100-1), however, the existence of covenants may enhance alienability because "they operate to protect the amenities of neighbourhoods and the competitiveness of businesses." Moreover, the system of land registration in Canada means that there should be no problem ascertaining what covenants may bind successors in title to the covenantor. Accordingly, the OLRC *Report on Covenants* considered the utility of positive covenants in subdivision developments, the fact that the burden of positive covenants has always run in leaseholds, and the enactment of legislation in some provinces permitting the running of positive covenants in condominiums. The OLRC *Report on Covenants* concluded (at 101-2):

> We have reached the conclusion that the present law, which prohibits the running of the burden of positive covenants upon a transfer of freehold land, operates to defeat the legitimate expectations of the parties. In our view, there can be no principled rationale for a rule that would preclude neighbours from agreeing, for example, to maintain a boundary fence, or, to keep certain drains clear, such that the covenant would run with the land ... . In addition, to the extent that a variety of methods have been developed to circumvent the undesirable effect of the present law, it has been productive of much uncertainty and confusion. For the foregoing reasons, the Commission recommends that the law should be reformed to permit the burden of affirmative obligations to run upon a transfer of freehold land.

The OLRC *Report on Covenants* defined legislative changes required to effect its recommendations for reform of the law of covenants (see 104ff). Do you agree that it would be appropriate to permit the running of the burden of positive covenants? Note that the OLRC *Report on Covenants* declined to recommend the creation of a single unified law of servitudes—comprising profits, easements, and covenants—concluding (at 103) that such an approach was "overly ambitious." Do you agree? What would be the advantage of a single law of servitudes? To date, there has been no legislative response to the OLRC's recommendations. Reassess, in this context, the majority and dissenting judgments in *Amberwood*, above. Which approach was more appropriate?

vi. The Requirement That the Covenantee Retain Land Benefited by the Covenant

In addition to requirements that the assignee of the covenantor have notice and that the covenant be negative in substance, the enforceability of the burden of a covenant in equity requires that the covenantee retain land benefited by the covenant. For example, in *Re British United Automobiles Ltd and Volvo Canada Ltd* (1980), 29 OR (2d) 725 (H Ct J), a homeowners' association was unable to enforce a restrictive covenant because it owned no land capable of benefiting from the covenant. This requirement distinguishes covenants "personal" to the covenantee from those that relate to the land owned by the covenantee and successors in title, and is reminiscent of the requirement of a dominant and servient tenement for a valid easement in English and Canadian law. Thus, just as there is no recognition of an "easement in gross" in these jurisdictions apart from statute, the burden of a negative covenant is not enforceable against an assignee of the covenantor's land unless the covenantee retains land benefited by the covenant. For other examples of the application of this requirement, see *Re Sekretov and City of Toronto*, [1973] 2 OR 161 (CA) and *Galbraith v Madawaska Club Ltd*, [1961] SCR 639. As Ziff argued, it is important for the covenantor and assigns of the covenantor to be able to identify precisely which lands are benefited by a covenant for purposes of both litigation and the negotiation of discharges of covenants. See Ziff at 405-10.

Consider these facts. A brewery located in Edmonton sold land that it owned in Calgary to a purchaser. The purchaser of the land in Calgary entered into a covenant not to use the land as a brewery; the covenant identified the land benefited by the covenant as the land owned by the brewery in Edmonton 200 miles away. The purchaser subsequently went bankrupt and the Calgary land passed to another company. The new owner of the Calgary land wished to ignore the covenant. Is the burden of the covenant enforceable against the new owner? In *880682 Alberta Ltd v Molson Breweries Properties Ltd* (2002), 324 AR 71, 9 Alta LR (4th) 256, 4 RPR (4th) 271 (QB), the court held that the covenant did not touch and concern the Edmonton lands because the dominant and servient tenements were not sufficiently proximate; in addition, the connection was collateral and incidental to the lands. How should geographical proximity affect this requirement for the running of the burden of covenants? Will anything other than immediately adjacent land ever be sufficient? How should this question be interpreted in relation to underlying policies about the enforceability of covenants? For another case in which a restrictive covenant was not enforceable, see *Thunder Bay (City) v 1013951 Ontario Ltd* (2000), 32 RPR (3d) 63 (Ont Sup Ct J).

This requirement has also created difficult problems for municipal authorities. In *London County Council v Allen*, [1914] 3 KB 642, for example, the English Court of Appeal held that the London County Council (LCC) could not enforce a restrictive covenant against the covenantor's successor in title because the LCC held no land for the benefit of which the covenant had been taken. Similarly, in *One Twenty-Five Varsity Road Ltd v Township of York* (1960), 23 DLR (2d) 465 (Ont CA), the court considered a covenant entered into by a municipality and a developer and held that it was not enforceable against the assignees of the developer because the municipality (the covenantee) did not retain lands capable of being benefited by the covenant. Counsel for the municipality argued that the case should be decided by reference to the basic principle in *Tulk v Moxhay*—that is, notice to assignees—without taking account of later developments, including the requirement that the covenantee retain land benefited by the covenant. Morden JA declined to accept this argument, stating (at 470):

> [T]he plaintiff in *Tulk v. Moxhay* had lands capable of being benefited by the covenant at the time he exacted it and when he sought to enforce it. Altogether apart from this consideration and assuming that the result in that case was based solely upon notice, it is, not only undesirable but in my opinion, too late now for this Court to return to the position as it was in 1849 and give countenance to a development of the doctrine along such substantially different lines; we ought, I think, to adhere to the greatly restricted scope of the doctrine in *Tulk v. Moxhay* as evidenced by the numerous decisions subsequent to that case. A restrictive covenant enforceable between persons other than the original parties is, in effect, an equitable interest in property. It is well recognized that decisions affecting real property upon the basis of which titles are passed and accepted should not lightly be disturbed; this is one branch of law which requires stability.

Is this reasoning consistent with the approach in *Tulk v Moxhay*? What are the underlying concerns of the court in *One Twenty-Five Varsity Road*? What options exist for a municipal authority that wishes to exert continuing control over development within its boundaries?

Compare the approach in *One Twenty-Five Varsity Road* with *Re Daly and City of Vancouver* (1956), 5 DLR (2d) 474 (BCSC), where the court held that the municipality's proprietary interest in its streets was sufficient as a "dominant tenement" to support a restrictive covenant. Is this approach consistent with *Tulk v Moxhay*? This problem has been overcome in some cases by precise legislative amendments permitting the burden of covenants to run on behalf of a municipal authority in the absence of land retained by the municipality—see e.g. *Ontario Water Resources Act*, RSO 1990, c O.40, s 27(1):

> A right or interest in ... any land or any covenant or condition relating thereto, in respect of water or sewage works, in favour of the Crown or any municipality ... is valid and enforceable ... notwithstanding that the right or interest ... is not appurtenant or annexed to or for the benefit of any land of the Crown or the municipality.

This requirement has also created problems in circumstances where the land to be benefited by a covenant is not clearly identified in the documents, so that there is a need for the court to interpret, perhaps through oral evidence, what land is benefited. In *Canadian Construction Co v Beaver (Alberta) Lumber Ltd*, [1955] SCR 682, the court held that the burden of a covenant in an agreement did not run because the land to be benefited was not identified in the agreement. There was some difference among the judges as to whether oral evidence could be admitted, but the majority stated that, even if the oral evidence were admitted, the agreement was personal to the covenantee and not intended to benefit land. For other examples, see *Guaranty Trust Co Canada v Campbelltown Shopping Centre Ltd* (1986), 44 Alta LR (2d) 270 (CA); *Sawlor v Naugle*, 1990 CanLII 4075, 101 NSR (2d) 160 (SC (TD)); *Canada Mortgage and Housing Corp v Hong Kong Bank of Canada* (1990), 75 DLR (4th) 307 (Alta CA), rev'd on other grounds *Hongkong Bank of Canada v Wheeler Holdings Ltd*, [1993] 1 SCR 167 (1993), 100 DLR (4th) 40; *Mt Matheson Conservation Society v 573132 BC Ltd*, 2002 BCSC 1254 (CanLII), 3 RPR (4th) 146; and *Piazza v Hopley* (2001), 46 RPR (3d) 133 (Ont Sup Ct J).

In England, a related issue was considered in *Re Ballard's Conveyance*, [1937] Ch 473 (Ch D), where the court held that the burden of a covenant could not run because the covenantee had retained 1,700 acres of land and it was not reasonable that the covenant could benefit such a large dominant tenement. More recently, however, in *Wrotham Park Estate Co Ltd v Parkside Homes Ltd*, [1974] 1 WLR 798, the court held that it would generally accept that a covenant benefited the covenantee's land unless there was evidence that it would be unreasonable to do so. What is the difference between the approaches of these two cases? Which is more likely to result in enforceable covenants? What explanation is there for these differences? To what extent are both these cases consistent with the approach of *Tulk v Moxhay*?

vii. The Need to Reassess Developments After Tulk v Moxhay

Related to the requirement that the covenantee retain land benefited by the covenant is a requirement that the covenant must touch and concern the land, and not be merely a personal covenant. The covenant must also be intended by the original parties to bind the heirs and assigns of the covenantor, not just the covenantor personally. Thus, in summary, the principles for the running of the burden of a covenant in equity now require:

1. notice on the part of the assignee of the covenantor;
2. a negative or restrictive covenant, in substance;
3. land benefited by the covenant retained by the covenantee;
4. a covenant that touches and concerns the land and not merely a personal covenant; and
5. intention on the part of the covenantor to bind successors and not just the covenantor personally.

Reconsider *Tulk v Moxhay* in relation to these principles. To what extent is the case consistent with these principles, some of which were developed after *Tulk v Moxhay* was decided? To what extent are these principles appropriate in the early 21st century? Some experts have argued that if there is inconsistency in the application of the principles, it is because courts have become frustrated by a lack of legislative initiative, just as may have occurred at the time when *Tulk v Moxhay* was decided. In this context, how should we assess *Tito v Waddell*, discussed above? In thinking about these questions, consider the following comment:

> [A] creative tension exists between the need to render land alienable and the need to allow private ordering by consensual arrangement. The stability and convenience of land use secured by durably binding covenants often ensures, in practice, that enforceable covenants, far from sterilizing title, operate to enhance the market value of both the benefited and the burdened land. Thus, while a sense of cautious concern still remains today at the core of the legal response, it is also apparent that in recent times the [English] courts have adopted a more sympathetic view of restrictive covenants. This relaxation of approach may in part reflect a general change in community attitudes towards the importance of preserving the integrity and attractiveness of local environments.

(Gray & Gray at 263.) See also HWR Wade, "Covenants—A Broad and Reasonable View" (1972) 31 Cambridge LJ 157. As you read the materials that follow, consider whether the Canadian case law on restrictive covenants demonstrates the same sympathetic tendencies claimed by Gray & Gray for the English jurisprudence.

2. The Benefit of the Covenant

a. Assignment

In some situations, the assignee of a covenantee is unable to rely on the legal principles for the running of the benefit of a covenant. For example, if the assignee has only an equitable interest in the land, the legal principles will not be available. In addition, where the assignee wishes to enforce a covenant against the assignee of the covenantor—that is, where both the covenantee and the covenantor have assigned their interests—so that enforcement depends on equitable principles for the running of the burden of a covenant, the assignee of the covenantee must satisfy the equitable rules for the running of the benefit. As DAL Smout once suggested, these principles illustrate equity's "unnatural and uncharacteristic interest in sheer technicalities," requiring great accuracy in the drafting process. See DAL Smout, "Easements and Restrictive Covenants" in *Special Lectures of the Law Society of Upper Canada 1951: Conveyancing and Real Property* (Toronto: Richard DeBoo, 1951) 105 at 113. For a more recent overview, see Bruce Ziff, "Restrictive Covenants: The Basic Ingredients" in *Special Lectures 2002 Real Property Law: Conquering the Complexities* (Toronto: Irwin Law, 2003).

In order for the benefit of a covenant to pass to an assignee in equity, it must touch and concern the land, a requirement that is similar to the legal principles. The assignee must, in addition, demonstrate entitlement to the benefit. To do so, the assignee must show that either the covenant was annexed to the land—either expressly or, in some cases, by implication—and thus passed with the conveyance of the interest in land; the covenant was assigned in addition to the conveyance; or the covenant was between owners whose parcels of land comprise a building scheme (also known as a development scheme).

b. Annexation

Annexation of a covenant occurs when a deed expressly provides that a covenant is for the benefit of an identified parcel of land, or for the benefit of the present and subsequent owners of the benefited land. This requirement was considered in *Galbraith v Madawaska Club*, [1961] SCR 639. The case involved a rather unusual restriction—that lots in a particular summer colony on Georgian Bay could be owned only by graduates of or faculty at the University of Toronto. The clause had its origins in a plan developed in the 1890s by some professors at the University to found a holiday colony in a place that would also be suitable for conducting scientific research. They persuaded the Ontario government to grant them some Crown land at half the usual price, but the government wished to impose some restrictions to prevent the professors from speculating in the land. The province agreed to sell the land to the club founded by the professors, but it inserted a clause in the club's corporate charter restricting ownership of shares in the club to those with the University of Toronto affiliation; the charter also stated that when the club allotted sites to its members, the lots were not to be conveyed or leased to anyone without the same qualifications on pain of forfeiture of the lands.

Mr Galbraith, whose father was one of the founders of the club, acquired one of the lots through purchase from Mrs Firth, an initial grantee from the club, and as a condition of the purchase was required to sign a covenant stating that he would not transfer the property to anyone without the University of Toronto qualification and that he would demand a similar covenant from any future purchaser. He then transferred the lot to himself and his wife, a non-graduate of the University of Toronto, as joint tenants, and sought a declaration that the University of Toronto restrictions were invalid. His main goal was to have the restrictions struck down on the basis of public policy. As he protested to a friend: "To deny a widow or widower or a child the right of ownership because he or she is not a member of the 'party' is communism at its very worst. To carry on the by-laws as presently constituted is the antithesis of the ideals for which two wars have been fought" (cited in Philip Girard, "Cottages, Covenants, and the Cold War: Galbraith v Madawaska Club" in E Tucker, J Muir & B Ziff, eds, *Property on Trial: Canadian Cases in Context* (Toronto: Irwin Law for the Osgoode Society for Canadian Legal History, 2012) at 102.

Mr Galbraith succeeded in the Supreme Court of Canada, but not on the ground that he sought. The court found that the restrictions did not touch and concern the land, because they related to personal characteristics and were not related to use of the land. It also found that no dominant lands had been specified in the initial deed to Mrs Firth, such that there was nothing to which any benefit could be annexed. The court also referred to the need to define the lands to be benefited with reasonable precision in the deed itself, but under the circumstances its remarks were *obiter*. Nonetheless, this statement was taken up in subsequent cases and has come to be seen as the main principle for which *Galbraith* stands.

Thus, in *Re Sekretov and City of Toronto*, [1973] 2 OR 161 (CA), a covenant was held to be unenforceable because the dominant tenement could not be ascertained from the deed. Although there have been cases in England that have recognized implied annexation, where the parties' intentions have been clear, these principles have tended to be less accepted in Canada as a result of requirements of detailed descriptions in provincial registration statutes. There is also some continuing debate about statutory provisions in Canada and England that may affect issues of implied annexation—e.g. see *Law of Property Act 1925* (15 & 16 Geo 5), c 20, s 78; *Conveyancing and Law of Property Act*, RSO 1990, c C.34, s 24; *Federated Homes Ltd v Mill Lodge Properties Ltd*, [1980] 1 WLR 594 (CA); and D Hayton, "Revolution in Restrictive Covenants Law?" (1980) 43 Mod L Rev 445. Annexation also requires that a deed must specify whether the covenant is annexed to all or only part of the covenantee's land, although the *Federated Homes* decision seems to create a presumption that a covenant is annexed to all parts of the land unless a contrary intention appears. On the impact of *Federated Homes*, see Nigel P Gravells, "Federated Homes Ltd v Mill Lodge Properties Ltd (1979): Annexation and Intention" in *Landmark Cases in Land Law*. For further analysis, see the OLRC *Report on Covenants* at 34-37.

c. Express Assignment

An assignee of the benefit of the covenant may also be able to enforce it against an assignee of the burden, in the absence of annexation, if the covenant has been expressly assigned. Generally, it is necessary for an assignment of the benefit of the covenant to occur at the same time as the conveyance of the freehold estate from the covenantee to the assignee. Only covenants that benefit the dominant land, and not personal covenants, are enforceable.

As well, in Canada, the assignment must identify the benefited land clearly (although there is some relaxation of this requirement in England). For a more detailed analysis of the relationship between assignment and annexation, see the OLRC *Report on Covenants* at 38-39, and the cases cited there.

d. Development Schemes

The benefit of a covenant may also be enforced in equity through the creation of a development scheme. Traditionally, these were "building schemes" in which a developer imposed mutual covenants on the purchasers of all the lots in a defined area for the benefit of the development as a whole. The creation of such a community of interest among the purchasers of the lots in the development was held in equity to require reciprocity of obligation among the vendor and all the purchasers. Equity established clear requirements for recognizing a building scheme, including a common vendor who had clearly defined the land subject to the building scheme, made all the lots subject to similar covenants, and then sold lots with the intention that the covenants should be for the benefit of all the lots in the scheme. In addition, all the purchasers must have purchased their lots in expectation that the covenants applied to all the lots and were intended to benefit all of them. These traditional requirements were enunciated in *Elliston v Reacher*, [1908] 2 Ch 374 (Ch D), although they have been somewhat relaxed in English cases, such as *Re Dolphin's Conveyance*, [1970] Ch 654 (Ch D), and in Prince Edward Island in *Re Spike and Rocca Group Ltd* (1979), 107 DLR (3d) 62 (PEISC). This more flexible approach was rejected in Ontario in *Re Lakhani and Weinstein* (1980), 31 OR (2d) 65 (H Ct J), where there was no common owner. However, see *Dorrell v Mueller* (1977), 16 OR (2d) 795 (Dist Ct), where the court held that a common vendor may not be required where land is registered under the *Land Titles Act*, RSO 1990, c L.5. The recognition of a building scheme requires a clear description of the land subject to the scheme and clear notice to purchasers of its existence: see *McGregor v Boyd Builders Ltd*, [1966] 1 OR 424 (H Ct J); *Kirk v Distacom Ventures Inc* (1996), 4 RPR (3d) 240 (BCCA); and *Berry v Indian Park Association* (1999), 44 OR (3d) 301 (CA).

The advantage of finding that a building scheme exists is that the developer need not maintain any land to be benefited. Rather, all the lots in the building scheme become respectively dominant and servient tenements vis-à-vis each other. A breach of the covenant by the owner of any lot in the building scheme gives rise to a right of action in every other lot owner to seek a remedy for the breach. In modern residential subdivisions, the restrictions contained in building schemes can run to dozens of pages and regulate the most minute aspects of land use in order to create aesthetic uniformity and maintain land values. This practice has inspired a backlash in certain instances on two grounds. First, restrictive covenants can impose a stifling homogeneity on behaviour and housing patterns: see JL Winokur, "The Mixed Blessings of Promissory Servitudes: Toward Optimizing Economic Utility, Individual Liberty, and Personal Identity" (1989) Wis L Rev 1. In addition, such covenants may work against good environmental practices. For example, the Nova Scotia *Clothesline Act*, SNS 2010, c 34, states:

> 4(1) No Act, by-law, covenant, agreement or contract prevents or prohibits the installation, placement or use of a clothesline outdoors at a single family dwelling or on the ground floor of a multi-unit residential building.

This legislative intervention is justified in the preamble of the Act, which states that "the use of clotheslines to dry clothes reduces energy consumption, greenhouse gas and mercury emissions." Section 5 does, however, permit reasonable restrictions on the "installation, placement or use" of a clothesline. For further details about building schemes, see OLRC *Report on Covenants* at 41ff.

3. A Case Study: Restrictive Covenants and Business Competition

In considering the appropriate role of covenants in the 21st century, examine the reasoning in the following case, and especially the discussion about the requirement that the covenant must touch and concern the land.

Canada Safeway Ltd v Thompson (City)
(1996), 5 RPR (3d) 1 (Man QB)

[The lessor (Woolworth) owned land on which there was a shopping mall and also held an option to buy certain adjacent lands. In 1971, Woolworth agreed to a long-term lease with Safeway, a major tenant in the shopping mall. Among other clauses in the lease, clause 12.04 provided that, if Woolworth acquired the adjacent lands, it would

> refrain from leasing any individual store exceeding fifteen hundred (1500) square feet ... in the Shopping Centre and Phase II thereof for the purposes of carrying on all or any of the following businesses ... :
>
> (a) a retail food store;
> (b) a butcher shop;
> (c) a produce (green grocery) store;
> (d) a fish market;
> (e) a grocery store;
> (f) a frozen food store;
> (g) a delicatessen; [and]
> (h) a cheese shop.

The lease also constrained the lessor (Woolworth) from developing the adjacent lands except in accordance with the above clause. The parties agreed that the lease would benefit and be binding on successors and assigns. There were also clauses creating parking rights in the Phase II lands (clause 12.05) and requiring (clause 10.01) an interpretation of clause 12.04 prohibiting the listed uses.

In 1975, Woolworth exercised its option and acquired the adjacent lands (the Phase II lands), which were later transferred to the city in 1995. Safeway initiated an action for a declaration of its equitable interest in the Phase II lands. Although the case also required a review of issues of registration, the analysis of the covenant issue was its primary focus.]

CLEARWATER J:

The Issues

The law dealing with covenants that may or may not "run with the land" and be binding on subsequent owners of the land is complex. An application such as this brings many issues and sub-issues into play. The central question or issue to be determined may be summarized as follows:

Do any of the covenants contained in Safeway's lease of a portion of the shopping centre lands "run with" the Phase II lands thereby creating an interest in the Phase II lands now owned by the City? Alternatively (and as submitted by the City), are the covenants in question in the lease mere personal undertakings binding only on the parties to the lease and (or) merely a restriction on alienation as opposed to a restriction on use such that the City, as a successor or assign of Woolworth to title to the Phase II lands, does not bear the burden of the covenants?

Just as Safeway covenanted not to compete with certain other businesses leased by Woolworth to other tenants in the shopping centre, Woolworth granted reciprocating rights (covenants) to Safeway. It is these covenants that are the subject matter of this Application. …

There is no doubt that the City had, or should have had, notice of the contents of the Safeway caveat when it elected to purchase the Phase II lands from Woolworth and take title. Neither notice nor the adequacy of notice are issues in this proceeding.

Safeway's Position

Safeway submits that the covenants contained in the lease (most specifically, those covenants contained in Articles 10 and 12, supra) are properly described as "restrictive covenants" and that these covenants "run with" the Phase II lands, thereby giving Safeway an equitable interest in those lands.

The City's Position

The City maintains two positions against Safeway. These positions are not necessarily "alternate" but perhaps may best be described as "complimentary" [*sic*]. The City submits that the covenants in question, and in particular Article 12.04 are merely covenants obliging Woolworth to "refrain from leasing" the Phase II of Shopping Centre lands. The City describes these covenants as being mere "restrictions on alienation" as opposed to "restrictions on use." The City says these covenants, in the form and content as found in this lease, do not run with the land; at best they are personal covenants enforceable only as between Safeway and Woolworth. The City points out that nowhere in the lease document did the parties provide expressly that the covenants in question would "run with the land." Further, if Woolworth had not exercised its option and purchased the Phase II lands, then neither Woolworth (nor Safeway) could ever have had any control over what happened on the Phase II lands. This fact, the City submits, supports its position that the parties never intended (and never expressed any such intention) that the covenants would run with the Phase II lands.

Secondly, the City submits that even if the court were to disagree with its interpretation and find that the covenants in question do run with the land, and are not merely personal in nature, nevertheless the covenants ceased to be in effect upon the sale of the lands by Woolworth in 1982 to the numbered Ontario Corporation (subsequently renamed "Thompson Mall Inc."). The City points to clause 9.06 of the lease ... which relieves Woolworth, as landlord, from any and all liability under the lease when it sold the shopping centre and assigned its leases to Thompson Mall Inc. in April 1982. This, the City says, means that Safeway no longer has any rights which could be enforced against any successor in title to the landlord.

Decision

The preparation of an enforceable restrictive covenant, particularly one which purports to limit competition in the market place, is a difficult task for a lawyer. To read even a significant portion of what has been written and published on the topic, going back to at least the 16th century, is an almost impossible task. The late Chief Justice of Canada, Bora Laskin, in his 1958 text (Revised Edition, 1964), *Cases and Notes on Land Law*, quoted at p. 475 from *Spencer's Case* (1583), 5 Co. Rep. 16a, 77 ER 72 (KB), where the English judge commented on some of the problems which continue to beset practitioners today:

> And many differences taken and agreed concerning express covenants, and covenants in law, and which of them run with the land, and which of them are collateral, and do not go with the land, and where the assignee shall be bound without naming him, and where not; and where he shall not be bound although he be expressly named, and where not.

In this case, Safeway must turn to and rely on equity for the relief sought. There is no privity of contract between Safeway and the City. Although Safeway and the City each derive their respective interests in the lands in question from a common owner/vendor (Woolworth), this is not a situation where there is privity of estate between the parties. Safeway has a *leasehold interest* in the Shopping Centre lands and the City is *the owner* of the Phase II lands. Although the parties derived their respective interests from the same owner/vendor (Woolworth), the City does not stand in the shoes of the original parties to the lease; at least not in all respects. Woolworth's lease to Safeway was assigned by it (ultimately to the current owner of the Shopping Centre lands, Thompson Mall Inc.). Woolworth itself has no further responsibility to Safeway under the terms of the lease. ...

To a large extent Safeway relies upon the decision in *Tulk v. Moxhay* (1848), 2 Ph. 774, 41 ER 1143 (Ch.), and the law on the enforceability of restrictive covenants as it developed both before and after the *Tulk* decision. In *Tulk*, Lord Cottenham said (pp. 777-78):

> It is said that, the covenant being one which does not run with the land, this court cannot enforce it; but the question is, not whether the covenant runs with the land, but whether a party shall be permitted to use the land in a manner inconsistent with the contract entered into by his vendor, and with notice of which he purchased.

Mr. Justice Morse, in *Lorne Ritchie Enterprises Ltd. v. Canada Life Assurance Co.*, [1976] 5 WWR 130 (Man. QB), referred to (at p. 136) and relied on the majority judgment of the Ontario Court of Appeal in *White v. Lauder Developments Ltd.* (1975), 60 DLR (3d) 419 (Ont. CA), where Kelly JA, for the majority of the Ontario Court of Appeal, stated at p. 427:

For the creation of such a negative easement certain qualifying conditions must be present:

1. The covenant or agreement must be negative in essence.

2. It must affect, and to have been intended by the original parties to affect, the land itself by controlling its use.

3. Two plots of land must be concerned, one bearing the burden and one receiving the benefit, in a sense a servient and a dominant tenement.

Where any of these conditions is absent the covenant will be personal or collateral and will not impose a burden on the servient tenement nor confer a benefit on the dominant tenement.

In their brief, counsel for Safeway referred to and relied upon DiCastri, in his text, *Registration of Title to Land* ([Scarborough, ON:] Carswell, 1987), where he summarizes the conditions which must be fulfilled in order to create a restrictive covenant enforceable against the covenantor and his successors in title (pp. 10-3 to 10-5):

(a) The covenant must be negative in substance and constitute a burden on the covenantor's land analogous to an easement. No personal or affirmative covenant, requiring the expenditure of money or the doing of some act, can, apart from statute, be made to run with the land.

(b) The covenant must be one that touches and concerns the land; i.e., it must be imposed for the benefit, or to enhance the value of the benefited land. Further, that land must be capable of being benefited by the covenant at the time it is imposed. ...

(c) The benefitted as well as the burdened land must be defined with precision in the instrument creating the restrictive covenant. ...

(d) The conveyance or agreement should state the covenant is imposed on the covenantor's land for the protection of specified land of the covenantee. ...

(e) Unless the contrary is authorized by statute, the titles to both the benefited land and the burdened land are required to be registered. ...

(f) Apart from statute the covenantee must be a person other than the covenantor. ...

Counsel for the City submits that on the true construction of the lease in question, the covenants are merely personal to Safeway and Woolworth, do not run with the Phase II lands which it purchased from Woolworth, and are not, therefore, enforceable against the City. The determination as to whether or not the lease and covenants in question meet any or all of the foregoing criteria depends upon the true construction of the lease agreement of May 10, 1971. The City relies upon the dicta of Mr. Justice Cartwright of the Supreme Court of Canada in *Canadian Construction Co. v. Beaver (Alberta) Lumber Ltd.*, [1955] SCR 682. As Cartwright J observed at p. 687:

... [I]t may first be observed that it is a formal and carefully prepared instrument obviously intended to be a complete statement of the whole bargain between the parties. ...

The lease before me must be considered in the same light. In discussing the numerous cases dealing with the enforceability of covenants such as these, Cartwright J observed, at p. 688:

> … The question is whether, on the true construction of the agreement, the respondent and Henderson intended the restrictive covenant therein contained to be (a) for the vendor's own benefit and personal to it, or (b) for the protection or benefit of the vendor's land, Parcel B. …

He went on to refer to some of the numerous cases on this issue and stated:

> … In these cases and in the text books dealing with them the importance of the difference between covenants intended to be for purpose (a) and those intended to be for purpose (b) is repeatedly stressed, and can hardly be supposed to have been absent from the mind of the draftsman of the agreement under consideration when he made no mention of any lands retained by the vendor and inserted in paragraph 2 the words "the said restriction and condition shall be binding upon each of the lots hereby conveyed for the benefit of the vendor." …

Simply put, it is the function of this court to ascertain the true intention of the parties from the words used in the lease agreement.

I will deal with the six criteria or conditions which Safeway must satisfy to succeed. … Firstly, are the covenants negative in substance? On a plain reading of the covenants contained in Articles 10 and 12 of the lease, I am satisfied that the covenants are negative in substance, if not expressly negative. The last sentence in Article 10.01, with reference to the opening provisions of that Article, requires a reader of the document (and any successor or assign of Woolworth) to construe the document and the provisions of Article 12.04 in a manner such that certain uses of the Phase II lands are prohibited. These Articles are, in my opinion, clearly intended to restrict or limit the use of the Phase II lands for certain specific purposes during the currency of the Safeway lease.

Article 12.04 uses the words "refrain from leasing" with reference to future use of either the Shopping Centre lands or the Phase II lands. This can only be reasonably interpreted to be negative in substance; that is, Woolworth and its successors and assigns will not lease any individual stores on either of the lands except as permitted by the balance of this clause as it must be construed with reference to Article 10.

Secondly, do the covenants in question touch and concern the land? Whether or not the lease in question satisfies this criteria, having regard to the wording used, or not used, as the case may be, is perhaps the most difficult issue to determine in this fact situation.

The law as to whether or not any particular covenant "touches and concerns the land" is concisely summarized in DiCastri's text, *Registration of Title to Land* ([Scarborough, ON:] Carswell, 1987), pp. 10-3, para. 332(b) and somewhat more fully discussed by one of the editors of this text, Albert H. Oosterhoff, in his recent article entitled "The Law of Covenants: Background and Basic Principles" (1993), vol. 2, National Real Property Law Review, p. 166, at p. 173:

> A covenant touches and concerns the land or, as it is sometimes said, has reference to the subject-matter of the lease, if it "affects either the landlord qua landlord or the tenant qua tenant." This means that the covenant must be intimately involved in the lessor–lessee relationship and must directly concern or benefit the land. In other words, it must affect the nature, quality or value of the demised land or its mode of use.

When one considers the covenants in question (Articles 10 and 12, supra) in the context of the entire lease document, including the recital which clearly expresses the intention of the parties for "planning" and "merchandising unity," I am satisfied that the covenants in Articles 12.04 and 12.05, with the proviso contained in the last sentence of Article 10.01, do in fact touch and concern the demised land. The ability to restrict competition on the Phase II lands and to maintain parking rights for its customers on the Phase II lands clearly has a value to Safeway and adds value to its leasehold interest. It should be noted that pursuant to Article 4.03 of the lease, Safeway is generally prohibited from transferring or assigning its lease without the consent of Woolworth. However, Woolworth is obliged to consent to any assignment of the lease or a sublease of the whole of Safeway's leased premises to *another grocery supermarket*; that is, at any time during the currency of its lease Safeway has the right to sell its premises and its interest in the lease to another grocery supermarket. The value of this right is clearly enhanced if Safeway can restrict competition on the adjacent lands and maintain parking rights over the adjacent land.

In *Pacific International Equities Corp. v. Royal Trust Co.* (1994), 42 RPR (2d) 66, the Ontario Court of Justice (General Division) held that a restrictive covenant regarding parking "touched and concerned" the neighbouring leasehold estate because it would benefit a successor tenant of that leasehold estate. In *Merger Restaurants v. DME Foods Ltd.* (1990), 66 Man. R (2d) 22, Justice Philp for the Manitoba Court of Appeal stated, at p. 27:

> There can be no doubt that the extent and availability of parking spaces in a shopping plaza will directly affect the nature and value of the land. …

Clearly it would have been preferable if the parties would have used more precise or specific language to express their intention that the benefit and burden of these covenants have attached themselves to the lands, the benefit to the dominant land (Safeway's leasehold interest) and the burden to the Phase II lands (now owned by the City). However, on reading the lease in its entirety and with particular reference to the fact that both parties expressly agreed that the lease would enure to the benefit of and be binding upon Woolworth, its successors and assigns and upon the heirs, executors, administrators and other personal legal representatives, successors and assigns of the tenant (Article 9.04, supra), I am satisfied that the requisite intention to so annex the benefits (and the burden) of the covenants to the respective interests in the lands is found in the lease document itself.

The City relies heavily on the British Columbia Court of Appeal decision in *Nylar Foods Ltd. v. Roman Catholic Episcopal Corp. of Prince Rupert* (1988), 48 DLR (4th) 175 (BC CA). In the *Nylar* case one party leased certain lands to another party and covenanted not to lease other adjoining lands to competitive businesses. The covenant was termed a restrictive covenant and was registered against the adjoining lands. The adjoining lands were then subdivided and the applicant purchased lots in the subdivision, subject to the restrictive covenant. The applicant then brought an application for an order striking out the covenant. The British Columbia Court of Appeal found in favour of the applicant and struck out the covenant. McLachlin JA (as she then was) recited the wording of the covenants in question at p. 176 of the *Nylar* decision as follows:

> The Landlord shall not during the term hereof without the prior consent in writing of the tenant entered [*sic*] into or be a party to any Lease [of] its Lands or any part thereof described

as Lot A, except Plans 26624, 29151, and 30349, District Lot 753, Cariboo District, Plan 24027 under the terms of which the same would be used for a purpose competitive in nature with that set forth in Article XX hereof.

Article XX provides:

> The tenant shall use the Demised Premises for a combination convenience store and retail gas bar outlet.

She goes on to refer to authorities which support what she describes as "the policy of the courts to favour competition and alienability" leading "to a strict construction of restrictive covenants." Notwithstanding the apparent presumed intention of the parties to these covenants, she concludes that the covenant in question in *Nylar* did not create a charge on land but was confined to restricting the ability of the Episcopal Corporation to lease the land. She states (pp. 176-7):

> … The only prohibition found in these words is against entering a lease in the forbidden terms. The land can be sold, assigned or otherwise dealt with free of such restriction. In fact this is what happened when the land was subdivided and ultimately purchased by the appellants.
>
> This analysis of the covenant leads me to the conclusion that it is a personal covenant between the parties who made it and not a restrictive covenant running with the land. In order to create a valid restrictive covenant, clear language is required showing unambiguously that the parties intended to create an interest in land in favour of one of them. If it is not entirely clear from the language that the parties intended to create an equity and correlative burden on the land, the restrictive covenant will be treated merely as a personal covenant between the parties who made it.
>
> It has repeatedly and consistently been held that clauses restricting the right to alienate or deal with the land do not evince the necessary intention to create a charge on the land. In so concluding, the courts distinguish between restrictions on "use," which may be taken as running with the land, and restrictions on alienation or other incidental matters, which are viewed as collateral to the land itself. …

The covenants in question in the Safeway lease do not "simply control a party to the agreement" as McLachlin JA opined in her analysis of *White v. Lauder*, found at p. 179 of *Nylar*. It is clear from the decision in *Nylar* and the authorities referred to in *Nylar* that a covenant which is only a restriction on alienation (in *Nylar* it was a restriction on leasing) will not run with the land. That type of covenant will not control the land itself or the use of the land. If one were considering Article 12.04 only, *Nylar* would apply. However, when one considers the proviso in the last sentence of Article 10.01 combined with the prohibition "from leasing" in Article 12.04 and combined with the parking rights created in the Phase II lands if and when Woolworth acquired ownership of the Phase II lands (as it did—Article 12.05, supra), I find there is sufficient intention expressed to restrict the use of the Phase II lands and to prevent these covenants from being interpreted strictly as being a restriction on alienation. Here, the proviso in the last sentence of Article 10.01 *combined with* the prohibition "from leasing" in Article 12.04 *and combined with* the parking rights created (Article 12.05) in the Phase II lands if and when Woolworth acquired ownership of the Phase II lands (as it did) is, in my view, a sufficient expression of intention that these covenants are more than just a restriction on alienation or a simple restriction on leasing.

In a recent Article entitled "Covenants," vol. 1, CCH Ontario Real Estate Law Guide, 8589 (paras. 52,142 to 52,164) published in March 1966, C.S. Goldfarb, an editor of the report in question, makes an accurate observation at p. 8589:

> This area is highly technical and the cases are not easily reconcilable. How a particular set of facts is characterized may produce different results in similar situations. ...

The theme of "strict construction" to be applied to covenants such as this in support of a policy of the courts to favour competition and alienability is a theme which runs throughout the decision of the British Columbia Court of Appeal in *Nylar*. While recognizing and accepting this principle, the court should not, in my opinion, impose such a "strict construction" that the obvious and apparent commercial reasons for the existence of the covenants in a lease such as this are obviated. The decision of the British Columbia Court of Appeal does not specifically consider the commercial realities of the ownership, development, leasing and operation of shopping centres and malls in urban centres in Canada. Mr. Justice Spence, writing for a majority of the Supreme Court of Canada in *Russo v. Field*, [1973] SCR 466 at 477, in upholding a restrictive covenant that both affected competition and alienability in a somewhat similar situation (a small shopping centre serving a suburban residential area) considered the principle as follows (at p. 486):

> It has been said that covenants such as those under consideration in this action are covenants in the restraint of trade and therefore must be construed restrictively. I am quite ready to recognize that as a general proposition [of] law and yet I am of the opinion that it must be considered in the light of each circumstance in each individual case. The mercantile device of a small shopping centre in a residential suburban area can only be successful [if it] ... is planned on the basis that the various shops therein must not be competitive. Since the shopping centre is a local one and not a regional shopping centre, the prospective purchasers at the various shops which it is planned to attract are residents in the neighbourhood. They are, of necessity, limited in number and therefore the business which they bring to the shopping centre is limited in extent. The prospective purchaser attracted to shop A in the plaza may well turn from shop A to shop B to purchase some other kind of his or her needed goods or service but if the limited number of prospective purchasers are faced in the same small shopping centre with several prospective suppliers of the same kind of goods or service then there may not be enough business to support several suppliers. They will suffer and the operator of the shopping plaza will suffer.
>
> I am therefore of the opinion that the disposition as a matter of public policy to restrictively construe covenants which may be said to be in restraint of trade has but little importance in the consideration of the covenants in the particular case.

In my opinion, the same analysis can and should be applied to covenants which may also be a restraint or restriction on alienation in the context of a shopping centre developed in an urban community, as is the case before me. When one is required to ascertain the intention of the parties by the wording that they used in their written contract, the court should look at the entire factual situation as evidenced by the entire contract. To accept and apply *Nylar*, as the City urges, in the context of this shopping centre and this lease is to, in effect, find that both Safeway and Woolworth intended (although Safeway had committed itself, as a major tenant in this shopping centre for a minimum period of 20 years, paid or agreed to pay a minimum base rent in the area of $100,000 per year plus a percentage rent based on sales on top of the base rent, together with other expenses, and paid $50,000 on the execution of the lease and an additional $100,000 on the date the leased premises were certified by Woolworth's architect as ready for occupancy) that Woolworth could, on May 11, 1971 or any date thereafter, *if it acquired the Phase II lands as it did*, assign its interests in the Phase II lands to a major competitor of Safeway who in turn could immediately develop and operate a grocery supermarket in direct competition with Safeway. This analysis of the document simply ignores commercial reality and commercial reasonableness. It is true that Woolworth gave no undertaking whatsoever to either exercise its option and acquire the Phase II lands or, if it did, to develop them in any particular way. However, it did agree that if it acquired the Phase II lands neither it nor any of its successors and assigns (which include the City) would construe the lease (Article 10) to permit the operation of specified restrictive uses on these lands during the currency of the Safeway lease.

Provided the "exclusive rights" clauses or "non-competition" clauses are properly drafted and do not otherwise offend public policy as being "too restrictive" or "too broad as to distance or time" (and in my opinion that is not the case with the clauses in question in this lease; they are, *prima facie*, reasonable as to scope and time, although a finding or decision in that regard must be left to be dealt with upon any trial of such an issue with appropriate evidence), experienced and well-qualified solicitors have been negotiating and using similar clauses in commercial shopping centre leases since at least the 1970s in Canada. Specifically, in an article entitled, "Exclusive Rights and Non-Competition Clauses," written by Harvey M. Haber and Stephen J. Messinger, and found in the text entitled, *Shopping Centre Leases—A collection of articles and precedents*, edited by Harvey M. Haber, Canada Law Book (1976), these practitioners give numerous examples of similar clauses which they recommend for inclusion in shopping centre leases. At p. 418, the writers state:

> An example of a clause which would be the tenant's "ideal" type of clause might be worded as follows:
>
>> To the intent that this covenant shall run with and burden the lands comprising the Shopping Centre as described in Schedule "A" attached hereto and *any enlargement thereof or addition thereto or any lands within a radius of one (1) mile from the Shopping Centre which now or may hereafter be owned or controlled by the Landlord*. ... (italics supplied)

Prima facie, parties in the position of Woolworth and Safeway as they were in 1971 ought to be permitted, within reasonable parameters, to build and develop shopping centres to serve the citizens of a community and ought to be permitted, again within reasonable parameters, to control the use and the competition to be permitted on those lands. Moreover, and again within reasonable parameters, when the parties clearly contemplate a possible expansion on adjoining or adjacent lands, the parties ought to be able to contract to control uses and competition on these lands.

Authorities referred to by the City such as *Noble v. Alley* (1950), [1951] SCR 64, and *Canadian Construction* (supra), are distinguishable on their facts and in principle. In *Noble* the covenant in question was an attempt to prevent the sale of lands to persons of Jewish or Negro race. In *Canadian Construction*, there was no reference in the covenant to any specific land retained by the vendor (the dominant tenement in that situation) such that the covenant could run with the land; the mere fact that the vendor owned other lands which were capable of being regarded as a "dominant tenement" was not sufficient.

Here, Safeway's land (their leasehold interest in the shopping centre lands adjacent to the Phase II lands) is clearly identified and set out in the caveat and in the lease.

The City's submission to the effect that because Woolworth sold the Shopping Centre lands in 1982 and thus obtained a release from Safeway in terms of Safeway being able to enforce the covenant against Woolworth is, in my opinion, premised on the assumption or belief that there is no longer any "dominant tenement" in existence from and after that date to enjoy the benefit of the restrictive covenant. Applying the clear and concise analysis of H.M. Haber, QC in his most recent text, *The Commercial Lease, A Practical Guide* (2d ed., 1994), at p. 332, and acknowledging the principle stated by Kelly JA in *White v. Lauder Developments Ltd.* (supra) to the effect that two plots or parcels of land must be involved, one bearing the burden and one receiving the benefit, I find that Safeway's "leasehold interest" is an equitable, if not a legal, interest in a portion of the Shopping Centre lands which are clearly identified in the caveat and the lease. The Phase II lands are clearly identified. Safeway's leasehold interest, being an interest in land, receives the benefit of the covenants (and is the dominant tenement) and the City's lands (the Phase II lands) bear the burden of the covenants and are the servient tenement.

On the question of whether or not the fact that Safeway did not own the Shopping Centre lands (it only has a "leasehold interest") affects Safeway's ability to create an interest in the adjoining lands, the decision of the Ontario Supreme Court, Appellate Division, in *Besinnett v. White* (1925), [1926] 1 DLR 95 (Ont. CA), is instructive and, in my opinion, applicable to this situation. In *Besinnett* the party attempting to uphold or enforce a restrictive covenant in a deed of land had, at the time the covenant was taken, only a right under a verbal agreement to later acquire an interest in the land. Middleton JA, writing for the appellate division, analyzed the authority and the fact situation as follows (p. 98):

> From this I conclude that the question is in each case one of intention—was the covenant taken to protect or benefit land in which the covenantee had an interest, using this term in its widest sense, or was it merely personal and collateral to the conveyance? If the former, then so long as the interest intended to be protected remains, or is augmented as in the case in hand, there is no reason why the Court should not compel the covenantor, or those who claim under him, with notice of the covenant, to regard the terms of the covenant. The question in each case is one of substance and reality and not of technicality.
>
> Here there is no question that the plaintiff at the time the covenant was taken had a real and actual interest in the land, an interest that might have been defeated if the sister had chosen to repudiate her verbal contract, but it was nevertheless a real interest, and the covenant was taken unquestionably for the protection of that interest, and not as a collateral and personal covenant.

Middleton JA goes on to analyze an earlier leading English decision in *Millbourn v. Lyons*, [1914] 1 Ch. D 34, which stands for the principle that in order for a covenantor (in this case Woolworth) to bind lands by a covenant, the covenantor must own the lands. *Millbourn* is authority for the proposition that the equitable interest of a purchaser under an agreement for sale is not "ownership" so as to make the covenant run with the land. However, Middleton JA goes on to state in *Besinnett*, at p. 98, that:

… The obligation must depend upon the actual conveyance and the state of affairs at the date of the conveyance.

In the case before me, Woolworth did not purport to burden the Phase II lands, or create any interest in the Phase II lands, on the date that it entered into the lease with Safeway (May 10, 1971). However, it did intend to burden the Phase II lands *if* it ever exercised its option and acquired title to them. This occurred in 1975 and the lease agreement, as it affects the Phase II lands, comes into effect at that time. There is nothing inherently wrong or unenforceable about a contract between two competent parties to create an interest in land at a defined point in time in the future, upon the happening of a defined event; that is, if and when one acquires the land, the interest or right comes into being.

On this issue as to whether or not the covenants in question touch and concern the land and are, by the terms of the lease agreement, annexed to the land, the City referred to and relied on the decision of Danis J of the Ontario High Court in *Coast-to-Coast Industrial Developments Ltd. v. Gorhim Holdings Ltd.* (1960), 22 DLR (2d) 695 (Ont. HC). In that case, one parcel of the land in question (Lot 8) was not acquired by the covenantor until after the tenant (covenantee) had gone into possession. At p. 698, Danis J refers to that fact and goes on to add:

The grammatical and ordinary meaning of the language of the covenant is not such as to include after-acquired lands (11 Hals., 3d ed., p. 385).

I do not understand this decision to mean that in no circumstances can a covenantor (in this case Woolworth) create an interest in lands that it acquires at a later date, by virtue of an option to purchase or otherwise. Rather, it depends on the language of the agreement. In this case the lease expressly and clearly contemplates the later acquisition by Woolworth of the Phase II lands. Any ancient or technical rules which might suggest that the parties cannot agree to create an interest in land if and when one or other of them acquires the land is not, in my view, reasonable in today's market place. …

In my opinion, the City's position that Article 9.06 of the lease, which releases Woolworth from any obligation to Safeway when it sold the Shopping Centre lands in 1982, should be construed to mean (or be evidence of the fact) that the covenants could not or should not run with the Phase II lands, at least after 1982, misses the point. If these covenants touch and concern the Phase II lands, then whether or not Woolworth may be personally liable on the covenants to Safeway is irrelevant. If these covenants touch and concern the land and are annexed to the land, as I have found, they run with the land and they bind the successors and assigns of Woolworth if those successors and assigns acquired title or notice, actual or constructive, of the existence of the covenants.

In conclusion, I find and declare that Safeway has an equitable interest in the Phase II lands by virtue of its lease dated May 10, 1971 and the covenants contained therein. Accordingly, Safeway is entitled to maintain the registration of its caveat against the titles to the Phase II lands. Safeway will have its costs, on a Class III basis, to be taxed or spoken to if the parties cannot agree on the amount.

Application allowed.

[The decision of Justice Clearwater was affirmed by the Manitoba Court of Appeal: (1997), 11 RPR (3d) 65.]

DISCUSSION NOTE

"Non-Competition" Covenants and the "Touch and Concern" Requirement

Does the covenant in clause 12.04 meet the test of touching and concerning the land? Is the reasoning in *Canada Safeway* more persuasive than that in *Nylar Foods Ltd v Roman Catholic Episcopal Corp of Prince Rupert* (1988), 48 DLR (4th) 175 (BC CA), discussed in this case? In an annotation to the decision in *Canada Safeway*, Jeffrey Lem stated ((1996) 5 RPR (3d) 1 at 4):

> With utmost respect, this annotator finds it difficult to distinguish the two cases on their facts and would invite those further interested in the issue (and not bound by stare decisis) to critically compare the decisions and decide for themselves why the restriction in *Nylar* is really any different than the restrictive covenant in *Canada Safeway*. Even if one finds no material factual distinctions between the two competing cases, this annotator would nonetheless still lean towards *Canada Safeway* as the better view, and *Nylar* as the heretic.

Do you agree that *Canada Safeway* is preferable? Is Lem's view based on legal principles or policy concerns? Is it possible that the context of the modern shopping centre is so different from *Tulk v Moxhay* that new principles are required? For an analysis of some of these issues in the United States, see P Franzese, "'Out of Touch': The Diminished Viability of the Touch and Concern Requirement in the Law of Servitudes" (1991) 21 Seton Hall L Rev 235. In relation to non-competition covenants, Franzese argued (at 243):

> [The touch and concern requirement] suggests that one's fiscal interests exist wholly separate and apart from one's ownership interests, use and enjoyment of … land. Most fundamentally, it [is used as] a means to avoid covenants thought to restrain trade. At bottom, thinly disguised public policy concerns (and not some failure of the covenant to touch and concern the burdened parcel), oftentimes precluded the burden of an anticompetition covenant from running.

Why should non-competition covenants be permitted in shopping centres as a matter of policy? Whose interests are fostered by such covenants? What limits, if any, should be imposed? Consider these questions again after reviewing the next section and the cases about discriminatory covenants.

F. Covenants and Discrimination

The law of covenants provides an opportunity to consider the relationship between private contractual rights of landowners and public policies of non-discrimination. This issue is similar to the problems considered in Chapter 3 with respect to limits imposed by law on the freedom of grantors and testators to impose conditions in grants and devises. Recall, for example, the principles invalidating grants and devises as restraints on alienation or marriage, or because they were uncertain, or contrary to public policy. These principles are related to covenants because it is arguable that the form in which a limitation is drafted may affect its validity. For example, it may be important to decide whether a particular document contains a restrictive covenant or a determinable fee simple. Even if a restrictive covenant is merely personal, and does not touch and concern the land, it will still be enforceable between the covenantor and covenantee because of their relationship of privity of contract. In this way, the issue of characterization remains an important one.

In addition, issues about freedom of contract and public policy also require an examination of the public–private dichotomy in law. Throughout the 20th century, but especially after 1945, public policies of non-discrimination were increasingly legislated and enforced by courts, restricting the scope of private choice on the part of landowners and others. Some of the historical context is required to understand the cases concerning discriminatory covenants. Early on, for example, the *Innkeepers Act* (now RSO 1990, c I.7) required innkeepers to receive all travellers willing to pay for accommodation. A Borovoy described the rationale for this statutory requirement on the basis that the lack of communication systems in earlier times made advance bookings for travellers impossible so that "travellers who were denied accommodation endured great inconvenience, often hardship," and the legal principles were therefore designed "for the greater convenience and safety of travellers and wayfarers." Borovoy suggested a need in post-Second-World-War Canada to redefine the rationale for these principles in terms of public policies of non-discrimination, and examined in particular the extension of innkeepers' duties to restaurant proprietors. See A Borovoy, "The Fair Accommodation Practices Act: The 'Dresden' Affair" (1956) 14:1 UT Fac L Rev 13, and the cases reviewed there, including *Christie v The York Corporation*, [1940] SCR 139, [1940] 1 DLR 81; *R v Emerson* (1955), 113 CCC 69 (Ont Co Ct); and *R v McKay* (1955), 113 CCC 56 (Ont Co Ct). For a comment on *Christie*, see B Laskin "Comment" (1940) 18 Can Bar Rev 314. See also C Backhouse, "Racial Segregation in Canadian Legal History: Viola Desmond's Challenge, Nova Scotia, 1946" (1994) 17 Dal LJ 299. For a historical analysis of the public–private dichotomy in contractual relations in the United States, see M Horowitz, "The History of the Public/Private Distinction" (1982) 130 U Pa L Rev 1423. See also JW Singer, "No Right to Exclude: Public Accommodations and Private Property" (1995-96) 90 Nw UL Rev 1283.

In reading the two cases that follow, note the differences in characterization, and the extent to which each case illustrates the tension between "private" and "public" law issues.

Re Drummond Wren

[1945] 4 DLR 674 (Ont HC)

MacKAY J: This is an application brought by Drummond Wren, owner of certain lands registered in the Registry Office for the County of York, to have declared invalid a restrictive covenant assumed by him when he purchased these lands and which he agreed to exact from his assigns, namely,—"Land not to be sold to Jews or persons of objectionable nationality."

The application is made by way of special leave and pursuant to s. 60 of the *Conveyancing and Law of Property Act*, RSO 1937, c. 152, and Rules 603 and 604 of the Rules of Practice and Procedure.

Under s. 60 of the *Conveyancing and Law of Property Act*, a wide discretion is given to a Judge to modify or discharge any condition or covenant "where there is annexed to any land any condition or covenant that such land or any specified portion thereof is not to be built on or is to be or not to be used in a particular manner, or any other condition or covenant running with or capable of being legally annexed to land."

Rules 603 and 604 provide respectively that:

603(1) Where any person claims to be the owner of land, but does not desire to have his title thereto quieted under *The Quieting Titles Act*, he may have any particular question which would arise upon an application to have his title quieted determined upon an originating notice.

(2) Notice shall be given to all persons to whom notice would be given under *The Quieting Titles Act*, and the Court shall have the same power finally to dispose of and determine such particular question as it would have under the said Act, but this shall not render it necessary to give the notice required by Rule 705.

604. Where the rights of any person depend upon the construction of any deed, will or other instrument, he may apply by originating notice, upon notice to all persons concerned, to have his rights declared and determined.

While, pursuant to an order made by me, notice of this application was served upon various persons interested in this and in adjacent lands subject to the same or a similar restrictive covenant, no one appeared in Court upon the return of this motion to oppose it.

The restrictive covenant which is the subject of this proceeding and which by the deed aforesaid the grantee assumes and agrees to exact from his assigns, reads as follows: "Land not to be sold to Jews, or to persons of objectionable nationality." Counsel for the applicant seeks the discharge and removal of this covenant on these alternative grounds: first, that it is void as against public policy; secondly, that it is invalid as a restraint on alienation; thirdly, that it is void for uncertainty; and fourthly, that it contravenes the provisions of the *Racial Discrimination Act*, 1944 (Ont.), c. 51. The matter before me, so defined, appears to raise issues of first impression because a search of the case law of Great Britain and of Canada does not reveal any reported decision which would be of direct assistance in this proceeding.

Counsel for the applicant did refer me to three Ontario cases dealing with restrictive covenants similar to that here involved, but, in my view, he rightly took the position that in none of those cases was the Court called upon to pass on the validity of the particular restriction in the way in which I am obliged to do in this case. Garrow J in *Essex Real Estate Co. v. Holmes* (1930), 37 OWN 392, did not have to determine the validity of the restriction in that case because he found that the purchaser of the land was not within its terms. Again, in *Re Bryers and Morris* (1931), 40 OWN 572, which was a vendor's and purchaser's motion, Hodgins JA refrained from passing on the validity of the restrictive covenant there in question. The third case mentioned by counsel for the applicant is a recent decision of Chevrier J, *Re McDougall and Waddell*, [1945] 2 DLR 244, OWN 272, which arose out of a vendor's and purchaser's motion for an order that the particular restrictive covenant there objected to offended against the terms of the *Racial Discrimination Act*, 1944 (Ont.), c. 51. The issue raised in that case was a narrow one and I shall return to a discussion of it later in my judgment.

In this short canvass of the authorities directly applicable, it may not be amiss to point out that, according to an affidavit filed on behalf of the applicant, the present Master of Titles at Toronto has not knowingly permitted anyone to register deeds containing restrictive covenants of a character similar to that in question here, and has on several occasions refused to accept for registration documents containing such covenants, and in no case has an appeal been taken from such refusal.

The applicant's argument is founded on the legal principle, briefly stated in 7 Hals. (2d ed.), pp. 153-4: "Any agreement which tends to be injurious to the public or against the public good is void as being contrary to public policy." Public policy, in the words of Halsbury, "varies from time to time."

In "The Growth of Law," Mr. Justice Cardozo says: "Existing rules and principles can give us our present location, our bearings, our latitude and longitude. The inn that shelters for the night is not the journey's end. The law, like the traveller, must be ready for the morrow. It must have a principle of growth."

And Mr. Justice Oliver Wendell Holmes, in "The Common Law" says: "The very considerations which judges most rarely mention and always with an apology are the secret root from which the law draws all the juices of life. I mean, of course, what is expedient for the community concerned."

The matter of not creating new heads of public policy has been discussed at some length by Mr. Justice McCardie in *Naylor, Benzon & Co. v. Krainische Industrie Gesellschaft*, [1918] 1 KB 331, later affirmed by the Court of Appeal, [1918] 2 KB 486.

There he points out [at 342-43] that "the Courts have not hesitated in the past to apply the doctrine (of public policy) whenever the facts demanded its application." "The truth of the matter," he says, "seems to be that public policy is a variable thing. It must fluctuate with the circumstances of the time. This view is exemplified by the decisions which were discussed by the House of Lords in *Nordenfelt v. Maxim Nordenfelt Guns and Ammunition Co.*, [1894] AC 535 ... . The principles of public policy remain the same, though the application of them may be applied in novel ways. The ground does not vary. As it was put by Tindal CJ in *Horner v. Graves* (1831), 7 Bing. 735, 743 [131 ER 284], "Whatever is injurious to the interests of the public is void, on the ground of public policy.'"

It is a well-recognized rule that Courts may look at various Dominion and Provincial Acts and public law as an aid in determining principles relative to public policy: see *Walkerville Brewing Co. v. Mayrand*, [1929] 2 DLR 945, 63 OLR 573.

First and of profound significance is the recent San Francisco Charter, to which Canada was a signatory, and which the Dominion Parliament has now ratified. The preamble to this Charter reads in part as follows:

We the peoples of the United Nations determined to save succeeding generations from the scourge of war, which twice in our lifetime has brought untold sorrow to mankind, and to reaffirm faith in fundamental human rights, in the dignity and worth of the human person, in the equal rights of men and women and of nations large and small ... and for these ends to practice tolerance and live together in peace with one another as good neighbours. ...

Under Articles 1 and 55 of this Charter, Canada is pledged to promote "universal respect for, and observance of, human rights and fundamental freedoms for all without distinction as to race, sex, language, or religion."

In the Atlantic Charter to which Canada has subscribed, the principles of freedom from fear and freedom of worship are recognized.

Section 1 of the *Racial Discrimination Act* provides:

1. No person shall,
   (a) publish or display or cause to be published or displayed; or

(b) permit to be published or displayed on lands or premises or in a newspaper, through a radio broadcasting station or by means of any other medium which he owns or controls,

any notice, sign, symbol, emblem or other representation indicating discrimination or an intention to discriminate against any person or any class of persons for any purpose because of the race or creed of such person or class of persons.

The Provincial Legislature further has expressed itself in the *Insurance Act*, RSO 1937, c. 256, s. 99, as follows:

Any licensed insurer which discriminates unfairly between risks within Ontario because of the race or religion of the insured shall be guilty of an offence.

Moreover, under s. 6 of the Regulations passed pursuant to the *Community Halls Act*, now RSO 1937, c. 284, it is provided that

Every hall erected under this Act shall be available for any public gathering of an educational, fraternal, religious or social nature or for the discussion of any public question, and no organization shall be denied the use of the hall for religious, fraternal or political reasons.

Proceeding from the general to the particular, the argument of the applicant is that the impugned covenant is void because it is injurious to the public good. This deduction is grounded on the fact that the covenant against sale to Jews or to persons of objectionable nationality prevents the particular piece of land from ever being acquired by the persons against whom the covenant is aimed, and that this prohibition is without regard to whether the land is put to residential, commercial, industrial or other use. How far this is obnoxious to public policy can only be ascertained by projecting the coverage of the covenant with respect to both the classes of persons whom it may adversely affect, and to the lots or subdivisions of land to which it may be attached. So considered, the consequences of judicial approbation of such a covenant are portentous. If sale of a piece of land can be prohibited to Jews, it can equally be prohibited to Protestants, Catholics or other groups or denominations. If the sale of one piece of land can be so prohibited, the sale of other pieces of land can likewise be prohibited. In my opinion, nothing could be more calculated to create or deepen divisions between existing religious and ethnic groups in this Province, or in this country, than the sanction of a method of land transfer which would permit the segregation and confinement of particular groups to particular business or residential areas, or conversely, would exclude particular groups from particular business or residential areas. The unlikelihood of such a policy as a legislative measure is evident from the contrary intention of the recently enacted *Racial Discrimination Act*, and the judicial branch of government must take full cognizance of such factors.

Ontario, and Canada too, may well be termed a Province, and a country, of minorities in regard to the religious and ethnic groups which live therein. It appears to me to be a moral duty, at least, to lend aid to all forces of cohesion, and similarly to repel all fissiparous tendencies which would imperil national unity. The common law Courts have, by their actions over the years, obviated the need for rigid constitutional guarantees in our polity by their wise use of the doctrine of public policy as an active agent in the promotion of the public weal. While Courts and eminent Judges have, in view of the powers of our Legislatures, warned against inventing new heads of public policy, I do not conceive that

I would be breaking new ground were I to hold the restrictive covenant impugned in this proceeding to be void as against public policy. Rather would I be applying well-recognized principles of public policy to a set of facts requiring their invocation in the interest of the public good.

That the restrictive covenant in this case is directed in the first place against Jews lends poignancy to the matter when one considers that anti-semitism has been a weapon in the hands of our recently-defeated enemies and the scourge of the world. But this feature of the case does not require innovation in legal principle to strike down the covenant; it merely makes it more appropriate to apply existing principles. If the common law of treason encompasses the stirring up of hatred between different classes of His Majesty's subjects, the common law of public policy is surely adequate to void the restrictive covenant which is here attacked.

My conclusion therefore is that the covenant is void because [it is] offensive to the public policy of this jurisdiction. This conclusion is reinforced, if reinforcement is necessary, by the wide official acceptance of international policies and declarations frowning on the type of discrimination which the covenant would seem to perpetuate.

It may not be inexpedient or improper to refer to a few declarations made by outstanding leaders under circumstances that arrest the attention and demand consideration of mankind. I first quote the late President Roosevelt:

Citizens, regardless of religious allegiance, will share in the sorrow of our Jewish fellow-citizens over the savagery of the Nazis against their helpless victims. The Nazis will not succeed in exterminating their victims any more than they will succeed in enslaving mankind. The American people not only sympathize with all victims of Nazi crimes but will hold the perpetrators of these crimes to strict accountability in a day of reckoning which will surely come.

I express the confident hope that the Atlantic Charter and the just World Order to be made possible by the triumph of the United Nations will bring the Jews and oppressed people in all lands to four freedoms which Christian and Jewish teachings have largely inspired.

And of the Right Honourable Winston Churchill:

In the day of victory the Jew's sufferings and his part in the struggle will not be forgotten. Once again, at the appointed time, he will see vindicated those principles of righteousness which it was the glory of his fathers to proclaim to the world. Once again it will be shown that, though the mills of God grind slowly, yet they grind exceeding small.

And of General Charles de Gaulle:

Be assured that since we have repudiated everything that has falsely been done in the name of France after June 23d, the cruel decrees directed against French Jews can and will have no validity in Free France. These measures are not less a blow against the honour of France than they are an injustice against her Jewish citizens.

When we shall have achieved victory, not only will the wrongs done in France itself be righted, but France will once again resume her traditional place as a protagonist of freedom and justice for all men, irrespective of race or religion, in a new Europe.

Also, the resolution passed by the representatives of over 60,000,000 organized workers at the World Trade Union Congress recently held at London that "every form of political, economic or social discrimination based on race, creed or sex, shall be eliminated."

The resolution against discrimination adopted unanimously by the Latin American nations and the United States in Mexico City on March 6, 1945, at the time of the Act of Chapultepec, is that the governments of these nations "prevent with all the means in their power all that may provoke discrimination among individuals because of racial and religious reasons."

It is provided in Article 123 of The Constitution of the Union of Soviet Socialistic Republics, that:

> Equality of rights of citizens of the USSR, irrespective of their nationality or race, in all spheres of economic, state, cultural, social and political life, is an indefeasible law.
>
> Any direct or indirect restriction of the rights of, or, conversely, any establishment of direct or indirect privileges for, citizens on account of their race or nationality, as well as any advocacy of racial or national exclusiveness or hatred and contempt, is punishable by law.

The second point raised by counsel for the applicant is that the covenant is invalid as a restraint on alienation. It is unnecessary to quote authorities in support of the long-established principle of the common law that land should be freely alienable. True, a limited class of exceptions to this general principle has from time to time been recognized, as in *Re Macleay* (1875), LR 20 Eq. 186, though it may be pointed out that this decision runs counter to the earlier case of *Attwater v. Attwater* (1853), 18 Beav. 330, 52 ER 131. Moreover, in *Re Rosher, Rosher v. Rosher* (1884), 26 Ch. D 801, Pearson J stated that he failed to appreciate how the exception recognized in *Re Macleay* arose. It is not necessary to challenge the doctrine of *Re Macleay*, which has been followed in some Canadian cases, in order to find that the covenant with which I am concerned is invalid as a restraint on alienation. The particular covenant in the case before me is not limited either in time or to the life of the immediate grantee (see Sweet, Restraints on Alienation, 33 LQ Rev., 236, 342, particularly at p. 354), which would seem to be characteristic of the partial restraints which were enforced in the decided cases that I have been able to find. The principle of freedom of alienation has been too long and too well established in the jurisprudence of English and Canadian Courts to warrant me at this late stage in recognizing a limitation upon it of a character not hitherto the subject of any reported case, especially in view of my conclusions as to public policy.

Counsel for the applicant contended before me that the restrictive covenant here in question is void for uncertainty. So far as the words "persons of objectionable nationality" are concerned, the contention admits of no contradiction. The conveyancer who used these words surely must have realized, if he had given the matter any thought, that no Court could conceivably find legal meaning in such vagueness. So far as the first branch of the covenant is concerned, that prohibiting the sale of the land to "Jews," I am bound by the recent decision of the House of Lords in *Clayton v. Ramsden*, [1943] 1 All ER 16; to hold that the covenant is in this respect also void for uncertainty; and I may add, that I would so hold even if the matter were *res integra*. The Law Lords in *Clayton v. Ramsden* were unanimous in holding that the phrase "of Jewish parentage" was uncertain, and Lord Romer was of the same opinion in regard to the phrase "of Jewish faith." I do not see that the bare term "Jews" admits of any more certainty.

I should like, in conclusion, to refer to the judgment of Chevrier J in *Re McDougall and Waddell*, [1945] 2 DLR 244. The learned Judge there decided that the registration of a deed containing a covenant restricting the sale or user of land to "gentiles (non-semitic) of European or British or Irish or Scottish racial origin" did not constitute an infringement of the *Racial Discrimination Act*. He came to this conclusion by holding that registration of a deed was not among the proscribed means of publishing or displaying enumerated in s. 1 of the Act. Counsel for the applicant herein contended that those proscribed means related only to the terms of cl. (b) of s. 1, and that they did not qualify cl. (a) of s. 1 which reads as follows:

> 1. No person shall,
>   (a) publish or display or cause to be published or displayed; ...
> any notice, sign, symbol, emblem or other representation indicating discrimination or an intention to discriminate against any person or any class of persons for any purpose because of the race or creed of such person or class of persons.

Mr. Cartwright further submitted that if this section had been read by the learned Judge without this limitation, that registration in the Registry Office constituted publication of a notice or other representation as aforesaid, and that following Halsbury (2d ed.), vol. 29, p. 444, "registration constitutes actual notice to all the world," therefore he should have found that the particular clause was in breach of the said Act.

I do not deem it necessary for the purpose of this case to deal with this argument, except to say that it appears to me to have considerable merit. My opinion as to the public policy applicable to this case in no way depends on the terms of the *Racial Discrimination Act*, save to the extent that such Act constitutes a legislative recognition of the policy which I have applied; in fact my brother Chevrier, as I read his judgment in *Re McDougall and Waddell*, is in accord with me in this respect.

An order will therefore go declaring that the restrictive covenant attacked by the applicant is void and of no effect.

Order declaring covenant void.

Noble and Wolf v Alley
[1951] SCR 64

KERWIN J (Taschereau J concurring):

This is an appeal against a judgment of the Court of Appeal for Ontario [[1949] 4 DLR 375, OR 503] affirming the judgment of Schroeder J [[1948] 4 DLR 123, OR 579] on a motion under s. 3 of the *Vendors and Purchasers Act*, RSO 1937, c. 168. That section, so far as relevant, provides that a vendor of real estate may apply in a summary way to the Supreme Court in respect of any requisition or objection arising out of, or connected with, a contract for the sale or purchase of land. The motion was made by the present appellant, Mrs. Noble, as the vendor under a contract for the sale by her to the purchaser, her co-appellant Bernard Wolf, of land forming part of a summer resort development known as the Beach O'Pines.

This land had been purchased in 1933 by Mrs. Noble from the Frank S. Salter Co. Ltd., and in the deed from it to her appeared the following covenant:

AND the Grantee for himself, his heirs, executors, administrators and assigns, covenants and agrees with the Grantor that he will carry out, comply with and observe, with the intent that they shall run with the lands and shall be binding upon himself, his heirs, executors, administrators and assigns, and shall be for the benefit of and enforcible by the Grantor and/or any other person or persons seized or possessed of any part or parts of the land included in Beach O'Pines Development, the restrictions herein following, which said restrictions shall remain in full force and effect until the first day of August, 1962, and the Grantee for himself, his heirs, executors, administrators and assigns further covenants and agrees with the Grantor that he will exact the same covenants with respect to the said restrictions from any and all persons to whom he may in any manner whatsoever dispose of the said lands. ...

"(f) The lands and premises herein described shall never be sold, assigned, transferred, leased, rented, or in any manner whatsoever alienated to, and shall never be occupied or used in any manner whatsoever by any person of the Jewish, Hebrew, Semitic, Negro or coloured race or blood, it being the intention and purpose of the Grantor, to restrict the ownership, use, occupation and enjoyment of the said recreational development, including the lands and premises herein described, to persons of the white or Caucasian race not excluded by this clause."

Although the deed was not signed by Mrs. Noble, I assume that she is bound to the same extent as if she had executed it.

Each conveyance by the company to a purchaser of land in the development contained a covenant in the same form. The present respondents, being owners of other parcels of land in the development, were served with notice of the application either before Schroeder J or the Court of Appeal, and they and their counsel affirmed the validity of the covenant, its binding effect upon Mrs. Noble, and that any of the respondents are able to take advantage of the covenant so as to prevent by injunction its breach. While before the Judge of first instance the vendor and purchaser apparently took opposite sides, each of them appealed to the Court of Appeal and, there, as well as before this Court, attacked the contentions put forward on behalf of the respondents.

In the Courts below emphasis was laid upon the decision of MacKay J, in *Re Drummond Wren*, [1945] 4 DLR 674, OR 778, and it was considered that the motion was confined to the consideration of whether that case, if rightly decided, covered the situation. The motion was for an order declaring that the objection to the covenant made on behalf of the purchaser had been fully answered by the vendor and that the same did not constitute a valid objection to the title or for such further and other order as might seem just. The objection was: "REQUIRED in view of the fact that the purchaser herein might be considered as being of the Jewish race or blood, we require a release from the restrictions imposed in the said clause (f) and an order declaring that the restrictive covenant set out in the said clause (f) is void and of no effect."

The answer by the vendor was that the decision in *Re Drummond Wren* applied to the facts of the present sale with the result that cl. (f) was invalid and the vendor and purchaser were bound to observe it. In view of the wide terms of the notice of motion, the application is not restricted and it may be determined by a point taken before the Court of Appeal and this Court, if not before Schroeder J.

That point depends upon the meaning of the rule laid down in *Tulk v. Moxhay* (1848), 2 Ph. 774, 41 ER 1143. This was a decision of Lord Cottenham LC affirming a decision of the Master of the Rolls. The judgment of the Master of the Rolls appears in 18 LJ Ch. 83, and the judgment of the Lord Chancellor is more fully reported there than in Phillips' Reports. In the latter, the Lord Chancellor is reported as saying, p. 777: "That this Court has jurisdiction to enforce a contract between the owner of land and his neighbour purchasing a part of it, that the latter shall either use or abstain from using the land purchased in a particular way, is what I never knew disputed."

In the Law Journal, the following appears at pp. 87-8: "I have no doubt whatever upon the subject; in short, I cannot have a doubt upon it, without impeaching what I have considered as the settled rule of this Court ever since I have known it. That this Court has authority to enforce a contract, which the owner of one piece of land may have entered into with his neighbour, founded, of course, upon good consideration, and valuable consideration, that he will either use or abstain from using his land in any manner that the other party by the contract stipulates shall be followed by the party who enters into the covenant, appears to me the very foundation of the whole of this jurisdiction. It has never, that I know of, been disputed."

At p. 88 of the Law Journal the Lord Chancellor states that the jurisdiction of the Court was not fettered by the question whether the covenant ran with the land or not but that the question was whether a party taking property, the vendor having stipulated in a manner, binding by the law and principles of the Court of Chancery to use it in a particular way will be permitted to use it in a way diametrically opposite to that which the party has covenanted for. To the same effect is pp. 777-8 of Phillips's.

In view of these statements I am unable to gain any elucidation of the extent of the equitable doctrine from decisions at law such as *Congleton v. Pattison* (1808), 10 East 130, 103 ER 725, and *Rogers v. Hosegood*, [1900] 2 Ch. 388. It is true that in the Court of Appeal, Collins LJ, after referring to extracts from the judgment of Sir George Jessel MR in *London & South Western R Co. v. Gomm* (1882), 20 Ch. D 562 at p. 583, said at pp. 405-6: "These observations, which are just as applicable to the benefit reserved as to the burden imposed, shew that in equity, just as at law, the first point to be determined is whether the covenant or contract in its inception binds the land. If it does, it is then capable of passing with the land to subsequent assignees; if it does not, it is incapable of passing by mere assignment of the land."

This, however, leaves untouched the problem as to when a covenant binds the land.

Whatever the precise delimitation in the rule in *Tulk v. Moxhay* may be, counsel were unable to refer us to any case where it was applied to a covenant restricting the alienation of land to persons other than those of a certain race. Mr. Denison did refer to three decisions in Ontario: *Essex Real Estate Co. v. Holmes* (1930), 37 OWN 392 [aff'd 38 OWN 69]; *Re Bryers & Morris* (1931), 40 OWN 572; *Re McDougall & Waddell*, [1945] 2 DLR 244, OWN 272; but he was quite correct in stating that they were of no assistance. The holding in the first was merely that the purchaser of the land there in question did not fall within a certain prohibition. In the second an inquiry was directed, without more. In the third, all that was decided was that the provisions of s. 1 of the *Racial Discrimination Act*, 1944 (Ont.), c. 51, would not be violated by a deed containing a covenant on the part of the purchaser that certain lands or any buildings erected thereon should not at any time be sold to, let to or occupied by any person or persons other than Gentiles (non-semitic (*sic*)) of European or British or Irish or Scottish racial origin.

It was a forward step that the rigour of the common law should be softened by the doctrine expounded in *Tulk v. Moxhay* but it would be an unwarrantable extension of that doctrine to hold, from anything that was said in that case or in subsequent cases, that the covenant here in question has any reference to the use, or abstension from use, of land. Even if decisions upon the common law could be prayed in aid, there are none that go to the extent claimed in the present case.

The appeal should be allowed with costs here and in the Court of Appeal. There should be no costs of the original motions in the Supreme Court of Ontario.

RAND J (Kellock and Fauteux JJ concurring):

Covenants enforceable under the rule of *Tulk v. Moxhay*, 11 Beav. 571, 50 ER 937, are properly conceived as running with the land in equity and, by reason of their enforceability, as constituting an equitable servitude or burden on the servient land. The essence of such an incident is that it should touch or concern the land as contradistinguished from a collateral effect. In that sense, it is a relation between parcels, annexed to them and, subject to the equitable rule of notice, passing with them both as to benefit and burden in transmissions by operation of law as well as by act of the parties.

But by its language, the covenant here is directed not to the land or to some mode of its use, but to transfer by act of the purchaser; its scope does not purport to extend to a transmission by law to a person within the banned class. If, for instance, the grantee married a member of that class, it is not suggested that the ordinary inheritance by a child of the union would be affected. Not only, then, is it not a covenant touching or concerning the land, but by its own terms it fails in annexation to the land. The respondent owners are, therefore, without any right against the proposed vendor.

On its true interpretation, the covenant is a restraint on alienation. The grantor company which has disposed of all its holdings in the subdivision has admittedly ceased to carry on business and by force of the provisions of the *Companies Act*, RSO 1937, c. 251, s. 28, its powers have become forfeited; but by s-s. (4) they may, on such conditions as may be exacted, be revived by the Lieutenant-Governor in Council. Assuming the grantor would otherwise be entitled to enforce the covenant in equity against the original covenantor—and if he would not the point falls—it becomes necessary to deal with the question whether for the purposes of specific performance the covenant is unenforceable for uncertainty.

It is in these words: "The lands and premises herein described shall never be sold, assigned, transferred, leased, rented or in any manner whatsoever alienated to and shall never be occupied or used in any manner whatsoever by any person of the Jewish, Hebrew, Semitic, Negro or coloured race or blood, it being the intention and purpose of the Grantor, to restrict the ownership, use, occupation and enjoyment of the said recreational development including the lands and premises herein described, to persons of white or Caucasian race not excluded by this clause."

If this language were in the form of a condition, the holding in *Clayton v. Ramsden*, [1943] AC 320, would be conclusive against its sufficiency. In that case the House of Lords dealt with a condition in a devise by which the donee became divested if she should marry a person "not of Jewish parentage and of the Jewish faith" and held it void for uncertainty. I am unable to distinguish the defect in that language from what we have here: it is impossible to set such limits to the lines of race or blood as would enable a Court to say in all cases whether a proposed purchaser is or is not within the ban. As put by Lord Cranworth in *Clavering v. Ellison* (1859), 7 HLC 707 at p. 725, 11 ER 282, the condition "must be such that the Court can see from the beginning, precisely and distinctly, upon the happening of what event it was that the preceding vested estate was to determine."

The effect of the covenant, if enforceable, would be to annex a partial inalienability as an equitable incident of the ownership, to nullify an area of proprietary powers. In both cases there is the removal of part of the power to alienate; and I can see no ground of distinction between the certainty required in the one case and that of the other. The uncertainty is, then, fatal to the validity of the covenant before us as a defect of or objection to the title.

I would, therefore, allow the appeal and direct judgment to the effect that the covenant is not an objection to the title of the proposed vendor, with costs to the appellants in this Court and in the Court of Appeal.

[Estey J agreed that the appeal should be allowed, while Locke J dissented on the basis that it was not appropriate to decide the case on a point not raised in the original motion. As Locke J pointed out, the covenant had been attacked before Schroeder J on the basis that it contravened public policy, it was void for uncertainty, and it represented an unlawful attempt to restrain alienation. However, the appeal was allowed, Locke J dissenting.]

DISCUSSION NOTES

i. The Litigation Context

In *Noble and Wolf*, the vendor and purchaser had entered into an agreement for the sale of Annie Noble's cottage property in the Beach O'Pines Development. As part of the real estate transaction, the purchaser's solicitor forwarded a requisition in respect of title to the vendor's solicitor, as follows:

> Required, in view of the fact that the purchaser herein might be considered as being of the Jewish race or blood, we require a release from the restrictions imposed in the said cl. (f) and an order declaring that the restrictive covenant set out in the said cl. (f) is void and of no effect.

The vendor's solicitor responded to this request, stating:

> In our opinion the decision rendered in the case of *Re Drummond Wren* ... applies to the facts of the present sale, with the result that the clause (f) objected to is invalid and the vendor and purchaser are not bound to observe it.

When the purchaser's solicitor insisted on a declaratory order, the vendor initiated an application to determine the matter. The vendor claimed that the covenant was unenforceable because it was contrary to public policy, void for uncertainty and a restraint on alienation. The motion was heard by Schroeder J, who decided that the restrictive covenant in clause (f) was a valid and enforceable covenant, rejecting all the vendor's arguments, and that the vendor had thus not answered the purchaser's objection satisfactorily. The vendor and purchaser then appealed to the Court of Appeal, together arguing that the covenant was invalid as contrary to public policy, void for uncertainty and a restraint on alienation, and "unenforceable as a restraint upon the alienation, occupancy and user of land because of race or blood, such being a novel restraint unknown to and unrecognized by the Common Law." See [1949] 4 DLR 375 at 378-79. The respondents were most of the other owners of cottage properties at Beach O'Pines Development, and the Court of Appeal unanimously dismissed the appeal and confirmed the decision of Schroeder J. From this decision, the appellants appealed to the Supreme Court of Canada.

As is evident in the judgment of Kerwin J in the Supreme Court of Canada, the court concluded that the covenant in question did not touch and concern the land, and thus could not bind successors in title of the covenantor. Relying on the "wide terms of the notice of motion," Kerwin J decided that the Supreme Court of Canada could decide *Noble and Wolf* on a point that had not been raised or argued before Schroeder J, and which the Court of Appeal had apparently declined to consider; only Hogg JA in the Court of Appeal briefly mentioned the issue of whether the covenant touched and concerned the land (see [1949] 4 DLR 375 at 394-95), and he concluded that the appellate court could not consider it because it had not been raised or argued previously nor included as one of the grounds of appeal. In these circumstances, reliance on this issue in the Supreme Court of Canada is interesting. To what extent does this procedural issue suggest that the Supreme Court was seeking a "technical" basis for holding the covenant void, by contrast with the "policy" basis in *Re Drummond Wren*? In considering this question, note a contemporaneous comment about the two cases:

> [*Re Drummond Wren*] was of general interest to all lawyers because of the bold manner in which MacKay J sought out public policy without regard to previous judicial opinion on the subject. It was refreshing to find a judge trying to recapture some of the spirit that enabled the greatest of his judicial forebears to systematize the common law and yet leave it the elasticity necessary to keep it in harmony with changing social needs. On the other hand, in *Re Noble and Wolf*, the judges of the Ontario courts took a cautious approach and refused to take notice of any change in the public policy of Canada or Ontario.

(CB Bourne, "Comment" (1951) 29 Can Bar Rev 969 at 974.)

To what extent are there factual differences in the two cases that may justify differing approaches?

ii. Approaches to Interpreting Racially Restrictive Covenants

Although the two cases illustrate different approaches to reasoning about racially restrictive covenants in Ontario just after the Second World War, the covenants in both cases were held to be void and unenforceable. How different were the covenants in substance? In *Drummond Wren*, for example, the covenant prohibited sales to "Jews or persons of objectionable nationality," while in *Noble and Wolf* the clause prohibited sale, assignment, transfer, leasing, renting, use or occupation "in any manner whatsoever by any person of the Jewish, Hebrew, Semitic, Negro or coloured race or blood." Are the same groups excluded by both these covenants? Are they equally broad or narrow in the activities proscribed? Did the language of the covenants affect the reasoning in the two cases?

What were the grounds for concluding that the restrictive covenant in *Re Drummond Wren* was invalid? In technical terms, which part of the judgment of MacKay J was *ratio*, and which parts *obiter*? Why did MacKay J make voidness for reasons of public policy such a prominent part of his decision? Was the covenant clearly void as a restraint on alienation or on the ground of uncertainty? To what extent did the existence of the *Racial Discrimination Act*, SO 1944, c 51 influence the reasoning of MacKay J? To what extent did MacKay J focus on principles of law and equity concerning the enforceability of covenants on successors in title? Is this case about the running of the benefit or burden of a covenant? Is the covenant in *Re Drummond Wren* one that touches and concerns the land, or is it merely a personal covenant as is the covenant in *Noble and Wolf*?

The decision in *Re Drummond Wren* was clearly argued before Schroeder J in *Noble and Wolf*, and Schroeder J expressly decided to disagree with the reasoning of MacKay J. Schroeder J pointed out that MacKay J reached his conclusions in *Re Drummond Wren* without the benefit of opposing argument, while in *Noble and Wolf* the other cottagers were notified and joined the litigation. In addition, however, Schroeder J distinguished *Re Drummond Wren* as follows (at 133):

> Let it also be stated that in the case before my brother MacKay he was not concerned with a summer colony as in the case under consideration, but with a residential subdivision on O'Connor Drive in the City of Toronto, where the residents sought shelter rather than recreation. Also, the restriction in that case was unlimited in point of duration.

What is the difference between a racially restrictive covenant in an urban area and in a summer colony? Significantly, this point was also addressed in the reasons of Robertson CJO in the Court of Appeal in *Noble and Wolf* (at 386):

> It is common knowledge that, in the life usually led [in a summer community], there is much intermingling in an informal and social way, of the residents and their guests, especially at the beach. That the summer colony should be congenial is of the essence of a pleasant holiday in such circumstances. The purpose of cl. (f) here in question is obviously to assure, in some degree, that the residents are of a class who will get along well together. To magnify this innocent and modest effort to establish and maintain a place suitable for a pleasant summer residence into an enterprise that offends against some public policy, requires a stronger imagination that I possess ... . There is nothing criminal or immoral involved; the public interest is in no way concerned. These people have simply agreed among themselves upon a matter of their own personal concern that affects property of their own in which no one else has an interest. If the law sanctions [this action], then I know of no principle of public policy against which this is an offence.

To what extent does this reasoning depend on the existence of a dichotomy between private property and public policy? How should courts decide issues of public policy? To what extent does the Court of Appeal's reasoning result from an approach of non-intervention? In thinking about this question, consider the reasoning of Schroeder J in concluding (at 139) that it was not appropriate for him to adopt *Re Drummond Wren* as a precedent:

> It is trite law that common law rights are not to be deemed to be abrogated by statute unless the legislative intent to do so is expressed in very clear language. It follows logically, it seems to me, that for a Court to invent new heads of public policy and found thereon nullification of established rights or obligations—in a sense embarking upon a course of judicial legislation—is a mode of procedure not to be encouraged or approved.

To what extent do these views reflect typical concerns in the law of property? For an interesting assessment of *Noble and Wolf* in relation to international norms of public interest and private property rights, see Edward Morgan & Ofer Attias, "Rabbi Kahane, International

Law, and the Courts: Democracy Stands on Its Head" (1990) 4 Temp Int'l & Comp LJ 185 at 194-96. See also Karen Pearlston, "A Restricted Country? The Racist Legacy of Restrictive Covenants" (1996) [unpublished, archived at Osgoode Hall Law School, 1996]; W Tarnopolsky, "Discrimination and the Law in Canada" (1992) 41 UNBLJ 215 at 224; and J Walker, *"Race," Rights, and the Law in the Supreme Court of Canada: Historical Case Studies* (Toronto: Wilfrid Laurier University Press for the Osgoode Society for Canadian Legal History, 1997). On the significance of *Drummond Wren* and *Noble and Wolf* in the emergence of the movement for legislative protection of human rights in Ontario and Canada, see Philip Girard, *Bora Laskin: Bringing Law to Life* (Toronto: University of Toronto Press for the Osgoode Society for Canadian Legal History, 2005) ch 11.

iii. Restraints on Alienation and Legislative Action

Both *Re Drummond Wren* and *Noble and Wolf* addressed at length the issue of the validity of restraints on alienation, a problem that may occur in numerous situations other than those of covenants that run with the land. Interestingly, MacKay J held that the covenant in *Re Drummond Wren* was a restraint on alienation, and therefore void. By contrast, Schroeder J and the members of the Ontario Court of Appeal concluded that the covenant in *Noble and Wolf* was not a restraint on alienation. In both cases, the judges referred to *Re Macleay* (1875), LR 20 Eq 186, a case that considered a devise of land to the deceased's brother on condition that the brother should not sell out of the family. The family was a large one, and the court held that the condition was valid, apparently because there was a "large enough class of potential purchasers" to make the condition only a partial restraint on alienation. As DAL Smout commented further:

> The situation does not lack irony, for the first Jew to hold judicial office in England [Sir George Jessel, the judge who decided *Re Macleay*] thus provided the basis for the subsequent contention that, if such a condition conforms to the principles of common law, then a restraint forbidding alienation outside the racial or religious group approved by the testator or vendor must also necessarily be valid.

(DAL Smout, "An Inquiry into the Law on Racial and Religious Restraints on Alienation" (1952) 30 Can Bar Rev 863 at 866.) Smout provided an analysis of *Re Drummond Wren* and *Noble and Wolf*, suggesting (at 872) that even if "it is readily conceded that one cannot legislate tolerance, ... surely there is nothing worthless in legislating against certain intolerant practices .... There would seem to be no reason why the courts should wait for the intolerant to become tolerant before holding the discrimination covenant to be also unenforceable."

After the decision in the Ontario Court of Appeal, and prior to the hearing in the Supreme Court of Canada, the Ontario legislature enacted an amendment to the *Conveyancing and Law of Property Act* (now RSO 1990, c C.34, s 22) as follows:

> Every covenant made after the 24th day of March, 1950, that but for this section would be annexed to and run with land and that restricts the sale, ownership, occupation or use of land because of the race, creed, colour, nationality, ancestry or place of origin of any person is void and of no effect.

Consider the wording of this section in the context of the decision of the Supreme Court of Canada. To the extent that the court concluded that the covenant in *Noble and Wolf* was a personal covenant only and not one that touched and concerned the land, what impact would s 22, above, have on similar covenants involving racial restrictions? As Smout concluded (at 880), the legislative provision is very limited in its application:

> The choice of words ... is curious. The sections are expressly limited to covenants and thus have no effect upon any testamentary stipulation; a restraint set out in a will ... will be effective if expressed with certainty. In further emphasizing that the covenant must be one that but for the sections would be annexed to and run with the land, the amendments clearly do not affect the personal covenant ... . The language used by the legislature in these amendments is the language usually used to describe restrictive covenants. It may be wondered whether it does anything to prejudice a restraint on alienation or a determinable fee.

Is further legislative action necessary here? How would you draft an amendment to the *Conveyancing and Law of Property Act* that would be effective to invalidate racially restrictive covenants? To what extent is the reasoning in *Re Drummond Wren* or *Noble and Wolf* useful in the drafting process? Is it more effective to adopt a "technical" or a "policy" approach here? Why?

iv. Restrictive Covenants: Beyond Racial Restrictions

The problems of racially restrictive covenants are not confined to Canada, of course. In the United States, at about the same time as *Re Drummond Wren* and *Noble and Wolf* were being decided, the US Supreme Court considered similar issues in *Shelley v Kraemer*, 334 US 1 (1948). The court held that enforcement by state courts of restrictive agreements denied the equal protection of the laws pursuant to the 14th amendment of the US Constitution. For further analysis of US developments, see Chused at 161-250; Harvard Law Review Association, "Note: The Antidiscrimination Principle in the Common Law" (1989) 102 Harv L Rev 1993; Patricia Williams, "Spirit-Murdering the Messenger: The Discourse of Fingerpointing as the Law's Response to Racism" (1987) 42 U Miami L Rev 127; and C Harris, "Whiteness as Property" (1993) 106 Harv L Rev 1709.

In relation to these issues, how would you respond to a request to draft a covenant restricting parcels of land in a community to single-family use? In the United States, courts have held that single-family-use covenants prohibit occupancy of property by an extended family; a foster home for disabled children; a group of elderly citizens; two single men jointly owning a home; a group home for the mentally and developmentally disabled; a number of college students, boarders, and tenants; and religious groups. See G Korngold, "Single Family Use Covenants: For Achieving a Balance Between Traditional Family Life and Individual Autonomy" (1989) 22 UC Davis L Rev 951 at 953, and cases cited there. Korngold concluded (at 977-78) that part of the solution in these situations could be provided by the "touch and concern" test:

> Personal choices within the homes could not be regulated, while objective, disturbing actions outside the home that affect the neighbourhood could be prevented ... . To be sure, the touch and concern test has its flaws. Most notably, it is only a rough vehicle for addressing the contracts/antirestrictions conflict and does not straightforwardly examine the issues. Rather, it forces the problem into an arcane framework replete with jargon. The touch and concern test needs to be reformulated or replaced in a modern law of servitudes. However, it is better than nothing when it comes to single family use covenants.

For another analysis, see Dirk Hubbard, "Group Homes and Restrictive Covenants" (1988) 57:1 U Miss Kansas City L Rev 135.

In considering this comment, you may also want to take into account how "covenant communities" are increasing in number in the United States. Commentators often credit the Disney Development Company and its common-interest community "Celebration" with starting the trend to such communities. Using private covenants, such communities have created structures for providing services and amenities to residents:

> As community associations reach beyond their geographic boundaries to become more involved in the broader community, as they perform more community services for their own members, and as they build public and private alliances to provide many different services that were formerly public services, the legal, political, social, and economic consequences and effects increase and implicate corporate, municipal, constitutional, and other areas of law as well as social and public policy concerns.

(See Wayne S Hyatt, "Common Interest Communities: Evolution and Reinvention" (1998) 31 J Marshall L Rev 303 at 307-8.) For an assessment of relationships between planning and communities in the United Kingdom, see Rod Edmunds & Teresa Sutton, "Who's Afraid of the Neighbours?" in Elizabeth Cooke, ed, *Modern Studies in Property Law*, vol 1 (Oxford: Hart, 2001) 133. In Canada, the issue of age restrictions in housing developments was addressed briefly in *North Vancouver (District) v Fawcett* (1998), 162 DLR (4th) 402 (BCCA).

G. A Note on Breach of Covenant, Extinguishment, Waiver, and Discharge

In general, the remedy for breach of covenant is an injunction, restraining the continuing breach. In some cases in the 19th century in England, it was suggested that the court of equity had no discretion to exercise in granting an injunction—e.g. see *Doherty v Allman*, [1878] 3 AC 709 (HL). However, in *Shepherd Homes Ltd v Sandham*, [1971] Ch 340 (Ch D), Megarry J concluded that judicial discretion was required to avoid unfairness, and this approach was subsequently adopted in *Wrotham Park Estate v Parkside Homes*, [1974] 1 WLR 798 (Ch D). In *Wrotham Park*, developers began work on the construction of houses, in violation of a covenant prohibiting such development without the plaintiff's approval of the plans. The plaintiff brought action against the developers for a prohibitory injunction restraining building, and, more controversially, for a mandatory injunction to demolish the houses already built in violation of the covenant. The plaintiff did not seek an interlocutory injunction, however, so the developers continued to work pending the hearing in the matter. By the time of the hearing, 14 houses had been constructed and sold to purchasers, and the purchasers were added as defendants.

Brightman J concluded that there had been no financial damage to the plaintiff as a result of the breach and noted that the homes were already occupied and that there was a shortage of housing. As a result, he refused a mandatory injunction and instead ordered damages, assessed on the basis of an estimate of the sum that the plaintiff would have demanded to release the covenant. This approach was followed in a BC case, *Arbutus Park Estates Ltd v Fuller* (1976), 74 DLR (3d) 257 (BCSC). More recently, see *Federated Homes Ltd v Mill Lodge*, [1980] 1 WLR 594 (CA) and *Wakeham v Wood* (1981), 125 SJ 608. For an analysis of these and other cases, see Polden.

It is common for building schemes to include a broad power for the developer to waive the breach of any restrictive covenant, the exercise of which can lead to frustrated expectations on the part of homeowners. In *Rice v Condran*, 2012 NSSC 95, Mr and Mrs Rice sued their lawyer in negligence for not advising them of the possible impact of such a power with regard to two vacant lots they had purchased. The restrictive covenants in their subdivision prohibited the keeping of horses or other livestock. Shortly after purchasing the second lot, the Rices discovered that their neighbour was constructing a horse barn. The developer had waived the breach of the covenant pursuant to a power reserved to him in the document. In her defence, the lawyer relied on an expert witness who testified that the standard of care in such cases was to warn clients of any "unusual" provisions in the documents constituting the restrictive covenants, but that the waiver clause was not unusual. The lawyer thus argued that she had satisfied the relevant standard of care. The trial judge disagreed, finding "the practice of not pointing out to purchasers the potential effects of waiver clauses in subdivisions' restrictive covenants is not reasonable, nor defensible, given the tremendous power of such a clause" (at para 49). Liability was not established, however, because the judge was not persuaded that "but for" the failure to warn, the Rices, who were experienced in the real estate market, would not have bought the properties. He also found that no damages had been proven.

The parties to a covenant may release it expressly, and it is possible to provide for modification or discharge in the document creating a covenant as well. In some cases, an application to a court may be submitted pursuant to statutory provisions such as the *Conveyancing and Law of Property Act*, RSO 1990, c C.34, s 61. For a more detailed analysis, see the OLRC *Report on Covenants* at 49-57.

DISCUSSION NOTE

Remedies in Practice: McDonald's Restaurants of Canada Ltd v West Edmonton Mall Ltd

The West Edmonton Mall leased space in the mall to McDonald's Restaurants. The lease contained a covenant by which the mall undertook not to permit another "fast food restaurant" to operate in that phase of the mall property. The terminology of the covenant was further defined in the lease to preclude a restaurant primarily engaged in the sale of hamburgers and chicken products. The mall later leased space to another restaurant that, on the evidence of its menu, company brochures, and sales volumes, was primarily engaged in the sale of hamburgers, and the court concluded that the mall was in breach of the restrictive covenant. What remedy is appropriate in these circumstances—an injunction or damages? What factors should be considered by a court in determining what remedy to grant to McDonald's? See *McDonald's Restaurants of Canada Limited v West Edmonton Mall Ltd* (1994), 159 AR 120, 22 Alta LR (3d) 402, 42 RPR (2d) 215 (QB), where the court concluded that it was appropriate to grant the plaintiff's application for a permanent injunction.

H. Reforming the Law of Covenants

The rigid and highly technical character of the law of covenants has resulted in law reform proposals in a number of common law jurisdictions, including the United Kingdom and Canada as well as the United States. In Ontario, the OLRC *Report on Covenants* addressed both current issues and recommended reforms. After reviewing legal principles about covenants in a number of other jurisdictions, OLRC focused on the problem of positive covenants and recommended (at 102) that "the law should be reformed to permit the burden of affirmative obligations to run upon a transfer of freehold land." To implement this recommendation, OLRC recognized that a choice is required—either to reform the law of covenants only, or to "consolidate, to the extent possible, not only positive and restrictive covenants, but also easements and *profits à prendre*, into a single unified law of servitudes." After examining these alternative approaches, OLRC concluded (at 103) that reform of all the non-possessory interests as part of the law of servitudes generally would be "overly ambitious within the limited context of the … *Report*." Thus, OLRC's recommendations focused more specifically on the principles of covenants.

OLRC recommended (at 105) the creation of a new interest in land called a "land obligation," and argued that it should "comprehend both positive and restrictive obligations, and should permit both the benefit and the burden of such obligations to run upon a transfer of freehold land." The benefit of land obligations would be permitted to exist either as appurtenant to land or in gross. For further analysis, see the OLRC *Report on Covenants* at 105ff.

The Law Commission of England and Wales, in its 2011 report noted above, recommended a similar reform, but to date neither the Ontario nor the British proposals have resulted in legislation. The British Columbia Law Institute recently recommended significant reforms to the law of covenants, including the recognition of the running of positive covenants where they relate to "expenditures for work, provision of materials, or operations in, on, above or under the land [or] the carrying out [of] any work or operations, including maintenance, repair or replacement, of anything … in, on, above or under the land": *Report on Restrictive Covenants: A Report Prepared for the British Columbia Law Institute by the Members of the Real Property Reform (Phase 2) Project Committee* (Vancouver: British Columbia Law Institute, 2012) at 62.

By contrast, New Zealand enacted a simple reform statute in 1986 that reads in its current version:

> 302(1) This section applies to a covenant burdening the land of the covenantor, whether expressed in an instrument or implied by this Act or any other enactment in an instrument, and whether a positive covenant or a restrictive covenant.
>
> (2) Unless a contrary intention appears in the instrument, the covenant binds
>
>> (a) the covenantor; and
>>
>> (b) the covenantor's successors in title; and
>>
>> (c) persons claiming through the covenantor or the covenantor's successors in title.

(See *Property Act 2007* (NZ) 2007/91.)

In light of this reform, is it possible that observers are overstating the complexities that allegedly stand in the way of altering the law on the running of positive covenants?

Perhaps the most significant reform to the law of covenants in Canada has happened indirectly by the enactment of legislation concerning condominiums. Although the condominium property as a whole is registered in the name of a condominium corporation, each unit owner holds title to a unit in fee simple, together with an undivided interest (along with all other unit holders) in all the common elements. There are numerous positive and negative obligations to which unit holders are bound when they purchase a unit, but by statute these can all be enforced by the condominium corporation, thus circumventing the common law rules about the running of benefit and burden. This is a major advance over the functioning of restrictive covenants in residential subdivisions, where there is normally no corporate body to take on the task of enforcing covenants. In Ontario, see *Condominium Act*, RSO 1990, c C.26 and further discussion in Chapter 6 concerning shared property interests.

By contrast with the approach of OLRC and New Zealand, a more general reform process has been undertaken in the United States in relation to the American Law Institute's servitudes project. As S French has described the US project:

> The American Law Institute's current servitudes project began with a lofty mission—to simplify, clarify, and modernize the law—and a bold and sweeping design—to unify the heretofore separate bodies of law governing easements, profits, irrevocable licenses, equitable servitudes, and real covenants under the single conceptual heading of servitudes … . The new Restatement … continues long traditions of coupling private rearrangement of property rights with active judicial scrutiny of those arrangements. It creates a new conceptual framework for thinking about servitudes and achieves substantial simplification of the law by eliminating several overlapping servitude categories … . Traditional at the core, the new Restatement should provide substantial material for innovative evolution of the common law.

(S French, "Tradition and Innovation in the New Restatement of Servitudes: A Report from Midpoint" (1994) 27 Conn L Rev 119 at 119 and 129.) The "lofty mission" of the American Law Institute was realized in its final report on the subject, *Restatement of the Law, Third: Property—Servitudes* (St Paul, MN: ALI, 2000).

What are the advantages of the American approach to covenant reform? What are the limitations of such an approach? Do you agree that it was preferable for OLRC to make recommendations about covenants without taking a more comprehensive approach to the reform of non-possessory interests and other limits on the use of land? You may want to reconsider these questions in relation to the discussion of conservation easements and covenants in the next section.

I. Non-Possessory Interests: "Private" Planning, "Public" Planning, and Conservation

Although landowners have often used non-possessory interests, particularly covenants, as a means of accomplishing private planning goals within defined communities, the rigidity of common law requirements for their creation and enforcement has sometimes resulted in uncertainty and disappointment. Accordingly, as public regulation increased with the enactment of provincial planning statutes and municipal zoning and bylaws in the 20th century, the role of non-possessory interests as tools for planning became secondary. Thus, planning legislation and governmental agencies created and enforced a scheme of public regulation with respect to land use, leaving landowners less scope to engage in private planning by means of non-possessory interests, especially covenants. For a recent example, see *Ontario Planning and Development Act, 1994*, SO 1994, c 23. In the United States, although there were a number of constitutional challenges to zoning bylaws, with arguments about whether these statutes constituted an "unlawful taking" of private property, the priority of governmental regulation of community planning was confirmed in *Village of Euclid v Ambler Realty Company*, 272 US 365 (1926). For a full examination of the background to this case, see Chused at 1156ff. In the Australian context, see J Tooher, "Restrictive Covenants and Public Planning Legislation—Should the Landowner Feel 'Touched and Concerned'?" (1992) 9 Envtl & Planning LJ 63.

Two developments in recent decades, however, have created new interest in the use of covenants, as well as easements and *profits à prendre*, as planning tools. First, there has been increasingly widespread recognition of a need for individual and group action, in addition to governmental efforts, to foster protection of the environment, both in urban areas and in natural settings. In this context, for example, L Caldwell identified the problems of current land law reform as the result of tension between the traditional concept of "land ownership" and a more recent concept of "land stewardship":

> The absence of an ingrained ethic of stewardship has been a major deterrent to the shift toward responsible land management ... . Legal and economic circumstances place the power to decide land use policies in those people who have the greatest incentive to regard land as a commodity and to discount noneconomic and long-range considerations. People committed to an ethic of stewardship and ecological sustainability continue to collide with those who make land use decisions upon a very different ethic, an ethic that regards economic development and monetary return as evidence of the land's highest and best use.

(L Caldwell, "Land and the Law: Problems in Legal Philosophy" (1986) U Ill L Rev 319 at 329.) Caldwell noted that ideas about the relationship between natural objects and human beings are reflected in current legal debates about environmental protection. See also C Stone, "'Should Trees Have Standing?' Revisited: How Far Will Law and Morals Reach? A Pluralist Perspective" (1985) 59 S Cal L Rev 1, and E Freyfogle, "The Construction of Ownership" (1996) U Ill L Rev 173. These views express attitudes to property relationships that are reflected in traditional Aboriginal property concepts.

In addition to a growing sense of concern about the environment, a renewed interest in the use of non-possessory interests as planning tools has resulted from political changes in Canada and elsewhere that emphasize private, rather than public, methods of regulation. After noting the former priority enjoyed by governmental planning arrangements, a report of the North American Wetlands Conservation Council in 1995 stated bluntly:

> But the 1990s have changed all that. Now, there is a general malaise and disillusionment with government, significant financial constraints on once pervasive agencies, ongoing degradation of resources and loss of biodiversity, and a recognition that not all land of conservation could—or should—be owned by a public entity. In fact, many private landowners and their families have demonstrated good stewardship over the years, in contrast to some poor management examples on public lands.

(T Silver et al, *Canadian Legislation for Conservation Covenants, Easements and Servitudes: The Current Situation*, Report no 95-1 (Ottawa: North American Wetlands Conservation Council (Canada), 1995) [Silver et al] at i.) As the authors explained, one response to these changed circumstances is "private stewardship programs." For example, a landowner who wanted to preserve a woodlot could grant a *profit à prendre* to a conservation organization, entitling the organization to cut the trees. This grant would prevent any future group from harvesting the trees because the right to do so had been transferred. However, such an arrangement creates a situation of non-exercise of the right and is not really well-designed for widespread use. A more viable solution is the creation by legislation of statutory conservation covenants, easements, or servitudes.

Historically, conservation "easements" were used to protect parkways around Boston in the 1880s, and they have been used by the federal government in the United States for habitat preservation since the 1930s. However, in 1981, the United States adopted the *Uniform Conservation Easement Act*, and many states have enacted complementary legislation. See WJ Andrews & D Loukidelis, *Leaving a Living Legacy: Using Conservation Covenants in British Columbia* (Vancouver: West Coast Environmental Law Research Foundation, 1996) at 2. For an earlier assessment of conservation easements in Canada, see S Silverstone, "Open Space Preservation Through Conservation Easements" (1974) 12 Osgoode Hall LJ 105.

In Canada, a conservation covenant is a written agreement negotiated between a "qualified holder" (often an environmental organization or a governmental agency) and a landowner, pursuant to which the landowner agrees to protect the land in defined ways. The conservation covenant is registered and binds successive owners. Legislation enabling the creation and enforcement of conservation covenants generally permits departures from the common law requirements for enforceable covenants—for example, the covenants may be either positive or negative, there is no requirement for the covenantee to hold land, and the principles concerning the "touch and concern" requirement are relaxed. For examples, see Ontario's *Conservation Land Act*, RSO 1990, c C.28, as amended by SO 1994, c 27, s 128, SO 2000, Sched L, s 2, and Nova Scotia's *Conservation Easements Act*, SNS 2001, c 28. There are also statutes concerning heritage preservation that have similar provisions—see *Ontario Heritage Act*, RSO 1990, c O.18; *Heritage Conservation Act*, SNB 2009, c H-4.05; *Heritage Property Act*, RSNS 1989, c 199; *Museum Act*, RSPEI 1988, c M-14; and *Historic Resources Act*, RSNL 1990, c H-4. For a full account of provincial and territorial statutes and efforts to achieve beneficial tax arrangements for landowners who enter these agreements, see Silver et al.

The authors argue that private efforts to protect the environment using conservation covenants can succeed only if there is complementary public restructuring of institutional arrangements, including (at 42) "legal reforms to ensure effective, inexpensive and streamlined use of these legal tools." They also suggest a need for immediate action (at ii):

> But for now, we—conservationists, land professionals, and especially landowners—need to become more familiar with conservation covenants, easements and servitudes, understand their supporting legislation, and push for reforms where necessary. Then we need to get out there and make these tools work on the landscape. Time is short. Older landowners will be transferring much of their holdings over the next decade, creating a golden opportunity for land securement; and the wealth of biodiversity, especially in southern settled landscapes, is increasingly "losing ground." Conservation covenants, easements and servitudes provide a key new means for seizing this opportunity and stemming these losses.

Are conservation covenants private or public property? Are such covenants an appropriate tool for fostering environmental concerns? Compare the advantages and disadvantages of private and public or private–public arrangements. For further analysis, see the collection of essays in A Kwasniak, ed, *Private Conservancy: The Path to Law Reform* (Edmonton: Environmental Law Centre, 1994), and A Kwasniak, "Conservation Easements: Pluses and Pitfalls, Generally and for Municipalities" (2009) 46 Alta L Rev 651. For an interesting account of gender issues in relation to planning issues and the use of space, see Gillian Rose, *Feminism and Geography: The Limits of Geographical Knowledge* (Minneapolis, MN: University of Minnesota Press, 1993).

PROBLEMS

1. In 2000, Arthur Adams inherited 60 acres of land in the Niagara Peninsula. As an ardent conservationist, he was determined to preserve the land for farming purposes in spite of all the problems inherent in so doing. In 2002, he leased a 20-acre parcel for 30 years to his neighbour Ben Brooks, who wanted to increase his acreage for growing organic hops used in the brewing of specialty beers. In 1987, Adams sold a 10-acre parcel to another local farmer, Cathy Clayton, who wanted to grow organic peaches. In both transactions, Arthur Adams required the insertion of a special clause in the documents requiring that the land be used productively for purposes of agriculture. By 2010, however, Ben found that the market for organic hops had declined and Cathy's peach orchard became infested with blight. Both Brooks and Clayton advised Adams that they intended to transfer their interests to Toronto residents who wanted to purchase holiday property in the Niagara area. Adams wants advice about the enforceability of his special clause.

Advise Adams about whether he can enforce the clause against:

    a. the assignee of the parcel leased to Brooks, and

    b. the assignee of the parcel sold to Clayton.

2. In *Bruce and Bruce v Dixon*, [1957] OWN 489 (CA), Laidlaw JA stated:

Mr. Jones was the owner of the east half of Lot 27 in the 10th Concession in the Township of Otonabee in the County of Peterborough. The defendant Dixon owned an adjoining lot. There was no well on either lot. Both Jones and Dixon agreed that they would search for a well and if they found a supply of water that they would construct a well. They employed the method of "witching" for a well. They were successful in finding water at or near the boundary line between the two lots. They intended to build the well as near as possible to the boundary line. They entered on the joint undertaking of finding and constructing a well with the certain and mutual intention that the well was to be for the benefit of the owners of both lots and their successors in title. The location of the boundary line was not known precisely and it happened that the well as constructed was located wholly on the lands owned by Dixon. After construction of the well, Jones made use of the water from the well for a period of time and, in so doing, used a portion of the lands owned by Dixon as a right of way. Subsequently, Jones sold the land owned by him to the plaintiffs. The plaintiffs and the defendant became involved in a dispute as to the right of the plaintiffs to use any part of the defendant's land by way of an easement for the purpose of getting water from the well. The defendant denied the plaintiffs any right to such user, or to any easement over his land.

Explain the arguments that counsel for the plaintiffs can make to demonstrate that:

    a. the right of way is an easement; and

    b. the plaintiffs can enforce the easement against the defendants.

3. Merry and Pippin live on adjoining lots in the salubrious suburb of Downsview. They are good neighbours. There is a driveway between their lots that belongs to Merry. However, ever since Pippin moved into his house in 1975, he had used this driveway to get to the laneway at the rear of his lot. Merry had expressly agreed that Pippin could use the driveway anytime, so long as he did not block Merry's access to his garage at the far end of the driveway.

For some years, this amicable arrangement continued. However, in 1990, Merry was persuaded by energy conservationists to give up using an automobile and to ride a bicycle. Thus, in 1990, Merry told Pippin that he could use the driveway from that time forward without worrying about blocking Merry's access to his garage. Thereafter, Pippin parked his car in the driveway quite regularly.

In 1996, Pippin became interested in vintage cars, and he began to park these cars in the driveway. From that time, he generally parked his own car on the street, and there were usually three or four vintage cars parked in the driveway. Because Merry was interested in Pippin's hobby, he never objected. In 2007, however, Merry decided to move to Rosedale and Gandalf now wants to buy his house. Merry has told Gandalf that the driveway will also be available to Gandalf.

Gandalf wants advice about his right to use the driveway. (You may want to reconsider *Keefer v Arillotta*, Chapter 2.)

4. In 1989, a landowner granted to R Ltd "the sole and exclusive licence to remove all gravel" from his property for the economical lifetime of the gravel pit. Before R Ltd registered its interest, the bank registered a charge (mortgage) relating to a loan to the landowner. The bank subsequently brought an application for a declaration that its mortgage had priority over R Ltd's licence agreement. The bank's application required the court to decide whether the agreement was an "instrument" as defined by s 1 of the *Registry Act*, RSO 1990, c R.20, and the court concluded that the agreement met the *Registry Act* requirements. Did the agreement create a *profit à prendre*? What is the difference between a licence and a *profit à prendre*? The issue was discussed briefly in *Canadian Imperial Bank of Commerce v Rockway Holdings Ltd* (1996), 29 OR (3d) 350 at 352-53. See also OLRC *Report on Basic Principles* at 126.

CHAPTER REFERENCES

Alexander, Gregory S. "Freedom, Coercion, and the Law of Servitudes" (1988) 73 Cornell L Rev 883.

American Law Institute. *Restatement of the Law of Property* (Philadelphia, PA: American Law Institute, 1944).

American Law Institute. *Restatement of the Law, Third: Property—Servitudes* (St Paul, MN: ALI, 2000).

Anderson, S. "Easement and Prescription—Changing Perspectives in Classification" (1975) 38 Mod L Rev 641.

Andrews, WJ & D Loukidelis. *Leaving a Living Legacy: Using Conservation Covenants in British Columbia* (Vancouver: West Coast Environmental Law Research Foundation, 1996).

Aoki, Keith. "Race, Space, and Place: The Relation Between Architectural Modernism, Post-Modernism, Urban Planning, and Gentrification" (1993) 20 Fordham L Rev 699.

Atkinson, S. *The Theory and Practice of Conveyancing*, 2d ed (London: Sweet, 1839).

Backhouse, C. "Racial Segregation in Canadian Legal History: Viola Desmond's Challenge, Nova Scotia, 1946" (1994) 17 Dal LJ 299.

Battersby, Graham. "Informally Created Interests in Land" in Susan Bright & John Dewar, eds, *Land Law: Themes and Perspectives* (Oxford: Oxford University Press, 1998).

Berger, L. "A Policy Analysis of Promises Respecting the Use of Land" (1970) 55 Minn L Rev 167.

Borovoy, A. "The Fair Accommodation Practices Act: The 'Dresden' Affair" (1956) 14:1 UT Fac L Rev 13.

Bourne, CB. "Comment" (1951) 29 Can Bar Rev 969.

Bowden, MA. "Protecting Solar Access in Canada: The Common Law Approach" (1985) 9 Dal LJ 261.

Bradbrook, AJ. "Access to Landlocked Land: A Comparative Study of Legal Solutions" (1983) 10 Sydney L Rev 39.

Bradbrook, AJ & S MacCallum. *Easements and Restrictive Covenants in Australia*, 3d ed (Sydney: Butterworths, 2012).

Bright, Susan. "Of Estates and Interests: A Tale of Ownership and Property Rights" in Susan Bright & John Dewar, eds, *Land Law: Themes and Perspectives* (Oxford: Oxford University Press, 1998).

Bright, Susan & John Dewar, eds. *Land Law: Themes and Perspectives* (Oxford: Oxford University Press, 1998).

British Columbia Law Institute. *Report on Restrictive Covenants: A Report Prepared for the British Columbia Law Institute by the Members of the Real Property Reform (Phase 2) Project Committee* (Vancouver: British Columbia Law Institute, 2012).

Browder, OL. "Running Covenants and Public Policy" (1978) 77 Mich L Rev 12.

Caldwell, L. "Land and the Law: Problems in Legal Philosophy" (1986) U Ill L Rev 319.

Chused, R. *Cases, Materials and Problems in Property* (New York: Matthew Bender, 1988).

Cooke, Elizabeth, ed. *Modern Studies in Property Law* (Oxford: Hart, 2001).

Cooke, Elizabeth. "Re Ellenborough Park (1955): A Mere Recreation and Amusement" in Nigel P Gravells, ed, *Landmark Cases in Land Law* (Oxford and Portland, OR: Hart, 2013).

Crane, FR. "Comment" (1957) 21 Conveyancer and Property Lawyer 160.

Davis, Christine. "The Principle of Benefit and Burden" (1998) 57 Cambridge LJ 522.

Department of Education. *Easements and Restrictive Covenants* (Toronto: Law Society of Upper Canada, 1989).

Edmunds, Rod & Teresa Sutton. "Who's Afraid of the Neighbours?" in Elizabeth Cooke, ed, *Modern Studies in Property Law*, vol 1 (Oxford: Hart, 2001) 133.

Eekelaar, J & J Bell, eds. *Oxford Essays in Jurisprudence*, 3d series (Oxford: Clarendon Press, 1987).

Epstein, R. "Notice and Freedom of Contract in the Law of Servitudes" (1982) 55 S Cal L Rev 1353.

Franzese, P. "'Out of Touch': The Diminished Viability of the Touch and Concern Requirement in the Law of Servitudes" (1991) 21 Seton Hall L Rev 235.

Franzese, P. "Servitudes Reform and the New Restatement of Property: Creation Doctrines and Structural Simplification" (1988) 73 Cornell L Rev 928.

French, SF. "Tradition and Innovation in the New Restatement of Servitudes: A Report from Midpoint" (1994) 27 Conn L Rev 119.

Freyfogle, E. "The Construction of Ownership" (1996) U Ill L Rev 173.

Gaunt, Jonathan & Paul Morgan. *Gale on Easements*, 19th ed (London: Sweet & Maxwell, 2012).

George, SI. "Tulk v Moxhay Restored—To Its Historical Context" (1990) 12:2 Liverpool L Rev 173.

Girard, Philip. *Bora Laskin: Bringing Law to Life* (Toronto: University of Toronto Press for the Osgoode Society for Canadian Legal History, 2005) ch 11.

Girard, Philip. "Cottages, Covenants, and the Cold War: Galbraith v Madawaska Club" in E Tucker, J Muir & B Ziff, eds, *Property on Trial: Canadian Cases in Context* (Toronto: Irwin Law for the Osgoode Society for Canadian Legal History, 2012) 93.

Goodhart, AL & RE Megarry. "Jus Spatiandi in a Pleasure Ground" (1956) 72 Law Q Rev 16.

Gravells, Nigel P. "Federated Homes Ltd v Mill Lodge Properties Ltd (1979): Annexation and Intention" in Nigel P Gravells, ed, *Landmark Cases in Land Law* (Oxford and Portland, OR: Hart, 2013).

Gravells, Nigel P, ed. *Landmark Cases in Land Law* (Oxford and Portland, OR: Hart, 2013).

Gray, Kevin & Susan Francis Gray. *Elements of Land Law*, 5th ed (Oxford: Oxford University Press, 2009).

Gray, KJ & PD Symes. *Real Property and Real People: Principles of Land Law* (London: Butterworths, 1981).

Grunow, JO. "Comment: Wisconsin Recognizes the Power of the Sun: Prah v Maretti and the Solar Access Act" (1983) Wis L Rev 1263.

Harris, C. "Whiteness as Property" (1993) 106 Harv L Rev 1709.

Harvard Law Review Association. "Note: The Antidiscrimination Principle in the Common Law" (1989) 102 Harv L Rev 1993.

Hayton, D. "Revolution in Restrictive Covenants Law?" (1980) 43 Mod L Rev 445.

Hegi, AD. "The Easement in Gross Revisited: Transferability and Divisibility Since 1945" (1986) 39 Vand L Rev 109.

Horowitz, M. "The History of the Public/Private Distinction" (1982) 130 U Pa L Rev 1423.

Hubbard, Dirk. "Group Homes and Restrictive Covenants" (1988) 57:1 U Miss Kansas City L Rev 135.

Huff, P. "Overburdening the Right of Way: Where the Right of Way Ends" (1991) 4:5 Nat'l Real PLR 49.

Hyatt, Wayne S. "Common Interest Communities: Evolution and Reinvention" (1998) 31 J Marshall L Rev 303.

Johnston, Jeremy. "Easements, Covenants, Licences, and Profits as Servitudes in Canadian Common Law: Escaping the Quagmire" (York University, D Jur dissertation, 2013).

Jost, Timothy. "The Defeasible Fee and the Birth of the Modern Residential Subdivision" (1984) 49 Miss L Rev 695.

Korngold, G. "Single Family Use Covenants: For Achieving a Balance Between Traditional Family Life and Individual Autonomy" (1989) 22 UC Davis L Rev 951.

Kwasniak, A. "Conservation Easements: Pluses and Pitfalls, Generally and for Municipalities" (2009) 46 Alta L Rev 651.

Kwasniak, A, ed. *Private Conservancy: The Path to Law Reform* (Edmonton: Environmental Law Centre, 1994).

La Forest, Anne Warner. *Anger and Honsberger Law of Real Property* (Aurora, ON: Canada Law Book, 2006).

Laskin, B. "Comment" (1940) 18 Can Bar Rev 314.

Law Commission of England and Wales. *Making Land Work: Easements, Covenants, and Profits à Prendre* (London: Stationery Office, 2011).

Law Reform Commission of Saskatchewan. *Background Paper: Solar Access Legislation* (Regina: Commission, 2008).

Lem, Jeffrey W. "Annotation" (1996) 5 RPR (3d) 1.

Lem, Jeffrey W. "Annotation" (2002) 50 RPR (3d) 4.

Litman, MM & Bruce Ziff. "Easements and Possession: An Elusive Limitation"(1989) Conveyancer and Property Lawyer 296.

Litman, MM & Bruce Ziff. "The Road Not Taken: Some Important Questions About the Nature of Easements" (1988) 57 Alta LR (2d) 326.

Lloyd, WH. "Enforcement of Affirmative Agreements Respecting the Use of Land" (1928) 14 Va L Rev 419.

Lyon, N. "An Essay on Constitutional Interpretation" (1988) 26 Osgoode Hall LJ 95.

McClean, AJ. "The Nature of an Easement" (1966) 5 West LR 32.

McFarlane, Ben. "Keppell v Bailey (1834); Hill v Tupper (1863): The Numerus Clausus and the Common Law" in Nigel P Gravells, ed, *Landmark Cases in Land Law* (Oxford and Portland, OR: Hart, 2013).

McNeil, K. "The Constitutional Rights of the Aboriginal People of Canada" (1982) 4 Sup Ct L Rev 255.

Megarry, RE. "Note" (1957) 73 Law Q Rev 154.

Megarry, RE & HWR Wade. *The Law of Real Property*, 5th ed (London: Stevens & Sons, 1984).

Melnitzer, Julius. "The Most Important Decision on the Subject of Positive Covenants," *Law Times* (3 June 2002).

Melnitzer, Julius. "Ruling Clarifies Law on Easements," *Law Times* (28 October 2002) 10.

Mendes da Costa, D, R Balfour & E Gillese. *Property Law: Cases, Text and Materials*, 2d ed (Toronto: Emond Montgomery, 1990).

Moore, Marguerite E. *Title Searching & Conveyancing in Ontario*, 6th ed (Toronto: LexisNexis, 2010).

Morgan, Edward & Ofer Attias. "Rabbi Kahane, International Law, and the Courts: Democracy Stands on Its Head" (1990) 4 Temp Int'l & Comp LJ 185.

Mossman, MJ. "Developments in Property Law: The 1984-85 Term" (1986) 8 Sup Ct L Rev 319.

Ontario Law Reform Commission. *Report on Basic Principles of Land Law* (Toronto: Ontario Law Reform Commission, 1996).

Ontario Law Reform Commission. *Report on Covenants Affecting Freehold Land* (Toronto: Ministry of the Attorney General, 1989).

Ontario Law Reform Commission. *Report of the Ontario Law Reform Commission on the Limitation of Actions* (Toronto: Department of the Attorney General, 1969).

Palmer, V. *The Paths to Privity: A History of Third Party Beneficiary Contracts at English Law* (San Francisco: Austin & Winfield, 1992).

Pearlston, Karen. "A Restricted Country? The Racist Legacy of Restrictive Covenants" (1996) [unpublished, archived at Osgoode Hall Law School, 1996].

Pentney, W. "The Rights of the Aboriginal Peoples of Canada in the Constitution Act, 1982, Part II, Section 35: The Substantive Guarantee" (1988) 22 UBC L Rev 207.

Perell, Paul. "A Commentary on Amberwood Investments Ltd v Durham Condominium Corp No 123" (2002) 50 RPR (3d) 52.

Platt, R. *Land Use and Society: Geography, Law, and Public Policy* (Washington, DC: Island Press, 1996).

Polden, P. "Views in Perspective" (1984) 48 Conveyancer and Property Lawyer 429.

Prichard, A. "Making Positive Covenants Run" (1973) 37 Conveyancer and Property Lawyer (NS) 194.

Reichman, U. "Residential Private Governments: An Introductory Survey" (1976) 43 U Chicago L Rev 253.

Reichman, U. "Toward a Unified Concept of Servitudes" (1982) 55 S Cal L Rev 1177.

Rose, Gillian. *Feminism and Geography: The Limits of Geographical Knowledge* (Minneapolis, MN: University of Minnesota Press, 1993).

Rudden, B. "Economic Theory v Property Law: The 'Numerus Clausus' Problem" in J Eekelaar & J Bell, eds, *Oxford Essays in Jurisprudence*, 3d series (Oxford: Clarendon Press, 1987) 239.

Saunders, Phillip M. "Forum on R v Marshall—Getting Their Feet Wet: The Supreme Court and Practical Implementation of Treaty Rights in the Marshall Case" (2000) 23 Dal LJ 48.

Scott, K. "Comment" (1964) 22 Cambridge LJ 203.

Silver, T et al. *Canadian Legislation for Conservation Covenants, Easements and Servitudes: The Current Situation*, Report no 95-1 (Ottawa: North American Wetlands Conservation Council (Canada), 1995).

Silverstone, S. "Open Space Preservation Through Conservation Easements" (1974) 12 Osgoode Hall LJ 105.

Simm, Peter A. "Time to Drain the Swamp? Case Comment on Amberwood Investments Ltd v Durham Condominium Corp No 123" (2002) 50 RPR (3d) 63.

Simpson, AWB. "The Rule in Wheeldon v Burrows and the Code Civile" (1967) 83 Law Q Rev 240.

Singer, JW. "No Right to Exclude: Public Accommodations and Private Property" (1995-96) 90 Nw UL Rev 1283.

Slattery, B. "Understanding Aboriginal Rights" (1987) 66 Can Bar Rev 726.

Smith, RJ. "The Running of Covenants in Equitable Leases and Equitable Assignments of Legal Leases" (1978) Cambridge LJ 98.

Smout, DAL. "An Inquiry into the Law on Racial and Religious Restraints on Alienation" (1952) 30 Can Bar Rev 863.

Smout, DAL. "Easements and Restrictive Covenants" in *Special Lectures of the Law Society of Upper Canada 1951: Conveyancing and Real Property* (Toronto: Richard DeBoo, 1951) 105.

Special Lectures of the Law Society of Upper Canada 1951: Conveyancing and Real Property (Toronto: Richard DeBoo, 1951).

Special Lectures of the Law Society of Upper Canada 2002: Real Property Law—Conquering the Complexities (Toronto: Law Society of Upper Canada, 2003).

Sterk, S. "Neighbors in American Land Law" (1987) 87 Colum L Rev 55.

Stone, C. "'Should Trees Have Standing?' Revisited: How Far Will Law and Morals Reach? A Pluralist Perspective" (1985) 59 S Cal L Rev 1.

Sturley, MF. "Easements in Gross" (1980) 96 Law Q Rev 557.

Tarlo, H. "Forcing the Creation of Easements—A Novel Law" (1979) 53 Austl L J 254

Tarnopolsky, W. "Discrimination and the Law in Canada" (1992) 41 UNBLJ 215.

Tooher, J. "Restrictive Covenants and Public Planning Legislation—Should the Landowner Feel 'Touched and Concerned'?" (1992) 9 Envtl & Planning LJ 63.

Tucker, E, J Muir & B Ziff, eds. *Property on Trial: Canadian Cases in Context* (Toronto: Irwin Law for the Osgoode Society for Canadian Legal History, 2012).

Wade, HWR. "Covenants—A Broad and Reasonable View" (1972) 31 Cambridge LJ 157.

Walker, J. *"Race," Rights, and the Law in the Supreme Court of Canada: Historical Case Studies* (Toronto: Wilfrid Laurier University Press for the Osgoode Society for Canadian Legal History, 1997).

Williams, Patricia. "Spirit-Murdering the Messenger: The Discourse of Fingerpointing as the Law's Response to Racism" (1987) 42 U Miami L Rev 127.

Winokur, JL. "The Mixed Blessings of Promissory Servitudes: Toward Optimizing Economic Utility, Individual Liberty, and Personal Identity" (1989) Wis L Rev 1.

Ziff, Bruce H. "A Matter of Overriding Interest: Unregistered Easements Under Alberta's Land Titles System" (1991) 29 Alta L Rev 718.

Ziff, Bruce H. "Positive Covenants Running with Land: A Castaway on Ocean Island?" (1989) 27 Alta L Rev 354.

Ziff, Bruce H. *Principles of Property Law*, 5th ed (Scarborough, ON: Carswell, 2010).

Ziff, Bruce H. "Restrictive Covenants: The Basic Ingredients" in *Special Lectures of the Law Society of Upper Canada: Real Property Law—Conquering the Complexities* (Toronto: Irwin Law, 2003).

CHAPTER EIGHT

The Evolution of Aboriginal Title in Canada

I. LAND AND THE LAW: ABORIGINAL PROPERTY INTERESTS

In an ideal world, the process of reconciliation would take place outside the adversarial milieu of a courtroom. This case [*Tsilhqot'in Nation v British Columbia*] demonstrates how the Court, confined by the issues raised in the pleadings and the jurisprudence on Aboriginal rights and title, is ill equipped to effect a reconciliation of competing interests. That must be reserved for a treaty negotiation process. Despite this fact, the question remains: how can this Court participate in the process of reconciliation between the Tsilhqot'in people, Canada and British Columbia in these proceedings?

(Vickers J in *Tsilhqot'in Nation v British Columbia*, 2007 BCSC 1700 at para 1357.)

As this judicial comment explains, issues about Aboriginal title to land in Canada (as well as other Aboriginal rights) create unique and difficult challenges for 21st-century courts. Clearly, indigenous peoples were present in the lands that now form the jurisdiction of Canada at the time when Europeans first arrived in North America. Moreover, many of these First Nations peoples provided essential assistance to early explorers and traders, in a setting that was very different from their previous experiences in Europe. First Nations peoples also became involved in conflicts in North America between European powers, particularly during the Seven Years War between England and France. The North American dimension of this war ended with the British victory on the Plains of Abraham in 1759 and the capitulation of Mont-real in 1760. As a result, France ceded all the territory of New France to the British Crown in the *Treaty of Paris* in 1763. In this way, the British Crown asserted not only *sovereignty* over large areas of eastern Canada, but also *title to all the land*.

As discussed in Chapter 3, the *Treaty of Paris* recognized the pre-existing claims of French settlers in North America (and this commitment was later included in the *Quebec Act, 1774*, 14 Geo 3, c 83 (UK)). However, although the British Crown also enacted the *Royal Proclamation* in 1763, which attempted to address Aboriginal concerns about the encroaching European settlements, the situation for First Nations peoples increasingly worsened. As a result, much recent litigation has focused on claims by First Nations for recognition of both their sovereignty and the legal title to their traditional lands. Yet, as recently as 1990, for example, the Supreme Court of Canada held:

> It is worth recalling that while British policy towards the native population was based on respect for their right to occupy their traditional lands, a proposition to which the *Royal Proclamation* of 1763 bears witness, there was from the outset never any doubt that sovereignty and legislative power, and indeed the underlying title, to such lands vested in the Crown.

(*R v Sparrow*, [1990] 1 SCR 1075 at para 49.)

In the context of the *Royal Proclamation*, the issue of Aboriginal title to land resulted in negotiations of treaties in some, but not all, parts of Canada. Moreover, as the significant political power among First Nations in the 18th century increasingly waned in the 19th and early 20th centuries, particularly after the enactment of the federal *Indian Act* in 1876 and increasing efforts to promote policies of assimilation for First Nations peoples in Canada, the issues of sovereignty and title to land were rendered more invisible to many Canadians. Indeed, as Prime Minister Trudeau stated in 1969, even if there were historic wrongs committed against Aboriginal people, they were irrevocably in the past; in this context, the prime minister asserted that policy-makers should focus only on the present and future, stating: "We will be just in our time. This is all we can do. We must be just today." (PE Trudeau, "Remarks on Aboriginal and Treaty Rights" (Vancouver, 8 August 1969) in P Cumming & N Mickenberg, eds, *Native Rights in Canada* (Toronto: Indian-Eskimo Association of Canada, 1972) at 332. See also J Fortune, "Construing Delgamuukw: Legal Arguments, Historical Argumentation, and Philosophy of History" (1993) 51 UT Fac L Rev 80 [Fortune].)

In this context, s 35 of the *Constitution Act, 1982* has proved fertile ground for rethinking issues about Aboriginal claims to land—although it has not been used as successfully in relation to issues about First Nations sovereignty. This chapter provides an overview of early developments in the relations between First Nations and the British Crown after the *Royal Proclamation*, including judicial decisions about the nature of Aboriginal title to land, the process of negotiating treaties with First Nations peoples in some parts of Canada, and the enactment of the *Indian Act* and its arrangements for Aboriginal reserve lands. The chapter then focuses on the Supreme Court's more recent decisions in *Guerin v The Queen*, [1984] 2 SCR 335 and *Delgamuukw v British Columbia*, [1997] 3 SCR 1010, and the significance of these cases in redefining recognition of First Nations' entitlement to land. Finally, the chapter examines some post-*Delgamuukw* developments that reflect recent views about First Nations' entitlement to land (and ongoing issues about sovereignty) in Canada.

The Royal Proclamation and the Evolution of Aboriginal Title to Land

Although Aboriginal interests in land may be understood in a variety of non-legal ways, the legal conception of Aboriginal title has played a fundamental role in structuring the relationship between North America's Aboriginal and non-Aboriginal peoples. For many years, the prevailing conception of Aboriginal interests in land was a limited "personal or usufructuary" interest—that is, although Aboriginal communities may have been able to reside and perform sustenance activities on their ancestral lands, the underlying title in the land (as well as the natural resources) were reserved for the Crown.

In Canada, this sentiment was reflected in a series of 19th-century cases, most notably *St Catherine's Milling and Lumber Co v The Queen* (1888), 14 AC 46 (Ont PC). Although the case was launched in relation to the interaction of provincial and federal governments regarding lands surrendered by treaty, the Privy Council decided to address the larger issue of Aboriginal title in the lands prior to the treaty. The Privy Council held that any interests that Aboriginal communities had in the land were merely "personal and usufructuary" rights held at the will of the Crown, and that the underlying title was vested in the Crown. A similar result occurred in the American case of *Johnson & Graham's Lessee v McIntosh*, 21 US (8 Wheat) 543 (1823), discussed in Chapter 2 (in the excerpt from Carol Rose's analysis of the "clear act" theory of possession). *Johnson* involved the inability of Aboriginal communities to transfer their lands to private purchasers.

To understand the limitations on Aboriginal title to land in these judicial decisions, it is important to take account of the broader political context. Specifically, the early relationship between First Nations and European settlers in the 18th and 19th centuries was occurring during a period in which the power of Aboriginal communities was weakening in the face of ever-encroaching colonial settlements. In the extract that follows, Michael Jackson explained this dynamic by showing how the partnership framework apparently created in the *Royal Proclamation* of 1763 gradually gave way to a government policy of indigenous assimilation, a policy that had a significant impact on Aboriginal interests in land.

Michael Jackson, "The Articulation of Native Rights in Canadian Law"
(1984) 18 UBC L Rev 255 at 258-62 (footnotes omitted)

The evolution of the principle of consent in colonial law is well illustrated in the treaties which were negotiated in the seventeenth and eighteenth centuries on the eastern seaboard of what is now the United States. These treaties show the acceptance by certain of the Indian tribes of a formal protectorate relationship with the English Crown, reserving to the tribes important powers of tribal sovereignty and rights to sell or retain all or part of their traditional lands. The treaties and compacts concluded with the Iroquois Confederacy in the eighteenth century most clearly articulate the nature of native rights in colonial law. The westward expansion of settlement among the British colonies of New England during the eighteenth century and the violation of Indian territorial integrity became a major issue for the colonial authorities. By mid-century, the group of the Six Nations of the Iroquois Confederacy, because of its military strength and political organization, was viewed as the lynch-pin in the security of the British colonies. Their military support, to either the French in Canada or to the British colonies, would threaten the stability, if not the existence, of the other colonial empires. The onset of the Seven Years' War with France in 1754 heightened British awareness of the strategic role which the Indian nations played in relation to the two European combatants.

Recent research into the role of the Indian nations during the Seven Years' War between England and France not only documents the crucial role that the Indian nations played in the major campaigns of the war but also shows that negotiations with the Indians proceeded upon the assumption that they were independent nations capable of pursuing their own foreign policies. ...

In 1763, at the conclusion of the Seven Years' War, Britain acquired from the French, through the *Treaty of Paris*, the French colony of Canada as well as the islands of Cape Breton and St. John (Prince Edward Island). Following the signing of the *Treaty of Paris*, the British Government sought to address the issues arising from the peace, in particular the organization of the newly acquired territories and the establishment of a consolidated policy with the Indian nations. Both of these objectives were embodied in the *Royal Proclamation* of 1763. ... [T]he Proclamation acknowledges the protectorate obligation of the Crown towards the Indian nations and recognizes that lands possessed by the Indian nations anywhere in British North America are reserved to them unless and until ceded to the Crown. This territorial integrity is protected by restrictions on grants, settlements and purchases. The Proclamation also closes large parts of North America to settlement, reserving them for the use of Indian nations as their hunting territories, subject to the right of the Crown to acquire the land with Indian consent. ...

Recent research undertaken by the Indian nations themselves, with the help of social scientists, has revealed some of the continuities between the treaty negotiations involving the Indian nations of western Canada in the late nineteenth century and the negotiations involving the Iroquois Confederacy in the previous century in the eastern colonies. As with the treaties negotiated in the eighteenth century with the Iroquois, the post-confederation treaties negotiated by the Indian nations of western Canada were viewed by them as establishing compacts to deal with issues of territorial and political integrity within the framework of a protectorate relationship with the Crown. However, what had changed in the intervening century was the balance of power between the Indian nations and the colonial authorities, and the condition of the Indians as the result of encroachment of European civilization. More specifically, the Indians were facing increasing white settlement, devastating epidemics, the influx of whisky traders and the disappearance of buffalo, the staple of the tribes' economy. The protectorate role embodied in the treaties was accordingly not confined, in the Indians' eyes, to preserving their territorial and political integrity within the lands which they were not prepared to cede, but also extended to the protection of the traditional Indian economy and assistance in the development of new forms of Indians' economic self-sufficiency.

The Canadian Government had a different view of what the treaties were intended to accomplish. They did not regard them as anything like a social contract in which different ways of life were to be accommodated within mutually acceptable limits. The government regarded the treaties primarily as the surrender of Indian rights to their land so that settlement and development could proceed. The payment of annuities, the provision of agricultural implements, the offers of medical and educational services and the establishment of reserves were conceived in part as compensation but primarily as the means of change. The government's expectation was that a backward people would, in time, abandon their semi-nomadic ways and, with the benefit of the white man's religion, education and agriculture, take their place in the mainstream of the economic and political life of Canada.

By contrast with these governmental policies, First Nations remained committed to their understanding of a partnership relationship in the *Royal Proclamation*. In relation to the Six Nations Confederacy, for example, Darlene Johnston explained how a political compact was established at the time of the first arrival of Europeans, when the power relations required British envoys to adopt Iroquois council procedure and treaty protocol.

Darlene Johnston, "The Quest of the Six Nations Confederacy for Self-Determination"
(1986) 44 UT Fac L Rev 1 at 11-12, 17-19, and 23-24

The Iroquois perception of the nature of the alliance formed with the British is captured by the *Gus-Wen-Qah*, the Two-Row Wampum Belt. The first of these belts was delivered and explained at the *Treaty of Fort Albany*, in 1664, marking the commencement of formal relations between the British and the confederacy. It has remained an integral feature of Iroquois negotiations into the twentieth century. The Special Committee on Indian Self-Government received an explanation of the import of *Gus-Wen-Qah* by an authorized representative of the confederacy at a hearing in May 1983:

> [W]hen your ancestors came to our shores, after living with them for a few years, observing them, our ancestors came to the conclusion that we could not live together in the same way inside the circle … . So our leaders at that time, along with your leaders, sat down for many years to try to work out a solution. This is what they came up with. We call it *Gus-Wen-Qah*, or the two row wampum belt. It is on a bed of white wampum, which symbolizes the purity of the agreement. There are two rows of purple, and those two rows have the spirit of our ancestors; those two rows never come together in that belt, and it is easy to see what that means. It means that we have two different paths, two different people.
>
> The agreement was made that your road will have your vessel, your people, your politics, your government, your way of life, your religion, your beliefs—they are all in there. The same goes for ours … . They said there will be three beads of wampum separating the two, and they will symbolize peace, friendship, and respect.

The vessel metaphor was used to characterize the distinct jurisdictions: the British vessel and confederacy canoe. The two were to co-exist as independent entities, each respecting the autonomy of the other. The two rows of purple wampum, representing the two governments, ran parallel, never crossing. The two vessels travel together, as allies, but neither nation tries to steer the other's vessel. In the relationship envisioned by the Two-Row Wampum, neither government has the authority to legislate for the other. The vessels are always separated by the three white beads symbolizing peace, friendship, and respect. The principles captured by the Two-Row Wampum formed the basis of the alliance between the British and the confederacy. Perhaps the most striking feature of the Iroquois vision of diplomatic relations with the British is its consistency. For over three centuries, the confederacy has abided steadfastly in its "canoe" and has reminded the British nation of its obligation to do the same.

The commitment of the confederacy to its alliance with the British was demonstrated by its participation in the Seven Years' War.

[The author explained the *Royal Proclamation* of 1763, followed by governmental policies over the next century that resulted in the enactment of the federal *Indian Act* in 1876. She also identified how Six Nations delegates to a council in Sarnia in 1871 withdrew from the council when they discovered that its purpose was to obtain their approval for earlier legislation in 1868-69, legislation that was "acutely inconsistent" with Iroquois government, "especially with respect to the roles of the women and the chiefs." In particular, the delegates rejected the idea that the legislation would govern the internal affairs of the Six Nations. Even after the enactment of the *Indian Act* in 1876, "the fifty chiefs continued to sit and guard the council fire of the confederacy."]

"We Are Not Part of Canada"

In the last century, the Six Nations Confederacy has produced a series of formal protests and defiant assertions of independence and sovereignty. It must be understood that its persistence is not merely a jealous defence of political autonomy. In the *Great Law of Peace*, the constitution of the confederacy, the political principles are intimately connected with the spiritual and the social. For the Iroquois, the *Great Law* constitutes a way of life, going far beyond a formula for division of powers. This concept has been captured (as noted earlier) in the symbolism of the Covenant Circle Wampum. To choose to submit to the law of a foreign nation is to forsake the confederacy, to go outside the circle. As the wampum depicts: "[I]nside the Circle is our language and culture, our clans and the ways we organize ourselves socially, our laws and the way we organize ourselves politically, and our ceremonies which reflect our spirituality and our cycle of life." Those who leave the circle are alienated from all that it contains. Hence the resistance of the Six Nations to the Canadian government's assertion of jurisdiction assumes the proportion of a people struggling for their very existence. ...

In keeping with their laws and with the history of their relations with the Crown, the Six Nations directed their claims to the governor-general of Canada. In 1890, a formal petition, maintaining that the *Indian Act, per se*, constituted a violation of ancient treaties and covenants, was delivered to the governor-general. Because this petition captures the essence of the confederacy's continuing claim to sovereignty, it warrants quotation at length:

> We will address your Excellency according to our ancient Treaties as Brothers.
>
> Brother, We will now let you know our way of thoughts. You are the Governor of Canada sent by the Queen our Mother to whom we the allies of to keep the Treaty the same as of whom our forefathers and Your forefathers made in the ancient time. The treaty made whenever we see anything wrong to tell once. And now we will tell you that we are disappointed because there never was yet any treaty made between you and Us, the Five Nations Indians, that You would force any kind your laws that we did not like. And now in some cases we see you are doing so.

Brother, We have kept patience for a long time, because, knowing the Treaty of which our forefathers and your forefathers made in the year 1758 being durable to us. But in the way you have treated us thinking for to ask you if the sun and moon has gone out of your sight. But we see the sun and moon as when our forefathers and your forefathers made the agreement. The treaty whenever you or us the Indians see anything wrong or dissatisfaction, we are to renew brighten and strengthen the ancient Covenant. And we want to be always free and satisfied to be governed by our own laws and customs, for we have laws of our own. And those that are in favour of your laws and customs we have nothing to do with suppose they are to be governed by it. But we cannot help them in no way, for they broken our word rules and customs. Here is law of our forefathers laid down for us.

The dark blue wampum twenty five courses mixed with white represents the figures of men, and Chiefs of the Five Nations Indians hands joined together, and Union of the Five Nations. And if any man or child were to go through outside where these men stands in form of a circumference. Then the emblem of this Chiefship strikes on their arms and falls from him, thus it remains inside the circumference ... . So he is nothing but a man no more Chief and longer but *how does he goes through well that is if he receives the laws of other Nations to be governed by it accordingly.*

Wampum belt treaty having two white rows, parallel and represents the two Governments, namely the Five Nations and the British Government will exist and shall not interfere with each other. Of which the British made an illustration that the British will remain in their vessel, that is their government. While the Five Nations will also abide in their birch bark canoe, meaning their Government. The British will never make compulsory, and *door way laws for the Five Nations to enter in so that should become a British subject.* [Emphasis added.]

Although the English is halting and much of the construction awkward, the petition conveys the central concepts underlying the confederacy's understanding of its historical relationship with the Crown: the Covenant Circle Wampum and the Two-Row Wampum. The introductory paragraphs refer to the ancient tradition of renewing the alliance. Then, the theme of alienation through submission to foreign laws—anathema to the confederacy—is developed. In asking whether the sun and moon have gone from the governor's sight, the chiefs are referring to the understanding that the alliance would last as long as the sun and moon endure and implying that, in legislating "door way laws," the Crown has broken its covenant with the Six Nations Confederacy. ...

[The author explained subsequent developments, including legal challenges in Ontario and before international tribunals, and concluded:]

These unsuccessful attempts have not daunted the confederacy's intention to voice its grievances within the international forum. Rather, the confederacy has been encouraged by the dramatic evolution of self-determination from an abstract, idealistic theory to an articulate and forceful international right. Although the right to self-determination has achieved international recognition, the task of identifying the appropriate unit of self-determination has been highly problematical. An equally troublesome problem has been the interplay between the right of peoples to self-determination and the right of existing states to territorial integrity. These two obstacles must be addressed in order for the Six

Nations Confederacy to establish the legitimacy of its claim to exercise the right of self-determination.

Although the limited conception of Aboriginal title to land, illustrated in *St Catherine's Milling* and 19th-century legislative policies, changed significantly after the passage of the *Constitution Act, 1982*, courts in the second half of the 20th century were beginning to show some new approaches that would eventually allow for substantial Aboriginal interests in land. The most important Canadian example was the split decision handed down by the Supreme Court in *Calder et al v Attorney-General of British Columbia*, [1973] SCR 313. Although divided over the substantive issue of whether Aboriginal title had been extinguished in British Columbia after the province joined Confederation (a 3-3 vote by the judges) and the procedural issue of the necessity for permission from the lieutenant general to sue the Crown (a 4-3 vote by the judges), the judges were united in affirming that Aboriginal title is grounded in the history of Aboriginal occupation and self-organization that pre-dated European contact and the *Royal Proclamation* (at 328):

> Although I think that it is clear that Indian title in British Columbia cannot owe its origin to the Proclamation of 1763, the fact is that when the settlers came, the Indians were there, organized in societies and occupying the land as their forefathers had done for centuries. This is what Indian title means and it does not help one in the solution of this problem to call it a "personal or usufructuary right."

Although this judicial understanding of Aboriginal title may not be as well-developed as the definitions that were to come, *Calder's* affirmation of Aboriginal title helped to set the groundwork for the later findings in *Guerin v The Queen* and *Delgamuukw v British Columbia*, discussed below.

For an overview of these earlier legal approaches, see B Slattery, *Ancestral Lands, Alien Laws: Judicial Perspectives on Aboriginal Title*, Studies in Aboriginal Rights no 2 (Saskatoon, Sask: University of Saskatchewan Native Law Centre, 1983). See also R Ross, *Dancing with a Ghost: Exploring Indian Reality* (Markham, ON: Octopus Books, 1992); M Boldt & JA Long, eds, *The Quest for Justice: Aboriginal Peoples and Aboriginal Rights* (Toronto: University of Toronto Press, 1985); and B Morse, ed, *Aboriginal Peoples and the Law: Métis and Inuit Rights in Canada* (Ottawa: Carleton University Press, 1991).

DISCUSSION NOTES

i. Historical Treaties

Much of the land that now forms the jurisdiction of Canada is covered by the historical treaties. Much like the modern-day treaty process now occurring between various Aboriginal communities and non-Aboriginal governments (most notably in British Columbia), these agreements were meant to structure the relationship between the First Nations of the so-called New World and the British Crown. Beginning with the peace and friendship treaties in the Maritime provinces during the early to mid 19th century, these agreements eventually reached as far west as Vancouver Island, and that concluded in the early 20th century—for example, the *Williams Treaties* of 1923 encompassing a large swath of southern and central

Ontario. The largest of these treaty lands are the numbered treaties, with agreements covering Northern Ontario, all three of the Prairie provinces, most of the Northwest Territories, and small regions of Yukon, Nunavut, and northern British Columbia. The numbered treaties were first signed in southern Manitoba during the 1870s, and ended with Treaty 11 (covering much of the north), signed in 1921. For a more in-depth discussion on the content of these treaties, see Thomas Isaac & Kristyn Annis, *Treaty Rights in the Historic Treaties of Canada* (Saskatoon, Sask: Houghton Boston Printers, 2010).

As vast as these regions may be, however, significant parts of Canada were left out of these historical accords. Areas absent from these agreements include all of Quebec and Newfoundland and Labrador, most of British Columbia, Nunavut, and Yukon, as well as the easternmost parts of the Northwest Territories (see Canada, Indian and Northern Affairs Canada, *Historical Treaties of Canada* (Ottawa: Indian and Northern Affairs Canada [nd]). However, the negotiation of land claims agreements is an ongoing process in some parts of Canada: e.g. see the *Nisga'a Final Agreement Act*, SBC 1999, c 2.

For some examples of litigation about treaties, see *Simon v The Queen*, [1985] 2 SCR 387, 24 DLR (4th) 390, concerning treaty rights in Nova Scotia, and *Ontario (Attorney General) v Bear Island Foundation*, [1991] 2 SCR 570, 83 DLR (4th) 381. See also Christopher Alcantara, *Negotiating the Deal: Comprehensive Land Claims Agreements in Canada* (Toronto: University of Toronto Press, 2013).

ii. The Indian Act

Passed less than a decade after Confederation, the *Indian Act* (now RSC 1985, c I-5) is the single most important piece of legislation concerning the interactions between the federal government and Canada's Aboriginal population. By characterizing who is and is not an "Indian," the Act applies a series of rules and programs to certain indigenous populations, including regulations over reserve lands. Although the Act was amended in 1985 to soften some of its more contentious clauses, it is difficult to overstate the pervasiveness of this regulatory regime on the day-to-day lives of Canada's indigenous peoples:

> [The *Indian Act*] established a new regulatory regime, defining who could be an Indian, who could live on Indian reserves, what and how they could hold as property, what happened to their property at their death, who could do business on and in relation to reserve land, and so on. In 1996, the *Report of the Royal Commission on Aboriginal Peoples* characterized this regime as a "legislative straitjacket" that had "regulated almost every important aspect of the daily lives of people."

(Shelley AM Gavigan, *Hunger, Horses, and Government Men* (Vancouver: UBC Press, 2012) [Gavigan] at 123.)

Not only does the process of classification within the *Indian Act* work to include and exclude certain indigenous populations from protections and regulations, but, as D'Arcy Vermette has asserted, these systems of racial classification represent yet another way that a colonial state is able to exercise power over a colonized population:

> [O]ne could argue that legal rules exist within a specific legal context and should not be given effect outside the courtroom. I agree, but this doesn't change the relationship within law and society ... . The law, being largely about the definition of words, can have the effect of placing

those who study and work with it in a state of tunnel vision. Specifically, it is very easy to get so caught up in definitions and legal rules that the context is entirely discarded … . If the colonizer is attempting to control the behaviour of the colonized it will be a responsibility of the colonial courts to identify the colonized people. To this end, judges may rely on what they have learned "Indians" are in popular opinion or they may search for a definition in legislation. But the court's responsibility in identifying Aboriginal people is helped a great deal if colonial authority, such as an Indian agent, has an opinion on the matter … . Part of the blind adherence to colonial authority obviously stems from the rule of law. This principle values the colonial party over those who are to be colonized because it is the colonizer who makes the law.

(D'Arcy Vermette, "Colonialism and the Process of Defining Aboriginal People" (2008) 31 Dal LJ 211 at 227.)

In other words, by characterizing particular peoples and activities as being truly "Indian," the colonizer crafts the understanding for both non-Aboriginal and Aboriginal peoples of what it means to be a "true Indian." This process of social construction not only changes the way that the popular culture thinks of indigenous peoples, but also has the effect of structuring how the judicial system interacts with these communities. Moreover, even after amendments to the *Indian Act* in 1985, many Aboriginal peoples perceived little improvement or ameliorative aspects: see Ovide Mercredi & Mary Ellen Turpel, *In the Rapids: Navigating the Future of First Nations* (Toronto: Viking Penguin, 1993) at 89. See also Shin Imai, *The Structure of the Indian Act: Accountability in Governance* (National Centre for First Nations Governance, 2007).

The courts' reliance on the *Indian Act* is one example of the legal system's tendency to ignore the perspectives of Aboriginal peoples. Although courts have occasionally recognized Aboriginal interests in some cases—for example, the validation of pre-contact societies in *Calder*—common law courts have often disregarded the legitimacy of indigenous legal traditions. Thus, as John Borrows suggested:

Much of the history of Canadian law concerning Aboriginal peoples can be seen as a contest between ideas rooted in First Nations, English, US, and international legal regimes. The intersection of these various legal genealogies is sometimes portrayed as a conflict in which one source of law is incompatible with, or should gain pre-eminence over, the others. In such instances, the Aboriginal source of law is generally not applied because of its incompatibility with, or supposed inferiority within, the legal hierarchy.

(John Borrows, "With or Without You: First Nations Law (in Canada)" (1996) 41 McGill LJ 629 [Borrows, "With or Without You"] at 633.) While recognizing the immense challenge of shifting this perspective, Borrows advocated a better incorporation of Aboriginal legal perspectives and methodologies within the Canadian legal system. The paucity of Aboriginal perspectives in legal decisions is discussed in more detail below.

iii. Connecting Self-Government and Aboriginal Title to Land

For First Nations, issues about property reveal the connections between land claims and aspirations of self-government. As former National Chief of the Assembly of First Nations George Erasmus explained, it is difficult to separate negotiations about land rights from political issues about self-government and control of resources:

Land, and jurisdiction over land, go hand in hand. We have been pressing for fair land settlement to provide the basis for an economically viable life for our people, but we have also insisted on our right to aboriginal self-government over that land. By this we mean our right to exercise jurisdiction over our traditional lands, resources, and people. We must share in the benefits that come from the resources of the land, and we must make decisions in the best interests of our people, the land, and its resources.

(G Erasmus, "Twenty Years of Disappointed Hopes" in B Richardson, ed, *Drumbeat: Anger and Renewal in Indian Country* (Toronto: University of Toronto Press, 1989) 3 at 13.) The report of the Royal Commission on Aboriginal Peoples, *Bridging the Cultural Divide: A Report on Aboriginal People and Criminal Justice in Canada* (Ottawa: Minister of Supply and Services Canada, 1996) also noted (at 11) the link between self-government and land claims for First Nations:

[A] larger vision of justice, one that is linked to recognition of the Aboriginal right of self-government and to the resolution of treaty and Aboriginal rights based on claims to lands and resources, is one that our Commission shares and endorses, and it is one that forms the backbone of our recommendations in this report.

See also Kent McNeil, "Indigenous Land Rights and Self-Government: Inseparable Entitlements" in Lisa Ford & Tim Rowse, eds, *Between Indigenous and Settler Governance* (Oxford: Routledge, 2013) 135.

II. (RE)DEFINING ABORIGINAL TITLE TO LAND

A. Guerin v The Queen

Although once a protracted dispute over a golf course in Vancouver, *Guerin v The Queen*, [1984] 2 SCR 335 is now seen as one of the most significant moments in the relationship between non-Aboriginal governments and Aboriginal communities: see David Arnot, "The Honour of First Nations—The Honour of the Crown: The Unique Relationship of First Nations with the Crown" (Paper delivered at a policy conference on the role of the Crown in Canadian governance, Ottawa, "The Crown in Canada: Present Realities and Future Options," 10 June 2010) at 9, online: Queen's University <http://www.queensu.ca/iigr/conf/Arch/2010/ConferenceOnTheCrown/CrownConferencePapers/The_Crown_and_the_First_Nations.pdf>. Thus, as the Supreme Court ruled in *Guerin*, because Aboriginal title constitutes a burden on the Crown's underlying title and cannot be alienated other than by surrender to the Crown, the federal government has a fiduciary duty when managing Aboriginal lands.

The case began in the 1950s, when the Shaughnessy Heights Golf Course decided to expand its operations into a prime piece of real estate in the Musqueam First Nation Reserve. Because Aboriginal lands can be transferred only by way of the Crown, the golf club president approached the local branch of the Department of Indian Affairs to see if a deal could be struck. When a draft agreement was reached between the government and the golf club, the Indian Affairs official called a public meeting with the band council. After a series of long and tempestuous negotiations, the Council eventually agreed—orally—on a series of terms. However, when the band council later received a written copy of the lease signed by the government and the golf club, the Council concluded that the written terms were significantly different from the original oral terms on which the Council had voted (at 365-71).

lower courts

At trial, the judge found that the government had breached its role as a trustee to the band council, because it had willingly taken on responsibility for the transfer of lands, but had failed to live up to the Council's expectations (at 371). The Federal Court of Appeal overturned the decision, finding that s 18(1) of the *Indian Act* provided a high level of discretion to the federal government in relation to Aboriginal land transfers; thus, there could never be a real trust relationship between the Crown and the Musqueam First Nation (at 373).

Although Wilson J, writing for herself and two others, held that there was a trust in this case, Dickson J (writing for four of eight judges) at the Supreme Court of Canada concluded that there was no trust relationship, but rather a fiduciary relationship (at 376). That is, because Aboriginal lands could be transferred only through the Crown, Dickson J held that the government had an implicit duty to ensure that it acts in the best interests of Aboriginal communities (at 376):

> An Indian band is prohibited from directly transferring its interest to a third party. Any sale or lease of land can only be carried out after a surrender has taken place, with the Crown then acting on the band's behalf. The Crown first took this responsibility upon itself in the *Royal Proclamation* of 1763 … . It is still recognized in the surrender provision of the *Indian Act*. The surrender requirement, and the responsibility it entails, are the source of a distinct fiduciary obligation owed by the Crown to the Indians.

This "distinct fiduciary obligation" was explained in light of the ancient concept known as "the Honour of the Crown," which means that representatives of the sovereign must act in accordance with the solemnity and duty befitting their position. Therefore, because the relevant government officials had breached the Honour of the Crown through their inappropriate dealings with the Musqueam First Nation, the court awarded a cash settlement of $10 million to the First Nation (at 391).

In *Guerin*, the Supreme Court of Canada also began to redefine the concept of Aboriginal title to land. By first confirming the holding from *Calder* (that the *Royal Proclamation* reveals that Aboriginal title was not extinguished by the Crown declaring sovereignty over Canada), the court then stated that the inalienability aspect of Aboriginal title had the effect of creating a property interest that is unique to Canada's Aboriginal peoples. As opposed to both the near absolute control found in a fee simple estate or the limited nature of "personal and usufructuary right" from *St Catherine's Milling*, *Guerin* established a *sui generis* interest in the land that is shaped by both the historical occupation of Canada by First Nations and the relationship negotiated between these groups and the British Crown at the time of the *Royal Proclamation* (at 382):

> It is true that the *sui generis* interest which the Indians have in the land is personal in the sense that it cannot be transferred to the grantee, but it is also true … that the interest gives rise upon surrender to a distinctive fiduciary obligation on the part of the Crown to deal with the land for the benefit of the surrendering Indians. These two aspects of Indian title go together, since the Crown's original purpose in declaring the Indians' interest to be inalienable otherwise than to the Crown was to facilitate the Crown's ability to represent the Indians in dealings with third parties. *The nature of the Indians' interest is therefore best characterized by its general inalienability, coupled with the fact that the Crown is under an obligation to deal with the lands on the Indians' behalf when the interest is surrendered.* [Emphasis added.]

This case laid important groundwork for the subsequent Supreme Court decision in *Delgamuukw v British Columbia* in 1997, where the Supreme Court again described the content of Aboriginal title as a *sui generis* property interest in land in Canada.

Guerin is also important because of the way that the court skirted the question of exactly what legal basis was available to European colonial powers in relation to their original claim of sovereignty in North America. During a discussion about past cases dealing with the question of whether Aboriginal title still existed after the assertion of sovereignty by the British Crown, Justice Dickson noted (at 378) that

> the rights of Indians in the lands they traditionally occupied prior to European colonization both predated and survived claims to sovereignty made by various European nations in the territories of the North American continent. *The principle of discovery which justified these claims gave the ultimate title in the land in a particular area to the nation which discovered and claimed it.* [Emphasis added.]

In light of the significance of this assertion to the entire question of Aboriginal title, the brevity of similar judicial discussions has often been challenged by legal scholars, including Minnawaanagogiizhigook (Dawnis Kennedy):

> The Crown relies on the claim that Crown sovereignty has never been questioned, which is factually untrue: the Crown's assertions of sovereignty over Indigenous peoples and "under" Indigenous territories have been, and continue to be, subject to serious contestation by Indigenous peoples.

(Minnawaanagogiizhigook (Dawnis Kennedy), "Reconciliation Without Respect? Section 35 and Indigenous Legal Orders" in Law Commission of Canada, ed, *Indigenous Legal Traditions* (Vancouver: UBC Press, 2007) 77 at 83.) See also John Hurley, "The Crown's Fiduciary Duty and Indian Title: Guerin v The Queen" (1985) 30 McGill LJ 559. Other scholars have also assessed the concept of "the Honour of the Crown": see Brian Slattery, "Aboriginal Rights and the Honour of the Crown" (2005) 20 Sup Ct L Rev 433. In addition, Mariana Valverde critiqued this concept, describing it as "paternalist, premodern, crypto-Christian logic" in "'The Honour of the Crown Is at Stake': Aboriginal Land Claims Litigation and the Epistemology of Sovereignty" (2011) 1 UC Irvine L Rev 955 at 957. As Valverde noted, the concept of the "Honour of the Crown" provides very little support for Aboriginal conceptions of title to land or for their claims to sovereignty.

B. Delgamuukw v British Columbia: The Content of Aboriginal Title to Land

The relationship between self-government and land claims was addressed in *Delgamuukw v British Columbia* (1991), 79 DLR (4th) 185 (BCSC), (1993), 104 DLR (4th) 470 (BCCA), [1997] 3 SCR 1010.

In *Delgamuukw*, hereditary chiefs of the Gitksan (also spelled Gitxsan) and Wet'suwet'en peoples asserted claims to ownership of and jurisdiction over 58,000 square kilometres of territory in central British Columbia. The trial decision dismissed both claims, stating that the claim to self-government was extinguished by the exercise of British sovereignty over the mainland colony of British Columbia. As well, the trial decision concluded that the underlying assertion of Crown title in the land in colonial enactments prior to British Columbia's entry into Canada in 1871 extinguished Aboriginal title over all unceded territory in British

Columbia. Thus, there were no "existing rights" under s 35 of the Constitution for the Gitxsan and Wet'suwet'en peoples to assert. On appeal to the British Columbia Court of Appeal, however, the newly elected provincial government abandoned the argument that there had been a complete extinguishment of Aboriginal title by colonial enactments prior to 1871, and the Court of Appeal unanimously held in favour of the claimants, issuing a declaration that the plaintiffs held existing Aboriginal rights of occupation and use over much of the territory claimed, to be defined more precisely by negotiation between the parties. However, the trial judge's conclusion with respect to the self-government issue was affirmed by a majority of 3-2. On a further appeal to the Supreme Court of Canada, the court set aside the decision of the BC Court of Appeal and ordered a new trial. As Bruce Ryder suggested, "[o]n the long and tortuous path to justice for the First Nations of Canada, the case of *Delgamuukw v The Queen* is likely to become one of the most important landmarks": see Bruce Ryder, "Aboriginal Rights and Delgamuukw v The Queen" (1994) 5 Const Forum 43 at 43.

In reading the excerpt from the *Delgamuukw* decision, which follows, identify the elements that make Aboriginal title uniquely different from common law conceptions of property and possession and reflect on how these elements were included in the test for establishing Aboriginal title. Note also how Aboriginal traditions and storytelling were used to buffet and challenge common law conceptions of evidence. In addition, examine the extent to which the court differentiates between Aboriginal title and activity-specific Aboriginal rights in cases such as *Van der Peet*, [1996] 2 SCR 507. Finally, consider the ways in which the claims presented in *Delgamuukw* (once again) linked issues about Aboriginal title to land and First Nations' claims to sovereignty.

Delgamuukw v British Columbia
[1997] 3 SCR 1010

LAMER CJ:

I. Introduction

[1] This appeal is the latest in a series of cases in which it has fallen to this Court to interpret and apply the guarantee of existing aboriginal rights found in s. 35(1) of the Constitution Act, 1982. Although that line of decisions, commencing with *R v Sparrow*, [1990] 1 SCR 1075, proceeding through the *Van der Peet* trilogy (*R v. Van der Peet*, [1996] 2 SCR 507, *R v. N.T.C. Smokehouse Ltd.*, [1996] 2 SCR 672, and *R v. Gladstone*, [1996] 2 SCR 723), and ending in *R v. Pamajewon*, [1996] 2 SCR 821, *R v. Adams*, [1996] 3 SCR 101, and *R v. Côté*, [1996] 3 SCR 139, have laid down the jurisprudential framework for s. 35(1), this appeal raises a set of interrelated and novel questions which revolve around a single issue—the nature and scope of the constitutional protection afforded by s. 35(1) to common law aboriginal title.

[2] In *Adams*, and in the companion decision in *Côté*, I considered and rejected the proposition that claims to aboriginal rights must also be grounded in an underlying claim to aboriginal title. But I held, nevertheless, that aboriginal title was a distinct species of aboriginal right that was recognized and affirmed by s. 35(1). Since aboriginal title was not being claimed in those earlier appeals, it was unnecessary to say more. This appeal

demands, however, that the Court now explore and elucidate the implications of the constitutionalization of aboriginal title. The first is the specific content of aboriginal title, a question which this Court has not yet definitively addressed, either at common law or under s. 35(1). The second is the related question of the test for the proof of title, which, whatever its content, is a right *in land*, and its relationship to the definition of the aboriginal rights recognized and affirmed by s. 35(1) in *Van der Peet* in terms of *activities*. The third is whether aboriginal title, as a right in land, mandates a modified approach to the test of justification first laid down in *Sparrow* and elaborated upon in *Gladstone*.

[3] In addition to the relationship between aboriginal title and s. 35(1), this appeal also raises an important practical problem relevant to the proof of aboriginal title which is endemic to aboriginal rights litigation generally—the treatment of the oral histories of Canada's aboriginal peoples by the courts. In *Van der Peet*, I held that the common law rules of evidence should be adapted to take into account the *sui generis* nature of aboriginal rights. In this appeal, the Court must address what specific form those modifications must take.

· · ·

II. Facts

[5] At the British Columbia Supreme Court, McEachern CJ heard 374 days of evidence and argument. Some of that evidence was not in a form which is familiar to common law courts, including oral histories and legends. Another significant part was the evidence of experts in genealogy, linguistics, archeology, anthropology, and geography.

[6] The trial judge's decision (reported at [1991] 3 WWR 97) is nearly 400 pages long, with another 100 pages of schedules. Although I am of the view that there must be a new trial, I nevertheless find it useful to summarize some of the relevant facts, so as to put the remainder of the judgment into context.

A. The Claim at Trial

[7] This action was commenced by the appellants, who are all Gitksan or Wet'suwet'en hereditary chiefs, who, both individually and on behalf of their "Houses" claimed separate portions of 58,000 square kilometres in British Columbia. For the purpose of the claim, this area was divided into 133 individual territories, claimed by the 71 Houses. This represents all of the Wet'suwet'en people, and all but 12 of the Gitksan Houses. Their claim was originally for "ownership" of the territory and "jurisdiction" over it. (At this Court, this was transformed into, primarily, a claim for aboriginal title over the land in question.) The province of British Columbia counterclaimed for a declaration that the appellants have no right or interest in and to the territory or alternatively, that the appellants' cause of action ought to be for compensation from the Government of Canada.

B. The Gitksan and Wet'suwet'en Peoples

(1) Demography

[8] The Gitksan consist of approximately 4,000 to 5,000 persons, most of whom now live in the territory claimed, which is generally the watersheds of the north and central

Skeena, Nass and Babine Rivers and their tributaries. The Wet'suwet'en consist of approximately 1,500 to 2,000 persons, who also predominantly live in the territory claimed. This territory is mainly in the watersheds of the Bulkley and parts of the Fraser-Nechako River systems and their tributaries. It lies immediately east and south of the Gitksan.

[9] Of course, the Gitksan and Wet'suwet'en are not the only people living in the claimed territory. As noted by both McEachern CJ at trial (at p. 440) and Lambert JA on appeal (at p. 243), there are other aboriginals who live in the claimed territory, notably the Carrier-Sekani and Nishga peoples. Some of these people have unsettled land claims overlapping with the territory at issue here. Moreover, there are also numerous non-aboriginals living there. McEachern CJ found that, at the time of the trial, the non-aboriginal population in the territory was over 30,000.

(2) History

[10] There were numerous theories of the history of the Gitksan and Wet'suwet'en peoples before the trial judge. His conclusion from the evidence was that their ancestors migrated from Asia, probably through Alaska, and spread south and west into the areas which they found to be liveable. There was archeological evidence, which he accepted, that there was some form of human habitation in the territory and its surrounding areas from 3,500 to 6,000 years ago, and intense occupation of the Hagwilget Canyon site (near Hazelton), prior to about 4,000 to 3,500 years ago. This occupation was mainly in or near villages on the Skeena River, the Babine River or the Bulkley River, where salmon, the staple of their diet, was easily obtainable. The other parts of the territory surrounding and between their villages and rivers were used for hunting and gathering for both food and ceremonial purposes. The scope of this hunting and gathering area depended largely on the availability of the required materials in the areas around the villages. Prior to the commencement of the fur trade, there was no reason to travel far from the villages for anything other than their subsistence requirements.

(3) North American Exploration

[11] There was little European influence in western Canada until the arrival of Capt. Cook at Nootka on Vancouver Island in 1778, which led to the sea otter hunt in the north Pacific. This influence grew with the establishment of the first Hudson's Bay trading post west of the Rockies (although east of the territories claimed) by Simon Fraser in 1805-1806. Trapping for the commercial fur trade was not an aboriginal practice, but rather one influenced by European contact. The trial judge held that the time of direct contact between the Aboriginal Peoples in the claimed territory was approximately 1820, after the trader William Brown arrived and Hudson's Bay had merged with the North West Company.

(4) Present Social Organization

[12] McEachern CJ set out a description of the present social organization of the appellants. In his opinion, this was necessary because "one of the ingredients of aboriginal land claims is that they arise from long-term communal rather than personal use or possession of land" (at p. 147). The fundamental premise of both the Gitksan and the

Wet'suwet'en peoples is that they are divided into clans and Houses. Every person born of a Gitksan or Wet'suwet'en woman is automatically a member of his or her mother's House and clan. There are four Gitksan and four Wet'suwet'en clans, which are subdivided into Houses. Each House has one or more Hereditary Chief as its titular head, selected by the elders of their House, as well as possibly the Head Chief of the other Houses of the clan. There is no head chief for the clans, but there is a ranking order of precedence within communities or villages, where one House or clan may be more prominent than others.

[13] At trial, the appellants' claim was based on their historical use and "ownership" of one or more of the territories. The trial judge held that these are marked, in some cases, by physical and tangible indicators of their association with the territories. He cited as examples totem poles with the Houses' crests carved, or distinctive regalia. In addition, the Gitksan Houses have an "adaawk" which is a collection of sacred oral tradition about their ancestors, histories and territories. The Wet'suwet'en each have a "kungax" which is a spiritual song or dance or performance which ties them to their land. Both of these were entered as evidence on behalf of the appellants (see my discussion of the trial judge's view of this evidence, *infra*).

[14] The most significant evidence of spiritual connection between the Houses and their territory is a feast hall. This is where the Gitksan and Wet'suwet'en peoples tell and retell their stories and identify their territories to remind themselves of the sacred connection that they have with their lands. The feast has a ceremonial purpose, but is also used for making important decisions. The trial judge also noted the *Criminal Code* prohibition on aboriginal feast ceremonies, which existed until 1951.

· · ·

V. Analysis

· · ·

C. What is the content of aboriginal title, how is it protected by s. 35(1) of the Constitution Act, 1982, and what is required for its proof?

(1) Introduction

[109] The parties disagree over whether the appellants have established aboriginal title to the disputed area. However, since those factual issues require a new trial, we cannot resolve that dispute in this appeal. But factual issues aside, the parties also have a more fundamental disagreement over the content of aboriginal title itself, and its reception into the Constitution by s. 35(1). In order to give guidance to the judge at the new trial, it is to this issue that I will now turn.

[110] I set out these opposing positions by way of illustration and introduction because I believe that all of the parties have characterized the content of aboriginal title incorrectly. The appellants argue that aboriginal title is tantamount to an inalienable fee simple, which confers on aboriginal peoples the rights to use those lands as they choose and which has been constitutionalized by s. 35(1). The respondents offer two alternative formulations: first, that aboriginal title is no more than a bundle of rights to engage in activities which are themselves aboriginal rights recognized and affirmed by s. 35(1), and that the *Constitution Act, 1982*, merely constitutionalizes those individual rights, not the bundle itself, because the latter has no independent content; and second, that aboriginal

title, at most, encompasses the right to exclusive use and occupation of land in order to engage in those activities which are aboriginal rights themselves, and that s. 35(1) constitutionalizes this notion of exclusivity.

[111] The content of aboriginal title, in fact, lies somewhere in between these positions. Aboriginal title is a right in land and, as such, is more than the right to engage in specific activities which may be themselves aboriginal rights. Rather, it confers the right to use land for a variety of activities, not all of which need be aspects of practices, customs and traditions which are integral to the distinctive cultures of aboriginal societies. Those activities do not constitute the right *per se*; rather, they are parasitic on the underlying title. However, that range of uses is subject to the limitation that they must not be irreconcilable with the nature of the attachment to the land which forms the basis of the particular group's aboriginal title. This inherent limit, to be explained more fully below, flows from the definition of aboriginal title as a *sui generis* interest in land, and is one way in which aboriginal title is distinct from a fee simple.

(2) Aboriginal Title at Common Law

(a) General Features

[112] The starting point of the Canadian jurisprudence on aboriginal title is the Privy Council's decision in *St. Catherine's Milling and Lumber Co. v. The Queen* (1888), 14 AC 46, which described aboriginal title as a "personal and usufructuary right" (at p. 54). The subsequent jurisprudence has attempted to grapple with this definition, and has in the process demonstrated that the Privy Council's choice of terminology is not particularly helpful to explain the various dimensions of aboriginal title. What the Privy Council sought to capture is that aboriginal title is a *sui generis* interest in land. Aboriginal title has been described as *sui generis* in order to distinguish it from "normal" proprietary interests, such as fee simple. However, as I will now develop, it is also *sui generis* in the sense that its characteristics cannot be completely explained by reference either to the common law rules of real property or to the rules of property found in aboriginal legal systems. As with other aboriginal rights, it must be understood by reference to both common law and aboriginal perspectives.

[113] The idea that aboriginal title is *sui generis* is the unifying principle underlying the various dimensions of that title. One dimension is its *inalienability*. Lands held pursuant to aboriginal title cannot be transferred, sold or surrendered to anyone other than the Crown and, as a result, is inalienable to third parties. This Court has taken pains to clarify that aboriginal title is only "personal" in this sense, and does not mean that aboriginal title is a non-proprietary interest which amounts to no more than a licence to use and occupy the land and cannot compete on an equal footing with other proprietary interests: see *Canadian Pacific Ltd. v. Paul*, [1988] 2 SCR 654, at p. 677.

[114] Another dimension of aboriginal title is its *source*. It had originally been thought that the source of aboriginal title in Canada was the *Royal Proclamation, 1763*: see *St. Catherine's Milling*. However, it is now clear that although aboriginal title was recognized by the *Proclamation*, it arises from the prior occupation of Canada by aboriginal peoples. That prior occupation, however, is relevant in two different ways, both of which illustrate the *sui generis* nature of aboriginal title. The first is the physical fact of occupation, which derives from the common law principle that occupation is proof of possession in law: see

Kent McNeil, *Common Law Aboriginal Title* [Oxford: Clarendon Press, 1989] ... , at p. 7. Thus, in *Guerin, supra*, Dickson J described aboriginal title, at p. 376, as a "legal right derived from the Indians' historic occupation and possession of their tribal lands." What makes aboriginal title *sui generis* is that it arises from possession *before* the assertion of British sovereignty, whereas normal estates, like fee simple, arise afterward: see Kent McNeil, "The Meaning of Aboriginal Title," in Michael Asch, ed., *Aboriginal and Treaty Rights in Canada* (1997), 135, at p. 144. This idea has been further developed in *Roberts v. Canada*, [1989] 1 SCR 322, where this Court unanimously held at p. 340 that "aboriginal title pre-dated colonization by the British and survived British claims of sovereignty" (also see *Guerin*, at p. 378). What this suggests is a second source for aboriginal title—the relationship between common law and pre-existing systems of aboriginal law.

[115] A further dimension of aboriginal title is the fact that it is held *communally*. Aboriginal title cannot be held by individual aboriginal persons; it is a collective right to land held by all members of an aboriginal nation. Decisions with respect to that land are also made by that community. This is another feature of aboriginal title which is *sui generis* and distinguishes it from normal property interests.

(b) The Content of Aboriginal Title

[116] Although cases involving aboriginal title have come before this Court and Privy Council before, there has never been a definitive statement from either court on the *content* of aboriginal title. In *St. Catherine's Milling*, the Privy Council, as I have mentioned, described the aboriginal title as a "personal and usufructuary right," but declined to explain what that meant because it was not "necessary to express any opinion upon the point" (at p. 55). Similarly, in *Calder, Guerin*, and *Paul*, the issues were the extinguishment of, the fiduciary duty arising from the surrender of, and statutory easements over land held pursuant to, aboriginal title, respectively; the content of title was not at issue and was not directly addressed.

[117] Although the courts have been less than forthcoming, I have arrived at the conclusion that the content of aboriginal title can be summarized by two propositions: first, that aboriginal title encompasses the right to exclusive use and occupation of the land held pursuant to that title for a variety of purposes, which need not be aspects of those aboriginal practices, customs and traditions which are integral to distinctive aboriginal cultures; and second, that those protected uses must not be irreconcilable with the nature of the group's attachment to that land. For the sake of clarity, I will discuss each of these propositions separately.

ABORIGINAL TITLE ENCOMPASSES THE RIGHT TO USE THE LAND HELD PURSUANT TO THAT TITLE FOR A VARIETY OF PURPOSES, WHICH NEED NOT BE ASPECTS OF THOSE ABORIGINAL PRACTICES, CULTURES AND TRADITIONS WHICH ARE INTEGRAL TO DISTINCTIVE ABORIGINAL CULTURES

[118] The respondents argue that aboriginal title merely encompasses the right to engage in activities which are aspects of aboriginal practices, customs and traditions which are integral to distinctive aboriginal cultures of the aboriginal group claiming the right and, at most, adds the notion of exclusivity; i.e., the exclusive right to use the land for those purposes. However, the uses to which lands held pursuant to aboriginal title can be

put are not restricted in this way. This conclusion emerges from three sources: (i) the Canadian jurisprudence on aboriginal title, (ii) the relationship between reserve lands and lands held pursuant to aboriginal title, and (iii) the *Indian Oil and Gas Act*, RSC 1985, c. I-7. As well, although this is not legally determinative, it is supported by the critical literature. In particular, I have profited greatly from Professor McNeil's article, "The Meaning of Aboriginal Title," *supra*.

(i) CANADIAN JURISPRUDENCE ON ABORIGINAL TITLE

[119] Despite the fact that the jurisprudence on aboriginal title is somewhat under-developed, it is clear that the uses to which lands held pursuant to aboriginal title can be put is not restricted to the practices, customs and traditions of aboriginal peoples integral to distinctive aboriginal cultures. In *Guerin*, for example, Dickson J described aboriginal title as an "interest in land" which encompassed "a legal right to occupy and possess certain lands" (at p. 382). The "right to occupy and possess" is framed in broad terms and, significantly, is not qualified by reference to traditional and customary uses of those lands. Any doubt that the right to occupancy and possession encompasses a broad variety of uses of land was put to rest in *Paul*, where the Court went even further and stated that aboriginal title was "more than the right to enjoyment and occupancy" (at p. 678). Once again, there is no reference to aboriginal practices, customs and traditions as a qualifier on that right. Moreover, I take the reference to "more" as emphasis of the broad notion of use and possession.

(ii) RESERVE LAND

[120] Another source of support for the conclusion that the uses to which lands held under aboriginal title can be put are not restricted to those grounded in practices, customs and traditions integral to distinctive aboriginal cultures can be found in *Guerin*, where Dickson J stated at p. 379 that the same legal principles governed the aboriginal interest in reserve lands and lands held pursuant to aboriginal title:

> It does not matter, in my opinion, that the present case is concerned with the interest of an Indian Band in a reserve rather than with unrecognized aboriginal title in traditional tribal lands. *The Indian interest in the land is the same in both cases* ... . [Emphasis added.]

[121] The nature of the Indian interest in reserve land is very broad, and can be found in s. 18 of the *Indian Act*, which I reproduce in full:

> 18(1) Subject to this Act, reserves are held by Her Majesty for the *use and benefit* of the respective bands for which they were set apart, and subject to this Act and to the terms of any treaty or surrender, the Governor in Council may determine whether any purpose for which lands in a reserve are used or are to be used is for the use and benefit of the band.
>
> (2) The Minister may authorize the use of lands in a reserve for the purpose of Indian schools, the administration of Indian affairs, Indian burial grounds, Indian health projects or, with the consent of the council of the band, *for any other purpose for the general welfare of the band*, and may take any lands in a reserve required for those purposes, but where an individual Indian, immediately prior to the taking, was entitled to the possession of those lands, compensation for that use shall be paid to the Indian, in such amount as may be agreed

between the Indian and the Minister, or, failing agreement, as may be determined in such manner as the Minister may direct. [Emphasis added.]

The principal provision is s. 18(1), which states that reserve lands are held "for the use and benefit" of the bands which occupy them; those uses and benefits, on the face of the *Indian Act*, do not appear to be restricted to practices, customs and traditions integral to distinctive aboriginal cultures. The breadth of those uses is reinforced by s. 18(2), which states that reserve lands may be used "for any other purpose for the general welfare of the band." The general welfare of the band has not been defined in terms of aboriginal practices, customs and traditions, nor in terms of those activities which have their origin pre-contact; it is a concept, by definition, which incorporates a reference to the present-day needs of aboriginal communities. On the basis of *Guerin*, lands held pursuant to aboriginal title, like reserve lands, are also capable of being used for a broad variety of purposes.

(iii) INDIAN OIL AND GAS ACT

[122] The third source for the proposition that the content of aboriginal title is not restricted to practices, customs and traditions which are integral to distinctive aboriginal cultures is the *Indian Oil and Gas Act*. The overall purpose of the statute is to provide for the exploration of oil and gas on reserve lands through their surrender to the Crown. The statute presumes that the aboriginal interest in reserve land includes mineral rights, a point which this Court unanimously accepted with respect to the *Indian Act* in *Blueberry River Indian Band v. Canada (Department of Indian Affairs and Northern Development)*, [1995] 4 SCR 344. On the basis of *Guerin*, aboriginal title also encompass mineral rights, and lands held pursuant to aboriginal title should be capable of exploitation in the same way, which is certainly not a traditional use for those lands. This conclusion is reinforced by s. 6(2) of the Act, which provides:

6.(2) Nothing in this Act shall be deemed to abrogate the rights of Indian people or preclude them from negotiating for oil and gas benefits in those areas in which land claims have not been settled.

The areas referred to in s. 6(2), at the very least, must encompass lands held pursuant to aboriginal title, since those lands by definition have not been surrendered under land claims agreements. The presumption underlying s. 6(2) is that aboriginal title permits the development of oil and gas reserves.

[123] Although this is not determinative, the conclusion that the content of aboriginal title is not restricted to those uses with their origins in the practices, customs and traditions integral to distinctive aboriginal societies has wide support in the critical literature: Jocelyn Gagne, "The Content of Aboriginal Title at Common Law: A Look at the Nishga Claim" (1982-83), 47 *Sask. L Rev.* 309 at pp. 336-37; Kent McNeil, *Common Law Aboriginal Title, supra*, at p. 242; Kent McNeil, "The Meaning of Aboriginal Title," *supra*, at pp. 143-150; William Pentney, "The Rights of the Aboriginal Peoples of Canada in the *Constitution Act, 1982* Part II—Section 35: The Substantive Guarantee" (1988), 22 *UBC L Rev.* 207, at p. 221; *Report of the Royal Commission on Aboriginal Peoples*, vol. 2 (*Restructuring the Relationship*), at p. 561; Brian Slattery, "The Constitutional Guarantee of Aboriginal and Treaty Rights" (1982-83), 8 *Queen's LJ* 232, at pp. 268-9; Brian Slattery, *Ancestral Lands,*

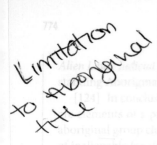

Perspectives on Aboriginal Title (1983), at p. 34; Brian Slattery, "Under-
~~l~~ Rights," 66 *Can. Bar Rev.* 727, at pp. 746-48.

...ion, the content of aboriginal title is not restricted to those uses which
...actice, custom or tradition integral to the distinctive culture of the
...iming the right. However, nor does aboriginal title amount to a form
...nple, as I will now explain.

(c) Inherent Limit: Lands Held Pursuant to Aboriginal Title Cannot Be Used in a
Manner That Is Irreconcilable with the Nature of the Attachment to the Land
Which Forms the Basis of the Group's Claim to Aboriginal Title

[125] The content of aboriginal title contains an inherent limit that lands held pursuant
to title cannot be used in a manner that is irreconcilable with the nature of the claimants'
attachment to those lands. This limit on the content of aboriginal title is a manifestation
of the principle that underlies the various dimensions of that special interest in land—it
is a *sui generis* interest that is distinct from "normal" proprietary interests, most notably
fee simple.

[126] I arrive at this conclusion by reference to the other dimensions of aboriginal
title which are *sui generis* as well. I first consider the source of aboriginal title. As I discussed earlier, aboriginal title arises from the prior occupation of Canada by aboriginal
peoples. That prior occupation is relevant in two different ways: first, because of the
physical fact of occupation, and second, because aboriginal title originates in part from
pre-existing systems of aboriginal law. However, the law of aboriginal title does not only
seek to determine the historic rights of aboriginal peoples to land; it also seeks to afford
legal protection to prior occupation in the present-day. Implicit in the protection of historic patterns of occupation is a recognition of the importance of the continuity of the
relationship of an aboriginal community to its land over time.

[127] I develop this point below with respect to the test for aboriginal title. The relevance of the continuity of the relationship of an aboriginal community with its land here
is that it applies not only to the past, but to the future as well. That relationship should
not be prevented from continuing into the future. As a result, uses of the lands that would
threaten that future relationship are, by their very nature, excluded from the content of
aboriginal title.

[128] Accordingly, in my view, lands subject to aboriginal title cannot be put to such
uses as may be irreconcilable with the nature of the occupation of that land and the relationship that the particular group has had with the land which together have given rise
to aboriginal title in the first place. As discussed below, one of the critical elements in the
determination of whether a particular aboriginal group has aboriginal title to certain
lands is the matter of the occupancy of those lands. Occupancy is determined by reference
to the activities that have taken place on the land and the uses to which the land has been
put by the particular group. If lands are so occupied, there will exist a special bond between the group and the land in question such that the land will be part of the definition
of the group's distinctive culture. It seems to me that these elements of aboriginal title
create an inherent limitation on the uses to which the land, over which such title exists,
may be put. For example, if occupation is established with reference to the use of the land
as a hunting ground, then the group that successfully claims aboriginal title to that land

may not use it in such a fashion as to destroy its value for such a use (e.g., by strip mining it). Similarly, if a group claims a special bond with the land because of its ceremonial or cultural significance, it may not use the land in such a way as to destroy that relationship (e.g., by developing it in such a way that the bond is destroyed, perhaps by turning it into a parking lot).

[129] It is for this reason also that lands held by virtue of aboriginal title may not be alienated. Alienation would bring to an end the entitlement of the aboriginal people to occupy the land and would terminate their relationship with it. I have suggested above that the inalienability of aboriginal lands is, at least in part, a function of the common law principle that settlers in colonies must derive their title from Crown grant and, therefore, cannot acquire title through purchase from aboriginal inhabitants. It is also, again only in part, a function of a general policy "to ensure that Indians are not dispossessed of their entitlements": see *Mitchell v. Peguis Indian Band*, [1990] 2 SCR 85, at p. 133. What the inalienability of lands held pursuant to aboriginal title suggests is that those lands are more than just a fungible commodity. The relationship between an aboriginal community and the lands over which it has aboriginal title has an important non-economic component. The land has an inherent and unique value in itself, which is enjoyed by the community with aboriginal title to it. The community cannot put the land to uses which would destroy that value.

[130] I am cognizant that the *sui generis* nature of aboriginal title precludes the application of "traditional real property rules" to elucidate the content of that title (*St. Mary's Indian Band v. Cranbrook (City)*, [1997] 2 SCR 657, at para. 14). Nevertheless, a useful analogy can be drawn between the limit on aboriginal title and the concept of equitable waste at common law. Under that doctrine, persons who hold a life estate in real property cannot commit "wanton or extravagant acts of destruction" (E.H. Burn, *Cheshire and Burn's Modern Law of Real Property* (14th ed. 1988), at p. 264) or "ruin the property" (Robert E. Megarry and H.W.R. Wade, *The Law of Real Property* (4th ed. 1975), at p. 105). This description of the limits imposed by the doctrine of equitable waste capture the kind of limit I have in mind here.

[131] Finally, what I have just said regarding the importance of the continuity of the relationship between an aboriginal community and its land, and the non-economic or inherent value of that land, should not be taken to detract from the possibility of surrender to the Crown in exchange for valuable consideration. On the contrary, the idea of surrender reinforces the conclusion that aboriginal title is limited in the way I have described. If aboriginal peoples wish to use their lands in a way that aboriginal title does not permit, then they must surrender those lands and convert them into non-title lands to do so.

[132] The foregoing amounts to a general limitation on the use of lands held by virtue of aboriginal title. It arises from the particular physical and cultural relationship that a group may have with the land and is defined by the source of aboriginal title over it. This is not, I must emphasize, a limitation that restricts the use of the land to those activities that have traditionally been carried out on it. That would amount to a legal straitjacket on aboriginal peoples who have a legitimate legal claim to the land. The approach I have outlined above allows for a full range of uses of the land, subject only to an overarching limit, defined by the special nature of the aboriginal title in that land.

(d) Aboriginal Title Under s. 35(1) of the Constitution Act, 1982

[133] Aboriginal title at common law is protected in its full form by s. 35(1). This conclusion flows from the express language of s. 35(1) itself, which states in full: "[t]he *existing* aboriginal and treaty rights of the aboriginal peoples of Canada are hereby recognized and affirmed" (emphasis added). On a plain reading of the provision, s. 35(1) did not create aboriginal rights; rather, it accorded constitutional status to those rights which were "existing" in 1982. The provision, at the very least, constitutionalized those rights which aboriginal peoples possessed at common law, since those rights existed at the time s. 35(1) came into force. Since aboriginal title was a common law right whose existence was recognized well before 1982 (e.g., *Calder, supra*), s. 35(1) has constitutionalized it in its full form.

[134] I expressed this understanding of the relationship between common law aboriginal rights, including aboriginal title, and the aboriginal rights protected by s. 35(1) in *Van der Peet*. While explaining the purposes behind s. 35(1), I stated that "it must be remembered that s. 35(1) did not create the legal doctrine of aboriginal rights; aboriginal rights existed and were recognized under the common law" (at para. 28). Through the enactment of s. 35(1), "a pre-existing legal doctrine was elevated to constitutional status" (at para. 29), or in other words, s. 35(1) had achieved "the constitutionalization of those rights" (at para. 29).

[135] Finally, this view of the effect of s. 35(1) on common law aboriginal title is supported by numerous commentators: Patrick Macklem, "First Nations Self-Government and the Borders of the Canadian Legal Imagination" (1991), 36 *McGill LJ* 382, at pp. 447-48; Kent McNeil, "The Constitutional Rights of the Aboriginal Peoples of Canada" (1982), 4 *Sup. Ct. L Rev.* 255, at pp. 256-57; James O'Reilly, "La *Loi constitutionnelle de 1982*, droit des autochtones" (1984), 25 *C. de D.* 125, at p. 137; William Pentney, "The Rights of the Aboriginal Peoples of Canada in the *Constitution Act, 1982* Part II—Section 35: The Substantive Guarantee," *supra*, at pp. 220-21; Douglas Sanders, "The Rights of the Aboriginal Peoples of Canada" (1983), 61 *Can. Bar Rev.* 314, at p. 329; Douglas Sanders, "Pre-Existing Rights: The Aboriginal Peoples of Canada," in Gérald-A. Beaudoin and Ed Ratushny, eds., *The Canadian Charter of Rights and Freedoms* (2nd ed. 1989), 707, at pp. 731-32; Brian Slattery, "The Constitutional Guarantee of Aboriginal and Treaty Rights," *supra*, at p. 254; Brian Slattery, *Ancestral Lands, Alien Laws: Judicial Perspectives on Aboriginal Title, supra*, at p. 45.

[136] I hasten to add that the constitutionalization of common law aboriginal rights by s. 35(1) does not mean that those rights exhaust the content of s. 35(1). As I said in *Côté, supra*, at para. 52:

> Section 35(1) would fail to achieve its noble purpose of preserving the integral and defining features of distinctive aboriginal societies if it only protected those defining features which were fortunate enough to have received the legal recognition and approval of European colonizers.

I relied on this proposition in *Côté* to defeat the argument that the possible absence of aboriginal rights under French colonial law was a bar to the existence of aboriginal rights under s. 35(1) within the historic boundaries of New France. But it also follows that the existence of a particular aboriginal right at common law is not a *sine qua non* for the proof of an aboriginal right that is recognized and affirmed by s. 35(1). Indeed, none of the decisions of this Court handed down under s. 35(1) in which the existence of an aboriginal right has been demonstrated has relied on the existence of that right at common law. The existence of an aboriginal right at common law is therefore sufficient, but not necessary, for the recognition and affirmation of that right by s. 35(1).

[137] The acknowledgement that s. 35(1) has accorded constitutional status to common law aboriginal title raises a further question—the relationship of aboriginal title to the "aboriginal rights" protected by s. 35(1). I addressed that question in *Adams, supra*, where the Court had been presented with two radically different conceptions of this relationship. The first conceived of aboriginal rights as being "inherently based in aboriginal title to the land" (at para. 25), or as fragments of a broader claim to aboriginal title. By implication, aboriginal rights must rest either in a claim to title or the unextinguished remnants of title. Taken to its logical extreme, this suggests that aboriginal title is merely the sum of a set of individual aboriginal rights, and that it therefore has no independent content. However, I rejected this position for another—that aboriginal title is "simply one manifestation of a broader-based conception of aboriginal rights" (at para. 25). Thus, although aboriginal title is a species of aboriginal right recognized and affirmed by s. 35(1), it is distinct from other aboriginal rights because it arises where the connection of a group with a piece of land "was of a central significance to their distinctive culture"

[at para. 26].

[138] The picture which emerges from *Adams* is that the aboriginal rights which are recognized and affirmed by s. 35(1) fall along a spectrum with respect to their degree of connection with the land. At the one end, there are those aboriginal rights which are practices, customs and traditions that are integral to the distinctive aboriginal culture of the group claiming the right. However, the "occupation and use of the land" where the activity is taking place is not "sufficient to support a claim of title to the land" (at para. 26). Nevertheless, those activities receive constitutional protection. In the middle, there are activities which, out of necessity, take place on land and indeed, might be intimately related to a particular piece of land. Although an aboriginal group may not be able to demonstrate title to the land, it may nevertheless have a site-specific right to engage in a particular activity. I put the point this way in *Adams*, at para. 30:

> Even where an aboriginal right exists on a tract of land to which the aboriginal people in question do not have title, that right may well be site specific, with the result that it can be exercised only upon that specific tract of land. For example, *if an aboriginal people demonstrates that hunting on a specific tract of land was an integral part of their distinctive culture then, even if the right exists apart from title to that tract of land, the aboriginal right to hunt is nonetheless defined as, and limited to, the right to hunt on the specific tract of land.* [Emphasis added.]

At the other end of the spectrum, there is aboriginal title itself. As *Adams* makes clear, aboriginal title confers more than the right to engage in site-specific activities which are aspects of the practices, customs and traditions of distinctive aboriginal cultures. Site-specific rights can be made out even if title cannot. What aboriginal title confers is the right to the land itself.

[139] Because aboriginal rights can vary with respect to their degree of connection with the land, some aboriginal groups may be unable to make out a claim to title, but will

nevertheless possess aboriginal rights that are recognized and affirmed by s. 35(1), including site-specific rights to engage in particular activities. As I explained in *Adams*, this may occur in the case of nomadic peoples who varied "the location of their settlements with the season and changing circumstances" (at para. 27). The fact that aboriginal peoples were non-sedentary, however (at para. 27)

> does not alter the fact that nomadic peoples survived through reliance on the land prior to contact with Europeans and, further, that many of the practices, customs and traditions of nomadic peoples that took place on the land were integral to their distinctive cultures.

(e) Proof of Aboriginal Title

(I) INTRODUCTION

[140] In addition to differing in the degree of connection with the land, aboriginal title differs from other aboriginal rights in another way. To date, the Court has defined aboriginal rights in terms of *activities*. As I said in *Van der Peet* (at para. 46):

> [I]n order to be an aboriginal right an *activity* must be an element of a practice, custom or tradition integral to the distinctive culture of the aboriginal group claiming the right. [Emphasis added.]

Aboriginal title, however, is a *right to the land* itself. Subject to the limits I have laid down above, that land may be used for a variety of activities, none of which need be individually protected as aboriginal rights under s. 35(1). Those activities are parasitic on the underlying title.

[141] This difference between aboriginal rights to engage in particular activities and aboriginal title requires that the test I laid down in *Van der Peet* be adapted accordingly. I anticipated this possibility in *Van der Peet* itself, where I stated that (at para. 74):

> *Aboriginal rights arise from the prior occupation of land, but they also arise from the prior social organization and distinctive cultures of aboriginal peoples on that land.* In considering whether a claim to an aboriginal right has been made out, courts must look at both the relationship of an aboriginal claimant to the land *and* at the practices, customs and traditions arising from the claimant's distinctive culture and society. Courts must not focus so entirely on the relationship of aboriginal peoples with the land that they lose sight of the other factors relevant to the identification and definition of aboriginal rights. [Emphasis added; "and" emphasized in original.]

Since the purpose of s. 35(1) is to reconcile the prior presence of aboriginal peoples in North America with the assertion of Crown sovereignty, it is clear from this statement that s. 35(1) must recognize and affirm both aspects of that prior presence—first, the occupation of land, and second, the prior social organization and distinctive cultures of aboriginal peoples on that land. To date the jurisprudence under s. 35(1) has given more emphasis to the second aspect. To a great extent, this has been a function of the types of cases which have come before this Court under s. 35(1)—prosecutions for regulatory offences that, by their very nature, proscribe discrete types of activity.

[142] The adaptation of the test laid down in *Van der Peet* to suit claims to title must be understood as the recognition of the first aspect of that prior presence. However, as

will now become apparent, the tests for the identification of aboriginal rights to engage in particular activities and for the identification of aboriginal title share broad similarities. The major distinctions are first, under the test for aboriginal title, the requirement that the land be integral to the distinctive culture of the claimants is subsumed by the requirement of occupancy, and second, whereas the time for the identification of aboriginal rights is the time of first contact, the time for the identification of aboriginal title is the time at which the Crown asserted sovereignty over the land.

(II) THE TEST FOR THE PROOF OF ABORIGINAL TITLE

[143] In order to make out a claim for aboriginal title, the aboriginal group asserting title must satisfy the following criteria: (i) the land must have been occupied prior to sovereignty, (ii) if present occupation is relied on as proof of occupation pre-sovereignty, there must be a continuity between present and pre-sovereignty occupation, and (iii) at sovereignty, that occupation must have been exclusive.

THE LAND MUST HAVE BEEN OCCUPIED PRIOR TO SOVEREIGNTY

[144] In order to establish a claim to aboriginal title, the aboriginal group asserting the claim must establish that it occupied the lands in question at the *time at which the Crown asserted sovereignty over the land subject to the title*. The relevant time period for the establishment of title is, therefore, different than for the establishment of aboriginal rights to engage in specific activities. In *Van der Peet*, I held, at para. 60 that "[t]he time period that a court should consider in identifying whether the right claimed meets the standard of being integral to the aboriginal community claiming the right is the period prior to contact … ." This arises from the fact that in defining the central and distinctive attributes of pre-existing aboriginal societies it is necessary to look to a time prior to the arrival of Europeans. Practices, customs or traditions that arose solely as a response to European influences do not meet the standard for recognition as aboriginal rights.

[145] On the other hand, in the context of aboriginal title, sovereignty is the appropriate time period to consider for several reasons. First, from a theoretical standpoint, aboriginal title arises out of prior occupation of the land by aboriginal peoples and out of the relationship between the common law and pre-existing systems of aboriginal law. Aboriginal title is a burden on the Crown's underlying title. However, the Crown did not gain this title until it asserted sovereignty over the land in question. Because it does not make sense to speak of a burden on the underlying title before that title existed, aboriginal title crystallized at the time sovereignty was asserted. Second, aboriginal title does not raise the problem of distinguishing between distinctive, integral aboriginal practices, customs and traditions and those influenced or introduced by European contact. Under common law, the act of occupation or possession is sufficient to ground aboriginal title and it is not necessary to prove that the land was a distinctive or integral part of the aboriginal society before the arrival of Europeans. Finally, from a practical standpoint, it appears that the date of sovereignty is more certain than the date of first contact. It is often very difficult to determine the precise moment that each aboriginal group had first contact with European culture. I note that this … approach has support in the academic literature: Brian Slattery, "Understanding Aboriginal Rights," *supra*, at p. 742; Kent McNeil, *Common Law Aboriginal Title*, *supra*, at p. 196. For these reasons, I conclude that aboriginals must

establish occupation of the land from the date of the assertion of sovereignty in order to sustain a claim for aboriginal title. McEachern C.J. found, at pp. 233-34, and the parties did not dispute on appeal, that British sovereignty over British Columbia was conclusively established by the Oregon Boundary Treaty of 1846. This is not to say that circumstances subsequent to sovereignty may never be relevant to title or compensation; this might be the case, for example, where native bands have been dispossessed of traditional lands after sovereignty.

[146] There was a consensus among the parties on appeal that proof of historic occupation was required to make out a claim to aboriginal title. However, the parties disagreed on how that occupancy could be proved. The respondents assert that in order to establish aboriginal title, the occupation must be the physical occupation of the land in question. The appellant Gitksan nation argue, by contrast, that aboriginal title may be established, at least in part, by reference to aboriginal law.

[147] This debate over the proof of occupancy reflects two divergent views of the source of aboriginal title. The respondents argue, in essence, that aboriginal title arises from the physical reality at the time of sovereignty, whereas the Gitksan effectively take the position that aboriginal title arises from and should reflect the pattern of land holdings under aboriginal law. However, as I have explained above, the source of aboriginal title appears to be grounded both in the common law and in the aboriginal perspective on land; the latter includes, but is not limited to, their systems of law. It follows that both should be taken into account in establishing the proof of occupancy. Indeed, there is precedent for doing so. In *Baker Lake* [*Baker Lake v Minister of Indian Affairs and Northern Development*, [1980] 1 FC 518], Mahoney J. held that to prove aboriginal title, the claimants needed both to demonstrate their "physical presence on the land they occupied" (at p. 561) and the existence "among [that group of] ... a recognition of the claimed rights ... by the regime that prevailed before" (at p. 559).

[148] This approach to the proof of occupancy at common law is also mandated in the context of s. 35(1) by *Van der Peet*. In that decision, as I stated above, I held at para. 50 that the reconciliation of the prior occupation of North America by aboriginal peoples with the assertion of Crown sovereignty required that account be taken of the "aboriginal perspective while at the same time taking into account the perspective of the common law" and that "[t]rue reconciliation will, equally, place weight on each." I also held that the aboriginal perspective on the occupation of their lands can be gleaned, in part, but not exclusively, from their traditional laws, because those laws were elements of the practices, customs and traditions of aboriginal peoples: at para. 41. As a result, if, at the time of sovereignty, an aboriginal society had laws in relation to land, those laws would be relevant to establishing the occupation of lands which are the subject of a claim for aboriginal title. Relevant laws might include, but are not limited to, a land tenure system or laws governing land use.

[149] However, the aboriginal perspective must be taken into account alongside the perspective of the common law. Professor McNeil has convincingly argued that at common law, the fact of physical occupation is proof of possession at law, which in turn will ground title to the land: *Common Law Aboriginal Title, supra*, at p. 73; also see *Cheshire and Burn's Modern Law of Real Property* [EH Burn, 14th ed (London: Butterworths, 1988)] at p. 28; and Megarry and Wade, *The Law of Real Property* [4th ed (London: Stevens, 1975)], at p. 1006. Physical occupation may be established in a variety of ways, ranging

from the construction of dwellings through cultivation and enclosure of fields to regular use of definite tracts of land for hunting, fishing or otherwise exploiting its resources: see McNeil, *Common Law Aboriginal Title*, at pp. 201-2. In considering whether occupation sufficient to ground title is established, "one must take into account the group's size, manner of life, material resources, and technological abilities, and the character of the lands claimed": Brian Slattery, "Understanding Aboriginal Rights," at p. 758.

· · ·

IF PRESENT OCCUPATION IS RELIED ON AS PROOF OF OCCUPATION PRE-SOVEREIGNTY, THERE MUST BE A CONTINUITY BETWEEN PRESENT AND PRE-SOVEREIGNTY OCCUPATION

[152] In *Van der Peet*, I explained that it is the pre-contact practices, customs and traditions of aboriginal peoples which are recognized and affirmed as aboriginal rights by s. 35(1). But I also acknowledged it would be "next to impossible" (at para. 62) for an aboriginal group to provide conclusive evidence of its pre-contact practices, customs and traditions. What would suffice instead was evidence of post-contact practices, which was "directed at demonstrating which aspects of the aboriginal community and society have their origins pre-contact" (at para. 62). The same concern, and the same solution, arises with respect to the proof of occupation in claims for aboriginal title, although there is a difference in the time for determination of title. Conclusive evidence of pre-sovereignty occupation may be difficult to come by. Instead, an aboriginal community may provide evidence of present occupation as proof of pre-sovereignty occupation in support of a claim to aboriginal title. What is required, in addition, is a *continuity* between present and pre-sovereignty occupation, because the relevant time for the determination of aboriginal title is at the time before sovereignty.

[153] Needless to say, there is no need to establish "an unbroken chain of continuity" (*Van der Peet*, at para. 65) between present and prior occupation. The occupation and use of lands may have been disrupted for a time, perhaps as a result of the unwillingness of European colonizers to recognize aboriginal title. To impose the requirement of continuity too strictly would risk "undermining the very purpose of s. 35(1) by perpetuating the historical injustice suffered by aboriginal peoples at the hands of colonizers who failed to respect" aboriginal rights to land (*Côté, supra*, at para. 53). In *Mabo* [*v Queensland* (1992), 107 ALR 1], the High Court of Australia set down the requirement that there must be "substantial maintenance of the connection" between the people and the land. In my view, this test should be equally applicable to proof of title in Canada.

· · ·

AT SOVEREIGNTY, OCCUPATION MUST HAVE BEEN EXCLUSIVE

[155] Finally, at sovereignty, occupation must have been exclusive. The requirement for exclusivity flows from the definition of aboriginal title itself, because I have defined aboriginal title in terms of the right to *exclusive* use and occupation of land. Exclusivity, as an aspect of aboriginal title, vests in the aboriginal community which holds the ability to exclude others from the lands held pursuant to that title. The proof of title must, in this respect, mirror the content of the right. Were it possible to prove title without demonstrating exclusive occupation, the result would be absurd, because it would be possible for

more than one aboriginal nation to have aboriginal title over the same piece of land, and then for all of them to attempt to assert the right to exclusive use and occupation over it.

[156] As with the proof of occupation, proof of exclusivity must rely on both the perspective of the common law and the aboriginal perspective, placing equal weight on each. At common law, a premium is placed on the factual reality of occupation, as encountered by the Europeans. However, as the common law concept of possession must be sensitive to the realities of aboriginal society, so must the concept of exclusivity. Exclusivity is a common law principle derived from the notion of fee simple ownership and should be imported into the concept of aboriginal title with caution. As such, the test required to establish exclusive occupation must take into account the context of the aboriginal society at the time of sovereignty. For example, it is important to note that exclusive occupation can be demonstrated even if other aboriginal groups were present, or frequented the claimed lands. Under those circumstances, exclusivity would be demonstrated by "the intention and capacity to retain exclusive control" (McNeil, *Common Law Aboriginal Title*, *supra*, at p. 204). Thus, an act of trespass, if isolated, would not undermine a general finding of exclusivity, if aboriginal groups intended to and attempted to enforce their exclusive occupation. Moreover, as Professor McNeil suggests, the presence of other aboriginal groups might actually reinforce a finding of exclusivity. For example, "[w]here others were allowed access upon request, the very fact that permission was asked for and given would be further evidence of the group's exclusive control" (at p. 204).

. . .

D. Has a Claim to Self-Government Been Made Out by the Appellants?

[170] In the courts below, considerable attention was given to the question of whether s. 35(1) can protect a right to self-government, and if so, what the contours of that right are. The errors of fact made by the trial judge, and the resultant need for a new trial, make it impossible for this Court to determine whether the claim to self-government has been made out. Moreover, this is not the right case for the Court to lay down the legal principles to guide future litigation. The parties seem to have acknowledged this point, perhaps implicitly, by giving the arguments on self-government much less weight on appeal. One source of the decreased emphasis on the right to self-government on appeal is this Court's judgment *Pamajewon*. There, I held that rights to self-government, if they existed, cannot be framed in excessively general terms. The appellants did not have the benefit of my judgment at trial. Unsurprisingly, as counsel for the Wet'suwet'en specifically concedes, the appellants advanced the right to self-government in very broad terms, and therefore in a manner not cognizable under s. 35(1).

[171] The broad nature of the claim at trial also led to a failure by the parties to address many of the difficult conceptual issues which surround the recognition of aboriginal self-government. The degree of complexity involved can be gleaned from the *Report of the Royal Commission on Aboriginal Peoples*, which devotes 277 pages to the issue. That report describes different models of self-government, each differing with respect to their conception of territory, citizenship, jurisdiction, internal government organization, etc. We received little in the way of submissions that would help us to grapple with these difficult and central issues. Without assistance from the parties, it would be imprudent for the

Court to step into the breach. In these circumstances, the issue of self-government will fall to be determined at trial.

· · ·

[186] Finally, this litigation has been both long and expensive, not only in economic but in human terms as well. By ordering a new trial, I do not necessarily encourage the parties to proceed to litigation and to settle their dispute through the courts. As was said in *Sparrow*, at p. 1105, s. 35(1) "provides a solid constitutional base upon which subsequent negotiations can take place." Those negotiations should also include other aboriginal nations which have a stake in the territory claimed. Moreover, the Crown is under a moral, if not a legal, duty to enter into and conduct those negotiations in good faith. Ultimately, it is through negotiated settlements, with good faith and give and take on all sides, reinforced by the judgments of this Court, that we will achieve what I stated in *Van der Peet*, *supra*, at para. 31, to be a basic purpose of s. 35(1)—"the reconciliation of the pre-existence of aboriginal societies with the sovereignty of the Crown." Let us face it, we are all here to stay.

DISCUSSION NOTES

i. Assessing Aboriginal Title in Delgamuukw

Kent McNeil, *Defining Aboriginal Title in the 90s: Has the Supreme Court Finally Got It Right?*
(Toronto: York University, Robarts Centre for Canadian Studies, 1998)
at 7-29 (footnotes omitted)

In my opinion, the most important aspect of the *Delgamuukw* decision for Aboriginal peoples is the part dealing with the content of Aboriginal title. For the first time, the Supreme Court stopped avoiding this issue and provided a clear picture of the title's nature. In so doing, the Court rejected the position of British Columbia and Canada that Aboriginal title is limited to historical uses of the land, but it also rejected the contention of the Gitxsan and Wet'suwet'en that it is equivalent to an inalienable fee simple estate. The Supreme Court affirmed earlier characterizations of Aboriginal title as *sui generis*; that is, as an interest in land that is in a class of its own. The fact that Aboriginal title cannot be sold or transferred is one aspect of this uniqueness. Another is the title's collective nature—it can only be held by a community of Aboriginal people, not by individuals. The source of Aboriginal title also distinguishes it from other land titles, which usually originate in Crown grants. Because the Aboriginal peoples were here before the Crown asserted sovereignty, their title is derived from the dual source of their prior occupation and their pre-existing systems of law.

These *sui generis* aspects of Aboriginal title do not restrict the uses that Aboriginal peoples can make of their lands. Chief Justice Lamer proclaimed emphatically that Aboriginal title is "a *right to the land* itself." It is not a mere collection of rights to pursue activities on the land that were integral to the distinctive cultures of the Aboriginal peoples before Europeans appeared on the scene, as British Columbia and Canada argued. Instead, Aboriginal title encompasses a full range of uses that need not be linked to past practices.

So Aboriginal nations can engage in mining, lumbering, oil and gas extraction, and so on, even if they did not use their lands in those ways in the past.

But the Chief Justice did not stop there—he declared as well that the right Aboriginal peoples have to use and occupy their lands is an exclusive right. This means that Aboriginal peoples are not just free to determine for themselves what uses they will make of their lands; they also have as much right as any landholder to prevent others—and this includes governments—from intruding on and using their lands without their consent. Indeed, they should have even greater protection against government intrusion than other landholders because their Aboriginal rights have been recognized and affirmed by the Constitution, whereas the property rights of other landholders have not. ...

While describing Aboriginal title as a right of exclusive use and occupation of land, the Supreme Court did place an inherent limitation on the purposes for which Aboriginal title lands can be used. The limitation is this:

> Lands held pursuant to Aboriginal title cannot be used in a manner that is irreconcilable with the nature of the attachment to the land which forms the basis of the group's claim to Aboriginal title [para. 124].

Chief Justice Lamer linked this limitation to the dual source of Aboriginal title in prior occupation of land and pre-existing systems of Aboriginal law. He emphasized the importance of maintaining the continuity between the historic patterns of occupation which are the basis of Aboriginal title and present-day uses. Thus Aboriginal peoples cannot use their lands in ways that would prevent their special relationship with the land from continuing into the future. The Chief Justice gave two examples to illustrate this point. First, if the occupation necessary for establishing Aboriginal title is proven by showing that the land was used as a hunting ground, it cannot be used today in ways that would destroy its value for hunting—so strip mining, for instance, would be precluded. Secondly [at para. 128],

> if a group claims a special bond with the land because of its ceremonial or cultural significance, it may not use the land in such a way as to destroy that relationship (e.g., by developing it in such a way that the bond is destroyed, perhaps by turning it into a parking lot).

These examples have added significance because they suggest that proof of a ceremonial or cultural connection with land, or of use of it as a hunting ground, can be sufficient to establish Aboriginal title ... .

To the extent that the inherent limitation on Aboriginal title precludes uses that would destroy the value of the land for future generations, it probably accords with the understanding Aboriginal people generally have of their own responsibilities. But the connection the Chief Justice made between their historic relationship to the land and uses they can make of it today concerns me because it suggests that Aboriginal peoples may be prisoners of the past. Lamer CJ tried to dispel this kind of concern by emphasizing that the limitation does not restrict use to activities traditionally carried out on the land. "That," he said, "would amount to a legal straitjacket on Aboriginal peoples who have a legitimate legal claim to the land." He added that his approach "allows for a full range of uses of the land, subject only to an overarching limit, defined by the special nature of the Aboriginal title in that land" [para. 132].

But to what extent is the "special nature" of Aboriginal title tied to the past? The Chief Justice did not answer this question directly. But if I understand him correctly, what he seems to have had in mind is this: On the one hand, present uses are not limited to historic uses, but on the other, present uses that would preclude historic uses, or destroy an Aboriginal people's special relationship with the land, are not permitted. In other words, present uses are not restricted to, but they are restricted by, past practices and traditions. …

[Noting that the Supreme Court had avoided the issue of self-government, McNeil then argued that the communal nature of Aboriginal title to land may require a community structure for making decisions—that is, some form of self-government.]

As suggested above, self-government provides a solution to the dilemma created by the inherent limitation Chief Justice Lamer placed on Aboriginal title. We have seen that this limitation prevents Aboriginal lands from being used in ways that are inconsistent with an Aboriginal nation's connection with the land. But the nature of that connection must be allowed to change over time so that Aboriginal peoples are not made prisoners of their own pasts. Canadian courts should not sit in judgment over social change in Aboriginal communities, deciding what is and what is not necessary for their cultural preservation. That kind of paternalism is self-defeating because it destroys the autonomy that is necessary for Aboriginal communities to thrive as dynamic cultural and political entities. Any internal limitations on Aboriginal title in the interests of cultural preservation should be determined by Aboriginal nations themselves through the exercise of self-government within their communities—they should not be imposed by Canadian courts. …

[McNeil concluded by suggesting that, in spite of achieving some success in this litigation, it was necessary to continue the process of negotiating land claims in future.]

… In my opinion, there are two reasons for doing so. First of all, after *Delgamuukw* Aboriginal people still have to prove that they have Aboriginal title. While the decision did remove the uncertainty over the meaning of Aboriginal title, it did not resolve the issue of which Aboriginal peoples have title to what lands. The decision did not even resolve that matter for the Gitxsan and Wet'suwet'en—that is why the case was sent back to trial. To avoid the protracted, expensive litigation that would be required to establish Aboriginal title in court, it is advisable for Aboriginal peoples to try to resolve the issues of the existence and geographical extent of their Aboriginal title through negotiations with the federal and provincial governments. If those governments refuse to take sufficient account of the *Delgamuukw* decision in the negotiations, or display other instances of bad faith, then the Aboriginal peoples always have the option of going to court.

A second reason for negotiating is that, although Aboriginal peoples are entitled to the resources on and under their lands, the inalienability of Aboriginal title may prevent them from developing those resources without the cooperation of the federal government. This feature of Aboriginal title may, for example, prevent Aboriginal titleholders from entering into leaseholds or resource extraction agreements with corporations that have the expertise and capital to develop the resources. While there would appear to be no legal impediment preventing Aboriginal peoples from developing these resources on their own (as long as they do not violate the inherent limitation on their title), this may not be a realistic option, at least in the short term, for Aboriginal peoples who do not have the necessary human and financial resources. So for Aboriginal peoples who are interested in developing the resources on their lands, negotiation of agreements with the federal and provincial governments may be unavoidable. ...

Negotiated agreements are the means by which Aboriginal land claims have been dealt with in Canada historically, originally by treaties and more recently by land claims agreements. This approach respects the Aboriginal peoples and their authority to make decisions regarding their lands, whereas non-consensual infringement of their Aboriginal title by federal legislation does not. Legislative infringement is a coercive act that should only be used in emergencies or as a last resort where a compelling and substantial objective is at stake, and the Aboriginal titleholders refuse good-faith negotiations. Moreover, there is no valid reason why negotiations need result in an absolute surrender of Aboriginal title. Aboriginal people should be able to participate in negotiations for the development of their lands without being compelled to give up their title.

Despite its shortcomings, the *Delgamuukw* decision could usher in a new era for Aboriginal rights in Canada. For the first time, the right of Aboriginal peoples to participate as equal partners in resource development on Aboriginal lands has been acknowledged. But for this new partnership to work, the federal and provincial governments will have to shed out-dated attitudes and accept the new legal landscape. This will take political courage, leadership, and imagination. The Canadian public as well needs to be aware of the unique position of the Aboriginal peoples in Canadian society, and accept the fact that they have special rights as the original inhabitants of this country. Over and over in his recent decisions on Aboriginal rights, Chief Justice Lamer has emphasized the need for reconciliation. Public support for governments that have the vision to negotiate just agreements with Aboriginal peoples for a sharing of this country's resources will help to achieve the kind of reconciliation he seems to have in mind.

––––––––––––––––––––

For other assessments of the Supreme Court's decision in *Delgamuukw*, see Kent McNeil, "Aboriginal Rights in Canada: From Title to Land to Territorial Sovereignty" (1998) 5 Tulsa J Comp & Int'l L 353; Catherine Bell, "New Directions in the Law of Aboriginal Rights" (1998) 77 Can Bar Rev 36; Gordon Christie, "Delgamuukw and the Protection of Aboriginal Land Interests" (2000-1) 32:1 Ottawa L Rev 85; and William F Flanagan, "Piercing the Veil of Real Property Law: Delgamuukw v British Columbia" (1998) 24 Queen's LJ 279. For assessments of the decisions at trial and on appeal, see BD Cox, "The Gitksan–Wet'suwet'en as 'Primitive' Peoples Incapable of Holding Proprietary Interests: Chief Justice McEachern's Underlying Premise in Delgamuukw" (1992) 1 Dal J Leg Stud 141; M Walters, "British Imperial Constitutional Law and Aboriginal Rights: A Comment on Delgamuukw v British Columbia" (1992) 17 Queen's LJ 350; and Fortune. More recently, see Kent McNeil, "Aboriginal Title and the Supreme Court: What's Happening?" (2006) 69 Sask L Rev 281, reproduced in part below.

ii. Delgamuukw and the Justification Test

The *Constitution Act, 1982* placed Aboriginal rights in s 35, outside the Charter. This placement appeared to make s 1 of the Charter (and especially its requirement of "reasonable limits") inapplicable to the interpretation of s 35 in relation to Aboriginal rights. However, the Supreme Court of Canada addressed this issue in *R v Sparrow*, [1990] 1 SCR 1075, and held that the words "recognized and affirmed" in s 35 indicated that Aboriginal rights could be infringed in certain circumstances. Though most commonly associated with the exercise of activity-specific rights, these infringements may also affect Aboriginal title to land.

After evidence establishes a *prima facie* infringement on an Aboriginal right by way of contact, the court must determine whether the infringement is reasonable. For the Court to meet this standard, it must first be shown that the infringement promotes a legislative goal that is pressing and substantial. The government must then demonstrate that the infringement was conducted in a manner consistent with the fiduciary duty that exists between Aboriginal peoples and the Crown. *Sparrow* originally identified only conservation as a pressing and substantial legislative goal that could meet this test; indeed, the court found that the "public interest" (cast broadly) would not conform to the spirit of s 35. However, the Supreme Court of Canada later lowered this high threshold in *R v Gladstone*, [1996] 2 SCR 723 at para 73, adding "the pursuit of economic and regional fairness" to the list of pressing and substantial legislative goals. This lowered standard was met with criticism, including the dissenting opinion of McLachlin J (as she was then) in *Van der Peet*:

> [306] … [T]he compelling objectives foreseen in *Sparrow* may be seen as united by a common characteristic; they constitute the essential pre-conditions of any civilized exercise of the right. … What are permitted are limitations of the sort that any property owner or right holder would reasonably expect—the sort of limitations which must be imposed in a civilized society if the resource is to be used now and in the future. They do not *negate* the right, but rather limit its exercise. The extension of the concept of compelling objective to matters like economic and regional fairness and the interests of non-aboriginal fishers, by contrast, would negate the very aboriginal right to fish itself, on the ground that this is required for the reconciliation of aboriginal rights and other interests and the consequent good of the community as a whole. This is not limitation required for the responsible exercise of the right, but rather limitation on the basis of the economic demands of non-aboriginals. It is limitation of a different order than the conservation, harm prevention type of limitation sanctioned in *Sparrow*.

In the following year, Chief Justice Lamer used his judgment in *Delgamuukw* to both extend the logic of *Gladstone* and put Aboriginal title under the purview of the *Sparrow* test:

> [165] The general principles governing justification laid down in *Sparrow*, and embellished by *Gladstone*, operate with respect to infringements of aboriginal title. In the wake of *Gladstone*, the range of legislative objectives that can justify the infringement of aboriginal title is fairly broad. Most of these objectives can be traced to the *reconciliation* of the prior occupation of North America by aboriginal peoples with the assertion of Crown sovereignty, which entails that "distinctive aboriginal societies exist within, and are a part of, a broader social, political and economic community" (at para. 73). In my opinion, the development of agriculture, forestry, mining, and hydroelectric power, the general economic development of the interior of British Columbia, protection of the environment or endangered species, the building of infrastructure and the settlement of foreign populations to support those aims, are the kinds of objectives that are consistent

with this purpose and, in principle, can justify the infringement of aboriginal title. [Emphasis in original.]

Yet, even though Lamer CJC subjected Aboriginal title to land to the same basic test as that for activity-specific rights, the unique discretionary and economic elements of Aboriginal title were held to impose additional responsibilities on the Crown—that is, because Aboriginal title is more than the right to perform a particular activity, but is rather the right to control the agenda and resources of a given area, infringements will be upheld only if the government can demonstrate that it adequately consulted affected First Nations and also provided compensation for such infringement.

Lamer CJC's comments about the duty to consult First Nations are particularly important because he identified the possibility that the potential consequences of an infringement on Aboriginal title may be so dire that the Aboriginal community should be given a veto over a proposed project. The duty on the part of the government to consult First Nations is addressed again below with respect to post-*Delgamuukw* developments. However, it is important to note that some scholars have rejected the court's rationale for both infringement of Aboriginal title and the test for justification:

> [B]y establishing that virtually any type of economic development can potentially infringe Aboriginal rights, the Court appears more concerned with protecting federal powers rather than protecting Aboriginal rights. The Court lost sight of the wording of section 35(1) and has maintained instead, its loyalty to the colonial state. There is nothing in the wording of section 35(1) demanding [that] the Court reconcile any competing claims. Recognition and affirmation do not, on their own, allow the Court to permit any infringement of Aboriginal rights. Quite the contrary. But, by crafting its own reconciliation doctrine, the Court has removed the impetus for a negotiated settlement of Aboriginal claims.

(See D'Arcy Vermette, "Dizzying Dialogue: Canadian Courts and the Continuing Justification of the Dispossession of Aboriginal Peoples" (2011) 29 Windsor YB Access Just 55 at 63.)

iii. Aboriginal Rights and Aboriginal Title to Land

When discussing the relationship between Aboriginal title to land and s 35 of the Constitution, it is important to remember that the courts view Aboriginal title as being a specific category of rights within the overall concept of "Aboriginal rights": see Kent McNeil, "Aboriginal Title and Aboriginal Rights: What's the Connection?" (1997) 36 Alta L Rev 117. That is, although the legal concept of Aboriginal title to land has developed by way of its own distinct line of case law, the larger jurisprudence of Aboriginal rights still plays a major role in structuring its scope and enforceability. Furthermore, even if a community is unable to make a sufficiently strong case for Aboriginal title to land, the courts may still issue a declaration that protects their right to perform a specific, traditional activity on land.

Section 35(1) recognizes and affirms "existing aboriginal and treaty rights of the Aboriginal peoples" (defined by s 35(2) to include "Indian, Inuit and Métis peoples of Canada"). In *R v Sparrow*, [1990] 1 SCR 1075 (briefly examined in Chapter 7), the Supreme Court of Canada held that s 35 of the *Constitution Act, 1982* provides constitutional protection to Aboriginal rights (including the accused's right to fish sought in *Sparrow*) that were not extinguished prior to the enactment of s 35 in 1982. For an overview of s 35 and *Sparrow* in relation to self-government, see K McNeil, "Envisaging Constitutional Space for Aboriginal Governments"

(1993-94) 19 Queen's LJ 95. See also P Macklem, "First Nations Self-Government and the Borders of the Canadian Legal Imagination" (1991) 36 McGill LJ 382, and John Borrows, "Constitutional Law from a First Nations Perspective: Self-Government and the Royal Proclamation" (1994) 28 UBC L Rev 1. See also *R v Van der Peet*, [1996] 2 SCR 507, 137 DLR (4th) 289 and *R v Nikal*, [1996] 1 SCR 1013, (1996), 133 DLR (4th) 658.

The interaction between Aboriginal title and rights was again considered in the cases of *R v Adams*, [1996] 3 SCR 101 and *R v Côté*, [1996] 3 SCR 139. In *Côté*, the Supreme Court held that an Aboriginal right to fish could stand alone, independently of a finding of Aboriginal title over particular fishing grounds. This finding was pushed even further in *Adams*, when Lamer CJC stated that—even without establishing Aboriginal title—a community might still be entitled to perform an activity-specific right on a particular tract of land. This distinction was addressed again by the Supreme Court of Canada in *R v Marshall; R v Bernard*, 2005 SCC 43, [2005] 2 SCR 220, explored later in this chapter.

iv. The "Limits" of Aboriginal Title to Land

In the context of the expanded land interests and the related notions of self-governance discussed in *Delgamuukw*, it is important to recognize the limits identified by the Supreme Court in relation to the *sui generis* nature of Aboriginal title to land. A number of cases reveal how the concept of "limits" may curtail some activities for Aboriginal peoples in relation to both "rights" and "title to land."

For example, in *R v Pamajewon*, [1995] CNLR 188 (Ont CA), aff'd [1996] 2 SCR 821, 4 CNLR 164, it was held that lottery activities that infringed sections of the *Criminal Code* were not protected by s 35, because the First Nations accused failed to demonstrate that the regulation of gambling was an integral part of their distinctive cultures according to the test for establishing Aboriginal rights set out in *R v Van der Peet*.

Section 35(4) has also been a site of conflict over indigenous autonomy, because its requirement for gender equality within the rights protected under s 35(1) has sometimes been inconsistent with traditional conceptions of gender relations. In *Sawridge Band v Canada*, [1995] 4 CNLR 121 (FCTD), the plaintiffs sought a declaration that the 1985 amendments to the *Indian Act* were inconsistent with s 35 because they required the community to practise gender equality when determining band membership, regardless of traditions within the community. That is, because the band had a marital custom that permitted an Indian husband, but not a wife, to bring a non-Indian spouse into residence on the reserve, the gender equality requirement was regarded as incompatible with the protection of traditional activities under s 35(1). At trial, Muldoon J did not limit his analysis to s 35(1), but instead interpreted this section in conjunction with s 35(4). Section 35(4) states that "[n]otwithstanding any other provision of this Act, the aboriginal and treaty rights referred to in subsection (1) are guaranteed equally to male and female persons." The judge therefore dismissed the plaintiffs' application, stating (at 141):

> The plaintiffs are firmly caught by the provisions of section 35 of the *Constitution Act, 1982* which they themselves invoke. The more firmly the plaintiffs bring themselves into and under subsection 35(1) the more surely subsection 35(4) acts upon their alleged rights pursuant to subsection 35(1) which, therefore, are modified so as to be guaranteed equally to the whole collectivity of Indian men and Indian women.

Clearly, as Turpel explained in the excerpt in Chapter 6 about matrimonial property on reserve land, the resolution of gender equality issues in this context is fraught with difficult challenges because of the need to take account of both historical traditions and the contemporary context. (An appeal from the decision of Muldoon J was granted by the Federal Court of Appeal in June 1997, when the appellate court concluded that there was a reasonable apprehension of bias (but no actual bias) on the part of the trial judge. A new trial was ordered.)

A few years later, in *Sawridge Band v Canada*, [2003] 3 CNLR 344 (FCTD), the court granted an injunction to prevent the band from denying that women were members of the band, holding that the inconvenience to the band in admitting the women was outweighed by the damage to the public interest in "flouting" federal law. The injunction was granted, pending a hearing of the band's application for a declaration that the federal law, enacted in 1985 (RSC 1985, c I-5) was unconstitutional. There have been a number of other disputes concerning gender equality and the *Indian Act*: e.g. see *Barry v Garden River Band of Ojibways* (1997), 33 OR (3d) 782 (CA). For another case involving a dispute about band membership, see *Hodgson v Ermineskin Indian Band No 942*, 1999 CanLII 8558, [1999] FCJ no 1428 (TD).

Finally, some courts have appeared reluctant to hand down declarations of Aboriginal title to land if the declarations conflict with titles held by non-Aboriginal individuals or communities.

In *Chippewas of Sarnia Band v Canada (Attorney General)*, [2001] 1 CNLR 56 (Ont CA), for example, the court confirmed the trial judge's decision that Aboriginal title had been extinguished, but not by voluntary surrender or by statute. In this case, there were non-Aboriginal persons, successors in title to the person to whom the lands had been granted by the Crown in 1853, and these non-Aboriginal persons had been in peaceful and innocent possession of the claimed lands for 140 years. In this context, the courts held that the current owners should not be displaced, in spite of the infirmity of their titles. After assessing the arguments accepted by the judges in this case to deny the Aboriginal claims, Kent McNeil concluded that this kind of "judicial constitutional wizardry" may send a message to Aboriginal people that

> *regardless of the legal validity of their claims*, judges will not necessarily allow those claims to prevail if they conflict with the claims of other Canadians who did not participate in and were not aware of the wrongs that were committed. Decisions like this will undoubtedly undermine the already shaky faith that Aboriginal people have in Canadian courts. This is particularly so when judges disregard or change well-established legal rules in order to deny Aboriginal claims. As this article has attempted to demonstrate, this is precisely what the Court of Appeal did in the *Chippewas of Sarnia* case. [Emphasis in original.]

(See Kent McNeil, "Extinguishment of Aboriginal Title in Canada: Treaties, Legislation, and Judicial Discretion" (2000-1) 33 Ottawa L Rev 301.) See also McNeil, "The Vulnerability of Indigenous Land Rights in Australia and Canada" (2004) 42 Osgoode Hall LJ 271 [McNeil, "Vulnerability of Land Rights"]; K Coates, ed, *Aboriginal Land Claims in Canada: A Regional Perspective* (Toronto: Copp Clark Pitman, 1992); J McLaren, AR Buck & N Wright, eds, *Despotic Dominion: Property Rights in British Settler Societies* (Vancouver: UBC Press, 2005); and John Borrows, *Canada's Indigenous Constitution* (Toronto: University of Toronto Press, 2010) [Borrows, *Canada's Indigenous Constitution*].

III. POST-DELGAMUUKW DEVELOPMENTS

A. R v Marshall; R v Bernard: Stepping Back from Delgamuukw?

Arising from two similar appeals over Mi'kmaq logging rights in Atlantic Canada, the *Marshall* and *Bernard* cases marked the first time a claim for Aboriginal title had been fully assessed by Canada's highest court. (Recall that *Delgamuukw* was sent back to trial without a final decision.) Both cases involved seemingly unlawful logging being conducted by Mi'kmaq persons in Nova Scotia and New Brunswick, with the accused admitting to the facts, but relying on either a treaty right to log in the areas or, as the following case extract highlights, a claim of Aboriginal title over the forest land in question. Although these claims were dismissed at trial, both the Nova Scotia and New Brunswick Courts of Appeal overturned the convictions by concluding that the Aboriginal perspective had not been properly considered in determining the question of Aboriginal title. In a split decision at the Supreme Court, Chief Justice McLachlin decided that the Aboriginal title tests adopted in the trial courts were appropriate, and therefore reinstated the trial judges' convictions. Agreeing with the final result, LeBel and Fish JJ nonetheless questioned the chief justice's new formulation of the *Delgamuukw* test— that is, one that greatly favoured the common law conception of property over the Aboriginal perspective.

R v Marshall; R v Bernard
2005 SCC 43, [2005] 2 SCR 220

McLACHLIN CJ (Major, Bastarache, Abella, and Charron JJ concurring):

I. Introduction

[1] Can members of the Mi'kmaq people in Nova Scotia and New Brunswick engage in commercial logging on Crown lands without authorization, contrary to statutory regulation? More precisely, do they have treaty rights or aboriginal title entitling them to do so? These are the central issues on this appeal.

· · ·

[6] I conclude that the trial judges in each case correctly held that the respondents' treaty rights did not extend to commercial logging and correctly rejected the claim for aboriginal title in the relevant areas. I would thus allow the appeals, dismiss the cross-appeal in *Marshall* and restore the convictions.

· · ·

III. Aboriginal Title

· · ·

B. Standard of Occupation for Title: The Law

[41] The trial judges in each of *Bernard* and *Marshall* required proof of regular and exclusive use of the cutting sites to establish aboriginal title. The Courts of Appeal held

that this test was too strict and applied a less onerous standard of incidental or proximate occupancy.

[42] Cromwell J.A. in *Marshall* ((2003), 218 N.S.R. (2d) 78, 2003 NSCA 105) adopted in general terms Professor McNeil's "third category" of occupation (*Common Law Aboriginal Title* (1989)), "actual entry, and some act or acts from which an intention to occupy the land could be inferred" (para. 136). Acts of "cutting trees or grass, fishing in tracts of water, and even perambulation, may be relied upon" (para. 136).

[43] Daigle J.A. in *Bernard* ((2003), 262 N.B.R. (2d) 1, 2003 NBCA 55) similarly concluded that it was not necessary to prove specific acts of occupation and regular use of the logged area in order to ground aboriginal title. It was enough to show that the Mi'kmaq had used and occupied an area near the cutting site at the confluence of the Northwest Miramichi and the Little Southwest Miramichi. This proximity permitted the inference that the cutting site would have been within the range of seasonal use and occupation by the Mi'kmaq (para. 119).

[44] The question before us is which of these standards of occupation is appropriate to determine aboriginal title: the strict standard applied by the trial judges; the looser standard applied by the Courts of Appeal; or some other standard? Interwoven is the question of what standard of evidence suffices; Daigle J.A. criticized the trial judge for failing to give enough weight to evidence of the pattern of land use and for discounting the evidence of oral traditions.

[45] Two concepts central to determining aboriginal rights must be considered before embarking on the analysis of whether the right claimed has been established. The first is the requirement that both aboriginal and European common law perspectives must be considered. The second relates to the variety of aboriginal rights that may be affirmed. Both concepts are critical to analyzing a claim for an aboriginal right, and merit preliminary consideration.

· · ·

[47] The difference between the common law and aboriginal perspectives on issues of aboriginal title is real. But it is important to understand what we mean when we say that in determining aboriginal title we must consider both the common law and the aboriginal perspective.

[The chief justice summarized her understanding of how the court reconciles Aboriginal and common law perspectives by discussing how this process is applied to Aboriginal rights in general. Essentially, by first understanding the "nature and extent" of the Aboriginal activity before European sovereignty is declared in a specific region, the court will then attempt to bring this pre-existing practice in line with a common law right. Once these two elements have been found and expanded on, the reconciliation of these perspectives can take place.]

[54] One of these rights is aboriginal title to land. It is established by aboriginal practices that indicate possession similar to that associated with title at common law. In matching common law property rules to aboriginal practice we must be sensitive to the context-specific nature of common law title, as well as the aboriginal perspective. The common law recognizes that possession sufficient to ground title is a matter of fact, depending on all the circumstances, in particular the nature of the land and the manner in

which the land is commonly enjoyed: *Powell v. McFarlane* (1977), 38 P. & C.R. 452 (Ch. D.), at p. 471. For example, where marshy land is virtually useless except for shooting, shooting over it may amount to adverse possession: *Red House Farms (Thorndon) Ltd. v. Catchpole*, [1977] E.G.D. 798 (Eng. C.A.). The common law also recognizes that a person with adequate possession for title may choose to use it intermittently or sporadically: *Keefer v. Arillotta* (1976), 13 O.R. (2d) 680 (C.A.), *per* Wilson J.A. Finally, the common law recognizes that exclusivity does not preclude consensual arrangements that recognize shared title to the same parcel of land: *Delgamuukw*, at para. 158.

[55] This review of the general principles underlying the issue of aboriginal title to land brings us to the specific requirements for title set out in *Delgamuukw*. To establish title, claimants must prove "exclusive" pre-sovereignty "occupation" of the land by their forebears: *per* Lamer C.J., at para. 143.

[56] "Occupation" means "physical occupation." This "may be established in a variety of ways, ranging from the construction of dwellings through cultivation and enclosure of fields to regular use of definite tracts of land for hunting, fishing or otherwise exploiting its resources": *Delgamuukw, per* Lamer C.J., at para. 149.

[57] "Exclusive" occupation flows from the definition of aboriginal title as "the right to *exclusive* use and occupation of land": *Delgamuukw, per* Lamer C.J., at para. 155 (emphasis in original). It is consistent with the concept of title to land at common law. Exclusive occupation means "the intention and capacity to retain exclusive control," and is not negated by occasional acts of trespass or the presence of other aboriginal groups with consent (*Delgamuukw*, at para. 156, citing McNeil, at p. 204). Shared exclusivity may result in joint title (para. 158). Non-exclusive occupation may establish aboriginal rights "short of title" (para. 159).

[58] It follows from the requirement of exclusive occupation that exploiting the land, rivers or seaside for hunting, fishing or other resources may translate into aboriginal title to the land if the activity was sufficiently regular and exclusive to comport with title at common law. However, more typically, seasonal hunting and fishing rights exercised in a particular area will translate to a hunting or fishing right. This is plain from this Court's decisions in *Van der Peet, Nikal, Adams* and *Côté*. In those cases, aboriginal peoples asserted and proved ancestral utilization of particular sites for fishing and harvesting the products of the sea. Their forebears had come back to the same place to fish or harvest each year since time immemorial. However, the season over, they left, and the land could be traversed and used by anyone. These facts gave rise not to aboriginal title, but to aboriginal hunting and fishing rights.

. . .

[60] In this case, the only claim is to title in the land. The issue therefore is whether the pre-sovereignty practices established on the evidence correspond to the right of title to land. These practices must be assessed from the aboriginal perspective. But, as discussed above, the right claimed also invokes the common law perspective. The question is whether the practices established by the evidence, viewed from the aboriginal perspective, correspond to the core of the common law right claimed.

[61] The common law, over the centuries, has formalized title through a complicated matrix of legal edicts and conventions. The search for aboriginal title, by contrast, takes us back to the beginnings of the notion of title. Unaided by formal legal documents and written edicts, we are required to consider whether the practices of aboriginal peoples at

the time of sovereignty compare with the core notions of common law title to land. It would be wrong to look for indicia of aboriginal title in deeds or Euro-centric assertions of ownership. Rather, we must look for the equivalent in the aboriginal culture at issue.

[62] Aboriginal societies were not strangers to the notions of exclusive physical possession equivalent to common law notions of title: *Delgamuukw*, at para. 156. They often exercised such control over their village sites and larger areas of land which they exploited for agriculture, hunting, fishing or gathering. The question is whether the evidence here establishes this sort of possession.

[63] Having laid out the broad picture, it may be useful to examine more closely three issues that evoked particular discussion here—what is meant by exclusion, or what I have referred to as exclusive control; whether nomadic and semi-nomadic peoples can ever claim title to land, as opposed to more restricted rights; and the requirement of continuity.

[64] The first of these sub-issues is the concept of exclusion. The right to control the land and, if necessary, to exclude others from using it is basic to the notion of title at common law. In European-based systems, this right is assumed by dint of law. Determining whether it was present in a pre-sovereignty aboriginal society, however, can pose difficulties. Often, no right to exclude arises by convention or law. So one must look to evidence. But evidence may be hard to find. The area may have been sparsely populated, with the result that clashes and the need to exclude strangers seldom if ever occurred. Or the people may have been peaceful and have chosen to exercise their control by sharing rather than exclusion. It is therefore critical to view the question of exclusion from the aboriginal perspective. ...

[65] It follows that evidence of acts of exclusion is not required to establish aboriginal title. All that is required is demonstration of effective control of the land by the group, from which a reasonable inference can be drawn that it could have excluded others had it chosen to do so. ...

[66] The second sub-issue is whether nomadic and semi-nomadic peoples can ever claim title to aboriginal land, as distinguished from rights to use the land in traditional ways. The answer is that it depends on the evidence. As noted above, possession at common law is a contextual, nuanced concept. Whether a nomadic people enjoyed sufficient "physical possession" to give them title to the land is a question of fact, depending on all the circumstances, in particular the nature of the land and the manner in which it is commonly used. Not every nomadic passage or use will ground title to land; thus this Court in *Adams* asserts that one of the reasons that aboriginal rights cannot be dependent on aboriginal title is that this would deny any aboriginal rights to nomadic peoples (para. 27). On the other hand, *Delgamuukw* contemplates that "physical occupation" sufficient to ground title to land may be established by "regular use of definite tracts of land for hunting, fishing or otherwise exploiting its resources" (para. 149). In each case, the question is whether a degree of physical occupation or use equivalent to common law title has been made out.

[67] The third sub-issue is continuity. The requirement of continuity in its most basic sense simply means that claimants must establish they are right holders. Modern-day claimants must establish a connection with the pre-sovereignty group upon whose practices they rely to assert title or claim to a more restricted aboriginal right. The right is based on pre-sovereignty aboriginal practices. To claim it, a modern people must show that the right is the descendant of those practices. Continuity may also be raised in this

sense. To claim title, the group's connection with the land must be shown to have been "of a central significance to their distinctive culture": *Adams*, at para. 26. If the group has "maintained a substantial connection" with the land since sovereignty, this establishes the required "central significance": *Delgamuukw, per* Lamer C.J., at paras. 150-51.

. . .

C. Application of the Legal Test

. . .

[72] The trial judge in each case applied the correct test to determine whether the respondents' claim to aboriginal title was established. In each case they required proof of sufficiently regular and exclusive use of the cutting sites by Mi'kmaq people at the time of assertion of sovereignty.

[73] In *Marshall*, Curran Prov. Ct. J. reviewed the authorities and concluded that the line separating sufficient and insufficient occupancy for title is between irregular use of undefined lands on the one hand and regular use of defined lands on the other. "Settlements constitute regular use of defined lands, but they are only one instance of it" (para. 141).

[74] In *Bernard*, Lordon Prov. Ct. J. likewise found that occasional visits to an area did not establish title; there must be "evidence of capacity to retain exclusive control" (para. 110) over the land claimed.

. . .

D. Assessment of the Evidence

[78] The question remains whether the trial judges, having applied essentially the right test, erred in their assessment of the evidence or application of the law to the evidence. ...

[79] Curran Prov. Ct. J. in *Marshall* reviewed the facts extensively and summarized his conclusions as follows:

a) The Mi'kmaq of 18th century Nova Scotia could be described as "moderately nomadic" as were the Algonquins in *Côté, supra*. The Mi'kmaq, too, moved with the seasons and circumstances to follow their resources. They did not necessarily return to the same campsites each year. Nevertheless, for decades before and after 1713 local communities on mainland Nova Scotia stayed generally in the areas where they had been.

b) On the mainland the Mi'kmaq made intensive use of bays and rivers and at least nearby hunting grounds. The evidence is just not clear about exactly where those lands were or how extensive they were. It is most unlikely all the mainland was included in those lands. There just weren't enough people for that.

c) As for Cape Breton, there simply is not enough evidence of where the Mi'kmaq were and how long they were there to conclude that they occupied any land to the extent required for aboriginal title.

d) In particular, there is no clear evidence that the Mi'kmaq of the time made any use, let alone regular use, of the cutting sites where these charges arose, either on the mainland or in Cape Breton. The [Respondents] have not satisfied me on

the balance of probability that their ancestors had aboriginal title to those sites.
[para. 142]

[80] Applying the law to these facts, Curran Prov. Ct. J. "concluded that the Mi'kmaq
of the 18th century on mainland Nova Scotia probably had aboriginal title to lands around
their local communities, but not to the cutting sites" (para. 143).

[A similar analysis was conducted by the lower court in *Bernard*.]

[83] I conclude that there is no ground to interfere with the trial judges' conclusions
on the absence of common law aboriginal title.

DISCUSSION NOTES

i. (Re)Thinking Delgamuukw?

As mentioned above, although the court was unanimous in its findings of guilt against the
appellants, the judges disagreed about what standard should be used for determining Aboriginal title. Writing about the disparity between the strong inclusion of Aboriginal perspectives in *Delgamuukw* and their limited inclusion in *Bernard; Marshall*, Kent McNeil used the
opinion of LeBel and Fish JJ to demonstrate how the court could better balance Aboriginal
traditions with the common law principles about title to land.

Kent McNeil, "Aboriginal Title and the Supreme Court: What's Happening?"
(2006) 69 Sask L Rev 281 at 303-4 (footnotes omitted)

Relying on passages from Lamer C.J.'s judgment in *Delgamuukw* that emphasized the *sui
generis* qualities of Aboriginal title, the relevance of Aboriginal law as a source of Aboriginal title, and the need to "give equal consideration to the aboriginal and common law
perspectives," LeBel J. stated that:

> Aboriginal conceptions of territoriality, land-use and property should be used to modify and
> adapt the traditional common law concepts of property in order to develop an occupancy
> standard that incorporates both the aboriginal and common law approaches. Otherwise, we
> might be implicitly accepting the position that aboriginal peoples had no right in land prior
> to the assertion of Crown sovereignty because their views of property or land use do not fit
> within Euro-centric conceptions of property rights (para. 127).

. . .

LeBel J. also took direct aim at McLachlin C.J.'s use of Aboriginal perspectives in a
limited way to assess Aboriginal practices in relation to land:

> The role of the aboriginal perspective cannot be simply to help in the interpretation of ab-
> original practices in order to assess whether they conform to common law concepts of title.
> The aboriginal perspective shapes the very concepts of aboriginal title. "Aboriginal law should
> not just be received as evidence that Aboriginal peoples did something in the past on a piece
> of land. It is more than evidence: it is actually law. And so, there should be some way to bring

to the decision-making process those laws that arise from the standards of the indigenous people before the court" (at para. 130, and quoting John Borrows, "Creating an Indigenous Legal Community" (2005), 50 *McGill Law Journal* 153, at 173).

This passage suggests as well that Aboriginal law is more than evidence of occupation and use of land. Law involves the exercise of jurisdiction, and when the law is in relation to land the jurisdiction is territorial. It is conceptually different from the site-specific physical occupation that the trial judges required and that McLachlin C.J. accepted as the appropriate standard. Disagreeing with the Chief Justice, LeBel J. said "[o]ccupation should therefore be proved by evidence not of regular and intensive use of the land but of the traditions and culture of the group that connect it with the land." For him, those traditions include "aboriginal conceptions of territoriality."

For additional perspectives on *Marshall* and *Bernard*, see (2006) 55 UNBLJ. Because the *Bernard* case involved a logging infraction in New Brunswick, the University of New Brunswick Law Journal dedicated this volume to interpreting the ruling through various disciplinary lenses: e.g. see Rusty Bittermann, "Mi'kmaq Land Claims and the Escheat Movement in Prince Edward Island" (at 172); a proposal for more effective adjudication of non-traditional forms of evidence in Shin Imai, "The Adjudication of Historical Evidence: A Comment and an Elaboration on a Proposal by Justice LeBel" (at 147); and an economic exploration of the Aboriginal and non-Aboriginal relationships promoted by the decision in Paul LAH Chartrand, "R v Marshall; R v Bernard: The Return of the Native" (at 133).

ii. Aboriginal Perspectives and the Common Law

As explained above in the discussion of the *Indian Act*, the differing views in the Supreme Court of Canada in *R v Marshall; R v Bernard* reveal how common law courts may not incorporate Aboriginal legal and cultural perspectives successfully. Because much of the disagreement among judges stems from their different understandings of Aboriginal conceptions of property and possession, these cases demonstrate that the necessity to include Aboriginal perspectives is more than an academic debate—indeed, it creates an ongoing struggle for reconciliation.

Scholars have suggested that it is important to frame this issue systemically, as opposed to assuming that problems arise solely from individual biases. For example, Linda Tuhiwai Smith argued that traditional Aboriginal "systems of order" came to be disregarded in law through a process of imperialism that negated indigenous humanity:

The fact that indigenous societies had their own systems of order was dismissed through what Albert Memmi referred to as a series of negations: they were not fully human, they were not civilized enough to have systems, they were not literate, their languages and modes of thought were inadequate. As [Frantz Fanon] and later writers such as [Ashis Nandy] have claimed, imperialism and colonialism brought complete disorder to colonized people, disconnecting them from their histories, their landscapes, their languages, their social relations and their own ways of thinking, feeling and interacting with the world. It was a process of systemic fragmentation which can still be seen in the disciplinary carve-up of the indigenous world: bones, mummies and skulls to the museum, art work to private collectors, languages to linguistics, "customs" to anthropologists, beliefs and behaviours to psychologists.

(See Linda Tuhiwai Smith, *Decolonizing Methodologies: Research and Indigenous Peoples* (London: Zed Books, 1999) at 28.)

Even with such a history and its persisting manifestations, however, some scholars continue to hope that a more thorough integration of common law and Aboriginal legal traditions may one day occur. John Borrows hesitantly cites s 35 as a possible guidepost for moving forward. However imperfect this jurisprudence may be, the courts are at least attempting to use First Nations' customs and concepts as a means of understanding how to institutionalize Aboriginal rights, particularly activity-specific rights. See Borrows, "With or Without You." For an analysis of the challenges and promises illustrated in s 35 jurisprudence, see Borrows, "Frozen Rights in Canada: Constitutional Interpretation and the Trickster" (1997) 22 Am Indian L Rev 37.

A more positive example in s 35 jurisprudence may have occurred in the reasoning of Bastarache J in the 2006 decision in *R v Sappier; R v Gray*, 2006 SCC 54, [2006] 2 SCR 686. In this case about Aboriginal logging rights in Atlantic Canada, the Supreme Court of Canada asserted that discussions about indigenous cultures and what makes them "distinct" (a necessary element of the test for demonstrating an activity-specific right) were inherently Eurocentric:

> [44] Culture, let alone "distinctive culture," has proven to be a difficult concept to grasp for Canadian courts. Moreover, the term "culture" as it is used in the English language may not find a perfect parallel in certain aboriginal languages. Barsh and Henderson note that "[w]e can find no precise equivalent of European concepts of 'culture' in Mi'kmaq, for example. How we maintain contact with our traditions is *tan'telo'tlieki-p*. How we perpetuate our consciousness is described as *tlilnuo'lti'k*. How we maintain our language is *tlinuita'sim*. Each of these terms connotes a process rather than a thing." Ultimately, the concept of culture is itself inherently cultural.

(Quoting RL Barsh & JY Henderson, "The Supreme Court's Van der Peet Trilogy: Naïve Imperialism and Ropes of Sand" (1997) 42 McGill LJ 993 at 1002, n 30.)

This approach also reflects past criticisms of the court's interaction with Aboriginal customs—most notably, in the dissenting opinions of Justice L'Heureux-Dubé and Justice McLachlin (as she was then) in *Van der Peet*. For a more thorough analysis of the changes in *Sappier*, see Constance MacIntosh, "Developments in Aboriginal Law: The 2006-2007 Term" (2007) 38 Sup Ct L Rev 1 at 18-37.

Scholars have also noted the willingness of some Aboriginal communities to integrate common law ideas and legal mechanisms into their own conceptions of law and justice. Although there continues to be resistance to any unilateral imposition of the Canadian justice system, these moments of voluntary, legal interplay may be a sign of the potential compatibility of competing legal systems. For example, in her analysis of British criminal law being introduced to the Canadian Prairies, Shelley Gavigan identified the continuing acceptance of certain common law ideas within Aboriginal legal systems:

> Contemporary Aboriginal legal scholars remind us of the importance of language in expressing and understanding different approaches to and concepts of justice, not least when one speaks of Aboriginal law or Aboriginal criminal law. *Mens rea* (the mental element, or guilty mind), so important, if imprecise and contested, in contemporary criminal law principles, appears not to

have been a prominent or even essential element of Aboriginal law. Some forms of harm that are central to Canadian criminal law norms formed no part of Aboriginal law; other forms, central to Aboriginal law, formed no part of Canadian criminal law. We are told that there are no indigenous words for criminal law concepts such as "guilty." Nonetheless, Freda Ahenakew and her colleagues have found that "pleading guilty has become so accepted by Aboriginal people ... it has become part of [contemporary] folklore."

(See Gavigan at 111-12.) In reviewing the cases and materials that follow, note the ways in which courts take account of Aboriginal legal perspectives, particularly with respect to issues about claims to land.

B. William v British Columbia: "Definite Tracts of Land"?

William v British Columbia, 2012 BCCA 285, [2012] 3 CNLR 333 involved an appeal from a ruling, based on a defect in the pleadings, that a declaration of Aboriginal title over a large area of central British Columbia could not be issued in favour of various bands from the Tsilhqot'in First Nation, despite the fact that the trial judge was of the opinion that they had proven title to a portion of the claim area. Starting with forestry licences being granted in the disputed area during the early 1980s, these historically semi-nomadic Aboriginal communities engaged in a long series of legal actions and blockades to stop logging from taking place in their traditional territory (paras 10-24). At trial, the *William* case took almost five years and resulted in a 400-page judgment calling on the federal and provincial governments and the Aboriginal communities to negotiate an "honourable settlement" (para 27). After a couple of years of failed negotiations, the appeal of the trial decision proceeded to the BC Court of Appeal.

The trial judge had granted a declaration that the communities had an Aboriginal right to fish and hunt on the lands in question, but had refused a declaration of Aboriginal title to the claim area because the case had been pleaded as an all-or-nothing claim to the entire area, whereas title had only been established on the evidence to a portion of that area. Although the BC Court of Appeal also dealt with appeals from the BC government concerning Aboriginal rights, the following extract from the decision focuses on the First Nation's appeal of the trial judge's decision on Aboriginal title. Notice how the Court of Appeal attempts to reconcile common law conceptions of possession with the goal of s 35 of the Constitution to achieve a compromise for Aboriginal and non-Aboriginal communities.

William v British Columbia

2012 BCCA 285, [2012] 3 CNLR 333

[1] These appeals concern the Aboriginal rights, including Aboriginal title, of the Xeni Gwet'in and the Tsilhqot'in First Nation in an area comprising approximately 438,000 ha. (4,380 km^2) in the Chilcotin region of the west central interior of British Columbia.

. . .

C. Canadian Law of Aboriginal Title

. . .

[182] The decision of the majority in *Van der Peet* marks the beginning of the Supreme Court of Canada's construction of a modern comprehensive framework dealing with Aboriginal rights and Aboriginal title. It defined the basic requirements for recognition of an Aboriginal right. The construction of the framework was further advanced in *R. v. Adams*, [1996] 3 S.C.R. 101, and *R. v. Côté*, [1996] 3 S.C.R. 139, which considered whether land-based Aboriginal rights could exist in places where claims to Aboriginal title could not be made out. The Court affirmed that they could.

. . .

[186] *Adams* stands for the proposition that traditional use of land will not necessarily found a claim to Aboriginal title—it may, instead, found an Aboriginal right to continue to use the land for specific activities or purposes. As the law recognized that usufructuary rights could be divorced from title, the rationale for describing Aboriginal title as being "usufructuary" in nature ceased to exist. I agree with the trial judge's conclusion, at para. 478, that it is no longer correct to describe Aboriginal title in this way.

[187] The Supreme Court of Canada first attempted a comprehensive discussion of Aboriginal title in *Delgamuukw*. Lamer C.J.C., speaking for the majority, described Aboriginal title as follows:

> [111] … Aboriginal title is a right in land and, as such, is more than the right to engage in specific activities which may be themselves aboriginal rights. Rather, it confers the right to use land for a variety of activities, not all of which need be aspects of practices, customs and traditions which are integral to the distinctive cultures of aboriginal societies. Those activities do not constitute the right per se; rather, they are parasitic on the underlying title. However, that range of uses is subject to the limitation that they must not be irreconcilable with the nature of the attachment to the land which forms the basis of the particular group's aboriginal title. This inherent limit … flows from the definition of aboriginal title as a *sui generis* interest in land, and is one way in which aboriginal title is distinct from a fee simple.

[188] Referring back to *Adams*, he considered the relationship between Aboriginal rights and Aboriginal title:

> [137] … [A]lthough aboriginal title is a species of aboriginal right recognized and affirmed by s. 35(1), it is distinct from other aboriginal rights because it arises where the connection of a group with a piece of land "was of a central significance to their distinctive culture" [citing para 26 of *Adams*].
>
> [138] The picture which emerges from *Adams* is that the aboriginal rights which are recognized and affirmed by s. 35(1) fall along a spectrum with respect to their degree of connection with the land. At the one end, there are those aboriginal rights which are practices, customs and traditions that are integral to the distinctive aboriginal culture of the group claiming the right. However, the *"occupation and use of the land"* where the activity is taking place is not *"sufficient to support a claim of title to the land"* [citing para 26 of *Adams*; emphasis in *Adams*]. Nevertheless, those activities receive constitutional protection. In the middle, there are activities which, out of necessity, take place on land and indeed, might be intimately related to a particular piece of land. Although an aboriginal group may not be able to demonstrate title to the land, it may nevertheless have a site-specific right to engage in a particular activity. … [Emphasis in original.]

[191] For the purposes of the present case, the question is what degree of occupation suffices to found a claim for Aboriginal title. There is some discussion of this question in *Delgamuukw* beginning at para. 149:

> [149] … Physical occupation may be established in a variety of ways, ranging from the construction of dwellings through cultivation and enclosure of fields to regular use of definite tracts of land for hunting, fishing or otherwise exploiting its resources: see McNeil, *Common Law Aboriginal Title*, at pp. 201-2. In considering whether occupation sufficient to ground title is established, "one must take into account the group's size, manner of life, material resources, and technological abilities, and the character of the lands claimed": Brian Slattery, "Understanding Aboriginal Rights," at p. 758.

[192] After discussing the requirement that occupancy be exclusive, the majority judgment concluded by noting that non-exclusive occupation can found rights other than Aboriginal title:

> [159] I should also reiterate that if aboriginals can show that they occupied a particular piece of land, but did not do so exclusively, it will always be possible to establish aboriginal rights short of title. These rights will likely be intimately tied to the land and may permit a number of possible uses. However, unlike title, they are not a right to the land itself. Rather, as I have suggested, they are a right to do certain things in connection with that land. If, for example, it were established that the lands near those subject to a title claim were used for hunting by a number of bands, those shared lands would not be subject to a claim for aboriginal title, as they lack the crucial element of exclusivity. However, they may be subject to site-specific aboriginal rights by all of the bands who used it. This does not entitle anyone to the land itself, but it may entitle all of the bands who hunted on the land to hunting rights.

[193] The Supreme Court further considered the issue of Aboriginal title in its judgment in *Marshall; Bernard* … . Technically, the title issue in each case only concerned the tract of land from which the logs had been cut. In asserting title, however, the defendants in each case contended that the relevant tract of land was, in fact, part of a large territory over which the Mi'kmaq held title.

· · ·

[197] The Supreme Court of Canada heard the two cases together. In both, it reinstated the convictions entered by the trial courts. McLachlin C.J.C., writing for the majority, began her discussion of the issue of common law Aboriginal title by referring to *Delgamuukw*. At para. 40 she noted that while *Delgamuukw* had established general principles governing proof of Aboriginal title, it had left many of the details to be developed in subsequent cases, including what level of occupation was necessary to found a claim to title.

[198] At para. 54, she held that in order to establish Aboriginal title, the claimant must demonstrate "possession similar to that associated with title at common law." She noted that that level of possession depends on all of the circumstances, including "the nature of the land and the manner in which the land is commonly enjoyed" as well as the actual nature of the occupation.

· · ·

[201] McLachlin C.J.C. summarized her legal conclusions at para. 70:

[70] In summary, exclusive possession in the sense of intention and capacity to control is required to establish aboriginal title. Typically, this is established by showing regular occupancy or use of definite tracts of land for hunting, fishing or exploiting resources: *Delgamuukw*, at para. 149. Less intensive uses may give rise to different rights. The requirement of physical occupation must be generously interpreted taking into account both the aboriginal perspective and the perspective of the common law: *Delgamuukw*, at para. 156. These principles apply to nomadic and semi-nomadic aboriginal groups; the right in each case depends on what the evidence establishes. Continuity is required, in the sense of showing the group's descent from the pre-sovereignty group whose practices are relied on for the right. On all these matters, evidence of oral history is admissible, provided it meets the requisite standards of usefulness and reasonable reliability. The ultimate goal is to translate the pre-sovereignty aboriginal right to a modern common law right. This must be approached with sensitivity to the aboriginal perspective as well as fidelity to the common law concepts involved.

[202] She found that, in each case, the trial judge had applied the correct test of Aboriginal title. While the trial decision in *Bernard* had turned in large measure on the question of whether occupation had been exclusive, the decision in *Marshall* had not. In his reasons for judgment in *R. v. Marshall*, 2001 NSPC 2, 191 N.S.R. (2d) 323, Curran P.C.J. specifically indicated that to the extent there was occupation, it was exclusive:

[137] The question of exclusiveness really does not arise in this case. There was no other aboriginal group in Nova Scotia in 1713 or 1763. On the mainland in 1713 there were a few Acadian enclaves and one small British outpost. In Cape Breton between the fall of Louisbourg and 1763 there was one small French community and some scattered French settlers. There is no reason to believe there was any European on any of the cutting sites, or for that matter on most of the mainland or in most of Cape Breton, at the relevant times. That leaves the question of occupancy.

[203] His analysis of the issue of sufficiency of occupation was as follows:

[139] The problem for the defendant is that mere occupancy of land does not necessarily establish aboriginal title: (See *Delgamuukw*, supra, at paragraph 138, where Lamer C.J. commented on *R. v. Adams*, [1996] 3 S.C.R. 101). If an aboriginal group has used lands only for certain limited activities and not intensively, the group might have an aboriginal right to carry on those activities, but it doesn't have title.

[140] The Supreme Court considered the question of sufficient occupancy for aboriginal title in *R. v. Côté*, supra. In paragraph 60 Lamer C.J. said, for the majority, that the superior court judge who heard the first appeal in the case had "made a finding of fact which was directed at the proper question before the court." The question was whether the ancestors of the appellants, the Algonquins, had "exercised sufficient occupancy" to prove aboriginal title. According to the evidence, the Algonquins were "a moderately nomadic people who settled only temporarily and moved frequently within the area of the Ottawa River basin." Their habits were the result of "the presence and movements of their sources of sustenance, ... governed by the changes of the seasons." Although the judge had found that the Algonquins frequented the territory at the relevant time, he decided that "in light of the itinerant hunting patterns and the thin population of the Algonquins" they had not "exercised real and exclusive possession" of the territory.

[141] … In paragraph 149 [of *Delgamuukw*] the Chief Justice referred to the book *Common Law Aboriginal Title* by Professor Kent McNeil and said:

> Professor McNeil has convincingly argued that at common law, the fact of physical occupation is proof of possession at law, which in turn will ground title to the land. … Physical occupation may be established in a variety of ways, ranging from the construction of dwellings through cultivation and enclosures of fields to regular use of definite tracts of land for hunting, fishing or otherwise exploiting its resources. …
>
> The line separating sufficient and insufficient occupancy for title seems to be between nomadic and irregular use of undefined lands on the one hand and regular use of defined lands on the other. Settlements constitute regular use of defined lands, but they are only one instance of it. There is no persuasive evidence that the Mi'kmaq used the cutting sites at all, let alone regularly.

[204] At paras. 73 and 75 of her reasons, McLachlin C.J.C. accepted this analysis as being correct in law, and quoted from it with approval.

D. Analysis

. . .

[206] In his argument, the plaintiff often treats the concept of "occupation" as if it is synonymous with "presence in the territory." He rejects the idea that proof of title depends on showing any intensive or regular use of specific plots of land. Rather, he says that proof that the Tsilhqot'in were present in the region and that there was a degree of exclusivity to that presence suffices to found a title claim. He points to the defendants' concession that the Tsilhqot'in were present in Tachelach'ed and the Trapline Territory in 1846, and to the judge's findings of fact to the effect that the Tsilhqot'in did, in fact, enjoy effective exclusive occupancy.

[207] To buttress his contention that the key criterion for a title claim is exclusivity of occupation, the plaintiff points to para. 159 of *Delgamuukw*, quoted above, arguing that only a lack of exclusivity will prevent a claim to land-based Aboriginal rights from being a claim to Aboriginal title.

. . .

[209] The plaintiff rejects the defendants' characterization of his claim as a "territorial" one. He points out that the Claim Area represents only a fraction of the traditional territory of the Tsilhqot'in. He also notes that the Claim Area is significantly smaller than the areas over which title was asserted in *Marshall* and *Bernard*.

[210] As at trial, the plaintiff emphasizes the semi-nomadic traditions of the Tsilhqot'in, and argues that requiring such a group to demonstrate intensive regular use of well-defined areas of land is to take a "postage stamp" approach to title. Such an approach, he contends, fails to give effect to the Aboriginal perspective from which the Tsilhqot'in claim arises.

[211] The defendants say that a claim to Aboriginal title can only be made out where definite boundaries can be established, and where there has been intensive occupation of a particular area. They emphasize Lamer C.J.C.'s comments in *Adams* and *Delgamuukw* doubting the ability of nomadic groups to prove title. They also place considerable weight on the examples of title land given at para. 149 of *Delgamuukw*: dwellings, cultivated areas,

enclosed fields, and definite tracts of land used for hunting, fishing, or other resource exploitation.

[212] The defendants also refer to passages from *Marshall; Bernard* that speak of a correspondence between the nature of the occupancy necessary to found an Aboriginal title claim and the common law requirements for title by virtue of possession.

. . .

[214] As I indicated when discussing the question of whether the claim in this case is an "all or nothing claim," I accept the defendants' characterization of the claim as being a "territorial" one. The plaintiff does not suggest that the Tsilhqot'in physically occupied the entire Claim Area, either at all times or seasonally. Rather, he says that they lived in various encampments in the Claim Area at different times, some of which have been identified. They hunted, trapped and fished at various places, some of which are in the Claim Area. On a seasonal basis, groups would transit over trails covering most regions of the Claim Area. He says that this type of presence in the Claim Area amounts to "occupation" for the purpose of claiming title, and allows a claim to title over the territory.

[215] Except in respect of a few specific sites, the evidence did not establish regular presence on or intensive occupation of particular tracts of land within the Claim Area. There were no permanent village sites, though there was evidence of encampments and wintering sites, including groupings of pit houses. Even among these, the evidence did not strongly point to occupation of particular sites in the period around 1846 except in three or four cases.

[216] The Tsilhqot'in did not cultivate or enclose fields. While they did hunt and fish in many parts of the Claim Area, there are only a few sites (primarily fishing sites) that can be said to be specifically delineated in the evidence. Only a few locations were referred to which may have been used intensively. As the defendants contend, the evidence and findings suggest that hunting, trapping and fishing occurred at many places in the Claim Area, more or less on an opportunistic basis. Gathering activities also appear to have been widespread, although the findings of fact suggest that some localized spots may exist where natural plants were harvested and, to a limited extent, managed.

[217] As I see it, the claim can only be described as being a "territorial" one rather than a site-specific claim to title. The fact that the territory being claimed, large as it is, is a fraction of the total area alleged to be the traditional territory of the Tsilhqot'in does not prevent the claim from being characterized in this way.

[218] Indeed, the plaintiff's often repeated statement that the Tsilhqot'in did not lead a "postage stamp" existence underlines the territorial nature of the claim—with a few exceptions, there are no definite tracts of land that were habitually occupied by the Tsilhqot'in at and around 1846.

[219] I also agree with the defendants that a territorial claim for Aboriginal title does not meet the tests in *Delgamuukw* and in *Marshall; Bernard*. Further, as I will attempt to explain, I do not see a broad territorial claim as fitting within the purposes behind s. 35 of the *Constitution Act, 1982* or the rationale for the common law's recognition of Aboriginal title. Finally, I see broad territorial claims to title as antithetical to the goal of reconciliation, which demands that, so far as possible, the traditional rights of First Nations be fully respected without placing unnecessary limitations on the sovereignty of the Crown or on the aspirations of all Canadians, Aboriginal and non-Aboriginal.

[220] As I read *Delgamuukw*, Aboriginal title cannot generally be proven on a territorial basis, even if there is some evidence showing that the claimant was the only group in a region or that it attempted to exclude outsiders from what it considered to be its traditional territory. I acknowledge that *Delgamuukw* did not fully address the quality of occupancy that was necessary to support a title claim, apart from indicating that the occupancy must have been exclusive. That said, several passages in *Delgamuukw* strongly suggest that an intensive presence at a particular site was what the Court had in mind.

[221] In particular, I note that the examples of title lands given at para. 149 of *Delgamuukw* are well-defined, intensively used areas. The reference to hunting, fishing and other resource extraction activities is coupled with a specific description of the lands so used as "definite" tracts of land. I agree with British Columbia's assertion that what was contemplated were specific sites on which hunting, fishing, or resource extraction activities took place on a regular and intensive basis. Examples might include salt licks, narrow defiles between mountains and cliffs, particular rocks or promontories used for netting salmon, or, in other areas of the country, buffalo jumps.

[222] The Court's specific references to the difficulty that nomadic peoples might face in proving title is also telling. While, as the Court pointed out in *Marshall; Bernard*, there is no reason that semi-nomadic or nomadic groups would be disqualified from proving title, their traditional use of land will often have included large regions in which they did not have an adequate regular presence to support a title claim. That is not to say, of course, that such groups will be unable to prove title to specific sites within their traditional territories.

. . .

[224] *Marshall; Bernard*, as I read it, is even stronger in showing that Aboriginal title must be demonstrated on a site-specific rather than territorial basis. The majority expressly dealt with the question of whether hunting or fishing or the taking of other resources from land could found a title claim. At para. 58, it agreed that such activities could, where they were sufficiently regular and exclusive, be a basis for title. It also cautioned, however, that more typically, such activities will found only claims to specific Aboriginal rights.

[225] The majority's equation of sufficient occupancy for Aboriginal title with the common law requirements to show title by virtue of possession is also important. It supports the views that title must be claimed on a site-specific basis, and that a certain regularity and intensity of presence is needed before it will count as "occupancy."

. . .

[230] As I have discussed, the case law does not support the idea that title can be proven based on a limited presence in a broad territory. Rather, as I read the jurisprudence, Aboriginal title must be proven on a site-specific basis. A title site may be defined by a particular occupancy of the land (e.g., village sites, enclosed or cultivated fields) or on the basis that definite tracts of land were the subject of intensive use (specific hunting, fishing, gathering, or spiritual sites). In all cases, however, Aboriginal title can only be proven over a definite tract of land the boundaries of which are reasonably capable of definition.

[231] The limitation of Aboriginal title to definite tracts of land is fully in keeping with the purpose of s. 35 of the *Constitution Act, 1982* and the rationale for common law recognition of Aboriginal rights and title. In order for an Aboriginal group to preserve

its culture and allow members of the group to pursue a traditional lifestyle, it is necessary for the group to have exclusive possession of those places that it traditionally occupied on a regular and intensive basis. The group must be given the opportunity to live where it lived traditionally, and to continue to use the land that it cultivated or intensively took resources from.

[232]   I do not doubt that the culture and traditions of a semi-nomadic group, like the Tsilhqot'in, depend on rights to use lands that extend well beyond the definite tracts that may be found to be subject to Aboriginal title. The Tsilhqot'in must be able to continue hunting and fishing throughout their traditional territory, and to have the right to pass and re-pass over the trails that they have used for hundreds of years. There will be other specific rights that must be recognized in order to preserve the rich traditions of the Tsilhqot'in people. It is not at all clear to me, however, that Tsilhqot'in culture and traditions cannot be fully respected without recognizing Aboriginal title over all of the land on which they roamed.

DISCUSSION NOTES

i. Rethinking "Sites" in Relation to Aboriginal Rights and Aboriginal Title to Land

The Supreme Court of Canada granted leave to appeal the decision in *Tsilhqot'in* in January 2013 (*William v BC*, [2012] SCCA no 339). In thinking about the arguments to be presented in the Supreme Court, consider the following critique of the decision of the BC Court of Appeal.

Douglas Lambert, "The Tsilhqot'in Case"
(2012) 70 Advocate 819 (footnotes omitted) at 819, 823-25

The reasons for judgment in *William v British Columbia* were given by the Court of Appeal on June 27, 2012, more than a year and a half after judgment was reserved. If the decision were correct, it would tilt the economic balance so far against First Nations that consultation would be virtually meaningless, accommodation an empty gesture, justification for infringement a trivial token, and the treaty process an expensive sham. However, I believe the decision is wrong. I propose to set out in this article my reasons for that conclusion. …

Site-Specific Title and Site-Specific Rights

The reasons of the Court of Appeal require that aboriginal title be required to be site-specific. This is the first time the concept of site-specificity has been applied to aboriginal title, though it is a familiar concept in relation to some aboriginal rights.

What the Supreme Court of Canada has said is that aboriginal title is held only over definite tracts of land which were, before 1846, occupied exclusively by the First Nation claiming them. The requirement that the tracts be definite is of course essential. Everyone must know at the end of a treaty process, a resource sharing agreement or a Court decision, what the boundaries are between the land the First Nation is entitled to control and the land it is not entitled to control. But the requirement that a tract of land be definite is not a requirement that it be tiny.

The concept of site-specificity is a concept about aboriginal rights and not about aboriginal title. It was clearly explained by Chief Justice Lamer in *Delgamuukw* (particularly at para. 159) and has been consistently applied in aboriginal rights jurisprudence. Where an aboriginal group cannot show general occupation of an area or cannot show that their use and presence in that area was exclusive, they may still show that they used a particular site for a regular, sometimes seasonal, practice and that it was integral to their distinctive culture to do so. Such sites may not be surrounded by aboriginal title land or widespread aboriginal rights land, but they may nonetheless ground a claim to a site-specific aboriginal right. A promontory where a fisherman can stand to net or gaff salmon may serve as an example.

The Court of Appeal reasons, at para. 221, refer to *Delgamuukw* at para. 149, where Chief Justice Lamer speaks of aboriginal title over "definite" tracts of land. The Court of Appeal reasons, but not Chief Justice Lamer's reasons, go on to conflate "definite tracts" with "specific sites" where hunting, fishing and resource extraction activities took place on a regular and intensive basis. The Court of Appeal, but not the Supreme Court of Canada, would then limit aboriginal title to such specific sites. The reasons of the Court of Appeal give examples of such lands as "salt licks, narrow defiles, rocks or promontories used for netting salmon or, in other areas of the country, buffalo jumps." Those examples are all examples of places where site-specific aboriginal rights could be located and exercised. But they are not examples of definite tracts of land occupied exclusively by an aboriginal people. A buffalo jump may be on aboriginal title land. But no one would think of it as being occupied exclusively as a buffalo jump by that aboriginal people. Now that the buffalo hunt is gone, do you show your continuity of occupation and your enjoyment of title at the top of the jump or at the bottom?

To think of aboriginal title as site-specific in the sense that the term has been used in aboriginal rights jurisprudence is simply wrong. And it is not a proposition derivable from the use of the phrase "definite tracts of land" by the Supreme Court of Canada.

The *Haida* case is illustrative of this point. The Haida Nation objected to the transfer without consultation of Tree Farm Licence 39, which covered spruce, hemlock and cedar forests on 241,000 hectares, about a quarter of Haida Gwaii. The chambers judge reached conclusions about the probability and possibility of aboriginal title being established to that forest land. Chief Justice McLachlin, for a unanimous Supreme Court of Canada, described the Haida title claim in these words, at para. 7: "*The Haida's claim to title to Haida Gwaii is strong, as found by the chambers judge.* But it is also complex and will take many years to prove" [emphasis added]. None of the members of the Supreme Court of Canada mentioned that aboriginal title is site-specific and confined to village sites and buffalo jumps. Had title been so limited, it would clearly have affected the court's opinion on consultation and on striving for accommodation. The reason why the court didn't mention it is because it simply isn't so.

ii. The Duty to Consult with First Nations

One of the most important developments in Aboriginal jurisprudence in the early 21st century has been the recognition of a "duty to consult" First Nations. First articulated in *Haida*

Nation v British Columbia (Minister of Forests), 2004 SCC 73, [2004] 3 SCR 511, the duty to consult requires the Crown to consult with and sometimes accommodate First Nations when actions of government or third parties may adversely affect Aboriginal interests in land. Though *Delgamuukw* identified a need for consultation in relation to projects that would affect established claims of Aboriginal title, consultation is required even when the Aboriginal community has not established title or activity-specific rights over the land in question. By assessing the *prima facie* case for Aboriginal title or rights, alongside the potential of harm that could arise from the actions of government or a third party, the court will determine what level of consultation is necessary for the Honour of the Crown to be upheld. Although *Taku River Tlingit First Nation v British Columbia (Project Assessment Director)*, 2004 SCC 74, [2004] 3 SCR 550 confirmed that the duty to consult does not result in a *de facto* veto for Aboriginal communities, the consultations necessary to fulfill this legal obligation may range from simply informing the community of the proposed plans to accommodating the community's interests throughout the life of the project.

For instance, *Haida Nation* involved logging activities on Haida Gwaii, a series of British Columbian islands claimed by the Aboriginal community as their traditional territory. Considering the strong case that the community could make for having their title to the land recognized, as well as the importance of red cedar to their culture, the Supreme Court of Canada therefore held that there was a strong need for consultation and accommodation in this conflict.

A year after the decision in *Haida Nation*, the Supreme Court extended the duty to consult First Nations not only for lands subject to Aboriginal rights and title claims but also to lands subject to treaty rights. In *Mikisew Cree First Nation v Canada (Minister of Canadian Heritage)*, 2005 SCC 69, [2005] 3 SCR 388, the court ordered the Canadian government to consult with the Mikisew Cree in relation to the construction of a winter road in an area of Wood Buffalo National Park that was subject to this First Nation's treaty rights to hunt, trap, and fish.

The jurisprudence surrounding the duty to consult continues to evolve. For example, the Ontario Court of Appeal recently overturned a decision of the Superior Court that would have required the province to work with the federal government when consulting indigenous peoples over treaty lands in Ontario (*Keewatin v Ontario (Natural Resources)*, 2013 ONCA 158). There was no debate over the province's legal obligation to conduct consultations with First Nations communities, but this decision clarified the necessary extent of these consultations by finding that "Ontario is not subject to federal supervision in carrying out its obligations" (at para 212). In *Behn v Moulton Contracting Ltd*, 2013 SCC 26, the broad doctrine of *Haida Nation* may have been diminished. In this case, the Supreme Court of Canada held that a group of individual members of the Fort Nelson First Nation could not order the Crown to fulfill its duty to consult after they had first blockaded a road leading to a disputed logging site. The court concluded that such a process of "self-help," followed by legal actions, amounted to an "abuse of process" (para 42). However, some questions remain after this decision, including whether the same outcome would have resulted if the plaintiffs had acted on behalf of the larger community—for example, had the band council held a democratic vote to decide whether to blockade the road.

Even in light of these recent clarifications, cases like *Wahgoshig First Nation v Ontario*, 2011 ONSC 7708 reveal the power of the legal duty to consult. In the context of a proposed gold mine on treaty lands, the Superior Court of Justice issued an injunction against a mining company to enforce the duty to consult that had apparently been delegated by the province of Ontario to the company. The mining company then attempted to appeal the order for an injunction, but new amendments to the *Mining Act* concerning consultation with Aboriginal communities caused the court to declare the matter moot (*Wahgoshig First Nation v Solid Gold Resources Corp*, 2013 ONSC 632). For one analysis of the duty to consult First Nations, see Dwight G Newman, *The Duty to Consult* (Saskatoon: Purich, 2009).

IV. TOWARD THE FUTURE: "WE ARE ALL TREATY PEOPLE"

As recent litigation about Aboriginal title to land reveals, there have been some significant developments in recent years in the courts. In addition, treaty negotiations have continued in several parts of Canada. In this context, it may be useful to reflect on fundamental issues at stake in the recognition of Aboriginal title to land. In the words of former Governor General of Canada Adrienne Clarkson:

> I recall again here that the treaty ends by stating that this bond "will hold as long as the sun shines, the rivers flow and the grass grows." Those treaties were entered into in good faith by the native peoples. I would like us, who came later, who live those treaties, to honour them. I believe that we will not be able to continue to deal with difference in our country until we have honestly dealt with the original promise to our Aboriginal peoples. …
>
> In every province, if you ask children in a class where there are Aboriginal children to identify themselves as treaty people, only those who are of native origin will put up their hands. *In fact, we are all treaty people because it takes two sides to make a treaty, and that's what we agreed to do.*

(See Adrienne Clarkson, "The Society of Difference" (Paper delivered at the 8th Annual LaFontaine-Baldwin Lecture, Vancouver, 2 March 2007) at 28, online: Institute for Canadian Citizenship <http://www.icc-icc.ca/en/lbs/docs/AdrienneClarkson-ASocietyofDifference8th LaFontaine-BaldwinLectureMarch22007.pdf>.) See also Borrows, *Canada's Indigenous Constitution*.

A. "Aboriginal" Status and the Métis: Recent Developments

Issues about Métis have become more significant in recent years. For example, in *R v Powley*, 2003 SCC 43, [2003] 2 SCR 207, the court applied s 35 of the Constitution to uphold the acquittal of Steve Powley and his son Roddy, members of the Métis community in Sault Ste Marie, Ontario who had been charged with hunting unlawfully. In applying the constitutional protection set out in *Van der Peet* for "Indian" communities, the court held that it was necessary in this case to establish an identifiable historic and contemporary Métis community with shared customs, traditions, and a collective identity, requirements that were met in *Powley* in relation to the Métis community in the area of Sault Ste Marie.

Furthermore, although s 35 of the *Constitution Act, 1982* specifically mentions Métis peoples within its definition of "Aboriginal peoples of Canada," a recent decision from the Federal Court suggests that the Métis may be included under the definition of Aboriginal peoples in the *Constitution Act, 1867* as well. For years, the federal government stated that the term "Indians" within s 91(24) did not include the Métis. This assertion allowed both the federal and the provincial officials to pass responsibility for Métis communities from one level of government to the other.

However, in *Daniels v Canada (Minister of Indian Affairs and Northern Development)*, 2013 FC 6, 223 ACWS (3d) 910, the Federal Court declared that the term "Indians" was not limited to status Indians, but that the federal government had jurisdiction over Métis and non-status Indians as well. Looking to the Supreme Court's decision that recognized Inuit peoples under s 91(24), *In re Eskimos Reference*, [1939] SCR 104, the court recognized the original purpose of the so-called Indian Power as being the control of indigenous populations during the British expansion into Western Canada (para 566). By citing the government's historical responsibility, this declaration was seen by the court as moving toward "a further level of respect and reconciliation by removing the constitutional uncertainty surrounding these groups" (para 568). The federal government has expressed its desire to appeal this decision to the Federal Court of Appeal (Aboriginal Affairs and Northern Development Canada, Media Release, "Statement from Minister Duncan Regarding Canada's Appeal of the Federal Court's Decision in Daniels v Canada" (6 February 2013), online: Market Wired News Room <http://www.marketwire .com/press-release/statement-from-minister-duncan-regarding-canadas-appeal-federal-courts-decision-daniels-1753995.htm>. Clearly, the outcome of this decision may result in some principles regarding Aboriginal title to land becoming applicable to Métis communities in the future.

Another significant development for Métis land rights is the recent case of *Manitoba Metis Federation Inc v Canada (Attorney General)*, 2013 SCC 14. Involving clauses of the *Manitoba Act, 1870*, SC 1870, c 3—that is, the statute used by the federal government to create the province of Manitoba—the Manitoba Métis Federation claimed that the federal government promised its people grants of land in s 31 of the Act, but reneged on that promise. Instead, these plots were scooped up by early, westward settlers, an issue that was only exacerbated by persistent government inaction. The applicants therefore sought a declaration stating that the federal Crown owed them a fiduciary duty because of the *Manitoba Act*, and that this duty had been breached. They also sought a declaration that the federal government had acted in a manner inconsistent with the Honour of the Crown when it was managing the lands that had been promised to their ancestors. Both of these claims were denied by the courts of Manitoba.

When the case reached the Supreme Court of Canada, the court concluded that the *Manitoba Act* had not created a fiduciary duty for the Crown in relation to the Métis. Essentially, the unique Aboriginal–Crown relationship outlined in *Guerin*—that is, the Crown undertakes a fiduciary obligation in dealing with a recognized Aboriginal interest—was not present during the drafting of the Act, because Métis conceptions of land did not adhere to the *sui generis* conception of Aboriginal title—for example, the Métis did not live communally. The court also held that a more traditional, equitable conception of the fiduciary duty did not even apply, because the relationship between the Crown and the Métis was directed toward the best interests of colonial expansion, as opposed to the best interests of the Métis community.

However, a majority of the court held that the continuing disregard for the promises in the Act constituted a violation of the Honour of the Crown, because s 31 of the *Manitoba Act* invoked the kind of solemn promises that engage the Honour of the Crown. The court clarified (at para 82) that not every violation of a solemn promise between an Aboriginal community and a non-Aboriginal government will put the Honour of the Crown at risk, but government officials who persistently fail to fulfill such promises diligently put this Honour in peril:

Not every mistake or negligent act in implementing a constitutional obligation to an Aboriginal people brings dishonour to the Crown. Implementation, in the way of human affairs, may be imperfect. However, a persistent pattern of errors and indifference that substantially frustrates the purposes of a solemn promise may amount to a betrayal of the Crown's duty to act honourably in fulfilling its promise.

The minority argued that any government violation (whether a fiduciary duty or solemn promise) was moot in light of statutory limitation periods and the equitable concept of laches. However, the majority rejected these arguments, citing the judiciary's role as protector of the Constitution's supremacy. Because the *Manitoba Act* comprises a part of Canada's constitutional documents (*Constitution Act, 1982* being Schedule B to the *Canada Act 1982* (UK), 1982, c 11, s 52(2)), the constitutional obligation of the Crown to fulfill solemn promises negates the effect of these statutory and equitable restrictions.

This judgment has changed the balance of power between Métis populations and the Crown, because it allows the Métis to invoke the Honour of the Crown during land negotiations. Even though Métis communities are unable to invoke the kind of fiduciary duty that governs the relationship between the Crown and other Aboriginal groups, this new constitutional obligation suggests the need for future developments to confront the unique historical circumstances and struggles of Métis peoples.

B. Aboriginal Title in a Commonwealth Context

Canada is not the only nation in which settlement has proceeded in indigenous territories, and thus it is not the only country to face conflicting property claims from Aboriginal and non-Aboriginal communities. To some extent, Canada and Australia share a similar history, and some Australian scholars have called for the Australian constitution to be amended to include a Canadian-style entrenchment of Aboriginal and treaty rights: see Margaret Stephenson, "Indigenous Lands and Constitutional Reform in Australia: A Canadian Comparison" (2011) 15:2 Austl Indigenous L Rev 87.

In *Mabo v Queensland*, [1992] 66 ALJR 408 (HC), the Australian High Court overturned the doctrine of "*terra nullius*" insofar as it applied to land in Australia. This doctrine permitted the British Crown to assert ownership of unoccupied land, but the common law doctrine had been extended to include inhabited lands if there were no recognizable laws or social organization, because they were too "barbaric" for English law to recognize: see *Cooper v Stuart*, [1889] 14 AC 286 (PC) and *Milirrpum v Nabalco Pty Ltd* (1971), 17 FLR 141 (N Terr SC). In *Mabo*, the Australian High Court rejected this approach and (at 422) confirmed legal recognition of land rights of the Meriam people, residents of the Murray Islands in Torres Strait. However, note that although native title was allowed to persist, the court affirmed the Crown's ability to retain the underlying title over the lands of Australia, due to its assertion of sovereignty:

> The fiction by which the rights and interests of indigenous inhabitants in land were treated as non-existent was justified by a policy which has no place in the contemporary law of this country ... . Whatever the justification advanced in earlier days for refusing to recognise the rights and interests in land of the indigenous inhabitants of settled colonies, an unjust and discriminatory doctrine of that kind can no longer be accepted. The expectations of the international community accord in this respect with the contemporary values of the Australian people.

The court analyzed the relationship between the acquisition of territorial sovereignty in international law and the acquisition of property according to common law principles. According to Brennan J (at 425), "[t]he Crown was invested with the character of Paramount Lord in the colonies by attributing to the Crown a title, adapted from feudal theory, that was called a radical, ultimate or final title," and this radical title permitted the Crown to grant lands in accordance with tenurial requirements. Yet, as Brennan J stated emphatically (at 425-26):

> [It] is not a corollary of the Crown's acquisition of a radical title to land in an occupied territory that the Crown acquired absolute beneficial ownership of that land to the exclusion of the indigenous inhabitants. If the land were desert and uninhabited, truly a *terra nullius*, the Crown would take an absolute beneficial title (an allodial title) to the land ... : there would be no *other* proprietor. But if the land were occupied by the indigenous inhabitants and their rights and interests in the land are recognised by the common law, the radical title which is acquired with the acquisition of sovereignty cannot itself be taken to confer an absolute beneficial title to the occupied land ... . Whether or not land is owned by individual members of a community, a community which asserts and asserts effectively that none but its members has any right to occupy or use the land has an interest in the land that must be proprietary in nature: there is no other proprietor ... . Where a proprietary title capable of recognition by the common law is found to have been possessed by a community in occupation of a territory, there is no reason why that title should not be recognised as a burden on the Crown's radical title when the Crown acquires sovereignty over that territory.

Thus the court concluded that the Crown's radical title could be subjected to a beneficial title on the part of the indigenous people of the Murray Islands. In reaching this conclusion, the court acknowledged that earlier precedent cases were being overruled, and Brennan J stated (at 429):

> To maintain the authority of those cases would destroy the equality of all Australian citizens before the law. The common law of this country would perpetuate injustice if it were to continue to embrace the enlarged notion of *terra nullius* and to persist in characterising the indigenous inhabitants of the Australian colonies as people too low in the scale of social organisation to be acknowledged as possessing rights and interests in land.

The decision in *Mabo* was "greeted by enthusiasm in many quarters committed to Aboriginal land rights," even though a close inspection of the reasoning in the case suggested that it raised a number of issues for subsequent claimants: see SB Phillips, "A Note: Eddie Mabo v The State of Queensland" (1993) 15 Sydney L Rev 121. For other assessments, see P Butt, "Native Land Rights in Australia: The Mabo Case" (1995) Conveyancer and Property Lawyer 33; G Nettheim, "The Mabo Response: Reconciliation or Continuing Conquest?" (1993) 3 UNSWLJ 19.

One commentator has contrasted the approach of the BC courts in *Delgamuukw* with the High Court judges in *Mabo*, suggesting that:

> [t]he *Mabo* decision lends credence to the idea that in contrast to the trial and Court of Appeal decisions in *Delgamuukw*, a "reverse weight of history" argument may be used to say that self-government is in existence today. This argument would say the following: the recognition in legislation and case law of continued aboriginal powers to govern themselves in certain spheres implies the contemporary existence of the aboriginal right of self-government.

(See B Freedman, "The Space for Aboriginal Self-Government in British Columbia: The Effect of the Decision of the British Columbia Court of Appeal in Delgamuukw v British Columbia" (1994) UBC L Rev 49 at 72-73.)

The federal government in Australia responded to *Mabo* by enacting the *Native Title Act 1993* (Cth). The statute permitted "validation" by government of pre-existing grants of free-hold; residential, pastoral, and tourist leasehold; and permanent public works. Validation extinguished native title, but compensation on "just terms" is payable. No grant over native land was possible after 31 December 1993 unless the government could do the same over freehold land (subject to limited provisions for mining and other leases). Native title was in-alienable, except for surrender to the relevant government, and the Federal Court could de-termine the existence of native title and compensation for its extinguishment. As well, a federal native-title tribunal could determine whether grants should be made over land sub-ject to native title, and judges of the Federal Court would be assisted by appropriately quali-fied mediators or assessors who were intended to be Aboriginal people. To what extent is such a legislative regime more appropriate than judicial decision making in the context of Aboriginal title?

The federal legislation was generally endorsed, sometimes with reservations, by all states in Australia except the state of Western Australia. Western Australia introduced state legisla-tion extinguishing native title and providing statutory rights of use and occupancy (not property rights), but the High Court held the legislation unconstitutional in *Western Australia v The Commonwealth* (1995), 128 ALR 1 (HC), reaffirming the principles outlined in *Mabo*: see K McNeil, "Racial Discrimination and Unilateral Extinguishment of Native Title" (1996) 1:2 Austl Indigenous L Rev 181 at 181-82; and R Bartlett, "Racism and Constitutional Protection of Native Title in Western Australia: The 1995 High Court Decision" (1995) 25 UWA L Rev 127. See also the collection of essays in R Bartlett & G Meyers, eds, *Native Title Legislation in Aus-tralia* (Perth: Centre for Commercial and Resources Law, University of Western Australia and Murdoch University, 1994).

In a later decision, *The Wik Peoples v Queensland* (1996), 141 ALR 129 (HC), the High Court held (4-3) that the grant of pastoral leases pursuant to state legislation (the *Land Act 1910* (Qld) and the *Land Act 1962-74* (Qld)) did not necessarily extinguish native title. The test was whether such grants were "inconsistent" with the continued existence of native title. In the face of widespread criticism from pastoral graziers, the federal government succeeded in passing the *Native Title Amendment Act* (1998), which tended to limit the nature and process of Aboriginal claims to land. According to Larissa Behrendt:

> These recent developments concerning Aboriginal property rights in Australia have been frus-trating for the Aboriginal community ... , as each incremental and piecemeal gain made within the judicial system has been truncated or extinguished by a legislature with a conflicting ideol-ogy and agenda. For Australia's indigenous peoples, the legacy of *terra nullius* may have been overturned by the *Mabo* case, but another ideological enemy remains.

(See Larissa Behrendt, "White Picket Fences: Recognizing Aboriginal Property Rights in Aus-tralia's Psychological Terra Nullius" (1999) 10:2 Const Forum 50.)

Do such views affect your conclusions about the need for legislative rather than judicial ac-tion in relation to issues of Aboriginal title? Do you agree, as McNeil argued, that questions of Aboriginal title and sovereignty for First Nations are intertwined? To what extent are principles about "private" property appropriate in this context? Is the issue of Aboriginal title to land a matter of "private" or "public" property?

For more detailed comparisons of Aboriginal title issues in Canada and Australia, see K Hazlehurst, *Legal Pluralism and Colonial Legacy: Indigenous Experiences of Justice in Canada, Australia and New Zealand* (Aldershot, UK: Avebury, 1995) and McNeil, "Vulnerability of Land Rights."

In a more recent decision, *Members of the Yorta Yorta Aboriginal Community v Victoria*, [2002] HCA 58, the Australian High Court appeared to retreat from the landmark decision in *Mabo*. Members of the Yorta Yorta Aboriginal community initiated a legal action to obtain a declaration of Aboriginal title to a large region of the Australian state of Victoria, but their claim was struck down at trial, with the High Court of Australia later upholding this decision. In essence, the High Court was not convinced by the community's demonstration of continuity between its current practices and the pre-sovereignty practices of its ancestors. Continuity is a necessary element arising from the *Mabo* ruling because, as Chief Justice Gleeson summarized during *Yorta Yorta* (at para 37):

> First, it follows from *Mabo (No 2)* [(1992), 175 CLR 1] that the Crown's acquisition of sovereignty over the several parts of Australia cannot be challenged in an Australian municipal court. Secondly, upon acquisition of sovereignty over a particular part of Australia, the Crown acquired a radical title to the land in that part, but native title to that land survived the Crown's acquisition of sovereignty and radical title. What survived were rights and interests in relation to land or waters. Those rights and interests owed their origin to a normative system other than the legal system of the new sovereign power; they owed their origin to the traditional laws acknowledged and the traditional customs observed by the indigenous peoples concerned.

Therefore, because evidence at trial seemed to suggest that there had been an abandoning of the Yorta Yorta's traditional way of life around the time of European conquest, even though the community had attempted to revive some of the old practices, the court stated (at para 53):

> When the society whose laws or customs existed at sovereignty ceases to exist, the rights and interests in land to which these laws and customs gave rise, cease to exist. If the content of the former laws and customs is later adopted by some new society, those laws and customs will then owe their new life to that other, later, society and they are the laws acknowledged by, and customs observed by, *that later society*; they are not laws and customs which can now properly be described as being the existing laws and customs of the earlier society. The rights and interests in land to which the re-adopted laws and customs give rise are rights and interests which are not rooted in pre-sovereignty traditional law and custom but in the laws and customs of the new society.

Fearing that this new articulation of societal continuity would deny the ability of Aboriginal peoples and cultures to evolve and change over time (particularly in the light of major events like colonialism), Australian author Simon Young commented:

> [T]he principal difficulty with the joint judgment lies in their Honours' interposition (and interpretation) of the notion of "society." The concept was apparently called upon in this rationalisation of the continuity of law and custom requirement to underline, or assist in demonstrating, the insufficiency of mere continuance of *knowledge* of traditional laws and customs combined with subse-

quent revival. However, their Honours' precise explanation seems to conflate two distinct issues of proof, thereby encouraging the restrictive approach to constancy and continuity. As noted previously, this book raises no objection to the presence of a continuity (and correlative constancy) of law and custom requirement. Nor does it take issue with the notion that, in the case of a communal interest, an inquiry into whether the "community" has continued may be appropriate … . However, logically the first requirement must be concerned simply with the law and custom in which the relevant interest is sourced; the survival or non-survival of peripheral features of the Aboriginal lifestyle can be of little relevance. And any requirement as the survival of a community or "society" must acknowledge the evolutionary nature and adaptability of such entities.

(Simon Young, *The Trouble with Tradition: Native Title and Cultural Change* (Sydney, Australia: Federation Press, 2008) at 325.)

In spite of this ruling, however, the case encouraged the Victorian government to enter into negotiations with the Aboriginal community, negotiations that ended in a "historic cooperative management agreement" covering parts of the disputed lands (Fergus Shiel, "Yorta Yorta Win Historic Deal," *The Age* (1 May 2004), online: The Age <http://www.theage.com.au/articles/2004/04/30/1083224579722.html>). The first of its kind in Australia, the agreement creates a joint land management committee that oversees development in the region. The minister of environment still holds the final say, but a majority of the voting members on this joint Aboriginal–governmental body are from the Yorta Yorta community.

As this Australian comparison indicates, there are a number of similarities in developments concerning Aboriginal rights to land in Australia and Canada. In reflecting on these issues, consider the following comparative assessment.

PG McHugh, *Aboriginal Title: The Modern Jurisprudence of Tribal Land Rights*
(Oxford: Oxford University Press, 2011) at 328-32 (footnotes omitted)

The impact that versions of common-law aboriginal title had in the new century in places like Belize, Malaysia, southern Africa, and (resurgent) in New Zealand suggested that it retained the capacity to shock governments and force the pace of their relations with indigenous peoples. Certainly, it jolted those relations out of an engrained culture of governmental inaction and required the political branch to take tribal peoples' land claims more seriously, confirming the doctrine's capacity to require higher prioritization of such claims. Yet, in those jurisdictions where the legal systems, having dealt with the initial shock, had acclimatized to the doctrine, its experience became more equivocal. In Canada and Australia, routed through the haphazard byways of the adjudicative processes, the doctrine did not fare strongly in its journey towards adulthood. …

One sign of that emergent caution appeared downstream as courts explored and amplified their breakthrough pronouncements. As this happened, it became plain that the post-breakthrough legalism was not relying entirely on the common law to describe its compass, pivotal as that source had been in punching the initial breakthrough. In part this was a result of judges stepping back into more accustomed reticence, out of the glare and the accusations of "activism" that accompanied those judgments. In Canada, aboriginal rights became a constitutional phenomenon housed inside section 35 of the *Constitu-*

tion Act, the set of "existing" rights extending beyond those entirely derived from the common law itself. In Australia the *Native Title Act 1993* (NTA) became the locus of juridical attention after the *Wik* case (1996), almost to the extent of disowning the common-law basis of native title entirely. If the road on which aboriginal title was travelling widened in Canada, it narrowed in Australia—which is not to say that its route in either jurisdiction was an uncluttered or easy one. ... The point is that after the breakthrough judgments the common law did not shoulder the entire juridical load as the sole mechanism for normative development. The courts of Canada and Australia turned to other sources to motor their emergent national jurisprudences.

Nonetheless, aboriginal title had been framed as an essentially cautious argument—although it did not seem that at first—situated inside the not unfamiliar or threatening paradigm of property. Inevitably, the implications of that location became plainer in the cut and thrust of litigation. Judges, some growing evidently weary of sequences of cases calling for laborious and deeper textured proprietary analysis and seemingly interminable hearings with mountains of detailed evidence, resiled from the boldness of the breakthrough era. Canadian courts boxed themselves in with a title/rights distinction and the Australian courts developed an onerous (and ungenerous) connection test and weak characterization of (the Aboriginal owners') right to exclude. These downstream developments compromised the initial effectiveness of the doctrine, especially as the probative elements became more elaborate and adversarial. Governments learned to live with aboriginal/native title and likewise developed strategies of litigation management and claims resolution that read negatively to aboriginal peoples as ruses for encompassment and curtailment. The doctrine became technically laden and its application by the Canadian and Australian courts much pickier. Microscopic and painstaking attention to the proof of key elements also became the means by which governments dragged their heels and pulled the land-claims processes (in court and negotiating room) back towards the older grinding pattern of inaction, or, at best, slow pace. Many politicians—with some honourable exceptions—seemed to fear the political fallout from appearing to concede too much to aboriginal claimants and sought tactically to keep claims-resolution below the public sightline and the negative media depiction that usually surrounded any attention to those processes.

Adversarialism was the manner of birth of the doctrine, and its dominance remained. It trellised and (mis)shaped growth of the legalism, bringing with it an infestation of lawyers and, on their coat-tails and playing attendant to their toilsome legalism, legions of other professionals like anthropologists and (ethno-)historians. This added to the spectacle—and, needless to say, cost—without necessarily gaining much headway for either Crown or claimant. ...

Despite the misshapen and unsympathetic results of litigation, the slow pace of consensus results remained, albeit with occasional quickening. In Canada and Australia the snail's pace was compounded by the nature of federalism, which typically impeded progress, largely because of the usual jurisdictional control by sub-national governments of the land and resources subject to claims. Governments preferred negotiation to litigation, understanding the desirability of incorporating indigenous consent into policy-making and implementation whilst also holding reservations about the way in which indigenous rights challenged deeply held notions of citizenship. The breakthrough court judgments certainly pushed governments towards more active dialogue and effort to engage the tribes, although it has recently been suggested that that might have happened even without the judgments (important catalysts as they nonetheless were). Certainly the shape of the jurisprudences of native title formed through the national adjudicative processes was, by any measure, ungainly and heavy on its feet.

At the beginning of the second decade of this century, however, there were some positive signs in these jurisdictions notwithstanding the unhelpful doctrinal state of legal art produced by rights-design through adjudication and the cumbersome machinery attending it. The Canadian courts seemed poised to leave the proprietary paradigm altogether, or at least keep it on the back-burner, as the Supreme Court amplified and extended the public law duty to consult. Lower judgments in Australia's federal courts wriggled against the High Court's constrictive framework and tests for native title, even as the number of consent determinations and [*Indigenous Land Use Agreements*] under the [*Native Title Act*] rose measurably. The State of Victoria legislated what seems a promising Settlement Framework mechanism (2010). The rising pace of agreed outcomes in Australia (the long-term durability of which remains another question) contrasted with the slow, almost stagnant state of the Canadian and the meandering one of historical claims resolution in New Zealand. In these settings the signal from the Canadian and Australian courts seemed to be that the renewed focus of juridical development would be on the procedural dimension of Crown–tribe relations. The doyen of aboriginal title, Brian Slattery, spoke of aboriginal rights as generative, emphasizing the consensual and relational rather than adversarial aspect of their design. One sensed a dawning though vague realization, and one not limited to the courtroom, that the proprietary paradigm had gone its distance in Canada, Australia, and in New Zealand … . In that regard, the modern history of aboriginal title had circled back to the emphasis and expectation of the mid-1980s that it would lead to negotiated settlements and consensus-led forms of engagement. By the beginning of this century's second decade there was no doubting the scrappy outcomes where rights-design was led by court judgment rather than shaped by the parties themselves. …

[The author contrasted the judicial treatment of Aboriginal title in Australia and Canada with the legislative changes that have been taking place in New Zealand over the past few years. Many of the changes in New Zealand have seemingly taken place because the current government was formed through a coalition that included a party composed of Aboriginal lawmakers.]

As it reached a kind of maturity, the pattern of the Canadian and Australian jurisprudence also signaled that mired in adversarialism the common-law doctrine was not very good at conferring *title* in the sense of full exclusive ownership and as the very title of the doctrine itself suggested (excuse the pun). No litigation for aboriginal title had succeeded in Canada where the few "successful" cases entailed reference back to the trial level. The Australian High Court's "bundle of rights" version of native title pitched the right to exclude in such a vulnerable and weak manner that exclusivity was all but impossible to attain … . In that way, the course of downstream doctrinal development frustrated—some would even say, betrayed—the hope of aboriginal peoples that the law would give them the equivalent of freehold ownership. …

Nonetheless, one sphere where aboriginal title has had some effectiveness has been in boosting tribes' claims over and to specific resources without necessarily involving an associated more encompassing claim to full ownership as the right to exclude all-comers from the particular zone. Fishing and hunting rights (inland and marine), sometimes presented as species-specific (such as the marine turtle, dugong, beluga, and bowhead whales), were the precursors of claims to rights to water and water-flow, minerals (including petroleum), flora and associated intellectual property rights (medicinal especially), aquaculture, tourist development (eco-tourism especially), and lumber. Often the claim based on the common law was the tribes' lever for negotiation and inclusion in development projects for such resources.

In the new century, ... aboriginal claims over sea country became particularly marked in Australia, New Zealand, and Canada's Pacific and, more recently, the Arctic coast. For the most part these claims were framed in terms of non-exclusive rights and thereby attracted greater judicial willingness to protect and preserve the particular right by qualifying the scope of non-indigenous activity and access. Recently a Canadian court granted an injunction to stop the government of Canada from conducting seismic testing in the waters of North Baffin Island in an area covered by the *Nunavut Land Claims Agreement* (and hence subject to unextinguished aboriginal title). [See *Qikiqtai Inuit Association v Canada (Minister of Natural Resources)*, 2010 NUCJ 12, [2010] 4 CNLR 190.] The applicant Qikiqtai Inuit Association (QIA) had expressed concern about the impact on marine mammals and dissatisfaction with the consultation process followed by the federal and territory governments. Despite these objections, the license was issued, so the QIA brought an action alleging that the governments of Canada and Nunavut had failed to meet their common law and constitutional duties to conduct meaningful consultations with Inuit, and if appropriate, accommodate Inuit interests. The successful outcome shows how the duty to consult is now being marshalled by Canadian courts to protect proprietary rights (including those built into land claims agreements).

To what extent does this comment accurately reflect the evolution of claims about Aboriginal title to land in Canada? Note how this comment suggests similar developments in Canada and Australia with respect to the courts' treatment of litigated claims, the trend to abandoning proprietary approaches, and increasing reliance on negotiation and consultation. In this context, how should the courts now define the public law duty to consult First Nations?

C. The Way Forward

In reflecting on the evolution of conceptions of Aboriginal title to land over several centuries, consider how the broader political and economic contexts have shaped legal principles—from "usufructuary interests" to a "right to the land itself" and the recent tests that justify "infringement" of Aboriginal claims to land. In this context, how might recent developments, including Aboriginal protests (such as the fasting protest of Chief Theresa Spence and others), the rise of the Idle No More movement, and other social and political factors contribute to the creation of new approaches to claims about Aboriginal title to land? In keeping with the idea that "we are all treaty people," reflect on how the following comment may assist Canadian governments (and Canadians) to support First Nations peoples. How should this goal be implemented in practice?

[T]he successful recognition of aboriginal claims must involve *the full and unstinting recognition of the historical reality of aboriginal title, the true scope and effects of indigenous dispossession, and the continuing links between an Indigenous people and its traditional lands.* So, for example, to maintain that "nomadic" or "semi-nomadic" peoples had historical aboriginal title to only a fraction of their ancestral hunting territories, or to hold that aboriginal title could be extinguished simply by Crown grant, is to rub salt into open wounds. However, by the same token, *the recognition of historical title, while a necessary precondition for modern reconciliation, is not in itself a sufficient basis for reconciliation, which must take into account a range of other factors.* So, for example, to suggest that historical aboriginal title gives rise to modern rights that automatically trump third party and public interests constitutes an attempt to remedy one grave injustice by committing another.

(B Slattery, "The Metamorphosis of Aboriginal Title" (2006) 85 Can Bar Rev 255 at 282 (emphasis in original; also quoted in *William v British Columbia* by Vickers J at trial).)

PROBLEMS

1. Consider the following explanation of Aboriginal title to land from *Delgamuukw v British Columbia* in 1997 (at para 125):

> The content of aboriginal title contains an inherent limit that lands held pursuant to title cannot be used in a manner that is irreconcilable with the nature of the claimants' attachment to those lands. This limit on the content of aboriginal title is a manifestation of the principle that underlies the various dimensions of that special interest in land—it is a *sui generis* interest.

Compare this explanation to a fee simple in common law property principles and identify how, and to what extent, Aboriginal title to land differs from fee simple entitlement in Canada. You may also want to consider the conditional fee simple in this context, a suggestion included in the extract from Leroy Little Bear's article in Chapter 1.

2. In 1997, in *Delgamuukw v British Columbia*, Lamer CJ stated (at para 113):

> The idea that aboriginal title is *sui generis* is the unifying principle underlying the various dimensions of [Aboriginal] title [to land].

Explain the content of Aboriginal title to land identified by the Supreme Court of Canada in *Delgamuukw*, and identify why, and to what extent, this decision of the Supreme Court of Canada represented a "turning point" for claims concerning Aboriginal title to land.

3. In a more recent assessment of developments in Canada relating to Aboriginal title to land, PG McHugh commented:

> The Canadian courts seemed poised to leave the proprietary paradigm altogether, or at least keep it on the back-burner.

By reference to judicial decisions after *Delgamuukw* in 1997, explain the extent to which this statement accurately reflects the pattern of decision making in Canadian courts with respect to issues about Aboriginal title to land. To what extent do recent judicial decisions explain the existence of protest actions, such as Idle No More?

CHAPTER REFERENCES

Aboriginal Affairs and Northern Development Canada. Media Release, "Statement from Minister Duncan Regarding Canada's Appeal of the Federal Court's Decision in Daniels v Canada" (6 February 2013), online: Market Wired News Room <http://www.marketwire.com/press-release/statement-from-minister-duncan-regarding-canadas-appeal-federal-courts-decision-daniels-1753995.htm>.

Alcantara, Christopher. *Negotiating the Deal: Comprehensive Land Claims Agreements in Canada* (Toronto: University of Toronto Press, 2013).

Arnot, David. "The Honour of First Nations—The Honour of the Crown: The Unique Relationship of First Nations with the Crown" (Paper delivered at a policy conference on the role of the Crown in Canadian governance, Ottawa, "The Crown in Canada: Present Realities and Future Options," Ottawa, 10 June 2010), online: Queen's University <http://www.queensu.ca/iigr/conf/Arch/2010/ConferenceOnTheCrown/CrownConferencePapers/The_Crown_and_the_First_Nations.pdf>.

Barsh, RL & JY Henderson. "The Supreme Court's Van der Peet Trilogy: Naïve Imperialism and Ropes of Sand" (1997) 42 McGill LJ 993.

Bartlett, R. "Racism and Constitutional Protection of Native Title in Western Australia: The 1995 High Court Decision" (1995) 25 UWA L Rev 127.

Bartlett, R & G Meyers, eds. *Native Title Legislation in Australia* (Perth: Centre for Commercial and Resources Law, University of Western Australia and Murdoch University, 1994).

Behrendt, Larissa. "White Picket Fences: Recognizing Aboriginal Property Rights in Australia's Psychological Terra Nullius" (1999) 10:2 Const Forum 50.

Bell, Catherine. "New Directions in the Law of Aboriginal Rights" (1998) 77 Can Bar Rev 36.

Bittermann, Rusty. "Mi'kmaq Land Claims and the Escheat Movement in Prince Edward Island" (2006) 55 UNBLJ 172.

Boldt, M & JA Long, eds. *The Quest for Justice: Aboriginal Peoples and Aboriginal Rights* (Toronto: University of Toronto Press, 1985).

Borrows, John. *Canada's Indigenous Constitution* (Toronto: University of Toronto Press, 2010).

Borrows, John. "Constitutional Law from a First Nations Perspective: Self-Government and the Royal Proclamation" (1994) 28 UBC L Rev 1.

Borrows, John. "Frozen Rights in Canada: Constitutional Interpretation and the Trickster" (1997) 22 Am Indian L Rev 37.

Borrows, John. "With or Without You: First Nations Law (in Canada)" (1996) 41 McGill LJ 629.

Butt, P. "Native Land Rights in Australia: The Mabo Case" (1995) Conveyancer and Property Lawyer 33.

Chartrand, Paul LAH. "R v Marshall; R v Bernard: The Return of the Native" (2006) 55 UNBLJ 133.

Christie, Gordon. "Delgamuukw and the Protection of Aboriginal Land Interests" (2000-1) 32:1 Ottawa L Rev 85.

Clarkson, Adrienne. "The Society of Difference" (Paper delivered at the 8th Annual LaFontaine-Baldwin Lecture, Vancouver, 2 March 2007), online: Institute for Canadian Citizenship <http://www.icc-icc.ca/en/lbs/docs/AdrienneClarkson-ASocietyofDifference8thLaFontaine-BaldwinLectureMarch22007.pdf>.

Coates, K, ed. *Aboriginal Land Claims in Canada: A Regional Perspective* (Toronto: Copp Clark Pitman, 1992).

Cox, BD. "The Gitksan–Wet'suwet'en as 'Primitive' Peoples Incapable of Holding Proprietary Interests: Chief Justice McEachern's Underlying Premise in Delgamuukw" (1992) 1 Dal J Leg Stud 141.

Cumming, P & N Mickenberg, eds. *Native Rights in Canada* (Toronto: Indian-Eskimo Association of Canada, 1972).

Erasmus, George. "Twenty Years of Disappointed Hopes" in B Richardson, ed, *Drumbeat: Anger and Renewal in Indian Country* (Toronto: University of Toronto Press, 1989) 3.

Flanagan, William F. "Piercing the Veil of Real Property Law: Delgamuukw v British Columbia" (1998) 24 Queen's LJ 279.

Ford, Lisa & Tim Rowse, eds. *Between Indigenous and Settler Governance* (Oxford: Routledge, 2013).

Fortune, J. "Construing Delgamuukw: Legal Arguments, Historical Argumentation, and Philosophy of History" (1993) 51 UT Fac L Rev 80.

Freedman, B. "The Space for Aboriginal Self-Government in British Columbia: The Effect of the Decision of the British Columbia Court of Appeal in Delgamuukw v British Columbia" (1994) UBC L Rev 49.

Gavigan, Shelley AM. *Hunger, Horses, and Government Men* (Vancouver: UBC Press, 2012).

Hazlehurst, K. *Legal Pluralism and Colonial Legacy: Indigenous Experiences of Justice in Canada, Australia and New Zealand* (Aldershot, UK: Avebury, 1995).

Hurley, John. "The Crown's Fiduciary Duty and Indian Title: Guerin v The Queen" (1985) 30 McGill LJ 559.

Imai, Shin. "The Adjudication of Historical Evidence: A Comment and an Elaboration on a Proposal by Justice LeBel" (2006) 55 UNBLJ 147.

Imai, Shin. *The Structure of the Indian Act: Accountability in Governance* (National Centre for First Nations Governance, 2007).

Indian and Northern Affairs Canada. *Historical Treaties of Canada* (Ottawa: Indian and Northern Affairs Canada [nd]).

Isaac, Thomas & Kristyn Annis. *Treaty Rights in the Historic Treaties of Canada* (Saskatoon, Sask: Houghton Boston Printers, 2010).

Jackson, Michael. "The Articulation of Native Rights in Canadian Law" (1984) 18 UBC L Rev 255.

Johnston, Darlene. "The Quest of the Six-Nations Confederacy for Self-Determination" (1986) 44 UT Fac L Rev 1.

Lambert, Douglas. "The Tsilhqot'in Case" (2012) 70 Advocate 819.

Law Commission of Canada, ed. *Indigenous Legal Traditions* (Vancouver: UBC Press, 2007).

MacIntosh, Constance. "Developments in Aboriginal Law: The 2006-2007 Term" (2007) 38 Sup Ct L Rev 1.

McHugh, PG. *Aboriginal Title: The Modern Jurisprudence of Tribal Land Rights* (Oxford: Oxford University Press, 2011).

McLaren, J, AR Buck & N Wright, eds. *Despotic Dominion: Property Rights in British Settler Societies* (Vancouver: UBC Press, 2005).

McNeil, Kent. "Aboriginal Rights in Canada: From Title to Land to Territorial Sovereignty" (1998) 5 Tulsa J Comp & Int'l L 353.

McNeil, Kent. "Aboriginal Title and Aboriginal Rights: What's the Connection?" (1997) 36 Alta L Rev 117.

McNeil, Kent. "Aboriginal Title and the Supreme Court: What's Happening?" (2006) 69 Sask L Rev 281.

McNeil, Kent. *Defining Aboriginal Title in the 90s: Has the Supreme Court Finally Got It Right?* (Toronto: York University, Robarts Centre for Canadian Studies, 1998).

McNeil, Kent. "Extinguishment of Aboriginal Title in Canada: Treaties, Legislation, and Judicial Discretion" (2000-1) 33 Ottawa L Rev 301.

McNeil, Kent. "Indigenous Land Rights and Self-Government: Inseparable Entitlements" in Lisa Ford & Tim Rowse, eds, *Between Indigenous and Settler Governance* (Oxford: Routledge, 2013) 135.

McNeil, Kent. "Racial Discrimination and Unilateral Extinguishment of Native Title" (1996) 1:2 Austl Indigenous L Rev 181.

McNeil, Kent. "The Vulnerability of Indigenous Land Rights in Australia and Canada" (2004) 42 Osgoode Hall LJ 271.

Mercredi, Ovide & Mary Ellen Turpel. *In the Rapids: Navigating the Future of First Nations* (Toronto: Viking Penguin, 1993).

Minnawaanagogiizhigook (Dawnis Kennedy). "Reconciliation Without Respect? Section 35 and Indigenous Legal Orders" in Law Commission of Canada, ed, *Indigenous Legal Traditions* (Vancouver: UBC Press, 2007) 77.

Morse, B, ed. *Aboriginal Peoples and the Law: Métis and Inuit Rights in Canada* (Ottawa: Carleton University Press, 1991).

Nettheim, G. "The Mabo Response: Reconciliation or Continuing Conquest?" (1993) 3 UNSWLJ 19.

Newman, Dwight G. *The Duty to Consult* (Saskatoon: Purich, 2009).

Phillips, SB. "A Note: Eddie Mabo v The State of Queensland" (1993) 15 Sydney L Rev 121.

Richardson, B, ed. *Drumbeat: Anger and Renewal in Indian Country* (Toronto: University of Toronto Press, 1989).

Ross, R. *Dancing with a Ghost: Exploring Indian Reality* (Markham, ON: Octopus Books, 1992).

Royal Commission on Aboriginal Peoples. *Bridging the Cultural Divide: A Report on Aboriginal People and Criminal Justice in Canada* (Ottawa: Minister of Supply and Services Canada, 1996).

Ryder, Bruce. "Aboriginal Rights and Delgamuukw v The Queen" (1994) 5 Const Forum 43.

Shiel, Fergus. "Yorta Yorta Win Historic Deal," *The Age* (1 May 2004), online: The Age <http://www.theage.com.au/articles/2004/04/30/1083224579722.html>.

Slattery, Brian. "Aboriginal Rights and the Honour of the Crown" (2005) 20 Sup Ct L Rev 433.

Slattery, B. *Ancestral Lands, Alien Laws: Judicial Perspectives on Aboriginal Title*, Studies in Aboriginal Rights no 2 (Saskatoon, Sask: University of Saskatchewan Native Law Centre, 1983).

Slattery, Brian. "The Metamorphosis of Aboriginal Title" (2006) 85 Can Bar Rev 255.

Stephenson, Margaret. "Indigenous Lands and Constitutional Reform in Australia: A Canadian Comparison" (2011) 15:2 Austl Indigenous L Rev 87.

Trudeau, PE. "Remarks on Aboriginal and Treaty Rights" (Vancouver, 8 August 1969) in P Cumming and N Mickenberg, eds, *Native Rights in Canada* (Toronto: Indian-Eskimo Association of Canada, 1972).

Tuhiwai Smith, Linda. *Decolonizing Methodologies: Research and Indigenous Peoples* (London: Zed Books, 1999).

Valverde, Mariana. "'The Honour of the Crown Is at Stake': Aboriginal Land Claims Litigation and the Epistemology of Sovereignty" (2011) 1 UC Irvine L Rev 955 at 957.

Vermette, D'Arcy. "Colonialism and the Process of Defining Aboriginal People" (2008) 31 Dal LJ 211.

Vermette, D'Arcy. "Dizzying Dialogue: Canadian Courts and the Continuing Justification of the Dispossession of Aboriginal Peoples" (2011) 29 Windsor YB Access Just 55.

Walters, M. "British Imperial Constitutional Law and Aboriginal Rights: A Comment on Delgamuukw v British Columbia" (1992) 17 Queen's LJ 350.

Young, Simon. *The Trouble with Tradition: Native Title and Cultural Change* (Sydney, Australia: Federation Press, 2008).